Everyman KT-227-862

THESAURUS OF ENGLISH
WORDS & PHRASES

A volume in
EVERYMAN'S REFERENCE LIBRARY

Everyman's Reference Library

DICTIONARY OF QUOTATIONS AND PROVERBS

THESAURUS OF
ENGLISH WORDS AND PHRASES

DICTIONARY OF SHAKESPEARE QUOTATIONS

DICTIONARY OF NON-CLASSICAL MYTHOLOGY

DICTIONARY OF DATES

DICTIONARY OF MUSIC

EVERYMAN'S ENGLISH DICTIONARY

ENGLISH PRONOUNCING DICTIONARY

DICTIONARY OF LITERARY BIOGRAPHY:
ENGLISH AND AMERICAN

DICTIONARY OF EUROPEAN WRITERS

CONCISE ENCYCLOPAEDIA OF ARCHITECTURE

CLASSICAL DICTIONARY

ATLAS OF ANCIENT AND CLASSICAL GEOGRAPHY

ENCYCLOPAEDIA OF GARDENING

FRENCH-ENGLISH—ENGLISH-FRENCH DICTIONARY

DICTIONARY OF ECONOMICS

DICTIONARY OF PICTORIAL ART (2 volumes)

EVERYMAN'S ENCYCLOPAEDIA (12 volumes)

Other volumes in preparation

Everyman's

THESAURUS OF ENGLISH WORDS AND PHRASES

Revised from

PETER ROGET

by

D. C. BROWNING

M.A. (Glasgow), B.A., B.Litt. (Oxon)

LONDON: J. M. DENT & SONS LTD
NEW YORK: E. P. DUTTON & CO. INC.

© Revisions, J. M. Dent & Sons Ltd, 1971
First published in Everyman's Library 1912
This edition compiled by D. C. Browning
First published 1952
Last revised edition 1971

ISBN: 0 460 03018 3

INTRODUCTION

It is just a hundred years since Roget's *Thesaurus of English Words and Phrases* was first published. In the course of that century of unprecedented development and change our language and vocabulary have undergone modifications and additions which have been dealt with from time to time in previous revisions of the work. But a new generation has grown up since the last recension, and the time seemed ripe for a more complete overhaul which would make it thoroughly up to date. Accordingly, the opportunity has been taken, in preparing this new single-volume edition, of giving the work as complete a revision as was possible, short of doing the whole compilation afresh. Every paragraph has been carefully reviewed, over 10,000 words and phrases have been added, and the articles have been 'tidied up' so that all additions follow the logical order which agrees with the original plan.

In the course of its century of use Roget's *Thesaurus* has come to be as widely accepted and as indispensable to writers as a dictionary, and its system and arrangement have become so familiar that any radical alteration of them would lessen the value of the book to those who know their way about it from constant use. For that reason no attempt has been made to modify the main scheme which Roget originally laid down, and except for a few very minor alterations of numbering where the order had become confused the arrangement is the same as in previous editions. Within this scheme the articles have been greatly amplified and expanded, some of the pages containing up to a hundred fresh insertions.

The list of contents at the beginning sets out the plan of classification, and indicates the general divisions of the book. Readers who are interested in the detailed subdivisions of the classification will find them in the different paragraph headings, and the general principles of the work are explained in Roget's original Introduction, now printed at the end of the volume.

Technical Terms.

In giving some account of the additions which have been made, it is natural to start off with those technical terms which have been coined to fit modern scientific, political, and cultural developments. The wide range of the subjects covered is shown by these typical examples taken at random: *air-condition, airgraph, allergy, antibiotic, Appleton layer, bathysphere, Dadaism, deviationist, diarchy, displaced person, electrolysis, existentialism, fifth column, Gallup poll, geriatrics, Heaviside layer, hydroponics, intercom, ionosphere, iron curtain, libido, liquidate, parapsychology, psychotherapist, quisling, radar, robot, rotor, stratosphere, surrealism, telekinesis, television, troposphere, weather station.*

Aviation.

Along with the previous section may be grouped the very numerous terms which deal with recent developments in aviation and aerial warfare. These represent new types of aircraft: *autogiro, flying fortress, flying wing, jet aircraft, stratocruiser, stratoliner*; new types of weapon: *atom bomb, buzz-bomb, doodlebug, flying bomb, guided missile, V1, V2*; new names for personnel: *group-captain, wing-commander, squadron-leader, flight-lieutenant*; and for their evolutions: *air lift, bunt.* Finally there are words for the yet untried adventure of interplanetary voyaging: *astronautics, spacecraft, space ship, space travel.*

Everyday Neologisms.

In addition to words marking scientific advance there are also, of course, many neologisms reflecting change or fashion in everyday affairs, such as *baby-sitter, bingle, blurb, bottle-neck, bottle party, bulldozer, cannibalize, cartophily, embus, exclosure, frogman, green belt, infrastructure, jive, lumberjacket, nylons, phillumenist, play-pen, plug* (repeat), *prefab, pullover, quiz, screen* (test), *stockpile, totalizator, zipper.*

Slang Terms.

New slang terms form a considerable proportion of our additions, and among them will be noted a large number of service, particularly Air Force Coinages; the newest arm seems to have eclipsed the Navy in fertility of etymological invention. A few of the more recent terms are: *blah, browned off, bunce, chokka, dippy, erk, flap* (fuss), *flat out, flicks* (cinema), *gen, good show, hush-hush, It, Joe Soap, loopy, mike* (microphone), *never-never system, oodles, popsy, scarper, scatty, shemozzle, smashing, sprog, toffee-nose, twerp, whodunit,* and such phrases as *get cracking, get weaving, gone for a Burton, in a spin, it's in the bag, a piece of cake, shoot down in flames, step on it, tear off a strip, couldn't care less.*

Americanisms.

So many of our slang and other new words are borrowed from across the Atlantic that they demand a separate paragraph. A number of the commoner Americanisms had already been incorporated in the work, but fresh additions include *attaboy, bobbysoxer, boloney, bonehead, bughouse, burp, calaboose, chipper, come-back, cutie, didoes, doll up, faze, floosy, 'fraid-cat, G-man, gander* (look), *goo, grip-sack, haywire, hick, high-hat, hoodlum, hooey, hophead, jeep, jinx, josh, juke box, mazuma, mortician, motel, oomph, once-over, pan* (face), *pep, pinch-hitter, punk, rube, scram, screwball, simoleons, simp, smog, snoop, soup-and-fish, spondulics, stand-in, stooge, stuffed shirt, teenager, tuxedo, upstage, wisecrack, wop, yegg,* along with phrases like *cut no ice, hit the hay, out of kilter, stick one's neck out, take a run-out powder, give the frozen mitt.*

Scotticisms.

The opportunity has also been taken to insert a few of the terms in most common use north of the Tweed or wherever there are colonies of

Scots.   Only the most familiar words have been inserted, such as *ben*, *brae*, *callant*, *canny*, *clachan*, *clarts*, *dander*, *dunt*, *fash*, *flyte*, *glaur*, *gowk*, *havers*, *hoots*, *jalouse*, *kenspeckle*, *kittle*, *kyle*, *kyte*, *lum*, *ooss*, *pech*, *ploy*, *quaich*, *scunner*, *shilpit*, *shoogle*, *siller*, *skelp*, *skirl*, *smeddum*, *smirr*, *snowk*, *sonsy*, *speer*, *stot* (bounce), *stour*, *stramash*, *thole*, *thrapple*, *thowless*, *tirrivee*, *wean* (child), *wersh*, *wheesht*.

Nouns of Assemblage.

Among the more interesting old-fashioned additions may be mentioned the collection of nouns of assemblage in paragraph 72.   In addition to the familiar *flock*, *herd*, *drove*, *pack*, there are listed the distinctive terms *sounder* (of swine), *skulk* (of foxes), *pride* (of lions), *charm* (of finches), *flush* (of mallards), *gaggle* (of geese), and *wedge* (of swans).   To old patrons of the work this list should make up for the omission of the tedious and pointless catalogue of different methods of divination, from aeromancy to sciomancy, which was formerly given as a footnote under *Prediction* (511).

Changes and Excisions.

Very few changes have been made in the original grouping.   The list of types of *tobacco-pipe* has been transferred from the *Air-pipe* paragraph to the *Tobacco* section, where it will naturally be more in keeping.   The account of religious terms towards the end of the book has been rearranged so that *dissenters* and *nonconformists* are no longer grouped with *idolaters*, *fire-worshippers*, and other *heathens* under the comprehensive but hardly explicit heading of *Heterodoxy*.   A number of foreign words and phrases have been omitted, particularly the more out-of-the-way Latin phrases, which are no longer so popular as in the days when Classics and culture were synonymous.   Finally, many words, like *caisson*, *chaperon*, *château*, which were formerly italicized as foreign are now printed in ordinary characters, having been accepted as English.

The Index.

A clear idea of the extent of the volume's expansion can be gathered from the size of the index, which occupies 744 columns as against 608 somewhat shorter columns in the last Everyman edition.   The opportunity has been taken of arranging the alphabetization of the references according to the up-to-date 'nothing-before-something' system set out in the pamphlet on Alphabetical Arrangement published by the British Standards Institution.   By this system phrases are inserted in order after their initial word, and hyphened words are reckoned as two except when the initial component is merely a prefix.   Every attempt has been made to render the index as complete as possible, and the process of hunting the required word in the body of the work has been further simplified by the insertion of numerous cross-references in those cases where one paragraph is closely related to others.

                                                                    D. C. B.

1952

NOTE

SINCE the first publication of the single-volume edition in Everyman's Reference Library in 1952 several reprints and a substantial revision in 1962 have taken account of recent developments in English vocabulary.

Two hundred words or meanings have been inserted in their appropriate places throughout the various sections, and corresponding references have been added to the index. In 1955 separate sections were allotted to *Aircraft, Cinema* and *Radio*. The revision of 1962 reflected progress in space travel, radio, transport and jazz music, with such words as *astronaut, lunik, orbital; newscast, teleprompter, transistor; clearway, speedway, traffic warden; bebop, rock-and-roll, skiffle.* Also included were examples of terms coined for types of pompous circumlocution (e.g. *officialese, gobbledygook*), and modern slang.

D. C. Browning having relinquished his editorship, the publishers' staff have continued the process of updating with numerous words in the same sections, and have added many more hitherto omitted from other sections. The present edition of the *Thesaurus* continues to record the neologisms of recent years in the *push-button* age, among them *bent, hippy, junkie, mini-, teach-in, whizz-kid* and everyday phrases such as *cliff-hanging, hive-off, industrial action, lean over backwards, steady as she goes,* and *at the end of the day.*

1971

CONTENTS

CLASS I

WORDS EXPRESSING ABSTRACT RELATIONS

1°. *Being in the Abstract*

1 EXISTENCE (*Substantives*), being, life, vital principle, entity, ens, essence, quiddity, subsistence; co-existence (120).

Reality, actuality, positiveness, absoluteness, fact, truth (494); actualization.

Presence; existence in space (186).

Science of existence, ontology; existentialism.

(*Phrases*) The sober reality; hard fact; matter of fact; the whole truth; no joke.

(*Verbs*) To be, to exist, have being, subsist, live, breathe, stand, abide, remain, stay, obtain, occur, prevail, be so, find itself, take place, eventuate, consist in, lie in; to vegetate, pass the time.

To come into existence, arise, come out, emerge, come forth, appear (448).

To bring into existence, produce, bring forth, discover (161), objectify.

(*Adjectives*) Existing, being, subsisting, subsistent, in being, in existence, extant, living, breathing, obtaining, prevailing, prevalent, current, afoot.

Real, actual, positive, absolute, essential, substantial, substantive, self-existing, self-existent; undestroyed, tangible, not ideal, not imagined, not suppositious, not potential, virtual, effective, unideal, true, authentic, genuine, mere, objective.

(*Adverbs*) Actually, really, absolutely, positively, etc., in fact, *de facto*, *ipso facto*.

(*Phrase*) *In esse*; *cogito ergo sum*.

2 INEXISTENCE (*Substantives*), non-existence, not-being, nonentity, *nihil*, nil, non-subsistence, nullity, vacuity, blank (4), negativeness, absence (187), removal (185).

Annihilation, abeyance, extinction (162); nirvana.

Philosophy of non-existence, nihilism.

(*Phrases*) No such thing; Mrs. Harris; 'men in buckram.'

(*Verbs*) Not to be, not to exist, etc.

To cease to be, pass away, perish, vanish, fade away, dissolve, melt away, disappear (449), to be annihilated, extinct, etc., to die (360), to die out.

(*Phrases*) To have no being; to have no existence; to be null and void; *non est*; to be no more; 'to leave not a rack behind'; to disappear into thin air; to be brought out of existence.

(*Adjectives*) Inexistent, non-existent, non-existing, etc., negative, blank, absent.

Unreal, potential, virtual, baseless, unsubstantial (4), imaginary, ideal, vain, fanciful, unpractical, shadowy, fabulous (515), suppositious (514).

Unborn, uncreated, unbegotten, unproduced, unmade.

Annihilated, destroyed, extinct, gone, lost, perished, melted, dissolved, faded, exhausted, vanished, missing, disappeared, departed, extinct, defunct (360).

(*Adverbs*) Negatively, virtually, etc.

(*Phrase*) *In nubibus.*

2°. Being in the Concrete

3 SUBSTANTIALITY (*Substantives*), hypostasis, person, thing, being, something, existence, entity, reification, corporeity, body, physique, substance, object, article, creature, matter, material, stuff (316), substratum, protoplasm.

Totality of existences, world (318), continuum, plenum.

(*Phrase*) Something or other.

(*Adjectives*) Substantive, substantial, personal, bodily, tangible, true, real, concrete, corporal, corporeal, material, objective, hypostatic.

(*Verbs*) Substantialize, actualize, materialize, reify, embody.

(*Adverbs*) Substantially, etc., essentially.

4 UNSUBSTANTIALITY (*Substantives*), insubstantiality, nothingness, nihility, nothing, naught, damn-all, *nihil*, nil, nix, love, zero, cipher, a duck, duck's-egg, pair of spectacles; nonentity, nobody, no one (187).

A shadow, phantom, phantasm, phantasmagoria, dream, mockery, air, thin air, idle dream, pipe dream, castle in Spain (515), idle talk, ignis fatuus, *fata morgana*, mirage.

Void, vacuum, vacuity, vacancy, voidness, vacuousness, inanity, emptiness, hollowness, blank, chasm, gap, hiatus (198); empty space, ether.

(*Phrases*) Nothing at all; nothing whatever; nothing on earth; nothing under the sun; not a particle.

A man of straw; *vox et praetera nihil*; 'such stuff as dreams are made on.'

(*Verbs*) To vanish, fade, dissolve, evaporate.

(*Adjectives*) Unsubstantial, immaterial, void, vacant, vacuous, blank, null, inane, idle, hollow, airy, visionary (515).

3°. Formal Existence

Internal Conditions

5 INTRINSICALITY (*Substantives*), inbeing, immanence, inherence, inhesion, essence; essentiality, essentialness, subjectiveness, subjectivity, essential part, soul, quintessence, quiddity, gist, pith, core, backbone, marrow, sap, lifeblood; incarnation.

Nature, constitution, character, type, quality (157), temperament, temper, manner, spirit, ethos, habit, humour, grain, endowment, capacity, capability, moods, declensions, features, aspects, specialities, peculiarities (79), particularities, idiosyncrasy, idiocrasy, diagnostics.

(*Verbs*) To be innate, inborn, etc.

(*Phrases*) To be in the blood; to be born like that.

External Conditions

6 EXTRINSICALITY (*Substantives*), extraneousness, objectiveness, objectivity, accident, superficiality, incident.

(*Adjectives*) Derived from without, objective, extrinsic, extrinsical, extraneous, modal, adventitious, adscititious, incidental, accidental, non-essential, outward (220).

Implanted, engrafted.

(*Adverb*) Extrinsically, etc.

(*Adjectives*) Derived from within, subjective, intrinsic, intrinsical, inherent, essential, natural, internal, implanted, inborn, innate, inbred, engrained, inherited, immanent, indwelling, radical, constitutional, congenital, connate, hereditary, instinctive, indigenous.

(*Phrases*) In the grain; in the blood; bred in the bone.

Characteristic, peculiar, qualitative, special, diagnostic (79), invariable.

(*Adverbs*) Intrinsically, subjectively, substantially, at bottom, *au fond*, at the core.

4°. Modal Existence

Absolute

7 STATE (*Substantives*), condition, category, class, kind, estate, lot, case, constitution, habitude, diathesis, mood, temper, morale.

Frame, fabric, structure, texture, contexture (329), conformation, organism.

Mode, modality, schesis, form, shape (240), figure, cut, cast, mould, stamp, set, fit, tone, tenor, trim, turn, guise, fashion, aspect, complexion, style, manner, character, kind, get-up, set-up, format, *genre*.

(*Verbs*) To be in a state, to be in condition, to be on a footing, etc.

To do, fare; to have, possess, enjoy, etc., a state, condition, etc.

To bring into a state, etc. (144).

(*Adjectives*) Conditional, modal, formal, structural, organic, textual.

(*Phrases*) As the matter stands; as things are; such being the case.

(*Adverb*) Conditionally, etc.

Relative

8 CIRCUMSTANCE (*Substantives*), situation, phase, position, posture, attitude, place, point, bearings, terms, fare, regime, footing, standing, status, predicament, contingency, occasion, juncture, conjuncture, emergency, exigence, exigency, crisis, pinch, impasse, pass, push, plight, fix.

(*Phrases*) How the land lies; how the wind blows; how the cat jumps.

(*Adjectives*) Circumstantial; given, conditional, provisional, modal, critical, contingent, incidental (6, 151), circumstanced, placed.

(*Verb Phrases*) To bow before the storm; to take things as they come; to cut one's coat according to the cloth.

(*Adverbs*) In or under the circumstances, conditions, etc.; thus, so; in such a case, contingency, etc.; accordingly, such being the case; since, sith, seeing that, as matters stand, as things go.

Conditionally, provided, if, an if, if so, if so be, if it be so, if it so prove, or turn out, or happen; in the event of, provisionally, unless, without.

(*Phrases*) According to circumstances; as it may happen, or turn out; as the case may be; *pro re nata*; wind and weather permitting; D.V.; rain or shine; sink or swim; at all events; other things being equal; *ceteris paribus*.

SECTION II—RELATION

1° Absolute Relation

9 RELATION (*Substantives*), relationship, bearing, reference, standing, concern, cognation, correlation (12), analogy, affinity, homology, alliance, homogeneity, connection, association, approximation, similarity (17), filiation, affiliation, etc. (11, 166), interest, habitude; relativity.

Relevancy, pertinency, fitness, etc. (646, 23).

Aspect, point of view, comparison (464); ratio, proportion.

Link, tie (45), homologue.

10 Want or absence of relation.

IRRELATION (*Substantives*), disconnection, dissociation, disassociation, misrelation, independence, isolation (44), multifariousness, disproportion; commensurability, irrelevancy; heterogeneity, irreconcilableness (24), impertinence.

(*Verbs*) To have no relation with, or to, to have nothing to do with, to have no business there, not to concern, not to admit of comparison.

(*Verbs*) To be related, have a relation, etc., to relate to, refer to, have reference to, bear upon, regard, concern, touch, affect, have to do with, pertain to, belong to, appertain to, answer to, interest.

To bring into relation with, correlate, associate, connect, affiliate, link (43), bring near (197), homologize; to bring to bear upon.

(*Phrase*) To draw a parallel with.

(*Adjectives*) Relative, correlative, cognate, relating to, relative to, relevant, in relation with, referable to, pertinent (23), germane, belonging to, pat, to the point, apposite, to the purpose, apropos, *ad rem,* just the thing, quite the thing; pertaining to, appertaining to, appurtenant, affiliated, allied, related, implicated, connected, associated, *en rapport,* in touch with, bound up with, homological, homologous.

Approximate, approximative, approximating, proportional, proportionate, proportionable, allusive, comparable, like, similar (17).

(*Adverbs*) Relatively, thereof, as to, about, connecting, concerning, touching, anent, as relates to, with relation to, relating to, as respects, with respect to, in respect of, respecting, as regards, with regard to, regarding, in the matter of, with reference to, according to, while speaking of, apropos of, in connection with, inasmuch as, whereas, in consideration of, in point of, as far as, on the part of, on the score of, under the head of, *in re*; pertinently, etc. (23).

To isolate, separate, detach, disconnect, segregate (44).

(*Adjectives*) Irrelative, irrespective, unrelated, without reference, etc., to, arbitrary, episodic, remote, far-fetched, forced, out of place, out of tune (414), inharmonious, malapropos, irrelevant, foreign to, alien, impertinent, inapposite, extraneous to, strange to, stranger to, independent, parenthetical, incidental, outlandish, exotic, unallied, unconnected, disconnected, unconcerned, adrift, detached, isolated, insular.

Not comparable, incommensurable, inapplicable (24), irreconcilable, heterogeneous (83), unconformable.

(*Phrases*) Foreign to the purpose; nothing to the purpose; having nothing to do with; *nihil ad rem*; neither here nor there; beside the mark; *à propos des bottes*; dragged in by the scruff of the neck.

(*Adverbs*) Parenthetically, by the way, by the by, *obiter dicta, en passant,* incidentally, irrespectively, irrelevantly, etc.

---

11 Relations of kindred.

CONSANGUINITY (*Substantives*), relationship, kindred, blood, parentage (166), filiation, affiliation, lineage, agnation, connection, alliance, family connection, family tie, nepotism.

A kinsman, kinswoman, kinsfolk, kith and kin, relation, relative, friend, sibling, one's people, clan, connection, one's own flesh and blood, brother, sister, father, mother, uncle, aunt, nephew, niece, stepfather, etc., brother-in-law, etc., guid-brother, etc., cousin, cousin-german; first, second cousin; cousin once, twice, etc., removed; grand- or great-grandfather, etc., great-uncle, etc., a near relation, a blood-relation, a distant relation or relative, congener, collateral.

Family, issue, fraternity, sisterhood, brotherhood, parentage, cousinhood, etc.; race, stock, generation, sept, clan, tribe, strain.

(*Verbs*) To be related, to have or claim relationship with.

(*Adjectives*) Related, akin, consanguineous, congeneric, family, kindred, affiliated, allied, collateral, sib, agnate, agnatic, fraternal, of the same blood, nearly or close related, remotely or distantly related.

(*Phrase*) Blood is thicker than water.

12 Double relation.

RECIPROCALNESS (*Substantives*), reciprocity, mutuality, correlation, correlativeness, interdependence, interchange, interaction, reciprocation, etc. (148), alternation (149), barter (794).

(*Verbs*) To reciprocate, alternate, interchange, interact, exchange, counterchange, interdepend.

(*Adjectives*) Reciprocal, mutual, common, correlative, alternate, alternative; interchangeable, interdependent, international.

(*Adverbs*) Reciprocally, mutually, etc.

(*Phrases*) *Mutatis mutandis*; each other; vice versa; turn and turn about.

---

13 IDENTITY (*Substantives*), sameness, oneness, coincidence, coalescence, convertibility; selfness, self, ego, oneself, number one; identification, monotony; equality (27), tautology (104).

Synonym; facsimile (21), counterpart (17).

(*Verbs*) To be identical, to be the same, etc., to coincide, to coalesce.

To render the same.

To recognize the identity of, to identify, recognize.

(*Adjectives*) Identical, identic, same, self, selfsame, very same, no other, ilk, one and the same, ditto, unaltered, coincident, coinciding, coessential, coalescing, coalescent, indistinguishable, tantamount, equivalent, equipollent, convertible, much the same.

(*Adverbs*) All one, all the same, *ibidem*, ibid, identically, likewise.

(*Phrases*) *Semper idem*; *toujours la même chose*; *alter ego*; on all fours; much of a muchness.

14 Non-coincidence.

CONTRARIETY (*Substantives*), contrast, foil, set-off, antithesis, contradiction, opposition, oppositeness, antagonism (179, 708), distinction (15).

Inversion, reversion (218).

The opposite, the reverse, inverse, converse, antonym, the antipodes (237).

(*Phrases*) The reverse of the medal; the other side of the shield; the tables being turned.

(*Verbs*) To be contrary, etc., to contrast with, contradict, contravene, oppose, negate, antagonize, invert, reverse, turn the tables, to militate against.

(*Adjectives*) Contrary, opposite, counter, converse, reverse, antithetical, opposed, antipodean, antagonistic, opposing, conflicting, inconsistent, contradictory, contrarious, contrariant, negative.

(*Phrases*) Differing *toto caelo*; diametrically opposite; as black to white; light to darkness; fire to water; worlds apart; poles asunder.

(*Adverbs*) Contrarily, contrariously, contrariwise, *per contra*, oppositely, *vice versa*, on the contrary, *tout au contraire*, quite the contrary, no such thing.

---

15 DIFFERENCE (*Substantives*), variance, variation, variety, diversity, modification, allotropy, shade of difference, nuance; deviation, divergence, divarication (291), disagreement (24), dissimilarity (18), disparity (28).

Distinction, contradistinction, differentiation, discrimination (465); a nice or fine or subtle distinction.

(*Phrases*) A very different thing; a *tertium quid*; a horse of a different colour; another pair of shoes.

(*Verbs*) To be different, etc., to differ, vary, mismatch, contrast, differ *toto caelo*.

To render different, etc., to vary, change, modify, varify, diversity, etc. (140).

To distinguish, differentiate, severalize (465), split hairs, discriminate.

(*Adjectives*) Different, differing, disparate, heterogeneous, heteromorphic, allotropic, varying, distinguishable, discriminative, varied, modified, diversified, deviating, diverging, devious, disagreeing (24), various, divers, all manner of, multifarious, multiform, variform (81), variegated (440), diacritical.

Other, another, other-guess, not the same.

Unmatched, widely apart, changed (140).

(*Phrase*) As different as chalk is from cheese.

(*Adverbs*) Differently, variously, otherwise.

2°. *Continuous Relation*

16 UNIFORMITY (*Substantives*), homogeneity, homogeneousness, consistency, connaturality, conformity (82), homology, accordance, agreement (23), regularity (58), routine, monotony, constancy.

(*Verbs*) To be uniform, etc., to accord with, harmonize with, hang together, go together.

To become uniform, conform with, fall in with, follow suit.

To render uniform, to assimilate, level, smooth (255).

(*Adjectives*) Uniform, homogeneous, homologous, of a piece, of a kind, consistent, connatural, monotonous, even, unvarying, flat, level, constant.

(*Adverbs*) Uniformly, uniformly with, conformably (82), consistently with, in unison with, in harmony with, in conformity with, according to (23).

Regularly, at regular intervals, invariably, constantly, always, without exception.

(*Phrases*) In a rut (or groove); *ab uno disce omnes*; 'forty feeding like one.'

16A Absence or want of uniformity. NON-UNIFORMITY (*Substantives*), variety, multiformity (81), diversity, unevenness, irregularity, unconformity (83).

(*Adjectives*) Multiform, multifarious, various (81), diversified, inconsistent, of various kinds.

3°. *Partial Relation*

17 SIMILARITY (*Substantives*), resemblance, likeness, similitude, affinity, semblance, approximation, parallelism (216), analogy, brotherhood, family likeness; alliteration, head-rhyme, rhyme, pun, assonance, repetition (104), reproduction.

An analogue, copy (21), the like, facsimile, match, double, pendant, fellow, pair, mate, twin, *alter ego*, parallel, counterpart, brother, sister; simile, metaphor (521), resemblance, imitation (19).

(*Phrases*) One's second self; *Arcades ambo*; birds of a feather; *et hoc genus omne*; a chip of the old block; the very spit (and image) of.

(*Verbs*) To be similar, like, resembling, etc., to look like, resemble, bear resemblance, favour, approximate, parallel, match, imitate, take

18 DISSIMILARITY (*Substantives*), unlikeness, dissimilitude, diversity, divergence, difference (15), novelty (123), originality (515), disparity (28).

(*Verbs*) To be unlike, etc., to vary (15, 20).

To render unlike, to diversify (140).

(*Phrase*) To strike out something new.

(*Adjectives*) Dissimilar, unlike, disparate, of a different kind, class, etc. (75); diversified, novel, new (123), unmatched, unique, unprecedented (83).

(*Phrases*) Nothing of the kind; far from it; cast in a different mould; as different as chalk is from cheese.

(*Adverb*) Otherwise.

after (19), **represent,** simulate, personate, savour of, have a flavour of, favour, feature.

To render similar, assimilate, approximate, reproduce, bring near, copy, plagiarize.

(*Adjectives*) Similar, like, alike, resembling, twin, analogous, analogical, parallel, allied to, of a piece, such as, connatural, congener, matching, conformable, on all fours with.

Near, something like, suchlike, mock, pseudo, simulating, representing, approximating, a show of, a kind of, a sort of.

Exact, accurate, true, faithful, close, speaking, lifelike, breathing.

(*Phrases*) True to nature; to the life; for all the world like; like as two peas; *comme deux gouttes d'eau*; cast in the same mould; like father, like son.

(*Adverbs*) As if, so to speak, as it were, quasi, as if it were, just as, after, in the fashion or manner of, *à la*.

19 IMITATION (*Substantives*), assimilation, copying, transcription, transcribing, following, repetition (104), duplication, reduplication, quotation, reproduction.

Mockery, mocking, mimicry, mimicking, echoing, reflection, simulation, counterfeiting, plagiarism, forgery, fake, fakement, acting, personation, impersonation, representation (554), copy (21), parody, paraphrase, travesty, burlesque, semblance, mimesis.

An imitator, mimic, impersonator, echo, cuckoo, parrot, ape, monkey, mocking-bird.

Plagiary, plagiarist, forger, counterfeiter.

(*Phrase*) *O imitatores, servum pecus.*

20 NON-IMITATION (*Substantives*), originality, inventiveness, novelty.

(*Adjectives*) Unimitated, uncopied, unmatched, unparalleled, inimitable, unique, original, novel.

(*Verb*) To originate.

VARIATION (*Substantives*), alteration, modification, difference (15), change (140), deviation (279), divergence (291); moods and tenses.

(*Verbs*) To vary, modify, change, alter, diversify (140).

(*Phrase*) To steer clear of.

(*Adjectives*) Varied, modified, diversified, etc.

(*Adverbs*) **Variously, in all manner of ways.**

(*Verbs*) To imitate, copy, plagiarize, forge, fake, reproduce, photograph, repeat (104), echo, re-echo, transcribe, match, parallel, emulate, do like, take off, hit off, reflect, mirror, model after (554).

To mock, mimic, ape, simulate, personate, impersonate (554), act, represent, adumbrate, counterfeit, parody, travesty, caricature, burlesque.

(*Phrases*) To take or catch a likeness; to take after; to follow or tread in the steps of, or in the footsteps of; to take a leaf out of another's book; to follow suit; to go with the stream; to be in the fashion.

(*Adjectives*) Imitated, copied, matched, repeated, paralleled, mock, mimic, parodied, etc., modelled after, moulded on, paraphrastic, imitative, mimetic, slavish, mechanical, synthetic, second-hand, imitable.

(*Adverbs*) Literally, verbatim, to the letter, *literatim, sic, totidem verbis*, so to speak, in so many words, word for word, *mot à mot* (562).

21 Result of imitation.

COPY (*Substantives*), facsimile, counterpart, effigies, effigy, form, likeness, similitude, semblance, reflex,

22 Thing copied.

PROTOTYPE (*Substantives*), original, model, pattern, standard, type, scale, scantling, archetype, protoplast,

portrait, photograph (556), photostat, microfilm, enlargement, miniature, study, cast, autotype, electrotype, imitation, replica, representation, adumbration.

Duplicate, transcript, transcription, repetition (104), réchauffé,
reflection, shadow, record, recording.

Rough copy, fair copy, revise, carbon copy, tracing, rubbing, squeeze,
draft or draught, proof, pull, reprint.

Counterfeit, parody, caricature, burlesque, travesty, paraphrase,
forgery.

(*Phrases*) A second edition; a twice-told tale.

antitype, module, exemplar, example,
ensample, protoplast, paradigm,
fugleman, lay figure.

Text, copy, design, plan, blue-
print, keynote.

Mould, matrix, last, plasm, proplasm, mint, die, seal, stamp, negative.

(*Verbs*) To set a copy, to set an
example.

4°. *General Relation*

23 AGREEMENT (*Substantives*),
accord, accordance, unison, uniformity, harmony, union, concord,
concert, concordance (714), cognation, conformity, conformance (82),
consonance, consentaneousness, consensus, consistency, congruity, con-
gruence, congeniality, correspondence
keeping, parallelism.

Fitness, pertinence, suitableness,
adaptation, meetness, patness, relevancy, aptness, aptitude, coaptation,
propriety, apposition, appositeness,
reconcilableness, applicability, appli-
cableness, admissibility, commensurability, compatibility, adaptability.

Adaptation, adjustment, graduation, accommodation, reconciliation,
reconcilement, concurrence (178),
consent (488), co-operation (709).

(*Verbs*) To be accordant, to agree,
accord (714), correspond, tally, jibe,
respond, harmonize, match, suit, fit,
befit, hit, fall in with, chime in with,
quadrate with, square with, cancel
with, comport with, assimilate, unite
with.

To render accordant, to adapt, accommodate, adjust, reconcile, fadge,
dovetail, dress, square, regulate, comport, graduate, gradate, grade.

(*Phrases*) To become one; to fit like
a glove; to suit one to a T.

(*Adjectives*) Agreeing, accordant,
concordant, consonant, congruous,
consentaneous, consentient, corresponding, correspondent, congenial,

24 DISAGREEMENT (*Substantives*),
discord, discordance, dissonance, dis-
harmony, dissidence, discrepancy,
unconformity, disconformity, nonconformity, incongruity, incongru-
ence, *mésalliance*, discongruity, jarring, clashing, jostling (713), inconsistency, inconsonance, disparity,
disproportion, disproportionateness,
variance, divergence, jar, misfit.

Unfitness, repugnance, unsuitable-
ness, unsuitability, unaptness, ineptitude, inaptness, impropriety,
inapplicability, inadmissibility, irreconcilableness, irreconcilability, in-
commensurability, inconcinnity, in-
compatability, inadaptability, interference, intrusion, irrelation (10).

(*Verbs*) To disagree, belie, clash,
jar, oppose (708), interfere, jostle
(713), intrude.

(*Phrase*) To have no business there.

(*Adjectives*) Disagreeing, discordant,
discrepant, jarring, clashing, repugnant, incompatible, irreconcilable,
intransigent, inconsistent with, unconformable, incongruous, dispropor-
tionate, disproportioned, unproportioned, inharmonious, inconsonant,
mismatched, misjoined, misjudged,
unconsonant, incommensurable, incommensurate, divergent (291).

Unapt, inapt, inept, inappropriate,
improper, unsuited, unsuitable, inapposite, inapplicable, irrelevant, not
pertinent, impertinent, malapropos,
ill-timed, intrusive, clumsy, unfit,

harmonizing, harmonious with, tallying with, conformable with, in accordance with, in harmony with, in unison with, in keeping with, squaring with, quadrating with, falling in with, of one mind, of a piece, consistent with, compatible, reconcilable with, commensurate.

Apt, apposite, pertinent, germane, relating to, pat, bearing upon (9), applicable, relevant, fit, fitting, suitable, happy, felicitous, proper, meet, appropriate, suiting, befitting, becoming, seasonable, deft, accommodating, topical.

(*Phrases*) The cap fits; to the point; to the purpose; *rem acu tetigisti*; at home; in one's element.

unfitting, unbefitting, unbecoming, misplaced, forced, unseasonable, far fetched, inadmissible, uncongenial, ill-assorted, ill-sorted, repugnant to, unaccommodating, irreducible.

(*Phrases*) Out of season; out of character; out of keeping; out of joint; out of tune; out of place; out of one's element; at odds; a fish out of water.

(*Adverbs*) Discordantly, etc.; at variance with, in defiance of, in contempt of, in spite of, despite.

Section III—Quantity

1°. *Simple Quantity*

25 Absolute quantity.

QUANTITY. (*Substantives*), magnitude (192), amplitude, size, mass, amount, volume, area, quantum, measure, substance.

Science of quantity, mathematics.

Definite or finite quantity, handful, mouthful, spoonful, bucketful, pailful, etc.; stock, batch, lot.

(*Adjective*) Quantitative.

(*Phrase*) To the tune of.

---

26 Relative quantity.

DEGREE (*Substantives*), grade, gradation, extent, measure, ratio, stint, standard, height, pitch, reach, sweep, radius, amplitude, magnitude, water, calibre, range, scope, shade, tenor, compass, sphere, rank, station, standing, rate, way, sort.

Point, mark, stage, step, position, slot, peg; term (71).

Intensity, might, fullness, strength (31), conversion (144), limit (233).

(*Adjectives*) Comparative, gradual, shading off.

(*Adverbs*) By degrees, gradually, *gradatim*, inasmuch, *pro tanto*, however, howsoever, step by step, rung by rung, bit by bit, little by little, by inches, inch by inch, by slow degrees, by little and little, in some degree, to some extent.

2°. *Comparative Quantity*

27 Sameness of quantity or degree.

EQUALITY (*Substantives*), parity, co-extension, evenness, equipoise, level, balance, equivalence, equipollence, equilibrium, poise, equiponderance, par, quits.

Equalization, equation, equilibration, co-ordination, adjustment, symmetry.

28 Difference of quantity or degree.

INEQUALITY (*Substantives*), disparity, imparity, imbalance, odds, handicap, bisque, difference (15), unevenness.

Preponderance, preponderation, inclination of the balance, advantage, prevalence, partiality.

Superiority (33), a casting vote; inferiority (34).

A drawn game or battle, a dead heat, a draw, a tie.

A match, peer, compeer, equal, mate, fellow, brother (17), equivalent, makeweight.

(*Phrases*) A distinction without a difference; a photo finish.

(*Verbs*) To be equal, etc., to equal, match, come up to, keep pace with; come to, amount to, balance, cope with.

To render equal, equalize, level, balance, equate, aequiparate, trim, dress, adjust, fit, accommodate, poise, square; to readjust, equipoise, equilibrate, set against.

(*Phrases*) To be or lie on a level with; to come to the same thing.

To strike a balance; to establish or restore equality; to stretch on the bed of Procrustes; to cry quits.

(*Verbs*) To be unequal, etc., to preponderate, outweigh, outbalance, overbalance, prevail, countervail, predominate, overmatch, outmatch (33).

To fall short of, to want (304), not to come up to.

(*Phrases*) To have or give the advantage; to turn the scale; to kick the beam; to topple over.

(*Adjectives*) Unequal, uneven, disparate, partial, unbalanced, overbalanced, top-heavy, lopsided, preponderating, outweighing, prevailing.

(*Phrases*) More than a match for; above par; below par; *haud passibus aequis.*

(*Adjectives*) Equal, even, quit, level, coequal, co-ordinate, equivalent, synonymous, tantamount, convertible, equipollent, equiponderant, equiponderous, square.

Rendered equal, equalized, equated, drawn, poised, levelled, balanced, symmetrical, trimmed, dressed.

(*Phrases*) On a par with; on a level with; much of a muchness; as broad as it is long; as good as; all the same; all one; six to one and half a dozen of the other; not a pin to choose between them; tarred with the same brush; diamond cut diamond.

(*Adverbs*) *Pari passu,* equally, symmetrically, *ad eundem,* practically, to all intents and purposes, neck and neck.

29 Mean (*Substantives*), medium, intermedium, compromise, average, norm, balance, middle (68), *via media, juste milieu.*

Neutrality, mediocrity, middle course, shuffling.

(*Phrases*) The golden mean; the average man; the man in the street.

(*Verbs*) To compromise, pair off, cancel out.

(*Phrases*) To sit on the fence; split the difference; strike a balance; take the average; reduce to a mean; to take a safe course.

(*Adjectives*) Mean, intermediate, middle, median, normal, average, mediocre, middling, ordinary (82), neutral.

(*Adverb phrases*) On an average; in the long run; half-way; taking the one with the other; taking all things together; in round numbers.

30 COMPENSATION (*Substantives*), equation, commutation, compromise (774), idemnification, neutralization, nullification, counteraction (179), recoil (277), atonement (952).

A set-off, offset, makeweight, counterpoise, ballast, indemnity, hush-money, amends, equivalent.

(*Phrases*) Measure for measure; give and take; *quid pro quo*; tit for tat.

(*Verbs*) To compensate, make up for, indemnify, countervail, counterpoise, balance, compromise, outbalance, overbalance, counterbalance, counteract, set off, hedge, redeem, neutralize (27), cover.

(*Phrases*) To make good; split the difference; fill up; make amends.

(*Adjectives*) Compensating, compensatory, countervailing, etc., equivalent, equipollent (27).

(*Phrase*) In the opposite scale.

(*Adverbs*) However, yet, but, still, all the same, for all that, nevertheless, none the less, notwithstanding, be that as it may, on the other hand, although, though, albeit, *per contra*.

(*Phrases*) As broad as it's long; taking one thing with another; it is an ill wind that blows nobody any good.

Quantity by Comparison with a Standard

31 GREATNESS (*Substantives*), largeness, magnitude, size (192), multitude (102), fullness, vastness, immensity, enormity, infinity (105), intensity (26), importance (642), strength.

A large quantity, deal, power, world, macrocosm, mass, heap (72), pile, sight, pot, volume, peck, bushel, load, stack, cart-load, wagon-load, truck-load, ship-load, cargo, lot, flood, spring tide, mobs, bags, oodles, abundance (639), wholesale, store (636).

The greater part (50).

(*Verbs*) To be great, etc., run high, soar, tower, transcend, rise, carry to a great height (305).

(*Phrases*) To know no bounds; to break the record.

(*Adjectives*) Great, gross, large, considerable, big, ample, above par, huge, full, saturated, plenary, deep, signal, extensive, sound, passing, goodly, famous, noteworthy, noble, heavy, precious, mighty (157), arch, sad, piteous, arrant, red-hot, downright, utter, uttermost, crass, lamentable, consummate, rank, thoroughpaced, thorough-going, sovereign, unparalleled, matchless, unapproached, extraordinary, intense, extreme, pronounced, unsurpassed, unsurpassable.

Vast, immense, enormous, towering, inordinate, severe, excessive, monstrous, shocking, extravagant, exorbitant, outrageous, whacking, thumping, glaring, flagrant, preposterous, egregious, overgrown, stupendous, monumental, prodigious, marked, pointed, remarkable, astonishing, surprising (870), incredible, marvellous, transcendent,

32 SMALLNESS (*Substantives*), littleness, minuteness (193), tenuity, scantness, scantiness, slenderness, meanness, mediocrity, insignificance (643), paucity, fewness (103).

A small quantity, modicum, atom, particle, molecule, corpuscle, microcosm, jot, iota, dot, speck, mote, gleam, scintilla, spark, ace, minutiae, thought, idea, suspicion, *soupçon*, whit, tittle, shade, shadow, touch, cast, taste, grain, scruple, spice, sprinkling, drop, droplet, driblet, globule, minim, dash, smack, nip, sip, scantling, dole, scrap, mite, slip, snippet, tag, bit, morsel, crumb, paring, shaving (51), trifle, thimbleful, toothful, spoonful, cupful, mouthful, handful, fistful.

Fineness, a finite quantity.

(*Phrases*) The shadow of a shade; a drop in a bucket or in the ocean.

(*Verbs*) To be small, etc., to run low, diminish, shrink, decrease (36), contract (195).

(*Phrases*) To lie in a nutshell; to pass muster.

(*Adjectives*) Small, little, wee, scant, inconsiderable, diminutive, minute (193), tiny, minikin, puny, petty, sorry, miserable, shabby, wretched, paltry (643), weak (160), slender, feeble, faint, slight, scrappy, fiddling, trivial, scanty, light, trifling, moderate, low, mean, mediocre, passable, passing, light, sparing.

Below par, below the mark, under the mark, at a low ebb, imperfect, unfinished, partial (651), inappreciable, evanescent, infinitesimal, atomic, homoeopathic.

Mere, simple, sheer, bare.

incomparable, tremendous, terrific, formidable, amazing, phenomenal, superhuman, titanic, immoderate.

Indefinite, boundless, unbounded, unlimited, incalculable, illimitable, immeasurable, infinite, unapproachable, unutterable, indescribable, unspeakable, inexpressible, beyond expression, swingeing, unconscionable, fabulous, uncommon, unusual (83).

Undiminished, unrestricted, unabated, unreduced, unmitigated, unredeemed, untempered.

Absolute, positive, decided, staring, unequivocal, serious, grave, essential, perfect, finished, completed, abundant (639).

(*Adverbs*) In a great degree, much, muckle, well, considerably, largely, grossly, greatly, very, very much, a deal, not a little, no end, pretty, pretty well, enough, richly, to a large extent, to a great extent, ever so, mainly, ever so much, on a large scale, insomuch, all lengths, wholesale, in a great measure.

In a positive degree, truly (494), positively, verily, really, indeed, actually, in fact, fairly, assuredly, decidedly, surely, clearly, obviously, unequivocally, purely, absolutely, seriously, essentially, fundamentally, radically, downright, in grain, altogether, entirely, completely.

In a comparative degree, comparatively, *pro tanto*, as good as, to say the least, above all, most, of all things, pre-eminently.

(*Adverbs*) In a small degree, on a small scale, to a small extent, a wee bit, something, somewhat, next to nothing, little, inconsiderably, slightly, so-so, minutely, faintly, feebly, lightly, imperfectly, scantily, shabbily, miserably, wretchedly, sparingly, weakly, slenderly, modestly.

In a limited degree, in a certain degree, to a certain degree or extent, partially, in part, some, somewhat, rather, in some degree, in some measure, something, simply, only, purely, merely, in a manner, at least, at most, ever so little, thus far, *pro tanto*, next to nothing.

Almost, nearly, well-nigh, all but, short of, not quite, close upon, near the mark.

In an uncertain degree, about, thereabouts, scarcely, hardly, barely, somewhere about, say, more or less, *à peu près*, there or thereabouts.

In no degree, noways, nowise, nohow, in no wise, by no means, not in the least, not at all, not a bit, not a bit of it, not a whit, not a jot, in no respect, by no manner of means, on no account.

(*Phrases*) As little as may be; after a fashion; in a way.

Within an ace of; on the brink of; next door to; a close shave (or call).

———

In a complete degree, completely (52), altogether, quite, entirely, wholly, totally, *in toto*, *toto coelo*, utterly, thoroughly, out and out, outright, out and away, fairly, clean, to the full, in every respect, *sous tous les rapports*, in all respects, on all accounts, nicely, perfectly, fully, amply, richly, wholesale, abundantly, consummately, widely, as . . . as . . . can be, every inch, *à fond*, *de fond*, far and wide, over head and ears, to the backbone, through and through, *ne plus ultra*.

In a greater degree, even, yea, *a fortiori*, still more.

In a high degree, highly, deeply, strongly, mighty, mightily, powerfully (157), profoundly, superlatively, ultra, in the extreme, extremely, exceedingly, excessively, consumedly, sorely, intensely, exquisitely, acutely, soundly, vastly, hugely, immensely, enormously, stupendously, passing, surpassing, supremely, beyond measure, immoderately, monstrously, inordinately, tremendously, over head and ears, extraordinarily, exorbitantly, indefinitely, immeasurably, unspeakably, inexpressibly, ineffably, unutterably, incalculably, infinitely, unsurpassably.

In a marked degree, particularly, remarkably, singularly, uncommonly, unusually, peculiarly, notably, *par excellence*, eminently, pre-eminently, superlatively, signally, famously, egregiously, prominently, glaringly, emphatically, strangely, wonderfully, amazingly, surprisingly, astonishingly, prodigiously, monstrously, incredibly, inconceivably, marvellously, awfully, stupendously.

In a violent degree, violently, severely, furiously, desperately, tremendously, outrageously, extravagantly, confoundedly, deucedly, devilishly, diabolically, with a vengeance, *à outrance*, like mad (173).

In a painful degree, sadly, grievously, woefully, wretchedly, piteously, sorely, lamentably, shockingly, frightfully, dreadfully, fearfully, terribly, horribly.

Quantity by Comparison with a Similar Object

33 SUPERIORITY (*Substantives*), majority, supremacy, primacy, advantage, preponderance, excess (641), prevalence, pre-eminence, championship.

Maximum, acme, climax, zenith, summit, utmost height, record, culminating point (210), the height of, lion's share, overweight.

(*Phrases*) A Triton among the minnows; cock of the walk; *ne plus ultra; summum bonum.*

(*Verbs*) To be superior, etc.; to exceed, surpass, excel, eclipse, transcend, top, overtop, o'ertop, cap, beat, cut out, outclass, override, outmatch, outbalance, overbalance, overweigh, overshadow, outdo; preponderate, predominate, prevail.

To render larger, magnify (194).

(*Phrases*) To have the advantage of; to have the upper hand; to bear the palm; to have one cold; to beat hollow; to take the shine out of; to throw into the shade; to be a cut above.

(*Adjectives*) Superior, greater, major, higher, surpassing, exceeding, excelling, passing, ultra, vaulting, transcending, transcendent, unequalled, unsurpassed, peerless, matchless, unparalleled, without parallel.

Supreme, greatest, utmost, paramount, pre-eminent, foremost, crowning, sovereign, culminating, superlative, topmost, top-hole, highest, first-rate, champion, A1, the last word, the limit.

(*Phrases*) *Facile princeps; nulli secundus; primus inter pares.*

(*Adverbs*) Beyond, more, over and above the mark, above par, over and above, at the top of the scale, at its height.

In a superior degree, eminently, pre-eminently, egregiously, prominently, superlatively, supremely, above all, of all things, principally, especially, particularly, peculiarly, *par excellence, a fortiori.*

34 INFERIORITY (*Substantives*), minority, subordination, shortcoming (304); deficiency, minimum.

(*Verbs*) To be less, inferior, etc., to fall or come short of, not to pass (304); to want, be wanting.

To become smaller, to render smaller (195); to subordinate.

(*Phrases*) To be thrown into the shade; to hide one's diminished head; to give a person best; to play second fiddle.

(*Adjectives*) Inferior, deficient, smaller, minor, less, lesser, lower, sub, subordinate, subaltern, secondary, second-rate, second-best.

Least, smallest, wee-est, minutest, etc., lowest.

(*Phrases*) Weighed in the balance and found wanting; not fit to hold a candle to.

(*Adverbs*) Less, under or below the mark, below par, at the bottom of the scale, at a low ebb, short of, at a disadvantage.

Changes in Quantity

35 INCREASE (*Substantives*), augmentation, enlargement, extension, dilatation (194), increment, accretion, development, rise, growth, swell, swelling, expansion, aggrandizement, aggravation, rise, exacerbation, spread, climax, exaggeration, diffusion (73), flood-tide; accession (37).

(*Verbs*) To increase, augment, enlarge, amplify, extend, dilate, swell, wax, expand, grow, stretch, shoot up, mushroom, rise, run up, sprout, burgeon, advance, spread, gather head, aggrandize, add, superadd, raise, heighten, strengthen, greaten, exalt, enhance, magnify, redouble, aggravate, exaggerate, exasperate, exacerbate, escalate,

(*Phrases*) To add fuel to the flame; to pour oil on the flames.

(*Adjectives*) Increased, augmented, enlarged, etc., undiminished; cumulative; additional (37).

(*Adverb*) Crescendo.

36 NON-INCREASE.

DECREASE (*Substantives*) diminution, depreciation, lessening, reduction, abatement, bating, declension, falling off, dwindling, contraction (195), shrinking, attentuation, extenuation, anticlimax, abridgment, curtailment (201), coarctation, narrowing; deduction (38).

Subsidence, wane, ebb, decrement,

(*Verbs*) To decrease, diminish, lessen, dwindle, decay, crumble, shrink, contract, shrivel, fall off, fall away, waste, wear, wane, ebb, subside, decline, languish, wear off, run low, grow downward.

To abridge, reduce, curtail, cut down, pare down, subtract, shorten, cut short, dock (201), bate, abate, fritter away, attenuate, extenuate, lower, weaken, dwarf; to mitigate (174), to throw in the shade.

(*Phrase*) To hide its diminished head.

(*Adjectives*) Decreased, diminished, lessened, etc., shorn, short by, decreasing, on the wane.

(*Adverbs*) *Diminuendo, decrescendo.*

3°. Conjunctive Quantity

37 ADDITION (*Substantives*) adjection, introduction, superinduction, annexation, superposition, superaddition, subjunction, supervention, increment, accession, superfetation, corollary, reinforcement, supplement, accompaniment (88), interposition (228), insertion (300).

(*Verbs*) To add, annex, affix, superadd, supplement, reinforce, subjoin, superpose, throw in, clap on, tack to, append, tag, engraft, saddle on, saddle with, superinduce, introduce, work in, interleave, extra-illustrate, grangerize.

To become added, to accrue, advene, supervene.

(*Phrase*) To swell the ranks of.

(*Adjectives*) Added, annexed, etc., additional, supplementary, supplemental, suppletory, subjunctive,

38 NON-ADDITION.

SUBDUCTION (*Substantives*), subtraction, abstraction, deduction, deducement, retrenchment, removal, elimination, ablation (789), purgation, curtailment, etc. (36), garbling, mutilation, truncation, abscission, excision, amputation, detruncation, sublation, castration, apocope.

Subtrahend, minuend; decrement, discount.

(*Verbs*) To subduct, exclude, deduct, subtract, abscind, retrench, remove, withdraw, eliminate, bate, detract, deduce, take away, deprive of, curtail (36), garble, truncate, mutilate, eviscerate, exenterate, detruncate, castrate, spay, geld, purge, amputate, cut off, excise, cut out, dock, lop, prune, pare, dress, clip, thin, shear, decimate, abrade (330).

adscititious, additive, accessory, cumulative.

(*Adverbs*) Additionally, in addition, more, *plus*, extra, and, also, likewise, too, furthermore, forby, item, and also, and eke, else, besides, to boot, etcetera, and so forth, into the bargain, over and above, moreover.

(*Adjectives*) Subtracted, deducted, etc., subtractive.

(*Adverbs*) In deduction, etc., less, *minus*, without, except, excepting, with the exception of, but for, barring, save, exclusive of, save and except (83).

With, together with, withal, along with, including, inclusive, as well as, not to mention, to say nothing of; jointly, conjointly (43).

---

39 Thing added.

ADJUNCT (*Substantives*), additament, addition, affix, appendage, annex, suffix, postfix, inflexion, augment, increment, augmentation, accessory, item, garnish, sauce, supplement, extra, bonus (810), adjective, addendum, complement, corollary, continuation, increment, reinforcement, pendant, apanage.

Sequel (65), postscript, codicil, envoy, rider, corollary, heel-piece, tag, tab, skirt, flap, lappet, trappings, tail, tailpiece (67), queue, train, suite, cortège, accompaniment (88).

(*Phrase*) More last words.

40 Thing remaining.

REMAINDER (*Substantives*), residue, remains, remnant, the rest, relics, leavings, heel-tap, odds and ends, cheese-parings, candle-ends, off-scourings, orts.

Residuum, *caput mortuum*, dregs, refuse (645), scum, recrement (653), ashes, dross, cinders, slag, sediment, silt, alluvium, stubble; slough, exuviae, result, educt.

Surplus, overplus, surplusage, superfluity, excess (641), balance, complement, fag-end, stump, butt, rump, wreck, wreckage, ruins, skeleton.

(*Verbs*) To remain, be left, be left behind, exceed, survive.

(*Adjectives*) Remaining, left, left behind, residual, exuvial, residuary, sedimentary, outstanding, net, cast off, odd, over, unconsumed, surviving, outlying.

Superfluous, over and above, exceeding, redundant (641), supernumerary.

---

41 Forming a whole without coherence.

MIXTURE (*Substantives*), admixture, commixture, commixtion, intermixture, alloyage, marriage, miscegenation.

Impregnation, infusion, infiltration, diffusion, suffusion, interspersion, transfusion, seasoning, sprinkling, interlarding, interpolation, interposition (228), intrusion; adulteration, sophistication.

Thing mixed, a touch, spice, tinge, tincture, dash, smack, sprinkling, seasoning, infusion, suspicion, *soupçon*, shade, bit, portion, dose.

Compound resulting from mixture, blend, alloy, amalgam, magma, *mélange*, half and half, hybrid, *tertium quid*, miscellany, medley,

42 Freedom from mixture.

SIMPLENESS (*Substantives*), singleness, purity, clearness, homogeneity.

Purification (652), elimination, sifting, winnowing.

(*Verbs*) To render simple, simplify, sift, winnow, bolt, screen, sort, eliminate; to separate, disjoin (44).

To purify (652).

(*Adjectives*) Simple, uniform, of a piece, homogeneous, single, pure, clear, sheer, blank, neat, absolute, elemental, elementary; unmixed, unmingled, untinged, unblended, uncombined, uncompounded, undecomposed, unadulterated, unsophisticated, undiluted, straight.

Free from, exempt from.

(*Phrase*) Pure and simple.

---

pastiche, pasticcio, patchwork, odds and ends; farrago, jumble (59), mess, salad, sauce, hash, hodge-podge or hotchpotch or hotchpot, mash, mish-mash, job lot, omnium gatherum, gallimaufry, olla podrida, olio, salmagundi, pot-pourri, Noah's ark, cauldron, marquetry, mosaic (440), complex.

A cross, hybrid, mongrel, half-breed, Eurasian, mulatto, quadroon, octoroon, sambo.

(*Phrases*) A mingled yarn; a scratch team.

(*Verbs*) To mix, commix, immix, intermix, associate, join (43), mingle, commingle, intermingle, bemingle, interlard, intersperse, interpose, interpolate (228); shuffle together, hash up, huddle together, deal, pound together, stir up, knead, brew, jumble (59); impregnate with.

To be mixed, to get among, to be entangled with.

To instil, imbue, infuse, infiltrate, dash, tinge, tincture, season, sprinkle, besprinkle, suffuse, transfuse, attemper, medicate, blend, alloy, amalgamate, compound (48), adulterate, sophisticate, infect, cross, intercross, interbreed, interblend.

(*Adjectives*) Mixed, mingled, intermixed, etc., motley, miscellaneous, promiscuous; complex, composite, mixed up with, half-and-half, linsey-woolsey, mongrel, heterogeneous; miscible.

---

43 JUNCTION (*Substantives*), joining, joinder, union, connection, connecting, hook-up, conjunction, conjugation, annexion, annexation, annexment, attachment, compagination, astriction, ligation, alligation, colligation, fastening, linking, accouplement, coupling, matrimony (903), grafting; infibulation, inosculation, symphysis, anastomosis, association (72), concatenation, communication, approach (197).

Joint, join, juncture, pivot, hinge, suture, articulation, commissure, mitre, seam, stitch, meeting, reunion, mortise.

Closeness, firmness, tightness, compactness, attachment, communication.

(*Verbs*) To join, conjoin, unite, connect, associate, put together, embody, re-embody, hold together, lump together, pack, fix together, attach, affix, saddle on, fasten, bind, secure, make fast, grapple, moor, clench (or clinch), catch, tie, pinion, strap, sew, lace, string, stitch, tack, knit, tat, crochet, knot, button, buckle, hitch, lash, truss, bandage, braid, splice, swathe, gird, tether, picket, harness, inspan, bridge over.

Chain, enchain, shackle, pinion, fetter, manacle, handcuff, lock, latch,

44 DISJUNCTION (*Substantives*), disconnection, disunity, disunion, disassociation, disengagement, abstraction, abstractedness, isolation, insularity, oasis, separateness, severalness, severality.

Separation, parting, detachment, divorce, sejunction, seposition, segregation, insulation, diduction, discerption, elision, caesura, division, subdivision, break, fracture, rupture, dismemberment, disintegration, dislocation, luxation, severance, disseverance, severing, fission, scission, rescission, abscission, laceration, dilaceration, wrenching, abruption, disruption, avulsion, divulsion, tearing asunder, section, cutting, resection, cleavage, fissure, breach, rent, split, crack, slit, tear, rip, dispersion (73), incision, dissection, vivisection anatomy.

Anatomist, prosector.

(*Phrase*) *Disjecta membra.*

(*Verbs*) To be disjoined, separated, etc., to come off, fall off, get loose, fall to pieces.

To disjoin, disconnect, disunite, part, dispart, detach, separate, space, space out, cut off, rescind, segregate, insulate, dissociate, isolate, disengage, set apart, liberate, loose, set free (750), unloose, unfasten, untie, unbind,

belay, brace, hook, clap together, leash, couple, link, yoke, bracket, hang together, pin, nail, bolt, hasp, clasp, clamp, screw, rivet, solder, weld, impact, wedge, rabbet, mortise, mitre, jam, dovetail, enchase, engraft, interlink, inosculate, entwine, enlace, interlace, intertwine, intertwist, interweave, interlock.

To be joined, etc., to hang or hold together, cohere (46).

(*Adjectives*) Joined, conjoined, coupled, etc., bound up together, conjunct, corporate, compact.

Firm, fast, close, tight, taut, secure, set, fixed, impacted, jammed, locked, etc., intervolved, intertwined, inseparable, indissoluble, inseverable, untearable.

(*Phrases*) Hand in hand; rolled into one.

(*Adverbs*) Conjointly, jointly, etc. With, along with, together with, in conjunction with.

Fast, firmly, closely, etc.

---

disband, unfix, unlace, unclasp, undo, unbutton, unbuckle, unchain, unfetter, untack, unharness, ungird, unpack, unbolt, unlatch, unlock, unlink, uncouple, unpin, unclinch, unscrew, unhook, unrivet, untwist, unshackle, unyoke, unknit, unsolder, ravel out, unravel, disentangle, unpick, unglue, switch off, shut off.

Sunder, divide, subdivide, divorce, sever, dissever, abscind, cut, scissor, incide, incise, snip, nib, cleave, rive, slit, split, split in twain, splinter, chip, crack, snap, burst, rend, break or tear asunder, shiver, crunch, chop, cut up, rip up, hack, hew, slash, whittle, haggle, hackle, discind, tear, lacerate, mangle, mince, gash, hash, knap.

Dissect, cut up, carve, slice, castrate, detruncate, anatomize; take, pull, or pick to pieces; unseam, tear to tatters, tear piecemeal, divellicate, disintegrate; dismember, disembowel, eviscerate, disbranch, dislocate, joint, disjoint, behead, mince, break up, crunch, gride, comminute (330), vivisect.

(*Phrase*) To tear limb from limb.

(*Adjectives*) Disjoined, disconnected, etc., snippety, disjointed, multipartite, abstract, disjunctive, isolated, insular, separate, discrete, apart, asunder, loose, free, liberated, disengaged, unattached, unannexed, distinct, unassociated, unconnected, adrift, straggling, dispersed, disbanded, segregated.

Cut off, rescinded, etc., rift, reft.

Capable of being cut, scissile, fissile, discerptible.

(*Adverbs*) Separately, etc., one by one, severally, apiece, apart, adrift, asunder; in the abstract, abstractedly.

45 Connecting medium.

VINCULUM (*Substantives*), link, connective, connection, junction (43), conjunction, copula, intermedium, hyphen, bridge, stepping-stone, isthmus, span, girder.

Bond, filament, fibre (205), hair, cordage, cord, thread, string, packthread, twine, twist, whipcord, tape, ferret, raffia, line, snood, ribbon, riband, rope, cable, hawser, painter, halyard, guy, guy-rope, wire, chain.

Fastening, tie, tendril, tendon, ligament, ligature, strap, tackle, rigging, traces, harness, yoke, band, withe, withy, brace, bandage, roller, fillet, thong, braid, inkle, girth, cinch, cestus, girdle, garter, halter, noose, lasso, lariat, surcingle, knot, running-knot, slip-knot, reef-knot, sailor's knot, grannyknot, etc.

Pin, corking-pin, safety-pin, nail, brad, tack, skewer, staple, clamp, vice, bracket, cramp, screw, button, buckle, brooch, clasp, slide, clip, hasp, hinge, hank, bolt, catch, latch, latchet, tag, hook, tooth, hook and eye, lock, locket, holdfast, padlock, rivet, anchor, grappling-iron, stake, post, gyve, shackle (752).

Cement, adhesive, mucilage, glue, gum, paste, size, goo, solder, lute, putty, bird-lime, mortar, stucco, plaster, grout.

46 COHERENCE (*Substantives*), cohesion, adherence, adhesion, accretion, concretion, agglutination, conglutination, aggregation, consolidation, set, cementation, soldering, welding, grouting.

Sticking, clinging, adhesiveness, stickiness, gumminess, gummosity, glutinosity (352), cohesiveness, density (321), inseparability, inseparableness, tenaciousness, tenacity.

Clot, concrete, cake, lump, conglomerate (321).

(*Verbs*) To cohere, adhere, stick, cling, cleave, hold, take hold of, hold fast, hug, grow or hang together, twine round.

To concrete, curdle, cake.

To glue, agglutinate, conglutinate, agglomerate, consolidate, solidify (321); cement, lute, paste, gum, grout, stick, solder, weld.

(*Phrases*) To stick like a leech; to stick like wax; to clink like ivy, like a bur, like a limpet.

(*Adjectives*) Cohesive, adhesive, cohering, tenacious, sticky, tacky, glutinous, gluey, gooey, gummy, viscous (352), agglutinatory.

United, unseparated, sessile, inseparable, inextricable, infrangible (321).

47 Want of adhesion.

INCOHERENCE (*Substantives*), non-adhesion, immiscibility, looseness, laxity, slackness, relaxation, freedom, disjunction.

(*Phrases*) A rope of sand; *disjecta membra*.

(*Verbs*) To loosen, make loose, slacken, relax, unglue, unsolder, etc., detach, untwist, unravel, unroll (44, 313), to comminute (330).

(*Adjectives*) Incoherent, immiscible, detached, non-adhesive, loose, slack, lax, relaxed, baggy.

Segregated, flapping, streaming, dishevelled, unincorporated, unconsolidated, uncombined.

(*Phrase*) Like grains of sand.

48 COMBINATION (*Substantives*), union, unification, synthesis, incorporation, amalgamation, coalescence, crasis, fusion, embodiment, conflation, absorption, blending, centralization; mixture (41).

Compound, composition, amalgam, impregnation, decompound, decomposite, resultant.

(*Verbs*) To combine, unite, unify, incorporate, amalgamate, synthesize, embody, unify, re-embody, blend, merge, fuse, absorb, melt into one, consolidate, coalesce, centralize; to impregnate, to put together, to lump together.

(*Adjectives*) Combined, compound, composite, coalescent, synthetic, synthetical, impregnated with, engrained.

49 DECOMPOSITION (*Substantives*), analysis, resolution, dissolution, disintegration, catalysis, electrolysis, corruption (653), dispersion (73), disjunction (44).

(*Verbs*) To decompose, rot, disembody, analyse, electrolyse, decompound, resolve, take to pieces, separate into its elements, dissect, unravel (313), break up.

(*Adjectives*) Decomposed, etc., catalytic, analytic, analytical, corrupted, dissolved.

4°. *Concrete Quantity*

50 WHOLE (*Substantives*), totality, integrity, integrality, allness, entireness, entirety, *ensemble*, collectiveness, individuality, unity (87), indivisibility, indiscerptibility, indissolubility; embodiment, integration.

All, the whole, total, aggregate, integer, gross amount, sum, sum total, *tout ensemble*, upshot, trunk, hull, skeleton, hulk, lump, heap (72).

The principal part, bulk, mass, tissue, staple, body, compages, the main, the greater part, major part.

(*Phrases*) The whole caboodle; the whole boiling.

(*Verbs*) To form or constitute a whole, to integrate, embody, aggregate, amass (72), to total, amount to, come to.

(*Adjectives*) Whole, total, integral, entire, one, unbroken, uncut, undivided, seamless, individual, unsevered, unclipped, uncropped, unshorn, undiminished, undemolished, undissolved, unbruised, undestroyed, indivisible, indissoluble, indissolvable, indiscerptible.

Wholesale, sweeping.

(*Adverbs*) Wholly, altogether, totally, entirely, all, all in all, as a whole, wholesale, in the aggregate, in the mass, *en masse*, in the lump, *en bloc*, on the whole, *in toto*, in the gross, *in extenso*, in the bulk, to the full, throughout, every inch.

(*Phrases*) The long and short of it; nearly or almost all; root and branch; lock, stock, and barrel; hook, line, and sinker; in the long run; in the main; neck and crop; from end to end; from beginning to end; from first to last; from head to foot; from top to toe; fore and aft; from alpha to omega.

51 PART (*Substantives*), portion, item, division, subdivision, section, chapter, verse, extract, passage, gobbet, sector, segment, fraction, fragment, frustum, detachment, piece, bit, lump, chunk, dollop, scrap, whit, swatch, morsel, mouthful, scantling, cantle, cantlet, slip, crumb (32), fritter, rag, tag, shred, tatter, splinter, snatch, cut, cutting, snip, snippet, snick, collop, slice, chip, chipping, shiver, sliver, matchwood, spillikin, smithereens, driblet, clipping, paring, shaving, debris, odds and ends, oddments, sundries, detritus, lamina, shadow, flotsam and jetsam, pickings.

Parcel, share, instalment, contingent, compartment, department, dividend, dose, particular, article, clause, paragraph.

Member, limb, lobe, lobule, arm, branch, scion, bough, joint, link, ramification (256), twig, bush, spray, sprig, offshoot, leaf, leaflet, stump, stub, butt, rump, torso.

(*Verbs*) To part, divide, subdivide, break (44); to partition, parcel out, portion, apportion (786), to ramify, branch, branch out.

(*Adjectives*) Part, fractional, fragmentary, scrappy, lobular, sectional, aliquot, divided, multifid, partitioned, isomeric.

(*Adverbs*) Partly, in part, partially, piecemeal, in detail, part by part, by driblets, bit by bit, little by little, by inches, inch by inch, foot by foot, drop by drop, in snatches, by fits and starts.

———

52 COMPLETENESS (*Substantives*), entirety, fullness, impletion, completion (729), perfection (650), solidity, stop-gap, makeweight, padding, filling up, integration, absoluteness, sufficiency; complement, supplement (39).

Fill, load, bumper, brimmer, bellyful, skinful.

53 INCOMPLETENESS (*Substantives*), deficiency, defectiveness, shortcoming (304), unreadiness, defalcation, failure, imperfection (651), hollowness, patchiness.

Part wanting, omission, defect, break, deficit, ullage, caret, lacuna, hiatus (198).

(*Verbs*) To be complete, etc., suffice (639).

To render complete or whole, to complete, exhaust, perfect, finish, make up, fill up, charge, load, replenish, make good, piece out, eke out.

(*Phrases*) To give the finishing touch; to supply deficiencies; to go to all lengths; to go the whole hog; to thrash out.

(*Adjectives*) Complete, entire, whole (50), absolute, perfect, full, plenary, solid, undivided, with all its parts, supplementary, adscititous, thorough, exhaustive, radical, sweeping, searching; consummate, thorough-paced, regular, sheer, unmitigated, unqualified.

Crammed, saturated, brimful, chock-full.

(*Adverbs*) Completely, entirely, to the full, outright, wholly, totally, thoroughly (31), *in toto, toto caelo,* in all respects.

(*Phrases*) To the top of one's bent; up to the ears; *à fond*; from first to last; from beginning to end; *ab ovo usque ad mala.*

(*Verbs*) To be incomplete, etc., to fail, fall short (304).

To dock, lop, mutilate, garble, truncate, castrate (38).

(*Adjectives*) Incomplete, unfinished, imperfect, defective, deficient, wanting, failing, short by, hollow, meagre, insufficient, half-baked, perfunctory, sketchy, scrappy, patchy.

Mutilated, garbled, docked, lopped, truncated; proceeding, in progress.

(*Phrase*) *Cetera desunt.*

---

54 COMPOSITION (*Substantives*), make-up, constitution, constituency, crasis.

Inclusion, admission, comprehension, reception.

(*Verbs*) To be composed of, to consist of, be made of, formed of, made up of, be resolved into.

To contain, include, hold, comprehend, take in, admit, embrace, involve, implicate.

To compose, constitute, form, make, make up, fill up, build up, put together, embody.

To enter into the composition of, to be or form part of (51), to merge in, be merged in.

(*Adjectives*) Comprehending, containing, including, comprising, etc.

Component, constituent, formative, forming, constituting, composing, etc., belonging to, appertaining to, inclusive.

55 EXCLUSION (*Substantives*), non-admission, omission, exception, rejection, proscription, repudiation, exile, banishment, excommunication.

Separation, segregation, elimination, seposition.

(*Verbs*) To be excluded from, etc., to be out of it.

To exclude, shut out, bar, leave out, omit, reject, repudiate, neglect, blackball; lay, put, or set apart or aside; segregate, pass over, throw overboard, slur over, neglect (460), excommunicate, banish, expatriate, extradite, deport, ostracize, relegate, rusticate, send down (297), rule out.

To eliminate, weed, winnow, screen, bar, separate (44), strike off.

(*Phrase*) 'Include me out.'

(*Adjectives*) Excluding, omitting, etc., exclusive.

Excluded, omitted, etc., unrecounted, inadmissible.

(*Adverbs*) Except, save, bar, barring, excepting.

---

56 COMPONENT (*Substantives*), component part, integral part, element, constituent, ingredient, member,

57 EXTRANEOUSNESS (*Substantives*), extrinsicality (5), exteriority (220).

limb (51), part and parcel, contents (190), appurtenance, feature, personnel.

A foreign body, alien, stranger, intruder, outsider, incomer, interloper, foreigner, dago, wop, *novus homo*, parvenu, immigrant, newcomer, new chum, pommy, greenhorn, tenderfoot.

(*Adjectives*) Extraneous, foreign, alien, tramontane, ultramontane, interloping.

(*Adverbs*) Abroad, in foreign parts, overseas.

SECTION IV—ORDER

1°. *Order in General*

58 ORDER (*Substantives*), regularity, orderliness, tidiness, uniformity, even tenor, symmetry.

Gradation, progression, pedigree, line, descent, subordination, course, series (69), array, routine.

Method, disposition, arrangement, system, economy, discipline, pattern, plan.

Rank, station, hierarchy, place, status, stand, scale, step, stage, period, term (71), footing; rank and file, pecking order.

(*Verbs*) To be or become in order, to form, fall in, arrange itself, place itself, range itself, fall into its place, fall into rank.

(*Adjectives*) Orderly, regular, in order, arranged, etc. (60), in its proper place, correct, tidy, shipshape, trim, *en règle*, well regulated, methodical, business-like, uniform, symmetrical, systematic, unconfused, undisturbed, untangled, unruffled, unravelled, still, etc. (265).

(*Phrases*) In apple-pie order; Bristol fashion.

(*Adverbs*) Systematically, methodically, etc., in turn, in its turn.

Step by step, by regular steps, gradations, stages, periods, or intervals, periodically (138).

At stated periods (138), *gradatim, seriatim.*

(*Phrase*) Like clockwork.

59 Absence, or want of Order, etc.

DISORDER (*Substantives*), irregularity, asymmetry, anomaly, confusion, confusedness, disarray, untidiness, jumble, huddle, litter, lumber, farrago, mess, hash, clutter, pie, muddle, mix-up, upset, hotchpotch, hugger-mugger, anarchy, anarchism, imbroglio, chaos, tohubohu, omnium gatherum (41), derangement (61).

Complexness, complexity, complication, intricacy, intricateness, implication, perplexity, involution, ravelling, tangle, entanglement, snarl, knot, coil, skein, sleave, network, labyrinth, Gordian knot, jungle.

Turmoil, *mêlée*, tumult, ferment, stew, fermentation, pudder, pother, riot, uproar, bobbery, rough-house, rumpus, scramble, fracas, vortex, whirlpool, maelstrom, hurly-burly, bear - garden, Babel, Saturnalia, Donnybrook, pandemonium.

Tumultuousness, riotousness, inquietude (173), derangement (61), topsyturvydom (218).

(*Phrases*) Wheels within wheels; confusion worse confounded; most admired disorder; *concordia discors*; hell broke loose.

A pretty kettle of fish; a fine state of things; a how-d'ye-do; the fat in the fire; a bull in a china shop; the devil to pay.

The cart before the horse; hysteron proteron.

(*Verbs*) To be out of order, irregular, disorderly, etc., to ferment.

To derange, put out of order (61).

(*Phrases*) To be at cross-purposes; to make hay of.

(*Adjectives*) Disorderly, orderless, out of order, disordered, misplaced, out of place, deranged, disarranged (61), irregular, desultory, anomalous, untidy, sloppy, slovenly, tousled, straggling, unarranged, immethodical, unsymmetrical, unsystematic, unmethodical, undigested, unsorted, unclassified, unclassed, asymmetrical.

Disjointed, out of joint, out of gear, out of kilter, confused, tangled, involved, intricate, complicated, inextricable, irreducible.

Mixed, scattered, promiscuous, indiscriminate, casual.

Tumultuous, turbulent, riotous, troublous, tumultuary (173), rough-and-tumble.

(*Adverbs*) Irregularly, etc., by fits and snatches, pell-mell; higgledy-piggledy, hugger-mugger; at sixes and sevens; helter-skelter, harum-scarum, anyhow.

60 Reduction to Order.

ARRANGEMENT (*Substantives*), disposal, disposition, collocation, allocation, distribution, sorting, assortment, allotment, apportionment, marshalling, alignment, taxis, taxonomy, gradation, organization, ordination; plan (626).

Analysis, sifting, screening, classification.

Result of arrangement, digest, synopsis, analysis, table, register (551).

Instrument for sorting, sieve, riddle, screen (260).

(*Verbs*) To order, reduce to order, bring into order, introduce order into.

To arrange, dispose, place, form; to put, set, place, etc., in order; to set out, collocate, pack, marshal, range, align (or aline), rank, group, parcel out, allot, distribute, assort, sort, sift, riddle.

To class, classify, categorize, file, string, thread, tabulate, pigeon-hole, catalogue, index, register, take stock.

To methodize, digest, regulate, size, grade, gradate, graduate, alphabetize, co-ordinate, systematize, organize, settle, fix, rearrange.

To unravel (246), disentangle, ravel, card, disembroil.

(*Phrases*) To put or set to rights; to assign places to.

(*Adjectives*) Arranged, methodical (58), embattled, in battle array.

(*Phrase*) A place for everything, and everything in its place.

61 Subversion of Order, bringing into disorder.

DERANGEMENT (*Substantives*), disarrangement, misarrangement, displacement, misplacement, dislocation, discomposure, disturbance, bedevilment, disorganization, perturbation, shuffling, rumpling, embroilment, corrugation (258), inversion (218), jumble, muddle, disorder (59).

(*Verbs*) To derange, disarrange, misarrange, misplace, mislay, discompose, disorder, embroil, unsettle, disturb, confuse, perturb, jumble, tumble, huddle, shuffle, muddle, toss, hustle, fumble; to bring, put, or throw into disorder, trouble, confusion, etc., break the ranks, upset.

To unhinge, put out of joint, dislocate, turn over, invert; turn topsy-turvy; turn inside out (218), bedevil, throw out of gear.

To complicate, involve, perplex, tangle, entangle, embrangle (or imbrangle), ravel, ruffle, tousle, rumple, dishevel, muss, litter, scatter, make a mess of, monkey with, make hay of.

(*Adjectives*) Deranged, etc., disordered (59).

2°. *Consecutive Order*

62 PRECEDENCE *(Substantives)*, coming before, antecedence, antecedency, anteposition, priority (116), anteriority, the *pas*, the lead.

Superiority (33), precession (280).

(Verbs) To precede, come before, lead, introduce, usher in.

To place before; to prefix, affix, premise, prelude, preface, prologize.

(Phrases) To have the *pas*; to take the lead; to have the start; set the fashion; to open the ball.

(Adjectives) Preceding, precedent, antecedent, anterior, prior, previous, before, ahead of, leading.

Former, foregoing; coming or going before; precursory, precursive, prevenient, inaugural, prodromal, prodromic, preliminary, aforesaid, said, aforementioned, prefatory, introductory, prelusive, prelusory, proemial, preparatory, preambulatory.

(Adverbs) In advance, ahead, in front of, before, in the van (234).

---

64 PRECURSOR *(Substantives)*, antecedent, precedent, predecessor, forerunner, pioneer, outrider, avant-courier, leader, bell-wether, herald, harbinger.

Prelude, preamble, preface, foreword, prologue, prodrome, protasis, prolusion, overture, premise, proem, prolepsis, prolegomena, prefix, introduction, heading, advertisement, frontispiece, groundwork (673).

(Adjectives) Precursory, prefatory (62).

66 BEGINNING *(Substantives)*, commencement, opening, outset, incipience, inception, inchoation, initiative, overture, exordium, introduction (64), inauguration, début, onset, brunt, alpha.

Origin, source, rise, conception, birth, infancy, bud, embryo, germ, egg, rudiment, *incunabula*, start, cradle, starting-point, starting-post (293); dawn, morning (125).

63 SEQUENCE *(Substantives)*, coming after, consecution, succession, posteriority (117), secondariness; following (281).

Continuation, order of succession, successiveness; alternation (138).

Subordination, inferiority (34).

(Phrase) *Proxime accessit.*

(Verbs) To succeed, come after, follow, come next, ensue, come on, tread close upon; to alternate.

To place after, to suffix, append.

(Phrases) To be in the wake or trail of; to tread on the heels of; to step into the shoes of; to assume the mantle of.

(Adjectives) Succeeding, coming after, following, subsequent, ensuing, sequent, sequacious, consequent, next; consecutive, amoebean, alternate (138).

Latter, posterior.

(Adverbs) After, subsequently, since, behind, in the wake of, in the train of, at the tail of, in the rear of (234).

---

65 SEQUEL *(Substantives)*, afterpart, aftermath, suffix, successor, tail, runner-up, queue, train, wake, trail, rear, retinue, suite, appendix (39), postscript, epilogue, peroration, excursus, after-piece, tailpiece, tag, colophon, afterthought, second thoughts, *arrière pensée*, codicil, continuation, sequela, apodosis.

(Phrases) More last words; to be continued.

(Adjectives) Subsequent, ensuing (63).

67 END *(Substantives)*, close, termination, desinence, conclusion, finish, finis, finale, period, term, terminus, limit, last, omega, extreme, extremity, butt-end, fag-end, stub, tail, nib, tip, after-part, rear (235), colophon, coda, tailpiece, tag, *cul-de-lampe*, peroration, swan-song.

Completion (729), winding-up, *dénouement*, catastrophe, consummation, expiration, expiry, finishing

Van, vanguard, title-page, heading, front (234), fore-part, head (210).

Opening, entrance, entry, inlet, orifice, porch, portal, portico, gateway, door, gate, postern, wicket, threshold, vestibule, mouth, *fauces*, lips.

Alphabet, A B C, rudiments, elements.

(*Phrase*) The rising of the curtain; the thin end of the wedge.

(*Verbs*) To begin, commence, inchoate, rise, arise, originate, initiate, open, dawn, set in, take its rise, enter upon, embark on, set out (293), recommence, undertake (676).

To usher in, lead off, lead the way, take the lead or the initiative; head, stand at the head, stand first; broach, set on foot, set a-going, set abroach, set up, handsel, institute, launch, strike up.

(*Phrases*) To make a beginning; to cross the Rubicon; to break ground; set the ball in motion; take the initiative; break the ice; fire away; open the ball; kick off; tee up; pipe up.

(*Adjectives*) Beginning, commencing, arising, initial, initiatory, initiative, inceptive, incipient, proemial, inaugural, inchoate, inchoative, embryonic, primigenial, aboriginal, rudimental, nascent, natal, opening, dawning, entering.

First, foremost, leading, heading, maiden.

Begun, commenced, etc.

(*Adverbs*) At, or in the beginning, at first blush, first, in the first place, *imprimis*, first and foremost, *in limine*, in the bud, in embryo.

From the beginning, *ab initio, ab ovo*.

stroke, knock-out, K.O., death-blow, *coup de grâce*, upshot, issue, fate, doom, Day of Judgment, doomsday.

(*Phrases*) The *ne plus ultra*; the fall of the curtain; '*le commencement de la fin*.'

(*Verbs*) To end, close, finish, expire, terminate, conclude; come or draw to an end, close or stop, be all over, pass away, give out, peter out, run its course; to say one's say, perorate, be through with.

To come last, bring up the rear.

To bring to an end, close, etc., to put a period, etc., to; to make an end of; to close, finish, seal, wind up, complete, achieve (729), crown, determine.

(*Phrases*) To cut the matter short; to shut up shop.

(*Adjectives*) Ending, closing, etc., final, terminal, eschatological, desistive, definitive, crowning.

Last, ultimate, penultimate, antepenultimate, hindermost, rear, caudal, conterminal, conterminous.

Ended, closed, terminated, etc., through.

Unbegun, fresh, uncommenced.

(*Adverbs*) Once for all, in fine, finally, at the end of the day, for good, for good and all.

---

68 MIDDLE (*Substantives*), midst, mean, medium, happy medium, *via media*, middle term, centre (223), *mezzo termine, juste milieu*, half-way house, hub, nave, navel, omphalos, bull's-eye, nucleus.

Equidistance, equator, diaphragm, midriff; bisection (91).

Intervenience, interjacence, intervention (228), mid-course (628).

(*Adjectives*) Middle, medial, median, mesial, mean, mid, middlemost, midmost, mediate, intermediate (29), intervenient, interjacent (228), central (222), equidistant, embosomed, merged.

Mediterranean, equatorial.

(*Adverbs*) In the middle, amid, amidst, midway, amidships, midships, half-way.

(*Phrases*) In the thick of; *in medias res*.

69 Uninterrupted sequence.

CONTINUITY (*Substantives*), consecution, consecutiveness, succession, suite, progression, series, train, chain, catenation, concatenation, scale, gradation, course, procession, column, retinue, cortège, cavalcade, rank and file, line of battle, array, pedigree, genealogy, lineage, race.

File, queue, echelon, line, row, rank, range, tier, string, thread, team, tandem, randem, suit, flush, colonnade.

(*Verbs*) To follow in, form, a series, etc.; to fall in.

To arrange in a series, to marshal (60); to string together, file, thread, graduate, tabulate.

(*Adjectives*) Continuous, sequent, consecutive, progressive, serial, successive, continued, uninterrupted, unbroken, entire, linear, in a line, in a row, etc., gradual, constant, unremitting, unintermitting, evergreen (110).

(*Adverbs*) Continuously, consecutively, etc., *seriatum*; in a line, row, series, etc., in succession, etc., running, gradually, step by step; uninterruptedly, at a stretch, at one go.

(*Phrase*) In Indian file.

70 Interrupted sequence.

DISCONTINUITY (*Substantives*), interruption, pause, period, interregnum, break, interval, interlude, episode, lacuna, cut, gap, fracture, fault, chasm, hiatus (198), caesura, parenthesis, rhapsody, anacoluthon.

Intermission, alternation (138); a broken thread, broken melody.

(*Verbs*) To be discontinuous, etc.; to alternate, intermit.

To discontinue, pause, interrupt, break, interpose (228); to break in upon, disconnect (44); to break or snap the thread.

(*Adjectives*) Discontinuous, inconsecutive, broken, interrupted, unsuccessive, desultory, disconnected, unconnected, fitful, spasmodic, sporadic, scattered.

Alternate, every other, intermitting, alternating (138).

(*Phrase*) Few and far between.

(*Adverbs*) At intervals, by snatches, *per saltum*, by fits and starts, *longo intervallo*.

---

71 TERM (*Substantives*), rank, station, stage, step, rung, round, degree (26), remove, grade, link, place, peg, mark, point, *pas*, period, pitch, stand, standing, status, footing, range.

(*Verbs*) To hold, occupy, find, fall into a place, station.

3°. *Collective Order*

72 ASSEMBLAGE (*Substantives*), collection, dozen, collocation, compilation, levy, gathering, ingathering, muster, round-up, colligation, contesseration, *attroupement*, association, concourse, conflux, convergence, meeting, assembly, congregation, at home (892), levee, club, reunion, gaudy, soirée, conversazione, accumulation, cumulation, array, mobilization.

Congress, convocation, convention, *comitium*, committee, quorum, conclave, synod, caucus, conventicle, eisteddfod, mass-meeting.

73 NON-ASSEMBLAGE.

DISPERSION (*Substantives*), scattering, dissemination, diffusion, dissipation, spreading, casting, distribution, apportionment, sprinkling, respersion, circumfusion, interspersion, divergence (291), demobilization.

Odds and ends, waifs and strays, flotsam and jetsam.

(*Verbs*) To disperse, scatter, sow, disseminate, diffuse, shed, spread, overspread, dispense, disband, disembody, distribute, dispel, cast forth; strew, bestrew, sprinkle, sparge, issue, deal out, utter, resperse, intersperse,

Miscellany, olla podrida, museum, *collectanea*, menagerie (636), Noah's ark, anthology, encyclopaedia, portfolio, file.

A multitude (102), crowd, throng, rabble, mob, press, crush, horde, posse, body, tribe, crew, gang, knot, band, party, swarm, school, shoal, bevy, galaxy, covey, flock, herd, drove, corps, troop, troupe, squad, squadron, phalanx, platoon, company, regiment, battalion, legion, host, army, division.

set abroach, circumfuse; to decentralize, demobilize; to hive-off.

(*Phrases*) To turn adrift; to scatter to the four winds; to sow broadcast; to spread like wildfire.

(*Adjectives*) Unassembled, uncollected, dispersed, scattered, diffused, sparse, spread, dispread, widespread, sporadic, cast, broadcast, epidemic, adrift.

(*Adverbs*) *Sparsim*, here and there, *passim*.

A sounder (of swine), skulk (of foxes), pride (of lions), charm (of finches), flush (of mallards), gaggle (of geese), wedge (of swans).

Clan, brotherhood, fraternity, sisterhood, party (712).

Volley, shower, storm, cloud, flood, deluge.

Group, cluster, clump, set, batch, battery, pencil, lot, pack, budget, assortment, bunch, parcel, packet, package, bundle, fascicle, fascicule, *fasciculus*, faggot, wisp, truss, tuft, rosette, shock, rick, fardel, stack, sheaf, stook, haycock.

Accumulation, congeries, heap, hoard, lump, pile, rouleau, tissue, mass, pyramid, bale, drift, snowball, acervation, cumulation, glomeration, agglomeration, conglobation, conglomeration, conglomerate, coacervation, coagmentation, aggregation, concentration (290), congestion, omnium gatherum.

Collector, tax-gatherer, whip, whipper-in.

(*Verbs*) To assemble, collect, muster, meet, unite, cluster, swarm, flock, herd, crowd, throng, associate, congregate, conglomerate, concentrate, congest, rendezvous, resort, flock together, get together, reassemble.

To bring, get or gather together, collect, draw together, group, convene, convoke, convocate, collocate, colligate, round up, scrape together, rake up, dredge, bring into a focus, amass, accumulate, heap up, pile, pack, do up, stack, truss, cram, pack together, congest, acervate, coagment, agglomerate, garner up, lump together, make a parcel of; to centralize; to mobilize.

(*Phrases*) To heap Pelion upon Ossa; to collect in a drag-net.

(*Adjectives*) Assembled, collected, etc., undispersed, met together, closely packed, dense, crowded, serried, huddled together, teeming, swarming, populous.

(*Phrases*) Packed like sardines; crowded to suffocation.

74 Place of meeting.

FOCUS (*Substantives*), point of convergence, corradiation, rendezvous, home, headquarters, club, centre (222), gathering-place, meeting-place, trysting-place, rallying-ground, haunt, howff, resort, museum, repository, depot (636).

4°. *Distributive Order*

75 CLASS (*Substantives*), division, category, predicament, head, order, section, department, domain, province.

Kind, sort, variety, type, genus, species, family, phylum, race, tribe, caste, sept, clan, *gens*, phratry, breed, kith, sect, set, assortment, feather, stripe, suit, range, run.

Gender, sex, kin, kidney, manner, nature, description, denomination, designation, character, stamp, stuff, *genre.*
(*Adjectives*) Generic, racial, tribal, etc.
(*Verbs*) To classify, catalogue (60).

76 INCLUSION (*Substantives*), comprehension under a class, reference to a class, admission, comprehension, reception, subsumption.
Inclusion in a compound, composition (54).
(*Verbs*) To be included in, to come under, to fall under, to range under; to belong, or pertain to, appertain; to range with, to merge in, to be of.
To include, comprise, comprehend, contain, admit, embrace, receive; to enumerate among, reckon among, reckon with, number among, refer to, place under, class with or among, arrange under or with, take into account, subsume.
(*Adjectives*) Including, inclusive, all-embracing, congener, congeneric, congenerous, *et hoc genus omne,* etcetera.
Included, merged, etc.
(*Phrase*) Birds of a feather.

77 EXCLUSION from a class (*Substantives*), rejection, proscription.
Exclusion from a compound (55).
(*Verbs*) To be excluded from, etc.; to exclude, proscribe, debar, rule out, set apart (55).
(*Phrase*) To shut the door upon.
(*Adjectives*) Exclusive, excluding, etc.

78 GENERALITY (*Substantives*), universality, catholicism, catholicity.
Every man, every one, everybody, all, all hands.
Miscellaneousness, miscellany, encyclopaedia, generalization, prevalence, drag-net.
(*Phrases*) The world and his wife; N or M.
(*Verbs*) To be general, common, or prevalent, to prevail.
To render general, to generalize.
(*Adjectives*) General, generic, collective, comprehensive, encyclopaedic, panoramic, bird's-eye, sweeping, radical, universal, world-wide, cosmopolitan, catholic, common, oecumenical, transcendental, prevalent, prevailing, all-pervading, epidemic, all-inclusive.
Unspecified, impersonal; every, all.
(*Adverbs*) Whatever, whatsoever, to a man; generally, universally, on the whole, for the most part.

79 SPECIALITY (*Substantives*), particularity, peculiarity, individuality, haecceity, thisness, personality, characteristic, mannerism, idiosyncrasy, trick, gimmick, specificness, specificity, eccentricity, singularity (83).
Version, reading (522).
Particulars, details, items, counts.
I, myself, self, I myself, *moi qui vous parle.*
(Phrases) *Argumentum ad hominem;* local colour.
(*Verbs*) To specify, particularize, individualize, realize, specialize, designate, determine.
(*Phrases*) To descend to particulars; to enter into detail.
(*Adjectives*) Special, particular, individual, specific, proper, appropriate, personal, private, respective, several, definite, determinate, especial, certain, esoteric, endemic, partial, party, peculiar, characteristic, distinctive, typical, unique, diagnostic, exlusive, *sui generis,* singular, exceptional (83).

This, that, yonder, yon, such and such.
(*Adverbs*) Specially, specifically, etc., in particular, respectively, personally, individually, *in propria persona.*
Each, apiece, one by one, severally, seriatim, namely, *videlicet,* viz., to wit.

5°. Order as regards Categories

80 RULE (*Substantives*), regularity, uniformity, constancy, standard, model, nature, principle, the order of things, routine, prevalence, practice, usage, custom, use, habit (613), regulation, precept (697), convention, *convenances*.

Form, formula, law, canon, principle, keynote, catchword.

Type, archetype, pattern, precedent, paradigm, the normal, natural, ordinary or model state or condition; norm, control.

(*Phrases*) A standing order; the bed of Procrustes; laws of the Medes and Persians.

(*Adjectives*) Regular, uniform, constant (82).

81 MULTIFORMITY (*Substantives*), variety, diversity, multifariousness, allotropy, allotropism.

(*Adjectives*) Multiform, variform, polymorphic, multifold, manifold, multifarious, multigenerous, omnifarious, omnigenous, heterogeneous, motley, epicene, indiscriminate, desultory, irregular, diversified, allotropic; different (15).

(*Phrase*) Of all sorts and kinds.

---

82 CONFORMITY (*Substantives*), conformance, observance, naturalization, harmony, convention (613).

Example, instance, specimen, sample, ensample, exemplar, exemplification, illustration, pattern (22), object lesson, case in point, quotation, the rule.

(*Phrases*) The order of the day; the common or ordinary run of things (23); a matter of course.

(*Verbs*) To conform to rule, be regular, orthodox, etc., to follow, observe, go by, bend to, obey rules; to be guided or regulated by, be wont, etc. (613), to comply or chime in with, to be in harmony with, follow suit; to standardize, naturalize.

To exemplify, illustrate, cite, quote, put a case, produce an instance, set an example.

(*Phrases*) To go with the crowd; to do in Rome as the Romans do; to follow the fashion; to swim with the stream; to keep one in countenance.

(*Adjectives*) Conformable to rule, regular, uniform, constant, steady, according to rule, *en règle, de rigueur,* normal, well regulated, formal, canonical, orthodox, conventional, strict, rigid, positive, uncompromising (23).

Ordinary, natural, usual, common, wonted, accustomed, habitual (613), household, average, everyday, current, rife, prevailing, prevalent, established,

83 UNCONFORMITY (*Substantives*), nonconformity, unconventionality, informality, arbitrariness, abnormity, abnormality, anomaly, anomalousness, lawlessness, peculiarity, exclusiveness; infraction, breach, violation, of law or rule; individuality, idiosyncracy, mannerism, eccentricity, aberration, irregularity, unevenness, variety, singularity, rarity, oddity, oddness, exemption, salvo.

Exception, nondescript, a character, original, nonesuch, monster, monstrosity, prodigy (872), *lusus naturae, rara avis,* freak, curiosity, crank, queer fish; half-caste, half-breed, cross-breed, mongrel, hybrid, mule, mulatto (41), *tertium quid,* hermaphrodite, sport.

Phoenix, chimera, hydra, sphinx, minotaur, griffin, centaur, hippocentaur, hippogriff, basilisk, cockatrice, tragelaph, kraken, dragon, wyvern, roc, sea-serpent, mermaid, merman, cyclops, unicorn.

(*Phrases*) Out of one's element; a fish out of water; neither one thing nor another; neither fish, flesh, nor fowl, nor good red herring; a law to oneself.

(*Verbs*) To be unconformable to rule, to be exceptional, etc.; to violate a law or custom, to stretch a point.

(*Phrases*) To have no business there; to beggar description.

(*Adjectives*) Unconformable, excep-

received, stereotyped, acknowledged, typical, accepted, recognized, representative, hackneyed, well-known, familiar, vernacular, commonplace, trite, banal, cut and dried, naturalized, orderly, shipshape, run of the mill.

Exemplary, illustrative, in point, of daily or everyday occurrence, in the order of things.

(*Phrases*) Regular as clockwork; according to Cocker (or Hoyle).

(*Adverbs*) Conformably, by rule, regularly, etc., agreeably to; in accordance, conformity, or keeping with.

Usually, generally, ordinarily, commonly, for the most part, as usual, *more solito, more suo, pro more*; of course, as a matter of course, *pro forma*.

Always, uniformly (16), invariably, without exception, never otherwise.

For example, for instance, *exempli gratia, inter alia*.

(*Phrases*) *Ab uno disce omnes; ex pede Herculem; ex ungue leonem*; birds of a feather.

———

tional, abnormal, anomalous, anomalistic, out of order, out of place, misplaced, irregular, unorthodox, uneven, arbitrary, informal, aberrant, stray, peculiar, funny, exclusive, unnatural, eccentric, unconventional, Bohemian, beatnik, hippy, yippy.

Unusual, unaccustomed, unwonted, uncommon, rare, singular, unique, curious, odd, extraordinary, strange, *outré*, out of the way, egregious, out of the ordinary, unheard of, queer, quaint, old-fashioned, unfashionable, nondescript, undescribed, unexampled, *sui generis*, unprecedented, unparalleled, unfamiliar, fantastic, newfangled, grotesque, bizarre, weird, eerie, outlandish, exotic, preternatural, unexampled, unrepresentative, uncanny, denaturalized.

Heteroclite, heteroclite, amorphous, out of the pale of, mongrel, amphibious, epicene, half-blood, hybrid (41), androgynous, betwixt and between.

(*Phrases*) 'None but himself could be his parallel'; caviare to the general.

(*Adverbs*) Unconformably, etc.; except, unless, save, barring, beside, without, but for, save and except, let alone, to say nothing of; however, yet, but.

SECTION V—NUMBER

1°. *Number in the Abstract*

84 NUMBER (*Substantives*), symbol, numeral, figure, cipher, digit, integer, counter, a round number, notation, a formula; series.

Sum, difference, subtrahend, complement, product, factorial, multiplicand, multiplier, multiplicator, coefficient, multiple, least common multiple, dividend, divisor, factor, highest common factor, greatest common measure, quotient, sub-multiple, fraction, vulgar fraction, mixed number, numerator, denominator, decimal, circulating decimal, recurring decimal, repetend, common measure, aliquot part, reciprocal, prime number; permutation, combination, election.

Ratio, proportion, progression (arithmetical, geometrical, harmonical), percentage.

Power, root, exponent, index, function, logarithm, antilogarithm; differential, integral, fluxion, fluent; incommensurable, surd.

(*Adjectives*) Numeral, complementary, divisible, aliquot, reciprocal, prime, fractional, decimal, factorial, fractional, mixed, incommensurable.

Proportional, exponential, logarithmic, logometric, differential, fluxional, integral.

Positive, negative, rational, irrational, surd, radical, real, imaginary, impossible.

85 NUMERATION (*Substantives*), numbering, counting, tale, telling, tally, calling over, recension, enumeration, summation, reckoning, computation, ciphering, calculation, calculus, algorism, dactylonomy, rhabdology.

Arithmetic, analysis, algebra, differential and integral calculus.

Statistics, dead reckoning, muster, poll, census, capitation, roll-call, muster-roll, account, score, recapitulation, demography.

Addition, subtraction, multiplication, division, proportion, rule of three, reduction, involution, evolution, practice, equations, extraction of roots, approximation, interpolation, differentiation, integration.

Abacus, logometer, ready-reckoner, slide-rule, sliding-rule, tallies, Napier's bones, calculating machine, tabulator, totalizator, totalizer, tote, cash-register.

(*Verbs*) To number, count, tell, tally, call over, take an account of, enumerate, muster, poll, run over, recite, recapitulate; sum, sum up, cast up, tell off, score, cipher, compute, calculate, reckon, estimate, figure up, tot up; add, subtract, multiply, divide; amount to.

Check, prove, demonstrate, balance, audit, overhaul, take stock.

(*Adjectives*) Numerical, arithmetical, logarithmic, numeral, analytic, algebraic, statistical, computable, calculable, commensurable, incommensurable, incommensurate.

86 LIST (*Substantives*), catalogue, inventory, schedule, register, census, return, statistics, record (551), account, registry, syllabus, roll, terrier, cadastre, cartulary, tally, file, muster-roll, roster, rota, bead-roll, panel, calendar, index, table, book, ledger, day-book, synopsis, bibliography, contents, invoice, bill of lading, bill of fare, menu, red book, peerage, baronetage, Almanach de Gotha, Debrett, Domesday Book, prospectus, programme, directory, gazetteer, who's who.

Registration, etc. (551).

2°. *Determinate Number*

87 UNITY (*Substantives*), unification, oneness, individuality, singleness, solitariness, solitude, isolation (893), abstraction; monism.

One, unit, ace, monad.

Someone, somebody, no other, none else, an individual; monist.

(*Verbs*) To be alone, etc.; to isolate (44), insulate, set apart.

To render one, unify.

(*Phrase*) To dine with Duke Humphrey.

(*Adjectives*) One, sole, single, individual, apart, alone, lone, isolated, solitary, lonely, lonesome, desolate, dreary, insular, insulated, disparate, discrete, detached; monistic.

Unaccompanied, unattended, *solus*, single-handed, singular, odd, unique, unrepeated, azygous.

Inseverable, irresolvable, indiscerptible, compact.

88 ACCOMPANIMENT (*Substantives*), coexistence, concomitance, company, association, companionship, partnership, collaboration, copartnership, coefficiency.

Concomitant, adjunct, context, accessory (39), coefficient, companion, attendant, fellow, associate, consort, spouse, colleague, collaborator, partner, copartner, side-kick, buddy, satellite, escort, hanger-on, parasite, shadow; travelling tutor, chaperon, duenna.

(*Verbs*) To accompany, chaperon, coexist, attend, associate or be associated with, keep company with, collaborate with, hang on, shadow, wait on, to join, tie together.

(*Phrases*) To go hand in hand with; to be in the same boat.

(*Adjectives*) Accompanying, coexisting, attending, attendant, concomi-

(*Adverbs*) Singly, etc., alone, by itself, *per se*, only, apart, in the singular number, in the abstract, one by one; one at a time.

One and a half, sesqui-.

tant, fellow, twin, joint, associated with, accessory.

(*Adverbs*) With, withal, together with, along with, in company with, collectively, hand in hand, together, in a body, cheek by jowl, side by side; therewith, herewith, moreover, besides, also, and (37), not to mention.

89 DUALITY (*Substantives*), dualism, duplicity, twofoldness, doubleness, biformity; polarity.

Two, deuce, couple, brace, pair, dyad (or duad), twins, Siamese twins, Castor and Pollux, Damon and Pythias, fellows, gemini, yoke, span, file, conjugation, twosome; dualist.

(*Verbs*) To unite in pairs, to pair, pair off, couple, match, mate, bracket, yoke.

(*Adjectives*) Two, twain, dual, binary, dualistic, duplex (90), duplicate, dyadic, binomial, twin, tête-à-tête, Janus-headed, bilateral, bicentric, bifocal.

Coupled, bracketed, paired, etc., conjugate.

Both, both the one and the other.

90 DUPLICATION (*Substantives*), doubling, gemination, reduplication, ngemination, repetition, iteration (104), renewal.

(*Verbs*) To double, redouble, geminate, reduplicate, repeat, iterate, re-echo, renew (660).

(*Adjectives*) Double, doubled, redoubled, second.

Biform, bifarious, bifold, bilateral, bifacial, twofold, two-sided, two-faced, duplex, duplicate, ingeminate.

(*Adverbs*) Twice, once more, over again, *da capo*, *bis*, *encore*, anew, as much again, twofold (104, 136).

Secondly, in the second place, again.

91 Division into two parts.

BISECTION (*Substantives*), bipartition, dichotomy, halving, dimidiation, bifurcation, forking, branching, ramification, divarication, splitting, cleaving.

Fork, prong, fold, branch, Y.

Half, moiety, semi-, demi-, hemi-.

(*Verbs*) To bisect, halve, divide, split, cut in two, cleave, dimidiate, dichotomize.

To separate, fork, bifurcate, branch out, ramify.

(*Phrases*) To go halves; to go fifty-fifty; to split the difference.

(*Adjectives*) Bisected, halved, divided, etc., bipartite, bicuspid, bind, bifurcated, bifurcate, cloven, cleft, split, etc.

92 TRIALITY (*Substantives*), trinity.

Three, triad, triangle, triplet, trey, trio, tern, trinomial, leash, threesome, trefoil, triquetra, *terza rima*, trilogy.

Third power, cube.

(*Adjectives*) Three, triform, trine, trinal, trinary, ternary, ternal, ternate (93), trinomial, tertiary, tri-.

93 TRIPLICATION (*Substantives*), triplicity, trebleness, trine.

(*Verbs*) To treble, triple, triplicate, cube.

(*Adjectives*) Treble, triple, tern, ternary, ternate, triplicate, trigeminal, threefold, third.

(*Adverbs*) Three times, thrice, threefold, in the third place, thirdly.

94 Division into three parts.

TRISECTION (*Substantives*), tripartition, trichotomy; third part, third.

(*Verbs*) To trisect, divide into three parts.

(*Adjectives*) Trifid, trisected, tripartite, trichotomous, trisulcate, triform.

95 QUATERNITY (*Substantives*), four, tetrad, quadruplet, quad, quartet, quaternion, foursome, square, tetragon, tetrahedron, tessara, quadrature; tetralogy.

(*Verbs*) To reduce to a square, to square.

(*Adjectives*) Four, quaternary, quaternal, quadratic, quartile, tetractic, tetra-, quadri-.

96 QUADRUPLICATION.

(*Verbs*) To multiply by four, quadruplicate, biquadrate.

(*Adjectives*) Fourfold, quadruple, quadruplicate, fourth.

(*Adverbs*) Four times, in the fourth place, fourthly, to the fourth degree.

97 Division into four parts.

QUADRISECTION (*Substantives*), quadripartition, quartering, a fourth, a quarter.

(*Verbs*) To quarter, to divide into four parts.

(*Adjectives*) Quartered, etc., quadrifid, quadripartite.

98 FIVE (*Substantives*), cinque, cinqfoil, quint, quincunx, pentad, pentagon, pentahedron, quintuplet, quin, quintet.

(*Adjectives*) Five, quinary, quintuple, fivefold, fifth.

SIX, half a dozen, hexad, hexagon, hexahedron, sextet.

(*Adjectives*) Senary, sextuple, sixfold, sixth.

SEVEN, heptad, heptagon, heptahedron, septet.

(*Adjectives*) Septenary, septuple, sevenfold, seventh.

EIGHT, octad, octagon, octahedron, octet, ogdoad.

(*Adjectives*) Octonary, octonal, octuple, eightfold, eighth.

NINE, ennead, nonagon, enneagon, enneahedron, novena.

(*Adjectives*) Enneatic, ninefold, ninth.

TEN, decad, decagon, decahedron, decade.

(*Adjectives*) Decimal, denary, decuple, tenfold, tenth.

TWELVE, a dozen.

(*Adjectives*) Duodenary, duodecimal, twelfth.

THIRTEEN, a long dozen, a baker's dozen.

TWENTY, a score, icosahedron.

(*Adjectives*) Vigesimal, twentieth.

FORTY, twoscore.

(*Adjective*) Quadragesimal.

FIFTY, twoscore and ten.

(*Adjective*) Quinquagesimal.

SIXTY, threescore.

(*Adjectives*) Sexagesimal, sexagenary.

SEVENTY, threescore and ten.

EIGHTY, fourscore.

99 QUINQUESECTION, etc.

(*Adjectives*) Quinquefid, quinquarticular, quinquepartite.

Sexpartite.

Septempartite.

Octopartite.

DECIMATION, tithe.

(*Verb*) To decimate.

NINETY, fourscore and ten.

HUNDRED, centenary, hecatomb, century. One hundred and forty-four, a gross.

(*Verb*) To centuriate.

(*Adjectives*) Centesimal, centennial, **centenary, centurial,** centuple, centuplicate, hundredfold, hundredth.

THOUSAND, chiliad, millennium.

(*Adjective*) Millesimal.

MYRIAD, lac, crore.

MILLION, billion, trillion, etc.

3°. *Indeterminate Number*

100 More than one.

PLURALITY (*Substantives*), a number, a certain number, a few, a wheen, a round number.

(*Adjectives*) Plural, more than one, upwards of, some, a few, one or two, two or three, umpteen, certain.

(*Adverb*) Etcetera.

102 MULTITUDE (*Substantives*), numerousness, numerosity, numerality, multiplicity, majority, profusion, legion, host, a great or large number, numbers, array, power, lot, sight, army, sea, galaxy, populousness (72), a hundred, thousand, myriad, million, etc.

A shoal, swarm, draught, bevy, flock, herd, drove, flight, covey, hive, brood, litter, mob, nest, crowd (72).

Increase of number, multiplication, multiple; greater number, majority.

(*Verbs*) To be numerous, etc., to swarm, teem, crowd, come thick upon, outnumber, multiply, to people.

(*Phrase*) To swarm like locusts or bees.

(*Adjectives*) Many, several, a wheen, sundry, divers, various, a great many, very many, full many, ever so many, no end of, numerous, profuse, manifold, multiplied, multitudinous, multiple, multinomial, endless (105), teeming, populous, peopled.

Frequent, repeated, reiterated, outnumbering, thick, crowding, crowded; galore.

(*Phrases*) Thick as hail; thick as leaves in Vallombrosa; plentiful as blackberries; in profusion; numerous as the sands on the seashore; their name is Legion.

101 ZERO (*Substantives*), nothing (4), nought (or naught), cipher; nobody, *nemo.*

(*Adjectives*) None, not one, not any, not a soul.

_____

103 FEWNESS (*Substantives*) paucity, a small number, handful, scantiness, rareness, rarity, thinness.

Diminution of number, reduction, weeding, elimination, thinning; smaller number, minority.

(*Verbs*) To be few, etc.

To render few; reduce, diminish in number, weed, weed out, prick off, eliminate, thin, thin out, decimate.

(*Adjectives*) Few, scanty, scant, rare, infrequent, sparse, scattered, hardly or scarcely any, reduced, thinned, etc.

(*Phrases*) Few and far between; you could count them on the fingers of one hand.

_____

104 REPETITION (*Substantives*), iteration, reiteration, harping, recapitulation, run, recurrence (136), recrudescence, tautology, monotony; cuckoo-note, chimes, repetend, echo, burden of a song, refrain, jingle, renewal, rehearsal, réchauffé, rehash, reproduction (19).

Cuckoo, mocking-bird, mimic, imitator, parrot.

Periodicity (138), frequency (136).

(*Phrase*) A twice-told tale.

(*Verbs*) To repeat, iterate, reiterate, recapitulate, renew, reproduce, echo, re-echo, drum, hammer, harp on, plug, rehearse, redouble, recrudesce, reappear, recur, revert, recommence.

(*Phrases*) Do or say over again; ring the changes on; to harp on the same string; to din or drum in the ear; to go over the same ground; to begin again.

(*Adjectives*) Repeated, repetitional, repetitionary, repetitive, recurrent, recurring, reiterated, renewed, ever-recurring, thick-coming, monotonous, harping, sing-song, mocking, chiming; above-mentioned, said, aforesaid.

(*Phrases*) It's that man again; cut and come again; *crambe repetita*.

(*Adverbs*) Repeatedly, often (136), again, anew, over again, afresh, ditto, *encore, de novo, da capo, bis* (90).

(*Phrases*) *Toties quoties*; again and again; in quick succession, over and over again; ever and anon; time after time; year after year; times out of number; *ad nauseam*.

105 INFINITY (*Substantives*), infiniteness, infinitude.

(*Adjectives*) Infinite, numberless, innumerable, countless, sumless, untold, unnumbered, unsummed, incalculable, unlimited, limitless, illimitable, immeasurable, unmeasured, measureless, unbounded, boundless, endless, interminable, unfathomable, exhaustless, termless, indefinite, without number, without limit, without end, unending.

(*Adverbs*) Infinitely, etc., without measure, limit, etc., *ad infinitum*, world without end.

SECTION VI—TIME

1°. *Absolute Time*

106 DURATION (*Substantives*), time, period, term, space, span, spell, season, era, epoch, decade, century, chiliad, age, cycle, aeon.

Intermediate time, while, interval, interim, pendency, intervention, intermission, interregnum, interlude, recess, break, intermittence, respite (265).

Long duration (110).

(*Phrases*) The enemy; the whirligig of time.

(*Verbs*) To continue, last, endure, remain, go on; to take, take up, fill or occupy time, to persist, to intervene.

107 TIMELESSNESS (*Substantives*), neverness, absence of time, no time, *dies non*.

Short duration (111).

(*Adverbs*) Never, ne'er, at no time, on no occasion, at no period, nevermore, *sine die*.

(*Phrases*) On Tib's eve; at the Greek Calends; *jamais de ma vie*; 'jam every other day.'

To pass, pass away, spend, employ, while away or consume time, waste time.

(*Adjectives*) Continuing, lasting, enduring, remaining, persistent, perpetual, permanent (150).

(*Adverbs*) While, whilst, so long as, during, pending, till, until, up to, during the time or interval, the whole time or period, all the time or while, in the long run, all along, throughout, from beginning to end (52).

Pending, meantime, meanwhile, in the meantime, in the interim, *ad interim, pendente lite*, from day to day, for a time, for a season, for good, yet, up to this time.

108 Definite duration, or portion of time.

PERIOD (*Substantives*), second, minute, hour, day, week, fortnight, month, lunation, quarter, year, leap-year, lustrum, quinquennium, decade, lifetime, generation, century, age, millennium, *annus magnus*.

(*Adjectives*) Hourly, horary; daily, diurnal, quotidian; weekly, hebdomadal, menstrual, monthly, annual, secular, centennial, bicentennial, etc., bissextile, seasonal.

(*Adverbs*) From day to day, from hour to hour.

Once upon a time; Anno Domini, A.D.; Before Christ, B.C.

108A CONTINGENT DURATION.
During pleasure, during good behaviour, *quamdiu se bene gesserit.*

110 Long duration.

DIUTURNITY (*Substantives*), a long time, an age, a century, an eternity, aeon.

(*Phrases*) *Temporis longinquitas*; a month of Sundays.

Durableness, durability, persistence, lastingness, continuance, permanence (150), longevity, survival.

Distance of time, protraction, extension or prolongation of time, delay (133).

(*Verbs*) To last, endure, stand, remain, continue, abide, tarry, protract, prolong, outlast, outlive, survive; spin out, draw out, eke out, temporize, linger, loiter, lounge (275), wait.

(*Phrase*) To live to fight another day.

(*Adjectives*) Durable, of long duration, permanent, enduring, chronic, intransient, intransitive, intransmutable, lasting, abiding, persistent; livelong, longeval, long-lived, macrobiotic, diuturnal, evergreen, perennial, unintermitting, unremitting, perpetual (112).

Protracted, prolonged, spun out, long-winded, surviving, lingering.

(*Adverbs*) Long, a long time, permanently.

(*Phrases*) As the day is long; all the

109 Indefinite duration.

COURSE (*Substantives*), progress, process, succession, lapse, flow, flux, stream, tract, current, tide, march, step, flight, etc., of time.

Indefinite time, aorist.

(*Verbs*) To elapse, lapse, flow, run, proceed, roll on, advance, pass, slide, press on, flit, fly, slip, glide, run its course.

(*Adjectives*) Elapsing, passing, etc.; aoristic.

(*Adverbs*) In course of time, in due time of season, in process of time, in the fullness of time.

(*Phrase*) *Labuntur anni.*

111 Short duration.

TRANSIENTNESS (*Substantives*), transitoriness, impermanence, evanescence, transitiveness, fugitiveness, fugacity, fugaciousness, caducity, mortality, span, shortness, brevity.

Quickness, promptness (132), suddenness, abruptness.

A *coup de main*, bubble, Mayfly, nine days' wonder.

(*Verbs*) To be transient, etc., to flit, pass away, fly, gallop, vanish, fade, intromit.

(*Adjectives*) Transitory, transient, transitive, passing, impermanent, evanescent, fleeting, momentary, fugacious, fugitive, flitting, vanishing, shifting, flying, temporary, temporal, makeshift, provisional, provisory, rough and ready, cursory, galloping, short-lived, ephemeral, deciduous, meteoric.

Brief, sudden, quick, prompt, brisk, abrupt, extemporaneous, summary, hasty, precipitate.

(*Adverbs*) Temporarily, etc., *en passant, in transitu*, extempore.

In a short time, soon, at once, awhile, anon, by and by, briefly, presently, apace, eftsoons, straight, straightway, quickly, speedily, promptly, presto, slapdash, directly,

day long; all the year round; the live-long day; hour after hour; morning, noon, and night; for good; for many a long day.

---

112 PERPETUITY (*Substantives*), eternity, sempiternity, immortality, athanasy, everlastingness, perpetuation.

(*Verbs*) To last or endure for ever, to have no end: to eternize, perpetuate.

(*Adjectives*) Perpetual, eternal, everlasting, sempiternal, coeternal; endless, unending, ceaseless, incessant, unceasing, uninterrupted, interminable, having no end, unfading, evergreen, never-fading, amaranthine, ageless, deathless, immortal, undying, never-dying, imperishable, indestructible.

(*Adverbs*) Always, ever, evermore, aye, for ever, for aye, for evermore, still, perpetually, eternally, etc., in all ages, from age to age.

(*Phrases*) For ever and a day; *esto perpetua*; for ever and ever; world without end; time without end; *in secula seculorum*; to the end of time; till Doomsday; till hell freezes; to a cinder.

---

114 Estimation, measurement, and record of time.

CHRONOMETRY (*Substantives*), chronology, horology, horometry, registry, date, epoch, style, era.

Greenwich, standard, mean, local, solar, sidereal time; summer time, double summer time.

Almanac, calendar, ephemeris, chronicle, annals, register, journal, diary, chronogram, time-book.

Instruments for the measurement of time, clock, watch, stop-watch, repeater, chronograph, chronometer, sextant, timepiece, dial, sun-dial, horologe, pendulum, hour-glass, water-clock, clepsydra; time signal.

Chronographer, chronologer, chronologist, time-keeper, annalist.

(*Verbs*) To chronicle, to fix or mark the time, date, register, etc., to bear date, to measure time, to beat time, to make time, to time.

(*Adjectives*) Chronological, chronometrical, chronogrammatical.

(*Adverb*) O'clock.

immediately, incontinently, forthwith; suddenly, *per saltum*, at one bound.

(*Phrases*) At short notice; the time being up; before the ink is dry; here to-day and gone to-morrow (149); *sic transit gloria mundi*.

113 Point of time.

INSTANTANEITY (*Substantives*), instantaneousness, moment, instant, second, split second, minute, twinkling, trice, flash, breath, span, jiffy, flash of lightning, suddenness (111).

(*Verbs*) To twinkle, flash, to be instantaneous.

(*Adjectives*) Instantaneous, push-button, sudden, momentary, extempore.

(*Phrases*) Quick as thought; quick as a flash; quick as lightning.

(*Adverbs*) Instantly, momentarily, *subito*, presto, instanter, suddenly, plump, slap, slapdash, in a moment, in an instant, in a second, in no time, in a trice, in a twinkling, at one jump, in a breath, extempore, *per saltum*, in a crack, out of hand.

(*Phrases*) Before one can say 'Jack Robinson'; in a brace of shakes; between the cup and the lip; on the spur of the moment; in the twinkling of an eye; in a jiffy; in two ticks; on the instant; in less than no time; at one fell swoop; no sooner said than done.

115 False estimate of time.

ANACHRONISM (*Substantives*), error in time, prolepsis, metachronism, prochronism, parachronism, anticipation.

Disregard or neglect of time.

(*Verbs*) To anachronize, misdate, antedate, postdate, overdate, anticipate.

(*Adjectives*) Anachronistic, anachronous, misdated, undated, overdue, postdated, antedated.

(*Phrases*) To take no note of time; to prophesy after the event.

2°. Relative Time

I. TIME WITH REFERENCE TO SUCCESSION

116 PRIORITY (*Substantives*), ante-cedence, anteriority, precedence, pre-existence.

Precursor, predecessor, prelude, forerunner (64), harbinger, antece-dent; the past (122).

(*Verbs*) To precede, come before, forerun, pre-exist, prelude, usher in, dawn, announce (511), foretell, antici-pate, forestall.

(*Phrases*) To be beforehand; to steal a march upon.

(*Adjectives*) Prior, previous, pre-ceding, precedent, anterior, ante-cedent, pre-existent, pre-existing, former, foregoing, aforesaid, said, above-mentioned, prehistoric, ante-diluvian, pre-Adamite.

Precursory, prelusive, prelusory, proemial, introductory, prefatory (62), prodromal, prodromic.

117 POSTERIORITY (*Substantives*), succession, sequence, subsequence, supervention, sequel, successor (65), postlude.

(*Verbs*) To follow, come or go after, succeed, supervene, ensue.

(*Phrases*) To tread on the heels of; to follow in the footsteps of.

(*Adjectives*) Subsequent, posterior, following, after, later, succeeding, post-glacial, post-diluvial, post-dilu-vian, puisne, posthumous, post-prandial, post-classical.

(*Adverbs*) Subsequently, after, after-wards, since, later, later on, at a subsequent or later period, proximo, next, in the sequel, close upon, there-after, thereupon, whereupon, upon which, eftsoons, below, *infra*.

(*Adverbs*) Before, prior to, previously, anteriorly, antecedently, aforetime, ere, ere now, erewhile, before now, heretofore, ultimo, yet, beforehand, above, *supra*.

(*Phrase*) Before the flood.

118 THE PRESENT TIME (*Substan-tives*), the existing time, the time being, the present moment, juncture, crisis, epoch, day, hour; the twentieth century.

Age, time of life.

(*Verb*) To strike while the iron is hot.

(*Adjectives*) Present, actual, current, existing, that is.

(*Adverbs*) At this time, moment, etc., now, at present, at this time of day, at the present time, day, etc., to-day, nowadays, instant, already, even now, but now, just now, upon which.

(*Phrases*) For the time being; for the nonce; *pro hac vice*; on the nail; on the spot; on the spur of the moment; now or never.

119 Time different from the present.

DIFFERENT TIME (*Substantives*), other time.

Indefinite time, aorist.

(*Adjective*) Aoristic.

(*Adverbs*) At that time, moment, etc., then, at which time, etc., on that occasion, upon, in those days.

When, whenever, whensoever, upon which, on which occasions, at another or a different time, etc., otherwhile, otherwhiles, at various times, ever and anon.

(*Phrases*) Once upon a time; one day; some other time; one of these days.

120 SYNCHRONISM (*Substantives*), synchronization, coinstantaneity, co-existence, coincidence, simultaneousness, coevality, contemporaneousness, contemporaneity, concurrence, concomitance.

Having equal times, isochronism.

A contemporary, coeval, coetanean.

(*Verbs*) To coexist, concur, accompany, synchronize.

(*Phrase*) To keep pace with.

(*Adjectives*) Synchronous, synchronal, synchronistic, simultaneous, coexisting, coincident, concomitant, concurrent, coeval, coetaneous, contemporary, contemporaneous, coeternal, isochronous.

(*Adverbs*) At the same time, simultaneously, etc., together, during the same time, etc., in the interim, in the same breath, in concert, *pari passu*; meantime, meanwhile (106), while, whilst.

121 Prospective time.

FUTURITY (*Substantives*), the future, futurition, the approaching time, hereafter, the time to come, posteriority (117), after time, after age, the coming time, the morrow, after days, hours, years, ages; after life, millennium, doomsday, the day of judgment, the crack of doom.

The approach of time, the process of time, advent, time drawing on, the womb of time.

Prospection, anticipation, prospect, perspective, expectation (507), horizon, outlook, look-out.

Heritage, heirs, progeny, issue, posterity, descendants, heir apparent, heir presumptive.

Future existence, future state, post-existence, after-life, beyond.

(*Verbs*) To look forward, anticipate, forestall (132), have in prospect, keep in view, expect (507).

To impend, hang over, lie over, approach, await, threaten, overhang, draw near, prepare.

(*Phrases*) Lie in wait for; bide one's time; to wait impatiently; kick one's heels.

To be in the wind; to be cooking; to loom in the future.

(*Adjectives*) Future, to come, coming, going to happen, approaching, impending, instant, at hand, about to be or happen, next, hanging, awaiting, forthcoming, near, near at hand, imminent, threatening, brewing, preparing, in store, eventual, ulterior, in view, in prospect, prospective, in perspective, in the offing, in the wind, on the cards, that will be, overhanging.

Unborn, in embryo, in the womb of time.

122 Retrospective time.

PRETERITION (*Substantives*), the past, past time, *status quo*, days of yore, time gone by, priority (116), former times, old times, the olden time, ancient times, antiquity, antiqueness, lang syne, time immemorial, prehistory.

Archaeology, palaeology, palaeontology, palaeography, archaism, retrospection, retrospect, looking back.

Archaeologist, antiquary, medievalist, palaeographer, palaeologist, Dr. Dryasdust.

Ancestry (166), pre-existence.

(*Phrases*) The good old days; the golden age; the rust of antiquity.

(*Verbs*) To pass, be past, lapse, go by, elapse, run out, expire, blow over; to look back, cast the eyes back, retrospect, trace back, dig up, exhume.

(*Phrases*) To have run its course; to have had its day.

(*Adjectives*) Past, gone, gone by, over, bygone, foregone, pristine, prehistoric, quondam, lapsed, elapsed, preterlapsed, expired, late, *ci-devant*, run out, blown over, that has been.

Former, foregoing, late, last, latter, recent, overnight, preterperfect, preterpluperfect, forgotten, irrecoverable, out of date.

Looking back, retrospective, retroactive, *ex post facto*; archaeological, etc.

Pre-existing, pre-existent.

(*Adverbs*) Formerly, of old, erst, whilom, erewhile, before now, time was, ago, over, in the olden time, anciently, in days of yore, long since, retrospectively, ere now, before now, till now, once, once upon a time, hitherto, heretofore, *ultimo*.

(*Adverbs*) Prospectively, hereafter, by and by, some fine day, one of these days, anon, in future, to-morrow, in course of time, in process of time, sooner or later, *proximo*, in after time.

On the eve of, ere long, at hand, near at hand, on the point of, beforehand, against the time.

After a time, from this time, henceforth, henceforwards, thence, thenceforth, thenceforward, whereupon, upon which.

(*Phrases*) All in good time; in the fullness of time.

The other day, yesterday, last night, week, month, year, etc.; just now, recently, lately, of late, latterly.

Long ago, a long while or time ago, some time ago.

(*Phrases*) Once upon a time; from time immemorial; in the memory of man; time out of mind.

Already, yet, at length, at last.

---

2. TIME WITH REFERENCE TO A PARTICULAR PERIOD

123 NEWNESS (*Substantives*), novelty, recentness, recency, modernity, freshness, greenness, immaturity, youth (127), rawness.

Innovation, renovation (660), renewal.

Nouveau riche, parvenu, upstart, mushroom; latest fashion, *dernier cri.*

(*Verbs*) Renew, renovate, restore (660), modernize.

(*Adjectives*) New, novel, recent, fresh, green, evergreen, raw, immature, untrodden, advanced, twentieth-century, modern, modernistic, avant-garde, neoteric, new-born, nascent, new-fashioned, up-to-date, new-fangled, vernal, renovated, brand-new, split-new, virgin.

(*Phrases*) Fresh as a rose; fresh as a daisy; fresh as paint; just out; spick and span.

(*Adverbs*) Newly, recently, lately, afresh, anew.

124 OLDNESS (*Substantives*), age (128), antiquity, eld, ancientry, primitiveness, maturity, decline, decay, obsolescence; seniority, eldership, primogeniture.

Archaism, relic, antique, fossil, eolith; elder, doyen.

(*Verbs*) To be or become old, mature, mellow; to age, fade, decay.

(*Adjectives*) Old, ancient, antique, antiquated, out-of-date, of long standing, time-honoured, venerable, hoary, primitive, diluvian, antediluvian, fossil, palaeozoic, preglacial, palaeolithic, neolithic, primeval, primordial, prime, pre-Adamite, prehistoric, antemundane, archaic, classic, medieval.

Immemorial, inveterate, rooted, traditional.

Senior, elder, eldest, oldest, first-born (128).

Obsolete, obsolescent, out-of-date, stale, time-worn, faded, decayed, effete, declining, played-out, crumbling, decrepit (128), *passé.*

(*Phrases*) Nothing new under the sun; old as the hills; old as Methuselah; old as Adam; before the Flood; time out of mind; since the year one.

125 MORNING (*Substantives*), morn, morrow, forenoon, a.m., prime, dawn, daybreak, dayspring, peep of day, break of day, matins, aurora, first blush of the morning, prime of the morning, twilight, crepuscule, sunrise, sun-up, cockcrow.

126 EVENING (*Substantives*), eve, e'en, decline of day, close of day, eventide, nightfall, curfew, vespers, evensong, dusk, twilight, gloaming, eleventh hour, sunset, sundown, afternoon, p.m., bedtime, midnight, autumn, Indian summer, St. Martin's

Noon, midday, noontide, meridian, noonday, prime; spring, summer, midsummer.

(*Adjectives*) Matutinal, auroral, vernal, midsummer.

summer, St. Luke's summer, winter the fall.

(*Phrases*) The witching time of night; the dead of night; blind-man's holiday.

(*Adjectives*) Nocturnal, vespertine, autumnal, hiemal, brumal.

---

127 YOUTH (*Substantives*), infancy, babyhood, boyhood, juvenility, childhood, youthhood, juniority, juvenescence, adolescence (131), minority, nonage, teens, tender age, bloom, heyday, boyishness, girlishness.

Cradle, nursery, leading strings, pupilage, pupilship, puberty.

(*Phrases*) Prime or flower of life; the rising generation; salad days; schooldays.

(*Adjectives*) Young, youthful, juvenile, callow, sappy, beardless, under age, in one's teens, boyish, girlish, junior, younger.

(*Phrase*) In statu pupillari.

128 AGE (*Substantives*), old age, senility, senescence, oldness, longevity, years, anility, grey hairs, climacteric, decrepitude, hoary age, caducity, crow's feet, superannuation, dotage, anecdotage, seniority, green old age, eldership.

(*Phrases*) The vale of years; decline of life; the sere and yellow leaf; second childhood.

(*Adjectives*) Aged, old, elderly, senile, matronly, anile, in years, ripe, mellow, grey, grey-headed, hoary, hoar, venerable, timeworn, declining, antiquated, *passé*, rusty, effete, decrepit, superannuated.

Patriarchal, ancestral, primitive, older, elder, senior; eldest, oldest, first-born, bantling, firstling.

(*Phrases*) With one foot in the grave; marked with crow's feet; advanced in life, or in years; stricken in years; no chicken; long in the tooth; old as the hills.

---

129 INFANT (*Substantives*), babe, baby, nursling, suckling.

Child, bairn, wean, little one, brat, toddler, kid, chit, urchin, bantling, bratling, papoose, elf, piccaninny.

Youth, boy, lad, laddie, stripling, youngster, teenager, callant, younker, gossoon, nipper, whipster, whippersnapper, schoolboy, young hopeful, hobbledehoy, cadet, minor.

Girl, lass, lassie, wench, miss, colleen, flapper, bobbysoxer, damsel, maid, maiden, *jeune fille*.

Scion, sapling, seedling, tendril, mushroom, nestling, chicken, larva, chrysalis, tadpole, whelp, cub, pullet, fry, foetus, calf, lamb, lambkin, colt, filly, pup, puppy, foal, kitten.

130 VETERAN (*Substantives*), old man, seer, patriarch, greybeard, gaffer, grandsire, grandam, dowager, matron, crone, beldam, hag, sexagenarian, octogenarian, centenarian, oldster, old-timer, old stager, old buffer, fogy, geezer.

Methuselah, Nestor; elders, forefathers, forbears, fathers, ancestors, ancestry.

(*Adjectives*) Veteran, aged, old, grey-headed (128).

(*Adjectives*) Infantine, infantile, puerile, boyish, girlish (127), virginal, childish, baby, babyish, unfledged, new-fledged, kittenish, callow.

(*Phrases*) In leading-strings; at the breast; in arms; in one's teens; tied to mother's apron-strings.

131 ADOLESCENCE (*Substantives*), puberty, pubescence, majority, adultness, maturity, ripeness, manhood, virility.

A man, adult (373), a woman, matron (374), *parti*; ephebe.

(*Phrases*) Prime of life; man's estate; flower of age; meridian of life; years of discretion; *toga virilis*.

(*Adjectives*) Adolescent, pubescent, of age, out of one's teens, grown up, mature, middle-aged, manly, virile, adult.

Womanly, matronly, nubile, marriageable, out.

3. TIME WITH REFERENCE TO AN EFFECT OR PURPOSE

132 EARLINESS (*Substantives*), timeliness, punctuality, readiness, promptness (682), promptitude, expedition, quickness, haste, acceleration, hastening, hurry, bustle, precipitation, anticipation, precociousness, precocity.

Suddenness, abruptness (111).

(*Phrases*) A stitch in time saves nine; the early bird catches the worm.

(*Verbs*) To be early, to be in time, keep time, be beforehand.

To anticipate, forestall, book, engage, bespeak, reserve.

To expedite, hasten, haste, quicken (274), press, dispatch, accelerate, precipitate, hurry, bustle (684).

(*Phrases*) To take time by the forelock; to steal a march upon; to be beforehand with; to be pressed for time.

(*Adjectives*) Early, prime, rathe, timely, timeous, punctual, matutinal, forward, ready, quick, expeditious, precipitate, summary, prompt, premature, precocious, prevenient, anticipatory, pre-emptive.

Sudden, abrupt, unexpected (508), subitaneous, extempore.

(*Adverbs*) Early, soon, anon, betimes, apace, eft, eftsoons, in time, ere long, presently, shortly, punctually, to the minute, on time, on the dot.

Beforehand, prematurely, before one's time, in anticipation.

Suddenly, abruptly, at once, extempore, instanter.

(*Phrases*) In good time; at sunrise; with the lark; early days.

On the point of; at short notice; on the spur of the moment; all at once; before you can say 'knife'; no sooner said than done.

133 LATENESS (*Substantives*), tardiness, slowness (275), delay, cunctation, procrastination, deferring, lingering, lagging, etc., postponement, dilatoriness, adjournment, shelving, prorogation, remand, moratorium.

Protraction, prolongation, leeway.

(*Phrase*) Fabian tactics.

(*Verbs*) To be late, etc., tarry, wait, stay, bide, take time, dally, dawdle, linger, loiter, lag, bide one's time, shuffle (275, 683).

To stand over, lie over, hang fire.

To put off, defer, delay, leave over, suspend, stave off, postpone, adjourn, carry over, shelve, procrastinate, temporize, stall, filibuster, prolong, protract, draw out, spin out, hold up, prorogue.

(*Phrases*) To tide it over; to bide one's time; to let the matter stand over; to sleep on it; to kick (or cool) one's heels.

(*Adjectives*) Late, tardy, slow, dilatory (275), posthumous, backward, unpunctual, procrastinatory, behindhand, belated, overdue.

Delayed, etc., suspended, pending, in abeyance.

(*Adverbs*) Late, after time, too late, behind time; at length, at last.

Slowly, leisurely, deliberately.

(*Phrases*) Late in the day; a day after the fair; at the eleventh hour; after death, the doctor.

134 Occasion (*Substantives*), opportunity, chance, opening, break, show, room, suitable or proper time or season, high time, opportuneness, tempestivity, seasonableness, crisis, turn, juncture, conjuncture.

Spare time, leisure, holiday (685), spare moments, hours, etc., time on one's hands.

(*Phrases*) Golden (or favourable) opportunity; the nick of time;

(*Verbs*) To use, make use of, employ, profit by, avail oneself of, lay hold of, embrace, catch, seize, snatch, clutch, pounce upon, grasp, etc., the opportunity.

To give, offer, present, afford, etc., the opportunity.

To time well; to spend or consume time.

(*Phrases*) To turn the occasion to account; to seize the occasion; to strike the iron while it is hot; to make hay while the sun shines; *carpe diem*; to take the tide at the flood; to furnish a handle for.

(*Adjectives*) Opportune, timely, well-timed, timeful, timeous, seasonable, happy, lucky, providential, fortunate, favourable, propitious, auspicious, critical.

135 Intempestivity (*Substantives*), untimeliness, unsuitable time, improper time, unseasonableness, inopportuneness, evil hour.

Hitch, impediment (706), check, *contretemps.*

(*Verbs*) To be ill-timed, etc., to mistime, intrude, come amiss.

To lose, omit, let slip, let go, neglect, pretermit, allow, or suffer the opportunity or occasion to pass, slip, go by, escape, lapse; to lose time, to fritter away time (683).

(*Phrase*) To let slip through the fingers; to lock the stable door when the steed is stolen.

(*Adjectives*) Ill-timed, untimely, untimeous, mistimed, unseasonable, out of season, unpunctual, inopportune, untoward, intrusive, too late (133), too early (132), malapropos, unlucky, inauspicious, unpropitious, unfortunate, unfavourable, unsuited, unsuitable.

(*Adverb*) Inopportunely, etc.

(*Phrases*) As ill luck would have it; in evil hour; after meat, mustard; a day before (or after) the fair.

(*Adverbs*) Opportunely, etc., on the spot, in proper or due time or season, high time, for the nonce.

By the way, by the by, *en passant, à propos*, parenthetically.

(*Phrases*) In the nick of time; on the spur of the moment (612); now or never; at the eleventh hour; time and tide wait for no man.

3°. Recurrent Time

136 Frequency (*Substantives*), oftness, recurrence, repetition (104), recrudescence, reiteration, iteration, run, reappearance, renewal, *ritornello, ritournelle*, burden.

Frequenter, *habitué*, fan, client.

(*Verbs*) To recur, revert, return, repeat, reiterate, reappear, renew, reword.

To frequent, resort to, visit, attend, haunt, infest.

(*Adjectives*) Frequent, common, not rare, repeated, reiterated, thick-coming, recurring, recurrent, incessant, everlasting, perpetual, rife; habitual (613).

137 Infrequency (*Substantives*), rareness, rarity, uncommonness, scarcity, fewness (103), seldomness.

(*Verb*) To be rare, etc.

(*Adjectives*) Infrequent, rare, scarce, unfrequent, uncommon, unprecedented, unheard-of.

(*Phrase*) In short supply.

(*Adverbs*) Seldom, rarely, scarcely, hardly, scarcely ever, ever, hardly ever, not often unfrequently.

Once, once for all, once in a way.

(*Phrases*) Once in a blue moon; angels' visits.

(*Adverbs*) Often, oft, oft-times, not infrequently, frequently, oftentimes, many times, several times, repeatedly.

Again, anew, afresh, *de novo*, ditto, over again, *da capo*, again and again, over and over, ever and anon, many times over, time after time, time and again, repeatedly (104).

Perpetually, continually, constantly, incessantly, everlastingly, without ceasing.

Sometimes, occasionally, at times, now and then, now and again, from time to time, at intervals, between whiles, once in a while, there are times when.

Most often, for the most part, generally, usually, commonly, most frequently, as often as not.

(*Phrases*) A number of times; many a time (and oft); times out of number.

138 REGULARITY of recurrence, punctuality.

PERIODICITY (*Substantives*), intermittence, beat, ictus, pulse, pulsation, rhythm, lilt, swing, alternation, alternateness, bout, round, revolution, rotation, turn.

Anniversary, jubilee; silver, golden, wedding; centenary, bicentenary, tercentenary, etc.; feast, festival, birthday.

139 IRREGULARITY of recurrence, uncertainty, unpunctuality, fitfulness.

(*Adjectives*) Irregular, uncertain, unpunctual, capricious, desultory, unrhythmic, unrhythmical, fitful, spasmodic, flickering, casual.

(*Adverbs*) Irregularly, etc., by snatches, by fits and starts, skippingly, now and then, occasionally.

Regularity of return, rota, cycle, period, stated time, routine.

(*Phrase*) The swing of the pendulum.

(*Verbs*) To recur in regular order or succession, to come round, return, revolve, alternate, come in its turn, beat, pulsate, intermit; to regularize.

(*Adjectives*) Periodic, periodical, recurrent, cyclical, revolving, intermittent, remittent, alternate, every other, alternating, rhythmic, rhythmical, steady, punctual.

Hourly, daily, diurnal, tertian, quotidian, weekly, hebdomadal, fortnightly, bi-monthly, monthly, biannual, annual, yearly, biennial, triennial, centennial.

(*Phrase*) Regular as clockwork.

(*Adverbs*) Periodically, at regular intervals, at stated times, at fixed periods, punctually, from day to day.

By turns, in turn, in rotation, alternately, in shifts, off and on, ride and tie, hitch and hike.

SECTION VII—CHANGE

1°. *Simple Change*

140 Difference at different times.

CHANGE (*Substantives*), alteration, mutation, permutation, variation, modification, modulation, inflexion, mood, qualification, innovation, metastasis, metabolism, deviation, turn, diversion, inversion, reversion, reversal, eversion, subversion (162),

141 Absence of change.

PERMANENCE (*Substantives*), persistence, endurance, *status quo*; maintenance, preservation, conservation, conservatism, *laissez-faire*, rest, sleep, establishment, truce, suspension, settledness (265), perdurability, stability (150).

bouleversement, upset, organic change, revolution (146), substitution (147), transposition (148), transit, transition.

Transformation, transmutation, transfiguration, metamorphosis, transmigration, transubstantiation, transmogrification, metempsychosis, avatar.

Vicissitude, flux, unrest (149); change of mind, tergiversation (607).

(*Phrase*) The wheel of fortune.

(*Verbs*) To change, alter, vary, modify, modulate, diversify, qualify, tamper with, edit, turn, shift, veer, tack, chop, shuffle, swerve, warp, deviate, turn aside, turn topsy-turvy, upset, invert, reverse, introvert, subvert, evert, turn inside out.

Form, fashion, mould, model, vamp, warp, work a change, superinduce, resume, disturb (61), innovate, reform, remodel, refound, new-model, modernize, revolutionize.

Transform, transume, transmute, transfigure, transmogrify, metamorphose, pass to, leap to, transfer.

(*Phrases*) To ring the changes; to turn over a new leaf; to introduce new blood; to shuffle the cards; to turn the corner; to wax and wane; to ebb and flow; *tempora mutantur; nous avons changé tout cela.*

(*Adjectives*) Changed, altered, new-fangled, warped, etc.; transitional, metamorphic, metabolic, metastatic.

(*Adverb*) *Mutatis mutandis.*

(*Phrase*) The law of the Medes and Persians.

(*Verbs*) To remain, stay, stop, persist, tarry, hold, last, endure, continue, dwell, bide, abide, maintain, keep, hold on, stand, subsist, live, stand still, outlive, survive.

To let alone, let be.

(*Phrases*) To keep one's footing; to hold one's ground; to stick to one's guns; to stand fast.

(*Adjectives*) Persisting, etc., permanent, established, unchanged, unmodified, unrenewed, unaltered, fixed, settled, unvaried, intact, inviolate, persistent, stagnant, rooted, monotonous, unreversed, conservative, unprogressive, undestroyed, unrepelled, unsuppressed, unfailing, stationary (265), stereotyped, perdurable.

(*Adverbs*) *In statu quo*, for good, finally, at a stand, at a standstill, *uti possidetis.*

(*Phrases*) *J'y suis, j'y reste ; plus cela change, plus cela est la même chose ; esto perpetua.*

---

142 Change from action to rest.

CESSATION (*Substantives*), discontinuance, desistance, quiescence.

Intermission, remission, suspension, interruption, suspense, stand, halt, closure, stop, stoppage, pause, rest, lull, breathing-space, respite, truce, drop, interregnum, abeyance.

Comma, colon, semicolon, period, full stop.

(*Verbs*) To discontinue, cease, desist, break off, leave off, hold, stop, pause, rest, drop, lay aside, give up, have done with, stick, hang fire, pull up, give over, shut down, knock off, relinquish (624), surcease.

To come to a stand, or standstill, suspend, cut short, cast off,

143 CONTINUANCE in action (*Substantives*), continuation, perseverance, repetition (104), persistence, run.

(*Verbs*) To continue, persist, go on, keep on, abide, keep, pursue, hold on, run on, follow on, carry on, keep up, uphold, sustain, perpetuate, persevere, keep it up, stick it, peg away, maintain, maintain one's ground, harp upon, repeat (104), take root.

(*Phrases*) To keep the pot boiling; to keep the ball rolling.

(*Adjectives*) Continual, continuous, continuing, etc., uninterrupted, inconvertible, unintermitting, unreversed, unstopped, unrevoked, unvaried, unshifting, perpetual (112).

---

go out, be at an end; intromit, interrupt, arrest, intermit, remit; put an end or stop to.

To pass away, go off, pass off, blow over, die away, wear away, wear off (122).

(*Phrases*) To shut up shop; to stay one's hand; to rest on one's oars; to rest on one's laurels.

(*Interjections*) Hold! hold on! stop! enough! avast! *basta !* have done! a truce to! stop it! drop it! cheese it! chuck it! stow it! cut it out!

144 Gradual change to something different.

CONVERSION (*Substantives*), reduction, transmutation, resolution, assimilation; chemistry, alchemy; growth, lapse, progress, becoming; naturalization.

Passage, transit, transition, transmigration, flux, shifting, sliding, running into, etc.; phase, conjugations; convertibility.

Laboratory, alembic, crucible (691).

Convert, pervert, vert, turncoat, renegade, apostate.

(*Verbs*) To be converted into; to become, get, wax, come to turn to, turn into, assume the form of, pass into, slide into, glide into, lapse, shift, run into, fall into, merge into, melt, grow, grow into, open into, resolve itself into, settle into, mature, mellow; assume the form, shape, state, nature, character, etc., of; illapse.

To convert into; to make, render, form, mould, reduce, resolve into; transume (140), fashion, model, remodel, reorganize, shape, modify, transmogrify; assimilate to; reduce to, bring to; refound, re-form, reshape.

(*Adjectives*) Converted into, become, etc., convertible, transitional.

(*Adverbs*) Gradually, *gradatim*, by degrees, step by step, by inches, inch by inch, by little and little, by slow degrees, consecutively, seriatim, *in transitu.*

145 REVERSION (*Substantives*), return, reconversion, relapse (661), recidivism, atavism, throwback, reaction, recoil (277), backlash, rebound, ricochet, revulsion, alternation (138), inversion, regression (283).

Reinstatement, re-establishment (660).

(*Phrases*) The turning-point; the turn of the tide; *status quo ante bellum.*

(*Verbs*) To revert, turn back, return to, relapse, recoil, rebound, react; to restore (660), to undo, unmake.

(*Phrase*) To turn the tables (719).

(*Adjectives*) Reverting, etc., restored, etc., regressive, retrogressive, atavistic, revulsive, reactionary.

(*Interjection*) As you were!

146 Sudden or violent change.

REVOLUTION (*Substantives*), counter-revolution, revolt, rebellion (742), transilience, jump, leap, plunge, jerk, start, spasm, convulsion, throe, storm, earthquake, catastrophe, cataclysm (173).

Legerdemain, conjuration, sleight of hand, hocus-pocus (545), harlequinade, witchcraft (992).

A revolutionary, revolutionist, counter-revolutionist, deviationist; the red flag.

(*Verbs*) To revolutionize, remodel, recast, refashion, reconstruct.

(*Adjectives*) Revolutionary, radical, extreme, intransigent, catastrophic, cataclysmic.

(*Adverbs*) Root and branch.

147 Change of one thing for another.

SUBSTITUTION (*Substantives*), commutation, supplanting, replacement, supersession, enallage, metonymy, synecdoche, antonomasia.

Thing substituted, substitute (634), succedaneum, makeshift, shift, apology, stand-in, pinch-hitter, locumtenens, representative, proxy; understudy, deputy (759), vice, double, dummy, changeling, scapegoat, stooge; stop-gap, jury-mast, palimpsest, metaphor (521).

(*Phrase*) Borrowing of or robbing Peter to pay Paul.

(*Verbs*) To substitute, put in place of, commute, supplant, cut out, change for, supersede, take over from.

To give place to; to replace.

(*Phrases*) To serve as a substitute, etc.; to do duty for; to stand in the shoes of; to take the place of.

(*Adjectives*) Substituted, etc., vicarious, subdititious, makeshift, provisional.

(*Adverbs*) Instead, in place of, in lieu of, in the room of, *faute de mieux*.

148 Double and mutual change.

INTERCHANGE (*Substantives*), exchange, commutation, intermutation, reciprocation, transposition, permutation, shuffling, castling (at chess), hocus-pocus, interchangeableness, interchangeability.

Reciprocity (12), retaliation (718), barter (794).

(*Phrases*) A Roland for an Oliver; tit for tat; *quid pro quo*.

(*Verbs*) To interchange, exchange, bandy, transpose, shuffle, change hands, swap, dicker, permute, reciprocate, commute, counterchange.

(*Phrases*) To play at puss in the corner; to play musical chairs; to return the compliment; to give and take; you scratch my back and I'll scratch yours.

(*Adjectives*) Interchanged, etc., reciprocal, mutual, commutative, interchangeable, intercurrent.

(*Adverbs*) In exchange, vice versa.

2°. *Complex Changes*

149 MUTABILITY (*Substantives*), changeableness, changeability, inconstancy, variableness, mobility, instability, unsteadiness, vacillation, unrest, restlessness, slipperiness, impermanence, fragility, fluctuation, vicissitude, alternation, vibration, oscillation (314), flux, ebbing and flowing, ebbs and flows, ups and downs, fidgets, fidgetiness, fugitiveness, disquiet, disquietude.

A Proteus, chameleon, quicksilver, weathercock, kaleidoscope, harlequin; the moon.

(*Phrases*) April showers; shifting sands; the wheel of fortune; the Cynthia of the minute.

(*Verbs*) To fluctuate, vary, waver, flounder, vibrate, flicker, flit, flitter, shift, shuffle, shake, totter, tremble, vacillate, ebb and flow, turn and turn about, change and change about.

150 IMMUTABILITY (*Substantives*), stability, unchangeableness, unchangeability, constancy, permanence, persistence (106), invariableness, durability, steadiness (604), immobility, fixedness, stableness, settledness, stabiliment, firmness, stiffness, anchylosis, solidity, aplomb, ballast, incommutability, insusceptibility, irrevocableness.

Rock, pillar, tower, foundation, fixture.

(*Phrase*) The law of the Medes and Persians.

(*Verbs*) To be permanent, etc. (265), to stand, stand fast, stand pat, remain.

To settle, establish, stablish, perpetuate, fix, set, stabilitate, retain, keep, hold, make sure, nail, clinch, rivet, fasten (43), settle down, set on its legs.

(*Phrases*) To build one's house on a rock; to weather the storm.

To fade, pass away like a cloud, shadow, or dream.

(*Adjectives*) Mutable, changeable, variable, ever-changing, inconstant, impermanent, unsteady, unstable, protean, proteiform, unfixed, fluctuating, vacillating, shifting, versatile, fickle, wavering, flickering, flitting, restless, erratic, unsettled, mobile, fluttering, oscillating, vibratory, vagrant, wayward, desultory, afloat, alternating, plastic, disquiet, alterable, casual, unballasted, volatile, capricious (608).

Frail, tottering, shaking, shaky, trembling, fugitive, ephemeral, transient (111), fading, fragile, deciduous, slippery, unsettled, irresolute (605), rocky, groggy.

Kaleidoscopic, prismatic, iridescent, opalescent, shot.

(*Phrases*) Unstable as water; changeable as the moon, or as a weathercock ; *sic transit gloria mundi*; here to-day and gone to-morrow.

Present events

151 EVENTUALITY (*Substantives*), event, happening, occurrence, incident, affair, transaction, proceeding, fact, matter of fact, phenomenon, advent.

Business, concern, circumstance, particular, casualty, accident, adventure, passage, crisis, episode, pass, emergency, contingency, consequence (154).

The world, life, things, doings, course of things, the course, tide, stream, current, run, etc., of events.

(*Phrases*) Stirring events; the ups and downs of life; a chapter of accidents; the cast of the dice (156).

(*Verbs*) To happen, occur, take place, take effect, come, come of, become of, come about, come off, pass, come to pass, fall, fall out, run, be on foot, fall in, befall, betide, bechance, turn out, go off, prove, eventuate, draw on, turn up, crop up, supervene, survene, issue, arrive, ensue, arise, spring, start, come into existence, fall to one's lot.

(*Adjectives*) **Immutable**, incommutable, unchangeable, unaltered, unalterable, not to be changed, constant, permanent, invariable, undeviating, stable, durable (265), perennial (110), valid.

Fixed, steadfast, firm, fast, steady, confirmed, immovable, irremovable, rooted, riveted, stablished, established, incontrovertible, stereotyped, indeclinable, settled, stationary, stagnant.

Moored, anchored, at anchor, on a rock, firmly seated, deep-rooted, ineradicable.

Stranded, aground, stuck fast, high and dry.

Indefeasible, irretrievable, intransmutable, irresoluble, irrevocable, irreversible, inextinguishable, irreducible, indissoluble, indissolvable, indestructible, undying, imperishable, indelible, indeciduous, insusceptible of change.

(*Phrases*) *J'y suis, j'y reste*; *stet*; can the Ethiopian change his skin, or the leopard his spots?

Future events

152 DESTINY (*Substantives*), fatality, fate, doom, destination, lot, fortune, star, planet, preordination, predestination, fatalism, inevitableness, kismet, karma, necessity (601), after life, futurity (121).

(*Phrases*) The decrees of fate; the wheel of fortune.

(*Verbs*) To impend, hang over, overhang, be in store, loom, threaten, await, come on, approach, stare one in the face, foreordain, preordain, predestine, doom, must be.

(*Phrase*) To dree one's weird.

(*Adjectives*) About to happen, impending, coming, destined, imminent, inevitable, ineluctable, inexorable, fated, doomed, devoted

(*Phrases*) On the cards; on the knees of the gods.

(*Adverbs*) Necessarily, inevitably.

(*Phrases*) What must be, must; *che sarà sarà*; 'It is written'; the die is cast.

To pass off, wear off, blow over.

To experience, meet with, go through, pass through, endure (821), suffer, fare.

(*Adjectives*) Happening, occurring, etc., going on, current, incidental, eventful, stirring, bustling.

(*Phrase*) The plot thickening.

(*Adverbs*) Eventually, in the event of, on foot, on the *tapis*, as it may happen, happen what may, at all events, sink or swim, come what may.

(*Phrases*) In the course of things; in the long run; as the world wags.

Section VIII—Causation

1°. *Constancy of Sequence in Events*

153 Constant antecedent.

Cause (*Substantives*), origin, source, principle, element, occasioner, prime mover, *primum mobile*, spring, mainspring, agent, seed, leaven, groundwork, basis (215), fountain, well, fount, fountain-head, spring-head, author (164), parent (166), *fons et origo, raison d'être*.

Pivot, hinge, turning-point, key, lever.

Final cause, proximate cause, immediate cause, ground, reason, the reason why, the why and the wherefore, rationale, occasion, derivation, provenance.

Rudiment, germ, embryo, bud, root, *radix*, radical, etymon, nucleus, seed, ovum, stem, stock, trunk, taproot.

Nest, cradle, womb, *nidus*, birthplace, hot-bed, forcing-bed.

Causality, origination, causation, production (161), aetiology.

Theories of causation, creationism; evolution, Lamarckism, Darwinism, Spencerism, orthogenesis.

(*Verbs*) To be the cause of, to originate, germinate, give origin to, cause, occasion, give rise to, kindle, suscitate, bring on, bring to pass, give occasion to, produce, bring about, institute, found, lay the foundation of, lie at the root of, procure, draw down, induce, realize, evoke, provoke, elicit, entail, develop, evolve, operate (161).

154 Constant sequent.

Effect (*Substantives*), consequence, product, result, resultant, resultance, upshot, issue, end (67), fruit, crop, aftermath, harvest, development, outgrowth, derivative, derivation.

Production, produce, work, handiwork, performance, creature, creation, offshoot, fabric, offspring, first-fruits, firstlings, output, *dénouement*, derivation, heredity, evolution (161).

(*Verbs*) To be the effect, work, fruit, result, etc., of; to be owing to, originate in or from, rise from, take its rise from, arise, spring, proceed, evolve, come of, emanate, come, grow, germinate, bud, sprout, stem, issue, flow, result, follow, accrue, etc., from; come to; to come out of, be derived from, be caused by, depend upon, hinge upon, turn upon, result from, to be dependent upon, hang upon; to pan out.

(*Phrase*) To take the consequences.

(*Adjectives*) Owing to, due to, attributable to, ascribable to, resulting from, through, etc., all along of, hereditary, genetic, derivative.

(*Adverbs*) Of course, consequently, necessarily, eventually.

(*Phrases*) *Cela va sans dire*; thereby hangs a tale.

To conduce, contribute, tend to (176); to determine, decide.

(*Phrases*) To have a hand in; to have a finger in the pie; to open the door to; to be at the bottom of; to sow the seeds of; to turn the scale.

(*Adjectives*) Caused, occasioned, etc., causal, original, primary, primordial, having a common origin, connate, radical, embryonic, embryotic, in embryo.

Evolutionary, Darwinian; aetiological.

(*Phrase*) Behind the scenes.

155 Assignment of cause.

ATTRIBUTION (*Substantives*), theory, aetiology, ascription, reference to, rationale, accounting for, imputation to, derivation from, filiation, affiliation, genealogy, pedigree, paternity, maternity (166), explanation (522), cause (153).

(*Verbs*) To attribute, ascribe, impute, refer to, derive from, lay to, point to, charge on, ground on, invest with, assign as cause, trace to, father upon, account for, theorize, ground, etc.

(*Phrases*) To put the saddle on the right horse; to point out the reason of; to lay at the door of.

(*Adjectives*) Attributable, imputable, assignable, traceable, ascribable, referable, owing to, derivable from.

Putative, attributed, imputed, etc.

(*Adverbs*) Hence, thence, therefore, because, from that cause, for that reason, on that account, owing to, thanks to, forasmuch as, whence, *propter hoc*, wherefore, since, inasmuch as.

Why? wherefore? whence? how comes it? how is it? how happens it? how does it happen?

In some way, somehow, somehow or other, in some such way.

(*Phrase*) *Hinc illae lacrimae.*

156 Absence of assignable cause.

CHANCE (*Substantives*), indetermination, accident, fortune, hazard, hap, haphazard, chance-medley, luck, lot, fate (152), casualty, contingency, adventure, venture, pot-luck, lucky dip, treasure trove, hit.

A lottery, toss-up, game of chance, *sortes Virgiliance, rouge et noir*, heads or tails, gambling (621), sweepstake.

Possibility, probability, odds, long odds, a near shave, bare chance.

(*Phrases*) The turn of the cards; a cast or throw of the dice; a pig in a poke; a blind date.

(*Verbs*) To chance, hap, turn up; to fall to one's lot, to be one's fate (152); to light upon; stumble upon.

To game, gamble, cast lots, raffle, play for.

(*Phrases*) To take one's chance; to toss up for; to chance one's arm; to take a flyer.

(*Adjectives*) Casual, fortuitous, random, accidental, adventitious, causeless, incidental, contingent, uncaused, undetermined, indeterminate, suppositional, possible (470); aleatory.

(*Adverbs*) By chance, by accident, perchance, peradventure, perhaps, maybe, mayhap, haply, possibly.

Casually, etc., at random, at a venture, as it may be, as it may chance, as it may turn up, as it may happen; as chance, luck, fortune, etc., would have it.

2°. *Connection between Cause and Effect*

157 POWER (*Substantives*), potentiality, potency, prepotence, prepotency, prepollence, puissance, strength, (159), might, force, energy, metal, dint, right hand, ascendancy, sway, control, almightiness, ability, ableness, competency, efficiency, effectiveness, efficacy, efficaciousness, validity, cogency, enablement; agency

158 IMPOTENCE (*Substantives*), inability, disability, disablement, impuissance, weakness (160), imbecility, paralysis, inaptitude, incapacity, incapability, invalidity, inefficacy inefficiency, inefficaciousness, ineffectualness, disqualification, helplessness, incompetence.

(*Phrases*) A dead letter; waste

(170), casualty (153), influence (175), authority (737).

Capability, capacity, faculty, quality, attribute, endowment, virtue, gift, property.

Pressure, high pressure, mechanical energy, applied force, motive power.

(*Verbs*) To be powerful, etc., to gain power; to exercise power, sway, etc., to constrain.

To be the property, virtue, attribute, etc., of; to belong to, pertain to, appertain to, to lie or be in one's power.

To give or confer power, to empower, enable, invest, endue, endow, arm, render strong (159).

(*Adjectives*) Powerful, high-powered, potent, puissant, potential, capable, able, equal to, cogent, valid, effective, effectual, efficient, efficacious, adequate, competent.

Forcible, energetic, vigorous, nervous, dynamic, vivid, sturdy, rousing, all-powerful, omnipotent, resistless, irresistible, inextinguishable, sovereign, invincible, unconquerable, indomitable.

(*Adverbs*) Powerfully, etc., by virtue of, in full force.

159 Degree of power.

STRENGTH (*Substantives*), energy (171), power (157), vigour, vitality, force, main force, physical force, brute force, spring, elasticity, tone, tension, tonicity.

Stoutness, sturdiness, lustiness, lustihood, stamina, physique, nerve, muscle, thews and sinews, backbone, pith, pithiness.

Feats of strength, athletics, gymnastics.

Strengthening, invigoration, bracing, recruital, recruitment, refreshment, refocillation (689).

Science of forces, dynamics, statics.

Adamant, steel, iron, oak, heart of oak.

An athlete, gymnast, acrobat; an Atlas, a Hercules, Sampson, Cyclops, Goliath.

(*Phrases*) A giant refreshed; a tower of strength.

paper; *brutum fulmen*; blank cartridge.

(*Verbs*) To be impotent, powerless, etc.; to collapse, fail, flunk, break down, fizzle out, fold up.

To render powerless, etc., to deprive of power, disable, disenable, incapacitate, disqualify, unfit, invalidate, nullify, deaden, cripple, cramp, paralyse, muzzle, hamstring, bowl over, render weak (160).

(*Phrases*) To go by the board; to end in smoke.

To clip the wings of; spike the guns; to tie a person's hands; to put a spoke in one's wheel; to take the wind out of one's sails.

(*Adjectives*) Powerless, impotent, unable, incapable, incompetent, inadequate, unequal to, inefficient, inefficacious, inept, ineffectual, ineffective, inoperative, nugatory, incapacitated, harmless, imbecile, disqualified, disabled, armless, disarmed, unarmed, weaponless, defenceless; unnerved, paralysed, palsied, disjointed, nerveless, adynamic, unendowed.

(*Phrases*) Laid on the shelf; *hors de combat*; not having a leg to stand on.

160 WEAKNESS (*Substantives*), feebleness, impotence (158), debility, atony, relaxation, helplessness, languor, slackness, enervation, nervousness, faintness, languidness, infirmity, emasculation, effeminacy, feminality, femineity, flaccidity, softness, defencelessness.

Childhood, etc. (127, 129); orphan, chicken.

Declension, loss, failure, etc., of strength, invalidation, delicacy, delicateness, decrepitude, asthenia, neurasthenia, anaemia, bloodlessness, palsy, paralysis, exhaustion, collapse, prostration, faintness, cachexy (or cachexia).

A reed, thread, rope of sand, house of cards; a weakling, sissy, jellyfish.

(*Verbs*) To be weak, etc., to droop, fade, faint, swoon, languish, decline, flag, fail, totter, drop, crock; to go by the board.

(*Verbs*) To be strong, etc., to be stronger, to overmatch.

To render strong, etc., to give strength, tone, etc., to strengthen, invigorate, brace, buttress, sustain, fortify, harden, case-harden, steel, gird up, screw up, wind up, set up, tone up.

To reinforce, refit, recruit, vivify, restore (660), refect, refocillate (689).

(*Phrase*) To set on one's legs.

(*Adjectives*) Strong, mighty, vigorous, stout, robust, sturdy, powerful, puissant, hard, adamantine, invincible, able-bodied, athletic, Herculean, muscular, brawny, sinewy, made of iron, strapping, well-set, well-knit, stalwart, doughty, husky, lusty, hardy, irresistible; strengthening, etc., invigorative, tonic.

Manly, manlike, masculine, male, virile, manful, full-blooded.

Unweakened, unallayed, unwithered, unshaken, unworn, unexhausted, unrelaxed, undiluted, unwatered, neat.

(*Phrases*) Made of iron; as strong as a lion, as a horse; in great form; fit as a fiddle.

(*Adverbs*) Strongly, forcibly, etc., by main force, *vi et armis*, by might and main, tooth and nail, hammer and tongs, for all one is worth.

To render weak, etc., to weaken, enfeeble, debilitate, devitalize, deprive of strength, relax, enervate, unbrace, unman, emasculate, castrate, geld, hamstring, disable, unhinge, cripple, cramp, paralyse, maim, sprain, exhaust, prostrate, blunt the edge of, deaden, dilute, water, water down.

(*Adjectives*) Weak, feeble, debile, strengthless, nerveless, imbecile, unnerved, relaxed, unstrung, unbraced, enervated, nervous, sinewless, spineless, lustless, effeminate, feminine, womanly, unmanned, emasculated, castrated.

Crippled, maimed, lamed, shattered, broken, frail, fragile, flimsy, gimcrack, halting, shaken, crazy, shaky, paralysed, palsied, paralytic, decrepit, puny, shilpit, drooping, languid, faint, sickly, flagging, dull, slack, limp, spent, effete, weatherbeaten, worn, seedy, exhausted, deadbeat, all in, whacked, done up, languishing, wasted, washy, vincible, untenable, laid low, run down, asthenic, neurasthenic, neurotic, rickety, invertebrate, feckless.

Unstrengthened, unsustained, unsupported, unaided, unassisted, defenceless, indefensible, unfortified, unfriended, fatherless, etc.

(*Phrases*) On one's last legs; the worse for wear; weak as a child, as a baby, as a kitten, as water; good or fit for nothing.

3°. *Power in Operation*

161 PRODUCTION (*Substantives*), creation, formation, construction, fabrication, manufacture, building, architecture, erection, edification, coinage, organization, putting together, establishment, setting up, performance (729), workmanship, output.

Development, breeding, evolution, flowering, genesis, generation, *epigenesis*, procreation, propagation, fecundation, impregnation, gestation, birth, bringing forth, parturition, growth, proliferation.

162 Non-production.

DESTRUCTION (*Substantives*), waste, dissolution, breaking up, disruption, consumption, disorganization, falling to pieces, crumbling, etc.

Fall, downfall, ruin, perdition, crash, smash, havoc, desolation, *bouleversement*, *débacle*, upset, wreck, shipwreck, cataclysm, extinction, annihilation; doom, destruction of life (360), prang (716, 732),

Demolition, demolishment, overthrow, subversion, suppression, dismantling, cutting up, corrosion,

Theory of development, Mendelism, eugenics.

(*Verbs*) To produce, effect, perform, operate, do, make, form, construct, fabricate, frame, contrive, manufacture, weave, forge, coin, carve, sculp, chisel, build, raise, edify, rear, erect, run up, establish.

To constitute, compose, organize, institute, work out, realize, bring to bear, bring to pass, accomplish, bring off.

To create, generate, engender, beget, bring into being, breed, propagate, proliferate, conceive, bear, procreate, give birth to, bring forth, yield, flower, fructify, hatch, develop, bring up.

To induce, superinduce, suscitate (153).

(*Phrases*) To be brought to bed of; to usher into the world.

(*Adjectives*) Produced, etc., producing, productive of, etc., creative, formative, parturient, pregnant, *enceinte*, genetic; eugenic.

(*Phrase*) In the family way.

---

163 REPRODUCTION (*Substantives*), renovation, restoration (660), reconstruction, revival, regeneration, revivication, resuscitation, reanimation, resurrection, resurgence, reappearance, palingenesis, reincarnation, multiplication; phoenix.

(*Verbs*) To reproduce, revive, renew, renovate, rebuild, reconstruct, regenerate, revivify, resurrect, resuscitate, reanimate, reincarnate, quicken; come again into life, reappear.

(*Phrase*) To spring up like a mushroom.

(*Adjectives*) Reproduced, etc., renascent, reappearing; hydra-headed.

---

erosion, crushing, upsetting, abolition, abolishment, sacrifice, immolation, holocaust, dilapidation, devastation, *razzia*, ravaging, extermination, eradication, extirpation, rooting out, averruncation, sweeping, etc., death-blow, *coup de grâce*, the crack of doom.

(*Verbs*) To be destroyed, etc., to perish, waste, fall to pieces, break up, crumble, break down, crack.

To destroy, do or make away with, demolish, overturn, upset, throw down, overthrow, overwhelm, subvert, put an end to, uproot, eradicate, extirpate, root out, grub up, break up, pull down, do for, dish, ditch, crumble, smash, crash, crush, quell, quash, squash, squelch, cut up, shatter, shiver, batter, tear or shake to pieces, tear to tatters, pick to pieces, put down, suppress, strike out, throw or knock down, cut down, knock on the head, stifle, dispel, fell, sink, swamp, scuttle, engulf, submerge, wreck, corrode, erode, consume, sacrifice, immolate, burke, blow down, sweep away, erase, expunge, liquidate, wipe out, mow down, blast.

To waste, lay waste, ravage, dilapidate, dismantle, disorganize, devour, swallow up, desolate, devastate, sap, mine, blow up, stifle, dispatch, exterminate, extinguish, quench, annihilate, kill (361), unroot, root out, rout out, averruncate, deracinate.

(*Phrases*) To go to the dogs, or to pot; to go to the devil, or to rack and ruin; to be all over with one.

To lay the axe to the root of; to make short work of; make a clean sweep of; to make mincemeat of; to scatter to the winds; cut up root and branch; knock on the head; to wipe the floor with; to knock into a cocked hat; to sap the foundations of; to nip in the bud; to strike at the root of; to pluck up by the root; to ravage with fire and sword.

(*Adjectives*) Destroyed, done for, dished, etc.; destructive, subversive, pernicious, ruinous, deadly, incendiary, demolitionary.

164 PRODUCER (*Substantives*), originator, author, artist, creator, prime mover, founder, workman, doer, performer, manufacturer, forger, agent (690), builder, architect, factor.

165 DESTROYER (*Substantives*), extinguisher, exterminator, assassin (361), executioner (975), ravager, annihilator, subverter, demolisher; iconoclast, vandal.

166 PATERNITY (*Substantives*), fatherhood, maternity, motherhood, parentage, parent, father, sire, paterfamilias, pater, dad, daddy, papa, pa; mother, mamma, ma, mummy, mum, dam, materfamilias, mater, procreator, pregenitor, begetter, ancestor, ancestry, forefathers, forbears, grandsire; house, parent stem, trunk, stock, pedigree.

(*Adjectives*) Paternal, maternal, parental, fatherly, motherly, family, ancestral, patriarchal.

167 POSTERITY (*Substantives*), progeny, breed, issue, offspring, brood, seed, litter, spawn, scion, offset, child, son, daughter, grandchild, grandson, granddaughter, etc., bantling, shoot, sprout, sprig, slip, branch, line, lineage, filiation, family, offshoot, ramification, descendant, heir, heiress, heir apparent, heir presumptive.

Straight descent, sonship, primogeniture, ultimogeniture.

(*Adjectives*) Filial, daughterly, dutiful, lineal, hereditary.

(*Phrase*) A chip of the old block; the rising generation.

168 PRODUCTIVENESS (*Substantives*), fecundity, fruitfulness, fertility, prolificness; creativeness, inventiveness.

Pregnancy, gestation, pullulation, fructification, multiplication, propagation, procreation.

A milch cow, rabbit, warren, hydra.

(*Phrase*) A land flowing with milk and honey.

(*Verbs*) To procreate (161), multiply, teem, pullulate, fructify, proliferate, generate, fertilize, impregnate, conceive.

(*Adjectives*) Productive, prolific, teeming, fertile, fruitful, luxuriant, fecund, pregnant, great, gravid, *enceinte*, with child, with young.

Procreant, procreative, generative, propagable, life-giving.

169 UNPRODUCTIVENESS (*Substantives*), infertility, barrenness, sterility, unfruitfulness, unprofitableness, infecundity, fruitlessness (645), nonagency.

(*Verbs*) To be unproductive, etc., to come to nothing.

To render unproductive, sterilize, castrate, spay, pasteurize.

(*Adjectives*) Unproductive, inoperative, barren, addle, infertile, unprolific, sterile, unfruitful, fallow, fruitless, infecund, issueless, unprofitable (645).

170 AGENCY (*Substantives*), operation, force, working, strain, function, office, hand, intervention, intercession, interposition, exercise, work, swing, play, causation (153), impelling force, mediation (631), action (680).

Modus operandi, quickening power, maintaining power.

(*Verbs*) To be in action, to operate, function, work, act, perform, play, support, sustain, strain, maintain, take effect, quicken, strike, strike hard, strike home, bring to bear.

(*Phrases*) To come into play; to make an impression.

(*Adjectives*) Acting, operating, etc., operative, practical, efficient, efficacious, effectual, in force.

Acted upon, wrought upon.

171 Physical ENERGY (*Substantives*), force, power, activity, keenness, intensity, sharpness, pungency, vigour, strength, edge, point, raciness, metal, mettle, vim, dash, fire, punch, go, pep.

Seasoning, mordant, pepper, mustard, cayenne, caviare (392).

Mental energy (604), mental excitation (824), voluntary energy (682).

Exertion, activity, stir, bustle, hustle, agitation, effervescence, fermentation, ferment, ebullition, splutter, perturbation, briskness, voluntary activity (682), quicksilver.

(*Verbs*) To give energy, energize, stimulate, invigorate, kindle, galvanize, electrify, intensify, excite, exert (173).

(*Adjectives*) Strong, energetic, emphatic, forcible, forceful, active, keen, vivid, intense, severe, sharp, acute, pungent, poignant, racy, brisk, ebullient, mettlesome, enterprising, go-ahead, double-edged, double-barrelled, double-distilled, drastic, intensive, trenchant.

(*Phrases*) *Fortiter in re*; with telling effect; with full steam; at high pressure; flat out.

172 Physical INERTNESS (*Substantives*) inertia, *vis inertiae*, inertion, passiveness, passivity, inactivity, torpor, latency, torpidity, dullness, stagnation, deadness, heaviness, flatness, slackness, tameness, slowness, languor, lentor, quiescence (265), sleep (683), intermission (141).

Mental inertness, indecision (605), placidity (826).

(*Verbs*) To be alert, inactive, passive, etc.; to hang fire, smoulder.

(*Phrase*) To sit on the fence.

(*Adjectives*) Inert, inactive, passive, torpid, flaccid, limp, lymphatic, sluggish, dull, heavy, flat, slack, tame, slow, supine, slothful, stagnant, blunt, lifeless, dead.

Latent, dormant, smouldering, unexerted, unstrained, uninfluential.

(*Adverbs*) Inactively, in suspense, in abeyance.

---

173 VIOLENCE (*Substantives*), inclemency, vehemence, might, impetuosity, boisterousness, abruptness, ebullition, turbulence, horseplay, bluster, uproar, shindy, row, riot, rumpus, fierceness, rage, wildness, fury, heat, exacerbation, exasperation, malignity, fit, paroxysm, orgasm, force, brute force, *coup de main*, strain, shock, spasm, convulsion, throe.

Outbreak, burst, outburst, dissilience, discharge, volley, explosion, blow-up, blast, detonation, rush, eruption, displosion, torrent.

Turmoil, tumult, storm, tempest, squall, hurricane, tornado, typhoon, cyclone, earthquake, volcano, thunder-storm.

A rowdy (949), berserk (or berserker), spitfire, fireater, hellhound, fury, termagant, virago, vixen, hellcat, dragon, demon, tiger, beldam, Tisiphone, Megaera, Alecto, Maenad.

174 MODERATION (*Substantives*), gentleness, temperateness, calmness, mildness, composure, sobriety, slowness, tameness, quiet (740), restfulness, reason.

Relaxation, remission, measure, golden mean, mitigation, tranquillization, assuagement, soothing, allaying, etc., contemperation, pacification (723), restraint, check (751), lullaby, sedative, lenitive, demulcent, palliative, opiate, anodyne, balm, opium.

Mental calmness (826).

(*Verbs*) To be moderate, etc., to keep within bounds or within compass, to settle down, to keep the peace, to sober down, remit, relent.

To moderate, soften, soothe, mitigate, appease, temper, attemper, contemper, mollify, lenify, tame, dull, take off that edge, blunt, obtund, tone down, subdue.

To tranquillize, assuage, appease, lull, cool, compose, still, calm, quiet,

(*Verbs*) To be violent, etc., to run high, ferment, effervesce, run wild, run riot, run amuck, rush, tear, rush headlong, bluster, rage, rampage, riot, storm, boil, fume, let off steam, foam, wreak, bear down.

To break out, fly out, bounce, go off, explode, displode, fly, fulminate, detonate, blow up, flash, flare, burst, burst out, shock, strain.

To render violent, sharpen, stir up, quicken, excite, incite, stimulate, kindle, lash, suscitate, urge, accelerate, foment, aggravate, exasperate, exacerbate, convulse, infuriate, madden, lash into fury, inflame, let off, discharge.

(*Phrases*) To break the peace; to see red; to out-herod Herod; add fuel to the flame.

(*Adjectives*) Violent, vehement, warm, acute, rough, rude, wild, boisterous, impetuous, ungentle, tough, brusque, abrupt, rampant, knock-about, rampageous, bluff, turbulent, blustering, riotous, rowdy, noisy, thundering, obstreperous, uproarious, outrageous, frantic, phrenetic, headstrong, rumbustious, disorderly (59).

hush, quell, sober, pacify, damp, lay, allay, rebate, slacken, smooth, soften, alleviate, rock to sleep, deaden (376), check, restrain, slake, curb, bridle, rein in, hold in, repress, smother, counteract (179).

(*Phrases*) To pour oil on the waves; to pour balm into; to throw cold water on.

(*Adjectives*) Moderate, gentle, mild, sober, temperate, measured, reasonable, tempered, calm, unruffled, tranquil, smooth, untroubled; unexciting, unirritating, soft, bland, oily, demulcent, lenitive, cool, quiet, anodyne, hypnotic, sedative, peaceful, peaceable, pacific, lenient, tame, halcyon, restful.

(*Phrases*) Gentle as a lamb; mild as milk.

(*Adverbs*) Moderately, gently, temperately, softly, etc.

(*Phrases*) Softly, softly, catchee monkey; *suaviter in modo*; *est modus in rebus*.

Savage, fierce, ferocious, fiery, fuming, excited, unquelled, unquenched, unextinguished, unrepressed, unbridled, unruly, boiling, boiling over, furious, outrageous, raging, running riot, storming, hysteric, hysterical, wild, running wild, ungovernable, unappeasable, immitigable, uncontrollable, insuppressible, irrepressible, raging, desperate, mad, rabid, infuriate, exasperated.

Tempestuous, stormy, squally, spasmodic, spastic, paroxysmal, convulsive, galvanic, bursting, explosive, detonating, volcanic, meteoric, seismic.

(*Phrases*) Fierce as a tiger; all the fat in the fire.

(*Adverbs*) Violently, etc., by force, by main force, like mad.

(*Phrases*) By might and main; tooth and nail; *vi et armis*; at the point of the sword, or bayonet.

4°. *Indirect Power*

175 INFLUENCE (*Substantives*), weight, pressure, prevalence, sway, ascendancy (or ascendency), preponderance, predominance, predominancy, dominance, prepotency, importance (642), reign, ableness, capability (157).

Footing, hold, foothold, purchase,

175A Absence of INFLUENCE, impotence (158), weakness (160), inertness (172).

(*Verb*) To have no influence.

(*Phrase*) To cut no ice.

(*Adjective*) Uninfluential.

----

fulcrum, stance, *point d'appui, pou sto, locus standi,* leverage, vantage-ground; aegis, protection, patronage, auspices.

(*Phrases*) A tower of strength; a host in himself.

(*Verbs*) To have influence, etc., to have a hold upon, to have a pull, to gain a footing, work upon, take root, take hold, permeate, penetrate, infiltrate, prevail, dominate, predominate, outweigh, overweigh, carry weight, weigh, tell, to bear upon.

(*Phrases*) To be in the ascendant; to cut some ice; to pull wires; to pull the strings; to set the fashion; to have a voice.

(*Adjectives*) Influential, valid, weighty, prevailing, prevalent, dominant, regnant, predominating, predominant, prepotent, ascendant, rife.

(*Adverb*) With telling effect.

176 TENDENCY (*Substantives*), aptness, proneness, proclivity, conduciveness, bent, bias, quality, inclination, trend, propensity, predisposition, leaning, drift, conducement, temperament, idiosyncrasy, vein, humour, mood.

(*Verbs*) To tend, contribute, conduce, lead, dispose, incline, trend, verge, bend to, affect, carry, promote, redound to, subserve to (644), bid fair to, make for, gravitate towards.

(*Adjectives*) Tending, contributing, conducing, conducive, working towards, calculated to, disposing, inclining, bending, leading, carrying to, subservient, subsidiary (644, 707); apt, liable, prone, disposed, predisposed.

(*Adverbs*) For, whither, in a fair way to.

177 LIABILITY (*Substantives*), subjection to, dependence on, exposure to, contingency, possibility (156), susceptivity, susceptibility.

(*Verbs*) To be liable, etc., incur, to lay oneself open to, lie under, expose oneself to, stand a chance, to open a door to.

(*Phrase*) To stick one's neck out.

(*Adjectives*) Liable, apt, prone, subject, open to, incident to, exposed to, dependent on; answerable, accountable, responsible.

Contingent, incidental, possible, casual.

(*Phrases*) Within range of; at the mercy of.

5°. *Combinations of Causes*

178 CONCURRENCE (*Substantives*), co-operation, collaboration (709), union, agreement, consent (488), pulling together, alliance; complicity, connivance, collusion.

Voluntary concurrence (709).

(*Verbs*) To concur, co-operate, conspire, agree, conduce, contribute, unite, to pull together, hang together, join forces.

(*Phrases*) To have a hand in; to be in the same boat; to go hand in hand (709).

(*Adjectives*) Concurring, concurrent, conjoined, concomitant, associate, co-operating, conspiring, agreeing, correspondent, conformable, pulling

179 COUNTERACTION (*Substantives*), opposition, antagonism, polarity, clashing, etc., collision, contrariety (14), resistance, interference, friction.

Neutralization, nullification, compensation (30).

Reaction, retroaction (277), repercussion, rebound, recoil, ricochet, counterblast.

Check, obstacle, hindrance (706); antidote, counter-irritant, preventive, corrective, remedy (662).

Voluntary counteraction (708).

(*Verbs*) To counteract, oppose, cross, contravene, antagonize, interfere or conflict with, collide with,

together, etc., of one mind, in alliance with, with one consent, of one mind, with one accord.

clash, neutralize, undo, nullify, render null; to militate against, withstand, resist (719), hinder (706), repress, control, curb, check, rein in (174).

To react (277), countervail, counterpoise (30), overpoise.

(*Adjectives*) Counteracting, opposing, etc., counteractive, antagonistic, conflicting, reactionary, recalcitrant, opposite, retroactive, cohibitive, counter, contrary (14).

(*Adverbs*) Counter, notwithstanding, nevertheless, nathless, none the less, yet, still, although, though, albeit, howbeit, maugre, at all events.

But, even, however, in defiance of, in the teeth of, in the face of, in spite of, in despite of (708).

(*Phrases*) For all that; all the same; be that as it may; even so.

CLASS II

WORDS RELATING TO SPACE

SECTION I—SPACE IN GENERAL

1°. *Abstract Space*

180 Indefinite space.
SPACE (*Substantives*), extension, extent, expanse, room, scope, range, purview, way, expansion, compass, sweep, play, amplitude, latitude, field, swing, spread, stretch; spare room, headway, elbow-room, freedom, house-room, stowage, roomage, margin.

Open space, void space, vacuity (4), opening, waste, wilderness, moor, moorland, campagna, tundra.

Abyss (198); unlimited space, infinity (105).

(*Adjectives*) Spatial, two-dimensional, three-dimensional.

Spacious, roomy, commodious, extensive, expansive, capacious, ample.

Boundless, unlimited, unbounded, limitless, illimitable, infinite, uncircumscribed, shoreless, trackless, pathless.

(*Adverbs*) Extensively, etc., wherever, everywhere.

(*Phrases*) The length and the breadth of the land; far and near, far and wide; all over; all the world over; from China to Peru; from Land's End to John o' Groat's; in every quarter; in all quarters; in all lands; every hole and corner; here, there, and everywhere; from pole to pole; throughout the world; to the four winds; under the sun.

181 Definite space.
REGION (*Substantives*), sphere, ground, area, realm, quarter, district, orb, circuit, circle, compartment, domain, tract, department, territory, country, canton, county, shire, township, riding, hundred, parish, bailiwick, province, satrapy, *arrondissement*, commune, enclave, principality, duchy, kingdom, empire, dominion, colony, protectorate, mandate.

Arena, precincts, *enceinte*, walk, patch, plot, paddock, enclosure, enclosure, field, compound.

Clime, climate, zone, meridian.

(*Adjectives*) Regional, territorial, provincial, parochial, local, etc.

Limited space, locality.
182 PLACE (*Substantives*), spot, point, nook, corner, recess, hole, niche, compartment, premises, precinct, station, pitch, venue, abode (189).

Indefinite place.

(*Adverbs*) Somewhere, in some place, wherever it may be.

———

2°. *Relative Space*

183 SITUATION (*Substantives*), position, locality, locale, status, latitude and longitude, footing, standing, post, stage, bearings, aspect, orientation, attitude, posture, lie, emplacement.

Place, site, station, pitch, seat, venue, whereabouts, direction, azimuth, etc. (278).

Topography, geography, chorography.

A map, chart, plan (554).

(*Verbs*) To be situated, to lie, to have its seat in.

(*Adjectives*) Local, topical; situate.

(*Adverbs*) *In situ*, here and there, *passim*, whereabouts.

184 LOCATION (*Substantives*), localization, lodgment, deposition, reposition, stowage, establishment, settlement, fixation, grafting, insertion (300), lading, encampment, billet, installation.

A colony, settlement, cantonment.

A habitation, residence, dwelling (189).

(*Phrases*) *Genius loci*; the spirit of the place.

(*Verbs*) To place, situate, locate, localize, put, lay, set, seat, station, lodge, park, post, install, house, settle, stow, dump, establish, fix, root, plant, graft, stick in, tuck in, insert, wedge in, shelve, pitch, camp, posit, deposit, reposit, cradle, encamp, moor, pack, embed (or imbed), vest, stock, populate, people, colonize, domicile.

To billet on, quarter upon.

To pocket, pouch, put up, bag, load.

To inhabit, reside (186), domesticate, put up at, colonize.

(*Phrase*) To pitch one's tent.

185 DISPLACEMENT (*Substantives*), dislodgment, eviction, ejectment (297), deportation, extradition, expatriation, banishment, exile.

Removal, remotion, transposition, relegation (270).

(*Verbs*) To displace, dislodge, unhouse, unkennel, break bulk, take off, eject, evict, chuck out, hoof out, expel, etc. (297), extradite, expatriate, banish, exile, relegate, oust, rusticate, ostracize, remove, transfer, transpose, transplant, transport (270), empty, clear, clear out, sweep off, sweep away, do away with, get rid of, root out, disestablish, unpeople, depopulate.

To vacate, leave (293), get out, heave out, bale out, lade out, pour out (297).

(*Phrase*) To make a clean sweep of.

(*Adjectives*) Displaced, etc., unhoused, houseless, homeless, stateless.

(*Phrase*) Like a fish out of water.

(*Adjectives*) Placed, located, etc., situate, situated, ensconced, nestled, embosomed, housed, moored, rooted, unremoved.

3°. *Existence in Space*

186 PRESENCE (*Substantives*), occupancy, occupation, attendance, whereness.

Diffusion, permeation, pervasion, interpenetration, dissemination (73).

Ubiquity, ubiety, ubiquitousness, omnipresence.

(*Verbs*) To exist in space, to be present, attend, remain.

To occur in a place, lie, stand, occupy, colonize.

To inhabit, dwell, reside, live, abide, sojourn, lodge, nestle, perch, roost, put up at, hang out at, stay at,

187 ABSENCE (*Substantives*), nonexistence (2), non-residence, nonattendance, alibi, absenteeism.

Emptiness, void, vacuum, voidness, vacuity, vacancy, vacuousness.

An absentee, truant, nobody, nobody on earth.

(*Verbs*) To be absent, not present, etc., vacate, to keep away, to keep out of the way.

(*Phrases*) Make oneself scarce; absent oneself; take oneself off; stay away; play truant; be conspicuous by one's absence.

stop at, squat, hive, burrow, camp, encamp, bivouac, anchor, settle, take up one's quarters, pitch one's tent, get a footing, frequent, haunt, tenant, take root, strike root, revisit.

To fill, pervade, permeate, penetrate, interpenetrate, infiltrate, be diffused through, be disseminated through, overspread, run through.

(*Adjectives*) Present, occupying, inhabiting, etc., moored, at anchor, resident, residentiary, domiciled.

Ubiquitous, omnipresent.

(*Adverbs*) Here, there, where? everywhere, in residence, aboard, on board, at home, afield, etc., on the spot.

(*Phrases*) Here, there, and everywhere; at every turn.

(*Adjectives*) Absent, not present, away, gone, from home, missing, non-resident.

Empty, void, vacant, vacuous, blank, untenanted, tenantless, uninhabited, deserted, devoid, unoccupied, unpeopled.

(*Phrases*) Nowhere to be found; A.W.O.L. (absent without leave); *non est inventus*; not a soul; nobody present; the bird being flown.

(*Adverbs*) Without, minus, nowhere, elsewhere, sans.

(*Phrases*) One's back being turned; behind one's back.

---

188 INHABITANT (*Substantives*), resident, residentiary, dweller, indweller, occupier, occupant, lodger, boarder, paying guest, inmate, tenant, sojourner, settler, squatter, backwoodsman, national, colonist, denizen, citizen, cit, cockney, townsman, burgess, countryman, villager, cottar, compatriot, garrison, crew, population, people.

N a t i v e, indigene, aborigines, autochthones, son of the soil.

A colony, settlement, household.

Newcomer (57).

(*Adjectives*) Indigenous, native, aboriginal, autochthonous, domestic, domiciliated, domesticated, domiciliary.

189 Place of habitation.

ABODE (*Substantives*), dwelling, lodging, domicile, residence, address, habitation, berth, seat, lap, sojourn, housing, quarters, accommodation, headquarters, throne, ark, tabernacle.

Nest, nidus, lair, haunt, eyrie (or aerie), den, hole, earth, warren, rookery, hive, habitat, haunt, resort, retreat, nidification, perch, roost.

Bivouac, camp, encampment, cantonment, castrametation, tent, marquee, teepee, igloo.

Cave, cavern, cell, grove, grot, grotto, alcove, bower, arbour, cove, chamber (191).

Home, fatherland, motherland, native land, country, homestead, homestall, fireside, snuggery, hearth, Lares and Penates, household gods, roof, household, housing; 'dulce domum,' Blighty.

Building, structure, edifice, fabric, erection, pile, tenement, messuage, farm, farmhouse, steading, grange.

Cot, cabin, hut, shack, chalet, croft, shed, hangar, penthouse, lean-to, booth, stall, hovel, outhouse, barn, kennel, sty, coop, hutch, cage, cote, stable, garage, offices.

House, mansion, villa, flat, flatlet, prefab, maisonnette, cottage, box, lodge, *pied-à-terre*, bungalow, hermitage, summer-house, gazebo, folly, rotunda, tower, temple (1000), château, castle, pavilion, court, hall, palace, kiosk, house-boat.

Inn, hostel, hotel, roadhouse, motel, tavern, caravansery, hospice, rest-house, dak-bungalow, barrack, lodging-house, guest-house, dosshouse, lodgings, apartments, diggings, digs.

Hamlet, village, clachan, thorp, dorp, kraal, borough, burgh, municipality, town, city, garden city, metropolis, suburb (227), conurbation, province, country.

Street, place, terrace, parade, road, avenue, row, lane, alley, court, wynd, close, yard, passage, rents, slum; square, polygon, quadrant, circus, crescent, mall, place, piazza, arcade, gardens.

Anchorage, roadstead, dock, basin, wharf, quay, port, harbour, haven.

(*Adjectives*) Urban, civic, metropolitan, municipal, provincial, rural, rustic, countrified; home-like, homy.

190 Things contained.

CONTENTS (*Substantives*), cargo, lading, filling, stuffing, freight, load, burden, ware (798).

191 RECEPTACLE (*Substantives*), recipient, receiver, reservatory, compartment (636).

Cell, cellule, loculus, follicle, hole, corner, niche, recess, nook, crypt, stall, pigeon-hole, lodging (189), bed, berth, bunk, doss, etc. (215), store-room, strong-room.

Capsule, vesicle, cyst, bladder, pod.

Stomach, belly, paunch, ventricle, crop, craw, maw, gizzard, bread-basket, kyte, ovary, womb (221).

Pocket, pouch, sporran, fob, sheath, scabbard, socket, bag, sac, sack, wallet, scrip, poke, kit, knapsack, rucksack, haversack, sabretache, satchel, cigar-case, cigarette-case, reticule, powder-box, flapjack, compact, vanity-case, vanity-bag, portfolio, budget.

Chest, box, hutch, coffer, case, casket, caddy, pyx (or pix), caisson, desk, davenport, escritoire, bureau, cabinet, reliquary; trunk, portmanteau, saratoga, grip-sack, grip, bandbox, valise, hold-all, attaché-case, dispatch-case, dispatch-box, writing-case, suit-case, dressing-case, kit-bag, brief-bag, brief-case, gladstone bag, boot, creel, crate, packing-case, snuff-box, mull.

Vessel, vase, bushel, barrel, canister, jar, can, pottle, basket, pannier, corbeille, punnet, hamper, tray, hod.

For liquids: cistern, reservoir, tank, vat, cauldron, barrel, cask, keg, runlet, firkin, kilderkin, demijohn, carboy, amphora, bottle, jar, decanter, carafe, tantalus, ewer, cruse, crock, kit, canteen, flagon, flask, flasket, thermos flask. vacuum flask, stoup, noggin, vial (or phial), cruet, caster, urn, samovar, billy.

Tub, bucket, pail, pot, tankard, beaker, jug, pitcher, mug, noggin, pipkin, gallipot, matrass, receiver, alembic, retort, test-tube, pipette, capsule, kettle, spittoon.

Bowl, basin, jorum, punch-bowl, cup, goblet, chalice, quaich, tumbler, glass, horn, can, pan, pannikin, plate, dish, trencher, tray, salver, patera, calabash, porringer, saucepan, skillet, casserole, tureen, saucer, platter, hod, scuttle, baikie, shovel, trowel, spoon, spatula, ladle.

Closet, cupboard, cellaret, chiffonier, wardrobe, bunker, locker, bin, buffet, press, safe, sideboard, whatnot, drawer, chest of drawers, tallboy, lowboy, till.

Chamber, flat, storey, apartment, room, cabin, bower, office, court, hall, saloon, *salon*, parlour, state-room, presence-chamber, reception-room, drawing-room, sitting-room, living-room, gallery, cabinet, nursery, boudoir, library, study, snuggery, adytum, sanctum, den, phrontistery, lumber-room (636), dormitory, bedroom, dressing-room, refectory, dining-room, breakfast-room, billiard-room, smoking-room, pew, harem, seraglio, zenana.

Attic, loft, garret, cockloft, belfry, cellar, vault, hold, cockpit, ground-floor, *rez-de-chaussée*, basement, kitchen, kitchenette, pantry, scullery, bath-room, lavatory, water-closet, w.c., urinal, latrine, rear, toilet, convenience, comfort station, heads, thunder-box, offices.

Portico, porch, veranda, piazza, stoop, lobby, court, hall, vestibule, foyer, lounge, corridor, loggia, passage, anteroom, antechamber.

(*Adjectives*) Capsular, saccular, sacculate, recipient, ventricular, cystic, vascular, celled, cellular, cellulous, cellulose, camerated, chambered, locular, multilocular, roomed, two-roomed, etc., polygastric, pouched, marsupial.

SECTION II—DIMENSIONS

1°. *General Dimensions*

192 SIZE (*Substantives*), magnitude, dimension, bulk, volume, largeness, bigness, greatness (31), expanse, amplitude, mass, massiveness.

Capacity, capaciousness, tonnage (or tunnage), calibre, scantling.

Average size, stock size.

Corpulence, adiposity, obesity, chubbiness, plumpness, *embonpoint*, stoutness, out-size; corporation, flesh and blood, brawn, brawniness.

Hugeness, vastness, enormousness, enormity, immensity, monstrousness, monstrosity; expansion (194), infinity (105).

A giant, Goliath, Brobdingnagian, Antaeus, Gargantua, monster, whale, leviathan, elephant, mammoth, colossus, tun, lump, chunk, bulk, block, boulder, mass, bushel, whacker, thumper, whopper, spanker, behemoth.

A mountain, mound, heap (72).

(*Phrases*) A Triton among the minnows; the lion's share.

(*Verbs*) To be large, etc., to become large (194).

(*Adjectives*) Large, big, great, considerable, bulky, voluminous, ample, massive, massy, capacious, comprehensive, mighty, king-sized.

Corpulent, obese, stout, fat, plump, rotund, buxom, sonsy, lusty, strapping, bouncing, portly, burly, brawny, fleshy, beefy, goodly, in good case, chopping, jolly, chubby, full-grown, chub-faced, lubberly, hulking, unwieldy, lumpish, husky, stalwart.

193 LITTLENESS (*Substantives*), smallness (32), minuteness, diminutiveness, exiguity, inextension, puniness, dwarfishness, epitome, duodecimo, rudiment, microcosm.

Leanness, emaciation, thinness, macilency, flaccidity, meagreness.

A dwarf, runt, pygmy, midget, Lilliputian, chit, bantam, urchin, elf, doll, puppet, skeleton, ghost, spindle-shanks, shadow, Tom Thumb, manikin, *homunculus*.

Animalcule, mite, insect, emmet, fly, gnat, midge, shrimp, minnow, worm, grub, tit, tomtit, mouse, small fry, smout, mushroom, pollard, millet-seed, mustard-seed, grain of sand, molehill.

Atom, point, speck, dot, mote, ace, jot, iota, tittle, whit, particle, corpuscle, electron, molecule, monad, granule, grain, crumb, globule, nutshell, minim, drop, droplet, mouthful, thimbleful, sprinkling, dash, suspicion, *soupçon*, minimum, powder (330), driblet, patch, scrap, chip, inch, mathematical point; minutiae.

(*Phrases*) The shadow of a shade; a drop in the ocean; chicken feed; tip of the ice-berg.

(*Verbs*) To be small, etc., to become small, contract (195).

(*Adjectives*) Little, small, minute, diminutive, inconsiderable, exiguous, puny, tiny, wee, weeny, teeny-weeny, petty, mini, minikin, hop-o'-my-thumb, miniature, bijou, *petite*, pygmy, undersized, half-pint, dwarf,

Squab, dumpy (202), tubby, roly-poly, pursy, blowsy.

Huge, immense, enormous, mighty, unbounded, vast, vasty, amplitudinous, stupendous, inordinate, herculean, thumping, whacking, whopping, spanking, thundering, monstrous, monster; gigantic, giant-like, colossal, titanic, mountainous, elephantine, mammoth, cyclopean, Antaean, Gargantuan, Falstaffian, Brobdingnagain; infinite, unbounded.

(*Phrases*) Large as life; plump as a partridge; fat as a pig; fat as butter; fat as bacon.

stunted, dwarfed, dwarfish, pollard, Lilliputian; pocket, thumb-nail, portative, portable, duodecimo.

Microscopic, infra-microscopic, evanescent, impalpable, imperceptible, invisible, inappreciable, infinitesimal, homoeopathic, atomic, corpuscular, molecular, rudimentary, rudimental.

Lean, thin, gaunt, meagre, emaciated, lank, macilent, ghostly, starved, starveling, fallen away, scrubby, reduced, shrunk, shrunken, attenuated, extenuated, shrivelled, tabid, flaccid, starved, skinny, wizen, wizened, scraggy, lanky, raw-boned, scrawny, spindle-shanked, lantern-jawed (203).

(*Phrases*) In a small compass; in a nutshell; on a small scale.

Worn to a shadow; skin and bone.

---

194 EXPANSION (*Substantives*), enlargement, extension, augmentation, increase of size, amplification, ampliation, aggrandisement, spread, increment, growth, development, pullulation, swell, dilatation, rarefaction, turgescence, turgidity, thickening, tumefaction, intumescence, swelling, tumour, diastole, distension, puffing, inflation.

Overgrowth, hypertrophy, over-distension, tympany.

Bulb, knot, knob (249).

Superiority of size.

(*Verbs*) To become larger, to expand, widen, enlarge, extend, grow, increase, swell (202), gather, fill out, deploy, dilate, stretch, largen, spread, mantle, bud, burgeon, shoot, spring up, sprout, germinate, vegetate, pullulate, open, burst forth, put on flesh, outgrow.

To render larger, to expand, aggrandize, etc., distend, develop, open out, broaden, thicken, largen, amplify, tumefy, magnify, rarefy, inflate, puff, blow up, stuff, cram, pad, fill out.

To be larger than, to surpass, exceed, be beyond, cap, overtop (206, 33).

(*Adjectives*) Expanded, enlarged, increased, etc., swelled out, swollen, distended, bulbous; exaggerated,

195 CONTRACTION (*Substantives*), reduction, diminution, decrease of size, defalcation, lessening, decrement, shrinking, shrivelling, systole, collapse, emaciation, attenuation, tabefaction, tabes, consumption, marasmus, atrophy; hour-glass, neck (203).

Condensation, compression, squeezing.

Inferiority of size.

Corrugation, contractility, astringency.

(*Verbs*) To become smaller, to lessen, diminish, decrease, dwindle, shrink, contract, shrivel, collapse, wither, wilt, lose flesh, wizen, fall away, decay, purse up, waste, wane, ebb, to grow less.

To render smaller, to contract, lessen, etc., draw in, to condense, reduce, clip, compress, constrict, cramp, squeeze, attenuate, chip, dwarf, bedwarf, stunt, cut short (201), corrugate, crumple, crush, purse up, pinch (203), deflate.

To be smaller than, to fall short of, not to come up to.

(*Phrases*) To grow 'small by degrees, and beautifully less' (659); to be on the wane; to hide its diminished head.

(*Adjectives*) Contracting, etc., astringent, styptic, tabid, contracted, lessened, etc., shrivelled, wasted,

bloated, tumid, turgid, puffy, full-blown, full-grown, full-formed, over-grown, hypertrophied, pot-bellied, swag-bellied, dropsical, oedematous.

(*Phrase*) 'A-swellin' wisibly.'

196 DISTANCE (*Substantives*), remoteness, farness, longinquity, elongation, offing, removedness, parallax, reach, span.

Antipodes, outpost, outskirts, aphelion, apogee, horizon.

Separation (44), transference (270). Diffusion, dispersion (73).

(*Phrases*) *Ultima Thule*; *ne plus ultra*; the uttermost parts of the earth; the back of beyond.

(*Verbs*) To be distant, etc.; to extend to, stretch to, reach to, spread to, go to, get to, stretch away to; outgo, outstep (303); to go great lengths.

To remain at a distance, keep away, stand off, keep off, keep clear, stand aloof, hold off.

(*Adjectives*) Distant, far, far off, remote, removed, distal, wide of, clear of, yon, yonder, at arm's length, apart, aloof, asunder, ulterior, trans-alpine, transatlantic, ultramundane, hyperborean, antipodean, hull down.

Inaccessible, un-get-at-able, out of the way, unapproachable, unreach-able; incontiguous.

(*Adverbs*) Far, away, far away, afar, off, a long way off, afar off, wide away, aloof, wide of, clear of, out of the way, a great way off, out of reach, abroad.

Apart, asunder, few and far between.

Yonder, farther, beyond, *longo intervallo*, wide apart, poles apart.

(*Phrases*) Far and near; far and wide; over the hills and far away; a far cry to; from end to end; from pole to pole; from Indus to the Pole; from China to Peru; from Dan to Beersheba; to the ends of the earth; out of the sphere of; wide of the mark.

wizened, stunted, **waning**, ebbing, etc., neap, condensed.

Unexpanded, contractile, **compres-sible.**

(*Phrase*) *Multum in parvo.*

197 NEARNESS (*Substantives*), nigh-ness, proximity, propinquity, vicinity, vicinage, neighbourhood, adjacency, closeness; perihelion, perigee.

A short distance, a step, an ear-shot, close quarters, a stone's throw, a hair's breadth, a span, bowshot, gunshot, pistol-shot.

Purlieus, neighbourhood, environs (227), vicinity, *alentours*, suburbs, whereabouts, *banlieue*, borderland.

A bystander, neighbour.

Approach, approximation, appro-pinquation, appulse (286), junction (43), concentration, convergence (290).

Meeting, *rencontre* (292).

(*Verbs*) To be near, etc., to adjoin, hang about, trench on, border upon, stand by, approximate, tread on the heels of, cling to, clasp, hug, crowd, get near, etc., to approach (287), to meet (290).

To bring near, **to crowd, pack,** huddle together.

(*Adjectives*) Near, nigh, close, close at hand, neighbouring, proximate, approximate, adjacent, adjoining, intimate, bordering upon, close upon, hard upon, trenching on, treading on the heels of, verging on, at hand, handy, near the mark, home, at the point of, near run, in touch with, nearish.

(*Adverbs*) Near, nigh, hard by, fast by, close to, next door to, within reach, within call, within hearing, within an ace of, close upon, at hand, on the verge of, near the mark, in the environs, round the corner, at one's door, at one's feet, at one's elbow, at close quarters; within range, pistol-shot, a stone's throw, etc.; cheek by jowl, beside, along-side, at the heels of, at the threshold.

About, hereabouts, thereabouts, in the way, in presence of, in round numbers, approximately, roughly, as good as, *à peu près* (32).

198 INTERVAL (*Substantives*), inter-space (70), break, gap, opening (260), chasm, hiatus, caesura, interstice, lacuna, cleft, fosse, mesh, crevice, chink, creek, cranny, crack, slit, fissure, scissure, chap, rift, flaw, gash, cut, leak, dike (350), ha-ha, fracture, breach, rent, oscitation, gaping, yawning, pandiculation, insertion (300), pass, gorge, defile, ravine, canyon (or cañon), crevasse, chimney, couloir, *bergschrund*, gulf, gully, gulch, nullah, strait, sound, kyle, frith, furrow (*see* 259).

Thing interposed, go-between, in-terjacence (228).

(*Verbs*) To separate (44), gape, yawn.

---

199 CONTIGUITY (*Substantives*), contact, proximity, apposition, juxta-position, touching, tangency, tangent, osculation, meeting (292), syzygy, coincidence, register, co-existence, adhesion (46).

Confine, frontier, demarcation, border (233).

(*Verbs*) To be contiguous, etc., to touch, meet, adhere (46), osculate, coincide, register, coexist, join, ad-join, abut on, graze, border, march with.

(*Adjectives*) Contiguous, touching, bordering on, meeting, in contact, conterminous, osculating, osculatory, tangential, proximate.

(*Phrases*) Hand to hand; end to end; tête-à-tête; next door to; with no interval; in juxtaposition, apposition, etc.; in register.

2°. Linear Dimensions

200 LENGTH (*Substantives*), longi-tude, span, stretch.

A line, bar, rule, stripe, spoke, radius.

Lengthening, elongation, prolonga-tion, production, producing, protrac-tion, extension, tension, stretching.

(*Verbs*) To be long, etc., to extend to, reach, stretch to.

To render long, lengthen, extend, elongate, prolong, produce, stretch, draw out, protract, spin out, drawl.

(*Phrase*) To drag its slow length along.

(*Adjectives*) Long, longsome, lengthy, tedious, tiresome, wiredrawn, out-stretched, lengthened, produced, etc., sesquipedalian, interminable, endless, unending, never-ending, there being no end of.

Linear, lineal, longitudinal, ob-long.

(*Phrases*) As long as my arm; as long as to-day and to-morrow.

(*Adverbs*) Lengthwise, longitudi-nally, in a line, along, from end to end, endways, from stem to stern, fore and aft, from head to foot, from top to toe, cap-à-pie.

201 SHORTNESS (*Substantives*), brevity, briefness, a span, etc., *see* Smallness (193).

Shortening, abbreviation, abbre-viature, abridgment, curtailment, reduction, contraction, compression (195), retrenchment, elision, ellipsis, compendium (596), conciseness (in style) (572).

(*Verbs*) To be short, brief, etc.

To render short, to shorten, cur-tail, abridge, abbreviate, epitomize, reduce, contract, compress, scrimp, skimp, boil down.

To retrench, cut short, cut down, pare down, whittle down, clip, dock, lop, poll, prune, pollard, crop, bob, shingle, bingle, snub, truncate, cut, hack, hew, foreshorten.

(*Adjectives*) Short, brief, curt, laconic, compendious, compact, stubby, squab, squabby, squat, chunky, stubby, stocky, dumpy, podgy, fubsy, skimpy, stumpy, pug, snub.

Oblate, elliptical.

Concise (572), summary.

202 BREADTH (*Substantives*), width, latitude, amplitude, diameter, bore, calibre, superficial extent, expanse.

THICKNESS, crassitude (192), thickening, expansion, dilatation, etc. (194).

(*Verbs*) To be broad, thick, etc.

To broaden, to swell, dilate, expand, outspread, etc. (194); to thicken, incrassate.

(*Adjectives*) Broad, wide, ample, extended, fan-like, outstretched, etc.

Thick, corpulent, fat (192), squab, squabby, squat, chunky, stubby, stocky, dumpy, podgy, fulsy, thickset.

(*Phrases*) Wide as a church door; thick as a rope.

---

203 NARROWNESS (*Substantives*), slenderness, closeness, scantiness, exility, lankness, lankiness, fibrousness.

A line (205), a hair's breadth, a finger's breadth, strip, streak, vein.

THINNESS, tenuity, leanness, meagreness.

A shaving, a slip (205), a mere skeleton, a shadow, an anatomy.

A middle constriction, stricture, neck, waist, isthmus, wasp, hourglass, bottle-neck, ridge, ravine, defile, gorge, pass (198).

Narrowing, coarctation, tapering, compression, squeezing, etc. (195).

(*Phrases*) A bag of bones; a living skeleton.

(*Verbs*) To be narrow, etc., to taper, contract, shrink.

To render narrow, etc., to narrow, contract, coarctate, attenuate, constrict, constringe, cramp, pinch, squeeze, compress, tweak, corrugate, warp.

To shave, pare, shear, etc.

(*Adjectives*) Narrow, strait, slender, thin, fine, tenuous, filiform, filamentary, filamentous, fibrous, funicular, capillary, stringy, wiredrawn, fine-spun, anguine, taper, dapper, slim, slight, gracile, scanty, scant, spare, delicate.

Meagre, lean, emaciated, lank, lanky, weedy, rangy, gangling, starveling, attenuated, pinched, skinny, scraggy, gaunt, cadaverous, skin and bone, raw-boned, scrawny, spindle-shanked (193), hatchet-faced, waspwaisted, herring-gutted, spidery, spindly, reedy.

(*Phrases*) Thin as a lath; thin as a whipping-post; lean as a rake; thin as a thread-paper; thin as a wafer; thin as a shadow.

---

204 LAYER (*Substantives*), stratum, bed, zone, substratum, slab, escarpment, floor, flag, stage, course, storey, tier.

Plate, lamina, lamella, sheet, flake, scale, coat, pellicle, membrane, film, slice, shive, cut, shaving, rasher, board, plank, platter, trencher, spatula, leaf.

Stratification, scaliness, a nest of boxes, coats of an onion.

(*Verbs*) To slice, shave, etc.

(*Adjectives*) Lamellar, laminated, lamelliform, laminiferous, scaly, squamous, filmy, membranous, flaky, foliated, foliaceous, stratified, stratiform, tabular, nested.

---

205 FILAMENT (*Substantives*), line, fibre, fibril, tendril, hair, gossamer, wire, thread, cord, funicle, rope, yarn, string, twine (45), cilium, gimp.

Strip (51), shred, slip, spill, list, string, band, fillet, fascia, ribbon (or riband); roll, lath, slat, splinter, sliver, shiver, shaving; arborescence (256); strand.

A hair-stroke.

(*Adjectives*) Filamentary, fibrous, hairy, capillary, thread-like, wiry, funicular, stringy.

206 HEIGHT (*Substantives*), altitude, elevation, eminence, pitch, loftiness, sublimity.

Stature, tallness, procerity, culmination (210).

A giant, grenadier, guardsman, colossus, giraffe.

Alp, mountain, mount, hill, butte, ben, brae, hillock, kopje, monticule, fell, moorland, hummock, knap, knoll, cape, headland, foreland, promontory, ridge, *arête*, peak, pike, uplands, highlands, rising ground, downs, dune, mound, mole, steep, bluff, cliff, crag, vantage-ground, tor, eagle's nest, aerie.

Orography, Orology.

Tower, pillar, column, obelisk, monument, steeple, spire, *flèche*, campanile, belfry, minaret, turret, cupola, pilaster, skyscraper.

Pole, pikestaff, maypole, flagstaff, topmast, topgallant mast, crow's nest.

Ceiling, roof, awning, canopy (*see* 210), attic, loft, garret, housetop.

Growth, upgrowth (194).

(*Verbs*) To be high, etc., to tower, soar, ride, beetle, hover, cap, overtop, culminate, overharg, hang over, impend, overlie, bestride, mount, surmount, to cover (222), perch.

To render high, to heighten, exalt (307).

To become high, grow, upgrow, soar, tower, rise (305).

(*Adjectives*) High, elevated, eminent, exalted, lofty, supernal, tall, towering, beetling, soaring, colossal, gigantic (192), Patagonian, culminating, raised, elevated, etc., perched up, hanging (gardens), crowning, coronary.

Upland, moorland, hilly, mountainous, cloud-touching, heaven-kissing, cloud-topt, cloud-capt, Alpine, subalpine, aerial; orographical.

Upper, uppermost (210), topgallant.

Overhanging, impending, incumbent, overlying, superincumbent, supernatant, superimposed, hovering.

(*Phrases*) Tall as a maypole; tall as a steeple; tall as a poplar.

(*Adverbs*) On high, high up, aloft, above, upstairs, overhead, in the clouds, on tiptoe, on stilts, on the shoulders of, over head and ears.

Over, upwards, from top to bottom, from top to toe, from head to foot, cap-à-pie.

(*Interjection*) Excelsior!

207 LOWNESS (*Substantives*), lowlands, depression, a molehill, recumbency, prostration.

Dwarf, pygmy bantam, Lilliputian. Lowlands; riclehill.

A ground-floor, basement, cellar, *rez de chaussée* (191), hold.

(*Verbs*) To be low, etc., lie low, grovel, wallow, crouch, slouch, lie flat.

To lower, depress (306), take down a peg, prostrate, subvert.

(*Adjectives*) Low, low-lying, neap, nether, prostrate, flat, level with the ground, grovelling, crouched, crouching, subjacent, underground, underlying, squat.

(*Adverbs*) Under, beneath, underneath, below, down, adown, downstairs, below stairs, over head and ears, downwards, underfoot, at the foot of, underground, at a low ebb.

---

208 DEPTH (*Substantives*), deepness, profundity, profoundness, depression, bathos, anti-climax, depth of water, draught.

A hollow, pit, shaft, well, crater, gulf, abyss, abysm, bottomless pit, hell.

209 SHALLOWNESS (*Substantives*), shoaliness, shoals.

(*Adjectives*) Shallow, skin-deep, superficial, shoaly.

Soundings, submersion, plunge, dive (310).

Plummet, lead, sounding-rod, probe; bathymetry.

Bathysphere, diving-bell, caisson, submarine; diver, frogman.

(*Verbs*) To be deep, etc.

To render deep, etc., to deepen, sink, submerge, plunge, dip, dive (310).

To dig, scoop out, hollow, sink, delve (252).

(*Adjectives*) Deep, deep-seated, profound, sunk, buried, submerged, etc., subaqueous, submarine, subterranean, underground, subterrene, abysmal; bathymetrical, bathymetric.

Bottomless, soundless, fathomless, unfathomed, unsounded, unplumbed, unfathomable.

(*Phrases*) Deep as a well; ankle-deep; knee-deep; breast-deep; chin-deep.

(*Adverbs*) Beyond one's depth, out of one's depth, underground.

(*Phrases*) Over head and ears; to Davy Jones's locker; in the bowels of the earth.

---

210 SUMMIT (*Substantives*), top, vertex, apex, zenith, pinnacle, acme, climax, culminating point, apogee, pitch, meridian, sky, pole, watershed.

Tip, tiptop, crest, crow's nest, mast-head, truck, peak, turning-point, pole.

Crown, brow, nib, head, nob, noddle, pate.

Capital, cornice, sconce, architrave, pediment, entablature, frieze.

Roof, ceiling, thatch, tiling, slating, awning, canopy (222).

(*Adjectives*) Top, topmost, uppermost, tiptop, culminating, meridian, capital, head, polar, supreme, crowning, coronary.

(*Phrase*) At the top of the tree.

211 BASE (*Substantives*), basement, plinth, foundation, substratum, ground, earth, pavement, floor, paving, flag, ground floor, deck, substructure, infrastructure, footing, groundwork.

The bottom, rock-bottom, nadir, foot, sole, toe, root, keel.

Dado, wainscot, skirting-board.

(*Adjectives*) Bottom, undermost, nethermost, fundamental, basic.

---

212 VERTICALITY (*Substantives*), erectness, uprightness, perpendicularity, aplomb, right angle, normal, plummet, plumb-line, azimuth, circle.

Wall, precipice, cliff.

Erection, raising, rearing.

(*Verbs*) To be vertical, etc., to stand up, to stand on end, to stand erect, to stand upright, to stick up.

To render vertical, to set up, stick up, erect, rear, raise up, cock up, prick up, raise on its legs.

(*Adjectives*) Vertical, upright, erect, perpendicular, sheer, normal, straight, standing up, etc., up on end, bolt upright, rampant.

213 HORIZONTALITY (*Substantives*), a level, plane, dead level, flatness (251).

Recumbency, lying, lying down, reclination, decumbence, decumbency, supination, resupination, prostration; spirit-level.

A plain, floor, level, flat, platform, bowling-green, billiard-table, plateau, terrace, estrade, esplanade, parterre, table-land (204, 215).

(*Verbs*) To be horizontal, recumbent, etc., to lie, recline, lie down, couch, sit down, squat, lie flat, lie prostrate, sprawl, loll.

To render horizontal, etc., to lay, lay down, lay out, level, flatten, prostrate, knock down, fell, floor.

(*Adverbs*) Up, vertically, etc., on end, up on end, endways, endwise.
(*Phrase*) Straight up and down.

(*Adverbs*) Horizontally, etc., on one's back, on all fours, on one's hunkers.
(*Phrases*) Like a millpond.

214 PENDENCY (*Substantives*), dependency, suspension, hanging.

A pendant, pedicel, peduncle, tail, train, flap, skirt, plait, pigtail, queue, tassel, earring, pendulum.

A peg, knob, button, stud, hook, nail, ring, fastener, zipper, clip, staple, knot (45), tenterhook.

(*Verbs*) To be pendant, etc., to hang, swing, dangle, swag, daggle, flap, trail.

To suspend, append, hang, sling, hook up, hitch, fasten to.

(*Adjectives*) Pendent, pendulous, pensile, hanging, dependent, swinging, etc., suspended, etc., loose, flowing, caudal.

Having a peduncle, etc., pedunculate, tailed, caudate.

(*Adverbs*) Dingle-dangle.
(*Phrase*) In the air.

(*Adjectives*) Horizontal, level, plane, flat, even, discoid.

Recumbent, decumbent, lying, prone, supine, couchant, couching, jacent, prostrate, squat, squatting, sitting, reclining.

215 SUPPORT (*Substantives*), ground, foundation, base, basis, *terra firma*, fulcrum, foothold, toehold, *point d'appui, pou sto, locus standi*, landing, landing-place, resting-place, ground-work, substratum, floor, bed, stall, berth, lap, mount.

A supporter, prop, stand, strut, stay, shore, boom, yard, outrigger, truss, sleeper, staff, stick, walking-stick, crutch, stirrups, stilts, alpenstock, baton, anvil.

Post, pillar, shaft, column, buttress, pedicle, pedestal, plinth (211), baluster, banister.

A frame, framework, scaffold, scaffolding, skeleton, cadre, beam, rafter, lintel, joist, jamb, mullion, corner-stone, stanchion, summer, girder, cantilever, sponson, tie-beam, (45), columella, backbone, keystone, axle, axle-tree, axis, fuselage, chassis.

A board, form, ledge, platform, floor, stage, shelf, hob, bracket, arbor, rack, mantel, mantelpiece, mantel-shelf, counter, slab, console, dresser, flange, corbel, table, trestle, shoulder, perch, truss, horse, easel, desk.

A seat, throne, dais, divan, musnud, chair, arm-chair, easy-chair, *chaise longue*, hammock-chair, deck-chair, bench, sofa, davenport, lounge, settee, chesterfield, couch, *fauteuil*, stool, tripod, footstool, *tabouret*, trivet, woolsack, ottoman, settle, squab, bench, saddle, pillion, dicky, hassock, pouffe, cushion, howdah.

Bed, bedstead, chair-bedstead, bedding, pillow, bolster, mattress, shake-down, tester, pallet, hammock, bunk, stretcher, crib, cradle, cot, palliasse, donkey's breakfast, sleeping-bag, flea-bag.

Atlas, Persides, Atlantes, Caryatides, Hercules, Yggdrasil.

(*Verbs*) To be supported, etc., to lie, sit, recline, lean, loll, lounge, abut, bear, rest, stand, step, repose, etc., on, be based on, bestride, straddle, bestraddle.

To support, bear, carry, hold, sustain, shoulder, uphold, hold on, upbear, prop, underprop, shore up, underpin, bolster up, pillow.

To give, furnish, afford, supply, lend, etc., support or foundations; to bottom, found, ground, base, embed.

(*Adjectives*) Supported, etc., astride, astraddle; fundamental, basic.

216 PARALLELISM (*Substantives*), coextension.

(*Verbs*) To be parallel, etc.

(*Adjectives*) Parallel, coextensive.

(*Adverbs*) Alongside, abreast, beside.

(*Phrases*) Side by side; cheek by jowl.

---

217 OBLIQUITY (*Substantives*), inclination, slope, leaning, slant, crookedness, bias, bend, bevel, tilt, list, dip, swag, cant, lurch, skew, skewness, bevelling, squint.

Acclivity, uphill, rise, ascent, gradient, rising ground, bank, ramp.

Declivity, downhill, fall, devexity.

A gentle or rapid slope, easy ascent or descent, chute, helter-skelter, switchback, *montagnes russes*.

Steepness, precipitousness, cliff, precipice, talus, scarp, escarp, escarpment; measure of inclination, clinometer.

Diagonal, zigzag, distortion, hypotenuse, angle (244).

(*Phrase*) The leaning tower of Pisa.

(*Verbs*) To be or render oblique, etc., to slope, slant, tilt, lean, incline, shelve, stoop, descend, bend, heel, careen, sag, swag, slouch, cant, sidle, skew, scarp, escarp, bevel, distort.

(*Adjectives*) Oblique, inclined, leaning, recumbent, sloping, shelving, skew, askew, skew-whiff, slant, aslant, slanting, slantendicular, plagioclastic, indirect, distorted, wry, awry, ajee, drawn, crooked, canted, tilted, biased, saggy, bevel, slouched, slouching, etc., out of the perpendicular, backhanded.

Uphill, rising, ascending, acclivitous.

Downhill, falling, descending, declining, declivitous, anticlinal.

Steep, abrupt, precipitous, break-neck.

Diagonal, transverse, athwart, transversal, antiparallel.

(*Adverbs*) Obliquely, etc., on one side, askew, edgewise, askant, askance, sideways, aslope, slopewise, all on one side, crinkum-crankum, asquint, at an angle.

(*Phrase*) *Facilis descensus Averni.*

---

218 INVERSION (*Substantives*), contraposition, overturn, somersault (or somerset), *culbute*, subversion, retroversion, reversion, reversal, introversion, eversion, transposition, pronation and supination.

Anastrophe, metathesis, hysteron, proteron, spoonerism, palindrome.

(*Verbs*) To be inverted, etc., to turn turtle, loop the loop, bunt.

To render inverted, etc., to invert, reverse, upset, overset, overturn, turn over, upturn, subvert, retrovert, transpose, turn topsy-turvy, tilt over, *culbuter*, keel over, topple over, capsize.

(*Adjectives*) Inverted, inverse, upside down, topsy-turvy, top-heavy.

(*Adverbs*) Inversely, topsy-turvy, etc., inside out.

(*Phrases*) To turn the tables; to put the cart before the horse; to the

---

219 CROSSING (*Substantives*), intersection, decussation, transversion, convolution.

Reticulation, network, inosculation, anastomosis, interweaving, twining, intertwining, matting, plaiting, interdigitation, mortise (or mortice).

Net, knot, plexus, web, mesh, twill, skein, hank, felt, lace, tulle, wattle, wicker, basket-work, basketry, mat, matting, plait, trellis, lattice, grille, *cancelli*, grid, griddle, grating, gridiron, tracery, fretwork, filigree, reticle, diaper.

Cross, chain, wreath, braid, cat's-cradle, dovetail, Greek cross, Latin cross, Maltese cross, cross of St. Anthony, St. Andrew's cross, cross of Lorraine, swastika, fylfot.

(*Verbs*) To cross, lace, intersect, decussate, interlace, intertwine, inter-

right about; bottom upwards; head over heels; the wrong side up; base over apex.

——————

twill, tangle, entangle, ravel, net, knot (43), dishevel, raddle.

twist, pleach, plash, **entwine, enlace,** enmesh, weave, interweave, inweave, twine, twist, wreathe, interdigitate, interlock, anastomose, inosculate, dovetail, splice (43).

To mat, plait, plat, braid, felt,

(*Adjectives*) Crossing, intersecting, etc., crossed, intersected, matted, etc., crucial, cruciform.

Retiform, reticulate, areolar, areolate, cancellated, grated, barred, streaked, traceried.

(*Adverbs*) Across, thwart, athwart, transversely, crosswise.

3°. *Centrical Dimensions*

I. GENERAL

220 EXTERIORITY (*Substantives*), externality, outness, outside, exterior, surface, superficies, superstratum, eccentricity, extremity, frontage.

Disk, face, facet, front (234), skin (222).

(*Verbs*) To be exterior, etc.

To place exteriorly, or outwardly, to turn out.

(*Adjectives*) Exterior, external, outer, outward, outlying, outdoor, outside, extramural, superficial, skin-deep, frontal, discoid, eccentric, extrinsic.

(*Adverbs*) Externally, etc., out, without, outwards, outdoors, abroad.

(*Phrases*) Out of doors; *extra muros*; *ab extra*; in the open air; *sub Jove*; *à la belle étoile*; al fresco.

——————

222 COVERING (*Substantives*), cover, roof, ceiling, slates, tiles, thatch, cowling, canopy, baldachin, awning, tarpaulin, tilt, tent (189), lid, hatch, operculum (263), shed.

Integument, skin, tegument, pellicle, fleece, cuticle, scarf-skin, epidermis, hide, pelt, peel, crust, bark, rind, cortex, husk, scale, shell, carapace, capsule, coat, tunic, tunicle, sheath, case, casing, calyx, theca,

221 INTERIORITY (*Substantives*), inside, interior, hinterland, back-blocks, interspace, substratum, sub-soil.

Vitals, viscera, pith, marrow, heart, bosom, breast, entrails, bowels, belly, intestines, guts, inwards, womb, lap, backbone, *penetralia*, inmost recesses, cave, cavern (191).

(*Verbs*) To be interior, internal, within, etc.

To place or keep within, to enclose, circumscribe (*see* 231, 232).

(*Adjectives*) Interior, internal, inner, inside, intramural, inward, inlying, inmost, innermost, deep-seated, intestine, intestinal, splanchnic, intercostal, inland, interstitial, subcutaneous, intrinsic.

Home, domestic, indoor.

(*Adverbs*) Internally, inwards, inwardly, within, inly, therein, *ab intra*, withinside, indoors, within doors, ben, at home, *chez soi*, up country.

——————

223 CENTRALITY (*Substantives*), centre (68), middle, focus, epicentre, hub, core, kernel, marrow, pith, nucleus, nucleolus, heart, pole, axis, bull's-eye, nave, navel, umbilicus, omphalos; concentration, centralization.

(*Verbs*) To be central, etc.

To render central, centralize, concentrate.

To bring to a focus.

(*Adjectives*) Central, centrical,

sheathing, scabbard, wrapping, wrapper, envelope, tarpaulin, cloth, table-cloth, blanket, rug, quilt, eiderdown, coverlet (or coverlid), counterpane, carpet, drugget, oilcloth, waxcloth, linoleum.

Superposition, coating, facing, veneer, paint, enamel, varnish, anointing, inunction, incrustation, plaster, stucco, wash, parget, patina.

(*Verbs*) To cover, superpose, superimpose, overspread, over-canopy, wrap, lap, overlap, face, case, encase, veneer, pave, upholster.

To coat, paint, enamel, varnish, pave, plaster, beplaster, daub, bedaub, encrust, stucco, dab, smear, besmear, anoint, spray, do over, gild, japan, lacquer (or lacker), plate, electroplate, parget.

(*Phrase*) To lay it on thick.

(*Adjectives*) Covering, etc., cutaneous, dermal, cortical, cuticular, tegumentary, skinny, scaly, squamous, imbricated, epidermal, loricated, armour-plated, iron-clad.

middle, middlemost, midmost, median, azygous, axial, focal, umbilical, concentric.

(*Adverbs*) Midway, centrally, etc.

224 LINING (*Substantives*), coating, facing, internal incrustation, puddle, stalactite, stalagmite, wainscot, dado, wall.

Filling, stuffing, wadding, padding.

(*Verbs*) To line, encrust, stuff, pad, wad, face, puddle, bush.

(*Adjectives*) Lined, encrusted, etc.

---

225 INVESTMENT (*Substantives*), dress, clothing, raiment, drapery, costume, attire, toilet, trim, rig, rig-out, fig, habiliment, vesture, apparel, underwear, full dress, evening dress, soup-and-fish, glad rags, dinner-jacket, tuxedo, fancy dress, accoutrement, outfit, wardrobe, trousseau, uniform, regimentals, battle-dress, kit, equipment, livery, gear, harness, turn-out, caparison, suit, dress suit, lounge suit, bathing suit, swim-suit, tweeds, flannels, rigging, trappings, slops, traps, duds, togs, clobber, frippery, bloomers, haberdashery, housing.

Dishabille, morning dress, dressing-gown, undress, mufti, civvies, rags, *négligé*, tea-gown.

Clothes, garment, garb, garniture, vestment, pontificals, robe, tunic, caftan, paletot, habit, gown, coat, dress-coat, claw-hammer, frock, stole, blouse, shirt-waist, toga, haik, smock-frock, kimono, bikini.

Cloak, opera-cloak, cape, mantle, mantlet, dolman, shawl, wrap, wrapper, veil, fichu, yashmak, tippet, kirtle, plaid, mantilla, tabard, burnous, overcoat, great-coat, British

226 DIVESTMENT (*Substantives*), nudity, bareness, nakedness, baldness, undress, dishabille, threadbareness.

Denuding, denudation, stripping, uncovering, decortication, peeling, flaying, excoriation, desquamation, moulting, exfoliation.

(*Verbs*) To divest, uncover, denude, bare, strip, unclothe, undress, unrobe, disrobe, disapparel, debag, disarray, take off, doff, cast off, peel, pare, decorticate, husk, uncoif, unbonnet, excoriate, skin, flay, expose, exfoliate, lay open, dismantle, unroof, uncase, unsheathe, moult, mew.

(*Adjectives*) Bare, naked, nude, stripped, denuded, undressed, unclothed, unclad, undraped, uncovered, unshod, barefoot, bareheaded, unbonneted, exposed, in dishabille, in buff, bald, threadbare, ragged, callow, roofless.

(*Phrases*) In a state of nature; stark-naked; *in puris naturalibus*; stripped to the buff; in one's birthday suit; bald as a coot; as bare as the back of one's hand; out at elbows.

---

warm, duffle coat, surtout, spencer, rain-coat, ulster, mackintosh, water-proof, oilskin, slicker, burberry, poncho, surplice, alb, cassock, pallium, etc., mask, domino, cardinal, pelerine.

Jacket, vest, under-vest, semmit, singlet, jerkin, lumberjacket, waist-coat, cardigan, sweater, jersey, pullover, slipover, jumper, windbreaker, windcheater, doublet, gaberdine, camisole, combinations, stays, corset, bodice, under-bodice, brassière, bra, corsage, cestus, petticoat, kilt, filibeg (or philibeg), stomacher, skirt, kirtle, crinoline, farthingale, underskirt, slip, apron, pinafore.

Trousers, trews, breeches, galligaskins, knickerbockers, plus-fours, knickers, drawers, scanties, pantaloons, pants, overalls, dungarees, boiler suit, rompers, unmentionables, inexpressibles, smalls, tights, bags, breeks, slacks, shorts, jeans, briefs.

Cap, hat, top-hat, silk hat, tile, bowler, panama, slouch-hat, trilby, Stetson, titfer, deerstalker, billycock, wide-awake, sou'wester, beaver, castor, bonnet, forage-cap, tam-o'-shanter, tammy, balmoral, glengarry, toque, sun-bonnet, hood, head-gear, head-dress, kerchief, scarf, muffler, comforter, boa, snood, coiffure, coif, skull-cap, calotte, biretta, cowl, chaplet, capote, calash, pelt, wig, peruke, periwig, toupee, transforma-tion, chignon, turban, puggaree, fez, helmet, topi, shako, busby, képi, casque, beret.

Shirt, smock, shift, chemise, chemisette, nightshirt, nightgown, nightdress, pyjamas, bed-jacket, bed-gown, collar, cravat, neck-cloth, neck-tie, stock, handkerchief.

Shoe, pump, high-low, Oxford shoe, sabot, brogue, sand-shoe, plim-soll, rubbers, sneakers, boot, jack-boot, top-boot, Wellington, gum-boot, slipper, mule, galosh, overshoe, legging, puttee, buskin, greaves, moccasin, gaiter, spatterdash, spat, stocking, sock, nylons, hose, sandal, clog, babouche.

Glove, gauntlet, mitten, sleeve, cuff, muff.

Outfitter, tailor, clothier, milliner, sempstress, costumier, hatter, hosier, shoemaker, cobbler.

(*Verbs*) To invest, cover, envelop, lap, involve, drape, enwrap, wrap up, lap up, sheathe, vest, clothe, array, enrobe, dress, dight, attire, apparel, accoutre, trick out, rig, fit out, fig out, caparison, adonize, dandify, titivate, don, put on, wear, have on, huddle on, slip on, roll up in, muffle, perk up, mantle, swathe, swaddle, equip, harness.

(*Adjectives*) Invested, clothed, arrayed, dight, etc., clad, shod, etc.; sartorial.

227 CIRCUMJACENCE (*Substantives*), circumambiency, encompassment, surroundings, environment, atmosphere, medium, setting, scene, out-post, skirt, outskirts, boulevards, suburbs, suburbia, rurbania, purlieus, precincts, faubourgs, environs, entourage, *banlieue*, green belt.

(*Verbs*) To lie around, surround, beset, set about, compass, encompass, environ, enclose, encircle, embrace, lap, gird, begird, engirdle, orb, enlace, skirt, twine round, hem in (231).

228 INTERJACENCE (*Substantives*), interlocation, intervention, insertion, interposition, interspersion, inter-penetration, interdigitation, inter-polation, interlineation, intercurrence, intrusion, obtrusion, insinuation, intercalation, insertion, intertwine-ment, interference, permeation, infiltration.

An intermedium, intermediary, a go-between, bodkin, intruder, interloper; interlude, episode; parenthesis, gag, flyleaf, *entresol* (68).

(*Adjectives*) Circumjacent, ambient, circumambient, surrounding, etc., circumfluent, circumferential, suburban, extramural, embosomed.

(*Adverbs*) Around, about, without, on every side, on all sides, right and left, all around, round about.

229 OUTLINE (*Substantives*), circumference, perimeter, periphery, ambit, circuit, lines, tournure, contour, profile, silhouette, sky-line.

Zone, belt, girth, band, baldric, zodiac, cordon, girdle, cingulum, clasp (247).

230 EDGE (*Substantives*), verge, brink, brow, brim, margin, marge, border, skirt, rim, side, mouth, jaws, lip, muzzle, door, porch, portal (260), kerb; shore, coast.

Frame, flounce, frill, ruffle, jabot, list, fringe, valance, edging, trimming, hem, selvedge, welt, furbelow.

(*Verbs*) To border, edge, skirt, coast, verge on.

(*Adjectives*) Border, marginal, coastal, skirting.

A partition, septum, panel, diaphragm, midriff, party-wall.

A half-way house, no-man's-land.

(*Verbs*) To lie, come, or get between, intervene, intrude, butt in, slide in, permeate, put between, put in, interpose, interject, chip in, throw in, wedge in, thrust in, foist in, insert, intercalate, interpolate, parenthesize, interline, interleave, interlard, interdigitate, dovetail, sandwich, worm in, insinuate, obtrude (300), intersperse, infiltrate; to gag.

(*Phrases*) To put one's oar in; to stick one's nose into; to have a finger in the pie.

(*Adjectives*) Interjacent, intervening, etc., intermediary, intermediate, intercalary, interstitial, parenthetical, mediterranean.

(*Adverbs*) Between, betwixt, 'twixt, among, amongst, amid, amidst, midst, betwixt and between, sandwich-wise, parenthetically, between the lines, in the thick of.

---

231 CIRCUMSCRIPTION (*Substantives*), limitation, enclosure, confinement shutting up, circumvallation, entombment.

Imprisonment, incarceration (751).

(*Verbs*) To circumscribe, limit, delimit, localize, bound, confine, enclose, surround (227), compass about, impound, restrict, restrain (751), shut in, shut up, lock up, bottle up, dam, hem in, hedge in, wall in, rail in, fence, picket, pen, enfold, coop, corral, encage, cage, mew, entomb, bury, immure, encase, pack up, seal up, wrap up (225), etc.

(*Adjectives*) Circumscribed, etc., imprisoned, pent up (754), landlocked.

(*Phrase*) Not room to swing a cat.

232 ENCLOSURE (*Substantives*), envelope, case, box (191), pen, penfold, fold, sheep-fold, pound, paddock, enclave, *enceinte*, corral, ring fence, wall, hedge, hedgerow, espalier, exclosure, play-pen.

Barrier, bar, gate, gateway, door, barricade, cordon.

Dike (or dyke), ditch, fosse, moat.

Fence, pale, paling, balustrade, rail, railing, hurdle, palisade, battlement, rampart, embankment, breakwater, mole, groyne (717), circumvallation, contravallation.

233 LIMIT (*Substantives*), boundary, bounds, confine, term, bourne, line of demarcation, termination, stint, frontier, border, precinct, marches, line of circumvallation, pillars of Hercules, Rubicon, turning-point, last word, *ne plus ultra*.

(*Adjectives*) Definite, conterminal, terminal, frontier.

(*Phrases*) To cross the Rubicon; thus far and no farther.

2. SPECIAL

234 FRONT (*Substantives*), face, anteriority, fore-part, front rank, foreground, van, vanguard, advanced guard, outpost, proscenium, façade, frontage, foreword, preface, frontispiece (64).

Forehead, visage, physiognomy, phiz, countenance, mug, dial, puss, pan, beak, rostrum, bow, stem, prow.

Pioneer, avant-courier (64).

(In a medal) obverse; (in a coin) head.

(*Verbs*) To be in front, etc., to front, face, envisage, confront, bend forward, etc.

(*Adjectives*) Fore, anterior, front, frontal, facial.

(*Adverbs*) Before, in front, ahead, right ahead, in the van, foremost, vis-à-vis, in the foreground, face to face, before one's eyes.

---

236 LATERALITY (*Substantives*), side, flank, quarter, hand, cheek, jowl, wing, profile, temple, loin, haunch, hip, broadside, lee-side, lee.

East, orient; West, occident.

(*Verbs*) To be on one side, etc., to flank, outflank, to sidle, skirt.

(*Adjectives*) Lateral, sidelong, collateral, sideling, bilateral, trilateral, quadrilateral, multilateral, many-sided, eastern, oriental, western, occidental, eastward, westward.

(*Adverbs*) Sideways, side by side (216), sidelong, abreast, abeam, alongside, aside, by the side of, to windward, to leeward.

(*Phrases*) Cheek by jowl; broadside on.

238 DEXTRALITY (*Substantives*), right, right hand, dexter, offside, starboard, recto.

(*Adjectives*) Dextral, right-handed; ambidextrous, ambidexter.

235 REAR (*Substantives*), back, posteriority, the rear rank, rear-guard, the background, heels, tail, scut, rump, croup, crupper, breech, backside, posterior, fanny, catastrophe, buttocks, haunches, hunkers, hurdies, hind quarters, *dorsum*, dorsal region, stern, poop, after-part, tail-piece, wake.

(In a medal) reverse; (in a coin) tail.

(*Verbs*) To be in the rear, behind, etc., to fall astern, to bend backwards, to back on,

(*Phrases*) Turn the back upon; bring up the rear.

(*Adjectives*) Back, rear, postern, hind, hinder, hindmost, sternmost, posterior, dorsal, after.

(*Adverbs*) Behind, in the rear, aft, abaft, astern, aback, rearward.

(*Phrases*) In the background; behind one's back; at the heels of; at the tail of; at the back of; back to back.

237 ANTIPOSITION (*Substantives*), opposite side, contraposition, reverse, inverse, antipodes, opposition, inversion (218)

Polarity, opposite poles, North and South.

(*Verbs*) To be opposite, etc., subtend.

(*Adjectives*) Opposite, reverse, inverse, antipodal, subcontrary.

Fronting, facing, diametrically opposite, vis-à-vis.

Northern, boreal, septentrional, arctic; southern, austral, antarctic.

(*Adverbs*) Over, over the way, over against, facing, against, fronting (234), face to face, vis-à-vis.

239 SINISTRALITY (*Substantives*), left, left hand, sinister, near side, port, larboard, verso.

(*Adjectives*) Sinistral, left-handed.

Section III—Form

1°. General Form

240 FORM (*Substantives*), figure, shape, configuration, make, formation, frame, construction, conformation, cut, set, trim, build, make, stamp, cast, mould, fashion, structure.

Feature, lineament, phase (448), turn, attitude, posture, pose.

Morphology, isomorphism.

Formation, figuration, efformation, sculpture.

(*Phrase*) The cut of one's jib.

(*Verbs*) To form, shape, figure, fashion, carve, cut, chisel, chase, emboss, hew, rough-hew, cast, roughcast, hammer out, block out, trim, work, lick into shape, knock together, mould, sculpture, sculp, grave, stamp.

241 Absence of form.

AMORPHISM (*Substantives*), amorphousness, formlessness, shapelessness, disfigurement, defacement, mutilation (846).

Vandalism, vandal, Goth.

(*Verbs*) To destroy form, deform, deface, disfigure, disfeature (846), mutilate.

(*Adjectives*) Shapeless, amorphous, formless, unhewn, rough, rude, Gothic, unfashioned, unshapen, misshapen, inchoate.

(*Adjectives*) Formed, graven, etc., receiving form, plastic, fictile.

Giving form, formative, plastic, plasmatic, plasmic.

---

242 Regularity of form.

SYMMETRY (*Substantives*), shapeliness, eurhythmy, uniformity, finish, beauty (845), proportion, balance.

(*Adjectives*) Symmetrical, regular, shapely, eurhythmic, well-set, uniform, finished, well-proportioned, balanced, chaste, classic.

(*Phrase*) *Teres atque rotundus.*

243 Irregularity of form.

DISTORTION (*Substantives*), twist, kink, wryness, asymmetry, gibbosity, contortion, malformation, ugliness, etc. (846), teratology.

(*Verbs*) To distort, twist, wrest, writhe, wring, contort, kink, buckle.

(*Adjectives*) Irregular, unsymmetrical, asymmetrical, distorted, twisted, wry, awry, askew, crooked, on one side, misshapen, deformed, ill-proportioned, ill-made, round-shouldered, pigeon-chested, humpbacked, hunchbacked, gibbous, gibbose; knock-kneed, bandy-legged, bow-legged, club-footed, splay-footed.

(*Phrases*) All manner of ways; all over the place.

2°. Special Form

244 ANGULARITY (*Substantives*), angulation, angle, cusp, bend, elbow, knee, knuckle, groin, crinkle-crankle, kink, crotch, crutch, crane, fluke, scythe, sickle, zigzag, anfractuosity, refraction; fold (258), corner (182).

Fork, bifurcation, dichotomy.

Right angle (212), salient angle, re-entrant angle, acute angle, obtuse angle.

A polygon, square, rectangle, triangle, pentagon, hexagon, heptagon, octagon, nonagon, decagon, lozenge, diamond, rhomb, rhombus, rhomboid, parallelogram, gore, gusset, wedge.

Cube, parallelepiped, pyramid, prism, rhombohedron, tetrahedron, pentahedron, hexahedron, octahedron, dodecahedron, icosahedron.

T-square, set-square, protractor, goniometer, theodolite, sextant, quadrant, clinometer.

(*Verbs*) To bend, refract, diffract, fork, bifurcate, angulate, crinkle, crankle, splay.

(*Adjectives*) Angular, triangular, quadrangular, rectangular, bent, crooked, hooked, aduncous, aquiline, jagged, serrated, falciform, falcated, furcated, forked, bifurcate, zigzag; dovetailed, knock-kneed, crinkled, akimbo, geniculated, polygonal, trigonal, pentagonal, etc., fusiform, sagittate, arrow-headed, wedge-shaped, cuneate, cuneiform, splayed, angulate, cubical, pyramidal, rhombohedral, tetrahedral, etc.

245 CURVATURE (*Substantives*), curvation, incurvity, incurvation, bend, flexure, flexion, hook, crook, camber, bending, deflexion, inflexion, arcuation, diffraction, turn, deviation, detour, sweep, sinuosity, curl, curling, winding, recurvature, recurvation, refraction, flexibility (324).

A curve, arc, circle, ellipse (247), parabola, hyperbola, catenary, festoon, arch, arcade, vault, bow, crescent, half-moon, lunette, horseshoe, loop, bight, crane-neck, conchoid, ogee.

(*Verbs*) To be curved, etc., to bend, curve, etc., decline, turn, trend, deviate, re-enter, sweep.

To render curved; to bend, curve, incurvate, camber, deflect, inflect, crook, hook, turn, round, arch, arcuate, bow, curl, recurve, loop, frizzle.

(*Adjectives*) Curved, vent, etc., curvilinear, curviform, recurved, recurvous, circular, oval (247), parabolic, hyperbolic, bowed, crooked, bandy, arched, vaulted, arcuated, camerated, hooked, falcated, falciform, crescent-shaped, semilunar, semicircular, conchoidal, lunular, lunulate, cordiform, heart-shaped, reniform, pear-shaped; bow-legged, bandy-legged, knock-kneed, devious.

246 STRAIGHTNESS (*Substantives*), rectilinearity, directness.

A straight line, a right line, a direct line; inflexibility (323).

(*Verbs*) To be straight, etc.

To render straight, to straighten, rectify, set or put straight, take the curl out of, unbend, unfold, uncurl, uncoil, unroll, unwind, unravel, untwist, unwreathe, unwrap.

(*Adjectives*) Straight, rectilinear (or rectilineal), direct, even, right, in a line; unbent; not inclining, not bending, not turning, not deviating to either side, undeviating, unturned, undistorted, unswerving.

(*Phrases*) Straight as an arrow; as the crow flies; in a bee line.

———

247 Simple circularity.

CIRCULARITY (*Substantives*), roundness, rotundity (249).

A circle, circlet, ring, areola, hoop, roundlet, *annulus*, annulet, bracelet, bangle, armlet, anklet, ringlet, eye, loop, wheel, cycle, orb, orbit, rundle, zone, belt, cordon, band, sash, girdle, cestus, cincture, baldric, bandolier, fillet, cummerbund, fascia, wreath, garland, crown, corona, coronal, coronet, chaplet, necklace, rivière; noose, lasso.

An ellipse, oval, ovule, ellipsoid,

248 Complex circularity.

CONVOLUTION (*Substantives*), winding, wave, undulation, circuit, tortuosity, anfractuosity, sinuosity, involution, sinuation, circumvolution, meander, circumbendibus, twist, twirl, squiggle, curl, curlicue, curliewurlie, tirlie-whirlie, crimp, frizz, frizzle, permanent wave, perm, windings and turnings, *ambages*, inosculation, peristalsis.

A coil, reel, roll, spiral, helix, corkscrew, worm, volute, scroll, cartouche, rundle, scallop (or scollop), escallop.

cycloid, epicycloid, epicycle, semi-circle, quadrant, sextant, sector, segment.

(*Verbs*) To make round, round, circle, encircle, environ (227).

(*Adjectives*) Round, rounded, circular, annular, orbicular.

Oval, elliptical, elliptic, ovate, egg-shaped; cycloidal, etc., moniliform.

———

Serpent, eel, maze, labyrinth.

(*Verbs*) To be convoluted, etc.

To wind, twine, twist, coil, roll turn and twist, weave, twirl, wave undulate, meander, scallop, curl crimp, frizz, frizzle, perm, inosculate, entwine (219), enlace, twist together, goffer.

(*Adjectives*) Convoluted, winding, twisting, contorted, waving, waved, wavy, curly, undulating, undulant, undulatory, undated, serpentine, anguilline, mazy, labyrinthine, Dae-dalian, tortuous, sinuous, flexuous, snaky, involved, sigmate, sigmoid, sigmoidal, vermiform, vermicular, peristaltic, meandrine; scalloped (or scolloped), wreathed, wreathy, crisped, crimped, frizzed, frizzy, frizzled, frizzly, ravelled, twisted, dishevelled (61).

Spiral, coiled, helical, turbinate.

(*Adverb*) In and out.

249 ROTUNDITY (*Substantives*), roundness, cylindricity; cylinder, barrel, drum, cylindroid, roll, roller, rouleau, column, rolling-pin, rundle.

Cone, conoid; pear-shape, bell-shape.

Sphericity, spheroidity, globosity; a sphere, globe, ball, spheroid, ellipsoid, drop, spherule, globule, vesicle, bulb, bullet, pellet, pill, clue, marble, pea, knob, pommel.

(*Verbs*) To form into a sphere, render spherical, to sphere, ensphere, to roll into a ball, round off, give rotundity, etc.

(*Adjectives*) Rotund, round, cylindric, cylindrical, cylindroid, columnar, lumbriciform; conic, conical, conoidal.

Spherical, spheral, spheroidal, globular, globated, globous, globose, ovoid, egg-shaped, gibbous, bulbiform, bulbous, bell-shaped, campaniliform, campaniform, campanulate, fungiform, bead-like, moniliform, pyriform, cigar-shaped.

(*Phrases*) Round as an apple; round as a ball; *teres atque rotundus.*

3°. *Superficial Form*

250 CONVEXITY (*Substantives*), prominence, projection, swelling, gibbosity, bulge, protuberance, intumescence, tumour, cancer, tuberosity, tubercle, tooth, knob, excrescence, elbow, process, condyle, bulb, nub, nubble, node, nodule, nodosity, tongue, *dorsum*, hump, hunch, hunk, bunch, boss, embossment, bump, lump, clump, sugarloaf, point (253), bow, bagginess.

Pimple, wen, papula, pustule, carbuncle, corn, wart, polyp, boil, furuncle, fungus, fungosity, bleb, blister, blain, chilblain, bunion.

Papilla, nipple, teat, pap, breast,

251 FLATNESS (*Substantives*), plane; horizontality (213), layer (204), smoothness (255); plate, platter, slab, table, tablet; level.

(*Verbs*) To render flat, flatten, smooth, level.

(*Adjectives*) Flat, plane, even, level, etc. (213), flush, scutiform, scutellate.

(*Phrases*) Flat as a pancake; flat as a flounder; flat as a board; flat as my hand; a dead flat; a dead level.

252 CONCAVITY (*Substantives*). depression, hollow, hollowness, indentation, intaglio, cavity, dent, dint, dimple, follicle, pit, sinus, alveolus,

ug, udder, mamilla, proboscis, nose,
eb, beak, snout, nozzle, belly,
aunch, corporation, kyte, back,
houlder, elbow, lip, flange.

Peg, button, stud, ridge, rib, jetty,
nag, eaves, mole, cupola, dome,
alcony.

Cameo, high and low relief, bas-
elief, *basso rilievo*, *alto rilievo*;
epoussé work.

Mount, hill (206); cape, promon-
ory, foreland, headland, ness, mull,
alient, point of land, hummock,
pur, hog's back, offset.

(*Verbs*) To be prominent, etc., to
roject, bulge, belly, jut out, bristle
p, to hang over, overhang, beetle,
end over, protrude, stand out, stick
ut, poke out, stick up, start up,
ock up, shoot up, swell.

To render prominent; to raise (307),
o emboss, chase, stud, bestud, ridge.

(*Adjectives*) Convex, prominent, projecting, bulging, etc., bold, bossed,
ossy, knobby, nubbly, lumpy, bumpy, nodose, embossed, chased,
ibbous, salient, mamilliform, in relief, bowed, arched, bellied, baggy,
ornute, odontoid, tuberous, tuberculous, ridged, ridgy.

lacuna, honeycomb, excavation,
trough (259).

Cup, basin, crater, etc. (191);
socket, thimble.

Valley, vale, dale, dell, dingle,
coombe, strath, bottom, corrie, glade,
glen, cave, cell, cavern, cove, grotto,
grot, alcove, gully (198), cul-de-sac.

(*Verbs*) To be depressed, etc., to
cave in, subside, retire.

To depress, hollow, scoop, gouge,
dig, delve, excavate, dent, dint,
stave in, mine, undermine, burrow,
tunnel.

(*Adjectives*) Depressed, concave,
hollow, stove in, retiring, retreating,
cavernous, honeycombed, alveolar,
cellular, funnel-shaped, infundibular,
bell-shaped, campaniliform, porous
(260).

---

253 SHARPNESS (*Substantives*),
eenness, pointedness, acuteness,
cuity, acumination, spinosity, prick-
ness.

A point, spike, spine, spicule,
eedle, bodkin (262), aiguille, pin,
rickle, prick, prong, tine, caltrop,
hevaux de frise, arrow, spear, bayo-
et, pike, sword, dagger (727), spur,
owel, barb, spit, cusp, horn, antler,

254 BLUNTNESS (*Substantives*),
obtuseness, dullness.

(*Verbs*) To be blunt, etc., to render
blunt, etc., to obtund, dull, take off
the point or edge, turn.

(*Adjectives*) Blunt, obtuse, dull,
bluff.

---

nag, tag, jag, thorn, brier, bramble, thistle, nib, tooth, tusk, denticle,
poke, cog, ratchet, comb, bristle, beard, awn, *arête*, crest, cone, peak,
pire, pyramid, steeple, porcupine, hedgehog.

Cutlery, blade, edge-tool, knife, jack-knife, penknife, clasp-knife,
owie, jocteleg, chisel, razor, scalpel, bistoury, lancet, axe, hatchet,
ole-axe, pick-axe, pick, mattock, spade, adze, coulter, ploughshare,
cythe, sickle, reaping-hook, bill, billhook, cleaver, scissors, shears,
écateurs.

Sharpener, knife-sharpener, strop, hone, grinder, grindstone, whet-
cone, steel, emery, carborundum.

(*Verbs*) To be sharp, etc., to taper to a point, to bristle with.

To render sharp, etc., to sharpen, point, aculeate, set, whet, strop,
one, grind, barb, bristle up.

(*Adjectives*) Sharp, keen, pointed, conical, acute, acicular, aculeated,
rrowy, needle-shaped, spiked, spiky, spicular, spiculate, mucronate,
ucronated, ensiform, peaked, acuminated, salient, cusped, cuspidate,
uspidated, cornute, prickly, spiny, spinous, thorny, jagged, bristling,

muricate, pectinated, studded, thistly, briery, snaggy, digitated, barbed, spurred, two-edged, tapering, fusiform, dentiform, denticular, denticulated, toothed, odontoid, cutting, trenchant, sharp-edged.

Starlike, stellated, stelliform.

(*Phrases*) Sharp as a needle, as a razor.

255 SMOOTHNESS (*Substantives*), evenness, level (213), polish, gloss, glossiness, sleekness, slipperiness, lubricity, lubrication (332), down, velvet, velveteen, velour, silk, satin, plush, glass, ice, enamel, macadam.

Burnisher, calender, mangle, iron, file, plane, sandpaper, emery-paper, roller.

(*Verbs*) To smooth, smoothen, plane, polish, burnish, calender, mangle, enamel, glaze, iron, file, roll, lubricate, macadamize.

(*Adjectives*) Smooth, even, level, plane, sleek, slick, polished, glazed, glossy, sleeky, silken, silky, satiny, velvety, glabrous, slippery, oily, soft, unwrinkled.

(*Phrases*) Smooth as glass, as velvet, as satin, as soil; slippery as an eel.

256 ROUGHNESS (*Substantives*), unevenness, asperity, rugosity, ruggedness, scabrousness, salebrosity, cragginess, craggedness, corrugation, nodosity, crispness, plumosity, villosity; grain, texture, nap, pile.

Arborescence, branching, ramification.

Brush, bur, beard, shag, whisker, dundreary, mutton-chop, sideboards, side-burns, down, goatee, imperial, moustache, feather, plume, crest, tuft, *panache*, byssus, hair, chevelure, toupee, wool, fur, mane, cilia, fringe, *fimbriae*, tress, moss, plush, velvet, velveteen, velour, stubble.

(*Verbs*) To be rough, etc.

To render rough, to roughen, crisp, crumple, corrugate, rumple.

(*Adjectives*) Rough, uneven, scabrous, gnarled, rugged, rugose, rugous, salebrous, unpolished, matt, frosted, rough-hewn, craggy, cragged, prickly, scrubby.

Arborescent, dendriform, arboriform, branching, ramose, ramulose, dendroid.

Feathery, plumose, plumous, plumigerous, tufted, fimbriated, hairy, ciliated, hirsute, flocculent, bushy, hispid, tomentous, downy, woolly, velvety, villous (or villose), bearded, pilous, shaggy, shagged, stubbly, fringed, befringed, setaceous, filamentous.

(*Phrases*) Rough as a nutmeg-grater; like quills upon the fretful porcupine; against the grain.

257 NOTCH (*Substantives*), dent, dint, nick, cut, indent, indentation, dimple.

Embrasure, battlement, machicolation, machicoulis, saw, tooth, sprocket, crenelle, scallop (or scollop).

(*Verbs*) To notch, nick, cut, dent, indent, dint, jag, scotch, slash, scallop (or scollop), crenelate.

(*Adjectives*) Notched, etc., jagged, crenate, crenated, crenelated, dented, dentated, denticulated, toothed, palmated, indented, serrated.

258 FOLD (*Substantives*), plication, plait, ply, crease, pleat, tuck, hem, flexion, flexure, joint, elbow, doubling, duplicature, gather, wrinkle, crow's-foot, rimple, crinkle, crankle, crumple, rumple, rivel, ruck, ruffle, ruche, dog's-ear, corrugation, flounce, frounce, lapel, pucker, crimp.

(*Verbs*) To fold, double, plicate, plait, crease, wrinkle, crinkle, crankle, curl, cockle up, cocker, rimple, frizz, frizzle, rumple, flounce, frounce, rivel,

will, corrugate, ruffle, crimp, crumple, pucker, to turn down, turn under,
uck, ruck.

(*Adjectives*) Folded, dog's-eared (or dog-eared), etc.

259 FURROW (*Substantives*), groove, rut, slit, scratch, streak, stria, crack,
core, rib.

Channel, gutter, trench, ditch, dike, moat, fosse, trough, kennel, chamfer,
avine (198), fluting.

(*Verbs*) To furrow, etc., flute, plough.

(*Adjectives*) Furrowed, etc., ribbed, striated, striate, sulcated, fluted,
canaliculate, bisulcate, trisulcate, etc., corduroy, corded, corrugated.

260 OPENING (*Substantives*), hole, foramen, perforation, eye, eyelet, keyhole, loophole, porthole, scuttle, mouse-hole, pigeon-hole, eye of a needle, pinhole, peep-hole, puncture.

Aperture, hiatus, yawning, osciancy, dehiscence, patefaction, slot, chink, crevice (198).

Window, light, fanlight, skylight, casement, lattice, embrasure.

Orifice, inlet, intake, outlet, mouth, throat, muzzle, gullet, weasand, nozzle, portal, porch, gate, lych-gate, wicket, postern, gateway, door, embouchure, doorway, exit, vomitory, hatch, hatchway, gangway, arcade.

Channel (350), passage, pass, tube, pipe, vessel, tubule, canal, thoroughfare, gut, fistula, ajutage, tap, faucet, chimney, flue, vent, funnel, gully, tunnel, main, adit, pit, shaft, gallery, alley, aisle, glade, vista, bore, mine, calibre, pore, follicle, porosity, porousness, lacuna.

Sieve, cullender, colander, strainer, tamis, riddle, screen, honeycomb.

261 CLOSURE (*Substantives*), occlusion, blockade, shutting up, filling up, plugging, sealing, obstruction, impassableness, blocking up, obstipation, constipation, blind alley, blind corner, cul-de-sac, impasse, caecum.

Imperforation, imperviousness, impermeability, imporosity.

(*Verbs*) To close, occlude, steek, plug, block up, fill up, blockade, obstruct, bar, stop, bung up, seal, clinch, plumb, cork up, shut up, choke, throttle, ram down, dam up, cram, stuff up.

(*Adjectives*) Closed, shut, unopened, occluded, etc., impervious, imperforate, caecal, impassable, invious, pathless, untrodden, unpierced, unventilated, impermeable, imporous, operculated, tight, water-tight, airtight, hermetic.

(*Phrase*) Hermetically sealed.

Apertion, perforation, piercing, boring, mining, terebration, drilling,
etc., impalement, pertusion, puncture, acupuncture, penetration
(302).

Opener, tin-opener, key, master-key.

(*Verbs*) To open, ope, gape, yawn.

To perforate, lay open, pierce, empierce, tap, bore, mine, drill, scoop
out, canalize, tunnel, transpierce, transfix, enfilade, rake, impale, spike,
spear, gore, stab, pink, stick, prick, lance, puncture, riddle, honeycomb,
punch, jab; uncover, unrip, stave in.

(*Phrase*) To cut a passage through.

(*Adjectives*) Open, pierced, perforated, etc., perforate, wide open,
ajar, unclosed, unstopped, patulous, gaping, yawning, patent.

Tubular, tubulous, tubulate, tubuliform, cannular, fistulous, fistular,
fistulate, pervious, permeable, foraminous, porous, follicular, cribriform,
honeycombed, infundibular, windowed, fenestrated.

(*Phrase*) Open sesame!

262 PERFORATOR (*Substantives*), borer, auger, gimlet, stylet, drill, wimble, awl, bradawl, brog, scoop, corkscrew, dibble, trepan, probe, bodkin, needle, stiletto, lancet, punch, spike, bit, brace and bit, gouge, fleam.

(*Verbs*) To spike, gouge, scoop, punch, lance.

263 STOPPER (*Substantives*), stopple, plug, cork, bung, spigot, spike, spile vent-peg, stopcock, tap, stopgap, rammer, ramrod, piston, wad, dossil wadding, tompion, stuffing, tourniquet.

Cover, lid, operculum, covering, covercle, door, etc. (222), valve.

A janitor, door-keeper, commissionaire, chucker-out, ostiary, concierge, porter, warder, beadle, Cerberus.

SECTION IV—MOTION

1°. *Motion in General*

264 MOTION (*Substantives*), movement, transit, transition, move, going, etc., passage, course, stir.

Step, gait, stride, tread, port, footfall, carriage, transference (270), locomotion, travel (266), voyage (267).

Mobility, restlessness, unrest, movability, movableness, inquietude, flux; kinematics.

(*Verbs*) To be moving, etc., to move, go, stir, hie, gang, budge, pass, flit, shift, glide, roll, roll on, flow (347, 348), sweep along, wander (279), change or shift one's place or quarters, dodge, keep going.

To put in motion, impel, etc. (276); to propel, project (284); to mobilize, motorize.

(*Adjectives*) Moving, in motion, on the move, going, transitional; kinematic.

Shifting, movable (270), mobile, restless, nomadic, wandering, vagrant, discursive, erratic (279), mercurial, unquiet.

(*Adverbs*) *In transitu*, under way, on the move.

265 QUIESCENCE (*Substantives*), rest, stillness, stagnation, stagnancy, fixedness, immobility, catalepsy, paralysis.

Quiet, quietness, quietude, tranquillity, calm, calmness, sedentariness, peace; steadiness, balance, equilibrium.

Pause, suspension, suspense, lull, stop, stoppage, interruption, stopping, stand, standstill, standing still, lying to, repose (687), respite.

Lock, deadlock, dead stop, embargo.

Resting-place, anchorage, moorings, bivouac, port (189, 666), bed, pillow, etc. (215).

(*Verbs*) To be quiescent, etc., to remain, stand, stand still, lie to, pull up, hold, halt, stop, anchor, stop short, stop dead, freeze, heave to, rest, pause, repose, keep quiet, take breath, stagnate, vegetate, settle; to mark time.

To stay, tarry, sojourn, dwell (186), pitch one's tent, cast anchor, settle, encamp, bivouac, moor, tether, picket, plant oneself, alight, land, etc. (292) ride at anchor.

(*Phrases*) Not to stir a peg (or step or inch); '*j'y suis, j'y reste*'; to come to a standstill; to come to a deadlock; to rest on one's oars or laurels.

To stop, suspend, arrest, lay to, hold one's hand, interrupt, intermit, discontinue (142), put a stop to, quell, becalm.

(*Phrases*) To bring to a standstill; to lay an embargo on.

(*Adjectives*) Quiescent, still, motionless, moveless, at rest, stationary, untravelled, stay-at-home, at a stand, at a standstill, stock-still, standing still, sedentary, undisturbed, unruffled, fast, stuck fast, fixed, transfixed, rooted, moored, aground, at anchor, tethered, becalmed, stagnant, quiet, calm, breathless, peaceful, unmoved, unstirred, immovable, immobile, restful, cataleptic, paralysed, frozen, irremovable, stable, steady, steadfast.

(*Phrases*) Still as a statue; still as a post; quiet or still as a mouse.

(*Interjections*) Soho! stop! stay! avast! belay! halt! as you were! hold hard! hold your horses! hold on! whoa!

266 Locomotion by land.

JOURNEY (*Substantives*), travel, travelling, excursion, expedition, tour, trip, trek, circuit, peregrination, discursion, ramble, outing, pilgrimage, Odyssey, course, ambulation, march, route march, marching, walk, walking, promenade, stroll, saunter, dander, turn, trot, tramp, hike, stalk, noctambulation, perambulation, ride, equitation, drive, jogtrot, airing, constitutional, spin, jaunt, joy-ride, change of scene.

Roving, vagrancy, flit, flitting, migration, emigration, immigration, intermigration; *Wanderlust*.

Map, plan, itinerary, road-book, guide, Baedeker, Bradshaw, A B C.

Procession, caravan, cavalcade, column, cortège.

Organs and instruments of locomotion, legs, feet, pins, stilt, skate, ski, snow-shoe, locomotive, vehicle (272, 273), velocipede, penny-farthing, bone-shaker, bicycle, cycle, bike, push cycle, tandem, tricycle, fairycycle, scooter.

(*Phrase*) Shanks's mare.

(*Verbs*) To travel, journey, trek, walk, ramble, roam, rove, course, wander, itinerate, perambulate, stroll, straggle, expatiate, range, gad about, gallivant, knock about, to go or take a walk, journey, tour, turn, trip, etc.; to prowl, stray, saunter, tour, make a tour, knock about, emigrate, flit, migrate.

To walk, march, counter-march, step, tread, pace, wend, wend one's way, promenade, perambulate, circumambulate, take a walk, go for a walk, take the air, trudge, trapes, stalk, stride, straddle, strut, foot it, hoof it, stump, clump, plod, peg along, bundle, toddle, patter, shuffle on,

267 Locomotion by water, or air, or through space.

NAVIGATION (*Substantives*), voyage, sail, cruise, Odyssey, circumnavigation, periplus, seafaring, yachting, boating; drifting, headway, sternway, leeway.

Natation, swimming, surf-riding.

Flight, flying, flip, volitation, aerostation, aeronautics, aerostatics, ballooning, aviation, gliding.

Space travel, astronautics.

Wing, pinion, fin, flipper; oar, scull, canvas, sail, rotor, paddle, punt-pole, paddle-wheel, screw, turbine, jet.

(*Verbs*) To sail, make sail, warp, put to sea, navigate, take ship, get under way, spread sail, spread canvas, carry sail, plough the waves, plough the deep, scud, boom, drift, course, cruise, coast, circumnavigate, aviate.

To row, pull, paddle, scull, punt, steam.

To swim, float, buffet the waves, skim, *effleurer*, dive, wade.

To fly, aviate, hedge-hop, be wafted, hover, soar, glide, wing; to flush.

(*Phrases*) To take wing; to take flight.

(*Adjectives*) Sailing, etc., seafaring, under way, under sail, on the wing, volant, nautical; airborne, aeronautic, aeronautical, aerostatic; astronautical.

(*Phrases*) In sail; under canvas.

tramp, hike, footslog, traverse, bend one's steps, thread one's way, make one's way, find one's way, tread a path, take a course, take wing, take flight, defile, file off.

Ride, jog on, trot, amble, canter, gallop, take horse, prance, frisk, tittup, caracole, have a run, ride and tie, hitch-hike, lorry-hop.

To drive, slide, glide, skim, skate, tobaggon, ski.

To go to, repair to, resort to, hie to.

(*Phrase*) To pad the hoof; to hump bluey.

(*Adjectives*) Travelling, etc., ambulatory, itinerant, wayfaring, peripatetic, discursive, vagrant, migratory, nomadic, on the wing, etc., circumforanean, overland.

(*Adverbs*) By the way, *chemin faisant*, on the road, *en passant*, *en route*, on foot, afoot.

268 TRAVELLER (*Substantives*), wayfarer, voyager, itinerant, passenger, commuter, tourist, tripper, excursionist, wanderer, rover, straggler, rambler, hiker, bird of passage, gad-about, globe-trotter, vagrant, tramp, hobo, bum, swagman, sundowner, vagabond, rolling-stone, nomad, pilgrim, hadji, palmer, runner, courier, pedestrian, peripatetic, emigrant, fugitive.

Rider, horseman, equestrian, cavalier, jockey, postilion, rough-rider, scout, motorist.

Mercury, Iris, Ariel.

269 MARINER (*Substantives*), navigator, seaman, sailor, seafarer, shipman, tar, old salt, bluejacket, marine, jolly, boatman, *voyageur*, ferryman, waterman, lighterman, bargee, gondolier, longshoreman, crew, oarsman.

An aerial navigator, aeronaut, balloonist, aviator, airman, flying man, pilot.

Astronaut, cosmonaut, spaceman.

270 TRANSFERENCE (*Substantives*), transfer, displacement, metathesis, transposition (148), remotion, removal (185), relegation, deportation, extradition, conveyance, draft, carriage, carrying, convection, conduction, export, import.

Transmission, passage, transit, transition, ferry, transport, gestation, portage, porterage, cartage, carting, shovelling, shipment, transhipment, air lift, air drop, freight, wafture, transportation, transumption, transplantation, transfusion, translation, shifting, dodging, dispersion (73), traction (285).

(*Verbs*) To transfer, convey, transmit, transport, transplant, transfuse, carry, bear, carry over, hand over, pass forward, remove (185), transpose (148), shift, export, import, convey, conduct, convoy, send, relegate, extradite, turn over to, deliver, waft, ship, tranship, ferry over.

To bring, fetch, reach, draft.

To load, lade, charge, unload, shovel, ladle, decant, empty, break bulk.

(*Adjectives*) Transferred, etc., movable, portable, portative.

(*Adverbs*) From hand to hand, on the way, *en route*, *en passant*, *in transitu*, from pillar to post.

271 CARRIER (*Substantives*), porter, bearer, coolie, *hammal*, conveyer, transport-worker, stevedore (690), conductor, locomotive (285).

Beast of burden, cattle, horse, blood-horse, arab, steed, nag, palfrey, galloway, charger, destrier, war-horse, courser, racer, racehorse, hunter, pony, filly, colt, foal, barb, jade, hack, *bidet*, pad, cob, tit, punch, roadster, goer, pack-horse, draught-horse, cart-horse, post-horse, shelty, jennet, bayard, mare, stallion, gelding, gee-gee, gee, stud.

Ass, donkey, moke, cuddy, jackass, mule, hinny, sumpter-mule.

Camel, dromedary, llama, zebra, reindeer, yak, elephant, carrier-pigeon.

272 VEHICLE (*Substantives*), conveyance.

Carriage, caravan, van, furniture van, pantechnicon, wagon, stage-wagon, wain, dray, cart, float, trolley, sledge, sleigh, bob-sleigh, *luge*, toboggan, truck, tumbril, pontoon, barrow, wheelbarrow, hand-barrow, lorry.

Train, railway train, goods train, freight train, rolling stock, Pullman car, parlour car, restaurant-car, dining-car, diner, buffet-car, sleeping-car, sleeper, horse-box, cattle-truck, rail-car, tender.

Equipage, turn-out, carriage, coach, chariot, chaise, post-chaise, phaeton, curricle, tilbury, whisky, victoria, landau, brougham, clarence, gig, calash, dog-cart, governess-cart, trap, buggy, carriole, jingle, wagonette, jaunting-car, shandrydan, droshky, kibitka, berlin, stage, stage-coach, diligence, car, omnibus, bus, charabanc, brake, cabriolet, cab, hackney cab, four-wheeler, growler, fly, hansom.

Motor-car, motor, automobile, autocar, touring-car, tourer, sports car, torpedo, landaulette, limousine, saloon, sedan, two-seater, runabout, coupé, jalopy, tricar, motor-cycle, side-car, autocycle, moped, corgi, motor-bus, motor-coach, autobus, taxi-cab, taxi, motor-van, jeep; trolley-bus, tram-car, tram, street-car.

Tank, armoured car, half-track, amtrac, duck.

Bath-chair, wheel-chair, sedan chair, palanquin (or palankeen), litter, jinricksha (or rickshaw), brancard, stretcher, perambulator, pram, mail-cart, bassinette, baby-carriage.

Shovel, spoon, spatula, ladle, hod.

273 SHIP (*Substantives*), vessel, bottom, craft, shipping, marine, fleet, flotilla, squadron, three-master, barque (or bark), barquentine, brig, brigantine, schooner, sloop, cutter, skiff, yawl, ketch, smack, dogger, hoy, lugger, barge, wherry, lighter, hulk, buss, packet, clipper, rotor ship.

Navy, armada, warship, man-of-war, ironclad, capital ship, super-dreadnought, dreadnought, battle-ship, battle-cruiser, cruiser, frigate, corvette, gunboat, aircraft-carrier, monitor, torpedo boat destroyer, destroyer, torpedo boat, mine-sweeper, mine-layer, submarine, Q-boat, troop-ship, trooper, transport, hsopital ship, flagship; ship of the line, first-rate, seventy-four, fireship.

Liner, merchantman, tramp, slaver, steamer, steamboat, steam-packet, paddle-steamer, stern-wheeler, screw-steamer, turbine, tender, tug, collier, whaler, coaster, tanker.

Argosy, bireme, trireme, quadri-reme, quinquereme, galley, galleon, carrack, caravel, galliot, polacca, tartan, junk, praam, saic, dhow, proa, sampan, xebec.

Boat, motor-boat, long-boat, pinnace, launch, cabin cruiser, yacht, shallop, jolly-boat, gig, funny, dinghy, bumboat, fly-boat, wherry, coble, cock-boat, punt, cog, kedge, outrigger, catamaran, fishing-boat, coracle, hooker, life-boat, gondola, felucca, dahabeeyah, caique, canoe, dug-out, raft, float.

(*Adverbs*) Afloat, aboard.

273A AIRCRAFT (*Substantives*), flying machine, aeroplane, monoplane, biplane, seaplane, hydroplane, plane, flyingboat, amphibian, air-liner, flying wing, stratocruiser, stratoliner, sky-master, jet aircraft, jet, turbo-jet, autogiro, helicopter, hoverplane, whirlybird, planicopter, glider; fighter, bomber, fighter-bomber, flying fortress, super-fortress.

Balloon, air-balloon, aerostat, Montgolfier, pilot balloon, blimp, kite, airship, dirigible, Zeppelin.

Space ship, rocket, sputnik, lunik, satellite.

(*Adjective*) Airborne; orbital.

2°. *Degrees of Motion*

274 VELOCITY (*Substantives*), speed, celerity, swiftness, rapidity, fleetness, expedition, speediness, quickness, nimbleness, briskness, agility, promptness, promptitude (682), dispatch, acceleration (684).

Gallop, full gallop, canter, trot, run, rush, scamper, scoot, scorch, handgallop, lope; flight, dart, bolt, dash, spurt, sprint.

Haste, hurry, scurry, bounce, bolt, precipitation, precipitancy (684), forced march, race, steeplechase, Marathon race.

Rate, pace, step, gait, course, progress.

Lightning, light, cannon-ball, bullet, wind, rocket, arrow, dart, quicksilver, telegraph, express train, clipper.

An eagle, antelope, doe, courser, racehorse, racer, gazelle, greyhound, hare, squirrel, bandersnatch.

Mercury, Ariel, Camilla.

Speed indicator, speedometer, tachometer, log, log-line.

(*Verbs*) To move quickly; to trip, speed, haste, hie, hasten, hurry, fly, press, press on, press forward, post, push on, whip, scamper, run, sprint, race, scud, scour, scurry, scuttle, spin, scoot, scorch, rip, clip, shoot, tear, whisk, sweep, skim, brush, glance, cut along, dash on, dash forward, trot, gallop, lope, rush, bound, bounce, flounce, frisk, tittup, bolt, flit, spring, boom, dart.

To hasten, accelerate, expedite, dispatch, urge, whip, forward, buck up, express, speed-up, hurry, precipitate, quicken pace, gather way, ride hard.

To keep up with, keep pace with, race, race with, outpace, outmarch, distance, outdistance, lap, leave behind, outrun, outstrip, gain ground.

(*Phrases*) To cover the ground; to clap on sail; take to one's heels; clap spurs to one's horse; to run like mad; ride hard; outstrip the wind; to make rapid strides; wing one's way; be off like a shot; run a race; stir one's stumps; do a scoot; get a move on; get cracking; step on it; give her the gun; let it rip.

275 SLOWNESS (*Substantives*), tardiness, dilatoriness, slackness, lentor, languor (683), drawl.

Hobbling, creeping, lounging, etc., shambling, claudication, halting, walk, amble, jog-trot, dog-trot, mincing steps, foot-pace, crawl.

A slow-goer, dawdle, dawdler, lingerer, slow-coach, lame duck, drone, tortoise, snail, slug, sluggard, slacker.

Retardation, slackening, slowing down, delay (133).

(*Verbs*) To move slowly, to creep, crawl, lag, slug, drawl, dawdle, linger, loiter (683), plod, trudge, flag, saunter, lounge, lumber, trail, drag, grovel, glide, laze, amble, steal along, inch along, jog on, rub on, bundle on, toddle, waddle, shuffle, halt, hobble, limp, claudicate, shamble, mince, falter, totter, stagger.

To retard, slacken, relax, check, rein in, curb, strike sail, reef, slow up, slow down.

(*Phrases*) To 'drag its slow length along'; to hang fire; to march in slow time, in funeral procession; to lose ground.

To put on the drag; apply the brake; clip the wings; take in sail; take one's time; ca' canny; *festina lente.*

(*Adjectives*) Slow, slack, tardy, dilatory, easy, gentle, leisurely, deliberate, lazy, languid, drowsy, sleepy, heavy, drawling, leaden, sluggish, snail-like, creeping, crawling, etc., dawdling, lumbering, hobbling, tardigrade.

(*Adverbs*) Slowly, etc., gingerly, softly, leisurely, deliberately, gradually, etc. (144), *piano, adagio, largo.*

(*Phrases*) In slow motion; just ticking over; under easy sail; at a snail's pace; with mincing steps; with clipped wings; by degrees; little by little; inch by inch.

(*Adjectives*) Fast, speedy, swift, rapid, full-drive, quick, double-quick, fleet, nimble, agile, expeditious, prompt, brisk, frisky, hasty, hurried, flying, etc., precipitate, furious, light-footed, nimble-footed, winged, eagle-winged, mercurial, electric, telegraphic, light-legged; accelerative.

(*Phrases*) Swift as an arrow, as a doe, as a lamplighter; off like a shot; quick as lightning; quick as thought.

(*Adverbs*) Swiftly, with speed, speedily, trippingly, etc., full-tilt, full speed, apace, post-haste, *presto*, tantivy, by express, by telegraph, slap, slap-dash, headlong, hurry-scurry, hand over hand, at a round trot.

(*Phrases*) Under press of sail, or canvas; *velis et remis*; on eagle's wings; at the double, in double-quick time; with giant, or gigantic steps; *à pas de géant*; in seven-league boots; whip and spur; *ventre à terre*; as fast as one's legs or heels will carry one; *sauve qui peut*; the devil take the hindmost; *vires acquirit eundo*; with rapid strides; at top speed; on top gear; flat out; all out; like greased lightning; like the wind.

3°. *Motion conjoined with Force*

276 IMPULSE (*Substantives*), momentum, impetus, push, impulsion, thrust, shove, fling, jog, jolt, brunt, throw, volley, explosion (173), propulsion (284).

Percussion, collision, concussion, impact, clash, encounter, cannon, carom, carambole, appulse, shock, crash, bump, charge, tackle (716), foul.

Blow, stroke, knock, tap, fillip, pat, rap, dab, dig, jab, smack, slap, hit, putt, cuff, bang, crack, whack, thwack, slog, belt, wipe, clout, swipe, clip, squash, dowse, punch, thump, pelt, kick, lunge, buffet, beating (972).

277 RECOIL (*Substantives*), retroaction, revulsion, reaction, rebound, bounce, stot, repercussion, ricochet, rebuff, reverberation, reflux, reflex, kick, springing back, ducks and drakes.

A boomerang, spring (325).

(*Verbs*) To recoil, react, spring back, fly back, bound back, rebound, stot, reverberate, repercuss.

(*Adjectives*) Recoiling, etc., on the recoil, etc., refluent, repercussive, reactionary, retroactive.

(*Phrase*) On the rebound.

Hammer, mallet, mall, maul, beetle, flail, cudgel, bludgeon, life-preserver, cosh, baton, truncheon, knobkerrie, shillelagh, staff, lathi, cane, stick, club, racket, bat, driver, brassy, baffy, spoon, putter, cleek, iron, mashie, niblick, ram, battering-ram, monkey-engine, catapult, pile-driver, rammer, sledge-hammer, steam hammer.

Dynamics; seismometer.

(*Verbs*) To impel, push, give impetus, etc., drive, urge, hurtle, boom, thrust, elbow, shoulder, charge, tackle, jostle, justle, hustle, shove, jog, jolt, encounter, collide, clash, cannon, foul.

To strike, knock, tap, slap, dab, pat, slam, hit, bat, putt, rap, prod, jerk, dig, cuff, smite, butt, impinge, thump, bethump, beat, bang, whang, biff, punch, thwack, whack, spank, skelp, swat, lay into, shin, slog, clout, wipe, swipe, batter, dowse, baste, pummel, pelt, patter, drub, buffet, belabour, cane, whip (972), poke at, hoof, jab, pink, lunge, kick, recalcitrate.

To throw, etc. (284), to set going, mobilize.

(*Adjectives*) Impelling, etc., impulsive, impellent, impelled, etc., dynamic, dynamical.

(*Interjections*) Bang! boom! wham!

4°. *Motion with reference to Direction*

278 DIRECTION (*Substantives*), bearing, course, route, bent, inclination, drift, tenor, tendency, incidence, set, leaning, bending, trend, dip, steerage, tack, steering, aim, alignment (or alinement), orientation, collimation.

A line, bee-line, path, road, aim, range, quarter, point of the compass, rhumb, great circle, azimuth, line of collimation.

(*Verbs*) To tend towards, go to, point to, or at; trend, verge, align (or aline), incline, conduct to, determine.

To make for, or towards, aim at, take aim, level at, steer for, keep or hold a course, be bound for, bend one's steps towards, direct or shape one's course.

To ascertain one's direction, orient (or orientate) oneself, to see which way the wind blows.

(*Adjectives*) Directed, etc., direct, straight, undeviating, unswerving, aligned (or alined) with, determinate, point-to-point.

(*Adverbs*) Towards, to, *versus*, thither, directly, straight, point-blank, full tilt at, whither, in a line with, as the crow flies.

By way of, via, in all directions, *quaquaversum*, in all manner of ways, to the four winds.

---

280 Going before.

PRECESSION (*Substantives*), leading, heading.

Precedence in order (62), priority (116), precursor (64), front (234).

(*Verbs*) To precede, forerun, lead, head, herald, introduce, usher in (62), go ahead.

(*Phrases*) Go in the van; take the lead; lead the way; open the ball; have the start; to get before; steal a march.

(*Adjectives*) Preceding, leading, etc.

(*Adverbs*) In advance, before (62), in the van, ahead.

279 DEVIATION (*Substantives*), swerving, aberration, obliquation, *ambages*, warp, bending, flexion, deflection, refraction, sidling, side-slip, skid, half-roll, barrel-roll, loop, straying, straggling, warping, etc., digression, circuit, detour, departure from, divergence (291), desultory motion; slice, pull, hook, leg-break, off-break, googly.

Motion sideways, side-step.

(*Verbs*) To alter one's course, divert, deviate, depart from, turn, bend, swerve, break, switch, skid, side-slip, zoom, bank, loop, bunt, jib, shift, warp, stray, straggle, sidle, diverge (291), digress, wander, meander, veer, wear, tack, yaw, turn aside, turn a corner, turn away from, face about, wheel, wheel about, steer clear of, ramble, rove, go astray, step aside, shunt, side-track , jay walk.

(*Phrases*) To fly off at a tangent; to face to the right-about; to go out of one's way; to lose one's way.

(*Adjectives*) Deviating, etc., aberrant, discursive, devious, desultory, erratic, vagrant, stray, undirected, circuitous, roundabout, crab-like, zigzag.

(*Adverbs*) Astray from, round about.

(*Phrases*) To the right-about; all manner of ways; like the knight's move in chess.

---

281 Going after.

SEQUENCE (*Substantives*), following, pursuit, chase, hunt (622).

A follower, pursuer, attendant, shadow, satellite, hanger-on, train.

Sequence in order (63), in time (117).

(*Verbs*) To follow, pursue, chase, hunt, hound, shadow, dog, tail, trail, lag.

(*Phrases*) Go in the rear, or in the wake of; tread in the steps of; tread on the heels of; go after; fly after; to follow as a shadow; to lag behind; to bring up the rear; to fall behind; to tail off.

(*Adjectives*) Following, etc.

(*Adverbs*) Behind, in the rear, etc.

282 Motion forwards.

PROGRESSION (*Substantives*), advance, advancement, progress (658), on-going, progressiveness, progressive motion, flood-tide, headway, advancing, etc., pursuit, steeplechase (622), journey, march (266).

(*Verbs*) To advance, proceed, progress, go, move, bend or pass forward, go on, move on, pass on, get on, get along, jog on, push on, go one's way, go ahead, forge ahead, make head, make way, make headway, work one's way, press forward, edge forward, get over the ground, gain ground, make progress, keep or hold on one's course, keep up with, get forward, distance.

(*Phrases*) To make up leeway; to go with the stream; to make rapid strides; to push or elbow or cleave one's way; to go full tilt at.

(*Adjectives*) Advancing, etc., progressive, go-ahead, avant-garde, profluent, undeviating.

(*Adverbs*) Forward, onward, forth, on, in advance, ahead, under way, straightforward.

(*Phrases*) *Vestigia nulla retrorsum; en avant.*

284 Motion given to an object in front.

PROPULSION (*Substantives*), push, pushing (276), projection, jaculation, ejaculation, throw, fling, fillip, toss, shot, discharge, shy.

Ballistics, gunnery; *vis a tergo.*

Missile, projectile, shot, shell, ball, bolt, dart, arrow, bullet, stone, shaft, brickbat, discus, quoit, caber.

Bow, sling, pea-shooter, catapult, etc. (727).

(*Verbs*) To propel, project, throw, fling, cast, pitch, chuck, bung, toss, lob, loft, jerk, jaculate, ejaculate, hurl, boost, bolt, drive, sling, flirt, flip, flick, shy, dart, send, roll, send off, let off, discharge, fire off, shoot, launch, let fly, dash, punt, volley, heave, pitchfork.

To bowl, trundle, roll along (312).

To put in motion, start, give an impulse, impel (276), expel (297).

(*Phrases*) To carry off one's feet; to put to flight.

(*Adjectives*) Propelling, etc., propulsive, projectile, etc.

283 Motion backwards.

REGRESSION (*Substantives*), regress, recess, retrogression, retrogradation, retreat, withdrawal, retirement, recession (287), refluence, reflux, retroaction, return, reflexion, reflex (277), ebb, countermovement, countermarch, veering, regurgitation, backwash.

(*Verbs*) To recede, retrograde, return, rebound, back, fall back, fall or drop astern, lose ground, put about, go back, turn back, hark back, double, countermarch, turn tail, draw back, get back, retrace one's steps, wheel about, back water, regurgitate, yield, give.

(*Phrases*) Dance the back step; beat a retreat.

(*Adjectives*) Receding, etc., retrograde, retrogressive, regressive, refluent, reflex, recidivous, resilient.

(*Adverbs*) Backwards, reflexively, to the right-about, about turn, *à reculons, à rebours.*

(*Phrase*) *Revenons à nos moutons.*

285 Motion given to an object behind.

TRACTION (*Substantives*), drawing, draught, pull, pulling, towage, haulage.

Traction engine, locomotive; hauler, haulyer, tractor, tug; trailer.

(*Phrase*) A long pull, a strong pull, and a pull all together.

(*Verbs*) To draw, pull, haul, lug, drag, tug, tow, trail, train, wrench, jerk, twitch, yank.

(*Phrase*) To take in tow.

(*Adjectives*) Drawing, etc., tractile.

286 Motion towards.

APPROACH (*Substantives*), approximation, appropinquation, access, appulse, afflux, affluxion, pursuit (622), collision (276), arrival (292).

(*Verbs*) To approach, draw near, approximate, to near; to come, get, go, etc., near; to set in towards, make up to, snuggle up to, gain upon, gain ground upon.

(*Phrases*) To tread on the heels of; to hug the shore.

(*Adjectives*), Approaching, etc., approximative.

287 Motion from.

RECESSION (*Substantives*), retirement, withdrawal, retreat, retrocession (283), departure (293), recoi (277), decampment, flight, stampede, skedaddle.

A runaway, a fugitive.

(*Verbs*) To recede, go, move or fly from, retire, retreat, withdraw, come away, go or get away, draw back shrink, move away.

To move off, stand off, draw off buzz off, fall back, turn tail, march off, decamp, absquatulate, skedaddle vamoose, sheer off, bolt, scram, hop it, beat it, slip away, run away, pack off, fly, remove, abscond, sneak off slink away.

(*Phrases*) To take French leave; to cut and run; take to one's heels to give leg-bail; take one's hook; *sauve qui peut*; the devil take the hindmost; beat a retreat; make oneself scarce; do a bolt; do a guy make tracks; cut one's lucky.

(*Adjectives*) Receding, etc., fugitive, runaway (671).

288 Motion towards, actively.

ATTRACTION (*Substantives*), drawing to, pulling towards, adduction, attractiveness, magnetism, gravity, gravitation.

A loadstone, magnet.

(*Verbs*) To attract, draw, pull, drag, etc., towards, adduce.

(*Adjectives*) Attracting, etc., adducent, attrahent, adductive, attractive, magnetic, gravitational.

(*Interjections*) Come! come here! approach! come near!

289 Motion from, actively.

REPULSION (*Substantives*), push (276), driving from, repulse, expulsion (297).

(*Verbs*) To repel, repulse; push drive, etc., from, drive away, cold shoulder, send packing.

(*Phrases*) To give the frozen mitt to; send away with a flea in one's ear; send to the right-about (678).

(*Adjectives*) Repelling, etc., repellent, repulsive, forbidding.

(*Interjections*) Get out! be off scram! avaunt! (293, 297).

290 Motion nearer to.

CONVERGENCE (*Substantives*), appulse, meeting, confluence, concourse, conflux, congress, concurrence, concentration.

Resort, assemblage, synod (72), focus (74), asymptote.

(*Verbs*) To converge, come together, unite, meet, fall in with, close in upon, centre in, enter in, meet, come across, come up against.

To gather together, unite, concentrate, etc.

291 Motion farther off.

DIVERGENCE (*Substantives*), aberration, peregrination, wandering, divarication, radiation, ramification separation (44), dispersion, diffusion dissemination (73); deviation (279).

(*Verbs*) To diverge, divaricate deviate, wander, stray (279), radiate, branch off, ramify, file off, draw aside.

To spread, disperse, scatter, distribute, decentralize, diffuse, disseminate, shed, sow broadcast, broadcast, sprinkle.

(*Adjectives*) Converging, etc., convergent, confluent, concurring, concurrent, centripetal, asymptotical.

---

292 Terminal motion at.
ARRIVAL (*Substantives*), advent, reception, welcome, return, disembarkation, debarkation, remigration.

Home, goal, resting-place, destination, journey's end, harbour, haven, port, dock, pier, landing-place, landing-stage, landing-ground, airfield, airstrip, airstop, airport, aerodrome, helidrome, terminus, station.

Meeting, rencontre, rencounter, encounter.

Caller, visitor, visitant, guest.

(*Verbs*) To arrive, get to, come, come to, reach, attain, come up with, come up to, catch up, make, fetch, overtake, overhaul.

To light, alight, land, dismount, disembark, debark, detrain, outspan, debus, put in, put into, visit, cast, anchor.

To come upon, light upon, pitch upon, hit, drop in, pop upon, bounce upon, plump upon, bump against, run against, run across, close with.

To come back, return, get back, get home, sit down.

To meet, encounter, rencounter, contact, come in contact (199).

(*Phrase*) To be in at the death.

(*Adjectives*) Arriving, etc., homeward bound.

(*Adverbs*) Here, hither.

(*Interjections*) Welcome! hallo! hail! all hail! good day! good morrow! *ave!*

To part, part company, turn away from, wander from, separate (44).

(*Phrase*) To go or fly off at a tangent.

(*Adjectives*) Diverging, etc., divergent, radiant, wandering, aberring, aberrant, centrifugal.

(*Adverb*) Broadcast.

293 Initial motion from.
DEPARTURE (*Substantives*), outset, removal, exit, exodus, decampment, embarkation, flight, hegira.

Valediction, adieu, farewell, goodbye, leave-taking, send-off; stirrup-cup, doch-an-doris, one for the road.

A starting point or post, place of departure or embarkation, airfield, terminus, etc. (292).

(*Phrase*) The foot being in the stirrup.

(*Verbs*) To depart, go, set out, set off, start, start off, issue, go forth, sally, debouch, sally forth, set forward, be off, move off, pack off, buzz off, scram, begone, get off, sheer off, clear out, vamoose, skedaddle, absquatulate.

To leave a place, quit, retire, withdraw, go one's way, take wing, flit, embus, inspan, entrain, embark, go on board, set sail, put to sea, weigh anchor, slip cable, decamp (671).

(*Phrases*) To take leave; bid or take adieu; bid farewell; to say goodbye; make one's exit; take a run-out powder.

(*Adjectives*) Departing, etc., valedictory, outward bound.

(*Adverbs*) Whence, hence, thence.

(*Interjections*) Be off! get out! clear out! scram! buzz off! hop it! beat it! begone! get you gone! go along! off with you! avaunt! away with you! go about your business!

Good-bye! bye-bye! 'bye! ta ta! farewell! fare you well! adieu! *au revoir! auf wiedersehen! a rivederci! bon voyage! vale! hasta la vista! sayonara!* so long! cheerio! chin-chin! tinkety-tonk! pip-pip! tootle-oo! bung-ho!

---

294 Motion into.
INGRESS (*Substantives*), ingoing, entrance, entry, introgression, admission, admittance, intromission,

295 Motion out of.
EGRESS (*Substantives*), exit, issue, emersion, emergence.

Exudation, extravasation, transu-

introduction, insinuation, insertion (300), intrusion, inroad, incursion, influx, irruption, invasion, penetration, interpenetration, infiltration, import, importation, illapse, immigration.

A mouth, door (260); an entrant.

(*Verbs*) To enter, go into, come into, set foot in, intrude, invade, flow into, pop into, insinuate itself, penetrate, interpenetrate, infiltrate, soak into; to put into, etc., bring in, insert, drive in, run in, wedge in, ram in (300), intromit, introduce, import, smuggle.

(*Phrases*) To find one's way into; creep into; worm oneself into; to darken one's door; have the *entrée*; to open the door to.

(*Adjectives*) Ingoing, incoming, penetrative, penetrant.

(*Adverb*) Inwards.

---

296 Motion into, actively.

RECEPTION (*Substantives*), admission, admittance, importation, immission, introduction, ingestion, imbibition, absorption, resorption, ingurgitation, inhalation (300).

Eating, swallowing, deglutition, devouring, gulp, gulping, gorge, gorging, carousal.

Drinking, potation, sipping, supping, suction, sucking, draught, libation; smoking, snuffing.

Mastication, manducation, rumination, chewing; hippophagy, ichthyophagy, anthropophagy.

(*Verbs*) To admit, receive, intromit, import, ingest, absorb, resorb, imbibe, inhale, let in, take in, readmit, resorb, reabsorb, snuff up, sop up, suck, suck in, swallow, take down, ingurgitate, engulf.

To eat, fare, feed, devour, tuck in, gulp, bolt, snap, get down, pick, peck, gorge, engorge, fall to, stuff, cram, gobble, guttle, guzzle, wolf, raven, eat heartily, do justice to, overeat, gormandize (957), dispatch, discuss.

To feed upon, live on, feast upon,

dation (348), leakage, seepage, percolation, distillation, oozing, effluence, efflux, effusion, drain, dropping, dripping, dribbling, drip, dribble, drainage, filtering, defluxion, trickling, eruption, outbreak, outburst, outpouring, gush (348), emanation, aura.

Export, expatriation, emigration, remigration, repatriation, exodus (293).

An outlet, vent, spout, tap, faucet, sluice, flue, chimney, pore, drain, sewer (350).

(*Verbs*) To emerge, emanate, issue, go, come, move, pass, pour, flow, etc., out of, find vent, pass off, evacuate.

To transude, exude, leak, seep, well out, percolate, transcolate, strain, distil, drain, ooze, filter, filtrate, dribble, trickle, drizzle, drip, gush, spout, run, flow out, effuse, extravasate, disembogue, debouch (348).

(*Adjectives*) Dripping, outgoing, etc., oozy, leaky, trickly, dribbly.

297 Motion out of, actively.

EJECTION (*Substantives*), emission, effusion, rejection, expulsion, detrusion, extrusion, eviction.

Discharge, egestion, evacuation, vomition, eructation, belch; bloodletting, venesection, phlebotomy, tapping.

Deportation, exile, rustication, banishment, relegation, extradition.

(*Phrases*) The rogue's march; the bum's rush.

(*Verbs*) To emit, eject, expel, export, reject, discharge, give out, let out, cast out, clear out, sweep out, clean out, gut, fillet, wipe off, turn out, chuck out, elbow out, kick out, hoof out, sack, dismiss, bounce, drive out, root out, pour out, ooze, shed, void, evacuate, disgorge, extrude, empty, detrude, throw off, spit, spit out, expectorate, spirt, spill, slop, drain.

To vomit, spue, cat, puke, cast up, keck, retch, spatter, splutter, slobber, slaver, slabber, squirt, eructate, belch, burp, give vent to, tap, broach, open the sluices, heave out, bale out, shake off.

regale, carouse, batten upon, fatten upon, dine, etc., browse, graze, crop, chew, champ, munch, gnaw, nibble, crunch, ruminate, masticate, manducate, mumble.

To drink, quaff, swill, swig, booze, drench, sip, sup, lap, drink up, drain up, toss off, drain the cup, tipple (959).

(*Phrases*) To give entrance or admittance to; open the door to; usher in.

To refresh the inner man; restore one's tissues; play a good knife and fork; get outside of; wrap oneself round.

To drink one's fill; wet one's whistle; empty one's glass; crook or lift one's elbow; crack a bottle.

(*Adjectives*) Admitting, etc., admitted, etc., admissible; absorbent, absorptive.

To throw, project (284); to push, thrust (276).

To unpack, unlade, unload (270).

To banish, exile, extradite, deport; ostracize, boycott, send to Coventry.

(*Phrases*) To send packing; to send to the right about; to send about one's business; to give the sack to; to show the door to; to turn out neck and crop; to make a clean sweep of; to send away with a flea in one's ear.

(*Adjectives*) Emitting, etc., emitted, etc.

(*Interjections*) Be off! get out! scram! (293), scat! fade! chase yourself! *allez-vous-en!*

Hippophagous, ichthyophagous, anthropophagous, herbivorous, graminivorous, granivorous, omnivorous.

---

298 FOOD (*Substantives*), pabulum, aliment, nourishment, nutriment, sustenance, sustentation, nurture, subsistence, provender, fodder, provision, prey, forage, pasture, pasturage, keep, fare, cheer, rations, diet, regimen.

Comestibles, eatables, victuals, prog, grub, chow, chuck, toke, eats, meat, bread, breadstuffs, cake, pastry, viands, cates, delicacy, delicatessen, dainty, creature comforts, bellytimber, staff of life, dish, flesh-pots, pottage, pudding, ragout, omelet, sundae, kickshaws.

299 EXCRETION (*Substantives*), discharge, emanation, exhalation, exudation, secretion, extrusion, effusion, extravasation, evacuation, faeces, excrement (653), perspiration, sweat, saliva, salivation, spittle, diaphoresis; bleeding, haemorrhage, flux.

(*Verbs*) To emanate, exhale, excern, excrete, exude, effuse, secrete, secern, extravasate, evacuate, urinate, discharge, etc. (297).

Table, board, commons, good cheer, bill of fare, menu, commissariat, table d'hôte, ordinary, cuisine.

Canteen, Naffy, restaurant, chop-house, café, cafeteria, eating-house, tea-room, tea-shop, coffee-house, coffee-stall, bar, milk bar, snack bar, public-house, pot-house, ale-house, wineshop, brasserie, bodega, tavern (189).

Meal, repast, feed, mess, spread, course, regale, regalement, entertainment, feast, banquet, junket, refreshment, refection; breakfast, *chota hazri*, elevenses, *déjeuner*, lunch, bever, luncheon, tiffin, tea, afternoon tea, five-o'clock tea, high tea, dinner, supper, whet, appetizer, aperitif, bait, dessert, *entremet, hors d'œuvre*, picnic, bottle-party, wayzgoose, beanfeast, blow-out, tuck-in, snack, pot-luck table d'hôte, *déjeuner à la fourchette*.

Mouthful, bolus, gobbet, sip, sup, sop, tot, snort, hoot, dram, peg, cocktail (615), nip, *chasse*, liqueur.

Drink, hard drink, soft drink, tipple, beverage, liquor, broth, soup, etc., symposium.

(Phrases) A good tuck-in; a modest quencher.

(Adjectives) Eatable, edible, esculent, comestible, alimentary, cereal, culinary, nutritious, nutritive, nutrient, nutrimental, succulent, potable, drinkable.

298A TOBACCO, the weed, bacca, baccy, honeydew, cavendish, bird's-eye, shag, virginia, latakia, perique, plug, twist.

Cigar, segar, cheroot, havana, manila, weed, whiff, cigarette, fag, gasper, stinker, coffin-nail.

Snuff, rappee.

A smoke, draw, puff, pinch, quid, chew, chaw.

Tobacco-pipe, pipe, briar, meerschaum, calabash, corncob, clay pipe, clay, churchwarden, dudeen (or dudheen), cutty, hookah, hubble-bubble, chibouque, narghile, calumet.

(Verbs) To smoke, chew, take snuff.

(Adjective) Nicotian.

300 Forcible ingress.

INSERTION *(Substantives)*, putting in, implantation, introduction, interjection, insinuation, planting, intercalation, embolism, injection, inoculation, vaccination, importation, intervention (228), dovetailing, tenon, wedge.

Immersion, dip, plunge, bath (337), submergence, submersion, souse, duck, soak.

Interment, burying, etc. (363).

(Verbs) To insert, introduce, intromit, put into, import, throw in, interlard, inject, interject, intercalate, infuse, instil, inoculate, vaccinate, pasteurize, impregnate, imbue, imbrue, graft, engraft, bud, plant, implant, embed, obtrude, foist in, worm in, thrust in, stick in, ram in, stuff in, tuck in, plough in, let in, dovetail, mortise (or mortice), insinuate, wedge in, press in, impact, drive in, run in, empierce (260).

301 Forcible egress.

EXTRACTION *(Substantives)*, taking out, removal, elimination, extrication, evulsion, avulsion, eradication, extirpation, wrench.

Expression, squeezing; ejection (297).

Extractor, corkscrew, pincers, pliers, forceps.

(Verbs) To extract, take out, draw, draw out, pull out, tear out, pluck out, extort, wring from, prise, wrench, rake out, rake up, grub up, root up, uproot, eradicate, extirpate, dredge, remove, get out (185), elicit, extricate, eliminate.

To express, squeeze out, wring out, pick out, disembowel, eviscerate, exenterate.

(Adjectives) Extracted, etc.

To immerse, dip, steep, immerge, merge, submerge, bathe, plunge, drop in, souse, douse, soak, duck, drown.

To inter, bury, etc. (363).

(Adjectives) Inserting, inserted, implanted, embedded, etc., ingrowing.

302 Motion through.

PASSAGE *(Substantives)*, transmission, permeation, penetration, interpenetration (294), filtration, infiltration, percolation, transudation, osmosis (or osmose), capillary attraction, endosmosis (or endosmose), exosmosis (or exosmose), intercurrence; way, path (627); channel, pipe (350).

Terebration, impalement, etc. (260).

(Verbs) To pass, pass through, traverse, terebrate, stick, pierce, impale, spear, spike, spit (260), penetrate, percolate, permeate, thread, thrid, enfilade,

go through, cross, go across, go over, pass over, get over, clear, negotiate, cut across, pass and repass; work, thread or worm one's way, force a passage; to transmit.

(*Adjectives*) Passing, intercurrent, penetrative, transudatory, etc.

303 Motion beyond.

TRANSCURSION (*Substantives*), transilience, transgression, trespass, encroachment, infringement, extravagation, transcendence, enjambement, overrunning.

(*Verbs*) To transgress, overstep, surpass, overpass, overrun, overgo, beat, outstrip, outgo, outstep, outrun, outdo, overreach, overleap, outleap, pass, go by, strain, overshoot the mark, overjump, overskip, overlap, go beyond, outpace, outmarch, transcend, distance, outdistance, lap, encroach, exceed, trespass, infringe, trench upon.

(*Phrases*) To stretch a point; to steal a march on; to pass the Rubicon; to shoot ahead of; to throw into the shade.

(*Adverbs*) Beyond the mark, out of bounds.

304 Motion short of.

SHORTCOMING (*Substantives*), failure, falling short (732), defalcation, default, backlog, leeway, incompleteness (53); imperfection (651); insufficiency (640).

(*Verbs*) To come or fall short of, not to reach, keep within bounds, keep within compass, to stop short, be wanting, lose ground, miss the mark.

(*Adjectives*) Unreached, deficient (53), short, minus.

(*Adverbs*) Within the mark, within compass, within bounds, etc., behindhand.

305 Motion upwards.

ASCENT (*Substantives*), rise, climb, ascension, upgrowth, leap (309).

A rocket, sky-rocket, lark, skylark; a climber, mountaineer, Alpinist, stegophilist.

(*Verbs*) To ascend, rise, mount, arise, uprise, go up, get up, climb, clamber, swarm, shin, scale, scramble, escalade, surmount, aspire.

To tower, soar, zoom, hover, spire, plane, swim, float, surge.

(*Phrase*) To make one's way up.

(*Adjectives*) Rising, etc., scandent, buoyant, floating, supernatant, superfluitant.

(*Adverbs*) Uphill, on the up grade.

(*Interjection*) Excelsior!

306 Motion downwards.

DESCENT (*Substantives*), fall, descension, declension, declination, drop, cadence, subsidence, lapse, downfall, tumble, tilt, toppling, trip, lurch, *culbute*, spill, cropper, purler, crash.

Titubation, shamble, shambling, stumble.

An avalanche, landslip, landslide, debacle, slump.

(*Phrase*) The fate of Icarus.

(*Verbs*) To descend, come or go down, fall, sink, gravitate, drop, drop down, droop, decline, come down, dismount, alight, light, settle, subside, slide, slip, slither, glissade, toboggan, coast, volplane, dive (310).

To tumble, slip, trip, stumble, pitch, lurch, swag, topple, topple over, swoop, tilt, sprawl, plump down, measure one's length, bite the dust, heel over, careen (217), slump, crash.

To alight, dismount, get down.

(*Adjectives*) Descending, etc., descendent, decurrent, decursive, deciduous.

(*Phrase*) Nodding to its fall.

(*Adverbs*) Downhill, on the down grade.

307 Elevation (*Substantives*), raising, lifting, erection, lift, uplift, upheaval, upcast.

Lift, elevator, hoist, escalator, crane, derrick, winch, windlass, jack, lever.

(*Verbs*) To elevate, raise, lift, uplift, upraise, set up, erect, stick up, rear, uprear, upbear, upcast, hoist, uphoist, heave, upheave, weigh, exalt, promote, give a lift, help up, prick up, perk up.

To drag up, fish up, dredge.

To stand up, rise up, ramp.

(*Phrases*) To set on a pedestal; to get up on one's hind legs.

(*Adjectives*) Elevated, etc., rampant.

(*Adverbs*) On stilts, on the shoulders of.

308 Depression (*Substantives*), lowering, abasement, abasing, detrusion, reduction.

Overthrow, upset, prostration, subversion, overset, overturn, precipitation.

Bow, curtsy (or curtsey), genuflexion, obeisance, kowtow, salaam.

(*Verbs*) To depress, lower, let down, take down, sink, debase, abase, reduce, demote, detrude, let fall, cast down, to grass, send to grass.

To overthrow, overturn, upset, overset, subvert, prostrate, level, raze, fell; cast, take, throw, fling, dash, pull, cut, knock, hew, etc., down.

To stoop, bend, bow, curtsy (or curtsey), bob, duck, kneel, crouch, cower, lout, kowtow, salaam, bend the head or knee; to recline, sit, sit down, couch, squat.

(*Phrases*) To take down a peg; to pull about one's ears; to trample in the dust.

(*Adjectives*) Depressed, sunk, prostrate.

309 Leap (*Substantives*), jump, hop, spring, bound, vault, saltation.

Dance, caper, curvet, caracole, *entrechat*, gambade, gambado, capriole, dido, demivolt.

Kangaroo, jerboa, chamois, goat, frog, grasshopper, flea, buck-jumper.

(*Phrases*) Hop, skip, and jump; on the light fantastic toe.

(*Verbs*) To leap, jump, bound, spring, take off, buck, buck-jump, hop, skip, vault, dance, bob, curvet, romp, caracole, caper, cut capers.

(*Adjectives*) Leaping, etc., saltatory, Terpsichorean, frisky.

310 Plunge (*Substantives*), dip, dive, ducking, header.

Diver, frogman.

(*Verbs*) To plunge, dip, souse, duck, dive, plump, plop, submerge, submerse, bathe, douse, sink, engulf, founder.

311 Curvilinear motion.

Circuition (*Substantives*), turn, wind, circuit, curvet, detour, excursion, circumbendibus, circumvention, circumnavigation, north-west passage, circulation.

Turning, winding, twist, twisting, wrench, evolution, twining, coil, circumambulation, meandering.

(*Verbs*) To turn, bend, wheel, put about, switch, circle, go round, or round about, circumnavigate, circumambulate, turn a corner, double a point, wind, meander, whisk, twirl, twist (248), twill; to turn on one's heel.

(*Phrases*) To lead a pretty dance; to go the round; to turn on one's heel.

(*Adjectives*) Turning, etc., circuitous, circumforaneous, circumfluent.

(*Adverb*) Round about.

312 Motion in a continued circle.

ROTATION (*Substantives*), revolution, gyration, roll, circumrotation, circumgyration, gurgitation, pirouette, circumvolution, convolution, turbination, whir, whirl, eddy, vortex, whirlpool, cyclone, anticyclone, tornado, typhoon, whirlwind, willy-willy, waterspout, surge, dizzy round, maelstrom, Charybdis.

A wheel, flywheel, screw, reel, whirligig, rolling stone, windmill, top, teetotum, merry-go-round, round-about, gyroscope, gyrostat.

313 Motion in a reverse circle.

EVOLUTION (*Substantives*), unfolding, etc., development, introversion, reversion, eversion.

(*Verbs*) To evolve, unfold, unroll, unwind, uncoil, untwist, unfurl, untwine, unravel, disentangle (44), develop, introvert, reverse.

(*Adjectives*) Evolving, evolved, etc.

(*Adverbs*) Against.

Axis, axle, spindle, pivot, pin, hinge, pole, swivel, gimbals, mandrel.

(*Verbs*) To rotate, roll, revolve, spin, turn, turn round, circumvolve, circulate, gyre, gyrate, gimble, wheel, reel, whirl, twirl, birl, thrum, trundle, troll, twiddle, bowl, roll up, furl, wallow, welter.

(*Phrases*) To box the compass; to spin like a top.

(*Adjectives*) Rotating, etc., rotatory, rotary, circumrotatory, turbinate, trochoid, vortiginous, vortical, gyratory.

(*Phrase*) Like a squirrel in a cage.

(*Adverbs*) Clockwise, with the sun, deiseal (or deisil); counter-clockwise, against the sun, withershins (or widdershins).

314 Reciprocating motion, motion to and fro.

OSCILLATION (*Substantives*), vibration, undulation, pulsation, pulse, systole, diastole, libration, nutation, swing, beat, shake, seesaw, alternation, wag, evolution, vibratiuncle, coming and going, ebb and flow, flux and reflux; vibratility.

Fluctuation, vacillation, dance, lurch, dodge, rolling, pitching, tossing, etc. A pendulum, seesaw, rocker, rocking-chair, rocking-horse, etc.

(*Verbs*) To oscillate, vibrate, undulate, librate, wave, rock, swing, sway, pulsate, beat, wag, waggle, wiggle, wobble, shoogle, nod, bob, tick, play, wamble, wabble, waddle, dangle, swag, curtsy.

To fluctuate, vacillate, alternate, dance, curvet, reel, quake, quiver, quaver, roll, top, pitch, flounder, stagger, totter, brandish, shake, flicker, flourish, seesaw, teeter, move up and down, to and fro, backwards and forwards, to pass, and repass, to beat up and down.

(*Adjectives*) Oscillating, etc., oscillatory, vibratory, vibratile, vibrant, vibrational, undulatory, pulsatory, pendulous, libratory, systaltic.

(*Adverbs*) To and fro, up and down, backwards and forwards, seesaw, zigzag, wibble-wabble.

315 Irregular motion.

AGITATION (*Substantives*), stir, tremor, shake, ripple, jog, jolt, jar, succussion, trepidation, quiver, quaver, dance, jactitation, jactitancy, restlessness, shuffling, twitter, flicker, flutter, bobbing.

Disturbance, perturbation, commotion, turmoil, welter, bobbery; turbulence, tumult, tumultuation, bustle, fuss, flap, tirrivee, jerk, throw, convulsion, spasm (173), twitch, tic, staggers, St. Vitus's dance, epilepsy, writhing, ferment, fermentation, effervescence, ebullition, hurly-burly, hubbub, stramash, *tohu-bohu*; tempest, storm, whirlwind, cyclone (312), ground swell.

(*Verbs*) To be agitated, to shake, tremble, quiver, quaver, shiver, dither, twitter, twire, writhe, toss about, tumble, stagger, bob, reel, sway, wag, waggle, wiggle, wobble, shoogle, dance, wriggle, squirm, stumble, flounder, shuffle, totter, dodder, shamble, flounce, flop, curvet, prance, cavort, throb, pulsate, beat, palpitate, go pit-a-pat, fidget, flutter, flitter, flicker, bicker, twitch, jounce, ferment, effervesce, boil.

To agitate, shake, convulse, toss, tumble, bandy, wield, brandish, flap, flourish, whisk, switch, jerk, hitch, jolt, jog, hoggle, jostle, hustle, disturb, shake up, churn.

(*Phrases*) To jump like a parched pea; to be in a spin; to shake like an aspen leaf; to drive from pillar to post.

(*Adjectives*) Shaking, etc., agitated, tremulous, shivery, tottery, jerky, shaky, shoogly, quivery, quavery, trembly, choppy, rocky, wriggly, desultory, subsultory, shambling, giddy-paced, saltatory.

(*Phrases*) All of a tremble or twitter; like a pea on a drum; like a cat on hot bricks; like a hen on a hot griddle.

(*Adverbs*) By fits and starts; subsultorily, *per saltum* (139).

CLASS III

WORDS RELATING TO MATTER

SECTION I—MATTER IN GENERAL

316 MATERIALITY (*Substantives*), corporeity, corporality, materialness, substantiality, physical, condition.

Matter, body, substance, brute matter, stuff, element, principle, parenchyma, material, substratum, frame, *corpus pabulum,* flesh and blood.

Thing, object, article, still life, stocks and stones.

Physics, somatology, somatics, natural philosophy, physiography, physical science, experimental philosophy, positivism, materialism.

(*Verbs*) To materialize, embody, incarnate, objectify, externalize.

(*Adjectives*) Material, bodily, corporeal, corporal, carnal, temporal, physical, somatic, somatological, materialistic, sensible, palpable, tangible, ponderable, concrete, impersonal, objective, bodied.

317 IMMATERIALITY (*Substantives*), incorporeity, spirituality, spirit, etc. (450), inextension.

Personality, I, me, myself, ego.

Spiritualism, spiritism, idealism, immaterialism.

(*Verbs*) To disembody, spiritualize, immaterialize.

(*Adjectives*) Immaterial, incorporeal, ideal, unextended, intangible, impalpable, imponderable, bodiless, unbodied, disembodied, extra-sensory, astral, psychical, psychic, extra-mundane, unearthly, supernatural, supranatural, transcendent, transcendental, pneumatoscopic, spiritualistic, spiritual (450).

Personal, subjective.

---

318 WORLD (*Substantives*), nature, creation, universe; earth, globe, wide world, cosmos, sphere, macrocosm.

The heavens, sky, welkin, empyrean, starry heaven, firmament, ether; vault or canopy of heaven; celestial spaces, starry host, heavenly bodies, star, constellation, galaxy, Milky Way, *via lactea,* nebula, etc., sun, moon, planet, asteroid, planetoid, satellite, comet, meteor, meteorite, shooting star.

Zodiac, ecliptic, colure, orbit.

Astronomy, astrophysics, uranography, uranology, cosmology, cosmography, cosmogony; planetarium, orrery.

An astronomer, star-gazer, cosmographer; observatory.

(*Adjectives*) Cosmic, cosmical, mundane, terrestrial, terraqueous, terrene, telluric, sublunary, under the sun, subastral, worldwide, global.

Celestial, heavenly, spheral, starry, stellar, nebular, etc., sidereal, sideral, astral, solar, lunar.

319 HEAVINESS (*Substantives*), weight, gravity, gravitation, ponderosity, ponderousness, avoirdupois, pressure, load, burden, ballast; a

320 LIGHTNESS (*Substantives*), levity, imponderability, subtlety, buoyancy, airiness, portability, volatility.

lump, mass, weight, counterweight, counterpoise; ponderability.

Lead, millstone, mountain.

Balance, spring balance, scales, steelyard, weighbridge.

Statics.

(*Phrase*) Pelion on Ossa.

(*Verbs*) To be heavy, to gravitate, weigh, press, cumber, load.

(*Adjectives*) Weighty, heavy, ponderous, gravitating, weighing, etc., ponderable, lumpish, cumbersome, hefty, massive, unwieldy, cumbrous, incumbent, superincumbent; gravitational.

(*Phrase*) Heavy as lead.

A feather, dust, mote, down, thistledown, flue, ooss, fluff, cobweb, gossamer, straw, cork, bubble; float, buoy; featherweight.

(*Verbs*) To be light, float, swim, be buoyed up.

(*Adjectives*) Light, subtle, airy, vaporous, imponderous, astatic, weightless, imponderable, ethereal, sublimated, floating, swimming, buoyant, air-borne, portable, uncompressed, volatile.

(*Phrases*) Light as a feather; light as thistledown; 'trifles light as air.'

SECTION II—INORGANIC MATTER

1°. *Solid Matter*

321 DENSITY (*Substantives*), denseness, solidness, solidity, impenetrability, incompressibility, cohesion, coherence, cohesiveness (46), imporosity, impermeability, closeness, compactness, constipation, consistence, spissitude, thickness.

Specific gravity; hydrometer, araeometer.

Condensation, consolidation, solidification, concretion, coagulation, conglomeration, petrifaction, lapidification, vitrification, crystallization, precipitation, inspissation, thickening, grittiness, knottiness, induration (323).

Indivisibility, indiscerptibility, indissolubility.

322 RARITY (*Substantives*), tenuity, absence of solidity, subtility, sponginess, compressibility; hollowness(252).

Rarefaction, expansion, dilatation, inflation, dilution, attenuation, subtilization.

Ether, vapour, air, gas (334).

(*Verbs*) To rarefy, expand, dilate, dilute, attenuate, subtilize, thin out.

(*Adjectives*) Rare, subtle, sparse, slight, thin, fine, tenuous, compressible.

Porous, cavernous, spongy, bibulous, spongious, spongeous.

Rarefied, expanded, dilated, subtilized, unsubstantial, hollow (252).

A solid body, mass, block, knot, lump, concretion, concrete, cake, clot, stone, curd, coagulum, clinker, nugget; deposit, precipitate.

(*Verbs*) To be dense, etc.

To become or render solid; solidify, solidate, concrete, set, consolidate, congeal, jelly, jell, coagulate, curdle, curd, fix, clot, cake, cohere, crystallize, petrify, vitrify, condense, incrassate, thicken, inspissate, compact, concentrate, compress, squeeze, ram down, constipate.

(*Adjectives*) Dense, solid, solidified, consolidated, etc., coherent, cohesive, compact, close, thick-set, serried, substantial, massive, lumpish, impenetrable, incompressible, impermeable, imporous, constipated, concrete, knotted, gnarled, crystalline, crystallizable, vitreous, coagulated, thick, incrassated, inspissated, curdled, clotted, grumous.

Undissolved, unmelted, unliquefied, unthawed.

Indivisible, indiscerptible, infrangible, indissolvable, indissoluble, insoluble, infusible.

323 HARDNESS (*Substantives*), rigidity, rigescence, firmness, renitence, inflexibility, stiffness, starchiness, starchedness, temper, callosity, durity, induration, grittiness, petrifaction, etc. (321), ossification, sclerosis.

A stone, pebble, flint, marble, rock, granite, brick, iron, steel, corundum, diamond, adamant, bone, callus.

(*Verbs*) To render hard, harden, stiffen, indurate, petrify, vitrify, temper, ossify.

(*Adjectives*) Hard, horny, corneous, bony, osseous, rigid, rigescent, stiff, firm, starch, stark, unbending, unyielding, inflexible, tense, indurate, indurated, gritty, stony, proof, adamantean, adamantine.

(*Phrases*) Hard as iron, etc.; hard as a brick; hard as a nail; hard as a deal board; 'as hard as a piece of the nether millstone'; stiff as buckram; stiff as a poker.

324 SOFTNESS (*Substantives*) tenderness, flexibility, pliancy, pliableness, pliantness, litheness, pliability, suppleness, sequacity, ductility, malleability, tractility, extensibility, plasticity, inelasticity, laxity, flaccidity, flabbiness, limpness.

Clay, wax, butter, dough; a cushion, pillow, featherbed, down, padding, wadding, cotton-wool.

Mollification, softening, etc.

(*Verbs*) To render soft, soften, mollify, relax, temper, mash, pulp, knead, squash.

To bend, yield, give, relent, relax.

(*Adjectives*) Soft, tender, supple, pliable, limp, limber, flexible, flexile, lithe, lissom, *svelte*, willowy, pliant, plastic, waxen, ductile, tractile, tractable, malleable, extensile, sequacious.

Yielding, bending, flabby, flaccid, lymphatic, flocculent, downy, flimsy, spongy, oedematous, doughy, argillaceous, mellow; emollient, softening, etc.

(*Phrases*) Soft as butter; soft as down; soft as silk; yielding as wax; tender as a chicken.

325 ELASTICITY (*Substantives*), springiness, spring, resilience, buoyancy, renitency, contractility (195), compressibility.

Indiarubber, rubber, caoutchouc, whalebone, elastic.

(*Verbs*) To be elastic, etc., to spring back, fly back, rebound, recoil (277).

(*Adjectives*) Elastic, tensile, springy, resilient, buoyant.

326 INELASTICITY (*Substantives*), want or absence of elasticity, softness, etc. (324).

(*Adjectives*) Inelastic, ductile, limber, etc. (324).

327 TOUGHNESS (*Substantives*), tenacity, strength, cohesion (46), stubbornness (606).

Leather, gristle, cartilage.

(*Verbs*) To be tenacious, etc., to resist fracture.

(*Adjectives*) Tenacious, tough, wiry, sinewy, stringy, stubborn, cohesive, strong, resisting, resistant, leathery, coriaceous.

(*Phrase*) Tough as leather.

328 BRITTLENESS (*Substantives*), fragility, crispness, friability, frangibility, fissility.

(*Verbs*) To be brittle, break, crack, snap, split, shiver, splinter, fracture, crumble, break short, fly.

(*Adjectives*) Brittle, frangible, fragile, frail, jerry-built, gimcrack, shivery, fissile, splitting, splintery, lacerable, crisp, friable, short, crumbling.

(*Phrases*) Brittle as glass; a house of cards.

329 TEXTURE (*Substantives*), structure, construction, organization, set-up, organism, anatomy, frame, mould, fabric, framework, carcass, architecture, *compages*; substance, stuff, parenchyma, constitution, intertexture, contexture, tissue, grain, web, warp, woof, nap (256).

Fineness or coarseness of grain.

Histology.

(*Adjectives*) Textural, structural, organic, anatomic, anatomical; fine, delicate, subtle, fine-grained; coarse, homespun, rough-grained, coarse-grained; flimsy, unsubstantial, gossamery, filmy, gauzy.

330 PULVERULENCE (*Substantives*), state of powder, powderiness, efflorescence, sandiness, friability.

Dust, stour (or stoor), powder, sand, shingle, sawdust, grit, meal, bran, flour, limature, filings, debris, detritus, moraine, scobs, crumb, seed, grain, spore, atom, particle (32), flocculence.

Reduction to powder, pulverization, comminution, granulation, disintegration, weathering, subaction, contusion, trituration, levigation, abrasion, detrition, filing, etc. (331).

Mill, quern, grater, nutmeg grater, rasp, file, pestle and mortar.

(*Verbs*) To reduce to powder, to pulverize, comminute, granulate, triturate, levigate, scrape, file, abrade, rub down, grind, grate, rasp, mill, pound, bray, bruise, contuse, contund, beat, crush, crunch, scrunch, crumble, disintegrate, weather.

(*Adjectives*) Powdery, granular, mealy, floury, branny, farinaceous, furfuraceous, flocculent, dusty, sandy, sabulous, arenaceous, gritty, efflorescent, impalpable; pulverizable, pulverulent, friable, crumbly, shivery, pulverized, etc., attrite.

331 FRICTION (*Substantives*), attrition, rubbing, massage, abrasion, rub, scouring, limature, filing, rasping, frication, elbow-grease.

Grindstone, whetstone, buff, hone, strop (253).

(*Verbs*) To rub, abrade, scratch, scrape, scrub, grate, fray, rasp, pare, scour, polish, massage, curry, shampoo, rub out.

332 Absence of friction.

LUBRICATION (*Substantives*), prevention of friction, oiling, etc., anointment.

Lubricant, oil, lard, grease, etc. (356); synovia, saliva.

(*Verbs*) To lubricate, oil, grease, anoint, wax; smooth (255).

(*Adjectives*) Lubricated, etc.

2°. *Fluid Matter*

I. FLUIDS IN GENERAL

333 FLUIDITY (*Substantives*), fluid (including both inelastic and elastic fluids).

Inelastic fluid.

Liquidity, liquidness, aquosity, a liquid, liquor, lymph, humour, juice, sap, blood, serum, serosity, gravy, chyle, rheum, ichor, sanies; solubility.

Hydrology, hydrostatics, hydrodynamics.

334 Elastic fluid.

Gaseity, vaporousness, flatulence, flatulency; gas, air, vapour, ether, steam, fume, reek, effluvium.

Smoke, cloud (353).

Pneumatics, aerostatics, aerodynamics; gas-meter, gasometer.

(*Verbs*) To be fluid or liquid, to flow, run (348).

(*Adjectives*) Liquid, fluid, fluent, running, flowing, serous, juicy, succulent, sappy, lush.

Liquefied, uncongealed, melted, etc. (335).

(*Verbs*) To emit vapour, evaporate, to steam, fume, reek, smoke, puff, smoulder.

(*Adjectives*) Gaseous, aeriform, ethereal, aerial, airy, vaporous, vapoury, flatulent, volatile, evaporable.

335 LIQUEFACTION (*Substantives*), liquescence, fusion, melting, thaw, deliquation, deliquescence, lixiviation.

Solution, dissolution, decoction, infusion, apozem, flux.

Solvent, menstruum, alkahest.

(*Verbs*) To render liquid, to liquefy, deliquesce, run, melt, thaw, fuse, solve, dissolve, resolve, to hold in solution.

(*Adjectives*) Liquefied, melted, unfrozen, molten, liquescent, liquefiable, deliquescent, diffluent, soluble, dissoluble.

336 VAPORIZATION (*Substantives*), gasification, volatilization, evaporation, distillation, sublimation, exhalation, volatility.

Vaporizer, retort, still.

(*Verbs*) To render gaseous, vaporize, volatilize, evaporate, exhale, distil, sublime, sublimate.

(*Adjectives*) Volatilized, etc., volatile, evaporable, vaporizable.

2. SPECIFIC FLUIDS

337 WATER (*Substantives*), heavy water, serum, lymph, rheum, whey.

Dilution, immersion, maceration, humectation, infiltration, sprinkling, washing, spraying, aspersion, affusion, irrigation, douche, balneation, bath, shower-bath, inundation, deluge (348), a diluent.

(*Verbs*) To be watery, etc., to reek.

To add water, to water, wet, moisten (339), dilute, dip, immerse, plunge, merge, immerge, steep, souse, duck, submerge, drown, soak, saturate, sop, macerate, pickle, blunge, wash, lave, springle, asperge, asperse, dabble, bedabble, affuse, splash, splatter, spray, swash, douse, drench, slop, slobber, irrigate, inundate, deluge, flood.

To take a bath, to tub, bathe, bath, paddle.

To syringe, inject, gargle.

(*Adjectives*) Watery (339), aqueous, aquatic, lymphatic, diluted, etc., reeking, dripping, sodden, drenched, soaking, sopping.

338 AIR (*Substantives*), common air, atmospheric air.

The atmosphere, troposphere, tropopause, stratosphere, ionosphere, Heaviside layer, Appleton layer; the sky, the ether, the open air, ozone, weather, climate.

Meteorology, climatology, isobar, barometer, aneroid barometer, weather-glass, weather-chart, weather station, weather ship.

Exposure to the air or weather, airing, weathering (330).

(*Verbs*) To aerate, oxygenate, arterialize, ventilate, air-condition.

(*Adjectives*) Containing air, windy, flatulent, aerated, effervescent.

Atmospheric, airy, open-air, *plein-air*, alfresco, aerial, aeriform; meteorological, barometric, weather-wise.

(*Adverbs*) In the open air, *à la belle étoile, sub Jove.*

Wet, washy, sloppy, squashy, splashy, soppy, soggy, slobbery, diluent, balneal.

(*Phrases*) Wet as a drowned rat; soaked to the skin; wet as a rag; wet through.

339 MOISTURE (*Substantives*), moistness, humidity, dampness, damp, wetness, wet, humectation, madefaction, dew, muddiness, marsh (345).

Hygrometer, hygrometry, hygrology.

(*Verbs*) To be moist, etc.

To moisten, wet, humectate, sponge, damp, dampen, bedew, imbue, infiltrate, imbrue; soak, saturate (337).

(*Adjectives*) Moist, damp, watery, humid, wet, dank, muggy, dewy, roral, rorid, roscid, juicy, swampy (345), humectant, sopping, dripping, sodden.

(*Phrase*) Wringing wet.

341 OCEAN (*Substantives*), sea, main, the deep, brine, salt water, blue water, high seas, offing, tide, wave, surge, ooze, etc. (348).

Hydrography, oceanography.

Neptune, Thetis, Triton, Oceanid, Nereid, sea-nymph, siren, mermaid, merman, dolphin; trident.

(*Phrases*) The vasty deep; the briny; the ditch; the drink.

(*Adjectives*) Oceanic, marine, maritime, thalassic, pelagic, pelagian, sea-going, hydrographic.

(*Adverbs*) At sea, on sea, afloat.

343 GULF (*Substantives*), bay, inlet, bight, estuary, roadstead, roads, arm of the sea, armlet, sound, frith, firth, fiord, lagoon, cove, creek, strait, belt, kyle, Euripus.

(*Adjective*) Estuarine.

LAKE (*Substantives*), loch, lough, mere, tarn, linn, plash, broad, pond, dew-pond, pool, puddle, well, reservoir, standing water, dead water, a sheet of water, fish-pond, ditch, dike, backwater.

(*Adjectives*) Lacustrine (or lacustrian), lacuscular.

340 DRYNESS (*Substantives*), siccity, aridity, drought.

Exsiccation, desiccation, arefaction, drainage.

(*Verbs*) To be dry, etc.

To render dry, to dry, dry up, sop up, swab, wipe, blot, exsiccate, desiccate, dehydrate, drain, parch.

(*Adjectives*) Dry, anhydrous, dehydrated, arid, dried, etc., unwatered, undamped, waterproof, husky, juiceless, sapless; siccative, desiccative.

(*Phrases*) Dry as a bone; dry as dust; dry as a stick; dry as a mummy; dry as a biscuit; dry as a limekiln.

342 LAND (*Substantives*), earth, ground, terra firma, continent, mainland, peninsula, delta, alluvium, polder, tongue of land, neck of land, isthmus, oasis.

Coast, shore, seaboard, seaside, sea-bank, strand, beach, bank, lea.

Cape, promontory, etc. (250), headland, point of land, highland (206).

Soil, glebe, clay, humus, loam, marl, clod, clot, rock, crag, chalk, gravel, mould, subsoil.

(*Adjectives*) Terrene, continental, earthy, terraqueous, terrestrial.

Littoral, riparian, alluvial, midland.

(*Adverbs*) Ashore, on shore, on land.

344 PLAIN (*Substantives*), tableland, open country, the face of the country, champaign country, basin, downs, waste, wild, weald, steppe, pampas, savanna, llano, prairie, tundra, heath, common, wold, moor, moorland, the bush; plateau, flat (213).

Meadow, mead, haugh, pasturage, park, field, lawn, green, plot, plat, terrace, esplanade, sward, turf, sod, heather, lea, grounds, pleasure-grounds, playing-fields, campus.

(*Phrase*) A weary waste.

(*Adjectives*) Campestrian, champaign, lawny.

345 MARSH (*Substantives*), marish, swamp, morass, moss, fen, bog, quag, quagmire, slough, sump, wash.

(*Adjectives*) Marshy, marish, swampy, boggy, quaggy, fenny, soft, plashy, poachy, paludal.

346 ISLAND (*Substantives*), isle, islet, ait, eyot, inch, holm, reef, atoll; archipelago.

(*Adjectives*) Insular, sea-girt.

---

3. FLUIDS IN MOTION

347 Fluid in motion.

STREAM (*Substantives*), flow, current, jet, undercurrent, course (348).

(*Verbs*) To flow, stream, issue, run.

348 Water in motion.

RIVER (*Substantives*), running water, jet, spurt, squirt, spout, splash, rush, gush, water-spout, sluice, linn, waterfall, cascade, force, catadupe, cataract, debacle, cataclysm, inundation, deluge, avalanche, spate.

Rain, shower, scud, driving rain, downpour, drencher, soaker, cloudburst, mizzle, drizzle, Scotch mist, smirr, dripping, stillicidium; flux, flow, profluence, effluence, efflux, effluxion, defluxion.

Irrigation (337).

Spring, fountain, fount, rill, rivulet, gill, gullet, rillet, streamlet, runnel, sike, burn, beck, brooklet, brook, stream, reach, torrent, rapids, race, flush, flood, swash.

Tide, spring tide, high tide, tidal wave, bore, eagre, freshet, current, indraught, reflux, eddy, whirlpool, vortex, maelstrom, regurgitation.

Tributary, confluent, effluent, billabong; corrivation, confluence, effluence.

Wave, billow, surge, swell, chop, ripple, ground swell, surf, breaker, roller, comber, white caps, white horses.

Irrigation (337); sprinkler, sprayer, spray, atomizer, aspergillum, aspersorium, water-cart, watering-pot, watering-can, pump, syringe, hydrant.

Hydraulics, hydrodynamics, hydrography; rain-gauge.

(*Verbs*) To flow, run, meander, gush, spout, roll, billow, surge, jet, well, drop, drip, trickle, dribble, ooze (295), percolate, distil, transude,

349 Air in motion.

WIND (*Substantives*), draught, current, breath, air, breath of air, puff, whiff, zephyr, blow, drift, aura.

Gust, blast, breeze, squall, gale, storm, tempest, hurricane, whirlwind, tornado, cyclone, typhoon, blizzard, simoom, samiel, harmattan, monsoon, trade wind, sirocco, mistral, *bise, tramontana, föhn,* pampero; windiness, ventosity.

Aeolus, Boreas, Auster, Euroclydon, the cave of Aeolus.

Bellows, blowpipe, fan, ventilator, punkah.

Anemometer, anemograph, windgauge, weathercock, vane.

Insufflation, sufflation, perflation, blowing, fanning, ventilation, blowing up, inflation, afflation; respiration, inspiration, expiration, sneezing, sternutation, cough, hiccup.

(*Phrase*) A capful of wind.

(*Verbs*) To blow, waft, blow hard, blow a hurricane, breathe, respire, inspire, expire, insufflate, puff, whiff, sough, whiffle, wheeze, gasp, snuffle, sniffle, sneeze, cough.

To fan, ventilate, inflate, perflate, blow up.

(*Phrase*) To blow great guns.

(*Adjectives*) Blowing, etc., rough, blowy, windy, breezy, gusty, squally, puffy, stormy, tempestuous, blustering.

---

stream, sweat, perspire (299), overflow, flow over, splash, swash, guggle, murmur, babble, bubble, purl, gurgle, sputter, spurt, regurgitate, surge.

To rain, rain hard, pour with rain, drizzle, spit, mizzle, set in.

To flow into, fall into, open into, drain into, discharge itself, disembogue, disgorge, debouch.

(*Phrases*) To rain cats and dogs; to rain in torrents.

To cause a flow, to pour, drop, distil, splash, squirt, spill, drain, empty, discharge, pour out, open the sluices or flood-gates; shower down, irrigate (337).

To stop a flow, to stanch, dam, dam up (261), intercept.

(*Adjectives*) Fluent, profluent, affluent, confluent, diffluent, tidal, flowing, etc., babbling, bubbling, gurgling, meandering, meandrous.

Fluviatile, fluvial, riverine, streamy, showery, drizzly, rainy, pluvial, pouring.

---

350 Channel for the passage of water.

CONDUIT (*Substantives*), channel, duct, watercourse, watershed, race, adit, aqueduct, canal, sluice, dike main, gully, moat, ditch, lode, leat, rhine, trough, gutter, drain, sewer, culvert, cloaca, sough, kennel, siphon, pipe (260), emunctory, gully-hole, artery, aorta, pore, spout, funnel, tap, faucet, scupper, adjutage (or ajutage), waste-pipe, hose, rose, gargoyle, artesian well.

Floodgate, dam, weir, levee, watergate, lock, valve.

351 Channel for the passage of air.

AIR-PIPE (*Substantives*), air-tube, shaft, flue, chimney, lum, funnel, smoke-stack, exhaust-pipe, exhaust, vent, blow-hole, nostril, nozzle, throat, weasand, trachea, larynx, windpipe, thrapple, spiracle, ventiduct.

Ventilator, louvre, register.

Tobacco-pipe, pipe, etc. (298A).

3°. *Imperfect Fluids*

352 SEMILIQUIDITY (*Substantives*), pulpiness, viscidity, viscosity, ropiness, sliminess, gumminess, glutinosity, gummosity, siziness, clamminess, mucosity, spissitude, lentor, thickness, crassitude.

Inspissation, thickening, incrassation.

Jelly, mucilage, gelatine, mucus, chyme, phlegm, gum, glue, gluten, goo, colloid, albumen, size, milk, cream, emulsion, soup, broth, starch, treacle, squash, mud, clart, glaur, slush, slime, ooze, dope, glycerine; lava.

Pitch, tar, bitumen, asphalt, resin, rosin, varnish, copal, mastic, wax, amber.

(*Verbs*) To inspissate, thicken, incrassate, jelly, jellify, mash, squash, churn, beat up, pulp.

(*Adjectives*) Semi-fluid, semi-liquid,

353 Mixture of air and water.

BUBBLE (*Substantives*), soda-water, aerated water, foam, froth, head, spume, lather, bleb, spray, spindrift, surf, yeast, barm, suds.

Cloud, vapour, fog, mist, smog, haze, steam, nebulosity (422); scud, rack, cumulus, cirrus, stratus, nimbus mare's tail, mackerel sky.

Nephelology; Fido.

Effervescence, foaming, mantling, fermentation, frothing, etc.

(*Verbs*) To bubble, boil, foam, froth, mantle, sparkle, guggle, gurgle, effervesce, fizz, ferment.

(*Adjectives*) Bubbling, etc., frothy, yeasty, barmy, nappy, effervescent, fizzy, up, boiling, fermenting, sparkling, mantling, *mousseux*.

Cloudy, foggy, misty, vaporous, nebulous.

milky, emulsive, creamy, lacteal, lacteous, curdy, curdled, soupy, muddy, slushy, clarty, thick, succulent, squashy.

Gelatinous, albuminous, gummy, colloid, amylaceous, mucilaginous, glairy, slimy, ropy, stringy, clammy, glutinous (46), viscid, viscous, sticky, gooey, slab, slabby, sizy, lentous, tacky.

Tarry, pitchy, resinous, bituminous.

354 PULPINESS (*Substantives*), pulp, paste, dough, curd, pap, pudding, poultice, soup, squash, mud, slush, grume, jam, preserve.

(*Adjectives*) Pulpy, pulpous, pultaceous, doughy, grumous.

————

355 UNCTUOUSNESS (*Substantives*), unctuosity, oiliness, greasiness, slipperiness, lubricity.

Lubrication (332), anointment, unction; ointment (356).

(*Verbs*) To oil, grease, anoint, wax, lubricate (332).

(*Adjectives*) Unctuous, oily, oleaginous, adipose, sebaceous, fat, fatty, greasy, waxy, butyraceous, soapy, saponaceous, pinguid, stearic, lardaceous.

356 OIL (*Substantives*), fat, butter, margarine, cream, grease, tallow, suet, lard, dripping, blubber, pomatum, pomade, stearin, lanoline, soap, soft soap, wax, beeswax, sealing-wax, ambergris, spermaceti, adipocere, ointment, unguent, liniment, paraffin, kerosene, gasolene, petroleum, petrol, mineral oil, vegetable oil, olive oil, castor oil, linseed oil, train oil.

SECTION III—ORGANIC MATTER

1°. *Vitality*

I. VITALITY IN GENERAL

357 ORGANIZATION (*Substantives*), the organized world, organized nature, living nature, animated nature, living beings; protoplasm, protein.

Biology, ecology (or oecology), natural history, organic chemistry, zoology (368), botany (369).

(*Adjectives*) Organic, animate.

358 INORGANIZATION (*Substantives*), the mineral world or kingdom; unorganized, inorganic, brute or inanimate matter.

Mineralogy, geognosy, petrology, lithology, geology, metallurgy, inorganic chemistry.

(*Adjectives*) Inorganic, azoic, mineral, inanimate.

359 LIFE (*Substantives*), vitality, animation, viability, the vital spark or flame or principle, the breath of life, life-blood; existence (1).

Vivification, revivification.

Physiology, biology; metabolism.

(*Phrase*) The breath of one's nostrils.

(*Verbs*) To be living, alive, etc., to live, subsist (1), breathe, fetch breath, respire, draw breath, to be born, be spared.

360 DEATH (*Substantives*), decease, dissolution, demise, departure, obit, expiration; termination, close or extinction of life, existence, etc.; mortality, fall, doom, fate, release, rest, end, quietus, loss, bereavement, euthanasia, katabolism.

Last breath, last gasp, last agonies, the death-rattle, dying breath, agonies of death, dying agonies.

Necrology, death-roll, obituary.

(*Phrases*) The ebb of life; the king

To come to life, to revive, come to.

To give birth to (161); to bring, restore, or recall to life, to vivify, revive, revivify, quicken, reanimate, vitalize.

(*Phrases*) To see the light; to come into the world; to walk the earth; to draw breath.

To keep body and soul together; to support life.

(*Adjectives*) Living, alive, in life, above ground, breathing, animated, quick, viable.

Vital, vivifying, vivified, Promethean, metabolic.

(*Phrases*) Alive and kicking; in the land of the living; on this side of the grave.

---

of terrors; the jaws of death; the swan-song; the Stygian shore; the sleep that knows no waking; a watery grave.

(*Verbs*) To die, perish, expire.

(*Phrases*) Breathe one's last; cease to live; depart this life; end one's days; be no more; go off; drop off; pop off; peg out; lose one's life; drop down dead; resign, relinquish, lay down, or surrender one's life; drop or sink into the grave; close one's eyes; break one's neck.

To give up the ghost; to be all over with one; to pay the debt to nature; to make the great change; to take one's last sleep; to shuffle off this mortal coil; to go to one's last home; to go the way of all flesh; to kick the bucket; to hop the twig; to turn up one's toes; to slip one's cable; to cross the Stygian ferry.

To snuff out; to go off the hooks; to go to one's account; to go aloft; to join the majority; to go west; to have had it; to be numbered with the dead; to die a natural death; to hand in one's checks; to pass away or over.

(*Adjectives*) Dead, lifeless, deceased, demised, gone, departed, defunct, exanimate, inanimate, *kaput*, out of the world, mortuary; still-born.

Dying, expiring, moribund, *in articulo mortis*, *in extremis*, in the agony of death, etc., going, life ebbing, going off, life failing, *aux abois*, booked, having received one's death warrant.

(*Phrases*) Dead and gone; dead as a door-nail, as mutton, as a door-post, as a herring; stone-dead; launched into eternity; gone to one's last home; gathered to one's fathers; gone to Davy Jones's locker; gone west; gone for a Burton; pushing up the daisies.

At death's door; on one's death-bed; in the jaws of death; death staring one in the face; one's hour being come; one's days being numbered; one's race being run; one foot in the grave; on one's last legs; life hanging by a thread; at one's last gasp.

(*Adverbs*) Post-mortem, post-obit.

361 Destruction of life, violent death.
KILLING (*Substantives*), homicide, parricide, matricide, fratricide, sororicide, infanticide, regicide, tyrannicide, vaticide, genocide, manslaughter, murder, assassination, blood, gore, bloodshed, slaughter, carnage, butchery, massacre, immolation, holocaust, fusillade, *noyade*, thuggee, thuggery, thuggism; casualty, fatality.

Death-blow, kiss of death, *coup de grâce*, grace-stroke, mercy killing, euthanasia.

Suicide, felo-de-se, hara-kiri, happy dispatch, suttee, martyrdom, execution.

Destruction of animals, slaughtering, battue, hecatomb.

Slaughter-house, shambles, abattoir.

A butcher, slayer, murderer, homicide, parricide, matricide, etc., assassin, cut-throat, bravo, thug, executioner (975).

(*Verbs*) To kill, put to death, do to death, slay, murder, assassinate, slaughter, butcher, immolate, massacre, decimate, take away or deprive of life, make away with, dispatch, burke, lynch, settle, do for, do in, bump off, brain, spiflicate.

To strangle, throttle, bowstring, choke, garrotte, stifle, suffocate, smother, asphyxiate, drown, hang, turn off, string up.

To cut down, sabre, cut to pieces, cut off, cut the throat, stab, knife, bayonet, shoot, behead, decapitate, stone, lapidate, execute (972).

To commit suicide, to make away with oneself.

(*Phrases*) To put to the sword; put to the edge of the sword; give no quarter to; run through the body; knock on the head; give one the works; put one on the spot; blow the brains out; give the death blow, the *coup de grâce*; put out of one's misery; launch into eternity; give a quietus to.

(*Adjectives*) Killing, etc., murderous, slaughterous, sanguinary, ensanguined, gory, bloody, blood-stained, blood-guilty, red-handed.

Mortal, fatal, deadly, lethal, internecine, suicidal, homicidal, fratricidal, etc.

362 CORPSE (*Substantives*), corse, carcass, bones, skeleton, carrion, defunct, relic, remains, ashes, earth, dust, clay, mummy.

Shade, ghost, *manes*; the dead, the majority, the great majority.

(*Phrases*) All that was mortal; this tenement of clay; food for worms or fishes.

(*Adjectives*) Cadaverous, corpse-like.

363 INTERMENT (*Substantives*), burial, sepulture, inhumation, obsequies, exequies, funeral, wake, lyke-wake, pyre, funeral pile, cremation.

Funeral rite or solemnity, knell, passing-bell, tolling, dirge, lament, coronach, keening (839), requiem, epicedium, obit, elegy, funeral oration, epitaph, death march, dead march, lying in state.

Grave-clothes, shroud, winding-sheet, cerecloth, cerement.

Coffin, casket, shell, sarcophagus, urn, pall, bier, hearse, catafalque.

Grave, pit, sepulchre, tomb, vault, catacomb, mausoleum, house of death, burial-place, cemetery, necropolis, churchyard, graveyard, God's acre, burial-ground, cromlech, dolmen, barrow, tumulus, cairn, ossuary, charnel-house, morgue, mortuary, crematorium, cinerator; Valhalla.

Monument, tombstone, gravestone, shrine, cenotaph.

Exhumation, disinterment; autopsy, necropsy, post-mortem.

Undertaker, mortician, mute, sexton, grave-digger.

(*Verbs*) To inter, bury, lay in the grave, consign to the grave or tomb, entomb, inhume, cremate, lay out, embalm, mummify.

To exhume, disinter.

(*Adjectives*) Buried, etc., burial, funereal, funebrial, funerary, mortuary, sepulchral, cinerary; elegiac.

(*Phrases*) *Hic jacet*; R.I.P.

2. SPECIAL VITALITY

364 ANIMALITY (*Substantives*), animal life, animality, animation, breath, animalization.

Flesh, flesh and blood, physique.

(*Verb*) To animalize.

(*Adjectives*) Fleshly, corporal, carnal.

365 VEGETABILITY (*Substantives*), vegetable life, vegetation.

(*Adjectives*) Lush, rank, luxuriant.

366 ANIMAL (*Substantives*), the animal kingdom, brute creation, fauna, avifauna.

A beast, brute, creature, created being; creeping or living thing, dumb creature, flocks and herds, live-stock.

Cattle, kine, etc.

Game, *fera natura*, wild life.

Mammal, quadruped, bird, reptile, fish, mollusc, worm, insect, zoophyte, animalcule, etc.

(*Phrases*) The beasts of the field; fowls of the air: denizens of the deep.

(*Adjectives*) Animal, zoological, piscatory, fishy, molluscous, vermicular, etc., feral.

---

368 The science of animals.

ZOOLOGY (*Substantives*), zoography, anatomy, zootomy, comparative anatomy, physiology, morphology.

Ornithology, ichthyology, herpetology, ophiology, malacology, helminthology, entomology; palaeontology.

370 The economy or management of animals.

TAMING (*Substantives*), domestication, domesticity; training, breaking-in, manège, breeding, pisciculture; veterinary art.

Menagerie, zoological garden, game reserve, aviary, apiary, vivarium, aquarium, fishery, fish-pond, duck-pond.

(*Verbs*) To tame, domesticate, train, tend, break in.

(*Adjectives*) Pastoral, bucolic.

---

367 PLANT (*Substantives*), vegetable, the vegetable kingdom, flora.

Tree, fruit-tree, shrub, bush, creeper, herb, herbage, grass, fern, fungus, lichen, moss, weed, seaweed, alga; annual, biennial, perennial; exotic.

Forest, wood, hurst, holt, greenwood, woodland, brake, grove, copse, coppice, hedgerow, boscage, plantation, thicket, spinney, underwood, undergrowth, brushwood, clump of trees, park, chase, weald, scrub, jungle, prairie.

Foliage, florescence, flower, blossom, branch, bough, spray, twig, leaf.

(*Adjectives*) Vegetable, vegetal, arboreal, herbaceous, herbal, botanic, sylvan, woodland, woody, wooded, well-wooded, shrubby, grassy, verdurous, verdant, floral, mossy.

369 The science of plants.

BOTANY (*Substantives*), phytography, phytology, vegetable physiology, herborization, dendrology, mycology, Pomona, Flora, Ceres.

Herbarium, herbal, *hortus siccus*, vasculum.

(*Verbs*) To botanize, herborize.

371 The economy or management of plants.

AGRICULTURE (*Substantives*), cultivation, culture, intensive cultivation, husbandry, agronomy, geoponics, hydroponics, georgics, tillage, gardening, horticulture, forestry, vintage, etc., arboriculture, floriculture, the topiary art.

Vineyard, vinery, garden, kitchen garden, market garden, nursery, bed, plot, herbaceous border, parterre, hothouse, greenhouse, conservatory, espalier, shrubbery, orchard, rock garden, rockery, winter garden, pinery, arboretum, allotment.

A husbandman, horticulturist, gardener, florist, agriculturist, agriculturalist, woodcutter, backwoodsman, forester, land girl, farmer, yeoman, cultivator.

(*Verbs*) To cultivate, till, garden, farm; delve, dibble, dig, sow, plant, graft; plough, harrow, rake, reap, mow, cut, weed.

(*Adjectives*) Agricultural, agrarian, arable, rural, country, rustic, agrestic.

372 Mankind (*Substantives*), the human race or species; man, human nature, humanity, mortality, flesh, generation; Everyman.

Anthropology, anthropography, ethnology, ethnography, demography, sociology, social economics; civics.

Anthropomorphism.

Human being, person, individual, type, creature, fellow creature, mortal, body, somebody, one, someone, a soul, living soul, earthling, party personage, inhabitant; *dramatis personae*.

People, persons, folk, population, public, world, race, society, community, the million, commonalty (876), nation, state, realm, community, commonwealth, republic, commonweal, polity, nationality; civilized society, civilization.

Anthropologist, ethnologist, sociologist, etc.

(*Phrases*) The lords of creation; the body politic.

(*Adjectives*) National, civic, public, human, mortal, personal, individual, social, cosmopolitan, ethnic, racial; sociological, anthropological, ethnological, anthropomorphic, anthropomorphous, anthropoid, manlike.

---

373 Man (*Substantives*), manhood, manliness, virility, he, menfolk.

A human being, man, male, mortal, person, body, soul, individual, fellow creature, one, someone, somebody, so-and-so.

Personage, a gentleman, sir, master, yeoman, citizen, denizen, burgess, burgher, cosmopolite, wight, swain, fellow, blade, bloke, beau, chap, guy, bod, type, cove, gossoon, buffer, gaffer, goodman; husband (903).

(*Adjectives*) Human, manly, male, masculine, manlike, mannish, virile, mannish, unwomanly, unfeminine.

(*Phrase*) The spear side.

---

374 Woman (*Substantives*), female, feminality, femininity, womanhood, muliebrity, girlhood, she, womenfolk.

Womankind, the sex, the fair, the fair sex, the softer sex, the weaker vessel, a petticoat, skirt.

Dame, madam, madame, ma'am, mistress, lady, gentlewoman, donna, belle, matron, dowager, goody, gammer, good woman, goodwife; wife (903).

Damsel, girl, lass, lassie, maid (209), maiden, *demoiselle*, flapper, miss, missie, nymph, wench, bint, floosy, popsy, pusher, jade, dona, grisette, colleen.

(*Adjectives*) Female, feminine, womanly, ladylike, matronly, maidenly, girlish; womanish, effeminate, unmanly, pansy.

(*Phrase*) The distaff side.

2°. *Sensation*

I. SENSATION IN GENERAL

375 Physical Sensibility (*Substantives*), sensitiveness, sensitivity, feeling, perceptivity, acuteness; allergy, idiosyncrasy; moral sensibility (822).

Sensation, impression, consciousness (490).

The external senses.

(*Verbs*) To be sensible of, to feel, perceive, be conscious of, respond to, react to.

---

376 Physical Insensibility (*Substantives*), obtuseness, dullness, paralysis, anaesthesia, analgesia, sleep, trance, stupor, coma, catalepsy; moral insensibility (823).

Anaesthetic, opium, ether, chloroform, chloral, cocaine, morphia, laudanum, nitrous oxide, laughing gas.

Anaesthetics.

(*Verbs*) To be insensible, etc. To

To render sensible, to sharpen, cultivate, train, tutor, condition.

To cause sensation; to impress, excite, or produce an impression.

(*Adjectives*) Sensible, conscious, sensitive, sensuous, aesthetic, perceptive.

Hypersensitive, thin-skinned, neurotic, hyperaesthetic, allergic.

Acute, sharp, keen, vivid, lively, impressive.

(*Adverb*) To the quick.

render insensible, to blunt, dull, obtund, benumb, deaden, stupefy, stun, paralyse, anaesthetize, dope, hocus, gas.

(*Adjectives*) Insensible, unfeeling, senseless, impercipient, impassable, thick-skinned, pachydermatous, hardened, proof, apathetic, obtuse, dull, anaesthetic, paralytic, palsied, numb, dead, unaffected, untouched.

(*Phrase*) Having a rhinoceros hide.

377 PHYSICAL PLEASURE (*Substantives*), bodily enjoyment, gratification, titillation, comfort, luxury, voluptuousness, sensuousness, sensuality; mental pleasure (827).

(*Phrases*) The flesh-pots of Egypt; creature comforts; a bed of roses; a bed of down; on velvet; in clover.

(*Verbs*) To feel, experience, receive, etc., pleasure, to enjoy, relish, luxuriate, revel, riot, bask, wallow in, feast on, gloat over, have oneself a ball.

To cause or give physical pleasure, to gratify, tickle, regale, etc. (829).

(*Adjectives*) Enjoying, etc., luxurious, sensual, voluptuous, comfortable, cosy, snug.

Pleasant, pleasing, agreeable, grateful, refreshing, comforting.

378 PHYSICAL PAIN (*Substantives*), bodily pain, suffering, sufferance, dolour, ache, aching, smart, smarting, shoot, shooting, twinge, twitch, gripe, headache, toothache, earache, sore, hurt, discomfort, malaise; mental pain (828).

Spasm, cramp, nightmare, crick, stitch, convulsion, throe.

Pang, anguish, agony, torment, torture, rack, cruciation, crucifixion, martyrdom.

(*Verbs*) To feel, experience, suffer, etc., pain; to suffer, ache, smart, bleed, tingle, shoot, twinge, lancinate, wince, writhe, twitch.

(*Phrases*) To sit on thorns; to sit on pins and needles.

To give or inflict pain; to pain, hurt, chafe, sting, bite, gnaw, pinch, tweak, grate, gall, fret, prick, pierce, gripe, etc., wring, torment, torture, rack, agonize, break on the wheel, put on the rack, convulse.

(*Adjectives*) In pain, in a state of pain; uncomfortable, pained, etc.

Painful, aching, etc., sore, raw, agonizing, excruciating.

2. SPECIAL SENSATION

(1) *Touch*

379 Sensation of pressure.

TOUCH (*Substantives*), taction, tactility, feeling, palpation, manipulation, tangibility, palpability.

Organ of touch: hand, finger, forefinger, thumb, paw, feeler, antenna.

(*Verbs*) To touch, feel, handle, finger, thumb, paw, fumble, grope, grabble, scrabble; pass, or run the fingers over, manipulate.

(*Phrase*) To throw out a feeler.

(*Adjectives*) Tactual, tangible, palpable, tactile.

380 SENSATIONS OF TOUCH (*Substantives*), itching, titillation, formication, etc., creeping, aura, tingling, thrilling.

(*Verbs*) To itch, tingle, creep, thrill; sting, prick, prickle, tickle, kittle, titillate.

(*Adjectives*) Itching, etc., ticklish, kittly.

381 Insensibility to touch.

NUMBNESS (*Substantives*), deadness, anaesthesia (376); pins and needles.

(*Verbs*) To benumb, paralyse, anaesthetize; to chloroform, inject with cocaine, etc. (376).

(*Adjectives*) Numb, benumbed; intangible, impalpable.

(2) *Heat*

382 HEAT (*Substantives*), caloric, temperature, warmth, fervour, calidity, incalescence, candescence, incandescence, glow, flush, hectic, fever, pyrexia, hyperpyrexia.

Fire, spark, scintillation, flash, flame, blaze, bonfire, firework, wildfire, pyrotechny, ignition (384).

Insolation, summer, dog-days, tropical heat, heat-wave, summer heat, blood heat, sirocco, simoom; isotherm.

Hot spring, thermal spring, geyser.

Pyrology, thermology, thermotics, calorimetry, thermodynamics; thermometer (389).

(*Phrase*) The devouring element.

(*Verbs*) To be hot, to glow, flush, sweat, swelter, bask, smoke, reek, stew, simmer, seethe, boil, burn, broil, bake, parch, fume, blaze, smoulder.

(*Phrases*) To be in a heat, in a glow, in a fever, in a blaze, etc.

(*Adjectives*) Hot, warm, mild, unfrozen, genial, tepid, lukewarm, blood-hot, thermal, thermotic, calorific, sunny, close, sweltering, stuffy, sultry, baking, boiling, broiling, torrid, tropical, aestival, canicular, glowing, piping, scalding, reeking, etc., on fire, afire, ablaze, alight, aglow, fervid, fervent, ardent, unquenched; isothermal, sotheral; feverish, pyretic, pyrexial, pyrexical.

Igneous, plutonic, fiery, candescent, incandescent, red-hot, white-hot, incalescent, smoking, blazing, unextinguished, smouldering.

(*Phrases*) Hot as fire; warm as toast; warm as wool; piping hot; like an oven; hot enough to roast an ox.

383 COLD (*Substantives*), coldness, frigidity, coolness, coolth, gelidity, chill, chilliness, freshness, inclemency; cold storage.

Frost, ice, snow, snowflake, sleet, hail, hailstone, rime, hoar-frost, icicle, iceberg, ice-floe, glacier, winter.

Sensation of cold : chilliness, shivering, shuddering, goose-skin, goose-pimples, goose-flesh, rigor, horripilation, chattering of teeth.

(*Verbs*) To be cold, etc., to shiver, quake, shake, tremble, shudder, dither, quiver, starve.

(*Adjectives*) Cold, cool, chill, chilly, gelid, frigid, algid, bleak, raw, inclement, bitter, biting, cutting, nipping, piercing, pinching, clay-cold, fresh, keen; pinched, starved, perished, shivering, etc., aguish, frozen, frostbitten, frost-nipped, frost-bound, unthawed, unwarmed; isocheimal, isochimenal.

Icy, glacial, frosty, freezing, wintry, brumal, hibernal, boreal, arctic, hiemal, hyperborean, icebound.

(*Phrases*) Cold as a stone; cold as marble; cold as a frog; cold as charity; cold as Christmas; cool as a cucumber; cool as a custard.

---

384 CALEFACTION (*Substantives*), increase of temperature, heating, tepefaction.

Melting, fusion, liquefaction, thaw,

385 REFRIGERATION (*Substantives*), infrigidation, reduction of temperature, cooling, freezing, congealing, congelation, glaciation.

liquescence (335), liquation, incandescence.

Burning, combustion, incension, accension, cremation, cautery, cauterization, roasting, broiling, frying, ustulation, torrefaction, scorification, branding, calcination, carbonization, incineration, cineration.

Boiling, coction, ebullition, simmering, scalding, decoction, smelting.

Ignition, inflammation, setting fire to, flagration, deflagration, conflagration, arson, incendiarism, fire-raising; *auto da fé*, suttee.

Inflammability, combustibility; incendiary, fire-bug, fire-ship, *pétroleur*.

Transmission of heat, diathermancy.

Fire-brigade, fire-extinguisher, fire-engine, fireman; incombustibility.

(*Verbs*) To cool, refrigerate, congeal, freeze, glaciate, ice, benumb, refresh, damp, slack, quench, put out, blow out, extinguish, starve, pinch, pierce, cut.

To go out.

(*Adjectives*) Cooled, frozen, benumbed, etc., shivery, frigorific, refrigerant.

Incombustible, non-inflammable, fire-proof.

(*Verbs*) To heat, warm, mull, chafe, fire, set fire to, set on fire, kindle, enkindle, light, ignite, relume, rekindle.

To melt, thaw, fuse, liquefy (335); defrost, de-ice.

To burn, inflame, roast, toast, broil, fry, grill, brander, singe, parch, sweal, scorch, brand, scorify, torrify, bake, cauterize, sear, char, carbonize, calcine, incinerate, smelt.

To boil, stew, cook, seethe, scald, parboil, simmer.

To take fire, catch fire, kindle, light, ignite.

(*Phrases*) To stir the fire; blow the fire; fan the flame; apply a match to; make a bonfire of; to take the chill off.

To consign to the flames; to reduce to ashes; to burn to a cinder.

(*Adjectives*) Combustible, inflammable, heating, etc., heated, warmed, melted, molten, unfrozen, boiled, stewed, sodden, adust.

386 FURNACE (*Substantives*), fire, gas fire, electric fire, stove, kiln, oven, bakehouse, hothouse, conservatory, fire-place, grate, hearth, radiator, register, reverberatory, range, hob, hypocaust, crematorium, incinerator, forge, blast-furnace, brasier, salamander, geyser, heater, hot-plate, hot-water bottle, electric blanket, warming-pan, stew-pan, boiler, cauldron, kettle, pot, urn, chafing-dish, gridiron, saucepan, frying-pan; sudatorium, sudatory, Turkish bath, *hammam*, vapour bath.

387 REFRIGERATORY (*Substantives*), refrigerator, frig, ice-pail, ice-bag, ice-house, freezing-mixture, cooler, freezer.

388 FUEL (*Substantives*), firing, coal, anthracite, coke, charcoal, briquette, peat, combustible, log, tinder, touchwood.

Lucifer, ingle, brand, match, vesuvian, vesta, safety-match, fusee, lighter, spill, embers, faggot, firebrand, incendiary, port-fire, fire-ball, fire-barrel.

389 THERMOMETER (*Substantives*), clinical thermometer, pyrometer, calorimeter, thermoscope, thermograph, thermostat, thermopile.

Fahrenheit, Centigrade, Celsius, Réaumur.

Thermometry, therm.

(3) *Taste*

390 TASTE (*Substantives*), flavour, gust, gusto, zest, savour, sapor, tang, twang, smack, relish, aftertaste, smatch, sapidity.

Tasting, gustation, degustation.

Palate, tongue, tooth, sweet tooth, stomach.

(*Verbs*) To taste, savour, smack, smatch, flavour, twang.

(*Phrases*) To tickle the palate; to smack the lips.

(*Adjectives*) Sapid, gustable, gustatory, saporific, strong, appetizing, palatable (394).

391 INSIPIDITY (*Substantives*), tastelessness, insipidness, vapidness, vapidity, mawkishness, wershness, mildness; wish-wash, milk and water, slops.

(*Verbs*) To be void of taste, tasteless, etc.

(*Adjectives*) Insipid, tasteless, savourless, mawkish, wersh, flat, vapid, *fade*, wishy-washy, watery, weak, mild; untasted.

---

392 PUNGENCY (*Substantives*), *haut-goût*, strong taste, twang, raciness, race, saltness, sharpness, roughness.

Ginger, caviare, cordial, condiment (393).

(*Verbs*) To be pungent, etc.

To render pungent, to season, spice, salt, pepper, pickle, brine, devil.

(*Adjectives*) Pungent, high-flavoured, high-tasted, high, sharp, strong, rough, stinging, piquant, racy, biting, mordant, spicy, seasoned, hot, peppery, gingery, high-seasoned, gamy, salt, saline, brackish.

(*Phrases*) Salt as brine; salt as a herring; salt as Lot's wife; hot as pepper.

393 CONDIMENT (*Substantives*), salt, mustard, pepper, cayenne, vinegar, curry, chutney, seasoning, spice, ginger, sauce, dressing, *sauce piquante*, caviare, pot-herbs, pickles, onion, garlic, sybo.

394 SAVOURINESS (*Substantives*), palatableness, toothsomeness, daintiness, delicacy, relish, zest.

A titbit, dainty, delicacy, ambrosia, nectar, *bonne-bouche*.

(*Verbs*) To be savoury, etc.

To render palatable, etc.

To relish, like, fancy, be partial to.

(*Adjectives*) Savoury, well-tasted, palatable, nice, good, dainty, delectable, toothsome, tasty, appetizing, delicate, delicious, exquisite, rich, luscious, ambrosial, meaty, fruity.

395 UNSAVOURINESS (*Substantives*), unpalatableness, bitterness, acridness, acridity, acrimony, roughness, acerbity, austerity; gall and wormwood, rue; sickener, scunner.

(*Verbs*) To be unpalatable, etc.

To sicken, disgust, nauseate, pall, turn the stomach.

(*Adjectives*) Unsavoury, unpalatable, ill-flavoured, bitter, acrid, acrimonious, unsweetened, rough, austere, uneatable, inedible.

Offensive, repulsive, nasty, fulsome, sickening, nauseous, nauseating, disgusting, loathsome, palling.

(*Phrases*) Bitter as gall; bitter as aloes.

---

396 SWEETNESS (*Substantives*), dulcitude, dulcification, sweetening.

Sugar, saccharine, glucose, syrup, treacle, molasses, honey, manna, confection, confectionery, candy,

397 SOURNESS (*Substantives*), acid, acidity, tartness, crabbedness, hardness, roughness, acetous fermentation.

Vinegar, verjuice, crab, alum.

(*Verbs*) To be sour, etc.

conserve, jam, jelly, marmalade, preserve, liquorice, julep, sugar-candy, toffee, caramel, butterscotch, plum, sugar-plum, lollipop, bonbon, jujube, lozenge, pastille, comfit, fudge, chocolate, sweet, sweetmeat, marzipan, marchpane, fondant, nougat; mead, nectar, hydromel, honeysuckle.

(*Verbs*) To be sweet, etc.

To render sweet, to sweeten, sugar, mull, edulcorate, candy, dulcify, saccharify.

(*Adjectives*) Sweet, saccharine, sacchariferous, sugary, dulcet, candied, honeyed, luscious, edulcorated, nectarous, nectareous, sweetish, sugary.

(*Phrases*) Sweet as a nut: sweet as honey.

To render or turn sour, to sour, acidify, acidulate.

(*Phrase*) To set the teeth on edge.

(*Adjectives*) Sour, acid, acidulous, acidulated, sourish, subacid, vinegary, tart, crabbed, acerb, acetic, acetous, acescent, acetose, styptic, hard, rough.

(*Phrases*) Sour as vinegar; sour as a crab.

---

(4) *Odour*

398 ODOUR (*Substantives*), smell, scent, effluvium, emanation, fume, exhalation, essence; trail, nidor, redolence.

The sense of smell, act of smelling.

(*Verbs*) To have an odour, to smell of, to exhale, to give out a smell, etc.

To smell, scent, snuff, sniff, inhale, nose, snowk.

(*Adjectives*) Odorous, odorant, odoriferous, smelling, strong-scented, graveolent, redolent, nidorous, pungent.

Relating to the sense of smell: olfactory, keen-scented.

399 INODOROUSNESS (*Substantives*), absence or want of smell; deodorization.

(*Verbs*) To be inodorous, etc., deodorize (652).

(*Adjectives*) Inodorous, odourless, scentless, smell-less, wanting smell.

---

400 FRAGRANCE (*Substantives*), aroma, redolence, perfume, savour, bouquet.

Incense, musk, myrrh, frankincense, ambrosia, attar (or otto), eau-de-Cologne, civet, castor, ambergris, bergamot, lavender, sandalwood, orris root, balm, pot-pourri, pulvil; scent-bag, scent-bottle, sachet, nosegay.

(*Phrase*) 'All the perfumes of Arabia.'

(*Verbs*) To perfume, scent, embalm.

(*Adjectives*) Fragrant, aromatic, redolent, balmy, scented, sweet-smelling, sweet-scented, ambrosial, perfumed, musky.

401 FETOR (*Substantives*), bad smell, empyreuma, stench, stink, mustiness, fustiness, frowziness, frowst, fug, rancidity, foulness, putrescence, putridity, mephitis.

A pole-cat, skunk, badger, teledu, asafoetida, cacodyl, stinkard, stink-bomb, stinkpot.

(*Verbs*) To smell, stink, hum, niff, pong.

(*Phrase*) To stink in the nostrils.

(*Adjectives*) Fetid, strong-smelling, smelly, whiffy, malodorous, noisome, offensive, rank, rancid, reasty, mouldy, fusty, musty, stuffy, frowsty, fuggy, foul, frowzy, olid, nidorous, stinking, rotten, putrescent, putrid, putrefying, tainted, high (653), mephitic, empyreumatic.

(5) Sound

(1) SOUND IN GENERAL

402 SOUND (*Substantives*), sonance, noise, strain, voice (580), accent, twang, intonation, tone, resonance (408); sonority, sonorousness, audibleness, audibility.

Acoustics, phonics, phonetics, phonology, diacoustics.

(*Verbs*) To produce sound; to sound, make a noise, give out or emit sound, to resound.

(*Adjectives*) Sonorous, sounding, soniferous, sonorific, sonoriferous, resonant, canorous, audible, distinct, phonic, phonetic.

403 SILENCE (*Substantives*), stillness, quiet, peace, calm, hush, lull; muteness (581).

A silencer, mute, damper, sordine.

(*Verbs*) To be silent, etc.

To render silent, to silence, still, hush, stifle, muffle, stop, muzzle, mute, damp, gag.

(*Phrases*) To keep silence; to hold one's tongue; to hold one's peace.

(*Adjectives*) Silent, still, stilly, noiseless, soundless, inaudible, hushed, etc., mute, mum, mumchance (581), solemn, awful, deathlike.

(*Phrases*) Still as a mouse; deathlike silence; silent as the grave; one might hear a pin drop.

(*Adverbs*) Silently, softly, etc., *sub silentio*.

(*Interjections*) Hush! silence! soft! mum! whist! chut! *tace!*

---

404 LOUDNESS (*Substantives*), clatter, din, clangour, clang, roar, uproar, racket, hubbub, flourish of trumpets, tucket, tantara, taratantara, fanfare, blare, alarum, peal, swell, blast, boom, echo, fracas, shindy, row, rumpus, bobbery, clamour, hullaballoo, chorus, hue and cry, shout, yell, whoop, charivari, shivaree, vociferation; Stentor, Boanerges.

Speaking-trumpet, megaphone, loud-speaker, microphone, mike, amplifier, resonator.

Artillery, cannon, thunder.

(*Verbs*) To be loud, etc., to resound, echo, re-echo, peal, swell, clang, boom, blare, thunder, fulminate, roar, whoop, shout (411).

(*Phrases*) To din in the ear; to pierce, split, or rend the ears, or head; to shout, or thunder at the pitch of one's breath, or at the top of one's voice; to make the welkin ring; to rend the air; *faire le diable à quatre*.

405 FAINTNESS (*Substantives*), lowness, faint sounds, whisper, undertone, breath, underbreath, murmur, mutter, hum, susurration, tinkle, rustle.

Hoarseness, huskiness, raucity.

(*Verbs*) To whisper, breathe, murmur, mutter, mumble, purl, hum, croon, gurgle, ripple, babble, tinkle.

(*Phrases*) Steal on the ear; melt, float on the air.

(*Adjectives*) Inaudible, scarcely audible, low, dull, stifled, muffled, hoarse, husky, gentle faint, breathed, etc., soft, floating, purling, etc., liquid, mellifluous, dulcet, flowing, soothing.

(*Adverbs*) In a whisper, with bated breath, under one's breath, *sotto voce*, between the teeth, from the side of one's mouth, aside, *piano, pianissimo, à la sourdine.*

(*Adjectives*) Loud, sonorous, resounding, etc., high-sounding, big-sounding, deep, full, swelling, clamorous, clangorous, multisonous, noisy, blatant, plangent, vocal, vociferous, stunning, piercing, splitting, rending, thundering, deafening, ear-deafening, ear-piercing, obstreperous, blaring, deep-mouthed, open-mouthed, trumpet-tongued, uproarious, rackety, stentorian.

(*Phrases*) Enough to split the head or ears; enough to wake the dead; enough to wake the Seven Sleepers.

(*Adverbs*) Loudly, aloud, etc., *forte, fortissimo.*

(*Phrases*) At the top of one's voice; in full cry.

(2) SPECIFIC SOUNDS

406 Sudden and violent sounds.

SNAP (*Substantives*), knock, rap, tap, click, clash, slam, clack, crack, crackle, crackling, crepitation, decrepitation, report, pop, plop, bang, thud, thump, ping, zip, clap, burst, explosion, discharge, crash, detonation, firing, salvo, atmospherics.

Squib, cracker, gun, pop-gun.

(*Verbs*) To snap, knock, etc.

(*Adjectives*) Snapping, etc.

407 Repeated and protracted sounds.

ROLL (*Substantives*), rumble, rumbling, hum, humming, shake, trill, whirr, chime, tick, beat, toll, ticking, tick-tack, patter, tattoo, ding-dong, drumming, quaver, tremolo, ratatat, tantara, rataplan, rat-tat, clatter, clutter, rattle, racket, rub-a-dub; reverberation (408).

(*Phrases*) The devil's tattoo; tuck of drum.

(*Verbs*) To roll, beat, tick, toll, drum, etc., rattle, clatter, patter, shake, trill, whirr, chime, beat; to drum or din in the ear.

(*Adjectives*) Rolling, rumbling, etc.

408 RESONANCE (*Substantives*), ring, ringing, jingle, chink, tinkle, ting, tink, tintinnabulation, gurgle, chime, toot, tootle, clang, etc. (404).

Reflection, reverberation, echo.

(*Verbs*) To resound, reverberate, re-echo, ring, jingle, clink, chime, tinkle, etc.

(*Adjectives*) Resounding, resonant, tintinnabular, ringing, etc.

(*Phrase*) Clear as a bell.

BASS (*Substantives*), low, flat or grave note, chest-note, baritone, contralto.

409 Hissing sounds.

SIBILATION (*Substantives*), hiss, swish, buzz, whiz, rustle, fizz, fizzle, wheeze, whistle, snuffle, sneeze, sternutation.

(*Verbs*) To hiss, buzz, etc.

(*Adjectives*) Sibilant, hissing, buzzing, etc., wheezy.

SOPRANO (*Substantives*), high note (410).

(*Adjectives*) Deep-toned, deep-sounding, deep-mouthed, hollow, sepulchral, *basso profondo.*

410 Harsh sounds.

STRIDOR (*Substantives*), jar, grating, creak, clank, twang, jangle, jarring, creaking, rustling, roughness, gruffness, sharpness, cacophony.

High note, shrillness, acuteness, soprano, falsetto, treble, alto, counter-tenor, penny trumpet, head-note.

(*Verbs*) To creak, grate, jar, burr, pipe, twang, jangle, rustle, clank; to shrill, shriek, screech, squeal, skirl (411), stridulate.

(*Phrases*) To set the teeth on edge; to grate upon the ear.

(*Adjectives*) Strident, stridulous, jarring, etc., harsh, hoarse, horrisonous, discordant, scrannel (414), cacophonous, rough, gruff, sepulchral, grating.

Sharp, high, acute, shrill, piping, screaming.

411 Human sounds.

CRY (*Substantives*), voice (580), vociferation, outcry, roar, shout, bawl, bellow, brawl, halloo, hullaballoo, hoop, whoop, yell, cheer, hoot, howl, chorus, scream, screech, screak, shriek, squeak, squawk, squeal, skirl, yawp, squall, whine, pule, pipe, grumble, plaint, groan, moan, snore, snort.

(*Verbs*) To vociferate, roar, shout, bawl, etc., sing out, thunder, raise or lift up the voice.

(*Adjectives*) Vociferating, etc., clamant, clamorous, vociferous, sterorous.

412 Animal sounds.

ULULATION (*Substantives*), latration, cry, roar, bellow, reboation, bark, yelp, howl, bay, baying, yap, growl, grunt, gruntle, snort, neigh, nicker, whinny, bray, croak, snarl, howl, caterwauling, mew, mewl, miaow, miaul, purr, pule, bleat, baa, low, moo, boo, caw, coo, croodle, cackle, gobble, quack, gaggle, squeak, squawk, squeal, chuckle, chuck, cluck, clack, chirp, chirrup, crow, woodnote, twitter, peep.

Insect cry, drone, buzz, hum.

Cuckoo, screech-owl.

(*Verbs*) To cry, bellow, rebellow, etc., bell, boom, trumpet, give tongue.

(*Phrases*) To bay the moon; to roar like a bull or lion.
(*Adjectives*) Crying, etc., blatant, latrant, remugient.

(3) MUSICAL SOUND

413 MELODY (*Substantives*), melodiousness, *melos*.

Pitch, note, interval, tone, intonation, timbre; high or low, acute or grave notes, treble, alto, tenor, bass, soprano, mezzo-soprano, contralto, counter-tenor, baritone, *basso profondo*.

Scale, gamut, diapason; diatonic, chromatic, enharmonic, whole-tone, etc., scales; key, clef; major, minor, Dorian, Phrygian, Lydian, etc., modes; tetrachord, hexachord, pentatonic scale; tuning, modulation, temperament; solmization, solfeggio, sol-fa.

Staff (or stave), lines, spaces, brace; bar, double bar, rest.

414 DISCORD (*Substantives*), discordance, dissonance, jar, jarring, caterwauling, cocophony.

Hoarseness, croaking, etc. (410).

Confused sounds, babel, Dutch concert, cat's concert, marrow-bones and cleavers, charivari (404).

(*Verbs*) To be discordant, etc., to croak, jar (410).

(*Adjectives*) Discordant, dissonant, out of tune, sharp, flat, tuneless, absonant, unmusical, inharmonious, unmelodious, untuneful, untunable, singsong.

Cacophonous, harsh, hoarse, croaking, jarring, stridulous, etc. (410).

Notes of the scale: sharps, flats, naturals, accidentals; breve, semibreve, minim, crotchet, quaver, semiquaver, demisemiquaver, etc.

Tonic, keynote, supertonic, mediant, subdominant, dominant, submediant, leading note, octave; primes, seconds, triads, etc.

Harmonic, overtone, partial, fundamental, note, hum-note.

Harmony, harmoniousness, concord, concordance, unison, homophony, chord, chime, consonance, concent, euphony; counterpoint, polyphony; tonality, atonality; thorough-bass, figured bass.

Rhythm, time, tempo; common, duple, triple, six-eight, etc., time; *tempo rubato*, syncopation, ragtime, jazz, swing, jive, boogie-woogie, bebop, skiffle, rock-and-roll.

(*Verbs*) To harmonize, chime, be in unison; put in tune, tune, accord.
(*Adjectives*) Harmonious, harmonic, harmonical, in harmony, in tune,

etc., unisonant, unisonal, univocal, symphonic, homophonous; contrapuntal, chordal; diatonic, chromatic, enharmonic, tonal, atonal.

Measured, rhythmical, in time, on the beat, hot.

Melodious, musical, tuneful, tunable, sweet, dulcet, canorous, mellow, mellifluous, silver-toned, silvery, euphonious, euphonic, euphonical; enchanting, ravishing, etc., Orphean.

415 MUSIC (*Substantives*), tune, air, lilt, melody, refrain, burden, cadence theme, motive, motif, *leit-motiv*, subject, counter-subject, episode, modulation introduction, finale, etc.

Composition, work, opus, score, full score, vocal score, etc.

Solo, duet, trio, quartet, etc., concerted music, chorus, chamber music.

Instrumental music: Symphony, *sinfonietta*, symphonic poem, tone-poem concerto, sonata, sonatina; *allegro, andante, largo*, scherzo, rondo, etc. overture, prelude, intermezzo, postlude, voluntary; ballade, nocturne, serenade, aubade, barcarolle, *berceuse*, etc.; fugue, fugato, canon; variations humoresque, rhapsody, caprice, *capriccio*, fantasia, impromptu; arrangement pot-pourri; march, pibroch, minuet, gavotte, waltz, mazurka, etc. (840) accompaniment, *obbligato*; programme music.

Vocal music: Chant, plain-song, Gregorian music, neume, psalmody, psalm hymn, anthem, motet, antiphon, canticle, introit, etc., service, song, ballad *lied, chanson*, cavatina, canzonet, serenade, lullaby, ditty, chanty, folk-song dithyramb; part-song, glee, catch, round, canon, madrigal, chorus, cantata oratorio, etc.; opera (599).

Dirge, requiem, *nenia*, knell, lament, coronach, dead march.

Musical ornament; grace-note, appoggiatura, trill, shake, turn, beat mordent, etc.; cadenza, roulade, bravura, colorature, *coloratura*.

Scale, run, arpeggio, chord; five-finger exercise, study, *étude*, toccata.

Performance, execution, technique, touch, expression, tone-colour, render ing, interpretation; voice-production, *bel canto*; *embouchure*, lipping, bowing

Concert, recital, performance, ballad concert, etc., musicale, sing-song.

Minstrelsy, musicianship, musicality, musicalness, an ear for music; composition, composing, orchestration, scoring, filling in the parts.

Composer, harmonist, contrapuntist.

Apollo, the Muses, Erato, Euterpe, Terpsichore.

(*Verbs*) To play, fiddle, bow, strike, strike up, thrum, strum, grind, touch tweedle, scrape, blow, pipe, tootle, blare, etc.; to execute, perform, render, interpret, conduct, accompany, vamp, arrange, prelude, improvise (612).

To sing, chant, vocalize, warble, carol, troll, lilt, hum, croon, chirp, chirrup, twitter, quaver, trill, shake, whistle, yodel.

To compose, set to music, score, harmonize, orchestrate.

To put in tune, tune, attune, accord, string, pitch.

(*Adjectives*) Musical, harmonious, etc. (413), instrumental, orchestral, pianistic, vocal, choral, operatic, etc.; musicianly, having a good ear.

(*Phrase*) *Fanatico per la musica.*

(*Adverbs*) *Adagio, largo, larghetto, andante, andantino, maestoso, moderato, allegretto, con moto, vivace, veloce, allegro, presto, prestissimo, strepitoso,* etc.; *scherzando, legato, staccato, crescendo, diminuendo, morendo, sostenuto, sforzando, accelerando, stringendo, più mosso, meno mosso, allargando, rallentando, ritenuto, a piacere,* etc.; *arpeggiando, pizzicato, glissando, martellato, da capo.*

416 MUSICIAN (*Substantives*), minstrel, performer, player, soloist, virtuoso, maestro.

Organist, pianist, violinist, fiddler, cellist, harper, harpist, flautist, fifer,

arinettist, trombonist, etc., trumpeter, bugler, piper, bagpiper, drummer,
mpanist; campanologist; band, orchestra, brass band, military band, string
and, pipe band, waits; conductor, bandmaster, drum-major, leader, *chef
orchestre*, etc., accompanist.

Vocalist, singer, songster, songstress, chanter, chantress, *cantatrice*, *lieder-
nger*, ballad-singer, etc.; troubadour, minnesinger, gleeman; nightingale,
hilomel, thrush, throstle, Orpheus.

Chorus, choir, chorister.

(*Phrase*) The tuneful Nine.

417 MUSICAL INSTRUMENTS.

1. Stringed instruments: Monochord, polychord, harp, lyre, lute, theorbo,
andolin, guitar, gittern, cithern, banjo, ukelele, balalaika.

Violin, fiddle, Cremona, Stradivarius (or Strad), kit, viola (or tenor),
ioloncello (or cello), double-bass (or bass-viol), viol, viola d'amore, viola da
amba, violone, rebeck, psaltery.

Pianoforte (or piano), harpsichord, clavier, clavichord, clavicembalo, spinet,
embalo, virginal, zither, dulcimer.

2. Wind instruments: Organ, siren, pipe, pitch-pipe, Pan-pipes; piccolo,
ute, bass-flute, oboe (or hautboy), oboe d'amore, cor anglais, clarinet, basset-
orn, bass-clarinet, bassoon, double-bassoon, saxophone, horn, French horn,
uba, trumpet, cornet, cornet-à-piston, trombone, euphonium; fife, flageolet,
vhistle, penny-whistle, ocarina, bugle, serpent, ophicleide, clarion, bagpipe,
ausette; harmonium, American organ, seraphina, concertina, accordion,
elodeon, mouth-organ, etc.; great, swell, choir, solo and echo organs.

3. Vibrating surfaces: Cymbal, bell, carillon, gong, tabor, tambourine,
imbrel, drum, side-drum, bass-drum, kettle-drum, timpano, military drum,
om-tom, castanet; musical glasses, harmonica, glockenspiel; sounding-board.

4. Vibrating bars: Tuning-fork, triangle, xylophone, Jew's harp.

5. Mechanical instruments: Musical box, hurdy-gurdy, barrel-organ, piano-
rgan, orchestrion, piano-player, pianola, etc.; gramophone, phonograph,
ape recorder, juke box, nickelodeon.

Key, string, bow, drumstick, bellows, sound-box, pedal, stop; loud or
ustaining pedal, soft pedal, mute, sordine, sourdine, damper, swell-box;
eyboard, finger-board, console; organ-loft, concert platform, orchestra, choir,
inging-gallery, belfry, campanile.

(4) PERCEPTION OF SOUND

418 Sense of sound.

HEARING (*Substantives*), audition,
uscultation, listening, eavesdrop-
ing; audibility.

Acuteness, nicety, delicacy, of ear.

Ear, auricle, acoustic organs, au-
litory apparatus, lug, ear-drum, tympanum.

Telephone, speaking-tube, ear-
rumpet, audiphone, audiometer, ear-
phone, phone, gramophone, phonograph, dictaphone, intercom, receiver.

Wireless telephony, broadcasting,
wireless, radio, transmitter, walkie-
talkie, radiogram, microphone, mike.

419 DEAFNESS (*Substantives*), hardness of hearing, surdity; inaudibility.

(*Verbs*) To be deaf, to shut, stop,
or close one's ears.

To render deaf, to stun, deafen.

(*Phrase*) To turn a deaf ear to.

(*Adjectives*) Deaf, stone deaf, tone
deaf, hard of hearing, earless, surd,
dull of hearing, deaf-mute, stunned,
deafened, having no ear.

Inaudible, out of earshot.

(*Phrases*) Deaf as a post; deaf as a
beetle; deaf as an adder.

A hearer, auditor, listener, eavesdropper, auditory, audience.

(*Verbs*) To hear, overhear, hark, listen, list, hearken, give or lend an ear, prick up one's ears, give a hearing or audience to, listen in.

To become audible, to catch the ear, to be heard.

(*Phrases*) To hang upon the lips of; to be all ears.

(*Adjectives*) Hearing, etc., auditory, auricular, acoustic.

(*Interjections*) Hark! list! hear! listen! oyez! (or oyes!)

(*Adverbs*) *Arrectis auribus*; with ears flapping.

(6) *Light*

(1) LIGHT IN GENERAL

420 LIGHT (*Substantives*), ray, beam, stream, gleam, streak, pencil, sunbeam, moonbeam, starbeam.

Day, daylight, sunshine, sunlight, moonlight, starlight, the light of day, the light of heaven, noontide, noonday, noontide light, broad daylight.

Glimmer, glimmering, glow, afterglow, phosphorescence, lambent flame, play of light.

Flush, halo, aureole, nimbus, glory, corona.

Spark, sparkle, scintilla, sparkling, scintillation, flame, flash, blaze, coruscation, fulguration, lightning, flood of light, glint.

Lustre, shine, sheen, gloss, tinsel, spangle, brightness, brilliancy, refulgence, dazzlement, splendour, resplendence, luminousness, luminosity, luminescence, lucidity, lucidness, incandescence, radiance, illumination, irradiation, glare, flare, flush, effulgence, fulgency, fluorescence, lucency, lambency.

Optics, photology, photometry, dioptrics, catoptrics.

Radioactivity, radiography, radiograph, radiometer, radioscopy, radiotherapy.

(*Verbs*) To shine, glow, glitter, glisten, glister, glint, twinkle, gleam, flicker, flare, glare, beam, radiate, shoot beams, shimmer, sparkle, scintillate, coruscate, flash, blaze, fizzle, daze, dazzle, bedazzle; to clear up, to brighten.

To illuminate, illume, illumine, lighten, enlighten, light, light up, irradiate, flush, shine upon, cast lustre upon; cast, throw, or shed a light upon, brighten, clear, relume.

421 DARKNESS (*Substantives*), night, midnight, obscurity, dusk (422), duskiness, gloom, gloominess, murk, mirk, murkiness, shadow, shade, umbrage, shadiness, umbra, penumbra, Erebus.

Obscuration, adumbration, obumbration, obtenebration, obfuscation, black-out, extinction, eclipse, gathering of the clouds, dimness (422).

(*Phrases*) Dead of night; darkness visible; darkness that can be felt; blind man's holiday.

(*Verbs*) To be dark, etc.; to lour (or lower).

To darken, obscure, shade, shadow, dim, bedarken, overcast, overshadow, obfuscate, obumbrate, adumbrate, cast in the shade, becloud, overcloud, bedim, put out, snuff out, blow out, extinguish, dout, douse.

To cast, throw, spread a shade or gloom.

(*Phrase*) To douse the glim.

(*Adjectives*) Dark, obscure, darksome, darkling, tenebrous, tenebrific, rayless, beamless, sunless, moonless, starless, pitch-dark, pitchy; Stygian, Cimmerian.

Sombre, dusky, unilluminated, unillumined, unlit, unsunned, nocturnal, dingy, lurid, overcast, louring (or lowering), cloudy, murky, murksome, shady, shadowy, umbrageous.

Benighted, noctivagant, noctivagous.

(*Phrases*) Dark as pitch; dark as a pit; dark as Erebus; dark as a wolf's mouth; the palpable obscure.

422 DIMNESS (*Substantives*), dimout, brown-out, paleness, glimmer, glimmering, owl-light, nebulousness,

(*Phrase*) To strike a light.

(*Adjectives*) Luminous, luminifer-us, shining, glowing, etc., lambent, lossy, lucid, lucent, luculent, lus-rous, lucific, glassy, clear, bright, cintillant, light, lightsome, un-louded, sunny, orient, noonday, noontide, beaming, beamy, vivid, light, splendent, radiant, radiating, cloudless, unobscured; radioactive, luorescent, phosphorescent.

Garish, resplendent, refulgent, ful-;ent, effulgent, in a blaze, ablaze, elucent, splendid, blazing, rutilant, neteoric, burnished.

(*Phrases*) Bright as silver, as day, as noonday.

nebulosity, nebula, cloud, film, mist, haze, fog, brume, smog, smoke, hazi-ness, eclipse, dusk, cloudiness, dawn, aurora, twilight, crepuscule, cockshut time, gloaming, daybreak, dawn, half-light, moonlight; moonshine, moonbeam, starlight, starshine, star-beam, candle-light.

(*Verbs*) To be dim, etc., to glimmer, loom, lour, twinkle.

To grow dim, to fade, to render dim, to dim, obscure, pale.

(*Adjectives*) Dim, dull, lack-lustre, dingy, darkish, glassy, faint, con-fused.

Cloudy, misty, hazy, foggy, brumous, muggy, fuliginous, nebulous, lowering, overcast, crepuscular, muddy, lurid, looming.

(*Phrase*) Shorn of its beams.

---

423 Source of light, self-luminous body.

LUMINARY (*Substantives*), sun, Phoebus, star, orb, meteor, galaxy, constellation, blazing star, glow-worm, firefly.

Meteor, northern lights, aurora borealis, aurora australis, fire-drake, ignis fatuus, jack-o'-lantern, will-o'-the-wisp, friar's lantern.

Artificial light, flame, gas-light, incandescent gas-light, electric light, limelight, acetylene, torch, candle, flash-lamp, flashlight, flambeau, link, light, taper, lamp, arc-lamp, mercury vapour lamp, neon lighting, lantern (or lanthorn), rushlight, farthing rushlight, night-light, firework, rocket, Very light, blue lights, fizgig, flare.

Chandelier, gaselier, electrolier, candelabra, girandole, lustre, sconce, gas-bracket, gas-jet, gas-burner, batswing; gas-mantle, electric bulb, filament.

Lighthouse, lightship, pharos, beacon, watch-fire, cresset, brand.

(*Adjectives*) Self-luminous, phosphoric, phosphorescent, radiant (420).

424 SHADE (*Substantives*), awning, parasol, sunshade, screen, curtain, veil, mantle, mask, gauze, blind, shutter, cloud, mist.

A shadow, chiaroscuro, umbrage, penumbra (421).

(*Adjectives*) Shady, umbrageous.

---

425 TRANSPARENCY (*Substantives*), transparence, diaphaneity, translu-cence, translucency, lucidity, pellu-cidity, limpidity, clarity.

Glass, crystal, mica, lymph, water.

(*Verbs*) To be transparent, etc., to transmit light.

(*Adjectives*) Transparent, pellucid,

426 OPACITY (*Substantives*), thick-ness, opaqueness, turbidity, turbid-ness, muddiness.

Cloud, film, haze.

(*Verbs*) To be opaque, etc., to ob-fuscate, not to transmit, to obstruct the passage of light.

(*Adjectives*) Opaque, turbid, roily,

lucid, diaphanous, translucent, relucent, limpid, clear, crystalline, vitreous, transpicuous, glassy, hyaline.
(*Phrase*) Clear as crystal.

thick, muddy, opacous, obfuscated, fuliginous, cloudy, hazy, misty, foggy, impervious to light.

---

427 SEMITRANSPARENCY, opalescence, pearliness, milkiness.
Film, gauze, muslin.

(*Adjectives*) Semitransparent, semi-diaphanous, semi-opaque, opalescent, gauzy, pearly, milky.

---

(2) SPECIFIC LIGHT

428 COLOUR (*Substantives*), hue, tint, tinge, dye, complexion, shade, spectrum, tincture, blazonry, cast, livery, coloration, glow, flush, tone, key.
Pure or positive colour, primary colour.
Broken colour, secondary or tertiary colour.
Chromatics; prism, spectroscope.
A pigment, colouring matter, medium, paint, dye, wash, stain, distemper, mordant.
(*Verbs*) To colour, dye, tinge, stain, tinct, tincture, paint, wash, illuminate, blazon, emblazon, bedizen, imbue, distemper.
(*Adjectives*) Coloured, colorific, chromatic, prismatic, full-coloured, lush, dyed; tinctorial.
Bright, deep, vivid, florid, fresh, high-coloured, unfaded, gay, showy, gaudy, garish, flaunting, vivid, gorgeous, glaring, flaring, flashy, tawdry, meretricious, raw, intense, double-dyed, loud, noisy.
Mellow, harmonious, pearly, light, quiet, delicate, pastel.

429 Absence of colour.
ACHROMATISM (*Substantives*), decoloration, discoloration, paleness, pallidity, pallidness, pallor, etiolation, anaemia, chlorosis, albinism, neutral tint, colourlessness; monochrome, black and white.
(*Verbs*) To lose colour, to fade, pale, blanch, become colourless.
To deprive of colour, discolour, bleach, tarnish, decolour, decolorate, decolorize, achromatize, tone down.
(*Adjectives*) Colourless, uncoloured, untinged, untinctured, achromatic, aplanatic, hueless, undyed, pale, pallid, pale-faced, pasty, etiolated, anaemic, chlorotic, faint, faded, dull, cold, muddy, wan, sallow, dead, dingy, ashy, ashen, cadaverous, glassy, lack-lustre, tarnished, bleached, discoloured.
(*Phrases*) Pale as death, as ashes, as a witch, as a ghost, as a corpse.

---

430 WHITENESS (*Substantives*), milkiness, hoariness.
Albification, etiolation.
Snow, paper, chalk, milk, lily, sheet, ivory, silver, alabaster.
(*Verbs*) To be white, etc.
To render white, whiten, bleach, whitewash, blanch, etiolate.
(*Adjectives*) White, milk - white, snow-white, snowy, niveous, chalky, hoary, hoar, silvery, argent.

431 BLACKNESS (*Substantives*), darkness (421), swarthiness, dinginess, lividity, inkiness, pitchiness, nigritude.
Nigrification.
Jet, ink, ebony, coal, pitch, charcoal, soot, sloe, smut, raven, crow; negro, nigger, darkie, coon, blackamoor.
(*Verbs*) To be black, etc.
To render black, to blacken, nigrify,

Whitish, off-white, cream-coloured, creamy, pearly, fair, blonde, etiolated, albescent.

(*Phrases*) White as the driven snow; white as a sheet.

---

denigrate, blot, blotch, smirch, smutch.

(*Adjectives*) Black, sable, swarthy, swart, sombre, inky, ebon, livid, coal-black, jet-black, pitch-black, fuliginous, dingy, dusky, Ethiopic, nigrescent.

(*Phrases*) Black as my hat; black as ink; black as coal; black as a crow; black as thunder.

432 Grey (*Substantives*), neutral tint, dun.

(*Adjectives*) Grey, etc., drab, dingy, sombre, leaden, livid, ashen, mouse-coloured, slate-coloured, stone-coloured, cinereous, cineritious, grizzly, grizzled.

---

433 Brown (*Substantives*), bistre, ochre, sepia.

(*Adjectives*) Brown, etc., bay, dapple, auburn, chestnut, nut-brown, umber, cinnamon, fawn, russet, olive, hazel, tawny, fuscous, chocolate, liver-coloured, tan, brunette, maroon, khaki, foxy, bronzed, sunburnt, tanned.

(*Phrases*) Brown as a berry, as mahogany, as a gipsy.

(*Verbs*) To render brown, embrown, to tan, bronze, etc.

Primitive Colours

434 Redness (*Substantives*), red, scarlet, vermilion, crimson, carmine, pink, lake, maroon, carnation, damask, ruby, rose, blush colour, peach colour, flesh colour, gules, solferino.

Rust, cinnabar, cochineal, madder, red lead, ruddle; blood, lobster, cherry, pillar-box.

Erubescence, rubescence, rubefaction, rosiness, rufescence, ruddiness, rubicundity.

(*Verbs*) To become red, to blush, flush, mantle, redden, colour.

435 Greenness (*Substantives*), verdure, viridescence, viridity.

Emerald, jasper, verd-antique, verdigris, beryl, aquamarine, malachite, grass.

(*Adjectives*) Green, verdant, pea-green, grass-green, apple-green, sea-green, turquoise-green, olive-green, bottle-green, glaucous, virescent, aeruginous, vert.

(*Phrase*) Green as grass.

To render red, redden, rouge, rubefy, rubricate, incarnadine.

(*Adjectives*) Red, scarlet, vermilion, carmine, rose, ruby, crimson, pink, etc., ruddy, rufous, florid, rosy, roseate, auroral, rose-coloured, blushing, mantling, etc., erubescent, blowzy, rubicund, stammel, blood-red, en-sanguined, rubiform, cardinal, cerise, *sang-de-bœuf*, murrey, carroty, sorrel, brick-coloured, brick-red, lateritic, cherry-coloured, salmon-coloured.

(*Phrases*) Red as fire, as blood, as scarlet, as a turkey-cock, as a cherry.

436 Yellowness (*Substantives*), buff colour, orpiment, yellow ochre, gamboge, crocus, saffron, xanthin, topaz.

437 Purple (*Substantives*), violet, plum, prune, lavender, lilac, peach colour, puce, gridelin, lividness, lividity, bishop's purple, magenta, mauve.

Lemon, mustard, jaundice, gold.

(*Adjectives*) Yellow, citron, gold, golden, aureate, citrine, fallow, tawny, flavous, fulvous, saffron, croceate, lemon, xanthic, xanthous, sulphur, amber, straw-coloured, sandy, lurid, Claude-tint, luteous, primrose-coloured, cream-coloured, buff, chrome.

Amethyst, murex.

(*Verb*) To empurple.

(*Adjectives*) Purple, violet, plum coloured, lilac, mauve, livid, etc.

(*Phrases*) Yellow as a quince, as a guinea, as a crow's foot.

---

438 BLUENESS (*Substantives*), bluishness, azure, indigo, ultramarine, Prussian blue, mazarine, bloom, bice.

Sky, sea, lapis lazuli, cobalt, sapphire, turquoise.

(*Adjectives*) Blue, cerulean, sky-blue, sky-coloured, sky-dyed, watchet, azure, bluish, sapphire, Garter-blue.

439 ORANGE (*Substantives*), gold flame, copper, brass, apricot colour aureolin, nacarat.

Ochre, cadmium.

(*Adjectives*) Orange, golden, ochreous, etc., buff, flame-coloured.

---

440 VARIEGATION (*Substantives*), dichroism, trichroism, iridescence, play of colours, *reflet*, variegatedness, patchwork, check, plaid, chess-board, tartan, maculation, spottiness, pointillism, parquetry, marquetry, mosaic, inlay, buhl, striae, spectrum.

A rainbow, iris, tulip, peacock, chameleon, butterfly, tortoise-shell, leopard, zebra, harlequin, motley, mother-of-pearl, nacre, opal, marble.

(*Verbs*) To be variegated, etc.

To variegate, speckle, stripe, streak, chequer, bespeckle, fleck, freckle, inlay, stipple, spot, dot, damascene, embroider, tattoo.

(*Adjectives*) Variegated, varicoloured, many-coloured, versicolour, many-hued, divers-coloured, particoloured, polychromatic, bicolour, tricolour, dichromatic.

Iridescent, prismatic, opaline, nacreous, pearly, opalescent, shot, watered, *chatoyant, gorge de pigeon*, all manner of colours, pied, piebald, skewbald, daedal, motley, mottled, veined, marbled, paned, dappled, clouded, cymophanous.

Mosaic, inlaid, tessellated, chequered, tartan, tortoiseshell.

Dotted, spotted, bespotted, spotty, speckled, bespeckled, punctate, maculated, freckled, fleckered, flecked, flea-bitten, studded, tattooed.

Striped, striated, streaked, barred, veined, brinded, brindled, tabby, roan, grizzled, listed, stippled.

(*Phrase*) All the colours of the rainbow.

(3) PERCEPTIONS OF LIGHT

441 VISION (*Substantives*), sight, optics, eyesight.

View, espial, glance, glimpse, peep, peek, look, squint, dekko, gander, the once-over, gaze, stare, leer, perlustration, contemplation, sight-seeing, regard, survey, reconnaissance, introspection, inspection, speculation,

442 BLINDNESS (*Substantives*), night-blindness, snow-blindness, cecity, amaurosis, cataract, ablepsy, nictitation, wink, blink.

A blinkard.

(*Verbs*) To be blind, etc., not to see, to lose sight of.

Not to look, to close or shut the

watch, *coup d'œil*, œillade, glad eye, po-peep, ocular demonstration, au-opsy, visualization, envisagement.

A point of view, gazebo, vista, oop-hole, peep-hole, look-out, belve-lere, field of view, watch-tower, observation post, crow's nest, theatre, amphitheatre, horizon, arena, com-nanding view, bird's-eye view, coign of vantage, observatory, periscope.

The organ of vision, eye, the naked or unassisted eye, retina, pupil, iris, cornea, white, optics, peepers.

Perspicacity, penetration, discern-ment.

Cat, hawk, lynx, eagle, Argus.

Evil eye; cockatrice, basilisk.

(*Verbs*) To see, behold, discern, have in sight, descry, sight, catch a sight, glance, or glimpse of, spy, espy, to get a sight of.

To look, view, eye, open one's eyes, glance on, cast or set one's eyes on, clap eyes on, look on or upon, turn or bend one's looks upon, turn the eyes to, envisage, visualize, peep, peer, peek, pry, scan, survey, reconnoitre, contemplate, regard, inspect, recognize, mark, discover, distinguish, see through, speculate; to see sights, lionize.

To look intently, strain one's eyes, be all eyes, look full in the face, look hard at, stare, gaze, pore over, gloat on, leer, to see with half an eye, to blink, goggle, ogle, make eyes at; to play at bo-peep.

(*Phrases*) To have an eye upon; keep in sight; look about one; glance round; run the eye over; lift up one's eyes; see at a glance, or with half an eye; keep a look-out for; to keep one's eyes skinned; to be a spectator of; to see with one's own eyes.

(*Adjectives*) Visual, ocular, optic, optical, ophthalmic.

Seeing, etc., the eyes being directed to, fixed, riveted upon.

Clear-sighted, sharp-sighted, quick-sighted, eagle-eyed, hawk-eyed, lynx-eyed, keen-eyed, Argus-eyed, piercing, penetrating.

(*Phrase*) The scales falling from one's eyes.

(*Adverbs*) Visibly, etc., at sight, in sight of, to one's face, before one's face, with one's eyes open, at a glance, at first sight, at sight.

(*Interjections*) Look! behold! see! lo! mark! observe! lo and behold!

eyes, to look another way, to turn away or avert the eyes, to wink, blink, nictitate.

To render blind, etc., to put out the eyes, to blind, blindfold, hood-wink, daze, dazzle.

(*Phrase*) To throw dust in the eyes.

(*Adjectives*) Blind, eyeless, sight-less, visionless, dark, stone-blind, sand-blind, stark-blind, mope-eyed, dazzled, hoodwinked, blindfolded, undiscerning.

(*Phrases*) Blind as a bat, as a buzzard, as a beetle, as a mole, as an owl.

(*Adverbs*) Blindly, etc., blindfold, darkly.

---

443 Imperfect vision.

DIM-SIGHTEDNESS (*Substantives*), purblindness, lippitude, confusion of vision, scotomy, failing sight, short-sightedness, near-sightedness, myopia, nictitation, long-sightedness, amblyopia, presbyopia, hypermetropia, nyctal-opia (or nyctalopy), nystagmus, astigmatism, squint, strabismus, wall-eye, swivel-eye, cast of the eye, double sight; an albino, blinkard.

Fallacies of vision: *deceptio visus*, refraction, false light, phantasm, anamor-phosis, distortion, looming, mirage, *fata morgana*, the spectre of the Brocken, ignis fatuus, phantasmagoria, dissolving views.

Colour-blindness, Daltonism.

Limitation of vision, blinker, screen.

(*Verbs*) To be dim-sighted, etc., to see double, to have a mote in the eye, to squint, goggle, look askance (or askant), to see through a prism, wink nictitate.

To glare, dazzle, loom.

(*Adjectives*) Dim-sighted, half-sighted, short-sighted, near-sighted, pur blind, myopic, long-sighted, hypermetropic, presbyopic, moon-eyed, mope eyed, blear-eyed, goggle-eyed, wall-eyed, one-eyed, nictitating, winking monoculous, amblyopic, astigmatic.

444 SPECTATOR (*Substantives*), looker-on, onlooker, watcher, sightseer bystander, *voyeur*, inspector, snooper, rubberneck (455), spy, beholder, witness, eye-witness, observer, star-gazer, etc., scout.

(*Verbs*) To witness, behold, look on at, spectate.

445 OPTICAL INSTRUMENTS (*Substantives*), lens, meniscus, magnifier, reading-glass, microscope, megascope, spectacles, specs, glasses, barnacles, goggles, pince-nez, lorgnette, folders, eye-glass, monocle, contact lens, peri- scope, telescope, spy-glass, monocular, binoculars, field-glass, night-glass, opera-glass, glass, view-finder, range-finder.

Mirror, reflector, speculum, looking-glass, pier-glass, cheval-glass, kaleido- scope.

Prism, camera, cine-camera, cinematograph (448), camera lucida, camera obscura, magic lantern, phantasmagoria, thaumatrope, chromatrope, stereo- scope, pseudoscope, bioscope.

Photometer, polariscope, spectroscope, collimator, polemoscope, eriometer, actinometer, exposure meter, lucimeter.

446 VISIBILITY (*Substantives*), per- ceptibility, conspicuousness, distinct- ness, conspicuity, appearance, ex- posure.

(*Verbs*) To be visible, etc., to appear, come in sight, come into view, heave in sight, open to the view, catch the eye, show its face, present itself, show itself, manifest itself, produce itself, discover itself, expose itself, come out, come to light, come forth, come forward, stand forth, stand out, arise, peep out, peer out, show up, turn up, crop up, start up, loom, burst forth, break through the clouds, glare, reveal itself, betray itself.

(*Phrases*) To show its colours; to see the light of day; to show one's face; to tell its own tale; to leap to the eye; *cela saute aux yeux*; to stare one in the face.

(*Adjectives*) Visible, perceptible, perceivable, discernible, in sight, ap- parent, plain, manifest, patent, obvious (525), clear, distinct, definite, well-defined, well-marked, recogniz- able, evident, unmistakable, palpable, naked, bare, barefaced, ostensible,

447 INVISIBILITY (*Substantives*), indistinctness, inconspicuousness, imperceptibility, nonappearance, de- litescence, latency (526), concealment (528).

(*Verbs*) To be invisible, escape notice, etc., to lie hidden, concealed, etc. (528), to be in or under a cloud, in a mist, in a haze, etc.; to lurk, lie in ambush, skulk.

Not to see, etc., to be blind to.

To render invisible, to hide, con- ceal (528).

(*Adjectives*) Invisible, impercep- tible, unseen, unbeheld, undiscerned, viewless, undiscernible, indiscernible, sightless, undescried, unespied, un- apparent, non-apparent, inconspicu- ous, unconspicuous, hidden, con- cealed, etc. (528), covert, eclipsed.

Confused, dim, obscure, dark, misty, hazy, foggy, indistinct, ill- defined, indefinite, ill-marked, blurred, shadowy, nebulous, shaded, screened, veiled, masked.

(*Phrases*) Out of sight; not in sight; out of focus.

conspicuous, prominent, staring, glaring, notable, notorious, overt; periscopic, panoramic, stereoscopic.

(Phrases) Open as day; clear as day; plain as a pikestaff; there is no mistaking; plain as the nose on one's face; before one's eyes; above-board; exposed to view; under one's nose; in bold relief; in the limelight.

448 APPEARANCE (Substantives), phenomenon, sight, spectacle, show, premonstration, scene, species, view, coup d'œil, look-out, prospect, out-look, vista, perspective, bird's-eye view, scenery, landscape, seascape, streetscape, picture, tableau, mise en scène, display, exposure, exhibition, manifestation.

Pageant, pageantry, peep-show, raree-show, panorama, diorama, cos-morama, georama, coup de théâtre, jeu de théâtre.

Bioscope, biograph, magic lantern, epidiascope, cinematograph (or kine-matograph).

Phantasm, phasma, phantom, spectrum, apparition, spectre, mirage, etc. (4, 443).

Aspect, phase, phasis, seeming, guise, look, complexion, shape, mien, air, cast, carriage, manner, bearing, deportment, port, demeanour, presence, expression.

Lineament, feature, trait, lines, outline, contour, face, countenance, physiognomy, visage, phiz, mug, dial, puss, pan, profile, tournure.

(Verbs) To seem, look, appear; to present, wear, carry, have, bear, exhibit, take, take on, or assume the appearance of; to play, to look like, to be visible, to reappear; to materialize.

To show, to manifest.

(Adjectives) Apparent, seeming, etc., ostensible.

(Adverbs) Apparently, to all appearance, etc., ostensibly, seemingly on the face of it, prima facie, at the first blush, at first sight.

449 DISAPPEARANCE (Substantives), evanescence, eclipse, occultation.

Dissolving views, fade-out.

(Verbs) To disappear, vanish, dis-solve, fade, melt away, pass, be gone, be lost, etc.

To efface, blot, blot out, erase, rub out, expunge (552).

(Phrase) To go off the stage.

(Adjectives) Disappearing, etc., lost, vanishing, evanescent, gone, missing.

Inconspicuous, unconspicuous (447).

(Phrases) Lost in the clouds; leaving no trace; out of sight.

(Interjections) Avaunt! vanish! disappear! (297).

CLASS IV

WORDS RELATING TO THE INTELLECTUAL FACULTIES

DIVISION I—FORMATION OF IDEAS

Section I—Operations of Intellect in General

450 INTELLECT (*Substantives*), mind, understanding, reason, thinking principle, nous, noesis, faculties, sense, common sense, consciousness, capacity, intelligence, percipience, intellection, intuition, instinct, conception, judgment, talent, genius, parts, wit, wits, shrewdness, intellectuality; the five senses; rationalism; ability, skill (698); wisdom (498).

Subconsciousness, subconscious mind, unconscious, id.

Soul, spirit, psyche, ghost, inner man, heart, breast, bosom.

Organ or seat of thought: *sensorium*, sensory, brain, head, headpiece, pate, noddle, nut, loaf, skull, brain-pan, grey matter, pericranium, cerebrum, cerebellum, cranium, upper storey, belfry.

Science of mind, phrenology, mental philosophy, metaphysics, psychology, psychics, psycho-analysis; ideology, idealism, ideality, pneumatology, immaterialism, intuitionism, realism; transcendentalism, spiritualism.

Metaphysician, psychologist, psychiatrist, psycho-analyst, psychotherapist.

(*Verbs*) Appreciate, realize, be aware of, be conscious of, take in, mark, note, notice.

(*Adjectives*) Intellectual, noetic, rational, reasoning, gnostic, mental, spiritual, subjective, metaphysical, psychical, psychological, noumenal, ghostly, immaterial (317), cerebral; subconscious, subliminal, Freudian.

450A ABSENCE or want of intellect, imbecility (499), materialism.

(*Adjectives*) Material, objective, unreasoning.

---

451 THOUGHT (*Substantives*), reflection, cogitation, cerebration, consideration, meditation, study, lucubration, speculation, deliberation, pondering, head-work, brain-work, application, attention (457).

Abstraction, contemplation, musing, brown study, reverie (458); depth of thought, workings of the mind, inmost thoughts, self-counsel, self-communing, self-examination, introspection; succession, flow, train,

452 Absence or want of thought.

INCOGITANCY (*Substantives*), vacancy, inanity, fatuity (499), thoughtlessness (458).

(*Verbs*) Not to think, to take no thought of, not to trouble oneself about, to put away thought; to inhibit, dismiss, discard, or discharge from one's thoughts, or from the mind; to drop the subject, set aside, turn aside, turn away from, turn

current, etc., of thought or of ideas, ɔrain-wave.

Afterthought, second thoughts, hindsight, reconsideration, retrospection, retrospect (505), examination (461), imagination (515).

Thoughtfulness, pensiveness, intentness.

Telepathy, thought-transference, mind-reading, extra-sensory perception, retrocognition, telekinesis.

(*Verbs*) To think, reflect, cogitate, excogitate, consider, deliberate, speculate, contemplate, mediate, introspect, ponder, muse, ruminate, think over, brood over, reconsider, animadvert, con, con over, mull over, study, discuss, hammer at, puzzle out, weigh, perpend, fancy, trow, dream of.

one's attention from, abstract oneself, dream.

To unbend, relax, divert the mind.

(*Adjectives*) Vacant, unintellectual (499), unoccupied, unthinking, inconsiderate, thoughtless, idealess, unidea'd, absent, *distrait*, abstracted, inattentive (458), diverted, distracted, distraught, unbent, relaxed.

Unthought-of, unconsidered, incogitable, undreamed-of, off one's mind.

(*Phrase*) *In nubibus.*

———

bend or apply the mind, digest, puzzle out, weigh, perpend, fancy, trow, dream of.

To occur, present itself, pass in the mind, suggest itself, strike one.

To harbour, entertain, cherish, nurture, etc., an idea, a thought, a notion, a view, etc.

(*Phrases*) Take into account; take into consideration; to take counsel; to commune with oneself; to collect one's thoughts; to advise with one's pillow; to sleep on or over it; to chew the cud upon; revolve in the mind; turn over in the mind; to rack or cudgel one's brains; to put on one's thinking-cap.

To flash on the mind; to flit across the view; to enter the mind; come into the head; come uppermost; run in one's head.

To make an impression; to sink or penetrate into the mind; fasten itself on the mind; to engross one's thoughts.

(*Adjectives*) Thinking, etc., thoughtful, pensive, meditative, reflective, ruminant, introspective, wistful, contemplative, speculative, deliberative, studious, abstracted, introspective, sedate, philosophical, conceptual.

Close, active, diligent, mature, deliberate, laboured, steadfast, deep, profound, intense, etc., thought, study, reflection, etc.

Intent, engrossed, absorbed, deep-musing, rapt (or wrapt), abstracted; sedate.

(*Phrases*) Having the mind on the stretch; lost in thought; the mind or head running upon.

453 Object of thought.

IDEA (*Substantives*), notion, conception, apprehension, concept, thought, fancy, conceit, impression, perception, apperception, percept, image, eidolon, sentiment, (484), fantasy, flight of fancy.

Point of view, light, aspect (448), field of view, standpoint; theory (514); fixed idea (481).

———

454 Subject of thought.

TOPIC (*Substantives*), subject, matter, theme, motif, thesis, text, subject-matter, point, proposition, theorem, business, affair, case, matter in hand, question, argument, motion, resolution, moot point (461), head, chapter; nice or subtle point, quodlibet.

(*Phrases*) Food for thought; mental pabulum.

(*Adverbs*) In question, under consideration, on the carpet, *sur le tapis*, relative to, *re, in re* (9), concerning, touching.

SECTION II—PRECURSORY CONDITIONS AND OPERATIONS

455 The desire of knowledge.
CURIOSITY (*Substantives*), curiousness, inquisitiveness, an inquiring mind.

A quidnunc, busybody, eavesdropper, snooper, rubberneck, Peeping Tom, Nosy Parker, Paul Pry, newsmonger, gossip.

(*Verbs*) To be curious, etc., to take an interest in, to stare, gape, pry, snoop, rubber, lionize.

(*Adjectives*) Curious, inquisitive, inquiring, inquisitorial, all agog, staring, prying, snoopy, gaping, agape, over-curious, nosy.

(*Adverbs*) With open mouth, on tiptoe, with ears flapping, *arrectis auribus*.

456 Absence of curiosity.
INCURIOSITY (*Substantives*), incuriousness, insouciance, nonchalance, want of interest, indifference (866).

(*Verbs*) To be incurious, etc., to have no curiosity, take no interest in, not to care, not to mind; to mind one's own business.

(*Phrases*) Not to trouble oneself about; one couldn't care less; the devil may care; san fairy ann.

(*Adjectives*) Incurious, uninquisitive, indifferent, *sans souci*, insouciant, nonchalant, aloof, detached, apathetic, uninterested.

---

457 ATTENTION (*Substantives*), advertence, advertency, observance, observation, interest, notice, heed, look, regard, view, remark, inspection, introspection, heedfulness, mindfulness, look-out, watch, vigilance, circumspection, surveillance, consideration, scrutiny, revision, revisal, recension, review, revise, particularity (459).

Close, intense, deep, profound, etc., attention, application, or study.

(*Verbs*) To be attentive, etc.; to attend, advert to, mind, observe, look, look at, see, view, look to, see to, remark, heed, notice, spot, twig, pipe, take heed, take notice, mark; give or pay attention to; give heed to, have an eye to; turn, apply, or direct the mind, the eye, or the attention to; look after, give a thought to, animadvert on, occupy oneself with, be interested in, devote oneself to, give oneself up to, see about.

To examine cursorily; to glance at, upon, or over; cast or pass the eyes over, run over, turn over the leaves, dip into, skim, perstringe.

To examine closely or intently, scrutinize, consider, give one's mind to, overhaul, pore over, perpend, note, mark, inspect, review, size up, take stock of, fix the eye, mind,

458 INATTENTION (*Substantives*), inconsideration, inconsiderateness, inadvertence, inadvertency, non-observance, inobservance, disregard, oversight, unmindfulness, giddiness, respectlessness, thoughtlessness (460), insouciance; wandering, distracted, etc., attention.

Absence of mind, abstraction, preoccupation, distraction, reverie, brown study, day-dream, day-dreaming, wool-gathering.

(*Phrases*) The wits going woolgathering; the attention wandering; building castle in the air, or castles in Spain.

(*Verbs*) To be inattentive, etc., to overlook, disregard, pass by, slur over, pass over, gloss over, blink, miss, skim, skim the surface, *effleurer* (460).

To call off, draw off, call away, divert, etc., the attention; to distract; to disconcert, put out, rattle, discompose, confuse, perplex, bewilder, bemuse, moider, bemuddle, muddle, dazzle, obfuscate, faze, fluster, flurry, flummox, befog.

(*Phrases*) To take no account of; to drop the subject; to turn a deaf ear to; to come in at one ear and go out of the other; to reckon without one's host.

houghts, or attention on, keep in riew, contemplate, revert to, etc. 451).

To fall under one's notice, observa-ion, etc., to catch the eye; to catch, awaken, wake, invite, solicit, attract, claim, excite, engage, occupy, strike, arrest, fix, engross, monopolize, pre-occupy, obsess, absorb, rivet, etc., he attention, mind, or thoughts; to nterest.

To call attention to, point out, ndicate (550).

(*Phrases*) To trouble one's head about; lend or incline an ear to; to take cognizance of; to prick up one's ears; to have one's eyes open; to keep one's eyes skinned.

To have one's wits about one; to bear in mind; to come to the point; to take into account; to read, mark, learn.

(*Adjectives*) Attentive, mindful, heedful, regardful, alive to, awake to, bearing in mind, occupied with, engaged, taken up with, interested, engrossed, wrapped in, absorbed, rapt.

Awake, watchful, on the watch (459), broad awake, wide awake, agape, intent on, with eyes fixed on, open-eyed, unwinking, undistracted, with bated breath, breathless, upon the stretch.

(*Interjections*) See! look! say! attention! hey! oy! mark! lo! behold! achtung! nota bene! N.B.

(*Adjectives*) Inattentive, mindless, unobservant, unmindful, uninter-ested, inadvertent, heedless, regard-less, respectless, careless (460), in-souciant, unwatchful, listless, cursory, blind, deaf, etc.

Absent, abstracted, *distrait*, absent-minded, lost, preoccupied, bemused, dreamy, moony, napping.

Disconcerted, put out, etc., dizzy, muzzy (460).

(*Phrase*) Caught napping.

(*Adverbs*) Inattentively, etc., cavalierly.

---

459 CARE (*Substantives*), caution, heed, heedfulness, attention (457), wariness, prudence, discretion, watch, watchfulness, alertness, vigil, vigil-ance, circumspection, watch and ward, deliberation, forethought (510), predeliberation, solicitude, precaution (673), scruple, scrupulousness, scru-pulosity, particularity, surveillance.

(*Phrases*) The eyes of Argus; *l'œil du maître*.

(*Verbs*) To be careful, etc., to take care, have a care, beware, look to it, reck, heed, take heed, provide for, see to, see after, keep watch, keep watch and ward, look sharp, look about one, set watch, take precau-tions, take tent, see about.

(*Phrases*) To have all one's wits about one; to mind one's P's and Q's; to speak by the card; to pick one's steps; keep a sharp look out; keep one's weather eye open; to keep an eye on.

(*Adjectives*) Careful, cautious,

460 NEGLECT (*Substantives*), negli-gence, omission, trifling, laches, heedlessness, carelessness, perfunc-toriness, remissness, imprudence, secureness, indiscretion, *étourderie*, incautiousness, indiscrimination, rashness (863), recklessness, non-chalance, inattention (458); slovenli-ness, sluttishness.

Trifler, flibbertigibbet, Micawber; slattern, slut, sloven.

(*Verbs*) To be negligent, etc., to neglect, scamp, pass over, cut, omit, pretermit, set aside, cast or put aside.

To overlook, disregard, ignore, slight, pay no regard to, make light of, trifle with, blink, wink at, con-nive at; take or make no ac-count of; gloss over, slur over, slip over, skip, skim, miss, shelve, sink, jump over, shirk (623), dis-count.

To waste time, trifle, frivol, fribble (683).

heedful, wary, canny, guarded, on one's guard, alert, on the alert, on the watch, watchful, on the look out, *aux aguets*, awake, vigilant, circumspect, broad awake, having the eyes open, Argus-eyed.

Discreet, prudent, sure-footed, provident, scrupulous, particular, meticulous.

(*Phrase*) On the *qui vive*.

(*Adverbs*) Carefully, etc., with care, etc., gingerly, considerately.

(*Phrases*) Let sleeping dogs lie; catching a weasel asleep.

(*Interjections*) Look out! mind your eye! watch! beware! cave! fore! heads!

To render neglectful, etc., to put or throw off one's guard.

(*Phrases*) To give to the winds; take no account of; turn a deaf ear to; shut one's eyes to; not to mind; think no more of; set at naught; give the go-by to.

(*Adjectives*) Neglecting, etc., unmindful, heedless, careless, *sans souci*, negligent, neglectful, slovenly, sluttish, remiss, perfunctory, thoughtless, unthoughtful, unheedful, off one's guard, unwary, incautious, unguarded, indiscreet, inconsiderate, imprudent, improvident, rash, headlong, reckless, heels over head, witless, hare-brained, giddy-brained, offhand, slapdash, happy-go-lucky, cursory, brain-sick, scatterbrained.

Neglected, missed, abandoned, shunted, shelved, unheeded, unperceived, unseen, unobserved, unnoticed, unnoted, unmarked, unattended to, untended, unwatched, unthought-of, overlooked, unmissed, unexamined, unsearched, unscanned, unweighed, unsifted, untested, unweeded, undetermined.

(*Phrases*) In an unguarded moment; buried in a napkin.

(*Adverbs*) Negligently, etc., anyhow, any old way.

(*Interjections*) Let it pass! never mind! no matter! I should worry! san fairy ann! *nichevo!*

---

461 INQUIRY (*Substantives*), **search**, research, quest, pursuit (622), examination, review, scrutiny, investigation, perquisition, perscrutation, referendum, straw vote, Gallup poll; discussion, symposium, inquest, inquisition, exploration, exploitation, sifting, screening, calculation, analysis, dissection, resolution, induction; the Baconian method.

Questioning, asking, interrogation, interpellation, interrogatory, the Socratic method, examination, cross-examination, cross-questioning, third degree, quiz, catechism.

Reconnoitring, reconnaissance, feeler, *ballon d'essai*, prying, spying, espionage, the lantern of Diogenes, searchlight.

QUESTION, query, difficulty, problem, proposition, desideratum, point to be solved; point or matter in dispute; moot point, question at issue,

462 ANSWER (*Substantives*), response, reply, replication, riposte, rejoinder, rebutter, surrejoinder, surrebutter, retort, come-back, repartee, rescript, antiphony, rescription, acknowledgment.

Explanation, solution, deduction, resolution, exposition, rationale, interpretation (522).

A key, master-key, open sesame, *passepartout*, clue.

Oedipus, oracle (513); solutionist.

(*Verbs*) To answer, respond, reply, rebut, retort, rejoin, return for answer, acknowledge, echo.

To explain, solve, resolve, expound, decipher, spell, interpret (522), to unriddle, unlock, cut the knot, unravel, fathom, pick or open the lock, discover, fish up, to find a clue to, to get to the bottom of.

(*Phrases*) To turn the tables upon; Q.E.D.

bone of contention, plain question, fair question, open question, knotty point, vexed question, crux.

Enigma, riddle, conundrum, crossword, bone to pick, quodlibet, Gordian knot.

(*Adjectives*) Answering, responding, etc., responsive, respondent.

(*Adverb*) On the right scent.

(*Interjection*) Eureka!

An inquirer, querist, questioner, heckler, inquisitor, scrutator, scrutineer, examiner, inspector, analyst, quidnunc, newsmonger, gossip (527, 532); investigator, detective, bloodhound, sleuth-hound, sleuth, inquiry agent, private eye, Sherlock Holmes, busy, dick, rozzer, flattie, G-man; secret police, Cheka, Ogpu, Gestapo.

(*Verbs*) To inquire, seek, search, look for, look about for, look out for, cast about for, beat up for, grope for, feel for, reconnoitre, explore, sound, rummage, fossick, ransack, pry, snoop, look round, look over, look through, scan, peruse.

To pursue, hunt, track, trail, mouse, dodge, trace, shadow, tail, dog (622), nose out, ferret out, unearth, hunt up.

To investigate; to take up, follow up, institute, pursue, conduct, carry on, prosecute, etc., an inquiry, etc.; to overhaul, examine, study, consider, fathom, take into consideration, dip into, look into, calculate, pre-examine, dive into, to delve into, rake, rake over, discuss, canvass, thrash out, probe, fathom, sound, scrutinize, analyse, anatomize, dissect, sift, screen, winnow, resolve, traverse, see into.

To ask, speer, question, query, demand; to put, propose, propound, moot, raise, stir, suggest, put forth, start, pop, etc., a question; to interrogate, catechize, pump, cross-question, cross-examine, grill, badger, heckle, dodge, require an answer.

(*Phrases*) To look, peer, or pry into every hole and corner, to beat the bushes; to leave no stone unturned; to seek a needle in a bundle of hay; to scratch the head.

To subject to examination; to grapple with a question; to put to the proof; pass in review; take into consideration; to ventilate a question; seek a clue; throw out a feeler.

To undergo examination; to be in course of inquiry; to be under consideration.

(*Adjectives*) Inquiring, etc., inquisitive, requisitive, requisitory, catechetical, inquisitorial, heuristic, analytic, in search of, in quest of, on the look out for, interrogative, zetetic.

Undetermined, untried, undecided, to be resolved, etc., in question, in dispute, under discussion, under consideration, *sub judice*, moot, proposed, doubtful.

(*Adverbs*) Why? wherefore? whence? *quaere?* how comes it? how happens it? how is it? what is the reason? what's in the wind? what's cooking?

---

463 EXPERIMENT (*Substantives*), essay, trial, tryout, tentative method, *tátonnement*, verification, probation, proof, criterion, test, acid test, reagent, check, control, touchstone, pyx, assay, ordeal; empiricism, rule of thumb method of trial and error.

A feeler, *ballon d'essai*, pilot-balloon, messenger-balloon; pilot-engine; straw to show the wind.

(*Verbs*) To experiment, essay, try, explore, grope, angle, cast about, beat the bushes; feel or grope one's way; to thread one's way; to make an experiment. make trial of.

To subject to trial, etc., to experiment upon, try over, rehearse, give a trial to, put, bring, or submit to the test or proof; to prove, verify, test, assay, touch, practise upon.

(Phrases) To see how the land lies; to see how the wind blows; to feel the pulse; to throw out a feeler; to have a try; to have a go.

(Adjectives) Experimental, crucial, tentative, probationary, empirical, *sub judtce*, under probation, on trial, on approval.

(Adverb) A tâtons.

464 COMPARISON *(Substantives)*, collation, contrast, antithesis, identification.

A comparison, simile, similitude, analogy, parallel, parable, metaphor, allegory (521).

(Verbs) To compare to or with; to collate, confront, place side by side or in juxtaposition, to draw a parallel, institute a comparison, contrast, balance, identify.

(Adjectives) Comparative, metaphorical, figurative, allegorical, comparable, compared with, pitted against, placed by the side of.

465 DISCRIMINATION *(Substantives)*, distinction, differentiation, perception or appreciation of difference, nicety, refinement, taste (850), judgment, discernment, nice perception, tact, critique.

(Verbs) To discriminate, distinguish, differentiate, draw the line, sift, screen.

(Phrases) To split hairs; to cut blocks with a razor; to separate the chaff from the wheat or the sheep from the goats.

465A INDISCRIMINATION *(Substantives)*, indistinctness, indistinction (460).

(Verbs) Not to distinguish or discriminate, to confound, confuse; to neglect, overlook, lose sight of a distinction.

(Adjectives) Indiscriminate, undistinguished, undistinguishable, unmeasured, sweeping, wholesale.

(Adjectives) Discriminating, etc., discriminative, distinctive, diagnostic, nice, judicial.

466 MEASUREMENT *(Substantives)*, admeasurement, mensuration, triangulation, survey, valuation, appraisement, assessment, assize, estimation, reckoning, evaluation, gauging; mileage, voltage, horse power.

Geometry, geodetics, geodesy, orthometry, altimetry, sounding, surveying, weighing, ponderation, trutination, dead reckoning, metrology.

A measure, standard, rule, yardstick, compass, callipers, dividers, gauge, meter, line, rod, plumb-line, plummet, log, log-line, sound, sounding-rod, sounding-line, lead-line, index, flood-mark, Plimsoll line (or mark), check.

Scale, graduation, graduated scale, vernier, quadrant, theodolite, slide-rule, balance, spring balance, scales, steelyard, beam, weather-glass, barometer, aneroid, barograph, araeometer, altimeter, clinometer, graphometer, goniometer, thermometer, speedometer, tachometer, pedometer, ammeter, voltmeter, micrometer, etc.

A surveyor, geometer, leadsman, etc.

(Verbs) To measure, mete, value, assess, rate, appraise, estimate, form an estimate, set a value on, appreciate, span, pace, step; apply the compass, rule, scale, etc., gauge, plump, probe, sound, fathom, heave the log, survey, weigh, poise, balance, hold the scales, take an average, graduate, evaluate, size up, to place in the beam, to take into account, price.

(Adjectives) Measuring, etc., metrical, ponderable, measurable, mensurable.

SECTION III—MATERIALS FOR REASONING

467 EVIDENCE, on one side, (*Substantives*), premises, data, grounds, *praecognita*, indication (550).

Oral, hearsay, internal, external, documentary, presumptive evidence.

Testimony, testimonial, deposition, declaration, attestation, testification, authority, warrant, warranty, guarantee, surety, handwriting, autograph, signature, endorsement, seal, sigil, signet (550), superscription, entry, finger-print.

Voucher, credential, certificate, deed, indenture, docket, dossier, probate, affidavit, diploma; admission, concession, allegation, deposition, citation, quotation, reference; admissibility.

Criterion, test, reagent, touchstone, check, control, prerogative, fact, argument, shibboleth.

A witness, eye-witness, indicator, ear-witness, deponent, telltale, informer, sponsor, special pleader.

Assumption, presumption, show of reason, postulation, postulate, lemma.

Reason, proof (478), circumstantial evidence.

Ex-parte evidence, one-sided view.

Secondary evidence, confirmation, corroboration, ratification, authentication, support, approval, compurgation.

(*Phrases*) A case in point; *ecce signum*; *ex pede Herculem*.

(*Verbs*) To be evidence, etc., to evidence, evince, show, indicate (550), imply, involve, entail, necessitate, argue, bespeak, admit, allow, concede, homologate, certify, testify, attest, bear testimony, depose, depone, witness, vouch for, sign, seal, set one's hand and seal to, endorse, confirm, ratify, corroborate, support, establish, uphold, bear upon, bear out, warrant, guarantee.

To adduce, cite, quote, refer to, appeal to, call, bring forward, produce, bring into court, confront witnesses, collect, bring together, rake up evidence, to make a case, make good, authenticate, substantiate, go bail for.

To allege, plead, assume, postulate, posit, presume; to beg the question.

468 Evidence on the other side, on the other hand.

COUNTER-EVIDENCE (*Substantives*), disproof, contradiction, rejoinder, rebutter, answer (462), weak point, conflicting evidence, refutation (479), negation (536).

(*Phrases*) A *tu quoque* argument; the other side of the shield.

(*Verbs*) To countervail, oppose, rebut, check, weaken, invalidate, contradict, contravene.

(*Phrases*) To tell another story; to cut both ways.

(*Adjectives*) Countervailing, etc., contradictory; unauthenticated, unattested, unvouched-for.

(*Adverbs*) Although, though, albeit, but, *per contra*.

(*Phrase*) *Audi alteram partem.*

469 QUALIFICATION (*Substantives*), limitation, modification, allowance, grains of allowance, consideration, extenuating circumstance, condition, proviso, saving clause, penalty clause, exception (83), assumption (514).

(*Verbs*) To qualify, limit, modify, tone down, colour, discount, allow for, make allowance for, take into account, introduce new conditions, admit exceptions, take exception.

(*Adjectives*) Qualifying, etc., conditional, exceptional (83), contingent, postulatory, hypothetical, supposititious (514).

(*Adverbs*) Provided, if, unless, but, yet, according as, conditionally, admitting, supposing, granted that; on the supposition, assumption, presumption, allegation, hypothesis, etc., of; with the understanding, even, although, for all that, at all events, after all.

(*Phrases*) With a grain of salt; *cum grano salis.*

(*Phrases*) To hold good, hold water; to speak volumes; to bring home to; to bring to book; to quote chapter and verse; to speak for itself; tell its own tale.

(*Adjectives*) Showing, etc., indicating, indicative, indicatory, evidential, evidentiary, following, deducible, consequential, collateral, corroborative, confirmatory, postulatory, presumptive.

Sound, logical, strong, valid, cogent, decisive, persuasive, persuasory, demonstrative, irrefragable, irresistible, etc. (578).

(*Adverbs*) According to, witness, admittedly, confessedly, *a fortiori*, still more, still less, all the more reason for.

Degrees of Evidence

470 POSSIBILITY (*Substantives*), potentiality, contingency (156), what may be, what is possible, etc.

Practicability, feasibility (705), compatibility (23).

(*Verbs*) To be possible, etc., to admit of, to bear.

To render possible, etc., to put into the way of.

(*Adjectives*) Possible, contingent (475), conceivable, credible.

Practicable, feasible, achievable, performable, viable, accessible, surmountable, attainable, obtainable, compatible.

(*Adverbs*) Possibly, by possibility, maybe, perhaps, mayhap, haply, perchance, peradventure, *in posse* (156).

(*Phrases*) Wind and weather permitting; within the bounds of possibility; on the cards; D.V.

471 IMPOSSIBILITY (*Substantives*), what cannot be, what can never be, imposs, no go, hopelessness (859).

Impracticability, incompatibility (704), incredibility.

(*Verbs*) To be impossible, etc., to have no chance whatever.

(*Phrases*) To make a silk purse out of a sow's ear; to wash a blackamoor white; to make bricks without straw; to get blood from a stone; to take the breeks off a highlandman; to square the circle; to eat one's cake and have it too.

(*Adjectives*) Impossible, contrary to reason, inconceivable, unreasonable, absurd, incredible, visionary, chimerical, prodigious (870), desperate, hopeless, unheard-of, unthinkable.

Impracticable, unattainable, unachievable, unfeasible, infeasible, beyond control, unobtainable, unprocurable, insuperable, unsurmountable, inaccessible, inextricable.

(*Phrases*) Out of the question; sour grapes; *non possumus*.

472 PROBABILITY (*Substantives*), likelihood, *vraisemblance*, verisimilitude, plausibility, show of, colour of, credibility, reasonable chance, favourable chance, fair chance, hope, prospect, presumption, presumptive evidence, circumstantial evidence, the main chance, a *prima facie* case.

Probabilism, probabiliorism.

(*Verbs*) To be probable, likely, etc.; to think likely, dare say, expect (507).

(*Phrases*) To bid fair; to stand fair for; to stand a good chance; to stand to reason.

473 IMPROBABILITY (*Substantives*), unlikelihood, unfavourable chances, small chance, off-chance, bare possibility, long odds, incredibility.

(*Verbs*) To be improbable, etc., to have or stand a small, little, poor, remote, etc., chance; to whistle for.

(*Adjectives*) Improbable, unheard-of, incredible, unbelievable, unlikely.

(*Phrases*) Contrary to all reasonable expectation; having scarcely a chance; a chance in a thousand.

(*Adjectives*) Probable, likely, hopeful, well-founded.

Plausible, specious, ostensible, colourable, standing to reason, reasonable, credible, tenable, easy of belief, presumable, presumptive, *ben trovato*.

(*Phrases*) Likely to happen; in a fair way; appearances favouring; according to every reasonable expectation; the odds being in favour.

(*Adverbs*) Probably, etc., belike, in all probability, or likelihood, apparently, to all appearance, on the face of it, in the long run, *prima facie*, very likely, like enough, arguably, ten to one.

(*Phrase*) All Lombard Street to a china orange.

474 CERTAINTY (*Substantives*), certitude, positiveness, a dead certainty, dead cert, infallibleness, infallibility, gospel, scripture, surety, assurance, indisputableness, moral certainty.

Fact, matter of fact, *fait accompli*. Bigotry, dogmatism, *ipse dixit*. Bigot, dogmatist, Sir Oracle.

(*Verbs*) To be certain, etc., to believe (484).

To render certain, etc., to ensure, to assure, clinch, determine, decide.

To dogmatize, lay down the law.

(*Phrases*) To stand to reason; to make assurance doubly sure.

(*Adjectives*) Certain, sure, assured, solid, absolute, positive, flat, determinate, categorical, unequivocal, inevitable, unavoidable, avoidless, unerring, infallible, indubitable, indubious, indisputable, undisputed, uncontested, undeniable, incontestable, irrefutable, unimpeachable, incontrovertible, undoubted, doubtless, without doubt, beyond a doubt, past dispute, unanswerable, decided, unquestionable, beyond all question, unquestioned, questionless, irrefragable, evident, self-evident, axiomatic, demonstrable (478), authoritative, authentic, official, unerring, infallible, trustworthy (939).

(*Phrases*) Sure as fate; and no mistake; sure as a gun; clear as the sun at noonday; sure as death (and taxes); bet your life; you bet; *cela va sans dire*; it's in the bag; that's flat.

(*Adverbs*) Certainly, assuredly, etc., for certain, *in esse*, sure, surely, sure enough, to be sure, of course, as a matter of course, yes (488), depend upon it, that's so, by all manner of means, beyond a peradventure.

475 UNCERTAINTY (*Substantives*), incertitude, doubt (485), doubtfulness, dubiety, dubiousness, suspense, precariousness, indefiniteness, indetermination, slipperiness, fallibility, perplexity, embarrassment, dilemma, ambiguity (520), hesitation, vacillation (605), equivoque, vagueness, peradventure, touch-and-go.

(*Phrases*) A blind bargain; a pig in a poke; a leap in the dark; a moot point; an open question.

(*Verbs*) To be uncertain, etc; to vacillate, hesitate, waver.

To render uncertain, etc., to perplex, embarrass, confuse, moider, confound, bewilder, disorientate.

(*Phrases*) To be in a state of uncertainty; not to know which way to turn; to be at a loss; to be at fault; to lose the scent.

To tremble in the balance; to hang by a thread.

(*Adjectives*) Uncertain, doubtful, dubious, precarious (665), chancy, casual, random, contingent, indecisive, dependent on circumstances, undecided, unsettled, undetermined, pending, pendent, vague, indeterminate, indefinite, ambiguous, undefined, equivocal, undefinable, puzzling, enigmatic, debatable, disputable, questionable, apocryphal, problematical, hypothetical, controvertible, fallible, fallacious, suspicious, fishy, slippery, ticklish.

Unauthentic, unconfirmed, undemonstrated, undemonstrable, unreliable, untrustworthy.

SECTION IV—REASONING PROCESSES

476 REASONING (*Substantives*), ratiocination, dialectics, induction, deduction, generalization; inquiry (461).

Argumentation, discussion, *pourparler*, controversy, polemics, debate, wrangling, logomachy, apology, apologetics, ergotism, disputation, disceptation.

The art of reasoning, logic, process, train or chain of reasoning, analysis, synthesis, argument, lemma, proposition, terms, premises, postulate, data, starting-point, principle, inference, result, conclusion.

Syllogism, prosyllogism, enthymeme, sorites, dilemma, *perilepsis*, pros and cons, a comprehensive argument.

Correctness, soundness, force, validity, cogency, conclusiveness.

A thinker, reasoner, disputant, controversialist, logician, dialectician, polemic, wrangler, arguer, debater.

(*Phrases*) A paper war; a war of words; a battle of the books; a full-dress debate.

The horns of a dilemma; *reductio ad absurdum*; *argumentum ad hominem*; *onus probandi*.

(*Verbs*) To reason, argue, discuss, debate, dispute, wrangle; bandy words or arguments; hold or carry on an argument, controvert, contravene (536), consider (461), comment upon, moralize upon, spiritualize.

(*Phrases*) To open a discussion or case; to moot; to join issue; to ventilate a question; to talk it over; to have it out; to take up a side or case.

To chop logic; to try conclusions; to impale on the horns of a dilemma; to cut the matter short; to hit the nail on the head; to take one's stand upon; to have the last word.

(*Adjectives*) Reasoning, etc., rational, rationalistic, ratiocinative, argumentative, controversial, dialectic, polemical, discursory, discursive, debatable, controvertible, disputatious; correct, just, fair, sound, valid,

477 The absence of reasoning.

INTUITION (*Substantives*), instinct, association, presentiment, insight, second sight, sixth sense.

False or vicious reasoning, show of reason.

Misjudgment, miscalculation (481).

SOPHISTRY (*Substantives*), paralogy, fallacy, perversion, casuistry, jesuitry, quibble, equivocation, evasion, chicanery, special pleading, quiddity, mystification; nonsense (497).

Sophism, solecism, paralogism, elenchus, fallacy, quodlibet, subterfuge, subtlety, quillet, inconsistency, antilogy.

Speciousness, plausibility, illusiveness, irrelevancy, invalidity; claptrap, hot air.

Quibbler, casuist, *advocatus diaboli*.

(*Phrases*) Begging the question; *petitio principii*; *ignoratio elenchi*; reasoning in a circle; *post hoc, ergo propter hoc*; *ignotum per ignotius*.

The meshes or cobwebs of sophistry; a flaw in an argument; an argument falling to the ground.

(*Verbs*) To envisage, to judge intuitively, etc.

To reason ill, falsely, etc.; to pervert, quibble, equivocate, mystify, evade, elude, gloss over, varnish, misjudge, miscalculate (481).

To refine, subtilize, cavil, sophisticate, mislead.

(*Phrases*) To split hairs; to cut blocks with a razor; throw off the scent; to beg the question; reason in a circle; beat about the bush; prove that black is white; not have a leg to stand on; lose one's reckoning.

(*Adjectives*) Intuitive, instinctive, impulsive, unreasoning, independent of or anterior to reason.

Sophistical, unreasonable, irrational, illogical, false, unsound, not following, not pertinent, inconsequent, inconsequential, unwarranted, untenable, inconclusive, incorrect, fallacious, inconsistent, groundless,

cogent, logical, demonstrative (478), relevant, pertinent (9, 23).

(*Phrases*) To the point; in point; to the purpose; *ad rem.*

(*Adverbs*) For, because, for that reason, forasmuch as, inasmuch as, since, hence, whence, whereas, considering, therefore, consequently, *ergo*, then, thus, accordingly, wherefore, *a fortiori, a priori, ex concesso.*

(*Phrases*) In consideration of; in conclusion; in fine; after all; *au bout du compte*; on the whole; taking one thing with another.

---

478 DEMONSTRATION (*Substantives*), proof, conclusiveness, probation, comprobation, clincher, *experimentum crucis*, test, etc. (463), argument (476).

(*Verbs*) To demonstrate, prove, establish, show, evince, verify, substantiate; to follow.

(*Phrases*) Make good; set at rest; settle the question; reduce to demonstration; to make out a case; to prove one's point; to clinch an argument; bring home to; bear out.

(*Adjectives*) Demonstrating, etc., demonstrative, probative, demonstrable, unanswerable, conclusive, final, apodictic (or apodeictic), irrefutable, irrefragable, unimpeachable, categorical, decisive, crucial.

Demonstrated, proved, proven, etc., unconfuted, unrefuted; evident, self-evident, axiomatic (474); deducible, consequential, inferential.

(*Phrases*) *Probatum est*; it stands to reason; it holds good; there being nothing more to be said; Q.E.D.

(*Adverbs*) Of course, in consequence, consequently, as a matter of course, no wonder.

fallible, unproved, indecisive, deceptive, illusive, illusory, specious, hollow, jesuitical, plausible, irrelevant.

Weak, feeble, poor, flimsy, trivial, trumpery, trashy, puerile, childish, irrational, silly, foolish, imbecile, absurd (499), extravagant, far-fetched, pettifogging, quibbling, fine-spun, hair-splitting.

(*Phrases*) *Non constat*; *non sequitur*; not holding water; away from the point; foreign to the purpose or subject; having nothing to do with the matter; not of the essence; *nihil ad rem*; not bearing upon the point in question; not the point; beside the mark.

---

479 CONFUTATION (*Substantives*), refutation, disproof, conviction, redargution, invalidation, exposure, exposition; demolition of an argument; answer, come-back, counter, retort.

(*Phrases*) *Reductio ad absurdum*; a knock-down argument; a *tu quoque* argument.

(*Verbs*) To confute, refute, disprove, redargue, expose, show the fallacy of, knock the bottom out of, rebut, parry, negative, defeat, overthrow, demolish, explode, riddle, overturn, invalidate, silence, reduce to silence, shut up, put down.

(*Phrases*) To cut the ground from one's feet; to give one a set-down.

(*Adjectives*) Confuting, etc., confuted, etc., capable of refutation, refutable, confutable, etc.; unproved, etc.

(*Phrases*) The argument falls to the ground; it won't hold water; that cock won't fight.

SECTION V—RESULTS OF REASONING

480 JUDGMENT (*Substantives*), conclusion, determination, deduction, inference, result, illation, corollary, rider, porism, consectary.

Estimation, valuation, appreciation, judication, adjudication, arbitrament, arbitration, assessment, award, ponderation.

Decision, sentence, verdict, moral, ruling, finding; detection, discovery, estimate; *chose jugée*.

Criticism, critique, review, report, notice; plebiscite, casting vote.

A judge, umpire, arbiter, arbitrator, assessor, censor, referee, critic, connoisseur, reviewer.

(*Verbs*) To judge, deduce, conclude, draw a conclusion, infer, make a deduction, draw an inference, put two and two together; come to, arrive or jump at a conclusion; to derive, gather, collect.

To estimate, appreciate, value, count, assess, rate, account, rank, regard, review, settle, decide, pronounce, arbitrate, perpend, size up.

(*Phrases*) To sit in judgment; to hold the scales; to pass an opinion; to pass judgment.

(*Adjectives*) Judging, etc., deducible (467); impartial, unbiased, unprejudiced, unwarped, unbigoted, equitable, fair, sound, rational, judicious, shrewd.

480A DETECTION (*Substantive*), discovery.

(*Verbs*) To ascertain, determine, find, find out, make out, detect, discover, elicit, recognize, trace, get at; get or arrive at the truth; meet with, fall upon, light upon, hit upon, fall in with, stumble upon, lay the finger on, spot, solve, resolve, unravel, fish out, worm out, ferret out, root out, nose out, disinter, unearth, grub up, fish up, investigate (461).

To be near the truth, to get warm, to burn.

(*Phrase*) To smell a rat.

(*Interjection*) Eureka!

481 MISJUDGMENT (*Substantives*), obliquity of judgment, misconception, error (495), miscalculation, miscomputation, presumption.

Prejudgment, prejudication, prejudice, prenotion, *parti pris*, prevention, preconception, predilection, prepossession, preapprehension, presentiment, *esprit de corps*, clannishness, party spirit, partisanship, partiality.

Bias, warp, twist, fad, whim, crotchet, fike; narrow-mindedness, bigotry, dogmatism, intolerance, tenacity, obstinacy (606); blind side; one-sided, partial, narrow or confined views, ideas, conceptions, or notions; *idée fixe*, fixed idea, obsession, monomania, infatuation.

(*Phrases*) A bee in one's bonnet; a mote in the eye; a fool's paradise.

(*Verbs*) To misjudge, misestimate, misconceive, misreckon, etc. (495).

To prejudge, forejudge, prejudicate, dogmatize, have a bias, etc., presuppose, presume.

To produce a bias, twist, etc.; to bias, warp, twist, prejudice, obsess, infatuate, prepossess.

(*Phrases*) To have on the brain; to look only at one side of the shield; to view with jaundiced eye; to run away with the notion; to jump to a conclusion.

(*Adjectives*) Prejudging, misjudging, etc., prejudiced, jaundiced, narrow-minded, dogmatic, intolerant, illiberal, blimpish, besotted, infatuated, fanatical, *entêté*, positive, obstinate (606), tenacious, pig-headed, having a bias, twist, etc., warped, partial, one-sided, biased, bigoted, hide-bound, tendentious, opinionated, opinionative, opinioned, self-opinioned, self-opinionated, crotchety, pernickety, faddy, fussy, fiky.

(*Phrases*) Wedded to an opinion; the wish being father to the thought.

———

482 OVERESTIMATION (*Substantive*), exaggeration.

(*Phrases*) Much ado about nothing; much cry and little wool; a storm in a tea-cup.

(*Verbs*) To overestimate, estimate too highly, overrate, overvalue, overprize, overpraise, overweigh, outreckon; exaggerate, extol, puff, boost, make too much of, overstrain.

(*Phrases*) To set too high a value upon; to make a mountain out of a molehill; *parturiunt montes, nascetur ridiculus mus*; to make two bites of a cherry; all his geese are swans.

(*Adjectives*) Overestimated, etc.

483 UNDERESTIMATION (*Substantives*), depreciation, disparagement, detraction (934), underrating, undervaluing, etc.

(*Verbs*) To depreciate, disparage, detract, underrate, underestimate, undervalue, underreckon, underprize, misprize, disprize, not to do justice to, make light of, slight, belittle, knock, slam, make little of, think nothing of, hold cheap, cheapen, disregard, to care nothing for, despise, set at naught, minimize, discount, deride, derogate, decry, cry down, crab, denigrate, smear, vilipend, run down (934).

To scout, deride, pooh-pooh, mock, scoff at, laugh at, whistle at, play with, trifle with, fribble, niggle, ridicule (856).

(*Phrases*) To snap one's fingers at; throw into the shade; not to care a pin, rush, hoot, tinker's cuss, etc., for; to damn with faint praise.
(*Adjectives*) Depreciating, etc., derogatory, cynical.
Depreciated, etc., unvalued, unprized.

484 BELIEF (*Substantives*), credence, faith, trust, troth, confidence, credit, dependence on, reliance, assurance.

Opinion, notion, idea (453), conception, apprehension, impression, conceit, mind, view, persuasion, conviction, convincement, sentiment, voice, conclusion, judgment (480), estimation, self-conviction.

System of opinions, creed, credo, religion (983, 987), doctrine, tenet, dogma, principle, school, ideology, articles of belief, way of thinking, popular belief, *vox populi*, public opinion, *esprit de corps*, partisanship; ism, doxy.

Change of opinion (607), proselytism, propagandism (537).

A convert, pervert, vert, proselyte.

(*Verbs*) To believe, credit, receive, give faith to, give credit to, rely upon, make no doubt, reckon, doubt not, confide in, count upon, depend upon, build upon, calculate upon, take upon trust, swallow, gulp down, take one's word for, take upon credit, swear by.

To be of opinion, to opine, presume;

485 UNBELIEF (*Substantives*), disbelief, misbelief, discredit, agnosticism, atheism (988), heresy (984), dissent (489).

DOUBT, dubitation, scepticism, *diaporesis*, misgiving, demur, cliff-hanging, suspense; shade or shadow of doubt, distrust, mistrust, misdoubt, suspicion, shyness, embarrassment, hesitation, uncertainty (475), scruple, qualm, dilemma; casuistry, paradox; schism (489), incredulity (487).

Unbeliever, sceptic (487); Doubting Thomas.

(*Verbs*) To disbelieve, discredit, not to believe; refuse to admit or believe; misbelieve, controvert; put or set aside; join issue, dispute, deny.

To doubt, be doubtful, etc., diffide, distrust, mistrust, suspect, scent, jalouse; have, harbour, entertain, etc., doubts; demur, stick at, pause, hesitate, scruple, question, query, call in question, look askance (or askant).

To cause, raise, suggest, or start a doubt; to pose, stagger, floor, startle, embarrass, puzzle (704); shake or stagger one's faith or belief.

(*Phrases*) Not to know what to

to have, hold, possess, entertain, adopt, imbibe, embrace, foster, nurture, cherish, etc., a notion, idea, opinion, etc.; to think, look upon, view, consider, take, take it, hold, trow, ween, conceive, fancy, apprehend, regard, esteem, deem, account; meseems, methinks.

To cause to be believed, thought, or esteemed; to satisfy, persuade, assure, convince, convert, bring over, win over, indoctrinate, proselytize (537), evangelize; to vert.

(*Phrases*) To pin one's faith to; to take at one's word.

To take it into one's head; to run away with the notion; to come round to an opinion.

To cram down the throat; to bring home to; to find credence; to carry conviction; pass current; pass muster; to hold water; to go down.

make of; to smell a rat; to hang in doubt; to have one's doubts; to float in a sea of doubts.

(*Adjectives*) Unbelieving, doubting, etc., incredulous, scrupulous, suspicious, sceptical, shy of belief, at sea, at a loss (487).

Unworthy or undeserving of belief, hard to believe, doubtful (475), dubious, unreliable, fishy, questionable, suspect, staggering, puzzling, etc., paradoxical, incredible, inconceivable.

(*Phrases*) With a grain of salt; *cum grano salis*; *timeo Danaos et dona ferentes*; all is not gold that glitters; the cowl does not make the monk.

(*Adjectives*) Believing, etc., impressed with, imbued with, wedded to, unsuspecting, unsuspicious, void of suspicion, etc., credulous (486), convinced, positive, sure, assured, cocksure, certain, confident.

Believed, etc., credited, accredited, unsuspected, received, current, popular.

Worthy or deserving of belief, commanding belief, believable, persuasive, impressive, reliable, dependable, trustworthy (939), credible, probable (572), fiducial, fiduciary; relating to belief, doctrinal.

(*Adverbs*) In the opinion of, in the eyes of, on the strength of, to the best of one's belief, *me judice*.

486 CREDULITY (*Substantives*), credulousness, gullibility, infatuation, self-delusion, self-deception, superstition, gross credulity, bigotry, dogmatism.

A credulous person, gull, gobemouche; dupe (547).

(*Verbs*) To be credulous, etc., to follow implicitly, swallow, take on trust, take for gospel.

To impose upon, practise upon, palm off upon, cajole, etc., deceive (545).

(*Phrases*) *Credo quia absurdum*; the wish being father to the thought.

(*Adjectives*) Credulous, gullible, confiding, trusting; easily deceived, cajoled, etc.; green, verdant, superstitious, simple, unsuspicious, etc. (484), soft, childish, silly, stupid, over-credulous, over-confident.

487 INCREDULITY (*Substantives*), incredulousness, scepticism, pyrrhonism, nihilism, suspicion (485), suspiciousness, scrupulousness, scrupulosity.

An unbeliever, sceptic, misbeliever, pyrrhonist; nihilist.

(*Verbs*) To be incredulous, etc., to distrust (485).

(*Adjectives*) Incredulous, hard of belief, sceptical, unbelieving, inconvincible, shy of belief, doubting, distrustful, suspicious (485).

(*Phrases*) Oh yeah? says you! a likely story! rats! that be hanged for a tale; tell that to the marines; it won't wash; that cock won't fight; *credat Judaeus Apella*.

488 ASSENT (*Substantives*), acquiescence, admission, assentation, nod, consent, concession, accord, accordance, agreement (23), concord (714), concordance, concurrence, ratification, confirmation, corroboration, approval, recognition, acknowledgment, acceptance, granting, avowal, confession.

Unanimity, chorus; affirmation (535), common consent, acclamation, consensus.

Yes-man, sycophant, echo.

(*Verbs*) To assent, acquiesce, agree, yield assent, accord, concur, consent, nod assent, accept, coincide, go with, go along with, be at one with, chime in with, strike in with, close with, vote for, conform with, defer to; say yes, ay, ditto, amen, etc.

To acknowledge, own, avow, confess, concede, subscribe to, abide by, admit, allow, recognize, grant, endorse, ratify, countersign, O.K., okay, approve, carry.

(*Phrases*) To go or be solid for; to come to an understanding; to come to terms; one could not agree more.

(*Adjectives*) Assenting, etc., acquiescent, content, consentient, willing; approved, agreed, carried; uncontradicted, unchallenged, unquestioned, uncontroverted; unanimous.

(*Phrase*) Of one mind.

(*Adverbs*) Affirmatively, in the affirmative (535).

Yes, yea, yeah, yep, ay, aye, uh-huh, sure, very well, even so, just so, quite so, to be sure, all right, right oh! right you are, you said it, definitely, absolutely, exactly, precisely, truly, certainly, assuredly, no doubt, doubtless, verily, very true (494), *ex concesso.*

Be it so, so be it, by all means, granted, O.K., okay, oke, okeydoke, by all manner of means, *à la bonne heure*, amen, willingly, etc. (602).

With one voice, with one accord, *una voce*, unanimously, in chorus, as one man, to a man, *nem. con.* or *nemine contradicente, nemine dissentiente*, *en bloc*, without a dissentient voice, one and all, on all hands.

489 DISSENT (*Substantives*), dissidence, discordance, denial (536), dissonance, disagreement; difference or diversity of opinion, recusancy, contradiction, nonconformity, schism (984), secession; protest.

A dissentient, dissenter, protestant, nonconformist, recusant, heretic; deviationist, nonjuror, schismatic, seceder.

(*Verbs*) To dissent, demur, deny, disagree, refuse assent, say no, differ, cavil, ignore, protest, contradict, secede, repudiate, refuse to admit.

(*Phrases*) To shake the head; to shrug the shoulders; to join issue; to give the lie; to differ *toto caelo.*

(*Adjectives*) Dissenting, etc., dissentient, dissident, discordant, protestant, nonconforming, recusant, nonjuring, non-content, schismatic, deviationist; unconvinced, unconverted, unavowed, unacknowledged.

Unwilling, reluctant, extorted, etc.

(*Adverbs*) Negatively, in the negative (536), at variance with.

No, nay, nope, nit, na, not, not so, not at all, nohow, nowise, not in the least, not a bit, not a whit, not a jot, by no means, by no manner of means, not for the world, on no account, in no respect.

(*Phrases*) Many men, many minds; *quot homines, tot sententiae*; *tant s'en faut*; the answer is in the negative; *il s'en faut bien.*

(*Interjections*) No sir! God forbid! I'll be hanged first! I'll see you far enough! not bloody likely! not on your nelly! not if I know it! over my dead body! pardon me! I beg your pardon!

---

490 KNOWLEDGE (*Substantives*), cognizance, cognition, cognoscence, awareness, gnosis, acquaintance, experience, ken, privity, insight,

491 IGNORANCE (*Substantives*), nescience, nescientness, unacquaintance, unconsciousness, darkness, blindness, incomprehension,

familiarity, apprehension, comprehension, understanding, recognition; discovery (480), appreciation; knowability.

Intuition, clairvoyance, consciousness, conscience, perception, precognition, light, enlightenment, glimpse, inkling, glimmer, dawn, scent, suspicion; conception, notion, idea (453).

Self-consciousness, self-knowledge, apperception.

System or body of knowledge, science, philosophy, pansophy, pandect, doctrine, ideology, theory, aetiology, literature, *belles-lettres*, *literae humaniores*, the humanities, humanism; ology.

Erudition, learning, lore, scholarship, letters, book-learning, bookishness, bibliomania, bibliolatry, education, instruction, information, acquisitions, acquirements, accomplishments, attainments, proficiency, cultivation, culture; a liberal education, encyclopaedic knowledge, omniscience.

Elements, rudiments, abecedary (542), cyclopaedia, encyclopaedia, school, academy, etc.

Depth, extent, profoundness, profundity, stores, etc., solidity, accuracy, etc., of knowledge.

(*Phrases*) The march of intellect; the progress, advance, etc., of science; the schoolmaster being abroad.

(*Verbs*) To know, be aware of, savvy, ken, wot, ween, trow, have, possess, perceive, conceive, apprehend, ideate, understand, comprehend, make out, recognize, be master of, know full well, possess the knowledge of, experience, discern, perceive, see, see through, have in one's head.

(*Phrases*) To know what's what; to know how the wind blows; to know the ropes; to have at one's fingertips or finger-ends.

(*Adjectives*) Knowing, aware of, etc., cognizant of, acquainted with, privy to, conscious of, no stranger to, *au fait*, *au courant*, versed in, hep,

incognizance, inexperience, emptiness.

Imperfect knowledge, smattering, sciolism, glimmering; bewilderment, perplexity (475); incapacity.

Affectation of knowledge, pedantry, charlatanry, quackery, dilettantism.

(*Phrases*) Crass ignorance; monumental ignorance.

A sealed book; unexplored ground; an unknown quantity; *terra incognita*.

(*Verbs*) To be ignorant, etc., not to know, to know nothing of, not to be aware of, to be at a loss, to be out of it, to be at fault, to ignore, to be blind to, etc., not to understand, etc.

(*Phrases*) To be caught tripping; not to know what to make of; to have no idea or notion; not to be able to make head or tail of; not to know a hawk from a handsaw; to lose one's bearings.

(*Adjectives*) Ignorant, unknowing, unconscious, unaware, unwitting, witless, a stranger to, unacquainted, unconversant, unenlightened, unilluminated, incognizant, unversed, uncultivated, clueless.

Uninformed, uninstructed, untaught, unapprised, untutored, unschooled, unguided.

Shallow, superficial, green, verdant, rude, half-learned, illiterate, unread, uneducated, unlearned, uncultured, Philistine, unlettered, empty-headed, having a smattering, etc., pedantic.

Confused, puzzled, bewildered, bemused, muddled, bemuddled, lost, benighted, belated, at sea, at fault, posed, blinded, abroad, distracted, in a maze, misinformed, hoodwinked, in the dark, at a loss, *désorienté*.

Unknown, novel, unapprehended, unexplained, unascertained, uninvestigated, unexplored, untravelled, uncharted, chartless, unheard-of, unperceived, unknowable.

(*Phrases*) Having a film over the eyes; wide of the mark; at cross purposes.

(*Adverbs*) Ignorantly, unwittingly,

up in, up to, alive to, wise to, conversant with, proficient in, read in, familiar with.

Apprised of, made acquainted with, informed of; undeceived.

Erudite, instructed, learned, well-read, lettered, literate, educated, cultivated, cultured, knowledgeable, enlightened, well-informed, shrewd, bookish, scholarly, scholastic, deep-read; self-taught, well-grounded, well-conned.

Known, etc., well-known, recognized, received, notorious, noted, proverbial, familiar; hackneyed, trite, commonplace; cognoscible, knowable; experiential.

(*Phrases*) Behind the scenes; in the know; at home in; the scales fallen from one's eyes.

(*Adverbs*) To one's knowledge, to the best of one's knowledge.

(*Phrase*) Experto crede.

unawares; for anything one knows; for aught one knows.

(*Phrase*) 'A little learning is a dangerous thing.'

---

492 SCHOLAR (*Substantives*), student (541), savant, scientist, humanist, grammarian, intellectual, pundit, schoolman, don, professor, lecturer, reader, demonstrator, graduate, doctor, master of arts, licentiate, wrangler, gownsman, philosopher, philomath, clerk, encyclopaedist.

Linguist; *littérateur, literati, illuminati*, intelligentsia.

Pedant, pedagogue, bookworm, *helluo librorum*, bibliomaniac, bibliophile, blue-stocking, *bas-bleu*, high-brow, bigwig, bookman; swot, grind.

(*Phrases*) Man of letters; man of learning; at the feet of Gamaliel; a walking dictionary.

(*Adjectives*) Erudite, learned, scholarly (490).

493 IGNORAMUS (*Substantives*), sciolist, smatterer, novice, greenhorn, half-scholar, schoolboy, booby, dunce (501); bigot (481); quack, mountebank, charlatan, dilettante, low-brow, amateur, Philistine, obscurant, obscurantist.

(*Phrase*) The wooden spoon.

(*Adjectives*) Bookless, shallow (499), ignorant, etc. (491), prejudiced (481), obscurantist.

---

494 Object of knowledge.

TRUTH (*Substantives*), verity, actual existence (1), reality, fact, matter of fact, actuality, nature, principle, orthodoxy, gospel, holy writ, substantiality, genuineness, authenticity, realism.

Accuracy, exactness, exactitude, precision, preciseness, nicety, delicacy, fineness, strictness, rigour, punctuality.

(*Phrases*) The plain truth; the honest truth; the naked truth; the sober truth; the very thing; a stubborn fact; not a dream, fancy, illusion, etc.; the exact truth; 'the truth, the whole truth, and nothing but the

495 Untruth (546).

ERROR (*Substantives*), mistake, miss, fallacy, misconception, misapprehension, misunderstanding, inaccuracy, incorrectness, inexactness, misconstruction (523), miscomputation, miscalculation (481).

Fault, blunder, *faux pas*, bull, Irish bull, Irishism, bloomer, howler, floater, clanger, boner, lapse, slip of the tongue, *lapsus linguae*, Spoonerism, slip of the pen, malapropism, equivoque, cross purposes, oversight, flaw, misprint, erratum; heresy, misstatement, misreport, bad shot.

Illusion, delusion, self-deceit, self-deception, hallucination, monomania,

truth'; 'a round unvarnished tale'; *ipsissima verba*; the real Simon Pure.

(*Verbs*) To be true, real, etc., to hold good, to be the case.

To render true, legitimatize, legitimize, substantiate, realize, actualize, to make good, establish.

To get at the truth (480).

(*Phrases*) *Vitam impendere vero*; *magna est veritas et praevalebit.*

(*Adjectives*) True, real, veritable, veracious, actual, certain, positive, absolute, existing (1), substantial, categorical, realistic, factual; unrefuted, unconfuted, unideal, unimagined.

Exact, accurate, definite, precise, well-defined, just, correct, right, strict, hard-and-fast, literal, rigid, rigorous, scrupulous, conscientious, religious, punctilious, nice, mathematical, axiomatic, demonstrable, scientific, unerring, constant, faithful, *bona fide*, curious, delicate, meticulous.

Genuine, authentic, legitimate, pukka, orthodox, official, *ex officio*, pure, sound, sterling, hall-marked, unsophisticated, unadulterated, unvarnished; solid, substantial, undistorted, undisguised, unaffected, unflattering, unexaggerated, unromantic.

(*Phrases*) Just the thing; neither more nor less; to a hair.

(*Adverbs*) Truly, verily, veritable, troth, certainly, certes, assuredly, in truth, in good truth, of a truth, really, indubitably, in sooth, forsooth, in verity, in fact, in point of fact, as a matter of fact, strictly speaking, *de facto*, indeed, in effect, actually, *ipso facto*, definitely, literally, positively, virtually, at bottom, *au fond*.

Precisely, accurately, *ad amussim*, etc., mathematically, to a nicety, to a hair, to a T, to an inch; to the letter, *au pied de la lettre*.

aberration; fable, dream, shadow, fancy, bubble, false light (443), the mists of error, will-o'-the-wisp, jack-o'-lantern, ignis fatuus, chimera (515), *maya*.

(*Verbs*) To be erroneous, false, etc., to cause error, to mislead, lead astray, lead into error, delude, give a false impression or idea, to falsify, misstate, misrelate, misinform, misrepresent (544), deceive (545), beguile.

To err, be in error, to mistake, to receive a false impression; to lie or labour under an error, mistake, etc., to blunder, be in the wrong, be at fault, to misapprehend, misconceive, misunderstand, misremember, misreckon, miscalculate, miscount, misestimate, misjudge, misthink, flounder, trip.

(*Phrases*) To take the shadow for the substance; to go on a fool's errand; to have the wrong sow by the ear; to put one's foot in it; to pull a boner; to drop a brick.

(*Adjectives*) Erroneous, untrue, false, fallacious, duff, unreal, unsubstantial, baseless, groundless, less, ungrounded, unauthenticated, untrustworthy, heretical.

Inexact, incorrect, wrong, illogical, partial, one-sided, unreasonable, absonous, absonant, indefinite, unscientific, inaccurate, aberrant.

In error, mistaken, etc., tripping, floundering, etc.

Illusive, illusory, ideal, imaginary, fanciful, chimerical, visionary, shadowy, mock, futile.

Spurious, apocryphal, bogus, illegitimate, phoney, pseudo, bastard, meretricious, deceitful, sophisticated, adulterated.

(*Phrases*) Wide of the mark; on the wrong scent; barking up the wrong tree; out of it; without a leg to stand upon.

———

In every respect, in all respects, *sous tous les rapports*, at any rate, at all events, by all means.

(*Phrases*) Joking apart; in good earnest; in sober earnest; sooth to say.

496 MAXIM (*Substantives*), aphorism, apophthegm, dictum, saying, *mot*, adage, gnome, saw, proverb, wisecrack, sentence, precept, rule, formula, tag, code, motto, slogan, catchword, word, byword, moral, sentiment, phylactery, conclusion, reflection, thought, golden rule, axiom, theorem, scholium, lemma, triusm.

Catechism, creed (484), profession of faith.

(*Adjectives*) Aphoristic, gnomic, proverbial, phylacteric, axiomatic; hackneyed, trite.

(*Phrases*) 'Wise saws and modern instances'; as the saying is or goes.

497 ABSURDITY (*Substantives*), absurdness, nonsense, folly, paradox, inconsistency, quibble, sophism (477), stultiloquy, stultiloquence, Irish bull, Irishism, Hibernicism, sciamachy, imbecility (499).

Jargon, gibberish, rigmarole, double-Dutch, fustian, rant, bombast, bathos, amphigouri, rhapsody, extravagance, rodomontade, romance; nonsense verse, limerick, clerihew.

Twaddle, claptrap, flapdoodle, bunkum, blah, fudge, rubbish, piffle, verbiage, trash, truism, stuff, balderdash, slipslop, *bavardage*, palaver, *baragouin*, moonshine, fiddlestick, wish-wash, platitude, cliché, flummery, inanity, fiddle-faddle, rot, tommy-rot, bosh, tosh, hot air, havers, blethers, tripe, bilge, bull, hooey, hokum, boloney.

Vagary, foolery, tomfoolery, mummery, monkey-trick, monkey-shine, dido, *boutade*, lark, escapade, ploy, rag.

(*Phrases*) A cock-and-bull story; a mare's-nest; a wild-goose chase; talking through one's hat; 'a tale told by an idiot, full of sound and fury, signifying nothing'; clotted nonsense; arrant rot.

(*Adjectives*) Absurd, nonsensical, foolish, senseless, preposterous (499), sophistical, inconsistent, extravagant, ridiculous, cock-and-bull, quibbling, trashy, washy, wishy-washy, twaddling, etc.; topsy-turvy, Gilbertian.

498 INTELLIGENCE (*Substantives*), capacity, nous, parts, talent, sagacity, sagaciousness, wit, mother-wit, *esprit*, gumption, comprehension, understanding, quick parts, grasp of intellect.

Acuteness, acumen, shrewdness, astuteness, arguteness, sharpness, aptness, aptitude, quickness, receptiveness, subtlety, archness, penetration, perspicacity, perspicaciousness, clear-sightedness, discrimination, discernment, flair, refinement (850).

Head, brains, headpiece, a long head.

WISDOM, sapience, sense, good sense, common sense, plain sense, horse-sense, reason, reasonableness, rationality, judgment, judiciousness, solidity, depth, profoundness, catholicity, breadth of view, enlarged views, reach or compass of thoughts.

Genius, inspiration, the fire of genius.

499 IMBECILITY (*Substantives*), incapacity, vacancy of mind, poverty of intellect, shallowness, dullness, stupidity, asininity, obtuseness, stolidity, hebetude, doltishness, muddle-headedness, vacuity, short-sightedness, incompetence.

Silliness, simplicity, childishness, puerility, babyhood; dotage, second childhood, anility, fatuity, idiocy, idiotism (503).

FOLLY, unwisdom, absurdity, infatuation, irrationality, senselessness, foolishness, frivolity, inconsistency, lip-wisdom, conceit, vanity, irresponsibility, giddiness, extravagance, oddity, eccentricity (503), ridiculousness, desipience.

Act of folly (497), imprudence (699), rashness, fanaticism.

(*Phrases*) A fool's paradise; apartments to let; one's wits going woolgathering; the meanest capacity.

Wisdom in action, prudence, discretion, self-possession, aplomb (698), sobriety, tact, ballast.

(*Phrase*) Discretion being the better part of valour.

(*Verbs*) To be intelligent, wise, etc., to reason (476), to discern (441), discriminate (465), to penetrate, to see far into.

(*Phrases*) To have all one's wits about one; to see as far through a brick wall as anybody.

(*Adjectives*) Applied to persons: Intelligent, sagacious, receptive, quick, sharp, acute, fly, smart, shrewd, gumptious, canny, astute, sharp-sighted, quick-sighted, quick-eyed, keen, keen-eyed, keen-sighted, keen-witted, sharp-witted, quick-witted, needle-witted, penetrating, piercing, clear-sighted, perspicacious, discerning, discriminating, discriminative, clever (698), knowledgeable.

Wise, sage, sapient, sagacious, reasonable, rational, sound, common-sense, sane, sensible, judicious, judgmatic, enlightened, impartial, catholic, broad-minded, open-minded, unprejudiced, unbiased, unprepossessed, undazzled, unperplexed, judicial, impartial, fair, progressive.

Cool, cool-headed, long-headed, hard-headed, long-sighted, calculating, thoughtful, reflective, oracular, heaven-directed.

Prudent, discreet, sober, staid, deep, solid, considerate, provident, politic, diplomatic, tactful.

Applied to actions: Wise, sensible, reasonable, judicious, well-judged, well-advised, prudent, prudential, politic (646), expedient.

(*Phrases*) Wise as a serpent; wise in one's generation; not born yesterday; up to snuff; no flies on him; wise as Solomon.

(*Verbs*) To be imbecile, foolish, etc., to trifle, drivel, ramble, dote, *radoter*, blether, haver; to fool, to monkey, to footle.

(*Phrases*) To play the fool; to play the giddy goat; to make an ass of oneself; to go on a fool's errand; to pursue a wild-goose chase; *battre la campagne*; Homer nods.

(*Adjectives*) Applied to persons: Unintelligent, unintellectual, witless, reasonless, not bright, imbecile, shallow, *borné*, weak, soft, simple, sappy, spoony, weak-headed, weak-minded, feeble-minded, half-witted, short-witted, half-baked, not all there, deficient, wanting, shallow-pated, shallow-brained, dull, dumb, dense, crass, stupid, heavy, obtuse, stolid, doltish, asinine, addle-headed, dull-witted, blunt, dull-brained, dim-sighted, vacuous.

Childish, infantine, infantile, babyish, childlike, puerile, callow; anile.

Fatuous, idiotic, lack-brained, drivelling, blatant, brainless, blunt-witted, beef-witted, fat-witted, fat-headed, boneheaded, insulse, having no head or brains, thick-skulled, ivory-skulled, blockish, Boeotian.

Foolish, silly, senseless, irrational, insensate, nonsensical, blunder-headed, chuckle-headed, puzzle-headed, muddle-headed, muddy-headed, undiscerning, unenlightened, unphilosophical; prejudiced, bigoted, purblind, narrow-minded, wrong-headed, tactless, crotchety, conceited, self-opinionated, pig-headed, mulish, unprogressive, one-ideaed, stick-in-the-mud, reactionary, blimpish, besotted, infatuated, unreasoning.

Wild, giddy, dizzy, thoughtless, eccentric, odd, extravagant, quixotic, light-headed, rantipole, high-flying, crack-brained, cracked, cranky, hare-brained, scatter-brained, scatter-pated, unballasted, ridiculous, frivolous, balmy (or barmy), daft (503).

Applied to actions: Foolish, unwise, injudicious, improper, imprudent, unreasonable, nonsensical, absurd, ridiculous, silly, stupid, asinine, ill-imagined, ill-advised, ill-judged, ill-devised, tactless, inconsistent, irrational, unphilosophical, extravagant, preposterous, egregious, footling, imprudent, indiscreet, improvident, impolitic, improper (645, 647).

(*Phrases*) Dead from the neck up; concrete above the ears.

Without rhyme or reason; penny-wise and pound-foolish.

500 SAGE (*Substantives*), wise man, master-mind, thinker, *savant*, expert, luminary, adept, authority, egghead.

Oracle, a shining light, *esprit fort*, intellectual, high-brow, pundit, academist, academician, philomath, schoolman, magi, a Solomon, Nestor, Solon, Socrates, a second Daniel.

(*Adjectives*) Venerable, reverend, authoritative.

(*Phrases*) 'A Daniel come to judgment'; the wise men of the East.

(*Ironically*) Wiseacre, know-all, bigwig.

501 FOOL (*Substantives*), blockhead, bonehead, idiot, tom-fool, lowbrow, simpleton, simp, sap, softy, sawney, witling, ass, donkey, goat, goose, ninny, dolt, booby, boob, noodle, muff, mug, muggins, juggins, owl, cuckoo, gowk, numskull, noddy, dumb-bell, gomeril, half-wit, imbecile, ninnyhammer, mutt, driveller, cretin, moron, natural, lackbrain, child, infant, baby, innocent, greenhorn, zany, zombie, gaby.

Dunce, lout, loon, oaf, dullard, duffer, calf, colt, buzzard, block, stick, stock, clod-poll, clot-poll, clodhopper, clod, lubber, bull-calf, bullhead, fat-head, thick-skull, dunderhead, addle-head, dizzard, hoddy-doddy, looby, Joe Soap, nincompoop, poop, put, *un sot à triple étage*, loggerhead, sot, shallow-brain, jobbernowl, changeling, dotard, driveller, moon-calf, giddy-head, gobemouche, rantipole, muddler, stick-in-the-mud, old woman, April fool.

(*Phrases*) One who is not likely to set the Thames on fire; one who did not invent gunpowder; one who is no conjurer; *qui n'a pas inventé la poudre*; who could not say 'Bo' to a goose; one with his upper storey to let; no fool like an old fool.

Men of Gotham; men of Boeotia.

502 SANITY (*Substantives*), rationality; being in one's senses, in one's right mind, in one's sober senses; sobriety, lucidity, lucid interval, sound mind, *mens sana*.

(*Verbs*) To be sane, etc., to retain one's senses, reason, etc.

To become sane, come to one's senses, sober down.

To render sane, bring to one's senses, to sober.

(*Adjectives*) Sane, rational, reasonable, *compos*, in one's sober senses, in one's right mind, sober-minded.

(*Phrase*) In full possession of one's faculties.

(*Adverbs*) Sanely, soberly, etc.

503 INSANITY (*Substantives*), lunacy, madness, unsoundness, derangement, psychosis, neurosis, alienation, aberration, schizophrenia, split personality, dementia, paranoia, mania, melancholia, hypochondria, calenture, frenzy, phrenitis, raving, monomania, megalomania, kleptomania, dipsomania, etc., disordered intellect, incoherence, wandering, delirium, hallucination, lycanthropy, eccentricity (499), dementation; Bedlam.

(*Phrases*) The horrors; the jim-jams; pink spiders; snakes in the boots.

(*Verbs*) To be or become insane, etc., to lose one's senses, wits, reason, faculties, etc., to run mad, run amuck, go off one's head, rave, dote, ramble, wander, drivel.

To render or drive mad; to madden, dementate, turn the brain, addl
the wits, turn one's head, befool, infatuate, craze.

(*Phrases*) *Battre la campagne; avoir le diable au corps.*

(*Adjectives*) Insane, mad, lunatic, crazy, crazed, *non compos*, cracked
cranky, loco, touched, deficient, wanting, out of one's mind, off one'
head or nut or onion, bereft of reason, unsettled in one's mind, unhinged
insensate, reasonless, beside oneself.

Demented, daft, dotty, potty, dippy, scatty, loopy, batty, bats
wacky, crackers, cuckoo, haywire, bughouse, bugs, nuts, possessed
maddened, moon-struck, mad-brained, maniac, maniacal, delirious
incoherent, rambling, doting, doited, gaga.

Wandering, frantic, phrenetic, paranoiac, schizophrenic, megalo
maniacal, kleptomaniacal, etc., raving, corybantic, dithyrambic, rabid
pixillated, light-headed, giddy, vertiginous, wild, haggard, flighty
neurotic, distracted, distraught, hag-ridden, *écervelé*, *tête montée*.

(*Phrases*) The head being turned; having a screw (or a tile) loose
far gone; stark staring mad; mad as a March hare; mad as a hatter; o
unsound mind; up the pole; bats in the belfry; the devil being in one
dizzy as a goose; candidate for Bedlam; like one possessed.

The wits going wool-gathering or bird's-nesting.

504 MADMAN (*Substantives*), lunatic, maniac, bedlamite, energumen, raver
monomaniac, paranoiac, schizophrenic, nut, screwball, crackpot, madcap
megalomaniac, dipsomaniac, kleptomaniac, psychopath, hypochondriac
malade imaginaire, crank, maenad.

SECTION VI—EXTENSION OF THOUGHT

1°. *To the Past*

505 MEMORY (*Substantives*), remembrance, reminiscence, recognition, anamnesis, retention, retentive-
ness, readiness, tenacity.

Recurrence, recollection, retrospection, retrospect, flash-back, afterthought, hindsight.

Token of remembrance, reminder,
memorial, memento, souvenir, keep-
sake, relic, reliquary, memorandum,
aide-mémoire, remembrancer,
prompter.

Things to be remembered, *memorabilia.*

Art of memory, artificial memory,
memoria technica, mnemonics;
Mnemosyne.

(*Phrases*) The tablets of the memory; *l'esprit de l'escalier.*

(*Verbs*) To remember, retain, mind,
bear or keep in mind, have or carry
in the memory, know by heart or by
rote; recognize.

506 OBLIVION (*Substantives*), for-
getfulness, amnesia, obliteration
(552), a short memory; a lapse o
memory; the memory failing, being in fault, or deserting one; the
waters of Lethe, Nepenthe, *tabula
rasa.*

(*Verbs*) To forget, lose, unlearn,
efface, expunge, blot out, etc. (552);
discharge from the memory.

To slip, escape, fade, die away
from the memory, to sink into
oblivion.

(*Phrases*) To cast behind one's
back; to have a short memory; to
put out of one's head: to apply the
sponge; to think no more of; to
consign to oblivion; to let bygones be
bygones.

(*Adjectives*) Forgotten, etc., lost,
effaced, blotted out, obliterated, discharged, sponged out, buried or sunk
in oblivion, out of mind, clean out

To be deeply impressed, live, remain, or dwell in the memory; to be ored up, bottled up, to sink in the ind, to rankle, etc.

To recollect, call to mind, bethink oneself, recall, call up, retrace, arry one's thoughts back, review, ok back, rake up, brush up, think upon, call to remembrance, tax the emory.

To suggest, prompt, hint, recall to mind, put in mind, remind, hisper, call up, summon up, renew, commend to.

To say by heart, repeat by rote, say one's lesson, repeat as a parrot.

To commit to memory, get or learn by heart or rote, memorize, con, n over, repeat; to fix, imprint, impress, stamp, grave, engrave, store, easure up, bottle up, embalm, enshrine, etc., in the memory; to load, ore, stuff, or burden the memory with; to commemorate (883).

(*Phrase*) To have at one's fingers' ends.

To jog or refresh the memory; to pull by the sleeve; to bring back to e memory; to keep the memory alive; to keep the wound green; to open old sores; to put in remembrance.

(*Adjectives*) Remembering, etc., mindful, remembered, etc., fresh, een, unforgotten, present to the mind; living in, being in, or within e's memory; indelible, ineffaceable, green in remembrance, reminisntial, commemorative.

(*Adverbs*) By heart, by rote, *memoriter*, without book; in memory of, memoriam.

of one's head or recollection, past recollection, unremembered.

Forgetful, oblivious, unmindful, mindless; Lethean.

2°. *To the Future*

507 EXPECTATION (*Substantives*), xpectance, expectancy, anticipation, orestalling, foreseeing (510); reckong, calculation.

Contemplation, prospect, look-out, utlook (121), perspective, horizon, ista, hope, trust (858), abeyance, aiting, suspense.

(*Phrase*) The torments of Tantalus.

(*Verbs*) To expect, look for, look ut for, look forward to, anticipate, ontemplate, flatter oneself, to dare o say, foresee (510), forestall, reckon pon, count upon, lay one's account , to calculate upon, rely upon, uild upon, make sure of, prepare neself for, keep in view, not to onder at.

To wait, tarry, lie in wait, watch r, abide, to bide one's time.

To hold out, raise, or excite exectation, to bid fair, to promise, to ugur, etc. (511).

(*Phrases*) To count one's chickens efore they are hatched.

508 INEXPECTATION (*Substantives*), non-expectation; blow, shock, surprise (870).

False or vain expectation, miscalculation.

(*Phrase*) A bolt from the blue.

(*Verbs*) Not to expect, not to look for, etc., to be taken by surprise, to start, come upon, to fall upon, not to bargain for, to miscalculate.

To be unexpected, etc., to crop up, pop up, to come unawares, suddenly, abruptly, like a thunderbolt, creep upon, burst upon, bounce upon; surprise, take aback, stun, stagger, startle.

(*Phrases*) To reckon without one's host; to trust to a broken reed.

To drop from the clouds; you could have knocked me down with a feather.

(*Adjectives*) Non-expectant, surprised, taken by surprise, unwarned, unaware, startled, etc., taken aback.

Unexpected, unanticipated, unlooked-for, unhoped-for, unforeseen,

To have in store for; to have a rod in pickle.

(*Adjectives*) Expectant, expecting, etc., prepared for, gaping for, ready for, agog, anxious, ardent, eager, breathless, sanguine.

Expected, anticipated, foreseen, etc., long expected, impending, prospective, in prospect.

(*Adverbs*) With breathless expectation, on tenterhooks.

(*Phrases*) On the tiptoe of expectation; on edge; looming in the distance; the wish father to the thought; we shall see; *nous verrons*.

---

beyond expectation, abrupt, sudden contrary to or against expectation unannounced, unheralded; back handed.

(*Adverbs*) Suddenly, abruptly, un expectedly, plump, pop, *à l'improviste* unawares, without notice or warning (113).

(*Phrases*) Like a thief in the night who would have thought it?

509 Failure of expectation.

DISAPPOINTMENT (*Substantives*) vain expectation, blighted hope, surprise, astonishment (870); balk, after clap, miscalculation.

(*Phrase*) 'There's many a slip 'twixt cup and lip.'

(*Verbs*) To be disappointed, etc., to miscalculate; to look blank, to look blue, to look or stand aghast.

To disappoint, balk, bilk, tantalize, let down, play false, stand up, dumbfound, dash one's hope (859), sell.

(*Adjectives*) Disappointed, disconcerted, aghast, blue, out of one's reckoning.

Happening, contrary to or against expectation.

(*Phrase*) *Parturiunt montes, nascetur ridiculus mus.*

---

510 FORESIGHT (*Substantives*), prospiscience, prescience, foreknowledge, forethought, forecast, prevision, prognosis, precognition, second sight, clairvoyance.

Anticipation, foretaste, prenotion, presentiment, foregone conclusion, providence, discretion, prudence, sagacity.

Announcement, prospectus, programme, policy (626).

(*Verbs*) To foresee, foreknow, forejudge, forecast, predict (511), anticipate, look forwards or beyond; look, peep, or pry into the future.

(*Phrases*) To keep a sharp look out for; to have an eye to the future; *respice finem*.

(*Adjectives*) Foreseeing, etc., prescient, weather-wise, far-sighted, far-seeing; provident, prudent, rational, sagacious, perspicacious.

---

511 PREDICTION (*Substantives*), announcement, prognosis, forecast, weird, prophecy, vaticination, mantology, prognostication, astrology, horoscopy, haruspicy, auguration, auspices, bodement, omination, augury, foreboding, abodement, aboding, horoscope, nativity, genethliacs, fortune-telling, crystal-gazing, palmistry, chiromancy, oneiromancy, sortilege, *sortes Virgilianae,* soothsaying, ominousness, divination (992).

Place of prediction, adytum, tripod.

(*Verbs*) To predict, prognosticate, prophesy, vaticinate, presage, augur, bode, forebode, divine, foretell, croak, soothsay, auspicate, to cast a horoscope or nativity, tell one's fortune, read one's hand.

To foretoken, betoken, prefigure, portend, foreshadow, foreshow, usher in, herald, signify, premise, announce, point to, admonish, warn, forewarn, advise.

(*Adjectives*) Predicting, etc., predictive, prophetic, fatidical, vaticinal, oracular, Sibylline.

Ominous, portentous, augural, auspicious, monitory, premonitory, significant of, pregnant with, weatherwise, bodeful, big with fate.

(*Phrase*) 'Coming events cast their shadows before.'

512 OMEN (*Substantives*), portent, presage, prognostic, augury, auspice, sign, forerunner, precursor (64), harbinger, herald, monition, warning, avant-courier, pilot-balloon, handwriting on the wall, rise and fall of the barometer, a bird of ill omen, a sign of the times, gathering clouds.

(*Phrases*) Touch wood! *absit omen.*

513 ORACLE (*Substantives*), prophet, seer, soothsayer, haruspex, fortune-teller, spaewife, palmist, gipsy, wizard, witch, geomancer, Sibyl, Python, Pythoness, *Pythia*, Pythian oracle, Delphic oracle, Old Moore, Zadkiel, Mother Shipton, Witch of Endor, Sphinx, Tiresias, Cassandra, Oedipus, Sibylline leaves.

SECTION VII—CREATIVE THOUGHT

514 SUPPOSITION (*Substantives*), conjecture, surmise, presurmise, speculation, inkling, guess, guess-work, shot, divination, conceit; assumption, postulation, hypothesis, presupposition, postulate, *postulatum*, presumption, theory, thesis; suggestion, proposition, motion, proposal, allusion, insinuation, innuendo.

(*Phrases*) A rough guess; a lucky shot.

(*Verbs*) To suppose, conjecture, surmise, guess, divine, theorize, give a guess, make a shot, hazard a conjecture, throw out a conjecture, etc., presuppose, fancy, wis, take it, dare to say, take it into one's head, assume, believe, postulate, posit, presume, presurmise.

To suggest, hint, insinuate, put forth, propound, propose, start, allude to, prompt, put a case, move, make a motion.

To suggest itself, occur to one, come into one's head; to run in the head; to haunt (505).

(*Phrases*) To put it into one's head; 'thereby hangs a tale.'

(*Adjectives*) Supposing, etc., supposed, supposititious, suppositious, suppositive, reputed, putative, suggestive, allusive, conjectural, presumptive, hypothetical, theoretical, warranted, authorized, mooted, conjecturable, supposable.

(*Adverbs*) If, if so be, an, gin, maybe, perhaps, on the supposition, in the event of, as if, *ex hypothesi, quasi.*

515 IMAGINATION (*Substantives*), fancy, conception, ideality, idealism, inspiration, afflatus, verve, dreaming, somnambulism, frenzy, ecstasy, excogitation, reverie, *Schwärmerei*, trance, imagery, vision; Pegasus.

Invention, inventiveness, originality, fertility, romanticism, utopianism, castle-building.

Conceit, maggot, figment, coinage, fiction, romance, novel (594), myth, Arabian Nights, fairyland, faerie, the man in the moon, dream, day-dream, pipe-dream, nightmare, vapour, chimera, phantom, phantasy, fantasia, whim, whimsy, vagary, rhapsody, extravaganza, air-drawn dagger, bugbear, men in buckram, castle in the air, air-built castle, castle in Spain, will-o'-the-wisp, ignis fatuus, jack-o'-lantern, Utopia, Atlantis, Shangri-la, land of Prester John, millennium, golden age, *fata morgana* (443).

A visionary, romancer, rhapsodist, high-flyer, enthusiast, idealist, energumen, dreamer, seer, fanatic, knight-errant, Don Quixote.

(*Phrases*) Flight of fancy; fumes of fancy; fine frenzy; thick-coming fancies; coinage of the brain; the mind's eye; a stretch of imagination; 'such stuff as dreams are made on.'

(*Verbs*) To imagine, fancy, conceive, ideate, idealize, realize, objectify; fancy or picture to oneself; create, originate, devise, invent, coin, fabricate, make up, mint, improvise, excogitate, conjure up.

(*Phrases*) To take into one's head; to figure to oneself; to strain or crack one's invention; to strike out something new; to give a loose to the fancy; to give the reins to the imagination; to set one's wits to work; to rack or cudgel one's brains.

(*Adjectives*) Imagining, imagined, etc.; ideal, unreal, unsubstantial, imaginary, *in nubibus*, fabulous, fictitious, legendary, mythological, chimerical, *ben trovato*, fanciful, faerie, fairylike, air-drawn, air-built, original, fantastic, fantastical, whimsical, high-flown.

Imaginative, inventive, creative, fertile, romantic, flighty, extravagant, high-flown, fanatic, enthusiastic, Utopian, Quixotic.

DIVISION II—COMMUNICATION OF IDEAS

SECTION I—NATURE OF IDEAS COMMUNICATED

516 Idea to be conveyed.

MEANING (*Substantives*), signification, sense, import, purport, significance, drift, gist, acceptation, acceptance, bearing, interpretation (522), reading, tenor, allusion, spirit, colouring, expression.

Literal meaning, literality, obvious meaning, grammatical sense, first blush, *prima facie* meaning; after-acceptation.

Equivalent meaning, synonym, synonymity.

Thing signified: Matter, subject, substance, pith, marrow, argument, text; sum and substance.

(*Verbs*) To mean, signify, express, import, purport, convey, breathe, imply, bespeak, speak of, tell of, touch on, bear a sense, involve, declare (527), insinuate, allude to, point to, indicate, drive at; to come to the point, give vent to; to stand for.

To take, understand, receive, or accept in a particular sense.

(*Adjectives*) Meaning, etc., significant, significative, significatory, literal, expressive, explicit, suggestive, allusive; pithy, pointed, epigrammatic, telling, striking, full of meaning, pregnant with meaning.

517 Absence of meaning.

UNMEANINGNESS (*Substantives*), empty sound, a dead letter, scrabble, scribble; inexpressiveness, vagueness (519).

Nonsense, stuff, balderdash (497), jabber, gibberish, palaver, rigmarole, twaddle, tosh, bosh, bull, rubbish, rot, empty babble, empty sound, verbiage, *nugae*, truism, moonshine, inanity.

(*Verbs*) To mean nothing, to be unmeaning, etc.; to scribble, jabber, gibber, babble.

(*Adjectives*) Unmeaning, meaningless, nonsensical, void of meaning, of sense, etc., senseless, not significant, undefined, tacit, not expressed.

Inexpressible, indefinable, undefinable, unmeant, unconceived.

Trashy, trumpery, twaddling, etc.

(*Phrases*) *Vox et praeterea nihil*; 'a tale told by an idiot, full of sound and fury, signifying nothing'; 'sounding brass and tinkling cymbal.'

(*Adverb*) Tacitly.

Synonymous, equivalent, tantamount; the same thing as.
Implied, tacit, understood, implicit, inferred, latent.
(*Adverbs*) Meaningly, literally, etc., *videlicet* (522), viz., i.e.
(*Phrases*) *Au pied de la lettre*; so to speak; to that effect; so to express oneself; as it were; that is to say; *façon de parler*.

518 INTELLIGIBILITY (*Substantives*), clearness, lucidity, perspicuity, explicitness, distinctness, plain speaking, expressiveness, legibility, visibility (446); precision (494).

Intelligence, comprehension, understanding, learning (539).

(*Phrases*) A word to the wise; *verbum sapienti*.

(*Verbs*) To be intelligible, etc.

To render intelligible, etc., to simplify, clear up, throw light upon.

To understand, comprehend, follow, take, take in, catch, catch on to, twig, dig, get the hang of, get wise to, grasp, sense, make out, get, collect; master, tumble to, rumble.

(*Phrases*) It tells its own tale; he who runs may read; to stand to reason; to speak for itself.

To come to an understanding; to see with half an eye.

(*Adjectives*) Intelligible, clear, lucid, understandable, explicit, expressive, significant, express, distinct, precise, definite, well-defined, perspicuous, transpicuous, striking, plain, obvious, manifest, palpable, glaring, transparent, above-board, unambiguous, unmistakable, legible, open, positive, expressive (516), unconfused, unequivocal, pronounced, graphic, readable.

(*Phrases*) Clear as day; clear as crystal; clear as noonday; not to be mistaken; plain to the meanest capacity; plain as a pikestaff; in plain English.

519 UNINTELLIGIBILITY (*Substantives*), incomprehensibility, inconceivability, darkness (421), imperspicuity, obscurity, confusion, perplexity, imbroglio, indistinctness, mistiness, indefiniteness, vagueness, ambiguity, looseness, uncertainty, mysteriousness (526), paradox, inexplicability, incommunicability, spinosity.

Jargon, gibberish, rigmarole, rodomontade, etc. (497); paradox, riddle, enigma, puzzle (533).

Double or High Dutch, Greek, Hebrew, etc.

(*Verbs*) To be unintelligible, etc., to pass comprehension.

To render unintelligible, etc., to perplex, confuse, confound, bewilder, darken, moither (475).

Not to understand, etc., to lose, miss, etc., to lose the clue.

(*Phrases*) Not to know what to make of; not to be able to make either head or tail of; to be all at sea; to play at cross purposes; to beat about the bush.

(*Adjectives*) Unintelligible, incognizable, inapprehensible, incomprehensible, inconceivable, unimaginable, unknowable, inexpressible, undefinable, incommunicable, above or past or beyond comprehension, inexplicable, illegible, undecipherable, inscrutable, unfathomable, beyond one's depth, paradoxical, insoluble, impenetrable.

Obscure, dark, confused, indistinct, indefinite, misty, nebulous, intricate, undefined, ill-defined, indeterminate, perplexed, loose, vague, ambiguous, disconnected, incoherent, unaccountable, puzzling, enigmatical, hieroglyphic, mysterious, mystic, mystical, at cross purposes.

Hidden, recondite, abstruse, crabbed, transcendental, far-fetched, *in nubibus*, searchless, unconceived, unimagined.

(*Phrases*) Greek to one; without rhyme or reason; *obscurum per obscurius; lucus a non lucendo*.

520 Having a double sense.

EQUIVOCALNESS (*Substantives*), double meaning, quibble, equivoque, equivocation, *double-entendre*, paragram, anagram, amphibology, amphiboly, ambiloquy, prevarication, white lie, mental reservation, tergiversation, slip of the tongue, *lapsus linguae*, a pun, play on words, homonym.

Having a doubtful meaning, ambiguity (475), homonymy.

Having a false meaning (544), *suggestio falsi*.

(*Verbs*) To be equivocal, etc., to have two senses, etc., to equivocate, prevaricate, tergiversate, palter to the understanding, to pun.

(*Adjectives*) Equivocal, ambiguous, amphibolous, amphibological, homonymous, double-tongued, double-edged, left-handed, equivocatory, paltering.

(*Adverb*) Over the left.

521 METAPHOR (*Substantives*), figure, metonymy, trope, catachresis, synecdoche, figure of speech, figurativeness, image, imagery, metalepsis, type (22), symbol, symbolism (550), tropology.

Personification, prosopopaeia, allegory, apologue, parable.

Implication, inference, allusion, application, adumbration, hidden meaning.

Allegorist, tropist, symbolist.

(*Verbs*) To employ metaphor, etc., to personify, allegorize, adumbrate, shadow forth, imply, understand, apply, allude to.

(*Adjectives*) Metaphorical, figurative, catachrestical, typical, tropical, parabolic, allegorical, allusive, symbolic (550), symbolistic, implied, inferential, implicit, understood.

(*Adverbs*) So to speak, as it were.

(*Phrases*) Where more is meant than meets the ear; in a manner of speaking; *façon de parler*; in a Pickwickian sense.

522 INTERPRETATION (*Substantives*), exegesis, explanation, meaning (516), explication, expounding, exposition, rendition, reddition.

Translation, version, rendering, construction, reading, spelling, restoration, metaphrase, literal translation, free translation, paraphrase.

Comment, commentary, inference, illustration, exemplification, definition, *éclaircissement*, elucidation, crib, cab, gloss, glossary, annotation, *scholium*, marginalia, note, clue, key, sidelight, master-key (631), rationale, denouement, solution, answer (462), object lesson.

Palaeography, dictionary, glossology, etc. (562), semantics, semasiology, oneirocritics, oneirocriticism, hermeneutics.

(*Verbs*) To interpret, expound, explain, clear up, construe, translate, render, English, do into, turn into, transfuse the sense of.

To read, spell, make out, decipher, decode, unfold, disentangle, elicit the

523 MISINTERPRETATION (*Substantives*), misapprehension, misunderstanding, misacceptation, misconstruction, misspelling, misapplication, catachresis, mistake (495), cross-reading, cross-purpose.

Misrepresentation, perversion, falsification, misquotation, garbling, exaggeration (549), false colouring, abuse of terms, parody, travesty, misstatement, etc. (544).

(*Verbs*) To misinterpret, misapprehend, misunderstand, misconceive, misdeem, misspell, mistranslate, misconstrue, misapply, mistake (495).

To misstate, etc. (544); to pervert, falsify, distort, misrepresent, torture, travesty; to stretch, strain, wring, or wrest the sense or meaning; to put a bad or false construction on; to misquote, garble, belie, explain away.

(*Phrases*) To give a false colouring to; to be or play at cross-purposes; to put a false construction on.

meaning of, make sense of, find the key of, unriddle, unravel, solve, resolve (480), restore.

To elucidate, throw light upon, illustrate, exemplify, expound, annotate, comment upon, define, unfold.

(*Adjectives*) Explanatory, expository, explicatory, explicative, exegetical, hermeneutic, constructive, inferential.

Paraphrastic, metaphrastic; literal, plain, simple, strict, synonymous; polyglot.

(*Adverbs*) That is to say, *id est* (or i.e.), *videlicet* (or viz.), in other words, in plain words, simply, in plain English.

Literally, word for word, verbatim, *au pied de la lettre*, strictly speaking (494).

(*Adjectives*) Misinterpreted, etc., untranslated, untranslatable.

(*Phrase*) *Traduttori traditori.*

———

524 INTERPRETER (*Substantives*), expositor, expounder, exponent, demonstrator, scholiast, commentator, annotator, metaphrast, paraphrast, palaeographer, spokesman, speaker, mouthpiece, guide, dragoman, cicerone, conductor, courier, showman, barker, oneirocritic; Oedipus (513).

SECTION II—MODES OF COMMUNICATION

525 MANIFESTATION (*Substantives*), expression, showing, etc., disclosure (529), presentation, indication, exposition, demonstration, exhibition, production, display, showing off.

An exhibit, an exhibitor.

Openness, frankness, plain speaking (543), publication, publicity (531).

(*Verbs*) To manifest, make manifest, etc., show, express, indicate, point out, bring forth, bring forward, trot out, set forth, exhibit, expose, produce, present, bring into view, set before one, hold up to view, lay open, lay bare, expose to view, set before one's eyes, show up, shadow forth, bring to light, display, demonstrate, unroll, unveil, unmask, disclose (529).

To elicit, educe, draw out, bring out, unearth, disinter.

To be manifested, etc., to appear, transpire, come to light (446), to come out, to crop up, get wind.

(*Phrases*) Hold up the mirror; draw, lift up, raise, or remove the curtain; show one's true colours; throw off the mask.

To speak for itself; to stand to reason; to stare one in the face; to tell its own tale; to give vent to.

526 LATENCY (*Substantives*), secrecy, secretness, privacy, invisibility (447), mystery, occultness, darkness, reticence, silence (585), closeness, reserve, inexpression; a sealed book, a dark horse, an undercurrent.

Retirement, delitescence, seclusion (893).

(*Phrases*) More is meant than meets the ear (or eye).

(*Verbs*) To be latent, etc., to lurk, underlie, escape observation, smoulder; to keep back, reserve, suppress, keep close, etc. (528).

To render latent (528).

(*Phrases*) Hold one's tongue; hold one's peace; leave in the dark; to keep one's own counsel; to keep mum; to seal the lips; not to breathe a syllable about.

(*Adjectives*) Latent, lurking, secret, close, unapparent, unknown (491), dark, delitescent, in the background, occult, cryptic, snug, private, privy, *in petto*, anagogic, sequestered, dormant, smouldering.

Inconspicuous, unperceived, invisible, (447) unseen, unwitnessed, **impenetrable, unespied, unsuspected.**

(*Adjectives*) Manifest, clear, apparent, evident, visible (446), prominent, in the foreground, salient, signal, striking, notable, conspicuous, palpable, patent, overt, flagrant, stark, glaring, open.

Manifested, shown, expressed, etc., disclosed (529), frank, capable of being shown, producible.

(*Phrases*) As plain as a pikestaff; as plain as the nose on one's face.

(*Adverbs*) Openly, before one's eyes, face to face, above-board, in open court, in open daylight, in the light of day, in the open streets, on the stage, on show.

Untold, unsaid, unwritten, unpublished, unmentioned, unbreathed, untalked-of, unsung, unpronounced, unpromulgated, unreported, unexposed, unproclaimed, unexpressed, not expressed, tacit, implicit, implied, undeveloped, embryonic, unsolved, unexplained, undiscovered, untraced, untracked, unexplored.

(*Phrase*) No news being good news.

(*Adverbs*) Secretly, etc., *sub silentio*.

(*Phrases*) In the background; behind one's back; under the table; behind the scenes; between the lines.

---

527 INFORMATION (*Substantives*), gen, pukka gen, low-down, enlightenment, communication, intimation, notice, notification, enunciation, announcement, annunciation, statement, specification, report, advice, monition, mention, acquaintance (490), acquainting, etc., outpouring, intercommunication, communicativeness.

An informant, teller, tipster, spy, nose, nark, stool-pigeon, intelligencer, correspondent, reporter, messenger, newsmonger, gossip (532).

Hint, suggestion (514), wrinkle, tip, pointer, insinuation, innuendo, wink, glance, leer, nod, shrug, gesture, whisper, implication, cue, office, byplay, eye-opener.

(*Phrases*) A word to the wise; *verbum sapienti*; a broad hint; a straight tip; a stage whisper.

(*Verbs*) To inform, acquaint, tell, mention, express, intimate, impart, communicate, apprise, post, make known, notify, signify to, let one know, advise, state, specify, give notice, announce, annunciate, publish, report, set forth, bring word, send word, leave word, write word, declare, certify, depose, pronounce, explain, undeceive, enlighten, put wise, set right, open the eyes of, convey the knowledge of, give an account of; instruct (537).

To hint, give an inkling of; give, throw out, or drop a hint, insinuate, allude to, glance at, touch on, make

528 CONCEALMENT (*Substantives*), hiding, occultation, etc., secrecy, stealth, stealthiness, slyness (702), disguise, incognito, privacy, masquerade, camouflage, smoke screen, mystery, mystification, freemasonry, reservation, suppression, secretiveness, reticence, reserve, uncommunicativeness; secret path.

A mask, visor, ambush, etc. (530), enigma, etc. (533).

(*Phrases*) A needle in a bundle of hay; a nigger in the woodpile; a skeleton in the cupboard; a family skeleton.

(*Verbs*) To conceal, hide, put out of sight, secrete, cover, envelop, screen, cloak, veil, shroud, enshroud, shade, muffle, mask, disguise, camouflage, ensconce, eclipse.

To keep from, lock up, bury, cache, sink, suppress, stifle, withhold, reserve, burke, hush up, keep snug or close or dark.

To keep in ignorance, blind, hoodwink, mystify, pose, puzzle, perplex, embarrass, flummox, bewilder, bamboozle, etc. (545).

To be concealed, etc., to lurk, skulk, smoulder, lie hid, lie in ambush, lie perdu, lie low, lie doggo, sneak, slink, prowl, gumshoe, retire, steal into, steal along.

To conceal oneself, put on a veil, etc. (530), masquerade.

(*Phrases*) To draw or close the curtain; not breathe a word about;

allusion to, to wink, to tip the wink, glance, leer, nod, shrug, give the cue, give the office, give the tip, wave, whisper, suggest, prompt, whisper in the ear, give one to understand.

To be informed, etc., of, made acquainted with; to hear of, get a line on, understand.

To come to one's ears, to come to one's knowledge, to reach one's ears.

(*Adjectives*) Informed, etc., of, made acquainted with, in the know, hep; undeceived.

Reported, made known (531), bruited.

Expressive, significant, pregnant with meaning, etc. (516), declaratory, enunciative, nuncupatory, expository, communicatory, communicative, insinuative.

(*Adverbs*) Expressively, significantly, etc.

(*Phrases*) A little bird told me; *on dit*; from information received.

let it go no farther; keep it under your hat.

To play at bo-peep; to play at hide-and-seek; to hide under a bushel; to throw dust in the eyes.

(*Adjectives*) Concealed, hid, hidden, etc., secret, clandestine, perdu, close, private, privy, furtive, surreptitious, stealthy, feline, underhand, sly, sneaking, skulking, hole-and-corner, undivulged, unrevealed, undisclosed, incognito, incommunicado.

Mysterious, mystic, mystical, dark, enigmatical, problematical, anagogical, paradoxical, occult, cryptic, gnostic, cabbalistic, esoteric, recondite, abstruse, unexplained, impenetrable, undiscoverable, inexplicable, unknowable, bewildering, baffling.

Covered, closed, shrouded, veiled, masked, screened, shaded, disguised, under cover, under a cloud, veil, etc., in a fog, haze, mist, etc., under an eclipse; inviolate, inviolable, confidential, under wraps.

Reserved, uncommunicative, secretive, buttoned up, taciturn (585).

(*Phrase*) Close as wax.

(*Adverbs*) Secretly, clandestinely, incognito, privily, in secret, *in camera*, with closed doors, *à huis clos*, *à la dérobée*, under the rose, *sub rosa*, privately, in private, aside, on the sly, *sub silentio*, behind one's back, under the counter, behind the curtain, behind the scenes.

Confidentially, between ourselves, between you and me, *entre nous*, *inter nos*, in strict confidence, on the strict q.t., off the record, it must go no farther.

(*Phrases*) Like a thief in the night; under the seal of secrecy, of confession; between you and me and the gate-post; 'tell it not in Gath'; nobody any the wiser.

529 DISCLOSURE (*Substantives*), revealment, revelation, disinterment, exposition, show-down, exposure, effusion, outpouring.

Acknowledgment, avowal, confession; an *exposé*, denouement.

A telltale, talebearer, informer, stool-pigeon, nark, nose.

(*Verbs*) To disclose, open, lay open, divulge, reveal, bewray, discover, unfold, let drop, let fall, let out, let on, spill, lay open, acknowledge, allow, concede, grant, admit, own, own up, confess, avow, unseal, unveil, unmask, uncover, unkennel, unearth (525).

530 AMBUSH (*Substantives*), hiding-place, hide, retreat, cover, lurking-hole, secret place, cubby-hole, recess, closet, priest's hole, crypt, cache, ambuscade, *guet-apens*, *adytum*, dungeon, oubliette.

A mask, veil, visor (or vizor), eye-shade, blinkers, cloak, screen, hoarding, curtain, shade, cover, disguise, masquerade dress, domino.

(*Verbs*) To lie in ambush, lurk, couch, lie in wait for, lay or set a trap for (545).

To blab, peach, squeal, let out, let fall, let on, betray, give away, tell tales, speak out, blurt out, vent, give vent to, come out with, round on, split; publish (531).

To make no secret of, to disabuse, unbeguile, undeceive, set right, correct.

To be disclosed, revealed, etc., to come out, to transpire, to ooze out, to leak out, to creep out, to get wind, to come to light.

(*Phrases*) To let into the secret; to let the cat out of the bag; to spill the beans; to unburden or disburden one's mind or conscience; to open one's mind; to unbosom oneself; to make a clean breast of it; to come clean; to give the show away; to own the soft impeachment; to tell tales out of school; to show one's hand; to turn Queen's (or King's or State's) evidence.

Murder will out.

(*Adjectives*) Disclosed, revealed, divulged, laid open, etc., unriddled, etc.; outspoken, etc. (543).

Open, public, exoteric.

(*Interjection*) Out with it!

531 PUBLICATION (*Substantives*), announcement, notification, enunciation, annunciation, advertisement, promulgation, circulation, propagation, edition, redaction, proclamation, hue and cry, the Press, journalism, wireless, radio, broadcasting, television.

Publicity, notoriety, currency, cry, bruit, rumour, fame, report (532), *on dit*, flagrancy, limelight, town-talk, small talk, table-talk, puffery, bally-hoo, *réclame*, the light of day, daylight.

Notice, notification, manifesto, propaganda, advertisement, blurb, circular, placard, bill, *affiche*, poster, newspaper, journal, daily, periodical, weekly, gazette; personal column, agony column.

Publisher (593), publicity agent, advertising agent: tout, barker, town crier.

(*Phrases*) An open secret; *un secret de Polichinelle*.

(*Verbs*) To publish, make known, announce, notify, annunciate, gazette, set forth, give forth, give out, broach, voice, utter, advertise, circularize, placard, *afficher*, circulate, propagate, spread, spread abroad, broadcast, edit, redact, rumour, diffuse, disseminate, celebrate, blaze about; blaze or noise abroad; bruit, buzz, bandy, hawk about, trumpet, proclaim, herald, puff, boost, splash, plug, boom, give tongue, raise a cry, raise a hue and cry, tell the world, popularize; bring, lay or drag before the public, give currency to, ventilate, bring out.

(*Phrases*) To proclaim from the house-tops; to publish in the gazette; to send round the crier; with beat of drum.

To be published, etc., to become public, to go forth, get abroad, get about, get wind, take air, get afloat, acquire currency, get in the papers, spread, go the rounds, buzz about, blow about.

To pass from mouth to mouth; to spread like wildfire.

(*Adjectives*) Published, etc., made public, in circulation, exoteric, rumoured, rife, current, afloat, notorious, flagrant, whispered, buzzed about, in every one's mouth, reported, trumpet-tongued; encyclical.

(*Phrases*) As the story runs; to all whom it may concern.

(*Interjections*) Oyez! O yes! notice is hereby given!

532 NEWS (*Substantives*), piece of information, intelligence, tidings, budget of news, word, advice, message, communication, errand, embassy, dispatch, bulletin.

533 SECRET (*Substantives*), *arcanum*, *penetralia*, profound secret, mystery, crux, problem, enigma, teaser, poser, riddle, puzzle, conundrum, charade, rebus, logograph,

Report, story, scoop, beat, rumour, canard, hearsay, *on dit*, fame, talk, gossip, tittle-tattle, *oui-dire*, scandal, buzz, bruit, *chronique scandaleuse*, town talk.

Letter, postcard, airgraph, telegram, wire, cable, wireless message, radiogram.

Newsmonger, scandalmonger, scaremonger, alarmist, talebearer, tattler, gossip (527), local correspondent, special correspondent, reporter (590).

anagram, acrostic, cross-word, cipher, code, cryptogram, monogram, paradox, maze, labyrinth, perplexity, chaos (528), the Hercynian wood; *terra incognita*.

Iron curtain, bamboo curtain, censorship, counter-intelligence.

(*Phrases*) The secrets of the prison-house; a sealed book.

(*Adjectives*) Secret, top secret, hush-hush, undercover, clandestine (528).

534 MESSENGER (*Substantives*), envoy, nuncio, internuncio, intermediary, go-between, herald, ambassador, legate, emissary, *corps diplomatique*.

Marshal, crier, trumpeter, pursuivant, *parlementaire*, courier, runner, postman, telegraph-boy, errand-boy, bell-boy, bell-hop, Mercury, Hermes, Iris, Ariel, carrier pigeon.

Narrator, etc., talebearer, spy, secret-service agent, scout.

Mail, post (592), post office, telegraph, telephone, wireless, radio; grapevine, bush telegraph.

535 AFFIRMATION (*Substantives*), statement, predication, assertion, declaration, word, averment, asseveration, protestation, swearing, adjuration, protest, profession, deposition, avouchment, affirmance, assurance, allegation, acknowledgment, avowal, confession, confession of faith, oath, affidavit; vote, voice.

Remark, observation, position, thesis, proposition, saying, dictum, theorem, sentence.

Positiveness (474), dogmatism, *ipse dixit*.

A dogmatist, doctrinaire.

(*Phrase*) The big bow-wow style.

(*Verbs*) To assert, make an assertion, etc., say, affirm, predicate, enunciate, state, declare, profess, aver, avouch, put forth, advance, express, allege, pose, propose, propound, broach, set forth, maintain, contend, pronounce, pretend, pass an opinion, etc.; to reassert, reaffirm, reiterate; quoth, *dixit*, *dixi*.

To vouch, assure, vow, swear, take oath, depose, depone, recognize, avow, acknowledge, own, confess, announce, hazard or venture an opinion.

To dogmatize, lay down, lay down the law; to call heaven to witness, protest, certify, warrant, posit, go bail for.

536 NEGATION (*Substantives*), abnegation, denial, denegation, disavowal, disclaimer, abjuration, contradiction, *démenti*, contravention, recusation, retraction, retractation, recantation, renunciation, palinode, recusancy, protest.

Qualification, modification (469); rejection (610); refusal (764).

(*Verbs*) To deny, disown, contradict, negative, gainsay, contravene, disclaim, withdraw, recant, disavow, retract, revoke, abjure, negate.

(*Phrases*) To deny flatly; eat one's words; go back from, or upon one's word.

To dispute, impugn, controvert, confute (479), question, call in question, give the lie to, rebut, belie.

(*Adjectives*) Denying, etc., denied, etc., negative, contradictory, recusant.

(*Adverbs*) No, nay, not, nohow, not at all, by no means (489), far from it, anything but, on the contrary, quite the reverse.

(*Phrases*) I doubt not; I warrant you; I 'll engage; take my word for it; depend upon it; I 'll be bound; I am sure; I have no doubt; sure enough; to be sure; what I have said, I have said; faith! that 's flat.

To swear till one is black in the face; to swear by all the saints in the calendar; to call heaven to witness.

(*Adjectives*) Asserting, etc., dogmatic, positive, emphatic, declaratory, affirmative, predicable, pronounced, unretracted.

Positive, broad, round, express, explicit, pointed, marked, definitive, distinct, decided, formal, solemn, categorical, peremptory, absolute, flat, pronounced.

(*Adverbs*) *Ex cathedra*, positively, avowedly, confessedly, broadly, roundly, etc.; ay, yes, indeed; by Jove, by George, by James, by jingo.

537 TEACHING (*Substantives*), instruction, direction, guidance, tuition, culture, inculcation, inoculation, indoctrination.

Education, co-education, initiation, preparation, practice, training, upbringing, schooling, discipline, exercise, drill, exercitation, breaking in, taming, drilling, etc., preachment, persuasion, edification, proselytism, propagandism.

A lesson, lecture, prolusion, prelection, exercise, task; curriculum, course.

Rudiments, ABC, elements, three Rs, grammar, text-book, vademecum, school-book (593).

Physical training, P.T., gymnastics, callisthenics.

(*Verbs*) To teach, instruct, enlighten, edify, inculcate, indoctrinate, instil, imbue, inoculate, infuse, impregnate, graft, infix, engraft, implant, sow the seeds of, infiltrate, give an idea of, cram, coach, put up to.

To explain, expound, lecture, hold forth, read a lecture or sermon, give a lesson, preach; sermonize, moralize, point a moral.

To educate, train, discipline, school, form, ground, tutor, prepare, qualify prime, drill, exercise, practise, bring up, rear, nurture, dry-nurse, breed, break in, tame, domesticate, condition.

To direct, guide, initiate, put in the way of, proselytize, bring round to an opinion, bring over, win over, brainwash, re-educate, persuade, convince, convict, set right, enlighten, give one new ideas, put one up to, bring home to.

538 MISTEACHING (*Substantives*) misdirection, misleading, misinformation, misguidance, perversion, false teaching, sophistry.

Indocility, incapacity, misintelligence, dullness, backwardness.

(*Verbs*) To misinform, misteach, mislead, misdirect, misguide, miscorrect, pervert, lead into error, bewilder, mystify (528), throw off the scent; to unteach.

(*Phrases*) To teach one's grandmother; *obscurum per obscurius*; the blind leading the blind.

(*Adjectives*) Misteaching, etc., unedifying.

539 LEARNING (*Substantives*), acquisition of knowledge, acquirement, attainment, scholarship, erudition, instruction, study, etc. (490).

Docility (602), aptitude (698), aptness to be taught, teachableness, persuasibility, capacity.

(*Verbs*) to learn; to acquire, gain, catch, receive, imbibe, pick up, gather, collect, glean, etc., knowledge or information.

To hear, overhear, catch hold of, take in, fish up, drink in, run away with an idea, to make oneself acquainted with, master, read, spell, turn over the leaves, pore over, run through, peruse, study, grind, cram, mug, swot, go to school; to get up a subject; to serve one's time or apprenticeship.

To be taught, etc.

(*Phrases*) **To teach** the young idea how to shoot; to sharpen the wits; to enlarge the mind.

(*Adjectives*) **Teaching**, etc., taught, etc., educational.

Didactic, academic, doctrinal, disciplinal, disciplinary, instructive, scholastic, persuasive.

540 TEACHER (*Substantives*), instructor, apostle, master, director, tutor, preceptor, institutor, mentor, adviser, monitor, counsellor, expositor, dry-nurse, trainer, coach, crammer, grinder, governor, bear-leader, disciplinarian, martinet, guide, cicerone, pioneer, governess, duenna.

Orator, speaker, mouthpiece (582).

Professor, lecturer, reader, demonstrator, praelector, prolocutor, schoolmaster, schoolmistress, schoolmarm, usher, pedagogue, monitor, pupilteacher, dominie, dame, moonshee; missionary, propagandist.

(*Adjectives*) **Tutorial**, professorial.

(*Adjectives*) **Docile**, apt, teachable, persuasible, studious, industrious, scholastic, scholarly.

(*Phrase*) **To burn** the midnight oil.

---

541 LEARNER (*Substantives*), scholar, student, alumnus, disciple, pupil, *élève*, schoolboy, schoolgirl, beginner, tyro (or tiro), abecedarian, novice, neophyte, chela, inceptor, probationer, apprentice, tenderfoot, freshman, bejan (or bejant), undergraduate, undergraduette, sophomore.

Proselyte, convert, catechumen, sectator; class, form.

Pupilage, pupilarity, pupilship, tutelage, apprenticeship, novitiate, leading-strings, matriculation.

(*Phrases*) Freshwater sailor; *in statu pupillari*.

542 SCHOOL (*Substantives*), day school, boarding school, public school, council school, national school, board school, private school, preparatory school, elementary school, primary school, secondary school, senior school, grammar school, high school, academy, university, Alma Mater, university extension, correspondence school, college, seminary, lyceum, polytechnic, nursery, institute, institution, palaestra, gymnasium, class, form, standard; nursery school, infant school, kindergarten, crèche; reformatory, Borstal, approved school.

Horn-book, rudiments, vade-mecum, abecedary, manual, primer, schoolbook, text-book.

Professorship, lectureship, readership, chair; pulpit, ambo, theatre, amphitheatre, forum, stage, rostrum, platform.

(*Adjectives*) **Scholastic**, academic, collegiate.

543 VERACITY (*Substantives*), truthfulness, truth, sincerity, frankness, straightforwardness, ingenuousness, candour, honesty, fidelity, bona fides, openness, unreservedness, bluntness, plainness, plain speaking, plain dealing; simplicity, bonhomie, naïveté, artlessness (703), love of truth.

A plain-dealer, truth-teller, man of his word.

(*Verbs*) **To speak** the truth, speak one's mind, open out, think aloud.

(*Phrases*) Tell the truth and shame the devil; to deal faithfully with; to show oneself in one's true colours.

544 FALSENESS (*Substantives*), falsehood, untruthfulness, untruth (546), falsity, mendacity, falsification, perversion of truth, perjury, fabrication, romance, forgery, prevarication, equivocation, shuffling, evasion, fencing, duplicity, doubledealing, unfairness, dishonesty, fraud, misrepresentation, *suggestio falsi*, *suppressio veri*, Punic faith, giving the go-by, disguise, disguisement, irony, understatement.

Insincerity, dissimulation, dissembling, deceit (545), shiftiness, hypocrisy, cant, humbug, gammon,

(*Adjectives*) Truthful, true, veracious, uncompromising, veridical, veridicous, sincere, candid, frank, open, outspoken, unreserved, free-spoken, open-hearted, honest, simple, simple-hearted, ingenuous, blunt, plain-spoken, true-blue, straightforward, straight, fair, fair-minded, single-minded, artless, guileless, natural, unaffected, simple-minded, undisguised, unfeigned, unflattering, warts and all.

(*Adverbs*) Truly, etc. (494), above-board, broadly.

(*Phrases*) In plain English; without mincing the matter; honour bright; honest Injun; boṇa fide; *sans phrase*.

jesuitry, pharisaism, mental reservation, lip-service, simulation, acting, sham, malingering, pretending, pretence, crocodile tears, false colouring, art, artfulness (702).

Deceiver (548).

(*Verbs*) To be false, etc., to play false, speak falsely, lie, fib, tell a lie or untruth, etc. (546), to mistake, misreport, misrepresent, misquote, belie, falsify, prevaricate, equivocate, quibble, palter, shuffle, fence, hedge, understate, mince the truth.

To forswear, swear false, perjure oneself, bear false witness.

To garble, gloss over, disguise, pervert, distort, twist, colour, varnish, cook, doctor, embroider, fiddle, wangle, gerrymander, put a false colouring or construction upon (523).

To invent, make up, fabricate, concoct, trump up, forge, fake, romance.

To dissemble, dissimulate, feign, pretend, assume, act or play a part, simulate, pass off for, counterfeit, sham, malinger, make believe, cant, put on.

(*Phrases*) To play the hypocrite; to give the go-by; to play fast and loose; to play a double game; to blow hot and cold; to lie like a conjurer; sham Abraham; to look as if butter would not melt in one's mouth; to sail under false colours; to ring false.

(*Adjectives*) False, dishonest, faithless, deceitful, mendacious, unveracious, truthless, trothless, unfair, uncandid, disingenuous, shady, shifty, underhand, underhanded, hollow, insincere, canting, hypocritical, jesuitical, sanctimonious, pharisaical, tartuffian, double, double-tongued, double-faced, smooth-spoken, smooth-tongued, plausible, mealy-mouthed, snide.

Artful, insidious, sly, designing, diplomatic, Machiavellian.

Untrue, unfounded, fictitious, invented, made up, *ben trovato*, forged, falsified, counterfeit, spurious, factitious, self-styled, bastard, sham, bogus, phoney, mock, pseudo, disguised, simulated, artificial, colourable, catchpenny, meretricious, tinsel, Brummagem, postiche, pinchbeck, illusory, elusory, supposititious, surreptitious, ironical, apocryphal.

(*Phrase*) All is not gold that glitters.

(*Adverbs*) Falsely, etc., slyly, stealthily, underhand.

---

545 DECEPTION (*Substantives*), falseness (544), fraud, deceit, imposition, artifice, juggle, juggling, sleight of hand, legerdemain, conjuration, hocus-pocus, jockeyship, trickery, coggery, fraudulence, imposture, *supercherie*, chicane, chicanery, covin, cozenage, circumvention, ingannation, prestidigitation, subreption, collusion, complicity, guile, gullery, hanky-panky, jiggery-pokery, rannygazoo.

Quackery, charlatanism, charlatanry, empiricism, humbug, hokum, eyewash, hypocrisy, gammon, flapdoodle, bunkum, *blague*, bluff, mummery, borrowed plumes.

Stratagem, trick, cheat, wile, artifice, cross, deception, take-in, camouflage, make-believe, ruse, manœuvre, finesse, hoax, canard, hum, kid, chouse, bubble, fetch, catch, spoof, swindle, plant, sell, hocus, dodge, bite, forgery, counterfeit, sham, fake, fakement, rig, delusion, stalking-horse.

Snare, trap, pitfall, decoy, gin, spring, noose, hook, bait, net, meshes, mouse-trap, trap-door, false bottom, ambush, ambuscade (530), masked battery, mine, mystery-ship, Q-boat.

(*Phrases*) A wolf in sheep's clothing; a whited (or painted) sepulchre; a pious fraud; a man of straw.

(*Verbs*) To deceive, mislead, cheat, impose upon, practise upon, circumvent, play upon, put upon, bluff, dupe, mystify, blind, hoodwink, best, outreach, trick, hoax, kid, gammon, spoof, hocus, bamboozle, hornswoggle, juggle, trepan, nick, entrap, beguile, lure, inveigle, decoy, lime, ensnare, entangle, lay a snare for, trip up, stuff the go-by.

To defraud, fiddle, take in, jockey, do, do brown, cozen, diddle, have, have on, chouse, welsh, bilk, bite, pluck, swindle, victimize, outwit, over-reach, nobble, palm upon, work off upon, foist upon, fob off, balk, trump up.

(*Phrases*) To throw dust in the eyes; to play a trick upon; to pull one's leg; to try it on; to cog the dice; to mark the cards; to live by one's wits; to play a part; to throw a tub to the whale.

(*Adjectives*) Deceiving, cheating, etc.; hypocritical, Pecksniffian; deceived, duped, done, had, etc., led astray.

Deceptive, deceitful, deceptious, illusive, illusory, delusory, prestigious, elusive, bogus, counterfeit, insidious, *ad captandum, ben trovato.*

(*Phrase*) *Fronti nulla fides; timeo Danaos et dona ferentes.*

546 UNTRUTH (*Substantives*), falsehood, lie, falsity, fiction, fabrication, fib, whopper, bouncer, cracker, crammer, tarradiddle, story, fable, novel, romance, flam, bull, gammon, flim-flam, *guet-apens*, white lie, pious, fraud, canard, nursery tale, fairy-tale, tall story.

Falsification, perjury, forgery, false swearing, misstatement, misrepresentation, inexactitude.

Pretence, pretext, subterfuge, irony, evasion, blind, disguise, plea, claptrap, shuffle, make-believe, shift, mask, cloak, visor, veil, masquerade, gloss, cobweb.

(*Phrases*) A pack of lies; a tissue of falsehoods; a cock-and-bull story; a trumped-up story; all my eye and Betty Martin; a mare's-nest.

547 DUPE (*Substantives*), gull (486), gudgeon, gobemouche, cully, victim, sucker, flat, greenhorn, puppet, cat's-paw, April fool, simple Simon, Joe Soap, pushover, soft mark.

(*Phrases*) To be the goat; to hold the baby; to carry the can; *qui vult decipi, decipiatur.*

548 DECEIVER (*Substantives*), liar, hypocrite, tale-teller, shuffler, shammer, dissembler, serpent, cockatrice; Janus, Tartuffe, Pecksniff, Joseph Surface, Cagliostro.

Pretender, impostor, knave, cheat, rogue, trickster, swindler, spiv, adventurer, humbug, sharper, jockey, welsher, leg, blackleg, rook, shark, confidence man, con man, confidence trickster, decoy, decoy-duck, stool-pigeon, gipsy.

Quack, charlatan, mountebank, empiric, quacksalver, *saltimbanco*, medicaster, *soi-disant.*

Actor, player, mummer, tumbler, posture-master, jack-pudding; illusionist, conjurer, (994).

(*Phrases*) A wolf in sheep's clothing; a snake in the grass; one who lives by his wits.

549 EXAGGERATION (*Substantives*), hyperbole, overstatement, stretch, strain, colouring, bounce, flourish, vagary, bombast (884), yarn, figure of speech, flight of fancy, *façon de parler*, extravagance, rhodomontade, heroics, sensationalism, highfalutin; tale of Baron Munchausen, traveller's tale.

(*Phrases*) A storm in a teacup; much ado about nothing.

(*Verbs*) To exaggerate, amplify, magnify, heighten, overcharge, overstate, overcolour, overlay, overdo, strain, stretch, bounce, flourish, embroider; to hyperbolize, aggravate, to make the most of.

(*Phrases*) To make a song about; spin a long yarn; draw the long bow; deal in the marvellous; out-herod Herod; lay it on thick; pile it on; make a mountain of a molehill.

(*Adjectives*) Exaggerated, etc., hyperbolical, turgid, tumid, fabulous, extravagant, magniloquent, bombastic, *outré*, highly coloured, high-flying, high-flown, high-falutin, sensational, blood-and-thunder, lurid.

(*Phrases*) All his geese are swans; much cry and little wool.

SECTION III—MEANS OF COMMUNICATING IDEAS

1°. *Natural Means*

550 INDICATION (*Substantives*), symbolization, symbolism, typification, notation, connotation, prefigurement, representation (554), exposition, notice (527), trace (551), name (564).

A sign, symbol, index, placard, exponent, indicator, pointer, mark, token, symptom, type, emblem, figure, cipher, code, device, epigraph, motto, posy.

Science of signs, sematology, semeiology, semeiotics.

Lineament, feature, line, stroke, dash, trait, characteristic, idiosyncracy, score, stripe, streak, scratch, tick, dot, point, notch, nick, asterisk, red letter, rubric, italics, print, stamp, impress, imprint, sublineation, underlining, display, jotting.

For identification: Badge, criterion, check, countercheck, countersign, stub, counterfoil, duplicate, tally, label, book-plate, *ex-libris*, ticket, billet, card, visiting-card, *carte de visite*, identity-card, passport, bill, bill-head, facia, signboard, witness, voucher, coupon, trade mark, hall-mark, signature, handwriting, sign manual, monogram, seal, sigil, signet, chop, autograph, autography, superscription, endorsement, *visé*, title, heading, caption, docket, watchword, password, shibboleth, *mot du guet*, catchword; fingerprint.

Insignia: Banner, banneret, flag, colours, bunting, streamer, standard, eagle, ensign, pennon, pennant, pendant, burgee, jack, ancient, labarum, oriflamme; gonfalon, banderole, Union Jack, Royal Standard, Stars and Stripes, Tricolour, etc.; crest, arms, coat of arms, armorial bearings, shield, scutcheon, escutcheon, uniform, livery, cockade, epaulet, chevron, cordon, totem.

Indication of locality: Beacon, cairn, post, staff, flagstaff, hand, pointer, vane, guide-post, finger-post, signpost, landmark, sea-mark, lighthouse, lightship, pole-star, lodestar, cynosure, guide, address, direction, rocket, bluelight, watch-fire, blaze.

Indication of an event: Signal, nod, wink, glance, leer, shrug, beck, cue, gesture, gesticulation, deaf-and-dumb alphabet, by-play, dumb-show, pantomime, touch, nudge, freemasonry, telegraph, heliograph, semaphore.

Indication of time: Time-signal, clock (114), alarm-clock, hooter, blower, buzzer, siren; tattoo, reveille, last post, taps.

Indication of danger: Alarm, alarum, alarm-bell, alert, fog-signal, detonator, red light, tocsin, fire-hooter, maroon, S O S, beat of drum, fiery cross, sound of trumpet, war-cry, war-whoop, slogan.

Indication of safety: all-clear, green light.

(*Verbs*) To indicate, point out, be the sign, etc., of, denote, betoken, connote, connotate, represent, stand for, typify, symbolize, shadow forth, argue, bear the impress of, witness, attest, testify.

To put an indication, mark, etc.; to note, mark, stamp, impress, earmark, brand, label, ticket, docket, endorse, sign, countersign; put, append, or affix a seal or signature; dot, jot down, book, score, dash, trace, chalk, underline, italicize, print, imprint, engrave, stereotype, rubricate, star, obelize, initial.

To make a sign, signal, etc., signalize; give or hang out a signal; give notice, gesticulate, beckon, beck, nod, wink, nudge, tip the wink; give the cue, tip, or office; wave, unfurl, hoist, or hang out a banner, flag, etc., show one's colours, give or sound an alarm, beat the drum, sound the trumpets, raise a cry, etc.

(*Adjectives*) Indicating, etc., indicatory, indicative, sematic, semeiological, denotative, representative, typical, typic, symbolic, symbolical, diacritical, connotative, pathognomic, symptomatic, exponential, emblematic, pantomimic, attesting; armorial, totemistic.

Indicated, etc., typified, impressed, etc.

Capable of being denoted, denotable, indelible.

(*Phrases*) *Ecce signum*; in token of.

---

551 RECORD (*Substantives*), trace, mark, tradition, vestige, footstep, footmark, footprint, footfall, wake, track, trail, slot, spoor, pug, scent.

Monument, relic, remains, trophy, hatchment, achievement, obelisk, monolith, pillar, stele, column, slab, tablet, medal, testimonial, memorial.

Note, minute, register, registry, index, inventory, catalogue, list (86), memorandum, jotting, document, account, score, tally, invoice, docket, voucher, protocol, inscription.

Paper, parchment, scroll, instrument, deed, indenture, debenture, roll, archive, schedule, file, dossier, cartulary, table, *procès verbal*, affidavit, certificate, attestation, entry, diploma, protest, round-robin, roster, rota, muster-roll, muster-book, note-book, commonplace-book, *adversaria*, portfolio.

552 Suppression of sign.

OBLITERATION (*Substantives*), erasure, rasure, cancel, cancellation, circumduction, deletion.

(*Verbs*) To efface, obliterate, erase, raze, expunge, cancel, delete, blot out, take out, rub out, scratch out, strike out, elide, wipe out, wash out, black out, write off, render illegible.

To be effaced, etc., to leave no trace.

(*Phrases*) To draw the pen through; to apply the sponge.

(*Adjectives*) Obliterated, effaced, etc., printless, leaving no trace.

Unrecorded, unattested, unregistered, intestate.

(*Interjections*) *Dele*; out with it!

Chronicle, annals, gazette, Hansard, history (594), newspaper, magazine, gazetteer, blue-book, almanac, calendar, ephemeris, diary, log, journal, day-book, ledger.

Registration, tabulation, enrolment, booking.

(*Verbs*) To record, note, register, chronicle, calendar, make an entry of, enter, book, take a note of, post, enrol, jot down, take down, mark, sign, etc. (550), tabulate, catalogue, file, index, commemorate (883).

(*Adjectives*) Registered, etc.

(*Adverbs*) Under one's hand and seal, on record.

553 RECORDER (*Substantives*), notary, clerk, registrar, registrary, register, prothonotary, secretary, stenographer, amanuensis, scribe, remembrancer, journalist, historian, historiographer, annalist, chronicler, biographer, bookkeeper.

Recordership, secretaryship, secretariat, clerkship.

---

554 REPRESENTATION (*Substantives*), delineation, representment, reproduction, depictment, personification.

Art, the fine arts, the graphic arts, design, designing, illustration, imitation (19), copy (21), portraiture, iconography, photography.

A picture, drawing, tracing, photograph.

An image, likeness, icon, portrait, effigy, facsimile, autotype, imagery, figure, puppet, dummy, lay figure, figurehead, doll, manikin, *mannequin*, mammet, marionette, *fantoccini* (599), statue (557), waxwork.

Hieroglyphic, hieroglyph, inscription, diagram, monogram, draught (or draft), outline, scheme, *schema*, schedule.

Map, plan, chart, ground-plan, projection, elevation, ichnography, atlas; cartography, chorography.

(*Verbs*) To represent, present, depict, portray, photograph, delineate, design, figure, adumbrate, shadow forth, copy, draft, mould, diagrammatize, schematize, map.

To imitate, impersonate, personate, personify, act, take off, hit off, figure as; to paint (556); carve (557); engrave (558).

(*Adjectives*) Representing, etc.; artistic, imitative, representative, illustrative, figurative, hieroglyphic, hieroglyphical, diagrammatic, schematic.

555 MISREPRESENTATION (*Substantives*), distortion (243), caricature, burlesque (856), a bad likeness, daub, scratch, sign-painting, anamorphosis; misprint, *erratum*.

(*Verbs*) To misrepresent, distort, falsify, caricature, wrest the sense (or meaning).

---

556 PAINTING (*Substantives*), depicting, drawing; perspective, composition, treatment.

Drawing in pencil, crayon, pastel, chalk, water-colour, etc.

Painting in oils, in distemper, in gouache, in fresco; encaustic painting, enamel painting, scene-painting; wash (428), body-colour, impasto.

A picture, drawing, painting, sketch, illustration, scratch, *graffito*, outline, tableau, cartoon, fresco, illumination; pencil, pen-and-ink, etc., drawing; oil, etc., painting; photograph; silver print; P.O.P., bromide, gaslight, bromoil, platinotype, carbon print; autochrome, Kodachrome; daguerreotype, calotype; mosaic, tapestry, etc., picture-gallery.

Portrait, portraiture, likeness, full-length, etc., miniature, kitcat, shade, profile, silhouette, still, snapshot.

Landscape, seascape, nocturne, view, still-life, *genre*, panorama, diorama.

Pre-Raphaelitism, impressionism, etc. (559).

(*Verbs*) To paint, depict, portray, limn, draw, sketch, pencil, scratch, scrawl, block in, rough in, dash off, chalk out, shadow forth, adumbrate, outline, illustrate, illuminate; to take a portrait, take a likeness, to photograph, snap, pan.

(*Phrases*) *Fecit, pinxit, delineavit.*

(*Adjectives*) Painted, etc.; pictorial, graphic, picturesque, Giottesque, Raphaelesque, Turneresque, etc.; like, similar (17).

557 SCULPTURE (*Substantives*), insculpture, carving, modelling.

A statue, statuary, statuette, figure, figurine, model, bust, image, high relief, low relief, alto-rilievo, mezzo-rilievo, basso-rilievo, bas-relief, cast, marble, bronze, intaglio, anaglyph; medallion, cameo.

(*Verbs*) To sculpture, sculp, carve, cut, chisel, model, mould, cast.

(*Adjectives*) Sculptured, etc., sculptural, sculpturesque, anaglyphic, ceroplastic, ceramic.

558 ENGRAVING (*Substantives*), etching, wood-engraving, process-engraving, xylography, chalcography, cerography, glyptography; poker-work.

A print, engraving, impression, plate, cut, wood-cut, steel-cut, linocut, vignette.

An etching, dry-point, stipple, roulette; copper-plate, mezzotint, aquatint, lithograph, chromolithograph, chromo, photo-lithograph, photogravure, anastatic-printing, collotype, electrotype, stereotype.

Matrix, flong.

(*Verbs*) To engrave, etch, lithograph, print, etc.

559 ARTIST (*Substantives*), painter, limner, draughtsman, black-and-white artist, cartoonist, caricaturist, drawer, sketcher, pavement artist, screever, designer, engraver, copyist, photographer.

Academician; historical, landscape, portrait, miniature, scene, sign, etc., painter; an Apelles.

Primitive, Pre-Raphaelite, old master, quattrocentist, cinquecentist, impressionist, post-impressionist, futurist, vorticist, cubist, surrealist, Dadaist, pointillist.

A sculptor, carver, modeller, goldsmith, silversmith, *figuriste*; a Phidias, Praxiteles, Royal Academician, R.A.

Implements of art: pen, pencil, brush, charcoal, chalk, pastel, crayon; paint (428); stump, graver, style, burin; canvas, easel, palette, maul-stick, palette-knife; studio, *atelier*.

2°. *Conventional Means*

I. LANGUAGE GENERALLY

560 LANGUAGE (*Substantives*), tongue, speech, lingo, vernacular, mother-tongue, native tongue, standard English, King's (or Queen's) English, the genius of a language.

Dialect, local dialect, class dialect, provincialism, vulgarism, colloquialism, Americanism, Scotticism, Cockney speech, brogue, patois, patter, slang, cant, argot, Anglic, Basic English, broken English, pidgin English, lingua franca.

Universal languages: Esperanto, Volapük, Ido, Interglossa.

Philology, etymology (562), linguistics, glossology, dialectology, phonetics.

Literature, letters, polite literature, belles-lettres, the muses, humanities, the republic of letters, dead languages, classics, *literae humaniores*.

Scholarship (490), linguist, scholar (492), writer (593), glossographer.

(*Verbs*) To express by words, to couch in terms, to clothe in language.

(*Adjectives*) Literary, belletristic, linguistic, dialectal, vernacular, colloquial, slang, current, polyglot, pantomimic.

(*Adverbs*) In plain terms, in common parlance, in household words.

561 LETTER (*Substantives*), alphabet, A B C, abecedary, spelling-book, horn-book, criss-cross-row; character (591), writing (590), hieroglyph, hieroglyphic; consonant, vowel, diphthong, triphthong; mute, liquid, labial, palatal, dental, guttural; spelling, orthography, phonetic spelling, misspelling; spelling-bee.

Syllable, monosyllable, dissyllable, trisyllable, polysyllable; anagram.

(*Verbs*) To spell, spell out.

(*Adjectives*) Literal, alphabetical, abecedarian, orthographic; syllabic, disyllabic, etc.

562 WORD (*Substantives*), term, vocable, terminology, part of speech (567), root, etymon.

Word similarly pronounced, homonym, homophone, paronym.

A dictionary, vocabulary, lexicon, index, polyglot, glossary, thesaurus, concordance, onomasticon, gradus; lexicography, lexicographer.

Derivation, etymology, glossology.

(*Adjectives*) Verbal, literal, titular, nominal, etymological, terminological.

Similarly derived, conjugate, paronymous.

(*Adverbs*) Nominally, etc., *verbatim*, word for word, in so many words, literally, *sic, totidem verbis, ipsissimis verbis, literatim*.

564 NOMENCLATURE (*Substantives*), nomination, naming, nuncupation.

A name, appellation, designation, appellative, denomination, term, expression, noun, byword, moniker, epithet, style, title, prenomen, forename, Christian name, baptismal name, given name, cognomen, agnomen, patronymic, surname, family name.

Synonym, namesake; euphemism, antonomasia, onomatopoeia.

Quotation, citation, chapter and verse.

(*Verbs*) To name, call, term, denominate, designate, style, clepe, entitle, dub, christen, baptize, characterize, specify, label (550).

To be called, etc., to take the name of, pass under the name of; to quote, cite.

563 NEOLOGY (*Substantives*), neologism, slang, cant, byword, hard word, jaw-breaker, dog Latin, monkish Latin, loan word, vogue word, nonce word, Gallicism.

A pun, play upon words, paronomasia, *jeu de mots, calembour*, palindrome, conundrum, acrostic, anagram (533).

Dialect (560).

Neologian, neologist.

(*Verbs*) To neologize, archaize, pun.

(*Phrase*) To coin or mint words.

(*Adjectives*) Neological, neologistic, paronomastic.

---

565 MISNOMER (*Substantives*), missaying, malaprop, malapropism, antiphrasis, nickname, sobriquet, byname, assumed name or title, alias, *nom de guerre, nom de plume*, penname, pseudonym, pet name, euphemism.

So-and-so, what's-his-name, thingummy, thingumbob, thingumajig, dingus, *je ne sais quoi*.

A Mrs. Malaprop.

(*Phrase*) *Lucus a non lucendo*.

(*Verbs*) To misname, missay, miscall, misterm, nickname.

To assume a name.

(*Adjectives*) Misnamed, etc., malapropian, pseudonymous, *soi-disant*, self-called, self-styled, so-called.

Nameless, anonymous, without a name, having no name, innominate, unnamed.

(*Phrases*) To call a spade a spade; to rejoice in the name of.

(*Adjectives*) Named, called, etc., hight, yclept, known as; nuncupatory, nuncupative, cognominal, titular, nominal.

Literal, verbal, discriminative.

566 PHRASE (*Substantives*), expression, phraseology, paraphrase, periphrasis, circumlocution (573), set phrase, round terms; mode or turn of expression; idiom, wording, *façon de parler*, mannerism, plain terms, plain English.

Sentence, paragraph, motto.

Figure, trope, metaphor (521), wisecrack, proverb (496).

(*Verbs*) To express, phrase, put; couch, clothe in words, give words to; to word.

(*Adjectives*) Expressed, etc., couched in, phraseological, idiomatic, paraphrastic, periphrastic, circumlocutory (573), proverbial.

(*Phrase*) As the saying is; in good set terms; *sans phrase*.

---

567 GRAMMAR (*Substantives*), accidence, syntax, parsing, analysis, praxis, punctuation, conjugation, declension, inflexion, case, voice, person, number; philology (560), parts of speech.

(*Phrase*) *Jus et norma loquendi.*

(*Verbs*) To parse, analyse, conjugate, decline, inflect, punctuate.

(*Adjectives*) Grammatical, syntactic, inflexional.

---

568 SOLECISM (*Substantives*), bad or false grammar, slip of the pen or tongue, bull, howler, floater, clanger, *lapsus linguae*, barbarism, vulgarism; dog Latin.

(*Verbs*) To use bad or faulty grammar, to solecize, commit a solecism.

(*Phrases*) To murder the king's English; to break Priscian's head.

(*Adjectives*) Ungrammatical, barbarous, slipshod, incorrect, faulty, inaccurate.

---

569 STYLE (*Substantives*), diction, phraseology, wording, turn of expression, idiom, manner, strain, composition, authorship; stylist.

(*Adjectives*) Stylistic, idiomatic, mannered.

(*Phrases*) Command of language; a ready pen; *le style, c'est l'homme même*.

Various Qualities of Style

570 PERSPICUITY (*Substantives*), lucidity, lucidness, clearness, clarity, perspicacity, plain speaking, intelligibility (518).

(*Adjectives*), Perspicuous, clear (525), lucid, intelligible, plain, transparent, explicit.

---

571 OBSCURITY (*Substances*), ambiguity (520), unintelligibility (519), involution, involvedness, vagueness.

(*Adjectives*) Obscure, confused, crabbed, ambiguous, vague, unintelligible, etc., involved, wiredrawn, tortuous.

---

572 CONCISENESS (*Substantives*), brevity, terseness, compression (195), condensation, concision, closeness, laconism, portmanteau word, telegraphese, pithiness, succinctness, quaintness, stiffness, ellipsis, ellipse, syncope.

Abridgment, epitome (596).

(*Verbs*) To be concise, etc., to condense, compress, abridge, abbreviate, cut short, curtail, abstract.

(*Phrase*) To cut the cackle and come to the horses.

---

573 DIFFUSENESS (*Substantives*), prolixity, verbosity, macrology, pleonasm, tautology, copiousness, exuberance, laxity, looseness, verbiage, flow, flow of words, fluency, *copia verborum*, loquacity (584), redundancy, redundance, digression, amplification, *longueur*, padding, circumlocution, ambages, periphrasis, officialese, commercialese, gobbledygook, episode, expletive.

(*Verbs*) To be diffuse, etc., to expatiate, enlarge, launch out, dilate, expand, pad out, spin out, run on,

(*Adjectives*) Concise, brief, crisp, curt, short, terse, laconic, sententious, gnomic, snappy, pithy, nervous, pregnant, succinct, *guindé*, stiff, compact, summary, compendious (596), close, cramped, elliptical, telegraphic, epigrammatic, lapidary.

(*Adverbs*) Concisely, briefly, etc., in a word, to the point, in short.

(*Phrases*) The long and short of it; *multum in parvo*; it comes to this; for shortness' sake; to make a long story short; to put it in a nutshell.

amplify, swell out, inflate, dwell on, harp on, descant, digress, ramble, maunder, rant.

(*Phrases*) To beat about the bush; to spin a long yarn; to make a long story of.

(*Adjectives*) Diffuse, wordy, verbose, prolix, copious, exuberant, flowing, fluent, bombastic, lengthy, long-winded, talkative (584), prosy, spun out, long-spun, loose, lax, slovenly, washy, slipslop, sloppy, frothy, flatulent, windy, digressive, discursive, excursive, tripping, rambling, ambagious, pleonastic, redundant, periphrastic, episodic, circumlocutory, roundabout.

Minute, detailed, particular, circumstantial.

(*Adverbs*) In detail, at great length, *in extenso*, about it and about, *currente calamo*, *usque ad nauseam*.

574 VIGOUR (*Substantives*), energy, power, force, spirit, point, vim, snap, punch, ginger, *élan*, pep, go, raciness, liveliness, fire, glow, verve, piquancy, pungency, spice, boldness, gravity, warmth, sententiousness, elevation, loftiness, sublimity, eloquence, individuality, distinction, emphasis, virility.

(*Phrase*) 'Thoughts that glow and words that burn.'

(*Adjectives*) Vigorous, energetic, powerful, strong, forcible, nervous, spirited, vivid, virile, expressive, lively, glowing, sparkling, racy, bold, slashing, incisive, trenchant, snappy, mordant, poignant, piquant, pungent, spicy, meaty, juicy, pointed, antithetical, sententious, emphatic, athletic, distinguished, original, individual, lofty, elevated, sublime, Miltonic, eloquent.

575 FEEBLENESS (*Substantives*), baldness, tameness, meagreness, coldness, frigidity, poverty, puerility, childishness, dullness, dryness, jejuneness, monotony.

(*Adjectives*) Feeble, bald, dry, flat, insipid, tame, meagre, invertebrate, weak, mealy-mouthed, wishy-washy, wersh, banal, uninteresting, jejune, vapid, cold, frigid, poor, dull (843), languid, anaemic, prosy, prosaic, pedestrian, platitudinous, conventional, mechanical, decadent, trashy, namby-pamby (866), puerile, childish, emasculate.

576 PLAINNESS (*Substantives*), simplicity, homeliness, chasteness, chastity, neatness, monotony, severity.

(*Adjectives*) Simple, unornamented, unvarnished, straightforward, artless, unaffected, downright, plain, unadorned, unvaried, monotonous, severe, chaste, blunt, homespun.

577 ORNAMENT (*Substantives*), floridness, floridity, flamboyance, richness, opulence, turgidity, tumidity, pomposity, inflation, altiloquence, spreadeagleism, pretension, fustian, affectation, euphuism, gongorism, mannerism, metaphor, preciosity, inversion, figurativeness, sesquipedalianism, *sesquipedalia verba*, rant, bombast, frothiness; flowers of speech, high-sounding words, well-rounded periods, purple patches.

A phrase-monger, euphuist.

(*Verbs*) To ornament, overcharge, overlay with ornament, lard or garnish with metaphors, lay the colours on thick, round a period, mouth.

(*Adjectives*) Ornamented, etc., ornate, florid, flamboyant, rich, opulent, golden-mouthed, figurative, metaphorical, pedantic, affected, pretentious, falsetto, euphuistic, Della Cruscan, pompous, fustian, high-sounding, mouthy, inflated, high-falutin (or high-faluting), bombastic, stilted, mannered, high-flowing, frothy, flowery, luscious, turgid, tumid, swelling, declamatory, rhapsodic, rhetorical, orotund, sententious, grandiose, grandiloquent, magniloquent, altiloquent, sesquipedalian, Johnsonian, ponderous.

(*Adverb*) Ore rotundo.

---

578 ELEGANCE (*Substantives*), grace, ease, naturalness, purity, concinnity, readiness, euphony; a purist.

(*Phrases*) A ready pen; flowing periods; *curiosa felicitas*.

(*Adjectives*) Elegant, graceful, Attic, Ciceronian, classical, natural, easy, felicitous, unaffected, unlaboured, chaste, pure, correct, flowing, mellifluous, euphonious, rhythmical, puristic, well-expressed, neatly put.

(*Phrases*) To round a period; 'to point a moral and adorn a tale.'

579 INELEGANCE (*Substantives*), stiffness, uncouthness, barbarism, archaism, rudeness, crudeness, bluntness, brusquerie, ruggedness, abruptness, artificiality, cacophony.

(*Phrases*) Words that dislocate the jaw, that break the teeth.

(*Verbs*) To be inelegant, etc.

(*Phrase*) To smell of the lamp.

(*Adjectives*) Inelegant, ungraceful, stiff, forced, laboured, clumsy, contorted, tortuous, harsh, cramped, rude, rugged, dislocated, crude, crabbed, uncouth, barbarous, archaic, archaistic, affected (577), artificial, abrupt, blunt, brusque, incondite.

---

2. SPOKEN LANGUAGE

580 VOICE (*Substantives*), vocality, vocalization, utterance, cry, strain, articulate sound, prolation, articulation, enunciation, delivery, vocalism, pronunciation, orthoepy, euphony.

Cadence, accent, accentuation, emphasis, stress, tone, intonation, exclamation, ejaculation, vociferation, ventriloquism, polyphonism.

A ventriloquist, polyphonist.

Phonetics, phonology; voice-production.

(*Verbs*) To utter, breathe, cry, exclaim, shout, ejaculate, vociferate; raise, lift, or strain the voice or lungs; to vocalize, prolate, articulate, enunciate, pronounce, accentuate, aspirate, deliver, mouth, rap out, speak out, speak up.

(*Phrase*) To whisper in the ear.

(*Adjectives*) Vocal, oral, phonetic, articulate.

Silvery, mellow, soft (413).

581 APHONY (*Substantives*), obmutescence, absence or want of voice, dumbness, muteness, mutism, speechlessness, aphasia, hoarseness, raucity; silence (585).

A dummy, a mute, deaf-mute.

(*Verbs*) To render mute, to muzzle, muffle, suppress, smother, gag (585); to whisper (405).

(*Phrases*) To stick in the throat; to close one's lips; to shut up.

(*Adjectives*) Aphonous, dumb, speechless, mute, tongueless, muzzled, tongue-tied, inarticulate, inaudible, unspoken, unsaid, mum, mumchance, lips close or sealed, wordless; raucous, hoarse, husky, sepulchral.

(*Phrases*) Mute as a fish; hoarse as a raven; with bated breath; *sotto voce*; with the finger on the lips; mum's the word.

582 SPEECH (*Substantives*), locution, talk, parlance, verbal intercourse, oral communication, word of mouth, palaver, prattle, effusion, narrative (594), tale, story, yarn, oration, recitation, delivery, say, harangue, formal speech, speechifying, sermon, homily, discourse (998), lecture, curtain lecture, pi-jaw, address, tirade, pep-talk, screed; preamble, peroration; soliloquy (589).

Oratory, elocution, rhetoric, declamation, eloquence, gift of the gab, *copia verborum*, grandiloquence, magniloquence.

A speaker, spokesman, prolocutor, mouthpiece, lecturer, orator, stump-orator, speechifier; a Cicero, a Demosthenes.

(*Verbs*) To speak, break silence, say, tell, utter, pronounce (580), open one's lips, give tongue, hold forth, make or deliver a speech, speechify, harangue, talk, discourse, declaim, stump, flourish, spout, rant, recite, rattle off, intone, breathe, let fall, whisper in the ear, expatiate, run on; to lecture, preach, address, sermonize, preachify; to soliloquize (589); quoth he.

(*Phrases*) To have a tongue in one's head; to have on the tip of one's tongue; to have on one's lips; to pass one's lips; to find one's tongue.

(*Adjectives*) Speaking, etc., oral, spoken, unwritten, elocutionary, oratorical, rhetorical, declamatory, outspoken.

(*Adverbs*) Viva voce; *ore rotundo*; by word of mouth.

583 Imperfect speech.

STAMMERING (*Substantives*), inarticulateness, stuttering, impediment in one's speech, titubancy, faltering, hesitation, lisp, drawl, jabber, gibber, sputter, splutter, mumbling, mincing, muttering, mouthing, twang, a broken or cracked voice, broken accents or sentences, tardiloquence, falsetto, a whisper (405), mispronunciation.

(*Verbs*) To stammer, stutter, hesitate, falter, hem, haw, hum and ha, mumble, lisp, jabber, gibber, mutter, sputter, splutter, drawl, mouth, mince, lisp, croak, speak through the nose, snuffle, clip one's words, mispronounce, missay.

(*Phrases*) To clip the King's (or Queen's) English; *parler à tort et à travers*; not to be able to put two words together.

(*Adjectives*) Stammering, etc., inarticulate, guttural, nasal, tremulous.

_____

584 LOQUACITY (*Substantives*), loquaciousness, talkativeness, garrulity, flow of words, prate, gas, jaw, gab, gabble, jabber, chatter, prattle, cackle, clack, clash, blether (or blather), patter, rattle, twaddle, bibble-babble, gibble-gabble, talkee-talkee, gossip.

Fluency, flippancy, volubility, verbosity, *cacoethes loquendi*, anecdotage.

A chatterer, chatterbox, blatherskite, babbler, wind-bag, gas-bag, rattle, ranter, tub-thumper, sermonizer, proser, driveller, gossip.

Magpie, jay, parrot, poll; Babel.

(*Phrases*) A twice (or thrice) told tale; a long yarn; the gift of the gab.

(*Verbs*) To be loquacious, etc., to prate, palaver, chatter, prattle, jabber,

585 TACITURNITY (*Substantives*), closeness, reserve, reticence (528), muteness, silence, curtness; aposiopesis; a clam, oyster.

(*Phrases*) A Quaker meeting; a man of few words.

(*Verbs*) To be silent, etc. (403), to hold one's tongue, keep silence, hold one's peace, say nothing, hold one's jaw, close one's mouth or lips, fall silent, dry up, shut up, stow it.

To render silent, silence, put to silence, seal one's lips, smother, suppress, stop one's mouth, gag, muffle, muzzle (581).

(*Adjectives*) Taciturn, silent, close, reserved, mute, sparing of words, buttoned up, curt, short-spoken, close-tongued, tight-lipped, reticent,

law, rattle, twaddle, blether, babble, gabble, gas, out-talk, descant, dilate, dwell on, reel off, expatiate, prose, launch out, yarn, gossip, wag one's tongue, run on.

(*Phrases*) To din in the ears; to drum into the ear; to spin a long yarn; to talk at random; to bum one's chat; to talk oneself out of breath; to talk nineteen to the dozen.

(*Adjectives*) Loquacious, talkative, garrulous, gassy, gabby, open-mouthed, chatty, chattering, etc.

Fluent, voluble, glib, flippant, long-tongued, long-winded, verbose, the tongue running fast.

(*Adverb*) Trippingly on the tongue.

secretive, uncommunicative, inconversable.

(*Phrases*) Not a word escaping one; not having a word to say.

(*Interjections*) Hush! silence! mum! *chut !* hist! whist! wheesht!

---

586 ALLOCUTION (*Substantives*), address, apostrophe, interpellation, appeal, invocation, alloquialism, salutation, accost, greeting (894).

Feigned dialogue, imaginary conversation; inquiry (461).

(*Phrase*) A word in the ear.

(*Verbs*) To speak to, address, accost, buttonhole, apostrophize, appeal to, invoke, hail, make up to, take aside, call to, halloo (or hallo), salute.

(*Phrases*) To talk with one in private; to break the ice.

(*Adjectives*) Accosting, etc., alloquial, invocatory, apostrophic.

(*Interjections*) Hallo! hello! hullo! I say! hoy! oi! hey! what ho! psst!

587 RESPONSE (*Substantives*), answer, reply (462).

(*Verbs*) To answer, respond, reply, etc.

(*Phrase*) To take up one's cue.

(*Adjectives*) Answering, responding, etc., responsive, respondent.

---

588 INTERLOCUTION (*Substantives*), collocution, colloquy, conversation, converse, confabulation, confab, talk, discourse, verbal intercourse, dialogue, duologue, logomachy, communication, intercommunication, commerce, debate.

Chat, chit-chat, crack, small talk, table-talk, tattle, gossip, tittle-tattle, babblement, clack, prittle-prattle, idle talk, town-talk, bazaar talk, *on dit*, causerie, *chronique scandaleuse.*

589 SOLILOQUY (*Substantives*), monologue, apostrophe, aside.

Soliloquist, monologist, monologuist.

(*Verbs*) To soliloquize, monologize; to say or talk to oneself, to say aside, to think aloud, to apostrophize.

(*Adjectives*) Soliloquizing, etc.

Conference, parley, interview, audience, tête-à-tête, reception, conversazione, palaver, pow-wow; council (686).

A talker, interlocutor, interviewer, gossip, tattler, chatterer, babbler (584), conversationalist, *causeur*; *dramatis personae.*

(*Phrases*) 'The feast of reason and the flow of soul'; a heart-to-heart talk.

(*Verbs*) To talk together, converse, collogue, commune, debate, discourse with, engage in conversation, interview; hold or carry on a conversation; chat, gossip, have a crack, put in a word, chip in, tattle, babble, prate, clack, prattle.

To confer with, hold conference, etc., to parley, palaver, commerce, hold intercourse with, be closeted with, commune with, have speech with, compare notes, intercommunicate.

(*Adjectives*) Conversing, etc., interlocutory, verbal, colloquial, discursive, chatty, gossiping, etc., conversable, conversational.

3. WRITTEN LANGUAGE

590 WRITING (*Substantives*), chirography, pencraft, penmanship, longhand, calligraphy, quill-driving, pen-pushing, typewriting, typing.

Scribble, scrawl, scratch, cacography, scribbling, etc., jotting, interlineation, palimpsest.

Uncial writing, court hand, cursive writing, picture writing, hieroglyphics, hieroglyph, cuneiform characters, demotic text, heiratic text, ogham, runes.

Pothooks and hangers.

Transciption, inscription, superscription, minute.

Shorthand, stenography, phonography, brachygraphy, tachygraphy, steganography.

Secret writing, writing in cipher, cryptography, polygraphy, stelography; cryptogram.

Automatic writing, planchette.

Composition, authorship, *cacoethes scribendi.*

591 PRINTING (*Substantives*), print, letterpress, text, context, note, page, proof, pull, revise; presswork.

Typography, stereotypography, type, character, black-letter, fount (or font), capitals, majuscules, lower-case letters, minuscules, etc.; roman, italic, type; braille.

Folio, quarto, octavo, etc. (593).

Printer, pressman, compositor, corrector of the press, proof-reader, copyholder; printer's devil.

Printing-press, linotype, monotype, etc.

(*Verbs*) To print, put to press, publish, edit, get out a work, etc.

(*Adjectives*) Printed, etc.

———

Manuscript, MS., copy, transcript, rough copy, fair copy, carbon, black, duplicate, flimsy, handwriting, hand, fist, script, autograph, signature, sign-manual, monograph, holograph, endorsement, paraph.

A scribe, amanuensis, scrivener, secretary, clerk, penman, calligraphist, copyist, transcriber, stenographer, typist.

Writer, author, scribbler, quill-driver, ink-slinger, pamphleteer, essayist, critic, reviewer, novelist (593), journalist, editor, subeditor, reporter, pressman, penny-a-liner, hack, free-lance; Grub Street, Fleet Street.

Pen, quill, fountain-pen, stylograph, stylo, ball-point, Biro, pencil, stationery, paper, parchment, vellum, tablet, slate, marble, pillar, table, etc.

(*Phrase*) A dash or stroke of the pen.

(*Verbs*) To write, pen, typewrite, type, write out, copy, engross, write out fair, transcribe, scribble, scrawl, scratch, interline; to sign, undersign, countersign, endorse (497), set one's hand to.

To compose, indite, draw up, draft, minute, jot down, dash off, make or take a minute of, put or set down in writing; to inscribe, to dictate.

(*Phrases*) To take up the pen; to spill ink; to sling ink; set or put pen to paper; put on paper; commit to paper.

(*Adjectives*) Writing, etc., written, in writing, penned, etc., scriptorial; uncial, cursive, cuneiform, runic, heiroglyphical; editorial, journalistic, reportorial.

(*Phrases*) Under one's hand; in black and white; pen in hand; *currente calamo.*

592 CORRESPONDENCE (*Substantives*), letter, epistle, note, line, air-graph, postcard, chit, billet, missive, circular, favour, *billet-doux*, dispatch, bulletin, memorial, rescript, rescription.

Letter-bag, mail, post; postage.

(*Verbs*) To correspond, write to, send a letter to.

(*Phrase*) To keep up a correspondence.

(*Adjectives*) Epistolary, postal.

---

593 BOOK (*Substantives*), writing, work, volume, tome, codex, opuscule, tract, manual, pamphlet, chap-book, booklet, brochure, enchiridion, circular, publication, part, issue, number, journal, album, periodical, magazine, digest, serial, ephemeris, annual, year-book.

Writer, author, publicist, scribbler, pamphleteer, poet, essayist, novelist, fabulist, editor (590).

Book-lover, bibliophile, bibliomaniac, paperback.

Bibliography, *incunabula*, Aldine, Elzevir, etc.; library.

Publisher, bookseller, bibliopole, bibliopolist, librarian.

Folio, quarto, octavo, duodecimo, sextodecimo, octodecimo.

Paper, bill, sheet, leaf, fly-leaf, page, title-page.

Chapter, section, paragraph, passage, clause.

(*Adjectives*) Auctorial, bookish, bibliographical, etc.

594 DESCRIPTION (*Substantives*), account, statement, report, return, delineation, specification, particulars, sketch, representation (554), narration, narrative, yarn, relation, recital, rehearsal, annals, chronicle, saga, *adversaria*, journal (551), itinerary, log-book.

Historiography; historicity, historic muse, Clio.

Story, history, memoir, tale, tradition, legend, folk-tale, folk-lore, anecdote, ana, analects (596), fable, fiction, novel, novelette, thriller, whodunit, romance, short story, *conte*, *nouvelle*, apologue, parable; word-picture; local colour.

Biography, necrology, obituary, life, personal narrative, adventures, autobiography, confessions, reminiscences.

A historian, historiographer, narrator, *raconteur*, annalist, chronicler, biographer, fabulist, novelist, fictionist, story-teller.

(*Verbs*) To describe, state (535), set forth, sketch, delineate, represent (554), portray, depict, paint, shadow forth, adumbrate.

To relate, recite, recount, sum up, run over, recapitulate, narrate, chronicle, rehearse, tell, give or render an account of, report, draw up a statement, spin a yarn, unfold a tale, novelize, actualize.

To take up or handle a subject; to enter into particulars, detail, etc., to characterize, particularize, detail, retail, elaborate, write up; to descend to particulars; to Boswellize.

(*Phrases*) To plunge *in medias res*; to fight one's battles over again.

(*Adjectives*) Descriptive, narrative, graphic, realistic, naturalistic, novelistic, historic, traditional, traditionary, legendary, storied, romantic, anecdotic, Boswellian, described, etc.

595 DISSERTATION (*Substantives*), treatise, tract, tractate, thesis, theme, monograph, essay, discourse, article, leading article, leader, leaderette, editorial, feuilleton, criticism, critique, review, memoir, prolusion, disquisition, exposition, exercitation, compilation, sermon, lecture, teach-in, homily, pandect, *causerie*, pamphlet (593).

Commentator, lecturer, critic, leader-writer, pamphleteer.

(*Verbs*) To dissert, descant, treat of, discuss, write, compile, touch upon, ventilate, canvass; deal with, do justice to a subject.

(*Adjectives*) Discursive, disquisitional, expository, compiled.

596 COMPENDIUM *(Substantives)*, compend, summary, abstract, précis, epitome, *aperçu*, analysis, digest, sum and substance, *compte rendu*, *procès verbal*, draft, *exposé*, brief, recapitulation, résumé, conspectus, abridgment, abbreviation, minute, note, synopsis, argument, plot, syllabus, contents, heads, prospectus.

Scrap-book, album, note-book, commonplace-book, compilation, extracts, cuttings, clippings, text-book, analects, *analecta*, excerpts, flowers, anthology, *collectanea*, memorabilia.

(Verbs) To abridge, abstract, excerpt, abbreviate, recapitulate, run over, make or prepare an abstract, etc. (201), epitomize, sum up, summarize, boil down, anthologize.

(Adjectives) Compendious, etc., synoptic, abridged, etc., analectic.

(Phrase) In a nutshell; in substance; in short.

597 POETRY *(Substantives)*, poetics, poesy, the Muse, the Nine, Calliope, Parnassus, Helicon, the Pierian spring.

Verse, metre, measure, foot, numbers, strain, rhyme (or rime), head-rhyme, alliteration, rhythm, heroic verse, Alexandrine, octosyllables, *terza rima*, blank verse, free verse, *vers libre*, sprung rhythm, assonance, versification, macaronics, doggerel, jingle, prosody, orthometry, scansion.

598 PROSE *(Substantives)*, prose-writer, proser, prosaist.

(Verb) To prose.

(Adjectives) Prosaic, prosaical, prosing, prosy, rhymeless, unrhymed, unpoetical, commonplace, humdrum.

Poem, epic, epopee, epic poem, ballad, ode, epode, idyll, lyric, eclogue, pastoral, bucolic, macaronic, dithyramb, anacreontic, sonnet, lay, roundelay, rondeau, rondel, ballade, villanelle, triolet, sestina, rhyme royal, madrigal, canzonet, libretto, posy, anthology; distich, stanza, stave, strophe, antistrophe, couplet, triplet, quatrain, cento, monody, elegy, *vers de société*.

Iambic (or iamb), trochee, spondee, dactyl, anapaest, amphibrach, amphimacer, tribrach, paeon, etc.

A poet, laureate, bard, scald, poetess, rhymer, rhymist, versifier, rhymester, sonneteer, poetaster, minor poet, minnesinger, meistersinger, troubadour, *trouvère*.

(Phrase) *Genus irritabile vatum.*

(Verbs) To rhyme, versify, sing, make verses, scan, poetize.

(Adjectives) Poetical, poetic, Castalian, Parnassian, Heliconian, lyric, lyrical, metrical, epic, heroic; catalectic, dithyrambic, doggerel, macaronic, leonine; Pindaric, Homeric, Virgilian, Shakespearian, Miltonic, Tennysonian, etc.

599 THE DRAMA *(Substantives)*, stage, theatre, the histrionic art, dramatic art, histrionics, acting; stage effect, *mise en scène*, stage production, setting, scenery; buskin, sock, cothurnus; Melpomene, Thalia, Thespis; play-writing, dramaturgy.

Play, stage-play, piece, tragedy, comedy, tragi-comedy, morality, mystery, melodrama, farce, knock-about farce, comedietta, curtain-raiser, interlude, after-piece, vaudeville, extravaganza, *divertissement*, burletta, burlesque, variety show, revue; opera, grand opera, music-drama, comic opera, *opéra bouffe*, operetta, ballad opera, *singspiel*, musical comedy; ballet, pantomime, harlequinade, charade, wordless play, dumb-show, by-play; monodrama, monologue, duologue; masque, pageant, show; scenario, libretto, book of words, part, role; matinée, benefit; act, scene, prologue, epilogue.

Theatre, playhouse, music-hall, variety theatre; stage, the boards, the footlights, green-room, foyer, proscenium, flies, wings, stalls, box, pit, circle, dress-circle, balcony, amphitheatre, gallery.

An actor, player, stage-player, performer, artiste, comedian, comedienne, tragedian, tragedienne, Thespian, Roscius, clown, harlequin, pantaloon, *buffo*, buffoon, pierrot, pierrette, impersonator, entertainer, etc., strolling player; ballet dancer, *ballerina*, figurant, mime, star; prima donna, *primo tenore*, etc., leading lady, heavy lead, juvenile lead, *ingénue*, soubrette; supernumerary, super, walking, gentleman or lady, chorus girl; *dramatis personae*, cast, company, stock company, touring company, repertory company; a star turn.

Mummer, guiser, masquer; dancer, nautch-girl, bayadère, geisha.

Stage manager, impresario, producer, prompter, stage hands, call-boy, etc.

Dramatic writer, pantomimist, playwright, play-writer, dramatist, dramaturge, librettist.

(*Phrase*) The profession.

(*Verbs*) To act, enact, play, perform, personate (554), play or interpret a part, rehearse, spout, rant, gag, star, walk on.

To produce, present, stage, stage-manager.

(*Phrases*) To strut and fret one's hour on the stage; to tread the boards.

(*Adjectives*) Dramatic, theatre, theatrical, scenic, histrionic, comic, tragic, buskined, farcical, knock-about, slapstick, tragi-comic, melodramatic, transpontine, stagy, operatic.

599A CINEMA (*Substantives*), picture theatre, picturedrome, film, motion picture, pictures, movies, flicks, pix, silver screen; silent film, sound film, talkie, flattie; three-dimensional film, 3-D, wide-screen film, deepie; documentary, trailer.

Close-up, flash-back, fade-out.

Scenario, star, vamp; cinema-goer, cinemaddict, film fan.

(*Verbs*) To feature, screen; dub.

599B RADIO (*Substantives*), wireless, receiving set, transistor, walkie-talkie; broadcast, radio play; teleprompter.

Announcer, listener.

Television, TV., video, telly; telecast, telefilm, newscast, script.

Looker-in, televiewer, viewer.

(*Verbs*) To broadcast, televise, telecast.

To listen in, look in, view, teleview.

(*Phrase*) On the air.

(*Adjective*) Telegenic.

CLASS V

WORDS RELATING TO THE VOLUNTARY POWERS

DIVISION I—INDIVIDUAL VOLITION

SECTION I—VOLITION IN GENERAL

1°. *Acts of Volition*

600 WILL (*Substantives*), volition, voluntariness, velleity, conation, free-will, spontaneity, spontaneousness, freedom (748).

Pleasure, wish, mind, animus, breast, mood, bosom, *petto*, heart, discretion, accord.

Libertarianism.

Determination (604), predetermination (611), intention (620), choice (609).

(*Verbs*) To will, list, think fit, see fit, think proper, determine, etc. (604), settle, choose (609), to take upon oneself, to have one's will, to do as one likes, wishes, or chooses; to use or exercise one's own discretion, to volunteer, lend oneself to.

(*Phrases*) To have a will of one's own; *hoc volo, sic jubeo, stet pro ratione voluntas*; to take the will for the deed; to know one's own mind; to know what one is about; to see one's way; to have one's will; to take upon oneself; to take the law into one's own hands.

(*Adjectives*) Voluntary, volitional, willing, content, minded, spontaneous, free, left to oneself, unconstrained, unfettered, autocratic, bossy, unbidden, unasked, unurged, uncompelled, of one's own accord, gratuitous, of one's own head, prepense, advised, express, designed, intended, calculated, premeditated, preconcerted, predetermined, deliberate.

(*Adverbs*) At will, at pleasure, *à volonté, à discrétion, ad libitum, ad*

601 NECESSITY (*Substantives*), instinct, blind impulse, necessitation, ἀνάγκη, fate, fatality, destiny, doom, kismet, weird (152), foredoom, destination, election, predestination, preordination, fore-ordination, compulsion (744), subjection (749), inevitability, inevitableness.

Determinism, necessitarianism, fatalism, automatism.

A determinist, necessarian, necessitarian; robot, automaton.

The Fates, Parcae, the Three Sisters, fortune's wheel, the book of fate, the stars, astral influence, spell (152).

(*Phrases*) Hobson's choice; what must be; a blind bargain; a *pis aller*.

(*Verbs*) To lie under a necessity, to be fated, doomed, destined, etc. (152), to need be, have no alternative.

To necessitate, destine, doom, foredoom, predestine, preordain.

To compel, force, constrain, etc. (744), cast a spell, etc. (992).

(*Phrases*) To make a virtue of necessity; to be pushed to the wall; to dree one's weird.

(*Adjectives*) Necessitated, fated, destined, predestined, foreordained, doomed, elect, spellbound.

Compelled, forced, etc., unavoidable, inevitable, irresistible, irrevocable.

Compulsory, involuntary, unintentional, undesigned, unintended, instinctive, automatic, blind, mechanical, impulsive, unconscious, reflex, unwitting, unaware.

arbitrium, spontaneously, freely, of one's own accord, voluntarily, advisedly, designedly, intentionally, expressly, knowingly, determinately, deliberately, pointedly, in earnest, in good earnest, studiously, purposely, *proprio motu, suo motu, ex mero motu; quo animo*.

(*Phrases*) With one's eyes open; in cold blood.

---

602 WILLINGNESS (*Substantives*), voluntariness, disposition, inclination, leaning, *penchant*, humour, mood, vein, bent, bias, propensity, proclivity, aptitude, predisposition, predilection (865), proneness, docility, pliability (324), alacrity, earnestness, readiness, assent (448).

(*Phrases*) A labour of love; *labor ipse voluptas.*

(*Verbs*) To be willing, etc., to incline to, lean to, not mind (865), to propend; to volunteer.

(*Phrases*) To find in one's heart; to set one's heart upon; to make no bones of; have a mind to; have a great mind to; 'Barkis is willin'.'

(*Adjectives*) Willing, fain, disposed, inclined, minded, bent upon, set upon, forward, predisposed, content, favourable, hearty, ready, wholehearted, cordial, genial, keen, prepense, docile, persuadable, persuasible, facile, tractable, easy-going, easily led.

Free, spontaneous, voluntary, gratuitous, unforced, unasked, unsummoned, unbiased, unsolicited, unbesought, undriven.

(*Adverbs*) Willingly, freely, readily, lief, heartily, with a good grace, without reluctance, etc., as soon, of one's own accord (600), certainly, be it so (488).

(*Phrases*) With all one's heart, *con amore*; with heart and soul; with a right good will; with a good grace; *de bon cœur*; by all means; by all manner of means; nothing loth; *ex animo*; to one's heart's content.

Deterministic, necessitarian, fatalistic.

(*Phrase*) Unable to help it.

(*Adverbs*) Necessarily, needs, of necessity, perforce, forcibly, compulsorily; on or by compulsion or force, willy-nilly, *nolens volens*; involuntarily, etc., impulsively (612), unwittingly (491).

(*Phrases*) It must be; it needs must be; it is written; one's fate is sealed; *che sarà sarà*; there is no help for it; there is no alternative; nothing for it but; necessity knows no law; needs must when the devil drives.

603 UNWILLINGNESS (*Substantives*), indisposition, indisposedness, backwardness, disinclination, averseness, aversion, reluctance, repugnance, demur, renitence, remissness, slackness, lukewarmness, indifference, nonchalance.

Hesitation, shrinking, recoil, suspense, dislike (867), scrupulousness, scrupulosity, delicacy, demur, scruple, qualm.

A recusant, pococurante.

(*Verbs*) To be unwilling, etc., to demur, stick at, hesitate (605), waver, hang in suspense, scruple, stickle, boggle, falter, to hang back, hang fire, fight shy of, jib, grudge.

To decline, reject, refuse (764), refrain, keep from, abstain, recoil, shrink, reluct.

(*Phrases*) To stick in the throat; to set one's face against; to draw the line at; I'd rather not.

(*Adjectives*) Unwilling, unconsenting, disinclined, indisposed, averse, reluctant, not content, laggard, backward, shy, remiss, slack, indifferent, lukewarm, frigid, scrupulous, repugnant, disliking (867).

Demurring, wavering, etc., refusing (764), grudging.

(*Adverbs*) Unwillingly, etc., perforce.

(*Phrases*) Against the grain; *invita Minerva; malgré lui; bon gré, mal gré; nolens volens*; in spite of one's teeth; with a bad grace; not for the world; willy-nilly.

604 RESOLUTION (*Substantives*), determination, decision, resolve, resolvedness, fixedness, steadiness, constancy, indefatigability, unchangeableness, inflexibility, decision, finality, firmness, doggedness, tenacity of purpose, pertinacity, perseverance, constancy, solidity, stability.

Energy, manliness, vigour, spirit, spiritedness, pluck, bottom, backbone, stamina, gameness, guts, grit, sand, will, iron will; self-reliance; self-mastery; self-control.

A devotee, zealot, extremist, ultra, enthusiast, fanatic, fan; bulldog, British lion.

(*Verbs*) To be resolved, etc., to have resolution, etc., to resolve, decide, will, persevere, determine, conclude, make up one's mind; to stand, keep, or remain firm, etc., to come to a determination, to form a resolution, to take one's stand, to stand by, hold by, hold fast, stick to, abide by, adhere to, keep one's ground, persevere, keep one's course, hold on, hang on, not to fail.

To insist upon, to make a point of.

(*Phrases*) To determine once for all; to form a resolution; to steel oneself; to pass the Rubicon; take a decisive step; to burn one's boats; to nail one's colours to the mast; to screw one's courage to the sticking-place; to take the bull by the horns; to mean business; to set one's teeth; to keep a stiff upper lip; to keep one's chin up.

(*Adjectives*) Resolved, resolute, game, firm, steady, steadfast, staunch, constant; solid, manly, stout.

Decided, strong-willed, determined, uncompromising, purposive, self-possessed, fixed, unmoved, unshaken, unbending, unyielding, unflagging, unflinching, inflexible, unwavering, unfaltering, unshrinking, undiverted, undeterred, immovable, not to be moved, unhesitating, unswerving.

605 IRRESOLUTION (*Substantives*), indecision, indetermination, demur, hesitation, suspense, uncertainty (475), hesitancy, vacillation, unsteadiness, inconstancy, wavering, fluctuation, flickering, changeableness, mutability, fickleness, caprice (608), levity, *légèreté*, trimming, softness, weakness, instability.

A weathercock, trimmer, timeserver, turncoat, shuttlecock, butterfly, harlequin, chameleon.

(*Verbs*) To be irresolute, etc., to hesitate, hang in suspense, demur, waver, vacillate, quaver, fluctuate, shuffle, boggle, flicker, falter, palter, debate, dilly-dally, shilly-shally, dally with, coquette with, swerve, etc.

(*Phrases*) To hang fire; to hum and ha; to blow hot and cold; not to know one's own mind; to leave '*ad referendum*'; letting 'I dare not' wait upon 'I would.'

(*Adjectives*) Irresolute, undecided, unresolved, undetermined, vacillating, wavering, hesitating, faltering, shuffling, etc., half-hearted, double-minded, indicisive.

Unsteady, unsteadfast, fickle, flighty, changing, changeable, versatile, variable, inconstant, mutable, protean, fluctuating, unstable, unsettled, unhinged, unfixed, weak-kneed, spineless.

Weak, feeble-minded, frail, soft, pliant, giddy, capricious, coquettish, volatile, fitful, frothy, freakish, lightsome, light-minded, invertebrate.

Revocable, reversible.

(*Phrases*) Infirm of purpose; without ballast; waiting to see which way the cat jumps, or the wind blows.

(*Adverbs*) Irresolutely, etc.; off and on.

Peremptory, inexorable, indomitable, persevering, pertinacious, persistent, irrevocable, irreversible, reverseless, decisive, final.

Strenuous, bent upon, set upon, intent upon, proof against, master of oneself, steeled, staid, serious, stiff, stiff-necked, obstinate (606).

(Phrases) Firm as a rock; game to the last; true to oneself; master of oneself; *in utrumque paratus.*
(Adverbs) Resolutely, etc., without fail.
(Phrases) Through thick and thin; through fire and water; at all hazards; sink or swim; *coûte que coûte; fortiter in re*; like grim death.

606 OBSTINACY *(Substantives)*, obstinateness, wilfulness, self-will, pertinacity, pertinaciousness, pervicacity, pervicaciousness, tenacity, tenaciousness, inflexibility, immovability, doggedness, stubbornness, steadiness (604), restiveness, contumacy, cussedness, obduracy, obduration, unruliness.

Intolerance, dogmatism, bigotry, opinionatedness, opiniativeness, fanaticism, zealotry, infatuation, monomania, indocility, intractability, intractableness (481), pig-headedness.

An opinionist, *opiniâtre*, crank, diehard, blimp, stickler, enthusiast, monomaniac, zealot, dogmatist, fanatic, mule.

A fixed idea, rooted prejudice, blind side, obsession (481), King Charles's head.

(Phrase) A bee in one's bonnet.

(Verbs) To be obstinate, etc., to persist, stickle, opiniate.

(Phrases) To stick at nothing; to dig in one's heels; not yield an inch.

(Adjectives) Obstinate, opinionative, opinative, opinionated, opinioned, wedded to an opinion, self-opinioned, prejudiced (481), cranky, wilful, self-willed, positive, tenacious.

Stiff, stubborn, stark, rigid, stiff-necked, dogged, pertinacious, restive, pervicacious, dogmatic, arbitrary, bigoted, unpersuadable, mulish, unmoved, uninfluenced, hard-mouthed, unyielding, inflexible, immovable, pig-headed, wayward, intractable, hide-bound, headstrong, restive, refractory, unruly, infatuated, *entêté*, wrong-headed, cross-grained, obdurate, contumacious, fanatical, rabid, inexorable, impracticable.

(Phrases) Obstinate as a mule; impervious to reason.

(Adverbs) Obstinately, etc.

(Phrases) *Non possumus; vestigia nulla retrorsum.*

607 Change of mind, intention, purpose, etc.

TERGIVERSATION *(Substantives)*, retractation, recantation, revocation, revokement, reversal, palinode, volteface, renunciation, disavowal (536), abjuration, abjurement, apostasy, relinquishment (624), repentance (950), vacillation, etc. (605).

A turncoat, rat, Janus, renegade, apostate, pervert, backslider, recidivist, trimmer, time-server, opportunist, Vicar of Bray, deserter, weathercock, etc. (605), Proteus.

(Verbs) To change one's mind, etc., to retract, recant, revoke, forswear, unsay, take back, abjure, renounce, apostatize, relinquish, trim, straddle, veer round, change sides, rat, go over; pass, change, or skip from one side to another; back out, back down, swerve, flinch, balance.

(Phrases) To eat one's words; turn over a new leaf; think better of it; play fast and loose; blow hot and cold; box the compass; swallow the leek; eat dirt.

(Adjectives) Changeful, changeable, mobile, unsteady (605), trimming, double-faced, ambidexter, fast and loose, time-serving, facing both ways.

Fugacious, fleeting (111), revocatory.

608 CAPRICE *(Substantives)*, fancy, fantasy, humour, whim, crotchet, fad, fike, craze, *capriccio*, quirk, freak, maggot, vagary, whimsy, whimwham, kink, prank, shenanigans, fit, flim-flam, escapade, ploy, dido, monkey-tricks, rag, monkey-shines, *boutade*, wild-goose chase, freakishness, skittishness, volatility, fancifulness, whimsicality, giddiness, inconsistency, contrariety; a madcap.

(Verb) To be capricious, etc.

(Phrases) To strain at a gnat and swallow a camel; to take it into one's head.

(*Adjectives*) Capricious, inconsistent, fanciful, fantastic, whimsical, full of whims, etc., erratic, crotchety, faddy, maggoty, fiky, perverse, humoursome, wayward, captious, contrary, contrarious, skittish, fitful.

(*Phrases*) The head being turned; the deuce being in him; by fits and starts.

609 CHOICE (*Substantives*), option, election, arbitrament, adoption, selection, excerption, co-optation, gleaning, eclecticism, lief, preference, predilection, preoption, discretion (600), fancy.

Decision, determination, adjudication, award, vote, suffrage, ballot, poll, plebiscite, referendum, verdict, voice, plumper.

Alternative, dilemma (704).

Excerpt, extract, cuttings, clippings; pick, *élite*, cream (650).

Chooser, elector, voter, constituent; electorate, constituency.

(*Verbs*) To choose, decide, determine, elect, list, think fit, use one's discretion, fancy, shape one's course, prefer, have rather, have as lief, take one's choice, adopt, select, fix upon, pitch upon, pick out, single out, vote for, plump for, co-opt, pick up, take up, catch at, jump at, cull, glean, pick, winnow.

(*Phrases*) To winnow the chaff from the wheat; to indulge one's fancy; to pick and choose; to take a decided step; to pass the Rubicon (604);

610 ABSENCE OF CHOICE (*Substantives*), Hobson's choice, necessity (601).

Indifference, indecision (605).

(*Phrase*) First come, first served.

(*Adjectives*) Neutral; indifferent, undecided.

(*Phrase*) To sit on the fence.

REJECTION (*Substantives*), refusal (764); declining, repudiation, exclusion.

(*Verbs*) To reject, refuse, etc., decline, give up, repudiate, exclude, lay aside, pigeon-hole, refrain, spare (678), abandon, turn down, blackball; to fail, plough, pluck, spin, cast.

(*Phrases*) To lay on the shelf; to return to store; to throw overboard; to draw the line at.

(*Adjectives*) Rejecting, etc., rejected, etc., not chosen, etc.

(*Phrases*) Not to be thought of; out of the question.

(*Adverbs*) Neither; neither the one nor the other, nothing to choose between them.

to hold out; offer for choice; commend me to; to swallow the bait; to gorge the hook; to yield to temptation.

(*Adjectives*) Optional, discretional, eclectic, choosing, etc., chosen, etc., decided, etc., choice, preferential; left to oneself.

(*Adverbs*) Discretionally, at pleasure, *à plaisir*, *a piacere*, at discretion, at will, *ad libitum*.

Decidedly, etc., rather; once for all, either the one or the other, for one's money, for choice.

611 PREDETERMINATION (*Substantives*), premeditation, predeliberation, foregone conclusion, *parti pris*.

(*Verbs*) To predetermine, premeditate, preconcert, resolve beforehand.

(*Adjectives*) Prepense, premeditated, predetermined, advised, predesigned, aforethought, calculated, studied, designed (620).

612 IMPULSE (*Substantives*), sudden thought, improvisation, inspiration, flash, spurt.

Improvisator, improvisatore, improvisatrice, creature of impulse.

(*Verbs*) To flash on the mind; to improvise, improvisate, make up, extemporize, vamp, ad-lib.

(*Adjectives*) Extemporaneous, extemporary, impulsive, unrehearsed,

(*Adverbs*) Advisedly, deliberately, &c., with the eyes open, in cold blood.

———

(*Adverbs*) Extempore, offhand, impromptu, *à l'improviste*, out of hand.

(*Phrases*) On the spur of the moment, or of the occasion.

unpremeditated (674), improvised, improvisatorial, improvisatory, unprompted, instinctive, spontaneous, natural, unguarded, unreflecting, precipitate.

---

613 HABIT (*Substantives*), habitude, wont, rule, routine, jog-trot, groove, rut.

Custom, consuetude, use, usage, practice, trick, run, run of things, way, form, prevalence, observance, fashion (852), etiquette, prescription, convention, *convenances*, red tape, red-tapery, red-tapism, routinism, conventionalism, vogue.

Seasoning, training, hardening, etc. (673), acclimatization, acclimation, acclimatation.

Second nature, *cacoethes*, taking root, diathesis.

A victim of habit, etc., an addict, junkie, *habitué*.

(*Verbs*) To be habitual, etc., to be in the habit of, be wont, be accustomed to, etc.

To follow, observe, conform to, obey, bend to, comply with, accommodate oneself to, adapt oneself to; fall into a habit, convention, custom, or usage; to addict oneself to, take to, get the hang of.

To become a habit, to take root, to gain or grow upon one, to run in the blood.

To habituate, inure, harden, season, form, train, accustom, familiarize, naturalize, acclimatize, conventionalize, condition.

To acquire a habit, to get into the way of, to learn, etc.

(*Phrases*) To follow the multitude; go with the current, stream, etc.; run on in a groove; do in Rome as the Romans do.

(*Adjectives*) Habitual, accustomed, prescriptive, habituated, etc.; in the habit, etc., of; used to, addicted to, attuned to, wedded to, at home in; usual, wonted, customary, hackneyed, commonplace, trite, ordinary, set, stock, established, accepted, stereotyped, received, acknowledged, recognized; groovy, fixed, rooted, permanent, inveterate, ingrained, running in the blood, hereditary, congenital, innate, inborn, besetting, natural, instinctive, etc. (5).

Fashionable, in fashion, in vogue, according to use, routine, conventional, etc.

(*Phrases*) Bred in the bone; in the blood.

(*Adverbs*) Habitually; as usual, as the world goes, *more suo*, *pro more*, *pro forma*, according to custom, *de rigueur*.

614 DESUETUDE (*Substantives*), disuse, want of habit or of practice, inusitation, newness to.

Non-observance (773), infraction, violation, infringement.

(*Phrase*) 'A custom more honoured in the breach than the observance.'

(*Verbs*) To be unaccustomed, etc., to be new to; to leave off, wean oneself of, break off, break through, infringe, violate, etc., a habit, usage, etc.; to disuse, to wear off.

(*Adjectives*) Unaccustomed, unused, unusual, unwonted, unpractised, unprofessional, unfashionable, non-observant, lax, disused, weaned.

Unseasoned, uninured, untrained, green.

Unhackneyed, unconventional, Bohemian (83).

———

2°. *Causes of Volition*

615 MOTIVE (*Substantives*), reason, ground, principle, mainspring, *primum mobile*, account, score, sake, consideration, calculation, *raison d'être*.

Inducement, recommendation, encouragement, attraction, allectation, temptation, enticement, bait, allurement, charm, witchery, bewitchment.

Persuasibility, softness, susceptibility, attractability, impressibility.

Influence, prompting, dictate, instance, impulse, impulsion, incitement, incitation, press, instigation, excitement, provocation, invitation, solicitation, advocacy, call, suasion, persuasion, hortation, exhortation, seduction, cajolery, tantalization, *agacerie*, seducement, fascination, blandishment, inspiration, honeyed words.

Incentive, stimulus, spur, fillip, urge, goad, rowel, provocative, whet, dram, cocktail, pick-me-up, appetizer.

Bribe, graft, sop, lure, decoy, charm, spell, magnetism, magnet, loadstone.

Prompter, tempter, seducer, seductor, siren, Circe, instigator, *agent provocateur*.

(*Phrases*) The pros and cons; the why and wherefore.

The golden apple; a red herring; a sop for Cerberus; the voice of the tempter; the song of the sirens.

(*Verbs*) To induce, move, lead, draw, draw over, carry, bring, to influence, to weigh with, bias, to operate, work upon, engage, incline, dispose, predispose, put up to, prompt, whisper, call, call upon, recommend, encourage, entice, invite, solicit, press, enjoin, entreat (765),

616 ABSENCE OF MOTIVE, caprice (608).

(*Adjectives*) Aimless, motiveless, pointless, purposeless (621); uninduced, unmoved, unactuated, uninfluenced, unbiased, unimpelled, unswayed, impulsive, wanton, unprovoked, uninspired, untempted, unattracted.

(*Phrase*) Without rhyme or reason.

DISSUASION (*Substantives*), dehortation, discouragement, remonstrance, expostulation, deprecation (766).

Inhibition, check, restraint, curb (752), bridle, rein, stay, damper, chill; deterrent, disincentive.

Scruple, qualm, demur (867), reluctance, delicacy (868); counterattraction.

(*Phrase*) A wet blanket.

(*Verbs*) To dissuade, dehort, discourage, disincline, indispose, dispirit, damp, choke off, dishearten, disenchant, disillusion, deter, keep back, put off, render averse, etc.

To withhold, restrain, hold, hold back, check, bridle, curb, rein in, keep in, inhibit, censor, repel (751).

To cool, blunt, calm, quiet, quench slake, stagger, remonstrate, expostulate, warn, deprecate (766).

To scruple, refrain, abstain, etc. (603).

(*Phrases*) To throw cold water on; to turn a deaf ear to.

(*Adjectives*) Dissuading, etc., dissuasive, dehortatory, expostulatory, deprecatory.

Dissuaded, discouraged, etc.

Repugnant, averse, scrupulous, etc. (867), unpersuadable (606).

———

court, plead, advocate, exhort, enforce, dictate, tantalize, bait the hook, tempt, allure, lure, seduce, decoy, draw on, captivate, fascinate, charm, bewitch, conciliate, wheedle, coax, speak fair, carny (or carney), cajole, pat on the back or shoulder, talk over, inveigle, persuade, prevail upon, get to do, bring over, procure, lead by the nose, sway, over-persuade, come over, get round, turn the head, enlist, retain, kidnap, bribe, suborn, tamper with.

To act upon, to impel, excite, suscitate, stimulate, key up, motivate, incite, animate, instigate, provoke, set on, urge, pique, spirit, inspirit,

nspire, **awaken,** buck up, give a fillip, light up, kindle, enkindle, rekindle, quicken, goad, spur, prick, edge, egg on, hurry on, stir up, work
ıp, fan, fire, inflame, set on fire, fan the flame, blow the coals, stir the
embers, put on one's mettle, set on, force, rouse, arouse, lash into fury,
get a rise out of.

(*Phrases*) To grease the palm; to gild the pill; to work the oracle.

To follow the bent of; to follow the dictates of; to yield to temptation;
to act on principle.

(*Adjectives*) Impulsive, motive, persuasive, hortative, hortatory,
seductive, carnying, suasory, suasive, honey-tongued, attractive, tempt-
ing, alluring, piquant, exciting, inviting, tantalizing, etc.

Persuadable, persuasible, suasible, soft, yielding, facile, easily
persuaded, etc.

Induced, moved, disposed, led, persuaded, etc., spellbound, instinct
with or by.

(*Adverbs*) Because, for, since, on account of, out of, from; by
reason of, for the sake of, on the score of.

As, forasmuch as, therefore, hence, why, wherefore; for all the
world.

(*Phrase*) *Hinc illae lacrimae.*

617 Ostensible motive, or reason assigned.

PLEA (*Substantives*), allegation, pretext, pretence, excuse, alibi, cue, colour,
gloss, salvo, loophole, handle, shift, quirk, guise, stalking-horse, makeshift,
white lie, evasion, get-out, special pleading (477), claptrap, advocation, soft
sawder, blarney (933), moonshine; a lame excuse or apology.

(*Verbs*) To make a pretext, etc., of; to use as a plea, etc.; to plead, allege,
pretend, excuse, make a handle, etc., of, make capital of.

(*Adjectives*) Ostensible, colourable, pretended, alleged, etc.

(*Phrases*) *Ad captandum*; *qui s'excuse s'accuse*; playing to the gallery.

3°. *Objects of Volition*

618 GOOD (*Substantives*), benefit,
advantage, service, interest, weal,
boot, gain, profit, velvet, good turn,
blessing, boon; behoof, behalf.

Luck, piece of luck, windfall, strike,
treasure trove, godsend, bonus, bunce,
bonanza, prize; serendipity.

Goodness (648), utility (644),
remedy (662).

(*Phrases*) The main chance; *summum bonum*; *cui bono ?*

(*Adjectives*) Good, etc. (648), gainful (644).

(*Adverbs*) Aright, well, favourably,
satisfactorily, for the best.

In behalf of, in favour of.

619 EVIL (*Substantives*), harm, ill,
injury,wrong,scathe,curse,detriment,
hurt,damage, disservice, ill-turn, bale,
grievance, prejudice, loss, mischief,
devilry (or deviltry), gravamen.

Disadvantage, drawback, trouble,
vexation (828), annoyance, nuisance,
molestation, oppression, persecution,
plague, corruption (659.

Blow, dunt, knock (276), bruise,
scratch, wound, mutilation, outrage,
spoliation, mayhem, plunder, pillage,
rapine, destruction (791), dilapidation, havoc, ravage, devastation,
inroad, sweep, sack, foray (716),
desolation, *razzia*, dragonnade.

Misfortune, mishap, woe, disaster,
calamity, affliction, catastrophe,
downfall, ruin (735), prostration,
curse, wrack, blight, blast; Pandora's
box; a plague-spot.

Cause of evil, bane (663).

(*Phrases*) Bad show; there's the devil to pay.

(*Adjectives*) Bad, hurtful, etc. (649).

(*Adverbs*) Amiss, wrong, evil, ill.

SECTION II—PROSPECTIVE VOLITION

1°. *Conceptional Volition*

620 INTENTION (*Substantives*), intent, purpose, design, purport, mind, meaning, drift (516), animus, view, set purpose, point, bent, turn, proposal, study, scope, purview.

Final cause, object, aim, end, motive (615), *raison d'être*; destination, mark, point, butt, goal, target, prey, quarry, game, objective; the philosophers' stone.

Decision, determination, resolve, resolution (604), predetermination (611); set purpose.

A hobby, ambition, wish (865).

Study of final causes, teleology; study of final issues, eschatology.

(*Verbs*) To intend, purpose, plan (626), design, destine, mean, aim at, propose to oneself.

To be at, drive at, be after, point at, level at, take aim, aspire at or after, endeavour after.

To meditate, think of, dream of, premeditate (611), contemplate, compass.

To propose, project, devise, take into one's head.

(*Phrases*) To have in view; to have an eye to; to take upon oneself; to have to do; to see one's way; to find in one's heart.

(*Adjectives*) Intended, etc., intentional, deliberate, advised, studied, minded, express, prepense (611), aforethought; set upon, bent upon, intent upon, in view, *in petto*, in prospect; teleological, eschatological.

(*Phrases*) In the wind; *sur le tapis*; on the stocks; in contemplation.

(*Adverbs*) Intentionally, etc., expressly, knowingly, wittingly, designedly, purposely, on purpose, with a view to, with an eye to, for the

621 Absence of purpose in the succession of events.

CHANCE (*Substantives*), fortune, accident, hazard, hap, haphazard (156), lot, fate (601), chance-medley, hit, fluke, casualty, contingency, exigency, fate, adventure, random shot, off chance, toss-up, gamble.

A godsend, luck, a run of luck, a turn of the dice or cards, a break, windfall, etc. (618).

Drawing lots, sortilege, *sortes Virgilianae*.

Wager, bet, flutter, betting, gambling; pitch-and-toss, *roulette*, *rouge-et-noir*.

(*Phrases*) A blind bargain; a pig in a poke.

(*Verbs*) To chance, hap, turn up; to stand a chance.

To risk, venture, hazard, speculate, stake; incur or run the risk; bet, wager, punt, gamble, plunge, raffle.

(*Phrases*) To take one's chance; to chance it; to chance one's arm; try one's luck; shuffle the cards; put into a lottery; lay a wager; toss up; spin a coin; cast lots; draw lots; stand the hazard.

To buy a pig in a poke; *alea jacta est*; the die being cast; to go nap on; to put one's shirt on.

(*Adjectives*) Casual, fortuitous, accidental, inadvertent, fluky, contingent, random, hit-or-miss, happy-go-lucky, adventitious, incidental.

Unintentional, involuntary, aimless, driftless, undesigned, undirected; purposeless, causeless, without purpose, etc., unmeditated, unpurposed, indiscriminate, promiscuous.

On the cards, possible (470), at stake.

(*Adverbs*) Casually, etc., by chance,

purpose of, with the view of, in order to, to the end that, on account of, in pursuance of, pursuant to, with the intent, etc.

(*Phrases*) In good earnest; with one's eyes open; to all intents and purposes.

622 Purpose in action.

PURSUIT (*Substantives*), pursuance, undertaking, enterprise (676), emprise, adventure, game, hobby, endeavour.

Prosecution, search, angling, chase, venery, quest, hunt, shikar, race, battue, drive, course, direction, wildgoose chase, steeplechase, point-to-point.

Pursuer, huntsman, hunter, Nimrod, shikari, hound, greyhound, foxhound, whippet, bloodhound, sleuthhound, beagle, harrier.

(*Verbs*) To pursue, undertake, engage in, take in hand, carry on, prosecute (461), endeavour.

To court, seek, angle, chase, give chase, course, dog, stalk, trail, hunt, drive, follow, run after, hound, bid for, aim at, take aim, make a leap at, rush upon, jump at, quest, shadow, tail, chivy.

(*Phrases*) Take or hold a course; tread a path; shape one's course; direct or bend one's steps or course; run a race; rush headlong; rush headforemost; make a plunge; snatch at, etc.; start game; follow the scent; to run or ride full tilt at.

(*Adjectives*) Pursuing, etc., in hot pursuit; in full cry.

(*Adverbs*) In order to, in order that, for the purpose of, with a view to, etc. (620); on the scent of.

(*Interjections*) Yoicks! tally-ho!

by accident, accidentally, etc., at haphazard, at a venture; heads or tails.

(*Phrase*) As luck would have it.

---

623 Absence of pursuit.

AVOIDANCE (*Substantives*), forbearance, abstention, abstinence, sparing, refraining.

Flight, escape (671), evasion, elusion.

Motive for avoidance, counter-attraction.

Shirker, slacker, quitter, truant, fugitive, runaway.

(*Verbs*) To avoid, refrain, abstain; to spare, hold, shun, fly, slope, flee, eschew, run away from, shrink, hold back, draw back (287), recoil from, flinch, blench, shy, elude, evade, shirk, blink, parry, dodge, let alone.

(*Phrases*) To give the slip or go-by; to part company; to beat a retreat; get out of the way; to give one a wide berth; steer clear of; fight shy of; to take to one's heels.

(*Adjectives*) Avoiding, etc., elusive, evasive, flying, fugitive, runaway, shy, retiring; unattempted, unsought.

(*Adverbs*) Lest, with a view to prevent.

(*Phrases*) *Sauve qui peut*; the devil take the hindmost.

624 RELINQUISHMENT (*Substantives*), dereliction, abandonment (782), renunciation, desertion (607), discontinuance (142).

Dispensation, riddance.

(*Verbs*) To relinquish, give up (782); lay, set, or put aside; drop, yield, resign, abandon, renounce, discard, shelve, pigeon-hole, waive, desist from, desert, defect, leave, leave off, back out of, quit, throw up, chuck up, give over, forgo, give up, forsake, throw over, forswear, swerve from (279), put away, discontinue (681).

(*Phrases*) To drop all idea of; to think better of it; to wash one's hands of; to turn over a new leaf; to throw up the sponge; to have other fish to fry; to draw in one's horns; to lay on the shelf; to move the previous question.

To give warning; to give notice; to ask for one's books.
(*Adjectives*) Relinquishing, etc., relinquished, etc., unpursued.
(*Interjections*) Hands off! keep off! give over! chuck it!

625 BUSINESS (*Substantives*), affair, concern, matter, task, work, job, job of work, assignment, darg, chore, stint, stunt, errand, agenda, commission, office, charge, part, duty, role; a press of business.

Province, department, beat, round, routine, mission, function, vocation, calling, avocation, profession, occupation, pursuit, cloth, faculty, trade, industry, commerce, art, craft, mystery, walk, race, career, walk of life, *métier*.

Place, post, orb, sphere, field, line, capacity, employment, engagement, exercise, occupation; situation, undertaking (676).

(*Verbs*) To carry on or run a business, ply one's trade, keep a shop, etc.; to officiate, serve, act, traffic.

(*Phrases*) To have to do with; have on one's hands; betake oneself to; occupy or concern oneself with; go in for; have on one's shoulders; make it one's business; go to do; act a part; perform the office of or functions of; to enter or take up a profession; spend time upon; busy oneself with, about, etc.

(*Adjectives*) Business-like, official, functional, professional, workaday, commercial, in hand.

(*Adverbs*) On hand, on foot, afoot, afloat, going.

(*Phrase*) In the swim.

626 PLAN (*Substantives*), scheme, device, design, project, proposal, proposition, suggestion.

Line of conduct, game, card course, tactics, strategy, policy, polity (692), craft, practice, campaign, platform, plank, ticket, agenda, orders of the day, gambit.

Intrigue, cabal, plot, conspiracy, complot, racket, machination, *coup d'état*.

Measure, step, precaution, proceeding, procedure, process, system, economy, set-up, organization, expedient, resource, contrivance, invention, artifice, shift, makeshift, gadget, stopgap, manœuvre, stratagem, fetch, trick, dodge, machination, intrigue, stroke, stroke of policy, masterstroke, great gun, trump card.

Alternative, loophole, counterplot, counter-project, side-wind, last resort, *dernier ressort, pis aller*.

Sketch, outline, blue-print, programme, draft (or draught), scenario, *ébauche*, rough draft, skeleton, forecast, prospectus, *carte du pays*, bill of fare, menu.

After-course, after-game, after-thought, *arrière-pensée*, under-plot.

A projector, designer, schemer, contriver, strategist, promoter, organizer, *entrepreneur*, artist, schematist, intriguant.

(*Verbs*) To plan, scheme, devise, imagine, design, frame, contrive, project, plot, conspire, cabal, intrigue (702), think out, invent, forecast, strike out, work out, chalk out, rough out, sketch, lay out, lay down, cut out, cast, recast, map out, countermine, hit upon, fall upon, arrange, mature, organize, systematize, concert, concoct, digest, pack, prepare, hatch, elaborate, make shift, make do, wangle.

(*Phrases*) To have many irons in the fire; to dig a mine; to lay a train; to spring a project; to take or adopt a course; to make the best of a bad job; to work the oracle.

(*Adjectives*) Planned, etc., strategic; planning, scheming, etc.

Well-laid, deep-laid, cunning, well-devised, etc., maturely considered, well-weighed, prepared, organized, etc.

(*Adverbs*) In course of preparation, under consideration, on the anvil, on the stocks, in the rough, *sur le tapis; faute de mieux*.

627 WAY (*Substantives*), method, manner, wise, form, mode, guise, fashion.

Path, road, gait, route, channel, walk, access, course, pass, ford, ferry, passage, line of way, trajectory, orbit, track, ride, avenue, approach, beaten track, pathway, highway, roadway, causeway, footway, pavement, sidewalk, *trottoir*, footpath, bridle path, corduroy road, cinder-path, turnpike road, high road, arterial road, *autobahn*, clearway, boulevard, the King's (or Queen's) highway, thoroughfare, street, lane, alley, gangway, hatchway, cross-road, crossway, flyover, cut, short cut, royal road, cross-cut, *carrefour*, promenade, subway.

Railway, railroad, tramway, tube, underground, elevated; canal.

Bridge, viaduct, stepping-stone, stair, corridor, aisle, lobby, staircase, moving staircase, escalator, companion-way, flight of stairs, ladder, step-ladder, stile, scaffold, scaffolding, lift, hoist, elevator; speedwalk, travolator.

Indirect way: By-path, by-way, by-walk, by-road, back door, backstairs.

Inlet, gate, door, gateway (260), portal, porch, doorway, adit, conduit, tunnel.

(*Phrase*) *Modus operandi.*

(*Adverbs*) How, in what way, in what manner, by what mode.

By the way, *en passant*, by the by, via, *in transitu, chemin faisant*.

One way or another, somehow, anyhow, by hook or by crook.

(*Phrases*) All roads lead to Rome; *hae tibi erunt artes*; where there's a will there's a way.

---

628 MID-COURSE (*Substantives*), middle course, middle (68), mean (29), golden mean, *juste milieu, mezzo termine.*

Direct, straight, straightforward, course or path; great-circle sailing.

Neutrality, compromise.

(*Verbs*) To keep in a middle course, etc.; to compromise, go half-way.

(*Adjectives*) Undeviating, direct, straight, straightforward.

(*Phrases*) *In medio tutissimus ibis;* to sit on the fence.

629 CIRCUIT (*Substantives*), roundabout way, zigzag, circuition, detour, circumbendibus (311), wandering, deviation (279), divergence (291).

(*Verbs*) To perform a circuit, etc., to deviate, wander, go round about, meander, etc. (279).

(*Phrases*) To beat about the bush; to make two bites of a cherry; to lead one a pretty dance.

(*Adjectives*) Circuitous, indirect, roundabout, tortuous, zigzag, etc.

(*Adverbs*) By a roundabout way, by an indirect course, etc.

---

630 REQUIREMENT (*Substantives*), requisition, need, occasion, lack, wants, requisites, necessities, desideratum, exigency, pinch, *sine qua non*, the very thing, essential, must.

Needfulness, essentiality, necessity, indispensability, urgency, call for.

(*Phrases*) Just what the doctor ordered; a crying need; a long-felt want.

(*Verbs*) To require, need, want, have occasion for, stand in need of, lack, desire, be at a loss for, desiderate; not to be able to do without or dispense with; to want but little.

To render necessary, to necessitate, to create a necessity for, demand, call for.

(*Adjectives*) Requisite, required, etc., needful, necessary, imperative, exigent, essential, indispensable, irreplaceable, prerequisite, that cannot be spared or dispensed with, urgent.

2°. *Subservience to Ends*

I. ACTUAL SUBSERVIENCE

631 INSTRUMENTALITY (*Substantives*), medium, intermedium, vehicle, channel, intervention, mediation, dint, aid (707), agency (170).

Minister, handmaid; obstetrician, midwife, *accoucheur*.

Key, master-key, passport, safe-conduct, passe-partout, 'open sesame'; a go-between, middleman (758), a cat's-paw, jackal, pander, tool, ghost, mainstay, trump card.

(*Phrase*) Two strings to one's bow.

(*Verbs*) To subserve, minister, intervene, mediate, devil, pander to.

(*Adjectives*) Instrumental, intervening, intermediate, intermediary, subservient, auxiliary, ancillary.

(*Adverbs*) Through, by, with, by means of, by dint of, *à force de*, along with, thereby, through the medium, etc., of, wherewith, wherewithal.

632 MEANS (*Substantives*), resources, wherewithal, appliances, ways and means, convenience, expedients, step, measure (626), aid (707), intermedium, medium.

Machinery, mechanism, mechanics, engineering, mechanical powers, automation, scaffolding, ladder, mainstay.

(*Phrases*) Wheels within wheels; a shot in the locker.

(*Adjectives*) Instrumental, accessory, subsidiary, mechanical.

(*Adverbs*) How, by what means, by all means, by all manner of means, by the aid of, by dint of.

(*Phrases*) By hook or by crook; somehow or other; for love or money; by fair means or foul; *quocumque modo*.

633 INSTRUMENT (*Substantives*), tool, implement, appliance, contraption, apparatus, utensil, device, gadget, craft, machine, engine, motor, dynamo, generator, mill, lathe.

Equipment, gear, tackle, tackling, rigging, harness, trappings, fittings, accoutrements, paraphernalia, equipage, outfit, appointments, furniture, material, plant, appurtenances.

A wheel, jack, clockwork, wheel-work, spring, screw, turbine, wedge, flywheel, lever, bascule, pinion, crank, winch, crane, capstan, windlass, pulley, hammer, mallet, mattock, mall, bat, racket, sledge-hammer, mace, club, truncheon, pole, staff, bill, crow, crowbar, poleaxe, handspike, crutch, boom, bar, pitchfork, etc.

Organ, limb, arm, hand, finger, claw, paw, talons, tentacle, wing, oar, paddle, pincer, plier, forceps, thimble.

Handle, hilt, haft, shaft, shank, heft, blade, trigger, tiller, helm, treadle, pummel, peg (214, 215), key.

Edge-tool, hatchet, axe, pickaxe, etc. (253), axis (312).

634 SUBSTITUTE (*Substantives*), shift, makeshift, succedaneum (147), stop-gap, expedient, *pis aller*, surrogate, understudy, pinch-hitter, stand-in, locum tenens, proxy, deputy (759).

635 MATERIALS (*Substantives*), material, matter, stuff, constituent, ingredient (56), pabulum, fuel, grist, provender, provisions, food (298).

Supplies, munition, ammunition, reinforcement, relay, contingents.

Baggage, luggage, bag and baggage, effects, goods, chattels, household stuff, equipage, paraphernalia, impedimenta, stock-in-trade, cargo, lading (780).

Metal, stone, ore, brick, clay, wood, timber, composition, compo, plastic.

636 STORE (*Substantives*), stock, fund, supply, reserve, relay, budget, quiver, *corps de réserve*, reserve fund, mine, quarry, vein, lode, fountain, well, spring, milch cow.

Collection, accumulation, heap (72), hoard, cache, stockpile, magazine, pile, rick, nest-egg, savings, bank (802), treasury, reservoir, repository, repertory, repertoire, album, depot, depository, treasure, thesaurus, museum, storehouse, promptuary, reservatory, conservatory, menagerie, aviary, aquarium, receptacle, warehouse, godown, *entrepôt*, dock, larder, cellar, garner, granary, store-room, box-room, lumber-room, silo, cistern, well, tank, gasometer, mill-pond, armoury, arsenal, coffer (191).

(*Verbs*) To store, stock, stockpile, treasure up, lay in, lay by, lay up, file, garner, save, husband, hoard, deposit, amass, accumulate (72).

To reserve, keep back, hold back.

(*Phrase*) To husband one's resources.

(*Adjectives*) Stored, etc., in store, in reserve, spare, surplus, extra.

637 PROVISION (*Substantives*), supply, providing, supplying, sustentation (707), purveyance, purveying, reinforcement, husbanding, commissariat, victualling.

Forage, pasture, food, provender (298).

A purveyor, caterer, contractor, commissary, quartermaster, sutler, victualler, *restaurateur*, feeder, batman; bum-boat.

(*Verbs*) To provide, supply, furnish, purvey, suppeditate, replenish, fill up, feed, stock with, recruit, victual, cater, find, fend, keep, lay in, lay in store, store, stockpile, forage, husband (636), upholster.

(*Phrase*) To bring grist to the mill.

638 WASTE (*Substantives*), consumption, expenditure, exhaustion, drain, leakage, wear and tear, dispersion (73), ebb, loss, misuse, prodigality (818), seepage, squandermania.

(*Verbs*) To waste, spend, expend, use, consume, spill, leak, run out, run to waste, disperse (73), ebb, dry up, impoverish, drain, empty, exhaust; to fritter away, squander.

(*Phrases*) to cast pearls before swine; to burn the candle at both ends; to employ a steam-hammer to crack nuts; to break a butterfly on a wheel; to pour water into a sieve.

(*Adjectives*) Wasted, spent, profuse, lavish, etc., at a low ebb.

(*Phrase*) Penny wise and pound foolish.

639 SUFFICIENCY (*Substantives*), adequacy, competence; enough, satiety.

Fullness, fill, plenitude, plenty, abundance, copiousness, amplitude, affluence, richness, fertility, luxuriance, uberty, foison.

Heaps, lots, bags, piles, lashings, oceans, oodles, mobs.

Impletion, repletion, saturation.

Riches (803), mine, store, fund, (636); a bumper, a brimmer, a bellyful, a cart-load, truck-load, ship-load; a plumper; a charge.

640 INSUFFICIENCY (*Substantives*), inadequacy, inadequateness, incompetence.

Deficiency, stint, paucity, defect, defectiveness, default, defalcation, deficit, shortcoming, falling short (304), too little, what will not do, scantiness, slenderness, a mouthful, etc. (32).

Scarcity, dearth, shortage, want, need, lack, exigency, inanition, indigence, poverty, penury (804), destitution, dole, pittance, short allowance, short commons, a banian day,

A flood, draught, shower, rain (347), stream, tide, spring tide, flush.

(*Phrases*) The horn of plenty; the horn of Amalthea; cornucopia; the fat of the land.

(*Verbs*) To be sufficient, etc., to suffice, serve, pass muster, to do, satisfy, satiate, sate, saturate, make up.

To abound, teem, stream, flow, rain, shower down, pour, swarm, bristle with.

To render sufficient, etc., to make up, to fill, charge, replenish, pour in; swim in, wallow in, roll in.

(*Adjectives*) Sufficient, enough, adequate, commensurate, what will just do.

Moderate, measured.

Full, ample, plenty, copious, plentiful, plenteous, plenary, wantless, abundant, abounding, flush, replete, laden, charged, fraught; well stocked or provided, liberal, lavish, unstinted, to spare, unsparing, unmeasured; *ad libitum*, wholesale.

Brimful, to the brim, chock-full, saturated, crammed, up to the ears, fat, rich, affluent, full up, luxuriant, lush.

Unexhausted, unwasted, exhaustless, inexhaustible.

(*Phrases*) Enough and to spare; cut and come again; full as an egg; ready to burst; plentiful as blackberries; flowing with milk and honey; enough in all conscience; enough to go round; *quantum sufficit*.

(*Adverbs*) Amply, etc., galore.

fast (956), a mouthful, starvation, malnutrition, famine, drought, depletion, emptiness, vacancy, flaccidity, ebb-tide, low water.

(*Phrase*) 'A beggarly account of empty boxes.'

(*Verbs*) To be insufficient, etc., not to suffice, to come short of, to fall short of, fail, run out of, stop short, to want, lack, need, require (630); caret.

To render insufficient, etc., to stint, grudge, hold back, withhold, starve, pinch, skimp, scrimp, famish.

(*Phrase*) To live from hand to mouth.

(*Adjectives*) Insufficient, inadequate, incompetent, too little, not enough, etc., scant, scanty, skimpy, scrimpy, deficient, defective, in default, scarce, empty, empty-handed, devoid, short of, out of, wanting, etc., hard up for.

Destitute, dry, drained, unprovided, unsupplied, unfurnished, unreplenished, unfed, unstored, untreasured, bare, meagre, poor, thin, spare, skimpy, stinted, starved, famished, pinched, fasting, starveling, jejune, without resources (735), shorthanded, undermanned, understaffed, etc.

(*Phrases*) In short supply; not to be had for love or money; at the end of one's tether; at one's last gasp.

---

641 REDUNDANCE (*Substantives*), superabundance, superfluity, superfluence, glut, exuberance, profuseness, profusion, plethora, engorgement, congestion, surfeit, gorge, load, turgidity, turgescence, dropsy.

Excess, nimiety, overdose, oversupply, overplus, surplus, surplusage, overflow, inundation, deluge, extravagance, prodigality (818), exorbitance, lavishness, immoderation.

An expletive (908), pleonasm.

(*Phrases*) *Satis superque*; a drug in the market; the lion's share.

(*Verbs*) To superabound, overabound, run over, overflow, flow over, roll in, wallow in.

To overstock, overdose, overlay, gorge, engorge, glut, sate, satiate, surfeit, cloy, load, overlord, surcharge, overrun, choke, drown, drench, inundate, flood, whelm, deluge.

(*Phrases*) To go begging; it never rains but it pours; to paint the lily; to carry coals to Newcastle.

(*Adjectives*) Redundant, superfluous, exuberant, superabundant, immoderate, extravagant, excessive, in excess, *de trop*, needless, unnecessary, uncalled-for, over and above (40), more than enough, buckshee, running to waste, overflowing, running over.

Turgid, gorged, plethoric, dropsical, replete, profuse, lavish, prodigal, supervacaneous, extra, spare, duplicate, supernumerary, supererogatory, expletive, surcharged, overcharged, sodden, overloaded, overladen, overburdened, overrun, overfed, overfull.

(*Phrase*) Enough and to spare.

(*Adverbs*) Over, over and above, too much, overmuch, over and enough, too far, without measure, without stint.

(*Phrase*) Over head and ears.

2. DEGREE OF SUBSERVIENCE

642 IMPORTANCE (*Substantives*), consequence, moment, weight, gravity, seriousness, consideration, concern, significance, import, influence (175), pressure, urgency, instancy, stress, emphasis, interest, preponderance, prominence (250), greatness (31).

The substance, essence, quintessence, core, kernel, nub, gist, pith, marrow, soul, point, gravamen.

The principal, prominent, or essential part.

A notability, somebody, personage (875), V.I.P., bigwig, toff, big pot, big gun, his nibs; great doings, *notabilia*, a red-letter day.

(*Phrases*) *A sine qua non*; a matter of life and death; no laughing matter.

(*Verbs*) To be important, or of importance, etc., to signify, import, matter, boot, weigh, count, to be prominent, etc., to take the lead.

To attach, or ascribe importance to; to value, care for, etc. (897); overestimate, etc. (482), exaggerate (549).

To mark, underline, italicize, score, accentuate, emphasize, stress, rub in.

(*Phrases*) To be somebody; to fill the bill; to make much of; to make a stir, a fuss, a piece of work, a song and dance; set store upon; to lay stress upon; to take *au grand sérieux*.

(*Adjectives*) Important, of importance, etc., grave, serious, material, weighty, influential, significant, emphatic, momentous, earnest, pressing, critical, preponderating, pregnant, urgent, paramount, essential, vital.

643 UNIMPORTANCE (*Substantives*), indifference, insignificance, triflingness, triviality, triteness; paltriness, emptiness, nothingness, inanity, lightness, levity, frivolity, vanity, frivolousness, puerility, child's play.

Poverty, meagreness, meanness, shabbiness, etc. (804).

A trifle, small matter, minutiae, bagatelle, cipher, moonshine, molehill, joke, jest, snap of the fingers, flea-bite, pinch of snuff, old song, *nugae*, fiddlestick, fiddlestick end, bubble, bulrush, nonentity, lay figure, nobody.

A straw, pin, fig, button, rush, feather, farthing, brass farthing, red cent, dime, dam, doit, peppercorn, pebble, small fry.

Trumpery, trash, codswallop, stuff, *fatras*, frippery, chaff, drug, froth, smoke, cobweb.

Toy, plaything, knick-knack, gimcrack, gewgaw, thingumbob, bauble, kickshaw, bric-à-brac, fal-lal, whimwham, whigmaleerie, curio, bibelot.

Refuse, lumber, junk, litter, orts, tares, weeds, sweepings, scourings, off-scourings; rubble, debris, dross, scoriae, dregs, scum, flue, dust (653).

(*Phrases*) 'Leather and prunella'; *peu de chose*; much ado about nothing; much cry and little wool; flotsam and jetsam; a man of straw; a stuffed shirt; a toom tabard.

(*Verbs*) To be unimportant, to be of little or no importance, etc.; not to signify, not to deserve, merit, or be

Great, considerable, etc. (31), capital, leading, principal, superior, chief, main, prime, primary, cardinal, prominent, salient, egregious, outstanding.

Signal, notable, memorable, remarkable, etc., grand, solemn, eventful, stirring, impressive; not to be despised, or overlooked, etc., unforgettable, worth while.

(*Phrases*) Being no joke; not to be sneezed at; no small beer.

worthy of notice, regard, consideration, etc.

(*Phrases*) To catch at straws; to make much ado about nothing; to cut no ice; *le jeu ne vaut pas la chandelle*.

(*Adjectives*) Unimportant, secondary, inferior, immaterial, inconsiderable, inappreciable, insignificant, unessential, non-essential, beneath notice, indifferent; of little or no account, importance, consequence, moment, interest, etc.; unimpressive, subordinate.

Trifling, trivial, trite, banal, mere, common, so-so, slight, slender, flimsy, trumpery, foolish, idle, puerile, childish, infantile, frothy, trashy, catchpenny, fiddling, frivolous, commonplace, contemptible, cheap.

Vain, empty, inane, poor, sorry, mean, meagre, shabby, scrannel, vile, miserable, scrubby, weedy, niggling, beggarly, piddling, peddling, pitiful, pitiable, despicable, paltry, ridiculous, farcical, finical, finicking, finicky, finikin, fiddle-faddle, wishy-washy, namby-pamby, gimcrack, twopenny, twopenny-halfpenny, two-by-four, one-horse, piffling, jerry, jerry built.

(*Phrases*) Not worth a straw; as light as air; not worth mentioning; not worth boasting about; no great shakes; nothing to write home about; small potatoes; neither here nor there.

(*Interjections*) No matter! pshaw! pooh! pooh-pooh! shucks! I should worry! fudge! fiddle-de-dee! nonsense! boloney! hooey! nuts! rats! stuff! *n'importe!*

(*Adverbs*) Meagrely, pitifully, vainly, etc.

---

644 UTILITY (*Substantives*), service, use, function, office, sphere, capacity, part, role, task, work.

Usefulness, worth, stead, avail, advantageousness, profitableness, serviceableness, merit, *cui bono*, applicability, adequacy, subservience, subserviency, efficacy, efficiency, help, money's worth.

(*Verbs*) To be useful, etc., of use, of service.

To avail, serve, subserve, help (707), conduce, answer, profit, advantage, accrue, bedstead.

To render useful, to use (677), to turn to account, to utilize, to make the most of.

(*Phrases*) To stand in good stead; to do yeoman service; to perform a function; to serve a purpose; to serve a turn.

645 INUTILITY (*Substantives*), uselessness, inefficacy, inefficiency, ineptness, ineptitude, inadequacy, inaptitude, unskilfulness, fecklessness, fruitlessness, inanity, worthlessness, unproductiveness, barrenness, sterility, vanity, futility, triviality, paltriness, unprofitableness, unfruitfulness rustiness, obsoleteness, discommodity, supererogation, obsolescence.

Litter, rubbish, lumber, trash, junk, punk, job lot, orts, weeds (643), bilge, hog-wash.

A waste, desert, Sahara, wild, wilderness.

(*Phrases*) The labour of Sisyphus; the work of Penelope; a slaying of the slain; a dead loss; a work of supererogation.

(*Verbs*) To be useless, etc., to be of no avail, use, etc. (644).

(*Adjectives*) Useful, beneficial, advantageous, serviceable, helpful, gainful, profitable, lucrative, worth while.

Subservient, conducive, applicable, adequate, efficient, efficacious, effective, effectual, seaworthy.

Applicable, available, handy, ready.

(*Adverbs*) Usefully, etc.; *pro bono publico*.

To render useless, etc.; to dismantle, disable, disqualify, cripple.

(*Phrases*) To use vain efforts; to beat the air; to fish in the air; to lash the waves; to plough the sands.

(*Adjectives*) Useless, inutile, inefficient, inefficacious, unavailing, inadequate, inoperative, bootless, supervacaneous, unprofitable, unremunerative, unproductive, sterile, barren, unsubservient, supererogatory.

Worthless, valueless, at a discount, gainless, fruitless, profitless, unserviceable, rusty, effete, vain, empty, inane, wasted, nugatory, futile, feckless, inept, withered, good for nothing, wasteful, ill-spent, obsolete, obsolescent, stale, dud, punk, dear-bought, rubbishy.

Unneeded, unnecessary, uncalled-for, unwanted, incommodious, discommodious.

(*Phrases*) Not worth having; leading to no end; no good; not worth while; of no earthly use; a dead letter.

(*Adverbs*) Uselessly, etc., to no purpose.

---

646 Specific subservience.

EXPEDIENCE (*Substantives*), expediency, fitness, suitableness, suitability, aptness, aptitude, appropriateness, propriety, pertinence, seasonableness (134), adaptation, congruity, consonance (23), convenience, eligibility, applicability, desirability, seemliness, rightness.

An opportunist, time-server.

(*Verbs*) To be expedient, etc.

To suit, fit, square with, adapt itself to, agree with, consort with, accord with, tally with, conform to, go with, do for.

(*Adjectives*) Expedient, fit, fitting, worth while, suitable, applicable, eligible, apt, appropriate, adapted, proper, advisable, politic, judicious, desirable, pertinent, congruous, seemly, consonant, becoming, meet, due, consentaneous, congenial, well-timed, pat, seasonable, opportune, apropos, befitting, happy, felicitous, auspicious, acceptable, etc., convenient, commodious, right.

(*Phrases*) Being just the thing; just as well.

648 Capability of producing good.

GOODNESS (*Substantives*), excellence, integrity (939), virtue (944),

647 INEXPEDIENCE (*Substantives*), inexpediency, disadvantageousness, unserviceableness, disservice, unfitness, inaptitude, ineptitude, ineligibility, inappropriateness, impropriety, undesirability, unseemliness, incongruity, impertinence, inopportuneness, unseasonableness.

Inconvenience, incommodiousness, incommodity, discommodity, disadvantage.

Inefficacy, inefficiency, inadequacy.

(*Verbs*) To be inexpedient, etc., to embarrass, cumber, lumber, handicap, be in the way, etc.

(*Adjectives*) Inexpedient, disadvantageous, unprofitable, unfit, unfitting, unsuitable, undesirable, amiss, improper, unapt, inept, impolitic, injudicious, ill-advised, unadvisable, ineligible, objectionable, inadmissible, unseemly, inopportune, unseasonable, inefficient, inefficacious, inadequate.

Inconvenient, incommodious, cumbrous, cumbersome, lumbering, unwieldy, unmanageable, awkward, clumsy.

649 Capability of producing evil.

BADNESS (*Substantives*), hurtfulness, disserviceableness, injurious-

merit, value, worth, price, preciousness, estimation, rareness, exquisiteness.

Superexcellence, superiority, supereminence, transcendence, perfection (650).

Mediocrity (651), innocuousness, harmlessness, inoffensiveness.

Masterpiece, *chef d'œuvre*, flower, pick, cream, *crême de la crême, élite*, gem, jewel, treasure; a good man (948).

(*Phrases*) One in a thousand (or in a million); the salt of the earth.

(*Verbs*) To be good, beneficial, etc.; to be superior, etc., to excel, transcend, top, vie, emulate (708).

To be middling, etc. (651); to pass, to do.

To produce good, benefit, etc., to benefit, to be beneficial, etc., to confer a benefit, etc., to improve (658).

(*Phrases*) To challenge comparison; to pass muster; to speak well for.

(*Adjectives*) Good, beneficial, valuable, estimable, serviceable, advantageous, precious, favourable, palmary, felicitous, propitious.

Sound, sterling, standard, true, genuine, household, fresh, in good condition, unfaded, unspoiled, unimpaired, uninjured, undemolished, undamaged, unravaged, undecayed, natural, unsophisticated, unadulterated unpolluted, unvitiated.

Choice, select, picked, nice, worthy, meritorious (944), fine, rare, unexceptionable, excellent, admirable, first-rate, splendid, swell, bully, wizard, priceless, smashing, super, topping, top-hole, clipping, ripping, nailing, prime, tiptop, crack, jake, cardinal, superlative, superfine, super-excellent, pukka, gradely, champion, exquisite, high-wrought, inestimable, invaluable, incomparable, transcendent, matchless, peerless, inimitable, unrivalled, *nulli secundus*, second to none, *facile princeps*, spotless, immaculate, perfect (650), *récherché*, first-class, first chop.

Moderately good (651).

Harmless, innocuous, innoxious,

ness, banefulness, mischievousness, noxiousness, malignancy, malignity, malevolence, tender mercies, venomousness, virulence, destructiveness, scathe, curse, pest, plague, bane (663), plague-spot, evil star, ill wind; evildoer (913).

Vileness, foulness, rankness, depravation, depravity; injury, outrage, ill treatment, annoyance, molestation, oppression; sabotage; deterioration (659).

(*Phrases*) A snake in the grass; a fly in the ointment; a nigger in the woodpile; a thorn in the side; a skeleton in the cupboard.

(*Verbs*) To be bad, etc.

To cause, produce, or inflict evil; to harm, hurt, injure, mar, damage, damnify, endamage, scathe, prejudice, stand in the light of, worsen.

To wrong, molest (830), annoy, harass, infest, grieve, aggrieve, trouble, oppress, persecute, weigh down, run down, overlay.

To maltreat, abuse, ill use, ill treat, bedevil, bruise, scratch, maul, mishandle, man-handle, strafe, knock about, strike, smite, scourge (972), wound, lame, maim, scotch, cripple, mutilate, hamstring, hough, stab, pierce, etc., crush, crumble, pulverize.

To corrupt, corrode, pollute, etc. (659).

To spoil, despoil, sweep, ravage, lay waste, devastate, dismantle, demolish, level, raze, consume, overrun, sack, plunder, destroy (162).

(*Phrases*) To play the deuce with; to break the back of; crush to pieces; crumble to dust; to grind to powder; to ravage with fire and sword; to knock the stuffing out of; to queer one's pitch; to let daylight into.

(*Adjectives*) Bad, evil, ill, wrong, prejudicial, disadvantageous, unprofitable, unlucky, sinister, left-handed, obnoxious, untoward, unadvisable, inauspicious, ill-omened.

Hurtful, harmful, injurious, grievous, detrimental, noxious, pernicious, mischievous, baneful, baleful.

Morbific, rank, peccant, malignant,

unoffending, inoffensive, unobjectionable.

(*Phrases*) The goods; the stuff to give them; a bit of all right; of the first water; precious as the apple of the eye; *ne plus ultra*; sound as a roach; worth its weight in gold; right as a trivet; up to the mark; an easy winner.

---

tabid, corroding, corrosive, virulent, cankering, mephitic, narcotic.

Deleterious, poisonous, venomous, envenomed, pestilent, pestilential, pestiferous, destructive, deadly, fatal, mortal, lethal, lethiferous, miasmal.

Vile, sad, wretched, sorry, shabby, scurvy, base, low, low-down (940), scrubby, lousy, stinking, horrid.

Hateful, abominable, loathsome, detestable, execrable, iniquitous, cursed, accursed, confounded, damnable, diabolic, devilish, demoniacal, infernal, hellish, Satanic, villainous, depraved, shocking (898).

(*Adverbs*) Wrong, wrongly, badly, to one's cost.

(*Phrases*) *Corruptio optimi pessima*; if the worst comes to the worst.

650 Perfection (*Substantives*), perfectness, indefectibility, impeccability, infallibility, unimpeachability, *beau idéal*, summit (210).

Masterpiece, *chef d'œuvre*, *magnum opus*, classic, model, pattern, mirror, phoenix, *rara avis*, paragon, cream, nonsuch (or nonesuch), nonpareil, *élite*.

Gem, bijou, jewel, pearl, diamond, ruby, brilliant.

A Bayard, a Galahad, an Admirable Crichton.

(*Phrases*) The philosophers' stone; the flower of the flock; the cock of the roost; the pink or acme of perfection; the pick of the bunch; the *ne plus ultra*.

(*Verbs*) To be perfect, etc., to excel, transcend, overtop, etc. (33).

To bring to perfection, to perfect, to ripen, mature, etc. (52, 729).

(*Phrases*) To carry everything before it; to play first fiddle; bear away the bell; to sweep the board.

(*Adjectives*) Perfect, best, faultless, finished, indeficient, indefectible, immaculate, spotless, impeccable, transcendent, matchless, peerless, unparagoned, etc. (648), inimitable, unimpeachable, superlative, superhuman, divine, classical.

(*Phrases*) Right as a trivet; sound as a bell; *ad unguem factus*; *sans peur et sans reproche*.

651 Imperfection (*Substantives*), imperfectness, unsoundness, faultiness, deficiency, disability, weak point, drawback, inadequacy, inadequateness (645), handicap.

Fault, defect, flaw, lacuna (198), crack, twist, taint, blemish, shortcoming (304), peccancy, vice.

Mediocrity, mean (29), indifference, inferiority.

(*Verbs*) To be imperfect, middling, etc., to fail, fall short, lie under a disadvantage, be handicapped.

(*Phrases*) To play second fiddle; barely to pass muster.

(*Adjectives*) Imperfect, deficient, defective, faulty, dud, inferior, inartistic, inadequate, wanting, unsound, vicious, cracked, warped, lame, feeble, frail, flimsy, sketchy, botched, gimcrack, gingerbread, tottering, wonky, decrepit, rickety, ramshackle, rattletrap, battered, worn out, threadbare, seedy, wormeaten, moth-eaten, played out, used up, decayed, mutilated, unrectified, uncorrected.

Indifferent, middling, mediocre, below par, so-so, *couci-couci*, secondary, second-rate, third-rate, etc., second-best, second-hand.

Tolerable, passable, bearable, pretty well, well enough, rather good, decent, fair, admissible, not bad, not amiss, not so dusty, unobjectionable, respectable, betwixt and between.

(*Phrases*) Having a screw loose; out of order; out of kilter; no great catch; milk and water; no great shakes; nothing to boast of; on its last legs; no class.

652 CLEANNESS (*Substantives*), cleanliness, asepsis, purity (960), neatness, tidiness, spotlessness, immaculateness.

Cleaning, purification, mundification, lustration, abstersion, depuration, expurgation, purgation, castration.

Washing, ablution, lavation, elutriation, lixiviation, clarification, defecation, edulcoration, filtration.

Fumigation, ventilation, antisepsis, decontamination, disinfection, soap; detergent, shampoo, antiseptic, disinfectant.

Washroom, wash-house, laundry; washerwoman, laundress, charwoman, cleaner, scavenger, dustman, sweep.

Brush, broom, besom, vacuum-cleaner, duster, handkerchief, napkin, face-cloth, towel, sponge, tooth-brush, nail-brush; mop, sieve, riddle, screen, filter.

(*Verbs*) To be clean, etc.

To render, clean, etc., to clean, to mundify, cleanse, wipe, mop, sponge, scour, swab, scrub, brush, sweep, vacuum, dust, brush up.

To wash, lave, sluice, buck, launder, steep, rinse, absterge, deterge, descale, clear, purify, depurate, defecate, elutriate, lixiviate, edulcorate, clarify, drain, strain, filter, filtrate, fine, fine down.

To disinfect, deodorize, fumigate, delouse, ventilate, purge, expurgate, bowdlerize.

To sift, winnow, pick, screen, weed.

(*Phrase*) To make a clean sweep of.

(*Adjectives*) Clean, cleanly, pure, spotless, unspotted, immaculate, unstained, stainless, unsoiled, unsullied, taintless, untainted, sterile, aseptic, uninfected.

Cleansing, etc., detergent, detersive, abstersive, abstergent, purgatory, purificatory, etc., abluent, antiseptic.

Spruce, tidy, washed, swept, etc., cleaned, disinfected, purified, etc.

(*Phrases*) Clean as a whistle; clean as a new penny; neat as ninepence.

653 UNCLEANNESS (*Substantives*), immundicity, uncleanliness, soilure, sordidness, foulness, impurity (961), pollution, nastiness, offensiveness, beastliness, muckiness, defilement, contamination, abomination, taint, tainture, corruption, decomposition (49).

Slovenliness, slovenly, untidiness, sluttishness, coarseness, grossness, dregginess, squalor.

Dirt, filth, soil, slop, dust, flue, ooss, cobweb, smoke, soot, smudge, smut, stour, clart, glaur, grime, *sordes*, mess, muck.

Slut, slattern, sloven, frump, mud-lark, riff-raff.

Dregs, grounds, sediment, lees, settlement, dross, drossiness, precipitate, scoriae, slag, clinker, scum, sweepings, off-scourings, garbage, *caput mortuum*, residuum, draff, fur, scurf, scurfiness, furfur, dandruff, vermin.

Mud, mire, slush, quagmire, slough, sludge, alluvium, silt, slime, spawn, offal, faeces, excrement, ordure, dung, droppings, guano, manure, compost, dunghill, midden, bog, laystall, sink, cesspool, sump, sough, *cloaca*, latrine, lavatory, water-closet, w.c., toilet, urinal, rear, convenience, privy, jakes, comfort station, heads, thunder-box, drain, sewer; hog-wash, bilge-water.

Sty, pigsty, dusthole, lair, den, slum.

Rottenness, corruption, decomposition, decay, putrefaction, putrescence, putridity, purulence, pus, matter, suppuration, feculence, rankness, rancidity, mouldiness, mustiness, mucidness, mould, mother, must, mildew, dry-rot, fetor, (401).

Scatology, coprology.

(*Phrases*) A sink of corruption; an Augean stable.

(*Verbs*) To be unclean, dirty, etc., to rot, putrefy, corrupt, decompose, go bad, mould, moulder, fester, etc.

To render unclean, etc., to dirt, dirty, soil, tarnish, begrime, smear, besmear, mess, smirch, besmirch, smudge, besmudge, bemire, spatter, bespatter, splash, bedaggle, bedraggle, daub, bedaub, slobber, beslobber, beslime, to cover with dust.

To foul, befoul, sully, pollute, defile, debase, contaminate, taint, corrupt, deflower, rot.

(*Adjectives*) Unclean, dirty, soiled, filthy, grimy, clarty, dusty, dirtied, etc., smutty, sooty, smoky, reechy, thick, turbid, dreggy, slimy, filthy, mucky.

Slovenly, untidy, sluttish, blowzy, draggle-tailed, dowdy, frumpish, slipshod, unkempt, unscoured, unswept, unwiped, unwashed, unstrained, unpurified, squalid.

Nasty, foul, impure, offensive, abominable, beastly, lousy.

Mouldy, musty, mildewed, fusty, rusty, mouldering, moth-eaten, reasty, rotten, rotting, tainted, rancid, high, fly-blown, maggoty, putrescent, putrid, putrefied, bad, festering, purulent, feculent, fecal, stercoraceous, excrementitious.

(*Phrases*) Wallowing in the mire; rotten to the core.

---

654 HEALTH (*Substantives*), sanity, soundness, heartiness, haleness, vigour, freshness, bloom, healthfulness, euphoria, incorruption, incorruptibility.

(*Phrases*) *Mens sana in corpore sano*; a clean bill.

(*Verbs*) To be in health, etc., to flourish, thrive, bloom.

To return to health, to recover, convalesce, recruit, pull through, to get the better of.

To restore to health, to cure, recall to life, bring to.

(*Phrases*) To keep on one's legs; to take a new or fresh lease of life; to turn the corner.

(*Adjectives*) Healthy, in health, well, sound, healthful, hearty, hale, fresh, whole, florid, staunch, flush, hardy, vigorous, chipper, spry, bobbish, blooming, weather-proof, fit.

Unscathed, uninjured, unmaimed, unmarred, untainted.

(*Phrases*) Sitting up and taking nourishment; being on one's legs; sound as a bell, or roach; fresh as a daisy or rose; in fine or high feather; in good case; fit as a fiddle; in the pink of condition; in the pink; in good form.

655 DISEASE (*Substantives*), illness, sickness, ailment, ailing, indisposition, complaint, disorder, malady, distemper.

Attack, visitation, seizure, stroke, fit.

Sickliness, sickishness, infirmity, diseasedness, tabescence, invalidation, delicacy, weakness, cachexy, witheredness, atrophy, marasmus, incurableness, incurability, palsy, paralysis, decline, consumption, prostration.

Taint, pollution, infection, septicity, epidemic, endemic, murrain, plague, pestilence, virus, pox.

A sore, ulcer, abscess, fester, boil, gathering, issue, rot, canker, cancer, carcinoma, sarcoma, caries, gangrene, mortification, eruption, rash, congestion, inflammation, fever.

A valetudinarian, invalid, patient, case, cripple.

Pathology, aetiology, nosology.

(*Verbs*) To be ill, etc., to ail, suffer, be affected with, etc., to complain of, to droop, flag, languish, halt, sicken, gasp; to malinger.

(*Phrases*) To be laid up; to keep one's bed.

(*Adjectives*) Diseased, ill, taken ill, seized, indisposed, unwell, sick, sickish, seedy, queer, crook, toutie, ailing, suffering, confined, bedridden, invalided.

Unsound, sickly, poorly, delicate, weakly, cranky, healthless, infirm, groggy, unbraced, drooping, flagging, withered, palsied, paralytic, paraplectic, decayed, decrepit, lame, crippled, battered, halting, worn out, used up, run down, off colour, moth-eaten, worm-eaten.

Morbid, tainted, vitiated, peccant, contaminated, tabid, tabescent, mangy, poisoned, immedicable, gasping, moribund (360).

(*Phrases*) Out of sorts; good for nothing; on the sick-list; on the danger list; in a bad way; *hors de combat*; on one's last legs; at one's last gasp.

656 SALUBRITY (*Substantives*), healthiness, wholesomeness, innoxiousness.

Preservation of health, prophylaxis, hygiene, sanitation.

A health resort, spa, hydropathic, sanatorium (662).

(*Verbs*) To be salubrious, etc., to agree with.

(*Adjectives*) Salubrious, wholesome, healthy, sanitary, hygienic, salutary, salutiferous, healthful, tonic, prophylactic, bracing, benign.

Innoxious, innocuous, harmless, uninjurious, innocent.

Remedial, restorative, sanatory (662), nutritious, alterative (660).

658 IMPROVEMENT (*Substantives*), melioration, amelioration, betterment, mend, amendment, emendation, advance, advancement, progress, elevation, promotion, preferment, convalescence, recovery, recuperation, curability.

Repair, reparation, cicatrization, correction, reform, reformation, rectification, epuration, purification, etc. (652), refinement, relief, redress, second thoughts.

New edition; *réchauffé, rifacimento*, revision, revise, recension, rehash, redaction.

(*Verbs*) To be, become, or get better, etc., to improve, mend, advance, progress (282), to get on, make progress, gain ground, make way, go ahead, pick up, rally, recover, get the better of, get well, get over it, pull through, convalesce, recuperate.

To render better, improve, amend, better, meliorate, ameliorate, advance, push on, promote, prefer, forward, enhance.

To relieve, refresh, restore, renew, redintegrate, heal (660); to palliate, mitigate.

To repair, refit, cannibalize,

657 INSALUBRITY (*Substantives*), unhealthiness, unwholesomeness, deadliness, fatality.

Microbe, germ, virus, etc. (663).

(*Adjectives*) Insalubrious, insanitary, unsanitary, unhealthy, ungenial, uncongenial, unwholesome, morbific, mephitic, septic, deleterious, pestilent, pestiferous, pestilential, virulent, poisonous, toxic, contagious, infectious, catching, epidemic, epizootic, endemic, pandemic, zymotic, deadly, pathogenic, pathogenetic, lowering, relaxing; innutritious (645).

(*Phrase*) 'There is death in the pot.'

659 DETERIORATION (*Substantives*), wane, ebb, debasement, degeneracy, degeneration, degradation, degenerateness, demotion, relegation.

Impairment, injury, outrage, havoc, devastation, inroad, vitiation, adulteration, sophistication, debasement, perversion, degradation, demoralization, corruption, prostitution, pollution, contamination, alloy, venenation.

Decline, declension, declination, going downhill, recession, retrogression, retrogradation (283), caducity, decrepitude, decadence, falling off, pejoration.

Decay, disorganization, damage, scathe, wear and tear, mouldiness, rottenness, corrosion, moth and rust, dry-rot, blight, marasmus, atrophy, emaciation, falling to pieces, *délâbrement*.

(*Verbs*) To be, or become worse, to deteriorate, worsen, disimprove, wane, ebb, degenerate, fall off, decline, go downhill, sink, go down, lapse, droop, be the worse for, recede, retrograde, revert (283), fall into decay, fade, break, break up, break down, fall to pieces, wither, moulder,

retouch, revise, botch, vamp, tinker, cobble, clout, patch up, touch up, cicatrize, darn, fine-draw, rub up, do up, furbish, refurbish, polish, bolster up, caulk, careen; to stop a gap, to staunch.

To purify, depurate (652), defecate, strain, filter, rack, refine, disinfect, chasten.

To correct, rectify, redress, reform, review, remodel, prune, restore (660), mellow, set to rights, sort, fix, put straight, straighten out, revise.

(*Phrases*) To turn over a new leaf; to take a new lease of life; to make the most of; to infuse new blood into.

(*Adjectives*) Improving, etc., improved, etc., progressive, corrective, reparatory, emendatory, revisory, sanatory, advanced.

Curable, corrigible, capable of improvement.

———

rot, rust, crumble, totter, shake, tumble, fall, topple, perish, die (360).

To render less good; to weaken, vitiate, debase, alloy, pervert.

To spoil, embase, defile, taint, infect, contaminate, sophisticate, poison, canker, corrupt, tamper with, pollute, deprave, demoralize, envenom, debauch, prostitute, defile, degrade, downgrade, demote, adulterate, stain, spatter, bespatter, soil, tarnish (653), addle.

To corrode, erode, blight, rot, wear away, wear out, gnaw, gnaw at the root of, sap, mine, undermine, shake, break up, disorganize, dismantle, dismast, lay waste, do for, ruin, confound.

To embitter, acerbate, aggravate.

To wound, stab, maim, lame, cripple, mutilate, disfigure, deface.

To injure, harm, hurt, impair, dilapidate, damage, endamage, damnify, etc. (649).

(*Phrases*) To go to rack and ruin; to have seen better days; to go to the dogs; to go to pot; to go on from bad to worse; to go farther and fare worse; to run to seed; to play the deuce with; to sap the foundations of.

(*Adjectives*) Deteriorated, worse, impaired, etc., degenerate, *passé*, on the decline, on the down-grade, deciduous, unimproved, unrecovered, unrestored.

Decayed, etc., moth-eaten, worm-eaten, mildewed, rusty, time-worn, moss-grown, effete, wasted, worn, crumbling, tumbledown, dilapidated, overblown.

(*Phrases*) Out of the frying-pan into the fire; the worse for wear; worn to a thread; worn to a shadow; reduced to a skeleton; the ghost of oneself; a hopeless case.

660 RESTORATION (*Substantives*), restoral, reinstatement, replacement, rehabilitation, instauration, re-establishment, rectification, revendication, redintegration, refection, reconstitution, cure, sanation, refitting, reorganization, recruiting, redress, retrieval, refreshment.

Renovation, renewal, reanimation, recovery, resumption, reclamation, reconversion, recure, resuscitation, revivification, reviviscence, revival, renascence, renaissance, rejuvenation, rejuvenescence, regeneration, regeneracy, regenerateness, palingenesis, redemption; a Phoenix.

661 RELAPSE (*Substantives*), lapse, falling back, backsliding, retrogression, reaction, set-back, recidivism, retrogradation, etc. (659).

Return to or recurrence of a bad state.

A recidivist, backslider, throwback.

(*Verbs*) To relapse, lapse, backslide, fall back, slide back, sink back, go back, return, retrograde.

———

Réchauffé, *rifacimento* (658), recast.

(*Phrases*) A new lease of life; second youth; new birth; 'Richard's himself again.'

(*Verbs*) To return to the original state, to right itself, come to, come round, rally, revive, recover.

To restore, replace, re-establish, reinstate, reseat, replant, reconstitute, redintegrate, set right, set to rights, sort, fix, rectify, redress, reclaim, redeem, recover, recoup, recure, retrieve, cicatrize.

To refit, recruit, refresh, refocillate, rehabilitate, reconvert, renew, renovate, revitalize, revivify, reinvigorate, regenerate, rejuvenesce, rejuvenate, resuscitate, reanimate, recast, reconstruct, rebuild, reorganize.

To repair, retouch, revise (658).

To cure, heal, cicatrize, remedy, doctor, physic, medicate.

(*Phrases*) Recall to life; set on one's legs.

(*Adjectives*) Restoring, etc., restored, etc., restorative, recuperative, reparative, sanative, remedial, curative (662).

Restorable, sanable, remediable, retrievable, recoverable.

(*Adverbs*) *In statu quo*; as you were; Phoenix-like.

662 REMEDY (*Substantives*), help, redress, cure, antidote, counter-poison, vaccine, antitoxin, antibiotic, antiseptic, specific, prophylactic, corrective, restorative, pick-me-up, bracer, sedative, anodyne, opiate, hypnotic, nepenthe, tranquillizer.

Febrifuge, diaphoretic, diuretic, carminative, purgative, laxative, emetic, palliative.

Physic, medicine, drug, tonic, medicament, nostrum, placebo, recipe, prescription, catholicon.

Panacea, elixir, *elixir vitae*, balm, balsam, cordial, cardiac, theriac, ptisan.

Pill, pilule, pellet, tablet, tabloid, pastille, lozenge, powder, draught, lincture, suppository.

Salve, ointment, plaster, epithem, embrocation, liniment, lotion, cataplasm, styptic, poultice, compress, pledget.

663 BANE (*Substantives*), scourge, curse, scathe, sting, fang, gall and wormwood.

Poison, virus, venom, toxin, microbe, germ, bacillus, miasma, mephitis, malaria, pest, rust, canker, cancer, canker-worm.

Hemlock, hellebore, nightshade, henbane, aconite, upas-tree.

Sirocco.

A viper, adder, serpent, cobra, rattlesnake, cockatrice, scorpion, wireworm, torpedo, hornet, vulture, vampire.

Science of poisons, toxicology.

(*Adjectives*) Poisonous, venomous, virulent, toxic, mephitic, pestilent, pestilential, miasmatic, baneful (649).

———

Treatment, diet, dieting, regimen.

Pharmacy, pharmacology, materia medica, therapeutics, homoeopathy, allopathy, radiotherapy, actinotherapy, heliotherapy, thalassotherapy, hydrotherapy, hydropathy, osteopathy, dietetics, dietary, chirurgery, surgery, gynaecology, midwifery, obstetrics, paediatrics, geriatrics; psycho-analysis, psychiatry, psychotherapy; faith-healing.

A hospital, infirmary, pest-house, lazaretto, madhouse, asylum, lunatic asylum, mental hospital, *maison de santé*, ambulance, clinic, dispensary, sanatorium, spa, hydropathic, nursing home.

A doctor, physician, general practitioner, G.P., surgeon, anaesthetist, dentist, aurist, oculist, specialist, alienist, psycho-analyst, psychiatrist, psycho-therapist; apothecary, druggist; midwife, nurse.

(*Verbs*) To dose, physic, attend, doctor, nurse.

(*Adjectives*) Remedial, medical, medicinal, therapeutic, surgical, chirurgical, sanatory, sanative, curative, salutary, salutiferous, healing, paregoric, restorative, tonic, corroborant, analeptic, balsamic, anodyne, sedative, lenitive, demulcent, emollient, depuratory, detersive, detergent, abstersive, disinfectant, antiseptic, corrective, prophylactic, antitoxic, febrifuge, alterative, expectorant; veterinary.

Dietetic, alexipharmic, nutritious, nutritive, peptic, alimentary.

3. CONTINGENT SUBSERVIENCE

664 SAFETY (*Substantives*), security, surety, impregnability, invulnerability, invulnerableness, escape (671).

Safeguard, guard, guardianship, chaperonage, protection, tutelage, wardship, wardenship, safe-conduct, escort, convoy, garrison.

Watch, watch and ward, sentinel, sentry, scout, watchman, patrol, vedette, picket, bivouac.

Policeman, policewoman, police officer, constable, cop, copper, bobby, peeler, slop, bull, dick, rozzer.

Watch-dog, bandog, Cerberus.

Protector, guardian, guard (717), defender, warden, warder, preserver, chaperon, tutelary saint, guardian angel, palladium.

Custody, safe-keeping (751).

Isolation, segregation, quarantine; insurance, assurance; cover.

(*Verbs*) To be safe, etc.

To render safe, etc., to protect, guard, ward, shield, shelter, flank, cover, screen, shroud, ensconce, secure, fence, hedge in, entrench, house, nestel.

To defend, forfend, escort, convoy, garrison, mount guard, patrol, chaperon, picket.

(*Phrases*) To save one's bacon; to light upon one's feet; to weather the storm; to bear a charmed life; to make assurance doubly sure; to take no chances.

To play gooseberry.

(*Adjectives*) Safe, in safety, in security, secure, sure, protected, guarded, etc., snug, fireproof, waterproof, seaworthy, airworthy.

Defensible, tenable; insurable.

665 DANGER (*Substantives*), peril, insecurity, jeopardy, risk, hazard, venture, precariousness, slipperiness.

Liability, exposure (177), vulnerability, vulnerable point, Achilles heel.

Hopelessness (859), forlorn hope, alarm (860), defencelessness.

(*Phrases*) The ground sliding from under one: breakers ahead; a storm brewing; the sword of Damocles.

(*Verbs*) To be in danger, etc., to be exposed to, to incur or encounter danger, run the danger of, run a risk.

To place or put in danger, etc., to endanger, expose to danger, imperil, jeopardize, compromise, adventure, risk, hazard, venture, stake.

(*Phrases*) To sit on a barrel of gunpowder; stand on a volcano; to engage in a forlorn hope.

(*Adjectives*) In danger, peril, jeopardy, etc., unsafe, insecure, unguarded, unscreened, unsheltered, unprotected, guardless, helpless, guideless, exposed, defenceless, vulnerable, at bay.

Unwarned, unadmonished, unadvised.

Dangerous, perilous, hazardous, parlous, risky, chancy, untrustworthy, fraught with danger, adventurous, precarious, critical, touch-and-go, breakneck, slippery, unsteady, shaky, tottering, top-heavy, harbourless, ticklish, dicky.

Threatening, ominous, alarming, minacious (909).

(*Phrases*) Not out of the wood; hanging by a thread; neck or nothing; in a tight place; between two fires; out of the frying-pan into the fire;

Invulnerable, unassailable, un-attackable, impregnable, inexpugnable.

Protecting, etc., guardian, tutelary.

Unthreatened, unmolested, un-harmed, scatheless, unhazarded.

(*Phrases*) Out of harm's way; safe and sound; under lock and key; on sure ground; under cover; under the shadow of one's wing; the coast being clear; the danger being past; out of the wood; proof against.

(*Interjections*) All's well! *salva est res!* safety first!

between the devil and the deep sea; between Scylla and Charybdis; on the rocks; hard bested.

---

666 Means of safety.

REFUGE (*Substantives*), asylum, sanctuary, fastness, retreat, ark, hiding-place, dug-out, funk-hole, fox-hole, loophole, shelter, lee, cover.

Roadstead, anchorage, break-water, mole, groyne, port, haven, harbour, harbour of refuge, pier.

Fort, citadel, fortification, strong-hold, strong point, keep, shield, etc. (717).

Screen, covert, wing, fence, rail, railing, wall, dike, ditch, etc. (232).

Anchor, kedge, grapnel, grappling-iron, sheet-anchor, prop, stay, main-stay, jury-mast, lifeboat, lifebuoy, lifebelt, plank, stepping-stone, um-brella, parachute, lightning-conduc-tor, safety-valve, safety curtain, safety-lamp.

667 Source of danger.

PITFALL (*Substantives*), rocks, reefs, sunken rocks, snags, sands, quick-sands, breakers, shoals, shallows, bank, shelf, flat, whirlpool, rapids, current, undertow, precipice, lee shore, air-pocket.

Trap, snare, gin, springe, deadfall, toils, noose, net, spring-net, spring-gun, masked battery, mine.

(*Phrases*) The sword of Damocles; a snake in the grass; trusting to a broken reed; a lion's den; a hornet's nest; an ugly customer.

---

668 WARNING (*Substantives*), caution, *caveat*, notice, premonition, pre-monishment, lesson, dehortation, monition, admonition (864); alarm (669).

Beacon, lighthouse, lightship, pharos, watch-tower, signal-post, guide-post (550).

Sentinel, sentry, watch, watchman, patrol, vedette (664); monitor, Cassandra.

(*Phrases*) The writing on the wall; the yellow flag; a red light; a stormy petrel; gathering clouds.

(*Verbs*) To warn, caution, forewarn, premonish, give notice, give warning, admonish, dehort, threaten, menace (909).

To take warning; to beware; to be on one's guard (864).

(*Phrases*) To put on one's guard; to sound the alarm.

(*Adjectives*) Warning, etc., monitory, premonitory, dehortatory, cautionary, admonitory.

Warned, etc., careful, on one's guard (459).

(*Interjections*) Beware! look out! mind what you are about! watch your step! let sleeping dogs lie! *foenum habet in cornu!* fore! heads! mind your back! cave!

669 Indication of danger.

ALARM (*Substantives*), alert, alarum, alarm-bell, horn, siren, maroon, fog-signal, tocsin, tattoo, signal of distress, S O S, hue and cry.

False alarm, cry of wolf, bugbear, bugaboo, bogy.
(*Verbs*) To give, raise, or sound an alarm, to alarm, warn, ring the tocsin, dial 999; to cry wolf.
(*Adjectives*) Alarming, etc., threatening.
(*Phrases*) Each for himself; *sauve qui peut*.

670 PRESERVATION (*Substantives*), conservation, maintenance (141), support, upkeep, sustentation, deliverance, salvation, rescue, redemption, self-preservation, continuance (143).
Means of preservation, prophylaxis, preservative, preserver.
(*Verbs*) To preserve, maintain, support, keep, sustain, nurse, save, rescue, file (papers).
To embalm, mummify, dry, dehydrate, cure, kipper, smoke, salt, pickle, marinade, season, kyanize, bottle, pot, can, tin.
(*Adjectives*) Preserving, conservative, prophylactic, preservatory, hygienic.
Preserved, intact, unimpaired, uninjured, unhurt, unsinged, unmarred.

671 ESCAPE (*Substantives*), getaway, flight, elopement, evasion, retreat, reprieve, reprieval, deliverance, redemption, rescue.
Narrow escape, hair's-breadth, escape, close shave, close call, narrow squeak.
Means of escape: Bridge, drawbridge, loophole, ladder, plank, stepping-stone, trap-door, fire-escape, emergency exit.
A fugitive, runaway, refugee, evacuee.
(*Verbs*) To escape, elude, evade, wriggle out of, make or effect one's escape, make off, march off, pack off, skip, skip off, slip away, steal away, slink away, flit, decamp, run away, abscond, levant, skedaddle, scoot, fly, flee, bolt, bunk, scarper, scram, hop it, beat it, vamoose, elope, whip off, break loose, break away, get clear.
(*Phrases*) To take oneself off; play truant; to beat a retreat; to give one the slip; to slip the collar; to slip through the fingers; to make oneself scarce; to fly the coop; to take to one's heels; to show a clean pair of heels; to take French leave; to do a bunk; to do a guy; to cut one's lucky; to cut and run; to live to fight another day; to run for one's life; to make tracks.
(*Interjections*) *Sauve qui peut!* the devil take the hindmost!
(*Adjectives*) Escaping, etc., escaped, etc., runaway.
(*Phrase*) The bird having flown.

672 DELIVERANCE (*Substantives*), extrication, rescue, reprieve, respite, redemption, salvation, riddance, release, liberation (750); redeemableness, redeemability.
(*Verbs*) To deliver, extricate, rescue, save, salvage, redeem, ransom, help out, bring off, *tirer d'affaire*, to get rid, to work off, to rid.
(*Phrases*) To save one's bacon; to find a hole to creep out of.
(*Adjectives*) Delivered, saved, etc., scot-free, scatheless.
Extricable, redeemable, rescuable.

3°. *Precursory Measures*

673 PREPARATION (*Substantives*), making ready, providing, provision, providence, anticipation, preconcertation, rehearsal, precaution; laying foundations, ploughing, sowing, semination, cooking, brewing, digestion,

674 NON-PREPARATION (*Substantives*), want or absence of preparation, inculture, inconcoction, improvidence.
Immaturity, crudeness, crudity, greenness, rawness, disqualification.

gestation, hatching, incubation, concoction, maturation, elaboration, predisposition, premeditation (611), acclimatization (613).

Physical preparation, training, drill, drilling, discipline, exercise, exercitation, gymnastics, callisthenics, eurhythmics, athletics, gymnasium, *palaestra*, prenticeship, apprenticeship, qualification, inurement, education, novitiate (537).

Putting or setting in order, putting to rights, clearance, arrangement, disposal, organization, adjustment, adaptation, disposition, accommodation, putting in tune, tuning, putting in trim, dressing, putting in harness, outfit, equipment, accoutrement, armament.

Groundwork, basis, foundation, pedestal, etc. (215), stepping-stone, first stone, scaffold, scaffolding, cradle, sketch (626).

State of being prepared, preparedness, ripeness, maturity, readiness, mellowness.

Preparer, pioneer, avant-courier, sappers and miners.

(*Phrases*) A stitch in time; clearing decks; a note of preparation; a breather; a trial bout; a practice swing.

(*Verbs*) To prepare, get ready, make ready, get up, anticipate, forecast, pre-establish, preconcert, settle preliminaries, to found.

To arrange, set or put in order, set or put to rights, organize, dispose, cast the parts, mount, adjust, adapt, accommodate, trim, tidy, fit, predispose, inure, elaborate, mature, mellow, season, ripen, nurture, hatch, cook, concoct, brew, tune, put in tune, attune, set, temper, anneal, smelt, undermine, brush up, get up.

To provide, provide against, discount, make provision, keep on foot, take precautions, make sure, lie in wait for (507).

Absence of art, state of nature, virgin soil.

An embryo, skeleton, rough copy, draft (626); germ, rudiment (153), raw material, rough diamond.

Tyro, beginner, novice, neophyte, greenhorn, new chum, pommy, recruit, sprog.

(*Verbs*) To be unprepared, etc., to want or lack preparation.

To improvise, extemporize (612).

To render unprepared, etc., to dismantle, dismount, dismast, disqualify, disable (645), unrig, undress (226).

(*Phrases*) To put *hors de combat*; to put out of gear; to spike the guns; to remove the sparking-plug.

(*Adjectives*) Unprepared, rudimentary, immature, embryonic, unripe, raw, green, crude, rough, roughcast, rough-hewn, unhewn, unformed, unhatched, unfledged, unnurtured, uneducated, unlicked, unpolished, natural, in a state of nature, *au naturel*, unwrought, unconcocted, undigested, indigested, unrevised, unblown, unfashioned, unlaboured, unleavened, fallow, uncultivated, unsown, untilled, untrained, undrilled, unexercised, unseasoned, disqualified, unqualified, out of order, unseaworthy.

Unbegun, unready, unarranged, unorganized, unfurnished, unprovided, unequipped, undressed, in dishabille, dismantled, untrimmed.

Shiftless, improvident, unguarded, happy-go-lucky, feckless, thoughtless, unthrifty.

Unpremeditated, unseen, off-hand (612), from hand to mouth, extempore (111).

(*Phrases*) Caught on the hop; with their trousers down.

To equip, arm, man, fit out, fit up, furnish, rig, dress, dress up, furbish up, accoutre, array, fettle, vamp up, wind up.

To train, drill, discipline, break in, cradle, inure, habituate, harden, case-harden, season, acclimatize, qualify, educate, teach.

(*Phrases*) To take steps; prepare the ground; lay or fix the foundations, the basis, groundwork, etc.; to clear the ground or way or course; clear decks; clear for action; close one's ranks; plough the ground; dress the ground; till the soil; sow the seed; open the way; pave the way; lay a train; dig a mine; prepare a charge; erect the scaffolding; *reculer pour mieux sauter.*

Put in harness; sharpen one's tools; whet the knife; shoulder arms; put the horses to; oil up; crank up; warm up.

To prepare oneself; lay oneself out for; get into harvest; gird up one's loins; buckle on one's armour; serve one's time or apprenticeship; be at one's post; gather oneself together.

To set on foot; to lay the first stone; to break ground.

To erect the scaffold; to cut one's coat according to one's cloth; to keep one's powder dry; to beat up for recruits; to sound the note of preparation.

(*Adjectives*) Preparing, etc., in preparation, in course of preparation, in hand, in train, brewing, hatching, forthcoming, in embryo, afoot, afloat, on the anvil, on the carpet, on the stocks, *sur le tapis.*

Preparative, preparatory, provisional, in the rough, rough and ready (111).

Prepared, trained, drilled, etc., forearmed, ready, in readiness, ripe, mature, mellow, fledged, ready to one's hand, on tap, cut and dried, annealed, concocted, laboured, elaborated, planned (626).

(*Phrases*) Armed to the teeth; armed cap-à-pie; booted and spurred; in full feather; *in utrumque paratus*; in working order.

(*Adverbs*) In preparation, in anticipation of, etc., against.

675 ESSAY (*Substantives*), endeavour, try, trial, experiment (463), probation, attempt (676), venture, adventure, tentative, *ballon d'essai, coup d'essai,* go, crack, whack, slap, shot, speculation.

(*Verbs*) To try, essay, make trial of, try on, experiment, make an experiment, endeavour, strive, attempt, grope, feel one's way; to venture, adventure, speculate, take upon oneself.

(*Phrases*) To put out or throw out a feeler; to tempt fortune; to fly a kite; to send up a pilot balloon; to fish for information, compliments, etc.; to have a crack at; to try one's luck; to chance it; to risk it.

(*Adjectives*) Essaying, etc., experimental, tentative, empirical, on trial, probative, probatory, probationary.

(*Adverbs*) Experimentally, etc., at a venture.

676 UNDERTAKING (*Substantives*), enterprise, emprise, quest, mission, endeavour, attempt, move, first move, the initiative, first step.

(*Verbs*) To undertake, take in hand, set about, go about, set to, fall to, set to work, engage in, launch into, embark in, plunge into, take on, set one's hand to, tackle, grapple with, volunteer, take steps, launch out.

To endeavour, strive, use one's endeavours; to attempt, make an attempt, tempt.

To begin, set on foot, set agoing, take the first step.

(*Phrases*) To break the neck of the business; take the initiative; to get cracking; to break ground; break the ice; break cover; to pass the Rubicon; to take upon oneself; to take on one's shoulders; to put one's shoulder to the wheel; *ce n'est que le premier pas qui coûte*; well begun is half done.

To take the bull by the horns; to rush *in medias res*; to have too many irons in the fire; to attempt impossibilities.

(*Adverbs*) Undertaking, attempting, etc.

677 USE (*Substantives*), employment, employ, application, appliance, adhibition, disposal, exercise, exercitation.

Recourse, resort, avail, service, wear, usage, conversion to use, usufruct, utilization.

Agency (170); usefulness (644).

(*Verbs*) To use, make use of, utilize, exploit, employ (134), apply, adhibit, dispose of, work, wield, manipulate, handle, put to use; turn or convert to use; avail oneself of, resort to, have recourse to, take up with, betake oneself to.

To render useful, serviceable, available, etc.; to utilize, draw, call forth, tax, task, try, exert, exercise, practise, ply, work up, consume, absorb, expend.

To be useful, to serve one's turn (644).

(*Phrases*) To take advantage of; to turn to account; to make the most of; to make the best of; to bring to bear upon; to fall back upon; to press or enlist into the service; to make shift with; make a cat's-paw of.

To pull the strings or wires; put in action; set to work; set in motion; put in practice.

(*Adjectives*) Used, employed, etc., applied, exercised, tried, etc.

678 DISUSE (*Substantives*), forbearance, abstinence, dispensation, desuetude (614), relinquishment, abandonment (624, 782).

(*Verbs*) To disuse, not to use, to do without, to dispense with, neglect, to let alone, to spare, waive.

To lay by; set, put, or lay aside, to discard, dismiss (756); cast off, throw off, turn off, turn out, turn away, throw away, scrap, dismantle, shelve (133), shunt, side-track, get rid of, do away with; to keep back (636).

(*Phrases*) To lay on the shelf; to lay up in a napkin; to consign to the scrap-heap; to cast, heave, or throw overboard; to cast to the winds; to turn out neck and crop; to send to the right-about; to send packing.

(*Adjectives*) Disused, etc., not used, unused, unutilized, done with, unemployed, unapplied, unspent, unexercised, kept or held back.

Unessayed, untouched, uncalled-for, ungathered, unculled, untrodden.

679 MISUSE (*Substantives*), misusage, misemployment, misapplication, misappropriation, abuse, profanation, prostitution, desecration.

Waste (818), wasting, spilling, exhaustion (638).

(*Verbs*) To misuse, misemploy, misapply, misappropriate, desecrate, abuse, profane, prostitute.

To waste, spill, fritter away, exhaust, throw or fling away, squander (818).

(*Phrases*) To waste powder and shot; cut blocks with a razor; cast pearls before swine.

(*Adjectives*) Misused, etc.

SECTION III.—VOLUNTARY ACTION

1°. *Simple Voluntary Action*

680 ACTION (*Substantives*), performance, work, operation, execution, perpetration, proceeding, procedure, *démarche*, process, handiwork, handicraft, workmanship, manœuvre, evolution, transaction, bout, turn,

681 INACTION (*Substantives*), abstinence from action, inactivity (683), non-intervention, non-interference, neutrality, strike, Fabian tactics.

(*Verbs*) Not to do, to let be, abstain from doing; let or leave alone, refrain,

job, doings, dealings, business, affair.

Deed, act, overt act, touch, move, strike, blow, *coup*, feat, stunt, exploit, passage, measure, step, stroke of policy, *tour de force*, *coup de main*, *coup d'état*.

(*Verbs*) To act, do, work, operate, do or transact business, practise, prosecute, perpetrate, perform, execute (729), officiate, exercise, commit, inflict, strike a blow, handle, take in hand, put in hand, run.

To labour, drudge, toil, ply, set to work, pull the oar, serve, officiate, go about, turn one's hand to, dabble; to have in hand.

(*Phrases*) To have a finger in the pie; to take or play a part; to set to work; to put into execution (729); to lay one's hand to the plough; to ply one's task; to get on with the job; to discharge an office.

(*Adjectives*) Acting, etc., in action, in operation, etc., operative, in harness, in play, on duty, on foot, at work, red-handed.

(*Interjection*) Here goes!

682 ACTIVITY (*Substantives*), briskness, quickness, promptness, promptitude, expedition, dispatch, readiness, alertness, smartness, sharpness, nimbleness, agility (274).

Spirit, ardour, animation, life, liveliness, vivacity, eagerness, *empressement*, *brio*, dash, *élan*, abandon, pep, go, alacrity, zeal, push, vim, energy (171), hustle, vigour, intentness.

Wakefulness, *pervigilium*, insomnia, sleeplessness.

Industry, assiduity, assiduousness, sedulity, sedulousness, diligence; perseverance, persistence, plodding, painstaking, drudgery, busyness, indefatigability, indefatigableness, patience, business habits.

Movement, bustle, commotion, stir, fuss, fluster, bother, pother, ado, fidget, restlessness, fidgetiness.

Officiousness, meddling, interference, interposition, intermeddling, tampering with, intrigue, *tripotage*, supererogation.

A man of action, busy bee, busybody, go-getter, zealot, devotee, meddler, hustler, whizz-kid.

(*Phrases*) The thick of the action; *in medias res*; too many cooks; new

desist, keep oneself from doing; let pass, lie by, let be, wait.

To undo, take down, take or pull to pieces, do away with.

(*Phrases*) To bide one's time; to let well alone; to cool one's heels; to stay one's hand; to wash one's hands of; to strike work; nothing doing; *nihil fit*; *dolce far niente*.

(*Adjectives*) Not doing, not done, let alone, undone, etc.; passive, neutral.

———

683 INACTIVITY (*Substantives*), inaction (681), idleness, sloth, laziness, indolence, inertness, inertia (172), lumpishness, supineness, sluggishness, segnitude, languor, torpor, quiescence, stagnation, lentor, limpness, listlessness, remissness, slackness.

Dilatoriness, cunctation, procrastination (133), relaxation, truancy, lagging, dawdling, rust, rustiness, want of occupation, resourcelessness.

Somnolence, drowsiness, doziness, nodding, oscitation, sleepiness, hypnosis.

Hypnology.

Sleep, nap, doze, slumber, shut-eye, bye-bye, snooze, dog-sleep, cat-nap, siesta, dream, faint, swoon, coma, trance, hypnotic state, snore, a wink of sleep, lethargy, hibernation, aestivation.

An idler, laggard, truant, do-nothing, lubber, sluggard, sleepy-head, slumberer, faineant, *flâneur*, loafer, drone, dormouse, slow-coach, stick-in-the-mud, lounger, slug, sundowner, bum, Weary Willie, lazy-bones, lotus-eater, slacker, trifler, dilettante.

brooms sweep clean; too many irons in the fire.

(*Verbs*) To be active, busy, stirring, etc., to busy oneself in, stir, bestir oneself, bustle, fuss, make a fuss, speed, hasten, push, make a push, go ahead, hustle; to industrialize.

To plod, drudge, keep on, hold on, persist, persevere, fag at, hammer at, peg away, stick to, buckle to, stick to work, take pains; to take or spend time in; to make progress.

To meddle, moil, intermeddle, interfere, interpose, kibitz, tamper with, fool with, get at, nobble, agitate, intrigue.

To overact, overdo, overlay, outdo, ride to death.

(*Phrases*) To look sharp; to lay about one; to have one's hands full; to kick up a dust; to stir one's stumps; to exert one's energies; to put one's best foot foremost; to do one's best; to do all one can; to leave no stone unturned; to have all one's eyes about one; make the best of one's time; not to let the grass grow under one's feet; to make short work of; to seize the opportunity; to come up to the scratch.

To take time by the forelock; to improve the shining hour; to make hay while the sun shines; to keep the pot boiling; to strike while the iron is hot; to kill two birds with one stone; to move heaven and earth; to go through fire and water; to do wonders; to go all lengths; to stick at nothing; to go the whole hog; to keep the ball rolling; to put one's back into it; to make things hum.

To have a hand in; to poke one's nose in; to put in one's oar; to have a finger in the pie; to mix oneself up with; steal a march upon.

(*Adjectives*) Active, brisk, quick, prompt, alert, on the alert, stirring, spry, sharp, smart, quick, nimble, agile, light-footed, tripping, ready, awake, broad awake, wide awake, alive, lively, live, animated, vivacious, frisky, forward, eager, strenuous, zealous, expeditious, enterprising, pushing, pushful, spirited, in earnest, up in arms, go-ahead.

Cause of inactivity (174), sedative, hypnotic, knock-out drops, hypnotism; lullaby.

(*Phrases*) The Castle of Indolence; *dolce far niente;* the Land of Nod; the Fabian policy; *laissez aller; laissez faire;* masterly inactivity; the thief o. time.

Sleeping partner; waiter on Providence.

(*Verbs*) To be inactive, etc., to do nothing, let alone, lie by, lie idle, stagnate, lay to, keep quiet, hang fire, relax, slouch, loll, drawl, slug, dally, lag, dawdle, potter, lounge, loiter, laze, moon, moon about, loaf, hang about, stooge, mouch; to waste, lose, idle away, kill, trifle away, fritter away or fool away time; trifle, footle, dabble, fribble, peddle, fiddle-faddle.

To sleep, slumber, nod, close the eyes, close the eyelids, doze, drowse, fall asleep, take a nap, go off to sleep, hibernate, aestivate, vegetate.

To languish, expend itself, flag, hang fire.

To render idle, etc.; to sluggardise.

(*Phrases*) To fold one's arms; to let well alone; play truant; while away the time; to rest upon one's oars; to burn daylight; to take it easy; slack off.

To get one's head down; to hit the hay; to have forty winks; to sleep like a top or like a log; to sleep like a dormouse; to swing the lead; to eat the bread of idleness; to twiddle one's thumbs.

(*Adjectives*) Inactive, unoccupied, unemployed, unbusied, doing nothing (685), resourceless.

Indolent, easy-going, lazy, slothful, idle, thowless, fushionless, slack, inert, torpid, sluggish, languid, supine, heavy, dull, stagnant, lumpish, soulless, listless, moony, limp, languorous, exanimate.

Dilatory, laggard, lagging, tardigrade, drawling, creeping, dawdling, faddling, rusty, lackadaisical, fiddle-faddle, shilly-shally, unpractical, unbusiness-like.

Sleepy, dozy, dopy, **dreamy,**

Working, on duty, at work, hard at work, intent, industrious, up and coming, assiduous, diligent, sedulous, painstaking, business-like, practical, in harness, operose, plodding, toiling, hard-working, fagging, busy, bustling, restless, fussy, fidgety.

Persevering, indefatigable, untiring, unflagging, unremitting, unwearied, ever-tiring, undrooping, unintermitting, unintermittent, unflinching, unsleeping, unslumbering, sleepless, persistent.

Meddling, meddlesome, pushing, intermeddling, tampering, etc., officious, over-officious, intriguing, managing.

(*Phrases*) Up and doing; up and stirring; busy as a bee; on the *qui vive*; nimble as a squirrel; the fingers itching; no sooner said than done; *nulla dies sine linea*; a rolling stone gathers no moss; the used key is always bright.

(*Adverbs*) Actively, etc. (684).

(*Interjections*) Look alive! look sharp! get a move on! get cracking! get busy! hump yourself! get weaving!

684 HASTE (*Substantives*), dispatch, precipitancy, precipitation, precipitousness, impetuosity, posthaste, acceleration, spurt, quickness (274).

Hurry, flurry, drive, bustle, fuss, splutter, scramble, brusquerie, fidget, fidgetiness (682).

(*Verbs*) To haste, hasten, urge, press on, push on, bustle, hurry, hustle, buck up, precipitate, accelerate; to bustle, scramble, scuttle, scurry, scoot, plunge, rush, dash on, press on, scorch, speed.

(*Phrases*) To make the most of one's time; to lose not a moment; *festina lente*.

(*Adjectives*) Hasty, hurried, precipitate, scrambling, etc., headlong, boisterous, impetuous, brusque, abrupt, slapdash, cursory.

(*Adverbs*) Hastily, etc., headlong, in haste, slapdash, slap-bang, amain, hurry-scurry, helter-skelter, head and shoulders, head over heels, by fits and starts, by spurts.

(*Phrases*) No sooner said than done; a word and a blow.

686 EXERTION (*Substantives*), labour, work, toil, fag, exercise, travail, swink, sweat, exercitation, duty, trouble, pains, ado, drudgery, fagging, slavery, operoseness.

Effort, strain, grind, tug, stress,

drowsy, somnolent, dormant, asleep, lethargic, comatose, napping, somniferous, soporific, soporous, soporose, somnific, hypnotic, narcotic, unawakened.

(*Phrases*) With folded arms; *les bras croisés*; with the hands in the pockets; at a loose end.

In the arms or lap of Morpheus.

———

685 LEISURE (*Substantives*), leisureliness, spare time, breathing-space, off-time, slack time, holiday, bank holiday, Sunday, sabbath, vacation, recess, red-letter day, relaxation, rest, repose, halt, pause (142), respite.

(*Phrases*) *Otium cum dignitate*; time to spare; time on one's hands.

(*Verbs*) To have leisure, take one's ease, repose (687), pause.

(*Phrase*) To shut up shop.

(*Adjectives*) Leisurely, undisturbed, quiet, deliberate, calm, slow (683).

(*Adverbs*) Leisurely, etc., at leisure.

———

687 REPOSE (*Substantives*), rest, halt, pause, relaxation, breathing-space, respite (685).

Day of rest, *dies non*, sabbath, holiday.

(*Verbs*) To repose, rest, relax, take

tension, throw, stretch, struggle, spell, heft.

Gymnastics, gym, physical jerks, P.T.

(*Phrases*) A stroke of work; the sweat of one's brow.

(*Verbs*) To labour, work, exert oneself, toil, strive, use exertion, fag, strain, drudge, moil, take pains, take trouble, trouble oneself, slave, pull, tug, ply the oar, rough it, sweat, bestir oneself, get up steam, get a move on, fall to work, buckle to, stick to.

(*Phrases*) To set one's shoulder to the wheel; to strain every nerve; to spare no pains; to do one's utmost or damnedest; to work day and night; to work one's fingers to the bone; to do double duty; to work double tides; to put forth one's strength; to work like a nigger or a horse; to go through fire and water; to put one's best foot forward (682); to do one's level best, grub along; to lay oneself out, lean over backwards.

(*Adjectives*) Labouring, etc., laborious, toilsome, troublesome, operose, herculean, gymnastic, palaestric.

Hard-working, painstaking, energetic, strenuous (682).

(*Adverbs*) Laboriously, lustily, roundly.

(*Phrases*) By the sweat of the brow; with all one's might; *totis viribus*; with might and main; *vi et armis*; tooth and nail; hammer and tongs; through thick and thin; heart and soul.

rest, breathe, take breath, take one' ease, gather breath, recover one' breath, respire, pause, halt, stay one' hand, lay to, lie by, lie fallow, recline lie down, go to rest, go to bed, go t sleep, etc., unbend, slacken.

(*Phrases*) To rest upon one's oars to take a holiday; to shut up shop.

(*Adjectives*) Reposing, resting, etc. restful, unstrained; sabbatical.

---

688 FATIGUE (*Substantives*), lassitude, weariness (841), tiredness, exhaustion, sweat, collapse, prostration, swoon, faintness, faint, *deliquium*, syncope, yawning, anhelation; overstrain.

(*Verbs*) To be fatigued, etc., to droop, sink, flag, wilt, lose breath, lose wind, gasp, pant, pech, puff, yawn, drop, swoon, faint, succumb.

To fatigue, tire, weary, fag, irk, jade, harass, exhaust, knock up, prostrate, wear out, strain, overtask, overwork, overburden, overtax, overstrain, drive, sweat.

(*Adjectives*) Fatigued, tired, unrefreshed, weary, wearied, jaded; wayworn; overworked, hard-driven, toilworn, done up.

689 REFRESHMENT (*Substantives*) recovery of strength, recruiting, repair, refection, refocillation, relief bracing, regalement, bait, restoration, revival; pick-up.

(*Phrase*) A giant refreshed.

(*Verbs*) To refresh, recruit, repair, refocillate, give tone, reinvigorate, reanimate, restore, recover.

To recover, regain, renew, etc., one's strength; perk up.

(*Adjectives*) Refreshing, etc., recuperative, tonic; refreshed, etc. untired, unwearied, etc. (682).

Breathless, out of breath, windless, out of wind, blown, winded, broken-winded.

Drooping, flagging, faint, fainting, done up, knocked up, exhausted, sinking, prostrate, spent, overspent, dead-beat, dog-tired, fagged out.

Worn out, played out, battered, shattered, weather-beaten, footsore, *hors de combat*, done for.

Fatiguing, etc., tiresome, irksome, wearisome, trying.

(*Phrases*) Ready to drop; tired to death; on one's last legs; run off one's legs; all in.

690 AGENT (*Substantives*), doer, performer, actor, perpetrator, practitioner, operator, hand, employee, commissionaire, executor, executrix, maker, effector, consignee, steward, broker, factor, middleman, jobber.

Artist, workman, workwoman, charwoman, worker, artisan, artificer, architect, craftsman, handicraftsman, mechanic, roustabout, machinist, machineman, manufacturer, operative, journeyman, labourer, navvy, stevedore, docker, smith, wright, day-labourer, co-worker; *dramatis personae*.

Drudge, hack, fag, man or maid of all work, hired man, hired girl, factotum, handy-man.

(*Phrase*) Hewers of wood and drawers of water.

691 WORKSHOP (*Substantives*), laboratory, manufactory, mill, shop, works, factory, mint, forge, smithy, loom, cabinet, office, bureau, studio, atelier, hive of industry, workhouse, nursery, hothouse, hotbed, kitchen, dock, slip, yard, foundry.

Crucible, alembic, cauldron, matrix.

2°. Complex Voluntary Action

692 CONDUCT (*Substantives*), course of action, practice, drill, procedure, business (625), transaction, dealing, ways, tactics, policy, polity, generalship, statesmanship, economy, strategy, husbandry, seamanship, stewardship, housekeeping, housewifery, *ménage*, regime, *modus operandi*, economy.

Execution, manipulation, handling, treatment, process, working-out, course, campaign, career, walk.

Behaviour, deportment, comportment, carriage, mien, air, demeanour, bearing, manner, observance.

(*Verbs*) To conduct, carry on, run, transact, execute, carry out, work out, get through, carry through, go through, dispatch, treat, deal with, proceed with, officiate, discharge, do duty, play a part or game, run a race.

To behave; to comport, acquit, demean, carry, hold, oneself.

(*Phrases*) To shape one's course; to paddle one's own canoe.

(*Adjectives*) Conducting, etc., strategical, business-like, practical, executive.

693 DIRECTION (*Substantives*), management, government, bureaucracy, statesmanship, conduct (692), regulation, charge, agency, senatorship, ministry, ministration, managery, directorate, directorship, chairmanship, guidance, steerage, pilotage, superintendence, stewardship, supervision, surveillance, proctorship, chair, portfolio, statecraft, politics, *haute politique*, kingcraft, cybernetics; council (696).

Helm, rudder, compass, needle, radar.

(*Phrase*) The reins of government.

(*Verbs*) To direct, manage, govern, guide, conduct, regulate, order, prescribe, brief, steer, con, pilot, have or take the direction, take the helm, have the charge of, administer, superintend, overlook, supervise, look after, see to, control, boss, run, preside, hold office, hold the portfolio.

To head, lead, show the way, etc.

(*Phrase*) To pull the wires.

(*Adjectives*) Directing, etc., managerial, gubernatorial, executive; dirigible.

694 DIRECTOR (*Substantives*), manager, executive, master (745), prime minister, premier, governor, statesman, legislator, controller, comptroller, intendant, superintendent, rector, matron, supervisor, president, preses, chairman, headman, supercargo, inspector, moderator, monitor, overseer, overlooker, shopwalker, taskmaster, leader, ringleader, demagogue, conductor, precentor, fugleman; official, jack-in-office, bureaucrat, minister, office-bearer, red-tapist, officer (726).

Conductor, steersman, helmsman, pilot, coxswain, guide, cicerone, guard, driver, engine-driver, motorman, whip, charioteer, coachman, Jehu, muleteer, teamster, chauffeur, postilion, *vetturino*.

Steward, factor, factotum, bailiff, landreeve, foreman, forewoman, gaffer, charge-hand, whipper-in, shepherd, proctor, procurator, housekeeper, major-domo, chef, master of ceremonies, M.C.

695 ADVICE (*Substantives*), counsel, suggestion, recommendation, advocacy, hortation, exhortation, dehortation, instruction, charge, monition, admonition (668), admonishment, caution, warning, expostulation (616), obtestation, injunction, persuasion.

Guidance, guide, handbook, chart, compass, manual, itinerary, road-book, reference.

An adviser, senator, counsellor, counsel, consultant, specialist, monitor, mentor, Nestor, guide, teacher (540), physician, leech, doctor.

Referee, arbiter, arbitrator, referendary, assessor.

(*Verbs*) To advise, counsel, give advice, recommend, advocate, admonish, submonish, suggest, prompt, caution, warn, forewarn.

To persuade, dehort, exhort, enjoin, expostulate, charge, instruct.

To deliberate, consult together, hold a council, etc., confer, call in, refer to, take advice, be closeted with.

(*Phrases*) To lay their heads together; to compare notes; to go into a huddle; to take counsel of one's pillow; to take one's cue from.

(*Adjectives*) Monitory, monitive, admonitory, recommendatory, hortatory, dehortatory, exhortatory, exhortative, warning, etc.

(*Phrases*) A word to the wise; *verb sap.*

(*Interjection*) Go to!

696 COUNCIL (*Substantives*), conclave, court, chamber, cabinet, cabinet council, house, committee, subcommittee, board, bench, brains trust, *comitia*, staff.

Senate, *senatus*, parliament, synod, soviet, convocation, convention, congress, consistory, conventicle, chapter, chapel, witenagemot, junta, states-general, diet, Cortes, Riksdag, Thing, Storthing, Reichsrat, Reichstag, Duma, Politburo, Presidium, Comintern, Sobranje, Skupshtina, Tynewald, divan, durbar, kgotla, indala, Areopagus, sanhedrim, directory.

A meeting, assembly, sitting, session, séance, sederunt.

(*Adjectives*) Senatorial, curule.

697 PRECEPT (*Substantives*), direction, instruction, charge, prescript, prescription, recipe, receipt, order (741).

Rule, canon, code, formula, formulary, law, statute, act, rubric, maxim, apophthegm, etc. (496).

698 SKILL (*Substantives*), skilfulness, cleverness, ability, talent, genius, ingenuity, calibre, capacity, competence, shrewdness, sagacity, parts, endowment, faculty, gift, forte, strong point, turn, invention, headpiece.

699 UNSKILFULNESS (*Substantives*), inability, incompetence, incompetency, improficience, improficiency, infelicity, inexpertness, indexterity, unaptness, ineptitude, lefthandedness, awkwardness, maladroitness, clumsiness, gaucherie, rawness,

Address, dexterity, adroitness, aptness, aptitude, facility, felicity, knack, expertness, quickness, sharpness, resourcefulness, smartness, readiness, excellence, habilitation, technique, virtuosity, artistry, ambidexterity, ambidextrousness, sleight of hand (545), know-how, knowingness.

Qualification, proficiency, panurgy, accomplishment, attainment, acquirement, craft, mastery, mastership.

Tact, knowledge of the world, *savoir faire*, discretion, finesse, worldly wisdom.

Prudence, discretion (864).

Art, science, management, tactics, manœuvring, sleight, trick, policy, strategy, jobbery, temporization, technology.

A masterstroke, *chef-d'œuvre*, a masterpiece, *tour de force*, a bold stroke, *coup de maître*, a good hit (650).

(*Verbs*) To be skilful, skilled, etc., to excel in, to specialize in, have the trick of, be master of; to temporize, manœuvre.

(*Phrases*) To play one's cards well; to stoop to conquer; to have all one's wits about one; to keep one's hand in; to know your stuff; to cut one's coat according to one's cloth; to know what one is about; to know what's what; to know the ropes.

(*Adjectives*) Skilled, skilful, etc., clever, able, accomplished, talented, versatile, many-sided, resourceful, ingenious, inventive, shrewd, gifted, hard-headed, sagacious, sharp-witted.

Expert, crack, dexterous, scientific, adroit, apt, sharp, handy, deft, fluent, facile, ready, quick, smart, slick, spry, yare, nimble, ambidextrous, neat-handed, fine-fingered.

Conversant, versed, proficient, efficient, capable, competent, qualified, good at, up to, master of, cut out for, at home in, knowing.

Experienced, practised, hackneyed, trained, initiated, prepared, primed, finished, schooled, thoroughbred, masterly, consummate.

slovenliness, greenness, inexperience, disability, disqualification.

Bungling, blundering, etc., blunder (495), *bêtise*; unteachableness, dumbness, dullness, stupidity (499).

Indiscretion, imprudence (863), thoughtlessness, giddiness, wildness, mismanagement, misconduct, maladministration, misrule, misgovernment, misapplication, misdirection.

(*Phrases*) Rule of thumb; a bad show.

(*Verbs*) To be unskilled, unskilful, etc.

To mismanage, bungle, blunder, botch, boggle, fumble, flounder, stumble, muff, foozle, miscue, muddle, murder, mistake, misapply, misdirect, misconduct; stultify.

(*Phrases*) To make a mess or hash of; to begin at the wrong end; to make sad work or a bad job of; to put one's foot in it; to lose or miss one's way; to lose one's balance; to stand in one's own light; to quarrel with one's bread and butter; to pay dear for one's whistle; to cut one's own throat; to kill the goose which lays the golden eggs; to reckon without one's host.

(*Adjectives*) Unskilled, etc., unskilful, bungling, etc., awkward, clumsy, unhandy, unworkmanlike, unscientific, shiftless, lubberly, *gauche*, maladroit, left-handed, hobbling, slovenly, sloppy, slatternly, giddy, gawky, dumb, dull, unteachable, at fault.

Unapt, unqualified, inhabile, incompetent, disqualified, untalented, ill-qualified, inapt, inept, inexpert, inartistic, raw, green, rusty.

Unaccustomed, unused, unhackneyed, unexercised, untrained, unpractised, undisciplined, uneducated, undrilled, uninitiated, unschooled, unconversant, unversed, inexperienced, unstatesmanlike, non-professional.

Unadvised, misadvised, ill-judged, ill-advised, unguided, misguided, foolish, wild, ill-devised, misconducted.

Technical, **artistic**, workmanlike, business-like, daedalian.

Discreet, politic, tactful, diplomatic, sure-footed, felicitous, strategic.

(*Phrases*) Up to snuff; sharp as a needle; no flies on him.

(*Adverbs*) Skilfully, etc., aright.

700 PROFICIENT (*Substantives*), adept, expert, specialist, genius, dab, crack, whiz, master, *maître*, masterhand, virtuoso, champion, first string, first fiddle, protagonist, ace, artist, tactician, marksman, old stager, veteran, top-sawyer, picked man, cunning man, conjurer, wizard, etc. (994); connoisseur (850); prodigy (872), an Admirable Crichton.

(*Phrases*) A man of the world; a practised hand; no slouch; a smart customer; an old file; an all-round man.

702 CUNNING (*Substantives*), craft, craftiness, wiliness, artfulness, subtlety, shrewdness, smartness, archness, insidiousness, slyness, opportunism, artificialness, artificiality.

Artifice, stratagem, wile, dodge, subterfuge, evasion, finesse, ruse, diplomacy, jobbery, backstairs influence.

Duplicity, guile, circumvention, chicane, chicanery, sharp practice, Machiavellism, legerdemain, trickery, etc. (545).

Net, toils, trap, etc. (667).

A slyboots, Ulysses, Machiavel, trickster, serpent, fox, intriguer, opportunist, time-server.

(*Verbs*) To be cunning, etc., to contrive, design, manœuvre, gerrymander, finesse, shuffle, wriggle, wangle, intrigue, temporize, overreach (545), circumvent, get round, nobble, undermine.

(*Phrases*) To play a deep game; to steal a march on; to know on which side one's bread is buttered.

(*Phrases*) His fingers are all thumbs; penny wise and pound foolish.

---

701 BUNGLER (*Substantives*), blunderer, marplot, greenhorn, lubber, landlubber, fumbler, muddler, duffer, butter-fingers, novice, no conjurer, flat, muff, babe.

(*Phrases*) A poor hand at; no good at; a fish out of the water; a freshwater sailor; the awkward squad; not likely to set the Thames on fire.

---

703 ARTLESSNESS (*Substantives*), nature, naturalness, simplicity, ingenuousness, *bonhomie*, frankness, naïveté, openness, *abandon*, candour, outspokenness, sincerity, straightforwardness, honesty (939), innocence (946).

(*Phrases*) *Enfant terrible*; a rough diamond; a mere babe.

(*Verbs*) To be artless, etc.

(*Phrases*) To call a spade a spade; not to mince one's words; to speak one's mind; to wear one's heart upon one's sleeve.

(*Adjectives*) Artless, natural, native, plain, simple-minded, ingenuous, candid, untutored, unsophisticated, simple, naïve, sincere, frank (543), open, frank-hearted, open-hearted, above-board, downright, unreserved, guileless, inartificial, undesigning, single-minded, honest, straightforward, outspoken, blunt, matter-of-fact.

(*Adjectives*) Cunning, crafty, artful, knowing, wily, sly, fly, pawky, smooth, sharp, smart, slim, feline, subtle, arch, designing, intriguing, contriving, insidious, canny, downy, leery, tricky, deceitful (545), artificial, deep, profound, diplomatic, vulpine, Machiavellian, time-serving.

(*Phrases*) Cunning as a fox; too clever by half; not born yesterday; not to be caught with chaff.

SECTION IV—ANTAGONISM

1°. *Conditional Antagonism*

704 DIFFICULTY (*Substantives*), hardness, toughness, hard work, up-hill work, hard task, troublesomeness, laboriousness.

Impracticability, infeasibility, intractability, toughness, perverseness (471).

Embarrassment, awkwardness, perplexity, intricacy, intricateness, entanglement, knot, Gordian knot, labyrinth, net, meshes, maze, etc. (248).

Dilemma, nice point, delicate point, knotty point, stumbling-block, snag, vexed question, crux; *pons asinorum*, poser, puzzle, floorer, teaser, nonplus, quandary, strait, pass, critical situation, crisis, trial, pinch, emergency, exigency, scramble.

Scrape, hobble, fix, hole, lurch, contretemps, hitch, how-d'ye-do, slough, quagmire, hot water, pickle, stew, imbroglio, mess, ado, false position, stand, deadlock, encumbrance, cul-de-sac, impasse.

(*Phrases*) A Herculean task; a labour of Sisyphus; a difficult role to play; a sea of troubles; horns of a dilemma; a peck of troubles; a kettle of fish; a pretty state of things; a handful; 'Ay, there's the rub.'

(*Verbs*) To be difficult, etc.

To meet with, experience, labour under, get into, plunge into, be surrounded by, be encompassed with, be entangled by, struggle, contend against or grapple with difficulties.

To come to a stand, to stick fast, to be set fast, to boggle, flounder, get left.

To render difficult, etc., to embarrass, perplex, put one out, bother, pose, puzzle, floor, nonplus, ravel, entangle, gravel, faze, flummox, run hard.

(*Phrases*) To come to a deadlock; to be at a loss; to get into hot water; to get into a mess; to be bunkered; to weave a tangled web; to fish in troubled waters; to buffet the waves;

705 FACILITY (*Substantives*), practicability, feasibility, practicableness (470).

Ease, easiness, smoothness, tractability, tractableness, ductility, flexibility, malleability, capability, disentanglement, freedom, advantage, vantage-ground.

A cinch, snap, cakewalk, walkover.

(*Phrases*) Plain sailing; smooth water; fair wind; a clear coast; a holiday task; a royal road; child's play; a soft job; a piece of cake.

(*Verbs*) To be easy, etc., to go, flow, swim, or drift with the tide or stream; to do with ease, to throw off.

To render easy, etc., to facilitate, popularize, smooth, ease, lighten, free, clear, disencumber, deobstruct, disembarrass, clear the way, smooth the way, disentangle, unclog, disengage, extricate, unravel, disburden, exonerate, emancipate, free from; to lubricate, etc. (332), relieve (834).

(*Phrases*) To have it all one's own way; to have a walk-over; to win in a canter; to make light (or nothing) of.

To leave a loophole; to open the door to; to pave the way to; to bridge over; to grease the wheels.

(*Adjectives*) Easy, facile, cushy, attainable, handy, practicable, feasible, achievable, performable, possible (470), superable, surmountable, accessible, come-at-able, get-at-able.

Easily managed or accomplished, etc., tractable, manageable, smooth, glib, pliant, yielding, malleable, ductile, flexible, plastic, submissive, docile.

At ease, free, light, unburdened, unencumbered, unloaded, disburdened, disencumbered, disembarrassed, exonerated, unrestrained, unobstructed, unimpeded, untrammelled, at home.

(*Phrases*) The coast being clear; as easy as falling off a log; like taking candy from a child.

to be put to one's shifts; not to know which way to turn; to skate over thin ice.

To lead one a pretty dance; to put a spoke in one's wheel; to leave in the lurch.

(*Adjectives*) Difficult, not easy, hard, stiff, troublesome, toilsome, formidable, laborious, onerous, operose, awkward, unwieldy, beset with or full of difficulties, Herculean, Sisyphean.

Unmanageable, tough, stubborn, hard to deal with, *difficile*, trying, provoking, ill-conditioned, refractory, perverse, crabbed, intractable, against the grain.

Embarrassing, perplexing, delicate, ticklish, pernickety, complicated, intricate, thorny, spiny, knotty, tricky, critical, pathless, trackless, labyrinthine.

Impracticable, not possible, impossible (471), not practicable, not feasible, unachievable, un-come-at-able, inextricable, impassable, innavigable, desperate, insuperable, insurmountable, unplayable.

In difficulty, perplexed, etc., beset, water-logged, put to it, hard put to it, run hard, hard pressed, thrown out, adrift, at fault, abroad, pushed.

Stranded, aground, stuck fast, at bay.

(*Phrases*) At a standstill; at a stand; up against it; up a gum-tree; out of one's depth; at the end of one's tether; in a cleft stick; on a wrong scent; driven from pillar to post; things being come to a pretty pass; at a pinch; between two stools; in the wrong box; in a fix; in a hole; in a tight place; in the cart; in the soup.

(*Adverbs*) With difficulty, hardly, etc., against the stream, against the grain, uphill.

Quite at home; in one's element in smooth water; on velvet.

(*Adverbs*) Easily, etc., swimmingly

2°. Active Antagonism

706 HINDRANCE (*Substantives*), prevention, preclusion, impedance, retardment, retardation.

Obstruction, stoppage, interruption, interclusion, oppilation, interception, restriction, restraint, inhibition, embargo, blockade, embarrassment.

Interference, interposition, obtrusion, discouragement, chill.

An impediment, hindrance, obstacle, obstruction, bunker, hazard, let, stumbling-block, snag, check, impasse, countercheck, *contretemps*, set-back, hitch, bar, barrier, barrage, barricade, turnpike, wall, dead wall, bulkhead, portcullis, etc. (717), dam, weir, broom, turnstile, tourniquet.

Drawback, objection.

An encumbrance, impedimenta, onus, clog, skid, drag, weight, dead weight, lumber, top-hamper, pack, millstone, incubus, nightmare; trammel, etc. (752).

707 AID (*Substantives*), assistance, help, succour, support, advocacy, relief, advance, furtherance, promotion.

Coadjuvancy, patronage, interest, championship, countenance, favour, helpfulness.

Sustentation, subvention, subsidy, alimentation, nutrition, nourishment, ministration, ministry, accommodation.

Supplies, reinforcements, succours, contingents, recruits; physical support (215); relief, rescue.

(*Phrases*) Corn in Egypt; a *deus ex machina*.

(*Verbs*) To aid, assist, help, succour, support, sustain, uphold, subscribe to, finance, promote, further, abet, advance, foster, cherish, foment; to give, bring, furnish, afford or supply support, etc., to reinforce, recruit, nourish, nurture.

A hinderer, marplot; killjoy, interloper, passenger; opponent (710).

(*Phrases*) A lion in the path; a millstone round one's neck; a wet blanket; the old man of the sea; *damnosa hereditas*; back to square one.

(*Verbs*) To hinder, impede, prevent, preclude, retard, slacken, obviate, forefend, avert, turn aside, ward off, draw off, cut off, counteract, undermine.

To obstruct, stop, stay, let, make against, bar, debar, inhibit, scotch, squash, cramp, restrain, check, stonewall, set back, discourage, discountenance, foreclose.

To thwart, traverse, contravene, interrupt, intercept, interclude, frustrate, defeat, disconcert, embarrass, baffle, undo, intercept; to balk, unsight, cushion, stymie, spoil, mar.

To interpose, interfere, intermeddle, obtrude (682).

To hamper, clog, cumber, encumber, saddle with, load with, overload, overlay, lumber, block up, incommode, hustle; to curb, shackle, fetter; to embog.

(*Phrases*) To lay under restraint; to tie the hands; to keep in swaddling-bands.

To stand in the way of; to take the wind out of one's sails; to break in upon; to run or fall foul of; to put a spoke in the wheel; to throw cold water on; to nip in the bud; to apply the closure.

(*Adjectives*) Hindering, etc., in the way of, impedimental, inimical, unfavourable, onerous, burdensome, cumbrous, intercipient, obstructive.

To favour, countenance, befriend, smile upon, encourage, patronize, make interest for.

To second, stand by, relieve, rescue, back, back up, take part with, side with, to come or pass over to, to join, to rally round, play up to.

To serve, do service, minister to, oblige, humour, cheer, accommodate, work for, administer to, pander to; to tend, attend, take care of, wait on, nurse, dry-nurse, entertain.

To speed, expedite, forward, quicken, hasten, set forward.

(*Phrases*) To take the part of; consult the wishes of; to take up the cudgels for; to espouse the cause of; to enlist under the banners of; to lend or bear a hand; to hold out a helping hand; to give one a lift; to do one a good turn; to see one through; to take in tow; to pay the piper; to help a lame dog over the stile; to give a leg-up.

(*Adjectives*) Aiding, helping, assisting, etc., auxiliary, adjuvant, ancillary, accessory, ministrant, subservient, subsidiary, helpful.

Friendly, amicable, favourable, propitious, well-disposed, neighbourly.

(*Adverbs*) On or in behalf of; in the service of; under the auspices of; hand in hand.

(*Interjections*) Help! save us! *à moi!*

Hindered, etc., wind-bound, storm-stayed, water-logged, heavy-laden.

Unassisted, unaided, unhelped, unsupported, single-handed, unbefriended.

(*Phrase*) Prevention is better than cure.

708 OPPOSITION (*Substantives*), antagonism, oppugnancy, oppugnation, counteraction (179), contravention, impugnment, control, clashing, collision, competition, conflict, rivalry, emulation.

Absence of aid, etc., counterplot (718).

(*Phrase*) A head wind.

709 CO-OPERATION (*Substantives*), coadjuvancy, collaboration, concert, collusion, participation, complicity, co-efficiency, concurrence (178).

Alliance, colleagueship, freemasonry, joint-stock, co-partnership, coalition, combine, syndicate (778), amalgamation, federation, confederation (712).

(*Verbs*) To oppose, antagonize, cross, counteract, control, contravene, countervail, counterwork, contradict, belie, controvert, oppugn, stultify, thwart, counter, countermine, run counter, go against, collide with, clash, rival, emulate, put against, militate against, beat against, stem, breast, encounter, compete with, withstand, to face, face down.

(*Phrases*) To set one's face against; to make a dead set against; to match (or pit) oneself against; to stand out against; to fly in the face of; to fall foul of; to come into collision with; to be or to play at cross-purposes; to kick against the pricks; to buffet the waves; to cut one another's throats; to join issue.

(*Adjectives*) Opposing, etc., adverse, antagonistic, opposed, conflicting, contrary, unfavourable, unfriendly, hostile, inimical; competitive, emulous.

(*Phrases*) Up in arms; at daggers drawn.

(*Phrases*) A helping hand; a long pull.

(*Verbs*) To co-operate, combine, concur, conspire, concert, collaborate, draw or pull together, to join with, collude, unite one's efforts, club together, fraternize, be in league, etc., with, be a party to, to side with.

(*Phrases*) To make common cause; to be in the same boat; to stand shoulder to shoulder; to play into the hands of; to hunt in couples; to hit it off together; to lay their heads together; to play ball.

(*Adjectives*) Co-operating, etc., co-operative, co-operant, in co-operation, etc., in concert, allied, clannish; favourable (707).

Unopposed, unobstructed, unimpeded.

(*Phrase*) Wind and weather permitting.

(*Adverbs*) As one man (488).

(*Adverbs*) Against, versus, counter to, against the grain; against the stream, tide, wind, etc., in the way of, in spite of, in despite of, in the teeth of, in the face of, *per contra*; single-handed.

Across, athwart, overthwart.

Though, although (179), even, *quand même*, all the same.

(*Phrases*) In spite of one's teeth; with the wind in one's teeth.

710 OPPONENT (*Substantives*), antagonist, adversary, adverse party, opposition, rival, competitor, pacemaker, enemy, foe (891), assailant; malcontent.

711 AUXILIARY (*Substantives*), assistant, adjuvant, adjunct, adjutant, help, helper, helpmate, helpmeet, colleague, partner, side-kick, *confrère*, coadjutor, co-operator, collaborator, co-belligerent, ally, aide-de-camp, accomplice, accessory, stand-in, stooge.

Friend (890), confidant, champion, partisan, right hand, stand-by; adherent, *particeps criminis*, confederate, bottle-holder, second, candle-holder, servant (746); *fidus Achates*.

(*Phrase*) *Deus ex machina*.

712 PARTY (*Substantives*), side, partnership, fraternity, sodality, company, society, firm, house, establishment, body, corporation, corporate body, union, association, syndicate, guild, tong, joint concern, combine, trust, cartel.

Fellowship, brotherhood, sisterhood, denomination, communion, community, clan, clanship, club, friendly society, clique, junto, coterie, faction, gang, ring, circle, *camarilla*, cabal, league, confederacy, confederation, federation; *esprit de corps*; alliance, partisanship.

Band, staff, crew, team, set, posse, phalanx, *dramatis personae*.

(*Verbs*) To unite, join, club together, join forces, federate, co-operate, befriend, aid, etc. (707), cement, form a party, league, etc., to be in the same boat.

(*Adjectives*) In partnership, alliance, etc., federal, federated, bounded, banded, linked, cemented, etc., together, embattled.

713 DISCORD (*Substantives*), disagreement (24), variance, difference, divergence, dissent, dissension, misunderstanding, jar, jarring, clashing, friction, odds, dissonance, disaccord.

Disunion, schism, breach, falling out, division, split, rupture, disruption, open rupture, *brouillerie*, feud, vendetta, contentiousness, litigiousness, strife, contention (720); enmity (889).

Dispute, controversy, polemics, quarrel, tiff, spat, *tracasserie*, altercation, imbroglio, bickering, snipsnap, chicanery, squabble, row, shemozzle, rumpus, racket, fracas, brawl, bear garden, Donnybrook, debate (476).

Litigation, words, war of words, battle of the books, logomachy, wrangling, wrangle, jangle, breach of the peace, declaration of war (722).

Subject of dispute, ground of quarrel, disputed point, vexed question, bone of contention, apple of discord, *casus belli*.

(*Verbs*) To be discordant, etc., to differ, dissent, disagree, clash, jar, to misunderstand one another.

714 CONCORD (*Substantives*), accord, agreement (23), unison, unity, union, good understanding, quiet, peace, conciliation, unanimity (488), harmony, amity, sympathy (897), *entente cordiale*, *rapprochement*, alliance.

(*Phrases*) The bonds of harmony; a happy family; kittens in a basket; a happy band of brothers.

(*Verbs*) To agree, accord, be in unison, etc., to harmonize with, fraternize, stand in with.

(*Phrases*) To understand one another; to see eye to eye with; to hit it off; to keep the peace; to pull together.

(*Adjectives*) Concordant, congenial, agreeing, etc., united, in unison, etc., harmonious, allied, cemented, friendly (888), amicable, fraternal, at peace, peaceful, pacific, tranquil.

(*Phrases*) At one with; with one voice.

———

To fall out, dispute, controvert, litigate, to quarrel, argue, wrangle, squabble, bicker, spar, jangle, nag, brawl; to break with; to declare war.

To embroil, entangle, disunite, set against, pit against; to sow dissension, disunion, discord, etc. among.

(*Phrases*) To be at odds with; to fall foul of; to have words with; to have a bone to pick with; to have a crow to pluck with; to have a chip on one's shoulder; to be at variance with; to be at cross purposes; to join issue; to pick a quarrel with; to part brass rags; to chew the fat or rag; to go to the mat with; to live like cat and dog.

To set by the ears; to put the cat among the pigeons; to sow or stir up contention.

(*Adjectives*) Discordant, disagreeing, differing, disunited, clashing, jarring, discrepant, divergent, dissentient, sectarian, at variance, controversial.

Quarrelsome, disputatious, litigious, litigant, factious, pettifogging, polemic, schismatic; unpacified, unreconciled.

(*Phrases*) At odds; on bad terms; in hot water; at daggers drawn; up in arms; out of tune; at sixes and sevens; at loggerheads; a house divided against itself; no love lost between them.

715 DEFIANCE (*Substantives*), challenge, dare, cartel, daring, war-cry, slogan, college yell, war-whoop.

(*Verbs*) To defy, challenge, dare, brave, beard, bluster, look big.

(*Phrases*) To set at naught; snap the fingers at; to cock a snook at; to bid defiance to; to set at defiance; to hurl defiance at; to double the fist; to show a bold front; to brave it out; to show fight; to throw down the gauntlet or glove; to call out.

(*Adjectives*) Defying, etc., defiant.

(*Adverbs*) In defiance of; with arms akimbo.

(*Interjections*) Come on! let 'em all come! do your worst!

(*Phrase*) *Nemo me impune lacessit.*

716 ATTACK (*Substantives*), aggression, offence, assault, charge, onset, onslaught, battue, brunt, thrust, pass, passado, cut, sally, inroad, invasion, irruption, incursion, excursion, sortie, *camisade*, storm, storming, boarding, escalade, foray, raid, air raid, *razzia*, dragonnade (619); siege, investment.

Fire, volley, cannonade, barrage, blitz, broadside, bombardment, stonk, hate, raking fire, platoon-fire, fusillade.

Kick, punch (276), lunge, a run at, a dead set at, carte and tierce, a back-hander.

An assailant, aggressor, invader.

(*Verbs*) To attack, assault, assail, go for, fall upon, close with, charge, bear down upon, set on, have at, strike at, run at, make a run at, butt, tilt at, poke at, make a pass at, thrust at, stab, bayonet, cut and thrust, pitch into, kick, buffet, bonnet, beat (972), lay about one, lift a hand against, come on, have a fling at, slap on the face, pelt, throw stones, etc., to round on.

To shoot, shoot at, fire at, fire upon, let fly at, brown, pepper, bombard, shell, bomb, dive-bomb, blitz, strafe, prang.

To beset, besiege, lay siege to, invest, beleaguer, open the trenches, invade, raid, storm, board, scale the walls.

To press one hard, be hard upon, drive one hard.

(*Phrases*) To draw the sword against; to launch an offensive; take the offensive; assume the aggressive; make a dead set at.

To give the cold steel to; to lay down a barrage; to pour in a broadside; to fire a volley.

717 DEFENCE (*Substantives*), self-defence, self-preservation, protection, ward, guard, guardianship, shielding, etc., resistance (719), safety (664).

Fence, wall, parapet, dike, ditch, fosse, moat (232), boom, mound, mole, outwork, trench, foxhole, dug-out, shelter, Anderson shelter, Morrison shelter, entrenchment, fortification, embankment, bulwark, barbican, battlement, stockade, laager, zareba, abattis, turret, barbette, casemate, muniment, vallum, circumvallation, contravallation, barbed-wire entanglement, sunk fence, ha-ha, buttress, abutment, breastwork, portcullis, glacis, bastion, redoubt, rampart.

Hold, stronghold, keep, donjon, palladium, fort, fortress, blockhouse, pillbox, hedgehog, sconce, citadel, tower, castle, capitol, fastness, asylum (666).

Anchor, sheet-anchor.

Shield, armour, buckler, aegis, breastplate, coat of mail, cuirass, hauberk, habergeon, *chevaux de frise*, screen, etc. (666), helmet, tin hat, battle bowler, casque, shako, bearskin, gas-mask, panoply; fender, torpedo-net, paravane, cow-catcher, buffer.

Defender, protector, guardian (664), champion, protagonist, knight errant; garrison, picket.

(*Verbs*) To defend, shield, fend, fence, entrench, guard (664), keep off, keep at bay, ward off, beat off, parry, repel, bear the brunt of, put to flight.

(*Phrases*) To act on the defensive; to maintain one's ground; to stand

(*Adjectives*) Attacking, etc., aggressive, offensive, up in arms.

at bay; to give a warm reception to.

(*Adjectives*) Defending, etc., defensive, defended, etc., armed, armoured, armour-plated, iron-clad, loopholed, sandbagged, castellated, panoplied, proof, bullet-proof, bomb-proof.

(*Phrases*) Armed cap-à-pie; armed to the teeth.

(*Adverbs*) Defensively, on the defence, on the defensive, at bay.

---

718 RETALIATION (*Substantives*), reprisal, retort, come-back, counter-stroke, reciprocation, *tu quoque*, recrimination, retribution, counterplot, counterproject, counterblast, *lex talionis*, revenge (919), compensation (30).

(*Phrases*) Tit for tat; a *quid pro quo*; a Roland for an Oliver; diamond cut diamond; the biter bit; catching a Tartar; a game two can play at; hoist with his own petard.

(*Verbs*) To retaliate, retort, cap, reciprocate, recriminate, counter, get even with one, pay off.

(*Phrases*) To turn the tables; to return the compliment; to pay off old scores; to pay in one's own coin; to give as good as one got.

(*Adjectives*) Retaliating, retaliatory, retaliative, recriminatory, recriminative.

(*Interjection*) You're another!

719 RESISTANCE (*Substantives*), stand, oppugnation, reluctation, front, repulse, rebuff, opposition (708), disobedience (742), recalcitration.

Strike, industrial action, lockout, tumult, riot, pronunciamento, *émeute*, mutiny.

Revolt, rising, insurrection, rebellion, *coup d'état*, *putsch*.

(*Verbs*) To resist, not to submit, etc., to withstand, stand against, stand firm, make a stand, repugn, reluct, reluctate, confront, grapple with, face down.

To kick, kick against, recalcitrate, lift the hand against (716), repel, repulse, rise, revolt, mutiny.

(*Phrases*) To show a bold front; to make head against; to stand one's ground; to stand the brunt of; to hold one's own; to keep at bay; to stem the torrent; to champ the bit; to sell one's life dearly.

To fly in the face of; to kick against the pricks; to take the bit between one's teeth.

(*Adjectives*) Resisting, etc., resistive, resistant, refractory, mutinous, recalcitrant, rebellious, up in arms, out.

Unyielding, unconquered, indomitable.

(*Interjections*) Hands off! keep off!

---

720 CONTENTION (*Substantives*), contest, struggle, contestation, debate (476), logomachy, paper war, litigation, high words, rivalry, corrivalry, corrivalship, competition, *concours*, gymkhana, race, heat, match, tie, bickering, strife (713).

Wrestling, jiu-jitsu, pugilism, boxing, fisticuffs, spar, prize-fighting, athletics, sports, gymnastics, set-to, round, fracas, row, shindy, scrap, dust, rumpus, shemozzle, stramash,

721 PEACE (*Substantives*), amity, truce, armistice, harmony (714), tranquillity.

(*Phrases*) Piping time of peace; a quiet life.

(*Verbs*) To be at peace, etc., to keep the peace, etc. (714), pacify (723).

(*Adjectives*) Pacific, peaceable, peaceful, tranquil, untroubled, bloodless, halcyon.

outbreak, clash, collision, shock, breach of the peace, brawl, Donnybrook (713).

Conflict, skirmish, rencounter, scuffle, encounter, velitation, tussle, scrimmage, scrummage, broil, fray, affray, *mêlée*, affair, brush, bout, fight, battle, combat, action, engagement, battle royal, running fight, free fight, joust, tournament, tourney, pitched battle, death struggle, Armageddon.

Naval engagement, naumachy, sea-fight; air duel, dogfight.

Duel, satisfaction, monomachy, single combat, passage of arms, affair of honour, a triangular duel.

(*Verbs*) To contend, contest, struggle, vie with, emulate, rival, race, race with, outvie, battle with, cope with, compete, join issue, bandy words with, try conclusions with, close with, square, buckle with, spar, box, tussle, fence, wrestle, joust, enter the lists, take up arms, take the field, encounter, struggle with, grapple with, tackle, engage with, pitch into, strive with, fall to, encounter, collide with.

(*Phrases*) Join battle; fall foul of; have a brush with; break the peace; take up the cudgels; unsheath the sword; break a lance; to run a tilt at; give satisfaction; measure swords; exchange shots; lay about one; cut and thrust; fight without the gloves; go on the warpath.

(*Adjectives*) Contending, etc., contentious, combative, bellicose (722); pugilistic, agonistic, competitive, rival, polemical (476), rough-and-tumble.

(*Phrases*) A word and a blow; pull devil, pull baker.

---

722 WARFARE (*Substantives*), war, hostilities, fighting, etc., arms, the sword, open war, *ultima ratio*, war to the knife.

Battle array, campaign, crusade, expedition, operation, mission, warpath.

Warlike spirit, military spirit, militarism, bellicosity.

The art of war, tactics, strategy, military evolutions, arms, service, campaigning, tented field; Mars, Bellona.

War-cry, slogan, fiery cross, trumpet, clarion, bugle, pibroch, warwhoop, beat of drum, tom-tom; mobilization.

(*Phrases*) The mailed fist; wager of battle.

(*Verbs*) To arm, fight, set to, spar, scrap, tussle, joust, tilt, box, skirmish, fight hand to hand, fence, measure swords, engage, combat, give battle, go to battle, join battle, engage in battle, raise or mobilize troops, declare war, wage war, go to war, come to blows, break a lance with, appeal to arms, appeal to the sword, give satisfaction, take the

723 PACIFICATION (*Substantives*), reconciliation, accommodation, arrangement, *modus vivendi*, adjustment, terms, amnesty.

Peace-offering, olive-branch, calumet or pipe of peace, preliminaries of peace.

Pacifism, pacificism, appeasement.

Truce, armistice, suspension of arms, of hostilities, etc., convention, *détente*.

Flag of truce, white flag, cartel.

(*Phrases*) Hollow truce; cold war; *pax in bello*.

(*Verbs*) To make peace, pacify, make it up, reconcile, conciliate, propitiate, appease, tranquillize, compose, allay, settle differences, restore harmony, heal the breach.

(*Phrases*) To put up the sword; to sheathe the sword; to beat swords into ploughshares; to bury the hatchet; to smoke the pipe of peace; to close the temple of Janus; to cry quits.

(*Adjectives*) Pacified, etc., pacific, conciliatory.

field, keep the field, fight it out, fight to a finish, spill blood, carry on war, carry on hostilities, to fight one's way, to serve, to fight like devils, to sell one's life dearly.

(*Phrases*) To see service; to smell powder; to go over the top.

(*Adjectives*) Contending, etc., unpeaceful, unpacific, contentious, belligerent, bellicose, jingo, chauvinistic, martial, warlike, military, militant, soldierly, soldierlike, gladiatorial, chivalrous, in arms, embattled.

(*Phrases*) Together by the ears; sword in hand.

(*Adverbs*) *Pendente lite*, the battle raging, in the cannon's mouth; in the thick of the fray.

(*Interjections*) To arms! the Philistines be upon thee!

724 MEDIATION (*Substantives*), intervention, interposition, interference, intermeddling, intercession, parley, negotiation, arbitration, conciliation, mediatorship, good offices, diplomacy, peace-offering, eirenicon.

A mediator, intermediary, go-between, intercessor, peacemaker, diplomat, diplomatist, negotiator, troubleshooter, ombudsman.

(*Verbs*) To mediate, intermediate, intercede, interpose, interfere, intervene, negotiate, arbitrate, compromise, meet half-way.

(*Phrase*) To split the difference.

725 SUBMISSION (*Substantives*), surrender, non-resistance, appeasement, deference, yielding, capitulation, cession.

Homage, obeisance, bow, curtsy, kneeling, genuflexion, prostration, kowtow.

(*Verbs*) To surrender, succumb, submit, yield, give in, bend, cringe, crawl, truckle to, knuckle down or under, knock under, capitulate, lay down or deliver up one's arms, retreat, give way, cave in.

(*Phrases*) Beat a retreat; strike one's flag or colours; surrender at discretion; make a virtue of necessity; to come to terms.

To eat humble pie; to eat dirt; to swallow the pill; to kiss the rod; to turn the other cheek; to lick a person's boots.

(*Adjectives*) Surrendering, etc., non-resisting, unresisting, submissive, downtrodden.

Undefended, untenable, indefensible.

726 COMBATANT (*Substantives*), belligerent, champion, disputant, controversialist, litigant, competitor, rival, corrival, assailant, bully, bruiser, fighter, duellist, fighting-man, pugilist, pug, boxer, the fancy, prize-fighter, fighting-cock, gladiator, swashbuckler, fire-eater, berserker; swordsman, wrestler, Amazon, Paladin, son of Mars; staff, *état-major*, brass hats; militarist.

726A NON-COMBATANT (*Substantives*), civilian; passive resister, conscientious objector, conchy, Cuthbert, pacifist, pacificist; non-effective.

Quaker, Quirites.

(*Adjectives*) Non-effective.

Warrior, soldier, campaigner, veteran, man-at-arms, redcoat, man in khaki, Tommy Atkins, tommy, doughboy, G.I., *poilu*, trooper, dragoon, hussar, grenadier, fusilier, guardsman, lifeguard, lancer, cuirassier, spearman, musketeer, carabineer, rifleman, sniper, sharpshooter, *bersagliere*;

ensign, standard-bearer, halberdier; private, subaltern, conscript, recruit, cadet; effectives, line, rank and file, cannon fodder, P.B.I.

Engineer, artilleryman, gunner, cannoneer, bombardier, sapper, miner; archer, bowman.

Paratrooper, aircraftman, erk, pilot, observer, aircrew.

Marine, jolly, leatherneck; seaman, bluejacket, tar, A.B.

Guerrilla, Maquis, partisan, cossack, sepoy, gurkha, spahi, janizary, zouave, bashi-bazouk.

Armed force, the army, the military, regulars, soldiery, infantry, mounted infantry, fencibles, volunteers, territorials, yeomanry, cavalry, artillery, guns, tanks, armour, commando.

Militia, irregulars, *francs-tireurs*, Home Guard, train-band.

Legion, phalanx, myrmidons, squadron, wing, group, troop, cohort, regiment, corps, platoon, battalion, unit, mob, company (72), column, detachment, brigade, division, garrison, battle array, order of battle.

727 ARMS (*Substantives*), weapons, armament, armour, armoury, quiver, arsenal, magazine, armature.

Mail, chain-mail, lorication; ammunition, powder, gunpowder, gun-cotton, dynamite, gelignite, T.N.T., cordite, lyddite, cartridge, cartouche (635).

Artillery, park, ordnance piece, gun, cannon, swivel, howitzer, carronade, culverin, field-piece, machine-gun, Gatling, Maxim, submachine-gun, tommy-gun, mitrailleuse, pom-pom, mortar, grenade, petronel, petard, falconet.

Fire-arms, side-arms, stand of arms, musketry, musket, smooth-bore, muzzle-loader, firelock, match-lock, flint-lock, fowling-piece, rifle, revolver, six-shooter, carbine, blunderbuss, pistol, gat, rod, betsy, automatic pistol, derringer, Winchester, Lee-Metford, Mauser, Bren gun, Bofors, Sten gun, Lewis gun, bazooka.

Bow, arquebus (or harquebus), cross-bow, sling, catapult.

Missile, projectile, shot, round-shot, ball, shrapnel; grape, grape-shot, chain-shot, bullet, stone, shell, gas-shell, bomb, land-mine, block-buster, flying bomb, buzz-bomb, doodlebug, guided missile, V1, V2, atomic bomb, hydrogen bomb, torpedo, rocket, ballistics.

Pike, lance, spear, javelin, assagai, dart, arrow, reed, shaft, bolt, boomerang, harpoon.

Bayonet, sword, sabre, broadsword, cutlass, falchion, scimitar, rapier, skean, toledo, tuck, claymore, kris (or creese), dagger, dirk, hanger, poniard, stiletto, stylet, dudgeon, axe, bill, pole-axe, battle axe, halberd, tomahawk, bowie-knife, snickersnee, yataghan, kukri.

Club, mace, truncheon, staff, bludgeon, cudgel, knobkerrie, life-preserver, knuckle-duster, shillelagh, bat, cosh, sandbag, lathi.

Catapult, battering-ram; tank.

728 ARENA (*Substantives*), field, walk, battle-field, field of battle, lists, palaestra, campus, playing field, recreation ground, playground, course, cinder-track, dirt-track, gridiron, diamond, pitch, links, rink, court, plat-form, stage, boards, racecourse, *corso*, circus, ring, cockpit, bear garden, scene of action, theatre of war, the enemy's camp, amphitheatre, hippodrome, coliseum (or colosseum), proscenium.

SECTION V—RESULTS OF VOLUNTARY ACTION

729 COMPLETION (*Substantives*), accomplishment, performance, fulfilment, fruition, execution, achievement, dispatch, work done, superstructure, finish, termination, denouement, catastrophe, conclusion, culmination, climax, consummation, *fait accompli*, winding up, the last stroke, finishing stroke, *coup de grâce*, last finish, final touch, crowning touch, coping-stone, end (67), arrival (292), completeness (52).

(*Verbs*) To complete, effect, perform, do, execute, go through, accomplish, fulfil, discharge, achieve, compass, effectuate, dispatch, knock off, close, terminate, conclude, finish, end (67), consummate, elaborate, bring about, bring to bear, bring to pass, get through, carry through, bring through, bring off, pull off, work out, make good, carry out, wind up, dispose of, bring to a close, termination, conclusion, etc.

To perfect, bring to perfection, stamp, put the seal to, polish off, crown.

To reach, arrive (292), touch, reach, attain the goal; to run one's race.

(*Phrases*) To give the last finish or finishing touch; to be through with; to get it over; to deliver the goods; to shut up shop.

(*Adjectives*) Completing, final, terminal, concluding, conclusive, exhaustive, crowning, etc., done, completed, wrought.

(*Phrases*) It is all over; *finis coronat opus; actum est.*

(*Adverbs*) Completely, etc. (52), out of hand, effectually, with a vengeance, with a witness.

730 NON-COMPLETION (*Substantives*), inexecution, shortcoming (304), non-fulfilment, non-performance, neglect; incompleteness (53); a drawn battle or game, a draw, a stalemate.

(*Phrase*) The web of Penelope; one swallow does not make a summer.

(*Verbs*) Not to complete, perform, etc., to fall short of, leave unfinished, let slip, lose sight of, neglect, leave undone, etc., draw.

(*Phrases*) To scotch the snake, not kill it; hang fire; do by halves.

(*Adjectives*) Not completed, etc., uncompleted, incomplete, unfinished, left undone (53), short, unaccomplished, unperformed, unexecuted.

In progress, in hand, proceeding, going on, on the stocks.

(*Adverbs*) *Re infecta; nihil fit.*

---

731 SUCCESS (*Substantives*), successfulness, speed, thrift, advance, luck, good fortune (734), godsend, prize, windfall, trump card, hit, stroke, lucky strike, break; lucky or fortunate hit; bold stroke, masterstroke, *coup de maître*, knock-out blow (698), checkmate.

Continued success, run of luck, time well spent, tide, flood, high tide, heyday.

Advantage over, ascendancy, mastery, conquest, subdual, victory, subjugation, triumph, exultation (884).

732 FAILURE (*Substantives*), unsuccess, non-success, disappointment, blow, frustration, inefficacy, discomfiture, abortion, miscarriage, lost trouble; vain, ineffectual, or abortive attempt or effort.

A mistake, error, blunder, fault, miss, oversight, blot, slip, trip, stumble, claudication, breakdown, false step, wrong step, howler, floater, clanger, boner, *faux pas, bêtise*, titubation, scrape, botch, bungle, foozle, mess, washout, stalemate, botchery, fiasco, flop, frost, sad work, bad job, bad show, want of skill.

A conqueror, victor, winner.

(*Phrase*) A feather in one's cap.

(*Verbs*) To succeed, to be successful, to come off successful, to be crowned with success, to come or go off well, catch on, to thrive, speed, prosper, bloom, blossom, flourish, go on well, be well off.

To gain, attain, carry, secure, or win a point or object; to triumph, be triumphant, etc.; to surmount, overcome, conquer, master, or get over a difficulty or obstacle; to score, make a hit.

To advance (282), come on, get on, gain ground, make one's way, make progress, progress, worry along, get by.

To bring to bear, to bring about, to effect, accomplish, complete (729), manage, contrive to, make sure; to reap, gather, etc., the benefit of.

To master, get the better of, conquer, subdue, subjugate, quell, reduce, overthrow, overpower, vanquish, get under; get or gain the ascendancy, obtain a victory; to worst, defeat, beat, lick, drub, trim, settle, floor, knock out, put down, trip up, beat hollow, checkmate, nonsuit, trip up the heels of, capsize, shipwreck, ruin, kibosh, do for, victimize, put to flight, drown, etc.; to roll in the dust, to trample under foot, to wipe the floor with.

To baffle, disconcert, frustrate, confound, discomfit, dish, foil, outgeneral, outmanœuvre, outflank, outwit, overreach, balk, outvote, circumvent, score off, catch napping.

To answer, succeed, work well, turn out well.

(*Phrases*) To sail before the wind; to swim with the tide; to stem the torrent; to turn a corner; to weather a point; to fall on one's legs or feet; *se tirer d'affaire*; to take a favourable turn; to turn up trumps; to have the ball at one's feet; to come off with flying colours; to win or gain the day; to win the palm; to win one's spurs; to breast the tape; to bear away the bell.

To get the upper hand; to gain an

Mischance, mishap, misfortune, misadventure, disaster, bad or hard luck (735).

Repulse, rebuff, set-down, defeat, fall, downfall, rout, discomfiture, collapse, smash, crash, wreck, perdition, shipwreck, ruin, subjugation, overthrow, death-blow, quietus, knock-out, destruction.

A victim, loser, bankrupt, insolvent (808).

(*Phrases*) A losing game; a flash in the pan; a wild-goose chase; a mare's-nest; a fool's errand.

(*Verbs*) To fail, to be unsuccessful, etc., to come off badly, go badly, go amiss, abort, go wrong, fall flat, flop, fall through, fizzle out, turn out ill, work ill, lose ground, recede (283), fall short of (304), prang (162, 176).

To miss, miss one's aim; to labour, toil, etc., in vain; to lose one's labour, flounder, limp, miss one's footing, miscarry, abort; to make vain, ineffectual, or abortive efforts; to make a slip; to make or commit a mistake, commit a fault, make a mess of; to botch, make a botch of, bungle, foozle.

To be defeated, overthrown, foiled, worsted, let down, etc.; to break down, sink, drown, founder, go to ruin, etc., fall, slip, tumble, stumble, falter, be capsized, run aground, pack up, crock up, collapse.

(*Phrases*) To come to nothing; to end in smoke; to slip through one's fingers; to hang fire; to miss fire; to miss stays; to flash in the pan; to split upon a rock; to go to the wall; to have had it; to take a back seat; to get the worst of it; to go to the dogs; to go to pot; to be all up with; to be in the wrong box; to stand in one's own light; to catch a Tartar; to get hold of the wrong sow by the ear; to burn one's fingers; to shoot at a pigeon and kill a crow; to beat the air; to tilt against windmills; to roll the stone of Sisyphus; to fall between two stools; to pull a boner; to come a cropper or mucker.

(*Adjectives*) Unsuccessful, failing, etc., unfortunate, in a bad way,

advantage; to get the whip-hand of; to have on the hip; to get the start of; to have a run of luck; to make a hit; to make a killing; to score a success; to reap or gather the harvest; to strike oil; to give a good account of oneself; to carry all before one; to put to rout; to cook one's goose; to settle one's hash.

(*Adjectives*) Succeeding, etc., successful, home and dry, prosperous, felicitous, blooming, etc., set up, triumphant, victorious, cock-a-hoop.

Unfoiled, unbeaten, unsubdued, etc. Effective, well-spent.

(*Phrases*) Flushed with success; one's star being in the ascendant; the spoilt child of fortune.

(*Adverbs*) Successfully, etc., triumphantly, with flying colours, in truimph, *à merveille*, to good purpose.

(*Phrase*) *Veni, vidi, vici*.

———

unlucky, luckless, out of luck, ill-fated, ill-starred, disastrous.

Unavailing, abortive, addle, still-born, fruitless, bootless, ineffectual, stickit, unattained, lame, hobbling, impotent, futile.

Aground, grounded, swamped, stranded, cast away, wrecked, on the rocks, foundered, capsized, torpedoed, shipwrecked.

Defeated, overcome, overthrown, overpowered, mastered, worsted, vanquished, conquered, subjugated, routed, silenced, distanced, foiled, unhorsed, baffled, befooled, dished, tossed about, stultified, undone, done for, down and out, ruined, circumvented, planet-struck, nonplussed.

(*Phrases*) At a loss; wide of the mark; not having a leg to stand upon; ruined root and branch; the sport of fortune; bitched, bothered, and bewildered; hoist by one's own petard; left in the lurch; out of the running.

(*Adverbs*) Unsuccessfully, etc., in vain, to no purpose, all up with.

(*Phrases*) The game is up; all is lost.

733 TROPHY (*Substantives*), laurel, palm, crown, bays, wreath, garland, chaplet, civic crown, medal, ribbon, cup, scalp, prize, award, oscar, triumphal arch, ovation, triumph (883), flourish of trumpets, flying colours.

(*Phrase*) A feather in one's cap.

734 PROSPERITY (*Substantives*), affluence (803), success (731), thrift, good fortune, welfare, well-being, felicity, luck, good luck, a run of luck, fair weather, sunshine, fair wind, a bed of roses, palmy days, the smiles of fortune, halcyon days, *Saturnia regna*, golden age.

An upstart, parvenu, *nouveau riche*, profiteer, skipjack, mushroom, self-made man.

A made man, a lucky dog.

(*Phrase*) A roaring trade.

(*Verbs*) To prosper, thrive, flourish, be well off; to flower, blow, blossom, bloom, fructify.

(*Phrases*) To feather one's nest; to line one's pockets; to make one's pile; to bask in the sunshine; to rise in the world; to make one's way; to better oneself; to light on one's feet.

735 ADVERSITY (*Substantives*), bad, ill, evil, adverse, etc., fortune, hap, or luck, tough luck, hard lines, reverse, set-back, come-down, broken fortunes, falling or going down in the world, hard times, iron age, evil day, rainy day.

Fall, ruin, ruination, ruinousness, undoing, mishap, mischance, misadventure, misfortune, disaster, calamity, catastrophe (619), failure (732); a hard life; trouble, hardship, blight, curse, evil star, evil genius, evil dispensation.

(*Phrases*) The frowns of fortune; the ups and downs of life; a black look-out; the time being out of joint.

(*Verbs*) To be ill off; to decay, sink, go under, fall, decline, come down in the world, lose caste; to have had it.

(*Adjectives*) Prosperous, fortunate, lucky, well-off, well-to-do, bein, affluent, solvent (803), thriving, set up, prospering, etc., blooming, palmy, halcyon.

Auspicious, propitious, in a fair way.

(*Phrases*) Born with a silver spoon in one's mouth; the spoilt child of fortune; in clover; on velvet; in luck's way.

(*Adverbs*) Prosperously, etc., swimmingly.

(*Adjectives*) Unfortunate, unlucky, luckless, untoward, ill-off, badly off, decayed, ill-fated, ill-starred, impecunious, necessitous (804), bankrupt (808), unprosperous, adverse, untoward.

Disastrous, calamitous, ruinous, dire, deplorable, etc.

(*Phrases*) Down on one's luck; in a bad way; in poor shape; having seen better days; born with a wooden ladle in one's mouth; one's star on the wane; from bad to worse; down and out.

---

736 MEDIOCRITY (*Substantives*), the golden mean, *aurea mediocritas*, moderation (174), moderate circumstances; the middle classes, bourgeoisie.

(*Adjectives*) Tolerable, fair, middling, passable, average, so-so, ordinary, mediocre; middle-class, bourgeois.

(*Verbs*) To keep a middle course, jog on, get along, get by.

(*Phrase*) *Medio tutissimus ibis*.

DIVISION II—INTERSOCIAL VOLITION

SECTION I—GENERAL INTERSOCIAL VOLITION

737 AUTHORITY (*Substantives*), influence, patronage, credit, power, prerogative, control, jurisdiction, censorship, authoritativeness, absoluteness, despotism, absolutism, tyranny.

Command, empire, sway, rule, dominion, domination, supremacy, sovereignty, suzerainty, lordship, headship, seigniory, seigniorship, mastery, mastership, office, government, administration, gubernation, empire, body politic, accession.

Hold, grasp, gripe, grip, reach, fang, clutches, talons, helm, reins.

Reign, dynasty, regime, directorship, proconsulship, prefecture, caliphate, seneschalship, magistrature, magistracy, presidency, presidentship, premiership.

Empire, autocracy, monarchy, kinghood, kingship, royalty, regality, kingcraft, aristocracy, oligarchy, feudalism, republic, republicanism, democracy, socialism, demagogy, ochlocracy, mobocracy, mob-rule, dictatorship of proletariat, ergatocracy, collectivism, communism, Bolshevism,

738 Absence of authority.

LAXITY (*Substantives*), laxness, licence, licentiousness, relaxation, looseness, loosening, slackness, toleration, *laissez-faire*, remission, liberty (748).

Misrule, anarchy, interregnum.

Deprivation of power, dethronement, deposition, usurpation.

Denial of authority: anarchism, nihilism; insubordination, mutiny (742).

Anarchist, nihilist, usurper, mutineer.

(*Phrases*) A dead letter; *brutum fulmen*.

(*Verbs*) To be lax, etc., to hold a loose rein, tolerate, to relax, to misrule.

To dethrone.

(*Phrases*) To give a loose rein to; to give rope enough.

(*Adjectives*) Lax, permissive, loose, slack, remiss, relaxed, licensed, reinless, unbridled, anarchic, anarchical, nihilistic.

Unauthorized (925).

bureaucracy, bumbledom, syndicalism, militarism, stratocracy, *imperium in imperio*, dictatorship, protectorate, protectorship, directorate, directory, executive, raj.

Limited monarchy, constitutional government, representative government, home rule, diarchy (or dyarchy), duumvirate, triumvirate.

Vicarious authority (755, 759).

Gynarchy, gynaecocracy, petticoat government, matriarchy; patriarchy, patriarchism.

(*Verbs*) To have, hold, possess, or exercise authority, etc.

To be master, etc.; to have the control, etc.; to overrule, override, overawe, dominate.

To rule, govern, sway, command, control, direct, administer, lead, preside over, boss; to dictate, reign, hold the reins; to possess or be seated on the throne; to ascend or mount the throne; to sway or wield the sceptre.

(*Phrases*) To have the upper hand; to have the whip-hand; to bend to one's will; to have one's own way; to rule the roast; to lay down the law; to be cock of the roost; to have under the thumb; to keep under; to lead by the nose; to wear the breeches; to have the ball at one's feet; to play first fiddle.

(*Adjectives*) Ruling, etc., regnant, dominant, paramount, supreme, authoritative, executive, gubernatorial, administrative, official.

Imperial, regal, sovereign, royal, royalist, kingly, monarchical, imperatorial, princely, baronial, feudal, seigneurial, seigniorial, aristocratic, democratic, etc.; totalitarian, ultramontane, absolutist.

Imperative, peremptory, arbitrary, absolute, overruling.

(*Adverbs*) In the name of, by the authority of, in virtue of, at one's command, under the auspices of, under the aegis of, *ex officio, ex cathedra*.

---

739 SEVERITY (*Substantives*), strictness, rigour, rigidity, rigidness, sternness, stringency, austerity, inclemency, harshness, acerbity, stiffness, rigorousness, inexorability.

Arbitrary power, absolutism, despotism, dictatorship, autocracy, domineering, tyranny; Moloch.

Assumption, usurpation.

A tyrant, disciplinarian, martinet, stickler, despot, oppressor, hard master; King Stork.

(*Phrases*) Iron rule; reign of terror; mailed fist; martial law; blood and iron; tender mercies; red tape.

740 LENITY (*Substantives*), mildness, lenience, leniency, gentleness, indulgence, clemency, tolerance, forbearance.

(*Verbs*) To be lenient, etc., to tolerate, indulge, spoil, bear with, to allow to have one's own way, to let down gently.

(*Adjectives*) Lenient, mild, gentle, soft, indulgent, tolerant, easy-going, clement.

(*Phrase*) Live and let live.

(*Verbs*) To be severe, etc.; to assume, usurp, arrogate, take liberties; to hold or keep a tight hand; to bear or lay a heavy hand on; to be down on; to dictate; to domineer, bully, oppress, override, tyrannize.

(*Phrases*) To lord it over; to carry matters with a high hand; to ride roughshod over; to rule with a rod of iron; to put on the screw; to deal faithfully with; to keep a person's nose to the grindstone.

(*Adjectives*) Severe, strict, rigid, stern, stiff, dour, strait-laced, rigorous, exacting, stringent, hard and fast, peremptory, absolute, positive, uncompromising, harsh, austere, arbitrary, haughty, overbearing, arrogant, autocratic, bossy, dictatorial, imperious, domineering, tyrannical, masterful, obdurate, unyielding, inflexible, inexorable, exigent, inclement, Spartan, Rhadamanthine, Draconian.

(*Adverbs*) Severely, etc., with a heavy hand.

741 COMMAND (*Substantives*), order, fiat, bidding, dictum, hest, behest, call beck, nod, message, direction, injunction, charge, instructions, appointment, demand, exaction, imposition, requisition, requirement, claim, reclamation, revendication.

Dictation, dictate, mandate, caveat, edict, decree, decretal, enactment, precept, prescript, writ, rescript, law, ordinance, ordination, bull, regulation, prescription, brevet, placet, ukase, firman, warrant, passport, mittimus, mandamus, summons, subpoena, interpellation, citation, word of command.

(*Verbs*) To command, to issue a command, order, give order, bid, require, enjoin, charge, claim, call for, demand, exact, insist on, make a point of, impose, entail, set, tax, prescribe, direct, brief, appoint, dictate, ordain, decree, enact; to issue or promulgate a decree, etc.

To cite, summon, call for, call up, send for, requisition, subpoena; to set or prescribe a task, to set to work, to give the word of command, to call to order.

(*Phrase*) The decree is gone forth.

(*Adjectives*) Commanding, etc., authoritative, peremptory, decretive, decretory (737).

(*Adverbs*) By order, with a dash of the pen.

(*Phrase*) *Le roy le veult.*

742 DISOBEDIENCE (*Substantives*), non-compliance, insubordination, contumacy, defection, infringement, infraction, violation; defiance (715), resistance (719), non-observance (773).

Rising, insurrection, revolt, *coup d'état*, *putsch*, rebellion, turn-out, strike, riot, riotousness, mutinousness, mutiny, tumult, sedition, treason, lese-majesty.

An insurgent, mutineer, rebel, rioter, traitor, apostate, renegade, seceder, quisling, fifth columnist; *carbonaro*, sansculotte, *frondeur*; agitator, demagogue, Jack Cade, Wat Tyler; ringleader.

(*Verbs*) To disobey, violate, infringe, resist (719), defy (715), turn restive, shirk, kick, strike, mutiny, rise, rebel, secede, lift the hand against, turn out, come out, go on strike.

(*Phrases*) To champ the bit; to kick over the traces; to unfurl the red flag.

(*Adjectives*) Disobedient, resisting, rebellious, unruly, unsubmissive, un-

743 OBEDIENCE (*Substantives*), submission, non-resistance, passiveness, resignation, cession, compliance, surrender (725), subordination, deference, loyalty, devotion, allegiance, obeisance, homage, fealty, prostration, kneeling, genuflexion, curtsy, kotow, salaam, submissiveness, obsequiousness (886), servitorship, subjection (749).

(*Verbs*) To be obedient, etc.; to obey, submit, succumb, give in, knock under, cringe, yield (725), comply, surrender, follow, give up, give way, resign, bend to, bear obedience to.

To kneel, fall on one's knees, bend the knee, curtsy, kowtow, salaam, bow, pay homage to.

To attend upon, tend; to be under the orders of, to serve.

(*Phrases*) To kiss the rod; to do one's bidding; to play second fiddle; to take it lying down; to dance attendance on.

(*Adjectives*) Obedient, submissive, resigned, passive, complying, compliant, loyal, faithful, devoted, yielding, docile, tractable, amenable,

overnable, **uncomplying**, uncom- | biddable, **unresisting**, henpecked;
liant, restive, insubordinate, con- | **restrainable**, unresisted.
umacious, mutinous, riotous, sedi-
ious, disaffected, recusant, recalci-
rant, refractory, naughty.
  Unbidden, unobeyed, a dead letter.
  (*Phrase*) The grey mare being the better horse.

---

744 COMPULSION (*Substantives*), coercion, coaction, force, constraint, enforcement, press, *corvée*, conscription, levy, duress, brute force, main force, *force majeure*, the sword, club law, *ultima ratio, argumentum baculinum.*

(*Verbs*) To compel, force, make, drive, coerce, constrain, steam-roller, enforce, put in force, oblige, force upon, press, conscribe, extort, put down, bind, pin down, bind over, impress, commandeer, requisition.

(*Phrases*) To cram down the throat; to take no denial; to insist upon; to make a point of.

(*Adjectives*) Compelling, etc., compulsory, compulsatory, obligatory, forcible, coercive, coactive, peremptory, rigorous, stringent, inexorable (739); being fain to do, having to do.

(*Adverbs*) By force, perforce, under compulsion, *vi et armis*, in spite of one's teeth; *bon gré, mal gré*; willy-nilly, *nolens volens*; *de rigueur*.

---

745 MASTER (*Substantives*), lord, laird, chief, leader, captain, skipper, mate, protagonist, coryphaeus, head, chieftain, commander, commandant, director (694), captain of industry, ruler, potentate, dictator, liege, sovereign, monarch, autocrat, despot, tyrant, *führer, duce*, demagogue, ringleader, boss, big shot, fugleman.

Crowned head, emperor, king, majesty, tetrarch, *imperator*, protector, president, stadtholder, governor.

Caesar, czar, sultan, soldan, caliph, sophy, khan, cacique, inca, lama, mogul, imam, shah, khedive, pasha (or bashaw), dey, cham, judge, aga, hospodar, mikado, shogun, tycoon, exarch.

Prince, seignior, highness, archduke, duke, marquis, earl, viscount, baron (875), margrave, landgrave, palatine, elector, doge, satrap, rajah, maharajah, emir, bey, effendi, nizam, nawab, mandarin, sirdar, ameer, sachem, sagamore.

Empress, queen, czarina, sultana, princess, duchess, marchioness, countess, viscountess, baroness, infanta, ranee, maharanee, margravine, etc.

Military authorities, marshal, field-marshal, *maréchal*, generalissimo,

746 SERVANT (*Substantives*), servitor, employee, attaché, secretary, subordinate, clerk, retainer, vassal, protégé, dependant, hanger-on, pensioner, client, emissary, *âme damnée.*

Retinue, cortège, staff, court, train, entourage, clientele, suite.

An attendant, squire, henchman, led captain, chamberlain, follower, usher, page, train-bearer, domestic, help, butler, footman, lackey, flunkey, parlour-man, valet, waiter, *garçon*, equerry, groom, jockey, ostler (or hostler), stable-boy, tiger, buttons, boot-boy, boots, livery servant, hireling, mercenary, underling, menial, gillie, under-strapper, journeyman, whipper-in, bailiff, castellan, seneschal, majordomo, cup-bearer, bottle-washer, scout, gyp.

Serf, villein, slave, galley-slave, thrall, peon, helot, bondsman, *adscriptus glebae*, wage-slave.

A maid, handmaid, abigail, chamber-maid, lady's maid, housekeeper, lady help, soubrette, *fille de chambre*, parlour-maid, housemaid, between-maid, kitchen-maid, nurse, *bonne*, scullion, laundress, bed-maker, skivvy, slavey, daily.

(*Verbs*) To serve, attend upon, dance attendance, wait upon, squire, valet.

commander-in-chief, admiral, commodore, general, lieutenant-general, major-general, brigadier, colonel, lieutenant-colonel, officer, captain, major, lieutenant, adjutant, midshipman, quartermaster, aide-de-camp, non-commissioned officer, drum-major, sergeant-major, sergeant, corporal, air-marshal, group-captain, wing-commander, squadron-leader, flight-lieutenant, centurion, *seraskier*, hetman, subahdar, *condottiere*.

(*Adverbs*) In one's pay or employ, in the train of.

Civil authorities, mayor, prefect, chancellor, provost, magistrate, syndic, alcade (or alcayde), burgomaster, *corregidor*, sheik, seneschal, burgrave, alderman, warden, constable (965), beadle, alguazil, kavass, tribune, consul, proconsul, quaestor, praetor, aedile, archon, polemarch.

Statesman, politician, statist, legislator, lawgiver.

President, chairman, speaker, moderator, vice-president, comptroller, director (694), monitor, monitress.

747 Ensign, or badge of authority.

SCEPTRE (*Substantives*), regalia, insignia (550), crown, coronet, rod of empire, orb, mace, *fasces*, wand, baton, truncheon, staff, insignia (550), portfolio.

A throne, chair, divan, dais, woolsack.

Diadem, tiara, ermine, purple, signet, seals, keys, talisman, cap of maintenance, toga, robes of state, decoration.

748 FREEDOM (*Substantives*), independence, liberty, licence (760), self-government, autonomy, scope, range, latitude, play, swing, free play, elbow-room, *lebensraum*, margin.

Franchise, immunity, exemption, emancipation (750), naturalization, denizenship.

Freeland, freehold, allodium (780).

A freeman, freedman, denizen.

(*Phrases*) The four freedoms; *liberté, egalité, fraternité*; a place in the sun; Liberty Hall.

(*Verbs*) To be free, to have scope, etc.

To render free, etc., to free, to emancipate, enfranchise (750), naturalize.

(*Phrases*) To have the run of; to have one's own way; to have one's fling; to stand on one's own feet; to stand on one's rights; to have a will of one's own; to paddle one's own canoe; to play a lone hand.

To take a liberty; to make free with; to take the bit between one's teeth.

749 SUBJECTION (*Substantives*), dependence, thrall, thraldom, subjugation, subordination, bondage, serfdom, servitude, slavery, vassalage, villeinage, service, clientship, liability (177), enslavement, tutelage, constraint (751).

Yoke, harness, collar.

(*Verbs*) To be subject, dependent, etc., to fall under, obey, serve (743).

To subject, subjugate, enthral, enslave, keep under, control, etc. (751), to reduce to slavery, mediatize, break in.

(*Phrases*) To drag a chain; not dare to call one's soul one's own; to be led by the nose; to be or lie at the mercy of.

To keep in leading strings.

(*Adjectives*) Subject, subordinate, dependent, subjected, in subjection to, in thrall to, feudatory, feudal, enslaved, a slave to, at the mercy of, downtrodden, overborne, henpecked, enthralled, controlled, constrained (751).

(*Phrases*) Under the thumb of; at the feet of; tied to the apron-

(*Adjectives*) Free, independent, loose, at large, unconstrained, unrestrained, unchecked, unobstructed, unconfined, unsubdued, unsubjugated, self-governed, autonomous, self-supporting, untrammelled, unbound, uncontrolled, unchained, unshackled, unfettered, uncurbed, unbridled, unrestricted, unmuzzled, unbuttoned, unforced, uncompelled, unbiased, spontaneous, unhindered, unthwarted, heart-whole, uncaught, unenslaved, unclaimed, ungoverned, resting.

Free and easy, at ease, *dégagé*, wanton, rampant, irrepressible, unprevented, unvanquished, exempt, freehold, allodial, enfranchised, emancipated, released, disengaged (750), out of hand.

(*Phrases*) Free as air; one's own master; *sui juris*; a law to oneself; on one's own; a cat may look at a king.

strings of; the puppet, sport, plaything of.

———

750 LIBERATION (*Substantives*), disengagement, release, enlargement, emancipation, affranchisement, enfranchisement, manumission, discharge, dismissal.

Escape (671), deliverance (672), redemption, extrication, absolution, acquittance, acquittal (970).

Licence, toleration; parole, ticket of leave.

(*Verbs*) To gain, obtain, acquire, etc., one's liberty, freedom, etc., to get off, get clear, to deliver oneself from.

To break loose, escape, slip away, make one's escape, cut and run, slip the collar, bolt (671).

To liberate, free, set free, set at liberty, release, loose, let loose, loosen, relax, unloose, untie, unbind, unhand, unchain, unshackle, unfetter, unclog, disengage, unharness (44).

To enlarge, set clear, let go, let out, disenchain, disimprison, unbar, unbolt, uncage, unclose, uncork, discharge, disenthral, dismiss, deliver, extricate, let slip, enfranchise, affranchise, manumit, denizen, emancipate, assoil (748).

To clear, acquit, redeem, ransom, get off.

(*Phrases*) To throw off the yoke; to burst one's bonds; to break prison.

To give one one's head.

(*Adjectives*) Liberated, freed, etc.

———

751 RESTRAINT (*Substantives*), constraint, coercion, cohibition, repression, clamp down, control, discipline.

Confinement, durance, duress, detention, imprisonment, incarceration, prisonment, internment, blockade, quarantine, coarctation, mancipation, entombment, 'durance vile,' limbo, captivity, penal servitude.

Arrest, arrestation, custody, keep, care, charge, ward.

Prison, fetter (752); *lettre de cachet*.

(*Verbs*) To be under restraint or arrest, to be coerced, etc.

To restrain, constrain, coerce, check, trammel, curb, cramp, keep under, enthral, put under restraint, restrict, repress, cohibit, detain, debar; to chain, enchain, fasten, tie up (43), picket, fetter, shackle, manacle, handcuff, bridle, muzzle, gag, suppress, pinion, pin down, tether, hobble.

To confine, shut up, shut in, clap up, lock up, cage, encage, impound, pen, coop, hem in, jam in, enclose, bottle up, cork up, seal up, mew, wall in, rail in, cloister, bolt in, close the door upon, imprison, incarcerate, immure, entomb, seclude, corral.

To take prisoner, lead captive, send or commit to prison, give in charge or in custody, arrest, commit, run in, lag; re-commit, remand.

(*Phrases*) To put in irons; to clap under hatches; to put in a straitwaistcoat.

(*Adjectives*) Restrained, coerced, etc., sewn up, pent up.

Held up, wind-bound, weather-bound, storm-stayed.
Coactive, stiff, restringent, strait-laced, hide-bound.
(*Phrases*) In limbo; under lock and key; laid by the heels; 'cabined cribbed, confined'; in quod; in durance vile; doing time; boun hand and foot.

752 Means of restraint.

PRISON (*Substantives*), jail (or gaol), prison-house, house of detention, lock-up the cells, clink, glasshouse, brig, jug, quod, cooler, choky, stir, calaboose cage, coop, den, cell, stronghold, fortress, keep, dungeon, bastille, oubliette bridewell, tollbooth, panopticon, hulks, galleys, penitentiary, guard-room hold, round-house, blackhole, station, enclosure, concentration camp, pen fold, pound, paddock, stocks, bilboes, nick.

Newgate, King's Bench, Fleet, Marshalsea, Pentonville, Holloway, Dart moor, Portland, Peterhead, Broadmoor, Sing Sing, the Bastille.

Fetter, shackle, trammel, bond, chain, irons, collar, cangue, pinion, gyve fetterlock, manacle, handcuff, darbies, strait waistcoat; yoke, halter, harness muzzle, gag, bridle, curb, bit, snaffle, rein, martingale, leading-strings swaddling-bands, tether, hobble, picket, band, brake.

Bolt, bar, lock, padlock, rail, wall, paling, palisade (232), fence, corral barrier, barricade.

753 KEEPER (*Substantives*), custodian, *custos*, warder, jailer (or gaoler), turnkey, castellan, guard, ranger, gamekeeper, watch, watchman, watch and ward, sentry, sentinel, coastguard, convoy, escort, *concierge*, caretaker, watch-dog.

Guardian, duenna, nurse, ayah, chaperon.

755 Vicarious authority.

COMMISSION (*Substantives*), delegation, consignment, assignment, devolution, procuration, deputation, legation, mission, agency, clerkship, agentship; power of attorney; errand, embassy, charge, brevet, diploma, exequatur, committal, commitment.

Appointment, nomination, ordination, installation, inauguration, return, accession, investiture, coronation.

Vicegerency, regency, regentship.

Deputy (759).

(*Verbs*) To commission, delegate, depute, devolve, send out, assign, consign, charge, encharge, entrust with, commit to, enlist.

To appoint, name, nominate, accredit, engage, bespeak, ordain, install, induct, inaugurate, invest, crown, return, enrol.

754 PRISONER (*Substantives*) prisoner-of-war, P.O.W., kriegie, captive, *détenu*, convict, jail-bird, lag; ticket-of-leave man.

(*Adjectives*) In custody, in charge, imprisoned, locked up, incarcerated, pent.

---

756 ABROGATION (*Substantives*), annulment, cancel, cancellation, revocation, repeal, rescission, rescinding, deposal, deposition, dethronement, defeasance, dismissal, sack, *congé*, demission, disestablishment, disendowment.

Abolition, abolishment, counter-order, countermand, repudiation, nullification, recantation, palinode, retractation (607).

(*Verbs*) To abrogate, annul, cancel, revoke, repeal, rescind, reverse, override, overrule, abolish, disannul, dissolve, quash, repudiate, nullify, retract, recant, recall, countermand, counter-order, break off, disclaim, declare null and void, disestablish, disendow, deconsecrate, set aside, do away with.

To dismiss, send off, send away, discard, turn off, turn away, cashier,

Employ, empower, set over.
To be commissioned, to represent.
(*Adverbs*) *Per procurationem per pro.*, p.p.

sack, fire, bounce, oust, unseat, unthrone, dethrone, depose, uncrown, unfrock, disbar, disbench.
(*Phrases*) Send about one's business; put one's nose out of joint; give one the mitten, the chuck, the sack, the boot, the push.

To get one's books or cards; to get the key of the street.
(*Adjectives*) Abrogated, etc.; *functus officio*.
(*Interjections*) Get along with you! clear out! be off! beat it!

757 RESIGNATION (*Substantives*), retirement, abdication, renunciation, abjuration.
(*Verbs*) To resign, give up, throw up, retire, abdicate, lay down, abjure, renounce, forgo, disclaim, retract (756); to tender one's resignation, send in one's papers.
(*Phrases*) To swallow the anchor; to be given one's bowler.
(*Adjective*) Emeritus.
(*Phrase*) 'Othello's occupation's gone.'

758 CONSIGNEE (*Substantives*), delegate, commissary, commissioner, vice-egent, legate, representative, secondary, nominee, surrogate, functionary, trustee, assignee.
Corps diplomatique, plenipotentiary, emissary, embassy, ambassador, diplomat(ist), consul, resident, nuncio, internuncio.
Agent, factor, attorney, broker, factotum, bailiff, man of business, go-between, intermediary, middleman, salesman, commission agent, commercial traveller, bagman, drummer, colporteur, commissionaire, employee, attaché, curator, clerk, placeman.

759 DEPUTY (*Substantives*), substitute, vice, proxy, locum tenens, baby-sitter, *chargé d'affaires*,, delegate, representative, *alter ego*, surrogate, understudy, stooge, stand-in, stopgap, pinch-hitter.
Regent, viceroy, vicegerent, vicar, satrap, exarch, vizier, minister, premier, commissioner, chancellor, prefect, warden, lieutenant, proconsul, legate.
(*Verbs*) To deputize; to be deputy, etc., for; to appear for; to understudy; to take duty for.
(*Phrase*) To hold a watching brief for.
(*Adjectives*) Acting, deputizing, etc.
(*Adverbs*) In place of, vice.

SECTION II—SPECIAL INTERSOCIAL VOLITION

760 PERMISSION (*Substantives*), leave, allowance, sufferance, tolerance, toleration, liberty, law, licence, concession, grant, vouchsafement, authorization, sanction, accordance, admission, favour, dispensation, exemption, connivance.
A permit, warrant, brevet, precept, authority, firman, pass, passport,

761 PROHIBITION (*Substantives*), inhibition, veto, disallowance, interdiction, estoppage, hindrance (706), restriction, restraints (751), embargo, an interdict, ban, injunction, taboo, proscription; *index librorum prohibitorum*.
(*Verbs*) To prohibit, forbid, inhibit, disallow, bar, debar, interdict, ban,

furlough, ticket, licence, charter, patent, *carte blanche*, exeat.

(*Verbs*) To permit; to give leave or permission; to let, allow, admit, suffer, tolerate, concede, accord, vouchsafe, humour, indulge, to leave it to one; to leave alone; to grant, empower, charter, sanction, authorize, warrant, license; to give licence; to give a loose to.

To let off, absolve, exonerate, dispense with, favour, wink, connive at.

(*Phrases*) To give *carte blanche*; to give rein to; to stretch a point; leave the door open; to let one have a chance; to give one a fair show.

To take a liberty; to use a freedom; to make so bold; to beg leave.

estop, veto, keep in, hinder, restrain (751), restrict, withhold, limit, circumscribe, keep within bounds.

To exclude, shut out, proscribe.

(*Phrase*) To clip the wings of; to forbid the banns.

(*Adjectives*) Prohibitive, restrictive, exclusive, prohibitory, forbidding, etc.

Not permitted, prohibited, etc., unlicensed, contraband, unauthorized.

(*Phrases*) Under the ban of; on the Index.

(*Interjections*) Hands off! keep off! God forbid!

(*Adjectives*) Permitting, etc., permissive, conceding, indulgent.
Allowable, permissible, lawful, legitimate, legal.
Unforbid, unforbidden, unconditional.

---

762 CONSENT (*Substantives*), compliance, acquiescence, assent (488), agreement, concession, yieldingness, acknowledgment, acceptance.
Settlement, ratification, confirmation.

(*Verbs*) To consent, give consent, assent, comply with, acquiesce, agree to, subscribe to, accede, accept.

To concede, yield, satisfy, grant, settle, acknowledge, confirm, homologate, ratify, deign, vouchsafe.

(*Phrase*) To take at one's word.

(*Adjectives*) Consenting, etc., having no objection, unconditional.

(*Adverbs*) Yes (488); if you please, as you please, by all means, by all manner of means, so be it, of course, certainly, sure, O.K.

(*Phrases*) Suits me; all right by me.

763 OFFER (*Substantives*), proffer, tender, present, overture, proposition, motion, proposal, invitation, candidature, presentation, offering, oblation, bid, bribe.

Sacrifice, immolation.

(*Verbs*) To offer, proffer, tender, present, invite, volunteer, propose, move, make a motion, start, press, bid, hold out, hawk about.

To sacrifice, immolate.

(*Phrases*) To be a candidate; to go a-begging.

(*Adjectives*) Offering, etc., in the market, for sale, on hire.

764 REFUSAL (*Substantives*), rejection, declining, non-compliance, declension, dissent (489), denial, repulse, rebuff, discountenance.

Disclaimer, recusancy, abnegation, protest.

Revocation, violation, abrogation (756), flat refusal, peremptory denial.

(*Verbs*) To refuse, reject, deny, decline, disclaim, repudiate, protest, resist, repel, veto, refuse or withhold one's assent; to excuse oneself, to negative, turn down, rebuff, snub, spurn, resist, cross, grudge, begrudge.

To discard, set aside, rescind, revoke, discountenance, forswear.

(*Phrases*) To turn a deaf ear to; to shake the head; not to hear of;

to send to the right-about; to hang fire; to wash one's hands of; to declare off.

(*Adjectives*) Refusing, etc., recusant, restive, uncomplying, unconsenting.

Refused, etc., out of the question, not to be thought of.

(*Adverbs*) No, by no means, etc. (489).

(*Phrases*) Excuse me; nix on that; not on your life; nothing doing.

765 REQUEST (*Substantives*), requisition, asking, petition, demand, suit, solicitation, craving, entreaty, begging, postulation, adjuration, canvass, candidature, prayer, supplication, impetration, imploration, instance, obsecration, obtestation, importunity, application, address, appeal, motion, invitation, overture, apostrophe, orison, incantation, imprecation, conjuration.

Mendicancy, begging letter, round robin.

Claim, reclamation, revendication.

766 Negative request.

DEPRECATION (*Substantives*), expostulation, intercession, mediation.

(*Verbs*) To deprecate, protest, expostulate; to enter a protest; to intercede for.

(*Adjectives*) Deprecating, etc., deprecatory, expostulatory, intercessory; deprecated, protested.

Unsought, unbesought.

(*Interjections*) God forbid! forbid it heaven! *absit omen!*

(*Verbs*) To request, ask, sue, beg, cadge, crave, pray, petition, solicit, beg a boon, demand, prefer a request or petition, ply, apply to, make application, put to, make bold to ask, invite, beg leave, put up a prayer.

To beg hard, entreat, beseech, supplicate, implore, plead, conjure, adjure, invoke, evoke, kneel to, fall on one's knees, impetrate, imprecate, appeal to, apply to, put to, address, call for, press, urge, beset, importune, dun, tax, besiege, cry to, call on.

To bespeak, canvass, tout, make interest, court; to claim, reclaim.

(*Phrases*) To send the hat round; to beg from door to door.

(*Adjectives*) Requesting, asking, beseeching, etc., precatory, suppliant, supplicatory, postulant, importunate.

(*Phrases*) Cap in hand; on one's knees.

(*Adverbs*) Do, please, kindly, be good enough, pray, prithee, be so good as, have the goodness, vouchsafe.

For heaven's sake, for goodness' sake, for God's sake, for the love of Mike.

767 PETITIONER (*Substantives*), solicitor, applicant, suppliant, supplicant, mendicant, beggar, mumper, suitor, candidate, aspirant, claimant, postulant, canvasser, tout, cadger, sponger.

SECTION III—CONDITIONAL INTERSOCIAL VOLITION

768 PROMISE (*Substantives*), word, troth, plight, profession, pledge, parole, word of honour, assurance, vow, oath.

Engagement, guarantee, undertaking, insurance, contract (769), obligation; affiance, betrothal, betrothment.

768A Release from engagement, disengagement, liberation (750).

(*Adjectives*) Absolute, unconditional, uncovenanted, unsecured.

(Verbs) To promise, give a promise, undertake, engage, assure; to give, pass, pledge or plight one's word, honour credit, faith, etc.; to covenant, warrant, guarantee (467); to swear, vow, be sworn; take oath, make oath, kiss the book; to attest, adjure; to betroth, plight troth, affiance.

To answer for, be answerable for, secure, give security (771).

(Phrases) To enter on, make or form an engagement, take upon oneself; to bind, tie, commit, or pledge oneself; to be in for it; to contract an obligation; to be bound; to hold out an expectation.

To call heaven to witness; to swear by bell, book, and candle; to put on one's oath; to swear a witness.

(Adjectives) Promising, etc., promised, pledged, sworn, etc.; votive, promissory.

(Phrases) Under one's hand and seal; as one's head shall answer for.

(Interjection) So help me God!

769 COMPACT *(Substantives)*, contract, agreement, understanding, bargain, bond, deal, pact, paction, stipulation, covenant, settlement, convention, cartel, protocol, charter, treaty, indenture, concordat, *zollverein*.

Negotiation, transaction, bargaining, haggling, chaffering; diplomacy.

Ratification, settlement, signature, endorsement, seal, signet.

A negotiator, diplomatist, diplomat, agent, contractor, underwriter, attorney, broker (758).

(Verbs) To contract, covenant, agree for, strike a bargain, engage (768); to underwrite.

To treat, negotiate, bargain, stipulate, haggle (or higgle), chaffer, stick out for, insist upon, make a point of, compound for.

To conclude, close, confirm, ratify, endorse, clench, come to an understanding, take one at one's word, come to terms.

To subscribe, sign, seal, indent, put the seal to, sign and seal.

(Phrase) *Caveat emptor.*

770 CONDITIONS *(Substantives)*, terms, articles, articles of agreement, clauses, proviso, provisions, salvo, covenant, stipulation, obligation, ultimatum, *sine qua non*.

(Verbs) To make it a condition, make terms; to stipulate, insist upon; to tie up.

(Adjectives) Conditional, provisional, guarded, fenced, hedged in.

(Adverbs) Conditionally, on the understanding; provided (469).

(Phrases) With a string tied to it; wind and weather permitting; God willing; D.V.; *Deo volente*.

771 SECURITY *(Substantives)*, surety, guaranty, guarantee, mortgage, warranty, bond, debenture, pledge, tie, plight, pawn, lien, caution, sponsion, hostage, sponsor, bail, parole.

Deed, instrument, deed-poll, indenture, warrant, charter, cartel, protocol, recognizance; verification, acceptance, endorsement, signature, execution, seal, stamp, I O U.

Promissory note, bill of exchange, bill.

Stake, deposit, pool, kitty, jack-pot, earnest, handsel.

Docket, certificate, voucher, verification, authentication.

(Verbs) To give security, go bail, pawn (787); guarantee, warrant, accept, endorse, underwrite, insure; execute, stamp.

To hold in pledge.

772 OBSERVANCE (*Substantives*), performance, fulfilment, satisfaction, discharge, compliance, acquittance, quittance, acquittal, adhesion, acknowledgment, fidelity (939).

(*Verbs*) To observe, perform, keep, fulfil, discharge, comply with, make good, meet, satisfy, respect, abide by, adhere to, be faithful to, act up to, acquit oneself.

(*Phrase*) To redeem one's pledge.

(*Adjectives*) Observant, faithful, true, honourable (939), strict, rigid, punctilious.

(*Adverb*) Faithfully, etc., to the letter.

(*Phrase*) As good as one's word.

773 NON-OBSERVANCE (*Substantives*), inobservance, evasion, omission, failure, neglect, laches, laxity, infringement, infraction, violation, forfeiture, transgression.

Retractation, repudiation, nullification, protest.

Informality, lawlessness, disobedience, bad faith (742).

(*Verbs*) To break, violate, fail, neglect, omit, skip, cut, forfeit, infringe, transgress.

To retract, discard, protest, go back upon or from one's word, repudiate, nullify, ignore, set at naught, wipe off, cancel, etc. (552), to fob off, palter, elude, evade.

(*Phrases*) To wash out; to shut one's eyes to; to drive a coach and six through.

(*Adjectives*) Violating, etc., elusive, evasive, transgressive, unfulfilled; compensatory (30).

774 COMPROMISE (*Substantives*), composition, middle term, *mezzo termine, modus vivendi*; bribe, hush-money.

(*Verbs*) To compromise, compound, commute, adjust, take the mean, split the difference, come to terms, come to an understanding, meet one half-way, give and take, submit to arbitration.

SECTION IV—POSSESSIVE RELATIONS

1°. *Property in general*

775 ACQUISITION (*Substantives*), obtainment, gaining, earning, procuration, procuring, procurement, gathering, gleaning, picking, collecting, recovery, retrieval, totting, salvage, find.

Book-collecting, book-hunting, etc., philately, cartophily, phillumeny.

Gain, profit, benefit, emolument, the main chance, pelf, lucre, loaves and fishes, produce, product, proceeds, return, fruit, crop, harvest, scoop, takings, winnings.

Inheritance, bequest, legacy.

Fraudulent acquisition, subreption, stealing (791).

Profiteering, pot-hunting.

A collector, book-collector, etc., bird-fancier, etc., philatelist,

776 LOSS (*Substantives*), perdition, forfeiture, lapse.

Privation, bereavement, deprivation (789), dispossession, riddance.

(*Verbs*) To lose; incur, experience, or meet with a loss; to miss, mislay, throw away, forfeit, drop, let slip, allow to slip through the fingers; to get rid of (782), to waste (638, 679).

To be lost, lapse.

(*Phrase*) To throw good money after bad.

(*Adjectives*) Losing, etc., lost, etc. Devoid of, not having, unobtained, unpossessed, unblest with.

Shorn of, deprived of, bereaved of, bereft of, rid of, quit of, dispossessed, denuded, out of pocket, minus, cut off.

cartophilist, phillumenist; a profit-eer, money-grubber, pot-hunter.

(*Verbs*) To acquire, get, gain, win, earn, realize, regain, receive (785), take (789), obtain, procure, derive, secure, collect, reap, gather, glean, come in for, step into, inherit, come by, rake in, scrape together, get hold of, scoop, pouch.

To profit, make profit, turn to profit, make money by, obtain a return, make a fortune, coin money, profiteer.

To be profitable, to pay, to answer.

To fall to, come to, accrue.

(*Phrases*) To turn an honest penny; to earn an honest crust; to bring grist to the mill; to raise the wind; to line one's pockets; to feather one's nest; to reap or gain an advantage; to keep the wolf from the door; to keep the pot boiling.

(*Adjectives*) Acquisitive, acquiring, acquired, etc., profitable, lucrative, remunerative, paying.

(*Phrase*) On the make.

Irrecoverable, irretrievable, irre mediable, irreparable.

(*Interjections*) Farewell to! adie to!

———

777 Possession (*Substantives*), ownership, proprietorship, tenure, tenancy, seisin, occupancy, hold, holding, preoccupancy.

Exclusive possession, impropria-tion, monopoly, inalienability.

Future possession, heritage, heir-ship, inheritance, reversion.

(*Phrases*) A bird in the hand; nine points of the law; the haves and the have-nots.

(*Verbs*) To possess, have, hold, own, be master of, be in possession of, enjoy, occupy, be seised of, be worth, to have in hand or on hand; to inherit (775).

To engross, monopolize, corner, forestall, absorb, preoccupy.

To be the property of, belong to, appertain to, pertain to, be in the hands of, be in the possession of.

(*Adjectives*) Possessing, etc., pos-sessed of, seised of, worth, endowed with, instinct with, fraught, laden with, charged with.

Possessed, etc., proprietary, pro-prietorial; on hand, in hand, in store, in stock, unsold, unshared; inalien-able.

778 Joint possession.

Participation (*Substantives*), joint stock, common stock, partnership, copartnership, possession in common, communion, community of posses-sions or goods, socialism, collectivism, communism, syndicalism.

Bottle party, share-out, picnic.

A syndicate, ring, corner, combine, cartel, trust, monopoly, pool.

A partner, co-partner, shareholder; co-tenant, co-heir; a communist, socialist.

(*Verbs*) To participate, partake, share, communicate, go snacks, go halves, share and share alike; to have or possess, etc., in common; to come in for a share, to stand in with, to socialize, to pool.

(*Adjectives*) Partaking, etc.; social-ist, socialistic, communist.

(*Adverbs*) Share and share alike, fifty-fifty, even Stephen.

———

779 Possessor (*Substantives*), owner, holder, proprietor, proprietress, proprietary, master, mistress, heritor, occupier, occupant, landlord, landlady, landowner, lord of the manor, squire, laird, landed gentry; tenant, renter, lessee, lodger.

Future possessor, heir, heiress, inheritor.

780 PROPERTY (*Substantives*), possession, ownership, proprietorship, seisin, tenancy, tenure, lordship, title, claim, stake, legal estate, equitable estate, fee simple, fee tail, *meum et tuum*, occupancy.

Estate, effects, assets, resources, means, belongings, stock, goods, chattels, fixtures, plant, movables, furniture, things, traps, trappings, paraphernalia, luggage, baggage, bag and baggage, cargo, lading.

Lease, term, settlement, remainder, reversion, dower, jointure, apanage, heritage, inheritance, patrimony, heirloom.

Real property, land, landed estate, manor, demesne, domain, tenement, holding, hereditament, household, freehold, farm, ranch, *hacienda, estancia*, fief, feoff, seigniority, allodium.

Ground, acres, field, close.

State, realm, empire, kingdom, principality, territory, sphere of influence.

(*Adjectives*) Predial, manorial, freehold, etc., copyhold, leasehold.

---

781 RETENTION (*Substantives*), keep, holding, keeping, retaining, detention, custody, grasp, gripe, grip, tenacity.

Fangs, teeth, clutches, hooks, tentacles, claws, talons, nails.

Forceps, pincers, pliers, tongs, vice.

Incommunicableness, incommunicability.

(*Phrase*) A bird in the hand.

(*Verbs*) To retain, keep, keep in hand, secure, detain, hold fast, grasp, clutch, clench, cinch, gripe, grip, hug, withhold, keep back.

(*Adjectives*) Retaining, etc., retentive, tenacious.

Unforfeited, undeprived, undisposed, uncommunicated, incommunicable, inalienable, not transferable.

782 RELINQUISHMENT (*Substantives*), cession, abandonment (624), renunciation, surrender, dereliction, rendition, riddance (776), resignation (758).

(*Verbs*) To relinquish, give up, let go, lay aside, resign, forgo, drop, discard, dismiss, waive, renounce, surrender, part with, get rid of, lay down, abandon, cede, yield, dispose of, divest oneself of, spare, give away, throw away, cast away, fling away, maroon, jettison, chuck up, let slip, make away with, make way for.

(*Phrases*) To lay on the shelf; to throw overboard.

(*Adjectives*) Relinquished, etc., derelict, left, residuary (40), unculled.

2°. *Transfer of Property*

783 TRANSFER (*Substantives*), interchange, exchange, transmission, barter (794), conveyance, assignment, alienation, abalienation, demise, succession, reversion; metastasis.

(*Verbs*) To transfer, convey, assign, consign, make over, pass, transmit, interchange, exchange (148).

To change hands, change from one to another, alienate, devolve.

To dispossess, abalienate, disinherit.

(*Adjectives*) Alienable, negotiable, transferable.

784 GIVING (*Substantives*), bestowal, donation, accordance, presentation, oblation, presentment, delivery, award, investment, granting.

Cession, concession, consignment, dispensation, benefaction, charity, liberality, generosity, munificence, almsgiving.

Gift, donation, bonus, boon, present, testimonial, presentation, fairing, benefaction, grant, subsidy, subvention, offering, contribution, subscription, whip-round, donative, meed, tribute, gratuity, tip, Christmas box, handsel, trinkgeld, *douceur, pourboire,* baksheesh, cumshaw, dash, bribe, free gift, favour, bounty, largess, allowance, endowment, charity, alms, dole, peace-offering, payment (807).

Bequest, legacy, demise, dotation.

Giver, grantor, donor, benefactor.

(*Phrase*) *Panem et circenses.*

(*Verbs*) To give, bestow, accord, confer, grant, concede, present, give away, deliver, deliver over, make over, consign, entrust, hand, tip, render, impart, hand over, part with, fork out, yield, dispose of, put into the hands of, vest in, assign, put in possession, settle upon, endow, subsidize.

To bequeath, leave, demise, devise.

To give out, dispense, deal, deal out, dole out, mete out.

To contribute, subscribe, put up a purse, send round the hat, pay (807), spend (809).

To furnish, supply, administer, afford, spare, accommodate with, indulge with, shower upon, lavish.

To bribe, suborn, grease the palm, square.

(*Adjectives*) Giving, etc., given, etc., charitable, eleemosynary, tributary.

(*Phrase*) *Bis dat qui cito dat.*

785 RECEIVING (*Substantives*), acquisition (775), reception, acceptance, admission.

A recipient, donee, assignee, legatee, grantee, stipendiary, beneficiary, pensioner, almsman.

(*Verbs*) To receive, take (789), accept, pocket, pouch, admit, catch, catch at, jump at, take in.

To be received, etc.; to accrue, come to hand.

(*Adjectives*) Receiving, etc., recipient; pensionary, stipendiary.

---

786 APPORTIONMENT (*Substantives*), distribution, dispensation, allotment, assignment, consignment, partition, division, deal, share-out.

Dividend, portion, contingent, share, whack, meed, allotment, lot, measure, dole, pittance, quantum, ration, quota, modicum, allowance, appropriation.

(*Phrase*) Cutting up the melon.

(*Verbs*) To apportion, divide, distribute, administer, dispense, billet, allot, cast, share, mete, parcel out, serve out, deal, partition, appropriate, assign.

(*Adjectives*) Apportioning, etc., respective.

(*Adverbs*) Respectively, severally.

---

787 LENDING (*Substantives*), loan, advance, mortgage, accommodation, lease-lend, subsistence money, sub, pawn, pignoration, hypothecation, investment; pawnshop, *mont de piété.*

Lender, pawnbroker, uncle.

788 BORROWING (*Substantives*), pledging, replevin, borrowed plumes, plagiarism, plagiary; a touch.

(*Verbs*) To borrow, hire, rent, farm, raise money, raise the wind; to plagiarize.

(*Verbs*) To lend, loan, advance, mortgage, invest, pawn, impawn, pop, hock, hypothecate, impignorate, place or put out to interest, entrust, accommodate with.

(*Adjectives*) Lending, etc., lent, etc., unborrowed.

(*Adverb*) In advance; up the spout.

(*Adjectives*) Borrowing, etc., borrowed, second-hand.

(*Phrases*) To borrow of Peter to pay Paul; to run into debt.

---

789 TAKING (*Substantives*), appropriation, prehension, capture, seizure, abduction, ablation, catching, seizing, apprehension, arrest, kidnapping, round-up.

Abstraction, subtraction, deduction, subduction.

Dispossession, deprivation, deprival, bereavement, divestment, sequestration, confiscation, disendowment.

Resumption, reprise, reprisal, recovery (775).

Clutch, swoop, wrench, catch, take, haul.

(*Verbs*) To take, capture, lay one's hands on; lay, take, or get hold of; to help oneself to; to possess oneself of, take possession of, make sure of, make free with.

To appropriate, impropriate, pocket, put into one's pocket, pouch, bag; to ease one of.

To pick up, gather, collect, round up, net, absorb (296), reap, glean, crop, get in the harvest, cull, pluck; intercept, tap.

To take away, carry away, carry off, bear off, hurry off with, abduct, kidnap, crimp, shanghai.

To lay violent hands on, fasten upon, pounce upon, catch, seize, snatch, nip up, whip up, jump at, snap at, hook, claw, clinch, grasp, gripe, grip, grab, clutch, wring, wrest, wrench, pluck, tear away, catch, nab, capture, collar, throttle.

To take from, deduct, subduct (38), subtract, curtail, retrench, abridge of, dispossess, expropriate, take away from, abstract, deprive of, bereave, divest, disendow, despoil, strip, fleece, shear, impoverish, levy, distrain, confiscate, sequester, sequestrate, commandeer, requisition, oust, extort, usurp, suck, squeeze, drain, bleed, milk, gut, dry, exhaust.

(*Phrases*) To suck like a leech; to be given an inch and take an ell; to sweep the board; to scoop the pool.

(*Adjectives*) Taking, etc., privative, prehensile, predatory, rapacious, raptorial, predial, ravenous.

790 RESTITUTION (*Substantives*), return, reddition, rendition, restoration, rehabilitation, remission, reinvestment, reparation, atonement.

Redemption, recovery, recuperation, release, replevin.

(*Verbs*) To return, restore, give back, bring back, derequisition, denationalize, render, refund, reimburse, recoup, remit, rehabilitate, repair, reinvest.

To let go, disgorge, regorge, regurgitate.

(*Adjectives*) Restoring, etc., recuperative.

(*Phrase*) *Suum cuique.*

---

791 STEALING (*Substantives*), theft, thieving, thievery, abstraction, appropriation, plagiarism, depredation, pilfering, rape, larceny, robbery, shoplifting, burglary, house-breaking, abaction (of cattle), cattle-lifting, kidnapping.

Spoliation, plunder, pillage, sack, rapine, brigandage, foray, raid, hold-up dragonnade, marauding.

Peculation, embezzlement, swindling (545), blackmail, *chantage*, smuggling black market; thievishness, rapacity, kleptomania; den of thieves, Alsatia.

Licence to plunder, letter of marque.

(*Verbs*) To steal, thieve, rob, abstract, appropriate, filch, pilfer, purloin, nab, nim, prig, grab, bag, lift, pick, pinch, knock off.

To convey away, carry off, make off with, run or walk off with, abduct, spirit away, kidnap, crimp, seize, lay violent hands on, etc. (789), abact, rustle (of cattle), shanghai.

To scrounge, wangle, win, crib, sponge, rook, bilk, diddle, swindle (545), peculate, embezzle, fiddle, flog, poach, run, smuggle, hijack.

To plunder, pillage, rifle, sack, ransack, burgle, spoil, spoliate, despoil, hold up, stick up, bail up, strip, fleece, gut, loot, forage, levy blackmail, pirate, plagiarize.

(*Phrases*) To live by one's wits; to rob Peter to pay Paul; to obtain under false pretences; to set a thief to catch a thief.

(*Adjectives*) Stealing, etc., thievish, light-fingered, larcenous, stolen, furtive, piratical, predaceous.

792 THIEF (*Substantives*), robber, spoiler, pickpocket, cutpurse, dip, depredator, yegg, yeggman, footpad, highwayman, burglar, house-breaker, larcener, larcenist, pilferer, filcher, sneak-thief, shop-lifter, poacher, rustler; swell mob; the light-fingered gentry; kleptomaniac.

Swindler, crook, spiv, welsher, smuggler, bootlegger, hijacker, gangster, cracksman, magsman, mobsman, sharper, blackleg, shark, trickster, harpy, *chevalier d'industrie*, peculator, plagiarist, blackmailer; receiver, fence.

Brigand, freebooter, bandit, pirate, viking, corsair, buccaneer, thug, dacoit, picaroon, moss-trooper, rapparee, maurauder, filibuster, wrecker, bushranger; Autolycus, Turpin, Macheath, Bill Sikes, Jonathan Wild.

(*Phrases*) A snapper-up of unconsidered trifles; *homo triarum literarum*.

793 BOOTY (*Substantives*), spoil, plunder, swag, loot, boodle, prey, pickings, grab, forage, blackmail, graft, prize.

3°. *Interchange of Property*

794 BARTER (*Substantives*), exchange, truck, swop (or swap), chop, interchange, commutation.

Traffic, trade, commerce, dealing, business, custom, negotiation, transaction, jobbing, agiotage, bargain, deal, package deal, commercial, enterprise, speculation, brokery.

(*Phrases*) A Roland for an Oliver, a *quid pro quo*; payment in kind.

(*Verbs*) To barter, exchange, truck, interchange, commute, swap (or swop), traffic, trade, speculate, transact, or do business with, deal with, have dealings with; open or keep an account with; to carry on a trade; to rig the market.

To bargain; drive, make, or strike a bargain; negotiate, bid for, haggle (or higgle), chaffer, dicker, stickle, cheapen, compound for, beat down, outbid, underbid, outbargain, come to terms, do a deal, quote, underquote.

(*Phrase*) To throw a sprat to catch a whale.

(*Adjectives*) Commercial, mercantile, trading, interchangeable, marketable, negotiable; wholesale, retail.

795 Purchase (*Substantives*), emption, buying, purchasing, shopping, hire-purchase, never-never; preemption, bribery, co-emption.

A buyer, purchaser, customer, emptor, shopper, patron, client, clientele.

(*Verbs*) To buy, purchase, procure, hire, rent, farm, pay, fee, repurchase, buy in, keep in one's pay; pre-empt; bribe, suborn, square, buy over; shop, market.

(*Adjectives*) Purchased, etc.

(*Phrase*) Caveat emptor.

796 Sale (*Substantives*), disposal, custom.

Auction, Dutch auction, roup.

Lease, mortgage.

Vendibility, salability.

A vendor, seller (797).

To sell, vend, dispose of, retail, dispense, auction, auctioneer, hawk, peddle, undersell.

To let, sublet, lease, mortgage.

(*Phrases*) Put up to sale or auction; bring under the hammer.

(*Adjectives*) Vendible, marketable, salable; unpurchased, unbought, on one's hands, unsalable.

797 Merchant (*Substantives*), trader, dealer, tradesman, buyer and seller, vendor, monger, chandler, shopkeeper, shopman, salesman, saleswoman, changer.

Retailer, chapman, hawker, huckster, regrater, higgler, pedlar, cadger, sutler, bumboatman, middleman, coster, costermonger; auctioneer, broker, money-broker, bill-broker, money-changer, jobber, factor, go-between, cambist, usurer, money-lender.

House, firm, concern, partnership, company, guild, syndicate.

798 Merchandise (*Substantives*), ware, mercery, commodity, effects, goods, article, stock, stock-in-trade, cargo (190), produce, freight, lading, ship-load, staple commodity.

799 Mart (*Substantives*), market, change (or 'change), exchange, bourse, market-place, fair, hall, staple, bazaar, guildhall, tollbooth (or tolbooth), custom-house.

Office, shop, counting-house, bureau, counter, stall, booth, chambers.

Warehouse, depot, store (636), *entrepôt*, emporium, godown.

4°. *Monetary Relations*

800 Money (*Substantives*), funds, treasure, capital, stock, proceeds, assets, cash, bullion, ingot, nugget; sum, amount, balance.

Currency, soft currency, hard currency, circulating medium, legal tender, specie, coin, hard cash, sterling, pounds shillings and pence, L.S.D.

Ready, rhino, blunt, oof, lolly, splosh, chink, dibs, plunks, bucks, bones, siller, dust, tin, dough, jack, spondulicks, simoleons, mazuma, ducats, the needful, the wherewithal.

Gold, silver, copper, nickel, rouleau, dollar, etc.

Finance, gold standard, monometallism, bimetallism.

Pocket-money, pin money, chicken feed, petty cash, change, small coin; doit, farthing, bawbee, penny, shilling, stiver, mite, sou; plum, grand, monkey, pony, tenner, fiver, quid, wheel, bob, tanner, two bits.

Sum, amount, balance.

Paper money, note, bank-note, treasury note, greenback, note of hand, promissory note, I O U.

Cheque (or check), bill, draft (or draught), order, remittance, postal order, money order, warrant, coupon, debenture, bill of exchange, exchequer bill, treasury bill, assignat.

A drawer, a drawee.

False money, base coin, flash note, kite, stumer.

Science of coins, numismatics.

(*Phrases*) The sinews of war; the almighty dollar.

(*Verbs*) To draw, draw upon, endorse, issue, utter; to amount to, come to.

(*Adjectives*) Monetary, pecuniary, fiscal, financial, sumptuary; monometallic, bimetallic; numismatical.

(*Phrases*) To touch the pocket; *argumentum ad crumenam.*

801 TREASURER (*Substantives*), purse-bearer, purser, bursar, banker, moneyer, paymaster, cashier, teller, accountant, steward, trustee, almoner. Chancellor of the Exchequer, minister of finance, Queen's Remembrancer.

802 TREASURY (*Substantives*), bank, savings-bank, exchequer, coffer, chest, money-box, money-bag, strong-box, strong-room, safe, bursary, till, note-case, wallet, purse, *porte-monnaie*, purse-strings, pocket, fisc.

Consolidated fund, sinking fund, the funds, consols, government securities, war loan, savings certificates.

803 WEALTH (*Substantives*), fortune, riches, opulence, affluence, independence, solvency, competence, easy circumstances, command of money; El Dorado, Golconda, plutocracy.

Means, provision, substance, resources, capital, revenue, income, alimony, livelihood, subsistence, loaves and fishes, pelf, mammon, lucre, dower (810), pension, superannuation, annuity, unearned increment, pin-money.

A rich man, capitalist, plutocrat, financier, money-bags, millionaire, a Nabob, Dives, Croesus, Midas; *rentier.*

(*Phrases*) The golden calf; a well-lined purse; the purse of Fortunatus; a mint or pot of money.

(*Verbs*) To be rich, etc., to afford. To enrich, fill one's coffers, etc.; to capitalize.

(*Phrases*) To roll in riches; to wallow in wealth; to make one's pile; to feather one's nest; to line one's pockets; to keep one's head above water.

(*Adjectives*) Wealthy, rich, well-off, affluent, opulent, flush, oofy, solvent (734), moneyed, plutocratic.

(*Phrases*) Made of money; in

804 POVERTY (*Substantives*), indigence, penury, pauperism, destitution, want, need, lack, necessity, privation, distress, an empty purse; bad, reduced, or straitened circumstances; narrow means, straits, insolvency, impecuniosity, beggary, mendicancy, mendicity.

A poor man, pauper, mendicant, beggar, tramp, bum, vagabond, gangrel, starveling; the proletariat; *un pauvre diable.*

Poorhouse, workhouse, the institution.

(*Phrases*) *Res angusta domi*; the wolf at the door.

(*Verbs*) To be poor, etc., to want, lack, starve.

To render poor, etc., to reduce, to impoverish, reduce to poverty, depauperate, ruin; to pauperize.

(*Phrases*) To live from hand to mouth; come upon the parish; not to have a penny; to have seen better days; to beg one's bread.

(*Adjectives*) Poor, indigent, penniless, moneyless, impecunious, short of money, out of money, out of cash, out of pocket, needy, destitute, necessitous, distressed, hard up, in need, in want, poverty-stricken,

funds; rich as Croesus; rolling in riches; one's ship come home.

———

badly off, in distress, pinched, straitened, dowerless, fortuneless, reduced, insolvent (806), bereft, bereaved, fleeced, stripped, stony broke, stony, stumped.

(*Phrases*) Unable to make both ends meet; out at elbows; in reduced circumstances; not worth a sou; poor as Job; poor as a church mouse; down at heels; on one's uppers; on the rocks.

805 CREDIT (*Substantives*), trust, tick, score, account.

Letter of credit, duplicate, traveller's cheque (or check); mortgage, lien, debenture.

A creditor, lender, lessor, mortgagee, debenture-holder; a dun, usurer, gombeen-man, Shylock.

(*Verbs*) To keep an account with, to credit, accredit.

To place to one's credit or account, give credit.

(*Adjective*) Crediting.

(*Adverbs*) On credit, on tick, on account, to pay, unpaid-for.

———

806 DEBT (*Substantives*), obligation, liability, debit, indebtment, arrears, deficit, default, insolvency.

Interest, usance, usury.

Floating debt, bad debt, floating capital, debentures; deferred payment, hire system, never-never system.

A debtor, debitor, borrower, lessee, mortgagor; a defaulter (808).

(*Verbs*) To be in debt, to owe, to answer for, to incur a debt, borrow (788).

(*Phrases*) To run up a hill; to go on tick; to outrun the constable.

(*Adjectives*) In debt, indebted, owing, due, unpaid, outstanding, in arrear, being minus, out of pocket, encumbered, involved, in difficulties, liable, chargeable, answerable for, insolvent, in the red.

Unrequited, unrewarded.

807 PAYMENT (*Substantives*), defrayment, discharge, quittance, acquittance, settlement, clearance, liquidation, satisfaction, remittance, instalment, stake, reckoning, arrangement, composition, acknowledgment, release.

Repayment, reimbursement, retribution, reward (973).

Bill, cheque, cash, ready money (800).

(*Phrase*) A *quid pro quo*.

(*Verbs*) To pay, defray, discharge, settle, quit, acquit oneself of, reckon with, remit, clear, liquidate, release; repay, refund, reimburse.

(*Phrases*) To honour a bill; to strike a balance; to settle, balance, or square accounts with; to be even with; to wipe off old scores; to satisfy all demands; to pay one's way or shot; to pay in full.

808 NON-PAYMENT (*Substantives*), default, defalcation, repudiation, protest.

Insolvency, bankruptcy, failure, whitewashing, application of the sponge.

Waste paper, dishonoured bills.

A defaulter, bankrupt, welsher, levanter, insolvent debtor, man of straw, lame duck.

(*Verbs*) Not to pay, to fail, break, become insolvent or bankrupt, default, defalcate.

To protest, dishonour, repudiate, nullify; hammer.

(*Phrases*) To run up bills; to tighten the purse-strings.

(*Adjectives*) Not paying, in debt, behindhand, in arrear, insolvent, bankrupt, gazetted.

(*Phrases*) Being minus or worse than nothing; plunged or over head

(*Adjectives*) Paying, etc., paid, owing nothing, out of debt.

(*Adverbs*) On the nail, money down, C.O.D.

809 EXPENDITURE (*Substantives*), money going out; outgoings, expenses, disbursement, outlay.

Pay, payment, fee, hire, wages, perquisites, vails, allowance, stipend, salary, screw, divided, tribute, subsidy, batta, bat-money, shot, scot.

Remuneration, recompense, reward (973), tips, *pourboire*, largess, honorarium, refresher, bribe, *douceur*, hush-money, extras, commission, rake-off.

Advance, subsistence money, sub, earnest, handsel, deposit, prepayment, entrance fee, entrance.

Contribution, donation, subscription, deposit, contingent, dole, quota.

Investment, purchase (795), alms (748).

(Verbs) To expend, spend, pay, disburse, lay out, lay or pay down, to cash, to come down with, brass up, shell out, fork out, bleed, make up a sum, to invest, sink money, prepay, tip.

(*Phrases*) To unloose the purse-strings; to pay the piper; to pay through the nose.

(*Adjectives*) Expending, etc., expended, etc., sumptuary.

810 RECEIPT (*Substantives*), money coming in, incomings.

Income, revenue, earnings (775), rent, rental, rent-roll, rentage, return, proceeds, premium, bonus, gate-money, royalty.

Pension, annuity, tontine, jointure, dower, dowry, dot, alimony, compensation.

Emoluments, perquisites, recompense (809), sinecure.

(*Verbs*) To receive, pocket (789), to draw from, derive from.

To bring in, yield, return, afford, pay, accrue.

(*Phrases*) To get what will make the pot boil; keep the wolf from the door; bring grist to the mill.

(*Adjectives*) Receiving, etc., received, etc.

Gainful, profitable, remunerative, lucrative, advantageous (775).

811 ACCOUNTS (*Substantives*), money matters, finance, budget, bill, score, reckoning, balance-sheet, books, account-books, ledger, day-book, cash-book, cash account, current acount, deposit account, pass-book.

Book-keeping, audit, double entry.

An accountant, C.A., auditory, actuary, book-keeper.

(*Verbs*) To keep accounts, to enter, post, credit, debit, tot up, carry over; balance, make up accounts, take stock, audit.

To falsify, garble, cook, or doctor accounts.

812 PRICE (*Substantives*), cost, expense, amount, figure, charge, demand, damage, fare, hire.

Dues, duty, toll, tax, supertax, pay-as-you-earn, P.A.Y.E., rate, impost, cess, levy, gabelle, octroi, assessment, benevolence, custom, tithe, exactment, ransom, salvage, excise, tariff, brokerage, demurrage.

Bill, account, score, reckoning.

Worth, rate, value, valuation,

813 DISCOUNT (*Substantives*), abatement, reduction, deduction, depreciation, allowance, drawback, poundage, *agio*, percentage, rebate, set-off, backwardation, contango, tare and tret, salvage.

(*Verbs*) To discount, bate, abate, rebate, reduce, take off, allow, give, discount, tax.

(*Adjectives*) Discounting, etc.

(*Adverb*) At a discount.

and ears in debt; in the gazette; in Queer Street.

evaluation, appraisement, market price, quotation; money's worth, pennyworth; price-current, price list.

(*Verbs*) To set or fix a price, appraise, assess, value, evaluate, price, charge, demand, ask, require, exact.

To fetch, sell for, cost, bring in, yield, make, change hands for, go for, realize, run into, stand one in; afford.

(*Phrases*) To run up a bill; to amount to; to set one back.

(*Adjectives*) Priced, charged, etc., to the tune of, *ad valorem*; mercenary, venal.

(*Phrases*) No penny, no paternoster; *point d'argent, point de Suisse*.

814 DEARNESS (*Substantives*), costliness, high price, expensiveness, rise in price, overcharge, surcharge, extravagance, exorbitance, extortion.

(*Phrase*) A pretty penny.

(*Verbs*) To be dear, etc., to cost much, to come expensive; to overcharge, surcharge, bleed, fleece (791).

To pay too much, to pay through the nose.

(*Adjectives*) Dear, high, high-priced, expensive, costly, dear-bought, precious, unreasonable, extortionate, extravagant, exorbitant, steep, stiff.

(*Adverbs*) Dear, at great cost, at a premium.

815 CHEAPNESS (*Substantives*), low price, inexpensiveness, drop in price, undercharge, bargain; absence of charge, gratuity, free admission.

(*Phrases*) A labour of love; the run of one's teeth; a drug in the market.

(*Verbs*) To be cheap, etc., to cost little, to come down or fall in price, to cut prices.

(*Phrase*) To have one's money's worth.

(*Adjectives*) Cheap, low, moderate, reasonable, inexpensive, unexpensive, low-priced, dirt-cheap, worth the money, half-price; catchpenny.

Gratuitous, gratis, free, for nothing, given away, free of cost, without charge, not charged, untaxed, scot-free, shot-free, expenseless, free of expense, free of all demands, honorary, unpaid.

(*Phrases*) Cheap as dirt; for a mere song; given away with a pound of tea; at cost price; at a reduction; at a sacrifice.

816 LIBERALITY (*Substantives*), generosity (942), bounty, munificence, bounteousness, bountifulness, charity (906), hospitality.

(*Verbs*) To be liberal, etc., spend freely, lavish, shower upon.

(*Phrases*) To loosen one's purse-strings; to give *carte blanche*; to spare no expense.

(*Adjectives*) Liberal, free, generous, charitable, hospitable, bountiful, bounteous, handsome, lavish, ungrudging, free-handed, open-handed, open-hearted, free-hearted, munificent, princely.

Overpaid.

817 ECONOMY (*Substantives*), frugality, thrift, thriftiness, care, husbandry, good housewifery, austerity, retrenchment; parsimony (819).

(*Verbs*) To be economical, etc., to save, economize, skimp, scrimp, scrape, meet one's expenses, retrench; to lay by, put by, save up, invest, bank, hoard, accumulate.

(*Phrases*) To cut one's coat according to one's cloth; to make ends meet; to pay one's way; to look at both sides of a shilling; to provide for a rainy day.

(*Adjectives*) Economical, frugal, thrifty, canny, careful, saving, chary, spare, sparing, cheese-paring.

(*Phrase*) Take care of the pence and the pounds will take care of themselves.

818 Prodigality (*Substantives*), unthriftiness, thriftlessness, unthrift, waste, profusion, profuseness, extravagance, dissipation, squandering, squandermania, malversation.

A prodigal, spendthrift, squanderer, waster, wastrel.

(*Verbs*) To be prodigal, etc., to squander, lavish, waste, dissipate, exhaust, run through, spill, misspend, throw away money, drain.

(*Phrases*) To burn the candle at both ends; to make ducks and drakes of one's money; to spend money like water; to outrun the constable; to fool away, potter, muddle away, fritter away, etc., one's money; to pour water into a sieve; to go the pace.

(*Adjectives*) Prodigal, profuse, improvident, thriftless, unthrifty, wasteful, extravagant, lavish, dissipated.

(*Phrases*) Penny wise and pound foolish; money burning a hole in one's pocket.

---

819 Parsimony (*Substantives*), parsimoniousness, stint, stinginess, niggardliness, cheese-paring, extortion, illiberality, closeness, penuriousness, avarice, tenacity, covetousness, greediness, avidity, rapacity, venality, mercenariness, cupidity.

A miser, niggard, churl, screw, skinflint, money-grubber, codger, muckworm, hunks, curmudgeon, harpy.

(*Phrase*) *Auri sacra fames.*

(*Verbs*) To be parsimonious, etc., to grudge, begrudge, stint, pinch, screw, dole out.

(*Phrases*) To skin a flint; to drive a hard bargain; to tighten one's purse-strings.

(*Adjectives*) Parsimonious, stingy, miserly, mean, mingy, penurious, shabby, near, niggardly, cheese-paring, close, close-fisted, close-handed, chary, illiberal, ungenerous, churlish, sordid, mercenary, venal, covetous, avaricious, greedy, grasping, griping, pinching, extortionate, rapacious.

(*Phrases*) Having an itching palm; with a sparing hand.

CLASS VI

WORDS RELATING TO THE SENTIENT AND MORAL POWERS

Section I—Affections in General

820 Affections (*Substantives*), character, qualities, disposition, nature, spirit, mood, tone, temper, temperament; cast or frame of mind or soul; turn, bent, idiosyncrasy, bias, turn of mind, predisposition, diathesis, predilection, propensity, proneness, proclivity, vein, humour, grain, mettle.

Soul, heart, breast, bosom, the inner man, inmost heart, heart's core, heart-strings, heart's-blood, heart of hearts, *penetralia mentis*.

Passion, pervading spirit, ruling passion, master-passion.

(*Phrases*) Flow of soul; fullness of the heart; the cockles of one's heart; flesh and blood.

(*Verbs*) To have or possess affections, etc.; be of a character, etc.; to breathe.

(*Adjectives*) Affected, characterized, formed, moulded, cast, tempered, attempered, framed, disposed, predisposed, prone, inclined, having a bias, etc., imbued or penetrated with; inbred, inborn, engrained (or ingrained).

821 Feeling (*Substantives*), endurance, experience, suffering, tolerance, sufferance, experience, sensibility (822), passion (825).

Impression, sensation, affection, response, emotion, pathos, warmth, glow, fervour, fervency, heartiness, effusiveness, effusion, gush, cordiality, ardour, exuberance, zeal, eagerness, *empressement*, *élan*, enthusiasm, verve, inspiration.

Blush, suffusion, flush, tingling, thrill, kick, excitement (824), turn, shock, agitation (315), heaving, flutter, flurry, fluster, twitter, stew, tremor, throb, throbbing, panting, palpitation, trepidation, perturbation, hurry of spirits, the heart swelling, throbbing, thumping, pulsating, melting, bursting; transport, rapture, ecstasy, ravishment (827).

(*Verbs*) To feel, receive an impression, etc.; to be impressed with, affected with, moved with, touched with, keen on.

To bear, bear with, suffer, endure, brook, tolerate, stomach, stand, thole, experience, taste, meet with, go through, put up with, prove; to harbour, cherish, support, abide, undergo.

To blush, change colour, mantle, tingle, twitter, throb, heave, pant, palpitate, go pit-a-pat, agitate, thrill, tremble, shake, quiver, wince, simmer, burble.

To swell, glow, warm, flush, redden, look blue, look black, catch the flame, catch the infection, respond, enthuse.

To possess, pervade, penetrate, imbue, absorb, etc., the soul.

(*Phrases*) To bear the brunt of; to come home to one's feelings or bosom; to strike a chord.

(*Adjectives*) Feeling, suffering, enduring; sentient, emotive, emotional.

Impressed, moved, touched, affected with, etc., penetrated, imbued.

Warm, quick, lively, smart, strong, sharp, keen, acute, cutting, incisive, piercing, pungent, racy, piquant, poignant, caustic.

Deep, profound, indelible, ineffaceable, impressive, effective, deep-felt, home-felt, heart-felt, warm-hearted, hearty, cordial, swelling, thrilling, rapturous, ecstatic, soul-stirring, emotive, deep-mouthed, heart-expanding, electric.

Earnest, hearty, eager, exuberant, gushing, effusive, breathless, glowing, fervent, fervid, ardent, soulful, burning, red-hot, fiery, flaming, boiling, boiling over, zealous, pervading, penetrating, absorbing, hectic, rabid, fanatical; the heart being big, full, swelling, overflowing, bursting.

Wrought up, excited, passionate, enthusiastic (825).

(*Phrase*) Struck all of a heap.

(*Adverbs*) Heartily, cordially, earnestly, etc.

(*Phrases*) From the bottom of one's heart; *de profundis*; heart and soul; over head and ears.

---

822 SENSIBILITY (*Substantives*), impressibility, sensibleness, sensitiveness, hyperaesthesia (825), responsiveness, affectibility, susceptibleness, susceptibility, susceptivity, excitability, mobility, vivacity, vivaciousness, tenderness, softness, sentimentality, sentimentalism, schmalz.

Physical sensibility (375).

(*Verbs*) To be sensible, etc., to shrink, have a tender heart.

(*Phrases*) To be touched to the quick; to feel where the shoe pinches; to take it hard; to take to heart.

(*Adjectives*) Sensible, sensitive, impressible, impressionable, susceptive, susceptible, responsive, excitable, mobile, thin-skinned, touchy, alive, vivacious, lively, mettlesome, high-strung, intense, emotional, tender, soft, sentimental, maudlin, sloppy, romantic, enthusiastic, neurotic.

(*Adverbs*) Sensibly, etc., to the quick.

---

823 INSENSIBILITY (*Substantives*), insensibleness, inertness, insensitivity, impassibility, impassibleness, impassivity, apathy, phlegm, dullness, hebetude, coolness, coldness, supineness, stoicism, insouciance, nonchalance, indifference, lukewarmness, frigidity, cold blood, sang-froid, dry eyes, cold heart, deadness, torpor, torpidity, ataraxia, pococurantism.

Lethargy, coma, trance, stupor, stupefaction, amnesia, paralysis, palsy, catalepsy, suspended animation, hebetation, anaesthesia (381), stock and stone, neutrality.

Physical insensibility (376).

(*Verbs*) To disregard, be insensible, not to be affected by, not to mind, to vegetate, *laisser aller*, not to care; to take it easy.

To render insensible (376), numb, benumb, paralyse, deaden, render callous, sear, inure, harden, steel, case-harden, stun, daze, stupefy, brutalize, hebetate.

(*Phrases*) To turn a deaf ear to; not care a straw (or a fig).

(*Adjectives*) Insensible, unconscious, impassive, unsusceptible, insusceptible, impassible, unimpressionable, unresponsive, unfeeling, blind to, deaf to, dead to, passionless, spiritless, soulless, apathetic, listless, phlegmatic, callous, hard-boiled, thick-skinned, pachydermatous, obtuse, proof against, case-hardened, inured, steeled against, stoical, dull, frigid, cold, cold-blooded, cold-hearted, flat, inert, bovine, supine, sluggish, torpid, languid, tame, tepid, numb, numbed, sleepy, yawning, comatose, anaesthetic.

Indifferent, insouciant, lukewarm, careless, mindless, regardless, disregarding, nonchalant, unconcerned, uninterested, pococurante; taking no interest in.

Unfelt, unaffected, unruffled, unimpressed, unmoved, unperturbed, uninspired, untouched, etc.; platonic, imperturbable, vegetative, automatic.

(*Adverbs*) Insensibly, etc., *aequo animo*, with dry eyes, with withers unwrung.

(*Phrases*) No matter; never mind; *n'importe*; it matters not; it does not signify; it is of no consequence or importance (643); it cannot be helped; nothing coming amiss; it is all the same or all one to; what's the odds? *nichevo.*

824 EXCITATION (*Substantives*), of feeling, excitement, galvanism, stimulation, provocation, calling forth, infection, animation, inspiration, agitation, perturbation, subjugation, fascination, intoxication, enravishment, unction; a scene, sensation, tableau, shocker, thriller.

(*Verbs*) To excite, affect, touch, move, stir, wake, awaken, raise, raise up, evoke, call up, summon up, rake up.

To impress, strike, hit, quicken, swell, work upon.

To warm, kindle, stimulate, pique, whet, animate, hearten, inspire, impassion, inspirit, spirit, provoke, irritate, infuriate, sting, rouse, work up, hurry on, ginger up, commove.

To agitate, ruffle, flutter, fluster, flush, shake, thrill, penetrate, pierce, cut; to work oneself up, to simmer, bubble, burble.

To soften, subdue, overcome, master, overpower, overwhelm, bring under.

To shock, stagger, jar, jolt, stun, astound, electrify, galvanize, give one a shock, petrify.

To madden, intoxicate, fascinate, transport, ravish, enrapture, enravish, entrance, send.

(*Phrases*) To come home to one's feelings; to make a sensation; to prey on the mind; to give one a turn; to cut to the quick; to go through one; to strike one all of a heap; to make one's blood boil; to lash to a fury; to make one sit up.

(*Adjectives*) Excited, affected (825), wrought up, worked up, strung up, lost, *éperdu*, wild, haggard, feverish, febrile.

Exciting, etc., impressive, pathetic, sensational, provocative, piquant, aphrodisiac, dramatic, warm, glowing, fervid, swelling.

(*Phrases*) Being all of a twitter; all of a flutter; the head being turned.

825 Excess of sensitiveness.

EXCITABILITY (*Substantives*), intolerance, impatience, wincing, perturbation, trepidation, disquiet, disquietude, restlessness, fidgets, fidgetiness, fuss, hurry, agitation, flurry, fluster, flutter, irritability (901), hypersensitiveness, hyperaesthesia.

Passion, excitement, vehemence, impetuosity, flush, heat, fever, fire, flame, fume, wildness, turbulence, boisterousness, tumult, effervescence, ebullition, boiling, boiling over, whiff, gust, storm, tempest, outbreak, outburst, burst, explosion, fit, paroxysm, brain-storm, the blood boiling.

Fierceness, rage, fury, furore, tantrum, hysteria, hysterics, raving, delirium, frenzy, intoxication, fascination, infection, infatuation, fanaticism, Quixotism, *la tête montée.*

826 Absence of excitability.

INEXCITABILITY (*Substantives*), hebetude, tolerance, patience.

Coolness, composure, calmness, imperturbability, sang-froid, collectedness, tranquillity, quiet, quietude, quietness, sedateness, soberness, poise, staidness, gravity, placidity, sobriety, philosophy, stoicism, demureness, meekness, gentleness, mildness.

Submission, resignation, sufferance, endurance, longanimity, long-sufferance, forbearance, fortitude, equanimity.

Repression, restraint (174), hebetation, tranquillization.

(*Phrases*) Patience of Job; even temper; cool head; Spartan endurance; a sober-sides.

(*Verbs*) To be composed, etc., to

(*Verbs*) To be intolerant, etc., not to bear, to bear ill, wince, chafe, fidget, fuss, not to be able to bear, stand, tolerate, etc.

To break out, fly out, burst out, explode, run riot, boil, boil over, fly off, flare up, fire, take fire, fume, rage, rampage, rave, run mad, run amuck, raise Cain.

(*Phrases*) To fly off at a tangent; to be out of all patience; to go off the deep end; to get the wind up; to make a scene; to go up in a blue flame.

(*Adjectives*) Excitable, etc., excited, etc.

Intolerant, impatient, unquiet, restless, restive, fidgety, irritable, mettlesome, chafing, wincing, etc.

Vehement, boisterous, impetuous, demonstrative, fierce, fiery, flaming, boiling, ebullient, over-zealous, passionate, impassioned, enthusiastic, rampant, mercurial, high-strung, skittish, overwrought, overstrung, hysterical, hot-headed, hurried, turbulent, furious, fuming, boiling, raging, raving, frantic, phrenetic, rampageous, wild, heady, delirious, intoxicated, demoniacal; hypersensitive.

Overpowering, overwhelming, uncontrolled, madcap, reckless, stanchless, irrepressible, ungovernable, uncontrollable, inextinguishable, volcanic.

(*Phrases*) More than flesh and blood can stand; stung to the quick; all hot and bothered.

(*Interjections*) Pish! pshaw! botheration!

bear, to bear well, tolerate, put up with, bear with, stand, bide, abide, aby, take easily, rub on, rub along, make the best of, acquiesce, submit, yield, bow to, resign oneself, suffer, endure, support, go through, reconcile oneself to, bend under; subside, calm down, pipe down.

To brook, digest, eat, swallow, pocket, stomach, brave, make light of.

To be borne, endured, etc., to go down.

To allay, compose, calm, still, lull, pacify, placate, quiet, tranquillize, hush, smooth, appease, assuage, mitigate, soothe, soften, temper, chasten, alleviate, moderate, sober down, mollify, lenify, tame, blunt, obtund, dull, deaden (823), slacken, damp, repress, restrain, check, curb, bridle, rein in, smother (174).

(*Phrases*) To take things as they come; to submit with a good grace; to shrug the shoulders.

To set one's heart at rest or at ease.

(*Adjectives*) Inexcitable, unexcited, calm, cool, temperate, composed, collected, placid, quiet, tranquil, unstirred, undisturbed, unruffled, serene, demure, sedate, staid, sober, dispassionate, unimpassioned, passionless, good-natured, easy-going, platonic, philosophic, stoical, imperturbable, cold-blooded, insensible (823).

Meek, tolerant, patient, submissive, unoffended, unresenting, content, resigned, subdued, bearing with, longsuffering, gentle, mild, sober-minded, cool-headed.

(*Phrases*) Gentle or meek as a lamb; mild as milk; patient as Job; armed with patience; cool as a cucumber.

SECTION II—PERSONAL AFFECTIONS

1°. *Passive Affections*

827 PLEASURE (*Substantives*), gratification, delectation, enjoyment, fruition, relish, zest, gusto, kick.

Well-being, satisfaction, complacency, content (831), ease, comfort, bed of roses, bed of down, velvet.

828 PAIN (*Substantives*), suffering; physical pain (378).

Displeasure, dissatisfaction, discontent, discomfort, discomposure, malaise.

Uneasiness, disquiet, inquietude,

Joy, gladness, delight, glee, cheer, sunshine.

Physical pleasure (377).

Treat, refreshment, feast, luxury, voluptuousness, clover.

Happiness, felicity, bliss, beatitude, beatification, enchantment, transport, rapture, ravishment, ecstasy, heaven, *summum bonum*, paradise, Eden, Arcadia, nirvana, elysium, empyrean (981).

Honeymoon, palmy days, halcyon days, golden age, *Saturnia regna.*

(*Verbs*) To be pleased, etc., to feel, receive, or derive pleasure, etc.; to take pleasure or delight in; to delight in, joy in, rejoice in, relish, like, enjoy, take to, take in good part.

To indulge in, treat oneself, solace oneself, revel, riot, luxuriate in, gloat over; to be on velvet, in clover, in heaven, etc.; to enjoy oneself; to congratulate oneself, hug oneself.

(*Phrases*) To slake the appetite; to bask in the sunshine; to tread on enchanted ground; to have a good time; to make whoopee.

(*Adjectives*) Pleased, enjoying, relishing, liking, gratified, glad, gladdened, rejoiced, delighted, overjoyed, charmed.

Cheered, enlivened, flattered, tickled, indulged, regaled, treated.

Comfortable, at ease, easy, cosy, satisfied, content (831), luxurious, on velvet, in clover, on a bed of roses, *sans souci.*

Happy, blest, blessed, blissful, overjoyed, enchanted, captivated, fascinated, transported, raptured, rapt, enraptured, in raptures, in ecstasies, in a transport, beatified, in heaven, in the seventh heaven, in paradise.

(*Phrases*) With a joyful face; with sparkling eyes; happy as a king; pleased as Punch; in the lap of luxury; happy as the day is long; *ter quaterque beatus.*

(*Adverbs*) Happily, etc.

weariness (841), dejection (837).

Annoyance, irritation, plague, bore, bother, botheration, worry, infliction, stew.

Care, anxiety, concern, mortification, vexation, chagrin, trouble, trial, solicitude, cark, dole, dule, load, burden, fret.

Grief, sorrow, distress, affliction, woe, bitterness, heartache, a heavy heart, a bleeding heart, a broken heart, heavy affliction.

Unhappiness, infelicity, misery, wretchedness, desolation, tribulation.

Dolour, sufferance, ache, aching, hurt, smart, cut, twitch, twinge, stitch, cramp, spasm, nightmare, convulsion, throe, angina.

Pang, anguish, agony, torture, torment, rack, crucifixion, martyrdom, purgatory, hell (982).

A sufferer, victim, prey, martyr.

(*Phrases*) Vexation of spirit; a peck of troubles; a sea of troubles; the ills that flesh is heir to; *mauvais quart d'heure*; the iron entering the soul.

(*Verbs*) To feel, suffer, or experience pain, etc.; to suffer, ache, smart, ail, bleed, twinge, tingle, gripe, wince, writhe.

To grieve, fret, pine, mourn, bleed, worry oneself, chafe, yearn, droop, sink, give way, despair (859).

(*Phrases*) To sit on thorns; to be on pins and needles; to labour under afflictions; to have a bad or thin time; to drain the cup of misery to the dregs; to fall on evil days.

(*Adjectives*) In pain; feeling, suffering, enduring, etc., pain; in a state of pain, of suffering, etc., sore, aching, suffering, ailing, etc., pained, hurt, stung (830).

Displeased, annoyed, dissatisfied, discontented, weary (832), uneasy, ungratified, uncomfortable, ill at ease.

Crushed, stricken, victimized, illused.

Concerned, afflicted, in affliction, sorry, sorrowful, in sorrow, cut up, bathed in tears (839).

Unhappy, unfortunate, hapless, unblest, luckless, unlucky, ill-fated, ill-starred, fretting, wretched, miserable, careworn, disconsolate, inconsolable, woebegone, poor, forlorn, comfortless, a prey to grief, etc., despairing, in despair (859), heart-broken, broken-hearted, the heart bleeding, doomed, devoted, accursed, undone.

829 Capability of giving pleasure.

PLEASURABLENESS (*Substantives*), pleasantness, gratefulness, welcomeness, acceptableness, acceptability, agreeableness, delectability, deliciousness, daintiness, sweetness, luxuriousness, lusciousness, voluptuousness, eroticism.

Charm, attraction, attractiveness, sex-appeal, S.A., It, oomph, fascination, witchery, prestige, loveliness, takingness, winsomeness, likableness, invitingness, glamour.

A treat, dainty, titbit, bonbon, *bonne bouche*, sweet, sweetmeat, sugarplum, nuts, *sauce piquante*.

(*Verbs*) To cause, produce, create, give, afford, procure, offer, present, yield, etc., pleasure, gratification, etc.

To please, take, gratify, satisfy, indulge, flatter, tickle, humour, regale, refresh, interest.

To charm, rejoice, cheer, gladden, delight, enliven (836), to transport, captivate, fascinate, enchant, entrance, bewitch, ravish, enrapture, enravish, beatify, enthral, imparadise.

(*Phrases*) To do one's heart good; to tickle one to death; to take one's fancy.

(*Adjectives*) Causing or giving pleasure, etc., pleasing, agreeable, grateful, gratifying, pleasant, pleasurable, acceptable, welcome, glad, gladsome, comfortable.

Sweet, delectable, nice, jolly, palatable, dainty, delicate, delicious, dulcet, savoury, toothsome, tasty, luscious, luxurious, voluptuous, genial, cordial, refreshing, comfortable, scrumptious.

Fair, lovely, favourite, attractive, engaging, winsome, winning, taking, prepossessing, inviting, captivating, bewitching, fascinating, magnetic, seductive, killing, stunning, ripping, smashing, likable.

Charming, delightful, exquisite, enchanting, enthralling, ravishing,

830 Capability of giving pain.

PAINFULNESS (*Substantives*), disagreeableness, unpleasantness, irksomeness, displeasingness, unacceptableness, bitterness, vexatiousness, troublesomeness.

Trouble, care, cross, annoyance, burden, load, nuisance, pest, plague, bore, bother, botheration, vexation, sickener, pin-prick.

Scourge, bitter pill, worm, canker, cancer, ulcer, curse, gall and wormwood, sting, pricks, scorpion, thorn, brier, bramble, hornet, whip, lash, rack, wheel.

A mishap, misadventure, mischance, pressure, infestation, grievance, trial, crosses, hardship, blow, stroke, affliction, misfortune, reverse, infliction, dispensation, visitation, disaster, undoing, tragedy, calamity, catastrophe, adversity (735).

Provocation, infestation, affront, aggravation, indignity, outrage (900, 929).

(*Phrases*) A thorn in one's side; a fly in the ointment; a sorry sight; a bitter pill; a crumpled rose-leaf.

(*Verbs*) To cause, produce, give, etc., pain, uneasiness, suffering, etc.

To pain, hurt, wound, sting, pinch, grate upon, irk, gall, jar, chafe, gnaw, prick, lacerate, pierce, cut, cut up, stick, gravel, hurt one's feelings, mortify, horrify, shock, twinge, gripe.

To wring, harrow, torment, torture, rack, scarify, cruciate, crucify, convulse, agonize.

To displease, annoy, incommode, discompose, trouble, disquiet, grieve, cross, tease, rag, josh, bait, tire, vex, worry, try, plague, fash, faze, fret, haunt, obsess, bother, pester, bore, gravel, flummox, harass, importune, tantalize, aggravate.

To irritate, provoke, nettle, pique, rile, ruffle, aggrieve, enchafe, enrage.

rapturous, heart-felt, thrilling, beatific, heavenly, celestial, elysian, empyrean, seraphic, ideal.

Palmy, halcyon, Saturnian, Arcadian.

(*Phrases*) To one's heart's content; to one's taste.

———

To maltreat, bite, assail, badger, infest, harry, persecute, haze, roast.

To sicken, disgust, revolt, turn the stomach, nauseate, disenchant, repel, offend, shock.

To horrify, prostrate.

(*Phrases*) To barb the dart; to set the teeth on edge; to stink in the nostrils; to stick in one's throat; to add a nail to one's coffin; to plant a dagger in the breast; to freeze the blood; to make one's flesh creep; to make one's hair stand on end; to break or wring the heart.

(*Adjectives*) Causing, occasioning, giving, producing, creating, inflicting, etc., pain, etc., hurting, etc.

Painful, dolorific, dolorous, unpleasant, unpleasing, displeasing, unprepossessing, disagreeable, distasteful, uncomfortable, unwelcome, unsatisfactory, unpalatable, unacceptable, thankless, undesirable, untoward, unlucky, undesired, obnoxious.

Distressing, bitter, afflicting, afflictive, cheerless, joyless, comfortless, depressing, depressive, mournful, dreary, dismal, bleak, melancholy, grievous, pathetic, woeful, disastrous, calamitous, ruinous, sad, tragic, tragical, deplorable, dreadful, frightful, lamentable, ill-omened.

Irritating, provoking, provocative, stinging, biting, vexatious, annoying, unaccommodating, troublesome, fashious, wearisome, tiresome, irksome, plaguing, plaguy, teasing, pestering, bothering, bothersome, carking, mortifying, galling, harassing, worrying, tormenting, aggravating, racking, importunate, insistent.

Intolerable, insufferable, insupportable, unbearable, unendurable, shocking, frightful, terrific, grim, appalling, dire, heart-breaking, heart-rending, heart-wounding, heart-corroding, dreadful, horrid, harrowing, horrifying, horrific, execrable, accursed, damnable.

Odious, hateful, unpopular, repulsive, repellent, uninviting, offensive, nauseous, disgusting, sickening, nasty, execrable, revolting, shocking, vile, foul, abominable, loathsome, rotten.

Sharp, acute, sore, severe, grave, hard, harsh, bitter, cruel, biting, caustic, corroding, consuming, racking, excruciating, grinding, agonizing.

(*Phrase*) More than flesh and blood can bear.

(*Adverbs*) Painfully, etc.

---

831 CONTENT (*Substantives*), contentment, contentedness, satisfaction, peace of mind, complacency, serenity, sereneness, ease.

Comfort, snugness, well-being.

Moderation, patience (826), endurance, resignation, reconciliation.

(*Verbs*) To be content, etc.; to rest satisfied, to put up with; to take up with; to be reconciled to.

To render content, etc., to set at ease, to conciliate, reconcile, disarm, propitiate, win over, satisfy, indulge, slake, gratify.

832 DISCONTENT (*Substantives*), discontentment, dissatisfaction, disappointment, mortification.

Repining, taking on, inquietude, heart-burning, regret (833).

Nostalgia, home-sickness, *maladie du pays.*

Grumbler, grouser, croaker.

(*Verbs*) To be discontented, dissatisfied, etc.; to repine, regret (833), grumble (839).

To cause discontent, etc., to disappoint, dissatisfy, mortify.

(*Phrases*) To take in bad part; to

(*Phrases*) To make the best of; to let well alone; to take in good part; to set one's heart at ease or at rest.

(*Adjectives*) Content, contented, satisfied, at ease, easy, snug, comfortable, cosy.

Patient, resigned to, reconciled to, unrepining; disarming, conciliatory.

Unafflicted, unvexed, unmolested, unplagued, etc., serene, at rest, *sine cura, sans souci.*

(*Phrases*) To one's heart's content; like patience on a monument.

(*Interjections*) Very well, all right, suits me.

833 REGRET (*Substantives*), bitterness, repining; lamentation (839); self-reproach, penitence (950).

(*Verbs*) To regret, deplore, repine, lament, rue, repent (950).

(*Phrase*) To rue the day.

(*Adjectives*) Regretting, etc., regretful, regretted, regrettable, lamentable.

(*Phrase*) What a pity!

835 AGGRAVATION (*Substantives*), heightening, exacerbation, exasperation.

(*Verbs*) To aggravate, render worse, heighten, intensify, embitter, sour, acerbate, envenom, exacerbate, exasperate.

(*Phrase*) To add fuel to the flame.

(*Adjectives*) Aggravating, etc., aggravated, etc., unrelieved; aggravable.

(*Phrases*) Out of the frying-pan into the fire; from bad to worse.

836 CHEERFULNESS (*Substantives*), gaiety, cheer, spirits, high spirits, high glee, light-heartedness, joyfulness, joyousness, good humour, geniality, hilarity, exhilaration, liveliness, sprightliness, briskness, vivacity, buoyancy, sunniness, jocundity, joviality, levity, sportiveness, playfulness, jocularity.

Mirth, merriment, merrymaking, laughter (838), amusement (840); nepenthe, Euphrosyne.

Gratulation, rejoicing, exultation,

have the hump; to quarrel with one's bread and butter.

(*Adjectives*) Discontented, dissatisfied, unsatisfied, malcontent, mortified, disappointed, cut up.

Repining, glum, grumbling, grousing, grouchy, exigent, *exigeant*, exacting; nostalgic, home-sick; disgruntled.

Disappointing, unsatisfactory.

(*Phrases*) Out of humour; in the dumps; in high dudgeon; down in the mouth.

———

834 RELIEF (*Substantives*), easement, alleviation, mitigation, palliation, solace, consolation, comfort, encouragement, refreshment (689), lullaby; deliverance, delivery.

Lenitive, balm, oil, restorative, cataplasm (662); cushion, pillow, bolster (215).

(*Phrases*) A crumb of comfort; balm in Gilead.

(*Verbs*) To relieve, ease, alleviate, mitigate, palliate, soften, soothe, assuage, allay, cheer, comfort, console, encourage, bear up, refresh, restore, remedy, cure.

(*Phrases*) To dry the tears; to pour balm into; to lay the flattering unction to one's soul; to temper the wind to the shorn lamb; to breathe again; to breathe freely.

(*Adjectives*) Relieving, etc., consolatory; balmy, balsamic, soothing, lenitive, anodyne (662), remedial, curative; easeful.

837 DEJECTION (*Substantives*), depression, low spirits, lowness or depression of spirits, dejectedness, sadness.

Heaviness, dullness, infestivity, joylessness, gloom, dolefulness, dolesomeness, weariness (841), heaviness of heart, heart-sickness.

Melancholy, melancholia, dismals, mumps, dumps, doldrums, blues, mulligrubs, blue devils, megrims, vapours, accidie, spleen, hypochondria; *taedium vitae; maladie du pays.*

jubilation, jubilee, triumph, paean, Te Deum, heyday; joy-bells.

(*Verbs*) To be cheerful, etc.; to be of good cheer, to cheer up, perk up, brighten up, light up; take heart, bear up.

To rejoice, make merry, exult, congratulate oneself, triumph, clap the hands, crow, sing, carol, lilt, frisk, prance, galumph, rollick, maffick, frivol.

To cheer, enliven, elate, exhilarate, entrance, inspirit, animate, gladden, buck up, liven up.

(*Phrases*) To drive dull care away; to make whoopee; to keep up one's spirits; care killed the cat; *ride si sapis*; laugh and grow fat.

(*Adjectives*) Cheerful, gay, blithe, cheery, jovial, genial, gleeful, of good cheer, in spirits, in good or high spirits, *allegro*, light, lightsome, buoyant, debonair, bright, glad, light-hearted, hearty, free and easy, airy, jaunty, canty, perky, spry, chipper, saucy, sprightly, lively, vivacious, sunny, breezy, chirpy, hopeful (858).

Merry, joyous, joyful, jocund, playful, waggish, frisky, frolicsome, sportive, gamesome, jokesome, joky, jocose, jocular, jolly, frivolous.

Rejoicing, elated, exulting, jubilant, hilarious, flushed, rollicking, cock-a-hoop.

(*Phrases*) In high feather; walking on air; with one's head in the clouds; gay as a lark; happy as a king or as the day is long; playful as a kitten; jolly as a sandboy; merry as a grig; full of beans.

(*Adverbs*) Cheerfully, cheerily, cheerly, etc.

(*Interjections*) Cheer up! never say die! hurrah! huzza!

———

Despondency, despair, pessimism, disconsolateness, prostration; the Slough of Despond (859).

Demureness, seriousness, gravity, solemnity, solemnness, sullenness.

A hypochondriac, self-tormentor, *malade imaginaire*, kill-joy, Job's comforter, wet blanket, pessimist, futilitarian.

(*Verbs*) To be dejected, sad, etc.; to grieve, take on, take to heart, give way, droop, sink, lour, look downcast, mope, mump, pout, brood over, fret, pine, yearn, frown, despond (859).

To depress, discourage, dishearten, dispirit, dull, deject, lower, sink, dash, unman, prostrate, over-cloud.

(*Phrases*) To look blue; to hang down the head; to wear the willow; to laugh on the wrong side of the mouth; to get the hump.

To prey on the mind or spirits; to dash one's hopes.

(*Adjectives*) Cheerless, unmirthful, mirthless, joyless, dull, glum, flat, dispirited, out of spirits, out of sorts, out of heart, in low spirits, spiritless, lowering, frowning, sulky.

Discouraged, disheartened, down-hearted, downcast, cast down, depressed, chap-fallen, crest-fallen, dashed, drooping, sunk, heart-sick, dumpish, mumpish, desponding, pessimistic.

Dismal, melancholy, sombre, tristful, *triste*, pensive, *penseroso*, mournful, doleful, moping, splenetic, gloomy, lugubrious, funereal, woe-begone, comfortless, forlorn, overcome, prostrate, cut up, care-worn, care-laden.

Melancholic, hipped, hypochondriacal, bilious, jaundiced, atrabilious, atrabiliar, saturnine, adust.

Disconsolate, inconsolable, despairing, in despair (859).

Grave, serious, sedate, staid, sober, solemn, grim, grim-faced, grim-visaged (846), rueful, sullen.

Depressing, preying upon the mind (830).

(*Phrases*) Down in the mouth; down on one's luck; sick at heart; with a long face; a prey to melancholy; dull as a beetle; dull as ditchwater; as melancholy as a gib-cat; grave as a judge.

838 Expression of pleasure.

REJOICING (*Substantives*), exultation, heyday, triumph, jubilation, jubilee (840), paean (990).

Smile, simper, smirk, grin, broad grin.

Laughter, giggle, titter, snigger, crow, cheer, chuckle, guffaw, shout, hearty laugh, horse-laugh, cachinnation; a shout, burst, or peal of laughter.

Derision, risibility (856).

Momus, Democritus the Abderite.

(*Verbs*) To rejoice, exult, triumph (884), hug oneself, sing, carol, dance with joy.

To smile, simper, smirk, grin, mock; to laugh, giggle, titter, snigger, chuckle, chortle, burble, crow, cackle; to burst out, shout, guffaw.

To cause, create, occasion, raise, excite, or produce laughter, etc.; to tickle, titillate.

(*Phrases*) To clap one's hands; to fling up one's cap; to laugh in one's sleeve; to shake one's sides; to hold both one's sides; to split one's sides; to die with laughter.

To tickle one's fancy; to set the table in a roar; to convulse with laughter; to be the death of one.

(*Adjectives*) Laughing, rejoicing, etc.; jubilant (836), triumphant.

Laughable, risible, ludicrous (853), side-splitting.

(*Phrases*) Ready to burst or split oneself; 'Laughter holding both his sides.'

(*Interjections*) Hurrah! three cheers!

---

839 Expression of pain.

LAMENTATION (*Substantives*), complaint, murmur, mutter, plaint, lament, wail, sigh, suspiration, heaving.

Cry, whine, whimper, sob, tear, moan, snivel, grumble, groan.

Outcry, scream, screech, howl, whoop, yell, roar, (414).

Weeping, crying, etc.; lachrymation, complaining, frown, scowl, sardonic grin or laugh.

Dirge (363), elegy, requiem, monody, threnody, jeremiad; coronach, wake, keen, keening.

Plaintiveness, querimoniousness, languishment, querulousness.

Mourning, weeds, willow, cypress, crape, sackcloth and ashes.

A grumbler, grouser, croaker, drip; Heraclitus, Niobe.

(*Phrases*) The melting mood; wringing of hands; weeping and gnashing of teeth.

(*Verbs*) To lament, mourn, grieve, keen, complain, murmur, mutter, grumble, grouse, belly-ache, beef, squawk, sigh; give, fetch, or heave a sigh.

To cry, weep, sob, greet, blubber, blub; snivel, whimper; to shed tears; pule, take on, pine.

To grumble, groan, grunt, croak, whine, moan, bemoan, wail, bewail, frown, scowl.

To cry out, growl, mew, mewl, squeak, squeal, sing out, scream, cry out lustily, screech, skirl, bawl, howl, holloa, bellow, yell, roar, yammer.

(*Phrases*) To melt or burst into tears; to cry oneself blind; to cry one's eyes out; to beat one's breast; to wring one's hands; to gnash one's teeth; to tear one's hair; to cry before one is hurt; to laugh on the wrong side of one's mouth.

(*Adjectives*) Lamenting, complaining, etc.; mournful, doleful, sad, tearful, lachrymose, plaintive, plaintful, querulous, querimonious, elegiac.

(*Phrases*) With tears in one's eyes; bathed or dissolved in tears; the tears starting from the eyes.

(*Interjections*) O dear! ah me! alas! alack! heigh-ho! ochone! well-a-day! well-a-way! alas the day! woe worth the day! *O tempora, O mores!*

---

840 AMUSEMENT (*Substantives*), diversion, entertainment, sport, divertissement, recreation, relaxation, distraction, avocation, pastime.

841 WEARINESS (*Substantives*), tedium, ennui, boredom, lassitude, fatigue (688), dejection (837).

Disgust, nausea, loathing, sickness,

Fun, frolic, pleasantry, drollery, jollity, joviality, jovialness, jocoseness, laughter (838).

Play, game, gambol, romp, prank, quip, quirk, rig, lark, fling, bat, spree, burst, binge, razzle-dazzle, escapade, dido, monkey-shines, ploy, jamboree.

Dance (309), ball, ballet (599), hop, shindig, jig, fling, reel, strathspey, cotillion, quadrille, lancers, rigadoon, saraband, lavolta, pavane, galliard, hornpipe, can-can, tarantella, cachucha, fandango, bolero, minuet, gavotte, polka, mazurka, schottische, waltz (or valse), fox-trot, tango, maxixe, rumba, samba, blues, two-step, one-step; folk-dance, morris-dance, square dance, round dance, country dance, step-dance, clog-dance, sword-dance, egg-dance, cakewalk, break-down.

Festivity, festival, jubilee, party (892), merrymaking, rejoicing, fête, gala, ridotto, revelry, revels, carnival, corroboree, saturnalia, high jinks, night out.

Feast, banquet, entertainment, carousal, bean-feast, beano, wayzgoose, jollification, junketing, junket, wake, field-day, regatta, fair, kermess, *fête champêtre*, symposium, wassail.

Buffoonery, mummery, tomfoolery, raree-show, puppet-show, masquerade.

disgust of life, *taedium vitae*, *Weltschmerz*.

Wearisomeness, irksomeness, tiresomeness, montony, sameness, treadmill, grind.

A bore, a buttonholer, proser, fossil, wet blanket.

(*Phrases*) A twice-told tale; time hanging heavily on one's hands; a thin time.

(*Verbs*) To tire, weary, fatigue, fag, jade, bore; set to sleep, send to sleep.

To sicken, disgust, nauseate.

(*Phrases*) To harp on the same string; to bore to tears; never hear the last of.

(*Adjectives*) Wearying, etc., wearisome, tiresome, irksome, uninteresting, devoid of interest, monotonous, humdrum, pedestrian, mortal, flat, tedious, prosy, prosing, slow, soporific, somniferous.

Disgusting, sickening, nauseating.

Weary, tired, etc.; aweary, uninterested, sick of, flagging, used up, blasé, bored, stale, fed up, browned off, brassed off, cheesed off, chokka, weary of life; drowsy, somnolent, sleepy (683).

(*Adverbs*) Wearily, etc.

(*Phrase*) *Ad nauseam.*

Bonfire, fireworks, *feu de joie.*

A holiday, gala day, red-letter day.

A place of amusement, theatre, music-hall, concert-hall, cinema, circus, hippodrome, ballroom, dance hall, arena, auditorium, recreation ground, playground, playing field, park.

Toy, plaything, bauble, doll, puppet, teddy-bear.

A master of ceremonies or revels; a sportsman, sportswoman, gamester, reveller; devotee, votary, enthusiast, fan.

(*Phrases*) A round of pleasure; a short life and a merry one; high days and holidays.

(*Verbs*) To amuse, divert, entertain, rejoice, cheer, recreate, enliven, solace; to beguile or while away the time; to drown care.

To play, sport, disport, make merry, take one's pleasure, make holiday, keep holiday; to game, gambol, revel, frisk, frolic, romp, jollify, skylark, dally; to dance, hop, foot it, jump, caper, cut capers, skip.

To treat, feast, regale, carouse, banquet.

(*Phrases*) To play the fool; to jump over the moon; to make a night of it; to make whoopee; to go on the bust; to have one's fling; *desipere in loco.*

(*Adjectives*) Amusing, amusive, diverting, entertaining, etc., amused, etc.

Sportive, jovial, festive, jocose, tricksy, rompish.

(*Phrases*) On with the dance! *vogue la galère! vive la bagatelle!*

842 WIT (*Substantives*), humour, comicality, imagination (515), fancy, fun, drollery, whim, jocularity, jocosity, facetiousness, waggery, waggishness, wittiness, salt, Atticism, Attic wit, Attic salt, *esprit*, smartness, banter, chaff, persiflage, badinage, farce, *espièglerie*.

Jest, joke, jape, conceit, quip, quirk, quiddity, crank, wheeze, side-splitter, *concetto*, witticism, gag, wisecrack, repartee, retort, come-back, *mot*, *bon mot*, pleasantry, funniment, flash of wit, happy thought, sally, point, dry joke, idle conceit, epigram, quibble, play upon words, pun (563), conundrum, anagram (533), quodlibet, *jeu d'esprit*, *facetiae*; a chestnut, a Joe Miller; an absurdity (497).

A practical joke, a rag.

(*Phrases*) The cream of the jest; the joke of it; *le mot pour rire*.

843 DULLNESS (*Substantives*), heaviness, stolidness, stolidity, dumbness, stupidity (499), flatness, prosiness, gravity (837), solemnity; prose, matter of fact, platitude, commonplace, bromide.

(*Verbs*) To be dull, prose, fall flat. To render dull, etc., damp, depress.

(*Phrase*) To throw cold water on.

(*Adjectives*) Dull, prosaic, prosing, prosy, unentertaining, dismal (837), uninteresting, boring, flat, pointless, stolid, humdrum (841), pedestrian, literal, unimaginative, matter-of-fact, commonplace.

Slow, stupid, dumb, plodding, Boeotian.

(*Phrases*) Dull as ditch-water; *Davus sum, non Oedipus*; *aliquando bonus dormitat Homerus*.

————

(*Verbs*) To joke, jest, jape, retort; to cut jokes, crack a joke, perpetrate a joke or pun.

To laugh at, banter, rally, chaff, josh, jolly, jeer (856), rag, guy, kid; to make fun of, make merry with.

(*Phrase*) To set the table in a roar.

(*Adjectives*) Witty, facetious, humorous, fanciful, quick-witted, ready-witted, nimble-witted, imaginative (515), sprightly, *spirituel*, smart, jocose, jocular, waggish, comic, comical, laughable, droll, ludicrous, side-splitting, killing, funny, risible, farcical, roguish, sportive, pleasant, playful, sparkling, entertaining, arch.

(*Adverbs*) In joke, in jest, in sport, for fun.

844 A HUMORIST (*Substantives*), wag, wit, funny man, caricaturist, cartoonist, epigrammatist, *bel esprit*, jester, joker, punster, wise-cracker.

A buffoon (599), comedian, *farceur*, merry-andrew, jack-pudding, tumbler, mountebank, harlequin, punch, punchinello, scaramouch, clown, pantaloon.

(*Phrase*) The life and soul of the party.

2°. *Discriminative Affections*

845 BEAUTY (*Substantives*), handsomeness, beauteousness, beautifulness, pulchritude, aesthetics.

Form, elegance, grace, symmetry, *belle tournure*; good looks.

846 UGLINESS (*Substantives*), deformity, inelegance, plainness, homeliness, uncomeliness, ungainliness, uncouthness, clumsiness, stiffness, disfigurement, distortion, contortion,

Comeliness, seemliness, shapeliness, fairness, prettiness, neatness, spruceness, attractiveness, loveliness, quaintness, speciousness, polish, gloss, nattiness; a good effect.

Bloom, brilliancy, radiance, splendour, magnificence, sublimity.

Concinnity, delicacy, refinement, charm, style.

A beautiful woman, belle, charmer, enchantress, goddess; Helen of Troy, Venus, Hebe, the Graces, Peri, Houri; Cupid, Apollo, Hyperion, Adonis, Antinous, Narcissus.

Peacock, butterfly, flower, rose, lily; the flower of, the pink of, etc.; a garden, a picture.

(*Phrases*) *Je ne sais quoi; le beau idéal;* a sight for sore eyes.

(*Verbs*) To be beautiful; to shine, beam, bloom.

To render beautiful, etc., to beautify, embellish, adorn, deck, bedeck, decorate, set out, set off, ornament (847), dight, bedight, array, garnish, furbish, smarten, trick out, rig out, fig out, dandify, dress up, prank, prink, perk, preen, trim, embroider, emblazon, adonize.

To polish, burnish, gild, varnish, japan, enamel, lacquer.

To powder, rouge, make up, doll up, titivate.

(*Adjectives*) Beautiful, handsome, good-looking, fine, pretty, lovely, graceful, elegant, delicate, refined, fair, personable, comely, seemly, bonny, braw, well-favoured, proper, shapely, well-made, well-formed, well-proportioned, symmetrical, sightly, becoming, goodly, neat, dapper, tight, trig, spruce, smart, stylish, chic, dashing, swagger, dandified, natty, sleek, quaint, jaunty, bright-eyed, attractive, seductive, stunning.

Blooming, rosy, brilliant, shining, beaming, splendid, resplendent, dazzling, gorgeous, superb, magnificent, sublime, grand.

Picturesque, statuesque, artistic, aesthetic, decorative, photogenic, well-composed, well-grouped.

malformation, monstrosity, misproportion, inconcinnity, want of symmetry, roughness, repulsiveness, squalor, hideousness, unsightliness, odiousness.

An eyesore, object, figure, sight, fright, guy, spectre, scarecrow, hag, harridan, satyr, sibyl, toad, baboon, monster, gorgon, Caliban, Hecate.

(*Phrases*) A forbidding countenance; a wry face; a blot on the landscape; no oil-painting; *'monstrum horrendum, informe, ingens, cui lumen ademptum.'*

(*Verbs*) To be ugly, etc.

To render ugly, etc., to deform, deface, distort, disfigure (241), disfeature, misshape, blemish, spot, stain, distain, soil, tarnish, discolour, sully, blot, daub, bedaub, begrime, blur, smear, besmear (653), bespatter, maculate, denigrate, uglify.

(*Phrase*) To make faces.

(*Adjectives*) Ugly, plain, homely, unsightly, unornamental, unshapely, unlovely, ill-looking, ordinary, unseemly, ill-favoured, hard-favoured, evil-favoured, hard-featured, hard-visaged, ungainly, uncouth, gawky, hulking, lumbering, slouching, ungraceful, clumsy, graceless, rude, rough, rugged, homespun, gaunt, raw-boned, haggard, scraggy.

Misshapen, shapeless, misproportioned, ill-proportioned, deformed, ill-made, ill-shaped, inelegant, disfigured, distorted, unshapen, unshapely, humpbacked, crooked, bandy, stumpy, dumpy, squat, stubby, bald, rickety.

Squalid, grim, grisly, gruesome, grooly, macabre, grim-faced, grim-visaged, ghastly, ghost-like, death-like, cadaverous, repellent, repulsive, forbidding, grotesque.

Frightful, odious, hideous, horrid, shocking, monstrous, unprepossessing.

Foul, soiled, tarnished, stained, distained, sullied, blurred, blotted, spotted, maculated, spotty, splashed, smeared, begrimed,

Passable, presentable, not amiss, undefaced, spotless, unspotted.

(*Phrases*) Easy to look at; dressed up to kill.

847 ORNAMENT (*Substantives*), ornamentation, adornment, decoration, embellishment, enrichment, illustration, illumination, ornature, ornateness, flamboyancy.

Garnish, polish, varnish, gilding, japanning, enamel, lacquer, ormolu.

Cosmetic, rouge, powder, lipstick, mascara, hair-oil, brilliantine.

Jewel, jewellery, bijouterie, spangle, trinket, locket, bracelet, bangle, anklet, necklace, earring, brooch, chain, chatelaine, carcanet, tiara, coronet, diadem.

Gem, precious stone, diamond, brilliant, emerald, sapphire, ruby, agate, garnet, beryl, onyx, topaz, amethyst, opal; pearl, coral.

Embroidery, broidery, brocade, galloon, lace, fringe, trapping, trimming, edging, border, chiffon, hanging, tapestry, arras.

Wreath, festoon, garland, lei, chaplet, tassel, knot, epaulette, frog, star, rosette, bow.

Feather, plume, *panache*, aigrette.

Nosegay, bouquet, posy, buttonhole.

Tracery, moulding, arabesque.

Frippery, finery, bravery, gewgaw, gaud, fal-lal, tinsel, spangle, clinquant, bric-à-brac, knick-knack.

spattered, bedaubed, besmeared; ungarnished.

(*Phrases*) Ugly as sin; not fit to be seen.

848 BLEMISH (*Substantives*), disfigurement, defacement, deformity, eyesore, defect, fault, deficiency, flaw, fleck.

Stain, blot, spot, speck, mote, blur, macula, blotch, speckle, spottiness; soil, tarnish, smudge, smut, dirt, soot (653); freckle, birthmark.

Excrescence, pimple, pustule (250).

(*Verbs*) To blemish, disfigure, deface (846).

(*Adjectives*) Blemished, disfigured, etc.; spotted, speckled, freckled, pitted.

849 SIMPLICITY (*Substantives*), plainness, undress, chastity, chasteness; freedom from ornament or affectation, homeliness.

(*Phrase*) *Simplex munditiis.*

(*Verbs*) To be simple, etc., to render simple, etc., to simplify.

(*Adjectives*) Simple, plain, ordinary, household, homely, homespun, chaste, unaffected, severe, primitive.

Unadorned, unornamented, undecked, ungarnished, unarrayed, untrimmed, unsophisticated, in dishabille.

Trope, flourish, flowers of rhetoric, purple patches (577).

Excess of ornament, tawdriness (851).

(*Verbs*) To ornament, embellish, illustrate, illuminate, enrich, decorate, adorn, beautify, garnish, polish, gild, varnish, enamel, paint, whitewash, stain, japan, lacquer, fume, grain; bespangle, bedeck, bedizen (845), embroider, work, chase, emboss, fret, tool; emblazon, illuminate.

(*Adjectives*) Ornamented, etc., beautified, rigged out, figged out, well-groomed, dolled up, ornate, showy, dressy, gaudy (851), garish, gorgeous, fine, gay, rich.

(*Phrases*) Fine as fivepence; in full fig; in one's Sunday best; dressed up to the nines.

850 Good taste.

TASTE (*Substantives*), delicacy, refinement, gust, gusto, *goût*, virtuosity, virtuosoship, nicety, finesse, grace, culture, virtu, τὸ πρέπον, polish, elegance.

851 Bad taste.

VULGARITY (*Substantives*), vulgarism, barbarism, Vandalism, Gothicism, *mauvais goût*, sensationalism, flamboyance.

Coarseness, grossness, indecorum,

Science of taste, aesthetics.

A man of taste, connoisseur, judge, critic, *cognoscente*, virtuoso, diletante, amateur, aesthete, purist, precision; an Aristarchus, Corinthian, *arbiter elegantiarum*.

(*Phrase*) Caviare to the general.

(*Verbs*) To appreciate, judge, discriminate, criticize (465).

(*Adjectives*) In good taste, tasteful, unaffected, pure, chaste, classical, attic, refined, aesthetic, cultivated, cultured, artistic, elegant.

(*Adverb*) Elegantly, etc.

(*Phrases*) To one's taste or mind; after one's fancy; *comme il faut*.

852 FASHION (*Substantives*), style, tonishness, *ton, bon ton*, mode, vogue, craze, rage, fad.

Manners, breeding, politeness, gentlemanliness, courtesy (894), decorum, *bienséance, savoir faire, savoir vivre*, punctilio, convention, conventionality, propriety, the proprieties, Mrs. Grundy, form, formality, etiquette, custom, demeanour, air, port, carriage, presence.

Show, equipage, turn-out (882).

The world, the fashionable world, the smart set, the *beau monde*, high life, society, town, court, gentility (875), civilization, civilized life, the *élite*.

(*Phrases*) The height of fashion; *dernier cri*; the latest thing.

(*Verbs*) To be fashionable, etc.

(*Phrases*) To cut a dash; to be in the swim.

(*Adjectives*) Fashionable, in fashion, in vogue, *à la mode*, modish, tony, tonish, stylish, smart, courtly, *recherché*, genteel, aristocratic, conventional, punctilious, *comme il faut*, well-bred, well-mannered, polished, gentlemanlike, ladylike, well-spoken, civil, presentable, *distingué*, refined, thorough-bred, county, *dégagé*, jaunty, swell, swagger, posh, dashing, unembarrassed; trendy.

(*Phrases*) Having a run; all the go.

(*Adverbs*) Fashionably, in fashion.

lowness, low life, *mauvais ton*, bad form, ribaldry, clownishness, rusticity, boorishness, brutishness, brutality, rowdyism, ruffianism, awkwardness, *gaucherie*, want of tact, tactlessness.

Excess of ornament, false ornament, tawdriness, loudness, gaudiness, flashiness, ostentation.

A rough diamond, a hoyden, tomboy, slattern, sloven, dowdy, frump, cub, unlicked cub, clown, cad, guttersnipe, ragamuffin (876); a Goth, Vandal.

(*Verbs*) To be vulgar, etc., to misbehave.

(*Adjectives*) In bad taste, vulgar, coarse, unrefined, gross, ribald, heavy, rude, unpolished, indecorous, home-spun, clownish, uncouth, awkward, *gauche*, ungraceful, slovenly, slatternly, dowdy, frumpish.

Ill-bred, ungenteel, impolite, ill-mannered, uncivil, tactless, underbred, caddish, ungentlemanly, unladylike, unfeminine, unmaidenly, unseemly, unpresentable, unkempt, uncombed.

Rustic, countrified, boorish, provincial, barbarous, barbaric, brutish, blackguardly, rowdy, raffish, Gothic, unclassical, heathenish, outlandish, untamed (876).

Obsolete, out of fashion, *démodé*, out of date, unfashionable, antiquated, fossil, old-fashioned, old-world, gone by.

New-fangled, odd, fantastic, grotesque, ridiculous (853), affected, meretricious, extravagant, sensational, monstrous, shocking, horrid, revolting.

Gaudy, tawdry, tinsel, bedizened, flamboyant, baroque, tricked out, gingerbread, loud, flashy, showy.

(*Phrase*) A back number.

853 RIDICULOUSNESS (*Substantives*), ludicrousness, risibility.

Oddness, oddity, whimsicality, comicality, drollery, grotesqueness, fanciful ness, quaintness, frippery, gawkiness, preposterousness, extravagance monstrosity, absurdity (497).

Bombast, bathos, fustian, doggerel, nonsense verse, amphigouri, extrava ganza, clerihew, bull, Irish bull, spoonerism.

(*Adjectives*) Ridiculous, absurd, extravagant, *outré*, monstrous, preposterous irrational, nonsensical.

Odd, whimsical, quaint, queer, rum, droll, grotesque, fanciful, eccentric bizarre, strange, out-of-the-way, outlandish, fantastic, baroque, rococo.

Laughable, risible, ludicrous, comic, serio-comic, mock-heroic, comical funny, derisive, farcical, burlesque, *pour rire*, quizzical, bombastic, inflated stilted.

Awkward, gawky, lumbering, lumpish, hulking, uncouth.

854 FOP (*Substantives*), dandy, exquisite, swell, toff, dude, nut, masher lady-killer, coxcomb, beau, macaroni, blade, blood, buck, spark, dog, popin jay, puppy, *petit-maître*, jackanapes, jack-a-dandy, tailor's dummy, man milliner, man about town.

855 AFFECTATION (*Substantives*), mannerism, pretension, airs, dandyism coxcombry, frills, side, swank, dog, conceit, foppery, affectedness, preciosity euphuism, charlatanism, quackery, foppishness, pedantry, acting a part pose, gush.

Prudery, Grundyism, demureness, coquetry, *minauderie*, sentimentality lackadaisicalness, stiffness, formality, buckram, mock modesty, *mauvaise honte*

Pedant, precisian, prig, square, bluestocking, *bas bleu*, formalist, *poseur* mannerist, *précieuse ridicule*; prude, Mrs. Grundy.

(*Phrases*) A lump of affectation; prunes and prisms.

(*Verbs*) To affect, to give oneself airs, put on side or frills, to swank, simper mince, to act a part, overact, attitudinize, gush, pose.

(*Adjectives*) Affected, conceited, precious, pretentious, stilted, pedantic pragmatical, priggish, smug, puritanical, prim, prudish, starchy, up-stage high-hat, stiff, formal, demure, goody-goody.

Foppish, namby-pamby, slip-slop, coxcombical, slipshod, simpering mincing, niminy-piminy, la-di-da, sentimental, lackadaisical.

Exaggerated (549), overacted, overdone, high-falutin, gushing, stagy theatrical.

856 RIDICULE (*Substantives*), derision, mockery, quiz, banter, chaff, badi nage, irony, persiflage, raillery, send-up.

Jeer, gibe, quip, taunt, satire, scurrility, scoffing.

A parody, burlesque, travesty, skit, farce, comedy, tragi-comedy, doggerel blunder, bull, *lapsus linguae*, slip of the tongue, malapropism, spoonerism anticlimax.

Buffoonery, vagary, antic, mummery, tomfoolery, grimace, monkey trick, escapade, prank, gambade, extravaganza, practical joke, booby-trap.

(*Verbs*) To ridicule, deride, laugh at (929), laugh down, scoff, mock, jeer banter, quiz, rally, fleer, flout, rag, rot, chaff, josh, guy, rib, razz, roast, twit taunt, point at, grin at.

To parody, caricature, burlesque, travesty, pillory, take off.

(*Phrases*) To raise a smile; to set the table in a roar; to make fun of; to poke fun at; to make merry with; to make a fool of; to make an ass of; to make game of; to make faces at; to make mouths at; to lead one a dance;

ɔ run a rig upon; to make an April fool of; to laugh out of court; to laugh
ɪ one's sleeve; to take the micky out of.

(*Adjectives*) Derisory, derisive, sarcastic, ironical, quizzical, mock, scurrilous,
ᴜurlesque, Hudibrastic.

857 Object and cause of ridicule.

Laughing-stock (*Substantives*), gazing-stock, butt, stooge, target, quiz; an
ᴜriginal, guy, oddity, card, crank, eccentric, monkey, buffoon, jester (844),
ᴍime, mimer (599), scaramouch, punch, punchinello, mountebank, golliwog.

(*Phrases*) A figure of fun; a queer fish; fair game.

3°. *Prospective Affections*

858 Hope (*Substantives*), trust,
ᴄonfidence, reliance, faith, assurance,
ᴄredit, security, expectation, affiance,
ᴘromise, assumption, presumption.

Hopefulness, buoyancy, reassur-
ance, optimism, enthusiasm, aspira-
ᴛion.

A reverie, day-dream, pipe-dream,
Utopia, millennium.

Anchor, mainstay, sheet-anchor,
ᴤtaff (215).

(*Phrases*) Castles in the air; castles
in Spain; a ray, gleam, or flash of hope;
ᴛhe silver lining of the cloud.

(*Verbs*) To hope; to feel, entertain,
ᴛarbour, cherish, feed, nourish, en-
ᴄourage, foster, etc., hope or confidence; to promise oneself.

To trust, confide, rely on, build
upon, feel or rest assured, confident,
ᴤecure, etc.; to flatter oneself, expect,
aspire, presume, be reassured.

To give or inspire hope; to augur
well, shape well, bid fair, be in a fair
way; to encourage, assure, promise,
flatter, buoy up, reassure, embolden,
raise expectations.

(*Phrases*) To see daylight; to live in
hopes; to look on the bright side; to
pin one's hope or faith upon; to catch
at a straw; to hope against hope.

(*Adjectives*) Hoping, etc., in hopes,
hopeful, confident, secure, buoyant,
buoyed up, in good heart, sanguine,
optimistic, enthusiastic, utopian.

Fearless, unsuspecting, unsuspicious; free or exempt from fear,
suspicion, distrust, etc., undespairing.

Auspicious, promising, propitious,
bright, rose-coloured, rosy, of good
omen, reassuring.

859 Absence, want, or loss of hope.

Hopelessness (*Substantives*), despair, desperation, despondency,
pessimism (837); forlornness, a forlorn
hope, the Slough of Despond.

(*Phrases*) A black look-out; a bad
business.

(*Verbs*) To despair, despond, give
up, be hopeless; to lose, give up,
abandon, relinquish, etc., all hope;
to yield to despair.

To inspire or drive to despair; to
dash, crush, or destroy one's hopes.

(*Phrases*) To trust to a broken
reed; '*lasciate ogni speranza voi ch'*
entrate.'

(*Adjectives*) Hopeless, having lost
or given up hope, losing, etc., hope,
past hope, despondent, pessimistic,
forlorn, desperate, despairing.

Incurable, irremediable, irreparable, irrevocable, incorrigible, beyond
remedy.

Inauspicious, unpropitious, unpromising, threatening, ill-omened.

860 Fear (*Substantives*), cowardice
(862), timidity, diffidence, nervousness, restlessness, inquietude, disquietude, solicitude, anxiety, care,
distrust, mistrust, hesitation, misgiving, suspicion, qualm, want of
confidence, nerves.

Apprehension, flutter, trepidation,
tremor, shaking, trembling, palpitation, jitters, the jumps, the creeps,
the needle, ague-fit, fearfulness, despondency; stage fright, cold feet,
wind up.

Fright, affright, alarm, dread, awe,
terror, horror, dismay, obsession,

(*Phrases*) *Nil desperandum*; while there's life there's hope; *dum spiro spero*; never say die; all for the best.

———

(*Phrases*) Raw head and bloody bones; fee-faw-fum; butterflies in the stomach.

(*Verbs*) To fear, be afraid, etc., to distrust, hesitate, have qualms misgiving, suspicions.

To apprehend, take alarm, start, wince, boggle, skulk, cower, crouch tremble, shake, quake, quaver, quiver, shudder, quail, cringe, turn pale, blench, flutter, flinch, funk.

To excite fear, raise apprehensions, to give, raise, or sound an alarm to intimidate, put in fear, frighten, fright, affright, alarm, startle scare, haunt, obsess, strike terror, daunt, terrify, unman, awe, horrify dismay, petrify, appal.

To overawe, abash, cow, browbeat, bully, deter, discourage.

(*Phrases*) To shake in one's shoes; to shake like an aspen leaf; to stand aghast; to eye askance.

To fright from one's propriety; to strike all of a heap; to make the flesh creep; to give one the creeps; to cause alarm and despondency.

(*Adjectives*) Fearing, timid, timorous, faint-hearted, tremulous, fearful, nervous, nervy, jumpy, funky, diffident, apprehensive, restless, haunted with the fear, apprehension, dread, etc., of.

Frightened, afraid, cowed, pale, alarmed, scared, terrified, petrified, aghast, awestruck, dismayed, horror-struck, horrified, appalled, panic-stricken.

Inspiring fear, fearsome, alarming, formidable, redoubtable, portentous, perilous (665), ugly, fearful, dreadful, dire, shocking, terrible, tremendous, horrid, horrible, horrific, ghastly, awful, awesome, horripilant, hair-raising, creepy, crawly.

(*Phrases*) White as a sheet; afraid of one's shadow; the hair standing on end; letting 'I dare not' wait upon 'I would'; more frightened than hurt; frightened out of one's senses or wits; in a blue funk.

panic, funk, flap, stampede, scare consternation, despair (859).

Intimidation, terrorism, reign of terror; an alarmist, scaremonger.

Object of fear, bugbear, bugaboo bogy, scarecrow, goblin (980), *bête noire*, nightmare, Gorgon, ogre.

861 Absence of fear.

COURAGE (*Substantives*), bravery, value, boldness, spirit, moral fibre, spiritedness, daring, gallantry, intrepidity, contempt of danger, self-reliance, confidence, fearlessness, audacity.

Manhood, manliness, nerve, pluck, grit, guts, sand, mettle, gameness, heart, spunk, smeddum, virtue, hardihood, fortitude, firmness, resolution, sportsmanship.

Prowess, derring-do, heroism, chivalry.

A hero, heroine, ace, paladin, *preux chevalier*, Hector, Hotspur, Amazon, Joan of Arc, *beau sabreur*, fire-eater (863).

862 Excess of fear.

COWARDICE (*Substantives*), fear (860), pusillanimity, cowardliness, timidity, fearfulness, spiritlessness, faint-heartedness, softness, effeminacy, funk.

Poltroonery, baseness, dastardliness, yellow streak, a faint heart.

A coward, poltroon, dastard, recreant, funk, mollycoddle, milksop, cry-baby, 'fraid-cat, chicken, cowardy custard.

(*Verbs*) To be cowardly, etc.; to quail (860), to flinch, fight shy, shy, turn tail, run away, cut and run, fly for one's life, stampede.

A lion, tiger, bulldog, gamecock, fighting-cock, sportsman.

(*Verbs*) To be courageous, etc., to face, front, affront, confront, despise, brave, defy, etc., danger; to take courage; to summon up, muster up, or pluck up courage; to rally.

To venture, make bold, face, dare, defy, brave (715), beard, hold out, bear up against, stand up to.

To give, infuse, or inspire courage; to encourage, embolden, inspirit, cheer, nerve.

(*Phrases*) To take the bull by the horns; to come up to the scratch; to face the music; to 'screw one's courage to the sticking-place'; to die game.

To pat on the back; to make a man of.

(*Adjectives*) Courageous, brave, valiant, valorous, gallant, intrepid.

Spirited, high-spirited, high-mettled, mettlesome, plucky, manly, manful, resolute, stout, stout-hearted, lion-hearted, heart of oak, firm, indomitable, game, sportsmanlike.

Bold, daring, audacious, fearless, unfearing, dauntless, undaunted, indomitable, unappalled, undismayed, unawed, unabashed, unalarmed, unflinching, unshrinking, unblenching, unblenched, unapprehensive, confident, self-reliant.

Enterprising, venturous, adventurous, venturesome, dashing, chivalrous, heroic, fierce, warlike (722).

Unfeared, undreaded, etc.

(*Phrases*) One's blood is up; brave as a lion; bold as brass; full of beans.

(*Phrases*) To show the white feather; to be in a sweat.

(*Adjectives*) Coward, cowardly, yellow, pusillanimous, shy, fearful, timid, skittish, timorous, poor-spirited, spiritless, weak-hearted, faint-hearted, chicken-hearted, white-livered.

Dastard, dastardly, base, craven, recreant, unwarlike, unheroic, un-soldierly, unmanly, womanish.

(*Phrase*) 'In face a lion, but in heart a deer.'

(*Interjections*) *Sauve qui peut!* the devil take the hindmost!

---

863 RASHNESS (*Substantives*), temerity, audacity, presumption, pre-cipitancy, precipitation, impetuosity, recklessness, overboldness, foolhardi-ness, desperation, knight-errantry, Quixotism; carelessness (460), want of caution, overconfidence.

Imprudence, indiscretion.

A desperado, madcap, bravo, dare-devil, *enfant perdu*, gambler, ad-venturer, knight errant; Hotspur, Don Quixote, Icarus.

(*Phrases*) A leap in the dark; a blind bargain; a wild-cat scheme.

(*Verbs*) To be rash, incautious, etc.

(*Phrases*) To buy a pig in a poke; to go on a forlorn hope; to go at it bald-headed; to play with fire; to tempt providence.

(*Adjectives*) Rash, temerarious,

864 CAUTION (*Substantives*), cau-tiousness, discretion, prudence, re-serve, wariness, heed, circumspection, calculation, deliberation (459).

Coolness, self-possession, aplomb, presence of mind, sang-froid, self-command, steadiness, the Fabian policy.

(*Phrases*) The better part of valour; masterly inactivity.

(*Verbs*) To be cautious, etc., to beware, take care, have a care, take heed, ca' canny, be on one's guard, look about one, take no chances.

(*Phrases*) To look before one leaps; to think twice; to let sleeping dogs lie; to see which way the wind blows; to see how the land lies; to feel one's way; to count the cost; to be on the safe side; steady as she goes.

headstrong, insane, foolhardy, slap-dash, dare-devil, devil-may-care, overbold, wild, reckless, desperate, hot-headed, hare-brained, headlong, hot-blooded, over-confident, precipitate, impetuous, venturesome, impulsive, Quixotic.

Imprudent, indiscreet, uncalculating, incautious, improvident.

(*Phrases*) Without ballast; neck or nothing.

(*Interjections*) *Vogue la galère!* come what may!

865 DESIRE (*Substantives*), wish, mind, inclination, leaning, bent, fancy, partiality, penchant, predilection, liking, love, fondness, relish.

Want, need, exigency.

Longing, hankering, solicitude, anxiety, yearning, yen, coveting, eagerness, zeal, ardour, aspiration, ambition, over-anxiety.

Appetite, appetence, appetency, the edge of appetite, keenness, hunger, stomach, thirst, thirstiness, drouth, mouth-watering, dipsomania, itch, itching, prurience, lickerishness, *cacoethes*, cupidity, lust, libido, concupiscence, greed.

Avidity, greediness, covetousness, craving, voracity, bulimia, rapacity.

Passion, rage, furore, mania, kleptomania, inextinguishable desire, vaulting ambition, impetuosity.

A gourmand, gourmet, glutton, cormorant (957).

An amateur, votary, devotee, fan, aspirant, solicitant, candidate.

Object of desire, desideratum, attraction, lure, allurement, fancy, temptation, magnet, loadstone, whim, whimsy (608), maggot, hobby, hobby-horse, pursuit.

(*Phrases*) The height of one's ambition; *hoc erat in votis*; the wish being father to the thought; the torments of Tantalus.

(*Verbs*) To desire, wish, long for, fancy, affect, like, have a mind to, be glad of, want, miss, need, feel the want of, would fain have, to care for.

To hunger, thirst, crave, lust after; to hanker after, itch for.

(*Adjectives*) Cautious, wary, careful, heedful, cautelous, chary, canny, cagey, circumspect, prudent, prudential, reserved, discreet, politic, non-committal.

Unenterprising, unadventurous, cool, steady, self-possessed.

(*Phrases*) Safety first; better be sure than sorry.

———

866 INDIFFERENCE (*Substantives*), coldness, coolness, unconcern, nonchalance, insouciance, inappetency, listlessness, lukewarmness, neutrality, impartiality; apathy (823), supineness (683), disdain (930).

(*Verbs*) To be indifferent, etc.; to have no desire, wish, taste, or relish for; to care nothing about, take no interest in, not mind, make light of; to disdain, spurn (930).

(*Phrase*) Couldn't care less.

(*Adjectives*) Indifferent, undesirous, cool, cold, frigid, unconcerned, insouciant, unsolicitous, unattracted, lukewarm, half-hearted, listless, lackadaisical, unambitious, unaspiring, phlegmatic.

Unattractive, unalluring, uninviting, undesired, undesirable, uncared-for, unwished, uncoveted, unvalued.

Vapid, tasteless, insipid (391), wersh, unappetizing, mawkish, namby-pamby, flat, stale, vain.

(*Phrases*) Never mind; all one to Hippocleides.

867 DISLIKE (*Substantives*), distaste, disrelish, disinclination, reluctance, backwardness, demur (603).

Repugnance, disgust, queasiness, turn, nausea, loathing, averseness, aversion, abomination, antipathy, abhorrence, horror, hatred, detestation (898), resentment (900); claustrophobia, agoraphobia, Anglophobia, Gallophobia.

(*Verbs*) To dislike, mislike, disrelish, mind, object to.

To desiderate, covet; to sigh, cry, gasp, pine, pant, languish, yearn for; to aspire after, catch at, jump at.

To woo, court, solicit, ogle, fish for.

To cause, create, raise, excite, or provoke, desire; to allure, attract, solicit, tempt, hold out temptation or allurement, to tantalize, appetize.

To gratify desire, slake, satiate (827).

(*Phrases*) To have at heart; to take a fancy to; to set one's heart upon; to make eyes at; to set one's cap at; to run mad after.

To whet the appetite; to make one's mouth water.

(*Adjectives*) Desirous, inclined, fain, keen, wishful, wishing, optative, desiring, wanting, needing, hankering after, dying for, partial to.

Craving, hungry, esurient, sharp-set, keen-set, peckish, thirsty, athirst, dry, drouthy.

Greedy, voracious, lickerish, open-mouthed, agog, covetous, ravenous, rapacious, extortionate; unsated, unslaked, insatiable, insatiate, omnivorous.

Eager, ardent, avid, fervent, bent on, intent on, aspiring, ambitious.

Desirable, desired, desiderated (829).

(*Phrases*) Pinched or perished with hunger; hungry as a hunter; parched with thirst; having a sweet tooth; nothing loth.

(*Interjections*) O for! would that!

To shun, avoid, eschew, withdraw from, shrink from, shrug the shoulders at, recoil from, shudder at.

To loathe, nauseate, abominate, detest, abhor, hate (898).

To cause or excite dislike; to disincline, repel, sicken, render sick, nauseate, disgust, shock, pall.

(*Phrases*) Not to be able to bear or endure or stand; to have no taste for; to turn up one's nose at; to look askance at.

To go against the grain; to turn one's stomach; to stink in the nostrils; to stick in one's throat; to make one's blood run cold.

(*Adjectives*) Disliking, disrelishing, etc., averse to, adverse, shy of, sick of, fed up with, queasy, disinclined.

Disliked, disagreeable, unpalatable, unpopular, offensive, loathsome, loathly, sickening, nauseous, nauseating, repulsive, disgusting, detestable, execrable, abhorrent, abhorred (830), disgustful.

(*Adverbs*) Disagreeably, etc.

(*Phrase*) *Usque ad nauseam.*

(*Interjections*) Faugh! Ugh!

868 FASTIDIOUSNESS (*Substantives*), nicety, daintiness, squeamishness, niceness, particularity, finicality, meticulosity, difficulty in being pleased, epicurism.

Excess of delicacy, prudery.

Epicure, gourmet, gourmand, *bon vivant*, gastronomer.

(*Verbs*) To be fastidious, etc., to discriminate, differentiate, disdain.

(*Phrases*) To split hairs; to mince one's words; to see spots in the sun.

(*Adjectives*) Fastidious, nice, difficult, dainty, delicate, finicky, lickerish, pernickety, squeamish, queasy, difficult to please, particular, choosy, punctilious, fussy, hypercritical; prudish, strait-laced.

869 SATIETY (*Substantives*), fullness, repletion, glut, saturation, surfeit.

A spoilt child; too much of a good thing.

(*Verbs*) To sate, satiate, satisfy, saturate, quench, slake, pall, glut, overfeed, gorge, surfeit, cloy, tire, spoil, sicken.

(*Adjectives*) Satiated, sated, blasé, used up, fed up, browned off, brassed off, cheesed off, chokka, sick of.

(*Phrases*) Enough is enough; *Toujours perdrix.*

(*Interjections*) Enough! that'll do!

4°. *Contemplative Affections*

870 WONDER (*Substantives*), surprise, marvel, astonishment, amazement, amazedness, wonderment, admiration, awe, bewilderment, stupefaction, fascination, thaumaturgy (992).

(*Verbs*) To wonder, marvel, be surprised, admire; to stare, gape, start.

To surprise, astonish, amaze, astound, dumbfound, dumbfounder, strike, dazzle, startle, take by surprise, take aback, strike with wonder, electrify, stun, petrify, flabbergast, confound, stagger, stupefy, bewilder, fascinate, boggle.

To be wonderful, etc.

871 Absence of wonder.

EXPECTANCE (*Substantives*), expectancy, expectation (507).

(*Verbs*) To expect, not to be surprised, not to wonder, etc., *nil admirari.*

(*Phrase*) To think nothing of.

(*Adjectives*) Expecting, etc., unamazed, astonished at nothing, blasé (841).

Common, ordinary (82); foreseen.

(*Phrases*) To open one's mouth or eyes; to look blank; to stand aghast; not to believe one's eyes; not to account for; not to know whether one stands on one's head or one's heels.

To make one sit up; to take one's breath away.

To beggar description; to stagger belief; imagination boggles at it.

(*Adjectives*) Surprised, astonished, amazed, astounded, struck, startled, taken by surprise, taken aback, struck dumb, awestruck, aghast, agape, dumbfounded, flabbergasted, thunder-struck, planet-struck, stupefied, open-mouthed, petrified.

Wonderful, wondrous, surprising, astonishing, amazing, astounding, startling, stunning, unexpected, unforeseen, strange, uncommon, unheard-of, unaccountable, incredible, inexplicable, indescribable, inexpressible, ineffable, unutterable, unspeakable, monstrous, prodigious, stupendous, marvellous, miraculous, passing strange, uncanny, weird, phenomenal.

(*Phrases*) Struck all of a heap; lost in wonder; like a dying duck in a thunder-storm; you could have knocked me down with a feather.

(*Adverbs*) Wonderingly, wonderfully, etc., with gaping mouth, all agog; *mirabile dictu.*

(*Interjections*) What! indeed! really! hallo! humph! you don't say so! my stars! good heavens! my goodness! good gracious! bless my soul! bless my heart! my word! O gemini! great Scott! gee! *wunderbar!* dear me! well, I'm damned! well, I never! lo! heyday! who'd have thought it!

872 PRODIGY (*Substantives*), phenomenon, wonder, cynosure, marvel, miracle, monster (83), unicorn, phoenix, gazing-stock, curiosity, *rara avis*, lion, sight, spectacle, wonderment, sign, portent (512), eye-opener; wonderland, fairyland.

Thunderclap, thunderbolt, bursting of a shell or bomb, volcanic eruption.

(*Phrases*) A nine days' wonder; *annus mirabilis.*

5°. *Extrinsic Affections*

873 REPUTE (*Substantives*), distinction, note, notability, name, mark, reputation, figure, *réclame*, *éclat*, celebrity, vogue, fame, famous-

874 DISREPUTE (*Substantives*), discredit, ingloriousness, derogation, abasement, degradation, odium, notoriety.

ness, popularity, renown, memory, immortality.

Glory, honour, credit, prestige, kudos, account, regard, respect, reputableness, respectability, respectableness, good name, illustriousness, gloriousness.

Dignity, stateliness, solemnity, grandeur, splendour, nobility, nobleness, lordliness, majesty, sublimity.

Greatness, highness, eminence, supereminence, pre-eminence, primacy, importance (642).

Elevation, ascent (305), exaltation, superexaltation, aggrandisement.

Rank, standing, condition, precedence, *pas*, station, place, status, order, degree, *locus standi*.

Dedication, consecration, enshrinement, glorification, beatification, canonization, deification, posthumous fame.

Chief, leader (745), hero, celebrity, notability, somebody, lion, cock of the roost, cock of the walk, man of mark, pillar of the state, prima donna.

A star, sun, constellation, galaxy, flower, pearl, paragon (650); honour, ornament, aureole.

(*Phrases*) A halo of glory; a name to conjure with; blushing honours; a feather in one's cap; the top of the tree; a niche in the temple of fame.

(*Verbs*) To glory in, to be proud of (878), to exult (884), to be vain of (880).

To be glorious, distinguished, etc., to shine, to figure, to make or cut a figure, dash, or splash; to rival, outrival, surpass, emulate, outvie, eclipse, outshine, overshadow, throw into the shade.

To live, flourish, glitter, flaunt.

To honour, lionize, dignify, glorify, ennoble, nobilitate, exalt, enthrone, signalize, immortalize, deify.

To consecrate, dedicate to, devote to, to enshrine.

To confer or reflect honour, etc., on; to do, pay, or render honour to; to redound to one's honour.

(*Phrases*) To acquire or gain honour, etc.; to bear the palm; to bear the bell; to take the cake; to win laurels;

Dishonour, shame, disgrace, disfavour, disapprobation (932), slur, scandal, obloquy, opprobrium, ignominy, baseness, turpitude, vileness, infamy.

Tarnish, taint, defilement, pollution.

Stain, blot, spot, blur, stigma, brand, reproach, imputation, slur, black mark.

(*Phrases*) A burning shame; *scandalum magnatum*; a badge of infamy; the bar sinister; a blot on the scutcheon; a byword of reproach; a bad reputation.

(*Verbs*) To be conscious of shame, to feel shame, to blush, to be ashamed, humiliated, humbled (879, 881).

To cause shame, etc.; to shame, disgrace, put to shame, dishonour; to throw, cast, fling, or reflect shame, etc., upon; to be a reproach to, to derogate from.

To tarnish, stain, blot, sully, taint, discredit, degrade, debase, defile.

To impute shame to, to brand, stigmatize, vilify, defame, slur, run down, knock.

To abash, humiliate, humble, dishonour, discompose, disconcert, shame, show up, put out, put down, snub, confuse, mortify; to obscure, eclipse, outshine.

(*Phrases*) To feel disgrace; to cut a poor figure; to hide one's face; to look foolish; to hang one's head; to laugh on the wrong side of the mouth; not to dare to show one's face; to hide one's diminished head; to lose caste; to be in one's black books.

To put to the blush; to put out of countenance; to put one's nose out of joint; to cast into the shade; to take one down a peg; to take the shine out of; to tread or trample under foot; to drag through the mud.

(*Adjectives*) Feeling shame, disgrace, etc.; ashamed, abashed, disgraced, blown upon, branded, tarnished.

Inglorious, mean, base (940), shabby, nameless, unnoticed, unnoted, unhonoured.

Shameful, disgraceful, despicable, discreditable, unbecoming, degrading,

to make a noise in the world; to go far; to make a sensation; to be all the rage; to have a run; to catch on.

To exalt one's horn; to leave one's mark; to exalt to the skies.

(*Adjectives*) Distinguished, *distingué*, noted, notable, respectable, reputable, celebrated, famous, famed, far-famed, honoured, renowned, popular, deathless, imperishable, immortal (112)

Illustrious, glorious, splendid, bright, brilliant, radiant, full-blown, heroic.

Eminent, prominent, conspicuous, kenspeckle, high, pre-eminent, peerless, signalized, exalted, dedicated, consecrated, enshrined.

humiliating, unworthy, disreputable, derogatory, vile, ribald, dishonourable, abject, scandalous, infamous, notorious.

(*Phrases*) Unwept, unhonoured and unsung; shorn of its beams; unknown to fame; in bad odour, under a cloud; down in the world.

(*Interjections*) Fie! shame! for shame! *O tempora! O mores!*

Great, dignified, proud, noble, worshipful, lordly, grand, stately, august, imposing, transcendent, majestic, kingly, queenly, princely, sacred, sublime, commanding.

(*Phrases*) Redounding to one's honour; one's name living for ever; *sic itur ad astra*.

(*Interjections*) Hail! all hail! *vive! viva!* glory be to! honour be to!

---

875 NOBILITY (*Substantives*) noblesse, aristocracy, peerage, gentry, gentility, quality, rank, blood, birth, donship, fashionable world (852), the *haute monde*, high life, the upper classes, the upper ten, the four hundred.

A personage, notability, celebrity, man of distinction, rank, etc.; a nobleman, noble, lord, peer, grandee, magnate, magnifico, hidalgo, don, gentleman, squire, patrician, lordling, nob, swell, dignitary, bigwig, big gun.

House of Lords, Lords Spiritual and Temporal.

Gentlefolk, landed proprietors, squirearchy, *optimates*.

Prince, duke, marquis, earl, viscount, baron, thane, banneret, baronet, knight, count, armiger, laird, esquire; nizam, maharajah, rajah, nawab, sultan, emir (or ameer), effendi, sheik, pasha.

Princess, duchess, marchioness, marquise, countess, viscountess, baroness, lady, dame, maharanee, ranee, sultana, begum.

(*Verbs*) To be noble, etc.

(*Adjectives*) Noble, exalted, titled,

876 COMMONALTY (*Substantives*) the lower classes or orders, the vulgar herd, the crowd, the people, the commons, the proletariat, the multitude, Demos, οἱ πολλοί, the populace, the million, the masses, the mobility, the peasantry.

The middle classes, bourgeoisie.

The mob, rabble, rabble-rout, ruck, *canaille*, the underworld, riff-raff, *profanum vulgus*.

A commoner, one of the people, a proletarian, *roturier*, plebeian; peasant, yeoman, crofter, boor, carle, churl, serf, kern, tyke, (or tike), chuff, ryot, fellah, cottar.

A swain, clown, hind, clodhopper, bog-trotter, chaw-bacon, hodge, joskin, yokel, bumpkin, hayseed, rube, hick, ploughman, plough-boy, gaffer, loon, looby, lout, *gamin*, street arab, guttersnipe, mudlark, slubberdegullion.

A beggar, tramp, vagrant, gangrel, gaberlunzie, bum, hobo, sundowner, panhandler, pariah, muckworm, sansculotte, raff, tatterdemalion, ragamuffin.

A Goth, Vandal, Hottentot, savage,

patrician, aristocratic, high-born, well-born, genteel, *comme il faut*, gentlemanlike, ladylike, princely, courtly, fashionable (852).

(*Phrases*) *Noblesse oblige*; born in the purple.

877 TITLE (*Substantives*), honour, princedom, principality, dukedom, marquisate, earldom, viscounty, baronetcy, lordship, knighthood.

Highness, excellency, grace, worship, reverence, esquire, sir, master, sahib, Mr., monsieur, signor, señor, Herr.

Decoration, laurel, palm, wreath, medal, gong, ribbon, cross, star, garter, feather, crest, epaulette, colours, cockade, livery; order, arms, shield, scutcheon.

(*Phrase*) A handle to one's name.

---

878 PRIDE (*Substantives*), haughtiness, loftiness, hauteur, stateliness, pomposity, vainglory, superciliousness, assumption, lordliness, stiffness, primness, arrogance, *morgue*, starch, starchiness, side, swank, uppishness; self-respect, dignity.

A proud man, etc., a highflier.

(*Verbs*) To be proud, etc., to presume, assume, swagger, strut, prance, peacock, bridle.

To pride oneself on, glory in, pique oneself, plume oneself, preen oneself.

(*Phrases*) To look big; give oneself airs; to ride the high horse; to put on side; to put on dog; to hold up one's head; to get one's tail up.

To put a good face upon.

(*Adjectives*) Proud, haughty, lofty, high, mighty, high-flown, high-minded, high-mettled, puffed up, flushed, supercilious, patronizing, condescending, disdainful, overweening, consequential, on stilts, swollen, arrogant, pompous.

Stately, dignified, stiff, starchy, prim, perked up, buckram, strait-laced, vainglorious, lordly,

barbarian, yahoo, rough diamond, unlicked cub.

An upstart, parvenu, skipjack, *novus homo, nouveau riche*, outsider, vulgarian, snob, mushroom.

Barbarousness, barbarism.

(*Phrases*) The man in the street; the submerged tenth; ragtag and bobtail; the swinish multitude; hewers of wood and drawers of water; the great unwashed.

(*Verbs*) To be ignoble, etc.

(*Adjectives*) Ignoble, common, mean, low, plebeian, proletarian, vulgar, bourgeois, untitled, homespun, homely, Gorblimey.

Base, base-born, low-bred, beggarly, earth-born, rustic, agrestic, countrified, provincial, parochial; banausic, menial, sorry, scrubby, mushroom, dunghill, sordid, vile, uncivilized, loutish, boorish, churlish, rude, brutish, raffish, unlicked, barbarous, barbarian, barbaric.

879 HUMILITY (*Substantives*), humbleness, meekness, lowness, lowliness, abasement, self-abasement, self-contempt, humiliation, submission, resignation, verecundity, modesty (881).

(*Verbs*) To be humble, etc.; to deign; vouchsafe, condescend; to humble or demean oneself; stoop, submit, knuckle under, look foolish, feel small.

To render humble; to humble, humiliate, set down, abash, abase, shame, mortify, crush, take down, snub.

(*Phrases*) To sing small; to pipe down; to draw in one's horns; to hide one's diminished head; to eat humble-pie; to eat dirt; to kiss the rod; to pocket an affront; to stoop to conquer.

To throw into the shade; to put out of countenance; to put a person in his place; to put to the blush; to take down a peg, cut down to size; to send away with a flea in one's ear.

(*Adjectives*) Humble, lowly, meek, sober-minded, submissive (725), resigned, self-contemptuous, under correction.

magisterial, purse-proud, stand-offish, up-stage, toffee-nose.

Unabashed (880).

(*Phrases*) High and mighty; proud as a peacock; proud as Lucifer.

(*Adverbs*) Proudly, haughtily, arrogantly, etc.

Humbled, humiliated, abashed, ashamed, chapfallen, crestfallen.

(*Phrases*) Out of countenance; on one's bended knees; humbled in the dust; not having a word to say for oneself.

(*Adverbs*) Humbly, meekly, etc.

880 VANITY (*Substantives*), conceit, conceitedness, self-conceit, self-confidence, self-sufficiency, self-esteem, self-approbation, self-importance, self-praise, self-laudation, self-admiration, complacency, self-complacency, swelled head, megalomania, *amour-propre*.

Pretensions, airs, mannerism, egotism, egoism, egomania, priggishness, coxcombry, gaudery, vainglory (943), elation, ostentation (882).

A coxcomb (854).

(*Verbs*) To be vain, etc., to egotize. To render vain, etc., to puff up, to inspire with vanity, turn one's head.

(*Phrases*) To have a high or overweening opinion of oneself; to think no small beer of oneself; to thrust oneself forward; to give oneself airs; to show off; to fish for compliments.

(*Adjectives*) Vain, conceited, overweening, forward, vainglorious, puffed up, high-flown, inflated, flushed, stuck-up.

Self-satisfied, self-confident, self-sufficient, self-flattering, self-admiring, self-applauding, self-opinionated, self-centred, egocentric, egoistic, egoistical, egotistic, egotistical, complacent, self-complacent, pretentious, priggish.

Unabashed, unblushing, unconstrained, unceremonious, free and easy.

(*Phrases*) Vain as a peacock; wise in one's own conceit.

(*Adverbs*) Vainly, etc., ostentatiously (882).

881 MODESTY (*Substantives*), humility (879), diffidence, timidity, bashfulness, shyness, coyness, sheepishness, *mauvaise honte*, shamefacedness, verecundity, self-consciousness.

Reserve, constraint, demureness.

(*Verbs*) To be modest, humble, etc.; to retire, keep in the background, keep private, reserve oneself.

(*Phrases*) To hide one's light under a bushel; to take a back seat.

(*Adjectives*) Modest, diffident, humble (879), timid, bashful, timorous, shy, skittish, coy, sheepish, shamefaced, blushing, self-conscious.

Unpretending, unpretentious, unassuming, unostentatious, unboastful, unaspiring.

Abashed, ashamed, dashed, out of countenance, crestfallen (879).

Reserved, constrained, demure, undemonstrative.

(*Adverbs*) Modestly, diffidently, quietly, privately, unostentatiously.

---

882 OSTENTATION (*Substantives*), display, show, flourish, parade, pomp, state, solemnity, pageantry, dash, splash, splurge, glitter, veneer, tinsel, magnificence, pomposity, showing off, swank, swagger, strut, *panache, coup de théâtre*, stage effect.

Flourish of trumpets, fanfare, salvo of artillery, salute, fireworks, *feu de joie*.

Pageant, spectacle, procession, march-past, review, promenade, turn-out, set-out, build-up, fête, gala, regatta, field-day.

Ceremony, ceremonial, mummery; formality, form, etiquette, ritual, protocol, punctilio, punctiliousness.

(*Verbs*) To be ostentatious, etc.; to display, exhibit, posture, attitudinize, show off, swank, come forward, put oneself forward, flaunt, emblazon, prink, glitter; make or cut a figure, dash, or splash.

To observe or stand on ceremony, etiquette, etc.

(*Adjectives*) Ostentatious, showy, gaudy, garish, flashy, dashing, pretentious, flaunting, jaunty, glittering, sumptuous, spectacular, ceremonial, stagy, theatrical, histrionic.

Pompous, solemn, stately, high-sounding, formal, stiff, ritualistic, ceremonious, punctilious.

(*Phrases*) With flourish of trumpets; with beat of drum; with flying colours; in one's Sunday best; in one's best bib and tucker.

883 CELEBRATION (*Substantives*), jubilee, jubilation, commemoration, festival, feast, solemnization, ovation, paean, triumph.

Triumphal arch, bonfire, illuminations, fireworks, salute, salvo, *feu de joie*, flourish of trumpets, fanfare.

Inauguration, installation, presentation, coronation, fête (882).

Anniversary, silver wedding, golden wedding, diamond wedding, diamond jubilee, centenary, bicentenary, tercentenary, quatercentenary, quingentenary (or quincentenary), sexcentenary, etc., millenary.

(*Verbs*) To celebrate, keep, signalize, do honour to, pledge, drink to, toast, commemorate, solemnize.

To inagurate, install.

(*Phrase*) To paint the town red.

(*Adjectives*) Celebrating, etc., in honour of, in commemoration of, in memoriam.

(*Interjections*) Hail! all hail! 'See the conquering hero comes.' 'For he's a jolly good fellow.'

884 BOASTING (*Substantives*), boast, vaunt, vaunting, brag, bounce, *blague*, swank, bluff, puff, puffing, puffery, flourish, fanfaronade, gasconade, braggadocio, bravado, tall talk, heroics, vapouring, rodomontade, bombast, exaggeration (549), self-advertisement, *réclame*; jingoism, Chauvinism, spread-eagleism.

Exultation, triumph, flourish of trumpets (883).

A boaster, braggart, braggadocio, Gascon, peacock; a pretender, charlatan.

(*Verbs*) To boast, make a boast of, brag, vaunt, puff, flourish, vapour, blow, strut, swagger, swank, skite, gas.

To exult, crow, chuckle, triumph, gloat, glory.

(*Phrases*) To talk big; to shoot a line; to blow one's own trumpet.

(*Adjectives*) Boasting, vaunting, etc., thrasonical, vainglorious, braggart, jingo, jingoistic, chauvinistic.

Elate, elated, flushed, jubilant.

(*Phrases*) On stilts; cock-a-hoop; in high feather.

885 Undue assumption of superiority.

INSOLENCE (*Substantives*), haughtiness, arrogance, imperiousness, contumeliousness, superciliousness, bumptiousness, bounce, swagger, swank.

Impertinence, sauciness, pertness, flippancy, petulance, malapertness.

Assumption, presumption, presumptuousness, forwardness, impudence, assurance, front, face, neck, cheek, lip, side, brass, shamelessness,

886 SERVILITY (*Substantives*), obsequiousness, suppleness, fawning, slavishness, abjectness, prostration, prosternation, genuflexion (900), abasement, subjection (749).

Fawning, mealy-mouthedness, sycophancy, flattery (833), humility (879).

A sycophant, parasite, gate-crasher, toad-eater, toady, spaniel, bootlicker, lickspittle, flunkey, sponger, snob, hanger-on, tuft-hunter, time-server, reptile, cur (941); Uriah Heep.

hardihood, a hardened front, effrontery, audacity, procacity, self-assertion, nerve, gall, crust.

(*Verbs*) To be insolent, etc.; to bluster, vapour, swagger, swank, swell, roister, arrogate, assume, bluff.

To domineer, bully, beard, snub, huff, outface, outlook, outstare, outbrazen, bear down, beat down, trample on, tread under foot, outbrave, hector.

To presume, take liberties or freedoms.

(*Phrases*) To give oneself airs; to lay down the law; to put on side; to ride the high horse; to lord it over; *traiter, ou regarder de haut en bas*; to ride roughshod over; to carry with a high hand; to throw one's weight about; to carry it off; to brave it out.

(*Verbs*) To cringe, bow, stoop, kneel, fall on one's knees, etc.

To sneak, crawl, crouch, cower, truckle to, grovel, fawn.

(*Phrases*) To pay court to; to dance attendance on; to do the dirty work of; to lick the boots of.

To go with the stream; to worship the rising sun; to run with the hare and hunt with the hounds.

(*Adjectives*) Servile, subservient, obsequious, sequacious, soapy, oily, unctuous, supple, mean, crouching, cringing, fawning, slavish, grovelling, snivelling, beggarly, sycophantic, parasitical, abject, prostrate.

(*Adverb*) Cap in hand.

(*Adjectives*) Insolent, etc.; haughty, arrogant, imperious, dictatorial, high-handed, contumelious, supercilious, snooty, uppish, self-assertive, bumptious, overbearing, intolerant, assumptive.

Flippant, pert, perky, cavalier, saucy, cheeky, fresh, forward, impertinent, malapert.

Blustering, swaggering, swanky, vapouring, bluff, roistering, rollicking, high-flown, assuming, presuming, presumptuous, self-assertive, impudent, free, brazen, brazen-faced, barefaced, shameless, unblushing, unabashed.

887 BLUSTERER (*Substantives*), bully, swaggerer, braggart (884), fire-eater, daredevil, roisterer, puppy, sauce-box, hussy, minx, malapert, jackanapes, jack-in-office, jingo, Drawcansir, Captain Bobadil, Sir Lucius O'Trigger, Bombastes Furioso, Hector, Thraso, Bumble.

(*Phrases*) The great Panjandrum himself; a cool hand.

SECTION III—SYMPATHETIC AFFECTIONS

1°. *Social Affections*

888 FRIENDSHIP (*Substantives*), amity, amicableness, amicability, friendliness, friendly regard, affection (897), goodwill, favour, brotherhood, fraternity, sodality, comradeship, *camaraderie*, confraternity, fraternization, cordiality, harmony, good understanding, concord (714), *entente cordiale*.

Acquaintance, introduction, intimacy, familiarity, fellowship, fellowfeeling, sympathy, welcomeness, partiality, favouritism.

889 ENMITY (*Substantives*), hostility, unfriendliness, antagonism, animosity, hate (898), dislike (867), malevolence (907), ill will, ill feeling, spite, bad blood, aversion, antipathy, alienation, estrangement; umbrage, pique.

(*Verbs*) To be inimical, etc.; to estrange, to fall out, alienate.

(*Phrases*) To keep at arm's length; to bear malice; to set by the ears.

(*Adjectives*) Inimical, unfriendly, hostile, antagonistic, adverse, at

(*Verbs*) To be friends, to be friendly, etc., to fraternize, sympathize with (897), to be well with, to be thick with, to befriend (707), to be in with, to keep in with.

To become friendly, to make friends with, to chum up with.

(*Phrases*) To take in good part; to hold out the right hand of fellowship; to break the ice; to scrape acquaintance with.

(*Adjectives*) Friendly, amical, amicable, brotherly, fraternal, harmonious, cordial, social, chummy, pally, neighbourly, on good terms, on a friendly footing, on friendly terms, well-affected, well-disposed, favourable.

Acquainted, familiar, intimate, thick, hand and glove, welcome.

Firm, staunch, intimate, familiar, bosom, cordial, devoted.

(*Phrases*) In one's good books; hail fellow well met.

(*Adverbs*) Friendly, amicably, etc., *sans cérémonie*.

variance, at loggerheads, at daggers drawn, on bad terms.

Estranged, alienated, irreconcilable.

---

890 FRIEND (*Substantives*), well-wisher, *amicus curiae*, *alter ego*, bosom friend, *fidus Achates*, partner (711); *persona grata*.

Partisan, sympathizer, ally, backer, patron, good genius, fairy godmother.

Neighbour, acquaintance, associate, compeer, comrade, companion, *confrère*, *camarade*, mate, messmate, shopmate, crony, cummer, confidant, chum, pal, buddy, side-kick, boon companion, pot-companion, schoolfellow, playfellow, playmate, bed-fellow, bed-mate, bunkie, room-mate.

Arcades ambo, Pylades and Orestes, Castor and Pollux, Nisus and Euryalus, Damon and Pythias, David and Jonathan, *par nobile fratrum*.

Host, guest, visitor, *habitué*, protégé.

891 ENEMY (*Substantives*), foe, opponent (710), antagonist.

Public enemy, enemy to society, anarchist, terrorist, Ishmael.

---

892 SOCIALITY (*Substantives*), sociability, sociableness, social intercourse, companionship, companionableness, consortship, intercommunication, intercommunion, consociation.

Conviviality, good fellowship, hospitality, heartiness, welcome, the glad hand, joviality, jollity, *savoir vivre*, festivity, merrymaking.

Society, association, union, co-partnership, fraternity, sodality, coterie, clan, club (72), circle, clique, knot.

Assembly-room, casino, clubhouse, common-room.

Esprit de corps, nepotism (11).

An entertainment, party, social gathering, reunion, gaudy, levee, soirée, conversazione, rout, *ridotto*,

893 SECLUSION (*Substantives*), privacy, retirement, withdrawal, reclusion, recess, retiredness, rustication.

Solitude, singleness, estrangement from the world, loneliness, lonesomeness, retiredness, isolation; hermitage, cloister, nunnery (1000); study, den; ivory tower, Shangri-la.

Wilderness, depopulation, desolation.

Agoraphobia, claustrophobia.

EXCLUSION (*Substantives*), excommunication, banishment, expatriation, exile, ostracism, cut, cut direct, dead cut, inhospitality, inhospitableness, unsociability.

A recluse, hermit, cenobite, anchoret (or anchorite), stylite, santon,

at-home, house-warming, bee, tea-party, bun-fight, picnic, garden-party, festival (840), interview, assignation, appointment, date, tryst, call, visit, visiting, reception (588).

A good fellow, good scout, boon companion, good mixer, *bon vivant*.

(*Verbs*) To be sociable, etc., to associate with, keep company with, to club together, sort with, hobnob with, consort, make advances, fraternize, make the acquaintance of.

To visit, pay a visit, interchange visits or cards, call upon, leave a card.

To entertain, give a party, dance, etc.; to keep open house; to receive, to welcome.

(*Phrases*) To make oneself at home; to crack a bottle with.

To be at home to; to do the honours; to receive with open arms; to give a warm reception to; to kill the fatted calf.

(*Adjectives*) Sociable, social, companionable, neighbourly, gregarious, clannish, clubbable, conversable, affable, accessible, familiar, on visiting terms, welcome, hospitable, convivial, jovial, festive.

(*Phrases*) Free and easy; hail fellow well met.

(*Adverbs*) *En famille*; in the family circle; in the social whirl; *sans façon*; *sans cérémonie*; *sans gêne*.

---

894 COURTESY (*Substantives*), good manners, good breeding, good form, mannerliness, manners, *bienséance*, urbanity, civilization, polish, politeness, gentility, comity, civility, amenity, suavity, discretion, diplomacy, good temper, easy temper, gentleness, mansuetude, graciousness, gallantry, affability, obligingness, *prévenance*, amiability, good humour.

Compliment, fair words, soft words, sweet words, honeyed phrases, attentions, *petits soins*, salutation, reception, presentation, introduction, *accueil*, greeting, regards, remembrances, welcome, *abord*, respect, devoir.

troglodyte, solitary, ruralist; displaced person, outcast, pariah; foundling, waif, wastrel, castaway; Timon of Athens, Simon Stylites.

(*Phrase*) 'A lone lorn creetur.'

(*Verbs*) To be secluded, etc., to retire, to live retired, secluded, etc.; to keep aloof, keep snug, shut oneself up, deny oneself.

To cut, refuse to associate with or acknowledge; repel, cold-shoulder, blackball, outlaw, proscribe, excommunicate, boycott, exclude, banish, exile, ostracize, rusticate, send down, abandon, maroon.

To depopulate, dispeople, unpeople.

(*Phrases*) To retire from the world; to take the veil; to sport one's oak.

To send to Coventry; to turn one's back upon; to give one the cold shoulder.

(*Adjectives*) Secluded, sequestered, retired, private, snug, domestic, claustral.

Unsociable, unsocial, aloof, eremitical, offish, stand-offish, unclubbable, inhospitable, cynical, inconversible, retiring, unneighbourly, exclusive, unforthcoming.

Solitary, lonely, lonesome, isolated, single, estranged, unfrequented, uninhabited, unoccupied, tenantless.

Unvisited, cut, blackballed, uninvited, unwelcome, friendless, deserted, abandoned, derelict, lorn, forlorn, homeless, out of it.

(*Phrase*) Left to shift for oneself.

---

895 DISCOURTESY (*Substantives*), ill-breeding; ill, bad, or ungainly manners; rusticity, inurbanity, impoliteness, ungraciousness, uncourtliness, insuavity, rudeness, incivility, tactlessness, disrespect, impertinence, impudence, cheek, barbarism, misbehaviour, *grossièreté*, brutality, blackguardism, roughness, ruggedness, brusqueness, brusquerie, bad form.

Bad or ill temper, churlishness, crabbedness, tartness, crossness, peevishness, moroseness, sullenness, sulkiness, grumpiness, grouchiness, acrimony, sternness, austerity, moodi-

Obeisance, reverence, bow, curtsy, scrape, salaam, kowtow, capping, shaking hands, embrace, hug, squeeze, accolade, salute, kiss, buss, kissing hands, genuflexion, prostration, obsequiousness.

Mark of recognition, nod, wave, valediction (293).

(*Verbs*) To be courteous, civil, etc., to show courtesy, civility, etc., to speak one fair; to make oneself agreeable; to unbend, thaw.

To visit, wait upon, present oneself, pay one's respects, kiss hands.

To receive, do the honours, greet, welcome, bid welcome, usher in, bid God speed; hold or stretch out the hand; shake, press, or squeeze the hand.

To salute, kiss, embrace, hug, drink to, pledge, hobnob; to wave to, nod to, smile upon, bow, curtsy, scrape, uncover, cap, present arms, take off the hat.

To pay homage or obeisance, kneel, bend the knee, prostrate oneself, etc.

To render polite, etc., to polish, civilize, humanize.

(*Phrases*) To mind one's p's and q's; to do the polite; to greet with open arms; to speed the parting guest.

(*Adjectives*) Courteous, courtly, civil, civilized, polite, Chesterfieldian, genteel, well-bred, well-mannered, mannerly, urbane, gentlemanly, ladylike, refined (850), polished, genial.

Gracious, affable, familiar, well-spoken, fair-spoken, soft-spoken, fine-spoken, suave, bland, mild, conciliatory, winning, obsequious, obliging, open-armed.

(*Phrases*) With a good grace; *suaviter in modo*; *à bras ouverts*.

(*Interjections*) Hail! welcome! good morning! good day! good afternoon! good evening! good night! well met! *pax vobiscum!*

ness, asperity, captiousness, sharpness, snappishness, perversity, cussedness, irascibility (901).

Sulks, dudgeon, mumps, scowl, frown, hard words, black looks.

A bear, brute, boor, blackguard, beast, cross-patch, grouch, sorehead.

(*Verbs*) To be rude, etc., frown, scowl, glower, lour, pout, snap, snarl, growl, nag; to cut, insult, etc.

To render rude, etc., to brutalize, decivilize, dehumanize.

(*Phrases*) To turn one's back upon; to turn on one's heel; to look black upon; to give one the cold shoulder, or the frozen face, or the frozen mitt; to take liberties with.

(*Adjectives*) Discourteous, uncourteous, uncourtly, ill-bred, ill-mannered, ill-behaved, unmannerly, mannerless, impolite, unpolished, ungenteel, ungentlemanly, unladylike, uncivilized.

Uncivil, rude, ungracious, cool, chilly, distant, stand-offish, offish, icy, repulsive, uncomplaisant, unaccommodating, ungainly, unceremonious, ungentle, rough, rugged, bluff, blunt, gruff, churlish, boorish, bearish, brutal, brusque, blackguardly, vulgar, stern, harsh, austere, cavalier.

Ill-tempered, out of temper or humour, cross, crusty, tart, sour, crabbed, sharp, short, snappish, testy, peevish, waspish, captious, grumpy, snarling, caustic, acrimonious, ungenial, petulant, pettish, pert.

Perverse, cross-grained, ill-conditioned, wayward, humoursome, naughty, cantankerous, intractable, curst, nagging, froward, sulky, glum, grim, morose, scowling, grouchy, glowering, surly, sullen, growling, splenetic, spleenful, spleeny, spleenish, moody, dogged, ugly.

(*Phrases*) Cross as two sticks; sour as a crab; surly as a bear.

(*Adverbs*) With a bad grace, grudgingly.

---

896 CONGRATULATION (*Substantives*), felicitation, wishing joy, the compliments of the season, good wishes.

(*Verbs*) To congratulate, felicitate, give or wish joy, tender or offer one's congratulations.

(*Adjectives*) Congratulatory, etc.

(*Phrases*) Many happy returns of the day! merry Christmas! happy New Year!

897 LOVE (*Substantives*), fondness, liking, inclination (865), regard, good graces, partiality, benevolence (906), admiration, fancy, tenderness, leaning, penchant, predilection; amativeness, amorousness.

Affection, sympathy, fellow-feeling, heart, affectionateness.

Attachment, yearning, amour, romance, gallantry, love-affair, *affaire de cœur*, passion, tender passion, *grande passion*, flame, pash, crush, rave, devotion, enthusiasm, fervour, enchantment, infatuation, adoration, idolatry, idolization.

Eros, Cupid, Aphrodite, Venus, Freya, the myrtle.

Maternal love, στοργή.

Attractiveness, etc., popularity.

Abode of love, love-nest, agape-mone.

A lover, suitor, follower, admirer, adorer, wooer, beau, fiancé, gallant, young man, boy friend, sweetheart, flame, love, true-love, leman, paramour, amorist, *amoroso, cavaliere servente, cicisbeo*; turtle-doves.

Girl friend, lady-love, fiancée, sweetie, cutie, mistress, *inamorata*, idol, doxy, dona, Dulcinea, goddess.

Betrothed, affianced.

(*Verbs*) To love, like, affect, fancy, care for, regard, revere, cherish, admire, dote on, adore, idolize, fall for, hold dear, prize.

To bear love to; to take to; to be in love with; to be taken, smitten, etc., with; to have, entertain, harbour, cherish, etc., a liking, love, etc., for; to be fond of, be gone on.

To excite love; to win, gain, secure, etc., the love, affections, heart, etc.; to take the fancy of, to attract, attach, seduce, charm, fascinate, captivate, enamour, enrapture.

To get into favour; to ingratiate oneself, insinuate oneself, curry favour with, pay one's court to, *faire l'aimable*.

(*Phrases*) To take a fancy to; to

898 HATE (*Substantives*), hatred, disaffection, disfavour, alienation, estrangement, odium, dislike (867), enmity (899), animus, animosity (900).

Umbrage, pique, grudge, dudgeon, spleen, bitterness, ill feeling, acrimony, acerbity, malice (907), implacability.

Disgust, repugnance, aversion, averseness, loathing, abomination, horror, detestation, antipathy, abhorrence.

Object of hatred, abomination, *bête noir*.

(*Verbs*) To hate, dislike, disrelish (867), loathe, nauseate, execrate, detest, abominate, shudder at, recoil at, abhor, shrink from.

To excite hatred, estrange, incense, envenom, antagonize, rile, alienate, disaffect, set against; to be hateful, etc.

(*Phrases*) To make one's blood run cold; to have a down on; to hate one's guts.

To sow dissension among; to set by the ears.

(*Adjectives*) Hating, etc., averse to, set against.

Unloved, disliked, unwept, unlamented, undeplored, unmourned, unbeloved, uncared-for, unvalued.

Crossed in love, forsaken, jilted, rejected, lovelorn.

Obnoxious, hateful, abhorrent, odious, repulsive, offensive, shocking, loathsome, sickening, nauseous, disgusting, abominable, horrid (830).

Invidious, spiteful, malicious (907), spleenful, disgustful.

Insulting, irritating, provoking.

(*Phrases*) Not on speaking terms; there being no love lost between them; at daggers drawn.

make a fuss of; to look sweet upon; to cast sheep's eyes at; to fall in love with; to set one's affections on; to lose one's heart to.

To set one's cap at; to turn one's head.

(*Adjectives*) Loving, liking, etc., attached to, fond of, taken with, struck with, gone on, sympathetic, sympathizing with, charmed, captivated, fascinated, smitten, bitten, *épris*, enamoured, lovesick, love-lorn.

Affectionate, tender, sweet upon, loving, lover-like, loverly, amorous, amatory, amative, spoony, erotic, uxorious, motherly, ardent, passionate, devoted, amatorial.

Loved, beloved, etc., dear, precious, darling, favourite (899), pet, popular.

Lovely, sweet, dear, charming, engaging, amiable, winning, winsome, lovesome, attractive, adorable, enchanting, captivating, fascinating, bewitching, taking, seductive (829).

(*Phrases*) Head over ears in love; to one's mind, taste, or fancy; in one's good graces; nearest to one's heart.

899 FAVOURITE (*Substantives*), pet, cosset, dear, darling, honey, duck, moppet, jewel, idol, minion, spoilt child, blue-eyed boy, *persona grata*.

(*Phrases*) The apple of one's eye; a man after one's own heart; the idol of the people; the answer to the maiden's prayer.

900 RESENTMENT (*Substantives*), displeasure, animus, animosity, anger, wrath, indignation.

Pique, umbrage, huff, miff, soreness, dudgeon, moodiness, acerbity, bitterness, asperity, spleen, gall, heart-burning, heart-swelling, rankling; temper (901), bad blood, ill blood, ill humour.

Excitement, irritation, exasperation, warmth, bile, choler, ire, fume, dander, passion, fit, tantrum, burst, explosion, paroxysm, storm, rage, wax, fury, desperation.

Temper, petulance, procacity, angry mood, taking, snappishness.

Cause of umbrage, affront, provocation, offence, indignity, insult (929).

The Furies; the Eumenides.

(*Phrases*) The blood being up or boiling; a towering passion; the vials of wrath; fire and fury.

A sore subject; a rap on the knuckles; *casus belli*.

(*Verbs*) To resent, take amiss, take offence, take umbrage, take huff, bridle up, bristle up, frown, scowl, lour, snarl, growl, gnash, snap.

To chafe, mantle, redden, colour, fume, froth up, kindle; get, fall, or fly into a passion, rage, etc.; fly out, take fire, fire up, flare up, boil, boil over, rage, storm, foam.

To cause or raise anger; to affront, offend, give offence or umbrage; hurt the feelings; discompose, fret, ruffle, nettle, excite, irritate, provoke, rile, chafe, wound, sting, incense, inflame, enrage, aggravate, embitter, exasperate, rankle, infuriate, peeve.

(*Phrases*) To take in bad part; to take it ill; to take exception to; to stick in one's gizzard; to take in dudgeon; to have a bone (or crow) to pick with one; to get up on one's hind legs; to show one's teeth; to lose one's temper; to stamp, quiver, swell, or foam with rage; to see red; to look as black as thunder; to breathe revenge; to cut up rough; to pour out the vials of one's wrath; to blaze up; to blow one's top; to go up in a blue flame; to go on the war-path; to raise Cain.

To put out of humour; to stir up one's bile; to raise one's dander or choler; to work up into a passion; to make one's blood boil; to lash into a fury; to drive one mad; to put one's monkey up; to get one's goat.

(*Adjectives*) Angry, wroth, irate, ireful, warm, boiling, fuming, raging, etc., nettled, sore, bitter, riled, ruffled, chafed, exasperated, wrought up, worked up, snappish.

Fierce, wild, rageful, furious, infuriate, mad, fiery, savage, rabid, waxy, shirty, boiling over, rankling, bitter, virulent, set against.

Relentless, ruthless, implacable, unpitying, pitiless (919), inexorable, remorseless, stony-hearted, immitigable.

(*Phrases*) One's back being up; up in arms; in a stew; the gorge rising; in the height of passion.

(*Interjections*) Hell's bells! zounds! damme! For crying out loud!

901 IRASCIBILITY (*Substantives*), susceptibility, excitability, temper, bad temper, procacity, petulance, irritability, fretfulness, testiness, grouchiness, tetchiness, touchiness, frowardness, peevishness, snappishness, hastiness, tartness, huffiness, resentfulness, vindictiveness, acerbity, protervity, aggressiveness, pugnacity (895).

A shrew, vixen, termagant, virago, scold, spitfire, Xanthippe; a tartar, fire-eater, fury; *genus irritabile*.

(*Verbs*) To be irascible, etc.; to take fire, fire up, flare up (900).

(*Adjectives*) Irascible, susceptible, excitable, irritable, fretful, fretty, on the fret, fidgety, peevish, hasty, over-hasty, quick, warm, hot, huffish, huffy, touchy, testy, tetchy (or techy), grouchy, restive, pettish, waspish, snappish, petulant, peppery, fiery, passionate, choleric, short-tempered.

Ill-tempered, bad-tempered, cross, churlish, sour, crabbed, cross-grained, sullen, sulky, grumpy, fractious, splenetic, spleenful, froward, shrewish.

Quarrelsome, querulous, disputatious, contentious, cranky, cantankerous, sarcastic (932), resentful, vindictive, pugnacious, aggressive.

(*Phrases*) Like touchwood or tinder; a word and a blow; as cross as two sticks.

902 Expression of affection or love.

ENDEARMENT (*Substantives*), caress, blandishment, fondling, billing and cooing, petting, necking, embrace, salute, kiss, buss, smack, osculation, deosculation.

Courtship, wooing, suit, addresses, attentions, *petits soins*, flirtation, coquetry, philandering, gallivanting, serenading, œillade, ogle, the glad eye, sheep's eyes, goo-goo eyes.

Love-tale, love-token, love-letter, *billet-doux*, valentine.

Flirt, coquette, gold digger, vamp; male flirt, masher, philanderer, lady killer, wolf, lounge lizard, cake eater, sheik.

(*Verbs*) To caress, fondle, wheedle, dandle, dally, cuddle, cockle, cosset, nestle, nuzzle, snuggle, clasp, hug, embrace, kiss, salute, bill and coo.

To court, woo, flirt, coquette, philander, spoon, canoodle, mash, spark, serenade.

(*Phrases*) To make much of; to smile upon; to make eyes at; to chuck under the chin; to pat on the cheek; to make love; to pay one's court or one's addresses to; to set one's cap at; to pop the question.

To win the heart, affections, love, etc., of.

(*Adjectives*) Caressing, etc., caressed, etc., flirtatious, spoony.

903 MARRIAGE (*Substantives*), matrimony, wedlock, union, bridal, match, intermarriage, coverture, cohabitation, bed, the marriage bond, the nuptial tie.

Wedding, nuptials, Hymen, spousals, espousals; leading to the altar;

904 CELIBACY (*Substantives*), singleness, misogamy; bachelorhood, bachelorship; virginity, maidenhood, maidenhead.

An unmarried man, bachelor, celibate, misogamist, misogynist.

An unmarried woman, spinster,

the torch of Hymen; nuptial benediction, marriage song, epithalamium.

Bride, bridegroom, groom, bridesmaid, maid of honour, matron of honour, bridesman, groomsman, best man.

Honeymoon, honeymooner.

A married man, a husband, spouse, benedick (or benedict), consort, goodman, lord and master, hubby.

A married woman, a wife, lady, matron, mate, helpmate, helpmeet, rib, better half, *femme couverte* (or *feme coverte*), squaw.

A married couple, wedded pair, Darby and Joan, man and wife.

A monogamist, bigamist, polygamist, a much-married man, a Turk, a Bluebeard, a Mormon.

Monogamy, bigamy, digamy, deuterogamy, trigamy, polygamy, polygyny, polyandry, endogamy, exogamy.

A morgantic marriage, left-handed marriage, marriage of convenience, *mariage de convenance*, companionate marriage, trial marriage, misalliance, *mésalliance*.

(*Verbs*) To marry, wed, espouse, wive.

To join, give away, handfast, splice.

(*Phrases*) To lead to the altar; to take to oneself a wife; to take for better for worse; to give one's hand to; to get spliced.

To tie the nuptial knot; to give in marriage.

(*Adjectives*) Matrimonial, conjugal, connubial, nuptial, wedded, hymeneal, spousal, bridal, marital, epithalamic.

Monogamous, bigamous, polygamous, etc.

maid, maiden, old maid, virgin, *feme sole*, bachelor girl.

(*Phrase*) Single blessedness.

(*Verb*) To live single.

(*Adjectives*) Unwedded, unmarried, single, celibate, wifeless, spouseless, lone.

905 DIVORCE (*Substantives*), dissolution of marriage, separation, divorcement.

A divorcee, co-respondent, cuckold.

(*Verbs*) To live separate, divorce, put away.

WIDOWHOOD, viduity, weeds.

Widow, relict, dowager, jointress, grass widow; widower, grass widower.

2°. *Diffusive Sympathetic Affections*

906 BENEVOLENCE (*Substantives*), goodwill, good nature, kindness, kindliness, benignity, brotherly love, beneficence, charity, humanity, fellow-feeling, sympathy, good feeling, kind-heartedness, amiability, complaisance, loving-kindness; toleration, consideration, generosity.

Charitableness, bounty, bounteousness, bountifulness, almsgiving, philanthropy (910), unselfishness (942).

Acts of kindness, a good turn, good works, kind offices, attentions, good treatment.

(*Phrases*) The milk of human kindness; the good Samaritan.

(*Verbs*) To be benevolent, etc., to do good to, to benefit, confer a benefit, be of use, aid, assist (707),

907 MALEVOLENCE (*Substantives*), ill will, unkindness, ill nature, malignity, malice, maliciousness, spite, spitefulness, despite, despitefulness.

Uncharitableness, venom, gall, rancour, rankling, bitterness, acerbity, harshness, mordacity, acridity, virulence, *acharnement*, misanthropy(911).

Cruelty, hardness of heart, obduracy, cruelness, brutality, brutishness, hooliganism, savageness, savagery, ferocity, barbarity, bloodthirstiness, immanity, pitilessness, truculence, devilry (or deviltry), devilment.

An ill turn, a bad turn, outrage, atrocity, affront (929).

(*Phrases*) A heart of stone; the evil eye; the cloven hoof.

render a service, treat well, to sympathize with.

(*Phrases*) To have one's heart in the right place; to enter into the feelings of others; to do a good turn to; to do as one would be done by.

(*Adjectives*) Benevolent, well-meaning, kind, obliging, accommodating, kind-hearted, tender-hearted, charitable, generous, beneficent, bounteous, bountiful, humane, clement, benignant, benign, considerate.

Good-natured, *bon enfant, bon diable*, a good sort, sympathizing, sympathetic, responsive, complaisant, accommodating, amiable, gracious.

Kindly, well-meant, well-intentioned, brotherly, fraternal, friendly (888).

(*Adverbs*) With a good intention, with the best intentions.

(*Interjections*) Good luck! God speed!

_____

(*Verbs*) To be malevolent, etc.; to injure, hurt, harm, molest, disoblige, do harm to, ill treat, maltreat (649), do an ill office or turn to, (830) to wrong.

To worry, harass, bait, oppress, grind, haze, persecute, hunt down, dragoon, hound.

(*Phrases*) To wreak one's malice on; to bear or harbour malice against; to do one's worst.

(*Adjectives*) Malevolent, malicious, ill-disposed, evil-minded, ill-intentioned, maleficent, malign, malignant.

Ill-natured, disobliging, inofficious, unfriendly, unsympathetic, unkind, uncandid, unaccommodating, uncharitable, ungracious, unamiable.

Surly, churlish (895), grim, spitefull, despiteful, ill-conditioned, foul-mouthed, acrid, rancorous, caustic, bitter, acrimonious, mordacious, vitriolic, venomous.

Cold, cold-blooded, cold-hearted, hard-hearted, iron-hearted, flint-hearted, marble-hearted, stony-hearted.

Pitiless, unpitying, uncompassionate, without bowels, ruthless, merciless, unmerciful, inexorable, relentless, unrelenting, virulent, dispiteous.

Cruel, brutal, savage, ferocious, atrocious, untamed, ferine, inhuman, barbarous, fell, Hunnish, bloody, blood-stained, bloodthirsty, bloody-minded, sanguinary, truculent (919), butcherly.

Fiendish, fiendlike, infernal, demoniacal, diabolical, devilish, hellish.

(*Adverbs*) Malevolently, etc., with bad intent or intention, despitefully.

908. MALEDICTION (*Substantives*), curse, malison, imprecation, denunciation, execration, anathema, ban, proscription, excommunication, commination, fulmination, *maranatha*.

Cursing, scolding, revilement, vilification, vituperation, invective, flyting, railing, Billingsgate, expletive, oath, bad language, unparliamentary language, ribaldry, scurrility.

(*Verbs*) To censure, curse, imprecate, damn, scold, swear at, flyte on, rail at or against, execrate.

To denounce, proscribe, excommunicate, fulminate against, anathematize, blaspheme.

(*Phrases*) To devote to destruction; to invoke or call down curses on one's head; to swear like a trooper; to rap out an oath; to curse with bell, book, and candle.

(*Adjectives*) Cursing, etc., accursed, cursed, etc., blue-pencil, asterisk; maledictory, imprecatory, blasphemous.

(*Interjections*) Curse! damn! blast! devil take it! dash! hang! blow! confound! plague on it! woe to! beshrew! *ruat coelum!* ill betide!

909 THREAT (*Substantives*), menace, defiance (715) abuse, minacity, intimidation, commination.

(*Verbs*) To threaten, threat, menace, fulminate, thunder, bluster, defy, snarl; growl, gnarl, mutter; to intimidate (860).

(*Phrases*) To hurl defiance; to throw down the gauntlet; to look daggers; to show one's teeth; to shake the fist at.

(*Adjectives*) Threatening, menacing, minatory, comminatory, minacious, abusive, sinister, ominous, louring, defiant (715).

(*Interjections*) Let them beware! You have been warned!

910 PHILANTHROPY (*Substantives*), humanity, humanitarianism, altruism, public spirit.

Patriotism, civicism, nationality, nationalism, love of country, *amor patriae*, sociology, socialism, utilitarianism.

A philanthropist, humanitarian, utilitarian, Benthamite, socialist, cosmopolitan, cosmopolite, citizen of the world, patriot, nationalist, lover of mankind.

911 MISANTHROPY (*Substantives*), egotism, egoism, incivism, want of patriotism, moroseness, selfishness (943); misogynism.

A misanthrope, egotist, cynic, man-hater, Timon, Diogenes.

Woman-hater, misogynist.

(*Adjectives*) Misanthropic, misanthropical, antisocial, unpatriotic, fish, egotistical, morose, sullen, maladjusted.

(*Adjectives*) Philanthropic, philanthropical, humanitarian, humane, utilitarian, patriotic, altruistic, public-spirited.

(*Phrases*) '*Humani nihil a me alienum puto*'; *pro bono publico*; the greatest happiness of the greatest number.

912 BENEFACTOR (*Substantives*), saviour, good genius, tutelary saint, guardian angel, fairy godmother, good Samaritan.

(*Phrase*) *Deus ex machina*.

913 Maleficent being.

EVILDOER (*Substantives*), wrongdoer, mischief-maker, marplot, anarchist, nihilist, terrorist, firebrand, incendiary, evil genius (980).

Frankenstein's monster.

Savage, brute, ruffian, blackguard, villain, scoundrel, cutthroat, barbarian, caitiff, desperado, jail-bird, hooligan, tough, rough, teddy boy, larrikin, hoodlum, gangster, crook, yegg, apache (949).

Fiend, tiger, hyena, bloodhound, butcher, blood-sucker, vampire, ogre, ghoul, serpent, snake, adder, viper, rattlesnake, scorpion, hell-hound, hag, hellbag, beldam, harpy, siren, fury, Jezebel.

Monster, demon, imp, devil (980), anthropophagi, Attila, vandal, Hun, Goth.

(*Phrases*) A snake in the grass; a scourge of the human race; a fiend in human shape; worker of iniquity.

3°. *Special Sympathetic Affections*

914 PITY (*Substantives*), compassion, commiseration, sympathy, fellow-feeling, tenderness, yearning.

Forbearance, mercy, humanity, clemency, leniency, ruth, long-suffering, quarter.

(*Phrases*) The melting mood; *coup de grâce*; bowels of compassion; *argumentum ad misericordiam*.

(Verbs) To pity, commiserate, compassionate, sympathize, feel for, yearn for, console, enter into the feelings of, have or take pity; show or have mercy; to forbear, relent, thaw, spare, relax, give quarter.

To excite pity, touch, soften, melt, propitiate, disarm.

To ask for pity, mercy, etc.; to supplicate, implore, deprecate, appeal to, cry for quarter, etc.; beg one's life, kneel, fall on one's knees, etc.

(Phrase) To put one out of one's misery.

(Adjectives) Pitying, commiserating, etc.

Pitiful, compassionate, tender, clement, merciful, lenient, relenting, etc.; soft-hearted, sympathetic, touched, weak, soft, melting, unhardened (740).

Piteous, pitiable, sorry, miserable.

(Phrases) Tender as a woman; one's heart bleeding for.

(Interjections) For pity's sake! mercy! God help you! poor thing! poor fellow!

915 CONDOLENCE *(Substantives)*, lamentation, lament (839), sympathy, consolation.

(Verbs) To condole with, console, solace, sympathize; express, testify, etc., pity; to afford or supply consolation, grieve for, lament with, weep with (839).

4°. *Retrospective Sympathetic Affections*

916 GRATITUDE *(Substantives)*, gratefulness, thankfulness, feeling of obligation.

Acknowledgment, recognition, thanksgiving, giving thanks.

Thanks, praise, benediction, grace, paean, Te Deum (990).

Requital, thank-offering.

(Verbs) To be grateful, etc.; to thank, to give, render, return, offer, tender thanks, acknowledgments, etc.; to acknowledge, appreciate, requite.

To lie under an obligation, to be obliged, beholden, etc.

(Phrases) To overflow with gratitude; to thank one's stars; never to forget.

(Adjectives) Grateful, thankful, obliged, beholden, indebted to, under obligation.

917 INGRATITUDE *(Substantives)*, ungratefulness, thanklessness, oblivion of benefits.

(Phrases) 'Benefits forgot'; a thankless task.

(Verbs) To be ungrateful, etc.; to forget benefits.

(Phrases) To look a gift-horse in the mouth; to bite the hand that fed one.

(Adjectives) Ungrateful, unmindful, unthankful, thankless, ingrate, inappreciative.

Forgotten, unacknowledged, unthanked, unrequited, unrewarded, ill-requited.

(Phrase) Thank you for nothing.

(Interjections) Thanks! many thanks! ta! *merci!* gramercy! much obliged! thank heaven! heaven be praised!

918 FORGIVENESS *(Substantives)*, pardon, condonation, grace, remission, absolution, amnesty, indemnity, oblivion, indulgence, reprieve.

Reconcilement, reconciliation, appeasement, mollification, shaking of hands, pacification (723).

919 REVENGE *(Substantives)*, vengeance, revengement, avengement, vendetta, feud, retaliation.

Rancour, vindictiveness, implacability.

Revenger, avenger, vindicator, Nemesis, Furies.

Excuse, exoneration, quittance, acquittal, propitiation, exculpation.

Longanimity, forbearance, placability.

(*Verbs*) To forgive, pardon, excuse, pass over, overlook, bear with, condone, absolve, pass, let off, remit, reprieve, exculpate, exonerate.

To allow for; to make allowance for.

To conciliate, propitiate, pacify, appease, placate, reconcile.

(*Phrases*) To make it up; to forgive and forget; to shake hands; to heal the breach; to kiss and be friends; to bury the hatchet; to wipe the slate clean; to let bygones be bygones.

(*Verbs*) To revenge, take revenge, avenge.

(*Phrases*) To wreak one's vengeance; to visit the sins on; to breathe vengeance; to have a bone to pick with; to have accounts to settle; to have a rod in pickle; to get one's knife into; to take one's change out of.

To harbour vindictive feelings; to rankle in the breast.

(*Adjectives*) Revengeful, revanchist, vindictive, vengeful, rancorous, unforgiving, pitiless, ruthless, remorseless, unrelenting, relentless, implacable, rigorous.

(*Adjectives*) Forgiving, etc., unreproachful, placable, conciliatory. Forgiven, etc., unresented.

920 JEALOUSY (*Substantives*), jealousness, heartburning.
(*Phrases*) A jaundiced eye; the green-eyed monster.
(*Verbs*) To be jealous, etc.; to view with jealousy.
(*Adjectives*) Jealous, jaundiced, yellow-eyed.
(*Phrase*) Eaten up with jealousy.

921 ENVY (*Substantives*), rivalry, emulation, covetousness; a Thersites, Zoilus.
(*Verbs*) To envy, rival, emulate, covet.
(*Adjectives*) Envious, invidious, covetous.
(*Phrase*) Bursting with envy.

SECTION IV—MORAL AFFECTIONS

1°. *Moral Obligation*

922 RIGHT (*Substantives*), what ought to be, what should be; goodness, virtue (944), rectitude, probity (939).

Justice, equity, equitableness, fitness, fairness, fair play, impartiality, reasonableness, propriety.

Astraea, Themis.

(*Phrases*) The scales of justice; even-handed justice; *suum cuique*; a fair field and no favour; *lex talionis*; '*Fiat justitia, ruat coelum.*'

Morality, morals, ethics, duty (926).

(*Verbs*) To stand to reason; to be right, just, etc.

To deserve, merit; to be worthy of, to be entitled to (924).

923 WRONG (*Substantives*), what ought not to be, badness, evil (945), turpitude, improbity (940).

Injustice, unfairness, inequity, foul play, partiality, favour, favouritism, leaning, bias, party spirit, undueness (925), unreasonableness, tort, unlawfulness (964), encroachment, imposition.

(*Verbs*) To be wrong, unjust, etc.; to favour, lean towards, show partiality, to encroach, impose upon.

(*Phrase*) To rob Peter to pay Paul.

(*Adjectives*) Wrong, wrongful, bad, unjust, unfair, undue, inequitable, unequal, partial, invidious, one-sided, improper, unreasonable, iniquitous, unfit, immoral (945).

(*Phrases*) To do justice to; to see justice done; to hold the scales even; to see fair play; to see one righted; to serve one right; to give the devil his due; to give and take; *audire alteram partem*.

(*Adjectives*) Right, just, equitable, fair, equal, even-handed, impartial, judicial, legitimate, justifiable, rightful, reasonable, fit, proper, becoming, decorous, decent (926).

Deserved, merited, condign (924).

(*Adverbs*) Rightly, in justice, in equity, fairly, etc., in reason, without distinction, without respect of persons.

(*Phrases*) *En règle*; *de jure*.

924 DUENESS (*Substantives*), due.

Right, privilege, prerogative, title, claim, qualification, pretension, birthright, prescription, immunity, exemption, licence, liberty, franchise, enfranchisement, vested interest.

Sanction, authority, warranty, tenure, bond, security, lien, constitution, charter, warrant (760), patent, letters patent, copyright, *imprimatur*.

A claimant, pretender, appellant, plaintiff (938).

Women's rights, feminism; feminist, suffragist, suffragette.

(*Verbs*) To be due, etc., to.

To have a right to, to be entitled to, to be qualified for, to have a claim upon, a title to, etc.; to deserve, merit, be worthy of.

To demand, claim, call upon, exact, insist on, challenge, to come upon one for, to revendicate, make a point of, enforce, put in force, use a right.

To appertain to, belong to, etc. (777).

To lay claim to, assert, assume, arrogate, make good, substantiate; to vindicate a claim, etc., to make out a case.

To give or confer a right; to entitle, authorize, warrant, sanction, sanctify, privilege, enfranchise, license, legalize, ordain, prescribe, allot.

(*Adjectives*) Having a right to, a claim to, etc.; due to, entitled to, deserving, meriting, worthy of, claiming, qualified.

Unjustified, **unjustifiable**, unwarranted, unauthorized, unallowable, unwarrantable.

(*Phrases*) In the wrong; in the wrong box.

(*Adverbs*) Wrongly, unjustly, etc., amiss.

(*Phrase*) It won't do.

———

925 Absence of right.

UNDUENESS (*Substantives*), unlawfulness, impropriety, unfitness, illegality (964).

Falseness, spuriousness, emptiness or invalidity of title, illegitimacy.

Loss of right, forfeiture, disfranchisement.

Usurpation, violation, breach, encroachment, stretch, imposition, relaxation.

(*Verbs*) Not to be due, etc., to; to be undue, etc.

Too infringe, encroach, violate, do violence to; to stretch or strain a point; to trench on, usurp.

To disfranchise, disentitle, disfrock, unfrock; to disqualify, invalidate, relax.

To misbecome, misbehave (945).

(*Adjectives*) Undue, unlawful, illicit, unconstitutional.

Unauthorized, unwarranted, unsanctioned, unjustified, unprivileged, illegitimate, bastard, spurious, supposititious, false, usurped, unchartered, unfulfilled, unofficial, unauthorized.

Unentitled, disentitled, unqualified, underprivileged; disfranchised, forfeit.

Undeserved, unmerited, unearned.

Improper, unmeet, unbecoming, unfit, misbecoming, unseemly, preposterous.

(*Phrases*) Not the thing; out of the question; not to be thought of; out of court.

———

Privileged, allowed, sanctioned, warranted, authorized, permitted, licit, ordained, prescribed, chartered, enfranchised, constitutional, official.

Prescriptive, presumptive, absolute, indefeasible, unalienable, inalienable, imprescriptible, inviolable, unimpeachable, unchallenged, sacred, sacrosanct.

Condign, merited, deserved.

Allowable, permissible, lawful, legitimate, legal, legalized (963), proper, square, equitable, unexceptionable, reasonable (922), right, correct, meet, fitting (926).

(*Adverbs*) Duly, by right, by divine right, *ex officio, Dei gratia, de jure.*

926 DUTY (*Substantives*), what ought to be done; moral obligation, accountableness, accountability, liability, onus, responsibility, bounden duty; dueness (924).

Allegiance, fealty, tie, office, function, province, post, engagement (768).

Morality, morals, conscience, accountableness, conscientiousness; the Decalogue, the Ten Commandments.

Dueness, propriety, fitness, decency, seemliness, decorum.

Observance, fulfilment, discharge, performance, acquittal, satisfaction, redemption, good behaviour.

Science of morals, ethics, deontology; moral or ethical philosophy, casuistry.

(*Phrases*) The thing; the proper thing; a case of conscience; the still small voice.

(*Verbs*) To be the duty of, to be due to, to be up to; ought to be; to be incumbent on, to behove, befit, become, beseem, belong to, pertain to, devolve on, to be on one's head; to be, or stand, or lie under an obligation; to have to answer for, to be accountable for, to owe it to oneself, to be in duty bound, to be committed to, to be on one's good behaviour.

To impose a duty or obligation; to enjoin, require, exact, bind, pin down, saddle with, prescribe, assign, call upon, look to, oblige.

927 DERELICTION OF DUTY (*Substantives*), guilt (947), sin (945), neglect, negligence, non-observance, failure, evasion, dead letter.

(*Verbs*) To violate, break, break through, infringe, set at naught, slight, neglect, trample on, evade, contravene, disregard, renounce, repudiate, quit, forswear, fail, transgress.

(*Phrase*) To wash one's hands of.

927A EXEMPTION (*Substantives*), freedom, irresponsibility, immunity, liberty, licence, release, exoneration, excuse, dispensation, absolution, franchise, renunciation, discharge.

(*Verbs*) To be exempt, free, at liberty, released, excused, exonerated, absolved, etc.

To exempt, release, excuse, exonerate, absolve, acquit, free, set at liberty, discharge, set aside, let off, remit, passover, spare, excuse, license, dispense with; to give dispensation.

(*Phrase*) To stretch a point.

(*Adjectives*) Exempt, free, released, at liberty, absolved, exonerated, excused, let off, discharged, licensed, acquitted, unencumbered, dispensed, scot-free, immune.

Irresponsible, unaccountable, unanswerable, unbound.

———

To do one's duty, to enter upon a duty; to perform, observe, fulfil, discharge, adhere to; acquit oneself of an obligation.

(*Phrases*) To be at one's post; to redeem one's pledge; to toe the mark or line.

(*Adjectives*) Dutiful, duteous, docile, obedient, compliant, tractable.

Obligatory, binding, imperative, peremptory, mandatory, behoving, incumbent on, chargeable on, meet, due to.

Being under obligation, under obedience, obliged by, beholden to, bound by, tied by, saddled with, indebted to.

Amenable, liable, accountable, responsible, answerable.

Right, proper, fit, due, correct, seemly, fitting, befitting, decent, meet.

Moral, ethical, casuistical, conscientious.

(*Adverbs*) Conscientiously, with a safe conscience; as in duty bound; on one's own responsibility.

2°. *Moral Sentiments*

928 RESPECT (*Substantives*), deference, reverence, regard, consideration, attention, honour, esteem, estimation, distance, decorum, veneration, admiration.

Homage, fealty, obeisance, genuflexion, kneeling, salaam, kowtow, presenting arms (896), prostration, obsequiousness, devotion, worship (990).

(*Verbs*) To respect, honour, reverence, regard, defer to, pay respect or deference to, render honour to, look up to, esteem, revere, think much of, think highly of, venerate, hallow.

To pay homage to, bow to, take off one's hat to, kneel to, bend the knee to, present arms, fall down before, prostrate oneself.

To command or inspire respect; to awe, overawe, dazzle.

(*Phrases*) To keep one's distance; to make way for; to observe due decorum.

(*Adjectives*) Respecting, etc., respectful, considerate, polite, attentive, reverential, obsequious, ceremonious, bare-headed, cap in hand, on one's knees, prostrate.

Respected, esteemed, honoured, hallowed, venerable, emeritus.

(*Phrases*) Saving your presence; begging your honour's pardon.

———

929 DISRESPECT (*Substantives*), irreverence, dishonour, disparagement, slight, neglect, disesteem, disestimation, superciliousness, contumely, indignity, insult, rudeness.

Ridicule (856), sarcasm, derision, scurrility, mockery, scoffing, sibilation.

A jeer, gibe, taunt, scoff, sneer (930), hiss, hoot, fling, flout.

(*Verbs*) To treat with disrespect, etc., to disparage, dishonour, misprise, vilipend, slight, insult, affront, disregard, make light of, hold in, no esteem, esteem of no account, set at naught, speak slightingly of, set down, pass by, overlook, look down upon, despise (930).

To deride, scoff, sneer at, laugh at, ridicule (856), roast, guy, rag, mock, jeer, taunt, twit, flout, gibe, hiss, hoot, boo.

(*Phrases*) To make game of; to point the finger at; to make a fool of; to turn into ridicule; to laugh to scorn; to turn one's back upon.

(*Adjectives*) Disrespectful, slighting, disparaging (934), dishonouring, scornful (940), irreverent, supercilious, contumelious, scurrilous, deriding, derisive, derisory.

Unrespected, unworshipped, unregarded, disregarded, ignored.

(*Adverbs*) Disrespectfully, cavalierly, etc.

930 CONTEMPT (*Substantives*), disdain, scorn, contumely, despisal, slight, sneer, spurn, sniff; a byword.

Scornfulness, disdainfulness, haughtiness, contemptuousness, superciliousness, derision (929).

The state of being despised, despisedness.

(*Verbs*) To despise, contemn, scorn, disdain, scout, spurn, look down upon, lisregard, slight, make light of, not mind, hold cheap, hold in contempt, >ooh-pooh, sneeze at, sniff at, whistle at, hoot, flout, trample upon.

(*Phrases*) Not to care a straw, fig, button, etc., for (643); to turn up one's nose at; to shrug one's shoulders; to snap one's fingers at; to take no account of; to laugh to scorn; to make light of; to tread or trample under foot; to set at naught; to point the finger of scorn at.

(*Adjectives*) Contemptuous, disdainful, scornful, contumelious, cavalier, derisive, supercilious, toplofty, upstage, sniffy, sardonic.

Contemptible, despicable, poor, paltry (643), downtrodden, unenvied.

(*Interjections*) A fig for! hoots! bah! pshaw! pish! shucks! pooh-pooh! fiddlestick! fiddle-de-dee! tush! tut!

931 APPROBATION (*Substantives*), approval, approvement, endorsement, sanction, esteem, admiration, estimation, good opinion, appreciation, regard, account, popularity, kudos.

Commendation, praise, laud, laudation, advocacy, good word; meed or tribute of praise, encomium, eulogium, eulogy, *éloge*, panegyric, puff, blurb, homage.

Applause, plaudit, cheer, clap, clapping, clapping of hands, acclamation; paean, benediction, blessing, benison, hosanna; claque.

(*Phrases*) A peal, shout, or chorus of applause; golden opinions; *succès d'estime*.

(*Verbs*) To approve, think well or highly of, esteem, appreciate, value, prize, admire, countenance, endorse.

To commend, speak well of, recommend, advocate, praise, laud, belaud, compliment, bepraise, clap, clap hands, applaud, cheer, panegyrize, celebrate, eulogize, cry up, root for, crack up, write up, extol, glorify, magnify, puff, boom, boost, exalt, swell, bless, give a blessing to.

To deserve praise, etc., to be praised, etc.

(*Phrases*) To set great store by; to sing the praises of; to extol to the skies; to applaud to the echo; to stick up for; to say a good word for; to pat on the back.

To redound to the honour or praise of; to do credit to.

To win golden opinions; to be in high favour; to bring down the house.

(*Adjectives*) Approving, etc., commendatory, complimentary, bene-

932 DISAPPROBATION (*Substantives*), disapproval, dislike (867), blame, censure, reprobation, obloquy, dispraise, contumely, odium, disesteem, depreciation, detraction (934), condemnation, ostracism.

Reprobation, exprobration, insinuation, innuendo, animadversion, reflection, stricture, objection, exception, criticism, critique, correction, discommendation.

Satire, sneer, fling, gibe, skit, squib, quip, taunt, sarcasm, lampoon, cavil, pasquinade, recrimination, castigation.

Remonstrance, reprehension, reproof, admonition, expostulation, reproach, rebuke, reprimand, talking-to, telling-off.

Evil speaking, hard words, foul language, personalities, ribaldry, Billingsgate, unparliamentary language.

Upbraiding, abuse, invective, vituperation, scolding, wigging, dressing-down, objurgation, jaw, railing, jobation, nagging, reviling, contumely, execration (908).

A set-down, trimming, rating, slap, snub, frown, scowl, black look.

A lecture, curtain lecture, diatribe, jeremiad, tirade, philippic; clamour, outcry, hue and cry, hiss, hissing, sibilation, cat-call.

(*Phrases*) A rap on the knuckles; a slap in the face; a left-handed compliment.

(*Verbs*) To disapprove, dislike (867), dispraise, find fault with, criticize, glance at, insinuate, cut up, carp at, cavil, point at, peck at, nibble at, object to, take exception

dictory, laudatory, panegyrical, eulo-gistic, encomiastic.

Approved, praised, uncensured, unimpeached, admired, popular, de-serving or worthy of praise, praise-worthy, commendable, estimable, plausible, meritorious.

(*Phrases*) Lavish of praise; lost in admiration.

(*Interjections*) Well done! good man! stout fellow! good show! atta-boy! bravo! bravissimo! *euge!* that's the stuff! hear, hear!

to, animadvert upon, protest against, frown upon, bar.

To disparage, depreciate, depre-cate, crab, knock, traduce, smear, speak ill of, decry, vilify, vilipend defame, detract (934), revile, satirize, sneer, gibe, lampoon, inveigh against, write down, scalp.

To blame; to lay or cast blame upon, reflect upon, cast a slur upon, censure, pass censure on, impugn show up, denounce, censure, brand, stigmatize, reprobate, improbate.

To reprehend, reprimand, ad-monish, remonstrate, expostulate, reprove, pull up, take up, set down snub, twit, taunt, reproach, load with reproaches, rebuke, come down upon, sit on, pitch into, get on to, tell off, tick off.

To chide, scold, wig, rate, objurgate, upbraid, vituperate, recriminate anathematize, abuse, call names, exclaim against, jaw, mob, trounce trim, rail at, nag, nag at, bark at, blackguard, revile, ballyrag, rag natter, blow up, roast, lecture; castigate, chastise, correct, lash, flay to fulminate against, fall foul of.

To cry out against, cry down, run down, clamour, hiss, hoot; to accuse (938), to find guilty, ostracize, blacklist, blackball.

To scandalize, shock, revolt, incur blame, excite disapprobation.

(*Phrases*) To set one's face against; to shake the head at; to take a poor or dim view of; to view with dark or jaundiced eyes; to pick holes in; to give a thing the bird; to damn with faint praise; to pluck a crow with; to have a fling at; to read a lecture; to put on the carpet (or mat); to take to task; to bring to book; to haul over the coals; to tear one off a strip; to shoot down in flames; to pull to pieces; to cut up; to cast in one's teeth; to abuse like a pickpocket; to speak or look daggers; to rail in good set terms; to give it one hot; to throw mud; to give a person the rough side of one's tongue.

To forfeit the good opinion of; to catch it; to be under a cloud; to carry the can; to stand corrected.

(*Adjectives*) Disapproving, disparaging, etc., condemnatory, damna-tory, denunciatory, reproachful, abusive, objurgatory, clamorous, vituperative, dyslogistic.

Censorious, critical, carping, satirical, sarcastic, sardonic, cynical, dry, hypercritical, captious; sharp, cutting, mordant, biting, withering, trenchant, caustic, severe, scathing; squeamish, fastidious, strait-laced (868).

Disapproved, chid, unapproved, blown upon, unblest, unlamented, unbewailed.

Blameworthy, uncommendable, exceptionable (649, 945).

(*Phrases*) Hard upon one; weighed in the balance and found wanting; not to be thought of.

(*Interjections*) Bad show! shame!

---

933 FLATTERY (*Substantives*), adu-lation, sycophancy, blandishment, cajolery, fawning, wheedling, coaxing,

934 DETRACTION (*Substantives*), obloquy, scurrility, scandal, vilifica-tion, smear, defamation, aspersion,

dunkeyism, toad-eating, toadyism, tuft-hunting, back-scratching, blandiloquence, schmalz.

Incense, honeyed words, flummery, soft sawder, soft soap, butter, applesauce, blarney, malarkey; mouthhonour, lip-service.

(*Verbs*) To flatter, wheedle, cajole, fawn upon, coax (615), humour, gloze, butter, toady, sugar, bespatter, beslaver, earwig, jolly, flannel, truckle to, pander to, court, pay court to.

(*Phrases*) To curry favour with; to lay it on thick; to lay it on with a trowel; to ingratiate oneself with; to bol to the top of one's bent.

(*Adjectives*) Flattering, adulatory, mealy-mouthed, smooth, honeyed, candied, soapy, oily, unctuous, fairspoken, plausible, servile, sycophantic, fulsome; courtier-like.

935 FLATTERER (*Substantives*), adulator, eulogist, encomiast, whitewasher, toady, sycophant, toad-eater, *prôneur*, touter, booster, *claqueur*, spaniel, back-scratcher, flunkey, lickspittle, pick-thank, earwig, tufthunter, hanger-on, courtier, parasite, doer of dirty work, *âme damnée*, *Graeculus esuriens*.

937 VINDICATION (*Substantives*), justification, exoneration, exculpation, acquittal, whitewashing.

Extenuation, palliation, mitigation, softening; extenuating circumstances.

Plea, excuse, apology, defence, gloss, varnish, salvo (617).

Vindicator, apologist, justifier, defender.

(*Verbs*) To vindicate, justify, warrant, exculpate, acquit, clear, set right, exonerate, disculpate, whitewash.

To extenuate, palliate, excuse, soften, apologize, varnish, slur, gloze, gloss over, bolster up.

To plead, advocate, defend, stand up for, stick up for, speak for, make good, bear out, say in defence, contend for.

traducement, slander, calumny, backbiting, criticism, slating, personality, evil-speaking, disparagement, depreciation (932).

Libel, lampoon, skit, squib, sarcasm.

(*Verbs*) To detract, criticize, asperse, depreciate, derogate, disparage, cheapen, blow upon, bespatter, blacken, denigrate, defame, brand, malign, decry, vilify, vilipend, backbite, libel, slate, lampoon, traduce, slander, calumniate, run down, write down.

(*Phrases*) To speak ill of one behind one's back; to damn with faint praise; to sell oneself short.

(*Adjectives*) Detracting, disparaging, libellous, scurrilous, abusive, cynical (932), foul-tongued, foulmouthed, slanderous, defamatory, calumnious, calumniatory.

936 DETRACTOR (*Substantives*), disapprover, critic, censor, caviller, carper, knocker, *frondeur*, defamer, backbiter, slanderer, traducer, libeller, calumniator, lampooner, satirist, candid friend, Thersites.

---

938 ACCUSATION (*Substantives*), charge, imputation, inculpation, exprobration, delation, crimination, recrimination, invective, jeremiad (932).

Denunciation, denouncement, challenge, indictment, libel, delation, citation, arraignment, impeachment, appeachment, bill of indictment, true bill, condemnation (971), scandal (934), *scandalum magnatum*.

Accuser, prosecutor, plaintiff, pursuer, informer, appellant, complainant.

Accused, defendant, prisoner, panel, respondent.

(*Phrases*) The gravamen of a charge; *argumentum ad hominem*.

(*Verbs*) To accuse, charge, tax, impute, twit, taunt with, slur, reproach, brand with, stigmatize, criminate,

(*Phrases*) To put in a good word for; to plead the cause of; to put a good face upon; to keep in countenance; to make allowance for.

(*Adjectives*) Vindicatory, vindicative, palliative, exculpatory; vindicating, etc.

Excusable, defensible, pardonable, venial, specious, plausible, justifiable, warrantable.

(*Phrases*) '*Honi soit qui mal y pense*'; *qui s'excuse s'accuse.*

incriminate, inculpate (932), implicate, saddle with.

To inform against; to indict, denounce, arraign, impeach, challenge, show up, pull up, cite, prosecute, summon.

(*Phrases*) To lay to one's door; to lay to one's charge; bring home to; to call to account; to bring to book; to take to task; to trump up a charge; to brand with reproach.

(*Adjectives*) Accusing, etc., accusatory, accusative, imputative, denunciatory, criminative, criminatory, incriminatory, accusable, imputable

Indefensible, inexcusable, unpardonable, unjustifiable (945).

3°. *Moral Conditions*

939 PROBITY (*Substantives*), integrity, uprightness, honesty, virtue (944), rectitude, faith, good faith, bona fides, fairness, honour, fair play, justice, principle, constancy, fidelity, incorruptibility.

Trustworthiness, trustiness, reliability, dependableness, grace, uncorruptedness, impartiality, equity, candour, veracity (545), straightforwardness, truth, equitableness, singleness of heart.

Conscientiousness, punctiliousness, nicety, scrupulosity, delicacy, sense of decency, strictness, punctuality.

Dignity, respectability, reputableness (873).

A man of honour, a gentleman, a man of his word, a sportsman, white man, trump, brick, *preux chevalier.*

(*Phrases*) The court of honour; a fair field and no favour; 'a verray parfit gentil knight.'

(*Verbs*) To be honourable, etc.; to keep one's word, to give and take, to deal honourably, squarely, impartially, fairly.

(*Phrases*) To hit straight from the shoulder; to play the game.

(*Adjectives*) Upright, honest, virtuous (944), honourable, fair, right, just, equitable, impartial, evenhanded, square, constant, faithful, loyal, staunch, straight.

940 IMPROBITY (*Substantives*) wickedness (945), bad faith, unfairness, infidelity, faithlessness, want of faith, dishonesty, disloyalty, falseness, falsity, one-sidedness, disingenuousness, shabbiness, littleness, meanness, caddishness, baseness, villainy, roguery, rascality, vileness, abjectness, turpitude, unreliability, untrustworthiness, insidiousness, knavery, knavishness, fraud (545), falsehood (544), shenanigans.

Disgrace, ignominy, infamy, tarnish, blot, stain, spot, slur, pollution, derogation, degradation (874).

Perfidy, perfidiousness, treason, high treason, perjury, apostasy (607), backsliding, breach of faith, defection, disloyalty, disaffection, foul play, sharp practice, graft, doubledealing, betrayal, treacherousness, treachery.

(*Phrases*) The kiss of Judas; divided allegiance; Punic faith.

(*Verbs*) To be of bad faith, dishonest, etc.; to play false, break one's word or faith, betray, forswear, shuffle (545).

To disgrace oneself, derogate, stoop, demean oneself, lose caste, dishonour oneself, sneak, crawl, grovel.

(*Phrases*) To seal one's infamy; to sell oneself; to go over to the enemy.

Trustworthy, trusty, reliable, dependable, tried, incorruptible, straightforward, ingenuous (703), frank, open-hearted, candid.

Conscientious, tender-conscienced, high-principled, high-minded, high-toned, scrupulous, strict, nice, punctilious, correct, punctual, inviolable, inviolate, unviolated, unbroken, unbetrayed.

Chivalrous, gentlemanlike, respectable, unbought, unbribed, unstained, stainless, untarnished, unsullied, untainted, unperjured, innocent (946).

(*Phrases*) Jealous of honour; as good as one's word; true to one's colours; *sans peur et sans reproche*; *integer vitae scelerisque purus*.

(*Adverbs*) Honourably, etc., bona fide; on the square; on the up and up.

(*Adjectives*) Dishonest, unfair, one-sided, fraudulent (545), bent, knavish, wicked (945), false, faithless, unfaithful, foul, disingenuous, trothless, trustless, untrustworthy, unreliable, slippery, double-faced, double-tongued, crooked, tortuous, unscrupulous, insidious, treacherous, perfidious, false-hearted, perjured, rascally.

Base, vile, grovelling, dirty, scurvy, scabby, low, low-down, abject, shabby, caddish, mean, paltry, pitiful, inglorious, scrubby, beggarly, putid, unworthy, disgraceful, dishonourable, derogatory, low-thoughted, disreputable, unhandsome, unbecoming (925), unbefitting, ungentlemanly, unmanly, unwomanly, undignified, base-minded, recreant, low-minded, blackguard, pettifogging, underhand, underhanded, unsportsmanlike.

(*Phrases*) Lost to shame; dead to honour.

(*Adverbs*) Dishonestly, etc., *mala fide*, on the crook.

941 KNAVE (*Substantives*), bad man (949), rogue, rascal, scoundrel, villain, spiv, sharper, shyster, blackleg, scab, trimmer, time-server, timist, turncoat, badmash, Vicar of Bray, Judas (607).

Apostate, renegade, pervert, black sheep, traitor, arch-traitor, quisling, fifth columnist, deviationist, betrayer, recreant, miscreant, cullion, outcast, mean wretch, slubberdegullion, snake in the grass, wolf in sheep's clothing.

942 UNSELFISHNESS (*Substantives*), selflessness, disinterestedness, generosity, high-mindedness, nobleness, elevation, liberality, greatness, loftiness, exaltation, magnanimity, chivalry, chivalrous spirit, heroism, sublimity, altruism, self-forgetfulness, unworldliness.

Self-denial, self-abnegation, self-sacrifice, self-restraint, self-control, devotion, stoicism.

(*Phrases*) To put oneself in the background, in the place of others; to do as one would be done by.

(*Adjectives*) Unselfish, selfless, self-forgetful, handsome, generous, liberal, noble, princely, great, high, high-minded, elevated, lofty, exalted, spirited, stoical, self-denying, self-sacrificing, self-devoted, magnanimous, chivalrous, heroic, sublime, unworldly.

943 SELFISHNESS (*Substantives*), egotism, egoism, self-regard, self-love, self-indulgence, worldliness, worldly-mindedness, earthly-mindedness, self-interest, opportunism.

Illiberality, meanness, baseness.

A time-server, tuft-hunter, fortune-hunter, gold-digger, jobber, worldling, self-seeker, opportunist, hog, road-hog.

(*Phrase*) A dog in the manger.

(*Verbs*) To be selfish, etc., to indulge oneself, coddle oneself.

(*Phrases*) To look after one's own interest; to take care of number one; to have an eye for the main chance.

(*Adjectives*) Selfish, egotistical, egoistical, self-indulgent, apolaustic, self-regarding, self-centred, illiberal, self-seeking, mercenary, venal, mean, ungenerous, interested.

Unbought, unbribed, pure, uncorrupted, incorruptible.

(*Adverb*) *En prince.*

---

944 VIRTUE (*Substantives*), virtuousness, goodness, righteousness, morals, morality (926), rectitude, correctness, dutifulness, conscientiousness, integrity, probity (939), uprightness, nobleness, nobility; innocence (946).

Merit, worth, worthiness, desert, excellence, credit, self-control, self-conquest, self-government, self-respect.

Well-doing, good actions, good behaviour, a well-spent life.

(*Verbs*) To be virtuous, etc.; to act well; to do, fulfil, perform, or discharge one's duty, to acquit oneself well, to practise virtue; to command or master one's passions (926).

(*Phrases*) To have one's heart in the right place; to keep in the right path; to fight the good fight; to set an example; to be on one's good behaviour.

(*Adjectives*) Virtuous, good, innocent (946), meritorious, deserving, worthy, correct, dutiful, duteous (926), moral, ethical, righteous, right-minded (939), laudable, well-intentioned, creditable, commendable, praiseworthy, excellent, admirable, sterling, pure, noble, well-conducted, well-behaved.

Exemplary, matchless, peerless, saintly, saint-like, heaven-born, angelic, seraphic, godlike.

(*Phrase*) *Mens sibi conscia recti.*

(*Adverb*) Virtuously, etc.

Worldly, earthly, mundane, time-serving, worldly-minded.

(*Phrases*) To serve one's private ends; from interested motives; charity begins at home; I'm all right, Jack.

945 VICE (*Substantives*), evildoing, wrongdoing, wickedness, sin, iniquity, unrighteousness, demerit, unworthiness, worthlessness, badness.

Immorality, impropriety, indecorum, laxity, looseness of morals, want of principle, obliquity, backsliding, recidivism, gracelessness, infamy, demoralization, pravity, depravity, depravation, obduracy, hardness of heart, brutality (907), corruption, pollution, dissoluteness, debauchery, grossness, baseness, knavery, roguery, rascality, villainy (940), profligacy, abandonment, flagrancy, atrocity, devilry (or deviltry), criminality, guilt (947).

Infirmity, weakness, feebleness, frailty, imperfection, error, weak side or point, blind side, foible, failing, failure, defect, deficiency, indiscretion, peccability.

(*Phrases*) The cloven hoof; the old Adam; the lowest dregs of vice; a sink of iniquity; the primrose path.

(*Verbs*) To be vicious, etc.; to sin, commit sin, do amiss, misdo, err, transgress, go astray, misdemean or misconduct oneself, misbehave; to fall, lapse, slip, trip, offend, trespass.

To render vicious, etc., to demoralize, corrupt, seduce, debauch, debase, vitiate.

(*Phrases*) To deviate from the line of duty or from the paths of virtue, rectitude, etc.; to blot one's copybook; to hug a sin or fault; to sow one's wild oats.

(*Adjectives*) Vicious, bad, sinful, wicked, evil, evil-minded, immoral, iniquitous, unprincipled, demoralized, unconscionable, worthless, unworthy, good for nothing, graceless, heartless, virtueless, undutiful, unrighteous, unmoral, amoral, guilty (947).

Wrong, culpable, naughty, incorrect, indictable, criminal, dissolute, debauched, disorderly, raffish, corrupt, profligate, depraved, degenerate, abandoned, graceless, shameless, recreant, villainous, sunk, lost, obdurate, reprobate, incorrigible, irreclaimable, ill-conditioned.

Weak, frail, lax, infirm, spineless, invertebrate, imperfect, indiscreet, erring, transgressing, sinning, etc., peccable, peccant.

Blamable, reprehensible, blameworthy, uncommendable, discreditable, disreputable, shady, exceptionable.

Indecorous, unseemly, improper, sinister, base, ignoble, scurvy, foul, gross, vile, black, felonious, nefarious, scandalous, infamous, villainous, heinous, grave, flagrant, flagitious, atrocious, satanic, satanical, diabolic, diabolical, hellish, infernal, stygian, fiendlike, fiendish, devilish, miscreated, misbegotten, hell-born, demoniacal.

Unpardonable, unforgivable, indefensible, inexcusable, irremissible, inexpiable.

(*Phrases*) Past praying for; of the deepest dye; not having a word to say for oneself; weighed in the balance and found wanting; *in flagrante delicto.*

(*Adverbs*) Wrongly, etc.; without excuse, too bad.

---

946 INNOCENCE (*Substantives*), guiltlessness, harmlessness, innocuousness, incorruption, impeccability, inerrability, blamelessness, sinlessness.

A newborn babe, lamb, dove.

(*Phrases*) Clean hands; a clear conscience.

(*Verbs*) To be innocent, etc.

(*Adjectives*) Innocent, guiltless, not guilty, faultless, sinless, clear, spotless, stainless, immaculate, unspotted, innocuous, unblemished, untarnished, unsullied, undefiled.

Inculpable, unblamed, blameless, unblamable, clean-handed, irreproachable, unreproached, unimpeachable, unimpeached, unexceptionable, inerrable, unerring.

Harmless, inoffensive, unoffending, dovelike, lamblike, pure, uncorrupted, undefiled, undepraved, undebauched, chaste, unhardened, unsophisticated, unreproved.

(*Phrases*) Innocent as an unborn babe; in the clear; above suspicion; more sinned against than sinning.

(*Adverbs*) Innocently, etc.

947 GUILT (*Substantives*), sin, guiltiness, culpability, criminality, criminousness, sinfulness.

Misconduct, misbehaviour, misdoing, malpractice, malefaction, malfeasance, misprision, dereliction, *corpus delicti.*

Indiscretion, peccadillo, lapse, slip, trip, *faux pas*, fault, error, flaw, blot, omission, failure.

Misdeed, offence, trespass, transgression, misdemeanour, delinquency, felony, sin, crime, enormity, atrocity.

Science of crime, criminology.

(*Phrases*) Besetting sin; deviation from rectitude; a deed without a name.

---

948 GOOD MAN (*Substantives*), trump, brick, worthy, example, pattern, mirror, model, paragon, phoenix (650), superman, hero, demigod, seraph, angel, saint (987).

A good fellow, good sort, sportsman, white man.

(*Phrases*) One of the best; one in a million; the salt of the earth.

949 BAD MAN (*Substantives*), wrongdoer, evildoer, culprit, delinquent, criminal, recidivist, malefactor, outlaw, felon, convict, lag, outcast, sinner (988).

Knave, rogue, rascal, scoundrel, spiv, scamp, scapegrace, black sheep, scallywag, spalpeen, varlet, *vaurien*, blighter, rotter, good-for-nothing, twerp, heel, jerk, creep, goon, son of a gun, dastard, blackguard, sweep, loose fish, bad egg, bad lot, hard case, lost soul, vagabond, bum, *mauvais sujet*, cur, sad dog, rip, rascallion, rapscallion, slubberdegullion, cullion, roisterer.

Mohock, rowdy, hooligan, larrikin, teddy boy, apache, thug, reprobate, *roué*, recreant, jail-bird, crook, tough, rough, roughneck, gangster, gunman, hoodlum, yegg, villain, ruffian, miscreant, caitiff, wretch, *âme damnée*, castaway, monster, Jonathan Wilde, Jack Sheppard, Lazarillo de Tormes, Scapin (941).

Cur, dog, hound, skunk, swine, rat, viper, serpent, cockatrice, basilisk, reptile, urchin, tiger, imp, demon, devil, devil incarnate, Mephistopheles (978), hellhound, son of Belial, cut-throat, *particep criminis*, incendiary.

Bad woman, hellcat, hellhag, bitch, witch, hag, harridan, trollop, jade, drab, hussy, minx, Jezebel.

Riff-raff, rabble, ragtag and bobtail, *canaille*.

(*Phrases*) A fiend in human shape; scum of the earth; poor white trash. (*Interjection*) Sirrah!

950 PENITENCE (*Substantives*), contrition, compunction, regret (833), repentance, remorse.

Self-reproach, self-reproof, self-accusation, self-condemnation.

Confession, acknowledgment, shrift, apology, recantation (607).

A penitent, prodigal, Magdalen.

(*Phrases*) The stool of repentance; the cutty-stool; sackcloth and ashes; qualms or prickings of conscience; a sadder and a wiser man.

(*Verbs*) To repent, regret, rue, repine, deplore, be sorry for.

To confess (529), acknowledge, apologize, shrive oneself, humble oneself, reclaim, turn from sin.

(*Phrases*) To have a weight on one's mind; to plead guilty; to sing small; to cry *peccavi*; to eat humble pie; to turn over a new leaf; to stand in a white sheet.

(*Adjectives*) Penitent, repentant, contrite, repenting, remorseful, regretful, sorry, compunctious, self-reproachful, self-accusing, self-convicted, conscience-stricken, conscience-smitten.

Not hardened, unhardened, reclaimed.

(*Adverb*) *Meâ culpâ*.

951 IMPENITENCE (*Substantives*), obduracy, recusance, irrepentance, hardness of heart, a seared conscience, induration.

(*Verbs*) To be impenitent, etc.; to steel or harden the heart.

(*Phrases*) To make no sign; to die game.

(*Adjectives*) Impenitent, uncontrite, obdurate, hard, callous, unfeeling, hardened, seared, recusant, relentless, unrepentant, graceless, shiftless, lost, incorrigible, irreclaimable, irredeemable, unatoned, unreclaimed, unreformed, unrepented.

952 ATONEMENT (*Substantives*), reparation, compromise, composition, compensation (30), quittance, quits; propitiation, expiation, redemption, conciliation.

Amends, *amende honorable*, apology, satisfaction, peace-offering, olive branch, sin-offering, scapegoat, sacrifice, burnt-offering.

Penance, fasting, maceration, flagellation, sackcloth and ashes, white sheet, lustration, purgation, purgatory.

(*Verbs*) To atone, expiate, propitiate, make amends, redeem, make good, repair, ransom, absolve, do penance, apologize, purge, shrive, give satisfaction.

(*Phrases*) To purge one's offence; to pay the forfeit or penalty.

(*Adjectives*) Propitiatory, piacular, expiatory, expiational.

4°. *Moral Practice*

953 TEMPERANCE (*Substantives*), moderation, forbearance, abnegation, self-denial, self-conquest, self-control, self-command, self-discipline, sobriety, frugality, vegetarianism.

Abstinence, abstemiousness, teetotalism, prohibition, asceticism (955), gymnosophy, system of Pythagoras.

An abstainer, ascetic, gymnosophist, vegetarian, teetotaller, Pythagorean.

(*Phrases*) The simple life; the blue ribbon.

(*Verbs*) To be temperate, etc.; to abstain, forbear, refrain, deny oneself, spare.

(*Phrases*) To sign the pledge; to go on the water wagon.

(*Adjectives*) Temperate, moderate, sober, frugal, sparing, abstemious, abstinent, Pythagorean, vegetarian, teetotal, dry.

954 INTEMPERANCE (*Substantives*), excess, immoderation, unrestraint; epicurism, epicureanism, hedonism, sensuality, luxury, luxuriousness, animalism, carnality, effeminacy; the lap of pleasure or luxury; indulgence, self-indulgence, voluptuousness; drunkenness (959).

Dissipation, licentiousness, debauchery, dissoluteness, crapulence, brutishness.

Revels, revelry, carousal, orgy, spree, jag, toot, drinking bout, debauch, jollification, saturnalia.

A sensualist, epicure, epicurean, voluptuary, rake, rip, *roué*, sybarite, drug addict, dope fiend, hophead.

(*Phrases*) The Circean cup; a fast life; wine, women, and song.

(*Verbs*) To be intemperate, sensual, etc.

To indulge, exceed, revel, dissipate; give a loose to indulgence, live hard.

To debauch, pander to, sensualize, animalize, brutalize.

(*Phrases*) To wallow in voluptuousness, luxury, etc.; to plunge into dissipation; to paint the town red; to live on the fat of the land; to sow one's wild oats.

(*Adjectives*) Intemperate, sensual, pampered, self-indulgent, fleshly, inabstinent, licentious, wild, dissolute, dissipated, fast, rakish, debauched, brutish, crapulous, hedonistic, epicurean, sybaritical, Sardanapalian, voluptuous, apolaustic, orgiastic, swinish, piggish, hoggish; indulged, pampered.

955 ASCETICISM (*Substantives*), austerity, puritanism, mortification, maceration, sackcloth and ashes, flagellation, martyrdom, yoga.

An ascetic, anchoret, yogi, martyr; a recluse, hermit (893); puritan, Cynic.

(*Adjectives*) Ascetic, ascetical, austere, puritanical.

956 FASTING (*Substantives*), fast, spare diet, meagre diet, Lent, Quadragesima, a lenten entertainment, famishment, starvation, banian day, Ramadan.

(*Phrases*) A Barmecide feast; a hunger strike; short commons.

(*Verbs*) To fast, starve, clem, famish.

(*Phrases*) To dine with Duke Humphrey; to perish with hunger.

957 GLUTTONY (*Substantives*), epicurism, greediness, good cheer, high living, edacity, voracity, gulosity, crapulence, hoggishness, piggishness.

Gastronomy; feast, banquet, good cheer, blow-out.

A glutton, epicure, *bon vivant*, cormorant, gourmand, gourmet, bellygod, pig, hog, Apicius, gastronome, gastronomer, gastronomist.

(*Adjectives*) Fasting, etc., unfed, famished, starved; lenten, Quadragesimal.

(*Verbs*) To gormandize, gorge, cram, stuff, guzzle, bolt, devour, gobble up, pamper.

(*Phrases*) To eat out of house and home; to have the stomach of an ostrich; to play a good knife and fork.

(*Adjectives*) Gluttonous, greedy, gormandizing, edacious, voracious, crapulent, swinish, piggish, hoggish, pampered, overfed; gastronomical.

958 SOBRIETY (*Substantives*), teetotalism, total abstinence, temperance (953).

Compulsory sobriety, prohibition.

A water-drinker, teetotaller, abstainer, total abstainer, blue-ribbonite, Rechabite, Band of Hope; prohibitionist.

(*Verbs*) To abstain, to take the pledge.

(*Adjectives*) Sober, abstemious, teetotal.

(*Phrases*) Sober as a judge; on the water wagon.

------

959 DRUNKENNESS (*Substantives*), insobriety, ebriety, inebriety, inebriation, intoxication, ebriosity, bibacity, drinking, toping, tippling, sottishness, tipsiness, bacchanals, compotation, intemperance (954); dipsomania, alcoholism, delirium tremens, D.T.

A drunkard, sot, toper, tippler, hard drinker, winebag, winebibber, dram-drinker, soak, soaker, sponge, tun, tosspot, pub-crawler, reveller, carouser, Bacchanal, Bacchanalian, Bacchant, a devotee to Bacchus; a dipsomaniac.

Drink, hard drinks, intoxicant, alcohol, liquor, spirits, booze, blue ruin, grog, cocktail, highball, dram, peg, stirrup-cup, doch-an-doris.

(*Phrases*) The flowing bowl; one for the road.

(*Verbs*) To drink, tipple, tope, booze; to guzzle, swill, soak, swig, get or be drunk, etc.; to take to drinking, drink hard, drink deep.

To inebriate, intoxicate, fuddle.

(*Phrases*) To liquor up; to wet one's whistle; to crack a bottle; to have a bucket; to look on the wine when it is red; to take a drop too much; to drink like a fish; to splice the main-brace; to crook or lift the elbow.

(*Adjectives*) Drunk, drunken, tipsy, intoxicated, in liquor, inebriated, fuddled, mellow, boozy, high, fou, boiled, tiddly, stinko, blotto, lit up, groggy, top-heavy, pot-valiant, glorious, overcome, overtaken, elevated, whiffled, sozzled, screwed, corned, raddled, sewed up, lushy, squiffy, muddled, oiled, canned, muzzy, maudlin, dead-drunk, disguised, tight, beery.

Bibacious, bibulous, sottish, Bacchanal, Bacchanalian.

(*Phrases*) In one's cups; *inter pocula;* the worse for liquor; half-seas-over; three sheets in the wind; under the table; drunk as a piper, as a fiddle, as a lord, as an owl, as David's sow; stewed to the eyebrows; pickled to the gills; one over the eight.

(*Interjections*) Cheers! here's to you! down the hatch! mud in your eye! skin off your nose! *prosit! slainte! skoal!*

960 PURITY (*Substantives*), modesty, decency, decorum, delicacy, continence, chastity, honesty, pudency, virtue, virginity.

961 IMPURITY (*Substantives*), immodesty, grossness, coarseness, indelicacy, impropriety, impudicity, indecency, obscenity, obsceneness,

A virgin, maiden, maid, vestal; Joseph, Hippolytus, Lucrece.

(*Phrase*) The white flower of a blameless life.

(*Adjectives*) Pure, immaculate, undefiled, modest, delicate, decent, decorous.

Chaste, continent, honest, virtuous; Platonic.

ribaldry, smut, smuttiness, bawdiness, bawdry, *double entendre*, equivoque, pornography.

Concupiscence, lust, carnality, flesh, salacity, lewdness, prurience, lechery, lasciviousness, voluptuousness, lubricity.

Incontinence, intrigue, gallantry, debauchery, libertinism, libertinage, fornication, liaison, wenching, whoring, whoredom, concubinage, hetaerism.

Seduction, defloration, violation, rape, adultery, defilement, *crim. con.*, incest, harlotry, stupration, procuration, white slave traffic.

A seraglio, harem, brothel, bagnio, stew, bawdy-house, disorderly house, house of ill fame, red lamp district, Yoshiwara.

(*Phrase*) The morals of the farmyard; the oldest profession.

(*Verbs*) To intrigue, debauch, defile, seduce, abuse, violate, force, rape, ravish, deflower, ruin, prostitute, procure.

(*Adjectives*) Impure, immodest, indecorous, indelicate, unclean, unmentionable, unseemly, improper, suggestive, indecent, loose, coarse, gross, broad, equivocal, risky, *risqué*, high-seasoned, nasty, smutty, scabrous, ribald, obscene, bawdy, lewd, pornographic, Rabelaisian, Aristophanic.

Concupiscent, prurient, lickerish, rampant, carnal, fleshy, sensual, lustful, lascivious, lecherous, libidinous, goatish, erotic, ruttish, salacious.

Unchaste, light, wanton, debauched, dissolute, carnal-minded, licentious, frail, riggish, incontinent, meretricious, rakish, gallant, dissipated, adulterous, incestuous, bestial.

(*Phrases*) On the streets; of easy virtue; no better than she should be. Near the knuckle; not for ears polite; four-letter words.

962 A LIBERTINE (*Substantives*), voluptuary, man of pleasure, sensualist (954), rip, rake, *roué*, debauchee, loose fish, intriguant, gallant, seducer, fornicator, lecher, satyr, whoremonger, *paillard*, adulterer, a gay deceiver, Lothario, Don Juan, Bluebeard.

A prostitute, courtesan, tart, call-girl, strumpet, harlot, whore, punk, *fille de joie*, cocotte, *lorette*, woman of the town, streetwalker, pick-up, piece, the frail sisterhood, the *demi-monde*, soiled dove, demirep, wench, trollop, trull, baggage, hussy, drab, jade, quean, slut, harridan, an unfortunate, Jezebel, Messalina, Delilah, Thais, Aspasia, Phryne, Lais.

Concubine, odalisque, mistress, doxy, kept woman, *petite amie*, hetaera. Pimp, pander, ponce, *souteneur*, bawd, procuress.

5°. *Institutions*

963 LEGALITY (*Substantives*), legitimateness, legitimacy, justice (922).

Law, legislature, code, constitution, pandect, enactment, edict, statute, charter, rule, order, ordinance, injunction, institution, precept, regulation, by-law, decree, firman, bull, ukase, decretal.

964 Absence or violation of law.

ILLEGALITY (*Substantives*), lawlessness, arbitrariness, antinomy, violence, brute force, despotism, outlawry.

Mob law, lynch law, club law, martial law.

Legal process, form, formula, formality, rite.

Science of law, jurisprudence, legislation, codification.

Equity, common law, *lex non scripta*, unwritten law, law of nations, international law, *jus gentium*, civil law, canon law, statute law, *lex mercatoria*, ecclesiastical law.

(*Phrase*) The arm of the law.

(*Verbs*) To legalize, enact, ordain, enjoin, prescribe, order, decree (741); to pass a law, issue an edict or decree; to legislate, codify.

(*Adjectives*) Legal, lawful, according to law, legitimate, constitutional, chartered, vested.

Legislative, statutable, statutory.

(*Adverbs*) Legally, etc.

(*Phrases*) In the eye of the law; *de jure*.

Camorra, Ku Klux Klan, Judge Lynch.

Informality, unlawfulness, illegitimacy, bastardy, the baton or bar sinister.

Smuggling, poaching, bootlegging, black market, grey market.

(*Verbs*) To smuggle, run, poach.

To invalidate, annual, illegalize abrogate, void, nullify, quash.

(*Phrases*) To take the law into one's own hands; to set the law at defiance; to drive a coach and six through the law.

(*Adjectives*) Illegal, unlawful, illicit, illegitimate, injudicial, unofficial, lawless, unauthorized, unchartered, unconstitutional, informal, contraband, hot.

Arbitrary, extrajudicial, despotic, autocratic, irresponsible, unanswerable, unaccountable.

(*Adverbs*) Illegally, with a high hand.

---

965 JURISDICTION (*Substantives*), judicature, soc (or soke), administration of justice.

Inquisition, inquest, coroner's inquest.

The executive, municipality, corporation, magistracy, police, police force, constabulary, posse, *gendarmerie*.

Lord lieutenant, sheriff, sheriff-substitute, deputy, officer, constable, policeman, state trooper, traffic warden, bailiff, tipstaff, bum-bailiff, catchpoll, beadle; *gendarme*, lictor, mace-bearer.

(*Adjectives*) Juridical, judicial, forensic, municipal, executive, administrative, inquisitorial, causidical.

(*Phrases*) *Coram judice; ex cathedra.*

966 TRIBUNAL (*Substantives*), court, guild, board, bench, judicatory, senate-house, court of law, court of justice, criminal court, police-court, Court of Chancery, of King's Bench; Probate, Divorce, Admiralty Court, court of appeal, justice-seat, judgment-seat, mercy-seat, Star Chamber, Judicial Committee of the Privy Council, U.S. Supreme Court, durbar.

City hall, town hall, theatre, bar, dock, forum, hustings, drum-head, woolsack, jury-box, witness-box.

Assize, sessions, quarter sessions, petty sessions, eyre, court-martial, wardmote.

967 JUDGE (*Substantives*), justice, justiciar, justiciary, chancellor, magistrate, beak, recorder, common serjeant, stipendiary, coroner, arbiter, arbitrator, umpire, referee, jury, Justice of the Peace, J.P., Lord Chancellor, Lord Chief Justice, Master of the Rolls.

Mullah, ulema, mufti, cadi (or kadi), kavass.

Prosecutor, plaintiff, accuser, appellant, pursuer.

Defendant, panel, prisoner, the accused.

(*Verbs*) Judge, try, pass judgment, give verdict.

968 LAWYER (*Substantives*), the bar, advocate, counsellor, counsel, queen's or king's counsel, Q.C., K.C., pleader, special pleader, conveyancer, bencher, proctor, civilian, barrister, barrister-at-law, jurist, jurisconsult, publicist, draughtsman, notary, notary public, scrivener, attorney, solicitor, legal adviser, writer to the signet, writer, marshal, pundit; pettifogger.

(*Phrases*) The gentlemen of the long robe; the learned in the law; a limb of the law.

(*Verbs*) To practise law, plead.

(*Phrases*) To be called to the bar; to take silk.

969 LAWSUIT (*Substantives*), suit, action, case, cause, trial, litigation.

Denunciation, citation, arraignment, prosecution, indictment, impeachment, apprehension, arrest, committal, imprisonment (751).

Pleadings, writ, summons, subpoena, plea, bill, affidavit, libel; answer, counterclaim, demurrer, rebutter, rejoinder, surrebutter, surrejoinder.

Verdict, sentence, judgment, finding, decree, arbitrament, adjudication, award, decision, precedent.

(*Verbs*) To denounce, cite, apprehend, sue, writ, arraign, summons, prosecute, indict, contest, impeach, attach, distrain; to commit.

To try, hear a cause, sit in judgment.

To pronounce, find, judge, adjudge, sentence, give judgment; bring in a verdict; to doom, arbitrate, adjudicate, award, report.

(*Phrases*) To go to law; to appeal to the law; to file a claim; to inform against; to lodge an information; to serve with a writ; to bring an action against; to bring to trial or the bar; to give in charge or custody; to throw into prison; to clap in jail.

(*Adjectives*) Litigious, litigant, litigatory.

(*Adverbial phrases*) *Sub judice; pendente lite.*

970 ACQUITTAL (*Substantives*), acquittal, absolution, exculpation, quietus, clearance, discharge, release, reprieve (918), respite, compurgation.

Exemption from punishment, impunity.

(*Verbs*) To acquit, absolve, whitewash, extenuate, exculpate, exonerate, clear, assoil, discharge, release, reprieve, respite.

(*Adjectives*) Acquitted, etc.

Uncondemned, unpunished, unchastised.

971 CONDEMNATION (*Substantives*), conviction, proscription, damnation, death-warrant.

Attainder, attainture, attaintment.

(*Verbs*) To condemn, convict, cast, find guilty, proscribe, ban, outlaw, attaint, damn, doom, sentence, confiscate, sequestrate, non-suit.

(*Adjectives*) Condemnatory, damnatory, condemned; self-convicted.

972 PUNISHMENT (*Substantives*), punition, chastisement, castigation, correction, chastening, discipline, infliction.

Retribution, requital (973), penalty (974), reckoning, Nemesis.

Imprisonment (751), transportation, exile (297), cucking-stool, ducking-stool, treadmill, crank, hulks, galleys, penal servitude, preventive detention.

A blow, slap, spank, skelp, swish, hit, knock, rap, thump, bang, buffet, stripe, stroke, cuff, clout, kick, whack, thwack, box, punch, pummel.

Beating, lash, flagellation, flogging, etc., dressing, lacing, tanning, knock-out, fustigation, leathering, lathering, jacketing, strap-oil, gruelling, spiflication, bastinado, strappado, pillory (975), running the gauntlet, *coup de grâce, peine forte et dure.*

Execution, capital punishment, hanging, beheading, decollation, decapitation, electrocution, guillotine, garrotte, *auto de fé*, *noyade*, crucifixion, impalement, *hara-kiri*, martyrdom.

(*Verbs*) To punish, chastise, castigate, chasten, correct, inflict punishment, pay, do for, serve out, pay out, visit upon, give it to, strafe, spiflicate.

To strike, hit, smite, knock, slap, flap, rap, bang, thwack, whack, thump, kick, punch, pelt, beat, buffet, thrash, swinge, pummel, clapperclaw, drub, trounce, baste, belabour, lace, strap, comb, lash, lick, whip, flog, scourge, knout, swish, spank, skelp, birch, tan, larrup, lay into, knock out, wallop, leather, flagellate, horsewhip, bastinado, lapidate, stone.

To execute, hang, behead, decapitate, decollate, electrocute, guillotine, garrotte, shoot, gibbet; to hang, draw, and quarter; break on the wheel; crucify, impale, torture, flay, keelhaul; lynch.

To banish, exile, transport, deport, expel, drum out, disbar, disbench, unfrock.

To be hanged, etc., to be spread-eagled.

(*Phrases*) To make an example of; to serve one out; to give it one; to dust one's jacket; to tweak or pull the nose; to box the ears; to beat to a jelly; to tar and feather; to give a black eye; to lay it on.

To come to the gallows; to swing for it; to go to the chair; to die in one's shoes.

(*Adjectives*) Punishing, etc., punitory, punitive, inflictive, penal, disciplinary, castigatory, borstal.

(*Interjection*) *A la lanterne!*

973 REWARD (*Substantives*), recompense, remuneration, meed, guerdon, premium, indemnity, indemnification, compensation, reparation, requital, retribution, quittance, hush-money, acknowledgment, amends, solatium, sop, atonement, redress, consideration, return, tribute, honorarium, perquisite, tip, vail; salvage.

Prize, purse, crown, laurel, bays, cross, medal, ribbon, decoration (877).

(*Verbs*) To reward, recompense, repay, requite, recoup, remunerate, compensate, make amends, indemnify, atone, satisfy, acknowledge, acquit oneself.

(*Phrase*) To get for one's pains.

(*Adjectives*) Remunerative, munerary, compensatory, retributive, reparatory.

---

974 PENALTY (*Substantives*), punishment (972), pain, penance.

Fine, mulct, amercement, forfeit, forfeiture, escheat, damages, deodand, sequestration, confiscation.

(*Phrases*) Pains and penalties; the devil to pay.

(*Verbs*) To fine, mulct, amerce, sconce, confiscate, sequester, sequestrate, escheat, estreat.

975 Instrument of punishment.

SCOURGE (*Substantives*), rod, cane, stick, rattan, switch, ferule, birch, cudgel.

Whip, lash, strap, thong, knout, cowhide, cat, cat-o'-nine-tails, sjambok, rope's end.

Pillory, stocks, cangue, whipping-post, ducking-stool, triangle, wooden horse, boot, thumbscrew, rack, wheel, treadmill.

Stake, tree, block, scaffold, gallows, halter, bowstring, gibbet, axe, maiden, guillotine, garrotte, electric chair, hot squat, lethal chamber.

Executioner, hangman, electrocutioner, firing squad, headsman, Jack Ketch.

Section V—Religious Affections

1°. *Superhuman Beings and Objects*

976 Deity (*Substantives*), Divinity, Godhead, Omnipotence, Omniscience, Providence.

Quality of being divine, divineness, divinity.

God, Lord, Jehovah, The Almighty; The Supreme Being; The First Cause, *Ens Entium*; The Author of all things, The Infinite, The Eternal, The All-powerful, The All-wise, The All-merciful, The All-holy.

Attributes and perfections, infinite power, wisdom, goodness, justice, mercy, omnipotence, omniscience, omnipresence, unity, immutability, holiness, glory, majesty, sovereignty, infinity, eternity.

The Trinity, The Holy Trinity, The Trinity in Unity, The Triune God.

God the Father, The Maker, The Creator.

Functions: creation, preservation, divine government, theocracy, thearchy, providence; the ways, dispensations, visitations of Providence.

God the Son, Christ, Jesus, The Messiah, The Anointed, The Saviour, The Redeemer, The Mediator, The Intercessor, The Advocate, The Judge, The Son of Man, The Lamb of God, The Word, The Logos, Emmanuel, The King of Kings and Lord of Lords, The King of Glory, The Prince of Peace, The Good Shepherd, The Way of Truth and Life, The Bread of Life, The Light of the World, The Sun of Righteousness, the Incarnation, the Word made Flesh.

Functions: salvation, redemption, atonement, propitiation, mediation, intercession, judgment.

God the Holy Ghost, The Holy Spirit, Paraclete, The Comforter, The Spirit of Truth, The Dove.

Functions: inspiration, unction, regeneration, sanctification, consolation.

(*Verbs*) To create, uphold, preserve, govern.

To atone, redeem, save, propitiate, mediate.

To predestinate, elect, call, ordain, bless, justify, sanctify, glorify.

(*Adjectives*) Almighty, all-powerful, omnipotent, omnipresent, omniscient, all-wise, holy, hallowed, sacred, divine, heavenly, celestial.

Superhuman, ghostly, spiritual, supernatural, theocratic.

---

977 Beneficent spirits.

Angel (*Substantives*), archangel.

The heavenly host; ministering spirits; the choir invisible.

Madonna, saint.

Seraphim, cherubim, thrones, principalities, powers, dominions.

(*Adjectives*) Angelic, angelical, seraphic, cherubic, celestial, heavenly, saintly.

---

978 Maleficent spirits.

Satan (*Substantives*), the Devil, Lucifer, Beelzebub, Belial, Mephistopheles, Mephisto, Abaddon, Apollyon, the Prince of the Devils.

His Satanic Majesty, the tempter, the evil one, the wicked one, the old Serpent, the Prince of darkness, the father of lies, the foul fiend, the arch-fiend, the common enemy, Old Harry, Old Nick, the Old Scratch, the Old Gentleman, Old Horny.

Diabolism, devilism, devilship; Satanism, the cloven hoof, the black mass.

Fallen angels, unclean spirits, devils, the powers of darkness, inhabitants of Pandemonium.

(*Adjectives*) Satanic, diabolic, devilish.

Gods of other Religions and Mythological Beings

979 GREAT SPIRIT (*Substantives*), deity, numen, god, goddess; Allah, Brahma, Vishnu, Siva, Krishna, Buddha, Mithra, Ormuzd, Isis, Osiris, Moloch, Baal, Asteroth.

Jupiter, Jove, Juno, Minerva, Apollo, Diana, Venus, Vulcan, Mars, Mercury, Neptune, Pluto; Zeus, Hera, Athena, Artemis, Aphrodite, Hephaestus, Ares, Hermes, Poseidon. Odin or Woden, Frigga, Thor.

Good genius, demiurge, familiar; fairy, fay, sylph, peri, kelpie, nymph, nereid, dryad, hamadryad, naiad, merman, mermaid (341), undine; Oberon, Mab, Titania, Puck, Robin Goodfellow; the good folk, the little people.

(*Adjectives*) Fairy, faery, fairy-like, sylph-like, sylphine.

Mythical, mythological, fabulous, legendary.

980 DEMON (*Substantives*), evil genius, fiend, unclean spirit, cacodemon, incubus, succubus, succuba, flibbertigibbet; fury, harpy, siren, faun, satur, Eblis, Demogorgon.

Vampire, werewolf, ghoul, afreet (or afrite), ogre, ogress, gnome, djinn, imp, genie (or jinnee), lamia, bogy, bogle, nix, nixie, kobold, brownie, leprechaun, elf, pixy, troll, sprite, gremlin, spandule.

Supernatural appearance, ghost, spectre, apparition, shade, vision, goblin, hobgoblin, banshee, spook, wraith, *revenant*, *doppelgänger*, poltergeist.

(*Phrases*) The powers of darkness.

(*Adjectives*) Supernatural, ghostly, apparitional, elfin, elfish, unearthly, uncanny, eerie, weird, spectral, spookish, spooky, ghostlike, fiendish, fiendlike, impish, demoniacal, haunted.

981 HEAVEN (*Substantives*), the kingdom of heaven; the kingdom of God, the heavenly kingdom; the throne of God, the presence of God.

Paradise, Eden, Zion, the Celestial City, the New Jerusalem, the abode of the blessed; celestial bliss or glory.

Mythological heaven, Olympus; mythological paradise, Elysium, the Elysian Fields, the garden of the Hesperides; Valhalla, Nirvana, happy hunting grounds.

Translation, apotheosis, deification, resurrection.

(*Adjectives*) Heavenly, celestial, supernal, unearthly, from on high, paradisaical, paradisical, paradisial, Elysian, beatific.

982 HELL (*Substantives*), bottomless pit, place of torment; the habitation of fallen angels, Pandemonium, Domdaniel.

Hell-fire, everlasting fire, the lake of fire and brimstone.

Purgatory, limbo, abyss.

Mythological hell, Tartarus, Hades, Pluto, Avernus, Styx, the Stygian creek, Acheron, Cocytus, Phlegethon, Lethe, Erebus, Tophet, Gehenna.

(*Phrases*) The fire that is never quenched; the worm that never dies.

The infernal or nether regions; the shades below; the realms of Pluto.

(*Adjectives*) Hellish, infernal, stygian, Tartarean, Plutonian.

2°. Religious Doctrines

983 Religious knowledge.

THEOLOGY (natural and revealed) (*Substantives*), divinity, religion, monotheism, hagiology, hagiography, hierography, theosophy; comparative religion, comparative mythology.

Creed, belief, faith, persuasion, tenet, dogma, articles of faith, declaration, profession or confession of faith.

Theologian, divine, schoolman, the Fathers.

(*Adjectives*) Theological, religious, patristic, ecumenical, denominational, sectarian.

983A CHRISTIAN RELIGION (*Substantives*), true faith, Christianity, Christianism, Christendom, Catholicism, orthodoxy.

A Christian, a true believer.

The Church, the Catholic or Universal Church, the Church of Christ, the body of Christ, the Church Militant.

The members of Christ, the disciples or followers of Christ, the Christian community.

Protestant, Church of England, Anglican, Church of Scotland; Church of Rome, Roman Catholic; Greek Church, Orthodox Church.

(*Adjectives*) Christian, Catholic, orthodox, sound, faithful, true, scriptural, canonical, schismless.

---

984 OTHER RELIGIONS (*Substantives*), paganism, heathenism, ethnicism, polytheism, ditheism, tritheism, pantheism, hylotheism.

Judaism, Gentilism, Mohammedanism (or Mahometanism), Islam, Buddhism, Hinduism, Taoism, Confucianism, Shintoism, Sufism.

A pagan, heathen, paynim, infidel, unbeliever, pantheist, etc.

A Jew, Mohammedan (or Mahometan), Mussulman, Moslem, Brahmin (or Brahman), Parsee, Sufi, Magus, Gymnosophist, Fire-worshipper, Buddhist, Rosicrucian.

(*Adjectives*) Pagan, heathen, ethnic, gentile, pantheistic, etc.

Judaical, Mohammedan, Brahminical, Buddhistic.

984A HERESY (*Substantives*), heterodoxy, false doctrine, schism, schismaticalness, latitudinarianism, recusancy, apostasy, backsliding, quietism, adiaphorism.

Bigotry, fanaticism, iconoclasm, bibliolatry, fundamentalism, puritanism, sabbatarianism.

Dissent, sectarianism, nonconformity, secularism, syncretism.

A heretic, deist, unitarian.

(*Adjectives*) Heretical, heterodox, unorthodox, unscriptural, uncanonical, schismatic, sectarian, nonconformist, recusant, latitudinarian.

Credulous, bigoted, fanatical, idolatrous, superstitious, visionary.

985 CHRISTIAN REVELATION (*Substantives*), Word, Word of God, Scripture, the Scriptures, Holy Writ, the Bible, the Holy Book.

Old Testament: Septuagint, Vulgate, Pentateuch, Hagiographa, the Law, the Prophets, the Apocrypha.

New Testament: the Gospel, the Evangelists, the Epistles, the Apocalypse, Revelations.

Talmud, Mishna, Masorah, Torah.

A prophet, seer, evangelist, apostle, disciple, saint, the Fathers.

(*Adjectives*) Scriptural, biblical, sacred, prophetic, evangelical, apostolic, apostolical, inspired, theopneustic, apocalyptic.

986 OTHER SACRED BOOKS (*Substantives*), the Koran (or Alcoran), Vedas, Upanishads, Puranas, Zend-Avesta.

Religious founders: Buddha (or Gautama), Zoroaster (or Zarathustra), Confucius, Lao-Tsze, Mohammed (or Mahomet).

Idols: Golden calf, Baal, Moloch, Dagon.

(*Adjectives*) Anti-scriptural, anti-christian, profane, idolatrous, pagan, heathen, heathenish.

3°. *Religious Sentiments*

987 PIETY (*Substantives*), religion, theism, faith, religiousness, godliness, reverence, humility, veneration, devoutness, devotion, spirituality, grace, unction, edification, unworldliness, other-worldliness; holiness, sanctity, sanctitude, sacredness, consecration; virtue (944).

Theopathy, beatification, adoption, regeneration, conversion, justification, salvation, inspiration.

A believer, convert, theist, Christian, saint, one of the elect, a devotee.

The good, righteous, faithful, godly, elect, just.

(*Phrases*) The odour of sanctity; the beauty of holiness; spiritual existence.

The children of God, of light.

(*Verbs*) To be pious, etc., to believe, have faith; to convert, edify, sanctify, hallow, beatify, regenerate, inspire; to consecrate, enshrine.

(*Phrases*) To work out one's salvation; to stand up for Jesus; to fight the good fight.

(*Adjectives*) Pious, religious, devout, reverent, reverential, godly, humble, heavenly-minded, pure, holy, spiritual, saintly, saint-like, unworldly, other-worldly.

Believing, faithful, Christian.

Sanctified, regenerated, born again, justified, adopted, elected, inspired, consecrated, converted, unearthly, sacred, solemn, not of the earth.

---

988 IMPIETY (*Substantives*), irreverence, profaneness, profanity, blasphemy, desecration, sacrilege, sacrilegiousness, sin (945); scoffing, ribaldry, reviling.

Assumed piety, hypocrisy, cant, pietism, lip-devotion, lip-service, lip-reverence, formalism, sanctimony, sanctimoniousness, pharisaism, precisianism, sabbatism, sabbatarianism, sacerdotalism, religiosity, religionism, *odium theologicum.*

Hardening, backsliding, declension, reprobation, perversion.

Sinner, outcast, castaway, lost sheep, reprobate.

A scoffer, hypocrite, pietist, pervert, religionist, precisian, formalist; son of darkness, son of Belial, blasphemer, Pharisee; bigot, devotee, fanatic, sabbatarian.

The wicked, unjust, ungodly, unrighteous.

(*Phrase*) The unco guid.

(*Verbs*) To be impious, etc., to profane, desecrate, blaspheme, revile, scoff, commit sacrilege.

To play the hypocrite, cant.

(*Adjectives*) Impious, profane, irreverent, sacrilegious, desecrating, blasphemous; unhallowed, unsanctified, hardened, perverted, reprobate.

Bigoted, priest-ridden, fanatical, churchy.

Hypocritical, canting, pietistical, sanctimonious, unctuous, pharisaical, over-righteous, righteous overmuch.

(*Phrases*) Under the mask, cloak, or pretence of religion.

---

989 IRRELIGION (*Substantives*), ungodliness, unholiness, gracelessness, impiety (989).

Scepticism, doubt, unbelief, disbelief, incredulity, incredulousness, faithlessness, want of faith or belief (485, 487).

Atheism, hylotheism, materialism, positivism.

Deism, infidelity, freethinking, rationalism, agnosticism, unchristianness, antichristianity, antichristianism.

An atheist, sceptic, unbeliever, deist, freethinker, rationalist, agnostic, nullifidian, infidel, alien, giaour, heathen.

(*Verbs*) To be irreligious, disbelieve, lack faith, doubt.

To dechristianize, rationalize.

(*Adjectives*) Irreligious, undevout, godless, atheistic, atheistical, ungodly, unholy, unhallowed, unsanctified, graceless, without God, carnal-minded.

Sceptical, unbelieving, freethinking, agnostic, rationalistic, incredulous, unconverted, faithless, lacking faith.

Deistical, antichristian, unchristian, worldly-minded, mundane, carnal, earthly-minded.

(*Adverbs*) Irreligiously, etc.

4°. *Acts of Religion*

990 WORSHIP (*Substantives*), adoration, devotion, cult, homage, service, humiliation, kneeling, genuflexion, prostration.

Prayer, invocation, supplication, rogation, petition, orison, litany, the Lord's prayer, paternoster, collect.

Thanksgiving, giving or returning thanks, praise, glorification, benediction, doxology, hosanna, hallelujah, paean, Te Deum, Magnificat, Ave Maria, De Profundis, Nunc dimittis, Non nobis, Domine.

Psalmody, psalm, hymn, plainsong, chant, antiphon, response, anthem, motet.

Oblation, sacrifice, incense, libation, burnt-offering, votive offering; offertory, collection.

Discipline, self-discipline, self-examination, self-denial, fasting.

Divine service, religious service, office, duty, prime, terce, sext, matins, mass (998), angelus, nones, evensong, vespers, vigils, lauds, compline; prayer meeting, revival.

Worshipper, congregation, communicant, celebrant.

(*Verbs*) To worship, adore, reverence, venerate, do service, pay homage, humble oneself, bow down, kneel, bend the knee, prostrate oneself.

To pray, invoke, supplicate, petition, put up prayers or petitions; to ask, mplore (765).

To return or give thanks; to say grace; to bless, praise, laud, glorify, magnify, sing praises, lead the choir, pronounce benediction.

To propitiate, offer sacrifice, fast, deny oneself; vow, offer vows, give alms.

(*Phrases*) To lift up the heart; to say one's prayers; to tell one's beads; to go to church; to attend divine service.

(*Adjectives*) Worshipping, etc., devout, solemn, devotional, reverent, pure, fervent, prayerful.

(*Interjections*) Hallelujah! alleluia! hosanna! glory be to God! *sursum corda!*

991 IDOLATRY (*Substantives*), idol-worship, idolism, demonism, demonolatry, fire-worship, devil-worship, fetishism.

Sacrifices, hecatomb, holocaust; human sacrifices, immolation, mactation, infanticide, self-immolation, suttee.

Idol, image, fetish, ju-ju, Mumbo-Jumbo, Juggernaut, joss.

(*Verbs*) To worship idols, pictures, relics, etc.; to idolize, idolatrize.

(*Adjectives*) Idolatrous, fetishistic.

992 OCCULT ARTS (*Substantives*), occultism, sorcery, magic, the black art, black magic, necromancy, theurgy, thaumaturgy, psychomancy, *diablerie*, bedevilment, witchcraft, witchery, bewitchment, wizardry, glamour, fetishism, vampirism, shamanism, voodooism, obeah (or obi), sortilege, conjuration, exorcism, fascination, mesmerism, hypnotism, animal magnetism, clairvoyance, telegnosis, telekinesis, psychokinesis, mediumship, spiritualism, extra-sensory perception, telepathy, parapsychology, second sight, spirit-rapping, table-turning, psychometry, crystal-gazing, divination, enchantment, hocus-pocus (545).

(*Verbs*) To practise sorcery, etc.; to conjure, exorcize, charm, enchant, bewitch, bedevil, hoodoo, entrance, mesmerize, hypnotize, fascinate; to taboo, wave a wand, cast a spell, call up spirits.

(*Adjectives*) Magic, magical, cabbalistic, talismanic, phylacteric, necromantic, incantatory, occult, mediumistic, charmed, exorcized, etc.

993 SPELL (*Substantives*), charm, fascination, incantation, exorcism, weird, cabbala, exsufflation, cantrip, runes, abracadabra, open sesame, mumbojumbo, taboo, counter-charm, evil eye, jinx, hoodoo, Indian sign.

Talisman, amulet, mascot, periapt, phylactery, philtre, fetish, wishbone, merrythought.

Wand, caduceus, rod, divining-rod, the lamp of Aladdin, magic ring, wishing-cap, seven-league boots.

994 SORCERER (*Substantives*), sorceress, magician, conjurer, necromancer, enchanter, enchantress, thaumaturgist, occultist, adept, Mahatma, seer, wizard, witch, warlock, charmer, exorcist, mage, archimage, soothsayer (513), shaman, medicine-man, witch-doctor, mesmerist, hypnotist, medium, spiritualist, clairvoyant; control.

(*Phrase*) *Deus ex machina.*

5°. *Religious Institutions*

995 CHURCHDOM (*Substantives*), ministry, apostleship, priesthood, prelacy, hierarchy, church government, Christendom, church; clericalism, sacerdotalism, priestcraft, theocracy, popery, papistry.

Monachism, monasticism, monkdom, monkhood, monkery.

Ecclesiastical offices and dignities: Pontificate, papacy, primacy, archbishopric, archiepiscopacy, bishopric, bishopdom, episcopate, episcopacy, see, diocese, prelacy, deanery, stall, canonry, canonicate, prebend, prebendaryship; benefice, incumbency, advowson, living, cure, rectorship, vicarship, vicariate, deaconry, deaconship, curacy, chaplaincy, chaplainship; cardinalate, abbacy.

Holy orders, ordination, institution, consecration, induction, preferment, translation.

Council, conclave, sanhedrim, synod, presbytery, consistory, chapter, vestry (696).

(*Verbs*) To call, ordain, induct, install, prefer, translate, consecrate, canonize, beatify; to take the veil, to take vows.

(*Adjectives*) Ecclesiastical, clerical, sacerdotal, priestly, prelatical, hierarchical, pastoral, ministerial, capitular, theocratic.

Pontifical, papal, episcopal, archidiaconal, diaconal, canonical; monastic, monachal, monkish; levitical, rabbinical.

996 CLERGY (*Substantives*), ministry, priesthood, presbytery.

A clergyman, cleric, parson, divine, ecclesiastic, churchman, priest, presbyter, hierophant, pastor, father, shepherd, minister, father in Christ, patriarch, padre, abbé, curé; skypilot, holy Joe, devil-dodger.

Dignitaries of the church: Primate, archbishop, bishop, prelate,

997 LAITY (*Substantives*), flock, fold, congregation, assembly, brethren, people.

Temporality, secularization.

A layman, parishioner.

(*Verb*) To secularize.

(*Adjectives*) Secular, lay, laical, civil, temporal, profane.

diocesan, suffragan; dean, subdean, archdeacon, prebendary, canon, capitular, residentiary, beneficiary; rector, vicar, incumbent, chaplain, curate, deacon, sub-deacon, preacher, reader, evangelist, revivalist, missionary, missioner.

Churchwarden, sidesman; clerk, precentor, choir, chorister, almoner, verger, beadle, sexton, sacrist, sacristan, acolyte.

Roman Catholic priesthood: Pope, pontiff, cardinal, confessor, spiritual director.

Cenobite, conventual, abbot, prior, father superior, monk, oblate, friar, lay brother, mendicant, Franciscan (or Grey Friars, Friars minor, Minorites), Observant, Capuchin, Dominican (or Black Friars), Carmelite (or White Friars), Augustin (or Austin Friars), Crossed or Crutched Friars, Benedictine, Jesuit (or Society of Jesus).

Abbess, prioress, canoness, mother, mother superior, *religieuse*, nun, novice, postulant.

Greek Church: Patriarch, metropolitan, archimandrite, pope.

Under the Jewish dispensation: Prophet, priest, high-priest, Levite, rabbi (or rabbin), scribe.

Moslem: Imam, mullah, mufti, dervish, fakir, santon, hadji; muezzin.

Hindu: Brahmin, pundit, guru, yogi.

Buddhist: Lama, bonze.

(*Phrase*) The cloth.

(*Adjectives*) Reverend, ordained, in orders.

998 RITE (*Substantives*), ceremony, ordinance, observance, cult, duty, form, formulary, ceremonial, solemnity, sacrament.

Baptism, immersion, christening, chrism, baptismal regeneration.

Confirmation, imposition or laying on of hands, ordination (995), consecration.

The Eucharist, the Lord's Supper, the communion, the sacrament, consubstantiation, celebration, consecrated elements, bread and wine.

Matrimony (903), burial (363), visitation of the sick, offertory.

Roman Catholic rites and ceremonies: Mass, high mass, low mass, dry mass; the seven sacraments, transubstantiation, impanation, extreme unction, viaticum, invocation of saints, canonization, transfiguration, auricular confession, maceration, flagellation, penance (952), telling of beads.

Relics, rosary, beads, reliquary, pyx (or pix), host, crucifix, *Agnus Dei*, thurible, censer, patera.

Liturgy, ritual, euchology, book of common prayer, litany, etc.; rubric, breviary, missal, ordinal; psalter, psalm book, hymn book, hymnal.

Service, worship (990), ministration, psalmody; preaching, predication; sermon, homily, lecture, discourse, exhortation, address.

Ritualism, ceremonialism, liturgics, liturgiology.

(*Verbs*) To perform service, do duty, minister, officiate; to baptize, dip, sprinkle; to confirm, lay hands on; to give or administer the sacrament; to take or receive the sacrament, communicate.

To preach, sermonize, predicate, lecture, harangue, hold forth, address the congregation.

(*Adjectives*) Ritual, ceremonial, baptismal, eucharistical, pastoral, liturgical.

999 VESTMENTS (*Substantives*), canonicals, robe, gown, pallium, surplice, cassock, alb, scapular (or scapulary), dalmatic, cope, soutane, chasuble, tonsure, cowl, hood, amice, calotte, bands, apron, biretta.

Mitre, tiara, triple crown, crosier.

1000 Place of worship, house of God.

TEMPLE (*Substantives*), cathedral, pro-cathedral, minster, church, kirk, chapel, meeting-house, tabernacle, conventicle, bethesda, little Bethel, basilica, fane, holy place, chantry, oratory.

Synagogue, mosque, pantheon, pagoda, joss-house, dagobah, tope.

Parsonage, rectory, vicarage, manse, presbytery, deanery, bishop's palace, the Vatican.

Altar, shrine, sanctuary, *sanctum sanctorum*, the Holy of Holies, sacristy, communion table, holy table, table of the Lord; piscina, baptistery, font, aumbry.

Chancel, choir, nave, aisle, transept, vestry, crypt, apse, belfry, stall, pew, pulpit, ambo, lectern, reading-desk, confessional, prothesis, credence.

Monastery, priory, abbey, convent, nunnery, cloister.

(*Adjectives*) Claustral, monastic, monasterial, conventual.

INDEX

Abominable, *hateful*, 898
  bad, 649
  foul, 653
  painful, 830
Abominate, *hate*, 898
  dislike, 867
Abomination, *foulness*, 653
* Abord, *courtesy*, 894
Aboriginal, *beginning*, 66
  native, 188
Aborigines, *inhabitants*, 188
Abortion, *failure*, 732
Abound, *sufficiency*, 639
About, *relative to*, 9
  near, 32, 197
  around, 227
Above, *height*, 206
  priority, 116
Above all, *greatness*, 31
Above-board, *visible*, 446
  plain, 518
  artless, 703
  true, 543
Above ground, *alive*, 359
Above par, *greatness*, 31
Abracadabra, *spell*, 993
Abrade, *subduct*, 38
Abrasion, *pulverulence*, 330
  friction, 331
Abreast, *lateral*, 236
  parallel, 216
Abridge, *shorten*, 201
  conciseness, 572
  lessen, 36
  deprive, 789
  in writing, 596
Abroach, *dispersion*, 73
Abroad, *extraneous*, 57
  exterior, 220
  distant, 196
  ignorant, 491
  perplexed, 704
Abrogation, *abrogation*,
    756, 764
  illegality, 964
Abrupt, *sudden*, 132
  hasty, 684
  violent, 173
  transient, 111
  steep, 217
  unexpected, 508
  style, 579
Abruption, *separation*, 44
Abscess, *disease*, 655
Abscission, *retrenchment*, 38
  division, 44
Abscond, *escape*, 671
  fly from, 287
Absence, *non-existence*, 2
  non-presence, 187
  inattention, 458
  thoughtlessness, 452

Absent-minded, *inattentive*,
    458
Absentee, *absence*, 187
* Absit omen, *deprecation*,
    766
Absolute, *not relative*, 1
  certain, 474, 31
  positive, 535
  true, 494
  unconditional, 768A
  simple, 42
  authoritative, 737
  severe, 739
  due, 924
  complete, 52
Absolutely, *assent*, 488
Absolve, *forgive*, 918
  exempt, 927A
  liberate, 750
  permit, 760
  acquit, 970
Absonant, *unreasonable*,
    495
  discordant, 414
Absorb, *combination*, 48
  take in, 296
  think, 451
  attend to, 457
  feel, 821
  possess, 777
  consume, 677
Absquatulate, *go away*, 287
Abstain, *refrain*, 603
  temperance, 953
  forbear, 623
Abstemious, *temperance*,
    953, 958
Absterge, *cleanness*, 652
Abstersive, *remedy*, 662
Abstinence, *disuse*, 678
  forbearance, 623, 953
Abstinent, *temperance*, 953
  sobriety, 958
Abstract, *separate*, 44
  deduct, 38
  idea, 451
  to abridge, 596, 572
  to take, 789
  to steal, 791
Abstraction, *inattention*,
    458
  deduction, 38
  disjunction, 44
  unity, 87
Abstruse, *recondite*, 519
  hidden, 528
Absurd, *nonsensical*, 497,
    499
  impossible, 471
  ridiculous, 853
Abundant, *copious*, 639
  great, 31

Abuse, *misuse*, 679
  ill treat, 649
  threat, 909
  upbraid, 932
  defame, 934
  debauch, 961
  deceive, 545
  of language, 523
Abut, *rest on*, 215
  touch, 199
Abyss, *depth*, 208
  space, 180
  hell, 982
Academic, *teaching*, 537
Academician, *artist*, 559
Academy, *school*, 542
Accede, *consent*, 762
Accelerate, *velocity*, 173,
    274
  earliness, 132
  haste, 684
Accension, *calefaction*, 384
Accent, *tone of voice*, 580
  sound, 402
Accept, *receive*, 785
  consent, 762
  assent, 488
Acceptable, *agreeable*, 829
  expedient, 646
Acceptance, *security*, 771
Acceptation, *meaning*,
    516
Accepted, *conformity*, 82
  habitual, 613
Access, *method*, 627
  approach, 286
Accessible, *facility*, 705
  possible, 470
  sociability, 892
Accession, *increase*, 35
  addition, 37
  commission, 755
  to power, 737
Accessory, *addition*, 37
  adjunct, 39
  means, 632
  auxiliary, 711
  aiding, 707
  accompanying, 88
Accidence, *grammar*, 567
Accident, *chance*, 156, 621
  event, 151
Accidental, *external*, 6
  music, 413
Accidie, *dejection*, 837
Acclamation, *approbation*,
    931
  assent, 488
Acclimatize, *inure*, 613
  train, 673
Acclivity, *obliquity*, 217
Accolade, *courtesy*, 894

Actuality, *truly*, 31
Actuary, *accounts*, 811
Actuate, *motive*, 615
*Actum est, *completion*, 729
Acuity, *sharpness*, 253
Aculeated, *sharpness*, 253
Acumen, *wisdom*, 494
Acuminated, *sharpness*, 253
Acupuncture, *opening*, 260
Acute, *pointed*, 253
　　violent (physically), 173
　　sensible (physically), 375
　　painful (morally), 830
　　strong feeling, 820
　　musical tone, 410
　　perspicacious, 498
Acutely, *much*, 31
* Ad arbitrium, *will*, 600
* Ad captandum, *plea*, 617
　　deception, 545
* Ad captandum vulgus,
　　ostentation, 852
* Ad eundem, *equality*, 27
* Ad infinitum, *infinity*, 105
* Ad interim, *duration*, 106
Ad-lib, *improvise*, 612
* Ad libitum, *will*, 600
　　choice, 609
　　sufficiency, 639
* Ad rem, *reasoning*, 473
* Ad unguem, *perfection*, 650
* Ad valorem, *price*, 812
Adage, *maxim*, 496
* Adagio, *slowness*, 275
　　music, 415
Adamant, *hard*, 323
　　strong, 159
Adapt, *fit*, 646
　　adjust, 673
　　agree, 23
Add, *addition*, 37
　　increase, 35
　　numerically, 85
Addendum, *adjunct*, 39
Adder, *viper*, 663
　　maleficent being, 913
Addict, *habit*, 613
Addition, *adjunction*, 37
　　thing added, 39
　　arithmetical, 85
Addle, *barren*, 169
　　abortive, 732
　　to spoil, 659
Addle-headed, *imbecile*, 499
Address, *speak to*, 586
　　skill, 698
　　request, 765
　　residence, 189
　　direction, 550
　　lecture, 582
　　preach, 998
Addresses, *courtship*, 902

Adduce, *bring to*, 288
　　evidence, 467
Adept, *proficient*, 700
　　sorcerer, 994
Adequate, *sufficient*, 639
　　power, 157
　　strength, 159
　　for a purpose, 644
Adhere, *stick*, 46
　　fidelity, 772
　　resoluteness, 604
Adherent, *follower*, 711
Adhesive, *coherence*, 46
　　connective, 45
Adhibit, *use*, 677
Adiaphorism, *heresy*, 984A
Adieu, *departure*, 293
Adipose, *unctuous*, 355
Adiposity, *corpulence*, 192
Adit, *conduit*, 350
　　orifice, 260
　　way, 627
Adjacent, *nearness*, 197
Adjection, *addition*, 37
Adjective, *adjunct*, 39
Adjoin, *nearness*, 197
　　contiguity, 199
Adjourn, *lateness*, 133
Adjudge, *lawsuit*, 969
Adjudication, *choice*, 609
　　judgment, 480
　　lawsuit, 969
Adjunct, *thing added*, 39
　　accompaniment, 88
　　aid, 707
Adjuration, *affirmation*, 535
Adjure, *request*, 765
　　promise, 768
Adjust, *fit*, 27
　　preface, 673
　　settle, 723
　　compromise, 774
Adjutage (or ajutage), *pipe*,
　　　　　　350
　　opening, 260
Adjutant, *auxiliary*, 711
　　military, 745
Adjuvant, *helper*, 707, 711
Admeasurement, *measure-*
　　ment, 466
Administer, *give*, 784
　　apportion, 786
　　manage, 693
　　govern, 737
Administration, *of justice*,
　　　　　　965
Admirable, *excellent*, 648
　　virtuous, 944
Admiral, *master*, 745
Admire, *approve*, 931
　　love, 897
　　wonder, 870

Admissible, *tolerable*, 651
Admission, *ingress*, 294,
　　　　　　296
　　inclusion, 76
Admit, *let in*, 296
　　accept, 785
　　include, 76
　　composition, 54
　　concede in argument, 467
　　disclose, 529
　　allow, 760
　　assent, 488
Admit of, *possibility*, 470
Admixture, *mixture*, 41
Admonish, *advise*, 695
　　warn, 668
　　reprove, 932
　　predict, 511
Ado, *exertion*, 686
　　activity, 682
　　difficulty, 704
Adolescence, *youth*, 131
Adonis, *beauty*, 845
Adopt, *choice*, 609
Adore, *love*, 897
　　worship, 990
Adorn, *beauty*, 845
Adown, *lowness*, 207
Adrift, *unrelated*, 10
　　dispersed, 73
　　at fault, 704
Adroit, *skill*, 698
Adscititious, *extrinsic*, 6
　　added, 37
　　supplementary, 52
* Adscriptus glebæ, *servant*
　　　　　　746
Adulation, *flattery*, 933
Adulator, *flatterer*, 935
Adult, *adolescence*, 131
Adulterate, *mix*, 41
　　deteriorate, 659
　　falsify, 495
Adulterer, *libertine*, 962
Adultery, *impurity*, 961
Adumbrate, *sketch*, 594
　　representation, 554
　　painting, 556
　　faint likeness, 21
　　imitate, 19
　　personify, 521
Adust, *burnt*, 384
　　gloomy, 837
Advance, *progress*, 282, 731
　　to promote, 658
　　forward, 707
　　increase, 35
　　lend, 787
　　expenditure, 809
　　assert, 535
Advanced, *progressive*, 658
　　modern, 123

Advantage, *good*, 618
  utility, 644
  goodness, 648
  superiority, 33
  inequality, 28
  success, 705, 731
Advene, *addition*, 37
Advent, *arrival*, 292
  event, 151
  futurity, 121
Adventitious, *extrinsic*, 6
  casual, 156, 621
Adventure, *event*, 151
  chance, 156, 621
  pursuit, 622
  trial, 675
Adventurer, *deceiver*, 548
  rashness, 863
Adventurous, *courageous*,
  dangerous, 665   [861
* Adversaria, *register*, 551
  chronicle, 594
Adversary, *opponent*, 710
Adverse, *opposed*, 708
  enmity, 889
  disliking, 867
  unprosperous, 735
Adversity, *adversity*, 735
Advert, *attention*, 457
Advertise, *publication*, 531
Advertisement, *preface*, 64
  information, 527
Advice, *counsel*, 695
  notice, 527; *news*, 532
Advisable, *expediency*, 646
Advise, *inform*, 527
  counsel, 695
  predict, 511
Advised, *voluntary*, 600
  intentional, 620
Adviser, *counsellor*, 695
  teacher, 540
Advocacy, *aid*, 707
Advocate, *counsellor*, 968
  advise, 695
  to prompt, 615
  commend, 931
  to vindicate, 937
  Saviour, 967
* Advocatus diaboli, *sophistry*, 477
Advowson, *churchdom*, 995
Adytum, *secret place*, 530
  room, 191
  prediction, 511
Aedile, *authority*, 745
Aegis, *defence*, 717
  patronage, 175
Aeolus, *wind*, 349
Aeon, *duration*, 106, 110
Aequiparate, *equate*, 27

* Aequo animo, *insensible*,
  823
Aerate, *air*, 338
Aerial, *aeriform*, 334, 338
  elevated, 206
Aerie, *abode*, 189
  height, 206
Aeriform, *gaseity*, 334, 338
Aerodrome, *destination*, 292
Aeronautics, *navigation*,
  267
Aeroplane, *aircraft*, 273A
Aerostat, *balloon*, 273A
Aerostatics, *gaseity*, 334
  navigation, 267
Aesthetic, *taste*, 850
  beauty, 845
  sensibility, 375
Aestival, *morning*, 125
Aestivate, *sleep*, 68
Aetiology, *knowledge*, 490
  attribution, 155
  disease, 655
Afar, *distance*, 196
Affable, *courteous*, 894
  sociable, 892
Affair, *business*, 625, 680
  event, 151
  topic, 454
  battle, 720
* Affaire de cœur, *love*, 897
Affect, *desire*, 865
  love, 897
  lend to, 176
  touch, 824
Affectability, *sensibility*,
  822
Affectation, *pretension*, 855
  in style, 577
Affection, *disposition*, 820
  love, 897
  friendship, 888
Affiance, *trust*, 858
  promise, 768
* Affiche, *publication*, 531
Affidavit, *evidence*, 467
  affirmation, 535
  record, 551
Affiliation, *relation*, 9
  kindred, 11
  attribution, 155
Affinity, *relation*, 9
  similarity, 17
Affirm, *assert*, 535
  confirm, 488
Affirmatively, *assent*, 488
Affix, *to join*, 43
  add, 37
  sequel, 39
  addition, 37
Afflatus, *inspiration*, 515
Afflict, *painfulness*, 830

Affliction, *calamity*, 619
  pain, 828
Afflictive, *painfulness*, 830
Affluent, *flowing*, 348
  sufficient, 639
  prosperous, 734
  wealthy, 803
Afflux, *approach*, 286
Afford, *supply*, 134, 784
  wealth, 803
  accrue, 810
Affranchise, *liberation*, 750
Affray, *contention*, 720
Affright, *fear*, 880
Affront, *insult*, 900, 929
  courage, 861
  molest, 830
Affuse, *water*, 337
Afire, *heat*, 382
Afloat, *at sea*, 341
  on shipboard, 273
  unstable, 149
  public, 531
Afoot, *walking*, 266
  existing, 1
  business, 625
  in preparation, 673
Afore, *priority*, 116
Aforementioned, *precedence*, 62
Aforesaid, *repetition*, 104
  precedence, 62
  priority, 116
Aforethought, *intention*,
  620
  premeditation, 611
Afraid, *fear*, 860
Afreet, *demon*, 980
Afresh, *new*, 123
  repeated, 104
  frequent, 136
Aft, *rear*, 235
After, *in order*, 63
  in time, 117
After all, *qualification*, 469
After-clap, *disappointment*,
  509
After-course, *plan*, 626
After-game, *plan*, 626
After-life, *futurity*, 121
After-part, *sequel*, 65
After-piece, *drama*, 599
After-time, *futurity*, 121
Afterglow, *light*, 420
Aftermath, *sequel*, 65
  effect, 154
Afternoon, *evening*, 126
Aftertaste, *taste*, 390
Afterthought, *sequel*, 65
  thought, 451
  memory, 505
  plan, 626

Afterwards, *posteriority*, 117
Aga, *master*, 745
* Agacerie, *motive*, 615
Again, *repeated*, 104
  frequent, 136
Against, *physical opposition*, 179
  voluntary opposition, 708
  anteposition, 237
  provision, 673
Agape, *wonder*, 870
  curiosity, 455
Agate, *ornament*, 847
Age, *period*, 108
  oldness, 124
  duration, 106
  present time, 118
  advanced life, 128
Aged, *veteran*, 130
Ageless, *perpetual*, 112
Agency, *physical*, 170
  instrumentality, 157, 631, 755
  direction, 693
Agenda, *business*, 625
  plan, 626
Agent, *physical*, 153
  voluntary, 690
  consignee, 758, 769
Agentship, *commission*, 755
Agglomerate, *assemblage*, 72
  coherence, 46
Agglutinate, *coherence*, 46
Aggrandize, *in degree*, 35
  in bulk, 194
  honour, 873
Aggravate, *increase*, 35
  vehemence, 173
  distress, 835
  render worse, 659
  exasperate, 900
  exaggerate, 549
  provoke, 830
Aggregate, *whole*, 50
  collection, 72
Aggregation, *coherence*, 46
Aggression, *attack*, 716
Aggressive, *pugnacious*, 901
Aggrieve, *distress*, 830
  injure, 649
Aghast, *with wonder*, 870
  with fear, 860
  disappointed, 509
Agile, *swift*, 274
  active, 682
Agio, *discount*, 813
Agiotage, *barter*, 794
Agitate, *motion*, 315
  activity, 682
  to affect the mind, 821
  to excite, 824

Aglow, *hot*, 382
Agnation, *consanguinity*, 11
Agnomen, *nomenclature*, 564
Agnosticism, *unbelief*, 485, 989
* Agnus Dei, *rite*, 998
Ago, *preterition*, 122
Agog, *curiosity*, 455
  expectation, 507
  desire, 865
Agonistic, *contention*, 720
Agonize, *painfulness*, 830
Agony, *physical*, 378
  mental, 828
Agoraphobia, *seclusion*, 893
  dislike, 866
Agrarian, *agriculture*, 371
Agree, *accord*, 23
  concur, 178
  assent, 488
  consent, 762
  concord, 714
Agreeable, *pleasant*, 377, 829
Agreeably, *conformably*, 82
Agreement, *bargain*, 769
Agrestic, *rural*, 371
  uncouth, 876
Agriculture, *agriculture*, 371
Agronomy, *agriculture*, 371
Aground, *stranded*, 265, 704
  fixed, 150
  failure, 732
Ague-fit, *fear*, 860
Aguish, *cold*, 383
Ahead, *in front*, 62, 234, 280
Ahead (go), *progression*, 282
  to improve, 658
Aid, *to help*, 707, 712
  charity, 606
Aide-de-camp, *auxiliary*, 711
  officer, 745
Aide-memoire, *memory*, 505
Aigrette, *ornament*, 847
Aiguille, *sharp*, 253
Ail, *sick*, 655
  in pain, 828
Ailment, *disease*, 655
Aim, *direction*, 278
  purpose, 620
Aimless, *chance*, 621
  motiveless, 616
Air, *gas*, 334
  atmospheric, 338
  wind, 349
  tune, 415
  appearance, 448
  conduct, 692
  unsubstantial, 4
  fashion, 852

Air, *affectation*, 855
  vanity, 880
Air-balloon, *aircraft*, 273A
Air-built, *imagination*, 515
Air-condition, *air*, 338
Air drop, *transference*, 270
Air lift, *transference*, 270
Air-liner, *aircraft*, 273A
Air Marshal, *master*, 745
Air-pipe, *air-pipe*, 351
Air-pocket, *pitfall*, 667
Air-raid, *attack*, 716
Air-tight, *closed*, 261
Airborne, *locomotion*, 267
  aircraft, 273A
  lightness, 320
Aircraft, *aeroplane*, 273A
Aircraft-carrier, *ship*, 273
Aircraftman, *fighter*, 726
Aircrew, *fighter*, 726
Airfield, *arrival*, 292
Airgraph, *news*, 532; *letter*, [592
Airiness, *levity*, 320
Airing, *journey*, 266
Airman, *navigation*, 269
Airport, *arrival*, 292
Airship, *aircraft*, 273A
Airstop, *arrival*, 292
Airstrip, *arrival*, 292
Airworthy, *safe*, 664
Airy, *atmosphere*, 338
  gay, 836
Aisle, *passage*, 260, 627
  church, 1000
Ajutage, *see*, Adjutage
Akimbo, *angular*, 244
Akin, *consanguinity*, 11
Alabaster, *whiteness*, 430
Alack! *lamentation*, 839
Alacrity, *activity*, 682
  cheerfulness, 836
Alarm, *fear*, 860
  notice of danger, 669
  signal, 550
  threatening, 665
Alarmist, *newsmonger*, 532
Alarum, *warning*, 669
  signal, 550; *loudness*, 404
Alas! *lamentation*, 839
Alb, *dress*, 225
  vestments, 999
Albeit, *counteraction*, 179
  counter-evidence, 468
  compensation, 30
Albescent, *white*, 430
Albification, *white*, 430
Albinism, *achromatism*, 429
Albino, *dim-sightedness*, 443
Album, *book*, 553
  compendium, 596
  repertoire, 636

Anthology, *poem*, 597
　　collection, 72, 596
Anthropology, *mankind*,
　　　　　　　　　372
Anthropomorphic, *man-
　　kind*, 372
Anthropophagi, *evil-doer*,
　　　　　　　　　913
Anthropophagous, *eat*, 296
Antibiotic, *remedy*, 662
Antic, *ridicule*, 856
Antichristian, *irreligion*,
　　　　　　　　　989
Anticipate, *early*, 132
　　future, 121
　　anachronism, 115
　　expect, 507
　　foresee, 510
　　prepare, 673
　　priority, 116
Anticlimax, *depth*, 208
　　bathos, 856
　　decrease, 36
Anticyclone, *rotation*, 312
Antidote, *remedy*, 662
　　counteraction, 179
Antilogarithm, *number*, 84
Antinomy, *illegality*, 964
Antinous, *beauty*, 845
Antiparallel, *obliquity*, 217
Antipathy, *enmity*, 889
Antiphon, *music*, 415
　　answer, 462
　　worship, 990
Antiphrasis, *misnomer*, 565
Antipodes, *distance*, 196
　　antiposition, 237
　　difference, 14
　　depth, 208
Antiposition, *antiposition*,
　　　　　　　　　237
Antiquary, *past*, 122
Antiquated, *vulgarity*, 851
Antique, *oldness*, 124
Anti-scriptural, *pagan*, 986
Antiseptic, *remedy*, 662
　　cleanness, 652
Antisocial, *misanthropy*, 911
Antistrophe, *poetry*, 597
Antithesis, *contrast*, 14
　　comparison, 464
　　style, 574
Antitoxin, *remedy*, 662
Antitype, *prototype*, 22
Antler, *sharpness*, 253
Antonomasia, *substitution*,
　　　　　　　　　147
　　nomenclature, 564
Antonym, *opposite*, 14
Anvil, *support*, 215
　　preparing, 673
　　(on the), *plan*, 626

Anxiety, *pain*, 828
　　fear, 860
　　desire, 865
Anyhow, *careless*, 460
Aorist, *indefinite time*, 119
Apace, *swift*, 274
　　short time, 111
　　early, 132
Apache, *ruffian*, 913, 949
Apanage, *adjunct*, 39
　　property, 780
Apart, *distance*, 196
　　singleness, 87
　　difference, 15
Apartment, *room*, 191
　　abode, 189
Apathy, *physical*, 376
　　moral, 823
　　indifference, 456, 866
Ape, *imitation*, 19
Apelles, *artist*, 559
* Aperçu, *compendium*, 596
Aperitif, *food*, 298
Aperture, *opening*, 260
Apex, *summit*, 210
Aphasia, *aphony*, 581
Aphelion, *distance*, 196
Aphony, *aphony*, 581
Aphorism, *maxim*, 496
Aphrodisiac, *excitation*, 824
Aphrodite, *goddess*, 979
　　love, 897
Apiary, *domestication*, 370
Apicius, *gluttony*, 957
Apiece, *disjunction*, 44
　　particularity, 79
Aplomb, *vertical*, 212
　　intelligence, 498
　　self-possession, 864
Apocalypse, *revelation*, 985
Apocryphal, *uncertain*, 475
　　false, 495, 544
Apodictic, *demonstration*,
　　　　　　　　　478
Apogee, *distance*, 196
　　summit, 210
Apolaustic, *self-indulgent*,
　　　　　　　　　943
Apollo, *god*, 979
　　music, 415
　　beauty, 845
Apologue, *description*, 521,
　　　　　　　　　594
Apology, *penitence*, 950
　　vindication, 937
　　reasoning, 476
　　atonement, 952
　　substitute, 147
Apophthegm, *maxim*, 496
Apoplexy, *weakness*, 160
Aposiopesis, *taciturnity*,
　　　　　　　　　585

Apostasy, *palinode*, 607
　　dishonour, 940
　　heterodoxy, 984A
Apostate, *knave*, 941
　　renegade, 144, 742
Apostatize, *tergiversation*,
　　　　　　　　　607
Apostle, *teacher*, 540
Apostolic, *revelation*, 985
Apostrophe, *appeal*, 765
　　address, 586, 589
Apothecary, *doctor*, 662
Apotheosis, *deification*, 981,
　　　　　　　　　991
Apozem, *solution*, 335
Appal, *fear*, 860
Appalling, *painfulness*, 830
Appanage, *see* Apanage
Apparatus, *instrument*, 633
Apparel, *vestment*, 225
Apparent, *visible*, 446
　　manifest, 525
Apparition, *ghost*, 980
　　appearance, 448
Appeal, *request*, 765
　　address, 586
Appear, *come into being*, 1,
　　　　　　　　　448
　　come to light, 525
　　come into view, 446
Appear for, *deputy*, 759
Appearance, *sight*, 448
　　probability, 472
Appease, *physically*, 174
　　morally, 826
　　conciliate, 918
Appeasement, *pacifism*, 723
　　submission, 725
Appellant, *plaintiff*, 924,
　　　　　　　　　938, 967
Appellation, *nomenclature*,
　　　　　　　　　564
Append, *addition*, 37
　　sequence, 63
　　hang, 214
Appendage, *adjunct*, 39
Appendix, *sequel*, 65
Apperception, *knowledge*,
　　　　　　　　　490
　　conception, 453
Appertain, *belong*, 777
　　related to, 9
　　right, 922
　　inclusion, 76
Appetence, *desire*, 865
Appetiser, *whet*, 298, 615
Appetite, *desire*, 865
Applaud, *approbation*, 931
Apple-green, *greenness*, 435
Apple of discord, *discord*,
　　　　　　　　　713
Apple-sauce, *flattery*, 933

Appleton layer, *air*, 338
Appliance, *means*, 632
    instrument, 633
Applicable, *to use*, 644
    expedient, 646
    relative, 23
Applicant, *petitioner*, 767
Application, *use*, 677
    request, 765
    metaphor, 521
    study, 457
* Appoggiatura, *music*, 415
Appoint, *commission*, 755
    command, 741
Appointment, *salary*, 809
    equipment, 633
    interview, 892
Apportion, *allot*, 786
    arrange, 60
    portion, 51
Apportionment, *dispersion*,
    73
Apposite, *agreeing*, 23
    relative, 9
Apposition, *agreement*, 23
    closeness, 199
Appraise, *value*, 812
    estimate, 466
Appreciate, *measure*, 466
    taste, 850
    realize, 450
    gratitude, 916
    judge, 480
    approve, 931
Apprehend, *know*, 490
    believe, 484
    fear, 860
    seize, 789, 969
Apprehension, *conception*,
    453
Apprentice, *learner*, 541
Apprenticeship, *learning*,
    539
    training, 673
Apprise, *information*, 527
Approach, *move*, 286
    nearness, 197
    path, 627
    of time, 121
Approbation, *approbation*,
    931
Appropinquation, *approach*,
    197, 286
Appropriate, *fit*, 23, 646
    special, 79
    to assign, 786
    to take, 789
    to steal, 791
Appropriation, *stealing*, 791
Approve, *commend*, 931
    corroborate, 467
    assent, 488

Approximate, *approach*, 286
    nearness, 197
    in mathematics, 85
    resemble, 17
    related to, 9
Appulse, *convergence*, 286,
    290
    collision, 276
Appurtenance, *part*, 51
    component, 56
Apricot, *colour*, 439
April fool, *fool*, 501
Apron, *dress*, 225
    vestments, 999
Apropos, *relation*, 9
    expedience, 646
    occasion, 134
Apse, *church*, 1000
Apt, *consonant*, 23
    clever, 698
    docile, 539
    willing, 602
    expedient, 646
    tendency, 176
Aptitude, *intelligence*, 498
    skill, 698
Aquarium, *domestication*,
    370
    collection, 636
Aquatic, *water*, 337
Aquatint, *engraving*, 558
Aqueduct, *conduit*, 350
Aqueous, *water*, 337
Aquiline, *angularity*, 244
Arabesque, *ornament*, 847
Arable, *agriculture*, 371
Araeometer, *density*, 321
    measure, 466
Arbiter, *judge*, 480, 967
    adviser, 695
* Arbiter   elegantiarum,
    taste, 850
Arbitrament, *sentence*, 969
    judgment, 480
    choice, 609
Arbitrary, *without law*, 964
    authority, 737
    obstinate, 606
    severity, 739
    irregular, 83
    without relation, 10
Arbitrate, *mediate*, 724, 969
    judge, 480
Arbor, *support*, 215
Arborescence, *branching*,
    205, 242, 256
Arboretum, *agriculture*, 371
Arboriculture, *agriculture*,
    371
Arbour, *abode*, 189
Arc, *curvature*, 245
Arc-lamp, *light*, 423

Arcade, *arch*, 245
    passage, 189
* Arcades ambo, *similarity*,
    17
    friend, 890
Arcadian, *delightful*, 829
Arcanum, *secret*, 533
Arch, *curve*, 245
    great, 31
    cunning, 702
    roguish, 842
    greatness, 31
Archaeology, *preterition*,
    122
Archaic, *oldness*, 124
Archaism, *inelegance*, 579
Archangel, *angel*, 977
Archbishop, *clergy*, 996
Archdeacon, *clergy*, 996
Archduke, *master*, 745
Archetype, *prototype*, 22
    model, 80
Arch-fiend, *Satan*, 978
Archiepiscopacy,   *church-
    dom*, 995
Archimage, *sorcerer*, 994
Archimandrite, *clergy*, 996
Archipelago, *island*, 346
Architect, *constructor*, 164
    agent, 690
Architecture, *construction*,
    161
    fabric, 329
Architrave, *summit*, 210
Archive, *record*, 551
Archness, *cunning*, 702
    cleverness, 498
    intelligence, 450
Archon, *master*, 745
Arch-traitor, *knave*, 941
Arctic, *polar*, 237
    cold, 383
Arcuation, *curvature*, 245
Ardent, *fiery*, 382
    feeling, 821
    desire, 865
    expectant, 507
Ardour, *activity*, 682
Arduous, *difficulty*, 704
Area, *region*, 181
    quantity, 25
Arefaction, *dryness*, 340
Arena, *field*, 181, 728
    amusement, 840
    workshop, 691
Arenaceous, *pulverulence*,
    330
Areolar, *crossing*, 219
Areopagus, *council*, 696
Ares, *god*, 979
* Arête, *height*, 206
    sharpness, 253

B

autochthonous, *inhabitant*,
        188
Autocracy, *severity*, 739
    authority, 737
Autocrat, *master*, 745
Autocratic, *arbitrary*, 739,
        964
    will, 600
Autocycle, *vehicle*, 272
Autogiro, *aircraft*, 273A
Autograph, *warranty*, 467
    signature, 550
    writing, 590
Autolycus, *thief*, 792
Automatic, *mechanical*, 601
    insensible, 823
Automation, *means*, 632
Automobile, *vehicle*, 272
Autonomy, *freedom*, 748
Autopsy, *vision*, 441
    disinter, 363
Autotype, *copy*, 21
* Aux abois, *death*, 360
* Aux aguets, *care*, 459
Auxiliary, *aid*, 707
    helper, 711
    intermediary, 631
Avail, *use*, 677
    utility, 644
Avalanche, *fall*, 306
    debacle, 348
Avant-courier, *pioneer*, 673
    precursor, 64
Avant-garde, *go-ahead*, 282
Avarice, *parsimony*, 819
Avast, *quiescence*, 265
    cessation, 142
Avaunt, *disappear*, 449
    depart, 293
    repulse, 289
* Ave, *arrival*, 292
Avenge, *revenge*, 919
Avenue, *street*, 189
    method, 627
Aver, *affirmation*, 535
Average, *mean*, 29
    ordinary, 82, 736
Avernus, *hell*, 982
Averse, *unwilling*, 603
    repugnant, 616
Aversion, *dislike*, 867
    enmity, 889; *hate*, 898
Avert, *hindrance*, 706
Aviary, *collection*, 636
    taming, 370
Aviation, *locomotion*, 267
Avidity, *desire*, 865
    avarice, 819
Avifauna, *animals*, 366
Avocation, *business*, 625
    diversion, 840

Avoid, *shun*, 623, 867
Avoirdupois, *weight*, 319
Avouch, *affirmation*, 535
Avow, *assert*, 535
    assent, 488
    disclose, 529
Avulsion, *separation*, 44
    extraction, 301
Await, *future*, 121
    impend, 152
Awake, *excite*, 824
    incite, 615
    active, 682
    attentive, 457
    careful, 459
Award, *lawsuit*, 969
    judgment, 480
    decision, 609
    giving, 784
    trophy, 733
Aware, *knowledge*, 490
Away, *absence*, 187
Awe, *wonder*, 870
    fear, 860
Aweary, *weariness*, 841
Awestruck, *fear*, 860
Awful, *great*, 31
    fearful, 860
Awhile, *transientness*, 111
Awkward, *unskilful*, 699
    vulgar, 851
    ridiculous, 853
    difficult, 704
Awl, *perforator*, 262
Awn, *bristle*, 253
Awning, *tent*, 222
    shade, 424
    top, 210
Awry, *oblique*, 217
    distorted, 243
Axe, *edge tool*, 253
    weapon, 727
    for beheading, 975
Axiom, *maxim*, 496
Axiomatic, *truth*, 494
    certain, 474
    demonstrable, 469, 478
Axis, *rotation*, 312
    length, 200
    support, 215
    centre, 223
Axle, *rotation*, 312
Ay, *yes*, 488
    affirmation, 535
Ayah, *keeper*, 753
Aye, *ever*, 112
Azimuth, *direction*, 278
    obliquity, 217
Azoic, *inanimate*, 358
Azure, *blueness*, 438
Azygous, *unity*, 87

B

Baa, *animal sound*, 412
Baal, *divinity*, 979
    idol, 986
Babble, *talk*, 584
    nonsense, 517
    faint sound, 405
    flow, 348
Babe, *infant*, 129
    innocent, 946
    novice, 701
Babel, *confusion*, 59
    discord, 414
Baboon, *ugliness*, 846
Baby, *fool*, 501
Baby-sitter, *deputy*, 759
Babyhood, *youth*, 127
Babyish, *folly*, 499
Bacca, *tobacco*, 298A
Bacchanals, *drunk*, 959
Bacchus, *drunkenness*, 959
Bachelor, *celibacy*, 904
Bacillus, *bane*, 663
Back, *rear*, 235
    convexity, 250
    to recede, 283; *to aid*, 707
Back-blocks, *interior*, 221
Back down, *revoke*, 607
Back out, *revoke*, 607
    relinquish, 624
Back to square one, *hind-
    rance*, 706
Back-scratcher, *flatterer*,
        935
Backbite, *traduce*, 932
    detract, 934
Backbiter, *detractor*, 936
Backbone, *frame*, 215
    interior, 221
    strength, 159
    decision, 604; *intrinsic*,
    5
Backer, *friend*, 891   [5
Backhanded, *oblique*, 717
    unexpected, 508
Backhander, *attack*, 716
Backlash, *recoil*, 145
Backlog, *leeway*, 304
Backsheesh, see Baksheesh
Backsliding, *dishonour*, 940
    delinquency, 945
    relapse, 661
    tergiversation, 607
    heresy, 984A
Backward, *regression*, 283
    traction, 285
    unwilling, 603
Backwardation, *discount*,
        813
Backwardness, *unwilling-
    ness*, 603
    indocility, 538

Backwardness, *dislike*, 867
Backwoodsman, *inhabitant*, 188
  forester, 371
Bacon, to save one's, *escape*, 671
Bad, *badness*, 649, 945
  evil, 619
  wrong, 923
  putrid, 653
Bad blood, *enmity*, 889
Bad show, *disapproval*, 932
  failure, 732
Badge, *indication*, 550
Badger, *to maltreat*, 830
  question, 461
  stink, 401
Badinage, *wit*, 842
  ridicule, 856
Badmash, *knave*, 941
Baedeker, *guide*, 266
Baffle, *thwart*, 706
  defeat, 731
Baffling, *bewildering*, 528
Baff, *club*, 276
Bag, *receptacle*, 191
  to take, 789, 791
  to receive, 810
  to pocket, 184
Bagatelle, *trifle*, 643
Baggage, *property*, 780
  materials, 634
  hussy, 962
Baggy, *loose*, 47
  bulging, 250
Bagman, *agent*, 758
Bagnio, *impurity*, 961
Bagpipe, *musical instrument*, 417
Bagpiper, *musician*, 416
Bags, *greatness*, 31
  plenty, 639
Bah, *contempt*, 930
Baikie, *receptacle*, 191
Bail, *security*, 771
Bail up, *rob*, 791
Bailiff, *director*, 694
  servant, 746
  officer, 965
  factor, 758
Bailiwick, *region*, 181
  tribunal, 966
Bairn, *infant*, 129
Bait, *allurement*, 615
  food, 298, 689
  harass, 907, 830
Bake, *heat*, 384
Bakehouse, *furnace*, 386
Baker's dozen, *thirteen*, 98
Baksheesh, *gratuity*, 784
Balance, *equality*, 27
  symmetry, 242

Balance, *remainder*, 40
  numeration, 85
  measure, 466
  weight, 319
  money, 800
  accounts, 811
  mean, 29
  steadiness, 265
Balcony, *convexity*, 250
  theatre, 599
Bald, *bare*, 226
  ugly, 846
  in style, 575
Baldachin, *canopy*, 222
Balderdash, *absurdity*, 497
  nonsense, 517
Baldric, *girdle*, 247
Bale, *bundle*, 72
  evil, 619
Bale out, *ejection*, 297
Baleful, *badness*, 649
Balk, *hinder*, 706
  fail, 731
  disappoint, 509
  deceive, 545
Ball, *globe*, 249
  missile, 284, 727
  dance, 840
Ball-point, *pen*, 590
Ballad, *song*, 415
  poem, 597
Ballad opera, *drama*, 599
Ballade, *poem*, 597
  music, 415
Ballast, *weight*, 319
  compensation, 30
  steadiness, 150
  wisdom, 498
Ballet, *amusement*, 840
Ballistics, *propulsion*, 284
* Ballon d'essai, *feeler*, 461, 463
Balloon, *aircraft*, 273A
Ballot, *choice*, 609
Ballyhoo, *publicity*, 531
Ballyrag, *abuse*, 932
Balm, *fragrance*, 400
  relief, 834
  lenitive, 174
  remedy, 662
Balmoral, *cap*, 225
Balmy, *foolish*, 499
Balsam, *see* Balm
Balsamic, *salubrious*, 656
Baluster, *support*, 215
Balustrade, *enclosure*, 232
Bamboo curtain, *secret*, 533
Bamboozle, *deception*, 545
Ban, *prohibition*, 761
  denunciation, 908
  condemnation, 971

Banal, *commonplace*, 82, 643
  feeble, 575
Banausic, *menial*, 876
Band, *ligature*, 45
  assemblage, 72
  party, 712
  of music, 416
  shackle, 752
Bandage, *ligature*, 45
  to lie, 43
Bandbox, *receptacle*, 191
Banderole, *flag*, 550
Bandersnatch, *swiftness*, 274
Bandit, *thief*, 792
Bandog, *warning*, 668
Bandolier, *roundness*, 247
Bands, *canonicals*, 999
Bandy, *agitate*, 315
  contest, 476, 720
  exchange, 148
  crooked, 245
  deformed, 876
Bandy-legged, *distorted*, 243
  curved, 245
Bane, *badness*, 649, 663
Bang, *sound*, 406
  to impel, 276
  to beat, 972
Bangle, *ornament*, 847
Banian day, *fast*, 956
  scanty, 640
Banish, *exclude*, 55, 297
  displace, 185
  seclude, 893
  punish, 972
Banister, *support*, 215
Banjo, *musical instrument*, 417
Bank, *side of river*, 342
  acclivity, 217
  store, 636
  money, 802
  deviate, 279
Banker, *treasurer*, 801
Bankruptcy, *failure*, 732
  non-payment, 808
* Banlieue, *nearness*, 197
Banner, *indication*, 550
Banneret, *nobility*, 875
Banquet, *meal*, 298
  feast, 840
  gluttony, 957
Banshee, *demon*, 980
Bantam, *small*, 193
  low, 207
Banter, *wit*, 842
  ridicule, 856
Bantling, *child*, 129
  offspring, 167
Baptism, *rite*, 998
Baptistery, *temple*, 1000

Bauble, *trifle*, 643
　toy, 840
Baulk, *see* Balk
* Bavardage, *absurdity*, 497
Bawbee, *money*, 800
Bawd, *libertine*, 962
Bawdy, *impurity*, 961
Bawl, *cry*, 411, 839
　to howl, 412
Bay, *gulf*, 343
　brown, 433
　to howl, 412
Bay, at, *defence*, 717
Bayadère, *dancer*, 599
Bayard, *carrier*, 271
　perfection, 650
Bayonet, *arms*, 727
　attack, 716
　kill, 361
Bays, *trophy*, 733
　reward, 973
Bazaar, *mart*, 799
Bazooka, *gun*, 727
Be, *existence*, 1
Be of, *inclusion*, 76
Be off, *departure*, 293
　ejection, 297
Beach, *land*, 342
Beacon, *sign*, 423, 550
　warning, 668
Bead-roll, *list*, 86
Beadle, *janitor*, 263
　officer, 745
　law officer, 965
　church, 996
Beads, *rite*, 998
Beak, *front*, 234
　nose, 250
　judge, 967
Beaker, *receptacle*, 191
Beam, *support*, 215
　of a balance, 466
　of light, 420
　beauty, 845
Beamless, *darkness*, 421
Bean-feast, *pleasure*, 827, 840
　meal, 298
Bear, *sustain*, 215
　produce, 161
　carry, 270
　suffer, 821
　admit, 470
　brute, 895
Bear down upon, *attack*, 716
Bear-garden, *arena*, 728
　brawl, 713
Bear-leader, *teacher*, 540
Bear off, *taking*, 789
Bear out, *confirm*, 467
　vindicate, 937
Bear up, *cheerfulness*, 836
Bear upon, *influence*, 175

Bear upon, *evidence*, 467
　to relate to, 9
Bear with, *indulge*, 740
Bearable, *tolerable*, 651
Beard, *spike*, 253
　rough, 256
　to defy, 715
　courage, 861
　insolence, 885
Beardless, *youth*, 127
Bearer, *carrier*, 271
Bearing, *support*, 215
　direction, 278
　meaning, 516
　appearance, 448
　demeanour, 692
　circumstance, 8
　situation, 183
Bearish, *discourtesy*, 895
Beast, *animal*, 366
　blackguard, 895
Beastly, *uncleanness*, 653
Beat, *strike*, 716, 972
　surpass, 33, 303
　periodic, 138
　oscillation, 314
　agitation, 315
　crush, 330; *sound*, 407
　succeed, 731
　line of pursuit, 625
　news, 532
Beat down, *chaffer*, 794
　insolent, 885
Beat hollow, *superiority*, 33
Beat it, go away, 293, 287
　escape, 671
Beat off, *defence*, 717
Beat time, *chronometry*, 114
Beat up for, *seek*, 461
Beatify, *enrapture*, 829
　honour, 873
　sanctify, 987, 995
Beating, *impulse*, 276
Beatnik, *hippy*, 183
Beatitude, *pleasure*, 827
Beau, *fop*, 854
　man, 373; *admirer*, 897
* Beau idéal, *beauty*, 845
　perfection, 650
* Beau monde, *fashion*, 852
　nobility, 875
* Beau sabreur, *hero*, 861
Beauty, *beauty*, 845
　ornament, 847
　symmetry, 242
Beaver, *hat*, 225
Bebop, *melody*, 413
Becalm, *quiescence*, 265
Because, *attribution*, 155
　reasoning, 476
　motive, 615

Bechance, *eventuality*, 151
Beck, *rill*, 348
　signal, 550
　mandate, 741
Beckon, *signal*, 550
Becloud, *darkness*, 421
Become, *change to*, 144
　behove, 926
Become of, *event*, 151
Becoming, *proper*, 646
　beautiful, 845
　just, 922
　apt, 23
Bed, *layer*, 204
　support, 215
　lodgment, 191
Bed-maker, *servant*, 746
Bedabble, *splash*, 337
Bedarken, *darkness*, 421
Bedaub, *cover*, 222
　dirt, 653
　deface, 846
Bedazzle, *light*, 420
Bedeck, *beauty*, 845
　ornament, 847
Bedevil, *derange*, 61
　bewitch, 992
Bedew, *moisture*, 339
Bedfellow, *friend*, 890
Bedight, *beauty*, 845
Bedim, *darkness*, 421
Bedizen, *beautify*, 845
　ornament, 851
Bedlam, *insanity*, 503
Bedlamite, *madman*, 504
Bedraggle, *soil*, 653
Bedridden, *disease*, 655
Bedstead, *support*, 215
Bedtime, *evening*, 126
Bee, *active*, 682
　party, 892
Bee-line, *direction*, 278
Bee-witted, *folly*, 499
Beef, *complain*, 839
Beefy, *corpulent*, 192
Beelzebub, *Satan*, 978
Beery, *drunken*, 959
Beeswax, *oil*, 356
Beetle, *high*, 206
　projecting, 250
　impact, 276
Befall, *eventuality*, 151
Befit, *agree*, 23
Befitting, *right*, 926
　expedient, 646
Befool, *deceive*, 503, 545
　baffle, 732
Before, *precedence*, 62
Before Christ, *period*, 108
Beforehand, *prior*, 116, 132
Befoul, *uncleanness*, 653
Beg, *request*, 765

Beg the question, *evidence*, 467
Beget, *produce*, 161
Begetter, *father*, 166
Beggar, *petitioner*, 767
   poor, 804
Beggarly, *mean*, 643
   vulgar, 876
   servile, 886
   vile, 940
Begilt, *ornament*, 847
Begin, *beginning*, 66
Begin again, *repetition*, 104
Beginner, *learner*, 541
   novice, 674
Beginning to end, from, *whole*, 50
   completeness, 52
   duration, 106
Begird, *encircle*, 227, 231
Begone, *depart*, 293
   repel, 289
Begrime, *soil*, 653
   deface, 846
Begrudge, *refusal*, 764
   parsimony, 819
Beguile, *deceive*, 545
   amuse, 840
Beguine, *nun*, 996
Begum, *nobility*, 875
Behalf, *advantage*, 618
   aid, 707
Behave, *conduct*, 692
Behead, *punish*, 972
   divide, 44
Behest, *command*, 741
Behind, *in order*, 63
   in space, 235
Behindhand, *late*, 133
   adversity, 735
   insolvent, 808
   shortcoming, 304
Behold, *vision*, 441
Beholden, *grateful*, 916
   obligatory, 926
Behoof, *good*, 618
Behove, *duty*, 926
Bein, *prosperous*, 734
Being, *abstract*, 1
   conduct, 3
Bejan, *learner*, 541
* Bel canto, *music*, 415
* Bel esprit, *humorist*, 844
Belabour, *thump*, 972
   buffet, 276
Belated, *late*, 133
   confused, 491
Belaud, *approbation*, 931
Belay, *junction*, 43
   stop, 265
Belch, *ejection*, 297

Beldam, *old woman*, 130
   hag, 913
Beleaguer, *attack*, 716
Belfry, *height*, 206
   church, 1000
   head, 450
Belie, *falsify*, 544
   misinterpret, 523
   deny, 536
   disagreement, 24
   oppose, 708
Belief, *credence*, 484
   supposition, 514
   religious creed, 983
Believer, *piety*, 987
Belike, *probability*, 472
Belittle, *disparage*, 483
Bell, *sound*, 417
   cry, 412
   funeral, 363
   alarm, 669
Bell-boy, *messenger*, 534
Bell-shaped, *globose*, 249
   concave, 252
Bell-washer, *precursor*, 64
Belle, *woman*, 374
   beauty, 845
Belles-lettres, *language*, 560
   knowledge, 490
Bellicose, *warlike*, 722
Belligerent, *warfare*, 722
Bellow, *cry*, 411, 412
   complain, 839
Bellows, *wind*, 349
Belly, *receptacle*, 191
   interior, 221
   to bulge, 250
Belly-ache, *complain*, 839
Belly-god, *glutton*, 957
Belly-timber, *food*, 298
Bellyful, *sufficiency*, 639
   fullness, 52
Belong, *related*, 9
   property, 717
   attribute, 157
   duty, 926
   inclusion, 76
Belongings, *property*, 780
Beloved, *lover*, 897, 899
Below, *lowness*, 207
   posterior, 117
Belt, *girdle*, 247
   gulf, 343
   outline, 229
   blow, 276
Belvedere, *vision*, 441
Bemire, *soil*, 653
Bemoan, *lament*, 839
Bemuddle, *bewilder*, 458
Bemuse, *bewilder*, 458
Ben, *height*, 206
   interior, 221

* Ben trovato, *probable*, 472
   falsehood, 544
   deception, 545
Bench, *support*, 215
   council, 696
   tribunal, 966
Bencher, *lawyer*, 968
Bend, *curve*, 245
   angularity, 244
   circle, 247
   yield, 324, 725
   circuit, 311
   obliquity, 217
   descent, 806
   deviation, 279
   bow, 308
   humble, 879
Bend to, *tend*, 176
   habit, 613
Bending, *pliant*, 324
Beneath, *under*, 207
   unbecoming, 940
Benedick, *marriage*, 903
Benedictine, *clergy*, 996
Benediction, *approval*, 931
   gratitude, 916
   worship, 990
Benefaction, *giving*, 784
Benefactor, *benevolence*, 912
   giver, 784
Benefice, *churchdom*, 995
Beneficent, *benevolence*, 906
Beneficial, *useful*, 644
   good, 648
Beneficiary, *clergy*, 996
Benefit, *advantage*, 618
   acquisition, 775
   benevolence, 906
Benevolence, *kindness*, 906
   love, 897; *tax*, 812
Benighted, *ignorance*, 491
   darkness, 421
Benignant, *benevolence*, 906
Benison, *approbation*, 931
Bent, *direction*, 278
   inclination, 602
   desire, 865
   tendency, 176
   intentions, 629
   affections, 820
   dishonest, 940
Bent on, *willing*, 602
   resolved, 604, 620
   desirous, 865
Benthamite, *philanthropy*, 910
Benumb, *cold*, 383
   general insensibility, 376
   tactual insensibility, 381
   apathy, 823
Beplaster, *cover*, 222
Bepraise, *approbation*, 931

Bijou, *gem*, 650
  little, 193
Bijouterie, *ornament*, 847
Bike, *bicycle*, 266
Bikini, *dress*, 225
Bilateral, *duplication*, 90
  side, 236
Bilbo, *arms*, 727
Bilboes, *prison*, 752
Bile, *resentment*, 900
Bilge, *trash*, 645
Bilge-water, *dirt*, 653
Bilious, *dejection*, 837
Bilk, *deception*, 545
  swindle, 791
  disappointment, 509
Bill, *money, account*, 811
  charge, 812
  money-order, 800
  security, 771
  in law, 969
  placard, 531
  ticket, 550
  instrument, 633
  weapon, 727
  sharpness, 253
Bill of fare, *food*, 298
  list, 86
  plan, 626
Billabong, *river*, 348
Billet, *epistle*, 592
  ticket, 550
  to apportion, 786
  to locate, 184
* Billet-doux, *epistle*, 592
  endearment, 902
Billiard-table, *level*, 213
Billingsgate, *scolding*, 932
  imprecatory, 908
Billion, *numbers*, 98
Billow, *wave*, 348
Billycock, *hat*, 225
Bimetallism, *money*, 800
Bimonthly, *periodical*, 138
Bin, *receptacle*, 191
Binary, *duality*, 89
Bind, *connect*, 43
  compel, 744
  obligation, 926
  condition, 770
Binge, *amusement*, 840
Bingle, *clip*, 201
Binoculars, *lens*, 445
Binomial, *duplication*, 90
Bint, *girl*, 374
Biograph, *spectacle*, 448
Biographer, *recorder*, 553
Biography, *description*, 594
Biology, *organization*, 357
  life, 359
Bioscope, *spectacle*, 448
Bipartition, *duplication*, 91

Biplane, *aircraft*, 273A
Birch, *scourge*, 975
  to punish, 972
Bird, *animal*, 366
Bird of passage, *traveller*,
             268
Bird-fancier, *collector*, 775
Bird-lime, *vinculum*, 45
Bird's-eye, *tobacco*, 298A
  general, 78
Bird's-eye view, *sight*, 448
Birds of a feather, *inclusion,*
  conformity, 82   [76
Bireme, *ship*, 273
Biretta, *cap*, 225
  vestments, 999
Biro, *pen*, 590
Birth, *beginning*, 66
  production, 161
  nobility, 875
Birthday, *anniversary*, 138
Birthmark, *blemish*, 848
Birthplace, *origin*, 153
Birthright, *dueness*, 924
* Bis, *duplication*, 89
  repetition, 104
* Bise, *wind*, 349
Bisection, *duality*, 91
Bishop, *clergy*, 996
Bishopric, *churchdom*, 995
Bissextile, *period*, 108
Bistoury, *sharpness*, 253
Bistre, *brown*, 433
Bisulcate, *fold*, 258, 259
Bit, *part*, 51
  mixture, 41
  small quantity, 32
  money, 800; *curb*, 752
Bit by bit, *part*, 51
  degree, 26
Bitch, *bad woman*, 949
Bite, *pain*, 378
  painful, 830
  cheat, 545
Biting, *cold*, 383
  pungent, 392
  painful, 830
Bitter, *taste*, 395
  cold, 383
  animosity, 898
  wrath, 900
  malevolence, 907
  regret, 833
  painful, 830
Bitumen, *semiliquid*, 352
Bivouac, *repose*, 265
  to encamp, 186
  camp, 189; *watch*, 664
Bizarre, *ridiculous*, 853
  unconformity, 83
Blab, *disclosure*, 529

Black, *colour*, 431
  crime, 945
  copy, 590
Black-and-white, *colourless*,
            429
Black art, *sorcery*, 992
Black hole, *prison*, 752
Black-letter, *printing*, 591
Black looks, *discourtesy*, 598
Black market, *illegality*, 964
  theft, 791
Black-out, *darkness*, 421
Black out, *obliterate*, 552
Black sheep, *bad man*, 949
Blackamoor, *blackness*, 431
Blackball, *exclude*, 55
  reject, 610
  seclude, 893
  disapprove, 932
Blacken, *disapprobation*,
            932
Blackguard, *rude*, 895
  vulgar, 851
  vagabond, 949
  evildoer, 913
  to revile, 932
Blackleg, *sharper*, 548
  thief, 792
  traitor, 941
Blacklist, *disapprove*, 932
Blackmail, *theft*, 791
  booty, 793
Bladder, *receptacle*, 191
Blade, *instrument*, 633
  sharpness, 253
  man, 372
  fop, 854
* Blague, *humbug*, 545
  boast, 884
Blah, *nonsense*, 497
Blain, *swelling*, 250
Blamable, *vice*, 945
Blame, *disapprobation*, 932
Blameless, *innocence*, 946
Blameworthy, *vice*, 945
  disapproval, 932
Blanch, *whiteness*, 430
Bland, *courteous*, 894
  mild, 174
Blandiloquence, *flattery*,
            933
Blandishment, *flattery*, 902,
            933
  motive, 615
Blank, *insubstantiality*, 2, 4
  simple, 42
  vacant, 187
  verse, 597
Blare, *loudness*, 404
Blarney, *flattery*, 933
  plea, 617
Blasé, *weariness*, 841

Blasé, *satiety*, 869
Blasphemy, *impiety*, 988
   malediction, 908
Blast, *wind*, 349
   sound, 404
   evil, 619
   curse, 908
   explosion, **173**
   destroy, 162
Blast-furnace, *furnace*, 386
Blatant, *cry*, **412**
   loud, 404
   silly, 499
Blatherskite, *chatter*, 584
Blaze, *light*, 420
   heat, 382
Blaze abroad, *publish*, 531
Blazon, *publication*, 531
Blazonry, *colour*, 428
Bleach, *discolour*, 429
   whiten, 430
Bleak, *cold*, 383
   dreary, 830
Blear-eyed, *dim-sighted*, 443
Bleat, *animal cry*, 412
Bleb, *swelling*, 250
   bubble, 353
Bleed, *physical pain*, 378
   moral pain, 828
   overcharge, 814
   despoil, 789
Bleeding, *excretion*, 299
Blemish, *ugly*, 846
   defect, 651, 848
Blench, *avoid*, 623
   fear, 860
Blend, *mix*, 41
   combine, 48
Bless, *approbation*, 931
Blessed, *happy*, 827
Blessing, *good*, 618
Blether, *nonsense*, 497, 499
   loquacity, 584
Blight, *evil*, 619
   adversity, 735
   decay, 659
Blighter, *knave*, 949
Blighty, *home*, 189
Blimp, *balloon*, 273A
   die-hard, 606
Blimpish, *prejudiced*, 481
   foolish, 499
Blind, *blindness*, 442
   ignorant, 491
   screen, 424
   falsehood, 546
   deception, 545
   concealment, 528
   necessity, 601
   heedless, 458
   pretext, 617
   imperforate, 261

Blind alley, *closure*, 261
Blind side, *obstinacy*, 606
   prejudice, 481
Blindfold, *sightless*, 442
   ignorant, 491
Blink, *wink*, 442
   neglect, 460
   overlook, 458
   shirk, 623
Blinkard, *dim-sighted*, 443
Blinkers, *mask*, 530
Bliss, *pleasure*, 827
Blister, *swelling*, 250
Blithe, *cheerfulness*, 836
Blitz, *attack*, 716
Blizzard, *wind*, 349
Bloated, *swollen*, 194
Block, *mass*, 192
   dense, 321
   fool, 501
   execution, 975
Block-buster, *bomb*, **727**
Block in, *sketch*, 556
Block out, *form*, 240
Block up, *plug*, 261
   impede, 706
Blockade, *closure*, 261
   hindrance, 706
   restraint, 751
Blockhead, *fool*, 501
Blockhouse, *defence*, **716**
Blockish, *folly*, 499
Bloke, *man*, 373
Blonde, *whiteness*, 430
Blood, *relation*, 11
   killing, 361
   fluid, 333
   affections, 820
   nobility, 875
   fop, 854
Blood-guilty, *killing*, 361
Blood-letting, *ejection*, 297
Blood-red, *redness*, 434
Blood-stained, *murderous*, 361
   maleficent, 907
Bloodhound, *evil-doer*, 913
   detective, 461
Bloodless, *weak*, 160
   peaceful, 721
Bloodshed, *killing*, 361
Bloodsucker, *evildoer*, 913
Bloodthirsty, *malevolence*, 907
Bloody, *malevolence*, 907
   killing, 361
Bloom, *youth*, 127
   prosperity, 734
   success, 731
   blueness, 438
Bloomer, *error*, 495
   dress, 225

Blooming, *beauty*, 845
   health, 654
Blossom, *plant*, 367
   success, 731
   prosperity, 734
Blot, *obliterate*, 552
   dry up, 340
   darken, 431
   disappear, 449
   discoloration, 429
   forget, 506
   ugly, 846
   blemish, 848
   disgrace, 874
   dishonour, 940
   guilt, 947
Blotch, *blackness*, 431
   blemish, 848
Blotto, *drunk*, 959
Blouse, *dress*, 225
Blow, *wind*, 349
   boast, 884
   knock, 276
   action, 680
   evil, 619
   expletive, 908
   pain, 828
   disappointment, 732
   inexpectation, 508
   mishap, 830
   to prosper, 734
Blow down, *destruction*, 162
Blow-hole, *air-pipe*, 351
Blow out, *extinguish*, 385, 421
   gluttony, 957
Blow over, *preterition*, 122
   cessation, 142
Blow up, *fan*, 615
   wind, 349
   inflame, 194
   eruption, 173
   objurgation, 932
Blow upon, *censure*, **934**
Blower, *signal*, 550
Blown, *fatigued*, 688
Blowpipe, *wind*, 349
Blowzy, *red*, 434
   sluttish, 653
Blubber, *cry*, 839
   fat, 356
Bludgeon, *club*, 276
   weapon, 727
Blue, *colour*, 438
   learned, 490
Blue-book, *record*, 551
Blue devils, *dejection*, 837
Blue lights, *firework*, 423
Blue-pencil, *expletive*, 908
Blue-print, *model*, 22
   plan, 626
Blue ruin, *drunkenness*, **959**

Bonnet, *hat*, 225
  to assault, 716
Bonny, *pretty*, 845
  cheerful, 836
Bonus, *advantage*, 618
  gift, 784
  money, 810
  addition, 39
Bony, *hard*, 323
Bonze, *clergy*, 996
Boo, *cry*, 412
  deride, 927
Boob, *fool*, 501
Booby, *fool*, 501
  ignoramus, 493
Boodle, *booty*, 793
Boogie-woogie, *rhythm*, 413
Book, *volume*, 593
  enter account, 811
  to record, 551
  to register, 86
  to bespeak, 132
Book-keeper, *recorder*, 553
Book-keeping, *accounts*, 811
Booked, *dying*, 360
Bookish, *erudite*, 490
  scholarly, 492
Bookless, *ignorant*, 493
Bookworm, *scholar*, 492
Boom, *bar*, 633
  defence, 717
  obstacle, 706
  support, 215
  to sail, 267
  rush, 274
  cry, 402
  sound, 404
  impact, 276
  praise, 931
Boomerang, *arms*, **727**
  recoil, 277
Boon, *giving*, 784
  good, 618
Boor, *clown*, 876
  discourteous, 895
  ridiculous, 851
Boost, *throw*, 284
  commend, 931
  publicity, 531
Boot, *addition*, 37
  dress, 225
  advantage, 618
  important, 642
  punishment, 975
Boot-boy, *servant*, 746
Booth, *abode*, 189
  shop, 799
Bootlegging, *illegality*, 964
Bootless, *useless*, 645
  failing, 732
Bootlicker, *toady*, 886
Boots, *servant*, 746

Booty, *plunder*, 793
Booze, *drunkenness*, 959
Bo-peep, *vision*, 441
Border, *edge*, 230
  limit, 233
  ornament, 847
  to be near, 197
Bore, *hole*, 260
  diameter, 202
  to trouble, 828
  to plague, 830
  to weary, 841
  dull, 843
  tide, 348
Boreal, *polar*, 237
  cold, 383
Boreas, *wind*, 349
Borer, *perforator*, 262
* Borné, *folly*, 499
Borough, *abode*, 189
Borrow, *borrowing*, 788
  debt, 806
Borstal, *school*, 542
  punishment, 972
Boscage, *vegetation*, 367
Bosh, *nonsense*, 517
Bosom, *breast*, 221
  mind, 450; *will*, 600
  affection, 820
Bosom friend, *friend*, 890
Boss, *convexity*, 250
  to direct, 693, 737
  master, 745
Bossy, *will*, 600
  severity, 739
Botanic, *plant*, 367
Botany, *botany*, 369
Botch, *to mend*, 658
  to fail, 732
  unskilful, 699
  imperfect, 651
Both, *duality*, 89
Bother, *trouble*, 828, 830
  fuss, 682
Bottle, *receptacle*, 191
Bottle-neck, *thinness*, 203
Bottle-party, *food*, 298
  sharing, 778
Bottle up, *preserve*, 670
  enclose, 231
  restrain, 751
  remember, 505
Bottle-washer, *servant*, 746
Bottom, *lowest part*, 211
  base, 215
  valley, 252
  ship, 273
  pluck, 604; *courage*, 861
Bottom, at, *intrinsicality*, 5
Bottomless, *depth*, 208
Boudoir, *room*, 191

Bough, *part*, **51**
  plant, 367
  curve, 245
Boulder, *mass*, 192
Boulevard, *circumjacence*,
              227
  way, 627
* Bouleversement, *change*,
              140
  destruction, 162
Bounce, *violence*, 173
  motion, 274
  recoil, 277
  eject, 297
  dismiss, 756
  boast, 884
  insolence, 885
  exaggeration, 549
Bounce upon, *arrival*, 292
  surprise, 508
Bouncer, *untruth*, 546
Bouncing, *large*, 192
Bound, *limit*, 233
  circumscribe, 231
  speed, 274
  leap, 309
Boundary, *limit*, 233
Bounder, *upstart*, 876
Boundless, *great*, 31
  infinite, 105
  space, 180
Bounteous, *benevolent*, 906
Bountiful, *liberal*, 816
Bounty, *gift*, 784
  liberality, 816
  benevolence, 906
Bouquet, *fragrance*, 400
  ornament, 847
Bourgeois, *middle class*,
           736, 876
Bourne, *limit*, 233
Bourse, *mart*, 799
Bout, *turn*, 138
  job, 680
  fight, 720
* Boutade, *absurdity*, 497
  caprice, 608
Bovine, *inert*, 172, 823
Bow, *curve*, 245
  ornament, 847
  fore-part, 234
  shot, 284
  arms, 727
  to stoop, 308
  reverence, 894
  submission, 725
  obeisance, 743
  servility, 886
  respect, 928
  prominence, 250
Bow-legged, *curvature*, 245
  distortion, 243

owdlerize, *expurgate*, 652
owels, *interior*, 221
  of compassion, 914
ower, *alcove*, 189
  chamber, 191
owie-knife, *arms*, **727**
  sharpness, 253
owl, *vessel*, 191
  hollow, 252
  to *propel*, 284
owler, *hat*, 225 '
owling-green, *horizontality*
           213
owshot, *nearness*, 197
owstring, *scourge*, 975
ox, *chest*, 191
  house, 189
  theatre, 599
  to *strike*, 972
  to *fight*, 720
oxer, *combatant*, **726**
oxing, *contention*, **720**
oy, *infant*, 129
oy friend, *love*, 897
oycott, *exclude*, 893
  eject, 297
oyhood, *youth*, **127**
ra, *dress*, 225
race, to *tie*, 43
  fastening, 45
  two, 89
  to *refresh*, 689
  to *strengthen*, 159
race and bit, *perforator*,262
racelet, *ornament*, 847
  circularity, 247
racer, *remedy*, 662
rachygraphy, *writing*, 590
racing, *strengthening*, 159
  refreshing, 689
racket, *tie*, 43
  support, 215
  vinculum, 45
  couple, 89
rackish, *pungent*, **392**
rad, *vinculum*, 45
radawl, *perforator*, 262
rae, *height*, 206
rag, *boasting*, 884
raggadocio, *boasting*, 884
raggart, *boasting*, 884
  bully, 887
rahma, *god*, 979
rahmin, *clergy*, **996**
  religious, 984
raid, to *tie*, 43
  ligature, 45
  intersection, 219
raille, *printing*, 591
rain, *intellect*, 450
  skill, 498
rain-sick, *giddy*, 460

Brain-storm, *excitability*,
           825
Brainless, *imbecile*, 499
Brains trust, *council*, 696
Brainwash, *teach*, 537
Brake, *copse*, 367
  curb, 752
  vehicle, 272
Bramble, *thorn*, 253
  painful, 830
Bran, *pulverulence*, 330
Bran-new, *see* Brand-new
Branch, *member*, 51
  plant, 367
  duality, 91
  posterity, 167
  ramification, 256
Branch off, *divergence*, 291
Branch out, *style*, 573
  divide, 91
Brand, to *burn*, 384
  fuel, 388
  to *stigmatize*, 932
  mark, 550
  to *accuse*, 938
  reproach, 874
Brand-new, *new*, 123
Brander, *roast*, 384
Brandish, *oscillate*, 314
  flourish, 315
* Bras croisés, *inactive*, 683
Brasier, *furnace*, 386
Brass, *insolence*, 885
  colour, 439
Brass up, *pay*, 809
Brassed off, *bored*, 641
  sated, 869
Brasserie, *food*, 298
Brassière, *dress*, 225
Brassy, *club*, 276
Brat, *infant*, 129
Bravado, *boasting*, 884
Brave, *courage*, 861
  to *defy*, 715
Bravery, *courage*, 861
  ornament, 847
Bravo, *assassin*, 361
  applause, 931
* Bravura, *music*, 415
Braw, *handsome*, 845
Brawl, *cry*, 411
  discord, 713
  contention, 720
Brawny, *strong*, 159
  stout, 192
Bray, *cry*, 412
  to *grind*, 330
Brazen-faced, *insolent*, 885
Breach, *crack*, 44
  quarrel, 713
  violation, 925
  exception, 83

Bread, *food*, 298
Breadstuffs, *food*, 298
Breadth, *thickness*, 202
  of mind, 498
Break, *fracture*, 44
  shatter, 162
  incompleteness, 53
  interval, 70, 106, 198
  opportunity, 134
  luck, 621, 731
  crumble, 328
  violation, 773
  bankruptcy, 808
  to *infringe*, 927
  to *disclose*, 529
  to *tame*, 749
  to *decline*, 659
  to *swerve*, 311
Break down, *fail*, 158, 732
Break ground, *undertaking*,
           676
Break in, *teach*, 537
  train, 370, 673
Break loose, *escape*, 671
  liberate, 750
Break off, *a habit*, 614
  leave off, 142
  abrogate, 756
Break out, *fly out*, 825
Break the ranks, *derange-*
  ment, 61
Break the record, *superior*
  ity, 33
Break up, *destroy*, 162
  deteriorate, 659
  decompose, 49
Break with, *discord*, 713
Breaker, *wave*, 348
  danger, 667
Breakfast, *food*, 298
Breakneck, *perilous*, 665
  precipitous, 217
Breakwater, *refuge*, 666
  enclosure, 232
Breast, *interior*, 221
  convexity, 250
  mind, 450
  will, 600
  soul, 820
  to *oppose*, 708
Breastplate, *defence*, 717
Breastwork, *defence*, 717
Breath, *air*, 349
  sound, 405
  life, 359, 364
Breathe, *exist*, 1
  live, 359
  blow, 349
  mean, 516
  utter, 580, 582
  repose, 687
Breather, *preparation*, **673**

Bruise, *hurt*, 619
  to injure, 649
  pound, 330
Bruiser, *fighter*, 726
Bruit, *publication*, 531
  news, 532
Brumal, *cold*, 383
  evening, 126
Brummagem, *spurious*, 544
Brumous, *foggy*, 422
Brunette, *brown*, 433
Brunt, *impulse*, 276
  attack, 716
Brush, *rapid motion*, 274
  to clean, 652
  painting, 559
  fight, 720
  rough, 256
Brush up, *memory*, 505
Brushwood, *plant*, 367
Brusque, *discourteous*, 895
  inelegant, 579
  rough, 173
Brutal, *vicious*, 945
  ill-bred, 895
  savage, 907
Brutalize, *harden*, 823, 895
Brute, *animal*, 366
  rude, 895
  maleficent, 913
Brute force, *illegality*, 964
Brute matter, *materiality*,
      316
  inanimate matter, 358
Brutish, *vulgar*, 851, 876
  intemperate, 954
* Brutum fulmen, *impotence*, 158
  laxity, 738
Bubble, *air*, 353
  light, 320
  trifle, 643
  error, 495
  vision, 515
  deceit, 545
  excitement, 824
  flow, 348
Buccaneer, *thief*, 792
Buck, *leap*, 309
  to wash, 652
  fop, 854
  money, 800
Buck up, *hasten*, 274
  stimulate, 615
  cheer, 836
Bucket, *receptacle*, 191
Bucketful, *quantity*, 25
Buckle, to tie, 43
  vinculum, 45
  distort, 243
Buckle to, *apply oneself*, 682
Buckle with, *grapple*, 720

Buckler, *defence*, 666, 717
Buckram, *hardness*, 323
  affectation, 855
Buckshee, *superfluous*, 641
Bucolic, *domestication*, 370
  poem, 597
Bud, *beginning*, 66
  to expand, 194
  effect, 154
  graft, 300
Buddha, *deity*, 979
  religious founder, 986
Buddhism, *religions*, 984
Buddy, *friend*, 891
  associate, 88
Budge, *move*, 264
Budget, *heap*, 72
  store, 636
  news, 532
  accounts, 811
Buff, *yellow*, 436
  grindstone, 331
Buffer, *defence*, 717
  fellow, 373
Buffet, *cupboard*, 191
  beat, 276, 972
Buffet car, *vehicle*, 272
* Buffo, *the drama*, 599
Buffoon, *humorist*, 844
  butt, 857
  actor, 599
Buffoonery, *amusement*, 840
  ridiculous, 856
Bugaboo, *fear*, 860
Bugbear, *fear*, 860
  alarm, 669
  imaginary, 515
Buggy, *vehicle*, 272
Bughouse, *insane*, 503
Bugle, *instrument*, 417
  war-cry, 722
Bugs, *insane*, 503
Buhl, *variegation*, 440
Build, *construct*, 161
  compose, 54
Build-up, *display*, 882
Build upon, *expect*, 507, 858
  count upon, 484
Builder, *producer*, 164
Building, *abode*, 189
Bulb, *knob*, 249, 250
Bulbous, *swollen*, 194
  rotund, 249
Bulge, *convexity*, 250
Bulimia, *desire*, 865
Bulk, *whole*, 50
  size, 192
Bulkhead, *hindrance*, 706
Bulky, *size*, 192
Bull, *absurdity*, 497, 853
  error, 495
  solecism, 568

Bull, *nonsense*, 497, 517
  law, 963
  ordinance, 741
  police, 664
Bull-calf, *fool*, 501
Bulldog, *courage*, 861
  resolution, 604
Bullet, *ball*, 249
  missile, 284
  arms, 727
  swiftness, 274
Bullet-proof, *defence*, 717
Bulletin, *message*, 532
Bullion, *money*, 800
Bull's-eye, *middle*, 68
Bully, *bluster*, 885
  blusterer, 887
  fight, 726
  domineer, 739
  frighten, 860
  good, 648
Bulrush, *unimportance*, 643
Bulwark, *defence*, 717
  refuge, 666
Bum, *tramp*, 268, 876
  loafer, 683
  pauper, 804
  rascal, 949
Bumbledom, *authority*, 737
Bumboat, *ship*, 273
  provision, 637
Bumboatman, *trader*, 797
Bump, *projection*, 250
  thump, 276
Bump off, *kill*, 361
Bumper, *sufficiency*, 639
  fullness, 52
Bumpkin, *commonalty*, 876
Bumptious, *insolent*, 885
Bun-fight, *party*, 892
Bunce, *profit*, 618
Bunch, *protuberance*, 250
  collection, 72
Bundle, *packet*, 72
  to move, 275
Bung, *stopper*, 263
  throw, 284
Bung-ho, *departure*, 293
Bungalow, *abode*, 189
Bungle, *unskilfulness*, 699
  failure, 732
Bungler, *unskilful*, 701
Bunion, *swelling*, 250
Bunk, *bed*, 191, 215
  escape, 671
Bunker, *receptacle*, 191
  obstruction, 706
Bunkie, *friend*, 891
Bunkum, *humbug*, 545
  nonsense, 497
Bunt, *inversion*, 218
  deviate, 279

Bunting, *flag*, 550
Buoy, *float*, 320
  to raise, 307
  to hope, 858
Buoyant, *floating*, **305**
  levity, 320
  elastic, 325
  hopeful, 858
  cheerful, 836
Bur, *rough*, 256
  clinging, 46
Burberry, *dress*, 225
Burden, *weight*, 319
  clog, 706
  chorus, 104, 415
  frequency, 136
  lading, 190
  care, 830
  oppression, 828
Bureau, *cabinet*, 691
  office, 799
Bureaucracy, *direction*, 693
  authority, 737
Burgee, *flag*, 550
Burgeon, *expansion*, 194
  increase, 35
Burgess, *citizen*, 188, 373
Burgher, *man*, 373
Burglar, *thief*, 792
Burglary, *stealing*, 791
Burgomaster, *master*, 745
Burgrave, *master*, 745
Burial, *corpse*, 362
Buried, *depth*, 208
Burin, *engraving*, 559
Burke, *kill*, 361
  destroy, 162
  suppress, 528
Burlesque, *imitation*, 19
  travesty, 21
  drama, 599
  ridicule, 856
  ridiculous, 853
Burletta, *the drama*, 599
Burly, *size*, 192
Burn, *heat*, 382
  consume, 384
  detection, 480A
  passions, 821
  rivulet, 348
Burnish, *polish*, 255
  beautify, 845
  shine, 420
Burnous, *dress*, 225
Burp, *belch*, 297
Burrow, *excavate*, 252
  lodge, 186
Bursar, *treasurer*, 801
Bursary, *treasury*, 802
Burst, *explosion*, 173
  sound, 406
  of anger, 900

Burst, *paroxysm*, 825
  spree, 840
  separate, 44
Burst forth, *appear*, 446
  sprout, 194
Burst out, *ejaculate*, 580
Burst upon, *inexpectation*,
    508
Bury, *inter*, 363
  conceal, 528
Bus, *vehicle*, 272
Busby, *hat*, 225
Bush, *branch*, 51
  shrub, 367
Bushel, *receptacle*, 191
Bushy, *roughness*, 256
Business, *occupation*, **625**
  event, 151
  topic, 454
  action, 680
  barter, 794
Business-like, *activity*, 682
  skilful, 698
  order, 58
Buskin, *dress*, 225
  drama, 599
Buss, *ship*, 272
  kiss, 902
Bustle, *activity*, 682
  agitation, 315
  haste, 684
  energy, 171
  earliness, 132
Busy, *activity*, 682
Busybody, *activity*, 682
  curiosity, 455
But, *exception*, 83, 179
  counter-evidence, 468
Butcher, *evildoer*, 913
Butchery, *killing*, 361
Butler, *servant*, 746
Butt, *aim*, 620
  laughing-stock, 857
  remnant, 40
  part, 51; *to push*, 276
  to attack, 716
Butt-end, *end*, 67
Butt in, *intervene*, 228
Butte, *height*, 206
Butter, *softness*, 324
  oiliness, 356
  to flatter, 933
Butter-fingers, *bungler*, **701**
Butterfly, *beauty*, 845
  fickleness, 605
  fear, 860
Butterscotch, *sweet*, 396
Button, *knob*, 250
  to fasten, 43
  fastening, 45
  hanging, 214
  trifle, 643

Buttoned up, *reserved*, 528
  taciturn, 585
Buttonhole, *ornament*, 847
  accost, 586
Buttonholer, *weariness*, 841
Buttons, *servant*, 746
Buttress, *support*, 215
  defence, 717
  strengthen, 159
Buxom, *plump*, 192
  cheerful, 836
Buy, *purchase*, 795
Buzz, *sound*, 409, 412
  to publish, 531
  news, 532
Buzz-bomb, *arms*, **727**
Buzz off, *depart*, 293
Buzzard, *fool*, 501
By and by, *transientness*,
    111
By fits and starts, *disorder*,
    59
  irregularity, 139
By jingo, *affirmation*, 535
By-law, *legality*, 963
By-name, *misnomer*, 565
By the by, *opportunity*, 134
Bye-bye, *departure*, 293
  sleep, 683
Bygone, *former*, 122
  forgotten, 506
Bypath, *road*, 627
Byplay, *gesture*, 550
Byssus, *roughness*, 256
Bystander, *spectator*, 444
  near, 197
Byway, *road*, 627
Byword, *maxim*, 496
  cant term, 563
  contempt, 930

C

C.A., *accounts*, 811
C.O.D., *payment*, 807
Ca' canny, *caution*, 864
Cab, *vehicle*, 272
  translation, 522
Cabal, *confederacy*, 712
  plan, 626
Cabbage, *purloin*, 791
Cabbala, *spell*, 993
Cabbalistic, *mysterious*, **528**
Caber, *missile*, 284
Cabin, *room*, 189
  receptacle, 191
Cabin cruiser, *ship*, 273
Cabinet, *receptacle*, 191
  workshop, 691
  council, 696
Cable, *vinculum*, 45

Cabriolet, *vehicle*, 272
Cache, *hiding-place*, 530
  conceal, 528
  store, 636
Cachexy, *disease*, 655
  weakness, 160
Cachinnation, *rejoicing*, 838
Cachucha, *dance*, 840
Cacique, *master*, 745
Cackle, *of geese*, 412
  talk, 588
  laughter, 838
Cacodemon, *demon*, 980
Cacodyl, *fetor*, 401
* Cacoethes, *habit*, 613
  itch, 865
  writing, 590
* Cacoethes loquendi,
  loquacity, 584
* Cacoethes scribendi,
  writing, 590
Cacography, *writing*, 590
Cacophony, *stridor*, 410
  discord, 414
  style, 579
Cad, *vulgarity*, 851
Cadastre, *list*, 86
Cadaverous, *corpse*, 362
  pale, 429
  thin, 203
  hideous, 846
Caddish, *mean*, 940
Caddy, *receptacle*, 191
Cadence, *accent*, 580
  music, 415
  descent, 306
Cadenza, *music*, 415
Cadet, *junior*, 129
  combatant, 726
  officer, 745
Cadge, *request*, 765
Cadger, *merchant*, 797
Cadi, *judge*, 967
Cadmium, *orange*, 439
Cadre, *framework*, 215
Caduceus, *spell*, 993
Caducity, *transientness*, 111
Caecum, *closure*, 261
Caesar, *master*, 745
Caesura, *break*, 70
  disjunction, 44
* Caetera desunt, *incomplete*, 53
* Caeteris paribus, *circumstance*, 8
  equality, 27
Café, *food*, 298
Cafeteria, *food*, 298
Caftan, *dress*, 225
Cage, *prison*, 231, 752
  to immure, 751
  abode, 189

Cagey, *cautious*, 864
Caique, *ship*, 273
Cairn, *grave*, 363
  sign, 550
Caisson, *receptacle*, 191
  depth, 208
Caitiff, *ruffian*, 913
  villain, 949
Cajole, *persuade*, 615
  flatter, 933
Cake, *cohesion*, 46
  density, 321
  food, 298
Cake eater, *philander*, 902
Cakewalk, *dance*, 840
  easy, 705
Calabash, *receptacle*, 191
  tobacco-pipe, 298A
Calaboose, *prison*, 752
Calamity, *evil*, 619
  adversity, 735
  suffering, 830
Calash, *vehicle*, 272
  cap, 225
Calcine, *calefaction*, 384
Calculate, *reckon*, 85
  expect, 507
  believe, 484
  investigate, 461
Calculated, *tending to*, 176
  premeditated, 600, 611
Calculating, *prudent*, 498
Calculation, *motive*, 615
  caution, 864
Calculus, *numeration*, 85
Caldron, *see* Cauldron
Calefaction, *heating*, 384
* Calembour, *pun*, 563
Calendar, *of time*, 114
  list, 86; *record*, 551
Calender, *to glaze*, 255
Calf, *fool*, 501
Caliban, *ugliness*, 846
Calibre, *size*, 192
  breadth, 202
  degree, 26
  opening, 260
  intellectual capacity, 698
Calidity, *heat*, 382
Caliph, *master*, 745
Caliphate, *authority*, 737
Call, *to name*, 564
  motive, 615
  visit, 892
  inspiration, 985
Call-boy, *theatre*, 599
Call down, *malediction*, 908
Call for, *order*, 741
  ask, 765
  require, 630
Call forth, *resort to*, 677

Call-girl, *prostitute*, 962
Call on, *ask*, 765
Call over, *numeration*, 85
Call up, *memory*, 505
  summon, 741
Call upon, *behove*, 926
  visit, 892
  claim, 924
Callant, *youth*, 129
Caller, *arrival*, 292
Calligraphy, *writing*, 590
Calling, *business*, 625
Callipers, *measurement*, 466
Callisthenics, *training*, 537, 673
Callosity, *hardness*, 323
Callous, *obtuse*, 376
  insensible, 823
  impenitent, 951
Callow, *infant*, 129
  young, 127
Calm, *physical*, 174
  moral, 826
  quiet, 265
  dissuade, 616
Calorific, *heat*, 382
Calorimeter, *thermometer*, 389
Calotte, *vestment*, 225, 999
Caltrop, *sharpness*, 253
Calumet, *pacification*, 723
  tobacco, 298A
Calumniator, *detractor*, 936
Calumny, *detraction*, 934
Calyx, *integument*, 222
* Camarade, *friend*, 890
* Camaraderie, *friendship*, 888
* Camarilla, *party*, 712
Camber, *curvature*, 250
Cambist, *merchant*, 797
Camel, *carrier*, 271
Cameo, *sculpture*, 557
Camera, *optical instrument*, 445
Camerated, *curved*, 245
* Camisade, *attack*, 716
Camisole, *dress*, 225
Camorra, *illegality*, 964
Camouflage, *conceal*, 528
  deception, 545
Camp, *to locate*, 184
  abode, 186
Campagna, *space*, 180
Campaign, *warfare*, 722
  plan, 626
  conduct, 692
Campaigner, *combatant*, 726
Campanile, *tower*, 206
Campaniliform, *bell-shaped*, 249
  cupped, 252

Cavern, *hollow*, 252
  cell, 191
  dwelling, 189
Cavernous, *hollow*, 252
  porous, 322
Caviare, *pungent*, 171, 392
Cavil, *censure*, 932
  dissent, 489
  split hairs, 477
Caviller, *detractor*, 936
Cavity, *concavity*, 252
Cavort, *prance*, 315
Caw, *animal cry*, 412
Cayenne, *condiment*, 393
  pungent, 171
Cease, *cessation*, 142
Ceaseless, *perpetuity*, 112
Cecity, *blindness*, 442
Cede, *relinquish*, 782
Ceiling, *height*, 206
  summit, 210
  covering, 222
* Cela va sans dire, *conformity*, 82
  effect, 154
Celebrant, *worship*, 990
Celebrate, *solemnize*, 883
  publish, 531
  praise, 931
Celebration, *fête*, 883
  rite, 998
Celebrity, *repute*, 873
  nobility, 875
Celerity, *velocity*, 274
Celestial, *physical*, 318
  moral, 829
  religious, 976, 981
  angelic, 977
Celibacy, *bachelor*, 904
Cell, *cavity*, 252
  receptacle, 191
  abode, 189
  prison, 752
Cellar, *room*, 191
  store, 636
  lowness, 207
Cellaret, *receptacle*, 191
Cellular, *concavity*, 252
Cellule, *receptacle*, 191
Celsius, *thermometer*, 389
Cembalo, *musical instrument*, 417
Cement, *connective*, 45
  to unite, 46
  concord, 714
Cemetery, *interment*, 363
Cenobite, *recluse*, 893
  anchoret, 996
Cenotaph, *interment*, 363
Censer, *temple*, 1000
Censor, *detractor*, 936
  inhibit, 616

Censorious, *disapprobation*, 932
Censorship, *authority*, 737
  secret, 533
Censure, *dissapprobation*, 932
Census, *counting*, 85
  list, 86
Centaur, *unconformity*, 83
Centenary, *numbers*, 98
  celebration, 883
Centennial, *numbers*, 98
  period, 108, 138
Centesimal, *hundred*, 98
Centigrade, *thermometer*, 389
Cento, *poetry*, 597
Central, *centrality*, 223
Centralize, *combine*, 48
  focus, 72
  concentrate, 223
Centre, *in order*, 68
  in space, 223
Centre in, *convergence*, 290
Centrifugal, *divergence*, 291
Centripetal, *convergence*, 290
Centuple, *number*, 98
Centurion, *master*, 745
Century, *period*, 108
  duration, 106
Ceramic, *sculpture*, 557
Cerberus, *janitor*, 263
  custodian, 664
Cerebration, *thought*, 451
Cerebrum, *intellect*, 450
Cerement, *interment*, 363
Ceremonious, *respect*, 928
Ceremony, *parade*, 882
  religious, 998
Ceres, *botany*, 369
Cerise, *red*, 434
Cerography, *engraving*, 558
Certain, *sure*, 474, 484
  special, 79
  indefinite number, 100
Certainly, *assent*, 488
Certificate, *voucher*, 551
  security, 771
  evidence, 467
Certify, *evince*, 467
  inform, 527
  vouch, 535
Certitude, *certainty*, 474
Cerulean, *blue*, 438
Cess, *tax*, 812
Cessation, *ceasing*, 142
Cession, *surrender*, 725, 782
  gift, 784
Cesspool, *uncleanness*, 633
Cestus, *girdle*, 225
  ligature, 45
  ring, 247

Chafe, *warm*, 384
  pain, 378
  irritate, 825, 828
  vex, 830
  incense, 900
Chaff, *trash*, 643
  wit, 842
  ridicule, 856
  vulgar, 876
Chaffer, *bargain*, 769
  sale, 794
Chafing-dish, *furnace*, 386
Chagrin, *pain*, 828
Chain, *series*, 69
  to fasten, 43
  vinculum, 45
  ornament, 847
  to imprison, 752
Chain-mail, *arms*, 727
Chain-shot, *arms*, 727
Chair, *support*, 215
  vehicle, 272
  direction, 693
  professorship, 542
  throne, 747
Chairman, *director*, 694, 745
Chairmanship, *direction*, 693
Chaise, *vehicle*, 272
* Chaise longue, *support*, 215
Chalcography, *engraving*, 558
Chalet, *abode*, 189
Chalice, *cup*, 191
  hollow, 252
Chalk, *mark*, 550
  drawing, 556, 559
  soil, 342
Chalk out, *plan*, 626
Chalky, *white*, 430
Challenge, *defy*, 715
  accuse, 938
  claim, 924
Cham, *master*, 745
Chamber, *room*, 191
  council, 696
  mart, 799
Chamber music, *music*, 415
Chamberlain, *servant*, 746
Chambermaid, *servant*, 746
Chameleon, *variegation*, 440
  inconstancy, 149, 605
Chamfer, *furrow*, 259
Champ, *eat*, 296
Champaign, *plain*, 344
Champion, *auxiliary*, 711
  proficient, 700
  good, 648
  defence, 717
  combatant, 726
Championship, *aid*, 707
  superiority, 33

Colourless, *achromatism*, 429
Colours, *standard*, 550
  decoration, 877
Colporteur, *agent*, 758
Colt, *fool*, 501
  horse, 271
Column, *series*, 69
  height, 206
  monument, 551
  cylinder, 249
  procession, 266
  troop, 726
Colure, *universe*, 318
Coma, *insensibility*, 376, 823
  inactivity, 683
Comb, *sharpness*, 253
Combat, *contention*, 720, 722
Combatant, *contention*, 726
Comber, *wave*, 348
Combination, *union*, 48
Combinations, *arithmetical*, 84
  dress, 225
Combine, *join*, 48
  co-operate, 709
  union, 712
  syndicate, 778
Combustible, *heating*, 384
  fuel, 388
Come, *arrive*, 292
  approach, 286
  happen, 151
Come about, *eventuality*, 151
Come after, *sequence*, 63
Come-at-able, *accessible*, 705
Come away, *recession*, 287
Come-back, *retort*, 462, 479, 842
  retaliation, 718
Come before, *precedence*, 62
Come by, *acquisition*, 775
Come down, *descend*, 306
  cheapness, 815
  pay, 809
Come-down, *adversity*, 735
Come forth, *existence*, 1
Come from, *effect*, 154
Come in for, *obtain*, 775
Come near, *approach*, 286
Come off, *disjunction*, 44
  take place, 151
Come on, *follow*, 63
  defy, 715
  prosper, 731
Come out, *egress*, 294
Come over, *induce*, 615
Come to, *whole*, 50

Come up to, *equal*, 27
Come up with, *arrival*, 292
Come upon, *arrival*, 292
Comedian, *the drama*, 599
  humorist, 844
Comedy, *drama*, 599
  ridicule, 856
Comely, *beauty*, 845
Comestible, *food*, 298
Comet, *wanderer*, 268
  universe, 318
Comfit, *sweetness*, 396
Comfort, *pleasure*, 377, 827
  content, 831
  relief, 834
Comfort station, *toilet*, 191, 653
Comfortable, *pleased*, 827
  pleasing, 829
Comforter, *deity*, 976
  dress, 225
Comfortless, *unhappy*, 828
  painful, 830
  dejected, 837
Comic, *witty*, 842
  ridiculous, 853
Comintern, *council*, 696
* Comitium, *assemblage*, 72
  council, 696
Comity, *courtesy*, 894
Comma, *stop*, 142
Command, *order*, 741
  authority, 737
Commandeer, *impress*, 744
  take, 789
Commander, *master*, 745
Commanding, *dignified*, 873
Commando, *combatant*, 726
* Comme il faut, *taste*, 850
  fashion, 852
Commemorate, *celebration*, 883
  record, 551
  memory, 505
Commence, *beginning*, 66
Commend, *approbation*, 931
Commendable, *virtuous*, 944
Commensurate, *accord*, 23
  adequate, 639
Comment, *reason*, 476
  interpret, 522
  dissertation, 595
Commerce, *intercourse*, 588
  business, 625
  barter, 794
Commercialese, *verbiage*, 573
Commination, *threat*, 909
Commingle, *mixture*, 41
Comminute, *pulverulence*, 330
  disjunction, 44
  incoherence, 47

Commiserate, *pity*, 914
Commissariat, *provision*, 298, 637
Commissary, *consignee*, 758
  deputy, 759
Commission, *business*, 625
  consignee, 755
  fee, 809
Commissionaire, *agent*, 690
  door-keeper, 263
Commissioner, *consignee*, 758
Commissure, *junction*, 43
Commit, *act*, 680
  delegate, 755
  imprison, 751
  arrest, 969
Committee, *council*, 696
  assemblage, 72
Commix, *mixture*, 41
Commodious, *spacious*, 180
  expedience, 646
Commodity, *merchandise*, 798
Commodore, *master*, 745
Common, *ordinary*, 82
  low, 876
  unimportant, 643
  general, 78
  reciprocal, 12
  frequent, 136
  plain, 344
Common-room, *sociality*, 892
Common sense, *intellect*, 450
  wisdom, 498
Commonalty, *common*, 876
  people, 372
Commoner, *commonalty*, 876
Commonplace, *unimportant*, 643
  habitual, 613
  dull, 843
Commons, *commonalty*, 876
  food, 298
Commonwealth, *man*, 373
Commotion, *agitation*, 315
Commune, *muse*, 451
  converse, 588
  territorial division, 181
Communicant, *worship*, 990
Communicate, *tell*, 527
  participate, 778
  join, 43
Communication, *information*, 527, 532
  connection, 43
Communion, *society*, 712
  participation, 778
  sacrament, 998

Communism, *participation*, 778
   authority, 737
Community, *man*, 373
   fellowship, 712
   participation, 778
Commute, *barter*, 794
   substitution, 147
   compensation, 30
   compromise, 774
   exchange, 148
Commuter, *traveller*, 268
Compact, *close*, 43
   dense, 321
   compendious, 201, 572
   bargain, 769
   unity, 87
   receptacle, 191
Compages, *whole*, 50
   texture, 329
Compagination, *junction*, 43
Companion, *friend*, 890
Companionable, *sociality*, 892
Companionship, *accompaniment*, 88
   sociality, 892
Company, *assembly*, 72
   accompaniment, 88
   partnership, 797
Comparable, *relation*, 9
Comparative, *degree*, 26
   magnitude, 31
Compare, *comparison*, 464
Compartment, *cell*, 191
   region, 181
   part, 51
   place, 182
Compass, *degree*, 26
   direction, 693
   space, 180
   surround, 227
   measure, 466
   to enclose, 231
   achieve, 729
   intend, 620
Compassion, *pity*, 914
Compatible, *consentaneous*, 23
   possible, 470
Compatriot, *inhabitant*, 188
Compeer, *equal*, 27
   friend, 890
Compel, *compulsion*, 744
Compendious, *compendium*, 596
   concise, 572
Compendium, *short*, 201
   writing, 596
Compensate, *make up for*, 30
   requite, 973

Compensation, *income*, 810
Compete, *oppose*, 708
   contend, 720
Competence, *power*, 157
   sufficiency, 639
   wealth, 803
   skill, 698
Competition, *opposition*, 708
   contention, 720
Competitor, *opponent*, 710
   combatant, 726
Compilation, *dissertation*, 595
   compendium, 596
   assemblage, 72
Complacent, *content*, 831
   pleased, 827
   self-satisfied, 880
Complainant, *accuser*, 938
Complaint, *murmur*, 839
   illness, 655
Complaisant, *benevolent*, 906
Complement, *adjunct*, 39
   remainder, 40
   part, 52
   arithmetical, 84
Complete, *entire*, 52
   great, 31
   end, 67
   to finish, 729
Complex, *mixture*, 41
   disorder, 59
Complexion, *state*, 7
   appearance, 448
Compliance, *observance*, 772
   consent, 762
   obedience, 743
   duty, 926
Complicated, *disorder*, 59
   difficult, 704
Complicity, *deceit*, 545
   concurrence, 178
   conspiring, 709
Compliment, *courtesy*, 894
   praise, 931
Compline, *worship*, 990
Comply, *consent*, 762
   obey, 743
   observe, 772
Component, *component*, 56
Comport, *conduct*, 692
Comport with, *agree*, 23
* Compos, *sanity*, 502
Compose, *make up*, 54
   produce, 161
   moderate, 174
   pacify, 723
   assuage, 826
   music, 415
   write, 590

Composed, *self-possessed*, 826
Composite, *mixture*, 41
Composition, *constitution*, 54
   combination, 48
   inclusion, 76
   music, 415
   painting, 556
   writing, 590
   style, 569
   compromise, 774
   atonement, 952
   materials, 635
Compositor, *printer*, 591
Compost, *manure*, 653
Composure, *inexcitability*, 826
   moderation, 174
Compotation, *drunkenness*, 959
Compound, *mix*, 41
   combination, 48
   compromise, 774
Compound for, *compact*, 769
   barter, 794
Comprehend, *include*, 76
   compose, 54
   understand, 518
   know, 490
Comprehension, *intelligence*, 498
Comprehensive, *general*, 78
   wide, 192
Compress, *condense*, 321, 572
   narrow, 203
   curtail, 201
   contract, 195
   remedy, 662
Comprise, *inclusion*, 76
Compromise, *compound*, 774
   atone, 952
   endanger, 665
   mean, 29, 628
   compensation, 30
* Compte rendu, *compendium*, 596
Comptroller, *director*, 694
   master, 745
Compulsion, *force*, 744
Compunction, *penitence*, 950
Compurgation, *acquittal*, 970
   evidence, 467
Compute, *numeration*, 85
Comrade, *friend*, 890
Con, *memory*, 505
   thought, 451
   to steer, 693

INDEX

363

Confirm, *corroborate*, 467
consent, 762
rites, 998
Confirmed, *fixed*, 150
Confiscate, *condemn*, 971
take, 789
Conflagration, *calefaction*,
384
Conflation, *combination*, 48
Conflict, *contention*, 720
disagreement, 24
Conflicting, *opposing*, 14,
179, 708
Confluence, *convergence*,
290
Conflux, *assemblage*, 72
Conform, *assent*, 488
accustom, 613
concur, 178
agree, 646
Conformation, *form*, 240
frame, 7
Conformity, *to rule*, 16, 82
Confound, *disorder*, 61
injure, 649
perplex, 475
baffle, 731
confuse, 519
astonish, 870
indiscriminate, 465A
expletive, 908
Confoundedly, *greatness*, 31
Confraternity, *friendship*,
888
* Confrère, *friend*, 890
Confront, *face*, 234
compare, 467
resist, 719
Confucianism, *religion*, 984
Confucius, *religious founder*,
986
Confuse, *derange*, 61
indiscriminate, 465A
obscure, 519
perplex, 458, 475
abash, 874
style, 571
Confusion, *disorder*, 59
shame, 874
Confutation, *disproof*, 479
Confute, *deny*, 536
* Congé, *dismissal*, 756
Congeal, *cold*, 385
Congealed, *dense*, 321
Congener, *consanguinity*, 11
similar, 17
included, 76
Congenial, *agreeing*, 23, 714
expedient, 646
Congenital, *intrinsic*, 5
habitual, 613
Congeries, *assemblage*, 72

Congestion, *collection*, 72
redundance, 641
disease, 655
Conglobation, *assemblage*,
72
Conglomerate, *assemblage*,
72
density, 321
Conglutinate, *coherence*, 46
Congratulate, *congratula-
tion*, 896
Congregate, *assemblage*, 72
Congregation, *laity*, 997
worship, 990
Congress, *assemblage*, 72,
290
council, 696
Congruous, *agreeing*, 23
expedient, 646
Conical, *round*, 249
pointed, 253
Conjecture, *supposition*,
514
Conjoin, *junction*, 43
concur, 178
Conjointly, *together*, 37, 43
Conjugal, *marriage*, 903
Conjugate, *word*, 562
Conjugation, *junction*, 43
pair, 89
phase, 144
grammar, 567
Conjunct, *junction*, 43
Conjunction, *vinculum*, 45
Conjuncture, *contingency*, 8
occasion, 134
Conjuration, *deception*, 545
sorcery, 992
Conjure, *entreat*, 765
exorcise, 992
Conjure up, *imagine*, 515
Conjurer, *sorcerer*, 994
adept, 700
Connate, *cause*, 153
intrinsic, 5
Connatural, *uniform*, 16
similar, 17
Connect, *relate*, 9
link, 43
Connection, *kindred*, 11
link, 45
Connective, *link*, 45
Connive, *overlook*, 460
concur, 178
allow, 760
Connoisseur, *taste*, 850
judge, 480
proficient, 700
Connotation, *indication*,
550
Connubial, *marriage*, 903
Conquer, *success*, 731

Conquered, *failure*, 732
Conquest, *success*, 731
Consanguinity, *kindred*, 11
Conscience, *moral sense*, 926
knowledge, 490
Conscience-smitten, *peni-
tence*, 950
Conscientious, *virtuous*, 944
scrupulous, 726A, 939
true, 494
Consciousness, *intuition*,
450
knowledge, 490
Conscript, *soldier*, 726
Conscription, *compulsion*,
744
Consecrate, *dedicate*, 873
sanctify, 987, 995, 998
Consectary, *corollary*, 480
Consecution, *sequence*, 63
Consecutive, *following*, 63
continuous, 69
Consecutively, *gradually*,
144
Consensus, *agreement*, 23
assent, 488
Consent, *grant*, 762
concur, 178
assent, 488
agreement, 23
Consentaneous, *agreeing*, 23
expedient, 646
Consequence, *effect*, 154
event, 151
importance, 642
Consequent, *sequence*, 63
Consequential, *arrogant*, 878
deducible, 467, 478
Consequently, *reasoning*,
154, 476
Conservation, *preservation*,
670
Conservative, *permanence*,
141
Conservatoire, *school*, 542
Conservatory, *store*, 636
hothouse, 386
Conserve, *sweet*, 396
Consider, *think*, 451
attend to, 457
inquire, 461
Considerable, *in degree*, 31
in size, 192
important, 642
Considerate, *judicious*, 498
benevolent, 906
respectful, 928
Consideration, *motive*, 615
qualification, 469
importance, 642
requital, 973
respect, 928

Costermonger, *merchant*, 797
Costly, *dearness*, 814
Costume, *dress*, 225
Cosy, *comfortable*, 377, 827, 829
Cot, *abode*, 189
Cote, *hut*, 189
Co-tenant, *partner*, 778
Coterie, *party*, 712
  sociality, 892
Cotillion, *amusement*, 840
Cottage, *abode*, 189
Cottar, *inhabitant*, 188
  peasant, 876
Cotton-wool, *softness*, 324
Couch, *bed*, 215
  to lie, 213
  recline, 308
  lie in wait, 530
  express, 566
Couchant, *horizontal*, 213
* Couci-couci, *imperfection*, 651
Cough, *puff*, 349
Couloir, *gully*, 198
Coulter, *sharpness*, 253
Council, *senate*, 696
  ecclesiastical, 995
Counsel, *advice*, 695
Counsellor, *adviser*, 695
  lawyer, 968
Count, *compute*, 85
  expect, 507
  believe, 484
  estimate, 480
  signify, 642
  lord, 875
Countenance, *face*, 234
  favour, 707
  appearance, 448
  to approve, 931
Counter, *contrary*, 14
  against, 179, 708
  retort, 479
  number, 84
  token, 550
  table, 215
  shopboard, 799
  to retaliate, 718
Counter-attraction, *dissuasion*, 616
  avoidance, 623
Counter-claim, *lawsuit*, 969
Counter-evidence, *contrary*, 468
Counter-intelligence, *secret*, 533
Counter-irritant, *counteraction*, 179
Counter-movement, *regression*, 283

Counter-order, *abrogation*, 756
Counter-project, *retaliation*, 718
  plan, 626
Counter-revolution, *revolution*, 146
Counter-stroke, *retaliation*, 718
Counter-subject, *music*, 415
Counter-tenor, *melody*, 413
  high note, 410
Counteract, *physically*, 179
  voluntarily, 708
  hinder, 706
  compensate, 30
Counterbalance, *compensation*, 30
Counterblast, *counteraction*, 179
  retaliation, 718
Counterchange, *reciprocality*, 12, 148
Countercharm, *spell*, 993
Countercheck, *hindrance*, 706
Counterfeit, *simulate*, 544, 545
  imitate, 19
  copy, 21
Counterfoil, *check*, 550
Countermand, *abrogation*, 756
Countermarch, *regression*, 283
  journey, 266
Countermark, *indication*, 550
Countermine, *opposition*, 708
Counterpane, *covering*, 222
Counterpart, *copy*, 21
  match, 17
Counterplot, *retaliation*, 718
  plan, 626
Counterpoint, *harmony*, 413
Counterpoise, *compensation*, 30
  weight, 319
Counterpoison, *remedy*, 662
Countersign, *indication*, 550
  assent, 488
Countervail, *compensate*, 28, 30
  oppose, 179, 708
  evidence, 468
Counterweight, *weight*, 319
Counterwork, *opposition*, 708
Countess, *noble*, 875
  chief, 745

Counting-house, *mart*, 799
Countless, *infinity*, 105
Countrified, *rural*, 185
  low, 876
Country, *definite region*, 181, 189
  agriculture, 371
Countryman, *inhabitant*, 185
Counts, *particulars*, 79
County, *region*, 181
  fashionable, 852
Coup, *action*, 680
* Coup de grâce, *death-blow*, 361
  destruction, 162
  completion, 729
  end, 67
  pity, 914
  punishment, 972
* Coup de main, *violence*, 173
  action, 680
* Coup de maître, *skill*, 698
  success, 731
* Coup d'essai, *essay*, 675
* Coup d'état, *action*, 680
  plan, 626
  revolt, 719, 742
* Coup de théâtre, *appearance*, 448
  ostentation, 882
* Coup d'œil, *vision*, 441
  appearance, 448
Coupé, *vehicle*, 272
Couple, *two*, 89
  to unite, 43
Couplet, *poetry*, 597
Coupon, *money*, 800
  ticket, 550
Courage, *bravery*, 861
Courier, *messenger*, 534
  interpreter, 524
Course, *order*, 58
  continuity, 69
  of time, 109
  layer, 204
  direction, 278
  motion, 264
  locomotion, 266
  effect, 154
  rapidity, 274
  pursuit, 622
  teaching, 537
  plan, 626
  way, 627
  conduct, 692
  arena, 728
  dinner, 298
Courser, *carrier*, 271
  swift, 274

Creation, *universe*, 318
Creationism, *causation*, 153
Creative, *productive*, 168
Creator, *deity*, 976
   producer, 164
Creature, *animal*, 366
   thing, 3
   effect, 154
Creature comforts, *food*, 298
Crèche, *nursery*, 542
Credence, *belief*, 484
Credential, *evidence*, 467
Credible, *probable*, 472, 484
   possible, 470
Credit, *belief*, 484
   authority, 737
   pecuniary, 805
   account, 811
   influence, 737
   hope, 858
   repute, 873
   desert, 944
Creditor, *credit*, 805
Credo, *belief*, 484
Credulity, *belief*, 486
   superstition, 984A
Creed, *belief*, 484, 496
   tenet, 983
Creek, *gulf*, 343
Creep, *crawl*, 275
   bad man, 949
Creeper, *plant*, 367
Creeping, *sensation*, 380
Creepy, *fearsome*, 860
Cremation, *burning*, 384
   of corpses, 363
* Crème de la crème, *goodness*, 648
Cremona, *musical instrument*, 417
Crenated, *notch*, 257
Crenelated, *notched*, 257
Crepitate, *snap*, 406
Crepuscule, *dawn*, 125
   dimness, 422
Crescendo, *increase*, 35
   music, 415
Crescent, *curve*, 245
   street, 189
Cresset, *torch*, 423
Crest, *summit*, 210
   tuft, 256
   armorial, 550, 877
Crestfallen, *dejected*, 837
   humiliated, 881, 879
Cretin, *fool*, 501
Crevasse, *interval*, 198
Crevice, *interval*, 198
   opening, 260
Crew, *assemblage*, 72
   party, 712
   inhabitants, 188

Crib, *bed*, 215
   to steal, 791
   interpretation, 522
Crick, *pain*, 378
Crier, *messenger*, 534
Crime, *guilt*, 947
Criminal, *culprit*, 949
   vicious, 945
Criminality, *guilt*, 947
Criminate, *accusation*, 938
Criminology, *crime*, 947
Crimp, *curl*, 248
   fold, 258
   to steal, 791
Crimson, *red*, 434
Cringe, *submit*, 725, 743
   servility, 886
   fear, 860
Crinkle, *fold*, 258
   angle, 244
Crinoline, *dress*, 225
Cripple, *weaken*, 160
   disable, 158
   injure, 649, 659
   disease, 655
Crisis, *conjuncture*, 8
   event, 151
   difficulty, 704
   opportunity, 134
Crisp, *brittle*, 328
   rough, 256
   rumpled, 248
   concise, 572
Criss-cross-row, *letter*, 561
Criterion, *trial*, 463
   evidence, 467
Critic, *taste*, 850
   judge, 480
   reviewer, 590
   dissertation, 595
   detractor, 936
Critical, *opportune*, 134
   important, 642
   difficult, 704
   dangerous, 665
Criticism, *disapprobation*, 932
   dissertation, 595
Criticize, *taste*, 850
Critique, *discrimination*, 465
   dissertation, 595
   disapprobation, 932
Croak, *cry*, 412
   stammer, 583
   complain, 839
   discontent, 832
   predict, 511
Croceate, *yellow*, 436
Crochet, *knit*, 43
Crock, *weakness*, 160
Crock up, *failure*, 732

Crocodile tears, *falsehood*, 544
Croesus, *wealth*, 803
Croft, *hut*, 189
Crofter, *peasant*, 876
Cromlech, *interment*, 363
Crone, *veteran*, 130
Crony, *friend*, 890
Crook, *curvature*, 245
   evildoer, 913
   swindler, 792
   ill, 655
Crooked, *angular*, 244
   distorted, 243, 846
   sloping, 217
   dishonourable, 940
Croon, *to hum*, 405, 415
Crop, *stomach*, 191
   to shorten, 201
   to gather, 775
   to take, 789
   to eat, 297
   harvest, 154
Crop up, *inexpectation*, 508
   event, 151
   appear, 446
Cropper, *fall*, 306
Crosier, *canonicals*, 999
Cross, *intersection*, 219
   passage, 302
   swindle, 545
   opposition, 179, 708
   refusal, 572
   vexation, 828
   vexatiousness, 830
   ill-tempered, 895
   fretful, 901
   failure, 732
   mixture, 41
   decoration, 877
   reward, 973
   rites, 998
Cross-breed, *unconformity*, 83
Cross-cut, *method*, 627
Cross-examine, *inquiry*, 461
Cross-grained, *obstinate*, 606
   ill-tempered, 895, 901
Cross-purposes, *error*, 495
   misinterpretation, 523
Cross-question, *inquiry*, 461
Cross-reading, *misinterpretation*, 523
Cross-road, *way*, 627
Crossbow, *arms*, 727
Crossing, *crossing*, 219
Crosspatch, *ill-tempered*, 895
Crossword, *puzzle*, 461, 533
Crotch, *angularity*, 244
Crotchet, *music*, 413
   prejudice, 481
   caprice, 608

Crotchety, *folly*, 499
Crouch, *stoop*, 308
  lower, 207
  servility, 886
  fear, 860
Croup, *rear*, 235
Crow, *cry*, 412
  laugh, 838
  boast, 884
  exult, 836
  lever, 633
  black, 431
Crowbar, *instrument*, 633
Crowd, *assemblage*, 72
  multitude, 102
  closeness, 197
  the vulgar, 876
Crown, *top*, 210
  end, 67
  circle, 247
  trophy, 733
  sceptre, 747
  reward, 973
  to complete, 729
Crowning, *superior*, 33
Crow's nest, *view*, 441
Crucial, *crossing*, 219
  experimental, 463
  demonstrative, 478
Crucible, *receptacle*, 191
  laboratory, 144, 691
Crucifix, *rite*, 998
  canonicals, 999
Cruciform, *crossing*, 219
Crucify, *torture (physical)*, 378
  agony (mental), 828
  painfulness, 830
  execution, 972
Crude, *unprepared*, 674
  inelegant, 579
Cruel, *painful*, 830
  inhuman, 907
Cruet, *receptacle*, 191
Cruise, *navigation*, 267
Cruiser, *ship*, 273
Crumb, *small part*, 51
  grain, 193
  powder, 330
  bit, 32
Crumble, *pulverize*, 330
  destroy, 162
  diminish, 36
  spoil, 659
  brittleness, 328
Crumple, *ruffle*, 256
  crease, 258
  contract, 195
Crunch, *bruise*, 44
  masticate, 297
  pulverize, 330
Crupper, *rear*, 235

Crusade, *warfare*, 722
Cruse, *vessel*, 191
Crush, *pulverize*, 330
  destroy, 162
  injure, 649
  humiliate, 879
  pain, 828
  contract, 195
  love, 897
Crust, *covering*, 222
  insolence, 885
Crusty, *discourtesy*, 895
Crutch, *support*, 215
  angle, 244
  instrument, 633
Crux, *question*, 461
  mystery, 533
Cry, *animal*, 412
  human, 411
  loudness, 404
  voice, 580
  publish, 531
  weep, 839
Cry down, *disapprove*, 932
Cry for, *desire*, 865
Cry to, *beseech*, 765
Cry up, *praise*, 931
Crypt, *cell*, 191
  hide, 530
  grave, 363
  altar, 1000
Cryptic, *latent*, 526, 528
Cryptogram, *cipher*, 533
Cryptography, *writing*, 590
Crystal-gazing, *prediction*, 511
Crystalline, *dense*, 321
  transparent, 425
Cub, *young*, 129
  clown, 876
Cube, *triality*, 92
  angularity, 244
Cubist, *artist*, 559
Cuckold, *divorce*, 905
Cuckoo, *repetition*, 104
  imitation, 19
  cry, 412
  fool, 501
  insane, 503
Cuddle, *caress*, 902
Cuddy, *carrier*, 271
Cudgel, *beat*, 975
  bludgeon, 276, 727
Cue, *hint*, 527
  watchword, 550
  plea, 617
Cuff, *beat*, 276, 972
  dress, 225
* Cui bono, *utility*, 644
Cuirass, *defence*, 717
Cuirassier, *combatant*, 726
Cuisine, *food*, 298

* Cul-de-lampe, *tail-piece*, 67
Cul-de-sac, *concavity*, 252
  closure, 261
  difficulty, 704
* Culbute, *inversion*, 218
  descent, 306
Culinary, *food*, 298
Cull, *choice*, 609
  take, 789
Cullender, *sieve*, 260
Cullion, *wretch*, 941, 949
Cully, *dupe*, 547
Culminate, *maximum*, 33
  height, 206, 210
Culmination, *completion*, 729
Culpability, *guilt*, 947
Culpable, *vice*, 945
Culprit, *sinner*, 949
Cult, *worship*, 990
  rite, 998
Cultivate, *improve*, 658
  sensitiveness, 375
  taste, 850
  till, 371
Culture, *tillage*, 371
  taste, 850
  teaching, 537
  knowledge, 490
Culverin, *arms*, 727
Culvert, *conduit*, 350
* Cum grano salis, *qualify*, 469
  unbelief, 485
Cumber, *load*, 319
  to incommode, 647
  to obstruct, 706
Cummer, *friend*, 891
Cummerbund, *girdle*, 247
Cumshaw, *gift*, 784
Cumulation, *assemblage*, 72
Cumulative, *increase*, 35
  addition, 37
Cumulus, *cloud*, 353
Cunctation, *delay*, 133
  inactivity, 683
Cuneiform, *angular*, 244
  writing, 590
Cunning, *art*, 702
  sagacity, 698
  well-planned, 626
Cup, *hollow*, 252
  vessel, 191
Cupboard, *receptacle*, 191
Cupid, *beauty*, 845
  love, 897
Cupidity, *avarice*, 819
  desire, 865
Cupola, *dome*, 250
  height, 206
Cur, *knave*, 949

Curable, *improvement*, 658
Curacy, *churchdom*, 995
Curate, *clergy*, 996
Curative, *remedial*, 834
Curator, *consignee*, 758
Curb, *restrain*, 751
  hinder, 706
  shackle, 752
  moderate, 174
  check, 826
  dissuade, 616
  counteract, 179
  slacken, 275
Curd, *mass*, 46
  density, 321
  pulp, 354
Curdle, *condense*, 321
  coagulate, 46, 352
Cure, *remedy*, 662, 834
  reinstate, 660
  religious, 995
  preserve, 670
  improve, 656
* Curé, *priest*, 996
Curfew, *evening*, 126
Curio, *toy*, 643
* Curiosa felicitas, *elegance*, 578
Curiosity, *curiosity*, 455
  phenomenon, 872
Curious, *true*, 494
  exceptional, 83
Curl, *bend*, 245, 248
  cockle up, 258
Curlicue, *convolution*, 248
Curliewurlie, *convolution*, 248
Curmudgeon, *parsimony*, 819
Currency, *publicity*, 531
  money, 800
Current, *existing*, 1
  present, 118
  happening, 151
  stream, 347
  river, 348
  wind, 349
  course, 109
  danger, 667
  opinion, 484
  public, 531
  prevailing, 82
* Currente calamo, *diffuseness*, 573
Curricle, *vehicle*, 272
Curriculum, *teaching*, 537
Curry, *condiment*, 393
  rub, 331
Curry favour, *flattery*, 933
Curse, *malediction*, 908
  bane, 663
  evil, 619

Curse, *adversity*, 735
  badness, 649
  painfulness, 830
Cursive, *writing*, 590
Cursory, *transient*, 111
  inattentive, 458
  neglecting, 460
  hasty, 684
Curst, *perverse*, 895
Curt, *short*, 201
  taciturn, 585
  concise, 572
Curtail, *shorten*, 201, 572
  retrench, 38
  decrease, 36
  deprive, 789
Curtain, *shade*, 424
  ambush, 530
Curtain lecture, *speech*, 582
Curtain-raiser, *play*, 599
Curtsy, *obeisance*, 743, 894
  submission, 725
  stoop, 308
Curule, *council*, 696
Curve, *curvature*, 245
Curvet, *leap*, 309
  oscillate, 314
  agitate, 315
Cushion, *pillow*, 215
  softness, 324
  to frustrate, 706
  relief, 834
Cushy, *easy*, 705
Cusp, *point*, 253
  angle, 244
Cussedness, *obstinacy*, 606
Custodian, *keeper*, 753
Custody, *captivity*, 664, 751, 781
  captive, 754
Custom, *rule*, 80
  habit, 613
  fashion, 852
  sale, 796
  barter, 794
  tax, 812
Custom-house, *mart*, 799
Customer, *purchaser*, 795
Cut, *divide*, 44
  bit, 51
  interval, 70, 198
  sculpture, 557
  curtail, 201
  cultivate, 371
  layer, 204
  notch, 257
  form, 240
  road, 627
  print, 558
  attach, 716
  pain, 828
  to give pain, 830

Cut, *affect*, 824
  ignore, 460, 893, 895
  neglect, 773
  state, 7; *cold*, 385
Cut across, *passage*, 302
Cut along, *velocity*, 274
Cut and dried, *ready*, 673
  trite, 82
Cut and run, *escape*, 671
Cut capers, *leap*, 309
  dance, 840
Cut down, *diminish*, 36
  destroy, 162
  shorten, 201
  lower, 308
  kill, 361
Cut down to size, *humiliate*, 879
Cut off, *kill*, 361
  subduct, 38
  impede, 706
  disjunction, 44
Cut out, *surpass*, 33
  retrench, 38; *plan*, 626
  supplant, 147
Cut short, *shorten*, 201, 572
  stop, 142; *decrease*, 36
  contract, 195
Cut-throat, *killing*, 361
  sinner, 913, 949
Cut up, *divide*, 44
  destroy, 162
  censure, 932
  unhappy, 828, 837
Cutaneous, *covering*, 222
Cuthbert, *pacifist*, 726A
Cuticle, *covering*, 222
Cutie, *sweetheart*, 897
Cutlass, *arms*, 727
Cutlery, *sharpness*, 253
Cutpurse, *thief*, 792
Cutter, *ship*, 273
Cutting, *cold*, 383
  affecting, 821
  censorious, 932
  extract, 596, 609
Cutty, *tobacco*, 298A
Cybernetics, *statecraft*, 693
Cycle, *period*, 138
  duration, 106
  circle, 247; *travel*, 266
Cycloid, *circularity*, 247
Cyclone, *violence*, 173
  rotation, 312
  agitation, 315
  wind, 349
Cyclopaedia, *knowledge*, 490
Cyclopean, *huge*, 192
Cyclops, *monster*, 83
Cylinder, *rotundity*, 249

Cymbal, *musical instrument*, 417

Cynical, *censorious*, 932
  detracting, 483
  unsociable, 893
  cross, 895

Cynosure, *indication*, 550
  prodigy, 872

Cypher, *see* Cipher

Cypress, *lamentation*, 839

Cyst, *receptacle*, 191

Czar, *master*, 745

D

D.T., *drunkenness*, 959

D.V., *conditions*, 770

* Da capo, *repetition*, 104
  duplication, 90
  frequency, 136

Dab, *clever*, 700
  to paint, 222
  to slap, 276

Dabble, *action*, 680
  trifle, 683
  moisten, 337

Dacoit, *thief*, 792

Dactyl, *verse*, 597

Dactylonomy, *numeration*, 85

Dad, *paternity*, 166

Dadaist, *artist*, 559

Dado, *lining*, 224
  base, 211

Daedal, *variegated*, 440

Daedalian, *skill*, 698
  convoluted, 248

Daft, *insane*, 503
  silly, 499

Dagger, *arms*, 727
  sharpness, 253

Daggers drawn, *discord*, 713
  enmity, 889

Daggle, *pendency*, 214

Dago, *alien*, 57

Dagon, *idol*, 986

Daguerreotype, *painting*, 556
  copy, 21

Dahabeeyah, *ship*, 273

Daily, *routine*, 138
  publication, 531
  servant, 746

Dainty, *savoury*, 394
  pleasing, 829
  fastidious, 868

Dais, *support*, 215

Dak-bungalow, *inn*, 189

Dale, *concavity*, 252

Dally, *irresolute*, 605
  delay, 133

Dally, *inactive*, 683
  amuse, 840
  fondle, 902

Dalmatic, *vestments*, 999

Dam, *parent*, 166
  lock, 350
  close, 261
  confine, 231
  obstruct, 348, 706
  trifle, 643

Damage, *evil*, 619
  to injure, 649
  to spoil, 659
  payment, 812

Damages, *penalty*, 974

Damascene, *variegate*, 440

Damask, *redness*, 434

Dame, *woman*, 374
  teacher, 540

Damn, *condemn*, 971
  expletive, 908

Damn-all, *nothing*, 4

Damnable, *execrable*, 830
  spoil, 659

Damnify, *damage*, 649

* Damnosa hereditas, *burden*, 706

Damp, *moist*, 339
  cold, 386
  to moderate, 174
  to dissuade, 616
  depress, 837
  calm, 826

Damper, *silencer*, 417

Damsel, *youth*, 129
  lady, 374

Dance, *oscillate*, 314
  agitate, 315
  jump, 309
  sport, 840

Dander, *resentment*, 900
  journey, 266

Dandify, *adorn*, 845
  dress, 225

Dandle, *endearment*, 902

Dandruff, *uncleanness*, 653

Dandy, *fop*, 854

Dandyism, *affectation*, 855

Danger, *danger*, 665

Dangle, *hang*, 214
  swing, 314

Dank, *moist*, 339

Dapper, *thin*, 203
  elegant, 845

Dapple, *brown*, 433

Dappled, *variegation*, 440

Darbies, *fetter*, 752

Dare, *defy*, 715
  face danger, 861

Dare-devil, *rashness*, 863
  blusterer, 887

Darg, *work*, 625

Daring, *courage*, 861

Dark, *obscure*, 421
  dim, 422
  invisible, 447
  unintelligible, 519
  mysterious, 528
  ignorant, 491
  blind, 442
  latent, 526

Darkie, *black*, 431

Darling, *favourite*, 899
  beloved, 897

Darn, *improve*, 658

Dart, *missile*, 727
  to propel, 284
  swift, 274

Darwinism, *causation*, 153

Dash, *sprinkling*, 32, 193
  to mix, 41
  throw down, 308
  display, 882
  depress, 837
  shine, 873
  mark, 550
  expletive, 908
  velocity, 274
  energy, 171
  vivacity, 682
  gift, 784

Dash off, *sketch*, 556

Dash out, *rush*, 274
  haste, 684

Dashing, *brave*, 861
  smart, 845
  fashionable, 852

Dastard, *coward*, 862

Data, *evidence*, 467
  reasoning, 476

Date, *chronometry*, 114
  party, 892

Daub, *cover*, 222
  dirt, 653
  bad painting, 555
  to deform, 846

Daughter, *posterity*, 167

Daunt, *frighten*, 860

Dauntless, *courage*, 861

Davenport, *receptacle*, 191
  support, 215

Dawdle, *slow*, 275
  tardy, 133
  inactive, 683

Dawn, *morning*, 125
  precursor, 116
  to begin, 66
  dim, 422
  glimpse, 490

Day, *period*, 108
  light, 420

Day-book, *list*, 86
  record, 551
  accounts, 811

Day-dream, *imagination*, 515
  hope, 858
  inattention, 458
Day-labourer, *workman*, 690
Day of Judgment, *end*, 67
Daybreak, *morning*, 125
  dim, 422
  beginning, 66
Daylight, *light*, 420
  publicity, 531
Dayspring, *morning*, 125
Daze, *light*, 420
  confuse, 442
  stupefy, 823
Dazzle, *light*, 420
  confuse, 442
* De bon cœur, *willingly*, 602
* De facto, *existence*, 1
  truth, 494
* De haut en bas, *contempt*, 930
* De jure, *right*, 922
  legal, 963
  dueness, 924
* De novo, *repetition*, 104
  frequency, 136
* De omnibus rebus, *multiformity*, 81
* De Profundis, *worship*, 990
* De règle, *rule*, 80
* De rigueur, *rule*, 80
* De trop, *redundance*, 641
Deacon, *clergy*, 996
Dead, *lifeless*, 360
  inert, 172
  insensible, 376, 823
  colourless, 429
Dead-beat, *fatigue*, 688
  weak, 160
Dead-drunk, *drunkenness*, 959
Dead heat, *equality*, 27
Dead weight, *hindrance*, 706
Deaden, *weaken*, 158, 160
  moderate, 174, 826
  benumb, 823
Deadfall, *trap*, 667
Deadlock, *stoppage*, 265
  hindrance, 706
Deadly, *mortal*, 361, 657
  destructive, 162
  pernicious, 649
Deadness, *numbness*, 381
  inertness, 172, 823
Deaf, *deafness*, 419
Deafening, *loud*, 404
Deal, *quantity*, 31
  mingle, 41

Deal, *give*, 784
  allot, 786
  barter, 794
Deal out, *distribute*, 73, 784
Dealer, *merchant*, 797
Dealings, *action*, 680
Dean, *clergy*, 996
Deanery, *office*, 995
  house, 1000
Dear, *loved*, 897, 899
  high-priced, 814
Dear-bought, *worthless*, 645
Dearth, *insufficiency*, 640
Death, *death*, 360
Death-blow, *end*, 67
  killing, 361
  failure, 732
Deathless, *perpetuity*, 112
  celebrated, 873
Deathlike, *hideous*, 846
  silence, 403
Debacle, *river*, 348
  descent, 306
  destruction, 162
Debag, *divest*, 226
Debar, *prohibit*, 761
  hinder, 751
  exclude, 77
Debark, *arrive*, 292
Debase, *depress*, 308
  deteriorate, 659
  foul, 653
  vicious, 945
Debatable, *uncertain*, 475
Debate, *reason*, 476
  dispute, 713, 720
  hesitate, 605
  talk, 588
Debauch, *spoil*, 659
  vice, 945
  intemperance, 954
  impurity, 961
Debenture, *certificate*, 551
  security, 771
  credit, 805
Debility, *weakness*, 160
Debit, *debt*, 806
  accounts, 811
Debonair, *cheerfulness*, 836
Debouch, *march out*, 292
  flow out, 295, 348
Debrett, *list*, 86
Debris, *part*, 51
  pulverulence, 330
  unimportance, 643
Debt, *debt*, 806
Debtor, *debt*, 806
Debus, *arrival*, 292
Début, *beginning*, 66
Decade, *number*, 98
  period, 108
  duration, 106

Decadence, *deterioration*, 659
Decadent, *feeble*, 575
Decagon, *number*, 98
  angularity, 244
Decahedron, *ten*, 98
Decalogue, *duty*, 926
Decamp, *move off*, 287, 293
  escape, 671
Decant, *transfer*, 270
Decanter, *receptacle*, 191
Decapitate, *kill*, 361, 972
Decay, *spoil*, 659
  disease, 655
  shrivel, 195
  decrease, 36
Decayed, *imperfect*, 651
  old, 124
  adversity, 735
Decease, *death*, 360
Deceit, *deception*, 544, 545
Deceiver, *deceiver*, 548
Decent, *modest*, 960
  tolerable, 651
  seemly, 926
  right, 922
Decentralize, *disperse*, 73
Deception, *deception*, 545
  sophistry, 477
Decide, *judge*, 480
  choose, 609
  make certain, 474
  cause, 153
Decided, *resolved*, 604
  positive, 535
  certain, 475
  great, 31
Deciduous, *transitory*, 111
  falling, 306
  spoiled, 659
Decimal, *number*, 84, 98
Decimate, *subduct*, 38, 103
  kill, 361
Decipher, *interpret*, 522
  solve, 462
Decision, *intention*, 620
  conclusion, 480
  resolution, 604
  verdict, 969
Decisive, *final*, 67
  evidence, 467
  resolution, 604
  demonstration, 478
Decivilize, *brutalize*, 895
Deck, *floor*, 211
  to beautify, 845
Declaim, *speech*, 582
Declamatory, *florid*, 577
Declare, *assert*, 535
  inform, 516, 527
Declension, *descent*, 306

Dégagé, *freedom*, 748
  fashion, 825
Degenerate, *deterioration*, 659
  vice, 945
Deglutition, *swallowing*, 296
Degradation, *shame*, 874
  dishonour, 940
  deterioration, 659
Degree, *quantity*, 26
  term, 71
  honour, 873
Degustation, *taste*, 390
Dehortation, *dissuasion*, 616
  advice, 695
  warning, 668
Dehumanize, *brutalize*, 895
Dehydrate, *dry*, 340
  preserve, 670
De-ice, *melt*, 384
* Dei gratiâ, *dueness*, 924
Deification, *heaven*, 981
  idolatry, 991
  honour, 873
Deign, *condescend*, 879
  consent, 762
Deiseal, *rotation*, 312
Deism, *irreligion*, 989
  heresy, 984A
Deity, *deity*, 976
  great spirit, 979
Dejection, *sadness*, 828, 837, 841
* Déjeuner, *food*, 298
Dekko, *look*, 441
* Délâbrement, *deterioration*, 659
Delation, *accusation*, 938
Delay, *lateness*, 133
  protraction, 110
  slowness, 275
Dele, *obliteration*, 552
Delectable, *savoury*, 394
  agreeable, 829
Delectation, *pleasure*, 827
Delegate, *consignee*, 758, 759
  to commission, 755
Deleterious, *pernicious*, 649
  unwholesome, 657
Deletion, *obliteration*, 552
Deliberate, *think*, 451
  cautious, 864
  slow, 275
  leisurely, 685
  advised, 620, 695
Deliberately, *slowly*, 133
  designedly, 600, 611
Delicacy, *of texture*, 329
  slenderness, 203
  weak, 160

Delicacy, *sickly*, 655
  savoury, 394
  dainty, 298
  of taste, 850
  fastidiousness, 868
  exactness, 494
  pleasing, 829
  beauty, 845
  honour, 939
  purity, 960
  difficulty, 704
  scruple, 603, 616
Delicatessen, *food*, 298
Delicious, *taste*, 394
  pleasing, 829
Delight, *pleasure*, 827
Delightful, *pleasurableness*, 829
Delilah, *temptress*, 615
Delimit, *circumscribe*, 231
Delineate, *describe*, 594
  represent, 554
* Delineavit, *painting*, 556
Delinquency, *guilt*, 947
Delinquent, *sinner*, 949
Delinquescent, *liquid*, 333
* Deliquium, *weakness*, 160
  fatigue, 688
Delirium, *raving*, 503
  passion, 825
Delirium tremens, *drunkenness*, 959
Delitescence, *latency*, 526
Deliver, *transfer*, 270
  give, 784
  liberate, 750
  relieve, 834
  utter, 582
  rescue, 672
  escape, 671
Dell, *concavity*, 252
Delouse, *disinfect*, 652
Delta, *land*, 342
Delude, *deceive*, 495, 545
Deluge, *flow*, 337, 348
  redundance, 641
  multitude, 72
Delusion, *error*, 495
  deceit, 545
Delve, *dig*, 252
  cultivate, 371
  depth, 208
Demagogue, *leader*, 745
  director, 694
  agitator, 742
Demagogy, *authority*, 737
Demand, *claim*, 924
  ask, 765
  require, 630
  inquire, 461
  order, 741
  price, 812

Demarcation, *limit*, 199, 233
* Démarche, *procedure*, 680
Dematerialize, *immateriality*, 317
Demean, *humble*, 879
  dishonour, 940
Demeanour, *conduct*, 692
  air, 448
  fashion, 852
Dementation, *insanity*, 503
* Démenti, *contradiction*, 536
Demerit, *vice*, 945
  inutility, 645
Demesne, *property*, 780
Demi, *bisection*, 91
Demigod, *hero*, 948
Demijohn, *receptacle*, 191
Demi-rep, *libertine*, 962
Demise, *death*, 360
  to transfer, 783
  to give, 784
Demiurge, *deity*, 979
Demivolt, *leap*, 309
Demobilize, *disperse*, 73
Democracy, *authority*, 737
* Démodé, *obsolete*, 851
Demogorgon, *demon*, 980
Demoiselle, *woman*, 374
Demolish, *destroy*, 162
  confute, 479
  damage, 649
Demolisher, *destroyer*, 165
Demon, *devil*, 980
  wretch, 913
  violent, 173
Demoniacal, *wicked*, 945
  furious, 825
  diabolic, 649, 980
Demonism, *idolatry*, 991
Demonolatry, *idolatry*, 991
Demonstrate, *prove*, 85, 478
  manifest, 525
Demonstrative, *evidential*, 467, 478
  excitable, 825
Demonstrator, *scholar*, 492
  teacher, 540
Demoralize, *vice*, 945
  degrade, 659
Demos, *commonalty*, 876
Demote, *abase*, 308
  degrade, 659
Demotic, *writing*, 590
Demulcent, *mild*, 174
  soothing, 662
Demur, *unwillingness*, 603
  hesitation, 605
  to disbelieve, 485
  dissent, 489
  dislike, 867

Demure, *grave*, 826
  modest, 881
  affected, 855
Demurrage, *charge*, 812
Demurrer, *lawsuit*, 969
Den, *lair*, 189
  room, 191, 893
  prison, 752
  sty, 653
Denary, *number*, 98
Denationalize, *restore*, 790
Denaturalized, *unconformity*, 83
Dendriform, *rough*, 256
Denegation, *negation*, 536
Denial, *negation*, 536
Denigrate, *blacken*, 431
  decry, 483, 934
Denization, *liberation*, 750
Denizen, *inhabitant*, 188
  man, 373
Denominate, *nomenclature*,
  564
Denomination, *class*, 75
  party, 712
Denominational, *theology*,
  983
Denominator, *number*, 84
Denote, *indication*, 550
Denouement, *result*, 154
  end, 67
  elucidation, 522
  completion, 729
Denounce, *accuse*, 297
  blame, 932
  cite, 965
Dense, *close*, 321
  crowded, 72
  stupid, 499
Density, *closeness*, 46, 321
Dent, *notch*, 257
  hollow, 252
Dental, *letter*, 561
Denticle, *sharpness*, 253
Denticulated, *sharp*, 253
Dentist, *doctor*, 662
Denude, *divest*, 226
  deprive, 776
Denunciation, *see* Denounce
Deny, *negative*, 536
  dissent, 489
  refuse, 764
* Deo volente, *conditions*,
  770
Deodand, *penalty*, 974
Deodorize, *disinfect*, 652
Deontology, *duty*, 926
Depart, *set out*, 293
  die, 360
Departed, *gone*, 2
Department, *class*, 75

Department, *part*, 51
  region, 181
  business, 625
Depauperate, *impoverish*,
  804
Depend, *hang*, 214
  be contingent, 475
Depend upon, *trust*, 484
  be the effect of, 154
  affirm, 535
Dependable, *belief*, 484
  probity, 939
Dependant, *servant*, 746
Dependence, *subjection*, 749
Dependent, *liable*, 177
Depict, *paint*, 556
  represent, 554
  describe, 594
Depletion, *insufficiency*, 640
Deplorable, *bad*, 649
  disastrous, 735
  painful, 830
Deplore, *regret*, 833
  complain, 839
  remorse, 950
Deploy, *expansion*, 194
Depone, *affirm*, 535
Deponent, *evidence*, 467
Depopulate, *displace*, 185
  desert, 893
Deportation, *displace*, 185
  exclusion, 55
  transfer, 270
  emigration, 297
  punishment, 972
Deportment, *conduct*, 692
  appearance, 448
Depose, *evidence*, 467
  tell, 527
  record, 551
  dethrone, 738, 756
  declare, 535
Deposit, *place*, 184
  secure, 771
  store, 636
  expenditure, 809
  solidify, 321
Depository, *store*, 636
Depot, *store*, 636
  focus, 74
  mart, 799
Deprave, *spoil*, 659
Depraved, *bad*, 649
  vicious, 945
Deprecate, *deprecation*, 766
  dissuade, 616
  disapproval, 932
  pity, 914
Depreciate, *detract*, 483
  censure, 932
  decrease, 36
Depreciation, *discount*, 813

Depredation, *stealing*, 791
Depredator, *thief*, 792
Depression, *lowering*, 308
  lowness, 207
  depth, 208
  concavity, 252
  dejection, 837
Deprive, *take*, 789
  subduct, 38
  lose, 776
Depth, *physical*, 208
  mental, 450, 490
Depurate, *clean*, 652
  improve, 658
Depuratory, *remedy*, 662
Depute, *commission*, 755
Deputy, *substitute*, 147, 634,
  759
  jurisdiction, 965
Derangement, *mental*, 503
  physical, 61
  disorder, 59
Derelict, *solitary*, 893
Dereliction, *relinquishment*,
  624, 782
  guilt, 947
Derequisition, *restore*, 790
Deride, *ridicule*, 856
  disrespect, 929
  contempt, 930
  trifle with, 643
  scoff, 483
Derisive, *ridiculous*, 853
Derivation, *origin*, 153
  verbal, 562
Derivative, *effect*, 154
Derive, *attribute*, 155
  receive, 785
  acquire, 775
  income, 810
Dermal, *covering*, 222
* Dernier cri, *fashion*, 852
  newness, 123
* Dernier ressort, *plan*, 626
Derogate, *detract*, 483, 934
  demean, 940
  shame, 874
Derrick, *raise*, 307
Derring-do, *courage*, 861
Derringer, *arms*, 727
Dervish, *clergy*, 996
Descale, *clean*, 652
Descant, *dissert*, 595
  dwell upon, 584
  diffuseness, 573
Descendant, *posterity*, 167
Descent, *slope*, 217
  motion downwards, 306
  order, 58
Describe, *set forth*, 594
Description, *kind*, 75
  narration, 594

escry, *vision*, 441
esecrate, *misuse*, 679
  profane, 988
esert, *solitude*, 101, 893
  waste, 645
  merit, 944
  to relinquish, 624
  to escape, 671
eserter, *apostate*, 607
  coward, 862
esertless, *vice*, 945
eserve, *merit*, 944
  right, 922, 924
Déshabillé, *see* Dishabille
esiccate, *dryness*, 340
esiderate, *desire*, 865
  require, 630
esideratum, *desire*, 865
  inquiry, 461
  requirement, 630
esign, *intention*, 620
  cunning, 702
  plan, 626
  delineation, 554
  prototype, 22
esignate, *specify*, 79, 564
esignation, *kind*, 75
esigned, *intended*, 600
esigner, *artist*, 559, 626
esigning, *false*, 544
  artful, 702
esirable, *expedient*, 646
esire, *longing*, 865
esist, *discontinue*, 142
  relinquish, 624
  inaction, 681
esk, *support*, 215
  receptacle, 191
esolate, *alone*, 87
  secluded, 893
  afflicted, 828
  to ravage, 162
esolation, *evil*, 619
Désorienté, *ignorance*, 491
espair, *hopelessness*, 859
  dejection, 837
espatch, *see* Dispatch
esperado, *rashness*, 863
esperate, *great*, 31
  violent, 173
  rash, 863
  difficult, 704
  impossible, 471
esperation, *hopelessness*,
  859
espicable, *shameful*, 874
  contemptible, 930
  trifling, 643
espise, *contemn*, 930
  deride, 483, 929
Despite, *notwithstanding*,
  179, 708

Despite, *malevolence*, 907
Despoil, *take*, 789
  rob, 791
  hurt, 649
Despondency, *sadness*, 837
  fear, 860
  despair, 859
Despot, *master*, 745
Despotism, *arbitrariness*,
  964
  authority, 737
  severity, 739
Desquamation, *divestment*,
  226
Dessert, *food*, 298
Destination, *fate*, 152, 601
  arrival, 292
  intention, 620
Destiny, *fate*, 601
  chance, 152
Destitute, *insufficient*, 640
  poor, 804
Destrier, *carrier*, 271
Destroy, *demolish*, 162
  injure, 649
  deface, 241
Destroyed, *inexistence*, 2
Destroyer, *ship*, 273
Destruction, *demolition*,
  162, 732
  evil, 619
Destructive, *hurtful*, 649
Desuetude, *disuse*, 614, 678
Desultory, *discontinuous*,
  70
  irregular in time, 139
  disordered, 59
  multiform, 81
  deviating, 149, 279
  agitated, 315
Detach, *separate*, 10, 44,
  47
Detached, *irrelated*, 10, 47
  indifferent, 456
  unity, 87
Detachment, *part*, 51
  army, 726
Detail, *to describe*, 594
  special portion, 79
Detain, *retention*, 781
Detection, *discovery*, 480A
Detective, *inquiry*, 461
Detention, *retention*, 781
  imprisonment, 751
* Détenu, *prisoner*, 754
Deter, *dissuasion*, 616
  fear, 860
Detergent, *remedy*, 662
  remedial, 656
  cleanness, 652
Deteriorate, *deterioration*,
  659

Determinate, *special*, 79
  exact, 474
  resolute, 604
Determination, *resolution*,
  604
  will, 600
  judgment, 480
Determine, *find out*, 480A
  intend, 620
  direction, 278
  make certain, 474
  cause, 153
  resolve, 604
  designate, 79
Determinism, *necessity*, 601
Deterrent, *restraint*, 616
Detersive, *cleanness*, 652
Detest, *hate*, 867, 898
Detestable, *bad*, 649, 867
Dethrone, *abrogation*, 756
Dethronement, *anarchy*,
  738
Detonate, *sound*, 406
  explode, 173
Detonator, *signal*, 550
Detour, *circuit*, 629
  curvature, 245
  deviation, 279
Detract, *subduct*, 38
  depreciate, 483
  censure, 932
  slander, 934
Detractor, *slanderer*, 936
Detrain, *arrival*, 292
Detriment, *evil*, 619
Detrimental, *hurtful*, 649
Detritus, *part*, 51
  pulverulence, 330
Detrude, *cast out*, 297
  cast down, 308
Detruncation, *subduction*,
  38
  disjunction, 44
Deuce, *duality*, 89
  demon, 980
Deuced, *great*, 31
* Deus ex machina, *helper*,
  707, 711
  wonder-worker, 994
Deuterogamy, *marriage*,
  903
Devastate, *destroy*, 162
  injure, 649
Devastation, *havoc*, 659
Develop, *cause*, 153
  produce, 161
  increase, 35
  expand, 194
  evolve, 313
Development, *effect*, 154
Deviate, *differ*, 15
  vary, 20

Dig, *cultivate*, 371
  deepen, 208
  poke, 276
  understand, 518
Dig up, *past*, 122
Digamy, *marriage*, 903
Digest, *arrange*, 60, 826
  think, 451
  plan, 626
  book, 593
  compendium, 596
Diggings, *abode*, 189
Dight, *dressed*, 225
Digit, *number*, 84
Digitated, *pointed*, 253
Dignify, *honour*, 873
Dignitary, *cleric*, 996
  personage, 875
Dignity, *glory*, 873
  pride, 878
  honour, 939
Digress, *deviate*, 279
  style, 573
Digs, *abode*, 189
Dike, *ditch*, 198, 232
  defence, 666, 717
Dilaceration, *disjunction*,
          44
Dilapidation, *wreck*, 162
  deterioration, 659
Dilate, *increase*, 35
  swell, 194
  lengthen, 202
  rarefy, 322
  style, 573
  discourse, 584
Dilatory, *slow*, 275
  inactive, 683
Dilemma, *difficulty*, 704
  logic, 476
  doubt, 475, 485
Dilettante, *ignoramus*, 493
  taste, 850
  idler, 683
Diligence, *coach*, 272
  activity, 682
Dilly-dally, *irresolution*, 605
  lateness, 133
Dilution, *weakness*, 160
  tenuity, 322
  water, 337
Diluvian, *old*, 124
Dim, *dark*, 421
  obscure, 422
  invisible, 447
Dim-out, *dim*, 422
Dim - sighted, *imperfect*
  vision, 443
  foolish, 499
Dime, *trifle*, 643
Dimension, *size*, 192
Dimidiation, *bisection*, 91

Diminish, *lessen*, 32, 36
  contract, 195
* Diminuendo, *music*, 415
Diminutive, *in degree*, 32
  in size, 193
Dimness, *dimness*, 422
Dimple, *concavity*, 252
  notch, 257
Din, *noise*, 404
  repetition, 104
  loquacity, 584
Dine, *to feed*, 297
Diner, *vehicle*, 272
Ding-dong, *noise*, 407
Dinghy, *boat*, 273
Dingle, *hollow*, 252
Dingus, *euphemism*, 565
Dingy, *dark*, 421, 431
  dim, 422
  colourless, 429
  grey, 432
Dining-car, *vehicle*, 272
Dinner, *food*, 298
Dinner-jacket, *dress*, 225
Dint, *power*, 157
  instrumentality, 631
  dent, 257
Diocesan, *clergy*, 996
Diocese, *churchdom*, 995
Diorama, *view*, 448
  painting, 556
Dip, *plunge*, 310
  direction, 278
  slope, 217
  depth, 208
  insert, 300
  immerse, 337
  thief, 792
Dip into, *examine*, 457
  investigate, 461
Diphthong, *letter*, 561
Diploma, *commission*, 755
  document, 551
Diplomacy, *mediation*, 724
  artfulness, 702
  courtesy, 894
  negotiation, 769
Diplomatic, *artful*, 544, 702
  tactful, 498, 698
Diplomat(ist), *messenger*,
  emissary, 758   [534
Dippy, *insane*, 503
Dipsomania, *drunkenness*,
          959
  insanity, 503, 504
  craving, 865
Dire, *fearful*, 860
  grievous, 830
  hateful, 649
Direct, *straight*, 246, 278,
  to order, 737   [628

Direct, *to command*, 741
  to teach, 537
  artless, 703
Direction, *tendency*, 278
  course, 622
  place, 183
  management, 693
  precept, 697
Directly, *soon*, 111
  towards, 278
Director, *manager*, 694
  master, 745
  teacher, 540
Directorship, *authority*, 737
Directory, *council*, 696
  list, 86
Dirge, *song*, 415
  lament, 839
  funeral, 363
Dirigible, *airship*, 273A
Dirk, *arms*, 727
Dirt, *uncleanness*, 653
  trifle, 643
  ugly, 846
  blemish, 848
Dirt-cheap, *cheap*, 815
Dirt-track, *arena*, 728
Dirty, *dishonourable*, 940
Disability, *impotence*, 158
  fault, 651
  unskilfulness, 698
Disable, *weaken*, 158, 160,
          674
Disabuse, *disclosure*, 529
Disadvantage, *evil*, 649
  inexpedience, 647
  badness, 649
Disaffection, *hate*, 898
  disobedience, 742
  disloyalty, 940
Disagreeable, *unpleasant*,
          830
  disliked, 867
Disagreement, *incongruity*,
          24
  difference, 15
  discord, 713
  dissent, 489
Disallow, *prohibit*, 761
Disannul, *abrogate*, 756
Disapparel, *divest*, 226
Disappear, *vanish*, 2, 449
Disappoint, *discontent*, 832
  fail, 732
  baulk, 509
Disapprobation, *blame*, 932
  disrepute, 874
Disarm, *incapacitate*, 158
  weaken, 160
  conciliate, 831
  propitiate, 914
Disarrange, *derange*, 61

Divellicate, *disjoin*, 44
Divergence, *variation*, 20
　dissimilarity, 18
　difference, 15
　discord, 713
　dispersion, 73
　separation, 291
　disagreement, 24
　deviation, 279
Divers, *many*, 102
　different, 15
　multiform, 81
Diversified, *varied*, 15, 16A,
　　　18, 20, 81
Diversion, *amusement*, 840
　change, 140
Diversity, *difference*, 15
　dissimilarity, 18
　multiform, 16A, 81
Divert, *turn*, 279
　amuse, 840
　abstract, 452
* Divertissement, *drama*,
　amusement, 840　　[599
Dives, *wealth*, 803
Divest, *denude*, 226
　take, 789
Divest oneself of, *leave*, 782
Divide, *separate*, 44
　part, 51, 91
　apportion, 786
Dividend, *part*, 51
　number, 84
　portion, 786
Dividers, *measure*, 466
Divination, *prediction*, 511
　occult arts, 992
Divine, *Diety*, 976
　clergyman, 996
　theologian, 983
　to guess, 514
　predict, 510, 511
　perfect, 650
Diving-bell, *depth*, 208
Divining-rod, *spell*, 993
Divinity, *Deity*, 976
　theology, 983
Division, *separation*, 44
　part, 51; *class*, 75
　troop, 72, 726
　arithmetical, 85
　discord, 713
　distribution, 786
Divisor, *number*, 84
Divorce, *matrimonial*, 905
　separation, 44
Divulge, *disclose*, 529
Divulsion, *disjoin*, 44
Dizzard, *fool*, 501
Dizzy, *confused*, 458
　vertigo, 503

Dizzy, *foolish*, 499
Djinn, *demon*, 980
Do, *act*, 680
　fare, 7
　produce, 161
　suffice, 639
　complete, 729
　cheat, 545
Do away with, *remove*, 185,
　　　678
　destroy, 162, 681
Do for, *injure*, 659
　defeat, 731
　kill, 361
　suit, 646
　punish, 972
Do in, *kill*, 361
Do into, *interpret*, 522
Do-nothing, *inactivity*, 683
Do over, *cover*, 222
Do up, *repair*, 658
　pack, 72
Doch-an-doris, *departure*,
　　　293
　intoxicant, 959
Docile, *teachable*, 539
　tractable, 705
　willing, 602
　obedient, 743
　dutiful, 926
Dock, *cut off*, 38
　diminish, 36
　incompleteness, 53
　shorten, 201
　port, 189
　yard, 636, 691
　tribunal, 966
Docker, *workman*, 690
Docket, *indication*, 467, 550
　record, 551
　security, 771
Doctor, *sage*, 492
　physician, 695
　to restore, 660
　amend, 658
　remedy, 662
　falsify, 544
Doctrinaire, *ignoramus*, 493
Doctrinal, *teaching*, 537
Doctrine, *tenet*, 484
　knowledge, 490
Document, *record*, 551
Documentary, *film*, 599A
Dodecahedron, *angle*, 244
Dodge, *oscillate*, 314
　pursue, 461
　deceive, 545
　avoid, 623
　shift, 264
　contrivance, 626
　cunning, 702
Doe, *swiftness*, 274

Doer, *agent*, 690
　originator, 164
Doff, *put off*, 226
Dog, *to pursue*, 622
　follow, 281
　affectation, 855
Dog-cart, *vehicle*, 272
Dog-days, *heat*, 382
Dog-ear, *fold*, 258
Dog Latin, *solecism*, 568
Dog-tired, *fatigue*, 688
Dog-trot, *slowness*, 275
Doge, *master*, 745
Dogfight, *contest*, 720
Dogged, *obstinate*, 606
　discourteous, 895
Dogger, *ship*, 273
Doggerel, *verse*, 597
　ridiculous, 853
Dogma, *tenet*, 484
　theological, 983
Dogmatic, *obstinate*, 606
　certainty, 474
　assertion, 535
　intolerant, 481
Dog's-eared, *fold*, 258
Doings, *actions*, 680
　events, 151
Doit, *trifle*, 643
　coin, 800
Doited, *insane*, 503
* Dolce far niente, *inac-*
　tivity, 638
Doldrums, *dejection*, 837
Dole, *small quantity*, 32
　to give, 784
　to allot, 786
　expenditure, 809
　grief, 828
Dole out, *parsimony*, 819
Doleful, *dejected*, 837
　lament, 839
Doll, *plaything*, 840
　image, 554
　small, 193
Doll up, *beautify*, 845
　adorn, 847
Dollar, *money*, 800
Dollop, *part*, 51
Dolman, *dress*, 225
Dolmen, *grave*, 363
Dolorous, *pain*, 830
Dolour, *physical*, 378
　moral, 828
Dolphin, *ocean*, 341
Dolt, *fool*, 501
Doltish, *folly*, 499
Domain, *region*, 181
　class, 75
　property, 780
Domdaniel, *hell*, 982
Dome, *convexity*, 250

Domesday Book, *list*, 86
Domestic, *interior*, 188, 221
   servant, 746
   secluded, 893
Domesticate, *tame*, 537
Domicile, *abode*, 189
Dominance, *influence*, 175
Dominant, *prevailing*, 737
   note in music, 413
Domination, *authority*, 737
Domineer, *tyrannize*, 739
   insolence, 885
Dominican, *clergy*, 996
Dominie, *teacher*, 540
Dominion, *region*, 181
   spirit, 977
Domino, *dress*, 225
   mask, 530
Don, *to put on*, 225
   noble, 875
   scholar, 492
Dona, *woman*, 374
   sweetheart, 897
Donation, *gift*, 784, 804
Done, *finished*, 729
   cheated, 547
Donee, *receive*, 785
Donjon, *defence*, 717
Donkey, *ass*, 271
   fool, 501
Donkey's breakfast, *bed*, 215
* Donna, *woman*, 374
Donnybrook, *disorder*, 59
   discord, 713
   contention, 720
Donor, *giver*, 784
Doodlebug, *bomb*, **727**
Doom, *fate*, 152
   necessity, 601
   destruction, 162, 360
   to sentence, 969
   condemn, 971
   end, 67
Doomed, *undone*, 828
   fated, 152, 601
Doomsday, *futurity*, 121
   end, 67
Door, *opening*, 260
   passage, 627
   brink, 230
   entrance, 66, 294
   barrier, 232
Door-keeper, *janitor*, 263
Doorway, *opening*, 260
Dope, *semiliquid*, 352
   stupefy, 376
Dope fiend, *intemperance*,
           954
* Doppelgänger, *ghost*, 980
Dopy, *sleepy*, 683
Dormant, *latent*, 526
   inert, 172, 683

Dormitory, *room*, 191
Dormouse, *inactivity*, 683
Dorsal, *rear*, 235
* Dorsum, *rear*, 235
   convexity, 250
Dose, *part*, 51
   mixture, 41
   remedy, 662
Doss-house, *inn*, 189
Dossier, *record*, 551
   evidence, 461
Dossil, *stopper*, 263
Dot, *speck*, 32, 193
   mark, 550
   dowry, 810
Dotage, *age*, 128
   folly, 499
Dotard, *fool*, 501
Dote, *drivel*, 499, 503
   love, 897
Dotted, *variegated*, 440
Double, *duplex*, 90
   turn, 283
   fold, 258
   false, 544
   similarity, 17
Double-dealing, *falsehood*,
           544
   dishonour, 940
Double Dutch, *jargon*,
           497
Double-edged, *energy*, 171
   equivocal, 520
* Double entendre, *equivo-*
   calness, 520
   indecency, 961
Double-faced, *deceitful*, 544
   trimming, 607
Double-quick, *speed*, 274
Double-tongued, *false*, 544
   equivocal, 520
Doublet, *dress*, 225
Doubt, *disbelief*, 485
   scepticism, 989
Doubtful, *uncertain*, 475
   incredulous, 485
Doubtless, *certainty*, 474
   assent, 488
* Douceur, *expenditure*,
           809
   giving, 784
Douche, *water*, 337
Dough, *pulp*, 354
   inelastic, 324
   money, 800
Doughboy, *fighter*, **726**
Doughty, *courageous*, 861
   strong, 159
Dour, *severe*, 739
Douse, *immerse*, 310
   splash, 337
Dove, *deity*, 976

Dovelike, *innocent*, 946
Dovetail, *intervene*, 228
   intersect, 219
   insert, 300
   angular, 244
   join, 43
   agree, 23
Dowager, *widow*, 905
   lady, 374
   veteran, 130
Dowdy, *vulgar*, 851
   dirty, 653
   ugly, 846
Dower, *wealth*, 803, 810
   property, 780
Dowerless, *poverty*, 804
Down, *levity*, 320
   smoothness, 255
   plumose, 256
   bed of, 377
   below, 207
Down-hearted, *dejection*,
           837
Downcast, *dejection*, 837
Downfall, *ruin*, 162, 732
   calamity, 619
Downgrade, *debase*, 659
Downhill, *obliquity*, 217
Downright, *absolute*, 31
   plain, 576
   sincere, 703
Downs, *plains*, 344
   uplands, 206
Downstairs, *lowness*, 207
Downtrodden, *contemptible*,
   submission, 725   [930
   subject, 749
Downwards, *lowness*, 207
Downy, *hairy*, 256
   soft, 324
   cunning, 702
Dowry, *wealth*, 803, 810
Doxology, *worship*, 990
Doxy, *belief*, 484
Doyen, *oldness*, 124
Doze, *inactivity*, 683
Dozen, *assemblage*, **72**
   number, 98
Drab, *colour*, 432
   hussy, 962, 949
Draconian, *severe*, 739
Draff, *uncleanness*, 653
Draft, *copy*, 21
   transfer, 270
   sketch, 554
   write, 590
   abstract, 596
   plan, 626
   cheque, 800
Drag, *traction*, 285
   attract, 288
   crawl, 275

Drop, *fall*, 306
  discontinue, 142
  expire, 360
  relinquish, 624, 782
  lose, 776
  faint, 160
  fatigue, 688
  flow out, 348
  spherule, 249
  small quantity, 32, 193
Drop astern, *regression*, 283
Drop in, *immerse*, 300
  arrive, 292
Drop off, *die*, 360
Droplet, *smallness*, 32
Dropsical, *swollen*, 194
  redundant, 641
Droshky, *vehicle*, 272
Dross, *dirt*, 653
  trash, 643
  remainder, 40
Drought, *insufficiency*, 640
Drouth, *thirst*, 865
Drove, *assemblage*, 72, 102
Drown, *kill*, 361
  immerse, 300
  water, 337
  surfeit, 641
  ruin, 731, 732
Drowsy, *slow*, 275
  inactive, 683
  weary, 841
Drub, *beat*, 276
  master, 731
  punish, 972
Drudge, *agent*, 690
  to work, 680
  to plod, 682
Drug, *remedy*, 662
  superfluity, 641
  trash, 643
Drugget, *covering*, 222
Drum, *cylinder*, 249
  music, 417
  sound, 407
  to repeat, 104
Drum-major, *master*, 745
Drum out, *punish*, 972
Drumhead, *tribunal*, 966
Drummer, *agent*, 758
Drunk, *intoxication*, 959
  intemperance, 954
Dry, *arid*, 340
  jejune, 575
  thirsty, 865
  teetotal, 953
  scanty, 640
  wit, 844
  cynical, 932
Dry-nurse, *tend*, 707
  teach, 537
  teacher, 540

Dry point, *engraving*, 558
Dry rot, *deterioration*, 653, 659
Dry up, *waste*, 638
  silent, 585
Dryasdust, *past*, 122
Duad, *duality*, 89
Duality, *duality*, 89
Dub, *name*, 465
  cinema, 599A
Dubious, *uncertain*, 475
Dubitation, *doubt*, 485
* Duce, *master*, 745
Duchess, *noble*, 875
Duchy, *region*, 181
Duck, *immerse*, 300
  plunge, 310
  wet, 337
  stoop, 308
  darling, 899
  nothing, 4
  vehicle, 272
Duck-pond, *taming*, 370
Ducking-stool, *punishment*, 975
Ducks and drakes, *recoil*, 277
Duct, *conduit*, 350
Ductile, *flexible*, 324
  easy, 705
  useless, 645
Dud, *defective*, 651
Dude, *fop*, 854
Dudeen, *tobacco-pipe*, 298A
Dudgeon, *anger*, 900
  discourteous, 895
  club, 727
Duds, *clothes*, 225
Due, *proper*, 924, 926
  owing, 806
  effect, 154
  expedient, 646
Duel, *contention*, 720
Duellist, *combatant*, 726
Dueness, *right*, 924
Duenna, *teacher*, 540
  accompaniment, 88
  keeper, 753
Dues, *price*, 812
Duet, *music*, 815
Duff, *false*, 495
Duffer, *fool*, 501
  bungler, 700
Duffle coat, *dress*, 225
Dug, *convexity*, 250
Dug-out, *refuge*, 666, 717
  canoe, 273
Duke, *noble*, 875
  ruler, 745
Dukedom, *title*, 877
Dulcet, *sound*, 405
  melodious, 413

Dulcet, *agreeable*, 829
Dulcify, *sweeten*, 396
Dulcimer, *musical instrument*, 417
Dulcinea, *favourite*, 899
Dull, *inert*, 172
  insensible, 376
  tame, 575
  callous, 823
  blunt, 254
  weak, 160
  moderate, 174
  colourless, 429
  dejected, 837
  inexcitable, 826
  stolid, 699
  prosing, 843
  unapt, 499
Dull-brained, *folly*, 499
Dull-witted, *folly*, 499
Dullard, *fool*, 501
Duma, *council*, 696
Dumb, *aphony*, 581
  stupid, 499, 843
  unskilful, 699
Dumb-bell, *fool*, 501
Dumb show, *the drama*, 599
Dumbfound, *astonish*, 870
  disappoint, 509
Dummy, *aphony*, 581
  effigy, 554
Dump, *deposit*, 184
Dumps, *sadness*, 837
  mortification, 832
Dumpy, *broad*, 202
  short, 200
  ugly, 846
Dun, *colour*, 432
  to importune, 765
  a creditor, 805
Dunce, *ignoramus*, 493
  fool, 501
Dunderhead, *fool*, 501
Dundreary, *whisker*, 256
Dune, *hillock*, 206
Dung, *uncleanness*, 653
Dungarees, *dress*, 225
Dungeon, *prison*, 752
  hide, 530
Dunghill, *vulgar*, 876
Dunt, *blow*, 619
Duodecimal, *twelve*, 98
Duodecimo, *littleness*, 193
  book, 593
Duodenary, *numbers*, 98
Duologue, *interlocution*, 588
  drama, 599
Dupe, *to deceive*, 545
  deceived, 547
  credulous, 486
Duplex, *double*, 89, 90

Empty-handed, *insufficient*, 640
Empty-headed, *ignorant*, 491
Empurple, *purple*, 437
Empyrean, *sky*, 318
    blissful, 827, 829
Emulate, *rival*, 708, 720
    envy, 921
    imitate, 19
    glory, 873
Emulsion, *semiliquidity*, 352
Emunctory, *conduit*, 350
* En bloc, *assent*, 488
    whole, 50
* En famille, *sociality*, 892
* En garçon, *celibacy*, 904
* En passant, *method*, 627
    transitoriness, 111
    irrelation, 10
    journey, 266
* En prince, *generosity*, 942
* En rapport, *agreement*, 23
    relation, 9
* En règle, *conformity*, 82
* En revanche, *compensation*, 30
* En route, *journey*, 266
Enable, *power*, 157
Enact, *order*, 741
    a law, 963
    drama, 599
Enamel, *painting*, 556
    covering, 222
    smooth, 255
    adorn, 845, 847
Enamour, *love*, 897
Encage, *circumscribe*, 231
    restrain, 751
Encamp, *locate*, 184, 265
    inhabit, 186
Encase, *circumscribe*, 231
Encaustic, *painting*, 556
* Enceinte, *region*, 181
    enclosure, 232
    pregnant, 168
Enchain, *bind*, 43, 751
Enchant, *please*, 829
    love, 897
    conjure, 992, 994
Enchantress, *beauty*, 845
    sorceress, 994
Encharge, *consign*, 755
Enchiridion, *book*, 593
Encircle, *begird*, 227
Enclave, *enclosure*, 232
    region, 181
Enclose, *circumscribe*, 231
Enclosure, *fence*, 752
    space, 181
Encomiast, *flatterer*, 935
Encomium, *approval*, 931

Encompass, *begird*, 227
Encore, *repetition*, 104
Encounter, *meet*, 292
    clash, 276
    contest, 720
    withstand, 708
Encourage, *animate*, 615
    aid, 707
    embolden, 861
    hope, 858
    comfort, 834
Encroach, *transgress*, 303
    infringe, 925
Encrust, *line*, 224
    coat, 222
Encumbered, *in debt*, 806
Encumbrance, *hindrance*, 704, 706
Encyclical, *publication*, 531
Encyclopaedia, *knowledge*, 490
    assembly, 72
    generality, 78
End, *termination*, 67, 154
    death, 360
    object, 620
Endamage, *injure*, 659
    harm, 649
Endanger, *danger*, 665
Endeavour, *attempt*, 675, 676
    pursue, 622
    intend, 620
Endemic, *special*, 79
    disease, 655, 657
Endless, *infinite*, 105
    multitudinous, 102
    long, 200
Endogamy, *marriage*, 903
Endorsement, *evidence*, 467
    sign, 550, 590
    voucher, 771
    ratification, 769
    approval, 931
Endosmosis, *passage*, 302
Endow, *confer power*, 157
Endowment, *gift*, 784
    capacity, 5
    power, 157
    talent, 698
Endue, *empower*, 157
Endure, *time*, 106
    to continue, 141
    to last, 110
    event, 151
    to bear, 821
    to submit, 826
Endways, *length*, 200
    vertical, 212
Enemy, *enemy*, 891
Energumen, *madman*, 503
    fanatic, 515

Energy, *physical*, 171
    strength, 159
    style, 574
    activity, 682
    exertion, 686
    resolution, 604
Enervate, *weakness*, 160
* Enfant perdu, *rashness*, 863
* Enfant terrible, *artlessness*, 703
Enfeeble, *weaken*, 160
Enfilade, *pierce*, 260
    pass through, 302
Enfold, *circumscribe*, 231
Enforce, *urge*, 615
    compel, 744
    require, 924
Enfranchise, *liberate*, 748, 750, 924
Engage, *induce*, 615
    the attention, 457
    in a pursuit, 622
    promise, 768, 769
    commission, 755
    undertake, 676
    book, 132
Engagement, *business*, 625
    contest, 720
    promise, 768
    duty, 926
Engaging, *pleasing*, 829
    amiable, 897
Engender, *produce*, 161
Engine, *instrument*, 633
Engine-driver, *director*, 694
Engineering, *means*, 632
Engirdle, *circumjacence*, 227
English, *translate*, 522
Engorge, *reception*, 296
Engorgement, *redundance*, 641
Engraft, *insert*, 301
    join, 43
    add, 37
    teach, 537
    implant, 6
Engrained, *imbued*, 5
    combined, 48
Engrave, *mark*, 550
    on the memory, 505
Engraving, *engraving*, 558
Engross, *possess*, 777
    write, 590
    the thoughts, 451
    the attention, 457
Engulf, *destroy*, 162
    plunge, 310
    swallow up, 296
Enhance, *increase*, 35
    improve, 658
Enharmonic, *harmony*, 413

Enigma, *secret*, 533
  question, 461
Enigmatic, *concealed*, 528
  obscure, 519
  uncertain, 475
Enjambement, *transcursion*, 303
Enjoin, *command*, 741
  induce, 615
  enact, 963
Enjoy, *physically*, 377
  morally, 827
  possess, 777
Enkindle, *induce*, 615
Enlace, *surround*, 227
  entwine, 219, 248
  join, 43
Enlarge, *increase*, 35
  swell, 194
  liberate, 750
  in writing, 573
Enlighten, *illuminate*, 420
  inform, 527
  instruct, 537
Enlightened, *wise*, 498
Enlightenment, *knowledge*, 490
Enlist, *commission*, 755
  engage, 615
Enliven, *amuse*, 840
  cheer, 836
  delight, 829
Enmesh, *entwine*, 219
Enmity, *hostility*, 889
  hate, 898
  discord, 713
Ennead, *nine*, 98
Enneagon, *nine*, 98
Ennoble, *glorify*, 873
Ennui, *weariness*, 841
Enormity, *crime*, 947
Enormous, *in degree*, 31
  in size, 192
Enough, *much*, 31
  sufficient, 639
  satiety, 869
Enquiry, *see* Inquiry
Enrage, *incense*, 900
  provoke, 830
Enrapture, *excite*, 824
  beatify, 829
  love, 897
Enravish, *beatify*, 829
Enrich, *wealth*, 803
  ornament, 847
Enrobe, *invest*, 225
Enrol, *record*, 551
  appoint, 755
Enrolment, *list*, 86
Ens, *essence*, 1
Ensanguined, *red*, 434
  murderous, 361

Ensconce, *settle*, 184
  render safe, 664
  conceal, 528
* Ensemble, *whole*, 50
Enshrine, *memory*, 505, 873
  sanctify, 987
Enshroud, *conceal*, 528
Ensiform, *sharpness*, 253
Ensign, *standard*, 550
  officer, 726
  master, 745
Enslave, *subjection*, 749
Ensnare, *cheat*, 545
Ensue, *follow*, 63, 117
  happen, 151
Ensure, *certainty*, 474
Entablature, *summit*, 210
Entail, *cause*, 153
  involve, 467
  impose, 741
Entangle, *derange*, 61
  entwine, 219
  disorder, 59
  embroil, 713
  perplex, 528
  mixture, 41
* Entente cordiale, *friendship*, 888
  concord, 714
Enter, *go in*, 294
  note, 551
  accounts, 811
Enter in, *converge*, 290
Enter into, *component*, 56
Enter upon, *begin*, 66
Enterprise, *pursuit*, 622
  attempt, 676
Enterprising, *active*, 682
  energetic, 171
  courageous, 861
Entertain, *amuse*, 840
  support, 707
  sociality, 892
  an idea, 451, 484
Entertainment, *repast*, 298
* Entêté, *obstinate*, 606
  prejudiced, 481
Enthral, *subdue*, 749
  delight, 829
Enthrone, *repute*, 873
Enthusiasm, *feeling*, 821
  imagination, 515
  love, 897
  hope, 850, 858
Enthusiast, *game*, 840
  zealot, 606
Enthusiastic, *sensibility*, 822
  excitability, 825
Enthymeme, *reasoning*, 476
Entice, *motive*, 615
Enticing, *pleasure*, 829

Entire, *whole*, 50
  complete, 52
Entirely, *greatness*, 31
Entitle, *name*, 564
  give a right, 924
Entity, *existence*, 1
Entomb, *inter*, 231, 363
  imprison, 751
* Entourage, *environment*, 227
  retinue, 746
* Entr'acte, *interval*, 106
Entrails, *interior*, 221
Entrain, *depart*, 293
Entrance, *beginning*, 66
  ingress, 294
  fee, 809
  to enrapture, 824, 829
  to conjure, 992
Entrap, *deceive*, 545
* Entre nous, *concealment*, 528
Entreat, *request*, 765
* Entrechat, *leap*, 309
Entrée, *ingress*, 294
* Entremet, *food*, 298
Entrench, *defence*, 717
* Entrepôt, *store*, 636
  mart, 799
* Entrepreneur, *organizer*, 626
* Entresol, *interjacence*, 228
Entrust, *consign*, 784
  lend, 787
  charge with, 755
Entry, *ingress*, 294
  beginning, 66
  record, 551
  evidence, 467
Entwine, *join*, 43
  intersect, 219
  convolve, 248
Enumerate, *number*, 85
Enunciate, *publish*, 531
  inform, 527
  affirm, 535
  voice, 580
Envelop, *invest*, 225
  conceal, 528
Envelope, *covering*, 222
  enclosure, 232
Envenom, *poison*, 649
  deprave, 659
  exasperate, 835, 898
Environs, *nearness*, 197
  circumjacence, 227
Envisage, *view*, 441
  confront, 234
  intuition, 477
Envoy, *messenger*, 534
  postscript, 39
Envy, *jealousy*, 921

Enwrap, *invest*, 225
Eolith, *oldness*, 124
Epaulet, *badge*, 550
  decoration, 877
  ornament, 847
* Éperdu, *excited*, 824
Ephemeral, *transient*, 111
  changeable, 149
Ephemeris, *calendar*, 114
  record, 551; book, 593
Epic, *poem*, 597
Epicedium, *interment*, 363
Epicene, *exceptional*, 83
  multiform, 81
Epicentre, *focus*, 223
Epicure, *sensual*, 954
  glutton, 957
  fastidious, 868
Epicycle, *circularity*, 247
Epicycloid, *circularity*, 247
Epidemic, *disease*, 655
  dispersed, 73
  general, 78
Epidermis, *covering*, 222
Epidiascope, *spectacle*, 448
Epigram, *wit*, 842
Epigrammatic, *pithy*, 516
  concise, 572
Epigrammatist, *humorist*,
  844
Epigraph, *indication*, 550
Epilepsy, *convulsion*, 315
Epilogue, *sequel*, 65
  drama, 599
Episcopal, *clergy*, 995
Episode, *event*, 151
  interjacence, 228
  interruption, 70
Episodic, *unrelated*, 10
  style, 573
Epistle, *letter*, 592
Epitaph, *interment*, 363
Epithalamium, *marriage*,
  903
Epithem, *remedy*, 662
Epithet, *nomenclature*, 564
Epitome, *compendium*, 596
  conciseness, 572
  miniature, 193
Epizootic, *insalubrity*, 657
Epoch, *time*, 113
  duration, 106
  period, 114
Epode, *poetry*, 597
Epopee, *poetry*, 597
* Épris, *love*, 897
Equable, *right*, 922
Equal, *equality*, 27
  equitable, 922
Equanimity, *inexcitability*,
  826
Equate, *equality*, 27

Equations, *numeration*, 85
Equator, *middle*, 68
Equerry, *servant*, 746
Equestrian, *traveller*, 268
Equidistant, *middle*, 68
Equilibrium, *equality*, 27
  steadiness, 265
Equip, *dress*, 225
  prepare, 673
Equipage, *vehicle*, 272
  instrument, 633
  materials, 635
Equipoise, *equal*, 27
Equipollent, *equal*, 27
  identical, 13
Equiponderant, *equal*, 27
Equitable, *just*, 922
  fair, 480, 939
  due, 924
Equitation, *journey*, 266
Equity, *justice*, 922
  law, 963; *honour*, 939
Equivalence, *equal*, 27
Equivalent, *identity*, 13
  compensation, 30
  synonymous, 516
Equivocal, *dubious*, 475
  double meaning, 520, 961
Equivocate, *pervert*, 477
  prevaricate, 520
Equivoque, *equivocal*, 520
  uncertainty, 475
  impurity, 961
  error, 495
Era, *duration*, 106
  chronology, 114
Eradicate, *destroy*, 162
  extract, 301
Erase, *efface*, 162, 499, 552
Ere, *priority*, 116
Ere long, *earliness*, 132
Erebus, *dark*, 421
  hell, 982
Erect, *raise*, 307
  build, 161
  vertical, 212
Erection, *house*, 189
Eremitical, *seclusion*, 893
Erewhile, *preterition*, 122
  priority, 116
Ergatocracy, *rule*, 737
* Ergo, *reasoning*, 476
Ergotism, *reasoning*, 476
Eriometer, *optical*, 445
Erk, *fighter*, 726
Ermine, *badge of authority*,
  747
Erode, *destroy*, 162
  injure, 659
Erotic, *amorous*, 897
  impure, 961
Eroticism, *pleasantness*, 829

Err, *in opinion*, 495
  morally, 945
Errand, *commission*, 755
  business, 625
  message, 532
Erratic, *capricious*, 149, 608
  wandering, 264, 279
Erratum, *error*, 495
  misprint, 555
Error, *false opinion*, 495
  failure, 732
  vice, 945
  guilt, 947
Erst, *preterition*, 122
Erubescence, *redness*, 434
Eructate, *eject*, 297
Erudite, *scholar*, 492
Erudition, *knowledge*, 490
Eruption, *egress*, 295
  violence, 173
  disease, 655
Escalade, *mount*, 305
  attack, 716
Escalate, *increase*, 35
Escalator, *way*, 627
  lift, 307
Escallop, *convolution*, 248
Escapade, *freak*, 608
  prank, 840
  vagary, 856
Escape, *flight*, 671
  liberate, 750
  evade, 927; *forget*, 506
Escarpment, *slope*, 217
Eschatology, *intention*, 620
  end, 67
Escheat, *penalty*, 974
Eschew, *avoid*, 623
  dislike, 867
Escort, *to accompany*, 88
  safeguard, 664
  keeper, 753
Escritoire, *desk*, 191
Esculent, *food*, 298
Escutcheon, *indication*, 550
Esoteric, *private*, 79
  concealed, 528
Espalier, *agriculture*, 371
Especial, *private*, 79
Esperanto, *language*, 560
Espial, *vision*, 441
* Espièglerie, *wit*, 842
Espionage, *inquiry*, 461
Esplanade, *flat*, 213
  plain, 344
Espousal, *marriage*, 903
* Esprit, *shrewdness*, 498
  wit, 842
* Esprit de corps, *party*, 712
  misjudgment, 781
  belief, 484
  sociality, 892

* Esprit fort, *sage*, 500
Espy, *vision*, 441
Esquire, *title*, 877
Essay, *try*, 463
  endeavour, 675
  dissertation, 595
Essayist, *writing*, 590
Essence, *nature*, 5
  existence, 1
  odour, 398
  pith, 642
Essential, *great*, 31
  requisite, 630
Establish, *fix*, 184
  demonstrate, 478
  evidence, 467
  create, 161
  substantiate, 494
  settle, 150
Established, *received*, 82
  habitual, 613
Establishment, *fixture*, 141
  party, 712
  location, 184
* Estancia, *property*, 780
Estate, *condition*, 7
  property, 780
Esteem, *judge*, 480
  believe, 484
  approve, 931
Estimable, *good*, 648
  commendable, 931
Estimate, *measure*, 466
  judge, 480
  count, 85
Estimation, *opinion*, 484
  respect, 928
  good, 648
Estoppage, *prohibition*, 761
Estrade, *horizontal*, 213
Estrange, *alienate*, 449
  hate, 898
  seclude, 893
Estreat, *penalty*, 974
Estuary, *gulf*, 343
Esurient, *hungry*, 865
* État-major, *combatant*,
  726
Etcetera, *addition*, 37
  inclusion, 76
  plurality, 100
Etch, *engraving*, 558
Eternal, *perpetuity*, 112
Ether, *sky*, 313, 338
  void, 4
  vapour, 334
Ethical, *virtue*, 944
Ethics, *duty*, 926
Ethiopic, *blackness*, 431
Ethnic, *heathen*, 984
  racial, 372
Ethnology, *mankind*, 372

Ethos, *nature*, 5
Etiolate, *bleach*, 429, 430
Etiquette, *fashion*, 852
  custom, 613
  ceremony, 882
* Étude, *music*, 415
Etymology, *word*, 562
  language, 560
Etymon, *origin*, 153
  verbal, 562
Eucharist, *rite*, 998
Euchology, *rite*, 998
Eugenics, *production*, 161
Eulogy, *approval*, 931
Euphemism, *misnomer*, 565
Euphonious, *musical*, 413
  style, 578
Euphony, *harmony*, 413
Euphoria, *health*, 654
Euphuism, *ornament*, 577
  affectation, 855
Eurasian, *mixture*, 41
Eureka, *judgment*, 480
  answer, 462
Eurhythmics, *training*, 673
Eurhythmy, *symmetry*, 242
Euroclydon, *wind*, 349
Euterpe, *music*, 415
Euthanasia, *death*, 360
  killing, 361
Evacuate, *emit*, 297
  excrete, 299
Evacuee, *escape*, 671
Evade, *avoid*, 623
  escape, 671
  sophistry, 477
  dereliction, 927
Evaluate, *appraise*, 466, 812
Evanescent, *transient*, 111
  minute, 32, 193
  disappearing, 449
Evangelist, *revelation*, 985
Evangelize, *convert*, 484
Evaporate, *vapour*, 336
  gas, 334
  unsubstantiality, 4
Evasion, *escape*, 623, 671
  sophistry, 477
  plea, 617
  falsehood, 544
  untruth, 546
  cunning, 702
  dereliction, 927
Eve, *evening*, 126
  priority, 116
Even, *equal*, 27
  uniform, 16
  level, 213
  flat, 251
  smooth, 265
  straight, 246
  although, 179, 469

Even-handed, *equitable*,
  922
  honourable, 939
Even so, *assent*, 488
Evening, *evening*, 126
Evening, *worship*, 990
  evening, 126
Event, *eventuality*, 151
Eventful, *stirring*, 151
  remarkable, 642
Eventide, *evening*, 126
Eventual, *futurity*, 121
Eventuate, *occur*, 1
Ever, *always*, 112
  seldom, 137
Ever and anon, *repetition*,
  104
Ever-changing, *mutability*,
  149
Ever-recurring, *repetition*,
  104
Evergreen, *newness*, 123
  diuturnity, 110
  continuous, 69
  perpetuity, 112
Everlasting, *perpetual*, 112,
  136
Evermore, *perpetual*, 112
Every, *generality*, 78
Everyday, *conformity*, 82
  perpetuity, 112
Everyman, *mankind*, 372
Everywhere, *space*, 180,
  186
Eviction, *displacement*, 185
Evidence, *evidence*, 467
Evident, *visible*, 446
  certain, 474
  demonstrable, 478
  manifest, 525
Evil, *harm*, 619
  wrong, 923
  vice, 945
  producing evil, 649
Evil day, *adversity*, 735
Evil eye, *malevolence*, 907
  glance, 441
Evil-minded, *malevolent*,
  907
  vicious, 945
Evil-speaking, *detraction*,
  934
Evildoer, *maleficent*, 913
  badness, 649
  culprit, 949
Evince, *show*, 467
  prove, 478
Eviscerate, *extract*, 301
  divide, 44
  mutilate, 38
Evoke, *call upon*, 765
  excite, 824

Exhaust, *drain*, 638, 789
  fatigue, 688
  weaken, 160
  misemploy, 679
  squander, 818
  complete, 52, 729
  tube, 351
Exhaustless, *infinite*, 105
  plentiful, 639
Exhibit, *show*, 525
  display, 882
Exhilarate, *cheer*, 836
Exhort, *advise*, 695
  induce, 615
  preach, 998
Exhume, *interment*, 363
  past, 122
Exigency, *crisis*, 8
  chance, 621
  difficulty, 704
  requirement, 630
  need, 865
  dearth, 640
Exigent, *severe*, 640
  exacting, 832
Exiguous, *little*, 193
Exile, *displace*, 185
  send out, 297
  seclude, 893
  punish, 972
Exility, *thinness*, 203
Existence, *being*, 1
  life, 359
  thing, 3
  in time, 118
  in space, 186
Exit, *departure*, 293
  egress, 295
  escape, 671
Exodus, *departure*, 293
  egress, 295
Exogamy, *marriage*, 903
Exonerate, *exempt*, 927
  vindicate, 937
  forgive, 918
  acquit, 970
  disburden, 705
  absolve, 760
  release, 756
Exorbitant, *enormous*, 31
  redundant, 641
  dear, 814
Exorcise, *conjure*, 992
Exorcism, *theology*, 993
Exorcist, *heterodoxy*, 994
Exordium, *beginning*, 66
Exosmosis, *passage*, 302
Exoteric, *disclosed*, 531
  public, 529
Exotic, *alien*, 10
  exceptional, 83
Expand, *swell*, 194

Expand, *increase*, 35
  in breadth, 202
  rarefy, 322
  in writing, 573
Expanse, *space*, 180, 202
  size, 192
Expansion, *space*, 180
Expatiate, *in writing*, 573
  in discourse, 582, 584
Expatriate, *deport*, 295
  displace, 185
  exclude, 55, 893
Expect, *look for*, 121, 507
  not wonder, 871
  hope, 858
Expectorant, *remedy*, 662
Expectorate, *eject*, 296
Expedience, *utility*, 646
Expedient, *means*, 632
  substitute, 634
  plan, 626
Expedite, *accelerate*, 274
  earliness, 132
  aid, 707
Expedition, *speed*, 274
  activity, 682
  warfare, 722
  march, 266
Expel, *displace*, 185
  eject, 297
  drive from, 289
  punish, 972
Expend, *use*, 677
  waste, 638
  pay, 809
Expense, *price*, 812
Expensive, *dear*, 814
Experience, *knowledge*, 490
  undergo, 821
  event, 151
Experienced, *skilled*, 698
Experiment, *trial*, 463
  endeavour, 675
* Experimentum crucis,
  demonstration, 478
Expert, *skill*, 698
  adept, 700
* Experto crede, *knowledge*,
    490
Expiate, *atonement*, 952
Expire, *death*, 360
  end, 67
  breathe out, 349
Explain, *expound*, 522
  inform, 527
  teach, 537
  answer, 462
Explain away, *misinterpret*,
    523
Expletive, *redundance*, 573,
    641
  malediction, 908

Explication, *interpret*, 522
Explicit, *distinct*, 516, 518,
    535
Explode, *burst*, 173
  sound, 406
  refute, 479
  passion, 825
  anger, 900
Exploit, *action*, 680
  to use, 677
Explore, *investigate*, 461
  experiment, 463
Explosion, *see* Explode
Exponent, *index*, 550
  numerical, 84
  interpreter, 522
Export, *transfer*, 270
  send out, 297
  thing sent, 295
* Exposé, *account*, 596
  disclosure, 529
Expose, *show*, 525
  interpret, 522
  confute, 479
  denude, 226
  endanger, 665
Exposition, *answer*, 462
  disclosure, 529
Expositor, *interpreter*, 524
  teacher, 540
Expository, *information*,
    527, 595
Expostulate, *deprecate*, 766
  reprehend, 932
  dissuade, 616
  advise, 695
Exposure, *disclosure*, 529
Exposure meter, *optical instrument*, 445
Exposure to, *liability*, 177
Expound, *interpret*, 522
  teach, 537
  answer, 462
Expounder, *interpreter*, 524
Express, *voluntary*, 600
  intentional, 620
  declare, 525
  mean, 516
  inform, 527
  phrase, 566
  intelligible, 518
  name, 564
  squeeze out, 301
  rapid, 274
Expression, *aspect*, 448
Expressive, *style*, 574
Exprobation, *disapproval*,
    932
Exprobration, *accusation*,
    938
Expropriate, *take*, 789
Expulsion, *see* Expel

Expunge, *efface*, 506, 552
  destroy, 162
  disappear, 449
Expurgation, *cleanness*,
                 652
Exquisite, *excellent*, 648
  pleasurable, 829
  savoury, 394
  fop, 854
Exquisitely, *great*, 31
Exsiccate, *dryness*, 340
Exsufflation, *sorcery*, 992
Extant, *being*, 1
Extempore, *instantly*, 113
  early, 132
  off-hand, 612
  unprepared, 674
Extend, *prolong*, 200
  expand, 194
  reach, 196
  increase, 35
Extensile, *pliable*, 324
Extension, *space*, 180
Extensive, *spacious*, 180
  considerable, 31
Extent, *degree*, 26
  space, 180
Extenuate, *decrease*, 36
  diminish, 192
  excuse, 937
  acquit, 970
Exterior, *exteriority*, 220
Exterminate, *destruction*,
                 162
Exterminator, *destroyer*,
                 165
External, *exteriority*, 220
Externalize, *materialize*,
                 316
Extinction, *destruction*, 162
  non-existence, 2
  of life, 360
Extinguish, *destroy*, 162
  darken, 421
  blow out, 385
Extinguisher, *destroyer*,
                 165
Extirpate, *destruction*, 162
  extraction, 301
Extol, *praise*, 931
  over-estimate, 482
Extort, *despoil*, 789
  extract, 301
  compel, 744
Extortionate, *greedy*, 865
  dear, 814
  parsimonious, 819
Extra, *additional*, 37, 39
  supernumerary, 641
  store, 636
* Extra muros, *exteriority*,
                 220

Extra-sensory, *occult*, 992
  thought, 451
  immaterial, 317
Extract, *take out*, 301
  part, 51
  choice, 609
  quotation, 596
Extradite, *deport*, 55, 270
  displace, 185
  eject, 297
Extrajudicial, *illegal*, 964
Extramundane, *immateri-
  ality*, 317
Extramural, *exterior*, 220
Extraneous, *extrinsic*, 6
  not related, 10
  foreign, 57
Extraordinary, *unconformity*, 83
  greatness, 31
Extravagant, *exaggerated*,
                 549
  irrational, 477
  absurd, 497
  ridiculous, 853
  foolish, 499
  redundant, 641
  high-priced, 814
  prodigal, 818
  vulgar, 851
  inordinate, 31
Extravaganza, *fanciful*, 515
  burlesque, 853
  the drama, 599
Extravasate, *excretion*, 299
Extreme, *greatness*, 31
  revolutionary, 146
Extremist, *zealot*, 604
Extremity, *end*, 67
  exterior, 220
Extricate, *take out*, 301
  liberate, 750
  deliver, 672
  facilitate, 705
Extrinsic, *extrinsicality*, 6
Extrude, *eject*, 297
Exuberant, *redundant*, 641
  style, 573
  feeling, 821
Exude, *excretion*, 299
  egress, 295
Exult, *crow*, 836
  rejoice, 838
  boast, 873, 884
Exuviae, *remainder*, 40
Eye, *organ of sight*, 441
  opening, 260
  circle, 247
Eye-opener, *enlightenment*,
                 527
  portent, 870
Eye-shade, *mask*, 530

Eye-witness, *evidence*, 467
  spectator, 444
Eyeglass, *optical instrument*,
                 445
Eyeless, *blind*, 442
Eyelet, *opening*, 260
Eyesight, *vision*, 441
Eyesore, *ugliness*, 846
Eyewash, *deception*, 545
Eyot, *island*, 346
Eyre, *jurisprudence*, 965
Eyrie, *abode*, 189

F

Fabian policy, *inactivity*,
                681, 683
  delay, 133
Fable, *fiction*, 546
  error, 495
  description, 594
Fabric, *texture*, 329
  house, 189
  effect, 154
  state, 7
Fabricate, *make*, 161
  invent, 515
  forge, 544
  falsify, 546
Fabulous, *imagination*, 515
  mythical, 979
  exaggerated, 549
  greatness, 31
  non-existent, 2
Façade, *front*, 234
Face, *exterior*, 220
  front, 234
  lining, 224
  impudence, 885
  confront, 861
  aspect, 448
Face about, *deviation*, 279
Face-cloth, *wash*, 652
Face down, *withstand*, 719
Face to face, *manifestation*,
                 525
Facet, *exterior*, 220
Facetious, *wit*, 842
Facia, *indication*, 550
Facile, *irresolute*, 605
  persuasible, 602, 615
  easy, 705
  skilful, 698
* Facile princeps, *superiority*, 33
  goodness, 648
Facility, *ease*, 705
  aid, 707
  skill, 698
Facing, *lining*, 224
  covering, 222

Fauna, *animal*, 366
* Faute de mieux, *shift*, 147
626
* Fauteuil, *support*, 215
* Faux pas, *failure*, 732
error, 495
vice, 945
Favour, *aid*, 707
permit, 760
friendship, 888
partiality, 923
gift, 784
letter, 592
to resemble, 17
Favourable, *good*, 648
willing, 602
friendly, 707, 888
co-operating, 709
Favourite, *pleasing*, 829
beloved, 897, 899
Favouritism, *wrong*, 923
Fawn, *colour*, 433
cringe, 886
flatter, 933
Fay, *fairy*, 979
Faze, *worry*, 830
discompose, 458
perplex, 704
Fealty, *duty*, 926
respect, 928
obedience, 743
Fear, *fear*, 860
cowardice, 862
Fearful, *great*, 31
Fearless, *hopeful*, 858
courageous, 861
Feasible, *possible*, 470
easy, 705
Feast, *repast*, 298
to devour, 296
gluttony, 957
revel, 840
enjoyment, 827
celebration, 883
anniversary, 138
Feast on, *enjoy*, 377
Feat, *action*, 680
Feather, *tuft*, 256
lightness, 320
trifle, 643
class, 75
ornament, 847
decoration, 877
Feather-bed, *softness*, 324
Feathery, *roughness*, 256
Feature, *character*, 5
form, 240
appearance, 448
lineament, 550
component, 56
to resemble, 17
cinema, 599A

Febrifuge, *remedy*, 662
* Fecit, *painting*, 556
Feckless, *feeble*, 160
improvident, 674
useless, 645
Feculence, *uncleanness*, 653
Fecund, *productive*, 168
Fecundation, *production*,
161
Fed up, *weariness*, 841
dislike, 867
satiety, 869
Federation, *co-operation*,
709
party, 712
Fee, *expenditure*, 795, 809
Fee simple, *property*, 780
Feeble, *weak*, 160
imperfect, 651
scanty, 32
silly, 477
style, 575
Feeble-minded, *foolish*, 499
irresolute, 605
Feed, *eat*, 296
supply, 637
meal, 298
Feel, *touch*, 379
sensibility, 375
moral, 821
Feel for, *seek*, 461
sympathize, 914
Feeler, *inquiry*, 461
Feet, *journey*, 266
Feign, *falsehood*, 544
Feint, *deception*, 545
Felicitate, *congratulate*, 896
Felicitous, *expedient*, 646
favourable, 648
skilful, 698
successful, 731
happy, 827
elegant, 578
apt, 23
Felicity, *happiness*, 827
prosperity, 734
skill, 698
Feline, *stealthy*, 528
sly, 702
Fell, *mountain*, 206
cut down, 308
knock down, 213
dire, 162
wicked, 907
Fellah, *commonalty*, 876
Fellow, *similar*, 17
equal, 27
companion, 88
man, 373
dual, 89
Fellow creature, *man*, 372,
373

Fellow-feeling, *love*, 897
friendship, 888
sympathy, 906, 914
Fellowship, *sociality*, 892
partnership, 712
friendship, 888
Felo-de-se, *killing*, 361
Felon, *sinner*, 949
Felonious, *vice*, 945
Felony, *guilt*, 947
Felt, *matted*, 219
Felucca, *ship*, 273
Female, *woman*, 374
Feminality, *feebleness*, 160
Feminine, *woman*, 374
Feminism, *rights*, 924
* Femme couverte, *mar-
riage*, 903
* Femme de chambre, *ser-
vant*, 746
Fen, *marsh*, 345
Fence, *circumscribe*, 231
enclose, 232
defence, 717
fight, 720, 722
safety, 664
refuge, 666
prison, 752
to evade, 544
Fencible, *combatant*, 726
Fend, *defence*, 717
provision, 637
Fenestrated, *windowed*,
260
Feoff, *property*, 780
Ferine, *malevolence*, 907
Ferment, *disorder*, 59
energy, 171
violence, 173
agitation, 315
effervesce, 353
Fern, *plant*, 367
Ferocity, *brutality*, 907
violence, 173
Ferret, *tape*, 45
Ferret out, *inquiry*, 461
discover, 480A
Ferry, *transference*, 270
way, 627
Fertile, *productive*, 168
abundant, 639
Ferule, *scourge*, 975
Fervent, *devout*, 990
Fervour, *heat*, 382
animation, 821
desire, 865
love, 897
Fester, *disease*, 655
corruption, 653
Festival, *celebration*, 883
anniversary, 138

Festive, *amusement*, 840
　sociality, 892
Festoon, *ornament*, 847
　curvature, 245
Fetch, *bring*, 270
　arrive, 292
　stratagem, 626
　evasion, 545
　price, 812
Fête, *amusement*, 840
　ostentation, 882
　celebration, 883
　convivial, 892
* Fête champêtre, *amusement*, 840
Fetid, *fetor*, 401
Fetish, *spell*, 993
Fetishism, *idolatry*, 991
　sorcery, 992
Fetter, *hinder*, 706
　restrain, 751
　shackle, 752
　join, 43
Fettle, *preparation*, 673
Fetus, *see* Foetus
Feud, *discord*, 713
　revenge, 919
Feudal, *authority*, 737
Feudatory, *subjection*, 749
* Feu de joie, *firework*, 840
　salute, 882
Feuilleton, *essay*, 595
Fever, *heat*, 382
　disease, 655
　excitement, 825
Few, *fewness*, 103
　plurality, 100
Fez, *cap*, 225
Fiancée, *love*, 897
Fiasco, *failure*, 732
Fiat, *command*, 741
Fib, *falsehood*, 544, 546
Fibre, *link*, 45
　filament, 205
Fibrous, *thin*, 203
Fichu, *dress*, 225
Fickle, *irresolute*, 605
Fictile, *form*, 240
Fiction, *untruth*, 546
　fancy, 515
　story, 594
Fictitious, *false*, 544
Fiddle, *to play*, 415
　violin, 417
　deceive, 545
　swindle, 791
　falsify, 544
Fiddle-de-dee, *trifling*, 643
　contemptible, 930
Fiddle-faddle, *trifle*, 643
　dawdle, 683
Fiddler, *musician*, 416

Fiddlestick, *contemptible*, 930
　absurd, 497
　trifling, 643
Fiddling, *trifling*, 643
Fidelity, *honour*, 939
　observance, 772
Fidget, *excitability*, 825
　irascibility, 901
　agitation, 315
　activity, 682
Fidgety, *changeable*, 149
Fido, *mist*, 353
Fiducial, *belief*, 484
* Fidus Achates, *auxiliary*, 711
Fie! *disrepute*, 874
Fief, *property*, 780
Field, *plain*, 344
　arena, 728
　scope, 180
　business, 625
　property, 780
Field-day, *pageant*, 882
　festivity, 840
Field-marshal, *master*, 745
Field of view, *vista*, 441
　idea, 453
Field-piece, *arms*, 727
Fiend, *demon*, 980
　ruffian, 913
Fiendish, *malevolent*, 907
　wicked, 945
Fierce, *violent*, 173
　passion, 825
　daring, 861
　angry, 900
Fiery, *violent*, 173
　excitable, 825
　hot, 382
　fervent, 821
Fiery cross, *warfare*, 722
Fife, *musical instrument*, 417
Fifth columnist, *traitor*, 742
Fig, *unimportant*, 643
　dress, 225
　adorn, 845, 847
Fight, *contention*, 720, 722
Fighter, *combatant*, 726
　aircraft, 273A
Fighter-bomber, *aircraft*, 273A
Figment, *imagination*, 515
* Figurante, *the drama*, 599
Figuration, *form*, 240
Figurative, *metaphorical*, 521
　style, 577
　comparison, 464
Figure, *state*, 7
　number, 84
　price, 812

Figure, *form*, 240
　metaphor, 521, 566
　imagine, 515
　represent, 550, 554
　reputation, 873
　ugliness, 846
　parade, 882
Figurehead, *effigy*, 554
　inaction, 683
Figurine, *sculpture*, 557
Fike, *whim*, 481
Filament, *slender*, 205
　ligature, 45
　light, 423
Filamentous, *thin*, 203
Filch, *steal*, 791, 792
File, *to smooth*, 255
　to pulverize, 330
　to string together, 60
　row, 69
　duality, 89
　collection, 72
　list, 86
　store, 636
　register, 551
File off, *march*, 266
　diverge, 291
Filial, *posterity*, 167
Filiation, *consanguinity*, 11
　posterity, 167
　derivation, 155
Filibeg, *dress*, 225
Filibuster, *thief*, 792
　delay, 133
Filigree, *crossing*, 219
Filings, *pulverulence*, 330
Fill, *occupy*, 186
　fullness, 52
Fill out, *expand*, 194
Fill up, *complete*, 52
　close, 261
　satisfy, 639
　composition, 54
　compensate, 30
* Fille de joie, *libertine*, 962
Fillet, *band*, 45
　circle, 247
　gut, 297
Filling, *contents*, 190
Fillip, *stimulus*, 615
　impulse, 276
　propulsion, 284
Filly, *horse*, 271
　young, 129
Film, *layer*, 204
　dimness, 421, 426
　semitransparency, 427
　cinema, 599A
Filmy, *texture*, 329
Filter, *clean*, 652
　percolate, 295
　amend, 658

Flagrant, *notorious*, 531
  manifest, 525
  great, 31
  atrocious, 945
Flagstaff, *sign*, 550
  high, 206
Flail, *impulse*, 276
Flair, *intelligence*, 498
Flake, *layer*, 204
Flam, *untruth*, 546
Flambeau, *luminary*, 423
Flamboyant, *vulgar*, 851
  ornamented, 577, 847
Flame, *light*, 420
  fire, 382
  luminary, 423
  passion, 825
  love, 897
  favourable, 899
Flame-coloured, *orange*, 439
Flaming, *excited*, 821, 825
* Flâneur, *idler*, 683
Flange, *support*, 215
Flank, *side*, 236
  safety, 664
Flannel, *flattery*, 933
Flannels, *dress*, 225
Flap, *adjunct*, 39
  hanging, 214
  move about, 315
  beat, 972
  fear, 860
Flapdoodle, *deception*, 546
  nonsense, 497
Flapjack, *receptacle*, 191
Flapper, *girl*, 129, 374
Flapping, *loose*, 47
Flare, *glare*, 420
  violence, 173
Flare up, *kindle*, 825
  anger, 900
Flaring, *colour*, 428
Flash, *instant*, 113
  fire, 382
  light, 420
  thought, 451
  sudden act, 612
  violence, 173
Flash-lamp, *light*, 423
Flash note, *money*, 800
Flashback, *memory*, 505
  cinema, 599A
Flashy, *gaudy colour*, 428
  bad taste, 851
  ostentatious, 882
Flask, *receptacle*, 191
Flat, *level*, 251
  uniform, 16
  horizontal, 213
  novice, 701
  dupe, 547
  low, 207

Flat, *vapid*, 391
  inert, 172, 823
  dull, 841, 843
  insipid, 575
  dejected, 837
  sound, 408
  indifferent, 866
  positive, 535
  abode, 189
  apartment, 191
Flatlet, *abode*, 189
Flatter, *pleasure*, 829
  encourage, 858
  adulation, 933
  servility, 886
Flatterer, *eulogist*, 935
Flattie, *detective*, 461
  cinema, 599A
Flatulent, *windy*, 338
  gaseous, 334
  style, 573
Flaunt, *display*, 873, 882
  gaudy, 428
  ornament, 847
Flautist, *musician*, 416
Flavour, *taste*, 390
Flavous, *yellow*, 436
Flaw, *crack*, 198
  error, 495
  imperfection, 651
  blemish, 848
  fault, 947
Flay, *divest*, 226
  punish, 972
Flea-bag, *bed*, 215
Flea-bite, *trifle*, 643
Flea-bitten, *variegated*, 440
Fleckered, *variegation*, 440
Fledged, *preparation*, 673
Flee, *escape*, 671
  avoid, 623
Fleece, *tegument*, 222
  to rob, 791
  to strip, 789
  impoverish, 804
Fleer, *ridicule*, 956
Fleet, *swift*, 274
  ships, 273
Fleeting, *transient*, 111
  changeful, 607
Flesh, *mankind*, 372
  carnality, 961
Flesh colour, *redness*, 434
Flesh-pots, *food*, 298
Fleshly, *sensual*, 954, 961
Fleshy, *corpulent*, 192
Flexible, *pliant*, 324
  tractable, 705
Flexion, *bending*, 245
  deviation, 279
  fold, 258
Flexuous, *convolution*, 248

Flexure, *bending*, 245
  fold, 258
Flibbertigibbet, *trifler*, 460
Flick, *propel*, 284
  cinema, 599A
Flicker, *flutter*, 315
  oscillate, 314
  waver, 149, 605
  shine, 420
Flickering, *irregular*, 139
Flight, *departure*, 287, 293
  escape, 671
  volitation, 267
  swiftness, 174
  multitude, 102
Flight-lieutenant, *master*,
                 745
Flight of Fancy, *imagina-*
  tion, 515
  idea, 453
Flighty, *insane*, 503
  fickle, 605
Flim-flam, *lie*, 546
  caprice, 608
Flimsy, *texture*, 329
  soft, 324
  irrational, 477
  trifling, 643
  frail, 160, 651
  manuscript, 590
Flinch, *fear*, 850, 862
  avoid, 623
  swerve, 607
Fling, *propel*, 284
  censure, 932
  attack, 716
  jeer, 929
  amusement, 840
Fling away, *relinquish*, 782
Flint, *hardness*, 323
Flint-hearted, *malevolence*,
                 907
Flip, *propel*, 284
  aviation, 267
Flippant, *pert*, 885
  fluent, 584
Flipper, *fin*, 267
Flirt, *propel*, 284
  coquette, 902
Flit, *move*, 264, 266
  fluctuate, 149
  depart, 293
  escape, 671
  swift, 274
  thought, 451
Flitter, *flutter*, 315
Flitting, *evanescent*, 111,
                 149
  roving, 266
Float, *navigate*, 267
  buoy up, 305
  lightness, 320

Float, *sound*, 405
 vehicle, 272
Floater, *error*, 495, 732
 solecism, 568
Flocculent, *soft*, 324
 pulverulent, 330
Flock, *herd*, 366
 assemblage, 72, 102
 laity, 997
Flog, *punishment*, 972
 steal, 791
Flong, *engraving*, 558
Flood, *water*, 348
 abundance, 639
 multitude, 72
 superfluity, 641
 increase, 35
 of light, 420
Floodgate, *conduit*, 350
Floor, *base*, 221
 level, 23
 horizontal, 213
 support, 215
 to puzzle, 485, 704
 to overthrow, 731
Floosy, *girl*, 374
Flop, *flutter*, 315
 failure, 732
Flora, *plant*, 367, 379
Florid, *colour*, 428
 red, 434
 health, 654
 style, 577
Flotilla, *ship*, 273
Flotsam, *fragments*, 51
 little, 643
Flounce, *quick motion*, 274
 agitation, 315
 trimming, 230
 fold, 258
Flounder, *toss*, 315
 waver, 314
 mistake, 495
 to blunder, 499, 699, 732
 struggle, 704
Flourish, *brandish*, 314
 succeed, 731, 734
 display, 873, 882
 boast, 884
 exaggerate, 549
 of speech, 577, 582
Flout, *mock*, 856, 929
 sneer, 929
Flow, *stream*, 347
 motion, 264
 course, 109
 result from, 154
Flow out, *egress*, 295
Flow over, *run over*, 348
 abound, 641
Flower, *plant*, 367
 beauty, 845

Flower, *perfection*, 648, 650
 prosper, 734
 produce, 161
 of life, 127
 of speech, 577
 honour, 873
Flowing, *style*, 573
 sound, 405
 abundant, 639
Fluctuate, *oscillate*, 314
 wavering, 605
Flue, *air-pipe*, 351
 egress, 295
 opening, 260
 down, 320
 dross, 643, 653
Fluent, *speech*, 584
 style, 573
 flowing, 348
 skilful, 698
Fluff, *lightness*, 320
Fluid, *liquidity*, 333
Fluke, *angularity*, 244
 chance, 621
Flummery, *vain*, 643
 flattery, 933
 absurd, 497
Flummox, *bewilder*, 458
Flunk, *break down*, 158
Flunkey, *lackey*, 746
 toady, 886
 flatterer, 935
Fluorescence, *light*, 420
Flurry, *hurry*, 684
 discompose, 458
 agitation, 821, 825
Flush, *flat*, 251
 flood, 348
 heat, 382
 light, 420
 redness, 434
 abundance, 639
 feeling, 821
 passion, 825
 series, 69
 flock, 72
 rich, 803
 in liquor, 959
Flushed, *elated*, 836, 884
 vain, 880
 proud, 878
Fluster, *excitement*, 824
 fuss, 682
 discompose, 458
Flustered, *tipsy*, 959
Flute, *musical*, 417
Fluted, *furrow*, 259
Flutter, *move*, 315
 fear, 860
 feeling, 821, 824, 825
Fluviatile, *river*, 348
Flux, *flow*, 109, 348

Flux, *excretion*, 299
 motion, 264
 oscillation, 314
 changes, 140
Fly, *depart*, 293
 take wing, 287
 speed, 274
 escape, 671
 recede, 287
 shun, 623
 run away, 862
 lose colour, 429
 minute, 193
 time, 109, 111
 burst, 173, 328
 vehicle, 272
 clever, 498
 cunning, 702
Fly at, *attack*, 716
Fly back, *recoil*, 277
 elastic, 325
Fly-down, *unclean*, 653
Fly-leaf, *insertion*, 228
 book, 593
Fly out, *burst*, 173
 passion, 825
 anger, 900
Fly-boat, *ship*, 273
Flying boat, *aircraft*, 273A
Flying bomb, *arms*, 727
Flying fortress, *aircraft*,
       273A
Flying wing, *aircraft*, 273A
Flyover, *way*, 627
Flyte, *curse*, 908
Flywheel, *instrument*, 633
 rotation, 312
Foal, *young*, 129
 carrier, 271
Foam, *spray*, 353
 passion, 173, 900
Fob, *pocket*, 191
 to cheat, 545
 evade, 773
Focus, *reunion*, 74
 centre, 223
Fodder, *food*, 298
Foe, *antagonist*, 710
 enemy, 891
Foetid, *see* Fetid
Foetus, *infant*, 129
Fog, *cloud*, 353
 dimness, 422
Foggy, *obscure*, 447
 shaded, 426
Fogy, *veteran*, 130
* Föhn, *wind*, 349
Foible, *vice*, 945
Foil, *contrast*, 14
 success, 731
Foiled, *failure*, 732
Foist in, *insert*, 228, 300

Foist upon, *deception*, 545
Fold, *plait*, 258
  enclosure, 232
  pen, 752
  congregation, 996
  bisect, 91
Foliaceous, *layer*, 204
Foliage, *plant*, 367
Foliated, *layer*, 204
Folio, *book*, 593
Folk, *man*, 373
Folk-dance, *dance*, 840
Folk-tale, *legend*, 594
Follicle, *hollow*, 252
  opening, 260
  cyst, 191
Follow, *in order*, 63
  in time, 117
  in motion, 281
  to imitate, 19
  pursue, 622
  result from, 154
  understand, 518
  demonstration, 478
  obey, 743
Follow on, *continue*, 143
Follow suit, *conformity*, 82
Follow up, *inquiry*, 461
Follower, *sequence*, 281
  partisan, 746
Folly, *irrationality*, 499
  nonsense, 497
  building, 189
Foment, *promote*, 707
  excite, 173
Fond, *love*, 897
Fondle, *endearment*, 902
Fondling, *favourite*, 899
Fondness, *love*, 897
  desire, 865
Font, *altar*, 1000
Food, *eatable*, 298
  materials, 635, 637
Fool, *silly*, 501
  to deceive, 548
Foolhardy, *rashness*, 863
Foolish, *unwise*, 499
  trifling, 643
  irrational, 477, 497
  misguided, 699
Foot, *stand*, 211
  metre, 597
Foot it, *walk*, 266
  dance, 840
Foot-pace, *slowness*, 275
Footfall, *motion*, 264
  trace, 551
Foothold, *influence*, 175
  support, 215
Footing, *situation*, 8, 183
  state, 7
  foundation, 211

Footing, *place*, 58
  rank, 71
  influence, 175
Footle, *trifle*, 683
Footlights, *drama*, 599
Footling, *silly*, 499
Footman, *servant*, 746
Footmark, *record*, 551
Footpad, *thief*, 792
Footpath, *way*, 627
Footprint, *record*, 551
Footslog, *journey*, 266
Footstep, *record*, 551
Footstool, *support*, 215
Foozle, *bungle*, 699, 732
Fop, *fop*, 854
Foppery, *affectation*, 855
For, *reason*, 476
  motive, 615
For good, *diuturnity*, 110
Forage, *provision*, 637
  booty, 793
  to steal, 791
  food, 298
Forage-cap, *dress*, 225
Foraminous, *opening*, 260
Forasmuch as, *reasoning*,
                 476
Foray, *attack*, 716
  robbery, 791
  havoc, 619
Forbear, *avoid*, 623
  spare, 678
  pity, 914
  abstain, 953
  lenity, 740
  forgiveness, 918
  sufferance, 826
Forbears, *ancestors*, 130, 166
Forbid, *prohibit*, 761
Forbidding, *repulsive*, 289,
                 846
Forby, *addition*, 37
Force, *power*, 157
  validity, 476
  strength, 159
  agency, 170
  energy, 171
  to compel, 744
  rape, 961
  to induce, 615
  of style, 574
  waterfall, 348
Forced, *out of place*, 10, 24
Forceps, *extraction*, 301
  retention, 781
Ford, *way*, 627
Fore, *front*, 234
  care, 459
Fore and aft, *whole*, 50
Forearmed, *preparation*,
                 673

Forebode, *prediction*, 511
Forecast, *foresee*, 510
  predict, 511
  plan, 626
  prepare, 673
Foreclose, *hindrance*, 706
Foredoom, *necessity*, 601
Forefather, *old*, 130
  ancestor, 166
Foregoing, *past*, 122
  preceding, 62
Foreground, *front*, 234
Forehead, *front*, 234
Foreign, *alien*, 10
  extraneous, 57
Forejudge, *misjudgment*,
                 481
Foreknow, *foresight*, 510
Foreland, *high*, 206
  projection, 250
Foreman, *director*, 694
Foremost, *front*, 234
  beginning, 66
  superior, 33
Forename, *name*, 564
Forenoon, *morning*, 125
Forensic, *jurisprudence*, 965
Foreordain, *predestine*, 152,
                 601
Forerun, *priority*, 116
  precession, 280
Forerunner, *in order*, 64
  in time, 116
  omen, 512
Foresee, *foreknow*, 510
  expect, 507, 871
Foreshadow, *prediction*, 511
Foreshorten, *shortness*, 201
Foresight, *foresight*, 510
Forest, *plant*, 367
Forestall, *early*, 132
  priority, 116
  futurity, 121
  expect, 507
  possess, 777
Forestry, *agriculture*, 371
Foretaste, *foresight*, 510
Foretell, *prediction*, 511
  priority, 116
Forethought, *care*, 459
Foretoken, *prediction*, 511
Forewarn, *warn*, 668
  advise, 695
  predict, 511
Foreword, *preamble*, 64
  front, 234
Forfeit, *lose*, 776
  fail, 773
  undueness, 925
  penalty, 974
Forfend, *guard*, 717
  hinder, 706

Forge, *produce*, 161
  furnace, 386
  workshop, 691
  trump up, 544
Forge ahead, *advance*, 282
Forgery, *untruth*, 546
  imitation, 19
Forget, *oblivion*, 506
Forgive, *forgiveness*, 918
Forgo, *relinquish*, 624, 782
  renounce, 757
Forgotten, *unremembered*,
    506
  ingratitude, 917
Fork, *angularity*, 244
  bisection, 91
Fork out, *give*, 784
  expend, 809
Forlorn, *abandoned*, 893
  dejected, 837
  woebegone, 828
Forlorn hope, *hopeless*, 859
  danger, 665
Form, *shape*, 240
  state, 7
  arrange, 60
  rule, 80
  to make up, 54
  produce, 161
  educate, 537
  habituate, 613
  bench, 215
  part, 569
  fashion, 852
  etiquette, 882
  law, 963
  rite, 998
  fours, 58
  manner, 627
  beauty, 845
  likeness, 21
  pupils, 541
Formal, *regular*, 82
  affected, 855
  positive, 535
Formalism, *hypocrisy*, 988
Formality, *ceremony*, 852
  parade, 882
  law, 963
Format, *style*, 7
Formation, *production*, 161
  shape, 240
Formed of, *composition*, 54
Former, *in order*, 62
  in time, 122
Formication, *itching*, 380
Formidable, *fear*, 860
  difficult, 704
  great, 31
Formless, *amorphism*, 241
Formula, *rule*, 80
  precept, 697

Formula, *law*, 963
  number, 84
Fornication, *impurity*, 961
Fornicator, *libertine*, 962
Forsake, *relinquish*, 624
Forsooth, *truth*, 494
Forswear, *renounce*, 624
  retract, 607
  refuse, 764
  perjure, 544, 940
  violate, 927
Fort, *defence*, 717
  refuge, 666
Forte, *excellence*, 698
* Forte, *loudness*, 404
Forth, *progression*, 282
Forthcoming, *futurity*, 121,
    673
Forthwith, *transient*, 111
Fortification, *defence*, 717
  refuge, 666
Fortify, *strength*, 159
Fortitude, *courage*, 861
  endurance, 826
Fortnight, *period*, 108, 138
Fortress, *defence*, 716
  prison, 752
Fortuitous, *chance*, 156,
    621
Fortunate, *opportune*, 134
  prosperous, 734
Fortune, *chance*, 156
  accident, 621
  wealth, 803
Fortune-teller, *oracle*, 513
Fortune-telling, *prediction*,
    511
Forum, *tribunal*, 966
  school, 542
Forward, *early*, 132
  to advance, 282
  to help, 707
  active, 682
  willing, 602
  vain, 880
  impertinent, 885
Fosse, *furrow*, 259
  gap, 198
  defence, 717
  enclosure, 232
Fossick, *inquiry*, 461
Fossil, *antiquated*, 851
  old, 124
  bore, 841
Foster, *aid*, 707
Fou, *drunken*, 959
Foul, *bad*, 649
  corrupt, 653
  odour, 401
  offensive, 830
  ugly, 846
  vicious, 945

Foul-mouthed, *malevolent*,
    907
Foul-tongued, *scurrilous*,
    934
Found, *cause*, 153
  prepare, 673
Foundation, *base*, 211
  support, 215
Founder, *originator*, 164
  sink, 310, 732
Foundling, *outcast*, 893
Fount, *origin*, 153
  spring, 348
  type, 591
Fountain, *cause*, 153
  river, 348
  store, 636
Fountain-pen, *writing*, 590
Four, *number*, 95
Four-square, *number*, 95
Fourfold, *number*, 96
Fourscore, *number*, 98
Fourth, *number*, 97
Fowl, *animal*, 366
Fowling-piece, *arms*, 727
Fox, *cunning*, 702
Fox-trot, *dance*, 840
Foxhole, *refuge*, 666
  defence, 717
Foxhound, *chase*, 622
Foyer, *room*, 191
Fracas, *contention*, 720
  brawl, 713
Fraction, *part*, 51
  numerical, 84
Fractious, *irascibility*, 901
Fracture, *disjunction*, 44
  discontinuity, 70, 198
  to break, 328
Fragile, *brittle*, 328
  frail, 149, 160
Fragment, *part*, 51
Fragrant, *fragrant*, 400
'Fraid-cat, *coward*, 862
Frail, *brittle*, 328
  mutable, 149
  weak, 160
  irresolute, 605
  imperfect, 651
  unchaste, 961
  failing, 945
Frame, *condition*, 7
  support, 215
  texture, 329
  form, 240
  substance, 316
  to construct, 161
  border, 230
* Franc-tireur, *fighter*, 726
Franchise, *right*, 924
  freedom, 748
  exemption, 927

Franciscan, *clergy*, 996
Frangible, *brittle*, 328
Frank, *artless*, 703
　open, 525
　sincere, 543
　honourable, 939
Frankincense, *fragrant*, 400
Frantic, *delirious*, 503
　violent, 173
　excited, 825
Fraternal, *brotherly*, 11
　friendly, 888, 906
Fraternity, *assemblage*, 72
　company, 712, 892
Fraternize, *co-operate*, 709
　harmonize, 714
Fratricide, *killing*, 361
Fraud, *deception*, 544, 545
　dishonour, 940
Fraught, *having*, 777
　full of, 639
Fray, *contention*, 720
　to abrade, 331
Freak, *caprice*, 608
　unconformity, 83
Freakish, *irresolution*, 605
Freckle, *blemish*, 848
Freckled, *variegation*, 440
Free, *detached*, 44
　at liberty, 748
　spontaneous, 600, 602
　exempt, 927
　unobstructed, 705
　liberal, 816
　gratuitous, 815
　insolent, 885
Free-born, *freedom*, 748
Free gift, *giving*, 784
Free play, *freedom*, 748
Free-spoken, *veracity*, 543
Free-thinking, *religion*, 989
Free will, *will*, 600
Freebooter, *thief*, 792
Freedom, *liberty*, 748
　looseness, 47
　full play, 705
　exemption, 927
　space, 180
Freehold, *property*, 780
　freedom, 748
Freelance, *writer*, 590
Freemasonry, *secrecy*, 528
　sign, 550
　fraternity, 712
　co-operation, 709
Freeze, *frigefaction*, 385
　stop dead, 265
Freight, *contents*, 190
　cargo, 798
　transfer, 270
Freight train, *vehicle*, 272
Frenzy, *insanity*, 503

Frequency, *repetition*, 104
Frequent, *in time*, 136
　in number, 102
　in space, 186
Fresco, *painting*, 556
Fresh, *new*, 123
　cold, 383
　colour, 428
　unforgotten, 505
　healthy, 654
　good, 648
　cheeky, 885
　tipsy, 959
Freshet, *flood*, 348
Freshman, *learner*, 541
Fret, *suffer*, 378
　grieve, 828
　to gall, 830
　sadness, 837
　to irritate, 900
　adorn, 847
Fretful, *irascibility*, 901
Fretwork, *crossing*, 219
Freya, *love*, 897
Friable, *pulverulence*, 330
Friar, *clergy*, 996
Friar's lantern, *light*, 423
Fribble, *trifle*, 460, 643
　dawdle, 683
Friction, *rubbing*, 331
　obstacle, 179
　discord, 713
Friend, *well-wisher*, 890
　relation, 11
　auxiliary, 711
Friendless, *seclusion*, 893
Friendly, *amical*, 714, 888
　helping, 707
Friendship, *amical*, 714,
　　　　　　　　888
Frieze, *summit*, 210
Frig, *refrigerator*, 387
Frigate, *ship*, 273
Frigga, *goddess*, 979
Fright, *alarm*, 860
　ugliness, 846
Frightful, *great*, 31
　hideous, 846
　dreadful, 830
Frigid, *cold*, 383
　callous, 823
　reluctant, 603
　indifferent, 866
Frigorific, *refrigeration*, 385
Frill, *border*, 230
Frills, *affectation*, 855
Fringe, *lace*, 256
　ornament, 847
Frippery, *dress*, 225
　trifle, 643
　ornament, 847
　ridiculous, 853

Frisk, *brisk*, 682
　gay, 836
　amuse, 840
Frisky, *nimble*, 274
　leap, 309
　in spirits, 836
Frith, *strait*, 343
　chasm, 198
Fritter, *small part*, 51
　waste, 135, 638, 683
　misuse, 679
　diminish, 36
Frivol, *trifle*, 460
Frivolous, *unimportant*, 643
　silly, 499
　frisky, 836
Frizzle, *curl*, 248
　fold, 258
Frock, *dress*, 225
Frog, *ornament*, 847
Frogman, *depth*, 208
　dive, 310
Frolic, *amusement*, 840
Frolicsome, *cheerful*, 836
Front, *fore-part*, 234
　precession, 280
　beginning, 66
　exterior, 220
　resistance, 719
Frontal, *beginning*, 66
　exterior, 220
Frontier, *limit*, 233
　vicinity, 199
Fronting, *antiposition*, 237
Frontispiece, *prefix*, 64
　front, 234
Frost, *cold*, 383
　failure, 732
Froth, *bubble*, 353
　trifle, 643
　style, 577
Frounce, *fold*, 258
Froward, *irascible*, 901
　discourteous, 895
Frown, *disapprove*, 932
　anger, 900
　scowl, 839, 895
　lower, 837
Frowzy, *fetor*, 401
Fructify, *production*, 161
　productiveness, 168
　prosper, 734
Frugal, *temperate*, 953
　economical, 817
Fruit, *result*, 154
　acquisition, 775
Fruitful, *productive*, 168
Fruition, *pleasure*, 827
　fulfilment, 729
Fruitless, *useless*, 645
　unproductive, 169
　abortive, 732

Glorify, *approve*, 931
   worship, 990
Glory, *honour*, 873
   light, 420
   boast, 884
   pride, 878
Gloss, *light*, 420
   smoothness, 255
   beauty, 845
   plea, 617
   falsehood, 546
   interpretation, 522
Gloss over, *neglect*, 460
   inattention, 458
   sophistry, 477
   vindication, 937
   falsehood, 544
Glossary, *interpretation*, 522
   verbal, 562
Glossy, *smooth*, 255
Glove, *cartel*, 715
Glow, *shine*, 420
   colour, 428
   warmth, 382
   passion, 821
   style, 574
Glow-worm, *luminary*, 423
Glower, *scowl*, 895
Gloze, *flatter*, 933
   palliate, 937
Glucose, *sweetness*, 396
Glue, *cement*, 45
   to stick, 46
   viscosity, 352
Glum, *discontented*, 832
   dejected, 837
   sulky, 895
Glut, *redundance*, 641
   satiety, 869
Glutinous, *coherence*, 46
   semiliquid, 352
Gluttony, *excess*, 957
   desire, 865
Glycerine, *semiliquid*, 352
Glyptography, *engraving*,
             558
Gnarled, *rough*, 256
Gnash, *anger*, 900
Gnat, *littleness*, 193
Gnaw, *eat*, 296
   corrode, 659
   pain, 378
   give pain, 830
Gnome, *demon*, 980
   maxim, 496
Gnomic, *sententious*, 572
Gnosis, *knowledge*, 490
Gnostic, *intellectual*, 450
   mystic, 528
Go, *move*, 264
   depart, 293
   vigour, 574

Go, *energy*, 171, 682
   try, 675
Go about, *undertake*, 676
Go across, *passage*, 302
Go ahead, *advance*, 282
   improve, 658
   activity, 682
Go-ahead, *energetic*, 171
Go bail, *security*, 771
Go-between, *intermedium*,
           228, 631
   messenger, 534
   agent, 758
Go by, *pass*, 303
Go-by, *evasion*, 623
Go down, *sink*, 306
   decline, 659
Go forth, *depart*, 293
   publish, 531
Go-getter, *activity*, 682
Go halves, *divide*, 91
Go hand in hand with,
   accompany, 88
Go in for, *business*, 625
Go near, *approach*, 286
Go off, *cease*, 142
   explode, 173
   die, 360
   fare, 151
Go on, *continue*, 143
Go over, *change sides*, 607
Go round, *circuition*, 311
Go through, *pass*, 302
   complete, 729
   endure, 821
Go to, *direction*, 278
   remonstrance, 695
Go under, *name*, 564
   sink, 310
   ruin, 735
Go up, *ascent*, 305
Go with, *assent*, 488
   suit, 646
Goad, *motive*, 615
Goal, *object*, 620
   reach, 292
Goat, *fool*, 501
Goatish, *impure*, 961
Gobbet, *piece*, 51
Gobble, *devour*, 296
   gluttony, 957
   cry, 412
Gobbledygook, *verbiage*, 573
* Gobemouche, *credulous,*
   fool, 501   [486
   dupe, 547
Goblin, *ghost*, 980
   bugbear, 860
GOD, *Deity*, 976
Goddess, *great spirit*, 979
   favourite, 899
   beauty, 845

Godless, *irreligion*, 989
Godlike, *virtue*, 944
Godliness, *piety*, 987
Godown, *store*, 636, 799
Godsend, *luck*, 621
   advantage, 618
   success, 731
Goer, *horse*, 271
Goggle, *optical instrument*,
           445
   to stare, 441
Goggle-eyed, *dimsighted*,
           443
Golconda, *wealth*, 803
Gold, *money*, 800
Gold-digger, *flirt*, 902
   selfishness, 943
Golden, *yellow*, 436
Golden age, *pleasure*, 827
   prosperity, 734
   imagination, 515
Golden calf, *idols*, 986
Golden-mouthed, *ornament*,
           577
Golden wedding, *celebra-
   tion*, 883
   anniversary, 138
Goldsmith, *artist*, 559
Goliath, *strength*, 159
   giant, 192
Gombeen-man, *usurer*, 805
Gomeril, *fool*, 501
Gondola, *ship*, 273
Gondolier, *mariner*, 269
Gone, *non-extant*, 2
   absent, 187
   dead, 360
Gone by, *past*, 123
Gone on, *loving*, 897
Gonfalon, *flag*, 550
Gong, *resonance*, 417
   decoration, 877
Goniometer, *angle*, 244
   measure, 466
Goo, *adhesive*, 45
   viscid, 352
Good, *advantage*, 618
   advantageous, 648
   virtuous, 944
   right, 922
   tasty, 394
Good-bye, *departure*, 293
Good day, *arrival*, 292
   salute, 894
Good-fellowship, 892
Good-for-nothing, *rascal,*
           949
Good humour, *cheerfulness,*
           836
Good-looking, *beauty*, 845
Good manners, *courtesy*, 894
Good morning, *salute*, 894

Good nature, *benevolence*, 906
  inexcitability, 826
Good show, *approval*, 931
Goodly, *large*, 192
  beautiful, 845
Goods, *effects*, 780
Goods train, *vehicle*, 272
Goodwill, *benevolence*, 906
  friendship, 888
  merchandise, 798
  materials, 635
Goody, *woman*, 374
Gooey, *sticky*, 46
Goo-goo eyes, *ogle*, 902
Goon, *rascal*, 949
Goose, *fool*, 501
Goose-skin, *cold*, 383
Gorblimey, *vulgar*, 876
Gordian knot, *problem*, 461
  difficulty, 704
Gore, *opening*, 260
  angularity, 244
Gorge, *ravine*, 198
  narrowness, 203
  to devour, 296
  full, 641; *satiety*, 869
  gluttony, 957
Gorgeous, *colour*, 428
  splendid, 845
  ornamented, 847
Gorgon, *fear*, 860
  ugliness, 846
Gormandize, *gluttony*, 957
  reception, 296
Gory, *killing*, 361
Gospel, *scripture*, 985
  truth, 494
  certainty, 474
Gossamer, *texture*, 329
  slender, 205
  light, 320
Gossip, *conversation*, 588
  chatterer, 584
  news, 532
Gossoon, *boy*, 129, 373
Goth, *barbarian*, 876
  evildoer, 913
Gothic, *vulgarity*, 851
  defacement, 241
* Gouache, *painting*, 556
Gouge, *concavity*, 252
Gourmand, *gluttony*, 957
  epicure, 868
Gourmet, *desire*, 865
  epicure, 868
  gluttony, 957
* Goût, *taste*, 850
Govern, *direct*, 693
  authority, 737
Governess, *teacher*, 540
Governess-cart, *vehicle*, 272

Governor, *director*, 694
  master, 745
  tutor, 540
Gowk, *fool*, 501
Gown, *dress*, 225
Grab, *snatch*, 789
  steal, 791
  booty, 793
Grabble, *fumble*, 379
Grace, *elegance*, 845
  polish, 850
  forgiveness, 918
  honour, 939
  title, 877
  piety, 987
  worship, 990
  thanks, 916
  style, 578
Grace-note, *music*, 415
Grace-stroke, *killing*, 361
Graceless, *ungraceful*, 846
  vicious, 945
  impenitent, 951
Gracile, *slender*, 203
Gracious, *courteous*, 894
  good-natured, 906
* Gradatim, *degree*, 26
  order, 58
  conversion, 144
Gradation, *degree*, 26
  order, 58
  arrangement, 60
  continuity, 69
Grade, *degree*, 26
  term, 71
Gradely, *good*, 648
Gradient, *obliquity*, 217
Gradual, *degree*, 26
  continuity, 69
Graduate, *to arrange*, 60
  to adapt, 23
  to measure, 466
  scholar, 492
Gradus, *dictionary*, 562
* Graffito, *drawing*, 556
Graft, *join*, 43
  insert, 300
  cultivate, 371
  locate, 184
  teach, 537
  bribe, 615
  improbity, 940
Grain, *essence*, 5
  minute, 32
  particle, 193
  texture, 329
  roughness, 256
  disposition, 820
  adorn, 847
Graminivorous, *eat*, 296
Grammar, *grammar*, 567
Grammar school, *school*, 542

Grammarian, *scholar*, 492
Grammercy, *gratitude*, 916
Gramophone, *reproduction*, 19
  music, 417
  hearing, 418
Granary, *store*, 636
Grand, *important*, 642
  beautiful, 845
  glorious, 873
  money, 800
Grandam, *veteran*, 130
Grandchild, *posterity*, 167
Grandee, *master*, 875
Grandeur, *repute*, 873
Grandiloquence, *eloquence*, 582
  style, 577
Grandiose, *style*, 577
Grandsire, *old*, 130
  ancestor, 166
Grandson, *posterity*, 167
Grange, *abode*, 189
Grangerize, *addition*, 36
Granite, *hardness*, 323
Granivorous, *eat*, 296
Grant, *give*, 784
  allow, 760
  consent, 762
  disclose, 529
  assent, 488
Grantee, *receive*, 785
Grantor, *give*, 784
Granulate, *pulverulence*, 330
Granule, *littleness*, 193
Grape-shot, *arms*, 727
Grapevine, *news*, 532
Graphic, *painting*, 556
  description, 594
  intelligible, 518
Grapnel, *anchor*, 666
Grapple, *contend*, 720
  undertake, 676
  join, 43
Grappling-iron, *fastening*, 45
  safety, 666
Grasp, *seize*, 789
  retain, 781
  comprehend, 518
  power, 737
Grasping, *parsimony*, 819
Grass, *plant*, 367
  green, 435
Grass widow, *divorce*, 905
Grate, *rub*, 330
  friction, 331
  harsh, 410, 414
  furnace, 386
  pain, physical, 378
  pain, moral, 830

Grateful, *thanks*, 916
  agreeable, 377, 829
Gratification, *animal*, 377
  moral, 827
Gratify, *pleasure*, 829
Grating, *noise*, 410
  lattice, 219
Gratis, *cheap*, 815
Gratitude, *thanks*, 916
Gratuitous, *spontaneous*,
                    600, 602
  cheap, 815
Gratuity, *giving*, 784
Gratulation, *rejoicing*, 836
Gravamen, *importance*, 642
  grievance, 619
Grave, *sad*, 836
  serious, 642
  distressing, 830
  heinous, 945
  great, 31
  engrave, 559
  impress, 505
  shape, 240
  tomb, 363
  sound, 408
Gravel, *offend*, 830
  puzzle, 704
  soil, 342
Graveolent, *odour*, 398
Graver, *artist*, 559
Gravestone, *interment*, 363
Graveyard, *interment*, 363
Gravid, *pregnant*, 168
Gravitate, *descent*, 306
Gravitation, *attraction*, 288
Gravity, *weight*, 319
  attraction, 288
  dullness, 843
  seriousness, 837
  importance, 642
  composure, 826
Gravy, *liquid*, 333
Graze, *browse*, 296
  touch, 199
Grease, *oil*, 332, 356
  unctuous, 355
Great, *much*, 31
  big, 192
  importance, 642
  glorious, 873
  magnanimous, 942
  pregnant, 168
Great circle, *direction*, 278
Greatcoat, *garment*, 225
Greaten, *enlarge*, 35
Greaves, *garment*, 225
Greedy, *voracious*, 957
  desirous, 865
  avaricious, 819
Greek Church, *Christian
religion*, 983A

Green, *colour*, 435
  meadow, 344
  new, 123
  unskilled, 699
  unprepared, 674
  unaccustomed, 614
  credulous, 484
  ignorant, 491
Green belt, *environs*, 227
Green-eyed, *jealousy*, 920
Green light, *signal*, 550
Greenback, *money*, 800
Greenhorn, *fool*, 501
  dupe, 547
  novice, 493, 674
  stranger, 57
  bungler, 701
Greenroom, *the drama*, 599
Greet, *hail*, 894
  weep, 839
Gregarious, *social*, 892
Gremlin, *demon*, 980
Grenade, *arms*, 727
Grenadier, *soldier*, 726
  tall, 206
Grey, *colour*, 432
  age, 128
Grey-headed, *age*, 128
  veteran, 130
Grey market, *illegality*, 964
Grey matter, *brain*, 450
Greybeard, *veteran*, 130
Greyhound, *swift*, 274
Grid, *lattice*, 219
Gridelin, *purple*, 437
Gridiron, *lattice*, 219
  arena, 728
Grief, *dejection*, 837
Grievance, *injury*, 619
  pain, 830
Grieve, *complain*, 828, 839
  afflict, 830
  injure, 649
Griffin, *unconformity*, 83
  keeper, 753
Grig, *cheerful*, 836
Grill, *calefaction*, 384
  question, 461
Grille, *lattice*, 219
Grim, *ugly*, 846
  frightful, 828
  discourteous, 895
  ferocious, 907
Grim-visaged, *grave*, 837
Grimace, *ridicule*, 856
Grime, *unclean*, 653
Grin, *laugh*, 838
  ridicule, 856
  scorn, 929
Grind, *pulverize*, 330
  an organ, 415
  oppress, 907

Grind, *learn*, 539
  sharpen, 253
  scholar, 492
Grinder, *teacher*, 540
Grinding, *painful*, 831
Grip, *power*, 737
  bag, 191
Grip-sack, *bag*, 191
Gripe, *seize*, 789
  retain, 781
  pain, 378, 828
  to give pain, 830
  power, 737
Griping, *avaricious*, 819
* Grisette, *woman*, 374
Grisly, *ugliness*, 846
Grist, *provision*, 637
  materials, 635
Gristle, *toughness*, 327
Grit, *pulverulence*, 330
  determination, 604
  courage, 861
Gritty, *hard*, 323
Grizzled, *variegation*, 440
Grizzly, *grey*, 432
Groan, *cry*, 411
  lament, 839
Groggy, *drunk*, 959
  ill, 655
Groin, *angular*, 244
Grooly, *ugly*, 845
Groom, *servant*, 746
  marriage, 903
Groomsman, *marriage*, 903
Groove, *furrow*, 259
  habit, 613
Grope, *feel*, 379
  experience, 463
  inquire, 461
  try, 675
Gross, *whole*, 51
  greatness, 31
  vulgar, 851
  vicious, 945
  impure, 961
* Grossièreté, *rudeness*, 895
Grot, *see* Grotto
Grotesque, *deformed*, 846
  ridiculous, 851, 853
  outlandish, 83
Grotto, *alcove*, 189
  hollow, 252
Grouchy, *discourteous*, 895
  bad-tempered, 901
Ground, *land*, 342
  support, 215
  base, 211
  region, 181
  cause, 153
  motive, 615
  plea, 617
  property, 780

Handsel, *give*, 784
 pay, 809
 begin, 66
Handsome, *beautiful*, 845
 liberal, 816
 disinterested, 942
Handspike, *instrument*, 633
Handwriting, *omen*, 512
 signature, 550
 autograph, 590
Handy, *near*, 197
 skilful, 698
 useful, 644
 attainable, 705
Hang, *pendency*, 214
 kill, 361
 execute, 972
 expletive, 908
Hang about, *loiter*, 275
Hang back, *hesitate*, 603
Hang fire, *reluctance*, 603
 vacillation, 605
 stop, 142
 refuse, 764
 lateness, 133
 slowness, 275
 inactivity, 683
Hang out, *reside*, 188
Hang over, *futurity*, 121
 destiny, 152
 height, 206
Hang together, *junction*, 43
Hang up, *defer*, 133
Hangar, *building*, 189
Hanger, *arms*, 727
Hanger-on, *servant*, 746
 accompany, 88
 follow, 281
 parasite, 886
 flatterer, 935
Hangings, *ornaments*, 847
Hangman, *executioner*, 975
Hank, *skein*, 219
Hanker, *desire*, 865
Hanky-panky, *fraud*, 545
Hansard, *record*, 551
Hansel, *see* Handsel
Hansom, *vehicle*, 272
Hap, *chance*, 156, 621
Haphazard, *chance*, 156, 621
Hapless, *hopeless*, 859
 miserable, 828
Haply, *chance*, 156
 possibly, 470
Happen, *event*, 151
Happy, *glad*, 827
 expedient, 646
 agreement, 23
Happy-go-lucky, *careless*, 460
 aimless, 621
 improvident, 674

Happy medium, *middle*, 68
Happy thought, *wit*, 842
Hara-kiri, *suicide*, 361
 execution, 972
Harangue, *speech*, 582
 preach, 998
Harass, *worry*, 907
 fatigue, 688
 vex, 830
Harbinger, *omen*, 512
 precursor, 64, 116
Harbour, *anchorage*, 189
 refuge, 666
 haven, 292
 to cherish, 821
Harbourless, *exposed*, 665
Hard, *dense*, 323
 difficult, 704
 grievous, 830
 strong, 159
 obdurate, 951
 sour, 397
Hard-and-fast, *exact*, 494
 strict, 739
Hard-boiled, *callous*, 823
Hard case, *bad man*, 949
Hard currency, *money*, 800
Hard-favoured, *ugly*, 846
Hard-headed, *skill*, 698
 wise, 498
Hard-hearted, *cruel*, 907
Hard lines, *adversity*, 735
Hard-mouthed, *obstinacy*, 606
Hard up, *poverty*, 804
Hard-working, *exertion*, 682, 686
Harden, *accustom*, 613
 train, 673
 render callous, 376, 823
 impious, 988
 impenitent, 951
Hardihood, *courage*, 861
 insolence, 885
Hardly, *scarcely*, 32
 infrequency, 137
Hardness of heart, *vice*, 945
Hardship, *pain*, 830
 adversity, 735
Hardy, *strong*, 159
 healthy, 654
Hare, *velocity*, 274
Hare-brained, *rash*, 460, 863
Harem, *apartment*, 191
 impurity, 961
Hark, *hearing*, 418
Hark back, *regression*, 283
Harlequin, *motley*, 440
 pantomimic, 599
 humorist, 844
Harlot, *libertine*, 962
Harlotry, *impurity*, 961

Harm, *evil*, 619
 badness, 649
 malevolence, 907
Harmattan, *wind*, 349
Harmless, *innocent*, 946
 innocuous, 648
 impotent, 158
Harmonic, *music*, 413
Harmonica, *musical*, 417
Harmonium, *musical instrument*, 417
Harmonize, *uniformity*, 16
Harmony, *agreement*, 23
 melody, 413
 concord, 714
 peace, 721
 conformity, 82
 friendship, 888
Harness, *fasten*, 43
 fastening, 45
 bond, 752
 accoutrement, 225
 instrument, 633
 subjection, 749
Harp, *musical instrument*, 417
 to repeat, 104
 to weary, 841
Harper, *musician*, 416
Harpoon, *arms*, 727
Harpsichord, *musical*, 417
Harpy, *demon*, 980
 evildoer, 913
 thief, 792
 miser, 819
Harquebus, *arms*, 727
Harridan, *hag*, 846
 trollop, 962
 bad woman, 949
Harrow, *pain*, 830
 cultivate, 371
Harry, *pain*, 830
Harsh, *severe*, 739
 morose, 895
 disagreeable, 830
 malevolent, 907
 sound, 410
Harum-scarum, *disorder*, 59
* Haruspex, *oracle*, 513
Harvest, *acquisition*, 775
 effect, 154
Hash, *mixture*, 41
 disorder, 59
 to cut, 44
Hasp, *lock*, 45
 to lock, 43
Hassock, *support*, 215
* Hasta la vista, *departure*, 293
Haste, *in time*, 132
 in motion, 274

Heaviness, *inertia*, 172
  dejection, 837
  dullness, 843
Heaviside layer, *air*, 338
Heavy, *weighty*, 319
  inert, 172, 682
  slow, 275
  stupid, 499
  rude, 851
  large, 31
Hebdomadal, *period*,
          108, 138
Hebe, *beauty*, 845
Hebetate, *insensible*, 823
Hecate, *hag*, 846
Hecatomb, *killing*, 361
Heckle, *question*, 461
Hectic, *fever*, 382
  feeling, 821
Hector, *courage*, 861
  bully, 885
Hedge, *enclosure*, 232
  to shuffle, 544
  to compensate, 30
Hedge-hop, *fly*, 267
Hedge in, *enclose*, 231
  safe, 664
Hedgehog, *sharpness*, 253
  defence, 717
Hedonism, *intemperance*,
          954
Heed, *attend*, 457
  care, 459
  caution, 864
Heedless, *inattentive*, 458
  neglectful, 460
Heel, *slope*, 217
  rascal, 949
Heel-tap, *remainder*, 40
Heels, *rear*, 235
Heels over head, *reckless*,
          460
Heft, *handle*, 633
  exertion, 686
Hefty, *heavy*, 319
Hegemony, *authority*, 737
Hegira, *departure*, 293
Heigh-ho! *lamentation*, 839
Height, *altitude*, 206
  degree, 26
  superiority, 33
Heighten, *increase*, 35
  exalt, 206
  exaggerate, 549
  aggravate, 835
Heinous, *vice*, 945
Heir, *possessor*, 779
  posterity, 167
  futurity, 121
Heirloom, *property*, 780
Heirship, *possess*, 777
Helen, *beauty*, 845

Helicon, *poetry*, 597
Helicopter, *aircraft*, 273A
Helidrome, *arrival*, 292
Heliograph, *signal*, 550
Heliotherapy, *remedy*,
          662
Helix, *convolution*, 248
Hell, *gehenna*, 982
  abyss, 208
Hell-born, *vice*, 945
Hellcat, *bad woman*, 949
  fury, 173
Hellebore, *bane*, 663
Hellhag, *bad woman*, 949
Hellhound, *miscreant*, 949
  ruffian, 173, 913
Hellish, *bad*, 649
  malevolent, 907
  vicious, 945
Hello, *see* Hallo
Helm, *handle*, 633
  direction, 693
  authority, 737
Helmet, *dress*, 225
  defence, 717
Helot, *servant*, 746
Help, *aid*, 707
  auxiliary, 711
  utility, 644
  remedy, 662
  servant, 746
Helpless, *weak*, 160
  incapable, 158
  exposed, 665
Helpmate, *auxiliary*, 711
  wife, 903
Helter-skelter, *disorder*, 59
  haste, 684
  slope, 217
Hem, *edge*, 230
  fold, 258
  to stammer, 583
Hem in, *enclose*, 231
  surround, 227
  restrain, 751
Hemlock, *bane*, 663
Henbane, *bane*, 663
Hence, *arising from*, 155
  deduction, 476
  motive, 615
Henceforth, *futurity*, 121
Henchman, *servant*, 746
Henpecked, *obedience*, 743
  subjection, 749
Hep, *knowing*, 490
  informed, 527
Hephaestus, *god*, 979
Heptad, *seven*, 98
Heptagon, *angularity*, 244
  seven, 98
Hera, *goddess*, 979
Herald, *messenger*, 534

Herald, *precursor*, 64
  omen, 512
  lead, 280
  to predict, 511
  to proclaim, 531
Herb, *plant*, 367
Herbarium, *botany*, 369
Herbivorous, *eat*, 296
Herculean, *strength*, 159
  huge, 192
  difficulty, 704
Herd, *animal*, 366
  flock, 72, 102
Here, *present*, 186
Hereabouts, *nearness*, 197
Hereafter, *futurity*, 121
Hereditament, *property*,
          780
Hereditary, *derivative*, 154
  posterity, 167
  habit, 613
  intrinsic, 5
Heredity, *paternity*, 166
Heresy, *error*, 495
  unbelief, 485
  religious, 984A
Heretic, *dissent*, 489
  heresy, 984A
Heretofore, *preterition*, 122
  priority, 116
Herewith, *accompaniment*,
          88
Heritage, *futurity*, 121
  possession, 777
  property, 780
Heritor, *possessor*, 779
Hermaphrodite, *incongru-
  ity*, 83
Hermeneutic, *interpreta-
  tion*, 522
Hermes, *god*, 979
  messenger, 534
Hermetically, *closure*, 261
Hermit, *seclusion*, 893
Hermitage, *abode*, 189
Hero, *brave*, 861
  saint, 948
Heroic, *brave*, 861
  glorious, 873
  magnanimous, 942
  verse, 597
Heroics, *exaggeration*, 549
  boast, 884
Herr, *title*, 877
Herring-gutted, *thin*, 203
Hesitate, *reluctant*, 603
  irresolute, 605
  uncertainty, 475
  fearful, 860
  sceptical, 485
  to stammer, 583
* Hetaera, *courtesan*, 962

Hook, *grip*, 781
  hang, 214
  curvature, 245
  deviation, 279
  take, 789
Hook-up, *junction*, 43
Hookah, *tobacco-pipe*, 298A
Hooker, *ship*, 273
Hooligan, *ruffian*, 913, 949
Hooliganism, *brutality*, 907
Hoop, *circle*, 247
Hoot, *cry*, 411
  deride, 929, 930, 932
  drink, 298
Hooter, *indication*, 550
Hoots, *contempt*, 930
Hop, *leap*, 309
  dance, 840
Hop it, *go away*, 293, 287
  escape, 671
Hop the twig, *die*, 360
Hope, *hope*, 858
  probability, 472
Hopeful, *probable*, 472
Hopeless, *desperate*, 859
  impossible, 471
Hophead, *intemperance*,
                            954
Horde, *assemblage*, 72
Horizon, *distance*, 196
  view, 441
  prospect, 507
  futurity, 121
Horizontal, *horizontality*,
                            213
Horn, *sharpness*, 253
  musical, 417
  alarm, 669
Horn-mad, *jealousy*, 920
Horn of plenty, *sufficient*,
                            639
Hornbook, *school*, 542
Hornet, *bane*, 663, 830
Hornpipe, *dance*, 840
Hornswoggle, *deceive*, 545
Horny, *hard*, 323
Horology, *chronometry*, 114
Horoscope, *prediction*, 511
Horrible, *great*, 31
  fearful, 860
Horrid, *noxious*, 649
  ugly, 846
  dire, 830
  vulgar, 851
  fearful, 860
  hateful, 898
Horripilation, *cold*, 383
  terror, 860
Horrisonous, *strident*, 410
Horror, *dislike*, 867
  hate, 898
  fear, 860

* Hors de combat, *impotence*, 158
  disease, 655
* Hors-d'œuvre, *food*, 298
Horse, *animal*, 271
  cavalry, 726
  stand, 215
Horse-box, *vehicle*, 272
Horse-laugh, *laugh*, 838
Horse-power, *measure*, 466
Horse-sense, *wisdom*, 498
Horse-shoe, *curvature*, 245
Horseman, *traveller*, 268
Horseplay, *violence*, 173
Horsewhip, *punishment*,
                            972
Hortation, *advice*, 615, 695
Horticulture, *agriculture*,
                            371
* Hortus siccus, *botany*, 369
Hosanna, *worship*, 990
Hose, *dress*, 225
  conduit, 350
Hospice, *abode*, 189
Hospitable, *social*, 892
  liberal, 816
Hospital, *remedy*, 662
Hospodar, *master*, 745
Host, *multitude*, 100
  collection, 72
  friend, 890
  religious, 999
Hostage, *security*, 771
Hostel, *inn*, 189
Hostile, *adverse*, 708
Hostilities, *warfare*, 722
Hostility, *enmity*, 889
Hot, *warm*, 382
  pungent, 392
  irascible, 901
  rhythm, 413
  contraband, 964
Hot air, *sophistry*, 477
Hot-bed, *workshop*, 691
  cause, 153
Hot-blooded, *rash*, 863
Hot-brained, *rash*, 863
  excited, 825
Hot-headed, *rash*, 863
  excited, 825
Hot-plate, *heater*, 386
Hot water, *difficulty*, 704
Hot-water bottle, *heater*,
                            386
Hotchpotch, *mixture*, 41
  confusion, 59
Hotel, *inn*, 189
Hothouse, *conservatory*, 386
  workshop, 691
Hotspur, *rashness*, 863
  courage, 861
Hottentot, *boor*, 876

Hough, *maltreat*, 649
Hound, *pursue*, 281, 622
  oppress, 907
  wretch, 949
Hour, *period*, 108
Hour-glass, *time*, 114
  form, 203
Houri, *beauty*, 845
Hourly, *routine*, 138
House, *abode*, 189
  to locate, 184
  safety, 664
  party, 712
  senate, 696
  partnership, 797
House-warming, *sociality*,
                            892
Houseboat, *abode*, 189
Housebreaker, *thief*, 792
Household, *abode*, 189
  conformity, 82
  plain, 849
  property, 780
Housekeeper, *director*, 694
  servant, 746
Housekeeping, *conduct*, 692
Houseless, *displaced*, 185
Housemaid, *servant*, 746
Housewifery, *conduct*, 692
  economy, 817
Housing, *lodging*, 189
Hovel, *abode*, 189
Hover, *soar*, 267
  rise, 305
  high, 206
Hoverplane, *aircraft*, 273A
How, *in what way*, 627
  by what means, 632
How-d'ye-do, *difficulty*, 704
Howbeit, *counteraction*, 179
Howdah, *seat*, 215
However, *except*, 83
  notwithstanding, 179
  degree, 23
  compensation, 30
Howff, *resort*, 74
Howitzer, *arms*, 727
Howl, *ululation*, 411, 412,
                            839
Howler, *error*, 495
  solecism, 568
Howsoever, *degree*, 26
Hoy, *ship*, 273
  salutation, 586
Hoyden, *vulgarity*, 851
Hub, *centre*, 223
  middle, 68
Hubble-bubble,   *tobacco-
  pipe*, 298A
Hubbub, *din*, 404
  discord, 713
  agitation, 315

Illapse, *entry*, 294
Illation, *judgment*, 480
Illegal, *illegality*, 964
Illegible, *unintelligible*, 519
Illegitimate, *undue*, 925
   illegal, 964
   erroneous, 495
Illiberal, *selfish*, 943
   stingy, 819
   intolerant, 481
Illicit, *illegality*, 964, 925
Illimitable, *infinite*, 105
   great, 31
Illiterate, *ignorance*, 491
Illness, *disease*, 655
Illogical, *sophistical*, 477
   erroneous, 495
Illuminate, *enlighten*, 420
   colour, 428
   adorn, 847
Illuminati, *scholar*, 492
Illumination, *drawing*, 556
   ornament, 847
   celebration, 883
Illusion, *error*, 495
   deceit, 545
Illusionist, *conjurer*, 548
Illusive, *erroneous*, 495
   sophistical, 477
   deceitful, 544
Illusory, *see* Illusive
Illustration, *interpretation*, 522
   drawing, 556
   representation, 554
   ornament, 847
   example, 82
Illustrious, *repute*, 873
Image, *representation*, 554
   idea, 453
   statue, 557
   idol, 991
   likeness, 17
Imagery, *metaphor*, 521
   fancy, 515
Imaginary, *non-existing*, 2
   erroneous, 495
   quantity, 84
Imagination, *fancy*, 515
   wit, 842
Imam, *clergy*, 996
   master, 745
Imbalance, *inequality*, 28
Imbecile, *foolish*, 477, 499
   absence of intellect, 450A
   weak, 160
   incapable, 158
Imbed, *see* Embed
Imbibe, *receive*, 296
   learn, 539
Imbrangle, *derange*, 61
Imbricated, *covering*, 222

Imbroglio, *unintelligibility*, 519
   discord, 713
Imbrue, *moisten*, 339
   impregnate, 300
Imbue, *mix*, 41
   tinge, 428
   impregnate, 300
   moisten, 339
   teach, 537
   feel, 821
Imitate, *to copy*, 19
   repetition, 104
   to represent, 554
Imitation, *copy*, 21
Immaculate, *excellent*, 648
   spotless, 652
   faultless, 650
   innocent, 946
   pure, 960
Immanent, *inherent*, 5
Immanity, *malevolence*, 907
Immaterial, *unsubstantial*, 4
   spiritual, 317
   mental, 450
   trifling, 643
Immature, *new*, 123
   unprepared, 674
Immeasurable, *infinite*, 105
   great, 31
Immediate, *transient*, 111
Immedicable, *incurable*, 655, 659
Immemorial, *old*, 124
Immense, *in degree*, 31
   in size, 192
Immerse, *introduce*, 300
   dip, 337
   baptism, 998
Immethodical, *disorder*, 59
Immigrant, *stranger*, 57
Immigration, *migration*, 266
   entrance, 294
Imminent, *futurity*, 121
   destiny, 152
Immiscibility, *incoherence*, 47
Immission, *reception*, 296
Immitigable, *ire*, 900
   violence, 173
Immobility, *immutability*, 150
   quiescence, 265
   resolution, 604
Immoderately, *greatness*, 31
Immoderation, *intemperance*, 954
Immodest, *impurity*, 961
Immolate, *destroy*, 162
   kill, 361
   offer, 763

Immolation, *sacrifice*, 991
Immoral, *vicious*, 945
   wrong, 923
Immortal, *perpetual*, 112
   glorious, 873
   celebrated, 883
Immovable, *unchangeable*, 150
   resolved, 604
   obstinate, 606
Immunity, *exemption*, 927A
   right, 924
   freedom, 748
Immure, *enclose*, 231
   imprison, 751
Immutable, *immutability*, 150
Imp, *demon*, 980
   ruffian, 913
   wretch, 943
Impact, *contact*, 43
   impulse, 276
   insertion, 300
Impair, *deterioration*, 659
Impale, *transfix*, 260
   pierce, 302
   execute, 972
Impalpable, *small*, 193
   powder, 330
   immaterial, 317
   intangible, 381
Impanation, *rite*, 998
Imparity, *inequality*, 28
Impart, *give*, 784
   inform, 527
Impartial, *just*, 922
   wise, 498
   indifferent, 866
   honourable, 939
Impassable, *closed*, 261, 704
Impasse, *hindrance*, 706
   situation, 8
   difficulty, 704
Impassible, *insensible*, 376, 823
Impassion, *excite*, 824
Impassive, *insensible*, 823
Impasto, *painting*, 556
Impatient, *excitable*, 825
Impawn, *lending*, 787
Impeach, *accuse*, 938
Impeccability, *perfection*, 650
Impecunious, *adversity*, 735
   poverty, 804
Impede, *hindrance*, 706
Impedimenta, *hindrance*, 706
   baggage, 635
Impel, *push*, 276, 284
   move, 264
   induce, 615

Impend, *future*, 121
  expectation, 507
  height, 206
  destiny, 152
Impenetrable, *latent*, 526
  hidden, 528
Impenitence, *impenitence*,
  951
Imperative, *authority*, 737
  duty, 926
  requirement, 630
* Imperator, *master*, 745
Imperceptible, *invisible*, 447
  minute, 193
Impercipient, *insensibility*,
  376
Imperfect, *incomplete*, 53
  failing, 651
  shortcoming, 304
  vicious, 945
  small, 32
Imperforate, *closure*, 261
Imperial, *authority*, 737
  beard, 256
Imperil, *endanger*, 665
Imperious, *stern*, 739
  insolent, 885
Imperishable, *external*, 112,
  150
  glorious, 873
Impermanent, *transitory*,
  111
Impermeable, *closed*, 261
  dense, 321
Impersonal, *generality*, 78
  material, 316
Impersonate, *represent*, 554
  imitate, 19
Impertinence, *inexpedience*,
  647
Impertinent, *irrelevant*, 10
  disagreeing, 24
  insolent, 885
  discourteous, 895
Imperturbable, *unruffled*,
  823, 826
Impervious, *closure*, 261
Impetrate, *beseech*, 765
Impetuous, *boisterous*, 173
  hot, 825
  hasty, 684
  rash, 863
  eager, 865
Impetus, *impulse*, 276
Impiety, *impiety*, 988
  irreligion, 989
Impignorate, *lending*, 787
Impinge, *impulse*, 276
Impish, *supernatural*, 980
Implacable, *hatred*, 898
  wrath, 900
  unforgiving, 919

Implant, *insert*, 300
  teach, 537
Implanted, *adventitious*, 6
  inborn, 5
Implement, *instrument*, 633
Impletion, *sufficiency*, 639
  fullness, 52
Implicate, *accuse*, 938
  involve, 54
Implication, *inference*, 521
Implicit, *understood*, 516
  metaphorical, 521
  untold, 526
Implore, *beseech*, 765
  pray, 990
  pity, 914
Imply, *mean*, 516
  latent, 526
  evidence, 467
  metaphor, 521
Impolite, *rude*, 895
  vulgar, 851
Impolitic, *folly*, 499
  inexpedient, 647
Imponderable, *light*, 320
  immaterial, 317
Import, *ingress*, 294
  transfer, 270
  insert, 300
  mean, 516
  be of consequence, 642
  receive, 296
Importance, *greatness*, 31
Important, *importance*, 642
  repute, 873
Importunate, *painfulness*,
  830
Importune, *ask*, 765
  pester, 830
Impose, *order*, 741
  cheat, 545
  be unjust, 923, 925
  palm off upon, 486
Imposing, *grand*, 873
Impossible, *incredible*, 471
  impracticable, 704
Impost, *price*, 812
Impostor, *deceiver*, 548
Imposture, *deception*, 545
Impotence, *impotence*, 158
  weakness, 160
  failure, 732
Impound, *enclose*, 231
  imprison, 751
Impoverish, *drain*, 638
  fleece, 789
  render poor, 804
Impracticable, *difficult*, 704
  impossible, 471
  obstinate, 606
Imprecation, *request*, 765
  malediction, 908

Impregnable, *safety*, 664
Impregnate, *insert*, 300
  produce, 161, 168
  mix, 41
  teach, 537
Imprescriptible, *dueness*,
  924
Impress, *mark*, 550
  memory, 505
  excite, 375, 824
  compel, 744
Impressario, *drama*, 599
Impressible, *sensibility*, 822
  motive, 615
Impression, *belief*, 375, 484
  idea, 453
  feeling, 821
  engraving, 558
Impressionist, *artist*, 559
Impressive, *exciting*, 824
  notable, 642
Imprimatur, *sanction*, 924
* Imprimis, *beginning*, 66
Imprint, *indication*, 550
Imprison, *shut up*, 751
  circumscribe, 231
Improbable, *improbability*,
  473
Improbity, *improbity*, 940
  wrong, 923
Improficiency, *unskilfulness*, 699
Impromptu, *impulse*, 612
  music, 415
Improper, *wrong*, 923, 925
  inexpedient, 499, 647
  incongruous, 24
  unseemly, 961
Impropriate, *take*, 789
  possess, 777
Improve, *improvement*, 658
Improvident, *careless*, 460
  not preparing, 674, 863
  prodigal, 818
Improvise, *impulse*, 612
  imagine, 515
Imprudent, *rash*, 863
  unwise, 699
  neglectful, 460
Impudent, *insolence*, 885
  discourtesy, 895
Impudicity, *impurity*, 961
Impugn, *blame*, 932
  deny, 536
  oppose, 708
Impuissance, *impotence*,
  158
Impulse, *push*, 276
  unpremeditation, 612
  necessity, 601
Impulsive, *instinctive*, 477
  motive, 615

Impulsive, *motiveless*, 616
   rash, 863
Impunity, *acquittal*, 970
Impure, *foul*, 653
   licentious, 961
Imputation, *disrepute*, 874
Impute, *ascribe*, 155
   accuse, 938
* In esse, *existence*, 1
* In extenso, *whole*, 50
   diffuse, 573
* In extremis, *death*, 360
In fine, *end*, 67
In hand, *possession*, 777
   business, 625
* In limine, *beginning*, 66
* In loco, *agreement*, 23
* In mediis rebus, *middle*,
             68
* In nubibus, *inexistence*, 2
   incogitancy, 452
   imagination, 515
   unintelligibility, 519
* In propria persona, *spec-
   iality*, 79
* In puris naturalibus, *di-
   vesiment*, 226
* In re, *relation*, 9
* In saecula saeculorum,
   perpetuity, 112
* In statu pupillari, *youth*,
             127
   learner, 541
* In statu quo, *permanence*,
             141
   restoration, 660
* In terrorem, *threat*, 909
* In toto, *whole*, 50
   greatness, 31
* In transitu, *transient*, 111
   conversion, 144
   motion, 264
   transference, 270
   method, 627
Inability, *want of power*, 158
   want of skill, 699
Inaccessible, *distance*, 196
   impossible, 471
Inaccurate, *error*, 495, 568
Inaction, *inaction*, 681
Inactivity, *inactivity*, 172,
             683
Inadaptability, *disagreement*, 24
Inadequate, *insufficient*,
         640, 645
   imperfect, 651
   weak, 158, 160
Inadmissible, *inexpedient*,
           647
   incongruous, 24
   excluded, 55

Inadvertence, *inattention*,
           458
   unintentional, 621
Inalienable, *right*, 924
   possession, 777
   retention, 781
* Inamorata, *love*, 897
Inane, *trivial*, 643
   useless, 645
   void, 4
Inanimate, *dead*, 360
   inorganic, 358
Inanition, *insufficiency*, 640
Inanity, *inutility*, 645
   absence of thought, 452
   absence of meaning, 517
   insignificance, 643
Inappetence, *indifference*,
           866
Inapplicable, *irrelation*, 10
   disagree, 24
Inapposite, *disagree*, 24
   irrelevant, 10
Inappreciable, *in size*, 193
   in degree, 32
   unimportant, 643
Inappreciative, *ungrateful*,
           917
Inapprehensible, *unknow-
able*, 519
Inappropriate, *discordant*,
           24
   inexpedient, 647
Inapt, *inexpedient*, 647
   incongruous, 24
Inaptitude, *impotence*, 158
Inarticulate, *stammering*,
           583
Inartificial, *artlessness*, 703
Inartistic, *unskilled*, 699
   imperfect, 651
Inattention, *indifference*,
           458
Inaudible, *silent*, 403, 405
   mute, 581
Inaugurate, *begin*, 66
   precedence, 62
   celebrate, 883
Inauguration, *commission*,
           755
Inauspicious, *hopeless*, 859
   untimely, 135
   untoward, 649
Inbeing, *intrinsicality*, 5
Inborn, *intrinsic*, 5, 820
   habitual, 613
Inbred, *intrinsic*, 5, 820
Inca, *master*, 745
Incalculable, *infinite*, 105
   much, 31
Incalescence, *heat*, 382
Incandescence, *heat*, 382

Incandescence, *light*, 420
Incantation, *invocation*, 765
   spell, 993
Incapable, *weak*, 160
   unable, 158
Incapacity, *impotence*, 158
   weakness, 160
   stupidity, 499
   indocility, 538
Incarcerate, *imprison*, 751
   surround, 231
Incarnadine, *red*, 434
Incarnate, *materialize*, 316
Incarnation, *intrinsic*, 5
   Deity, 976
Incautious, *neglectful*, 460
   rash, 863
Incendiary, *evildoer*, 913
   destructive, 162
Incense, *fragrance*, 400
   to provoke, 900
   hatred, 898
   flattery, 933
   worship, 990
Incentive, *motive*, 615
Inception, *beginning*, 66
Inceptor, *learner*, 541
Incertitude, *uncertain*, 475
Incessant, *perpetual*, 112
   frequency, 136
Incest, *impurity*, 961
Inch, *littleness*, 193
   slowness, 275
   island, 346
Inch by inch, *degree*, 26
Inchoate, *amorphous*, 241
Inchoation, *beginning*, 66
Incidence, *direction*, 278
Incident, *event*, 151
Incidental, *extrinsic*, 6, 8
   irrelative, 10
   liable, 177
   casual, 156, 621
Incinerate, *calefaction*, 384
Incipient, *beginning*, 66
   style, 574
Incision, *cut*, 44
Incisive, *style*, 574
   feeling, 821
Incite, *urge*, 615
   exasperate, 173
Incivility, *rudeness*, 895
Incivism, *misanthropy*, 911
Inclement, *cold*, 383
   severe, 739
Incline, *slope*, 217
   direction, 278
   tendency, 176
   willing, 602
   desire, 865
   love, 897
   induce, 615

Indenture, *evidence*, 467
  compact, 769
Independence, *irrelation*,
                       10
  wealth, 803
  freedom, 748
Indescribable, *wonder*, 870
  great, 31
Indestructible, *perpetual*,
                       112
Indeterminate, *uncertain*,
                       475
  obscure, 519
  chance, 156
Indetermination, *irresolution*, 605
Index, *sign*, 550
  list, 86, 562
  arrangement, 60
  record, 551
  numerical exponent, 84
Indian sign, *spell*, 993
Indian summer, *autumn*,
                       126
Indiarubber, *elasticity*, 325
Indicate, *point out*, 550
  manifest, 525
  mean, 516
  evidence, 467
Indict, *arraign*, 969
  accuse, 938
Indictable, *criminal*, 945
Indifference, *unconcern*, 866
  absence of choice, 610
  coldness, 823
  unwillingness, 603
  unimportance, 643
  imperfect, 651
Indigene, *inhabitant*, 188
Indigenous, *intrinsic*, 5
Indigent, *poor*, 804
  insufficient, 640
Indignation, *resentment*,
                       900
Indignity, *insult*, 929
  affront, 900
  outrage, 830
Indigo, *blueness*, 438
Indirect, *obliquity*, 217
Indiscernible, *invisible*, 447
Indiscerptible, *unity*, 50
  whole, 87
  dense, 321
Indiscreet, *unskilful*, 699
  blamable, 945
  neglectful, 460
  foolish, 499
Indiscretion, *guilt*, 947
Indiscriminate, *multiform*,
                       81
  unarranged, 59
  casual, 621

Indiscrimination, *neglect*,
                       460
  indistinction, 465A
Indispensable, *requirement*,
                       630
Indisposed, *disincline*, 603
  to dissuade, 616
  sick, 655
Indisputable, *certainty*, 474
Indissoluble, *whole*, 50
  dense, 321; *united*, 43
  unchangeable, 150
Indistinct, *vague*, 519
  dim, 447
Indistinguishable, *minute*,
  identical, 13   [447
Indite, *write*, 590
Individual, *special*, 79
  exceptional, 83
  unity, 87; *whole*, 50
  style, 574
Indivisible, *whole*, 50
  dense, 321
Indocility, *obstinacy*, 606
  incapacity, 538
Indoctrinate, *teach*, 484,
                       537
Indolence, *inactivity*, 683
Indomitable, *resolution*, 604
  courage, 861
  unyielding, 719
Indraught, *current*, 348
Indubitable, *certainty*, 474
Induce, *motive*, 615
  cause, 153
  produce, 161
Induction, *investigation*,
  reasoning, 476   [461
  of a priest, 995
  appointment, 755
Indulge, *allow*, 760
  give, 784; *lenity*, 740
  pleasure, 827
  pleasing, 829
  intemperance, 954
  satisfy, 831
Induration, *hardening*, 323
  impenitence, 951
Industrial action, *strike*,
                       719
Industry, *activity*, 682
  learning, 539
  business, 625
Indweller, *inhabitant*, 188
Inebriety, *drunkenness*, 959
Inedible, *unsavoury*, 395
Ineffable, *wonder*, 870
Ineffably, *greatness*, 31
Ineffaceable, *memory*, 505
  feeling, 821

Ineffectual, *incapable*, 158
  weak, 160
  useless, 645
  failing, 732
Inefficacious, *see* Ineffectual
Inefficient, *see* Ineffectual
Inelastic, *not elastic*, 326
  soft, 324
Inelegant, *ugly*, 846
  in style, 579
Ineligible, *inexpedience*,
                       647
Ineluctable, *destiny*, 152
Inept, *incapable*, 158, 699
  useless, 645
  unsuitable, 24
Inequality, *inequality*, 28
Inequitable, *wrong*, 923
Ineradicable, *fixed*, 150
Inerrable, *innocence*, 946
Inert, *physically*, 172, 683
  morally, 823
Inertia, *inertness*, 172
  inactivity, 683
Inestimable, *goodness*, 648
Inevitable, *destiny*, 152, 601
  certain, 474
Inexact, *error*, 495
Inexactitude, *lie*, 546
Inexcitability,   *inexcitabil-
ity*, 826
Inexcusable, *vice*, 938, 945
Inexecution,   *non-comple-
tion*, 730
Inexhaustible, *sufficiency*,
                       639
Inexistence, *inexistence*, 2
Inexorable, *resolved*, 604
  stern, 739
  compelling, 744
  wrathful, 900
  relentless, 907
Inexpectation,   *inexpecta-
tion*, 508
Inexpedient, *inexpedience*,
                       647
Inexpensive, *cheapness*, 815
Inexperience, *ignorance*,
                       491
  disqualification, 699
Inexpert, *unskilfulness*, 699
Inexpiable, *vice*, 945
Inexplicable, *unintelligible*,
                       519
  wonderful, 870
Inexpressible, *unmeaning*,
                       517
  wonder, 870
  great degree, 31
Inexpressive, *unmeaning*,
                       517, 519
Inexpugnable, *safety*, 664

Instalment, *portion,* 51
  payment, 807
Instance, *example,* 82
  solicitation, 765
  motive, 615
Instancy, *urgency,* 642
Instant, *moment,* 113
  present, 118
  future, 121
Instanter, *earlier,* 132
  instantaneity, 113
Instauration, *restoration,*
    600
Instead, *substitution,* 147
Instigate, *motive,* 615
Instil, *insert,* 300
  teach, 537
  mix, 41
Instinct, *intellect,* 450
  intuition, 477
  impulse, 601
  innate, 5
Instinctive, *habitual,* 613
  impulsive, 612
Institute, *school,* 542
  beginning, 66
  cause, 153
  organize, 161
Institution, *legality,* 963
  poorhouse, 804
Institutor, *teacher,* 540
Instruct, *teach,* 537
  advise, 695
  precept, 697
  command, 741
Instructor, *teacher,* 540
Instrument, *implement,* 633
  record, 551
  security, 771
Instrumental, *means,* 632
  music, 415
  subservient, 631
Instrumentality, *medium,*
    631
Insubordinate, *disobedience,*
    742
  anarchy, 738
Insubstantiality, *nothingness,* 4
Insufferable, *painfulness,*
    830
Insufficient, *insufficiency,*
    640
  shortcoming, 304
Insufflation, *wind,* 349
Insular, *island,* 346
  detach, 44
  single, 87
Insulate, *separate,* 44
Insult, *rudeness,* 895
  disrespect, 929
  offence, 900

Insuperable, *difficulty,* 704
  impossible, 471
Insupportable, *painfulness,*
    830
Insuppressible, *violence,*
    173
Insurance, *promise,* 768
  security, 771
  precaution, 664
Insurgent, *disobedience,* 742
Insurmountable, *difficulty,*
    704
  impossible, 471
Insurrection, *disobedience,*
    742
  resistance, 719
Insusceptible, *insensibility,*
    823
Intact, *permanence,* 141
  preserve, 669
Intaglio, *concavity,* 252
  sculpture, 557
Intake, *inlet,* 260
Intangible, *numbness,* 381
  immaterial, 317
Integer, *whole,* 50
Integral calculus, *number,*
    84
Integral part, *component,*
    56
Integrate, *consolidate,* 50
  complete, 52
Integration, *number,* 84
Integrity, *whole,* 50
  virtue, 944
  probity, 939
Integument, *covering,* 222
Intellect, *intellect,* 450
Intelligence, *mind,* 450
  news, 532
  wisdom, 498
Intelligible, *intelligibility,*
    518, 570
Intemperate, *intemperance,*
    954
  drunkenness, 957
Intempestivity, *unseason-
  ableness,* 135
Intend, *design,* 620
Intendant, *director,* 694
Intended, *will,* 600
Intensify, *energize,* 171
  aggravate, 835
Intensity, *degree,* 26
  greatness, 31
  energy, 171
Intent, *active,* 682
  thoughtful, 451, 457
Intention, *design,* 620
Intentional, *will,* 600
Intentness, *attention,* 457
  thought, 451

Inter, *bury,* 363
  insert, 300
* Inter alia, *conformity,* 82
Interaction, *reciprocal,* 12
Interblend, *mix,* 41
Interbreed, *mix,* 41
Intercalate, *insert,* 300
  intervene, 228
Intercede, *mediate,* 724
  deprecate, 766
Intercept, *hinder,* 706
  take, 789
Intercession, *deprecation,*
    766
Interchange, *interchange,*
    148
  reciprocate, 12
  barter, 794
  transfer, 783
Intercipient, *hinder,* 706
Interclude, *hindrance,* 706
Intercom, *hearing,* 418
Intercommunicate, *inter-
  locution,* 588
  information, 527
Intercommunion, *society,*
    892
Intercostal, *interiority,* 221
Intercourse, *converse,* 588
Intercross, *mix,* 41
Intercurrence, *passage,* 302
Interdict, *prohibition,* 761
Interdigitate, *intervene,* 228
  intersect, 219
Interest, *advantage,* 618
  concern, 9
  importance, 642
  curiosity, 455
  attention, 457
  aid, 707
  to please, 829
  debt, 806
Interested, *selfish,* 943
Interesting, *style,* 574
Interfere, *intervene,* 228
  meddle, 682
  disagree, 24
  counteract, 179
  thwart, 706
  mediate, 724
  activity, 682
Interglossa, *language,* 560
Interim, *duration,* 106
  synchronism, 120
Interior, *interiority,* 221
Interjacence, *coming be-
  tween,* 228
  middle, 68
Interject, *insert,* 300
  interpose, 228
Interlace, *twine,* 219
  join, 43

Jellyfish, *weakness*, 160
Jennet, *carrier*, 271
Jeopardy, *danger*, 665
Jeremiad, *invective*, 932, 938
   lamentations, 839
Jerk, *throw*, 146, 284
   draw, 285
   agitate, 315
   bad man, 949
Jerry, *flimsy*, 643
Jerry-built, *fragile*, 328
Jersey, *dress*, 225
Jest, *wit*, 842
   trifle, 643
Jester, *humorist*, 844
   buffoon, 857
Jesuit, *clergy*, 996
Jesuitry, *deception*, 544
   sophistry, 477
JESUS, *Deity*, 976
Jet, *water*, 347
   stream, 348
   aircraft, 273A
   blackness, 431
Jetsam, *fragments*, 51
   little, 643
Jettison, *abandon*, 782
Jetty, *convexity*, 250
* Jeu d'esprit, *wit*, 842
* Jeu de mots, *neology*, 563
* Jeu de théâtre, *appearance*, 448
* Jeune fille, *girl*, 129
Jew, *religions*, 984
Jewel, *gem*, 650
   ornament, 847
   goodness, 648
   favourite, 899
Jew's harp, *musical*, 417
Jezebel, *wretch*, 949
   courtesan, 962
Jib, *deviation*, 279
   demur, 603
Jibe, *accord*, 23
Jiffy, *instant*, 113
Jig, *dance*, 840
Jilt, *deception*, 545
   lovelorn, 898
Jimjams, *insanity*, 503
Jingle, *resonance*, 408
   vehicle, 272
Jingo, *warlike*, 722
   boasting, 884
   blusterer, 887
Jinnee, *demon*, 980
Jinx, *spell*, 993
Jitters, *fear*, 860
Jiu-jitsu, *contention*, 720
Jive, *rhythm*, 413
Job, *business*, 625
   action, 680
   unfairness, 940

Jobation, *upbraiding*, 932
Jobber, *merchant*, 797
   agent, 690
   trickster, 943
Jobbernowl, *fool*, 501
Jobbery, *cunning*, 702
Jobbing, *skill*, 698
   barter, 794
Jockey, *horseman*, 268
   servant, 746
   to deceive, 545
   deceiver, 548
Jocose, *witty*, 836, 840, 842
Jocular, *gay*, 836
   amusing, 840
Jocund, *cheerful*, 836
Joe Soap, *fool*, 501
   dupe, 547
Jog, *push*, 276
   shake, 315
Jog on, *advance*, 282
   slowness, 275
   trudge, 266
Jog-trot, *routine*, 613
Joggle, *agitation*, 315
Johnsonian, *style*, 577
Join, *junction*, 43
   contiguity, 199
Joint, *part*, 44, 51
   junction, 43
   flexure, 258
   accompanying, 88
Joint stock, *share*, 778
Jointly, *addition*, 37
Jointress, *widow*, 905
Jointure, *receipt*, 810
   property, 780
Joist, *support*, 215
Joke, *wit*, 842
   trifle, 643
Jollification, *spree*, 954
Jollity, *amusement*, 480
Jolly, *gay*, 836
   conviviality, 892
   pleasing, 829
   plump, 192
   joke, 842
   flatter, 933
Jolly-boat, *ship*, 273
Jolt, *impulse*, 276
   agitation, 315
   shock, 824
Jonathan Wild, *thief*, 792
Jorum, *receptacle*, 191
Josh, *tease*, 830
   joke, 842
   ridicule, 856
Joskin, *clown*, 876
Joss, *idolatry*, 991
Joss-house, *temple*, 1000
Jostle, *clash*, 24
   push, 276

Jostle, *agitate*, 315
Jot, *small quantity*, 32
   particle, 193
   to record, 551
Jotting, *writing*, 590
Jounce, *agitation*, 315
Journal, *annals*, 114
   record, 551
   description, 594
   book, 593
Journalism, *publication*, 531
Journalist, *recorder*, 553
   writer, 590
Journey, *journey*, 266
   progression, 282
Journeyman, *agent*, 690
   servant, 746
Joust, *contention*, 720
Jove, *god*, 979
Jovial, *gay*, 836
   convivial, 892
   amusement, 840
Jowl, *laterality*, 236
Joy, *pleasure*, 827
Joy-ride, *journey*, 266
Joyful, *cheerful*, 836
Joyless, *dejection*, 830, 837
Joyous, *cheerful*, 836
Jubilant, *joyous*, 836
   boastful, 884
Jubilation, *celebration*, 882
Jubilee, *rejoicing*, 836, 838
   festival, 840
   anniversary, 138
   celebration, 883
Judaism, *religions*, 984
Judge, *arbitrator*, 967
   master, 745
   taste, 850
Judgmatic, *wisdom*, 498
Judgment, *decision*, 480
   intellect, 450
   belief, 484
   wisdom, 498
   sentence, 969
Judgment-seat, *tribunal*, 966
Judicature, *law*, 965
Judicial, *discriminative*, 465
   impartial, 922
Judicious, *wisdom*, 498
   expedient, 646
Jug, *receptacle*, 191
   prison, 752
Juggernaut, *idol*, 991
Juggle, *deception*, 545
Juice, *liquid*, 333
Juicy, *moist*, 339
   style, 574
Ju-ju, *idol*, 991

Kingdom, *property*, 780
   region, 181
Kingly, *majestic*, 873
   authority, 737
King's Remembrancer,
   treasurer, 801
Kingship, *authority*, 737
King-sized, 192
Kink, *distortion*, 243
   angle, 244; *caprice*, 608
Kinsfolk, *consanguinity*, 11
Kinsman, *consanguinity*, 11
Kipper, *preservation*, 670
Kirk, *temple*, 1000
Kirtle, *dress*, 225
Kismet, *destiny*, 152, 601
Kiss, *endearment*, 902
   courtesy, 894
   of death, 361
Kit, *bag*, 191
   accoutrements, 225
   fiddle, 417
Kitcat, *painting*, 556
Kitchen, *workshop*, 691
   room, 191
Kitchen garden, *agri-
culture*, 371
Kitchen-maid, *servant*, 746
Kite, *flying*, 273A
   bill, 800
Kith and kin, *consanguin-
ity*, 11
Kittle, *sensation*, 380
Kitty, *stake*, 771
Kleptomania, *desire*, 865
   insanity, 503, 504
Knack, *skill*, 698; *toy*, 840
Knap, *ridge*, 206
   to break, 44
Knapsack, *receptacle*, 191
Knave, *deceiver*, 548
   rogue, 941
   dishonour, 949
Knavish, *improbity*, 940
Knead, *mix*, 41
   soften, 324
Knee, *angularity*, 244
Kneel, *beg*, 765
   respect, 928
   submission, 725
   stoop, 308; *pray*, 990
   servility, 886
Knell, *interment*, 363
Knick-knack, *unimportant*,
   ornament, 847   [643
Knife, *sharpness*, 253
   kill, 361
Knight, *noble*, 875
Knight errant, *defence*, 717
   rash, 863

Knighthood, *title*, 877
Knit, *junction*, 43
Knob, *protuberance*, 250
   ball, 249
Knobkerrie, *arms*, 727
   club, 276
Knock, *blow*, 276, 619
   sound, 406
   beat, 972
   disparage, 483, 932
   vilify, 874
Knock about, *maltreat*, 649
   wander, 266
   boisterous, 173
Knock down, *destroy*, 162
   overthrow, 308
Knock-kneed, *curved*, 245
   distorted, 243
Knock off, *finish*, 729
   cease, 142
   steal, 791
Knock out, *beating*, 972
   end, 67
   combine, 778
Knock under, *yield*, 725
   obey, 743
Knock up, *fatigue*, 688
   distorted, 243
Knoll, *height*, 206
Knot, *ligature*, 45
   to fasten, 43
   entanglement, 59
   group, 72, 892
   intersection, 219
   difficulty, 704
   ornament, 847
Knotted, *crossing*, 219
Knotty, *difficult*, 704
   dense, 321
Knout, *scourge*, 972, 975
Know-all, *sage*, 500
Know-how, *skill*, 698
Know no bounds, *greatness*,
   31
Knowing, *skill*, 698
   cunning, 702
Knowingly, *intentionally*,
   620
Knowledge, *know*, 490
Knuckle, *angularity*, 244
Knuckle-duster, *arms*, 727
Knuckle under, *submit*, 725
   humble, 879
Kobold, *gnome*, 980
Kodachrome, *photograph*,
   556
Kopje, *height*, 206
Koran, *sacred books*, 986
Kowtow, *bow*, 308, 894
   respect, 928
   submission, 725
   obedience, 743

Kraal, *abode*, 189
Kraken, *monster*, 83
Kriegie, *prisoner*, 753
Kris, *knife*, 727
Ku Klux Klan, *illegality*,
   964
Kudos, *repute*, 873, 931
Kukri, *arms*, 727
Kyanize, *preserve*, 670
Kyle, *gap*, 198
   gulf, 343
Kyte, *belly*, 191
   convexity, 250

L

L.S.D., *money*, 800
Laager, *defence*, 717
Labarum, *flag*, 550
Label, *indication*, 550
Labial, *letter*, 561
Laboratory, *workshop*, 691
Labour, *exertion*, 686
   work, 680
   difficulty, 704
Labourer, *agent*, 690
Labyrinth, *secret*, 533
   difficulty, 704
   disorder, 59
   convolution, 248
Lace, *tie*, 43
   net, 219
   to beat, 972
Lacerable, *fragile*, 328
Lacerate, *disjunction*, 44
   pain, 830
Laches, *neglect*, 460
   omission, 773
Lachrymation, *lamentation*,
   839
Lack, *insufficiency*, 640
   destitution, 804
   requisition, 630
   number, 98
Lack-brain, *fool*, 501
Lack-lustre, *dim*, 423
   discoloured, 429
Lackadaisical, *affected*, 855
   indifferent, 866
Lacker, see Lacquer
Lackey, *servant*, 746
Laconic, *conciseness*, 572
   shortness, 201
Lacquer, *varnish*, 22
   adorn, 845, 847
Lacteal, *semiliquid*, 352
Lacuna, *orifice*, 260
   pit, 252
   deficiency, 53
   interval, 198
   break, 70

Latent, *implied*, 516
  inert, 172
Later, *posterior*. 117
Lateral, *side*, 236
Lath, *strip*, 205
Lathe, *instrument*, 633
Lather, *foam*, 353
  to flog, 972
Lathi, *impact*, 276
  arms, 727
Latitude, *scope*, 180
  situation, 183
  breadth, 202
  freedom, 748
Latitudinarian, *heterodoxy*,
    984A
Latrine, *room*, 191
Latter, *sequent*, 63
  past, 122
Lattice, *crossing*, 219
  opening, 260
Laud, *praise*, 931
  worship, 990
Laudable, *virtue*, 944
Laudanum, *anaesthetic*, 376
Laudation, *approval*, 931
* Laudator temporis acti,
  oldness, 124
  permanence, 141
  discontent, 832
  lamentation, 839
Lauds, *worship*, 990
Laugh, *rejoice*, 838
Laugh at, *ridicule*, 856
  sneer, 929
  underestimate, 483
  joke, 842
Laughable, *ridiculous*, 853
Laughing gas, *anaesthetic*,
    376
Laughing-stock, *ridicule*,
    857
Laughter, *rejoice*, 836, 838,
    840
Launch, *propel*, 284
  begin, 66
  adventure, 876
Launch out, *expatiate*, 584
  style, 573
Laundress, *servant*, 746
Laundry, *cleanness*, 652
Laureate, *poetry*, 597
Laurel *trophy*, 733
  reward, 973
  glory, 873
  decoration, 877
Lava, *semiliquid*, 352
Lavatory, *room*, 191
  privy, 653
Lave, *cleanness*, 652
  water, 337
Lavender, *colour*, 437

Lavender, *fragrance*, 400
Lavish, *prodigal*, 818
  giving, 784
  profuse, 639, 641
  liberal, 816
Lavolta, *dance*, 840
Law, *rule*, 80, 697
  ordination, 963
  command, 741
  permission, 760
Lawful, *dueness*, 924
  allowable, 760
Lawless, *arbitrary*, 964
  irregular, 83
Lawn, *plain*, 344
Lawsuit, *law*, 969
Lawyer, *lawyer*, 968
Lax, *incoherent*, 47
  soft, 324
  diffuse, 573
  disuse, 614
  remiss, 738
  licentious, 945
Laxative, *remedy*, 662
Lay, *place*, 184
  assuage, physically, 174
  assuage, morally, 826
  bet, 151
  poetry, 597
  music, 415
  level, 213
  secular, 997
Lay aside, *relinquish*, 624
  give up, 782
  cease, 142
  reject, 610
Lay bare, *manifest*, 525
Lay brother, *clergy*, 996
Lay by, *store*, 636
  economize, 817
Lay down, *assert*, 535
  renounce, 757
Lay figure, *prototype*, 22
  effigy, 554
  nonentity, 643
Lay in, *store*, 636
Lay into, *punish*, 972
  buffet, 276
Lay open, *disclose*, 529
  show, 525
  divest, 226
Lay out, *level*, 213
Lay to, *stop*, 265
  be inactive, 683
  repose, 687
Lay up, *illness*, 655
  store, 636
Lay waste, *ravage*, 649
  disorganize, 659
Layer, *layer*, 204
Layman, *laity*, 997
Laystall, *unclean*, 653

Lazaretto, *remedy*, 662
Lazy, *inactive*, 683
  slow, 275
Lea, *plain*, 342, 344
Lead, *to precede in order*, 62
  precede in motion, 280
  to tend, 176
  to direct, 693
  to induce, 615
  authority, 737
  heaviness, 319
  depth, 208
Lead-line, *measurement*, 466
Lead off, *begin*, 66
  precursor, 64
Leader, *master*, 745
  director, 694
  dissertation, 595
Leading, *important*, 642
Leading strings, *subjection*,
    749
Leaf, *part*, 51
  plant, 367
  layer, 204
  of a book, 593
Leaflet, *part*, 51
League, *party*, 712
Leak, *dribble*, 295
  waste, 638
Lean, *thin*, 193
  narrow, 203
  oblique, 217
  recline, 215
Lean-to, *building*, 189
Leaning, *direction*, 278
  tendency, 176
  willingness, 602
Leap, *jump*, 309
Leap to, *change*, 140
Learned, *knowledge*, 490,
    492
Learner, *learner*, 541
Learning, *acquiring*, 539
  erudition, 490
Lease, *sale*, 796
  property, 780
Lease-lend, *lend*, 787
Leash, *tie*, 43
  three, 92
Least, *inferiority*, 34
Leat, *conduit*, 350
Leather, *to beat*, 972
  toughness, 327
Leatherneck, *fighter*, 726
Leave, *quit*, 293
  vacate, 185
  relinquish, 624
  permission, 760
  bequeath, 784
Leave off, *cessation*, 142,
    614, 624
Leave out, *exclusion*, 55

Line, *continuity*, 69
   direction, 278
   business, 625
   soldier, 726
   feature, 550
   appearance, 448
   posterity, 167
   epistle, 592
Lineage, *posterity*, **167**
   series, 69
   kindred, 11
Lineament, *appearance*, 448
   mark, 550
Linear, *length*, 200
Linger, *loiter*, 275
   delay, 133
   protract, 110
Lingo, *language*, 560
Lingua franca, *neology*, 563
Linguist, *scholar*, 492
   language, 560
Liniment, *unctuous*, 355
   remedy, 662
Lining, *lining*, 224
Link, *relation*, 9
   connecting, 45
   to connect, 43
   part, 51
   term, 71
   flambeau, 423
Links, *arena*, 728
Linn, *lake*, 343
Linocut, *engraving*, 558
Linoleum, *covering*, 222
Linotype, *printing*, 591
Linsey-woolsey, *mixed*, 41
Lion, *courage*, 861
   prodigy, 872
   celebrity, 873
Lip, *edge*, 230
   beginning, 66
   prominence, 250
   impudence, 885
Lip-devotion, *impiety*, 988
Lip-service, *insincerity*, 544
   flattery, 933
   impiety, 988
Lip-wisdom, *folly*, 499
Lipogram, *misnomer*, 565
Lippitude, *dim sight*, 443
Lipstick, *ornament*, 847
Liquation, *calefaction*, 384
Liquefaction, *soluble*, 335
   calefaction, 384
Liquescence, *calefaction*, 384
Liquescent, *soluble*, 335
Liquid, *fluid*, 333
   letter, 561
   sound, 405
Liquidate, *pay*, 807
   destroy, 162

Liquor, *liquid*, 333
   intoxicant, 959
   potable, 299
Liquorice, *sweet*, 396
Lisp, *stammering*, 583
Lissom, *soft*, 324
List, *catalogue*, 86
   record, 551
   strip, 205
   fringe, 230
   obliquity, 217
   hear, 418
   will, 600
   choose, 609
Listed, *variegation*, 440
Listen, *hearing*, 418
Listen in, *radio*, 599B
Listless, *inattentive*, 458
   inactive, 683
   impassive, 823
   indifferent, 866
Lists, *arena*, 728
Lit up, *drunk*, 959
Litany, *rite*, 998
* Literae humaniores, *language*, 560
Literal, *exact*, 19, 494
   meaning, 516
   unimaginative, 843
Literate, *knowledge*, 491
Literati, *scholar*, 492
* Literatim, *imitation*, 19
   word, 562
Literature, *learning*, 490
   language, 560
Lithe, *softness*, 324
Lithograph, *engraving*, 558
Litigant, *combatant*, 726
   lawsuit, 969
Litigate, *discord*, 713
   contention, 720
Litigious, *discord*, 713
   lawsuit, 969
Litter, *disorder*, 59
   to derange, 61
   trash, 643
   useless, 645
   vehicle, 272
   offspring, 167
Little, *in degree*, 32
   in size, 193
Littoral, *land*, 342
Liturgy, *rite*, 998
Live, *exist*, 1
   continue, 141
   dwell, 186
   fame, 873
Livelihood, *wealth*, 803
Livelong, *perpetuity*, 110
Lively, *sprightly*, 836
   acute, 821
   sensitive, 375, 822

Lively, *active*, 682
   style, 574
Liver-coloured, *brown*, 433
Livery, *badge*, 550, 877
   colour, 428
   suit, 225
Livid, *dark*, 431
   purple, 437
Living, *life*, 359
   benefice, 995
Lixiviate, *cleanness*, 652
   liquefaction, 335
Lixivium, *liquidity*, 333
Llama, *carrier*, 271
Llano, *plain*, 344
Lo! *see*, 441
   wonder, 870
Load, *weight*, 319
   cargo, 190
   quantity, 31
   redundance, 641
   hindrance, 706
   anxiety, 828
   fill up, 52
   to oppress, 830
Loadstone, *attraction*, 289, 865
   motive, 615
Loaf, *head*, 450
Loafer, *idler*, 683
Loam, *soil*, 342
Loan, *lending*, 787
Loathe, *dislike*, 867
   hate, 898
Loathing, *nausea*, 841
Loathsome, *hateful*, 649, 898
   abhorrent, 867
   nauseous, 395
Lob, *toss*, 284
Lobby, *room*, 191
   passage, 627
Lobe, *part*, 51
Lobster, *red*, 434
Local, *situation*, 183
   regional, 180
Locality, *situation*, 183
Localize, *location*, 184
   limit, 231
Locate, *location*, 184
Loch, *lake*, 343
Lock, *fasten*, 43
   confine, 229
   rest, 265
   enclose, 232
   barrier, 706
   canal, 350
   tuft, 256
Lock up, *concealment*, 528
   restraint, 751
Lock-up, *jail*, 752
Locker, *receptacle*, 191
Locket, *ornament*, 847

INDEX

Mab, *fairy*, 979
Macabre, *gruesome*, 846
Macadam, *smoothness*, 255
Macaroni, *fop*, 854
Macaronic, *poetry*, 597
Mace, *club*, 633
    weapon, 727
    sceptre, 747
Mace-bearer, *jurisprudence*,
                        965
Macerate, *water*, 337
Maceration, *asceticism*, 955
    atonement, 952
Machiavellian, *falsehood*,
                        544
Machiavellism, *cunning*,
                        702
Machicolation, *embrasure*,
                        257
Machination, *plan*, 626
Machine, *instrument*, 633
Machinist, *agent*, 690
Mackerel sky, *cloud*, 353
Mackintosh, *dress*, 225
Macrobiotic, *lasting*, 110
Macrocosm, *world*, 318
    greatness, 31
Macrology, *diffuseness*, 573
Mactation, *idolatry*, 991
Macula, *blemish*, 848
Maculated, *variegation*, 440
Maculation, *ugliness*, 846
Mad, *insane*, 503
    violent, 173
Madcap, *caprice*, 608
    rash, 863
    excitable, 825
Madden, *excite*, 824
Madder, *red*, 434
Made of, *composition*, 54
Madefaction, *moisture*, 339
Madhouse, *hospital*, 662
Madman, *madman*, 504
Madness, *insanity*, 503
Madrigal, *poetry*, 597
Maelstrom, *whirlpool*,
                    312, 348
    turmoil, 59
Maenad, *violence*, 173
Maffick, *make merry*, 836
Magazine, *store*, 636
    record, 551
    book, 593
Magdalen, *penitent*, 950
Mage, *sorcerer*, 994
Magenta, *purple*, 437
Maggot, *whim*, 608
    desire, 865
Maggoty, *uncleanness*, 653
Magi, *sage*, 500
    saint, 948
Magic, *sorcery*, 992

Magic lantern, *optical*, 445
    spectacle, 448
Magician, *sorcerer*, 994
Magisterial, *pride*, 878
Magistracy, *authority*, 737
    jurisdiction, 965
Magistrate, *justiciary*, 967
    ruler, 745
Magistrature, *authority*,
                        737
Magma, *mixture*, 41
Magnanimity, *disinterested-
    ness*, 942
Magnate, *nobility*, 875
Magnet, *attraction*, 288, 829
    desire, 865
    motive, 615
* Magnificat, *worship*, 990
Magnificent, *grand*, 882
    fine, 845
    magnanimous, 942
Magnifico, *nobility*, 875
Magnifier, *optical instru-
    ment*, 445
Magnify, *increase*, 35
    enlarge, 194
    exaggerate, 549
    praise, 990
    approve, 931
Magniloquent, *ornament*,
                        577
    extravagant, 549
    speech, 582
Magnitude, *quantity*, 25
    size, 192
Magpie, *loquacity*, 584
Magsman, *thief*, 792
Magus, *heathen*, 984
Maharajah, *master*, 745
    noble, 875
Maharanee, *noble*, 875
    chief, 745
Mahatma, *sorcerer*, 994
Mahogany colour, *brown*,
                        433
Mahomet, *religious founder*,
                        986
Mahometanism, *religions*,
                        984
Maid of honour, *marriage*,
                        903
Maiden, *girl*, 129, 374
    servant, 746
    spinster, 904
    purity, 960
    guillotine, 975
    first, 66
Mail, *letters*, 592
    news, 532
    defence, 717
    armoury, 727
Mail-cart, *vehicle*, 272

Maim, *injure*, 649, 659
    weaken, 160
Main, *whole*, 50
    tunnel, 260
    conduit, 350
    ocean, 341
    principal, 642
Mainland, *land*, 342
Mainly, *greatness*, 31
Mainspring, *cause*, 153
    motive, 615
Mainstay, *instrument*, 631
    refuge, 666
    hope, 858
Maintain, *continue*, 141, 143
    preserve, 670
    sustain, 170
    assert, 535
* Maison de santé, *remedy*,
                        662
* Maître, *expert*, 700
Majestic, *repute*, 873
Majesty, *king*, 745
    rank, 873
    Deity, 976
Major, *greater*, 33
    officer, 745
Majordomo, *director*, 694
    commissary, 746
Majority, *age*, 131
    greater number, 102
    dead, 362
Majuscules, *printing*, 591
Make, *produce*, 161
    constitute, 54
    form, 240
    arrive at, 292
    price, 812
Make-believe, *untruth*, 546
Make fast, *vinculum*, 43
Make for, *tend*, 176
Make good, *compensation*,
                        30
    substantiate, 467
Make it up, *forgive*, 918
Make known, *information*,
                        527
Make loose, *incoherence*, 47
Make out, *decipher*, 522
    understand, 518
    discover, 480A
Make over, *transfer*, 783
Make up, *complete*, 52
    compose, 54
    imagine, 515
    invent, 544
    improvise, 612
Make up for, *compensate*, 30
Make up to, *accost*, 586
    approach, 286
Make way, *progress*, 282
    improve, 658

Meteorology, *air*, 338
Methinks, *belief*, 484
Method, *order*, 58
   way, 627
Methodize, *arrange*, 60
Meticulous, *careful*, 459
Metonymy, *metaphor*, 521
   substitution, 147
Metre, *poetry*, 597
Metrical, *measurement*, 466
Metropolis, *abode*, 189
Mettle, *spirit*, 820
   courage, 861
Mettlesome, *excitable*, 822,
            825
   brave, 861
Mew, *enclose*, 231
   restrain, 751
   divest, 226
   complain, 839
Mewl, *ululation*, 412
* Mezzo-rilievo, *sculpture*,
           557
Mezzo-soprano, *melody*, 413
* Mezzo termine, *middle*, 68
   mid-course, 628
Mezzotint, *engraving*, 558
Miasma, *bane*, 663
Miasmal, *morbific*, 649
Micawber, *careless*, 460
Microbe, *bane*, 663
   insalubrity, 657
Microcosm, *little*, 32, 193
Microfilm, *copy*, 21
Microphone, *loudness*, 404
   hearing, 418
Microscope, *optical*, 445
Microscopic, *little*, 193
Mid, *middle*, 68
Mid-course, *middle*, 628
Midas, *wealth*, 803
Midday, *course*, 125
Midden, *uncleanness*, 653
Middle, *in order*, 68
   in degree, 29
   in space, 223
Middleman, *agent*, 690
   go-between, 631
   salesman, 797
Middling, *imperfect*, 651
   mean, 29
Midge, *littleness*, 193
Midget, *dwarf*, 193
Midland, *land*, 342
Midnight, *evening*, 126
   darkness, 421
Midriff, *interjacence*, 228
Midshipman, *master*, 745
Midst, *central*, 223
Midsummer, *morning*, 125
Midway, *middle*, 68
Midwife, *doctor*, 662

Mien, *appearance*, 448
   conduct, 692
Miff, *resentment*, 900
Might, *power*, 157
   degree, 26
   violence, 173
Mighty, *much*, 31
   large, 192
   powerful, 159
   haughty, 878
Migrate, *journey*, 266
Mikado, *master*, 745
Mike, *loudness*, 404
   hearing, 418
Milch cow, *store*, 636
Mild, *moderate*, 174
   insipid, 391
   lenient, 740
   calm, 826
   courteous, 894
   warm, 382
Mildew, *unclean*, 653
Mileage, *measurement*, 466
Militant, *contention*, 720
Militarism, *warfare*, 722
   authority, 737
Military, *combatant*, 726
Militate, *opposition*, 179, 608
Militia, *combatant*, 726
Milk, *to despoil*, 789
Milk-and-water, *imperfect*,
           651
Milk-white, *whiteness*, 430
Milksop, *coward*, 862
Milky, *semitransparent*, 427
   emulsive, 252
Milky Way, *world*, 318
Mill, *machine*, 330, 633
   workshop, 691
Mill-pond, *store*, 636
Millenary, *celebration*, 883
Millennium, *period*, 108
   thousand, 98
   futurity, 121
   Utopia, 515
   hope, 858
Millesimal, *thousand*, 98
Millet-seed, *littleness*, 193
Milliner, *dress*, 225
Million, *number*, 98
Millionaire, *wealth*, 803
Millstone, *incubus*, 706
   weight, 319
Miltonic, *sublime*, 574
   poetry, 597
Mime, *player*, 599
   buffoon, 856
Mimeograph, *imitation*, 19
Mimesis, *imitation*, 19
Mimic, *imitation*, 19
   repeat, 104
Minacity, *threat*, 909

Minaret, *height*, 206
Minatory, *threatening*, 909
   dangerous, 665
* Minauderie, *affected*, 855
Mince, *disjoin*, 44
   stammer, 583
Mincing, *slow*, 275
   affected, 855
Mind, *intellect*, 450
   will, 600
   desire, 865
   dislike, 867
   purpose, 620
   to attend to, 457
   believe, 484
   remember, 505
Minded, *willing*, 602
Mindful, *attentive*, 457
   remembering, 505
Mindless, *inattentive*, 458
   forgetful, 506
Mine, *store*, 636
   abundance, 639
   to hollow, 252
   open, 260; *snare*, 545
   sap, 162
   damage, 659
Mine-layer, *ship*, 273
Mine-sweeper, *ship*, 273
Mineral, *inorganic*, 358
Mineralogy, *inorganic*, 358
Minerva, *goddess*, 979
Mingle, *mix*, 41
Mingy, *parsimony*, 819
Mini, *small*, 193
Miniature, *portrait*, 556
   small, 193
Minikin, *small*, 193
Minim, *small*, 32, 193
Minimize, *moderate*, 174
   underestimate, 483
Minimum, *small*, 32, 193
Mining, *opening*, 260
Minion, *favourite*, 899
Minister, *deputy*, 759
   instrumentality, 631
   director, 694
   to aid, 707
   rites, 998
Ministry, *direction*, 693
   church, 995
Minnow, *littleness*, 193
Minor, *inferior*, 34
   infant, 129
Minority, *fewness*, 103
Minotaur, *unconformity*, 83
Minster, *temple*, 1000
Minstrel, *music*, 416
Minstrelsy, *musician*, 415
Mint, *workshop*, 691
   mould, 22
   wealth, 803

Minuend, *deduction*, 38

Minuet, *dance*, 840
  music, 415

Minus, *less*, 38
  in debt, 806
  deficient, 304

Minuscules, *printing*, 591

Minute, *in quantity*, 32
  in size, 193
  of time, 108
  instant, 113
  compendium, 596
  record, 551
  in style, 573

Minutest, *inferior*, 34

Minutiae, *small*, 32
  little, 193
  unimportant, 643

Minx, *impertinent*, 887
  bad woman, 949

* Mirabile dictu, *wonder*, 870

Miracle, *prodigy*, 872

Miraculous, *wonder*, 870

Mirage, *dim sight*, 443
  appearance, 448
  shadow, 4

Mire, *uncleanness*, 653

Mirk, *darkness*, 421

Mirror, *reflector*, 445
  perfection, 650
  saint, 948
  imitate, 19

Mirth, *cheerful*, 836

Mirthless, *dejected*, 837

Misadventure, *failure*, 732
  adversity, 735
  misfortune, 830

Misalliance, *marriage*, 903

Misanthrope, *recluse*, 893,
  911

Misapply, *misuse*, 679
  misinterpret, 523
  mismanage, 699

Misapprehend, *mistake*, 495
  misinterpret, 523

Misappropriate, *misuse*, 679

Misarrange, *derange*, 61

Misbecome, *vice*, 945

Misbegotten, *vice*, 945

Misbehaviour, *discourtesy*,
  895
  vulgarity, 852
  guilt, 947

Misbelief, *doubt*, 495

Miscalculate, *sophistry*, 477
  disappoint, 509

Miscall, *misnomer*, 565

Miscarriage, *failure*, 732

Miscegenation, *mixture*, 41

Miscellany, *mixture*, 41
  collection, 72
  generality, 78

Mischance, *misfortune*, 830
  adversity, 735
  failure, 732

Mischief, *evil*, 619

Mischievous, *badness*, 649

Miscible, *mix*, 41

Miscompute, *mistake*, 495

Misconceive, *mistake*, 495
  misinterpret, 481, 523

Misconduct, *guilt*, 947
  bungling, 699

Misconstrue, *misinterpret*,
  523

Miscount, *error*, 495

Miscreant, *wretch*, 949
  apostate, 941

Miscreated, *vice*, 945

Miscue, *unskilfulness*, 699

Misdate, *anachronism*, 115

Misdeed, *guilt*, 947

Misdeem, *misinterpret*, 523

Misdemean, *vice*, 945

Misdevotion, *impiety*, 988

Misdirect, *misteaching*, 538
  bungle, 699

Misdoing, *guilt*, 947

* Mise en scène, *appearance*,
  448

Misemploy, *misuse*, 679

Miser, *parsimony*, 819

Miserable, *contemptible*,
  643
  unhappy, 828
  pitiable, 914
  small, 32

Miserly, *parsimony*, 819

Misery, *pain*, 828

Misestimate, *error*, 495

Misfit, *disparity*, 24

Misfortune, *evil*, 619
  failure, 732
  adversity, 735
  unhappiness, 830

Misgiving, *fear*, 860
  doubt, 485

Misgovern, *unskilful*, 699

Misguide, *misteaching*, 538

Misguided, *foolish*, 699

Mishandle, *maltreat*, 649

Mishap, *evil*, 619
  failure, 732
  adversity, 735
  disaster, 830

Mishmash, *mixture*, 41

Misinform, *misteach*, 538
  ignorance, 491
  error, 495

Misintelligence, *misteach*,
  538

Misinterpret, *misinterpret*,
  523

Misjoined, *disagreement*, 24

Misjudge, *err*, 495
  sophistry, 477

Mislay, *lose*, 776
  derange, 61

Mislead, *deceive*, 477, 545
  misteach, 538
  error, 495

Mislike, *dislike*, 867

Mismanage, *unskilful*, 699

Mismatch, *difference*, 15

Mismatched, *disagreement*,
  24

Misname, *misnomer*, 565

Misnomer, *misnomer*, 565

Misogamy, *celibacy*, 904

Misogynist, *celibacy*, 904

Misplace, *disorder*, 59
  unconformity, 83

Misplaced, *unsuitable*, 24

Misprint, *error*, 495

Mispronounce, *speech*, 583

Misproportioned, *ugliness*,
  846

Misquote, *misinterpret*, 523
  false, 544

Misreckon, *error*, 495

Misrelate, *error*, 495

Misremember, *error*, 495

Misreport, *err*, 495
  falsify, 544

Misrepresent, *untruth*, 546

Misrepresentation, *perversion*, 523
  falsehood, 544
  caricature, 555

Misrule, *misconduct*, 699
  laxity, 738

Miss, *lose*, 776
  fail, 732
  inattention, 458, 460
  want, 865
  girl, 374

Missal, *rite*, 998

Missay, *stammer*, 583
  misnomer, 565

Misshapen, *ugliness*, 846
  distortion, 243

Missile, *thing thrown*, 284
  arms, 727

Missing, *absence*, 187

Mission, *commission*, 755
  undertaking, 676
  business, 625
  warfare, 722

Missionary, *clergy*, 996

Missive, *correspond*, 592

Misspell, *misinterpret*, 523

Misspend, *prodigal*, 818

Misstate, *misinterpret*, 523
  falsify, 544

Misstatement, *error*, 495
  falsehood, 544

Misstatement, *untruth,* 546
    perversion, 523
Mist, *dimness,* 422
Mistake, *error,* 495
    failure, 732
    mismanagement, 699
    misconstrue, 523
Misteach, *misteach,* 538
Misterm, *misnomer,* 565
Misthink, *error,* 495
Mistime, *intempestivity,* 135
Mistral, *wind,* 349
Mistranslate, *misinterpret,*
    523
Mistress, *lady,* 374
    sweetheart, 897
    concubine, 962
Mistrust, *doubt,* 485
Misty, *opaque,* 426
    dim, 422
    invisible, 447
Misunderstanding, *error,*
    495
    misinterpretation, 523
    discord, 713
Misuse, *misuse,* 679
    waste, 638
Mite, *small,* 193
    bit, 32
    money, 800
Mitigate, *abate,* 36, 174
    relieve, 834
    calm, 826
    improve, 658
    extenuate, 937
* Mitrailleuse, *gun,* 727
Mitre, *canonicals,* 999
    joint, 43
Mitten, *dress,* 225
Mittimus, *command,* 741
Mix, *mix,* 41
Mixed, *disorder,* 59
Mixture, *mix,* 41
Mizzle, *rain,* 348
Mnemonics, *memory,* 505
Mnemosyne, *memory,* 505
Moan, *lamentation,* 839, 411
Moat, *enclosure,* 232
    ditch, 350
    defence, 717
Mob, *crowd,* 72, 31
    multitude, 102
    troop, 726
    plenty, 639
    vulgar, 876
    to scold, 932
Mob law, *illegal,* 964
Mobile, *movable,* 264
    sensible, 822
    inconstant, 607
Mobilization, *warfare,* 722
    move, 264

Mobility, *commonalty,* 876
Mobocracy, *authority,* 737
Mobsman, *thief,* 792
Moccasin, *dress,* 225
Mock, *imitate,* 17
    repeat, 104
    erroneous, 495
    false, 544
    to ridicule, 483, 856
    laugh at, 838
Mock-heroic, *ridiculous,*
    853
Modal, *extrinsic,* 6
    state, 7
    circumstance, 8
Mode, *fashion,* 852
    method, 627
Model, *prototype,* 22
    to change, 140, 144
    rule, 80
    example, 82
    to copy, 19
    sculpture, 557
    perfection, 650
    saint, 948
Modeller, *artist,* 559
Moderate, *small,* 32
    to allay, 174
    to assuage, 826
    temperate, 953
    cheap, 815
Moderation, *temperateness,*
    174
    mediocrity, 736
* Moderato, *music,* 415
Moderator, *master,* 745
    director, 694
Modern, *newness,* 123
Modernize, *change,* 140
Modesty, *humility,* 881
    purity, 960
Modicum, *little,* 33
    allotment, 786
Modification, *difference,* 15
    variation, 20
    change, 140
    qualification, 469
Modify, *convert,* 144
Modish, *fashion,* 852
Modulation, *change,* 140
    harmony, 413
* Modus operandi, *method,*
    627
    conduct, 692
* Modus vivendi, *arrange-*
    ment, 723
    compromise, 774
Mogul, *master,* 745
Mohammed, *religious*
    founder, 986
Mohammedanism, *religions,*
    984

Mohock, *roisterer,* 949
Moider, *bewilder,* 475
    inattention, 458
Moiety, *bisection,* 91
Moil, *action,* 680
    work, 686
Moist, *wet,* 337
    humid, 339
Moke, *carrier,* 271
Molasses, *sweetness,* 396
Mole, *mound,* 206
    defence, 717
    refuge, 666
Molecule, *small,* 32, 193
Molehill, *lowness,* 207
    trifling, 643
Molestation, *evil,* 619
    damage, 649
    malevolence, 907
Mollify, *allay,* 174
    soften, 324
    conciliate, 918
    assuage, 826
Mollusc, *animal,* 366
Mollycoddle, *cowardice,*
    862
Moloch, *tyranny,* 739
    divinity, 979
    idol, 986
Molten, *liquid,* 335
Moment, *of time,* 113
    importance, 642
Momentary, *transient,* 111
Momentum, *impulse,* 276
Momus, *rejoicing,* 838
Monachism, *church,* 995
Monad, *littleness,* 193
    unity, 87
Monarch, *master,* 745
Monarchy, *authority,* 737
Monastery, *temple,* 1000
Monastic, *churchdom,* 995
Monetary, *money,* 800
Money, *money,* 800
Money-bag, *treasury,* 802
Money-changer, *merchant,*
    797
Money-grubber, *miser,* 819
    acquisition, 775
Moneyed, *wealth,* 803
Moneyer, *treasurer,* 801
Moneyless, *poverty,* 804
Monger, *merchant,* 797
Mongrel, *mixture,* 41
    anomalous, 83
Moniker, *name,* 564
Moniliform, *circular,* 247
Monism, *unity,* 87
Monition, *advice,* 695
    warning, 668
    information, 527
    omen, 512

Monitor, *teacher*, 540
  director, 694
  master, 745
  ship, 723
Monitory, *prediction*, 511
  warning, 668
Monk, *clergy*, 996
Monkery, *churchdom*, 995
Monkey, *imitative*, 19
  engine, 276
  ridiculous, 856
  laughing-stock, 857
  to play the fool, 499
  money, 800
Monkey-shines, *prank*, 840
  foolery, 497
  caprice, 608
Monkish, *clergy*, 995
Monochord, *musical*, 417
Monochrome, *colourless*, 429
Monocular, *lens*, 445
Monody, *lamentation*, 839
Monogamy, *marriage*, 903
Monogram, *sign*, 550
  cipher, 533
  diagram, 554
Monograph, *dissertation*, 595
Monolith, *record*, 551
Monologue, *soliloquy*, 589
Monomania, *insanity*, 503
  error, 495
  obstinacy, 606
Monomaniac, *madman*, 504
Monometallism, *money*, 800
Monoplane, *aircraft*, 273A
Monopolize, *possess*, 777
  engross, 457
Monopoly, *syndicate*, 778
Monosyllable, *letter*, 561
Monotheism, *theology*, 983
Monotonous, *unchanging*, 141
Monotony, *identity*, 13
  uniformity, 16
  repetition, 104, 141
  in style, 575
  weariness, 841
Monotype, *printing*, 591
* Monsieur, *title*, 877
Monsoon, *wind*, 349
Monster, *exception*, 83
  prodigy, 872
  size, 192
  ugly, 846
  evildoer, 913
  ruffian, 949
Monstrous, *greatness*, 31
  huge, 192
  wonderful, 870
  ugly, 846
  ridiculous, 853

* Mont de piété, *lending*, 787
Montgolfier, *balloon*, 273A
Month, *period*, 108
Monthly, *periodical*, 138
Monticule, *height*, 206
Monument, *record*, 551
  interment, 363
  tallness, 206
Monumental, *great*, 31
Mood, *nature*, 5
  state, 7
  temper, 820
  will, 600
  tendency, 176
  disposition, 602
  affections, 820
  variations, 20
  change, 140
Moody, *sullen*, 895
  fretful, 900
  furious, 825
Moon, *inaction*, 681
  changeable, 149
Moon-eyed, *dim sight*, 443
Moonbeam, *light*, 420
  dimness, 422
Mooncalf, *fool*, 501
Moonless, *dark*, 421
Moonlight, *light*, 420
Moonshine, *nonsense*, 497, 517
  excuse, 617
  trumpery, 643
  dimness, 422
Moonstruck, *insanity*, 503
Moony, *dreamy*, 458
  foolish, 499
  listless, 683
Moor, *open space*, 180
  plain, 344
  locate, 184
  join, 43; *rest*, 265
Moorland, *space*, 180
  plain, 344
Moot, *inquire*, 461
  argue, 476
  conjecture, 514
Moot point, *topic*, 454, 461
Mop, *clean*, 652
Mope, *dejection*, 837
Mope-eyed, *dim sight*, 443
Moped, *vehicle*, 272
Moppet, *darling*, 899
Moraine, *debris*, 330
Moral, *right*, 922
  duty, 926
  virtuous, 944
  maxim, 496
Moral fibre, *courage*, 861
Morale, *state*, 7
Moralize, *reason*, 476
  teach, 537

Morality, *drama*, 599
Morass, *marsh*, 345
Moratorium, *delay*, 133
Morbid, *bad*, 649
  diseased, 655
  noxious, 657
Morbific, *bad*, 649
  diseased, 655
  noxious, 657
Mordacity, *malevolence*, 907
Mordant, *pungent*, 392
  vigorous, 574
  sarcastic, 932
Mordent, *grace-note*, 415
More, *addition*, 37
  superiority, 33
More or less, *smallness*, 32
  equality, 27
* More suo, *conformity*, 82
Moreover, *addition*, 37
  accompaniment, 88
Morganatic, *marriage*, 903
* Morgue, *pride*, 878
  dead-house, 363
Moribund, *dying*, 360
  sick, 655
Mormon, *polygamist*, 903
Morning, *morning*, 125
Moron, *fool*, 501
Morose, *discourtesy*, 895
Morphia, *anaesthetic*, 376
Morphology, *form*, 240
Morris-dance, *dance*, 840
Morrison, *shelter*, 717
Morrow, *futurity*, 121
  morning, 125
Morsel, *small quantity*, 32
  portion, 51
Mortal, *man*, 373
  fatal, 361
  bad, 649
  weariness, 841
Mortality, *death*, 360
  evanescence, 111
  mankind, 372
Mortar, *cement*, 45
  artillery, 727
  pulverization, 330
Mortgage, *sale*, 796
  lend, 787
  security, 771
  credit, 805
Mortgagee, *credit*, 805
Mortgagor, *debt*, 806
Mortice, see Mortise
Mortician, *interment*, 363
Mortify, *pain*, 828
  to vex, 830
  to discontent, 832
  to humiliate, 874, 879
  disease, 655
  asceticism, 955

Mullion, *support*, 215
Multifarious, *multiform*, 81
  various, 15
Multifid, *divided*, 51
Multifold, *multiform*,
  16A, 81
Multiform, *diversified*,
  16A, 81
Multigenerous, *multiform*,
  81
Multilateral, *side*, 236
Multipartite, *disjunction*,
  44
Multiple, *numerous*, 102
  product, 84
Multiplicand, *number*, 84
Multiplication, *arithmetical*, 85
  reproduction, 163
Multiplicator, *number*, 84
Multiplicity, *multitude*, 102
Multiplier, *number*, 84
Multisonous, *loud*, 404
Multitude, *number*, 102
  greatness, 31; *mob*, 876
  assemblage, 72
Multitudinous, *multitude*,
  102
* Multum in parvo, *contraction*, 195
  conciseness, 572
Mum, *silence*, 403
  aphony, 581
  mother, 166
Mumble, *eat*, 296
  mutter, 405, 583
Mumbo Jumbo, *idol*, 991
  spell, 993
Mumchance, *silent*, 403
  mute, 581
Mummer, *the drama*, 599
Mummery, *absurdity*, 497
  ridicule, 856
  parade, 882
  imposture, 545
  masquerade, 840
Mummify, *preserve*, 670
  bury, 363
Mummy, *corpse*, 362
  dryness, 340
  mother, 166
Mump, *dejection*, 837
Mumper, *beggar*, 767
Mumps, *sullenness*, 895
Munch, *eat*, 296
Munchausen, *exaggerate*,
Mundane, *world*, 318 [549
  selfishness, 943
  irreligion, 989
Munerary, *reward*, 973
Municipal, *law*, 965
  distinct, 189

Munificent, *liberality*, 816
  giving, 784
Muniment, *record*, 551
  defence, 717
  refuge, 666
Munition, *material*, 635
Murder, *killing*, 361
  to bungle, 699
Murex, *purple*, 437
Muricate, *sharpness*, 253
Murky, *darkness*, 421
Murmur, *sound*, 405
  complaint, 839
  flow, 348
Murrain, *disease*, 655
Murrey, *redness*, 434
Muscle, *strength*, 159
Muse, *to reflect*, 451
  poetry, 597
  language, 560
Musette, *musical instrument*, 415
Museum, *store*, 636
  collection, 72
  focus, 74
Mushroom, *small*, 193
  newness, 123
  low-born, 876
  upstart, 734; *increase*, 35
Music, *music*, 415
Music-hall, *theatre*, 599
  amusement, 840
Musical, *melodious*, 413
Musician, *musician*, 416
Musk, *fragrance*, 400
Musket, *arms*, 727
Musketeer, *combatant*, 726
Muslin, *semitransparent*,
Muss, *dishevel*, 61 [427
Mussulman, *religions*, 984
Must, *mucor*, 653
  necessity, 152
  obligation, 926
  compulsion, 744
  essential, 630
Mustard, *condiment*, 393
  yellow, 436
Mustard-seed, *little*, 193
Muster, *collect*, 72
  numeration, 85
Muster-roll, *record*, 551
  list, 86
Musty, *foul*, 653
  rank, 401
Mutable, *changeable*, 149
  irresolute, 605
Mutation, *change*, 140
*Mutatis mutandis, *reciprocalness*, 12
  substitution, 147
* Mutato nomine, *substitution*, 147

Mute, *silent*, 403
  letter, 561
  silencer, 417
  speechless, 581
  taciturn, 585
  interment, 363
Mutilate, *retrench*, 38
  deform, 241
  garble, 651
  incomplete, 53
  injure, 649, 659
  spoliation, 619
Mutineer, *disobey*, 742
Mutiny, *disobey*, 742
  misrule, 738
  revolt, 719
Mutt, *fool*, 501
Mutter, *speak*, 583
  murmur, 405
  threaten, 909
Mutual, *reciprocal*, 12, 148
Muzzle, *opening*, 260
  edge, 230
  to silence, 403, 581
  taciturn, 585
  to incapacitate, 158
  restrain, 751
  imprison, 752
Muzzle-loader, *gun*, 727
Muzzy, *confused*, 458
  in liquor, 959
Myopic, *dim sight*, 443
Myriad, *number*, 98
  multitude, 102
Myrmidon, *troop*, 726
Myrrh, *fragrance*, 400
Myrtle, *love*, 897
Mysterious, *concealed*, 528
  obscure, 519
Mystery, *secret*, 533
  latency, 526
  concealment, 528
  craft, 625
  drama, 599
Mystery-ship, *deception*,
Mystic, *concealed*, 528 [545
  obscure, 519
Mystify, *to deceive*, 545
  hide, 528
  falsify, 477
  misteach, 538
Myth, *imagination*, 515
Mythological, *god*, 979
  imaginary, 515

N

N.B., *attention*, 457
N or M, *generality*, 78
Na, *dissent*, 489
Nab, *seize*, 789
Nabob, *wealth*, 803

Nacreous, *variegation*, 440
Nadir, *base*, 211
Naffy, *food*, 298
Nag, *carrier*, 271
  be rude, 895
  discord, 713
  to scold, 932
Naiad, *mythological*, 979
Nail, *to fasten*, 43
  fastening, 45
Nail-brush, *clean*, 652
Nailing, *good*, 648
Naïveté, *artless*, 703
Naked, *denuded*, 226
  visible, 446
Namby-pamby, *affected*, 855
  insipid, 866
  trifling, 643
  style, 575
Name, *appellation*, 564
  fame, 873
  to appoint, 755
Nameless, *anonymous*, 565
  obscure, 874
Namely, *conformity*, 82
  specifically, 79
Namesake, *name*, 564
Nap, *sleep*, 683
  down, 256
  texture, 329
Napkin, *clean*, 652
Napping, *inattentive*, 458
Nappy, *frothy*, 353
Narcissus, *beauty*, 845
Narcotic, *noxious*, 649
  somniferous, 683
Narghile, *tobacco-pipe*, 298A
Nark, *informer*, 527, 529
Narrate, *description*, 594
Narrow, *thinness*, 203
Narrow-minded, *bigoted*, 499
  prejudiced, 481
Nasal, *accent*, 583
Nascent, *begin*, 66
  new, 123
Nasty, *foul*, 653
  unsavoury, 395
  offensive, 830
  ugly, 846
Natal, *beginning*, 66
Natation, *navigation*, 267
Nathless, *counteraction*, 179
Nation, *mankind*, 372
National, *inhabitant*, 188
Nationality, *philanthropy*, 910
Native, *inhabitant*, 188
  artless, 703
Nativity, *prediction*, 511
Natter, *nag*, 932
Natty, *spruce*, 845

Natural, *intrinsic*, 5
  regular, 82
  true, 543
  artless, 703
  a fool, 501
  style, 578
Natural history, *organize*, 357
Natural philosophy, *materiality*, 316
Naturalistic, *description*, 594
Naturalization, *conversion*, 144
Naturalized, *habitual*, 613
  established, 82
Nature, *essence*, 5
  world, 318
  organization, 357
  affections, 820
  reality, 494
  rule, 82
  artlessness, 703
  unfashioned, 674
  spontaneous, 612
  class, 75
  style, 578
Naught, *nothing*, 4
  zero, 101
Naughty, *vicious*, 945
  disobedient, 742
  perverse, 895
Naumachy, *conflict*, 720
Nausea, *disgust*, 867
  weariness, 841
  hatred, 898
  unsavoury, 395
Nautch-girl, *dancer*, 599
Nautical, *navigation*, 267
Nave, *middle*, 68
  centre, 223
  church, 1000
Navel, *middle*, 68
  centre, 223
Navigation, *ship*, 267
Navigator, *mariner*, 269
Navvy, *workman*, 690
Navy, *ship*, 273
Nawaub, *master*, 745
Nay, *negation*, 536
* Ne plus ultra, *greatness*, 31
  end, 67
  distance, 196
  superiority, 33
  goodness, 648
  perfection, 650
Neap, *lowness*, 207
Near, *in space*, 197
  in time, 121
  approach, 286
  stingy, 817
  likeness, 17

Near side, *sinistrality*, 239
Near-sighted, *dim sight*, 443
Nearly, *small*, 32
Neat, *spruce*, 845
  clean, 652
  in writing, 576
Neat-handed, *skilful*, 698
Neb, *convexity*, 250
Nebula, *stars*, 318
  dimness, 422
  misty, 353
  invisible, 447
  obscure, 519
Nebulosity, *see* Nebula
Necessitate, *evidence*, 467
Necessitous, *adversity*, 735
Necessity, *fate*, 601
  indigence, 804
  requirement, 630
Neck, *contraction*, 195
  narrow, 203
  insolence, 885
  caress, 902
Neck and crop, *whole*, 50
Neck-cloth, *dress*, 225
Necklace, *ornament*, 847
  circularity, 247
Necrology, *description*, 594
  death, 360
Necromancer, *sorcerer*, 994
Necromancy, *sorcery*, 992
Necropsy, *disinter*, 363
Nectar, *sweet*, 394, 396
Need, *requirement*, 630
  insufficiency, 640
  indigence, 804
  desire, 865
Needle, *sharpness*, 253
  perforator, 262
  fear, 860
  compass, 693
Needless, *redundance*, 641
Needs, *necessity*, 601
Nefarious, *vice*, 945
Negation, *negation*, 536
Negative, *inexisting*, 2
  contrariety, 14
  quantity, 84
  denial, 536
  confute, 479
  refusal, 764
  prototype, 22
Neglect, *disregard*, 460
  disuse, 678
  non-observance, 773
  to leave undone, 730
  to slight, 929
  to evade, 927
Negotiable, *transferable*, 783
Negotiate, *bargain*, 769
  traffic, 794
  mediate, 724

Obeisance, *worship*, 990
  fealty, 743
Obelisk, *monument*, 551
  tall, 206
Obelize, *indicate*, 550
Oberon, *sprite*, 980
Obesity, *size*, 192
Obey, *obedience*, 743, 749
Obfuscate, *darken*, 421, 426
  bewilder, 458
Obit, *death*, 360
* Obiter dictum, *irrelation*,
  10
Obituary, *description*, 594
  death, 360
Object, *thing*, 3, 316
  intention, 620
  ugly, 846
  to disapprove, 932
Object lesson, *explanation*,
  522
Object to, *dislike*, 867
Objectify, *existence*, 1
Objective, *extrinsic*, 6
  material, 316, 450A
Objurgate, *disapprobation*,
  932
Oblate, *shortness*, 201
  monk, 996
Oblation, *gift*, 789
  proffer, 763
  worship, 990
Obligation, *duty*, 926
  promise, 768
  conditions, 770
  debt, 806
  gratitude, 916
Oblige, *compel*, 744
  benefit, 707
Obliging, *kind*, 906
  courteous, 894
Oblique, *obliquity*, 217
Obliquity, *vice*, 945
Obliterate, *efface*, 552
Oblivion, *oblivion*, 506
Oblong, *length*, 200
Obloquy, *censure*, 932
  disgrace, 874
Obmutescence, *aphony*, 581
Obnoxious, *hateful*, 898
  unpleasing, 830
  pernicious, 649
Oboe, *musical instrument*,
  417
Obscene, *impurity*, 961
Obscurantist, *ignoramus*,
  493
Obscure, *dark*, 421
  unseen, 447
  unintelligible, 519
  style, 571
  to eclipse, 874

* Obscurum per obscurius,
  unintelligibility, 519
  misteaching, 538
Obsecration, *request*, 765
Obsequies, *interment*, 363
Obsequious, *respectful*, 928
  courteous, 894
  servile, 886
Observance, *fulfilment*, 772
  rule, 82
  habit, 613
  practice, 692
  rites, 998
Observatory, *universe*, 318
Observe, *note*, 457
  conform, 926
  remark, 535
Observer, *spectator*, 444
  fighter, 726
Obsess, *preoccupy*, 457
  worry, 830
  haunt, 860
Obsession, *misjudgment*, 481
  fixed idea, 606
Obsolete, *old*, 124
  effete, 645
  vulgar, 851
Obstacle, *physical*, 179
  moral, 706
Obstetrician, *instrumentality*, 631
Obstinate, *stubborn*, 606
  resolute, 604
  prejudiced, 481
Obstreperous, *violent*, 173
  loud, 404
Obstruct, *hinder*, 706
  close, 261
Obtain, *exist*, 1
  acquire, 775
Obtainable, *possibility*, 470
Obtestation, *entreaty*, 765
  injunction, 695
Obtrude, *intervene*, 228
  insert, 300
  obstruct, 706
Obtund, *blunt*, 254
  deaden, 376
  paralyse, 826
Obtuse, *blunt*, 254
  stupid, 499
  dull, 823
Obverse, *front*, 234
Obviate, *hindrance*, 706
Obvious, *visible*, 446
  clear, 518
Ocarina, *musical instru-
ment*, 417
Occasion, *juncture*, 8
  opportunity, 134
  cause, 153
Occasionally, *frequency*, 136

Occidental, *lateral*, 236
Occlusion, *closure*, 261
Occult, *latent*, 526
  hidden, 528
  supernatural, 992
Occupancy, *presence*, 18
  property, 780
  possession, 777
Occupant, *dweller*, 188
  proprietor, 779
Occupation, *business*, 625
  presence, 186
Occupier, *dweller*, 188
  possessor, 779
Occupy, *station*, 71
  place, 186
  attention, 457
Occur, *exist*, 1
  happen, 151
  be present, 186
  to the mind, 451
Ocean, *ocean*, 341
  plenty, 639
Ochlocracy, *authority*, 737
Ochone, *lamentation*, 839
Ochre, *brown*, 433
  orange, 439
O'clock, *time*, 114
Octad, *number*, 98
Octagon, *angularity*, 244
  eight, 98
Octahedron, *angularity*, 244
  eight, 98
Octavo, *book*, 593
Octodecimo, *book*, 593
Octonary, *eight*, 98
Octoroon, *mixture*, 41
Octroi, *tax*, 812
Octuple, *number*, 98
Ocular, *vision*, 441
Oculist, *doctor*, 662
Odalisque, *concubine*, 962
Odd, *exception*, 83
  single, 87
  remaining, 40
  eccentric, 499
  ludicrous, 853
  vulgar, 851
Oddity, *folly*, 499
  laughing-stock, 857
Oddments, *part*, 51
Odds, *inequality*, 28
  chance, 156
  discord, 713
Odds and ends, *portions*, 51
  dispersion, 73
  mixture, 41
Ode, *poetry*, 597
Odin, *god*, 979
Odious, *ugly*, 846
  hateful, 898
  offensive, 830

Odium, *blame*, 932
  disgrace, 874
  hatred, 898
Odontoid, *sharpness*, 253
Odour, *odour*, 398
Odourless, *inodorous*, 399
Odyssey, *journey*, 266
  navigation, 267
Oecology, *organization*, 357
Oecumenical, *generality*, 78
Oedematous, *soft*, 324
  swollen, 194
Oedipus, *expounder*, 524
  answer, 462
Œillade, *ogle*, 441, 902
Off, *distance*, 196
Off-break, *deviation*, 279
Off-chance, *chance*, 621
Off-white, *white*, 430
Offal, *uncleanness*, 653
Offence, *attack*, 716
  guilt, 947
Offend, *affront*, 900
Offensive, *unsavoury*, 395
  fetid, 401
  foul, 653
  displeasing, 830
  distasteful, 867
  obnoxious, 898
Offer, *proposal*, 763
  gift, 784
Offering, *worship*, 990
Offertory, *worship*, 990
Offhand, *spontaneous*, 612, 674
  careless, 460
Office, *function*, 644
  duty, 926
  business, 625
  mart, 799
  room, 191
  bureau, 691
  authority, 737
  worship, 990
Office-bearer, *director*, 694
Officer, *director*, 694
  constable, 965
  master, 745
Official, *authority*, 474, 737
  business, 625
  authorized, 924
Officialese, *verbiage*, 573
Officiate, *conduct*, 692
  act, 625, 680
  religious, 998
Officious, *activity*, 682
Offing, *distance*, 196
  sea, 341
Offish, *unsocial*, 893
  discourteous, 895
Offscourings, *remains*, 40
  dirt, 653

Offscourings, *trash*, 643
Offset, *compensation*, 30
  ridge, 250
Offshoot, *part*, 51
  posterity, 167
Offspring, *posterity*, 167
  produce, 154
Often, *frequency*, 136
Ogee, *curve*, 245
Ogham, *writing*, 590
Ogle, *vision*, 441
  desire, 865
  courtship, 902
Ogpu, *detective*, 461
Ogre, *demon*, 980
  bugbear, 860
  evildoer, 913
Oil, *unctuosity*, 355, 356
  lubricate, 332
  smooth, 255
  flattery, 933
  servility, 886
  bland, 894
  relief, 834
  to assuage, 174
Oilcloth, *covering*, 222
Oiled, *drunk*, 959
Oilskin, *dress*, 225
Okay, *assent*, 488
Old, *oldness*, 124
  veteran, 130
Old-fashioned, *obsolete*, 851
  quaint, 83
Old Harry, Old Horny, Old Nick, *Satan*, 978
Old-timer, *veteran*, 130
Oleaginous, *unctuous*, 355
Olfactory, *odour*, 398
Olid, *fetor*, 401
Oligarchy, *authority*, 737
Olio, *mixture*, 41
Olive, *brown*, 433
Olive-branch, *pacify*, 723
Olive-green, *greenness*, 435
Olla podrida, *mixture*, 41
  miscellany, 72
Olympus, *heaven*, 981
Ombudsman, *mediator*, 724
Omega, *end*, 67
Omelet, *food*, 298
Omen, *omen*, 512
Ominous, *prediction*, 511
  danger, 665
  threat, 909
Omission, *neglect*, 460
  exclusion, 55
  incomplete, 53
  non-fulfilment, 773
  guilt, 947
Omnibus, *vehicle*, 272
Omnifarious, *multiformity*, 81

Omnigenous, *multiform*, 81
Omnipotence, *Deity*, 976
Omnipotent, *powerful*, 157
Omnipresence, *presence*, 186
  Deity, 976
Omniscience, *knowledge*, 490
  divine, 976
*Omnium gatherum, *mixture*, 41
  confusion, 59
  assemblage, 72
Omnivorous, *voracious*, 865
Omphalos, *middle*, 68
  centre, 223
On, *forwards*, 282
On end, *verticality*, 212
* On dit, *publication*, 531
  news, 532
  interlocution, 588
Once, *preterition*, 122
  infrequency, 137
Once for all, *end*, 76, 137
Once-over, *look*, 441
Once upon a time, *different time*, 119
  period, 108
One, *unity*, 87
One by one, *disjunction*, 44
  unity, 87
One-ideaed, *folly*, 499
One-sided, *prejudiced*, 481
  partial, 940
  incorrect, 495
One-step, *dance*, 840
Oneiromancy, *prediction*, 511
Oneness, *unity*, 87
  identity, 13
Onerous, *difficulty*, 704
Onion, *condiment*, 393
Onlooker, *spectator*, 444
Onomasticon, *dictionary*, 562
Onset, *attack*, 716
  beginning, 66
Onslaught, *attack*, 716
Ontology, *existence*, 1
Onus, *duty*, 926
* Onus probandi, *reasoning*, 476
Onward, *progression*, 282
Onyx, *ornament*, 847
Oodles, *greatness*, 31
  plenty, 639
Oof, *money*, 800
Oomph, *charm*, 829
Ooss, *lightness*, 320
  dirt, 653
Ooze, *distil*, 295, 297
  river, 348
  sea, 341

Overweight, *overrate*, 482
    exceed, 33
    influence, 175
Overwhelm, *destroy*, 162
    affect, 824
Overwhelming, *excitability*,
825
Overwork, *fatigue*, 688
Overwrought, *excited*, 825
Ovoid, *rotundity*, 249
Ovule, *circularity*, 247
Owe, *debt*, 806
Owing to, *attribution*, 155
Owl-light, *dimness*, 422
Own, *assent*, 488, 535
    divulge, 529
    possess, 777
Owner, *possessor*, 779
Ownership, *property*, 780
Oxygenate, *air*, 338
Oy, *attention*, 457
Oyez, *hearing*, 418
Oyster, *taciturnity*, 585

P

P.A.Y.E., *tax*, 812
P.B.I., *soldier*, 725
p.m., *evening*, 126
P.O.P., *photograph*, 556
P.O.W., *prisoner*, 754
p.p., *commission*, 755
P.T., *teaching*, 537
    exertion, 686
Pa, *father*, 166
Pabulum, *food*, 298
Pace, *speed*, 274
    step, 266
    measure, 466
Pachydermatous, *insen-*
    sible, 376, 823
Pacific, *concord*, 714, 721
Pacifism, *pacification*, 723
Pacifist, *non-combatant*,
726A
Pacify, *allay*, 174
    compose, 826
    give peace, 723
    forgive, 918
Pack, *to join*, 43
    arrange, 60
    bring close, 197
    locate, 184
    assemblage, 72
Pack-horse, *carrier*, 271
Pack off, *depart*, 293
    recede, 287
    decamp, 671
Pack up, *circumscribe*, 231
    fail, 732
Package, *parcel*, 72

Packet, *parcel*, 72
    ship, 273
Packing-case, *receptacle*,
191
Packthread, *vinculum*, 45
Pact, *agreement*, 769
Pactolus, *wealth*, 803
Pad, *carrier*, 271
    line, 224
    expand, 194
    diffuse, 573
Padding, *softness*, 324
Paddle, *oar*, 267, 633
    to bathe, 337
Paddle-steamer, *ship*, 273
Paddle-wheel, *navigation*,
267
Paddock, *arena*, 181
    enclosure, 232, 752
Padlock, *fastening*, 45
    fetter, 752
Padre, *clergy*, 996
Paean, *thanks*, 916
    rejoicing, 836
    worship, 990
Paediatrics, *remedy*, 662
Paeon, *verse*, 597
Paganism, *heathen*, 984, 996
Page, *attendant*, 746
    of a book, 593
Pageant, *spectacle*, 448
    the drama, 599
    show, 882
Pagoda, *temple*, 1000
Pail, *receptacle*, 191
Pailful, *quantity*, 25
* Paillard, *libertine*, 962
Pain, *physical*, 378
    moral, 828
    penalty, 974
Painful, *painfulness*, 830
Pains, *exertion*, 686
Painstaking, *active*, 682
    laborious, 686
Paint, *coat*, 222
    colour, 428
    adorn, 847
    delineate, 556
    describe, 594
Painter, *artist*, 559
    rope, 45
Painting, *painting*, 556
Pair, *couple*, 89
    similar, 17
Pair off, *average*, 29
Pal, *friend*, 890
Palace, *abode*, 189
Paladin, *courage*, 861
Palaeography, *interpreta-*
    tion, 522
Palaeolithic, *oldness*, 142
Palaeology, *preterition*, 122

Palaeontology, *zoology*, 368
    past, 122
Palaestra, *school*, 542
    arena, 728
    training, 673
Palaestric, *exertion*, 686
Palanquin, *vehicle*, 272
Palatable, *savoury*, 394
    pleasant, 829
Palatal, *letter*, 561
Palate, *taste*, 390
Palatine, *master*, 745
Palaver, *speech*, 582
    colloquy, 588
    council, 696
    nonsense, 497, 517
    loquacity, 584
Pale, *dim*, 422
    colourless, 429
    enclosure, 232
Palfrey, *carrier*, 271
Palimpsest, *substitution*, 147
    writing, 590
Palindrome, *neology*, 563
    inversion, 218
Paling, *prison*, 752
    enclosure, 232
Palingenesis, *restore*, 660
Palinode, *denial*, 536
    recantation, 607
Palisade, *prison*, 752
    enclosure, 232
Pall, *funeral*, 363
    disgust, 395, 867
    satiate, 869
Palladium, *defence*, 664, 717
Pallet, *support*, 215
Palliasse, *support*, 215
Palliate, *mend*, 658
    relieve, 834
    moderate, 174
    extenuate, 937
Palliative, *remedy*, 662
Pallid, *achromatism*, 429
Palling, *unsavouriness*, 395
Pallium, *dress*, 225
    canonicals, 999
Pally, *friendship*, 888
Palm, *trophy*, 733
    glory, 873
    laurel, 877
    deceive, 545
    impose upon, 486
Palmer, *traveller*, 268
Palmist, *fortune-teller*, 513
Palmistry, *prediction*, 511
Palmy, *prosperous*, 734
    halcyon, 827, 829
Palpable, *tactile*, 379
    tangible, 316
    obvious, 446, 525
    intelligible, 518

Palpitate, *tremble,* 315
  emotion, 821
  fear, 860
Palsy, *disease,* 655
  weakness, 160
  incapacity, 158
  insensibility, 376, 823
Palter, *falsehood,* 544
  shift, 605
  elude, 773
Paltry, *mean,* 940
  despicable, 643, 930
  little, 32
Paludal, *marsh,* 345
Pampas, *plain,* 344
Pamper, *indulge,* 954
  gorge, 957
Pampero, *wind,* 349
Pamphlet, *book,* 593
Pamphleteer, *writing,* 590
  dissertation, 595
Pan, *receptacle,* 191
  face, 234, 448
Panacea, *remedy,* 662
* Panache, *plume,* 256
  ornament, 847
Pandect, *code,* 963
  compendium, 596
  erudition, 490
Pandemic, *insalubrity,* 657
Pandemonium, *hell,* 982
  disorder, 59
Pander, *flatter,* 933
  indulge, 954
  mediate, 631
  help, 707
Pandora, *evil,* 619
Paned, *variegation,* 440
Panegyric, *approbation,* 931
Panel, *list,* 86
  partition, 228
  accused, 938
  legal, 967
* Panem et circenses, *giving,*
  784
Pang, *physical,* 378
  moral, 828
Panhandler, *tramp,* 876
Panic, *fear,* 860
Pannier, *receptacle,* 191
Panoply, *defence,* 717
Panopticon, *prison,* 752
Panorama, *view,* 448
  painting, 556
Panoramic, *general,* 78
Pansophy, *knowledge,* 490
Pansy, *effeminate,* 374
Pant, *breathless,* 688
  desire, 865
  agitation, 821
Pantaloon, *buffoon,* 844
  dress, 225

Pantechnicon, *vehicle,* 272
Pantheism, *heathen,* 984
Pantheon, *temple,* 1000
Pantograph, *imitation,* 19
Pantomime, *sign,* 550
  language, 560
  drama, 599
Pantry, *receptacle,* 191
Pap, *pulp,* 354
  teat, 250
Papa, *father,* 166
Papacy, *churchdom,* 995
Paper, *writing,* 590
  book, 593
  record, 551
  white, 430
Paperback, *book,* 593
Papilla, *convexity,* 250
Papoose, *infant,* 129
Pappy, *semiliquidity,* 352
Par, *equality,* 27
Parable, *metaphor,* 521
  analogy, 464
  story, 594
Parabolic, *metaphor,* 521
  curve, 245
Parachronism, *anachronism,* 115
Parachute, *refuge,* 666
Paraclete, *Deity,* 976
Parade, *walk,* 189
  ostentation, 882
Paradigm, *prototype,* 22
  example, 80
Paradise, *heaven,* 981
  bliss, 827
Paradox, *obscurity,* 519
  absurdity, 497
  mystery, 528
  enigma, 533
Paragon, *perfection,* 650
  saint, 948
  glory, 873
Paragraph, *phrase,* 566
  part, 51
  article, 593
Paralipsis, *neglect,* 460
Parallax, *distance,* 196
Parallel, *position,* 216
  similarity, 17
  to imitate, 19
  agreement, 23
  comparison, 464
Parallelepiped, *angularity,*
  244
Parallelogram, *angularity,*
  244
Paralogism, *sophistry,* 477
Paralyse, *weaken,* 160
  benumb, 381
  deaden, 823
  insensibility, 376

Paralyse, *impassivity,* 823
  stillness, 265
  disqualify, 158
  disease, 655
Paramount, *essential,* 642
  in degree, 33
  authority, 737
Paramour, *love,* 897
Paranoia, *insanity,* 503,
  504
Parapet, *defence,* 717
Paraph, *writing,* 590
Paraphernalia, *machinery,*
  633
  materials, 635
  property, 780
Paraphrase, *interpretation,*
  522, 524
  phrase, 566
  imitation, 19, 21
Paraplectic, *disease,* 655
Parapsychology, *occult,* 992
Parasite, *flatterer,* 935
  servile, 886
  follow, 88
Parasol, *shade,* 424
Paratrooper, *fighter,* 726
Paravane, *defence,* 717
Parboil, *calefaction,* 384
Parcel, *group,* 72
  portion, 51
Parcel out, *arrange,* 60
  allot, 786
Parch, *dry,* 340
  heat, 382
  bake, 384
Parchment, *manuscript,*
  590
  record, 551
Pardon, *forgiveness,* 918
Pardonable, *vindication,*
  937
Pare, *scrape,* 38, 226, 331
  shorten, 201
  decrease, 36
Paregoric, *salubrity,* 656
Parenchyma, *texture,* 329
Parent, *paternity,* 166
Parentage, *kindred,* 11
Parenthesis, *interjacence,*
  228
  discontinue, 70
Parenthetical, *irrelation,* 10
  occasion, 134
* Par excellence, *greatness,*
  31
  superiority, 33
* Pari passu, *equality,* 27
Pariah, *commonalty,* 876
  outcast, 892
Paring, *part,* 51
  smallness, 32

Parish, *region*, 181
Parishioner, *laity*, 997
Parity, *equality*, 27
Park, *plain*, 344
  vegetation, 367
  amusement, 840
  artillery, 727
  locate, 184
Parlance, *speech*, 582
* Parlementaire, *messenger*, 534
Parley, *talk*, 588
  mediation, 724
Parliament, *council*, 696
Parlour, *room*, 191
Parlour-car, *vehicle*, 272
Parlourmaid, *servant*, 746
Parnassus, *poetry*, 597
Parochial, *regional*, 181
  ignoble, 876
Parody, *imitation*, 19
  copy, 21
  travesty, 856
  misinterpret, 523
Parole, *promise*, 768
Paronomasia, *pun*, 563
Paronymous, *word*, 562
Paroxysm, *violence*, 173
  emotion, 825
  anger, 900
Parquetry, *variegation*, 440
Parricide, *killing*, 361
Parrot, *imitation*, 19
  loquacity, 584
  repetition, 104
Parry, *avert*, 623
  confute, 479
  defend, 717
Parse, *grammar*, 567
Parsee, *religions*, 984
Parsimony, *parsimony*, 819
Parson, *clergy*, 996
Parsonage, *temple*, 1000
Part, *portion*, 51
  component, 56
  to diverge, 291
  to divide, 44
  business, 625
  function, 644
Part with, *relinquish*, 782
  give, 784
Partake, *participation*, 778
Parterre, *agriculture*, 371
* Parti, *adolescence*, 131
* Parti pris, *prejudgment*, 481
  predetermination, 611
Partial, *unequal*, 28
  special, 79
  one-sided, 481
  unjust, 923
  love, 897

Partial, *friendship*, 888
  desire, 865
  erroneous, 495
  smallness, 32
  harmonic, 413
* Particeps criminis, *auxil-iary*, 711
  bad man, 949
Participation, *participation*, 778
  co-operation, 709
Particle, *quantity*, 32
  size, 193
Particoloured, *variegation*, 440
Particular, *special*, 79
  event, 151
  careful, 459
  capricious, 608
  fastidious, 868
  item, 51
  detail, 79
  description, 594
Particularly, *greatness*, 31
Parting, *disjunction*, 44
Partisan, *auxiliary*, 711
  friend, 891
  fighter, 726
Partition, *allot*, 51, 786
  wall, 228
Partner, *auxiliary*, 711
Partnership, *participation*, 778
  company, 797
  companionship, 88
Parts, *intellect*, 450
  wisdom, 498
  talents, 698
Party, *assemblage*, 72
  association, 712
  society, 892
  merry-making, 840
  special, 79
Party-wall, *interjacence*, 228
Parvenu, *upstart*, 876
  intruder, 57
  successful, 734
* Pas, *rank*, 873
  precedence, 62
  term, 71
Pash, *love*, 897
Pasha, *master*, 745
  noble, 875
Pasquinade, *satire*, 932
Pass, *move*, 264
  move out, 295
  move through, 302
  exceed, 303
  be superior, 33
  happen, 151
  lapse, 122

Pass, *vanish*, 449
  passage, 260
  gap, 198
  defile, 203
  way, 627
  difficulty, 704
  conjuncture, 8
  forgive, 918
  thrust, 716
  passport, 760
  time, 106
Pass away, *cease*, 2, 142
Pass-book, *accounts*, 811
Pass by, *disregard*, 929
Pass for, *falsehood*, 544
Pass in the mind, *thought*, 451
Pass over, *disregard*, 458
  neglect, 460
  forgive, 918
  exclude, 55
  exempt, 927A
  traverse, 302
Pass the time, *duration*, 106
Pass through, *experience*, 151
Passable, *imperfection*, 651
  tolerable, 736
Passage, *passage*, 302
  motion, 264
  opening, 260
  eventuality, 151
  method, 627
  transfer, 270
  text, 593
  part, 50
  act, 680
  assault, 720
* Passage d'armes, *conten-tion*, 720
* Passé, *age*, 128
  deterioration, 659
Passe-partout, 462
  instrumentality, 631
Passenger, *traveller*, 268
  hindrance, 706
* Passim, *dispersion*, 73
  situation, 183
Passing, *exceeding*, 33
  transient, 111
  greatness, 31
Passion, *emotion*, 820, 821
  desire, 865
  love, 879
  anger, 900
Passionate, *warm*, 825
  irascible, 901
Passionless, *insensibility*, 823
Passive, *inert*, 172
  inactive, 681
  submissive, 743

Pedantic, *half-learned,* 491
 style, 577
Peddle, *trifle,* 683
 sell, 796
Pedestal, *support,* 215
Pedestrian, *traveller,* 268
 dull, 842, 843
 style, 573
Pedicel, *pendency,* 214
Pedigree, *ancestry,* 155, 166
 continuity, 69
Pediment, *capital,* 210
 base, 215
Pedlar, *merchant,* 797
Peduncle, *pendency,* 214
Peek, *look,* 441
Peel, *skin,* 222
 to uncover, 226
Peeler, *police,* 664
Peep, *vision,* 441
Peep-hole, *opening,* 260
 view, 441
Peep out, *visibility,* 446
Peep-show, *spectacle,* 448
Peeping Tom, *curiosity,* 455
Peer, *equal,* 27
 nobleman, 875
 pry, 441
 inquire, 461
 appear, 446
Peerage, *list,* 86
Peerless, *perfect,* 650
 excellent, 648, 873
 superior, 33
 virtuous, 944
Peeve, *irritate,* 900
Peevish, *cross,* 895
 irascible, 901
Peg, *degree,* 26, 71
 project, 250
 hang, 214
 jog on, 266
 drink, 298
 intoxicant, 959
Peg away, *persist,* 143
 activity, 682
Peg out, *die,* 360
Pegasus, *imagination,* 515
* Peine forte et dure,
 punishment, 972
Pejoration, *deterioration,*
 659
Pelagic, *ocean,* 341
Pelerine, *dress,* 225
Pelf, *money,* 803
 materials, 635
 gain, 775
Pellet, *rotundity,* 249
 remedy, 662
Pellicle, *film,* 205
 skin, 222
Pell-mell, *disorder,* 59

Pellucid, *transparency,* 425
Pelt, *skin,* 222
 throw, 276
 attack, 716
 beat, 972
Pen, *surround,* 231
 enclose, 232
 restrain, 751
 imprison, 752
 draw, 559
 write, 590
Pen-and-ink, *drawing,* 556
Pen-name, *misnomer,* 565
Penal, *punishment,* 972
Penalty, *penalty,* 974
Penance, *atonement,* 952
 rite, 998
 penalty, 974
* Penchant, *inclination,* 865
 love, 897
Pencil, *bundle,* 72
 of light, 420
 artist, 556, 559, 590
Pencraft, *writing,* 590
Pendant, *adjunct,* 39
 flag, 550
 pendency, 214
 match, 17
Pendent, *during,* 106
 hanging, 214
 uncertain, 485
* Pendente lite, *warfare,*
 722
 lawsuit, 969
Pending, *duration,* 106
 lateness, 133
 uncertain, 475
Pendulous, *pendency,* 214
Pendulum, *clock,* 114
 oscillation, 314
Penetralia, *interiority,* 221
 secret, 533
Penetrate, *fill,* 186
 influence, 175
Penetrating, *affecting,* 821
Penetration, *ingress,* 294
 passage, 302
 discernment, 441
 sagacity, 498
Penfold, *enclosure,* 232
Peninsula, *land,* 342
Penitent, *penitence,* 950
Penitentiary, *prison,* 752
Penmanship, *writing,* 590
Penniless, *poverty,* 804
Pennon, *indication,* 550
Penny-a-liner, *writer,* 590
Penny-farthing, *bicycle,* 266
Pennyworth, *price,* 812
* Penseroso, *dejection,* 837
Pensile, *pendency,* 214
Pension, *wealth,* 803, 810

Pensioner, *servant,* 746
 recipient, 785
Pensive, *thoughtful,* 451
 sad, 837
Pent, *imprisoned,* 754
Pentad, *five,* 98
Pentagon, *angularity,* 244
 five, 98
Pentahedron, *angularity,*
 244
 five, 98
Pentatonic, *melody,* 413
Penthouse, *building,* 189
Penultimate, *end,* 67
Penumbra, *darkness,*
 421, 424
Penurious, *parsimony,* 819
Penury, *poverty,* 804
 scantiness, 640
People, *man,* 373
 inhabitant, 188
 commonalty, 876
 to colonize, 184
Pep, *energy,* 171, 682
 vigour, 574
Pep-talk, *speech,* 582
Pepper, *hot,* 171
 pungent, 392
 condiment, 393
 attack, 716
Peppercorn, *unimportance,*
 643
Peppery, *irascibility,* 901
Peptic, *remedy,* 662
* Per contra, *contrariety,* 14
 opposition, 708
* Per procurationem, *com-*
 mission, 755
* Per saltum, *discontinuity,*
 70
 transientness, 111
 instantaneity, 113
* Per se, *unity,* 87
Peradventure, *chance,* 156
 possibly, 470
 uncertainty, 475
Perambulate, *journey,* 266
Perceivable, *visible,* 446
Percentage, *proportion,* 84
 discount, 813
Perceptible, *visibility,* 446
Perception, *idea,* 453
 of touch, 380
Perceptivity, *sensibility,*
 375
Perch, *support,* 215
 to alight, 186
 tall, 206
 habitation, 189
Perchance, *chance,* 156
 possibly, 470
Percipience, *intellect,* 450

INDEX

Pertinent, *relevant*, 476
  applicable, 646
Perturb, *derange*, 61
  agitate, 315
  emotion, 821
  excitability, 825
  ferment, 171
Peruke, *dress*, 225
Peruse, *learning*, 539
  examine, 461
Pervade, *extend*, 186
  affect, 821
Perverse, *crotchety*, 608
  difficult, 704
  wayward, 895
Perversion, *injury*, 659
  sophistry, 477
  falsehood, 544
  misinterpretation, 523
  misteaching, 538
  impiety, 988
Pervert, *apostate*, 144, 941
  turncoat, 607
  blasphemer, 988
Pervicacious, *obstinacy*, 606
* Pervigilium, *activity*, 682
Pervious, *opening*, 260
Pessimism, *dejection*, 837
  hopelessness, 859
Pest, *bane*, 663
  badness, 649
  bother, 830
Pest-house, *remedy*, 662
Pester, *painfulness*, 830
Pestiferous, *insalubrity*, 657
Pestilent, *badness*, 649
  poison, 663
Pestle, *pulverulence*, 330
Pet, *plaything*, 840
  favourite, 899
  passion, 900
  to love, 897
  to fondle, 902
Petard, *arms*, 727
Peter out, *end*, 67
Peterhead, *prison*, 752
* Petit-maître, *fop*, 854
* Petite, *little*, 193
* Petite amie, *mistress*, 962
* Petitio principii, *sophistry*, 477
Petition, *ask*, 765
  pray, 990
Petitioner, *petitioner*, 767
* Petits soins, *courtesy*, 894
  courtship, 903
* Pétri, *feeling*, 821
Petrify, *dense*, 321
  hard, 323
  affright, 860
  astonish, 870
  thrill, 824

Petroleum, *oil*, 356
* Pétroleur, *incendiary*, 384
Petronel, *arms*, 727
Petticoat, *dress*, 225
Pettifogger, *lawyer*, 968
Pettifogging, *discord*, 713
  hair-splitting, 477
Pettish, *irascibility*, 895, 901
Petty, *in degree*, 32
  in size, 193
Petulant, *insolent*, 885
  snappish, 895
  angry, 900
  irascible, 901
Pew, *temple*, 1000
Phaeton, *carriage*, 272
Phalanx, *army*, 726
  party, 712
  assemblage, 72
Phantasm, *unreal*, 4
  appearance, 448
  delusion, 443
Phantasmagoria, *optical*, 445
Phantom, *vision*, 448
  unreal, 4
  imaginary, 515
Pharisaical, *falsehood*, 544
Pharmacology, *remedy*, 662
Pharmacy, *remedy*, 662
Pharos, *warning*, 668
  indication, 550
Phase, *aspect*, 8
  appearance, 448
  change, 144
  form, 240
Phenomenal, *great*, 31
  apparent, 448
  wonderful, 870
Phenomenon, *appearance*, 448
  event, 151
  prodigy, 872
Phial, *receptacle*, 191
Phidias, *artist*, 559
Philanderer, *flirt*, 902
Philanthropy, *philanthropy*, 910
Philatelist, *collector*, 775
Philibeg, *dress*, 225
Philippic, *disapproval*, 932
Philistine, *uncultured*, 491, 493
Phillumenist, *collector*, 775
Philology, *grammar*, 567
Philomath, *scholar*, 492
  sage, 500
Philomel, *musician*, 416
Philosopher, *scholar*, 492
Philosophy, *calmness*, 826
  thought, 451
  knowledge, 490

Philtre, *charm*, 993
Phiz, *appearance*, 448
Phlebotomy, *ejection*, 297
Phlegethon, *hell*, 982
Phlegm, *insensibility*, 823
  semiliquid, 352
Phoenix, *prodigy*, 872
  exception, 83
  paragon, 650
  saint, 948
  renovation, 163, 660
Phonetics, *sound*, 402
  speech, 580
Phoney, *false*, 495, 544
Phonic, *sound*, 402
Phonograph, *musical instrument*, 417
  hearing, 418
Phonography, *shorthand*, 590
Phosphorescent, *light*, 420, 423
Photo-lithograph, *engraving*, 558
Photogenic, *beauty*, 845
Photograph, *copy*, 21
  representation, 554
Photography, *painting*, 556
Photogravure, *engraving*, 558
Photology, *light*, 420
Photometer, *optical instrument*, 445
Photostat, *copy*, 21
Phrase, *phrase*, 566
Phrase-monger, *floridity*, 577
Phraseology, *style*, 569
Phratry, *class*, 75
Phrenetic, *see* Frantic
Phrenitis, *insanity*, 503
Phrenology, *intellect*, 450
Phrontistery, *room*, 191
Phylactery, *spell*, 993
Phylum, *class*, 75
Physic, *remedy*, 662
  to cure, 660
Physical, *materiality*, 316
Physician, *advice*, 695
Physics, *materiality*, 316
Physiognomy, *appearance*, 448
  face, 234
Physiology, *life*, 359
Physique, *substance*, 3
  animality, 364
Phytography, *botany*, 369
Phytology, *botany*, 369
Piacular, *atonement*, 952
* Pianissimo, *faint*, 405
Pianist, *musician*, 416
Piano, *instrument*, 417

Pneumatology, *intellect*, 450
Poach, *steal*, 791, 964
Poacher, *thief*, 792
Poachy, *marsh*, 345
Pocket, *pouch*, 191
  to place, 184
  take, 789
  receive, 785
  endure, 826
  receipts, 810
  treasury, 802
  diminutive, 193
Pococurante, *indifferent*,
  603
Pod, *receptacle*, 191
Podgy, *broad*, 202
  short, 200
Poem, *poetry*, 597
Poet, *poetry*, 597
  writer, 593
Poetic, *metrical*, 597
Poignant, *physical*, 171
  moral, 821
  vigorous, 574
Point, *condition*, 8
  degree, 26
  term, 71
  place, 182
  question, 461
  topic, 454
  prominence, 250
  mark, 550
  intention, 620
  wit, 842
  style, 574
  punctilio, 939
  speck, 193
  poignancy, 171
  sharp, 253
Point-blank, *direction*, 278
* Point d'appui, *influence*,
  175
Point of view, *aspect*, 441
  idea, 453
  relation, 9
Point to, *indicate*, 550
  show, 525
  mean, 516
  predict, 511
Point-to-point, *direction*,
  278
  chase, 622
Pointed, *explicit*, 535
  great, 31
Pointer, *index*, 550
  hint, 527
Pointillism, *variegation*,
  440
Pointillist, *artist*, 559
Pointless, *dullness*, 843
  motiveless, 616
Poise, *balance*, 27

Poise, *measure*, 466
  composure, 826
Poison, *bane*, 663
  to injure, 659
Poisonous, *deleterious*, 657
  injurious, 649
Poke, *push*, 276
  project, 250
  pocket, 191
Poker, *stiff*, 323
Polacca, *ship*, 273
Polar, *summit*, 210
Polariscope, *optical*, 445
Polarity, *duality*, 89
  antagonism, 179, 237
Polder, *land*, 342
Pole, *lever*, 633
  axis, 223
  summit, 210
  tallness, 206
Pole-axe, *arms*, 727
Pole-star, *indication*, 550
  sharpness, 253
Polecat, *fetor*, 401
Polemarch, *master*, 745
Polemics, *discussion*, 476
  discord, 713
Polemoscope, *optical*, 445
Police, *jurisdiction*, 965
  safety, 664
Policy, *plan*, 626
  conduct, 692
  skill, 698
Polish, *smooth*, 255
  to rub, 331
  urbanity, 894
  furbish, 658
  beauty, 845
  ornament, 847
  taste, 850
Politburo, *council*, 696
Politeness, *manners*, 852
  urbanity, 894
  respect, 928
Politic, *wise*, 498
  expedient, 646
  skilful, 698
  cautious, 864
  cunning, 702
Politician, *statesman*, 745
Politics, *government*, 693
Polity, *plan*, 626
  conduct, 692
  community, 372
Polka, *dance*, 840
Poll, *count*, 85
  choice, 609
  crop, 201
  parrot, 584
Pollard, *clip*, 201.
Pollute, *corrupt*, 659
  soil, 653

Pollute, *disgrace*, 874
  dishonour, 940
Pollution, *vice*, 945
  disease, 655
Poltergeist, *demon*, 980
Poltroon, *cowardice*, 862
Polychord, *musical*, 417
Polychromatic, *variegation*,
  440
Polygamy, *marriage*, 903
Polyglot, *word*, 562
  interpretation, 522
Polygon, *figure*, 244
  building, 189
Polygraphy, *writing*, 590
Polygyny, *marriage*, 903
Polymorphic, *multiform*, 81
Polyp, *convexity*, 250
Polyphonism, *voice*, 580
Polyphony, *melody*, 413
Polysyllable, *letter*, 561
Polytechnic, *school*, 542
Polytheism, *heathen*, 984
Pomade, *oil*, 356
Pomatum, *oil*, 356
Pommel, *rotundity*, 249
Pommy, *stranger*, 57
  greenhorn, 674
Pomp, *ostentation*, 882
Pom-pom, *gun*, 727
Pomposity, *pride*, 878
  style, 577
Ponce, *libertine*, 962
Poncho, *dress*, 225
Pond, *lake*, 343
Ponder, *thought*, 451
Ponderation, *judgment*, 480
Ponderous, *gravity*, 319
  style, 577
Pong, *stink*, 501
Poniard, *arms*, 727
* Pons asinorum, *difficulty*,
  704
Pontiff, *clergy*, 996
Pontifical, *churchdom*, 995
Pontificals, *dress*, 225
Pony, *carrier*, 271
  money, 800
Pooh-pooh, *trifle*, 643
  contempt, 930
  to make light of, 483
Pool, *lake*, 343
  participation, 778
Poop, *rear*, 235
  fool, 501
Poor, *indigent*, 804
  afflicted, 828
  weak, 160
  insufficient, 640
  trifling, 643
  contemptible, 930
  style, 575

Pot-companion, *friend*, 890
Pot-hooks, *writing*, 590
Pot-hunting, *acquisition*, 775
Pot-luck, *food*, 298
Pot-pourri, *mixture*, 41
  fragrance, 400
  music, 415
Pot-valiant, *drunk*, 959
Potable, *drinkable*, 298
Potation, *drink*, 296
Potency, *power*, 157
Potentate, *master*, 745
Potential, *virtual*, 2
  possible, 470
  power, 157
Pother, *to worry*, 830
  fuss, 682
  confusion, 59
Pottage, *food*, 298
Potter, *idle*, 683
Pottle, *receptacle*, 191
Potty, *mad*, 503
* Pou sto, *influence*, 175
Pouch, *receptacle*, 191
  insert, 184
  receive, 785
  take, 789
  acquire, 775
Pouffe, *support*, 215
Poultice, *soft*, 354
  remedy, 662
Pounce upon, *taking*, 789
Pound, *bruise*, 330
  mix, 41
  enclose, 232
  imprison, 752
Poundage, *discount*, 813
Pounds, *money*, 800
Pour, *egress*, 295
Pour out, *eject*, 185, 297, 248
* Pour rire, *ridicule*, 853
* Pourboire, *giving*, 784
  expenditure, 809
* Pourparler, *discussion*, 476
Pout, *sullen*, 895
  sad, 837
Poverty, *indigence*, 804
  scantiness, 640
  trifle, 643
Powder, *pulverulence*, 330
  ornament, 845, 847
Powder-box, *receptacle*, 191
Power, *efficacy*, 157
  physical energy, 171
  authority, 737
  spirit, 977
  much, 31
  multitude, 102
  numerical, 84
  of style, 574

Powerful, *strength*, 159
Powerless, *weakness*, 160
Pow-wow, *conference*, 588
Pox, *disease*, 655
  expletive, 908
Praam, *ship*, 273
Practicable, *possible*, 470
  easy, 705
Practical, *activity*, 672
  agency, 170
Practice, *act*, 680
  conduct, 692
  use, 677
  habit, 613
  teaching, 537
  rule, 80
  proceeding, 626
Practise, *deceive*, 645
Practised, *skill*, 698
Practitioner, *agent*, 690
* Praecognita, *evidence*, 467
Praenomen, *name*, 564
Praetor, *master*, 745
Pragmatical, *pedantic*, 855
  vain, 880
Prairie, *plain*, 344
  plaint, 367
Praise, *commendation*, 931
  thanks, 916
  worship, 990
Praiseworthy, *commendable*, 931
  virtuous, 944
Prance, *dance*, 315
  swagger, 878
  move, 266
Prang, *bomb*, 162, 716, 732
Prank, *caprice*, 608
  amusement, 840
  vagary, 856
  to adorn, 845
Prate, *babble*, 584, 588
Prattle, *talk*, 582, 588
Pravity, *badness*, 649
Pray, *request*, 765
Prayer, *request*, 765
  worship, 990
Preach, *teach*, 537
  speech, 582
  predication, 998
Preacher, *clergy*, 996
Preachify, *speech*, 582
Preamble, *precursor*, 64
  speech, 582
Preapprehension, *misjudgment*, 481
Prebendary, *clergy*, 996
Prebendaryship, *churchdom*, 995
Precarious, *uncertain*, 475
  perilous, 665
Precatory, *request*, 764

Precaution, *care*, 459
  expedient, 626
  preparation, 673
Precede, *in order*, 62
  in time, 116
  lead, 280
Precedence, *rank*, 873
Precedent, *rule*, 80
  verdict, 969
Precentor, *clergy*, 996
  director, 694
Precept, *maxim*, 697
  order, 741
  rule, 80
  permit, 760
  decree, 963
Preceptor, *teacher*, 540
Precession, *in oder*, 62
  in motion, 280
* Précieuse ridicule, *affectation*, 855
  style, 577
Precincts, *environs*, 227
  boundary, 233
  region, 181
  place, 182
Preciosity, *affectation*, 855
Precious, *excellent*, 648
  valuable, 814
  beloved, 897
Precipice, *slope*, 217
  vertical, 212
  danger, 667
Precipitancy, *haste*, 274, 684
Precipitate, *rash*, 863
  impulse, 612
  early, 132
  transient, 111
  to sink, 308
  refuse, 653
  consolidate, 321
  swift, 274
Precipitous, *obliquity*, 217
Précis, *compendium*, 596
Precise, *exact*, 494
  definite, 518
Precisely, *assent*, 488
Precisian, *formalist*, 855
  taste, 850
Preclude, *hindrance*, 706
Precocious, *early*, 132
  immature, 674
Precognition, *foresight*, 510
  knowledge, 490
Preconception, *misjudgment*, 481
Preconcert, *preparation*, 673
  predetermine, 611
Preconcerted, *will*, 600
Precursor, *forerunner*, 64
  precession, 280
  harbinger, 512

Precursory, *in order, 62*
  in time, 116
Predacious, *stealing,* 791
Predatory, *stealing,* 791
Predecessor, *in order,* 64
  in time, 116
Predeliberation, *care,* 459
Predestination, *fate,* 152
  necessity, 601
Predetermination, *predeter-mination,* 611
Predetermined, *will,* 600
  predetermination, 611
Predial, *property,* 780
Predicament, *situation,* 8
  class, 75
Predicate, *affirmation,* 535
Predication, *rite,* 998
Prediction, *prediction,* 511
Predilection, *love,* 897
  desire, 865
  choice, 609
  prejudice, 481
  inclination, 602
  affections, 820
Predisposition, *proneness,*
  602
  tendency, 176
  motive, 615
  affection, 820
  preparation, 673
Predominance, *influence,*
  175
  inequality, 28
  superiority, 33
Pre-eminent, *famed,* 873
  superior, 31, 33
Pre-emption, *purchase,* 795
Pre-emptive, *early,* 132
Preen, *adorn,* 845
Pre-establish, *preparation,*
  673
Pre-examine, *inquiry,* 461
Pre-exist, *priority,* 116
  past, 122
Prefab, *abode,* 189
Preface, *precedence,* 62
  precursor, 64
  front, 234
Prefatory, *in order, 62,* 64
  in time, 106
Prefect, *ruler,* 745
  deputy, 759
Prefecture, *authority,* 737
Prefer, *choose,* 609
  a petition, 765
Preferment, *improvement,*
  658
  ecclesiastical, 995
Prefiguration, *indication,*
  prediction, 510   [550

Prefix, *precedence,* 62
  precursor, 64
Pregnant, *productive,* 161,
  168
  predicting, 511
  important, 642
  concise, 572
Prehension, *taking,* 789
Prehistoric, *preterition,* 122
  old, 124
Prejudge, *misjudgment,* 481
Prejudice, *evil,* 619
  detriment, 649
Prelacy, *churchdom,* 995
Prelate, *clergy,* 996
Prelection, *teaching,* 537
Prelector, *teacher,* 540
Preliminary, *preceding, 62*
  precursor, 64
  priority, 116
Prelude, *preceding, 62*
  precursor, 64
  priority, 116
  music, 415
Prelusory, *preceding, 62*
  precursor, 64
  priority, 116
Premature, *earliness,* 132
Premeditate, *intend,* 630
  predetermine, 611
Premeditated, *will,* 600
Premier, *director,* 694,
  759
Premiership, *authority,* 737
Premise, *prefix,* 62
  precursor, 64
  announce, 511
Premises, *ground,* 182
  evidence, 467
Premisses, *see* Premises
Premium, *reward,* 973
  receipt, 810
Premonition, *warning,* 668
Prenticeship, *preparation,*
  673
Preoccupied, *inattentive,*
  458
Preoccupy, *possess,* 777
  the attention, 457
Preoption, *choice,* 609
Preordain, *necessity,* 601
Preordination, *destiny,* 152
Preparatory, *precedence,* 62
Prepare, *mature,* 673
  plan, 626
  instruct, 537
Prepared, *ready,* 698
Prepay, *expenditure,* 809
Prepense, *advised,* 611
  spontaneous, 600
  intended, 620
Prepollence, *power,* 157

Preponderant, *unequal,* 28
  superior, 33
  important, 642
  influential, 175
Prepossessing, *pleasurable-ness,* 829
Prepossession, *misjudgment,*
  481
Preposterous, *in degree,* 31
  ridiculous, 853
  absurd, 497, 499
Prepotency, *power,* 157
Pre-Raphaelite, *artist,* 559
Prerequisite, *requirement,*
  630
Prerogative, *right,* 924
  authority, 737
Presage, *omen,* 512
  to predict, 511
Presbyopic, *dim-sighted-ness,* 443
Presbytery, *parsonage,* 1000
Prescient, *foresight,* 510
Prescribe, *order,* 741
  direct, 693
  entitle, 924
  duty, 926
Prescript, *decree,* 741
  precept, 697
  law, 963
Prescription, *remedy,* 662
  convention, 613
Prescriptive, *dueness,* 924
Presence, *in space,* 186
  existence, 1
  appearance, 448
  carriage, 852
Presence of mind, *caution,*
  864
Present, *in time,* 118
  in place, 186
  in memory, 505
  give, 784
  offer, 763
  show, 525
  represent, 554
  introduce, 894
  to the mind, 451
Presentable, *fashion,* 852
  beauty, 845
Presentation, *offer,* 763
  manifestation, 525
  gift, 784
  celebration, 883
Presentiment, *prejudgment,*
  481
  instinct, 477
  foresight, 510
Presently, *soon,* 111, 132
Preservation, *continuance,*
  141
  conservation, 670

Preserve, *sweet*, 396
Preses, *director*, 694
Preside, *command*, **737**
  direct, 693
Presidency, *authority*, **737**
President, *master*, 694, 745
Presidium, *council*, 696
Press, *hasten*, 132, 684
  beg, 765; *compel*, 744
  offer, 763
  weigh, 319
  solicit, 615
  crowd, 72
  closet, 191; *velocity*, 274
Press in, *insertion*, 300
Pressing, *urgent*, 642
Pressman, *writer*, 590
  printer, 591
Pressure, *weight*, 319
  influence, 175
  urgency, 642
  affliction, 830
Prestidigitation, *deception*,
    545
Prestige, *attractiveness*, 829
  repute, 873
Prestigious, *delusive*, 545
* Prestissimo, *music*, 415
* Presto, *transientness*, 111
  velocity, 274
  music, 415
Presume, *suppose*, 514
  hope, 858
  believe, 484
  prejudge, 481
  take liberties, 885
Presumption, *probable*, 472
  right, 924
  rashness, 863
  insolence, 885
Presumptive, *conjectural*,
    514
  rightful, 924
  probable, 472
  indicative, 467
Presumptuous, *rash*, 863
  insolent, 885
Presuppose, *prejudge*, 481
  conjecture, 514
Presurmise, *prejudge*, 481
  conjecture, 514
Pretence, *untruth*, 544, 546
  excuse, 617
Pretend, *simulate*, 544
  assert, 535
Pretender, *boaster*, 884
  claimant, 924
  deceiver, 548
Pretension, *claim*, **924**
  affectation, 855
  vanity, 880, 884

Pretension, *ostentation*, 882
Preterition, *preterition*, 122
Preterlapsed, *preterition*,
    122
Pretermit, *omit*, 460
Preternatural, *irregular*, 83
Pretext, *excuse*, 617
  falsehood, 546
Pretty, *beauty*, 845
Pretty well, *much*, 31
  imperfect, 651
Prevail, *influence*, 175
  be general, 78
  be superior, 33
  exist, 1
Prevail upon, *motive*, 615
Prevailing, *preponderating*,
    28
  usual, 82
Prevalence, *influence*, 175
  usage, 613
  superiority, 33
Prevaricate, *falsehood*, 544
  equivocate, 520
* Prévenance, *courtesy*, 894
Prevenient, *precedence*, 62
Prevention, *hindrance*, 706
  counteraction, 179
  prejudice, 481
Previous, *in order*, 62
  in time, 116
Prevision, *foresight*, 510
Prey, *food*, 298
  booty, 793
  object, 620
  victim, 828
Price, *money*, **812**
  value, 648
Priceless, *goodness*, 648
Prick, *sharpness*, 253
  to incite, 615
  sensation, 380
  pain, 378, 830
Prick off, *weed*, 103
Prick up, *raise*, 212
Prickle, *sharpness*, 253
  sensation, 380
Pride, *loftiness*, 878
Priest, *clergy*, 996
Priest-ridden, *impiety*, 988
Priestcraft, *churchdom*, 995
Priesthood, *clergy*, 996
Prig, *affectation*, 855
  to steal, 791
Priggish, *affectation*, 855
  vanity, 880
Prim, *affectation*, 855, 878
Prima donna, *the drama*,
    599
  repute, 873
* Prima facie, *appearance*,
    448

Primacy, *churchdom*, 995
  pre-eminence, 33
  repute, 873
Primary, *importance*, 642
Primate, *clergy*, 996
Prime, *early*, 132
  primeval, 124
  excellent, 648, 650
  important, 642
  to prepare, 673
  teach, 537
  number, 84
  worship, 990
Primed, *prepared*, 698
Primer, *school*, 542
Primeval, *oldness*, 124
Primigenial, *beginning*, 66
Primitive, *old*, 124
  simple, 849
Primogeniture, *posterity*,
    167
Primordial, *oldness*, 124
Primrose-coloured, *yellow-
    ness*, 436
* Primum mobile, *cause*,
    153
Prince, *master*, 745
  noble, 875
Princedom, *title*, 877
Princely, *authoritative*, **737**
  liberal, 816
  generous, 942
  noble, 873, 875
Princess, *noble*, 875
Principal, *importance*, 642
  money, 800
Principality, *property*, 780
  spirit, 977
  title, 877
Principle, *element*, 316
  cause, 153
  truth, 494
  reasoning, 476
  law, 80
  tenet, 484
  motive, 615
Prink, *adorn*, 845
  show off, 882
Print, *mark*, 550
  record, 551
  engraving, 558
  letterpress, 591
Printless, *obliteration*, 552
Prior, *in order*, 62
  in time, 116
  religious, 996
Prioress, *clergy*, 996
Priory, *temple*, 1000
Prise, *extract*, 301
Prism, *optical instrument*,
    445
  angularity, 244

Prismatic, *colour*, 428, 440
  changeable, 149
Prison, *prison*, 752
  restraint, 751
Prisoner, *captive*, 754
  defendant, 967
Pristine, *preterition*, 122
Prithee, *request*, 765
Prittle-prattle, *interlocution*, 588
Privacy, *secrecy*, 526
  concealment, 528
  seclusion, 893
Private, *special*, 79
Private eye, *inquiry agent*, 461
Privateer, *combatant*, 726
Privation, *loss*, 776
  poverty, 804
Privative, *taking*, 789
Privilege, *dueness*, 924
Privity, *knowledge*, 490
Privy, *concealed*, 528
Prize, *booty*, 793
  reward, 973
  success, 731
  palm, 733
  good, 618
  love, 897
  approve, 931
Prize-fighter, *combatant*, 726
Pro and con, *reasoning*, 476
* Pro bono publico, *utility*, 644
  philanthropy, 910
* Pro forma, *habit*, 613
* Pro hac vice, *present*, 118
* Pro more, *conformity*, 62
  habit, 613
* Pro rata, *relation*, 9
* Pro re nata, *circumstance*, 8
  occasion, 134
* Pro tanto, *greatness*, 31
  smallness, 32
Proa, *ship*, 273
Probable, *probability*, 472
  chance, 156
Probate, *evidence*, 467
Probation, *trial*, 463
  essay, 675
  demonstration, 478
Probationer, *learner*, 541
Probe, *stiletto*, 262
  measure, 466
  depth, 208
  investigate, 461
Probity, *virtue*, 944
  right, 922
  integrity, 939
Problem, *enigma*, 533

Problem, *inquiry*, 461
Problematical, *uncertain*, 475
  hidden, 528
Proboscis, *convexity*, 250
Procedure, *conduct*, 692
  action, 680
  plan, 626
Proceed, *advance*, 282
  from, 154
  elapse, 109
  happen, 151
Proceeding, *action*, 680
  event, 151
  plan, 626
  incomplete, 53
Proceeds, *money*, 800
  receipts, 810
  gain, 775
Procerity, *height*, 206
* Procès-verbal, *compendium*, 596
Process, *projection*, 250
  plan, 626
  action, 680
  conduct, 692
  engraving, 558
  time, 109
Procession, *train*, 69
  ceremony, 882
Prochronism, *anachronism*, 115
Proclaim, *publication*, 531
Proclivity, *disposition*, 602
  proneness, 176, 820
Proconsul, *deputy*, 759
  master, 745
Proconsulship, *authority*, 737
Procrastination, *delay*, 133, 683
Procreant, *productiveness*, 168
Procreate, *production*, 161
Procreator, *paternity*, 166
Proctor, *officer*, 694
  law, 968
Proctorship, *direction*, 693
Procumbent, *horizontality*, 213
Procuration, *commission*, 755
  pimping, 961
Procurator, *director*, 694
Procure, *get*, 775
  cause, 153
  buy, 795
  pimp, 962
Prod, *poke*, 276
Prodigal, *extravagant*, 818
  lavish, 641
  penitent, 950

Prodigious, *wonderful*, 870
  much, 31
Prodigy, *prodigy*, 872
Prodromal, *precedence*, 62
Prodrome, *precursor*, 64
Produce, *cause*, 153
  create, 161
  prolong, 200
  show, 525, 599
  evidence, 467
  result, 154
  fruit, 775
  ware, 798
Product, *effect*, 154
  acquisition, 775
  multiple, 84
Productive, *productiveness*, 168
Proem, *precursor*, 64
Proemial, *preceding, in order*, 62
  in time, 106
  beginning, 66
Profane, *impious*, 988
  pagan, 986
  desecrate, 679
  laical, 997
Profess, *affirmation*, 535
Profession, *business*, 625
  promise, 768
Professor, *teacher*, 540
Proffer, *offer*, 763
Proficiency, *skill*, 698
Proficient, *adept*, 700
  knowledge, 490
  skilful, 698
Profile, *lateral*, 236
  outline, 229
  appearance, 448
Profit, *acquisition*, 775
  advantage, 618
Profitable, *useful*, 644
  gainful, 810
Profiteer, *acquisition*, 775
  upstart, 734
Profitless, *inutility*, 645
Profligacy, *vice*, 945
Profluent, *advancing*, 282
  flowing, 348
Profound, *deep*, 208
  sagacity, 702
  feeling, 821
  thought, 451
Profoundly, *great*, 31
Profuse, *prodigal*, 818
  lavish, 641
Prog, *food*, 298
Progenitor, *paternity*, 166
Progeny, *posterity*, 121, 167
Prognostic, *omen*, 512
Prognosticate, *prediction*, 511

Programme, *catalogue*, 86
  announcement, 510
  plan, 626
Progress, *advance*, 282
  speed, 274
  of time, 109
  improvement, 658
  success, 731
Progression, *series*, 69
  gradation, 58
  numerical, 84
  motion, 282
Prohibit, *forbid*, 761
Prohibition, *sobriety*, 953,
  958
Project, *bulge*, 250
  propel, 284
  eject, 297
  move, 264
  plan, 626
  intend, 620
Projectile, *missile*, 284
  weapon, 727
Projection, *map*, 554
Prolegomena, *precursor*, 64
Prolepsis, *anachronism*, 115
* Prolétaire, *commonalty*,
  876
Proletarian, *commonalty*,
  876
Proliferate, *reproduction*,
  161
Prolific, *productive*, 168
Prolix, *diffuse*, 573
Prolocuter, *teacher*, 540
  speaker, 582
Prologue, *precursor*, 64
  drama, 599
Prolong, *lengthen*, 200
  protract, 110, 133
Prolusion, *beginning*, 64
  lesson, 537
  dissertation, 595
Promenade, *journey*, 266
  causeway, 627
  display, 882
Promethean, *life*, 359
Prominent, *convex*, 250, 252
  conspicuous, 446, 525
  important, 642
  famous, 873
Prominently, *great*, 31
Promiscuous, *irregular*, 59
  casual, 621
Promise, *engage*, 768
  augur, 507
  hope, 858
Promissory, *pledged*, 768
Promissory note, *security*,
  771
  money, 800
Promontory, *cape*, 206, 342

Promontory, *projection*, 250
Promote, *aid*, 707
  plan, 626
Promotion, *improvement*,
  658
Prompt, *in time*, 111
  early, 132
  quick, 274
  suggest, 514, 695
  tell, 527
  remind, 505
  induce, 615
  active, 682
Promptuary, *store*, 636
Promulgate, *publication*,
  531
Pronation, *inversion*, 218
Prone, *horizontal*, 213
  tending, 176
  inclined, 602
  disposed, 820
Prong, *sharpness*, 253
Pronounce, *articulate*, 580
  speak, 582
  assert, 535
  judge, 480
  sentence, 969
Pronounced, *great*, 31
  obvious, 518
  emphatic, 535
Pronunciamento, *revolt*, 719
Proof, *demonstration*, 478
  test, 463
  copy, 21
  defence, 717
  insensible, 376
Prop, *support*, 215
  help, 707
  refuge, 666
Propagable, *productive*, 168
Propaganda, *publicity*, 531
Propagandism, *teaching*,
  537
  proselytism, 484
Propagate, *produce*, 161
  publish, 531
Propel, *propulsion*, 284
  move, 264
Propensity, *tendency*, 176
  disposition, 602
  affections, 820
Proper, *special*, 79
  right, 922, 926
  expedient, 646
  consonant, 23
  handsome, 845
Property, *possession*, 780
  power, 157
Prophecy, *prediction*, 511
  scriptural, 985
Prophesy, *predict*, 511
Prophet, *oracle*, 513

Prophylactic, *remedy*, 662
  preservative, 670
Prophylaxis, *preservation*,
  670
  salubrity, 656
Propinquity, *nearness*, 197
Propitiate, *conciliate*, 831,
  918
  pacify, 723
  atone, 952
  pity, 914
  religious, 976
  worship, 990
Propitious, *favouring*, 707
  opportune, 134
  prosperous, 734
  auspicious, 858
Proplasm, *prototype*, 22
Proportion, *relation*, 9
  mathematical, 84, 85
  symmetry, 242
Proposal, *plan*, 626
Propose, *offer*, 763
  intend, 620
  suggest, 514
  broach, 535
  ask, 461
Proposition, *reasoning*, 476
  problem, 461
  supposition, 454
Propound, *broach*, 535
  inquire, 461
  suggest, 514
* Propria persona, *speciality*, 79
Proprietary, *possessor*, 779
Proprietor, *possessor*, 779
Proprietorship, *possession*,
  777
  property, 780
Propriety, *consonance*, 23
  expedience, 646
  taste, 850
  duty, 922, 926
* Proprio motu, *will*, 600
* Propter hoc, *attribution*,
  155
Propulsion, *propulsion*, 284
  impulse, 276
Prorogue, *lateness*, 133
Prosaic, *dull*, 843
  style, 575, 598
Proscenium, *front*, 234
Proscribe, *interdict*, 761
  curse, 908
  condemn, 971
  denounce, 938
  exclude, 77, 893
Prose, *not verse*, 598
  dullness, 843
  to prate, 584
  to weary, 841

Prosector, *anatomist*, 44
Prosecute, *pursue*, 622
   accuse, 938
   arraign, 969
   action, 680
Prosecutor, *judge*, 967
Proselyte, *learner*, 541
   convert, 484
Proselytism, *teaching*, 537
   belief, 484
Prosit, *drink*, 959
Prosody, *poetry*, 597
Prosopopoeia, *metaphor*, 521
Prospect, *view*, 448
   probability, 472
   futurity, 121, 507
Prospectus, *scheme*, 626
   compendium, 596
   programme, 86
Prosperity, *success*, 731, 734
Prostitute, *to corrupt*, 659
   misuse, 679
   dishonour, 961, 962
Prostrate, *low*, 207
   level, 213
   to depress, 308
   weak, 160
   exhausted, 688
   laid up, 655
   dejected, 837
   heart-broken, 830
Prostration, *ruin*, 619
   disease, 655
   servility, 886
   obeisance, 725, 743, 928
   worship, 990
Prosy, *diffuse*, 573
   dull, 575, 843
Prosyllogism, *reasoning*, 476
Protagonist, *leader*, 745
   champion, 711
   proficient, 700
Protasis, *precursor*, 64
Protean, *mutable*, 149, 605
Protect, *shield*, 664
   defend, 717
Protection, *influence*, 175
Protector, *master*, 745
Protectorate, *region*, 181
   authority, 737
Protégé, *servant*, 746
   friend, 890
Protein, *living beings*, 357
Protervity, *petulance*, 901
Protest, *dissent*, 489
   denial, 536
   affirmation, 535
   refusal, 764
   deprecate, 766
   censure, 932

Protest, *non-observance*, 773
   non-payment, 808
Protestant, Christian *religion*, 983A
Proteus, *change*, 149
Prothonotary, *recorder*, 553
Protocol, *document*, 551
   compact, 769
   warrant, 771
   etiquette, 613
   ceremony, 882
Protoplasm, *substance*, 3
   living beings, 357
Protoplast, *prototype*, 22
Prototype, *thing copied*, 22
Protract, *time*, 110, 133
   length, 200
Protractor, *angularity*, 244
Protrude, *convexity*, 250
Protuberance, *convexity*, 250
Proud, *lofty*, 878
   dignified, 873
Prove, *demonstrate*, 85, 478
   try, 463
   turn out, 151
   affect, 821
Provenance, *cause*, 153
Provender, *food*, 298
   materials, 635
   provision, 637
Proverb, *maxim*, 496
Proverbial, *knowledge*, 490
Provide, *furnish*, 637
   prepare, 673
Provided, *qualification*, 469
   condition, 770
   conditionally, 8
Providence, *foresight*, 510
   divine government, 976
Provident, *careful*, 459
   foresight, 510
   wise, 498
   prepared, 673
Providential, *opportune*, 134
Province, *region*, 181
   department, 75
   office, 625
   duty, 926
Provincialism, *language*, 560
   vulgarity, 851, 876
Provision, *supply*, 637
   materials, 635
   preparation, 673
   wealth, 803
   food, 298
Provisional, *preparing*, 673
   substituted, 147
   temporary, 111
   conditional, 8

Proviso, *qualification*, 469
   condition, 770
Provoke, *incite*, 615
   cause, 153
   excite, 824
   vex, 830
   hatred, 898
   anger, 900
Provoking, *difficult*, 704
Provost, *master*, 745
Prow, *front*, 234
Prowess, *courage*, 861
Prowl, *journey*, 266
   conceal, 528
Proximity, *nearness*, 197
   contiguity, 199
Proximo, *futurity*, 121
   posterior, 117
Proxy, *deputy*, 759
   substitute, 634
Prude, *affectation*, 855
Prudent, *cautious*, 864
   foresight, 510
   careful, 459
   wise, 498
   discreet, 698
Prudery, *affectation*, 855
Prune, *shorten*, 201
   correct, 658
   purple, 437
Prunella, *unimportance*, 643
Prurient, *desire*, 865
   lust, 961
Pry, *inquire*, 461
   curiosity, 455
   look, 441
Psalm, *worship*, 990
Psalmody, *music*, 415
Psalter, *rite*, 998
Pseudo, *spurious*, 495
   sham, 544
Pseudonym, *misnomer*, 565
Pseudoscope, *optical*, 445
Pshaw, *contempt*, 930
Psst, *accost*, 586
Psyche, *soul*, 450
Psychiatrist, *mind*, 450
   remedy, 662
Psychical, *immaterial*, 317
   intellectual, 450
Psycho-analysis, *remedy*, 662
Psychokinesis, *occult*, 992
Psychology, *intellect*, 450
Psychomancy, *divination*, 992
Psychopath, *madman*, 504
Psychosis, *insanity*, 503
Psycho-therapist, *intellect*, 450
   remedy, 662
Ptisan, *remedy*, 662

Pub-crawler, *drunkard,* 959
Puberty, *youth,* 127
Public, *people,* 373
   open, 529, 531
Public-house, *drink,* 298
Public-spirited, *philan-*
   thropy, 910
Publication, *promulgation,*
              531
   showing, 525
   printing, 591
   book, 593
Publicist, *writer,* 593
   lawyer, 968
Publicity, *publication,* 531
Publish, *inform,* 527
Puce, *purple,* 437
Puck, *imp,* 980
Pucker, *fold,* 258
Pudder, *disorder,* 59
Pudding, *food,* 298
Puddle, *lakelet,* 343
   lining, 224
Pudency, *purity,* 960
Puerile, *boyish,* 127, 129
   trifling, 643
   foolish, 499
   weak, 477, 575
Puff, *wind,* 349
   vapour, 334
   tobacco, 298A
   inflate, 194
   commendation, 931
   advertisement, 531
   boast, 884
   pant, 688
Puffed up, *vain,* 770
   proud, 878
Puffy, *swollen,* 194
   wind, 349
Pug, *shortness,* 201
   footprint, 551
   boxer, 726
Pugilism, *contention,* 720
Pugilist, *combatant,* 726
Pugnacity, *anger,* 901
Puisne, *posterior,* 117
Puissant, *strong,* 157, 159
Puke, *ejection,* 297
Pukka, *true,* 494
   goodness, 648
Pulchritude, *beauty,* 845
Pule, *cry,* 411, 412
   weep, 839
Pull, *draw,* 285
   attract, 288
   row, 267
   swerve, 279
   advantage, 33
   proof, 21, 591
Pull down, *destroy,* 162
   lay low, 308

Pull off, *accomplish,* 729
Pull out, *extract,* 301
Pull through, *recover,* 658
Pull together, *concord,* 714
Pull up, *stop,* 142, 265
   accuse, 938
Pullet, *infant,* 129
Pulley, *instrument,* 633
Pullman car, *vehicle,* 272
Pullover, *dress,* 225
Pullulate, *grow,* 194
   multiply, 168
Pulp, *pulpiness,* 354
   soften, 324
   semiliquid, 352
Pulpit, *rostrum,* 542
   church, 1000
Pulsate, *see* Pulse
Pulse, *oscillate,* 314
   agitate, 315
   periodically, 138
Pultaceous, *pulpy,* 354
Pulverize, *maltreat,* 649
Pulverulence, *powder,* 330
Pulvil, *fragrance,* 400
Pummel, *handle,* 633
   beat, 276, 972
Pump, *inquire,* 461
   spray, 348
   reservoir, 636
Pun, *verbal,* 520, 563
   wit, 842
   similarity, 17
Punch, *to perforate,* 260
   perforator, 262
   to strike, 276
   punish, 972
   energy, 171
   vigour, 574
   buffoon, 857
   humorist, 844
   puppet, 599
   horse, 271
Punctate, *spotted,* 440
Punctilio, *ostentation,* 882
Punctilious, *correct,* 494
   fashionable, 852
   observant, 772
   fastidious, 868
   scrupulous, 939
Punctual, *early,* 132
   periodical, 138
   scrupulous, 939
Punctuation, *grammar,* 567
Puncture, *opening,* 260
Pundit, *scholar,* 462
   sage, 500
   clergy, 996
Pungent, *taste,* 392
   caustic, 171
   feeling, 821
Punic faith, *improbity,* 940

Punish, *punishment,* 972
Punk, *prostitute,* 962
   trash, 645
Punka, *fan,* 349
Punnet, *receptacle,* 191
Punster, *humorist,* 844
Punt, *ship,* 273
   propel, 267, 284
   gamble, 621
Puny, *in degree,* 32
   in size, 193
   weak, 160
Pup, *infant,* 129
Pupil, *learner,* 541
   eye, 441
Puppet, *subjection,* 749
   effigy, 554
   plaything, 840
   dupe, 547
   little, 193
Puppet-show, *the drama,*
              599
   amusement, 840
Puppy, *fop,* 854
   blusterer, 887
Puranas, *sacred books,* 986
Purblind, *dim-sighted,* 443
   undiscerning, 499
Purchase, *buy,* 795
   leverage, 175
Pure, *simple,* 42
   true, 494
   good taste, 850
   clean, 652
   innocent, 946
   virtuous, 944
Purely, *smallness,* 32
   greatness, 31
Purgation, *cleansing,* 652
   atonement, 952
Purgative, *remedy,* 662
Purgatory, *suffering,* 828
   atonement, 952
   hell, 982
Purge, *clean,* 652
   improve, 658
   atone, 952
   subduction, 38
Purify, *cleanse,* 652
   improve, 658
Purist, *style,* 578
   taste, 850
Puritanical, *ascetic,* 955
   pedantic, 855
Puritanism, *heterodoxy,*
              984A
Purity, *purity,* 960
   of style, 578
Purl, *gargle,* 405
   flow, 348
Purler, *fall,* 306
Purlieus, *suburbs,* 197, 227

* Quantum sufficit, *suffi-ciency*, 639
* Quaquaversum, *direction*, 278
Quarantine, *safety*, 664
  confinement, 751
Quarrel, *discord*, 713
Quarrelsome, *enemy*, 901
Quarry, *mine*, 636
  object, 620
Quarter, *fourth*, 97
  region, 181
  side, 236
  direction, 278
  to place, 184
  mercy, 914
Quartering, *number*, 97
Quartermaster, *provision*, 637
  master, 745
Quarters, *abode*, 189
Quartet, *number*, 95
Quarto, *book*, 593
Quash, *destroy*, 162
  annul, 756, 964
Quasi, *similarity*, 17
Quatercentenary, *celebration*, 883
Quaternal, *number*, 95
Quaternity, *number*, 95
Quatrain, *poetry*, 597
Quaver, *oscillate*, 314
  shake, 315
  sound, 407
  music, 413
  hesitate, 605
  fear, 860
  shiver, 383
Quay, *abode*, 189
Quean, *libertine*, 962
Queasiness, *dislike*, 867
  fastidious, 868
Queen, *master*, 745
Queenly, *majestic*, 873
Queer, *unconformity*, 83
  sick, 655
  whimsical, 853
Quell, *destroy*, 162
  hush, 265
  calm, 826
  moderate, 174
  subdue, 732
Quench, *cool*, 385
  dissuade, 616
  extinguish, 162
  satiate, 869
Querimonious, *lament*, 839
Querist, *inquiry*, 461
Quern, *mill*, 330
Querulous, *complaining*, 839
  quarrelsome, 901

Query, *inquiry*, 461
  to doubt, 485
Quest, *inquiry*, 461
  pursuit, 622
  undertaking, 676
Question, *inquiry*, 461
  topic, 454
  to doubt, 485
  to deny, 536
Questionable, *uncertainty*, 475, 485
Questionless, *certainty*, 474
Questor, *treasurer*, 801
Queue, *appendix*, 39, 214
  sequel, 65
  row, 69
Quibble, *sophistry*, 477
  equivocate, 544
  absurdity, 497
  wit, 842
Quick, *rapid*, 274
  transient, 111
  active, 682
  haste, 684
  early, 132
  skilful, 698
  irascible, 901
  feeling, 821, 822
Quick-sighted, *quick-eyed*, 441
  sagacious, 498
Quick-witted, *wit*, 842
  clever, 498
Quicken, *hasten*, 132
  animate, 163
  vivify, 359
  operate, 170
  urge, 615
  excite, 824
  promote, 907
  violence, 173
Quicksand, *pitfall*, 667
Quicksilver, *velocity*, 274
Quid, *tobacco*, 298A
  money, 800
* Quid pro quo, *compensation*, 30
  payment, 807
  exchange, 794
  interchange, 148
Quiddity, *essence*, 1, 5
  quibble, 477
  wit, 842
Quidnunc, *curiosity*, 455
Quiescence, *cessation*, 142
  inertness, 172
  inactivity, 683
  rest, 265
Quiet, *rest*, 265
  silent, 403
  calm, 174, 826
  dissuade, 616

Quiet, *peace*, 714
Quietism, *piety*, 987
  heresy, 984A
Quietus, *death*, 360
  downfall, 732
Quill, *writing*, 590
Quill-driver, *writing*, 590
Quinary, *number*, 98
Quincentenary, *see* Quingentenary
Quincunx, *number*, 98
Quingentenary, *celebration*, 883
Quinquagesimal, *fifty*, 98
Quinquefid, *number*, 99
Quinquereme, *ship*, 273
Quinquesection, *number*, 99
Quint, *number*, 98
Quintessence, *essence*, 5
  importance, 642
Quintet, *five*, 98
Quintuple, *number*, 98
Quip, *wit*, 842
  amusement, 840
  ridicule, 856
  satire, 932
Quirites, *non-combatant*, 726A
Quirk, *caprice*, 608
  evasion, 617
  wit, 842
Quisling, *traitor*, 742
Quit, *depart*, 293
  relinquish, 624
  loss, 776
  neglect, 927
  pay, 807
Quite, *greatness*, 31
Quits, *equality*, 27
  atonement, 952
Quittance, *forgiveness*, 918
  atonement, 952
  reward, 973
  payment, 807
  observance, 772
Quitter, *coward*, 862
  shirker, 623
Quiver, *agitate*, 315
  vibrate, 314
  shiver, 383
  fear, 860
  affect, 821
  store, 636
  arm, 727
Quixotic, *imaginary*, 515
  rash, 863
  enthusiastic, 825
Quiz, *to ridicule*, 856
  inquiry, 461
Quizzical, *ridiculous*, 853
* Quocumque modo, *means*, 632

Quod, *prison*, 752
Quodlibet, *sophism*, 477
　　subtle point, 454
　　enigma, 461
　　wit, 842
Quondam, *preterition*, 122
Quorum, *assembly*, 72
Quota, *apportionment*, 786
Quotation, *imitation*, 19
　　citation, 82
　　price, 812
Quote, *cite*, 82, 467
　　bargain, 794
Quotidian, *period*, 108, 138
Quotient, *number*, 84

R

R.A., *artist*, 559
R.I.P., *burial*, 363
Rabbet, *junction*, 43
Rabbi, *clergy*, 996
Rabble, *mob*, 876
　　bad man, 949
　　assemblage, 72
Rabelaisian, *coarse*, 961
Rabid, *insanity*, 503
　　headstrong, 606
　　angry, 900
　　feeling, 821
Race, *to run*, 274
　　contest, 720
　　course, 622
　　career, 625
　　torrent, 348
　　lineage, 11, 69
　　kind, 75
　　people, 372
Racehorse, *horse*, 271
　　fleetness, 274
Racer, *horse*, 271
　　fleetness, 274
Racial, *ethnic*, 372
Rack, *frame*, 215
　　physical pain, 378
　　moral pain, 828
　　to torture, 830
　　punish, 975
　　purify, 652
　　refine, 658
　　cloud, 353
Racket, *noise*, 402, 404
　　brawl, 713
　　roll, 407
　　bat, 633
　　plan, 626
* Raconteur, *narrator*, 594
Racy, *strong*, 171
　　pungent, 392
　　feeling, 821
　　style, 574

Radar, *direction*, 693
Raddle, *weave*, 219
　　red, 434
Radiant, *diverging*, 291
　　light, 420, 423
　　beauty, 845
　　glory, 873
Radiator, *fire*, 386
Radical, *cause*, 153
　　algebraic root, 84
　　complete, 52
　　intrinsic, 5
　　reformer, 658
　　revolution, 146
Radically, *thorough*, 31
Radio, *hearing*, 418
　　publication, 531
　　news, 532
　　wireless, 599B
Radioactivity, *light*, 420
Radiogram, *hearing*, 418
　　news, 532
Radioscopy, *light*, 420
Radiotherapy, *light*, 420
Radius, *length*, 200
　　degree, 26
Radix, *cause*, 153
Raff, *refuse*, 653
　　rabble, 876
Raffia, *tape*, 45
Raffish, *vulgar*, 851
Raffle, *chance*, 156, 621
Raft, *ship*, 273
Rafter, *support*, 215
Rag, *shred*, 51
　　clothes, 225
　　escapade, 497
　　to tease, 830
　　joke, 842
　　deride, 929
　　revile, 932
Ragamuffin, *rabble*, 876
Rage, *violence*, 173
　　fury, 825
　　wrath, 900
　　desire, 865
　　fashion, 852
Ragged, *bare*, 226
Ragout, *food*, 298
Ragtag, *commonalty*, 876
　　bad man, 949
Raid, *attack*, 716
　　robbery, 791
Rail, *enclosure*, 232
　　fence, 666
　　imprison, 752
Rail at, *disapprove*, 932
Rail-car, *vehicle*, 272
Rail in, *circumscribe*, 231
Raillery, *ridicule*, 856
Railroad, *way*, 627
Railway, *road*, 627

Raiment, *dress*, 225
Rain, *river*, 348
Rainbow, *variegation*, 440
Raise, *elevate*, 307
　　increase, 35
　　produce, 161
　　excite, 824
* Raison d'être, *cause*, 153
　　motive, 615, 620
Raj, *authority*, 737
Rajah, *master*, 745
Rake, *cultivate*, 371
Rake-off, *payment*, 809
Rake up, *collect*, 72
　　extract, 301
　　recall, 504
　　excite, 824
Rakehell, *intemperate*, 954
Rakish, *intemperate*, 954
　　licentious, 961
Rally, *ridicule*, 856
　　joke, 842
　　recover, 658
　　stand by, 707
　　pluck up courage, 861
Ram, *impel*, 276
　　press in, 261
　　insert, 300
Ram down, *condense*, 321
　　fill up, 261
Ramadan, *fasting*, 956
Ramble, *stroll*, 266
　　wander, 279
　　diffuse, 572
　　delirium, 503
　　folly, 499
Rambler, *traveller*, 268
Ramification, *branch*, 51, 256
　　divergence, 291
　　posterity, 167
Rammer, *plug*, 263
　　impeller, 276
Ramp, *rise up*, 307
　　slope, 217
Rampage, *violence*, 173
　　excitement, 825
Rampant, *violent*, 173
　　vehement, 825
　　licentious, 961
　　free, 748
　　rearing, 307
Rampart, *defence*, 717
Ramrod, *stopper*, 263
Ramshackle, *imperfect*, 651
Ranch, *farm*, 780
Rancid, *fetid*, 401
　　rotten, 653
Rancour, *malevolence*, 907
　　revenge, 919
Randem, *row*, 69
Random, *casual*, 156, 621

Recognizance, *security*, 771
Recognize, *see*, 441
  know, 490
  assent, 488
  remember, 505
  discover, 480A
  acknowledge, 535
Recognized, *received*, 82
  habitual, 613
Recoil, *repercussion*,
           277, 325
  revert, 145
  shun, 623
  reluctance, 603
  dislike, 867
  hate, 898
  reaction, 179
Recollect, *remember*, 505
Recommence, *repetition*,
           104
Recommend, *advise*, 695
  approve, 931
  induce, 615
Recompense, *reward*, 973
  payment, 809
Reconcile, *agree*, 23
  content, 831
  pacify, 723
  forgive, 918
Recondite, *obscure*, 519
  hidden, 529
Reconnaissance, *survey*, 441
Reconnoitre, *see*, 441
  inquire, 461
Reconsideration, *thought*,
           451
Reconstitute, *restore*, 660
Reconstruct, *reproduce*, 164
  remodel, 146
  restore, 660
Reconvert, *restore*, 660
Record, *note*, 551
  list, 86
Recorder, *recorder*, 553
  judge, 967
Recording, *copy*, 21
Recount, *description*, 594
Recoup, *restore*, 660, 790
  reward, 973
Recourse, *use*, 677
Recovery, *reinstatement*,
           660
  improvement, 658
  recruit, 689
Recreant, *coward*, 862
  base, 940, 945
  apostate, 941
  wretch, 949
Recreation, *amusement*, 840
Recrement, *unclean*, 653
Recrimination, *accusation*,
           938

Recrimination, *reprobation*,
           932
  retaliation, 718
Recrudescence, *recurrence*,
        104, 136
Recruit, *refresh*, 689
  reinstate, 660
  health, 654
  repair, 658
  aid, 707
  provide, 637
  strengthen, 159
  beginner, 674
  fighter, 726
Rectangle, *angularity*, 244
Rectify, *straighten*, 246
  improve, 658
  re-establish, 660
Rectilinear, *straightness*,
           246
Rectitude, *virtue*, 944
  right, 922
  probity, 939
Recto, *dextrality*, 228
Rector, *clergy*, 996
  director, 694
Rectory, *office*, 995
  house, 1000
* Reculons, *regression*, 283
Recumbent, *horizontal*, 213
  oblique, 217
Recuperation, *restitution*,
           790
  improvement, 658
  restore, 660
  refresh, 689
Recur, *repeat*, 104
  frequent, 136
  periodic, 138
Recurvation, *curvature*, 245
Recusant, *denying*, 536
  dissenting, 489
  disobedient, 742
  unwilling, 603
  refusing, 764
  heterodox, 984A
  impenitent, 951
Red, *redness*, 434
Red book, *list*, 86
Red cent, *trifle*, 643
Red-handed, *murderous*,
           361
  action, 681
Red-hot, *heat*, 382
Red lamp, *brothel*, 961
Red letter, *indication*, 550
Red light, *signal*, 550
Red tape, *custom*, 613
Red-tapist, *director*, 695
Redaction, *publication*, 531
  improvement, 658
Redargue, *confute*, 479

Redcoat, *combatant*, 726
Redden, *flush*, 821
Reddition, *restoration*, 790
Redeem, *reinstate*, 660
  deliver, 672
  liberate, 750
  fulfil, 772
  atone, 952
  compensate, 30
  restore, 790
Redemption, *salvation*, 976
Redintegrate, *reinstate*, 660
  renovate, 658
Redolence, *odour*, 398
  fragrance, 400
Redouble, *duplication*, 90
  repeat, 104
  increase, 35
Redoubt, *defence*, 717
Redoubtable, *fear*, 860
Redound, *conduce*, 176
Redress, *remedy*, 662
  rectify, 658
  restore, 660
  reward, 873
Reduce, *lesson*, 36
  contract, 195
  shorten, 201
  lower, 308
  weaken, 160
  convert, 144
  subdue, 731
  impoverish, 804
  in number, 103
* Reductio ad absurdum,
  confutation, 479
Reduction, *arithmetical*, 85
Redundant, *ample*, 641
  diffuse, 573
  remaining, 40
Reduplication, *imitation*, 19
  doubling, 90
Re-echo, *imitate*, 19
  repeat, 104
  reduplication, 90
  sound, 404, 408
Reechy, *uncleanness*, 653
Reed, *musical instrument*,
           417
Re-educate, *teach*, 537
Reef, *slacken*, 275
  shoal, 346
  danger, 667
Reek, *hot*, 382
  fume, 334
Reel, *rock*, 314
  agitate, 315
  rotate, 312
  cinema, 599
  dance, 840
Re-embody, *combine*, 43
  junction, 48

Re-entrant, *angle*, 244
Re-establishment, *restoration*, 145, 660
Refashion, *remodel*, 146
Refection, *refreshment*, 689
  meal, 298
Refectory, *room*, 191
Refer, *attribute*, 155
  relate, 9
Referee, *judge*, 480, 967
  adviser, 695
Referendum, *vote*, 609
  inquiry, 461
Refinement, *elegance*, 845
  fashion, 852
  taste, 850
  discrimination, 465
  improvement, 658
  wisdom, 498
  sophistry, 477
Refit, *repair*, 658
  reinstate, 660
Reflect, *think*, 451
  imitation, 19
Reflect upon, *blame*, 932
Reflecting, *thoughtful*, 498
Reflection, *maxim*, 496
  likeness, 21
  imitation, 19
  blame, 932
Reflector, *optical instrument*, 445
* Reflet, *variegation*, 440
Reflex, *regress*, 283
  recoil, 277
Reflux, *regress*, 283
  recoil, 277
Refocillate, *refresh*, 689
  restore, 660
Reform, *improve*, 658
  change, 140
Reformatory, *school*, 542
Refraction, *deviation*, 279
  angularity, 244
Refractor, *optical instrument*, 445
Refractory, *resisting*, 719
  obstinate, 606
  disobedient, 742
  difficult, 704
Refrain, *avoid*, 623
  reject, 610
  unwilling, 603
  abstain, 616, 681
  temperance, 953
  repetition, 104, 415
Refresh, *cool*, 385
  relieve, 834
  refit, 658
  restore, 660
  strengthen, 159
Refresher, *fee*, 809

Refreshing, *pleasing*, 377, 829
Refreshment, *food*, 298
  pleasure, 827
  recruiting, 689
Refrigeration, *refrigerate*, 385
Refrigeratory, *cold*, 387
Reft, *disjoin*, 44
Refuge, *refuge*, 666
Refugee, *escape*, 671
Refulgence, *light*, 420
Refund, *restore*, 790
  pay, 807
Refurbish, *improve*, 658
Refuse, *decline*, 764
  reject, 610
  remains, 40
  offscourings, 643
Refute, *confute*, 479
Regain, *acquisition*, 775
Regal, *authority*, 737
Regale, *feast*, 298
  pleasing, 377, 829
Regalia, *sceptre*, 747
Regard, *esteem*, 931
  respect, 928
  love, 897
  compliment, 894
  view, 441
  judge, 480
  conceive, 484
  credit, 873
Regarding, *relation*, 9
Regardless, *inattention*, 458
Regatta, *amusement*, 840
Regency, *commission*, 755
Regenerate, *reproduce*, 163
  restore, 660
  piety, 987
Regent, *deputy*, 759
  governor, 745
Regicide, *killing*, 361
Regime, *authority*, 737
  circumstance, 8
  conduct, 692
Regimen, *diet*, 298
  remedy, 662
Regiment, *army*, 726
  assemblage, 72
Regimentals, *dress*, 225
Region, *region*, 181
Register, *record*, 551
  list, 86
  to arrange, 60
  range, 26
  to coincide, 199
  ventilator, 351
  fire-place, 386
Registrar, *recorder*, 553
Regorge, *restitution*, 790
Regrater, *merchant*, 797

Regress, *regression*, 283
Regressive, *reversion*, 145
Regret, *sorrow*, 833
  penitence, 950
Regular, *orderly*, 58
  complete, 52
  rule, 80, 82
  symmetric, 242
  periodic, 138
  soldier, 726
Regulation, *arrangement*, 60
  direction, 693
  usage, 80
  order, 741
  law, 963
Regurgitate, *return*, 283
  flow, 348
  restore, 790
Rehabilitate, *reinstate*, 660
  restore, 790
Rehash, *repetition*, 104
  improvement, 658
Rehearse, *repeat*, 104
  trial, 463
  describe, 594
  prepare, 673
  dramatic, 599
Reify, *materialize*, 3
Reign, *authority*, 175, 737
Reimburse, *restore*, 790
  pay, 807
Rein, *moderate*, 174
  check, 179
  slacken, 275
  restrain, 616
  hold, 737
Reincarnation, *reproduction*, 163
Reindeer, *carrier*, 271
Reinforce, *strengthen*, 159
  aid, 707
  add, 37, 39
Reinforcement, *supplies*, 635, 637
Reinstate, *restore*, 660
Reinvigorate, *restore*, 660
  refresh, 689
Reiterate, *frequent*, 136
  repeat, 104, 535
  multitude, 102
Reject, *decline*, 610
  refuse, 764
  exclude, 55
  eject, 297
Rejoice, *exult*, 838
  gratify, 829
  cheer, 836
  amuse, 840
Rejoinder, *answer*, 462
  evidence, 468
  lawsuit, 969

INDEX

Rider, *equestrian,* 268
  corollary, 480
  appendix, 39
Ridge, *narrowness,* 203
  projection, 250
Ridicule, *deride,* 856
  depreciate, 483
  disrespect, 929
Ridiculous, *grotesque,* 853
  vulgar, 851
  absurd, 497
  silly, 499
  trifling, 643
Riding, *region,* 181
* Ridotto, *gala,* 840
  rout, 892
* Rifacimento, *recast,* 660
Rife, *ordinary,* 82
  frequent, 136
  prevailing, 175
Riff-raff, *rabble,* 876, 949
  dirt, 653
Rifle, *to plunder,* 791
  arms, 727
Rifleman, *combatant,* 726
Rift, *separation,* 44
  fissure, 198
Rig, *dress,* 225
  prepare, 673
  frolic, 840
  deception, 545
  adorn, 845
Rigadoon, *dance,* 840
Rigescence, *hardness,* 323
Rigging, *gear,* 225
  cordage, 45
Right, *just,* 922
  privilege, 924
  duty, 926
  honour, 939
  straight, 246
  true, 494
  suitable, 646
Righteous, *virtuous,* 944
  just, 922
Rigid, *hard,* 323
  exact, 494
  strict, 772
  severe, 739
  stubborn, 606
  regular, 82
Rigmarole, *nonsense,*
            497, 517
  unintelligible, 519
Rigour, *severity,* 739
  compulsion, 744
  exactness, 494
Rile, *irritate,* 830, 900
  alienate, 898
Rill, *river,* 348
Rim, *edge,* 230
Rime, *cold,* 383

Rind, *covering,* 222
Ring, *circle,* 247
  sound, 408
  arena, 728
  party, 712
  syndicate, 778
Ring-fence, *enclosure,* 232
Ringleader, *master,* 745
  director, 694
Ringlet, *circle,* 247
Rink, *arena,* 728
Rinse, *cleanness,* 652
Riot, *violence,* 173
  revolt, 719, 742
  confusion, 59
  luxuriate, 377, 827
Rip, *tear,* 44
  rush, 274
  sensualist, 954
  rascal, 949
Riparian, *land,* 342
Ripe, *preparation,* 673
Riposte, *answer,* 462
Ripping, *excellent,* 648
  delightful, 827
Ripple, *shake,* 315
  murmur, 405
  wave, 348
Rise, *ascend,* 206, 305
  slope, 217
  resist, 719
  revolt, 742
  spring, 154
  grow, 35
Risible, *laughable,* 828
  ridiculous, 853
  witty, 842
Risk, *danger,* 665
  chance, 621
Risky, *improper,* 961
Rite, *law,* 963
  religious, 998
* Ritornello, *frequency,* 136
Ritual, *rite,* 998
  ceremony, 882
Rival, *emulate,* 720
  envy, 921
  oppose, 708
  competitor, 710, 726
Rive, *disjoin,* 44
Rivel, *fold,* 258
River, *water,* 348
Rivet, *to fasten,* 43, 150
  fastening, 45
Rivulet, *water,* 348
Road, *way,* 189, 627
  direction, 278
Road-hog, *selfishness,* 943
Roadhouse, *inn,* 189
Roadstead, *anchorage,* 189
  gulf, 343
  refuge, 666

Roadster, *carrier,* 271
Roadway, *way,* 627
Roam, *journey,* 266
Roan, *variegation,* 271
Roar, *sound,* 404
  cry, 411
  weep, 839
Roast, *heat,* 384
  ridicule, 856
  deride, 929
  persecute, 830
  censure, 932
Rob, *plunder,* 791
Robber, *thief,* 792
Robe, *dress,* 225
Robin Goodfellow, *imp,* 980
Robot, *automaton,* 601
Robust, *strength,* 159
Roc, *monster,* 83
Rock, *hardness,* 323
  land, 342
  to oscillate, 314
  pitfall, 667
Rock-and-roll, *melody,* 413
Rock-bottom, *base,* 211
Rockery, *garden,* 371
Rocket, *signal,* 550
  arms, 727
  light, 423
  space ship, 273A
  rise, 305
  rapid, 274
Rocky, *unsteady,* 149
Rococo, *fantastic,* 853
Rod, *sceptre,* 747
  scourge, 975
  bane, 663
  measure, 466
  divining, 992
  gun, 727
Rodomontade, *rant,* 497
  unintelligible, 519
  boasting, 884
Rogation, *worship,* 990
Rogue, *cheat,* 548
  knave, 941
  scamp, 949
Roguery, *vice,* 945
  dishonour, 940
Roguish, *sportive,* 842
Roily, *opaque,* 426
Roister, *insolence,* 885
Role, *business,* 625
  drama, 599
Roll, *rotate,* 312
  move, 264
  push, 284
  flow, 348
  smooth, 255
  sound, 407
  cylinder, 249
  convolution, 248

Roll, *fillet*, 205
   record, 551
   list, 86
Roll-call, *number*, 85
Roll in, *abound*, 639
Roller, *rotundity*, 249
Rollicking, *frolicsome*, 836
   blustering, 885
Rolling-stock, *vehicle*, 292
Rolling stone, *traveller*, 268
Roly-poly, *size*, 192
Roman, *type*, 591
Roman Catholic, *Christian religion*, 983A
Romance, *fiction*, 515
   falsehood, 544
   absurdity, 497
   fable, 594
   love, 897
Romantic, *sentimental*, 822
Romp, *leap*, 309
Rompers, *dress*, 225
Rondeau, *poem*, 597
Rondo, *music*, 415
Roof, *summit*, 210
   height, 206
   cover, 222
   house, 189
Roofless, *divestment*, 226
Rook, *deceiver*, 548
   swindle, 791
Rookery, *abode*, 189
Room, *space*, 180
   occasion, 124
   chamber, 191
Roommate, *friend*, 891
Roomy, *space*, 180
Roost, *abode*, 186, 189
Root, *cause*, 153
   base, 211
   word, 562
   algebraic, 84
   to place, 184
Root for, *commend*, 931
Root out, *destroy*, 162
   displace, 185
   eject, 301
   discover, 480A
Rooted, *fixed*, 265
   permanent, 141
   old, 124
   habitual, 613
Rope, *cord*, 205
   fastening, 45
Ropy, *semiliquidity*, 352
Roral, *moisture*, 339
Rosary, *rite*, 998
   garden, 371
Roscid, *moisture*, 339
Roscius, *actor*, 599
Rose, *redness*, 434
   beauty, 845

Rose, *spout*, 350
Rosette, *cluster*, 72
   ornament, 847
Rosicrucian, *heathen*, 984
Rosin, *semiliquid*, 352
Roster, *list*, 86
   record, 551
Rostrum, *beak*, 234
   pulpit, 542
Rosy, *red*, 434
   auspicious, 858
Rot, *disease*, 655
   decay, 659
   decompose, 48
   putrefy, 653
   nonsense, 497, 517
   to banter, 856
Rota, *periodicity*, 138
   list, 86
   record, 551
Rotate, *rotation*, 312
Rote, *memory*, 505
Rotor, *navigation*, 267
   ship, 273
Rotten, *foul*, 653
   fetid, 401
Rotter, *knave*, 949
Rotund, *fat*, 192
   round, 249
Rotunda, *abode*, 189
Rotundity, *roundness*, 249
* Roturier, *commonalty*, 876
* Roué, *scoundrel*, 949
   sensualist, 954
   libertine, 962
Rouge, *red*, 434
   ornament, 847
* Rouge-et-noir, *chance*, 156, 621
Rough, *uneven*, 256
   shapeless, 241
   pungent, 392
   sour, 397
   austere, 395
   violent, 173
   windy, 349
   sound, 410
   unprepared, 674
   ugly, 846
   churlish, 895
   brute, 913
   bad man, 949
   to fag, 686
Rough and ready, *transient*, 111
   provisional, 673
Rough-grained, *texture*, 329
Rough-hewn, *rugged*, 256
   unprepared, 674
Rough-house, *disorder*, 59
Roughcast, *unprepared*, 674
Roughly, *near*, 197

Roughneck, *ruffian*, 949
Rouleau, *cyclinder*, 249
   money, 800
Roulette, *engraving*, 558
   gambling, 621
Round, *circular*, 247
   rotund, 249
   assertion, 535
   periodicity, 138
   song, 415
   fight, 720
   rung, 71
   work, 625
Round-house, *prison*, 752
Round on, *attack*, 716
   peach, 529
Round robin, *record*, 551
   request, 765
Round-shot, *arms*, 727
Round-shouldered, *distorted*, 243
Round up, *assemblage*, 72
   capture, 789
Roundabout, *circuitous*, 31
   way, 629
   circumlocutory, 566, 573
Roundelay, *poetry*, 597
Roundlet, *circular*, 247
Roundly, *exertion*, 686
Roup, *sale*, 796
Rouse, *stimulate*, 615
   passion, 824
Roustabout, *labourer*, 690
Rout, *discomfort*, 732
   assembly, 892
   rabble, 876
Rout out, *destruction*, 162
Route, *method*, 627
   direction, 278
Route march, *journey*, 266
Routine, *order*, 58
   uniformity, 16
   cycle, 138; *rule*, 60
   custom, 613
   work, 625
Rove, *wander*, 266, 279
Rover, *traveller*, 268
Row, *series*, 69
   navigate, 267
   violence, 173
   brawl, 713
   riot, 720; *din*, 404
Rowdy, *violent*, 173
   vulgar, 851
Rowel, *sharpness*, 253
   stimulus, 615
Royalty, *authority*, 737
   receipt, 810
Rozzer, *police*, 664
Rub, *friction*, 331
   difficulty, 703

Rub-a-dub, roll, 407
Rub down, *pulverulence*, 330
Rub out, *disappear*, 449
  efface, 552
Rub up, *improve*, 658
Rubber, *elasticity*, 325
  shoe, 225
  pry, 455
Rubberneck, *spectator*, 444
  curiosity, 455
Rubbing, *copy*, 21
Rubbish, *inutility*, 645
  nonsense, 497, 517
Rubble, *unimportance*, 643
Rube, *peasant*, 876
Rubefy, *red*, 434
Rubicon, *limit*, 233
  passage, 303
  undertaking, 676
Rubicund, *red*, 434
Rubric, *precept*, 697
  liturgy, 998
Rubricate, *red*, 434
Ruby, *red*, 434
  gem, 650
  ornament, 847
Ruche, *fold*, 258
Ruck, *fold*, 258
  commonalty, 876
Rucksack, *receptacle*, 191
Rudder, *guidance*, 693
Ruddle, *red*, 434
Ruddy, *red*, 434
Rude, *violent*, 173
  vulgar, 851
  uncivil, 895
  disrespectful, 929
  ugly, 846
  shapeless, 241
  uncivilized, 876
Rudiment, *beginning*, 66
  cause, 153
  smallness, 193
  non-preparation, 674
Rudiments, *elementary*
  knowledge, 490
  beginning, 66
  school, 542
Rue, *regret*, 833
  repent, 950
Rueful, *doleful*, 837
Ruffian, *maleficent*, 913
  scoundrel, 949
  vulgarity, 851
Ruffle, *derange*, 61
  fold, 258
  edge, 230
  discompose, 830
  excite, 824
  anger, 900
Rufous, *red*, 434

Rug, *covering*, 222
Rugged, *rough*, 256
  ugly, 846
  churlish, 895
  style, 579
Rugose, *wrinkled*, 256
Ruin, *decay*, 659
  failure, 732
  evil, 619
  debauch, 961
  impoverish, 804
  adversity, 735
  ruins, 40
Ruinous, *painful*, 830
Rule, *regularity*, 80
  length, 200
  measure, 466
  government, 737
  precept, 697
  custom, 613
  law, 963
  to decide, 480
Rule out, *exclude*, 77
Ruler, *master*, 745
Rum, *odd*, 853
Rumba, *dance*, 840
Rumble, *noise*, 407
  understand, 518
Rumbustious, *violent*, 173
Ruminate, *thought*, 451
  chew, 296
Rummage, *seek*, 461
Rumour, *publicity*, 531
  report, 532
Rump, *rear*, 235
  remnant, 40
  part, 51
Rumple, *fold*, 258
  derange, 61
  rough, 256
Rumpus, *confusion*, 59
  din, 404
  violence, 173
  brawl, 713
  contention, 720
Run, *move quickly*, 274
  move out, 295
  recurrence, 104, 136
  flow, 109, 333
  continue, 143
  operate, 680
  conduct, 692, 693
  smuggle, 791
Run across, *encounter*, 292
Run after, *pursue*, 622
Run away, *escape*, 671
  avoid, 623
  from fear, 862
  recede, 287
Run down, *censure*, 932
  depreciate, 483
  weakness, 160

Run high, *violence*, 173
Run in, *insert*, 300
  arrest, 751
Run into, *become*, 144
Run low, *decrease*, 36
Run on, *continue*, 143
Run out, *elapse*, 122
  waste, 638
Run over, *redundant*, 641
  describe, 594
  count, 85
  examine, 457, 596
Run riot, *violence*, 173
Run through, *peruse*, 539
  squander, 818
Run up, *expend*, 809
  increase, 35
Runabout, *vehicle*, 272
Runaway, *fugitive*, 623,
Rundle, *circle*, 247 [671
  convolution, 248
  rotundity, 249
Rune, *writing*, 590
Runlet, *receptacle*, 191
Runnel, *river*, 348
Runner, *courier*, 268
  messenger, 534
Runner-up, *sequel*, 65
Running, *continuously*, 69
Runt, *littleness*, 193
Rupture, *break*, 44, 713
Rural, *country*, 189, 371
Ruralist, *recluse*, 893
Rurbania, *suburbs*, 227
Ruse, *cunning*, 702
  deception, 545
Rush, *rapidity*, 274
  haste, 684
  violence, 173
  to pursue, 622
  trifle, 643
Rushlight, *light*, 423
Russet, *red*, 433
Rust, *decay*, 659
  sluggishness, 683
  canker, 663; *red*, 434
Rustic, *rural*, 189, 371
  clown, 876; *vulgar*, 851
Rusticate, *expel*, 185
  exclude, 55
Rustication, *seclusion*, 895
Rusticity, *inurbanity*, 895
Rustle, *noise*, 405, 409, 410
  rob, 791
Rustler, *robber*, 792
Rusty, *sluggish*, 683
  old, 128
  unserviceable, 645
  dirty, 653
  deteriorated, 659

Sands, *pitfall*, 667
Sandwich, *interpose*, 228
Sandy, *pulverulence*, 330
Sane, *intelligent*, 498
  rational, 502
Sang-froid, *insensibility*, 823
  inexcitability, 826
  caution, 864
Sanguinary, *brutal*, 907
Sanguine, *expectant*, 507
  hopeful, 858
Sanhedrim, *tribunal*, 696
Sanies, *fluidity*, 333
Sanitary, *salubrity*, 656
Sanity, *rationality*, 502
  health, 654
Sans, *absence*, 187
* Sans cérémonie, *modesty*, 881
  sociality, 892
  friendship, 888
* Sans façon, *modesty*, 881
  sociality, 892
* Sans pareil, *superiority*, 33
* Sans phrase, *frankness*, 543, 566
* Sans souci, *pleasure*, 827
  content, 831
Sansculotte, *rebel*, 742
  commonalty, 876
Santon, *hermit*, 893
  priest, 996
Sap, *juice*, 333
  inbeing, 5
  to destroy, 162
  damage, 659
  fool, 501
Sapid, *tasty*, 390
Sapient, *wisdom*, 498
Sapless, *dry*, 340
Sapling, *youth*, 129
Saponaceous, *soapy*, 355
Sapor, *flavour*, 390
Sapphire, *ornament*, 847
Sappy, *juicy*, 333
  foolish, 499
Saraband, *dance*, 840
Sarcasm, *satire*, 932
  disrespect, 929
Sarcastic, *irascible*, 901
  derisory, 856
Sarcoma, *disease*, 655
Sarcophagus, *interment*, 363
Sardonic, *contempt*, 838
Sartorial, *dress*, 225
Sash, *central*, 247
Satan, *devil*, 978
Satanic, *evil*, 649
  hellish, 982
  vicious, 945
Satchel, *bag*, 191

Sate, *see* Satiate
Satellite, *follower*, 281
  companion, 88
  space ship, 273A
Satiate, *sufficient*, 639
  redundant, 641
  cloy, 869
Satiety, *see* Satiate
Satin, *smooth*, 255
Satire, *ridicule*, 856
  censure, 932
Satirist, *detractor*, 936
Satisfaction, *duel*, 720
  reward, 973
Satisfactorily, *well*, 618
Satisfy, *content*, 831
  gratify, 827, 829
  convince, 484
  fulfil a duty, 926
  an obligation, 772
  reward, 973
  pay, 807; *suffice*, 639
  satiate, 869
  grant, 762
Satrap, *ruler*, 745
  deputy, 759
Satrapy, *province*, 181
Saturate, *fill*, 52, 639
  soak, 337
  moisten, 339
  satiate, 869
Saturated, *greatness*, 31
Saturnalia, *amusement*, 840
  intemperance, 954
  disorder, 59
Saturnian, *halcyon*, 734, [829
Saturnine, *grim*, 837
Satyr, *ugly*, 846
  demon, 980
  rake, 961
Sauce, *mixture*, 41
  adjunct, 39
  abuse, 832
Sauce-box, *impudence*, 887
Saucepan, *stove*, 386
Saucer, *receptacle*, 191
Saucy, *insolent*, 885
  flippant, 895
  cheerful, 836
Saunter, *ramble*, 266
  dawdle, 275
* Sauve qui peut, *speed*, 274
  recession, 287
  avoidance, 623
  escape, 671
  cowardice, 862
Savage, *violent*, 173
  brutal, 876; *angry*, 900
  malevolent, 907
  a wretch, 913

Savanna, *plain*, 344
Savant, *scholar*, 492
  wisdom, 500
Save, *except*, 38, 55, 83
  to preserve, 670
  deliver, 672
  lay by, 636
  economize, 817
Savings certificates, *treasury*, 802
Saviour, *Deity*, 976
  benefactor, 912
* Savoir faire, *tact*, 698
  manners, 852
* Savoir vivre, *sociality*, 892
  breeding, 852
Savour, *taste*, 390
  fragrance, 400
Savour of, *similarity*, 17
Savourless, *insipid*, 391
Savoury, *palatable*, 394
  delectable, 829
Savvy, *know*, 490
Saw, *jagged*, 257
  saying, 496
Sawder, *flattery*, 933
Sawdust, *pulverulence*, 330
Sawney, *fool*, 501
Saxophone, *musical instrument*, 417
Say, *speak*, 582
  assert, 535
  attention, 457
  about, 32
Saying, *assertion*, 535
  maxim, 496
* Sayonara, *departure*, 293
Scab, *traitor*, 941
Scabbard, *receptacle*, 191, 222
Scabby, *improbity*, 940
Scabrous, *rough*, 256
  indelicate, 961
Scaffold, *frame*, 215
  preparation, 673
  way, 627
  execution, 975
Scald, *burn*, 384
  poet, 597
Scalding, *hot*, 382
  burning, 384
Scale, *slice*, 204
  skin, 222
  order, 58
  measure, 466
  weight, 319
  series, 69
  gamut, 413
  to mount, 305
  attack, 716
Scale, on a large, *greatness*, 31

Scotch, *maltreat*, 649
  stop, 706
  notch, 257
Scotch mist, *rain*, 348
Scotomy, *dim-sightedness*, 443
Scotticism, *language*, 560
Scoundrel, *vice*, 949
  evildoer, 913
Scour, *rub*, 331
  run, 274
  clean, 652
Scourge, *whip*, 972, 975
  bane, 663
  painful, 830
  bad, 649
Scourings, *refuse*, 643
Scout, *messenger*, 534
  servant, 746
  watch, 664
  to disdain, 930
  deride, 643
Scowl, *frown*, 895
  complain, 839
  anger, 900
Scrabble, *fumble*, 379
  nonsense, 517
Scraggy, *narrow*, 203
  ugly, 846
Scram, *go away*, 293, 287
  escape, 671
  repel, 289
  ejection, 297
Scramble, *confusion*, 59
  haste, 684
  difficulty, 704
  mount, 305
Scrannel, *stridulous*, 410
  meagre, 643
Scrap, *piece*, 51
  small portion, 32, 193
  disuse, 678
  contention, 720
  to fight, 722
Scrap-book, *collection*, 596
Scrape, *difficulty*, 704
  mischance, 732
  abrade, 330, 331
  bow, 894
  save, 817
Scrape together, *collect*, 72
  get, 775
Scratch, *groove*, 259
  mark, 550
  write, 590
  daub, 555
  abrade, 331
  hurt, 619
  to wound, 649
Scratch out, *obliteration*, 552
Scrawl, *write*, 590

Scrawny, *lean*, 193, 203
Scream, *cry*, 410
  complain, 839
Screech, *cry*, 410
  complain, 839
Screech-owl, *noise*, 412
Screed, *speech*, 582
Screen, *concealment*, 528
  asylum, 666, 717
  ambush, 530
  to shield, 664
  sieve, 260
  sift, 652
  inquire, 461
  discriminate, 465
  sort, 42, 60
  exclude, 55
  shade, 424
  cinema, 599A
Screened, *safe*, 664
  invisible, 447
Screever, *artist*, 559
Screw, *fasten*, 43
  joining, 45
  instrument, 267, 633
  rotation, 312
  salary, 809
  miser, 819
Screw-steamer, *ship*, 273
Screw up, *strengthen*, 159
Screwball, *madman*, 504
Screwed, *drunk*, 959
Scribble, *write*, 590
  unmeaning, 517
Scribe, *writer*, 553, 590
  priest, 996
Scrimp, *shorten*, 201
  stint, 640
  save, 817
Scrip, *receptacle*, 191
Script, *writing*, 590
  radio, 599B
Scriptural, *Christian*, 983A
Scripture, *revelation*, 985
  certain, 474
Scrivener, *writing*, 590
Scroll, *record*, 551
  convolution, 248
Scrounge, *steal*, 791
Scrub, *clean*, 652
  plant, 367
Scrubby, *vulgar*, 876
  shabby, 940
  bad, 649
  trifling, 643
  small, 193
  rough, 256
Scrumptious, *pleasing*, 829
Scrunch, *pulverulence*, 330
Scruple, *doubt*, 485
  dissuasion, 616
  smallness, 32

Scrupulous, *careful*, 459
  incredulous, 487
  exact, 494
  reluctant, 603
  punctilious, 939
  virtuous, 944
Scrutator, *inquiry*, 461
Scrutinize, *examine*, 457, 461
Scud, *speed*, 274
  sail, 267
  shower, 348
  haze, 353
Scuffle, *contention*, 720
Scull, *navigation*, 267
Scullery, *room*, 191
Scullion, *servant*, 746
Sculp, *produce*, 161
Sculptor, *artist*, 559
Sculpture, *carving*, 557
  form, 240
Scum, *dregs*, 643, 653
Scunner, *disgust*, 395
Scupper, *conduit*, 350
Scurf, *uncleanness*, 653
Scurrility, *ridicule*, 856
  malediction, 908
  detraction, 934
  disrespect, 929
Scurry, *hasten*, 274, 684
Scurvy, *bad*, 649
  base, 940, 945
Scut, *tail*, 235
Scutcheon, *standard*, 550
  honour, 877
Scuttle, *tray*, 191
  opening, 260
  to destroy, 162
  hasten, 274, 684
Scythe, *angularity*, 244
  sharpness, 253
Sea, *water*, 341
  blue, 438
Sea-nymph, *sea*, 341
Seaboard, *edge*, 342
Seal, *to close*, 67, 261
  sigil, 550
  mould, 22
  evidence, 467
  record, 551
  compact, 769
  security, 771
  authority, 747
Seal up, *shut up*, 231, 751
Seam, *junction*, 43
Seaman, *mariner*, 269
Seamanship, *conduct*, 603
Seamstress, *see* Sempstress
Séance, *council*, 696
Seaplane, *aircraft*, 273A
Sear, *burn*, 384
  deaden, 823

Search, *seek*, 461
  pursuit, 622
Searching, *thorough*, 52
Searchless, *unintelligible*,
                519
Seared, *impenitent*, 951
Seascape, *spectacle*, 448
Seaside, *edge*, 342
Season, *time*, 106
  opportunity, 134
  pungent, 392, 393
  to preserve, 670
  prepare, 673
  accustom, 613
Seasonable, *opportune*, 134
  expedient, 646
  agreement, 23
Seasonal, *period*, 108
Seasoning, *mixture*, 41
  pungency, 171, 393
Seat, *abode*, 189
  position, 183
  to place, 184
  support, 215
Seaworthy, *useful*, 644
  fit, 673
Sebaceous, *unctuous*, 355
Secateurs, *sharpness*, 253
Secede, *dissent*, 489
  disobedience, 742
Seclude, *restrain*, 751
Seclusion, *retirement*, 526,
                893
Second, *of time*, 108
  instant, 113
  abet, 707
  auxiliary, 711
  duplication, 90
Second-best, *imperfection*,
                651
  inferiority, 34
Second-hand, *borrowed*, 788
  indifferent, 651
  imitated, 19
Second-rate, *imperfection*,
                651
  inferiority, 34
Second sight, *prediction*, 510
  intuition, 477
  witchcraft, 992
Secondary, *following*, 63
  consignee, 758
  deputy, 759
  inferior, 34, 643
  imperfect, 651
Secondly, *bisection*, 91
Secret, *latent*, 526
  hidden, 528
  riddle, 533
Secretary, *recorder*, 553
  writer, 590
Secrete, *hide*, 528

Secretive, *reserved*, 528
Sect, *division*, 75
Sectarian, *dissenter*, 984A
  theology, 983
Section, *part*, 51
  division, 44
  class, 75
  chapter, 593
Sector, *part*, 51
  circularity, 247
Secular, *number*, 99
  laity, 997
Secularism, *heterodoxy*,
              984A
Secure, *fasten*, 43
  safe, 664
  engage, 768
  gain, 775
  retain, 781
  confident, 858
Security, *pledge*, 771
  warranty, 924
Sedan, *vehicle*, 272
Sedan chair, *vehicle*, 272
Sedate, *thoughtful*, 451
  calm, 826
  grave, 837
Sedative, *calming*, 174
  sleep, 683
  remedy, 662
Sedentary, *quiescence*, 265
Sederunt, *council*, 696
Sediment, *dregs*, 653
  remainder, 40
Sedition, *disobedience*, 742
Seduce, *entice*, 615
  vice, 945
  impurity, 961
  love, 897
Seducer, *libertine*, 962
Seducing, *charming*, 829
Seduction, *impurity*, 961
Seductive, *attractive*, 829,
          845, 897
Sedulous, *active*, 682
See, *view*, 441
  look, 457
  bishopric, 995
See to, *manage*, 693
Seed, *cause*, 153
  posterity, 167
Seedling, *youth*, 129
Seedy, *weak*, 160
  ailing, 655
  worn, 651
Seek, *inquire*, 461
  pursue, 622
Seem, *appear*, 448
Seeming, *semblance*, 448
Seemly, *expedient*, 646
  proper, 927
  handsome, 845

Seepage, *egress*, 295
Seer, *veteran*, 130
  oracle, 513
  sorcerer, 994
Seesaw, *oscillation*, 314
Seethe, *boil*, 382, 384
Segar, *tobacco*, 298A
Segment, *part*, 51
  circularity, 247
Segnitude, *inactivity*, 683
Segregate, *exclude*, 55
  separate, 44
  safety, 664
  not related, 10
  incoherent, 47
Seignior, *master*, 745
Seisin, *possession*, 777
Seismometer, *impulse*, 276
Seize, *take*, 789
  rob, 791
  possess, 777
Seizure, *weakness*, 160
  disease, 655
Seldom, *infrequency*, 137
Select, *choose*, 609
  good, 648
Selection, *part*, 51
Self, *special*, 13
Self-abasement, *humility*,
              87
Self-accusation, *penitence*,
              95
Self-admiration, *pride*, 88
Self-advertisement,
  boasting, 884
Self-applause, *vanity*, 880
Self-assertion, *effrontery*,
              88
Self-centred, *selfish*, 943
Self-communing, *thought*,
              45
Self-complacency, *conceit*,
              88
Self-conceit, *conceit*, 880
Self-confidence, *conceit*, 880
Self-conquest, *restraint*, 953
Self-consciousness, *know-*
  ledge, 490
  modesty, 881
Self-contempt, *humility*,
              879
Self-control, *restraint*, 942
Self-deceit, *error*, 495
Self-defence, *defence*, 717
Self-delusion, *credulity*, 486
Self-denial, *disinterested-*
  ness, 942
  temperance, 953
Self-evident, *clear*, 478
  certain, 474
Self-examination, *thought*,
              451

Sermon, *dissertation*, 595
   lesson, 537
   speech, 582
   pastoral, 998
Serosity, *fluidity*, 333
Serpent, *tortuous*, 248
   Satan, 978
   deceiver, 548
   cunning, 702
   evil, 663
Serpentine, *convolution*, 248
Serrated, *angular*, 244
   notched, 257
Serried, *crowded*, 72
   dense, 321
Serum, *lymph*, 333
   water, 337
Servant, *servant*, 711, 746
Serve, *aid*, 707
   obey, 743, 749
   work, 625, 680
   suffice, 639
Serve out, *apportion*, 786
   punish, 972
Service, *good*, 618
   use, 677
   utility, 644
   worship, 990
   servitude, 749
   warfare, 722
Serviceable, *useful*, 644
   good, 648
Servile, *obsequious*, 886
   flattery, 933
Servitor, *servant*, 746
Servitude, *subjection*, 749
Sesqui-, *number*, 87
* Sesquipedalia verba, *ornament*, 577
Sesquipedalian, *long*, 200
Sessions, *legal*, 966
   council, 696
Sestina, *poetry*, 597
Set, *condition*, 7
   group, 72
   class, 75
   firm, 43
   to place, 184
   establish, 150
   prepare, 673
   sharpen, 253
   solidify, 321
   leaning, 278
   gang, 712
   lease, 796
   habitual, 613
Set about, *begin*, 676
Set apart, *disjoin*, 55
Set aside, *disregard*, 460
   annul, 756
   release, 927A
Set-back, *hindrance*, 706

Set-back, *adversity*, 735
   relapse, 661
Set down, *humiliate*, 879
   censure, 932
   slight, 929
   rebuff, 732
Set fire to, *burn*, 384
Set foot in, *ingress*, 294
Set forth, *publish*, 531
   tell, 527
   show, 525
   assert, 535
   describe, 594
Set forward, *depart*, 293
Set in, *begin*, 66
   tide, 348
   approach, 286
Set off, *depart*, 293
   compensate, 30
   adorn, 845
Set-off, *foil*, 14
Set on, *attack*, 615
Set out, *begin*, 66
   depart, 293
   decorate, 845
Set right, *reinstate*, 660
Set sail, *depart*, 293
Set-square, *angularity*, 244
Set-to, *combat*, 720
Set to work, *begin*, 676
Set up, *raise*, 307
   prosperous, 734
Set-up, *state*, 7
   structure, 329
   plan, 626
Set upon, *attack*, 716
   desire, 865
   willing, 602
   determined, 604, 620
Setaceous, *rough*, 256
Settee, *support*, 215
Setting, *surroundings*, 227
Settle, *decide*, 480
   be fixed, 141
   be stationary, 265
   place, 184
   dwell, 186
   sink, 306
   arrange, 60
   pacify, 723
   defeat, 731
   consent, 762
   pay, 807
   give, 784
   bench, 215
Settlement, *location*, 184
   colony, 188
   dregs, 653
   compact, 762, 769
   property, 780
Settler, *inhabitant*, 188
Seven, *number*, 98

Seventy-four, *ship*, 273
Sever, *disjoin*, 44
Several, *repetition*, 102
   special, 79
Severally, *one by one*, 44, 79
   sharing, 786
Severe, *harsh*, 739
   energetic, 171
   painful, 830
   unadorned, 576, 849
   critical, 932
   greatness, 31
Sew, *join*, 43
Sewer, *drain*, 295, 350
   cloaca, 653
Sex, *kind*, 75
   women, 374
Sex-appeal, *charm*, 829
Sexagesimal, *sixty*, 98
Sexcentenary, *celebration*, 883
Sext, *worship*, 990
Sextant, *angularity*, 244
   roundness, 247
Sextet, *number*, 98
Sextodecimo, *book*, 593
Sexton, *church*, 996
   interment, 363
Sextuple, *number*, 98
* Sforzando, *music*, 415
Sgraffito, *see* Graffito
Shabby, *mean*, 819, 874
   bad, 649
   disgraceful, 940
   trifling, 643
   smallness, 32
Shack, *abode*, 189
Shackle, *to tie*, 43
   hinder, 706
   restrain, 751
   fetter, 752
Shade, *darkness*, 421
   shadow, 424
   colour, 428
   degree, 26
   difference, 15, 41
   small quantity, 32
   screen, 530
   manes, 362
   ghost, 980
   decrease, 36
Shaded, *invisible*, 447
Shades, *hell*, 982
Shading off, *degree*, 26
Shadow, *darkness*, 421
   shade, 424
   error, 495
   phantom, 4
   little, 193, 203
   small in degree, 32
   part, 51
   sequence, 281

Shut up, *confute*, 479
Shutter, *shade*, 424
Shuttlecock, *irresolute*, 605
Shy, *avoid*, 623
  suspicious, 485
  unwilling, 603
  modest, 881
  fearful, 862
  propel, 276, 284
Shylock, *usurer*, 805
Shyster, *knave*, 941
Sib, *relation*, 11
Sibilant, *hiss*, 409
Sibilation, *decry*, 929
  censure, 932
Sibling, *relation*, 11
Sibyl, *oracle*, 513
  ugly, 846
Sibylline, *prediction*, 511
* Sic, *imitation*, 19
  word, 562
Sick, *ill*, 655
  tired, 841
Sicken, *weary*, 841
  nauseate, 395
  fall ill, 655
  disgust, 830, 867
  hate, 898
Sickle, *instrument*, 244
  sharpness, 253
Sickly, *ill*, 655
  weak, 160
Sickness, *disease*, 655
Side, *laterality*, 236
  party, 712
  affectation, 855
  insolence, 878, 885
Side-car, *vehicle*, 272
Side-kick, *friend*, 890
  associate, 88
  partner, 711
Side-slip, *deviation*, 279
Side-track, *set aside*, 678
Side with, *aid*, 707
Sideboard, *receptacle*, 191
  whisker, 256
Sideburns, *whiskers*, 256
Sidelight, *interpretation*, 522
Sidelong, *lateral*, 236
Sidereal, *world*, 318
Sideways, *oblique*, 217
  lateral, 236
Sidle, *oblique*, 217
  deviate, 279, 291
  lateral, 236
Siege, *attack*, 716
Siesta, *inactivity*, 683
Sieve, *perforation*, 260
  to sort, 60
Sift, *to sort*, 60
  winnow, 42
  clean, 652

Sift, *inquire*, 461
  discriminate, 465
Sigh, *lament*, 839
Sigh for, *desire*, 865
Sight, *vision*, 441
  spectacle, 448
  prodigy, 872
  large quantity, 31
Sightless, *blind*, 442
  invisible, 447
Sightly, *beauty*, 845
Sightseer, *spectator*, 444
Sigil, *seal*, 550
  evidence, 467
Sigmoidal, *convolution*, 248
Sign, *indication*, 550
  omen, 512
  record, 551
  write, 590
  prodigy, 872
  evidence, 467
  compact, 769
Sign manual, *sign*, 550
Signal, *sign*, 550
  manifest, 525
  important, 642
  greatness, 31
Signalize, *celebrate*, 883
  glory, 873
Signally, *great*, 31
Signature, *mark*, 550
  writing, 590
Signboard, *indication*, 550
Signet, *evidence*, 467
  signature, 550
  sign of authority, 747
Significant, *meaning*, 516, 527
  clear, 518
  foreboding, 511
  important, 642
Signify, *mean*, 516
  inform, 527
  forebode, 511
* Signor, *title*, 877
Silence, *no sound*, 403
  aphony, 581
  confute, 479
  taciturn, 585
  to check, 731
Silhouette, *portrait*, 556
  outline, 229
Silk, *smooth*, 255
Silk hat, *dress*, 225
Siller, *money*, 800
Silly, *irrational*, 477
  credulous, 486
  foolish, 499
Silt, *dirt*, 653
  dregs, 50
Silver, *money*, 800
Silver-toned, *harmony*, 413

Silver wedding, *celebration*, 883
  anniversary, 138
Silversmith, *artist*, 559
Silvery, *colour*, 430
  voice, 580
Similar, *relation*, 9
  resembling, 17
  comparison, 464
Simile, Similitude, *see* Similar
Simmer, *heat*, 382, 384
  excitement, 824
Simoleons, *money*, 800
Simon Stylites, *hermit*, 893
Simony, *churchdom*, 995
Simoon, *blast*, 349
  heat, 382
Simp, *fool*, 501
Simper, *smile*, 838
  affectation, 855
Simple, *unmixed*, 42
  unadorned, 576, 849
  small, 32
  credulous, 486
  silly, 499
  true, 543
Simpleton, *fool*, 501
Simplify, *meaning*, 518
Simulate, *resemble*, 17
  imitate, 19
  cheat, 544
Simultaneous, *contemporary*, 120
Sin, *guilt*, 947
  vice, 945
Sin-offering, *atonement*, 952
Since, *in order*, 8, 63
  in time, 117
  because, 155, 476, 615
Sincere, *veracious*, 543
  ingenuous, 703
Sinecure, *receipt*, 810
* Sine die, *neverness*, 107
  long duration, 110
* Sine qua non, *condition*, 770
  importance, 642
  requirement, 630
Sinewy, *strong*, 159
  tough, 327
* Sinfonietta, *music*, 415
Sinful, *evil*, 947
Sing, *music*, 415
  poetry, 597
  cheerful, 836
  rejoice, 838
Sing out, *cry*, 411
Sing-song, *untuneful*, 414
  concert, 415
  repetition, 104

Singe, *burn*, 384
Singer, *musician*, 416
Single, *unit*, 87
  unmixed, 42
  secluded, 893
  unmarried, 904
Single-handed, *unaided*, 708
Single-minded, *honest*, 543
Single out, *select*, 609
Singlet, *dress*, 225
Sing Sing, *prison*, 752
* Singspiel, *drama*, 599
Singular, *exceptional*, 79, 83
  one, 87
  remarkable, 31
Sinister, *left*, 239
  bad, 649
  discourtesy, 895
  menacing, 909
  vicious, 945
Sink, *descend*, 306
  lower, 308
  submerge, 310
  deep, 208
  fail, 732
  destroy, 162
  decay, 659
  fatigue, 688
  cloaca, 653
  depressed, 837
  droop, 828
  conceal, 528
  neglect, 460
  in the memory, 505
Sinless, *good*, 946
Sinner, *sinner*, 949
  impiety, 988
Sinuous, *curved*, 245
  convoluted, 248
Sinus, *concavity*, 252
Sip, *drink*, 296
  smallness, 32
Siphon, *conduit*, 350
Sir, *respect*, 877
Sirdar, *master*, 745
Sire, *elder*, 166
Siren, *musician*, 416
  indication, 550
  alarm, 669
  seducing, 615
  sea, 341
  demon, 980
  evildoer, 913
Sirocco, *wind*, 349
  heat, 382
Sissy, *weakness*, 160
Sister, *kindred*, 11
  likeness, 17
Sisterhood, *assembly*, 72
  party, 712
Sisyphean, *difficulty*, 704

Sit, *repose*, 215
  lie, 213
  lowering, 308
Site, *situation*, 183
Sitting, *consultation*, 696
Situate, *location*, 184
Situation, *circumstances*, 8
  place, 183
  business, 625
Siva, *deity*, 979
Six, *number*, 98
Six-shooter, *gun*, 727
Sixth sense, *intuition*, 477
Size, *magnitude*, 31, 192
  grade, 60
  glue, 45, 352
  quantity, 25
Size up, *measure*, 466
  estimate, 480
  scrutinize, 457
Sizy, *sticky*, 350
Sjambok, *scourge*, 975
Skate, *locomotion*, 266
Skean, *arms*, 727
Skedaddle, *escape*, 671
  go away, 293, 287
Skein, *knot*, 219
  disorder, 59
Skeleton, *corpse*, 362
  frame, 626
  small, 193
  lean, 203
  imperfect, 651
  essential part, 50
Skelp, *impact*, 276
  punishment, 972
Sketch, *painting*, 556
  description, 594
  plan, 626
Sketcher, *artist*, 559
Sketchy, *imperfect*, 53, 651
Skew, *obliquity*, 217
Skew-whiff, *oblique*, 217
Skewbald, *variegation*, 440
Skewer, *vinculum*, 45
Ski, *locomotion*, 266
Skid, *deviation*, 279
  hindrance, 706
Skiff, *boat*, 273
Skiffle, *melody*, 413
Skill, *ability*, 450, 698
Skim, *move*, 266
  rapid, 274
  attend lightly, 458, 460
Skimp, *shorten*, 201
  stint, 640
  save, 817
Skin, *tegument*, 222
  to peel, 226
Skin-deep, *shallow*, 220
Skinflint, *miser*, 819
Skinful, *fullness*, 52

Skinny, *small*, 193
  slender, 203
  tegumentary, 222
Skip, *jump*, 309
  neglect, 460
  omit, 773
  escape, 671
  dance, 840
Skipjack, *upstart*, 734, 876
Skipper, *master*, 745
Skirl, *shriek*, 410, 411
  lamentation, 839
Skirmish, *fight*, 720, 722
Skirt, *edge*, 230
  appendix, 39
  pendent, 214
  circumjacent, 227
  woman, 374
Skirting-board, *base*, 211
Skit, *parody*, 856
  satire, 932
Skite, *boast*, 884
Skittish, *capricious*, 608
  bashful, 881
  excitable, 825
  timid, 862
Skivvy, *servant*, 746
* Skoal, *drink*, 959
Skulk, *hide*, 447, 528
  coward, 860
  flock, 72
Skull, *head*, 450
Skunk, *fetid*, 401
  bad man, 949
Sky, *world*, 318
  air, 338
  summit, 210
Sky-line, *outline*, 229
Sky-rocket, *ascent*, 350
Skylark, *frolic*, 840
Skylight, *opening*, 260
Skymaster, *aircraft*, 273A
Skyscraper, *height*, 206
Slab, *layer*, 204
  flatness, 251
  record, 551
Slabber, *ejection*, 297
Slack, *loose*, 47
  weak, 160
  slow, 275
  inert, 172
  inactive, 683
  unwilling, 603
  laxity, 738
  to moderate, 174
  retard, 706
  calm, 826
Slacken, *relax*, 687
Slacker, *evasion*, 623
Slacks, *dress*, 225
Slag, *refuse*, 40
  dirt, 653

Somewhere, *place*, 182
Somnambulism, *imagination*, 515
Somniferous, *sleepy*, 683
  weary, 841
Somnolence, *sleepy*, 683
  weary, 841
Son, *relation*, 167
Sonance, *sound*, 402
Sonata, *music*, 415
Song, *music*, 415
Song, old, *unimportant*, 643
Songster, *musician*, 416
Soniferous, *sound*, 402
Sonnet, *poetry*, 597
Sonorous, *sound*, 402
  loud, 404
Sonsy, *fat*, 102
Soon, *early*, 132
  transient, 111
Soot, *black*, 431
  dirt, 653
  blemish, 846
Sooth, *truth*, 494
Soothe, *allay*, 174
  calm, 826
  relieve, 834
Soothsay, *predict*, 511
Soothsayer, *omen*, 513
  magician, 994
Sop, *bribe*, 615
  reward, 973
  wet, 337
Sophism, *bad logic*, 477
  absurdity, 497
Sophisticate, *mix*, 41
  mislead, 477
  debase, 659
Sophistry, *false reasoning*, 477
  misteaching, 538
Sophomore, *learner*, 541
Sophy, *ruler*, 745
Soporific, *sleepy*, 683
  boring, 841
Sopping, *moist*, 339
Soprano, *music*, 413
  high note, 409, 410
Sorcerer, *sorcerer*, 994
Sorcery, *occult arts*, 992
* Sordes, *uncleanness*, 653
Sordid, *mean*, 819
  base, 876
Sordine, *silencer*, 417
  damper, 403
Sore, *pain*, 378
  grievance, 828
  painful, 830
  angry, 900
Sorehead, *discourtesy*, 895
Sorely, *greatness*, 31
Sorites, *reasoning*, 476

Sororicide, *killing*, 361
Sorrel, *redness*, 434
Sorrow, *pain*, 828
Sorry, *grieved*, 828
  penitent, 950
  pitiful, 914
  bad, 649
  mean, 876
  trifling, 643
  smallness, 32
Sort, *kind*, 75
  degree, 26
  rectify, 658, 660
  to arrange, 60
  simplify, 42
* Sortes, *chance*, 156, 621
  prediction, 511
Sortie, *attack*, 716
Sortilege, *sorcery*, 992
  prediction, 511
  chance, 621
Sorting, *arrangement*, 60
* Sostenuto, *music*, 415
Sot, *fool*, 501
  drunkard, 959
* Sotto voce, *faintness*, 405
  aphony, 581
  stammering, 583
Sou, *money*, 800
Soubrette, *actress*, 599
  servant, 746
Sough, *conduit*, 350
  cloaca, 653
  wind, 349
Soul, *intrinsic*, 5
  intellect, 450
  affections, 820
  man, 373
  important part, 50, 642
Soulful, *feeling*, 821
Soulless, *insensible*, 823
Sound, *noise*, 402
  healthy, 654
  perfect, 650
  good, 648
  great, 31
  to measure, 466
  to investigate, 461
  true, 494
  wise, 498
  orthodox, 983A
  bay, 343
  gap, 198
Sounder, *herd*, 72
Sounding-rod, *depth*, 208
Soundings, *deep*, 208
Soundless, *deep*, 208
  silent, 403
Soundly, *great*, 31
Soup, *food*, 298
  pulp, 354
Soup-and-fish, *dress*, 225

* Soupçon, *little*, 32, 193
  mixture, 41
Sour, *acid*, 397
  uncivil, 895
  misanthropic, 901
  to embitter, 835
Source, *origin*, 66, 153
Sourdine, *silencer*, 417
Souse, *immerse*, 300
  water, 337
Soutane, *canonicals*, 999
* Souteneur, *libertine*, 962
South, *opposite*, 237
Souvenir, *memory*, 505
Sou'wester, *dress*, 225
Sovereign, *great*, 31
  superiority, 33
  strong, 157
  ruler, 745
Sovereignty, *authority*, 737
Soviet, *council*, 696
Sow, *scatter*, 73
  cultivate, 371
  prepare, 673
Sozzled, *drunk*, 959
Spa, *salubrity*, 656
  remedy, 662
Space, *room*, 180
  separate, 44
Space ship, *aircraft*, 273A
Space travel, *voyage*, 267
Spacious, *roomy*, 180
Spade, *sharpness*, 253
Spaewife, *oracle*, 513
Spahi, *combatant*, 726
Spalpeen, *bad man*, 949
Span, *distance*, 196
  nearness, 197
  length, 200
  measure, 466
  time, 106
  duality, 89
Spandule, *demon*, 980
Spangle, *spark*, 420
  ornament, 847
Spaniel, *servile*, 886
  flatterer, 935
Spank, *impact*, 276
  beat, 972
Spanking, *size*, 192
Spar, *discord*, 713
  contention, 720, 722
Spare, *meagre*, 203
  scanty, 640
  to give, 784
  relinquish, 782
  disuse, 678
  exempt, 927A
  refrain, 623
  pity, 914
  frugal, 953
  economic, 817

Spare, *superfluous*, 641
in reserve, 636
Spare time, *leisure*, 685
Sparge, *sprinkle*, 73
Sparing, *temperate*, 953
small, 32
economic, 817
Spark, *light*, 420
fire, 382
fop, 854
court, 902
Sparkle, *glisten*, 420
bubble, 353
Sparkling, *vigorous*, 574
Sparse, *scattered*, 73
tenuous, 322
few, 103
* Sparsim, *non-assemblage*, 73
Spartan, *severe*, 739
Spasm, *fit*, 173
throe, 146
pain, 378, 828
Spasmodic, *fitful*, 139
Spat, *quarrel*, 713
Spatial, *space*, 99
Spatter, *dirt*, 653
damage, 659
Spatterdash, *dress*, 225
Spatula, *layer*, 204
trowel, 191
Spawn, *dirt*, 653
offspring, 167
Spay, *sterilize*, 169
Speak, *speech*, 582
Speak fair, *conciliate*, 615
Speak of, *mean*, 516
Speak to, *allocution*, 586
Speak out, *disclose*, 529
Speaker, *speech*, 582
teacher, 540
interpreter, 524
president, 745
Spear, *lance*, 727
to pierce, 260
pass through, 302
Spearman, *combatant*, 726
Special, *particular*, 79
peculiar, 5
Special pleading, *sophistry*, 477
Specialist, *adviser*, 695
doctor, 662
proficient, 700
Speciality, *intrinsic*, 5
particular, 79
Specie, *money*, 800
Species, *kind*, 75
appearance, 448
Specific, *special*, 79
Specification, *description*, 594

Specify, *name*, 564
tell, 527
Specimen, *example*, 82
Specious, *probable*, 472
sophistical, 477
plausible, 937
Speck, *dot*, 193
small quantity, 32
blemish, 848
Speckle, *variegated*, 400
blemish, 848
Spectacle, *appearance*, 448
show, 882
prodigy, 872
Spectacles, *optical instrument*, 445
Spectator, *spectator*, 444
Spectre, *vision*, 448
ugly, 846
ghost, 980
Spectroscope, *optical*, 445
colour, 428
Spectrum, *colour*, 428
appearance, 448
Speculate, *think*, 451
suppose, 514
chance, 621
venture, 675
traffic, 794
view, 441
Speculum, *mirror*, 445
Speech, *speech*, 582
Speechless, *silence*, 581
Speed, *velocity*, 274
activity, 682
haste, 684
to help, 707
succeed, 731
Speedometer, *velocity*, 274
measure, 466
Speedwalk, *way*, 627
Speer, *ask*, 461
Spell, *interpret*, 522
read, 539
period, 106
charm, 993
necessity, 601
motive, 615
exertion, 686
Spellbound, *motive*, 615
Spelling, *letters*, 561
Spencer, *dress*, 225
Spencerism, *causation*, 153
Spend, *expend*, 809
waste, 638
Spendthrift, *prodigal*, 818
Spent, *exhausted*, 688
Spermaceti, *oil*, 356
Spew, *ejection*, 297
Sphere, *ball*, 249
region, 181
world, 318

Sphere, *rank*, 26
business, 625
Spheroid, *round*, 249
Spherule, *round*, 249
Sphinx, *oracle*, 513
monster, 83
Spice, *small quantity*, 32
mixture, 41
pungent, 392
condiment, 393
Spick and span, *clean*, 123
Spicule, *sharp*, 253
Spidery, *narrowness*, 203
Spiflicate, *trounce*, 972
Spike, *to pierce*, 260
plug, 263
pass through, 302
sharp, 253
Spile, *stopper*, 263
Spill, *filament*, 205
fuel, 388
to shed, 297
waste, 638
splash, 348
disclose, 529
lavish, 818
misuse, 679
fall, 306
Spin, *rotation*, 312
excursion, 266
velocity, 274
reject, 610
Spin out, *prolong*, 200
protract, 110, 133
style, 573
Spindle, *rotation*, 312
Spindle-shanked, *thin*, 193, 203
Spindrift, *spray*, 353
Spine, *sharpness*, 253
Spineless, *vicious*, 945
weak, 160
irresolute, 605
Spinet, *musical instrument*, 417
Spinney, *plant*, 367
Spinster, *celibacy*, 904
Spiracle, *air-pipe*, 351
Spiral, *convolution*, 248
Spire, *peak*, 253
height, 206
soar, 305
Spirit, *essence*, 5
immateriality, 317
intellect, 450
affections, 820
resolutions, 604
courage, 861
ghost, 980
style, 576
activity, 682
to stimulate, 824

Spirit-level, *horizontal,* 213
Spirited, *brave,* 861
　generous, 942
Spiritless, *torpid,* 823
　dejected, 837
　timid, 862
Spirits, *cheerfulness,* 836
　intoxicant, 959
Spiritual, *immaterial,* 317
　mental, 450
　divine, 976
　piety, 987
Spiritualism, *occult arts,*
　　　　　　　992
* Spirituel, *witty,* 842
* Spirituoso, *music,* 415
Spirt, *see* Spurt
Spissitude, *density,* 321, 352
Spit, *eject,* 297
　pierce, 302
　rain, 348
　bar, 253
Spite, *malevolence,* 907
　enmity, 889
　notwithstanding, 179
Spitfire, *fury,* 173, 901
Spittle, *excretion,* 299
Spittoon, *receptacle,* 191
Spiv, *knave,* 941
　bad man, 949
　cheat, 548
　swindler, 792
Splanchnic, *interior,* 221
Splash, *affuse,* 337
　spill, 348
　spatter, 653
　sully, 846
　parade, 882
　publicity, 531
Splatter, *wet,* 337
Splay, *angularity,* 244
Splay-footed, *distorted,* 243
Spleen, *melancholy,* 837
　hatred, 898
　anger, 900
　discourteous, 895
Spleenless, *good-natured,*
　　　　　　　906
Splendid, *beautiful,* 845
　glorious, 873
　excellent, 648
Splendour, *light,* 420
Splenetic, *sad,* 837
　ill-tempered, 895
　irascible, 901
Splice, *join,* 43
　entwine, 219
　marry, 903
Splinter, *divide,* 44
　brittle, 328
　bit, 51, 205
Split, *divide,* 44, 91

Split, *quarrel,* 713
　fail, 732
　laugh, 838
Split hairs, *argue,* 465
　sophistry, 477
Split-new, *new,* 123
Splosh, *money,* 800
Splurge, *ostentation,* 882
Splutter, *stammer,* 583
　haste, 684
　energy, 171
　spitting, 297
Spoil, *vitiate,* 659
　hinder, 706
　plunder, 791
　booty, 793
　injure, 649
　indulge, 740
　satiate, 869
Spoke, *tooth,* 253
　radius, 200
　obstruct, 706
Spokesman, *interpreter,* 524
　speaker, 582
Spoliate, *plunder,* 791
　evil, 619
Spondulicks, *money,* 800
Sponge, *clean,* 652
　despoil, 791
　porous, 322
　oblivion, 506
　petitioner, 767
　parasite, 886
Spongy, *soft,* 324
Sponsion, *security,* 771
Sponson, *support,* 215
Sponsor, *security,* 771
　evidence, 467
Spontaneous, *voluntary,*
　　　　　　600, 602
　free, 748
　impulsive, 612
Spoof, *deception,* 545
Spook, *ghost,* 980
Spoon, *receptacle,* 191
　ladle, 272
　club, 276
　to make love, 902
Spoonerism, *blunder,* 495
　inversion, 218
　ridiculousness, 853, 856
Spoonful, *quantity,* 25
Spoony, *fool,* 499
　amorous, 897
Spoor, *track,* 551
Spore, *particle,* 330
Sporran, *pouch,* 191
Sport, *amusement,* 840
　gaiety, 836
　wit, 842
　enjoyment, 827
　contention, 720

Sport, *subjection,* 749
　abnormality, 83
Sports car, *vehicle,* 272
Sportsman, *courage,* 861
　game, 840
　good man, 948
Spot, *place,* 182
　decoloration, 429
　blemish, 848
　to sully, 846
　blot, 874
　disgrace, 940
　to detect, 457, 480A
Spotless, *innocent,* 946
　clean, 652
　good, 648, 650
　fair, 845
Spotty, *spotted,* 440
Spousals, *marriage,* 903
Spouse, *married,* 903
　companion, 88
Spouseless, *celibacy,* 904
Spout, *conduit,* 350
　egress, 295
　flow out, 348
　speak, 582
　act, 599
Sprain, *strain,* 160
Sprawl, *lie,* 213
　leap, 309
Spray, *sprig,* 51
　plant, 367
　cover, 222
　sprinkle, 337
　sprinkler, 348
Spread, *enlarge,* 35
　expand, 194
　disperse, 73
　diverge, 291
　expanse, 180
　publish, 531
Spread-eagleism, *boasting,*
　　　　　　　884
　bombast, 577
Spree, *frolic,* 840
　intemperance, 954
Sprig, *part,* 51
　scion, 167
Sprightly, *cheerful,* 836
　witty, 842
Spring, *early,* 125
　cause, 153
　arise from, 154
　ensue, 151
　strength, 159
　velocity, 274
　leap, 309
　rivulet, 348
　instrument, 633
　store, 636
Spring back, *elastic,* 325
　recoil, 277

Stake, *payment,* 807
  danger, 665
  security, 771
  property, 780
  execution, 975
Stalactite, *lining,* 224
Stalagmite, *lining,* 224
Stale, *old,* 124
  vapid, 866
  weary, 841
Stalemate, *non-completion,*
       730
Stalk, *follow,* 266
  pursue, 622
Stalking-horse, *plea,* 617
  deception, 545
Stall, *lodge,* 189
  mart, 799
  theatre, 599
  cathedral, 1000
  delay, 133
Stallion, *horse,* 271
Stalwart, *strong,* 159
  large, 192
Stamina, *strength,* 159
  resolution, 604
Stammel, *redness,* 434
Stammer, *stutter,* 583
Stamp, *character,* 7
  form, 240
  mould, 22
  to impress, 505
  mark, 550
  record, 551
  complete, 729
  security, 771
Stampede, *flight,* 287
  fear, 860, 862
Stance, *footing,* 175
Stanch, *dam up,* 348
  stop, 658
Stanchion, *support,* 215
Stand, *to be,* 1
  rest, 265
  be present, 186
  to continue, 141, 143
  endure, 110
  station, 58
  rank, 71
  support, 215
  resistance, 719
Stand against, *resist,* 719
Stand by, *near,* 197
  be firm, 604
  befriend, 707
  auxiliary, 711
Stand for, *represent,* 550
  signify, 516
Stand-in, *substitute,* 147,
       634
  deputy, 759
  assistant, 711

Stand in with, *participation,*
       778
Stand off, *distance,* 196, 287
Stand-offish, *unsociable,*
       893
Stand on, *support,* 215
Stand out, *project,* 250
  appear, 446
  opposition, 708
Stand still, *stop,* 265
  remain, 141
Stand over, *lateness,* 133
Stand up, *vertical,* 212
  elevation, 307
  disappoint, 509
Stand up for, *vindicate,* 937
Stand up to, *courage,* 861
Standard, *rule,* 80
  measure, 466
  degree, 26
  pupil, 541
  colours, 550
  good, 648
  prototype, 22
Standard-bearer, *combatant,*
       726
Standardize, *conformity,* 82
Standing, *footing,* 8
  term, 71
  situation, 183
  degree, 26
  repute, 873
  vertical, 212
Standpoint, *aspect,* 453
Stanza, *poetry,* 597
Staple, *whole,* 50
  peg, 214
  mart, 799
Star, *luminary,* 423
  decoration, 877
  ornament, 847
  glory, 873
  actor, 599, 599A
Star Chamber, *jurispru-
  dence,* 966
Star-gazer, *astronomer,* 318
Starbeam, *light,* 420
  dimness, 422
Starboard, *dextrality,* 238
Starch, *viscidity,* 352
Starchy, *stiff,* 323
  proud, 878
  affected, 855
Stare, *look,* 441
  curiosity, 455
  wonder, 870
Staring, *visible,* 446
Stark, *stiff,* 323
  stubborn, 606
Starless, *dark,* 421
Starlight, *light,* 420
  dimness, 422

Stars, *celestial,* 318
  necessity, 601
Stars and Stripes, *flag,* 550
Start, *depart,* 293
  begin, 66
  desultory, 139
  jump, 139; *arise,* 151
  suggest, 514
  from surprise, 508
  from fear, 860
  from wonder, 870
Start up, *project,* 250
  appear, 446
Starting-point, *beginning,*
  departure, 293 [66
Startle, *unexpected,* 508
  wonder, 870
  fear, 860
  doubt, 485
Starve, *fast,* 956
  with cold, 383, 385
  want, 804
Starved, *lean,* 193
  insufficient, 640
Starveling, *pinched,* 203
  poor, 804
  famished, 640
State, *condition,* 7
  nation, 372
  ostentation, 882
  property, 780
  to inform, 527
  assert, 535
  describe, 594
State trooper, *police,* 965
Stateless, *displaced,* 185
Stately, *pompous,* 882
  proud, 878
  grand, 873
Statement, *information,*
       527
  assertion, 535
Stateroom, *chamber,* 191
Statesman, *master,* 745
Statesmanship, *direction,*
Statics, *gravity,* 319 [694
Station, *stage,* 58
  term, 71
  place, 182, 183
  to locate, 184
  stopping-place, 292
  rank, 26, 873
Stationary, *quiescence,* 265
Stationery, *writing,* 590
Statist, *statesman,* 745
Statistics, *numeration,* 85
  list, 86
Statue, *sculpture,* 557
  representation, 554
Stature, *height,* 206

Status, *standing*, 8, 71
   situation, 183
   order, 58
   rank, 873
* Status quo, *reversion*, 145
Statute, *law*, 697, 963
Staunch, *spirited*, 604
   trusty, 939
   healthy, 654
Stave, *verse*, 597
Stave in, *open*, 260
   concavity, 252
Stave off, *defer*, 133
Stay, *wait*, 133
   continue, 141
   exist, 1; *support*, 215
   refuge, 666
   rest, 265; *prevent*, 706
   dissuade, 616
   corset, 225
Stead, *utility*, 644
Steadfast, *resolved*, 604
   stable, 150
   quiescent, 265
   thought, 451
Steading, *farm*, 189
Steady, *resolved*, 604
   cautious, 864
   still, 265
   constant, 138, 150
   normal, 82
Steady as she goes, *caution*,
Steal, *rob*, 791   [864
   creep, 275, 528
Steal away, *evade*, 671
Stealth, *concealment*, 528
Steam, *vapour*, 334, 353
   to sail, 267
Steamboat, *ship*, 273
Steamer, *ship*, 273
Steam-roller, *compel*, 744
Stearic, *unctuous*, 355
Stearin, *fat*, 356
Steed, *horse*, 271
Steek, *close*, 261
Steel, *strength*, 159
   sharpener, 253
   inure, 823
Steel-cut, *engraving*, 558
Steeled, *resolved*, 604
Steelyard, *scale*, 466
   weight, 319
Steep, *slope*, 217
   height, 206
   immerse, 300
   soak, 337; *clean*, 652
Steeple, *spire*, 253
   high, 206
Steeplechase, *race*, 274
   pursuit, 282, 622
Steer, *guide*, 693

Steer for, *direction*, 278
Steersman, *director*, 694
Steganography, *writing*, 590
Stegophilist, *climber*, 305
Stele, *record*, 551
Stellar, *heavens*, 318
Stem, *origin*, 153
   result, 154
   front, 234
   to oppose, 708
   to resist, 718
Sten, *gun*, 727
Stench, *fetor*, 401
Stencil, *copy*, 556
Stenographer, *secretary*, 553
Stenography, *writing*, 590
Stentorian, *loud*, 404
Step, *degree*, 26
   station, 58
   term, 71
   near, 197
   support, 215
   motion, 264, 266
   measure, 466
   expedient, 626
   means, 632
   action, 680
Steppe, *plain*, 344
Stepping-stone, *link*, 45
   way, 627
   preparation, 763
   resource, 666
Stercoraceous, *unclean*, 653
Stereoscope, *optical*, 445
Stereoscopic, *visible*, 446
Stereotype, *printing*, 591
   engraving, 558
Stereotyped, *ordinary*, 82
   habitual, 613
   fixed, 141, 150
Sterile, *unproductive*, 169
   useless, 645
   clean, 652
Sterling, *true*, 494
   good, 648
   virtuous, 944
   money, 800
Stern, *back*, 235
   severe, 739
   forbidding, 895
Stern-wheeler, *ship*, 273
Sternutation, *sneeze*, 349
   sound, 409
Sternway, *navigation*, 267
Stertorous, *sound*, 411
* Stet, *unchanged*, 150
Stetson, *hat*, 225
Stevedore, *doer*, 271, 690
Stew, *confusion*, 59
   fluster, 821
   difficulty, 704
   heat, 382

Stew, *cook*, 384
   perplex, 828
   bagnio, 961
Steward, *director*, 694
   agent, 690
   treasurer, 801
Stewardship, *charge*, 693
   conduct, 692
Stick, *adhere*, 46
   stop, 142
   continue, 143
   staff, 215
   to stab, 260, 830
   pierce, 302
   difficulty, 704
   fool, 501
   scourge, 975
Stick at, *demur*, 603
Stick in, *insert*, 300
   locate, 184
Stick-in-the-mud,   *in-*
   activity, 683
Stick out, *project*, 250
   erect, 212
Stick up, *project*, 250
   erect, 212, 307
   rob, 791
Stickit, *failure*, 732
Stickle, *haggle*, 769
   barter, 794
   reluctant, 603
Stickler, *obstinacy*, 606
   severity, 739
Sticky, *cohering*, 46
   semiliquid, 352
Stiff, *rigid*, 323
   resolute, 604
   difficult, 704
   restrained, 751
   severe, 739
   dear, 814
   affected, 855
   haughty, 878
   pompous, 882
   ugly, 846
   style, 572, 579
Stiff-necked, *obstinate*, 606
   resolute, 604
Stifle, *silence*, 403
   conceal, 528
   destroy, 162
   kill, 361
   sound, 405
Stigma, *disgrace*, 874
   blame, 932
Stigmatize, *accuse*, 938
Stile, *way*, 627
Stiletto, *piercer*, 262
   dagger, 727
Still, *ever*, 112
   silent, 403
   quiet, 174

Strain, *effort*, 686
   violence, 173
   fatigue, 688
   sound, 402
   melody, 413
   clean, 652
   to clarify, 658
   percolate, 295
   transgress, 304
   poetry, 597
   voice, 580
   misinterpret, 523
   kindred, 11
   style, 569
Strainer, *sieve*, 260
Strait, *maritime*, 343
   gap, 198
   difficulty, 704
   want, 804
   narrow, 203
Strait-laced, *severe*, 739
   censorious, 932
   haughty, 878
   stiff, 751
   fastidious, 868
Strait waistcoat, *restraint*,
   752
Straitened, *poor*, 804
Stramash, *agitation*, 315
   contention, 720
Strand, *shore*, 342
Stranded, *difficulty*, 704
   fixed, 150
   failure, 732
Strange, *exceptional*, 83
   wonderful, 870
   ridiculous, 853
Stranger, *extraneous*, 57
   ignorant, 491
Strangle, *choke*, 361
Strap, *to tie*, 43
   ligature, 45
   scourge, 975
Strap-oil, *punishment*, 972
Strappado, *punishment*, 972
Strapping, *large*, 192
   strong, 159
Stratagem, *plan*, 626
   artifice, 702
   deception, 545
Strategy, *conduct*, 692
   skill, 698
   warfare, 722
   plan, 626
Strath, *valley*, 252
Strathspey, *dance*, 840
Stratification, *layer*, 204
Stratocracy, *authority*, 737
Stratocruiser, *aircraft*, 273A
Stratoliner, *aircraft*, 273A
Stratosphere, *air*, 338
Stratum, *layer*, 204

Straw, *light*, 320
   trifling, 643
Straw-coloured, *yellow*, 436
Straw vote, *inquiry*, 461
Stray, *wander*, 266
   deviate, 279
   exceptional, 83
Streak, *colour*, 420
   stripe, 440
   furrow, 259
   narrow, 203
   intersection, 219
Stream, *flow*, 347
   river, 348
   of light, 420
   of time, 109
   of events, 151
   abundance, 639
Streamer, *flag*, 550
Streaming, *incoherent*, 47
Streamlet, *river*, 348
Street, *buildings*, 189
   way, 627
Street arab, *commonalty*,
   876
Street-car, *vehicle*, 272
Streetscape, *spectacle*, 448
Streetwalker, *libertine*, 962
Strength, *vigour*, 159
   power, 157
   greatness, 31
   energy, 171
   tenacity, 327
   degree, 26
Strengthen, *to increase*, 35
Strenuous, *active*, 682, 686
   resolved, 604
* Strepitoso, *music*, 415
Stress, *weight*, 642
   intonation, 580
   strain, 686
Stretch, *increase*, 35
   expand, 194
   lengthen, 200
   space, 180
   distance, 196
   exertion, 686
   encroachment, 925
   misinterpret, 523
   exaggeration, 549
Stretcher, *vehicle*, 272
   support, 215
Strew, *spread*, 73
Stria, *spot*, 440
   furrow, 259
Striate, *furrowed*, 259
   spotted, 440
Stricken, *hurt*, 828
Strict, *severe*, 739
   exact, 494
Stricture, *disapprobation*,
   932

Stride, *walk*, 266
   motion, 264
Strident, *harsh*, 410
Stridulous, *shrill*, 410
Strife, *quarrel*, 713, 720
Strike, *hit*, 276
   luck, 618
   beat, 972, 649
   revolt, 719, 742
   inaction, 681
   impress, 824
   wonder, 870
   operate, 170
   music, 415
Strike off, *exclude*, 55
Strike out, *invent*, 515
   plan, 626
   efface, 552
Strike up, *begin*, 66
Striking, *manifest*, 525
String, *continuity*, 69
   to tie, 43
   fibre, 205
   ligature, 45
   to arrange, 60
String up, *kill*, 361
* Stringendo, *music*, 415
Stringent, *severe*, 739
   compulsory, 744
Stringy, *narrow*, 203
   tough, 327
   viscous, 352
Strip, *to divest*, 226
   rob, 789, 791
   narrowness, 203
   filament, 205
Stripe, *length*, 200
   blow, 972
   mark, 550
   type, 75
   variegation, 440
Stripling, *youth*, 129
Stripped, *poor*, 804
Strive, *exert*, 686
   endeavour, 675, 676
   contend, 720
Stroke, *impulse*, 276
   mark, 550
   work, 680
   expedient, 626
   success, 731
   disease, 655
Stroll, *walk*, 266
Strong, *powerful*, 159
   energetic, 171
   vigorous, 574
   tenacious, 327
   pungent, 390, 392
   cogent, 467
   feeling, 821
Strong-box, *treasury*, 802
Strong-room, *treasury*, 802

Sublimation, *see* Sublimate
Sublime, *high*, 206
  beauty, 845
  glory, 873
  lofty, 574
  magnanimous, 942
Subliminal, *subconscious*, 450
Sublunary, *world*, 318
Submachine-gun, *arms*, 727
Submarine, *depth*, 208
  ship, 273
Submerge, *immerse*, 300
  steep, 337
  sink, 162, 208
  plunge, 310
Submission, *surrender*, 725, 879
Submissive, *humble*, 725, 879
  enduring, 826
Submit, *surrender*, 725
  obey, 743
Subordinate, *inferior*, 34
  unimportant, 643
  servant, 746
  subjection, 749
Subordination, *order*, 58
Suborn, *hire*, 795
  bribe, 784
Subpoena, *mandate*, 741
Subscribe, *assent*, 488
  agree to, 762, 769
  give, 707, 784
Subscription, *donation*, 809
Subsequent, *in time*, 117
  in order, 63, 65
Subservient, *utility*, 644
  intermediate, 631
  aiding, 707
  servility, 886
Subside, *sink*, 306
  cave in, 252
  decrease, 36
  calm down, 826
Subsidiary, *tending*, 176
  means, 632
  auxiliary, 707
Subsidy, *pay*, 809
  gift, 784
  aid, 707
Subsist, *existence*, 1
  life, 359
  continuance, 141
Subsistence, *food*, 298
  livelihood, 803
Subsistence money, *loan*, 787
  advance, 809
Subsoil, *earth*, 342
  interior, 221

Substance, *thing*, 3
  matter, 316
  interior, 221
  quantity, 25
  texture, 329
  compendium, 596
  meaning, 516
  important, 642
  wealth, 803
Substantial, *dense*, 321
  existence, 1
  true, 494
Substantially, *intrinsically*, 5
Substantiate, *demonstrate*, 478
  make good, 494, 924
Substantive, *substance*, 3
Substitute, *means*, 634
  deputy, 759
Substitution, *change*, 147
Substratum, *substance*, 3
  interior, 221
  layer, 204
  base, 211
  support, 215
  materiality, 316
Subsumption, *inclusion*, 76
Subterfuge, *lie*, 546
  sophistry, 477
  cunning, 702
Subterranean, *underground*, 208
Subtilize, *sophistry*, 477
Subtle, *cunning*, 702
  wise, 498
  rare, 322
  light, 320
  texture, 329
Subtract, *retrench*, 38
  diminish, 36
  arithmetical, 84
  to take, 789
Subtrahend, *deduction*, 38
  number, 84
Suburban, *environs*, 227
  distance, 197
Subvention, *aid*, 707
  gift, 784
Subvert, *invert*, 218
  depress, 308
  change, 140
  destroy, 162
Subway, *road*, 627
Succedaneum, *substitute*, 147, 634
Succeed, *answer*, 731
  follow, 63
* Succès d'estime, *approbation*, 931
Success, *success*, 731
Succession, *sequence*, 63

Succession, *transfer*, 783
  continuity, 69
  of time, 109
  lateness, 117
Successor, *sequel*, 65
  posterior, 117
Succinct, *concise*, 572
Succour, *help*, 707
Succubus, *demon*, 980
Succulent, *juicy*, 333
  edible, 298
  semiliquid, 352
Succumb, *yield*, 725
  obey, 743
  fatigue, 688
Such, *similarity*, 17
Suck, *imbibe*, 296
  deprive, 789
Sucker, *dupe*, 547
Suckling, *youth*, 129
Suction, *imbibition*, 296
Sudatorium, *furnace*, 386
Sudden, *early*, 132
  abrupt, 508
  transient, 111
Suds, *froth*, 353
Sue, *demand*, 765
  at law, 969
Suet, *fat*, 356
Suffer, *physical pain*, 378
  moral pain, 828
  to endure, 821
  to allow, 760
  disease, 655
  experience, 151
Sufferance, *permission*, 760
Sufficient, *enough*, 639
Suffix, *sequel*, 65
  adjunct, 39
Sufflation, *wind*, 349
Suffocate, *choke*, 361
Suffragan, *church*, 996
Suffrage, *vote*, 609
  prayer, 990
Suffragist, *dueness*, 924
Suffuse, *mix*, 41
  feel, 821
  blush, 874
Sufism, *religions*, 984
Sugar, *sweet*, 396
  to flatter, 933
Sugarloaf, *convexity*, 250
Suggest, *suppose*, 514
  advise, 695
  inform, 527
  recall, 505
  occur, 451
* Suggestio **falsi**, *equivocalness*, 520
  falsehood, 544
Suggestion, *plan*, 626
Suggestive, *impure*, 961

Supplies, *materials*, 635
  aid, 707
Supply, *give*, 784
  provide, 637
  store, 636
Support, *sustain*, 215
  operate, 170
  evidence, 467
  aid, 707
  preserve, 670
  endure, 821, 826
Supporter, *prop*, 215
Suppose, *supposition*, 514
Supposing, *provided*, 469
Supposition, *supposition*, 514
Supposititious, *false*, 544, 925
  non-existing, 2
Suppository, *remedy*, 662
Suppress, *conceal*, 528
  silence, 581
  destroy, 162
Suppurate, *fester*, 653
* Supra, *priority*, 116
Supranatural, *spiritual*, 317
Supremacy, *superior*, 33
  authority, 737
  summit, 210
Supremely, *great*, 31
Surcease, *cessation*, 142
Surcharge, *redundance*, 641
  dearness, 814
Surcingle, *fastening*, 45
Surd, *number*, 84
Sure, *certain*, 474
  assent, 488
  consent, 762
  safe, 664
Sure-footed, *careful*, 459
  skilful, 698
Surely, *wonder*, 870
Surety, *security*, 771
  evidence, 467
Surf, *foam*, 353
  tide, 458
Surf-riding, *navigation*, 267
Surface, *exterior*, 220
Surfeit, *satiety*, 869
  redundance, 641
Surge, *ocean*, 341
  rotation, 312
  swell, 305
  wave, 348
Surgery, *remedy*, 662
Surly, *gruff*, 895
  unkind, 907
Surmise, *supposition*, 514
Surmount, *rise*, 305
  tower, 206
  overcome, 731

Surmountable, *facility*, 705
  possible, 470
Surname, *nomenclature*, 564
Surpass, *superior*, 33
  grow, 194
  go beyond, 303
  repute, 873
Surpassing, *greatness*, 31
Surplice, *gown*, 225
  canonical, 999
Surplus, *remainder*, 40
  store, 326
  redundance, 641
Surprise, *wonder*, 870
  non-expectation, 508
  disappoint, 509
Surprisingly, *great*, 31
Surrealist, *artist*, 559
Surrebutter, *lawsuit*, 969
  reply, 462
Surrejoinder, *lawsuit*, 969
  reply, 462
Surrender, *submit*, 725
  obey, 743
  relinquish, 782
Surreptitious, *false*, 544
  furtive, 528
Surrogate, *consignee*, 758
  deputy, 634, 759
Surround, *circumjacence*, 227, 231
Surtout, *dress*, 225
Surveillance, *care*, 459
  direction, 693
Survey, *view*, 441
  measure, 466
Survive, *remain*, 40
  continue, 141
  endure, 110
Susceptible, *liable*, 177
  impressible, 822
  excitable, 901
Suscitate, *cause*, 153
  produce, 161
  induce, 615
  excite, 825
  stir up, 173
Suspect, *doubt*, 485
  suppose, 514
Suspend, *hang*, 214
  continue, 141
  discontinue, 142
  defer, 133
  stop, 265
Suspense, *doubt*, 485
  uncertainty, 475
  expectancy, 507
  hesitation, 603
  irresolution, 605
Suspicion, *doubt*, 485
  incredulity, 487
  uncertainty, 475

Suspicion, *fear*, 860
  particle, 193, 32
  mixture, 41
Suspiration, *lamentation*, 839
Sustain, *support*, 215
  strengthen, 159
  aid, 707
  operate, 170
  preserve, 670
  continue, 143
Sustenance, *food*, 298
Sustentation, *provision*, 637
Susurration, *whisper*, 405
Sutler, *trader*, 797
  provision, 637
Suttee, *religion*, 991
  burning, 384
  killing, 361
Suture, *joint*, 43
Suzerainty, *authority*, 737
* Svelte, *lissom*, 324
Swab, *cleanness*, 562
  dry, 340
Swaddle, *dress*, 225
Swag, *hang*, 214
  lean, 217
  oscillation, 314
  drop, 306
  booty, 793
Swag-bellied, *swollen*, 194
Swagger, *boast*, 884
  bluster, 885
  smart, 845
Swaggerer, *blusterer*, 887
Swagman, *tramp*, 268
Swain, *rustic*, 876
Swallow, *gulp*, 296
  believe, 484
  destroy, 162
Swamp, *marsh*, 345
  destroy, 162
Swamped, *failure*, 732
Swan-song, *end*, 67
  death, 360
Swank, *ostentation*, 882
  boasting, 884
  pride, 878
  affectation, 855
Swap, *interchange*, 148
  barter, 794
Sward, *plain*, 344
Swarm, *crowd*, 72
  sufficiency, 639
  multitude, 102
  to climb, 305
Swarthy, *black*, 431
Swash, *spurt*, 348
  affuse, 337
Swashbuckler, *fighter*, 726
Swastika, *cross*, 219
Swat, *blow*, 276

Swatch, *part*, 51
Swathe, *clothe*, 225
  fasten, 43
Sway, *power*, 157
  influence, 175
  authority, 737
  induce, 615
  oscillate, 314
  agitate, 315
Sweal, *calefaction*, 384
Swear, *promise*, 768
  affirm, 535
  malediction, 908
Sweat, *transude*, 348
  heat, 382
  excretion, 299
  labour, 686
  to fatigue, 688
Sweater, *dress*, 225
Sweep, *space*, 180
  degree, 26
  curve, 245
  rapidity, 274
  clean, 652
  displace, 185
  destroy, 162
  devastation, 619, **649**
  blackguard, 949
Sweeping, *wholesale*, 50
  complete, 52
  indiscriminate, 465A
Sweepings, *refuse*, 653
  trifle, 643
Sweet, *saccharine*, 396
  agreeable, 829
  lovely, 897
  melodious, 413
Sweetheart, *love*, 897
Sweetie, *sweetheart*, 897
Sweetmeat, *sweet*, 396
Swell, *increase*, 35
  expand, 194, **202**
  bulge, 250
  tide, 348
  fop, 854
  personage, 875
  emotion, 821, 824
  extol, 931
  swagger, 885
  good, 648
Swell mob, *thief*, 792
Swelled head, *vanity*, 880
Swelling, *bombastic*, 577
Swelter, *heat*, 382
Swerve, *deviate*, 279
  diverge, 291
  irresolution, 605
  tergiversation, 607
Swift, *velocity*, 274
Swig, *drink*, 296
  tope, 959
Swill, *drink*, 296

Swill, *tope*, 959
Swim, *float*, 305
  navigate, 267
  vertigo, 503
Swim in, *abound*, 639
Swim-suit, *dress*, 225
Swimming, *successful*, 731
  buoyant, 320
Swimmingly, *easily*, 705
  prosperously, 734
Swindle, *peculate*, 791
  cheat, 545
Swindler, *defrauder*, 792
  sharper, 548
Swing, *space*, 180
  hang, 214
  play, 170
  oscillate, 314
  rhythm, 138, 413
  freedom, 748
Swinge, *punish*, 972
Swingeing, *great*, 31
Swinish, *intemperance*, 954
  gluttony, 957
Swink, *work*, 686
Swipe, *blow*, 276
Swish, *hiss*, 409
Switch, *scourge*, 975
  shift, 279
  whisk, 311, 315
Switchback, *obliquity*, 217
Swivel, *hinge*, 312
  cannon, 727
Swivel-eye, *squint*, 443
Swollen, *proud*, 878
  expanded, 194
Swoon, *fainting*, 160
  inactivity, 683
  fatigue, 688
Swoop, *seizure*, 789
  descent, 306
Swop, *see* Swap
Sword, *arms*, 722, 727
  sharpness, 253
Swordsman, *combatant*, 726
Swot, *to study*, 539
  scholar, 492
Sybarite, *intemperance*, 954
Sybo, *condiment*, 393
Sycophant, *servility*, 886
  assent, 488
  adulation, 933
  flatterer, 935
Syllable, *word*, 561
Syllabus, *list*, 86
  compendium, 596
Syllogism, *logic*, 476
Sylph, *sprite*, 979
Sylvan, *woody*, 367
Symbol, *sign*, 550
  metaphor, 521
  mathematical, 84

Symmetry, *form*, **252**
  order, 58
  beauty, 845
  equality, 27
Sympathy, *kindness*, 906
  love, 897
  friendship, 888, 891
  pity, 914
Symphonic, *harmony*, 413
Symphony, *music*, 415
Symposium, *feast*, 299
  festivity, 840
  discussion, 461
Symptom, *sign*, 550
Synagogue, *temple*, 1000
Synchronism, *time*, 120
Syncopate, *shorten*, 201
Syncopation, *rhythm*, 413
Syncope, *cut*, 160
  conciseness, 572
Syncretism, *heresy*, 984A
Syndic, *master*, 745
Syndicalism, *participation*, 778
Syndicate, *partnership*, 712, 797
  co-operation, 709
Synecdoche, *metaphor*, 521
  substitution, 147
Synod, *council*, 696
  church, 995
  assemblage, 72
Synonym, *nomenclature*, 564
  identity, 13
Synonymous, *equal*, 27
  interpretation, 522
Synopsis, *arrangement*, 60
  compendium, 596
Synovia, *lubricant*, 332
Syntax, *grammar*, 567
Synthesis, *combination*, 48
  reasoning, 476
Synthetic, *imitation*, 19
Syphon, *see* Siphon
Syren, *see* Siren
Syringe, *spray*, 348
Syrup, *sweet*, 396
Systaltic, *pulse*, 314
System, *order*, 58, 60
  plan, 626
Systole, *pulse*, 314
  contraction, 195
Syzygy, *contiguity*, 199

T

T.N.T., *arms*, 727
T-square, *angularity*, 244
T.V., *radio*, 599B
Ta, *thanks*, 917

Ta ta, *departure,* 293
Tab, *adjunct,* 39
Tabby, *variegated,* 440
Tabernacle, *temple,* 1000
Tabid, *morbid,* 655
   shrivelled, 195
   noxious, 649
Table, *stand,* 215
   layer, 204
   flatness, 251
   list, 86
   record, 551
   repast, 298
Table-cloth, *covering,* 222
Table-d'hôte, *food,* 298
Table-talk, *talk,* 588
Table-turning, *occult,* 992
Tableau, *painting,* 556
   scene, 824
Tableland, *plain,* 344
   flat, 213
Tablet, *record,* 551
   layer, 204
   flatness, 251
Taboo, *spell,* 992, 993
   prohibition, 761
Tabor, *music,* 417
Tabouret, *support,* 215
* Tabula rasa, *oblivion,* 506
Tabulate, *arrange,* 60, 69
   register, 86
* Tace, *silence,* 403
Tachometer, *velocity,* 274
Tachygraphy, *writing,* 590
Tacit, *hidden,* 526
Taciturn, *silent,* 585
Tack, *direction,* 278
   nail, 45
   to turn, 279
   change course, 140
Tack to, *add,* 37
   join, 43
Tackle, *gear,* 633
   fastening, 45
   to undertake, 676
   encounter, 720
   impact, 276
Tacky, *sticky,* 46
Tact, *skill,* 698
   wisdom, 498
   taste, 850
   discrimination, 465
Tactician, *proficient,* 700
Tactics, *conduct,* 692
   plan, 626
   skill, 698
   warfare, 722
Tactile, *touch,* 379
Taction, *touch,* 379
Tactless, *foolish,* 499
   discourteous, 895
Tactual, *touch,* 379

Tadpole, *young,* 129
Tag, *add,* 37, 39
   fastening, 45
   part, 51
   smallness, 32
   end, 67
   sequel, 65
   point, 253
   maxim, 496
Tail, *end,* 67
   back, 235
   adjunct, 37, 214
   sequel, 65
   follow, 281, 461
Tailor, *dress,* 225
Tailpiece, *rear,* 235
   sequel, 65
   end, 67
   adjunct, 39
Taint, *disease,* 655
   decay, 659
   dirt, 653
   stink, 401
   fault, 651
   disgrace, 874
Taintless, *pure,* 652
Take, *to appropriate,* 789
   receive, 785
   eat, 296
   believe, 484
   understand, 518
   please, 829
Take aback, *surprise,* 508, 870
Take after, *similarity,* 17
Take away, *remove,* 38, 789
Take back, *retract,* 607
Take care, *caution,* 864
Take down, *swallow,* 296
   note, 551
   lower, 308
   humiliate, 879
Take effect, *agency,* 170
Take heed, *attention,* 457
Take hold, *taking,* 789
Take in, *include,* 64
   admit, 296
   realize, 450
   understand, 518
   cheat, 545
Take it, *believe,* 484
   suppose, 514
Take off, *remove,* 185
   divest, 226
   imitate, 19
   personate, 554
   ridicule, 856
   jump, 305
Take on, *anger,* 837
   undertake, 676
Take out, *extract,* 301
   obliterate, 552

Take part with, *aid,* 707
Take place, *happen,* 151
Take root, *dwell,* 186
Take tent, *care,* 459
Take the mickey out of, *ridicule,* 856
Take to, *like,* 827
Take up, *inquire,* 461
Take up with, *sociality,* 892
Take wing, *departure,* 293
Taking, *vexation,* 828
   anger, 900
   acquisition, 775
   pleasing, 829, 897
Tale, *narrative,* 582, 594
   counting, 85
Tale-teller, *tell,* 534
Talebearer, *tell,* 534
Talent, *skill,* 698
   intellect, 450
   intelligence, 498
Talisman, *spell,* 993
Talk, *speak,* 582
   rumour, 532
   conversation, 588
Talkative, *talk,* 584
   prolix, 573
Talkie, *cinema,* 599A
Tall, *height,* 206
Tallboy, *receptacle,* 191
Tallow, *fat,* 356
Tally, *agreement,* 23
   numeration, 85
   record, 551; *check,* 550
Talmud, *revelation,* 985
Talons, *claw,* 633
   authority, 737
Talus, *slope,* 217
Tam-o'-shanter, *hat,* 225
Tambourine, *music,* 417
Tame, *inert,* 172
   moderate, 174
   feeble, 575; *calm,* 826
   domesticate, 370
   teach, 537
Tamis, *strainer,* 260
Tammy, *hat,* 225
Tamper with, *change,* 140
   meddle, 682; *bribe,* 615
Tan, *yellow,* 433
   to thrash, 972
Tandem, *journey,* 266
   sequence, 69
Tang, *taste,* 390
Tangent, *contiguity,* 199
Tangible, *touch,* 379
   real, 1; *material,* 316
Tangle, *derange,* 61
Tangled, *disordered,* 59
   matted, 219

Tango, *dance*, 840
Tank, *recipient*, 191
   reservoir, 636
   fighter, 726
   arms, 727
   vehicle, 272
Tankard, *receptacle*, 191
Tanker, *ship*, 273
Tanner, *money*, 800
Tantalize, *entice*, 615
   disappoint, 509
   tease, 830
   tempt, 865
Tantalus, *receptacle*, 191
   desire, 865
Tantamount, *equal*, 27
   identical, 13
   synonymous, 516
Tantara, *loudness*, 404
   roll, 407
Tantrum, *passion*, 900
   excitability, 825
Taoism, *religions*, 984
Tap, *hit*, 276
   opening, 260
   channel, 350
   plug, 263
   noise, 406
   to let out, 297
   to intercept, 789
Tape, *joint*, 45
Tape recorder, *mechanical instruments*, 417
Taper, *narrow*, 203
   sharp, 253
   candle, 423
Tapestry, *art*, 556
   ornament, 847
Taps, *signal*, 550
Tar, *mariner*, 269
   semiliquid, 352
Taradiddle, *untruth*, 546
Tarantella, *dance*, 840
Tardy, *dilatory*, 133
   slow, 275
Tare and tret, *discount*, 813
Target, *object*, 620
   laughing-stock, 857
Tariff, *price*, 812
Tarn, *lake*, 343
Tarnish, *discoloration*, 429
   deface, 846
   spoil, 659
   dirt, 653
   disgrace, 874, 940
Tarpaulin, *covering*, 222
Tarry, *remain*, 110
   continue, 141
   late, 133
   expect, 507
   rest, 265
Tart, *acid*, 397

Tart, *rude*, 895
   irascible, 901
   courtesan, 962
Tartan, *dress*, 225
   variegated, 440
   ship, 273
Tartar, *irascible*, 901
Tartarus, *hell*, 982
Tartuffe, *hypocrite*, 544, 548
   impiety, 989
Task, *business*, 625
   to put to use, 677
   function, 644
Taskmaster, *director*, 694
Tassel, *ornament*, 847
   pendant, 214
Taste, *sapidity*, 390
   to experience, 821
   discrimination, 850
   small quantity, 32
Tasteless, *vapid*, 391
   unattractive, 866
Tasty, *savoury*, 394
   delicious, 829
Tat, *knit*, 43
* Tâtonnement, *trial*, 463
Tatter, *part*, 51
Tatterdemalion, *commonalty*, 876
Tattle, *talk*, 588
Tattler, *newsmonger*, 532
Tattoo, *roll*, 407
   variegate, 440
Taunt, *reproach*, 938
   ridicule, 856
   hoot, 929
Tautology, *repetition*, 104
   identity, 13
   diffusiveness, 573
Tavern, *inn*, 189
Tawdry, *vulgar*, 851
   colour, 428
Tawny, *yellow*, 436
   brown, 433
Tax, *impost*, 812
   to accuse, 938
   require, 765
   impose, 741; *employ*, 677
Taxi, *vehicle*, 272
Tea, *food*, 298
Tea-gown, *dress*, 225
Tea-room, *food*, 298
Teach, *teaching*, 537
Teach-in, *lecture*, 595
Teachable, *learning*, 539
Teacher, *instructor*, 540
Team, *group*, 69
   party, 712
Teamster, *director*, 694
Tear, *separate*, 44
   destroy, 162

Tear, *violence*, 173
   move rapidly, 274
   weeping, 839
Tear out, *extract*, 301
Tease, *annoy*, 830
Teaser, *poser*, 533, 704
Teat, *convexity*, 250
Technique, *skill*, 698
   musical, 415
Technology, *skill*, 698
Techy, see Tetchy
Teddy bear, *plaything*, 840
Teddy boy, *bad man*, 913, 949
Tedium, *fatigue*, 841
Teem, *abound*, 639
   numerous, 102
   productiveness, 168
Teeming, *assemblage*, 72
Teenager, *youngster*, 129
Teeny-weeny, *little*, 193
Teepee, *abode*, 189
Teeter, *oscillate*, 314
Teetotalism, *sobriety*, 958
   temperance, 953
Teetotum, *rotation*, 840
Tegument, *covering*, 222
Telecast, *radio*, 599B
Teledu, *stink*, 401
Telegenic, *radio*, 599B
Telegnosis, *occult*, 992
Telegraph, *signal*, 550
   news, 532
Telegraphic, *concise*, 572
   velocity, 274
Telekinesis, *occult*, 992
   thought, 451
Teleology, *intention*, 620
Telepathy, *occult*, 992
   thought, 451
Telephone, *hearing*, 418
   news, 532
Teleprompter, *radio*, 599B
Telescope, *optics*, 445
Teleview, *radio*, 599B
Television, *publication*, 531
   radio, 599B
Tell, *inform*, 527
   count, 85
   influence, 175
   speak, 582
   describe, 594
Tell of, *mean*, 516
Tell off, *count*, 85
   reprimand, 932
Telltale, *evidence*, 467
   divulge, 529
Telly, *radio*, 599B
Temerity, *rashness*, 863
Temper, *nature*, 5
   state, 7
   elasticity, 323
   affections, 820

Temper, *to moderate*, 174
  soften, 324, 826
  prepare, 673
  irascibility, 901
Temperament, *nature*, 5
  tendency, 176
  disposition, 820
  music, 413
Temperance, *moderation*,
                        953
Temperate, *moderate*, 174
  mild, 826
Temperature, *heat*, 382
Tempest, *violence*, 173
  wind, 349; *agitation*, 315
  excitement, 825
Tempestivity, *occasion*, 134
Temple, *church*, 1000
  side, 236
* Tempo, *melody*, 413
Temporal, *transient*, 111
  material, 316
  laical, 997
Temporary, *transient*, 111
Temporize, *cunning*, 702
  policy, 698
  diuturnity, 110
  delay, 133
  opportunity, 134
Tempt, *entice*, 615
  desire, 865; *try*, 676
Ten, *number*, 98
Tenable, *probable*, 472
Tenacious, *retentive*, 781
  avaricious, 819
  resolved, 604
  obstinate, 606
  prejudiced, 481
Tenacity, *toughness*, 327
Tenancy, *possession*, 777
Tenant, *occupier*, 188
  possessor, 779
  present, 186
Tenantless, *empty*, 187
  solitary, 893
Tend, *aid*, 107
  train, 370
  contribute, 153
  conduce, 176
  direct to, 278
Tendentious, *misjudgment*,
Tender, *soft*, 324   [481
  susceptible, 822
  loving, 897
  compassionate, 914
  to offer, 763; *ship*, 273
  vehicle, 272
Tenderfoot, *stranger*, 57
  learner, 541
Tendon, *fastening*, 45

Tendril, *infant*, 129
  filament, 205
  fastening, 45
Tenebrific, *darkness*, 421
Tenement, *house*, 189
  property, 780
Tenet, *belief*, 484
  creed, 983
Tenner, *money*, 800
Tennysonian, *poetry*, 597
Tenon, *dovetail*, 300
Tenor, *course*, 7
  degree, 26
  direction, 278
  meaning, 516
  musical, 413
Tense, *hard*, 323
Tensile, *elasticity*, 325
Tension, *strength*, 159
  length, 200
  hardness, 323
  strain, 686
Tent, *receptacle*, 189
  covering, 222
Tentacle, *instrument*, 633
  grip, 781
Tentative, *experimental*,
                        463
  essaying, 675
Tenterhooks, *expectation*,
                        507
Tenuity, *rarity*, 322
  thinness, 203
  smallness, 32
Tenure, *dueness*, 924
  possession, 777
Tepefaction, *heating*, 384
Tepid, *warm*, 382
  passionless, 823
Terce, *worship*, 990
Tercentenary, *period*, 138
  celebration, 883
Terebration, *opening*, 260
  piercing, 302
Tergiversation, *change*, 140,
                        607
  equivocation, 520
Term, *place in series*, 71
  end, 67
  limit, 233
  period of time, 106
  property, 780
  word, 562
  name, 564
Termagant, *irascibility*, 901
  fury, 173
Terminal, *end*, 67
Terminate, *completion*, 729
Terminology, *word*, 562
Terminus, *end*, 67
Termless, *infinity*, 105
Terms, *conditions*, 770

Terms, *circumstances*, 8
  reasoning, 476
Ternary, *number*, 92, 93
Terpsichore, *music*, 415
Terpsichorean, *leap*, 309
Terrace, *plain*, 344
  level, 213
  buildings, 189
Terra firma, *support*, 215
* Terra incognita, *ignor-*
  ance, 491
Terraqueous, *land*, 342
  world, 318
Terrene, *land*, 342
  world, 318
Terrestrial, *land*, 342
  world, 318
Terrible, *fearful*, 860
  great, 31
Terrier, *list*, 86
Terrific, *frightful*, 830
  great, 31
Terrify, *affright*, 860
Territory, *region*, 181
  realm, 780
Terror, *fear*, 860
Terrorist, *enemy*, 891
  evildoer, 913
Terse, *concise*, 572
Tertian, *periodicity*, 138
Tertiary, *triality*, 92
* Tertium quid, *difference*,
                        15
  mixture, 41
* Terza rima, *poetry*, 597
  three, 92
Tessara, *four*, 95
Tessellated, *variegation*, 440
Test, *experiment*, 463
Test-tube, *receptacle*, 191
Testament, *revelation*, 985
Tester, *support*, 215
Testify, *evidence*, 467, 560
Testimonial, *record*, 551
  gift, 784
Testimony, *evidence*, 467
Testy, *irascible*, 901
  rude, 895
Tetchy, *irascible*, 901
Tête-à-tête, *duality*, 89
  chat, 588
Tether, *fasten*, 43
  moor, 265
  restrain, 751
Tetrad, *number*, 95
Tetragon, *four*, 95
Tetrahedron, *angularity*,
                        244
  four, 95
Tetralogy, *four*, 95
Tetrarch, *master*, 745
Text, *meaning*, 516

Thresh, *see* Thrash

Threshold, *beginning,* **66**

Thrice, *number,* 93

Thrift, *success,* 731
   prosperity, 734
   economy, 817

Thriftless, *prodigal,* **818**

Thrill, *touch,* 379
   affect, 821, 824

Thriller, *story,* 594

Thrilling, *tingling,* 380
   charming, 829

Thrive, *succeed,* 731
   prosper, 734
   health, 654

Throat, *opening,* 260
   air-pipe, 351

Throb, *agitate,* 315
   emotion, 821

Throe, *violence,* 173
   agitation, 146, 315
   pain, 378, 828

Throne, *seat,* 215
   abode, 189
   authority, 747

Throng, *assembly,* **72**

Throttle, *seize,* 789
   occlude, 261
   suffocate, 361

Through, *passage,* **302**
   instrument, 631
   owing to, 154
   end, 66

Throughout, *totality,* **50**
   time, 106

Throw, *propel,* **284**
   eject, 297
   exertion, 686

Throw away, *lose,* 776
   relinquish, 782

Throw-back, *reversion,* 145

Throw down, *destroy,* 162
   overthrow, 308

Throw in, *add,* 300

Throw off, *eject,* 297
   do with ease, 705

Throw over, *desert,* 624

Throw up, *resign,* 757
   desert, 624

Thrum, *music,* 415

Thrush, *musician,* 416

Thrust, *push,* 276
   eject, 297
   attack, 716

Thrust in, *insert,* **300**
   interpose, 228

Thud, *noise,* 406

Thug, *thief,* 792
   bad man, 949

Thuggism, *killing,* 361

Thumb, *finger,* 379

Thumb-nail, *little,* 193

Thumbscrew, *scourge,* **975**

Thump, *beat,* 276
   punish, 972
   noise, 406

Thumping, *great,* **31**

Thunder, *noise,* 404
   roar, 411
   violence, 173
   threaten, 909

Thunder-box, *toilet,* **191**,
                653

Thunder-storm, *violence,* 173

Thunder-struck, *awe,* 870

Thunderbolt, *prodigy,* 872

Thunderclap, *prodigy,* 872

Thundering, *size,* 192

Thurible, *rite,* 998

Thus, *reasoning,* 470

Thus far, *smallness,* 32

Thwack, *beat,* 276
   punish, 972

Thwart, *obstruct,* 706
   intersect, 219

Tiara, *diadem,* 747
   ornament, 847
   canonicals, 999

Tick, *sound,* 407
   oscillation, 314
   indicate, 550
   credit, 805

Tick off, *reprimand,* 932

Ticket, *indication,* 550
   permission, 760
   plan, 626

Tickle, *touch,* 380
   please, 377, 829
   laugh, 838

Tickled, *amused,* 827

Ticklish, *difficult,* 704
   uncertain, 475
   dangerous, 665

Tiddly, *drunk,* 959

Tide, *ocean,* 341
   flood, 348
   abundance, 639

Tidings, *news,* 532

Tidy, *clean,* 652
   trim, 673

Tie, *relation,* 9
   fasten, 43, 45
   security, 771
   equality, 27
   obligation, 926
   contention, 720

Tie-beam, *support,* 215

Tier, *continuity,* 69
   layer, 204

Tiff, *discord,* 713
   anger, 900

Tiffin, *food,* 298

Tiger, *violence,* 173
   courage, 861

Tiger, *servant,* 746
   wretch, 913
   miscreant, 949

Tight, *fast,* 43
   closed, 261
   smart, 845
   drunk, 959

Tight-lipped, *taciturn,* **585**

Tike, *commonalty,* 876

Tile, *covering,* 222
   hat, 225

Till, *to cultivate,* 371
   coffer, 191, 802
   up to the time, 108

Tilt, *slope,* 217
   tumble, 306
   cover, 222

Tilt at, *attack,* 716

Tilt over, *obliquity,* 218

Timber, *materials,* 635

Timbre, *music,* 413

Timbrel, *musical instru-*
   ment, 417

Time, *period,* 106

Time-ball, *indication,* 550

Time-server, *servility,* **886**
   apostate, 941
   cunning, 702
   expedient, 646
   irresolution, 605
   versatile, 607
   selfish, 943

Time-worn, *old,* **124**
   exhausted, 659

Timelessness, *never,* **107**

Timely, *early,* 132
   opportune, 134

Timepiece, *chronometer,* **114**

Timid, *fearful,* 860
   cowardly, 862
   humble, 881

Timon of Athens, *recluse,*
              893

Timorous, *see* Timid

Timpanist, *musician,* **416**

Tin, *money,* 800
   to preserve, 670

Tin hat, *defence,* 717

Tin-opener, *open,* 260

Tinct, *colour,* 428

Tincture, *mixture,* 41
   to colour, 428

Tinder, *burn,* 388

Tine, *sharpness,* 253

Ting, *ring,* 408

Tinge, *colour,* 428
   mix, 41

Tingle, *pain,* 378, 828
   feeling, 821

Tingling, *titillation,* 380

Tink, *resonance,* 408

Tinker, *improve,* 658

Tinkety-tonk, *departure*, 293

Tinkle, *resonance*, 408
　faint sound, 405

Tinsel, *ornament*, 847
　glitter, 420
　display, 882
　tawdry, 851
　false, 544

Tint, *colour*, 428

Tintinnabulation, *resonance*, 408

Tiny, *little*, 32
　small, 193

Tip, *summit*, 210
　end, 67; *hint*, 527
　to give, 784, 809
　reward, 973
　of iceberg, 193

Tippet, *dress*, 225

Tipple, *drink*, 296, 298
　drunkenness, 959

Tipstaff, *police*, 965

Tipsy, *drunk*, 959

Tiptoe, *high*, 206
　curiosity, 455

Tiptop, *summit*, 210
　first-rate, 648

Tirade, *disapproval*, 932
　declamation, 582

Tire, *weary*, 841
　worry, 830
　fatigue, 688

Tiresome, *wearisome*, 841

Tiro, *see* Tyro

Tirrivee, *agitation*, 315

Tissue, *texture*, 329

Tit, *small*, 193
　pony, 271

Tit for tat, *retaliation*, 718
　compensation, 30

Titanic, *greatness*, 31, 192

Titbit, *dainty*, 829

Tithe, *tenth*, 99
　dues, 812

Titillate, *touch*, 380
　please, 377, 838

Titivate, *dress*, 225
　beautify, 845

Title, *distinction*, 877
　name, 564
　mark, 550
　property, 780
　right, 924

Title-page, *beginning*, 66, 593

Titter, *laugh*, 838

Tittle, *small quantity*, 32
　little, 192

Tittle-tattle, *chat*, 588
　news, 532

Tittup, *frisk*, 266, 274

Titubation, *fall*, 306
　failure, 732

Titular, *title*, 564

Toad, *ugliness*, 846

Toad-eater, *servile*, 886
　flatterer, 935

Toady, *to flatter*, 933

Toast, *roast*, 384
　celebrate, 883

Toccata, *music*, 415

Tocsin, *alarm*, 669
　indication, 550

Toddle, *walk*, 266
　limp, 275

Toddler, *child*, 129

Toe, *base*, 211

Toehold, *support*, 215

Toff, *notability*, 642
　fop, 854

Toffee, *sweet*, 396

Toffee-nose, *proud*, 878

Toga, *dress*, 225

Together, *added*, 37
　simultaneous, 120
　accompanying, 88

* Tohu-bohu, *tumult*, 315

Toil, *exertion*, 682, 686
　trap, 667

Toilet, *dress*, 225
　room, 191

Toilsome, *difficult*, 704

Token, *sign*, 550

Toledo, *arms*, 727

Tolerable, *endurable*, 651

Tolerant, *patient*, 826

Tolerate, *endure*, 821
　permit, 760
　licence, 750
　lenity, 740
　laxity, 738

Toll, *sound*, 407
　tax, 812

Tollbooth, *mart*, 799
　prison, 752

Tolling, *interment*, 363

Tomahawk, *arms*, 727

Tomb, *interment*, 363

Tomboy, *vulgar*, 851

Tome, *volume*, 593

Tomfoolery, *absurdity*, 497
　ridiculous, 856
　amusement, 840

Tommy, *soldier*, 726

Tommy-gun, *arms*, 727

Tompion, *stopper*, 263

Tom-tom, *drum*, 416, 722

* Ton, *taste*, 852

Tonality, *melody*, 413

Tone, *state*, 7
　affections, 820
　strength, 159

Tone, *sound*, 402
　melody, 413
　minstrelsy, 415
　colour, 428

Tone down, *modify*, 174, 469
　discoloration, 429

Tone-poem, *music*, 415

Tong, *guild*, 712

Tongs, *grip*, 781

Tongue, *language*, 560

Tongue-tied, *dumb*, 581

Tongueless, *dumb*, 581

Tonic, *remedy*, 662, 656
　refresh, 689
　music, 413

Tonnage, *size*, 192

Tonsure, *canonicals*, 999

Tontine, *income*, 810

Too, *addition*, 37

Too much, *redundance*, 641

Tool, *instrument*, 631, 633
　adorn, 847

Toot, *sound*, 408
　intemperance, 954

Tooth, *projection*, 250
　notch, 257
　sharp, 253
　link, 45
　taste, 390

Toothache, *pain*, 378

Toothbrush, *clean*, 652

Toothful, *smallness*, 32

Toothsome, *savoury*, 394
　agreeable, 829

Tootle-oo! *departure*, 293

Top, *summit*, 210
　good, 648
　to surpass, 33

Top-boot, *dress*, 225

Top-hamper, *hindrance*, 706

Top-heavy, *inverted*, 218
　dangerous, 665
　tipsy, 959
　unbalanced, 28

Top-hole, *excellent*, 648

Top-sawyer, *proficient*, 700

Topaz, *yellow*, 436
　ornament, 847

Toper, *drunkard*, 959

Tophet, *hell*, 982

Topi, *hat*, 225

Topic, *topic*, 454

Topical, *situation*, 183
　apt, 23

Toplofty, *contempt*, 930

Topmast, *height*, 200

Topmost, *great*, 33
　high, 210

Topography, *situation*, 183

Topping, *excellent*, 648

Topple, *fall*, 306
　ruin, 659

Trooper, *combatant*, 726
  ship, 273
Trope, *metaphor*, 521
Trophy, *triumph*, 733
  record, 551
Tropical, *heat*, 382
  metaphor, 520
Tropology, *metaphor*, 520
Tropopause, *air*, 338
Troposphere, *air*, 338
Trot, *run*, 266
  velocity, 274
Trot out, *manifestation*, 525
Troth, *truth*, 494
  promise, 768
  belief, 484
Trothless, *faithless*, 940
  false, 544
Troubadour, *musician*, 416
Trouble, *derange*, 61
  evil, 619, 649
  adversity, 735
  pain, 828, 830
  exertion, 686
Troubleshooter, *mediator*, 724
Troublesome, *difficulty*, 704
Troublous, *disorder*, 59
Trough, *conduit*, 250
  trench, 259
  hollow, 252
Trounce, *censure*, 932
  punish, 972
Trousers, *dress*, 225
Trousseau, *dress*, 225
Trow, *think*, 451, 484
  know, 490
Trowel, *instrument*, 191
Truant, *absent*, 187
  fugitive, 623
  idle, 683
Truce, *pacification*, 723
  suspension, 141, 142
Truck, *vehicle*, 272
  barter, 794
  summit, 210
Truckle to, *submission*, 725
Truculent, *malevolence*, 907
Trudge, *slowness*, 275
True, *real*, 1, 3
  veracious, 543
  good, 648
  faithful, 772
  orthodox, 983A
True-love, *love*, 897
Truepenny, *probity*, 939
Truism, *absurdity*, 497
Trull, *impurity*, 962
Truly, *really*, 31
  assent, 488
  verily, 494, 543
Trump, *good man*, 939, 948

Trump card, *device*, 626
  success, 731
Trump up, *falsehood*, 544
Trumpery, *unimportance*, 643
  nonsense, 517
Trumpet, *musical instrument*, 417
  to publish, 531
  roar, 412
  war-cry, 722
Trumpet-tongued, *publication*, 531
Trumpeter, *messenger*, 534
Truncate, *shorten*, 201
  incomplete, 53
  subduct, 38
Truncheon, *club*, 727
  staff of office, 747
  mace, 633
Trundle, *roll*, 312
  propel, 284
Trunk, *whole*, 50
  origin, 153
  paternity, 166
  box, 191
Truss, *join*, 43
  support, 215
  packet, 72
Trust, *credit*, 805
  belief, 484
  credulity, 486
  hope, 858
Trustee, *consignee*, 758
  treasurer, 801
Trustless, *improbity*, 940
Trustworthy, *probity*, 939
  certainty, 474
Trusty, *probity*, 939
Truth, *truth*, 494
Truthful, *veracity*, 543
Truthless, *falsehood*, 544
Try, *experiment*, 463
  endeavour, 675
  use, 677
  annoy, 830
  judge, 967
Try-out, *trial*, 463
Trying, *difficult*, 704
Tryst, *party*, 892
Tsar, *see* Czar
* Tu quoque, *retaliation*, 718
Tub, *vessel*, 191
  to bathe, 337
Tub-thumper, *ranter*, 584
Tuba, *wind instrument*, 417
Tubby, *corpulent*, 192
Tube, *opening*, 260
  way, 627
Tubercle, *convexity*, 250
Tuberosity, *convexity*, 250
Tubular, *opening*, 260

Tuck, *fold*, 258
  dagger, 727
Tuck in, *insert*, 300
  eat, 296
  locate, 184
Tuft, *rough*, 256
  collection, 72
Tuft-hunter, *sycophant*, 886
  flatterer, 935
  time-server, 943
Tug, *pull*, 285
  effort, 686
  ship, 273
Tuition, *teaching*, 537
Tulip, *variegation*, 440
Tumble, *fall*, 306
  derange, 61
  spoil, 659
  fail, 732
  agitate, 315
Tumbledown, *deterioration*, 659
Tumbler, *glass*, 191
  buffoon, 844
Tumbrel, *vehicle*, 272
Tumefaction, *expansion*, 194
Tumid, *swollen*, 194
  bombastic, 549, 577
Tumour, *swelling*, 194
  convexity, 250
Tumult, *disorder*, 59
  violence, 173
  agitation, 315, 825
  resistance, 719
  revolt, 742
  emotion, 825
Tumultuous, *disorder*, 59
Tumulus, *interment*, 363
Tun, *large*, 192
  drunkard, 959
Tunable, *harmony*, 413
Tundra, *space*, 180
  plain, 344
Tune, *music*, 415
  melody, 413
  to prepare, 673
Tune, out of, *irrelation*, 10
  disagreement, 24
Tuneful, *harmony*, 413
Tuneless, *discord*, 414
Tunic, *cover*, 222
  dress, 225
Tuning-fork, *musical*, 417
Tunnage, *size*, 192
Tunnel, *opening*, 260
  way, 627
Turban, *dress*, 225
Turbid, *opaque*, 416
  foul, 653
Turbinate, *convolution*, 248
  rotation, 312

Turbine, *navigation*, 267
  ship, 273
  instrument, 633
Turbo-jet, *aircraft*, 273A
Turbulence, *disorder*, 59
  violence, 173
  agitation, 315
  excitation, 825
Tureen, *receptacle*, 191
Turf, *plain*, 344
Turgescent, *expanded*, 194
  exaggerated, 549
  redundant, 641
Turgid, *swollen*, 194
  exaggerated, 549, 577
  redundant, 641
Turkish bath, *furnace*, 386
Turmoil, *confusion*, 59
  agitation, 315
  violence, 173
Turn, *state*, 7
  juncture, 134
  form, 240
  period of time, 138
  curvature, 245
  deviation, 279
  circuition, 311
  rotation, 312
  journey, 266
  change, 140, 144
  translate, 522
  purpose, 630
  bout, 680
  aptitude, 698
  emotion, 820
  nausea, 867
Turn away, *diverge*, 291
  dismiss, 756
Turn down, *reject*, 610
Turn off, *dismiss*, 756
  execute, 361
Turn out, *happen*, 151
  eject, 297
  strike, 742
  equipage, 852
Turn over, *invert*, 218
  reflect, 451
Turn round, *rotation*, 312
Turn tail, *retreat*, 283, 287
Turn the scale, *superiority*, 33
Turn the tables, *contrariety*, 14
Turn turtle, *inversion*, 218
Turn up, *happen*, 151
  chance, 156, 621
  arrive, 292
  appear, 446
Turncoat, *tergiversation*, 607
  irresolution, 605
  renegade, 144
  knave, 941

Turnkey, *keeper*, 753
Turnpike, *hindrance*, 706
Turnpike road, *way*, 627
Turnstile, *hindrance*, 706
Turpitude, *dishonour*, 940
  wrong, 923
  disgrace, 874
Turquoise, *blue*, 438
Turret, *height*, 206
  defence, 717
Turtle-dove, *love*, 897
Tush, *contempt*, 930
Tusk, *sharpness*, 253
Tussle, *contention*, 720
Tutelage, *safety*, 664
  subjection, 749
  learner, 541
Tutelary, *safety*, 664
Tutor, *teacher*, 540
  to teach, 537
  cultivate, 375
Tuxedo, *dress*, 225
Twaddle, *absurdity*, 497
  nonsense, 517
  loquacity, 584
Twain, *duplication*, 90
Twang, *taste*, 390
  sound, 402, 410
  voice, 583
Tweak, *squeeze*, 195, 203
  punish, 972
Tweeds, *dress*, 225
Twelve, *number*, 98
Twenty, *number*, 98
Twerp, *bad man*, 949
Twice, *duplication*, 90
Twiddle, *rotation*, 312
Twig, *part*, 51
  plant, 367
  to notice, 457
  comprehend, 518
Twilight, *morning*, 125
  evening, 126
  grey, 432
Twill, *fold*, 258
Twilled, *crossing*, 219
Twin, *duplicate*, 90
  accompaniment, 88
  similar, 17
Twine, *thread*, 45
  fibre, 205
  intersect, 219
  convolution, 248
  cling, 46
Twinge, *bodily pain*, 378
  mental, 828, 830
Twinkle, *light*, 420
Twinkling, *moment*, 113
Twirl, *agitation*, 315
  convolution, 248
  turn, 311, 312
Twist, *cord*, 45

Twist, *distort*, 243
  falsehood, 544
  obliquity, 217
  convolution, 248
  bend, 311
  imperfection, 651
  prejudice, 481
Twit, *disapprove*, 932
  ridicule, 856
  slight, 929
Twitch, *pull*, 285
  convulsion, 315
  pain, 378
  mental, 828
Twitter, *agitation*, 315
  cry, 412
  music, 415
  emotion, 821
Two, *duality*, 89
Two-by-four, *trifling*, 643
Two-seater, *vehicle*, 272
Two-step, *dance*, 840
Twofold, *duplication*, 89, 90
Twopenny, *paltry*, 643
Tycoon, *master*, 745
Tyke, *commonalty*, 876
Tympanum, *hearing*, 418
Tympany, *expansion*, 194
Tynewald, *council*, 696
Type, *pattern*, 22
  class, 75
  nature, 5
  person, 372
  man, 373
  rule, 80
  indication, 550
  printing, 591
Typewriting, *writing*, 590
Typhoon, *violence*, 173
  rotation, 312
  wind, 349
Typical, *ordinary*, 82
  special, 79
Typify, *indication*, 550
Typography, *printing*, 591
Tyrannicide, *killing*, 361
Tyranny, *severity*, 739
  authority, 737
Tyrant, *master*, 745
Tyro, *learner*, 541
  novice, 674

U

Uberty, *sufficiency*, 639
Ubiety, *presence*, 186
Ubiquitous, *presence*, 186
Udder, *teat*, 250
Ugly, *ugliness*, 846
  cantankerous, 895
  formidable, 860
Uh-huh, *assent*, 488

Ukase, *order*, 741
  law, 963
Ukelele, *stringed instrument*,
  417
Ulcer, *disease*, 655
  care, 830
Ulema, *judge*, 967
Ullage, *deficiency*, 53
Ulster, *coat*, 225
Ulterior, *in space*, 196
  in time, 121
Ultimate, *end*, 67
Ultimatum, *conditions*, 770
Ultimo, *priority*, 116
Ultimogeniture, *descent*, 167
Ultra, *superiority*, 33
  greatness, 31
  extremist, 604
Ultramarine, *blueness*, 438
Ultramontane, *authority*,
  737
  alien, 57
Ululation, *cry*, 412
Ulysses, *cunning*, 702
Umber, *brown*, 433
Umbilical, *centrality*, 223
Umbra, *darkness*, 421
Umbrage, *shade*, 424
  darkness, 421
  offence, 900
  enmity, 889
  grudge, 898
Umbrella, *shelter*, 666
Umpire, *judge*, 480, 967
Umpteen, *plurality*, 100
Unabashed, *bold*, 861
  haughty, 873, 878
  insolent, 885
  conceited, 880
Unabated, *great*, 31
Unable, *impotence*, 158
Unacceptable, *painfulness*,
  830
Unaccommodating, *dis-
  agreeing*, 24
  uncivil, 895
  disobliging, 907
Unaccompanied, *alone*, 87
Unaccomplished, *incom-
  plete*, 730
Unaccountable, *obscure*, 519
  wonderful, 870
  arbitrary, 964
  irresponsible, 927A
Unaccustomed, *unused*, 614
  unskilled, 699
  unusual, 83
Unachievable, *difficult*, 704
  impossible, 471
Unacknowledged, *ignored*,
  489
  unrequited, 917

Unacquainted, *ignorant*,
  491
Unactuated, *unmoved*, 616
Unadmonished, *unwarned*,
  665
Unadorned, *simple*, 849
  style, 575
Unadulterated, *simple*, 42
  genuine, 494, 648
Unadventurous, *quiet*, 864
Unadvisable, *inexpedient*,
  647
Unadvised, *unwarned*, 665
  foolish, 699
Unaffected, *callous*, 376
  genuine, 494
  sincere, 543
  simple, 576, 849
  elegant, 578
  in good taste, 850
Unafflicted, *serene*, 831
Unaided, *weak*, 160
Unalarmed, *courage*, 861
Unalienable, *dueness*, 924
Unallayed, *strength*, 159
Unallied, *irrelative*, 10
Unallowable, *wrong*, 923
Unalluring, *indifference*, 866
Unalterable, *identical*, 13
  unchanged, 141
  unchangeable, 150
Unamazed, *expectance*, 871
Unambiguous, *intelligi-
  bility*, 518
Unambitious, *indifference*,
  866
Unamiable, *ill-natured*, 907
Unanimity, *accord*, 714
  assent, 488
Unannexed, *disjoined*, 44
Unannounced, *inexpecta-
  tion*, 508
Unanswerable, *demonstra-
  tive*, 478
  certain, 474
  irresponsible, 927A
  arbitrary, 964
Unappalled, *courage*, 861
Unapparent, *invisible*, 447
  latent, 526
Unappeasable, *violence*, 173
Unapplied, *disuse*, 678
Unapprehended, *unknown*,
  491
Unapprehensive, *courage*,
  861
Unapprised, *ignorance*, 491
Unapproachable, *distant*,
  196
  great, 31
Unapproved, *disapproba-
  tion*, 932

Unapt, *incongruous*, 24
  inexpedient, 647
  unskilful, 699
Unarmed, *weak*, 158, 160
Unarranged, *in disorder*, 59
  unprepared, 674
Unarrayed, *simplicity*, 849
Unascertained, *ignorance*,
  491
Unasked, *voluntary*, 602
Unaspiring, *indifferent*, 866
  modest, 881
Unassailable, *safety*, 664
Unassailed, *freedom*, 748
Unassembled, *non-assem-
  blage*, 73
Unassociated, *disjunction*,
  44
Unassuming, *modesty*, 881
Unatoned, *impenitence*, 951
Unattached, *disjunction*, 44
Unattackable, *safety*, 664
Unattainable, *difficult*, 704
  impossible, 471
Unattained, *failure*, 732
Unattempted, *avoidance*,
  623
Unattended, *alone*, 87
Unattended to, *neglect*, 460
Unattested, *counter-evi-
  dence*, 468
  unrecorded, 552
Unattracted, *dissuasion*,
  616
Unattractive, *indifference*,
  866
Unauthentic, *uncertainty*,
  475
Unauthenticated, *counter
  evidence*, 468
  erroneous, 495
Unauthorized, *undue*, 738,
  925
  wrong, 923
  lawless, 964
  prohibited, 761
Unavailing, *useless*, 645
  failure, 732
Unavoidable, *necessary*, 601
  certain, 474
Unavowed, *dissent*, 489
Unawakened, *inactivity*,
  683
Unaware, *ignorant*, 491
  unexpecting, 508
  impulsive, 601
Unawed, *courage*, 861
Unbalanced, *inequality*, 28
Unballasted, *mutable*, 149
  foolish, 499
Unbar, *liberate*, 750
Unbearable, *pain*, 830

Unguarded, *neglected*, 460
   improvident, 674
   dangerous, 665
   spontaneous, 612
Unguent, *oil*, 356
Unguided, *ignorant*, 491
   unskilful, 699
Unhackneyed, *desuetude*,
               614
Unhallowed, *irreligion*, 989
   profane, 988
Unhand, *liberation*, 750
Unhandsome, *ugly*, 940
Unhandy, *unskilfulness*,
               699
Unhappy, *pain*, 828
Unhardened, *tender*, 914
   penitent, 950
   innocent, 946
Unharmed, *safety*, 664
Unharness, *disjoin*, 44
   liberate, 750
Unhatched, *non-prepara-
tion*, 674
Unhazarded, *safety*, 664
Unhealthy, *ill*, 655
   unwholesome, 657
Unheard-of, *ignorant*, 491
   exceptional, 83, 137
   impossible, 471
   improbable, 473
   wonderful, 870
Unheeded, *neglected*, 460
Unheralded, *inexpectation*,
               507
Unheroic, *cowardly*, 862
Unhesitating, *resolution*,
               604
Unhewn, *formless*, 241
   unprepared, 674
Unhindered, *free*, 748
Unhinge, *weaken*, 169
   derange, 61
Unhinged, *unsettled*, 605
   insane, 503
Unholy, *evil*, 989
Unhonoured, *disrespect*, 874
Unhook, *disjoin*, 44
Unhoped, *unexpected*, 508
Unhouse, *displace*, 185
Unhurt, *uninjured*, 670
Unicorn, *monster*, 83
   prodigy, 872
Unidea'd, *unthinking*, 452
Unideal, *true*, 494
   existing, 1
Uniform, *homogeneous*, 16
   simple, 42
   orderly, 58
   regular, 82
   symmetrical, 242
   livery, 225

Uniform, *insignia*, 550
   uniformity, 23
Unify, *combine*, 48
   make one, 87
Unilluminated, *dark*, 421
   ignorant, 491
Unimaginable, *inconceiv-
able*, 519
Unimaginative, *dull*, 843
Unimagined, *truth*, 494
Unimitated, *original*, 20
Unimpaired, *preserved*, 670
   sound, 648
Unimpassioned, *inexcitable*,
               826
Unimpeachable, *innocent*,
               946
   irrefutable, 474, 478
   inalienable, 924
   perfect, 650
Unimpeded, *facility*, 705
Unimpelled, *uninduced*, 616
Unimportant, *insignificant*,
               643
Unimpressionable, *insen-
sible*, 823
Unimproved, *deterioration*,
               659
Uninfluenced, *unbiased*, 616
   obstinate, 606
Uninfluential, *inert*, 172
Uninformed, *ignorance*, 491
Uninhabited, *empty*, 187
   solitary, 893
Uninitiated, *unschooled*, 699
Uninjured, *good*, 648
   preserved, 670
   healthy, 644
Uninquisitive, *indifferent*,
               456
Uninspired, *unexcited*, 823
   unactuated, 616
Uninstructed, *ignorant*, 491
Unintellectual, *ignorant*,
               452
   imbecile, 499
Unintelligent, *foolish*, 499
Unintelligible, *difficult*, 519
   style, 571
Unintentional, *change*, 621
Uninterested, *incurious*, 456
   inattentive, 458
   indifferent, 823
   weary, 841
Uninteresting, *wearisome*,
               841
   dull, 843
Unintermitting, *unbroken*,
               69
   durable, 110
   continuing, 143
   active, 682

Uninterrupted, *continuous*,
               69
   unremitting, 143
Uninvestigated, *unknown*,
               491
Uninvited, *exclusion*, 893
Uninviting, *unattractive*,
               866
   unpleasant, 830
Union, *junction*, 43
   combination, 48
   concord, 23, 714
   concurrence, 178
   marriage, 903
Union Jack, *flag*, 550
Unique, *special*, 79
   alone, 87
   exceptional, 83
   dissimilarity, 18
   non-imitation, 20
Unison, *agreement*, 23
   concord, 714
   uniformity, 16
   melody, 413
Unisonant, *harmony*, 413
Unit, *number*, 87
   troop, 726
Unitarian, *heterodoxy*, 984A
Unite, *join*, 43
   agree, 23
   concur, 178
   assemble, 72
   converge, 290
   league, 712
Unity, *singleness*, 87
   integrity, 50
   concord, 714
Universal, *general*, 78
Universe, *world*, 318
University, *school*, 542
Unjust, *wrong*, 923
Unjustified, *undue*, 925
Unkempt, *careless*, 653
   slovenly, 851
Unkennel, *turn out*, 185
   disclose, 529
Unkind, *malevolent*, 907
Unknit, *disjoin*, 44
Unknowable, *concealment*,
               528
Unknown, *ignorant*, 491
   latent, 526
   to fame, 874
Unlaboured, *unprepared*,
               674
   style, 578
Unlace, *disjoin*, 44
Unlade, *ejection*, 297
Unladylike, *vulgar*, 851
   rude, 895
Unlamented, *disliked*, 898
   unapproved, 932

Unpierced, *closure*, 261

Unpin, *disjunction*, 44

Unpitying, *ruthless*, 907

angry, 900

Unplagued, *content*, 831

Unplayable, *difficult*, 704

Unpleasant, *pain*, 830

Unplumbed, *deep*, 208

Unpoetical, *prose*, 598

Unpolished, *rude*, 895

vulgar, 851

unprepared, 674

Unpolluted, *goodness*, 648

Unpopular, *disliked*, 830

Unpossessed, *loss*, 776

Unpractical, *inactivity*, 683

Unpractised, *unskilfulness*,
699

disuse, 614

Unprecedented, *unconformity*, 83

dissimilarity, 18

infrequency, 137

Unprejudiced, *judicious*,
480

wise, 498

Unpremeditated, *impulsive*, 612

unprepared, 674

Unprepared, *non-preparation*, 674

Unprepossessed, *wisdom*,
498

Unprepossessing, *unpleasing*, 829

ugly, 846

Unpresentable, *vulgarity*,
851

Unpretending, *modesty*, 881

Unpretentious, *modest*, 881

Unprincipled, *vice*, 945

Unprivileged, *undueness*,
925

Unproclaimed, *latency*, 526

Unprocurable, *impossibility*, 471

Unproduced, *non-existent*, 2

Unproductive, *barren*, 169

useless, 645

Unprofessional, *non-observance*, 614

Unprofitable, *useless*, 645

inexpedient, 647

bad, 649

unproductive, 169

Unprogressive, *unchanged*,
141

Unprolific, *barren*, 169

Unpromising, *hopeless*, 859

Unprompted, *impulse*, 612

Unpromulgated, *latent*, 526

Unpronounced, *latent*, 526

Unpropitious, *hopeless*, 859

inauspicious, 135

Unproportioned, *disagreement*, 24

Unprosperous, *adversity*,
735

Unprotected, *danger*, 665

Unproved, *sophistry*, 477

Unprovided, *scanty*, 640

unprepared, 674

Unprovoked, *uninduced*,
616

Unpublished, *latency*, 526

Unpunctual, *tardy*, 133

untimely, 135

irregular, 139

Unpunished, *exempt*, 960

Unpurified, *uncleanness*,
653

Unpurposed, *chance*, 621

Unpursued, *relinquishment*,
624

Unqualified, *inexpert*, 699

unentitled, 925

unprepared, 674

complete, 52

Unquelled, *violence*, 173

Unquenched, *violence*, 173

burning, 382

Unquestionable, *certainty*,
474

Unquestioned, *certainty*,
474

assent, 488

Unquiet, *excitement*, 825

Unravaged, *undamaged*, 648

Unravel, *untie*, 44

straighten, 246

unfold, 313

decompose, 49

solve, 462, 480A

interpret, 522

disembarrass, 705

arrange, 60

Unravelled, *arranged*, 58

Unreachable, *distance*, 196

Unreached, *shortcoming*,
304

Unread, *ignorance*, 491

Unready, *non-preparation*,
674

incompleteness, 53

Unreal, *non-existing*, 2

erroneous, 495

imaginary, 515

Unreasonable, *foolish*, 499

exorbitant, 814

unjust, 923

impossible, 471

erroneous, 495

Unreasoning, *material*, 450A

instinctive, 477

Unreclaimed, *impenitence*,
951

Unreconciled, *discord*, 713

Unrecorded, *obliteration*,
552

Unrecounted, *exclusion*, 55

Unrecovered, *deterioration*,
659

Unrectified, *imperfection*,
651

Unredeemed, *greatness*, 31

Unreduced, *greatness*, 31

Unrefined, *vulgarity*, 851

Unreflecting, *impulse*, 612

Unreformed, *impenitence*,
951

Unrefreshed, *fatigue*, 688

Unrefuted, *demonstrated*,
478

true, 494

Unregarded, *neglected*, 460

unrespected, 929

Unregistered, *unrecorded*,
552

Unrehearsed, *impulse*, 612

Unrelated, *irrelation*, 10

Unrelaxed, *unweakened*, 159

Unrelenting, *malevolent*,
907

revengeful, 919

Unreliable, *dubious*, 475,
485

untrustworthy, 940

Unrelieved, *aggravation*,
835

Unremarked, *neglected*, 460

Unremembered, *forgotten*,
506

Unremitting, *continuing*,
69, 110

industrious, 682

Unremoved, *location*, 184

Unremunerative, *inutility*,
645

Unrenewed, *unchanged*, 141

Unrepealed, *unchanged*, 141

Unrepeated, *fewness*, 103

unity, 87

Unrepentant, *impenitent*,
951

Unrepining, *patient*, 831

Unreplenished, *insufficient*,
640

Unreported, *untold*, 526

Unrepressed, *violent*, 173

Unreproached, *innocence*,
946

Unreproachful, *forgiveness*,
918

Unreproved, *innocence*, 946

Unrequited, *owing*, 806

ingratitude, 917

Unresented, *forgiven*, 918
Unresenting, *enduring*, 826
Unreserved, *frank*, 543
Unresisting, *obedience*, 743
Unresolved, *irresolute*, 605
Unrespected, *disrespect*, 929
Unresponsive, *insensibility*, 823
Unrest, *moving*, 264
  change, 140
  changeable, 149
Unrestored, *deterioration*, 659
Unrestrained, *free*, 748
  unencumbered, 705
Unrestraint, *intemperance*, 954
Unrestricted, *undiminished*, 31
  free, 748
Unretracted, *affirmation*, 535
Unrevealed, *concealed*, 528
Unrevenged, *jealousy*, 920
Unreversed, *permanence*, 141
  continuance, 143
Unrevoked, *continuance*, 143
Unrewarded, *debt*, 806
  ingratitude, 917
Unrhymed, *prose*, 598
Unriddle, *solve*, 462
  interpret, 522
  disclose, 529
Unrighteous, *evil*, 945
Unrip, *uncover*, 260
Unripe, *unprepared*, 674
Unrivalled, *goodness*, 648
Unrivet, *disjoin*, 44
Unrobe, *divest*, 226
Unroll, *straighten*, 246
  evolve, 313
  display, 525
  unravel, 47
Unromantic, *true*, 494
Unroof, *divest*, 226
Unroot, *pull up*, 162
Unruffled, *calm*, 174
  placid, 826
  unaffected, 823
  quiet, 265
  orderly, 58
Unruly, *disobedient*, 742
  obstinate, 606
  violent, 173
Unsafe, *dangerous*, 665
Unsaid, *unspoken*, 581
  untold, 526
Unsanctified, *unholy*, 988, 989
Unsanctioned, *undue*, 925

Unsanitary, *insalubrious*, 657
Unsated, *desire*, 865
Unsatisfactory, *discontent*, 832
  displeasing, 830
Unsatisfied, *discontent*, 832
Unsavoury, *unsavouriness*, 395
Unsay, *retract*, 607
Unscanned, *neglected*, 460
Unscathed, *health*, 654
Unschooled, *illiterate*, 491
  uneducated, 699
Unscientific, *ignorant*, 495
  unskilled, 699
Unscoured, *unclean*, 653
Unscreened, *danger*, 665
Unscrew, *disjoin*, 44
Unscriptural, *heterodoxy*, 984A
Unscrupulous, *evil*, 940
Unseal, *disclosure*, 529
Unseam, *disjoin*, 44
Unsearched, *neglect*, 460
Unseasonable, *intempestivity*, 135
  inexpedient, 647
  inappropriate, 24
Unseasoned, *unprepared*, 674
  unaccustomed, 614
Unseat, *dismiss*, 756
Unsecured, *uncovenanted*, 768A
Unseemly, *undue*, 925
  vicious, 945, 961
  vulgar, 851
  ugly, 846
  inexpedient, 647
Unseen, *invisible*, 447
  unprepared, 674
  neglected, 460
Unselfish, *generous*, 942
Unserviceable, *useless*, 645
Unset, *disjoin*, 44
Unsettle, *derange*, 61
  irresolute, 475, 605
  mutable, 149
  insane, 503
Unsevered, *whole*, 50
Unshackle, *free*, 748
  liberate, 750
  untie, 44
Unshaken, *strong*, 159
  resolute, 604
Unshapely, *ugly*, 846
Unshapen, *amorphous*, 241
  ugly, 846
Unshared, *possession*, 777
Unsheathe, *uncover*, 226
Unsheltered, *danger*, 665

Unshifting, *continuance*, 143
Unshocked, *unmoved*, 823
Unshod, *divestment*, 226
Unshorn, *whole*, 50
Unshrinking, *resolution*, 604
  courage, 861
Unsifted, *neglected*, 460
Unsight, *hinder*, 706
Unsightly, *ugly*, 846
Unsinged, *uninjured*, 670
Unskilful, *unskilled*, 699
  useless, 645
Unslaked, *desire*, 865
Unsleeping, *activity*, 682
Unsociable, *exclusive*, 893
Unsocial, *exclusive*, 893
Unsoiled, *clean*, 652
Unsold, *possessed*, 777
Unsolder, *disjoin*, 47
Unsoldierly, *cowardly*, 862
Unsolicited, *willing*, 602
Unsolicitous, *indifferent*, 866
Unsolved, *secret*, 526
Unsophisticated, *genuine*, 494
  simple, 42, 849
  good, 648
  innocent, 946
Unsorted, *unarranged*, 59
Unsought, *avoided*, 623
  unrequested, 766
Unsound, *imperfect*, 651
  unhealthy, 655
  sophistical, 477
Unsounded, *deep*, 208
Unsown, *unprepared*, 674
Unsparing, *ample*, 639
Unspeakable, *great*, 31
  wonderful, 870
Unspecified, *general*, 78
Unspent, *unused*, 678
Unspoiled, *goodness*, 648
Unspoken, *unsaid*, 581
Unsportsmanlike, *improbity*, 940
Unspotted, *clean*, 652
  innocent, 946
  beautiful, 845
Unstable, *mutable*, 149
  irresolute, 605
Unstained, *untouched*, 652
  honourable, 939
Unstatesmanlike, *unskilful*, 699
Unsteadfast, *irresolute*, 605
Unsteady, *mutable*, 149
  irresolute, 605, 607
  dangerous, 665
Unstinted, *plenteous*, 639

Unstirred, *unmoved*, 826
  calm, 265
Unstitch, *disjoin*, 44
Unstopped, *open*, 260
  continuing, 143
Unstored, *unprovided*, 640
Unstrained, *unexerted*, 172
  relaxed, 687
  turbid, 653
Unstrengthened, *weak*, 160
Unstrung, *weak*, 160
Unsubdued, *free*, 748
Unsubjugated, *free*, 748
Unsubmissive, *disobedient*,
  742
Unsubstantial, *unsubstantiality*, 4
  rare, 322
  texture, 329
  imaginary, 515
  erroneous, 495
Unsubstantiated, *erroneous*,
  495
Unsuccessful, *failure*, 732
Unsuccessive, *discontinuous*, 70
Unsuitable, *incongruous*, 24
  inexpedient, 647
  time, 135
Unsuited, *see* Unsuitable
Unsullied, *clean*, 652
  honourable, 939
  guiltless, 946
Unsummed, *infinity*, 105
Unsummoned, *voluntary*,
  600
Unsung, *untold*, 526
Unsunned, *dark*, 421
Unsupplied, *insufficiency*,
  640
Unsupported, *weak*, 160
Unsuppressed, *persisting*,
  141
Unsurpassed, *great*, 31
  superior, 33
Unsusceptible, *unfeeling*,
  823
Unsuspected, *latent*, 526
Unsuspicious, *credulous*,
  484, 486
  hopeful, 858
Unsustained, *weak*, 160
Unswayed, *uninfluenced*,
  616
Unsweetened, *unsavoury*,
  395
Unswept, *dirty*, 653
Unswerving, *straight*, 246
  direct, 278
  determined, 604
Unsymmetrical, *disorder*, 59
  distortion, 243

Unsympathetic, *unfriendly*,
  907
Unsystematic, *disorder*, 59
Untack, *disjoin*, 44
Untainted, *healthy*, 654
  pure, 652
  honourable, 939
Untalented, *unskilled*, 699
Untalked-of, *latency*, 526
Untamed, *rude*, 851
  ferocious, 907
Untangled, *order*, 58
Untarnished, *probity*, 939
  innocence, 946
Untasted, *taste*, 391
Untaught, *ignorant*, 491
Untaxed, *cheap*, 815
Unteach, *misteach*, 538
Unteachable, *unskilled*, 699
Untempered, *greatness*, 31
Untempted, *uninfluenced*,
  616
Untenable, *weak*, 160
  undefended, 725
  sophistical, 477
Untenanted, *empty*, 187
Untended, *neglected*, 460
Untested, *neglected*, 460
Unthanked, *ingratitude*, 917
Unthankful, *ungrateful*, 917
Unthawed, *solid*, 321
  cold, 383
Unthinkable, *impossible*,
  471
Unthinking, *thoughtless*, 452
Unthought-of, *neglected*,
  460
  unconsidered, 452
Unthoughtful, *neglectful*,
  460
Unthreatened, *safe*, 664
Unthrifty, *prodigal*, 818
  unprepared, 674
Unthrone, *dismiss*, 756
Unthwarted, *unhindered*,
  748
Untidy, *in disorder*, 59
  slovenly, 653
Untie, *loose*, 44
  liberate, 750
Until, *time*, 106, 108
Untilled, *unprepared*, 674
Untimely, *ill-timed*, 135
Untinged, *simple*, 42
  uncoloured, 429
Untired, *refreshed*, 689
Untiring, *active*, 682
Untitled, *commonalty*, 876
Untold, *secret*, 526, 528
  countless, 105
Untouched, *disused*, 678
  insensible, 376, 823

Untoward, *bad*, 649
  inopportune, 135
  unprosperous, 735
  unpleasant, 830
Untraced, *latency*, 526
Untracked, *latency*, 526
Untrained, *unskilled*, 699
  unprepared, 674
  unaccustomed, 614
Untrammelled, *free*, 705,
  748
Untranslated, *misinterpretation*, 523
Untravelled, *quiescent*, 265
  unknown, 491
Untreasured, *unstored*, 640
Untried, *undetermined*, 461
Untrimmed, *simple*, 849
  unprepared, 674
Untrodden, *new*, 123
  not used, 678
  impervious, 261
Untroubled, *calm*, 174, 721
Untrue, *false*, 544
Untrustworthy, *dishonest*,
  940
  erroneous, 495
  uncertain, 475
  dangerous, 665
Untruth, *falsehood*, 544,
  546
Untunable, *discord*, 414
Unturned, *straight*, 246
Untutored, *ignorant*, 491
Untwine, *unfold*, 313
Untwist, *straighten*, 246
  evolve, 313
  separate, 44, 47
Unurged, *spontaneous*, 600
Unused, *unaccustomed*, 614,
  699
  untouched, 678
Unusual, *unconformity*, 83
  greatness, 31
Unutilized, *disuse*, 678
Unutterable, *wonderful*, 870
  great, 31
Unvalued, *depreciated*, 483
  undesired, 866
  disliked, 898
Unvanquished, *free*, 748
Unvaried, *permanent*, 141
  continued, 143
  monotonous, 576
Unvarnished, *truth*, 494
Unvarying, *uniform*, 16
Unveil, *manifest*, 525
  disclose, 529
Unventilated, *close*, 261
Unveracious, *false*, 544
Unverified, *indiscrimination*, 465A

Vestige, *record*, 551
Vestments, *canonicals*, 999
Vestry, *conclave*, 995
  church, 1000
Vesture, *dress*, 225
Veteran, *old*, 130
  adept, 700
  fighter, 726
Veterinary, *remedy*, 662
  taming, 370
Veto, *prohibit*, 761
  refuse, 764
* Vetturino, *director*, 694
Vex, *painful*, 830
Vexation, *pain*, 828
Vexatious, *painful*, 830
Via, *way*, 627
  direction, 278
* Via media, *mean*, 29
  middle, 68
Viability, *life*, 359
Viable, *practicable*, 470
Viaduct, *way*, 627
Vial, *bottle*, 191
  wrath, 900
Viands, *food*, 298
Viaticum, *rite*, 998
Vibrate, *fluctuate*, 149
  oscillate, 314
Vicar, *clergy*, 996
  deputy, 759
Vicarage, *office*, 995
  house, 1000
Vicarious, *substituted*, 149,
  755
Vice, *guiltiness*, 945
  imperfection, 651
  deputy, 759
  grip, 781
  vinculum, 45
Vice versa, *correlation*, 12
  contrariety, 14
  interchange, 148
Vicegerency, *agency*, 755
Vicegerent, *consignee*, 758
  deputy, 759
Vice-president, *master*, 745
Viceroy, *deputy*, 759
Vicinity, *nearness*, 197
Vicious, *fallacious*, 477
  faulty, 651
  immoral, 945
Vicissitude, *change*, 140
  mutable, 149
Victim, *injured*, 732
  dupe, 547
  sufferer, 828
Victimize, *deceive*, 545
  baffle, 731
Victoria, *vehicle*, 272
Victory, *success*, 731
Victualling, *provision*, 637

Victuals, *food*, 298
* Videlicet, *namely*, 522
  specification, 79
Video, *radio*, 599B
Viduity, *widowhood*, 905
Vie, *emulate*, 648
  contend, 720
View, *sight*, 441
  appearance, 448
  to attend to, 457
  landscape, 556
  opinion, 484
  intention, 620
  radio, 599B
View-finder, *optical*, 445
Viewless, *invisible*, 447
Viewy, *caprice*, 608
Vigesimal, *twenty*, 98
Vigil, *watch*, 459
  eve, 116
Vigilance, *attention*, 457
  care, 459
Vigils, *worship*, 990
Vignette, *engraving*, 558
Vigour, *strong*, 159
  healthy, 654
  activity, 683
  energy, 171
  style, 574
Viking, *pirate*, 792
Vile, *bad*, 649
  odious, 830
  valueless, 643
  disgraceful, 874, 940
  plebeian, 876
Vilify, *censure*, 932
  defame, 934
  scold, 908
  shame, 874
Vilipend, *censure*, 932
  defame, 934
  shame, 874
  disrespect, 929
Villa, *abode*, 189
Village, *abode*, 189
Villager, *inhabitant*, 188
Villain, *vice*, 945
  knave, 941
Villainage, *subjection*, 749
Villainy, *vice*, 945
  improbity, 940
Villanelle, *poetry*, 597
Villous, *roughness*, 256
Vim, *energy*, 171, 682
  style, 574
Vincible, *weakness*, 160
Vinculum, *junction*, 45
Vindicate, *justify*, 924, 937
Vindictive, *revengeful*, 919
  irascible, 901
Vinegar, *sourness*, 397
  condiment, 393

Vineyard, *agriculture*, 371
Vintage, *agriculture*, 371
Viola, *musical instrument*,
  417
Violate, *disobey*, 742
  engagement, 773
  right, 925
  duty, 927
  a usage, 614
Violence, *physical*, 173
  arbitrariness, 964
Violently, *great*, 31
Violet, *purple*, 437
Violin, *musical instrument*,
  417
Violinist, *musician*, 416
Violoncello, *musical instrument*, 417
Viper, *bane*, 663, 913
  miscreant, 949
Virago, *irascibility*, 901
  fury, 173
Virescent, *green*, 435
Virgin, *girl*, 129
  celibacy, 904
  purity, 960
Virginal, *musical instrument*, 417
Virginia, *tobacco*, 298A
Viridescent, *green*, 435
Viridity, *green*, 435
Virile, *manly*, 373
  adolescent, 131
  strong, 159
  style, 574
Virtu, *taste*, 850
Virtual, *real*, 1
  potential, 2
Virtually, *truth*, 494
Virtue, *goodness*, 944
  right, 922
  probity, 939
  purity, 960
  power, 157
  courage, 861
Virtueless, *vice*, 945
Virtuosity, *taste*, 850
  skill, 698
Virtuoso, *taste*, 850
  performer, 416
  proficient, 700
Virulence, *insalubrity*,
  657
  poison, 663
  malignity, 649
  page, 900
  malevolence, 907
Virus, *poison*, 663
  disease, 655
  insalubrity, 657
Visage, *front*, 234
  appearance, 448

ORIGINAL INTRODUCTION

By Peter Roget

THE present work is intended to supply, with respect to the English language, a desideratum hitherto unsupplied in any language; namely, a collection of the words it contains and of the idiomatic combinations peculiar to it, arranged, not in alphabetical order, as they are in a dictionary, but according to the *ideas* which they express.[1] The purpose of an ordinary dictionary is simply to explain the meaning of words; and the problem of which it professes to furnish the solution may be stated thus: The word being given, to find its signification, or the idea it is intended to convey. The object aimed at in the present undertaking is exactly the converse of this; namely, the idea being given, to find the word, or words, by which that idea may be most fitly and aptly expressed. For this purpose, the words and phrases of the language are here classed, not according to their sound or their orthography, but strictly according to their *signification.*

The communication of our thoughts by means of language, whether spoken or written, like every other object of mental exertion, constitutes a peculiar art, which, like other parts, cannot be acquired in any perfection but by long and continued practice. Some, indeed, there are, more highly gifted than others with a facility of expression, and naturally endowed with the power of eloquence; but to none is it at all times an easy process to embody in exact and appropriate language the various trains of ideas that are passing through the mind, or to depict in their true colours and proportions the diversified and nicer shades of feeling which accompany them. To those who are unpractised in the art of composition, or unused to extempore speaking, these difficulties present themselves in their most formidable aspect. However distinct may be our views, however vivid our conceptions, or however fervent our emotions, we cannot but be often conscious that the phraseology we have at our command is inadequate to do them justice. We seek in vain the words we need, and strive ineffectually to devise forms of expression which shall faithfully portray our thoughts and sentiments. The appropriate terms, notwithstanding our utmost efforts, cannot be conjured up at will. Like 'spirits from the vasty deep,' they come not when we call; and we are driven to the employment of a set of words and phrases either too general or too limited, too strong or too feeble, which suit not the occasion, which hit not the mark we aim at; and the result of our prolonged exertion is a style at once laboured and obscure, vapid and redundant, or vitiated by the still graver faults of affectation or ambiguity.

[1] See note on p. 571.

It is to those who are thus painfully groping their way and struggling with the difficulties of composition, that this work professes to hold out a helping hand. The assistance it gives is that of furnishing on every topic a copious store of words and phrases, adapted to express all the recognizable shades and modifications of the general idea under which those words and phrases are arranged. The inquirer can readily select, out of the ample collection spread out before his eyes in the following pages, those expressions which are best suited to his purpose, and which might not have occurred to him without such assistance. In order to make this selection, he scarcely ever need engage in any elaborate or critical study of the subtle distinctions existing between synonymous terms; for if the materials set before him be sufficiently abundant, an instinctive tact will rarely fail to lead him to the proper choice. Even while glancing over the columns of this work, his eye may chance to light upon a particular term, which may save the cost of a clumsy paraphrase, or spare the labour of a tortuous circumlocution. Some felicitous turn of expression thus introduced will frequently open to the mind of the reader a whole vista of collateral ideas, which could not, without an extended and obtrusive episode, have been unfolded to his view; and often will the judicious insertion of a happy epithet, like a beam of sunshine in a landscape, illumine and adorn the subject which touches it, imparting new grace, and giving life and spirit to the picture.

Every workman in the exercise of his art should be provided with proper implements. For the fabrication of complicated and curious pieces of mechanism the artisan requires a corresponding assortment of various tools and instruments. For giving proper effect to the fictions of the drama, the actor should have at his disposal a well-furnished wardrobe, supplying the costumes best suited to the personage he is to represent. For the perfect delineation of the beauties of nature, the painter should have within reach of his pencil every variety and combination of hues and tints. Now the writer, as well as the orator, employs for the accomplishment of his purposes the instrumentality of words; it is in words that he clothes his thoughts; it is by means of words that he depicts his feelings. It is therefore essential to his success that he be provided with a copious vocabulary, and that he possess an entire command of all the resources and appliances of his language. To the acquisition of this power no procedure appears more directly conducive than the study of a methodized system such as that now offered to his use.

The utility of the present work will be appreciated more especially by those who are engaged in the arduous process of translating into English a work written in another language. Simple as the operation may appear, on a superficial view, of rendering into English each of its sentences, the task of transfusing, with perfect exactness, the sense of the original, preserving at the same time the style and character of its composition, and reflecting with fidelity the mind and the spirit of the author, is a task of extreme difficulty. The cultivation of this useful department of literature was in ancient times strongly recommended both by Cicero and by Quintilian as essential to the formation of a good writer and accomplished orator. Regarded simply as a mental exercise, the practice of translation is the best training for the attainment of that mastery of language and felicity of diction which are the sources of the highest oratory and are requisite for the possession of a graceful and persuasive eloquence. By rendering ourselves the faithful interpreters of the thoughts and feelings of others, we are rewarded with the acquisition of greater readiness and facility in correctly expressing our own; as he who has best learned to execute the orders of a commander becomes himself best qualified to command.

In the earliest periods of civilization, translations have been the agents for propagating knowledge from nation to nation, and the value of their labours has been inestimable; but, in the present age, when so many different languages have become the depositories of the vast treasures of literature and of science which have been accumulating for centuries, the utility of accurate translations has greatly increased, and it has become a more important object to attain perfection in the art.

The use of language is not confined to its being the medium through which we communicate our ideas to one another; it fulfils a no less important function as an *instrument of thought*, not being merely its vehicle, but giving it wings for flight. Metaphysicians are agreed that scarcely any of our intellectual operations could be carried on to any considerable extent without the agency of words. None but those who are conversant with the philosophy of mental phenomena can be aware of the immense influence that is exercised by language in promoting the development of our ideas, in fixing them in the mind, and detaining them for steady contemplation. In every process of reasoning, language enters as an essential element. Words are the instruments by which we form all our abstractions, by which we fashion and embody our ideas, and by which we are enabled to glide along a series of premises and conclusions with a rapidity so great as to leave in the memory no trace of the successive steps of the process; and we remain unconscious how much we owe to this potent auxiliary of the reasoning faculty. It is on this ground, also, that the present work founds a claim to utility. The review of a catalogue of words of analogous signification will often suggest by association other trains of thought, which, presenting the subject under new and varied aspects, will vastly expand the sphere of our mental vision. Amidst the many objects thus brought within the range of our contemplation, some striking similitude or appropriate image, some excursive flight or brilliant conception, may flash on the mind, giving point and force to our arguments, awakening a responsive chord in the imagination or sensibility of the reader, and procuring for our reasonings a more ready access both to his understanding and to his heart.

It is of the utmost consequence that strict accuracy should regulate our use of language, and that every one should acquire the power and

the habit of expressing his thoughts with perspicuity and correctness.
Few, indeed, can appreciate the real extent and importance of that
influence which language has always exercised on human affairs, or can
be aware how often these are determined by causes much slighter than
are apparent to a superficial observer.   False logic, disguised under
specious phraseology, too often gains the assent of the unthinking
multitude, disseminating far and wide the seeds of prejudice and error.
Truisms pass current, and wear the semblance of profound wisdom,
when dressed up in the tinsel garb of antithetical phrases, or set off by
an imposing pomp of paradox.   By a confused jargon of involved and
mystical sentences, the imagination is easily inveigled into a transcendental region of clouds, and the understanding beguiled into the
belief that it is acquiring knowledge and approaching truth.   A mis-
applied or misapprehended term is sufficient to give rise to fierce and
interminable disputes: a misnomer has turned the tide of popular
opinion; a verbal sophism has decided a party question; an artful
watchword, thrown among combustible materials, has kindled the
flames of deadly warfare, and changed the destiny of an empire.

In constructing the following system of classification of the ideas
which are expressible by language, my chief aim has been to obtain the
greatest amount of practical utility.   I have accordingly adopted such
principles of arrangement as appeared to me to be the simplest and
most natural, and which would not require, either for their comprehension or application, any disciplined acumen, or depth of metaphysical
or antiquarian lore.   Eschewing all needless refinements and subtleties,
I have taken as my guide the more obvious characters of the ideas for
which expressions were to be tabulated, arranging them under such
classes and categories as reflection and experience had taught me would
conduct the inquirer most readily and quickly to the object of his
search.   Commencing with the ideas expressing mere abstract relations,
I proceed to those which relate to the phenomena of the material world,
and lastly to those in which the mind is concerned, and which comprehend intellect, volition, and feeling; thus establishing six primary Classes
of Categories.

1. The first of these classes comprehends ideas derived from the
more general and ABSTRACT RELATIONS among things, such as *Existence,
Resemblance, Quantity, Order, Number, Time, Power*.

2. The second class refers to SPACE and its various relations, including
Motion, or change of place.

3. The third class includes all ideas that relate to the MATERIAL
WORLD; namely, the *Properties of Matter*, such as *Solidity, Fluidity,
Heat, Sound, Light,* and the *Phenomena* they present, as well as the
simple *Perceptions* to which they give rise.

4. The fourth class embraces all ideas of phenomena relating to the
INTELLECT and its operations, comprising the *Acquisition*, the *Retention*,
and the *Communication of Ideas*.

5. The fifth class includes the ideas derived from the exercise of VOLITION, embracing the phenomena and results of our *Voluntary and Active Powers*, such as *Choice, Intention, Utility, Action, Antagonism, Authority, Compact, Property*, etc.

6. The sixth and last class comprehends all ideas derived from the operation of our SENTIENT AND MORAL POWERS, including our *Feelings, Emotions, Passions*, and *Moral and Religious Sentiments*.[1]

The object I have proposed to myself in this work would have been but imperfectly attained if I had confined myself to a mere catalogue of words, and had omitted the numerous phrases and forms of expression, composed of several words, which are of such frequent use as to entitle them to rank among the constituent parts of the language.[2] Very few of these verbal combinations, so essential to the knowledge of our native tongue, and so profusely abounding in its daily use, are to be met with in ordinary dictionaries. These phrases and forms of expression I have endeavoured diligently to collect and to insert in their proper places, under the general ideas they are designed to convey. Some of these conventional forms, indeed, partake of the nature of proverbial expressions; but actual proverbs, as such, being wholly of a didactic character, do not come within the scope of the present work, and the reader must therefore not expect to find them here inserted.

For the purpose of exhibiting with greater distinctness the relations

[1] It must necessarily happen in every system of classification framed with this view, that ideas and expressions arranged under one class must include also ideas relating to another class; for the operations of the *Intellect* generally involve also those of the *Will*, and vice versa; and our *Affections* and *Emotions*, in like manner, generally imply the agency both of the *Intellect* and the *Will*. All that can be effected, therefore, is to arrange the words according to the principal or dominant idea they convey. *Teaching*, for example, although a Voluntary act, relates primarily to the Communication of Ideas, and is accordingly placed at No. 537, under Class IV, Division II. On the other hand, *Choice, Conduct, Skill*, etc., although implying the co-operation of Voluntary with Intellectual acts, relate principally to the former, and are therefore arranged under Class V.

It often happens that the same word admits of various applications, or may be used in different senses. In consulting the Index the reader will be guided to the number of the heading under which that word, in each particular acceptation, will be found, by means of *supplementary words*, printed in italics; which words, however, are not to be understood as explaining the meaning of the word to which they are annexed, but only assisting in the required reference. I have also, for shortness' sake, generally omitted words immediately derived from the primary one inserted, which sufficiently represents the whole group of correlative words referable to the same heading. Thus the number affixed to *Beauty* applies to all its derivatives, such as *Beautiful, Beauteous, Beautify, Beautifulness, Beautifully*, etc., the insertion of which was therefore needless.

[2] For example: To take time by the forelock; to turn over a new leaf; to show the white feather; to have a finger in the pie; to let the cat out of the bag; to take care of number one; to kill two birds with one stone, etc.

between words expressing opposite and correlative ideas, I have, whenever the subject admitted of such an arrangement, placed them in two parallel columns in the same page, so that each group of expressions may be readily contrasted with those which occupy the adjacent column, and constitute their antitheses. By carrying the eye from the one to the other, the inquirer may often discover forms of expression of which he may avail himself advantageously to diversify and infuse vigour into his phraseology. Rhetoricians, indeed, are well aware of the power derived from the skilful introduction of antitheses in giving point to an argument, and imparting force and brilliancy to the diction. A too frequent and indiscreet employment of this figure of rhetoric may, it is true, give rise to a vicious and affected style; but it is unreasonable to condemn indiscriminately the occasional and moderate use of a practice on account of its possible abuse.

The study of correlative terms existing in a particular language may often throw valuable light on the manners and customs of the nations using it. Thus Hume has drawn important inferences with regard to the state of society among the ancient Romans, from certain deficiencies which he remarked in the Latin language.[1]

In many cases, two ideas, which are completely opposed to each other, admit of an intermediate or neutral idea, equidistant from both: all these being expressible by corresponding definite terms. Thus, in the following examples, the words in the first and third columns,

---

[1] 'It is an universal observation,' he remarks, 'which we may form upon language, that where two related parts of a whole bear any proportion to each other, in numbers, rank, or consideration, there are always correlative terms invented which answer to both the parts and express their mutual relation. If they bear no proportion to each other, the term is only invented for the less, and marks its distinction from the whole. Thus *man* and *woman*, *master* and *servant*, *father* and *son*, *prince* and *subject*, *stranger* and *citizen*, are correlative terms. But the words *seaman*, *carpenter*, *smith*, *tailor*, etc., have no correspondent terms which express those who are no seamen, no carpenters, etc. Languages differ very much with regard to the particular words where this distinction obtains; and may thence afford very strong inferences concerning the manners and customs of different nations. The military government of the Roman emperors had exalted the soldiery so high, that they balanced all the other orders of the state: hence *miles* and *paganus* became relative terms; a thing, till then, unknown to ancient, and still so to modern, languages.' 'The term for a slave, born and bred in the family, was *verna*. As *servus* was the name of the genus, and *verna* of the species without any correlative, this forms a strong presumption that the latter were by far the least numerous: and from the same principles I infer that if the number of slaves brought by the Romans from foreign countries had not extremely exceeded those which were bred at home, *verna* would have had a correlative, which would have expressed the former species of slaves. But these, it would seem, composed the main body of the ancient slaves, and the latter were but a few exceptions.'—HUME, *Essay on the Populousness of Ancient Nations*.

The warlike propensity of the same nation may in a like manner be inferred from the use of the word *hostis* to denote both a *foreigner* and an *enemy*.

which express opposite ideas, admit of the intermediate terms contained in the middle column having a neutral sense with reference to the former:

Identity	*Difference*	*Contrariety*
Beginning	*Middle*	*End*
Past	*Present*	*Future*

In other cases, the intermediate word is simply the negative to each of two opposite positions; as, for example:

Convexity	*Flatness*	*Concavity*
Desire	*Indifference*	*Aversion*

Sometimes the intermediate word is properly the standard with which each of the extremes is compared; as in the case of

Insufficiency	*Sufficiency*	*Redundance*

For here the middle term, *Sufficiency*, is equally opposed on the one hand to *Insufficiency* and on the other to *Redundance*.

These forms of correlative expressions would suggest the use of triple, instead of double, columns for tabulating this threefold order of words; but the practical inconvenience attending such an arrangement would probably overbalance its advantages.

It often happens that the same word has several correlative terms, according to the different relations in which it is considered. Thus to the word *Giving* are opposed both *Receiving* and *Taking*; the former correlation having reference to the *persons* concerned in the transfer, while the latter relates to the *mode* of transfer. *Old* has for opposite both *New* and *Young*, according as it is applied to *things* or to *living beings*. *Attack* and *Defence* are correlative terms, as are also *Attack* and *Resistance*. *Resistance*, again, has for its other correlative *Submission*. *Truth in the abstract* is opposed to *Error*, but the opposite of *Truth communicated* is *Falsehood*. *Acquisition* is contrasted both with *Deprivation* and with *Loss*. *Refusal* is the counterpart both of *Offer* and of *Consent*. *Disuse* and *Misuse* may either of them be considered as the correlative of *Use*. *Teaching*, with reference to what is taught, is opposed to *Misteaching*, but with reference to the act itself, its proper reciprocal is *Learning*.

Words contrasted in form do not always bear the same contrast in their meaning. The word *Malefactor*, for example, would, from its derivation, appear to be exactly the opposite of *Benefactor*, but the ideas attached to these two words are far from being directly opposed; for while the latter expresses one who confers a benefit, the former denotes one who has violated the laws.

Independently of the immediate practical uses derivable from the arrangement of words in double columns, many considerations, interesting in a philosophical point of view, are presented by the study of correlative expressions. It will be found, on strict examination, that there seldom exists an exact opposition between two words which may at first sight appear to be the counterparts of one another; for, in general, the one will be found to possess in reality more force or extent of meaning than the other with which it is contrasted. The correlative term sometimes assumes the form of a mere negative, although it is really endowed with a considerable positive force. Thus *Disrespect* is not merely the absence of *Respect*; its signification trenches on the opposite idea, namely, *Contempt*. In like manner, *Untruth* is not merely the negative of *Truth*; it involves a degree of *Falsehood*. *Irreligion*, which is properly *the want of Religion*, is understood as being nearly synonymous with *Impiety*. For these reasons, the reader must not expect that all the words which stand side by side in the two columns shall be the precise correlatives of each other; for the nature of the subject, as well as the imperfections of language, renders it impossible always to preserve such an exactness of correlation.

There exist comparatively few words of a general character to which no correlative term, either of negation or of opposition, can be assigned, and which therefore require no corresponding second column. The correlative idea, especially that which constitutes a sense negative to the primary one, may, indeed, be formed or conceived; but, from its occurring rarely, no word has been framed to represent it; for in language, as in other matters, the supply fails when there is no probability of a demand. Occasionally we find this deficiency provided for by the contrivance of prefixing the syllable *non*; as, for instance, the negatives of *existence, performance, payment*, etc., are expressed by the compound words, *non-existence, non-performance, non-payment*, etc. Functions of a similar kind are performed by the prefixes *dis-*,[1] *anti-*, *contra-, mis-, in-*, and *un*.[2] With respect to all these, and especially the last, great latitude is allowed according to the necessities of the case, a latitude which is limited only by the taste and discretion of the author.

On the other hand, it is hardly possible to find two words having in all respects the same meaning, and being therefore interchangeable; that is, admitted of being employed indiscriminately, the one or the other, in all their applications. The investigation of the distinctions to be drawn between words apparently synonymous forms a separate branch of inquiry which I have not presumed here to enter upon; for the subject has already occupied the attention of much abler critics than myself, and its complete exhaustion would require the devotion of a whole life. The purpose of this work, it must be borne in mind, is not to explain the signification of words, but simply to classify and arrange them according to the sense in which they are now used, and which I presume to be already known to the reader. I enter into no inquiry into the changes of meaning they may have undergone in the

---

[1] The word *disannul*, however, had the same meaning as *annul*.
[2] In the case of adjectives, the addition to a substantive of the terminal syllable *less*, gives it a negative meaning: as *taste, tasteless; care, careless; hope, hopeless; friend, friendless; fault, faultless*, etc.

course of time.[1] I am content to accept them at the value of their present currency, and have no concern with their etymologies, or with the history of their transformations; far less do I venture to thrid the mazes of the vast labyrinth into which I should be led by any attempt at a general discrimination of synonyms. The difficulties I have had to contend with have already been sufficiently great without this addition to my labours.

The most cursory glance over the pages of a dictionary will show that a great number of words are used in various senses, sometimes distinguished by slight shades of difference, but often diverging widely from their primary signification, and even, in some cases, bearing to it no perceptible relation. It may even happen that the very same word has two significations quite opposite to one another. This is the case with the verb *to cleave*, which means *to adhere tenaciously*, and also *to separate by a blow*. *To propugn* sometimes expresses *to attack*; at other times, *to defend*. *To ravel* means both *to entangle* and *to disentangle*. The alphabetical index at the end of this work sufficiently shows the multiplicity of uses to which, by the elasticity of language, the meaning of words has been stretched so as to adapt them to a great variety of modified significations in subservience to the nicer shades of thought which, under peculiarity of circumstances, require corresponding expression. Words thus admitting of different meanings have therefore to be arranged under each of the respective heads corresponding to these various acceptations. There are many words, again, which express ideas compounded of two elementary ideas belonging to different classes. It is therefore necessary to place these words respectively under each of the generic heads to which they relate. The necessity of these repetitions is increased by the circumstance that ideas included under one class are often connected by relations of the same kind as the ideas which belong to another class. Thus we find the same relations of *order* and of *quantity* existing among the ideas of *Time* as well as those of *Space*. Sequence in the one is denoted by the same terms as sequence in the other, and the measures of time also express the measures of space. The cause and the effect are often designated by the same word. The word *Sound*, for instance, denotes both the impression made upon the ear by sonorous vibrations, and also the vibrations themselves, which are the cause or source of that impression. *Mixture* is used for the act of mixing, as well as for the product of that operation. *Taste* and *Smell* express both the sensations and the

---

[1] Such changes are innumerable; for instance, the words *tyrant, parasite, sophist, churl, knave, villain*, anciently conveyed no opprobrious meaning. *Impertinent* merely expressed *irrelative*, and implied neither *rudeness* nor *intrusion*, as it does at present. *Indifferent* originally meant *impartial*; *extravagant* was simply *digressive*; and *to prevent* was properly to *precede* and *assist*. The old translations of the Scriptures furnish many striking examples of the alterations which time has brought in the signification of words. Much curious information on this subject is contained in Trench's *Lectures on the Study of Words*.

qualities of material bodies giving rise to them. *Thought* is the act of thinking, but the same word denotes also the idea resulting from that act. *Judgment* is the act of deciding, and also the decision come to. *Purchase* is the acquisition of a thing by payment, as well as the thing itself so acquired. *Speech* is both the act of speaking and the words spoken; and so on with regard to an endless multiplicity of words. Mind is essentially distinct from Matter, and yet, in all languages, the attributes of the one are metaphorically transferred to those of the other. Matter, in all its forms, is endowed by the figurative genius of every language with the functions which pertain to intellect; and we perpetually talk of its phenomena and of its powers as if they resulted from the voluntary influence of one body on another, acting and reacting, impelling and being impelled, controlling and being controlled, as if animated by spontaneous energies and guided by specific intentions. On the other hand, expressions of which the primary signification refers exclusively to the properties and actions of matter are metaphorically applied to the phenomena of thought and volition, and even to the feelings and passions of the soul; and in speaking of a *ray of hope*, a *shade of doubt*, a *flight of fancy*, a *flash of wit*, the *warmth of emotion*, or the *ebullitions of anger*, we are scarcely conscious that we are employing metaphors which have this material origin.

As a general rule, I have deemed it incumbent on me to place words and phrases which appertain more especially to one head also under the other heads to which they have a relation, whenever it appeared to me that this repetition would suit the convenience of the inquirer, and spare him the trouble of turning to other parts of the work; for I have always preferred to subject myself to the imputation of redundance, rather than incur the reproach of insufficiency.[1] When, however, the divergence of the associated from the primary idea is sufficiently marked, I have contented myself with making a reference to the place where the modified signification will be found. But in order to prevent needless extension, I have, in general, omitted *conjugate words*[2] which are so obviously derivable from those that are given in the same place, that the reader may safely be left to form them for himself. This is the

---

[1] Frequent repetitions of the same series of expressions, accordingly, will be met with under various headings. For example, the word *Relinquishment*, with its synonyms, occurs as a heading at No. 624, where it applies to *intention*, and also at No. 782, where it refers to *property*. The word *Chance* has two significations, distinct from one another: the one implying the *absence of an assignable* cause, in which case it comes under the category of the relation of Causation, and occupies the No. 156; the other, the *absence of design*, in which latter sense it ranks under the operations of the Will, and has assigned to it the place No. 621. I have, in like manner, distinguished *Sensibility, Pleasure, Pain, Taste*, etc., according as they relate to *Physical* or to *Moral Affections*; the former being found at Nos. 375, 377, 378, 390, etc., and the latter at Nos. 822, 827, 828, 850, etc.

[2] By '*conjugate* or *paronymous* words is meant, correctly speaking, different parts of speech from the same root, which exactly correspond in point of meaning.'—*A Selection of English Synonyms*, edited by Archbishop Whately.

case with adverbs derived from adjectives by the simple addition of the terminal syllable -*ly*, such as *closely, carefully, safely*, etc., from *close, careful, safe*, etc., and also with adjectives or participles immediately derived from the verbs which are already given. In all such cases, an 'etc.' indicates that reference is understood to be made to these roots. I have observed the same rule in compiling the index, retaining only the primary or more simple word, and omitting the conjugate words obviously derived from them. Thus I assume the word *short* as the representative of its immediate derivatives *shortness, shorten, shortening, shortened, shorter, shortly*, which would have had the same references, and which the reader can readily supply.

The same verb is frequently used indiscriminately either in the active or transitive, or in the neuter or intransitive sense. In these cases I have generally not thought it worth while to increase the bulk of the work by the needless repetition of that word, for the reader, whom I suppose to understand the use of the words, must also be presumed to be competent to apply them correctly.

There are a multitude of words of a specific character, which although they properly occupy places in the columns of a dictionary, yet, having no relation to general ideas, do not come within the scope of this compilation, and are consequently omitted. The names of objects in Natural History, and technical terms belonging exclusively to Science or to Art, or relating to particular operations, and of which the signification is restricted to those specific objects, come under this category. Exceptions must, however, be made in favour of such words as admit of metaphorical application to general subjects with which custom has associated them, and of which they may be cited as being typical or illustrative. Thus the word *Lion* will find a place under the head of *Courage*, of which it is regarded as the type. *Anchor*, being emblematic of *Hope*, is introduced among the words expressing that emotion; and, in like manner, *butterfly* and *weathercock*, which are suggestive of fickleness, are included in the category of *Irresolution*.

With regard to the admission of many words and expressions which the classical reader might be disposed to condemn as vulgarisms, or which he, perhaps, might stigmatize as pertaining rather to the slang than to the legitimate language of the day, I would beg to observe that, having due regard to the uses to which this work was to be adapted, I did not feel myself justified in excluding them solely on that ground, if they possessed an acknowledged currency in general intercourse. It is obvious that, with respect to degrees of conventionality, I could not have attempted to draw any strict lines of demarcation, and far less could I have presumed to erect any absolute standard of purity. My object, be it remembered, is not to regulate the use of words, but simply to supply and to suggest such as may be wanted on occasion, leaving the proper selection entirely to the discretion and taste of the employer. If a novelist or a dramatist, for example, proposed to delineate some vulgar personage, he would wish to have the power of putting into the mouth of the speaker expressions that would accord with his character, just as the actor, to revert to a former comparison, who had to personate a peasant, would choose for his attire the most homely garb, and would have just reason to complain if the theatrical wardrobe furnished him with no suitable costume.

Words which have, in process of time, become obsolete, are, of course, rejected from this collection. On the other hand, I have admitted a considerable number of words and phrases borrowed from other languages, chiefly the French and Latin, some of which may be considered as already naturalized; while others, though avowedly foreign, are frequently introduced in English composition, particularly in familiar style, on account of their being peculiarly expressive, and because we have no corresponding words of equal force in our own language.[1] The rapid advances which are being made in scientific knowledge, and consequent improvement in all the arts of life, and the extension of those arts and sciences to so many new purposes and objects, create a continual demand for the formation of new terms to express new agencies, new wants, and new combinations. Such terms, from being at first merely technical, are rendered, by more general use, familiar to the multitude, and having a well-defined acceptation, are eventually incorporated into the language, which they contribute to enlarge and to enrich. *Neologies* of this kind are perfectly legitimate, and highly advantageous; and they necessarily introduce those gradual and progressive changes which every language is destined to undergo.[2] Some modern writers, however, have indulged in a habit of arbitrarily fabricating new words and a new-fangled phraseology without any necessity, and with manifest injury to the purity of the language. This vicious practice, the offspring of indolence or conceit, implies an ignorance or neglect of the riches in which the English language already abounds, and which would have supplied them with words of recognized legitimacy, conveying precisely the same meaning as those they so recklessly coin in the illegal mint of their own fancy.

A work constructed on the plan of classification I have proposed might, if ably executed, be of great value in tending to limit the fluctuations to which language has always been subject, by establishing an authoritative standard for its regulation. Future historians, philologists, and lexicographers, when investigating the period when new words were introduced, or discussing the import given at the present time to the old, might find their labours lightened by being enabled to appeal to such a standard, instead of having to search for data among

---

[1] All these words and phrases are printed in italics.

[2] Thus in framing the present classification I have frequently felt the want of substantive terms corresponding to abstract qualities or ideas denoted by certain adjectives, and have been tempted to invent words that might express these abstractions; but I have yielded to this temptation only in the four following instances: having framed from the adjectives *irrelative, amorphous, sinistral*, and *gaseous* the abstract nouns *irrelation, amorphism, sinistrality*, and *gaseity*. I have ventured also to introduce the adjective *intersocial* to express the active voluntary relations between man and man.

the scattered writings of the age. Nor would its utility be confined to a single language, for the principles of its construction are universally applicable to all languages, whether living or dead. On the same plan of classification there might be formed a French, a German, a Latin, or a Greek Thesaurus, possessing, in their respective spheres, the same advantages as those of the English model. Still more useful would be a conjunction of these methodized compilations in two languages, the French and the English, for instance; the columns of each being placed in parallel juxtaposition. No means yet devised would so greatly facilitate the acquisition of the one language by those who are acquainted with the other: none would afford such ample assistance to the translator in either language; and none would supply such ready and effectual means of instituting an accurate comparison between them, and of fairly appreciating their respective merits and defects. In a still higher degree would all those advantages be combined and multiplied in a *Polyglot Lexicon* constructed on this system.

Metaphysicians engaged in the more profound investigation of the Philosophy of Language will be materially assisted by having the ground thus prepared for them in a previous analysis and classification of our ideas, for such classification of ideas is the true basis on which words, which are their symbols, should be classified.[1] It is by such

[1] The principle by which I have been guided in framing my verbal classification is the same as that which is employed in the various departments of natural history. Thus the sectional divisions I have formed correspond to natural families in botany and zoology, and the filiation of words presents a network analogous to the natural filiation of plants or animals.

The following are the only publications that have come to my knowledge in which any attempt has been made to construct a systematic arrangement of Ideas with a view to their expression. The earliest of these, supposed to be at least nine hundred years old, is the AMERA CÓSHA, or *Vocabulary of the Sanscrit Language*, by Amera Sinha, of which an English translation, by the late Henry T. Colebrooke, was printed at Serampoor in the year 1808. The classification of words is there, as might be expected, exceedingly imperfect and confused, especially in all that relates to abstract Ideas or mental operations. This will be apparent from the very title of the first section, which comprehends '*Heaven, Gods, Demons, Fire, Air, Velocity, Eternity, Much*'; while '*Sin, Virtue, Happiness, Destiny, Cause, Nature, Intellect, Reasoning, Knowledge, Senses, Tastes, Odours, Colours*, are all included and jumbled together in the fourth section. A more logical order, however, pervades the sections relating to natural objects, such as *Seas, Earth, Towns, Plants*, and *Animals*, which form separate classes, exhibiting a remarkable effort at analysis at so remote a period of Indian literature.

The well-known work of Bishop Wilkins, entitled *An Essay towards a Real Character and a Philosophical Language*, published in 1668, had for its object the formation of a system of symbols which might serve as a universal language. It professed to be founded on a 'scheme of analysis of the things or notions to which names were to be assigned'; but notwithstanding the immense labour and ingenuity expended in the construction of this system, it was soon found to be far too abstruse and recondite for practical application.

In the year 1797 there appeared in Paris an anonymous work, entitled *Pasigraphie, ou Premiers Éléments du nouvel Art-Science d'écrire et d'imprimer*

analysis alone that we can arrive at a clear perception of the relation which these symbols bear to their corresponding ideas, or can obtain a correct knowledge of the elements which enter into the formation of compound ideas, and of the exclusions by which we arrive at the abstractions so perpetually resorted to in the process of reasoning and in the communication of our thoughts.

Lastly, such analyses alone can determine the principles on which a strictly *Philosophical Language* might be constructed. The probable result of the construction of such a language would be its eventual adoption by every civilized nation, thus realizing that splendid aspiration of philanthropists—the establishment of a Universal Language. However Utopian such a project may appear to the present generation, and however abortive may have been the former endeavours of Bishop Wilkins and others to realize it,[1] its accomplishment is surely not beset with greater difficulties than have impeded the progress to many other beneficial objects which in former times appeared to be no less visionary, and which yet were successfully achieved, in later ages, by the continued and persevering exertions of the human intellect. Is there at the present day, then, any ground for despair that, at some future stage of that higher civilization to which we trust the world is gradually tending, some new and bolder effort of genius towards the solution of this great problem may be crowned with success, and compass an object of such vast and paramount utility? Nothing, indeed, would conduce more directly to bring about a golden age of union and harmony among the several nations and races of mankind than the removal of that barrier to the interchange of thought and mutual good understanding between man and man which is now interposed by the diversity of their respective languages.

---

une langue de manière à être lu et entendu dans toute autre langue sans traduction, of which an edition in German was also published. It contains a great number of tabular schemes of categories, all of which appear to be excessively arbitrary and artificial, and extremely difficult of application, as well as of apprehension.

[1] 'The languages,' observes Horne Tooke, 'which are commonly used throughout the world, are much more simple and easy, convenient and philosophical, than Wilkins's scheme for a *real character*; or than any other scheme that has been at any other time imagined or proposed for the purpose.' —῎Επεα Πτερόεντα, p. 125.